# THE OXFORD

## New Essential
## Thesaurus

**AMERICAN EDITION**

# THE OXFORD
# New Essential
# Thesaurus

AMERICAN EDITION

BERKLEY BOOKS, NEW YORK

**THE BERKLEY PUBLISHING GROUP**
**Published by the Penguin Group**
**Penguin Group (USA) Inc.**
**375 Hudson Street, New York, New York 10014, USA**
Penguin Group (Canada), 90 Eglinton Avenue East, Suite 700, Toronto, Ontario M4P 2Y3, Canada
(a division of Pearson Penguin Canada Inc.)
Penguin Books Ltd., 80 Strand, London WC2R 0RL, England
Penguin Group Ireland, 25 St. Stephen's Green, Dublin 2, Ireland (a division of Penguin Books Ltd.)
Penguin Group (Australia), 250 Camberwell Road, Camberwell, Victoria 3124, Australia
(a division of Pearson Australia Group Pty. Ltd.)
Penguin Books India Pvt. Ltd., 11 Community Centre, Panchsheel Park, New Delhi—110 017, India
Penguin Group (NZ), 67 Apollo Drive, Rosedale, North Shore 0632, New Zealand
(a division of Pearson New Zealand Ltd.)
Penguin Books (South Africa) (Pty.) Ltd., 24 Sturdee Avenue, Rosebank, Johannesburg 2196,
South Africa

Penguin Books Ltd., Registered Offices: 80 Strand, London WC2R 0RL, England

THE OXFORD® NEW ESSENTIAL THESAURUS

A Berkley Book / published by arrangement with Oxford University Press, Inc.

PRINTING HISTORY
Berkley mass-market edition / July 2008

Copyright © 1998, 2008 by Oxford University Press
Oxford is a registered trademark of Oxford University Press, Inc.
Published in 1998 as *The Oxford Essential Thesaurus*

ISBN: 978-0-425-22242-3

BERKLEY®
Berkley Books are published by The Berkley Publishing Group,
a division of Penguin Group (USA) Inc.,
375 Hudson Street, New York, New York 10014.
BERKLEY is a registered trademark of Penguin Group (USA) Inc.
The "B" design is a trademark belonging to Penguin Group (USA) Inc.

PRINTED IN THE UNITED STATES OF AMERICA

10   9   8   7   6   5

# Contents

# Project Staff

|                       |                                         |
| --------------------: | --------------------------------------- |
|              *Editor:* | Christine L. Stevens                    |
|       *Project Editors:* | Nancy LaRoche, Laurie H. Ongley         |
| *Editorial Assistant:* | Deborah Argosy                          |
|         *Proofreaders:* | Linda Costa, Adrienne Makowski, Ruth Handlin Manley, Julie Marsh |
|           *Data Entry:* | Kimberly Roberts                        |
|                        |                                         |
|       *Editor-in-chief:* | Frank R. Abate                          |
|       *Managing Editor:* | Elizabeth J. Jewell                     |

# Guide to
# *The New Oxford Essential Thesaurus: American Edition*

## HEADWORDS

The text of *The Oxford Essential Thesaurus: American Edition* is organized under headwords, which are printed in bold type. The headwords are listed in strict alphabetical order.

Many English words have two or more acceptable spellings; in this book, the one used is the one regarded as being the most common. Occasionally, two spellings share nearly equal usage; in such cases, the headwords include both forms. For example:

> **cagey, cagy** adjective guarded, secretive, noncommittal, cautious, chary, wary, careful, shrewd, wily.

## PARTS OF SPEECH

A headword is always followed by its part of speech. When a word has two or more different parts of speech, it is listed more than once with separate entries for each. For example:

> **obscure** adjective **1** *obscure references* unclear, indeterminate, opaque . . . .

> **obscure** verb **1** *obscure the main issue* confuse, blur, muddle . . . .

Not all parts of speech of a word are necessarily included as headwords. For example, many words that function as adjectives can also function as adverbs. In such cases, the adverbial senses are included only when they have useful sets of synonyms.

## HOMOGRAPHS

Certain words have the same spelling but different meanings and different etymologies (origins). Such words, known as homographs, are treated as separate headwords, even when they have the same part of speech. For the purposes of cross-referencing, homograph numbers are included in order to distinguish identical headwords with the same part of speech. For example,

> **bank**[1] noun **1** *a grassy bank* slope, rise, incline, . . . .

> **bank**[2] noun **1** *empty the child's bank* piggy bank, cashbox, safe, . . . .

If two or more headwords are identical in spelling but have different parts of speech, homograph numbers are not used. This does not necessarily imply that these entries share the same etymology.

## ENTRIES

Each entry contains a list of words that are synonyms of the headword: i.e., the words can be used in place of the headword in most (although not all) contexts. When a word has more than one meaning, the different senses of the word are numbered. In many instances, example phrases (in italic type) indicate the particular sense and illustrate the use of the word. In some cases, two or more examples are given; these are separated by a vertical bar (|). For example:

> **contribute** verb **1** *contribute money/time to the charity | happy to contribute* give, donate, hand out, . . . .

Note that a slash (/) is used to separate alternative words in order to save space. The slash applies only to the two words it separates; thus "contribute time/money" can be read as "contribute time" and "contribute money."

## SUBENTRIES

Verb phrases are included as subentries (in bold type) under a main entry. For example:

> **chance** verb **1** *it chanced that they arrived last* happen, occur, take place, come about. **2** *have to chance it* risk, hazard, gamble . . . .
> **chance on/upon** come across, stumble on, come upon, encounter; *inf.* bump into, run into.

## GROUPS WITHIN SENSES

In general, the synonyms in an entry are separated by commas. However, there are cases in which the words fall naturally into two or more distinct groups, which are separated by semicolons. There are various reasons for subdividing a sense in this way:

### Grammatical Differences

Within a given sense, some synonyms may function differently from others. For example:

> **acclaim** noun . . . praise, commendation, approval, approbation, homage, tribute; cheers, congratulations, plaudits, bouquets.

In the **acclaim** entry, the semicolon separates the singular nouns from the plural nouns. There are other grammatical reasons for subdividing synonym groups; for instance, a headword may function as both a transitive verb (taking a direct object) and an intransitive verb (without an object), whereas some of the synonyms may be only intransitive or only transitive.

### Relationship of Meanings

Within a given sense, there sometimes are synonyms whose meanings share a relationship that sets them apart from the other synonyms in that sense. For example:

> **age** verb mature, ripen, grow up, come of age; grow old, decline, wither, fade.

> **bag** noun receptacle; handbag, pocketbook,
> purse, shoulder bag; suitcase, grip, flight
> bag, . . . .

In the entry for **age**, a semicolon is used to separate the "maturing" senses of *age* from the "growing old" senses. In the **bag** entry, semicolons separate the general synonym "receptacle" from the specific synonyms, which themselves are separated into categories of bags.

### Restricted Usage

Some synonyms are separated into labeled groups of restricted usage. Such groups are always set off by semicolons. For example:

> **acquit** verb . . . vindicate, liberate, free,
> deliver; *fml.* exculpate.

> **work** noun . . . effort, exertion, labor, toil,
> sweat, drudgery, trouble, industry; *lit.*
> travail; *inf.* grind, elbow grease.

The usage labels used in this thesaurus are abbreviated as follows:

| | |
|---|---|
| *derog.* | derogatory |
| *fml.* | formal |
| *inf.* | informal |
| *lit.* | literal |
| *Med.* | Medicine |
| *TM* | trademark |

## CROSS-REFERENCES

A cross-reference to a main entry is indicated by small capitals and is preceded by "See." Where necessary, the part of speech and sense number are also given. For example:

> **abridge** verb shorten, cut down, con-
> dense, contract, compress. *See* ABBRE-
> VIATE.

> **alternate** adjective every other, every se-
> cond; . . . .*See* ALTERNATIVE adjective 1.

A cross-reference to a subentry follows the same format but also includes the main entry (given in parentheses). For example:

> **transcend** verb. . . . **2** *her performance*
> *transcended that of her opponents* surpass,
> excel. *See* TOWER ABOVE (TOWER) verb.

# Aa

**abandon** verb **1** *abandon one's family* desert, leave, forsake, depart from, leave behind, cast aside, jilt; *inf.* run out on. **2** *abandon hope* give up, renounce, relinquish, dispense with, forgo. **3** *abandon a country to the enemy* yield, surrender, give up, cede, deliver up. **4** *abandon smoking* stop, give up, cease, drop, forgo, desist from, dispense with.

**abandon** noun recklessness, lack of restraint/inhibition, unrestraint, carelessness, wildness, impulse, impetuosity, immoderation, wantonness.

**abandoned** adjective **1** *an abandoned child* deserted, forsaken, cast aside. **2** *an abandoned ship* vacated, evacuated, deserted, unoccupied, empty, unused.

**abase** verb humiliate, humble, belittle, lower, degrade, disparage, debase, demean, discredit.

**abashed** adjective embarrassed, ashamed, shamefaced, mortified, humiliated; taken aback, disconcerted, nonplussed, discomfited.

**abate** verb **1** *the storm/pain abated* die down, lessen, ease, subside, let up, decrease, diminish, moderate, decline, fade, slacken, wane. **2** *abate the pain/noise* ease, lessen, decrease, diminish, moderate, soothe, relieve, dull, blunt, alleviate, mitigate, allay, assuage, palliate, appease, reduce, lower.

**abbreviate** verb shorten, reduce, cut, contract, condense, compress, abridge, truncate, clip, crop, shrink, summarize, abstract, synopsize.

**abbreviation** noun shortening, reduction, cutting, contraction, condensation, compression, abridgment.

**abdicate** verb **1** *the king abdicated due to illness* resign, stand down, retire, quit. **2** *abdicate the throne* give up, renounce, resign from, relinquish. **3** *abdicate responsibility* reject, disown, waive, yield, forgo, refuse, abandon, turn one's back on, wash one's hands of.

**abduct** verb kidnap, carry off, run away/off with, make off with, seize, hold as hostage.

**aberrant** adjective deviant, divergent, anomalous, abnormal, irregular, atypical, freakish.

**aberration** noun **1** *a statistical aberration* deviation, divergence, anomaly, abnormality, variation, freak. **2** *in a moment of aberration* abnormality, irregularity, eccentricity, deviation, straying, aberrancy. **3** *a mental aberration* disorder, disease, irregularity, instability.

**abet** verb assist, aid, help, support, back, second, encourage, promote, cooperate with, connive at, endorse, sanction, succor.

**abhor** verb detest, loathe, hate, abominate, feel aversion to, shrink/recoil from.

**abhorrent** adjective detestable, loathsome, hated, abominable, repellent, repugnant, repulsive, revolting, disgusting, distasteful, horrible, horrid, heinous.

**abide** verb **1** *abide by the rules* keep to, comply with, observe, follow, obey, agree to, hold to, stick to. **2** *I cannot abide his smoking* stand, tolerate, bear, put up with, endure, stomach.

**abiding** adjective lasting, everlasting, eternal, unending, constant, enduring, persisting, unchanging, steadfast, immutable.

**ability** noun **1** *a person of outstanding ability* talent, competence, competency, proficiency, skill, expertise, expertness, adeptness, aptitude, cleverness, flair, gift, knack, *savoir faire; inf.* know-how. **2** *the ability to cope* capacity, capability, potential, potentiality, power, aptness, facility, faculty, propensity.

**abject** adjective **1** *abject poverty* wretched, miserable, hopeless, pathetic, pitiable. **2** *an abject coward* base, low, vile, worthless, contemptible, despicable. **3** *an abject apology* obsequious, groveling, servile, cringing, ingratiating, sycophantic, submissive.

**ablaze** adjective **1** *the house was ablaze* on fire, burning, blazing, flaming; *lit.* afire, aflame. **2** *the house was ablaze with lights* lit up, alight, gleaming, glowing, aglow, illuminated, radiant, shimmering, sparkling.

**able** adjective competent, capable, talented, skillful, skilled, clever, intelligent, accomplished, gifted, proficient, apt, fit, expert, adept, efficient.

**able-bodied** adjective healthy, fit, robust, strong, sound, sturdy, vigorous, hardy, hale and hearty, muscular, strapping, rugged, burly, stalwart.

**abnormal** adjective unusual, strange, odd, peculiar, uncommon, curious, queer, weird, eccentric, extraordinary, unexpected, exceptional, irregular, unnatural, erratic, singular, atypical, nontypical, anomalous, deviant, deviating, divergent, aberrant; *inf.* oddball, off the wall, wacko.

**abode** noun home, house, dwelling place, domicile, dwelling, accommodations, quarters; *inf.* pad.

**abolish** verb do away with, put an end to, end, stop, terminate, eliminate, eradicate, exterminate, destroy, annihilate, stamp out, obliterate, wipe out, extinguish, quash, expunge, extirpate, annul, cancel, invalidate, nullify, void, rescind, repeal, revoke.

**abolition** noun ending, termination, elimination, extermination, destruction, annihilation, obliteration, extirpation, annulment, cancellation, nullification, invalidation, repeal.

**abominable** adjective hateful, loathsome, detestable, odious, obnoxious, base, despicable, contemptible, damnable, cursed, disgusting, revolting, repellent, repulsive, repugnant, abhorrent, reprehensible, foul, vile.

**aboriginal** adjective indigenous, native, original, earliest, first, ancient, primitive.

**abort** verb **1** *abort a pregnancy/plan* terminate, halt, stop, end, arrest. **2** *the space mission aborted* come to a halt, end, terminate, fail, miscarry.

**abound** verb be plentiful, proliferate, thrive, flourish. **abound with/in** be full of, overflow with, teem with, be alive with, swarm with; *inf.* be crawling/lousy with.

**aboveboard** adverb/adjective honest, fair, open, frank, straight, overt, candid, forthright, unconcealed.

**abrasion** noun **1** *skin abrasion* graze, scrape, scratch, sore, ulcer. **2** *the abrasion of the rock* erosion, wearing down/away, corrosion, rubbing, scraping.

**abrasive** adjective **1** *an abrasive substance* erosive, eroding, corrosive, chafing, rubbing, coarse, harsh. **2** *an abrasive manner* caustic, cutting, grating, biting, rough, harsh, irritating.

**abridge** verb shorten, cut down, condense, contract, compress. *See* ABBREVIATE.

**abridgment** noun summary, synopsis, précis, abstract, digest, shortening, cutting, condensation, summarization.

**abroad** adverb **1** *go abroad for the summer* overseas, out of the country, across the ocean. **2** *spread a rumor abroad* far and wide, everywhere, publicly, extensively.

**abrupt** adjective **1** *an abrupt ending* sudden, quick, hurried, hasty, swift, rapid, headlong, instantaneous, surprising, unexpected, unanticipated. **2** *an abrupt manner* curt, blunt, brusque, gruff, snappish, unceremonious, rough, rude. **3** *an abrupt slope* steep, sheer, precipitous, sudden, sharp. **4** *an abrupt writing style* jerky, disconnected, rough.

**abscess** noun ulcer, ulceration, boil, pustule, carbuncle, pimple.

**abscond** verb *abscond with the funds* run away, bolt, clear out, flee, make off, escape, take flight, fly, decamp, disappear, take to one's heels, make a quick getaway.

**absence** noun **1** *the teacher noted their absence* nonattendance, nonappearance, truancy, absenteeism. **2** *an absence of proof* lack, want, nonexistence, unavailability.

**absent** adjective **1** *the workers are absent* away, off, out, gone, missing, truant, unavailable. **2** *an absent expression* absentminded, distracted, preoccupied, faraway, blank, empty, vacant, inattentive, vague, absorbed.

**absentminded** adjective forgetful, oblivious. *See* ABSENT 2.

**absolute** adjective **1** *absolute trust* complete, total, utter, out and out, perfect, entire, undivided, unqualified. **2** *the absolute truth* certain, positive, definite, unquestionable, undoubted, unequivocal, decisive, unconditional, infallible. **3** *an absolute standard* fixed, rigid, established, set, definite. **4** *absolute power* unlimited, unrestricted, unrestrained, ultimate, total, supreme, unconditional, sovereign, omnipotent, despotic, dictatorial, autocratic, tyrannical, authoritarian.

**absolutely** adverb **1** *absolutely correct* completely, totally, utterly, perfectly, entirely, wholly, fully, thoroughly. **2** *absolutely the worst driver* certainly, positively, definitely, unquestionably, without a doubt, unequivocally, unconditionally, conclusively, unreservedly, actually, in actual fact, really, in truth. **3** *ruling absolutely* despotically, dictatorially, autocratically, tyrannically.

**absolve** verb **1** *absolve from blame* acquit, exonerate, discharge, release, free, deliver, liberate, let off, clear, exculpate. **2** *absolve sinners* forgive, pardon, excuse, reprieve, clear, set free, vindicate.

**absorb** verb **1** *absorb liquid* soak up, suck up, draw up/in, take up/in, blot up, mop, sponge up, sop up. **2** *absorb their attention* occupy, engage, preoccupy, captivate, engross, monopolize, rivet.

**absorbent** adjective porous, spongy, permeable, pervious, penetrable, receptive, blotting.

**absorbing** adjective fascinating, gripping, interesting, captivating, engrossing, riveting, spellbinding.

**abstain** verb *abstain from voting/pleasure/drinking* refrain, decline, hold back, keep from, refuse, renounce, avoid, shun, eschew; teetotal, be/stay sober, take the pledge; *inf.* be on the wagon.

**abstinence** noun teetotalism, temperance, sobriety, refraining, forbearing, renunciation.

**abstract** adjective **1** *abstract beliefs* theoretical, conceptual, notional, intellectual, metaphysical, philosophical. **2** *abstract theories* complex, abstruse, recondite, obscure, deep.

**abstract** noun summary, synopsis, précis, abridgment, condensation, digest.

**absurd** adjective ridiculous, foolish, silly, idiotic, stupid, nonsensical, senseless, inane, crazy, ludicrous, funny, laughable, comical, preposterous, farcical, harebrained, asinine; *inf.* daft.

**absurdity** noun ridiculousness, foolishness, silliness, idiocy, stupidity, inanity, folly, incongruity, irrationality, ludicrousness, funniness, comedy, humor, joke, farce; nonsense, rubbish, gibberish, drivel.

**abundance** noun plenty, profusion, copiousness, amplitude, affluence, lavishness; *inf.* heaps, lots, tons, oodles.

**abundant** adjective plentiful, large, great, huge, ample, well-supplied, well-provided, profuse, copious, lavish, bountiful, teeming, overflowing; *inf.* galore.

**abuse** verb **1** *abuse power/alcohol* misuse, misapply, misemploy, mishandle, exploit. **2** *abuse children* mistreat, maltreat, ill-use, ill-treat, injure, hurt, harm, beat, wrong, oppress, torture. **3** *abuse trespassers* insult, swear at, curse, scold, rebuke, upbraid, reprove, castigate, revile, vilify, slander.

**abuse** noun **1** *the abuse of power/alcohol* misuse, misapplication, misemployment, mishandling, exploitation. **2** *child abuse* mistreatment, maltreatment, ill-use, ill-treatment, manhandling, injury, hurt, harm, beating, oppression. **3** *torrents of abuse* swearing, cursing, scolding, upbraiding, vilification, vituperation, defamation, slander, insults, curses, expletives, swearwords.

**abusive** adjective insulting, rude, blasphemous, offensive, vulgar, vituperative, reproachful, reproving, derisive.

**abut** verb adjoin, border, verge on, join, touch, meet, impinge on.

**abysmal** adjective extreme, utter, complete, thorough, profound, deep, endless, unfathomable, bottomless.

**abyss** noun chasm, gorge, cavity, void, pit, bottomless pit, hole, hellhole, gulf, depth, depths, ravine, canyon, crevasse.

**academic** adjective **1** *academic considerations* educational, scholastic, instructional, pedagogical. **2** *an academic turn of mind* scholarly, studious, intellectual, erudite, learned, pedantic, professorial, cerebral; *inf.* brainy. **3** *an academic solution* theoretical, hypothetical, notional, impractical, unrealistic, speculative, ivory-towerish.

**academic** noun scholar, lecturer, teacher, tutor, professor, fellow, pedant, pedagogue; *inf.* bookworm, egghead.

**accede** verb **accede to 1** *accede to the request* agree to, consent to, accept, assent to, acquiesce to, comply with, go along with, concur with, grant. **2** *accede to the throne* succeed to, assume, attain, inherit.

**accentuate** verb **1** *the black dress accentuated her paleness* emphasize, stress, highlight, underline, draw attention to, give prominence to, heighten, point up, underscore, accent. **2** *accentuate the pulse of the music* stress, put the stress/emphasis on, emphasize, accent.

**accept** verb **1** *accept the award* receive, take, get, gain, obtain, acquire. **2** *accept the decision* accede to, agree to, consent to, acquiesce in, concur with, comply with, go along with, defer to. **3** *accept the responsibility* take on, undertake, assume, bear, tackle. **4** *accept their story* believe, trust, credit, have faith in. **5** *accepted as one of the family* welcome, receive, embrace, integrate.

**acceptable** adjective **1** *an acceptable present* welcome, agreeable, delightful, pleasing, desirable. **2** *an acceptable standard of work* satisfactory, good enough, adequate, passable, tolerable. **3** *an acceptable risk* allowable, tolerable, admissible, bearable.

**access** noun **1** *access to the building* entry, entrance, way in; admittance, admission. **2** *access to the prisoner | access to information* admission, admittance, entrée, right of entry, permission/opportunity to enter; accessibility, attainability.

**accessory** noun **1** *his accessory in the raid* accomplice, associate, confederate, abettor, helper, assistant, partner. **2** *bicycle accessories* attachment, extra, addition, adjunct, appendage, supplement. **3** *clothing accessories* adornment, ornament, ornamentation, embellishment, trappings.

**accident** noun **1** *an industrial/automobile accident* mishap, casualty, misfortune, misadventure, injury, disaster, tragedy; crash, collision; *inf.* pileup. **2** *met by accident* chance, fate, twist of fate, fortune, luck; *inf.* fluke.

**accidental** adjective **1** *accidental death | an accidental meeting* chance, unintentional, unintended, inadvertent, unexpected, unforeseen, unlooked-for, fortuitous, unanticipated, unplanned. **2** *an accidental* *consideration* nonessential, inessential, incidental, extraneous, extrinsic, supplementary, subsidiary, subordinate, secondary, irrelevant.

**acclaim** verb **1** *acclaim his victory* applaud, cheer, celebrate, salute, welcome, approve, honor, praise, commend, hail, extol. **2** *acclaim her queen* declare, announce, proclaim.

**acclaim** noun *the acclaim of the crowd* applause, ovation, praise, commendation, approval, approbation, homage, tribute; cheers, congratulations, plaudits, bouquets.

**acclimate** verb adjust, adapt, accustom, get used, accommodate, accustom/habituate oneself, become seasoned, familiarize oneself.

**accommodate** verb **1** *we can accommodate four people* put up, house, cater for, board, lodge, provide shelter for, shelter, harbor, billet. **2** *accommodate our plans to suit yours* adapt, adjust, modify, reconcile, fit, harmonize, conform. **3** *accommodate you with a loan* provide, supply, furnish, grant. **4** *accommodate her whenever possible* help, assist, aid, lend a hand to, oblige.

**accommodating** adjective obliging, cooperative, helpful, adaptable, pliable, compliant, complaisant, considerate, willing, kindly, hospitable, kind.

**accommodations** plural noun housing, lodging, board, shelter; residence, house, billet; rooms, quarters; *inf.* digs.

**accompany** verb **1** *accompany her to the dance* escort, go with, squire, usher. **2** *vegetables accompany the meat* go with, go together with, coexist/occur/coincide with, supplement.

**accomplice** noun confederate, accessory, collaborator, abettor, associate, partner, ally, assistant, helper, henchman, right hand, right-hand man, fellow conspirator, partner in crime; *inf.* sidekick.

**accomplish** verb **1** *accomplish an aim* achieve, carry out, fulfill, perform, attain, realize, succeed in, bring off, bring about. **2** *accomplish a task* finish, complete, carry through, do, conclude, effect, execute, consummate.

**accomplished** adjective **1** *an accomplished player* skilled, skillful, expert, gifted, talented, proficient, adept, masterly, polished, practiced, capable, able, competent, experienced, professional, deft, consummate. **2** *an accomplished aim* achieved, fulfilled, realized. **3** *an accomplished task* finished, completed, executed.

**accomplishment** noun **1** *a woman of accomplishment* talent, ability, attainment, achievement, proficiency. **2** *the army's proud accomplishments* achievement, act,

deed, exploit, performance, attainment, feat. **3** *the accomplishment of aims* achievement, fulfillment, attainment, realization. **4** *the accomplishment of tasks* completion, conclusion, execution, consummation.

**accord** verb **1** *his statement does not accord with hers* agree, concur, fit, correspond, match, conform, harmonize, be in tune. **2** *accord them permission/welcome* give, grant, confer, bestow, tender, offer, present.

**accord** noun agreement, harmony, rapport, unison, concord, amity, sympathy, unanimity, accordance. **of one's own accord** of one's own free will, volition, voluntarily, willingly, freely, unforced. **with one accord** unanimously, with one mind, of one voice.

**according** adverb **according to 1** *according to the manager* as stated/maintained by, as claimed by, on the authority of, on the report of. **2** *acting according to their principles* in accordance with, in agreement with, in line with, in keeping with, in compliance with, in harmony with, in conformity with, in obedience to. **3** *salary according to experience* in proportion to, commensurate with, in relation to.

**accordingly** adverb **1** *know the truth and act accordingly* appropriately, correspondingly, suitably, properly, fitly, consistently. **2** *they could not pay the rent and accordingly left* as a result, consequently, therefore, so, thus.

**accost** verb address, speak to, confront, approach, solicit, importune.

**account** noun **1** *a full account of the accident* statement, report, description, record, narration, narrative, story, recital, explanation, tale, chronicle, history. **2** *pay your account on time* bill, invoice; charges, debts. **3** *the firm's accounts are in good order* ledger, balance sheet, financial statement, books. **4** *of no account* importance, consequence, significance. **on account of** because of, owing to, on (the) grounds of. **on no account** not under any circumstances, under no circumstances, certainly not, absolutely not.

**account** verb *account her guilty* consider, regard, reckon, believe, think, look upon, view as, judge, count, deem. **account for 1** *he must account for the delay* explain, explain away, give reasons for, show grounds for, justify. **2** *oil accounts for most of their exports* be responsible for, make up, supply, provide.

**accountable** adjective **1** *accountable for one's actions* responsible, answerable, liable. **2** *accountable to the manager* responsible, answerable. **3** *his actions are not accountable* explicable, explainable, understandable, comprehensible.

**accredit** verb **1** *accredited with the invention* credit with, have ascribed/attributed to, receive the credit for. **2** *accredited to Shakespeare* ascribe, attribute.

**accredited** adjective **1** *our accredited representative* official, authorized, legal, appointed, approved, recognized, certified. **2** *accredited theories* accepted, recognized, believed, endorsed, orthodox. **3** *an accredited day-care center* certified, licensed.

**accrue** verb **1** *bank interest accrued* accumulate, build/mount up, amass, collect, gather, grow, increase. **2** *medical advances accrued from the new technology* arise, follow, ensue, result/emanate from.

**accumulate** verb **1** *dust accumulated over the weeks* gather, pile/build up, collect, increase, accrue. **2** *accumulate antiques* amass, gather, collect, stockpile, pile/heap up, store, hoard.

**accumulation** noun stockpile, pile, heap, mass, collection, buildup, gathering, stock, store, hoard, stack; amassing, building up, stockpiling.

**accuracy** noun correctness, precision, exactness, rightness, validity, closeness, faithfulness, truth, truthfulness, authenticity, factuality, veracity, carefulness, meticulousness.

**accurate** adjective correct, precise, exact, right, errorless, without error, valid, close, faithful, true, truthful, authentic, factual, literal, careful, meticulous, painstaking.

**accusation** noun charge, allegation, attribution, incrimination, imputation, denouncement, indictment, arraignment, impeachment, citation.

**accuse** verb *accuse of* charge with, indict for, arraign for, impeach for, summon with/for, cite for, inculpate for, blame for, lay the blame on, hold responsible/accountable/answerable for.

**accustom** verb *accustom to* adapt to, adjust to, acclimatize to, get used to, make familiar/acquainted with, habituate to.

**ace** noun expert, champion, master, star, winner, genius, virtuoso; *inf.* whiz, pro.

**ace** adjective expert, champion, brilliant, great, superb, outstanding, excellent, first-rate, fine, skillful, adept; *inf.* crack, A-1, tip-top, hotshot.

**acerbic** adjective **1** *an acerbic wit* harsh, sarcastic, sharp, biting, stinging, caustic, trenchant, bitter, vitriolic, mordant. **2** *an acerbic taste* sour, tart, bitter, acid, sharp, acrid, pungent.

**ache** noun **1** *an ache in my back* pain, dull pain, soreness; pang, throb, twinge, smarting, gnawing, stabbing, spasm. **2** *an ache in my heart* suffering, sorrow, misery, distress, grief, anguish, affliction, woe, mourning. **3** *an ache for old times* longing, yearning, craving, desire, hunger, hungering, pining, hankering.

**ache** verb **1** *my head aches* hurt, be sore, be painful, be in pain, pain; throb, pound, twinge, smart. **2** *my heart aches* grieve, be sorrowful, be distressed, be in distress, be miserable, mourn, agonize, suffer. **ache for** *he aches for sunshine* long for, yearn for, crave, desire, hunger for, pine for.

**achieve** verb **1** *achieve success* attain, reach, arrive at, gain, earn, realize, win, acquire, obtain, procure, get, wrest. **2** *achieve all the tasks begun* complete, fulfill, perform. *See* ACCOMPLISH 2.

**achievement** noun **1** *the achievement of success* attainment, gaining, realization. **2** *the achievement of tasks begun* completion, finishing. *See* ACCOMPLISHMENT 4. **3** *proud of their child's achievement* accomplishment, feat, performance, deed, effort.

**acid** adjective **1** *an acid taste* sour, tart, bitter, sharp, biting, acrid, pungent, acerbic, vinegary, vinegarish, acetic, acetous, acidulous. **2** *an acid wit* biting, sarcastic. *See* ACERBIC 1.

**acknowledge** verb **1** *acknowledge the need for reform* admit, grant, allow, recognize, accept, concede. **2** *acknowledge him with a wave* greet, recognize, notice. **3** *acknowledge a letter* answer, reply to, respond to, react to. **4** *acknowledge help* show appreciation for/of, express gratitude for, give thanks for, thank.

**acknowledgment** noun **1** *acknowledgment of the need for reform* admission, granting, recognition, acceptance, agreement. **2** *acknowledgment of his presence* recognition, notice. **3** *acknowledgment of a letter* answer, reply, response. **4** *acknowledgment of help* expression of appreciation/gratitude, thanks.

**acme** noun peak, pinnacle, zenith, climax, culmination, height, high point, crown, summit, optimum, apex.

**acquaint** verb familiarize, make familiar/conversant, make known to, make aware of, advise of, inform, apprise of, enlighten, let know.

**acquaintance** noun **1** *an acquaintance, not a close friend* associate, colleague, contact. **2** *our acquaintance with them* association, relationship, contact, fellowship, companionship. **3** *have some acquaintance with his poetry* familiarity, knowledge, awareness, understanding, cognizance.

**acquiesce** verb consent, agree, accept, concur, approve, assent, allow, comply, conform, concede, go along with, bow to, yield.

**acquiescent** adjective **1** *an acquiescent response* consenting, concurrent, compliant, concessionary. **2** *an acquiescent personality* submissive, servile, subservient, obsequious, ingratiating, self-effacing; *inf.* bootlicking.

**acquire** verb obtain, come by, get, receive, gain, procure, earn, win, secure, take possession of, gather, collect, pick up, achieve, attain, appropriate, amass.

**acquisition** noun **1** *the museum's recent acquisition* purchase, buy, possession, accession, addition, accretion, property. **2** *the acquisition of money* obtaining, procurement, collecting, collection.

**acquit** verb *acquit the suspect* clear (of charges), absolve, exonerate, discharge, release, vindicate, liberate, free, deliver; *fml.* exculpate. **acquit oneself** *they acquitted themselves well* perform, act, behave, conduct oneself, comport oneself.

**acrid** adjective **1** *an acrid taste* pungent, sharp, sour, bitter, tart, harsh, acid, stinging, burning, irritating, vinegary, acerbic, acetic. **2** *an acrid wit* acerbic, sarcastic, sharp, stinging, caustic, astringent, trenchant, vitriolic, virulent.

**acrimonious** adjective bitter, caustic, cutting, sarcastic, harsh, sharp, acid, acerbic, virulent, trenchant, stringent, spiteful, crabbed, vitriolic, venomous.

**acrimony** noun bitterness, sarcasm, harshness, sharpness, acidity, acerbicity, virulence, spitefulness.

**act** noun **1** *acts of bravery/cowardice* deed, action, feat, performance, undertaking, operation, execution, exploit, enterprise, achievement, accomplishment. **2** *acts of Congress* bill, law, decree, statute, edict, dictum, enactment, resolution, ruling, judgment, ordinance, measure. **3** *a music hall act* performance, turn, routine, show, sketch, skit. **4** *putting on an act* pretense, sham, fake, make-believe, show, feigning, affectation, counterfeit, front, posture, pose.

**act** verb **1** *you must act now* take action, do, move, be active, perform, function, react, behave, be employed, be busy. **2** *the painkiller will act soon* work, take effect, operate, function, be efficacious. **3** *she's acting in a play* perform, play, play a part; portray, enact, represent, characterize, personify, stage. **4** *he's not ill but just acting* pretend, fake, feign, pose. **act on/upon 1** *alcohol acts on the brain* affect, have an effect on, influence, alter. **2** *act on instructions* act in accordance with, follow, obey, comply with. **act up** misbehave, give/cause trouble, malfunction.

**acting** noun **1** *a career in acting* the theater, drama, the performing arts, dramatics, stagecraft, theatricals, performing, portraying. **2** *acting now will save trouble* taking action, moving, functioning, reacting. **3** *the quick acting of the pills* action, working, taking effect. **4** *the acting of the cast* performance, playing, portrayal, enacting. **5** *his acting fools no one* pretending, pretense, faking, feigning, play-acting, posturing.

**acting** adjective *an acting head of the department* deputy, substitute, temporary, interim, provisional, pro tem, *pro tempore.*

**action** noun **1** *their prompt action saved lives* act, deed, move, effort, operation, performance, undertaking, maneuver, exploit. **2** *put ideas into action* activity, doing, motion, operation, work, functioning, performance, effort, exertion. **3** *men of action* activity, energy, vitality, vigor, forcefulness. **4** *the action of acid on metal* effect, influence, power, result, consequence. **5** *the action of the play is set in Spain* events, happenings, incidents, episodes. **6** *a piece of the action* activity, excitement, bustle, happenings, incidents; *inf.* goings-on. **7** *soldiers seeing action* conflict, combat, warfare, fighting, battle. **8** *the military action at Gettysburg* battle, engagement, clash, encounter, skirmish, affray.

**actions** plural noun behavior, conduct, activity, comportment, deportment, ways.

**activate** verb switch on, turn on, start, set going, trigger, set in motion, energize.

**active** adjective **1** *an active member of the team | an active volcano* working, functioning, operating, operative, in action, in operation, in force, effective. **2** *people leading active lives* mobile, energetic, vigorous, vital, sprightly, lively, spry, busy, bustling, occupied, involved; *inf.* on the go/move. **3** *active ingredients* effective, effectual, operational, nonpassive, noninert.

**activity** noun **1** *markets are places of great activity* business, bustle, hustle and bustle, liveliness, movement, life, stir, animation, commotion, flurry, tumult; *inf.* comings and goings. **2** *schoolwork and outside activities* interest, hobby, pastime, pursuit, occupation, venture, undertaking, enterprise, project.

**actor, actress** noun performer, player, dramatic artist, thespian, film star, starlet, leading man/woman, trouper, tragedian.

**actual** adjective real, true, factual, genuine, authentic, verified, confirmed, veritable, existing.

**actually** adverb really, in fact, in point of fact, as a matter of fact, in reality, indeed, truly, in truth.

**acumen** noun astuteness, shrewdness, sharpness, cleverness, smartness, judgment, discernment, wisdom, perspicacity, ingenuity, insight, sagacity.

**acute** adjective **1** *an acute sense of hearing | an acute mind* sharp, keen, penetrating, discerning, sensitive, incisive, astute, shrewd, clever, smart, perceptive, perspicacious, discriminating, sagacious, judicious. **2** *an acute shortage* severe, critical, crucial, grave, serious, urgent, pressing. **3** *an acute pain* sharp, shooting, piercing, keen, penetrating, stabbing, intense, excruciating, fierce, racking.

**adage** noun saying, maxim, axiom, proverb, aphorism, saw, dictum, precept, truism, platitude; *fml.* apothegm.

**adamant** adjective resolute, determined, firm, immovable, unshakable, uncompromising, unrelenting, unyielding, unbending, inflexible, obdurate, inexorable, intransigent.

**adapt** verb **1** *adapt a dress/novel* adjust, tailor, convert, change, alter, modify, transform, remodel, reshape. **2** *adapt to a new environment* adjust, conform, acclimatize, accommodate, familiarize oneself with, habituate oneself.

**adaptable** adjective **1** *an adaptable design* adjustable, convertible, alterable, modifiable, variable, versatile. **2** *try to be adaptable* flexible, pliant, compliant, malleable, versatile, resilient, easygoing, conformable.

**adaptation** noun **1** *the adaptation of a dress/novel* adjustment, tailoring, converting, alteration, changing, modification, remodeling, reshaping. **2** *adaptation to a new environment* adjustment, conformity, acclimatization, accommodation, familiarization, habituation.

**add** verb **1** *he added an extra sentence* include, put on/in, attach, append. **2** *add all the numbers* add up, add together, total, count, count up, compute; *inf.* tot up. **3** *"That's fine," he added* go on to say, state further; *inf.* tack on. **add to** increase, magnify, amplify, augment, intensify, aggravate, exacerbate. **add up** *it doesn't add up* make sense, hold water, seem reasonable, be/seem plausible; *inf.* ring true, hold water, stand to reason. **add up to 1** *it adds up to $100* amount to, come to, total. **2** *it all adds up to a disaster* amount to, constitute, comprise, signify; *inf.* spell, spell out.

**addendum** noun addition, appendix, codicil, postscript, appendage.

**addict** noun **1** *a drug/heroin addict* abuser, user; *inf.* junkie, head, fiend. **2** *a movie addict* fan, enthusiast, devotee, follower, adherent; *inf.* buff, freak, nut.

**addiction** noun dependency, craving, devotion, obsession, dedication, enslavement, habit.

**addition** noun **1** *the addition of an extra sentence* inclusion, attachment, appendage. **2** *the addition of a row of figures | check*
*my addition* adding up, counting, totaling, computation, calculation. **3** *an addition to the family* increase, increment, extension, augmentation, gain, supplement, appendage. **in addition** additionally, besides, as well, as well as.

**additional** adjective extra, supplementary, further, more, other, over and above.

**address** noun **1** *the address on the envelope* inscription, label, superscription. **2** *a new address* house, home, location, place, residence, abode, domicile, dwelling. **3** *an address to the crowd* speech, lecture, talk, discourse, oration, sermon, harangue, diatribe.

**address** verb **1** *address an envelope* direct, label, inscribe, superscribe. **2** *address the audience* talk to, speak to, give a talk to, make a speech to, lecture, preach to, declaim to, harangue; *inf.* spout to. **3** *address someone across the street* greet, speak to, hail, salute. **4** *how to address the mayor* name, call, speak to, write. **5** *address any remarks to the manager* direct, send, communicate, convey, forward, remit. **6** *address the golf ball* take aim at, aim at, face. **address oneself** apply oneself to, attend to, turn to, get down to, devote oneself to, concentrate on.

**adept** adjective proficient, skillful; *inf.* top-notch, A-1. *See* ACCOMPLISHED 1.

**adequate** adjective **1** *an adequate salary* sufficient, enough, ample, reasonable, satisfactory, requisite. **2** *your work is adequate* passable, tolerable, acceptable, fair, middle-of-the-road, mediocre, unexceptional, indifferent, average, so-so. **adequate to** *he did not feel adequate to the task* up to, equal to, capable of (doing/performing), competent for, suited to.

**adhere** verb **adhere to** stick to, stick fast to, cling to, hold fast to, cohere to, be fixed to, be pasted/glued to; hold to, abide by, comply with, stand by, be faithful to, follow, obey, fulfill.

**adherent** noun supporter, follower, upholder, advocate, disciple, votary, partisan, sectary, member; fan, admirer, follower, enthusiast, devotee, lover, addict, aficionado; *inf.* buff, freak, fiend.

**adherent** adjective sticky, adhering. *See* ADHESIVE adjective.

**adhesive** adjective sticky, sticking, adhering, adherent, clinging, tacky, gluey, gummy, cohesive, viscous, viscid, glutinous, mucilaginous.

**adhesive** noun glue, fixative, gum, paste, cement, mucilage.

**adjacent** adjective adjoining, neighboring, next door, abutting, bordering, alongside, contiguous, attached, touching, conjoining.

**adjoining** adjective connected, connecting. *See* ADJACENT.

**adjourn** verb break off, discontinue, interrupt, suspend, dissolve, postpone, put off, defer, delay, shelve; break, pause, take a recess; withdraw, retire, retreat, repair.

**adjournment** noun discontinuation, interruption, suspension, postponement, deferral, delay; breaking-off, break, pause, recess; withdrawing, retirement, retreat; *fml.* repairing.

**adjudicate** verb judge, arbitrate, referee, umpire; decide on, settle, determine, pronounce on, give a ruling on.

**adjunct** noun extra, addition, attachment, accessory, appendage, add-on.

**adjust** verb adapt, become accustomed, get used (to), accommodate, acclimatize, reconcile oneself, habituate oneself, assimilate; rearrange, alter, modify, change, remodel, regulate, fix, repair, rectify.

**adjustable** adjective alterable, adaptable, modifiable, movable, accommodating, amenable, obliging, flexible.

**adjustment** noun adaptation, accommodation, acclimatization, alteration, modification, regulating, fixing, repair, change, rearrangement.

**ad lib** verb extemporize, improvise, speak off the cuff, speak impromptu.

**administer** verb 1 *administer the firm's financial affairs* manage, direct, control, conduct, run, govern, operate, superintend, supervise, oversee, preside over. 2 *administer justice* dispense, hand out, allot, deal, distribute, mete out, disburse, provide. 3 *administer a remedy* apply, give, dispense.

**administration** noun 1 *he's in hospital administration* management, direction, operation, supervision. 2 *the Nixon administration* government, regime, term of office. 3 *the administration of justice* dispensation, discharge, allotment, dealing, distribution. 4 *the administration of a remedy* application, dispensation, provision.

**administrative** adjective managerial, management, directorial, executive, organizational, supervisory, regulatory.

**administrator** noun manager, director, executive, head, chief, superintendent, supervisor.

**admirable** adjective worthy, commendable, praiseworthy, laudable, good, excellent.

**admiration** noun approval, regard, high regard, respect, approbation, appreciation, praise, esteem, veneration.

**admire** verb approve of, respect, think highly of, appreciate, applaud, praise, hold in high regard/esteem, venerate, like, sing the praises of, be taken with, adore, love, idolize.

**admirer** noun enthusiast, fan, devotee, aficionado, supporter, follower; suitor, wooer, beau, sweetheart, lover, boyfriend, girlfriend.

**admissible** adjective allowable, allowed, permissible, permitted, acceptable.

**admission** noun 1 *admission to the university* admittance, entry, right of entry, entrance, access, entrée. 2 *admission is $3* entrance fee, ticket, cover charge. 3 *an admission of guilt* acknowledgment, confession, revelation, disclosure, divulgence.

**admit** verb 1 *one ticket admits two people* let in, allow/permit entry to, give access to. 2 *they admitted their guilt* acknowledge, confess, reveal, make known, disclose, divulge, declare, avow. 3 *admit that you may be right* concede, accept, grant, agree, allow, concur.

**admittance** noun entry, access. *See* ADMISSION 1.

**admonish** verb 1 *admonish the boys for smoking* reprimand, rebuke, scold, reprove, upbraid, chide, censure, berate. 2 *she admonished us to seek help* advise, urge, counsel, exhort.

**admonition** noun 1 *deliver an admonition to the culprits* reprimand, rebuke, scolding. 2 *gave them an admonition to seek help* piece of advice, warning, exhortation; advice.

**ado** noun fuss, trouble, bother, commotion, upset, agitation, hubbub, confusion, disturbance, flurry, to-do.

**adolescent** adjective teenage, youthful, pubescent, immature, juvenile, childish, puerile.

**adolescent** noun teenager, youngster, young person, youth.

**adopt** verb 1 *adopt Eastern customs* assume, take on, affect, embrace, espouse, appropriate. 2 *adopt a candidate* select, choose, vote for. 3 *adopt the new measures* approve, endorse, accept, ratify.

**adoption** noun 1 *the adoption of Asian customs* assumption, taking on, affecting, espousal, appropriation. 2 *the adoption of the candidate* selection, choosing, voting for. 3 *the adoption of the new measures* approval, endorsement, acceptance, ratification.

**adorable** adjective lovable, appealing, charming, sweet, enchanting, captivating, dear, darling, delightful, attractive, winsome, winning, fetching.

**adoration** noun 1 *the adoration of their children* love, doting, devotion, idolization. 2 *the adoration of God* worship, glorification, praise, homage, exaltation, veneration. 3 *their adoration of travel* love, liking, enjoyment.

**adore** verb **1** *adore their children* love, be devoted to, dote on, cherish, hold dear, idolize. **2** *let us adore God* worship, glorify, praise, revere, reverence, exalt, magnify, laud, extol, venerate. **3** *they adore ice cream* like, love, be fond of, enjoy, delight in, relish.

**adorn** verb decorate, embellish, ornament, trim, enhance, beautify, bedeck, deck, array, grace, emblazon.

**adornment** noun decoration, embellishment, ornamentation, trimming, enhancement, beautification, enrichment, ornament, frills, accessories, trimmings.

**adrift** adjective drifting, unmoored, unanchored, aimless, purposeless, directionless, awry, amiss, astray, off course.

**adroit** adjective skillful, skilled, expert, adept, dexterous, deft, clever, able, capable, competent, masterly, proficient, quick-thinking, quick-witted, cunning, astute, shrewd.

**adulation** noun worship, hero-worship, idolization, adoration, glorification; praise, flattery, blandishments.

**adult** adjective **1** *an adult tree* mature, grown-up, full-grown, fully developed; *fml.* of age. **2** *adult magazines* sexually explicit, obscene, pornographic.

**adulterate** verb debase, degrade, spoil, contaminate, taint, doctor, water down.

**advance** verb **1** *the army advanced* move forward, proceed, go ahead, move along, press on, push forward, make headway, forge ahead, gain ground. **2** *advance the building schedule* speed up, accelerate, step up, hasten, expedite, hurry, quicken, forward. **3** *advance his chances of promotion* further, forward, help, assist, facilitate, boost, improve. **4** *her career advanced rapidly* progress, develop, improve. **5** *advance a theory* put forward, suggest, propose, submit. **6** *the company advanced him $500* lend, supply on credit.

**advance** noun **1** *the advance of the army* movement forward, progress, headway. **2** *the advance of civilization* progress, development, advancement, improvement, betterment, furtherance. **3** *recent medical advances* development, discovery, breakthrough, finding, invention.

**advance** adjective **1** *the advance party* sent ahead, leading, first. **2** *advance warning* early, previous, prior, beforehand.

**advanced** adjective progressive, forward, highly developed, modern, ultramodern, avant-garde, ahead of the times.

**advances** plural noun approaches, overtures, moves, proposals, propositions.

**advantage** noun **1** *its main advantage is size* benefit, asset, good point, boon, blessing. **2** *the advantage of age* benefit, superiority, dominance, supremacy, power, mastery, upper hand, trump card. **3** *not to one's advantage* benefit, profit, gain, good.

**advantageous** adjective **1** *an advantageous position* favorable, superior, dominant, powerful. **2** *advantageous to your career* beneficial, helpful, useful, valuable, profitable.

**advent** noun arrival, coming, appearance, approach, occurrence.

**adventure** noun **1** *a spirit of adventure* risk, hazard, danger, peril, gamble, gambling. **2** *the sailor's adventures* exploit, deed, feat, experience.

**adventurous** adjective daring, daredevil, bold, intrepid, audacious, adventuresome, venturesome, risky, dangerous, perilous, hazardous.

**adversary** noun opponent, antagonist, rival, enemy, foe, competitor.

**adverse** adjective **1** *adverse circumstances* unfavorable, unlucky, disadvantageous, inauspicious, unpropitious. **2** *adverse criticism* hostile, unfriendly, unfavorable, antagonistic, negative. **3** *adverse to health* harmful, dangerous, injurious, detrimental, hurtful.

**adversity** noun misfortune, ill luck, bad luck, trouble, hardship, distress, disaster, suffering, affliction, sorrow, misery, tribulation, woe, hard times, mishap, accident, shock, reverse, setback, catastrophe, calamity.

**advertise** verb **1** *advertise the results* make known, publicize, announce, broadcast, proclaim, call attention to, promulgate. **2** *advertise a product* promote, publicize, give publicity to, display, tout; *inf.* push, plug.

**advertisement** noun **1** *a newspaper advertisement* notice, announcement; *inf.* ad; display ad, want ad, classified ad. **2** *a television advertisement* promotion, commercial, blurb; *inf.* ad, plug. **3** *product advertisement* advertising, promotion, publicizing, touting; *inf.* plugging, pushing.

**advice** noun guidance, counseling, counsel, help, recommendations, suggestions, hints, tips.

**advisable** adjective desirable, sensible, sound, prudent, proper, appropriate, suitable, fitting, apt, judicious, expedient, politic.

**advise** verb **1** *cannot advise you on your affairs | advise caution* guide, counsel, instruct; suggest, recommend, urge. **2** *advise you of the facts* inform, notify, apprise, acquaint with, warn.

**adviser, advisor** noun counselor, mentor, guide, consultant, coach, teacher, therapist.

**advocate** verb recommend, advise, favor, support, uphold, back, subscribe to, champion, speak for, campaign on behalf of, argue/plead/press for, urge, promote.

**advocate** noun **1** *an advocate of political freedom* supporter, upholder, backer, champion, spokesman, spokeswoman, speaker, campaigner, pleader, promoter, proponent, exponent, apostle, apologist. **2** *the defendant's advocate* counsel, lawyer, attorney.

**aegis** noun protection, guardianship, support, patronage, sponsorship, auspices.

**affable** adjective friendly, amiable, genial, congenial, cordial, pleasant, agreeable, easygoing, good-humored, good-natured, sociable.

**affair** noun **1** *that's my own affair* concern, business, matter, responsibility. **2** *forget the sad affair* event, happening, occurrence, incident, episode, circumstance, adventure, case. **3** *an informal affair* party, function, reception, gathering; *inf.* get-together, do. **4** *an affair with a married man* love affair, relationship, romance, liaison, affair of the heart, intrigue, amour.

**affect** verb **1** *it affected his health* have an effect on, influence, act on, work on, have an impact on, change, alter, transform. **2** *the disease affected his lungs* attack, strike at, infect. **3** *the experience deeply affected us* move, touch, upset, disturb.

**affectation** noun pretense, pretension, pretentiousness, affectedness, artificiality, insincerity, posturing.

**affected** adjective **1** *an affected style of writing* pretentious, artificial, unnatural, assumed, high-flown, ostentatious, contrived, pompous, mannered. **2** *an affected politeness* pretended, feigned, fake, counterfeit, sham, simulated.

**affection** noun love, liking, fondness, warmth, devotion, caring, attachment, friendship, amity, warm feelings.

**affectionate** adjective loving, fond, devoted, caring, tender, doting.

**affiliate** verb associate, unite, combine, join, ally.

**affiliation** noun connection, link, bond, tie, relationship.

**affirm** verb state, assert, declare, aver, proclaim, pronounce, swear, attest.

**afflict** verb trouble, burden, distress, beset, harass, oppress, torment, plague, rack, smite.

**affliction** noun trouble, distress, pain, misery, suffering, wretchedness, hardship, misfortune, sorrow, torment, tribulation, woe, disorder, disease, trial, ordeal, scourge, plague.

**affluence** noun wealth, prosperity, opulence, fortune, richness, riches, resources.

**affluent** adjective rich, wealthy, prosperous, opulent, well off, moneyed, well-to-do, comfortable; *inf.* well-heeled, in the money, loaded.

**afford** verb **1** *afford a house* pay for, meet the expense of, spare the price of. **2** *afford the loss* bear, sustain, stand. **3** *the tree affords shade/fruit* provide, supply, offer, give, impart, bestow, furnish, yield, produce, bear.

**affront** noun insult, offense, indignity, slight, snub, outrage; *inf.* slap in the face.

**afraid** adjective **1** *noises made them afraid* frightened, scared, terrified, apprehensive, fearful, nervous, alarmed (at), intimidated (by), terror-stricken. **2** *I'm afraid I can't help* sorry, regretful, apologetic, unhappy.

**aftermath** noun aftereffects, effects, consequences, results; end result, outcome, upshot, issue, end.

**against** preposition **1** *people against the movement* opposed to, in opposition to, hostile to, at odds with, in disagreement with, versus. **2** *rowing against the tide* in opposition to, counter to, resisting. **3** *leaning against the fence* touching, in contact with, close up to, up against, abutting. **4** *his age is against him* disadvantageous to, unfavorable to, damaging to, detrimental to, prejudicial to.

**age** noun **1** *what is his age?* number of years, lifetime, duration, stage of life, generation. **2** *wisdom comes with age* maturity, seniority, elderliness, old age, advancing years, declining years, senescence. **3** *the Elizabethan age* era, epoch, period, time.

**age** verb mature, ripen, grow up, come of age; grow old, decline, wither, fade.

**aged** adjective old, elderly, superannuated; *fml.* senescent; *inf.* as old as the hills.

**agency** noun **1** *advertising agency* business, organization, company, firm, office, bureau, concern. **2** *brought together through the agency of friends* mediation, intervention, intercession.

**agenda** noun program, schedule, timetable, plan, list, scheme.

**agent** noun **1** *an insurance agent* representative, negotiator, emissary; *inf.* rep. **2** *an enemy agent* spy, secret agent; *inf.* mole. **3** *a cleansing agent* factor, cause, instrument, vehicle, means, power, force.

**ages** plural noun a long time, an eternity, an eon; hours, days, months, years, eons, hours/days/months on end.

**aggravate** verb **1** *aggravate the situation* worsen, exacerbate, inflame, intensify, increase, heighten, magnify. **2** *aggravate the* *teacher irritate*, irk, get on one's nerves, rub the wrong way; *inf.* needle. *See* ANGER verb.

**aggravation** noun **1** *the aggravation of the situation* worsening, exacerbation, intensification. **2** *the aggravation of the teacher* annoyance, irritation, angering, exasperation, provocation. **3** *just one more aggravation* irritant, nuisance, pest, thorn in the flesh; *inf.* headache.

**aggression** noun attack, assault, injury, encroachment, offense, onslaught, foray, raid, sortie, offensive, invasion.

**aggressive** adjective **1** *an aggressive person/act* quarrelsome, argumentative, belligerent, pugnacious, militant, warring, hostile, combative, bellicose, invasive, intrusive. **2** *aggressive sales promotion* assertive, forceful, insistent, vigorous, energetic, dynamic, bold, enterprising, zealous; *inf.* pushy.

**aggressor** noun attacker, assaulter, invader, assailant, provoker, instigator, initiator.

**agile** adjective active, nimble, spry, lithe, fit, supple, sprightly, in good condition, lively, quick-moving, limber.

**agility** noun activeness, nimbleness, litheness, fitness, suppleness.

**agitate** verb **1** *she was agitated by the delay* upset, work up, perturb, fluster, ruffle, disconcert. **2** *agitate the mixture* stir, whisk, beat, churn, shake, toss. **3** *agitate the crowd* stir up, rouse, arouse, excite, inflame, incite, foment.

**agitator** noun troublemaker, instigator, agent provocateur, inciter, rabble-rouser, provoker, fomenter, firebrand, revolutionary, demagogue.

**agonizing** adjective excruciating, harrowing, racking, painful, acute, insufferable, torturous.

**agony** noun suffering, pain, hurt, distress, torture, torment, anguish, misery, woe; pangs, throes.

**agree** verb **agree on** settle on, arrange, arrive at, decide on. **agree to** consent to, accept, approve, acquiesce in, assent to, concede to, allow, admit, grant. **agree with 1** *agree with you* concur with, be of the same mind/opinion with, see eye to eye with. **2** *the statements do not agree with each other* match, correspond to, conform to, harmonize with. **3** *the warm climate agrees with me* suit, be good for.

**agreeable** adjective **1** *agreeable occasion/manner* pleasant, pleasing, delightful, enjoyable, pleasurable, likable, charming, amiable, nice, friendly, good-natured. **2** *if you want us to go, we are agreeable* willing, amenable, compliant.

**agreement** noun **1** *in total agreement* accord, assent, concurrence, harmony, unity, concord. **2** *a business agreement* contract, compact, treaty, covenant, concordat, pact; *inf.* deal. **3** *the agreement of the statements* correspondence, conformity, harmony.

**aid** verb **1** *aid us in our effort* help, assist, support, lend a hand, succor, sustain. **2** *aid recovery* hasten, facilitate, promote.

**aid** noun **1** *give aid to a motorist* help, assistance, support, a helping hand, succor, encouragement. **2** *foreign aid* contribution, subsidy, gift, donation.

**aide** noun assistant, helper, help; *inf.* right arm, girl/man Friday.

**ailing** adjective ill, unwell, sick, sickly, poorly, weak, indisposed, under the weather.

**ailment** noun illness, disease, disorder, sickness, complaint, infection.

**aim** verb **1** *aim a gun* point, direct, take aim, train, sight, focus, position. **2** *aim to increase profits* plan, intend, resolve, propose. **aim at/for** set one's sights on, try for, strive for, work toward, aspire to.

**aim** noun **1** *the archer's aim* pointing, directing, training; line of sight. **2** *our aim is to win* goal, ambition, objective, object, end, target, intention, plan, purpose.

**aimless** adjective purposeless, pointless, goalless, undirected, unambitious, drifting, wandering.

**air** noun **1** *propelled through the air* atmosphere, sky, heavens, aerospace. **2** *let's get some air* breeze, breath of air, gust/movement of wind, zephyr, draft. **3** *an air of peace* impression, appearance, look, atmosphere, mood, ambience, aura, manner, feeling. **4** *playing an old air* tune, melody, song, theme, strain.

**air** verb **1** *air the room* ventilate, aerate, freshen. **2** *air one's views* express, voice, publish, vent, communicate, reveal, proclaim.

**airs** plural noun affectedness, posing, posturing; affectations, pretensions.

**airy** adjective **1** *an airy day* breezy, windy, gusty. **2** *an airy office* well-ventilated, spacious, open. **3** *an airy being* delicate, insubstantial, ethereal, flimsy, wispy, incorporeal. **4** *an airy reply* lighthearted, breezy, flippant, blithe, nonchalant.

**akin** adjective **akin to** related to, similar to, corresponding to.

**alarm** noun **1** *a burglar alarm* warning, signal, bell, siren, alert. **2** *rumors causing alarm* fear, fright, terror, apprehension, panic, trepidation, nervousness, anxiety.

**alarm** verb **1** *crowds alarm her* frighten, scare, terrify, panic, unnerve, distress, intimidate. **2** *saw the fire and alarmed the neighborhood* warn, alert, arouse, signal.

**alarming** adjective frightening, disturbing, terrifying, startling, shocking, distressing.

**alcohol** noun liquor, spirits; *inf.* booze, firewater, hooch, rotgut, hard stuff.

**alcoholic** adjective intoxicating, inebriating, strong, hard.

**alcoholic** noun hard/heavy drinker, dipsomaniac, drunk, drunkard, tippler, sot, toper, inebriate, imbiber; *inf.* boozer, lush, alky, tosspot, wino.

**alert** adjective wide awake, sharp, bright, quick, keen, perceptive; *inf.* on the ball, on one's toes. **alert to** wide awake to, on the lookout for, aware of, heedful of, watchful of, attentive to, wary of, on one's guard for; *fml.* on the qui vive for.

**alias** noun assumed/false name, pseudonym, stage name, nom de plume, sobriquet, nom de guerre.

**alibi** noun defense, plea, justification, explanation, reason, vindication, excuse, pretext.

**alien** adjective **1** *an alien culture* foreign, overseas, nonnative, strange, unfamiliar, unknown, remote, exotic. **2** *alien to his principles* opposed, conflicting, contrary, adverse, incompatible, inimical.

**alien** noun **1** *aliens deported in wartime* foreigner, outsider, stranger. **2** *aliens from Mars* extraterrestrial, *inf.* E.T., little green man.

**alienate** verb estrange, set against, turn away, make hostile, sever, divorce, separate, cut off, divide.

**align** verb **1** *align the books on the shelves* line up, arrange, put in order. **2** *align with a political party* affiliate, ally, associate, join, side, sympathize, agree.

**alike** adjective like, similar, the same, indistinguishable.

**alike** adverb *think alike* similarly, the same, identically, in like manner.

**alive** adjective **1** *the captives are still alive* living, live, breathing; *inf.* in the land of the living, alive and kicking; *fml.* animate. **2** *interest is still very much alive* active, continuing, going on, existing, in the air/wind, in operation. **3** *seeming very much alive today* lively, active, energetic, alert, animated, vivacious, vigorous, vital, spirited. **4** *alive to the possibilities* alert to, awake to, aware/cognizant of. **5** *alive with vermin* overflowing, teeming, crowded, packed, swarming; *inf.* crawling, hopping.

**all** noun everyone, everybody, every/each person/thing, everything, the whole/total amount, the entirety; *inf.* the whole lot; lock, stock, and barrel.

**allay** verb *allay suffering* lessen, diminish. *See* ASSUAGE 1.

**allegation** noun claim, charge, accusation, declaration, statement, assertion.

**allege** verb claim, profess, declare, state, assert, aver, avow, affirm.

**alleged** adjective supposed, so-called, claimed, designated.

**allegiance** noun loyalty, obedience, fidelity, faithfulness, duty, devotion, constancy, adherence, homage; *fml.* fealty.

**alleviate** verb *alleviate poverty* reduce, ease, abate. *See* ASSUAGE 1.

**alley** noun alleyway, lane, passage, passageway, path, pathway, corridor, backstreet.

**alliance** noun **1** *form an alliance* union, association, coalition, league, confederation, federation, partnership. **2** *the alliance between physics and math* affinity, association, relationship.

**allocate** verb allot, assign, distribute, give out, share/mete/parcel out, dispense, apportion.

**allot** verb **1** *we allotted money for expenses* set aside, designate, earmark, assign, appropriate. **2** *allot portions to everyone* distribute, dispense. *See* ALLOCATE.

**allow** verb **1** *allow them to enter* permit, let, authorize, sanction; *inf.* give the go-ahead to, give the green light to. **2** *allow $50 for expenses* allocate, allot, assign. **3** *I allow that you won* admit, acknowledge, concede, grant. **allow for** *allow for wastage* plan for, take into consideration/account, make provision for, provide for.

**allowable** adjective permissible, admissible, authorized, sanctioned, justifiable, legitimate; *inf.* legit.

**allowance** noun **1** *father gives her an allowance* remittance, payment, subsidy, grant, contribution. **2** *our book allowance* allocation, quota, share, ration, portion. **3** *tax/business allowances* rebate, discount, deduction, reduction, concession. **make allowances for** take into consideration/account, bear in mind, have regard to; make excuses for, excuse, forgive, pardon.

**alloy** noun compound, mixture, amalgam, blend, combination, admixture, composite.

**all right** adjective **1** *the children are all right* safe, safe and sound, secure, unharmed, well, fine; *inf.* OK. **2** *the coffee's all right?* satisfactory, acceptable, adequate, passable; *inf.* OK.

**all right** adverb **1** *reached home all right* safely; *inf.* OK. **2** *worked out all right* satisfactorily, acceptably, fine; *inf.* OK.

**allude** verb **allude to** refer to, mention, touch upon, mention in passing, cite.

**allure** verb attract, fascinate, entice, seduce, charm, enchant, bewitch, beguile, captivate, tempt, lure.

**allusion** noun reference, citation, mention, hint, intimation, suggestion.

**ally** noun confederate, partner, associate, accomplice, colleague, helper, accessory, abettor.

**almost** adverb nearly, close to, just about, not quite, all but, not far from, approximately, practically, as good as, virtually, approaching, verging on, bordering on.

**alone** adjective/adverb **1** *be alone in the house* by oneself, solitary, unaccompanied, unattended, unescorted, companionless. **2** *succeed alone* single-handed, single-handedly, unassisted, unaided. **3** *left (all) alone* solitary, lonely, deserted, abandoned, forsaken, forlorn, desolate, isolated. **4** *house standing alone* separate, detached, apart, unconnected. **5** *in his field the professor stands alone* unique, unparalleled, unequaled, unsurpassed, matchless, peerless. **6** *you alone can help* only, solely, just, exclusively, no one else but, nothing but.

**aloof** adjective distant, detached, unresponsive, remote, unapproachable, standoffish, indifferent, unsympathetic, unsociable, unfriendly, cold, chilly.

**alter** verb change, make different, adjust, adapt, modify, convert, remodel, vary, transform, metamorphose.

**alteration** noun change, adjustment, adaptation, modification, revision, transformation, metamorphosis.

**alternate** adjective every other, every second; in rotation, rotating, occurring in turns, following in sequence, sequential; different. *See* ALTERNATIVE adjective 1.

**alternate** verb take turns, rotate, interchange, oscillate.

**alternative** adjective **1** *an alternative route* another, other, second, different. **2** *alternative medicine* nonstandard, unconventional, nonconventional.

**alternative** noun choice, option, preference, election, substitute.

**altitude** noun height, elevation; tallness, loftiness.

**altogether** adverb **1** *altogether content* completely, thoroughly, totally, entirely, absolutely, fully, utterly. **2** *altogether the day was fine* on the whole, all things considered, all in all, by and large. **3** *nine of us altogether* in all, all told, *in toto*, taken together.

**altruistic** adjective unselfish, selfless, public-spirited, philanthropic, humanitarian, benevolent, charitable.

**always** adverb **1** *he always comes early* every time, on every occasion, consistently, invariably, without exception, unfailingly. **2** *she's always complaining* continually, constantly, forever, repeatedly, perpetually, incessantly. **3** *he will love her always* forever, forever and ever, evermore, eternally, ever.

**amass** verb accumulate, pile/heap up, hoard, store up, assemble, garner; *inf.* stash away.

**amateur** noun nonprofessional, dilettante, layman, tyro, dabbler.

**amateurish** adjective unprofessional, inexperienced, incompetent, clumsy, bungling.

**amaze** verb astonish, astound, surprise, dumbfound, flabbergast, shock, stun, startle, stupefy; *inf.* bowl over.

**amazement** noun astonishment, surprise, shock, bewilderment, stupefaction, wonder.

**ambassador** noun diplomat, consul, envoy, emissary, legate, attaché, plenipotentiary.

**ambiguity** noun doubtfulness, obscurity, vagueness, uncertainty, abstruseness, equivocation, double-talk, puzzle, enigma, paradox.

**ambiguous** adjective equivocal, two-edged; cryptic, obscure, doubtful, unclear, vague, abstruse, puzzling, enigmatic.

**ambition** noun **1** *ambition to succeed* desire, aspiration, drive, eagerness, zeal, longing; *inf.* get-up-and-go. **2** *an ambition to be boss* goal, aim, objective, wish, dream.

**ambitious** adjective **1** *an ambitious man* aspiring, forceful, enterprising, zealous, purposeful, assertive. **2** *an ambitious task* challenging, demanding, exacting, formidable, arduous, difficult, bold.

**ambivalent** adjective *an ambivalent attitude* uncertain, doubtful, fluctuating, vacillating, opposing, conflicting, clashing.

**amenable** adjective **1** *amenable to suggestion* agreeable, responsive, pliant, flexible, adaptable, manageable. **2** *amenable to the law* accountable, answerable, subject, liable, responsible.

**amend** verb **1** *amend a text* revise, alter, correct, modify. **2** *amend the situation* improve, remedy, ameliorate, better, fix, set right.

**amendment** noun **1** *amendment of the text* revision, alteration, correction, modification. **2** *amendment of the situation* improvement, amelioration, betterment, fixing. **3** *amendment to the bylaws* alteration, addendum, attachment, appendage.

**amends** plural noun *make amends for the mistake* compensation, recompense, reparation.

**amiable** adjective friendly, pleasant, agreeable, pleasing, charming, delightful, good-natured.

**amicable** adjective *an amicable settlement* friendly, civil, harmonious, nonhostile.

**amiss** adjective *something was amiss* wrong, awry, faulty, out of order, unsatisfactory, inappropriate.

**ammunition** noun **1** *ammunition for the guns* bullets, cartridges, shells, shot, slugs, grenades, gunpowder, bombs, missiles. **2** *his speech ran out of ammunition* information, data, points, arguments.

**amnesty** noun pardon, reprieve, absolution, forgiveness, dispensation.

**amorous** adjective loving, passionate, sexual, lustful, erotic, amatory.

**amorphous** adjective formless, shapeless, unstructured, indeterminate, ill-organized, vague, nebulous; *fml.* inchoate.

**amount** noun **1** *a large amount of experience* quantity, measure, mass, volume, bulk, expanse. **2** *calculate the (full) amount* total, grand/sum total; *inf.* whole kit and caboodle, whole shebang.

**amount** verb **amount to 1** *the bill amounted to $50* add up to, total, come to, run to. **2** *their silence amounts to a confession* equal, add up to, be equivalent to. **3** *he never amounted to anything* become, grow/develop/mature into, progress/advance to.

**ample** adjective **1** *ample food to live on* enough, sufficient, adequate, more than enough. **2** *an ample supply of wine* plentiful, abundant, copious, generous, liberal, bountiful, plenteous. **3** *an ample bed* substantial, extensive, wide, spacious, roomy, capacious, commodious.

**amplify** verb increase, boost, magnify, intensify, heighten, augment, expand, enlarge on, elaborate on, add to, develop, flesh out, expound on.

**amuse** verb **1** *the clowns amused them* entertain, gladden, cheer, please, charm, delight, divert, beguile. **2** *amuse yourselves when I'm out* occupy, interest, entertain, divert, absorb, engross.

**amusement** noun **1** *smile with amusement* mirth, laughter, fun, merriment, gaiety, hilarity, enjoyment, pleasure, delight. **2** *a range of amusements* entertainment, diversion, interest, recreation, sport, pastime, hobby.

**amusing** adjective humorous, funny, comical, witty, entertaining, facetious, droll, jocular.

**analogy** noun similarity, parallel, correspondence, likeness, resemblance, correlation.

**analysis** noun breakdown, dissection, examination, study, investigation, review, evaluation, interpretation.

**analytical, analytic** adjective investigative, inquiring, dissecting, inquisitive, critical.

**analyze** verb break down, dissect, separate out, examine, study, investigate, inquire into, review, evaluate, interpret.

**anarchist** noun revolutionary, nihilist, rebel, insurgent, terrorist.

**anarchy** noun lawlessness, misgovernment, misrule, revolution, riot, disorder, chaos, rebellion, mutiny, tumult, mayhem.

**anatomy** noun **1** *the anatomy of dogs* structure, makeup, composition, framework. **2** *the anatomy of crime* analysis, examination, study, investigation, scrutiny, research, inquiry.

**ancestor** noun forebear, progenitor, forerunner, precursor, prototype.

**ancestry** noun lineage, descent, extraction, parentage, origin, derivation, genealogy, pedigree, blood, stock, ancestors, antecedents, forefathers, forebears, progenitors, family tree.

**anchor** noun mooring, stability, security, mainstay, support, protection.

**anchor** verb secure, fasten, moor, attach, connect, bind.

**ancient** adjective **1** *ancient times* earliest, early, primeval, prehistoric, primordial. **2** *an ancient custom* age-old, time-worn, antique, long-lived. **3** *ancient ideas* antiquated, old-fashioned, outmoded, archaic, obsolete, passé, superannuated, atavistic.

**anecdote** noun story, tale, narrative, yarn, sketch, reminiscence.

**anemic** adjective weak, pale, wan, colorless, pallid, ashen, feeble, powerless, impotent, ineffective, ineffectual, enervated.

**anesthetic** noun narcotic, opiate, soporific, stupefacient, painkiller, sedative, analgesic.

**anesthetic** adjective numbing, deadening, dulling, narcotic, soporific, stupefacient, painkilling, sedative, analgesic.

**anew** adverb again, afresh, once more, once again.

**angel** noun **1** *heavenly angels* messenger of god, heavenly messenger, archangel, seraph, cherub. **2** *thanks! you're an angel* darling, dear, gem, saint. **3** *the play depends on angels* backer, supporter, benefactor, promoter.

**angelic** adjective celestial, heavenly, ethereal, virtuous, innocent, pure, good, saintly.

**anger** noun annoyance, rage, fury, indignation, temper, wrath, exasperation, irritation, vexation, ire, outrage, pique, spleen, choler.

**anger** verb annoy, infuriate, enrage, exasperate, irritate, incense, madden, vex, outrage, provoke, nettle, rile, pique, gall.

**angle** noun **1** *the angle of the walls* intersection, projection, corner, bend, fork, recess, elbow. **2** *a news angle* slant, spin, approach, viewpoint.

**angry** adjective annoyed, furious, infuriated, indignant, enraged, irate, wrathful, exasperated, irritated, heated, incensed, maddened, ill-humored, hot-tempered, choleric, outraged, vexed, provoked; *inf.* mad, hot under the collar.

**angst** noun anxiety, fear, apprehension, foreboding, disquiet.

**anguish** noun suffering, sorrow, grief. *See* AGONY.

**animate** verb give life to, enliven, liven up, cheer up, gladden, vitalize; encourage, hearten, inspire, fire, rouse, stir, energize; *inf.* pep up.

**animate** adjective living, alive, live, moving, breathing.

**animated** adjective lively, energetic, active, vigorous, excited, enthusiastic, spirited, fiery, forceful, vital, vivacious.

**annex** verb **1** *annex a garage to the house* add, attach, join, connect. **2** *annex a country* take over, occupy, seize, conquer.

**annex** noun *a school annex* extension, wing, ell.

**annihilate** verb destroy, wipe out, exterminate, decimate, eliminate, liquidate, abolish, obliterate, eradicate, extinguish, erase.

**announce** verb **1** *announce the results* make known/public, give out, declare, proclaim, report, disclose, reveal, divulge, publicize, broadcast, publish, advertise, promulgate. **2** *announce a guest* name, herald, usher in. **3** *cigar smoke announced his approach* signal, indicate, signify, give notice of, warn, foretell, herald.

**announcement** noun declaration, proclamation, disclosure, report, statement, bulletin, communiqué, message.

**announcer** noun commentator, presenter, newscaster, broadcaster, reporter, anchor, master of ceremonies, emcee.

**annoy** verb irritate, exasperate, vex, ruffle, rile, irk, provoke, displease, anger, madden, rub one the wrong way, get on one's nerves, bother, disturb, pester, worry, harry, get to; *inf.* bug.

**annul** verb nullify, declare null and void, quash, cancel, invalidate, rescind, revoke, repeal, abrogate, void, negate.

**anonymous** adjective unnamed, nameless, unidentified, unknown, unspecified, undesignated.

**answer** noun **1** *receive an answer* reply, response, acknowledgment, rejoinder, retort, riposte; *inf.* comeback. **2** *the answer to the clue* solution, explanation, resolution. **3** *his answer to the charge* defense, plea, refutation, rebuttal, vindication.

**answer** verb **1** *answer a letter* reply to, respond to, acknowledge, react to. **2** *answer our requirements* meet, satisfy, fulfill, fill, measure up to. **3** *answer for her crimes* pay, suffer, atone. **4** *cannot answer for my sister* vouch for, be responsible for, be liable for, take the blame for; *inf.* take the rap for. **answer back** talk back, be impertinent, contradict, argue with, disagree with. **answer to** fit, match, correspond to, be similar to, conform to, correlate to.

**answerable** adjective responsible, accountable, liable.

**antagonism** noun hostility, opposition, animosity, antipathy, enmity, rivalry, competition, dissension, friction, conflict.

**antagonist** noun adversary, enemy, foe, opponent, rival, competitor, contender.

**antagonistic** adjective hostile, ill-disposed, opposed, dissenting, adverse, antipathetic, inimical, at odds with.

**antagonize** verb alienate, put against, estrange.

**anthem** noun hymn, psalm, song of praise, paean, chorale, chant, canticle.

**anthology** noun collection, compendium, treasury, compilation, miscellany; *lit.* garland.

**anticipate** verb **1** *anticipate trouble* expect, foresee, predict, forecast; count on, look for, prepare for, await; look forward to, look toward. **2** *anticipate his chess move* forestall, intercept, prevent. **3** *anticipate the invention of radio* antedate, predate.

**anticipation** noun expectation, prediction, preparation, awaiting, expectancy, hope, hopefulness.

**antics** plural noun pranks, capers, larks, tricks, romps, frolics, horseplay.

**antidote** noun cure, remedy, corrective, countermeasure, counteragent, antitoxin.

**antiquated** adjective out-of-date, old-fashioned, outmoded, passé, archaic, obsolete, antediluvian.

**antique** adjective **1** *antique furniture* antiquarian, old, vintage. **2** *antique customs* age-old, timeworn, early, earliest, prehistoric, primeval, primordial. **3** *antique attitudes* old-fashioned, passé.

**antique** noun heirloom, relic, curio, collectible, collector's item.

**antiseptic** adjective **1** *antiseptic surface* sterile, germ-free, uncontaminated, aseptic, sanitary, hygienic. **2** *antiseptic surroundings* clinical, characterless, undistinguished, unexciting.

**antithesis** noun opposite, converse, reverse, inverse, reversal.

**anxiety** noun **1** *anxiety about the future* worry, concern, uneasiness, apprehension, disquiet, nervousness, tenseness, misgiving, angst. **2** *full of anxiety to win* eagerness, desire, longing.

**anxious** adjective **1** *anxious about the future* worried, concerned, uneasy, apprehensive, fearful, nervous, disturbed, tense. **2** *anxious to please* eager, keen, avid.

**apart** adverb **1** *a person/house standing apart* to one side, aside, to the side, distant, isolated. **2** *blow/break apart* to pieces, in pieces, to bits, asunder. **apart from** *no one apart from him* except, but, other than, aside from, excluding.

**apartment** noun quarters, rooms, suite, flat; *inf.* pad, digs.

**apathetic** adjective uninterested, unconcerned, unfeeling, unemotional, unresponsive, indifferent, impassive, passive, listless.

**apathy** noun unconcern, unresponsiveness, indifference, impassivity, passivity, dispassion, dispassionateness, listlessness.

**ape** verb imitate, mimic, copy, echo, mock, parody, parrot.

**aperture** noun opening, gap, hole, orifice, window, crack, slit, space, chink, fissure, eye, interstice.

**apex** noun top, summit, peak, pinnacle, tip, crest, vertex, acme, zenith, apogee.

**aplomb** noun poise, assurance, self-confidence, self-assurance, composure, equanimity, levelheadedness, sang-froid.

**apocryphal** adjective unverified, unsubstantiated, spurious, debatable, questionable, dubious, doubtful, mythical, fictitious, false.

**apologetic** adjective sorry, regretful, contrite, remorseful, penitent, repentant, rueful.

**apologize** verb express regret, ask forgiveness, beg pardon; *inf.* eat humble pie.

**apology** noun **1** *deliver an apology* expression of regret; regrets. **2** *the apology for their beliefs* defense, justification, argument, apologia. **apology for** *an apology for a man* travesty of, poor excuse for, substitute for.

**appall** verb shock, dismay, horrify, outrage, astound, alarm.

**appalling** adjective shocking, horrifying, frightful, outrageous, dreadful.

**apparatus** noun **1** *gymnastic apparatus* equipment, gear, tackle, mechanism, appliance, machine, device, contraption, instruments, tools. **2** *government apparatus* structure, system, organization, network, setup.

**apparel** noun clothing, dress, attire, outfit, wear, costume, garb, habit; clothes, garments, robes, vestments; *inf.* gear, togs.

**apparent** adjective **1** *apparent from the start* clear, plain, obvious, evident, perceptible, manifest, patent. **2** *apparent calmness* seeming, ostensible, outward, superficial.

**apparition** noun **1** *frightened of the apparition* ghost, specter, phantom, spirit; *inf.* spook. **2** *the sudden apparition of the figure* manifestation, visitation. *See* APPEARANCE 1.

**appeal** noun **1** *an appeal for help* request, call, plea, entreaty, petition, supplication. **2** *an appeal of the decision* reconsideration, reexamination, review. **3** *hold little appeal* attraction, attractiveness, allure, charm, interest.

**appeal** verb **appeal for** *appeal for money* ask for, request, put in a plea for, entreat, beg/beseech/plead for, implore. **appeal to 1** *appeal to a higher authority* seek reconsideration/reexamination/review/another opinion from. **2** *appeals to her* attract, charm, interest, engage, fascinate.

**appear** verb **1** *a messenger/solution appeared* come into view/sight, emerge, come forth, arrive, turn/show/crop up, materialize, surface, loom. **2** *she appeared sad* seem, look, have the appearance/air of being. **3** *the new line of spring fashions has appeared* come into being/existence, come out, become available, come on the market.

**appearance** noun **1** *the appearance of the messenger/solution* emergence, arrival, advent, materialization, attendance, presence. **2** *an appearance of sadness* look, air, expression, manner, demeanor, bearing, mien. **3** *the appearance of being rich* semblance, guise, show, pretense, image, impression.

**appease** verb **1** *appease the enemy* placate, pacify, conciliate, tranquilize, soothe, quiet down, mollify, propitiate. **2** *appease one's appetite* satisfy, assuage, blunt, relieve, quench, diminish.

**append** verb add, attach, affix, adjoin.

**appendix** noun *appendix to a book* supplement, addendum, postscript, extension, codicil.

**appetite** noun hunger, taste, palate, desire, relish, thirst, need, liking, inclination, passion, longing, craving.

**appetizer** noun starter, hors d'oeuvre, antipasto, canapé.

**appetizing** adjective mouthwatering, tasty, succulent, delicious, palatable, tempting, inviting, enticing, appealing, alluring.

**applaud** verb **1** *the audience applauded* clap, cheer, whistle; *inf.* give someone a big hand. **2** *applaud their courage* praise, admire, compliment on, commend, acclaim, extol, laud.

**applause** noun **1** *the applause of the audience* clapping, handclapping, cheering, whistling, standing ovation; cheers, whistles, encores, bravos, curtain calls. **2** *won the applause of the neighborhood* praise, admiration, approval, approbation, acclaim; compliments, accolades, plaudits.

**applicable** adjective appropriate, pertinent, apposite, fitting, suitable, useful.

**applicant** noun candidate, interviewee, competitor, petitioner, suitor.

**application** noun **1** *the application of force* use, exercise, administration, employment, practice. **2** *a remark having no application to the case* relevance, bearing, significance, pertinence, aptness. **3** *an application for a job* request, claim, appeal, petition, entreaty.

**apply** verb **1** *apply the brakes* use, put to use, employ, utilize, administer, exercise. **2** *the remark did not apply to the situation* be relevant/significant/pertinent, be apt/apposite/germane. **3** *apply ointment* put on, rub in, cover with, spread, smear. **apply for** *apply for tax relief* put in for, try for, inquire after, request, seek, solicit. **apply oneself** be industrious/diligent/assiduous, study, work hard, make an effort.

**appoint** verb **1** *appoint him manager* name, designate, nominate, select, choose, elect. **2** *appoint a time* set, fix, arrange, establish, assign, designate, allot.

**appointment** noun **1** *cancel an appointment* meeting, engagement, date, interview, rendezvous, assignation, tryst. **2** *his appointment as manager* job, post, position, situation, place, office, station.

**appraise** verb *appraise his ability* assess, evaluate, sum up, estimate, gauge, judge, review; *inf.* size up.

**appreciable** adjective considerable, substantial, significant, sizable, visible, goodly.

**appreciate** verb **1** *appreciate your help* be thankful/grateful for, be indebted/beholden for. **2** *appreciate good work* value, prize, cherish, treasure, rate highly, respect, think highly of. **3** *appreciate its importance* recognize, acknowledge, realize, know, be aware of, be conscious/cognizant of, comprehend. **4** *appreciate in value* increase, gain, grow, rise, mount, inflate, escalate.

**appreciation** noun **1** *appreciation for their help* gratitude, thankfulness, indebtedness, obligation, thanks. **2** *appreciation of its importance* recognition, acknowledgment, realization, knowledge, awareness, cognizance. **3** *the appreciation of housing values* increase, rise, growth, inflation, escalation.

**appreciative** adjective grateful, thankful, indebted; responsive, supportive, sympathetic.

**apprehend** verb **1** *apprehend the criminal* arrest, catch, seize, capture, take prisoner, take into custody, haul in, detain; *inf.* collar, nab, nail, run in, bust. **2** *apprehend the significance* understand, grasp, realize, recognize, appreciate, comprehend.

**apprehension** noun **1** *full of apprehension* anxiety, dread, alarm, worry, unease, nervousness, fear, misgiving, disquiet, concern, trepidation, foreboding, presentiment, angst; *inf.* butterflies in the stomach, the willies, the heebie-jeebies. **2** *the apprehension of criminals* arrest, seizure, capture, detention.

**apprehensive** adjective anxious, alarmed, worried, uneasy, nervous, frightened, fearful.

**apprentice** noun trainee, learner, beginner, probationer, cub, greenhorn, tyro, novice, neophyte; *inf.* rookie.

**apprise** verb inform, notify, tell, let know; *inf.* clue in, fill in.

**approach** verb **1** *approach the house* draw near/nearer, come/go close/closer, draw nigh, catch up, gain on, near, advance. **2** *don't approach strangers* talk/speak to, greet, address, salute, hail. **3** *approach them for a contribution* broach the matter to, make advances/overtures to, make a proposal to, sound out. **4** *approach the task with care* set about, tackle, begin, start, commence, embark on, undertake. **5** *a price approaching $600* approximate, be comparable/similar to.

**approach** noun **1** *the approach of footsteps* advance, advent, arrival. **2** *the approach to the estate* driveway, drive, access, road, avenue, street, passageway. **3** *make an approach to|make approaches* appeal, proposal, proposition; advances, overtures. **4** *a new approach to teaching* method, procedure, technique, manner, modus operandi.

**appropriate** adjective suitable, fitting, befitting, proper, seemly, right, apt, relevant, pertinent, apposite, applicable, germane.

**appropriate** verb **1** *appropriate a country* take possession of, take over, seize, commandeer, expropriate, annex, arrogate. **2** *appropriate money for education* set apart/aside, assign, allot, allocate, earmark. **3** *appropriate company money* embezzle, misappropriate, steal, pilfer, pocket; *inf.* pinch, swipe; *fml.* peculate.

**approval** noun **1** *look on with approval* favor, liking, approbation, admiration. **2** *give approval to the plan* acceptance, agreement, consent, assent, sanction, endorsement, blessing, permission, confirmation, ratification; *inf.* the go-ahead, the green light, the OK.

**approve** verb accept, pass, agree to, sanction, consent/assent to, ratify, authorize, validate, accede to, acquiesce in, concur in; *inf.* give the go-ahead to, give the OK to, give the green light to, buy. **approve of** think well of, look on with favor, give one's blessing to, be pleased with.

**approximate** adjective rough, estimated, near, close, inexact.

**approximate** verb come close/near to, approach, border on, verge on, resemble, be similar to.

**approximately** adverb roughly, about, just about, around, circa, or so, more or less, in the neighborhood of, nearly, almost.

**approximation** noun **1** *200 is an approximation* guess, estimate, conjecture, rough idea, guesswork; *inf.* guesstimate. **2** *an approximation to the truth* semblance, similarity, likeness, correspondence.

**apropos** adjective appropriate, pertinent, relevant, apposite, apt, applicable, germane. **apropos of** concerning, with reference to, regarding, on the subject of, re.

**apt** adjective **1** *an apt remark* suitable, fitting, appropriate, felicitous, apropos. **2** *apt to get angry* inclined, given, likely, liable, disposed, prone. **3** *an apt student* quick, bright, sharp, clever. *See* ABLE.

**aptitude** noun talent, bent. *See* ABILITY 1, 2.

**aquatic** adjective water, sea, river, marine, maritime, fluvial.

**arable** adjective plowable, tillable, cultivable, farmable; fertile, productive, fruitful, fecund.

**arbitrary** adjective **1** *an arbitrary decision* discretionary, subjective, random, chance, whimsical, capricious, unreasonable, unsupported, irrational. **2** *an arbitrary ruler* despotic, tyrannical, tyrannous, absolute, autocratic, dictatorial, imperious, domineering, high-handed.

**arbitrate** verb adjudicate, judge, referee, umpire, settle, decide, determine.

**arc** noun curve, bow, arch, bend, crescent, half-moon, semicircle, curvature.

**arcane** adjective secret, mysterious, hidden, concealed, recondite, covert, enigmatic, inscrutable, abstruse, esoteric, cryptic, occult.

**arch-** prefix *archbishop / archenemy* chief, foremost, principal, leading, main, prime, primary, first, top, highest, greatest, preeminent.

**archaic** adjective old, obsolete, out-of-date, old-fashioned, outmoded, bygone, passé, antiquated, antique; *inf.* old hat.

**architect** noun designer, planner, author, engineer, creator, originator, deviser, instigator, founder, prime mover.

**archives** plural noun records, annals, chronicles, papers, documents, registers, rolls; history, documentation.

**arctic** adjective polar, freezing, frigid, frozen, icy, gelid, glacial, frosty, chilly, cold.

**ardent** adjective passionate, avid, impassioned, fervent, zealous, enthusiastic, intense, fierce, fiery, profound, consuming.

**ardor** noun passion, fervor, zeal, eagerness, enthusiasm, intensity, fierceness, fire.

**arduous** adjective taxing, difficult, hard, onerous, heavy, laborious, burdensome, exhausting, wearying, fatiguing, tiring, strenuous, grueling, punishing, Herculean.

**area** noun **1** *the area around the city* region, district, zone, sector, territory, tract, stretch, domain, realm, sphere. **2** *the area of the room* extent, size, expanse, scope, compass, range, measurements. **3** *in the area of finance* field, sphere, discipline, realm, domain.

**arena** noun **1** *circus/boxing arena* grounds, field, stadium, ballpark, ring, stage, amphitheater, coliseum; *inf.* park, bowl. **2** *the political arena* battleground, battlefield, area, scene, sphere, realm, domain.

**argue** verb **1** *please don't argue* disagree, quarrel, squabble, bicker, fight, dispute, feud. **2** *argue that they are right* assert, declare, maintain, insist, hold, claim, contend. **3** *argue the point* debate, dispute, discuss.

**argument** noun **1** *the couple had an argument* disagreement, quarrel, squabble, fight, difference of opinion, dispute, clash, altercation, controversy, feud; *inf.* tiff, falling out. **2** *stick to the argument that they are right* assertion, declaration, claim, plea, contention. **3** *the argument against capital punishment* reasoning, logic, case, defense, evidence, argumentation, polemic; reasons, grounds.

**argumentative** adjective quarrelsome, disputatious, contentious, combative, litigious.

**arid** adjective **1** *arid areas* dry, dried up, desert, parched, baked, scorched, barren. **2** *arid discussion* uninspiring, unstimulating, dull, dreary, drab, dry, colorless, flat, boring, uninteresting, lifeless, tedious.

**arise** verb **1** *a difficulty arose* appear, come to light, crop/turn up, spring up, emerge, occur. **2** *accidents arising from carelessness* result, proceed, follow, stem, originate. **3** *arise and go* rise, stand up, get up. **4** *birds arising* ascend, mount, climb, fly, soar.

**aristocrat** noun noble, nobleman, noblewoman, lord, lady, peer, peeress, patrician, Brahmin; *inf.* blue blood.

**aristocratic** adjective **1** *an aristocratic family* noble, titled, blue-blooded, highborn, upper-class, patrician, elite. **2** *aristocratic bearing* well-bred, dignified, courtly, refined, elegant, stylish, gracious, fine.

**arm** noun **1** *arms and legs* limb, forelimb, member, appendage. **2** *arm of the sea* inlet, estuary, channel, strait. **3** *an arm of the civil service* branch, offshoot, section, department, division.

**arm** verb **1** *arm with information* provide, supply, equip, furnish, issue. **2** *arm oneself against criticism* prepare, forearm, make ready, brace, steel, fortify, gird one's loins.

**armistice** noun truce, ceasefire, peace, suspension of hostilities.

**arms** plural noun **1** *carrying arms* weapons, firearms, guns, armaments, weaponry. **2** *the family arms* coat of arms, emblem, crest, insignia, escutcheon, shield, blazonry.

**army** noun **1** *the invading army* armed/military force, soldiery, infantry, troops, soldiers, land forces, military. **2** *an army of tourists* horde, pack, host, multitude, mob, crowd, swarm, throng, array.

**aroma** noun smell, scent, odor, bouquet, fragrance, perfume, redolence.

**aromatic** adjective fragrant, sweet-smelling, perfumed, balmy, spicy, savory, pungent, odoriferous.

**around** preposition **1** *around the tree* on all sides of, on every side of, circling, encircling, surrounding, encompassing. **2** *thrown around the room* about, here and there, all over, everywhere, in all parts of. **3** *around 9 o'clock* about, roughly. *See* APPROXIMATELY. **4** *turn around* in the opposite direction, in reverse, backward, to the rear.

**arouse** verb **1** *arouse them at dawn* rouse, awaken, waken, wake, wake up. **2** *arouse panic* cause, induce, stir up, inspire, kindle, provoke, foster, sow the seeds of. **3** *arouse the crowd* rouse, incite, excite, provoke, goad, prompt, spur on, egg on, animate, inflame.

**arrange** verb **1** *arrange the books* put in order, order, set out, group, sort, organize, tidy, dispose, align, line up, rank, file, classify, categorize, array, systematize. **2** *arrange to meet* settle on, decide, determine, agree, schedule, devise, contrive, make preparations, prepare, plan. **3** *music arranged for the piano* score, adapt, orchestrate.

**arrangement** noun **1** *the arrangement of flowers* order, ordering, grouping, organization, positioning, system, marshalling, alignment, classification, categorization, array. **2** *make an arrangement* preparation, plan, provision; agreement, contract, compact. **3** *a musical arrangement* score, adaptation, orchestration, instrumentation, harmonization.

**array** noun **1** *an array of bottles* collection, arrangement, assemblage, formation, disposition, muster, amassing, display, aggregation. **2** *in silken array* attire, apparel, clothing, dress, garments, garb, finery.

**array** verb **1** *array the troops* assemble, arrange, draw up, group, order, line up, place, position, dispose, muster, amass, agglomerate, aggregate. **2** *she arrayed herself in silk* attire, clothe, dress, fit out, garb, deck, robe, apparel, accoutre.

**arrest** verb **1** *arrest the thief* apprehend, take into custody, take prisoner, detain, seize, capture, catch, lay hold of, haul in; *inf.* run in, nab, pinch, collar, bust, nail, pick up. **2** *arrest the spread of disease* stop, halt, end, check, block, hinder, prevent, obstruct, inhibit, stay. **3** *arrest their attention* attract, capture, catch, catch hold of, grip, engage, absorb.

**arrest** noun **1** *the arrest of the thieves* apprehension, detention, seizure, capture. **2** *the arrest of the disease* stoppage, halt, ending, end, check, prevention, obstruction.

**arrival** noun **1** *the arrival of winter* coming, advent, appearance, entrance, entry, occurrence, approach. **2** *several recent arrivals* newcomer, visitor, visitant, guest.

**arrive** verb **1** *arrive on time* come, appear, enter, happen, occur, turn/show up; *inf.* blow in. **2** *the actor has really arrived* succeed, make good, reach the top, prosper, flourish, become famous, achieve recognition; *inf.* make it.

**arrogance** noun haughtiness, pride, self-importance, conceit, egotism, snobbishness, snobbery, pomposity, superciliousness, high-handedness, condescension, disdain, imperiousness, lordliness, presumption, pretentiousness; *inf.* uppitiness.

**arrogant** adjective haughty, proud, self-important, conceited, egotistic, snobbish, pompous, supercilious, overbearing, overweening, high-handed, condescending, disdainful, imperious, lordly, presumptuous, pretentious, insolent; *inf.* stuck-up, uppity, high and mighty.

**arrow** noun **1** *bow and arrow* shaft, bolt, dart. **2** *follow the arrows* pointer, indicator, marker.

**arsenal** noun arms depot, magazine, armory, ammunition dump, ordnance depot, repository; store, supply, stock, stockpile, storehouse.

**art** noun **1** *study art* painting, drawing, design, visual arts. **2** *the art of conversation* skill, craft, artistry, mastery.

**artful** adjective cunning, deceitful, wily, sly, crafty, duplicitous, designing, shrewd, politic.

**article** noun **1** *three black articles* object, thing, item; *inf.* thingamajig, thingama-bob, watchamacallit. **2** *a newspaper article* item, piece, story, feature, report, account, write-up. **3** *an article in the document* clause, section, paragraph, division.

**articulate** adjective **1** *an articulate speaker* eloquent, fluent, coherent, lucid, expressive, silver-tongued. **2** *an articulate speech* eloquent, clear, intelligible, comprehensible, lucid.

**articulate** verb enunciate, pronounce, voice, say, utter, express, vocalize.

**artifice** noun **1** *an artifice to mislead* trick, stratagem, ruse, dodge, subterfuge, machination, tactic, contrivance. **2** *win by using artifice* trickery, cunning, deceit, craftiness, artfulness, wiliness, duplicity, guile, chicanery.

**artificial** adjective **1** *artificial flowers* man-made, manufactured, synthetic, imitation, simulated, pseudo, ersatz, plastic, mock, sham, fake, bogus, counterfeit; *inf.* phony. **2** *an artificial smile* feigned, false, affected, unnatural, assumed, insincere, forced, strained.

**artist** noun painter, drawer, sculptor, craftsman, craftswoman, expert, adept, genius, past master, maestro.

**artistic** adjective **1** *an artistic person* creative, talented, gifted, imaginative, sensitive, cultivated. **2** *an artistic flower arrangement* decorative, beautiful, attractive, lovely, tasteful, graceful, stylish, elegant, aesthetic.

**artistry** noun art, skill, ability, talent, genius, brilliance, expertness, flair, gift, creativity, proficiency, virtuosity, craftsmanship, workmanship.

**artless** adjective natural, simple, childlike, naïve, ingenuous, guileless, sincere.

**ascend** verb climb, go/move up, mount, scale, rise, levitate, fly up, soar, slope upward.

**ascertain** verb find out, establish, discover, learn, determine, settle, verify, confirm; *inf.* pin down.

**ascetic** noun recluse, hermit, solitary, anchorite, abstainer, celibate, nun, monk, dervish, yogi.

**ascetic** adjective self-denying, abstinent, abstemious, self-disciplined, austere, frugal, rigorous, strict, celibate, spartan, puritanical.

**ascribe** verb attribute, assign, credit, put/set down to, chalk up to, impute, charge with, lay on, blame.

**ashamed** adjective **1** *ashamed of his conduct* humiliated, conscience-stricken, sorry, mortified, abashed, crestfallen, shame-faced, remorseful, discomfited, embarrassed, distressed, sheepish, red-faced. **2** *ashamed to say* reluctant, unwilling, hesitant.

**ashen** adjective pale, pale-faced, pallid, wan, white, colorless, anemic, washed out, bleached, ghostly, deathlike.

**asinine** adjective stupid, silly, idiotic, foolish, brainless, nonsensical, senseless, half-witted, fatuous, inane, imbecilic, moronic; *inf.* daft, dopey, balmy.

**ask** verb **1** *ask about it* inquire, question, query, interrogate, quiz, cross-examine; *inf.* grill, pump. **2** *ask the boss for a raise* request, demand, appeal to, entreat, beg, implore, beseech, plead, supplicate. **3** *ask them to dine* invite, bid, summon.

**askew** adverb/adjective sideways, awry, out of line.

**asleep** adjective/adverb sleeping, fast/sound asleep, slumbering, napping, catnapping, dozing, resting, dormant, comatose; *inf.* snoozing, dead to the world; *lit.* in the arms of Morpheus.

**aspect** noun **1** *every aspect of the problem* feature, facet, side, angle, slant, viewpoint, standpoint, light. **2** *a fierce aspect* appearance, look, expression, countenance, demeanor, bearing, features, mien. **3** *the southern aspect of the house* direction, situation, position, location, exposure. **4** *affording a pleasant aspect* outlook, view, scene, prospect.

**aspersions** plural noun *cast aspersions* disparagement, deprecation, denigration, defamation, slander.

**asphyxiate** verb choke, suffocate, smother, stifle, throttle, strangle, strangulate.

**aspiration** noun desire, longing, yearning, hankering, wish, ambition, hope, dream.

**aspire** verb desire, long to/for, yearn to/for, dream of, hunger for, seek, pursue.

**assail** verb **1** *assail the enemy with blows* attack, assault, set about, lay into, set upon, accost; *inf.* jump. **2** *assail with insults* bombard, berate, lash, abuse, criticize, harangue, revile, lambaste.

**assailant** noun attacker, mugger, aggressor, assaulter, accoster.

**assassin** noun murderer, killer, slayer, executioner, liquidator; *inf.* hit man, contract man.

**assassinate** verb murder, kill, slay, execute, liquidate, eliminate; *inf.* hit.

**assault** noun attack, onslaught, onset, charge, offensive.

**assault** verb attack, charge, strike, hit, mug, molest, rape.

**assemble** verb **1** *assemble the children* bring together, gather, collect, round up, marshal, muster, summon, accumulate, amass. **2** *the crowd assembled* come together, meet, congregate, convene. **3** *assemble the parts* put together, piece/fit together, build, fabricate, construct, connect, join.

**assembly** noun *talking to a crowded assembly* gathering, meeting, group, crowd, throng, congregation.

**assent** noun agreement, concurrence, acceptance, approval, consent, acquiescence, compliance, approbation, permission, sanction.

**assert** verb **1** *assert her innocence* declare, state, maintain, proclaim, contend, aver, swear, affirm, allege, claim. **2** *assert one's rights* uphold, press/push for, insist upon, stand up for, defend.

**assertive** adjective confident, self-assured, aggressive, forceful, dominant; *inf.* pushy.

**assess** verb **1** *assess the quality* evaluate, judge, gauge, rate, estimate, appraise. **2** *assess taxes* fix, evaluate, levy, impose.

**assessment** noun **1** *the assessment of quality* evaluation, judgment, gauging, estimation, appraisal. **2** *tax assessment* levy, charge, rate, toll, tariff, fee.

**asset** noun advantage, benefit, blessing, strong point, strength, boon, aid, help.

**assets** plural noun property, estate, capital, wealth, resources, holdings, possessions, effects, goods, belongings, chattels.

**assign** verb **1** *assign duties to all* allocate, allot, distribute, give out, dispense, apportion. **2** *assign him to the post* appoint, select, install, designate, nominate, name, delegate. **3** *assign Thursdays for trips* fix, appoint, decide on, determine, set aside/apart, stipulate, appropriate. **4** *assign her behavior to jealousy* ascribe, put down, attribute.

**assignment** noun **1** *carry out an assignment* task, job, duty, commission, charge, mission, responsibility, obligation. **2** *the assignment of duties* allocation, allotment, apportionment. **3** *his assignment to the post* appointment, selection, installation, nomination.

**assimilate** verb *assimilate food/facts* absorb, take in, incorporate, digest, ingest.

**assist** verb *assist the police* help, aid, lend a hand, succor, support, cooperate/collaborate with, abet, work with, play a part, help out, support, back, second.

**assistance** noun help, aid, succor, support, reinforcement, cooperation; a helping hand.

**assistant** noun **1** *her assistant is in charge* subordinate, deputy, auxiliary, second in command; *inf.* right-hand man/woman. **2** *an assistant in the project* helper, colleague, associate, partner, confederate, accomplice, accessory.

**associate** verb **1** *associate wine with France* link, connect, relate, think of together, couple. **2** *associate with criminals* mix, keep company, mingle, socialize, hobnob, fraternize; *inf.* run around, hang out.

**assorted** adjective mixed, varied, miscellaneous, diverse, motley, sundry, heterogeneous.

**assortment** noun mixture, variety, miscellany, selection, medley, mélange, jumble, mishmash, hodgepodge, potpourri.

**assuage** verb **1** *assuage the pain* relieve, ease, alleviate, soothe, mitigate, lessen, allay, moderate, diminish, calm, palliate, abate. **2** *assuage their thirst* appease, satisfy, relieve, slake, quench, dull, blunt, take the edge off.

**assume** verb **1** *assume he's coming* suppose, take for granted, presuppose, presume, imagine, expect, suspect, understand, gather, guess. **2** *assume a thorough knowledge* feign, pretend, simulate, put on. **3** *assume an air of authority* adopt, take on, acquire, come to have. **4** *assume a position of responsibility* undertake, set about, take on/up, embark on, take upon oneself, accept, shoulder. **5** *the invaders assumed power* seize, appropriate, usurp, commandeer.

**assumed** adjective *an assumed name* false, fictitious, fake, made-up, bogus; *inf.* phony.

**assumption** noun **1** *on the assumption that you're right* supposition, presupposition, presumption, premise, theory, hypothesis. **2** *the invaders' assumption of power* seizure, appropriation, usurpation. **3** *amazed at his assumption* arrogance, presumption, conceit, impertinence.

**assurance** noun **1** *you have my assurance that I'll be there* word of honor, word, guarantee, promise, pledge, affirmation. **2** *no assurance of her success* certainty, guarantee.

**assure** verb **1** *I assure you that he's wrong* declare to, affirm to, give one's word to, guarantee, promise, swear to, certify to, pledge to, vow to, attest to. **2** *they assured him of their ability* convince, persuade, reassure, prove to. **3** *assure their success* ensure, secure, guarantee, seal, clinch, confirm.

**astonish** verb amaze, astound, dumbfound, stagger, surprise, stun, take aback, confound, take one's breath away, flabbergast; *inf.* floor.

**astonishing** adjective amazing, astounding, staggering, surprising, breathtaking, striking, impressive, bewildering, stunning.

**astound** verb amaze, surprise. *See* ASTONISH.

**astounding** adjective amazing, surprising. *See* ASTONISHING.

**astute** adjective shrewd, sharp, perceptive, discerning, crafty, wily, perspicacious, sagacious.

**asylum** noun *seek political asylum* refuge, sanctuary, shelter, safety, safekeeping, protection; haven, retreat, harbor, port in a storm.

**atheist** noun nonbeliever, unbeliever, heretic, heathen, freethinker, nihilist, infidel.

**athletic** adjective muscular, powerful, robust, able-bodied, sturdy, strong, strapping, brawny.

**atmosphere** noun *a friendly atmosphere* environment, surroundings, milieu, medium, background, setting, air, ambience, aura, climate, feeling, character, tone.

**atom** noun iota, jot, bit, whit, particle, scrap, shred, trace, speck, spot, grain, morsel, mite.

**atone** verb make amends/reparation, compensate, recompense, expiate, do penance.

**atonement** noun reparation, compensation, recompense, redress, indemnity, restitution, expiation, penance, redemption.

**atrocious** adjective **1** *atrocious crimes* brutal, barbaric, barbarous, savage, vicious, wicked, cruel, ruthless, merciless, villainous, murderous, heinous, monstrous, fiendish, diabolical, flagrant, outrageous. **2** *atrocious weather* unpleasant, appalling, dreadful.

**atrocity** noun *the atrocity of war* abomination, enormity, outrage, horror, evil, monstrosity, brutality, cruelty, barbarity.

**attach** verb **1** *attach a label to the briefcase* fasten, fix, affix, join, connect, couple, link, secure, tie, stick, adhere, pin, hitch, bond. **2** *attach no significance to it* ascribe, assign, attribute, accredit. **3** *attaching their property* seize, confiscate, appropriate.

**attack** verb **1** *attack the enemy* assault, set/fall upon, strike at, rush, storm, charge, pounce upon, beset, besiege, beleaguer; strike, begin hostilities; *inf.* lay into, let one have it. **2** *attack the writer* criticize, censure, berate, reprove, rebuke, impugn, revile, fulminate against, vilify; *inf.* knock, slam. **3** *attack the work* set about, get/go to work on, get started on, undertake, embark on.

**attack** noun **1** *an attack on the enemy* assault, onslaught, offensive, onset, strike, charge, foray, rush, incursion, inroad. **2** *an attack on his writing* criticism, censure, rebuke, reproval, blame, revilement, vilification. **3** *an asthmatic attack* fit, bout, seizure, spasm, convulsion, paroxysm, stroke.

**attacker** noun assailant, aggressor, assaulter, mugger.

**attain** verb achieve, accomplish, obtain, gain, procure, secure, get, grasp, win, earn, acquire, reach, realize, fulfill, bring off.

**attempt** verb try, strive, aim, venture, endeavor, seek, undertake, essay, tackle, have a go/shot at; *inf.* have a crack at, give it a whirl.

**attempt** noun effort, try, endeavor, venture, trial, experiment, essay.

**attend** verb **1** *attend a meeting* appear, put in an appearance, turn up, visit, frequent, haunt; *inf.* show up, show. **2** *attend the sick* look after, care for, tend, nurse, mind, minister to. **3** *the president attended by top aides* accompany, escort, guard; chaperon, squire, convoy. **attend to** *attend to this matter* deal/cope with, see to, handle, take care of.

**attendance** noun **1** *attendance is not compulsory* presence, appearance. **2** *attendances vary* turnout, crowd, audience, house, gate.

**attendant** noun **1** *parking attendant* assistant, helper, auxiliary, steward, waiter, servant, menial. **2** *the queen and her attendants* companion, escort, aide, guard, custodian, guide.

**attention** noun **1** *give more attention to the problem* concentration, attentiveness, observation, heed, regard, contemplation, deliberation, scrutiny, thought. **2** *attract their attention* notice, awareness, observation, consciousness, recognition. **3** *for the personal attention of the manager* consideration, action, notice, investigation.

**attentive** adjective **1** *keen and attentive* alert, aware, awake, watchful, observant, heedful, mindful, vigilant, on guard, on the qui vive. **2** *an attentive host* considerate, thoughtful, courteous, gracious, conscientious, obliging, accommodating.

**attest** verb affirm, aver, asseverate, confirm, testify to, vouch for, bear witness to, bear out, endorse, back up, support, corroborate, verify, authenticate. **attest to** prove, demonstrate, evince, display, exhibit, show, manifest.

**attire** noun clothing, ensemble, costume, array, habiliments, accoutrements; *inf.* threads, glad rags. *See* APPAREL.

**attire** verb dress, clothe, dress up, garb, robe, array, deck out, costume; *inf.* doll up.

**attitude** noun *his attitude toward marriage* point of view, viewpoint, opinion, frame of mind, outlook, perspective, stance, position, thoughts, ideas.

**attract** verb **1** *magnets attract iron filings* draw, pull, magnetize. **2** *attracted by beauty* allure, entice, tempt, fascinate, charm, engage, enchant, captivate, bewitch.

**attractive** adjective **1** *an attractive proposal* appealing, agreeable, pleasing, inviting, tempting. **2** *an attractive woman/man* good-looking, striking, beautiful, handsome, pretty, stunning, gorgeous, prepossessing, fetching, comely, captivating, charming, fascinating, interesting, appealing, enchanting, alluring.

**attribute** noun quality, feature, characteristic, property, mark, trait.

**attribute** verb ascribe, assign, accredit, put down, chalk up.

**audacious** adjective **1** *an audacious scheme* bold, daring, fearless, intrepid, brave, courageous, adventurous, plucky, daredevil, reckless; *inf.* gutsy, spunky. **2** *an audacious youth* impudent, impertinent, insolent, presumptuous, forward, rude, brazen.

**audacity** noun **1** *the audacity of the scheme* boldness, daring, fearlessness, bravery, courage, pluck, recklessness; *inf.* guts, spunk. **2** *the child had the audacity to swear* impudence, impertinence, insolence, rudeness, brazenness.

**audience** noun **1** *a concert audience* listeners, spectators, viewers, onlookers; assembly, gathering, house, turnout, congregation, gallery. **2** *publications aimed at a wide audience* public, market, following. **3** *an audience with the pope* interview, meeting, hearing, reception.

**audit** verb inspect, examine, go over/through, scrutinize, investigate, review, check.

**augment** verb increase, boost, build up, enlarge, grow, add to, expand, extend, amplify, raise, enhance, heighten, multiply, magnify, elevate, swell, inflate, escalate, intensify.

**augur** verb foretell, forecast, predict, prophesy, bode, foreshadow, promise, presage, portend, herald, betoken.

**august** adjective dignified, solemn, majestic, stately, magnificent, imposing, impressive, exalted, awe-inspiring.

**aura** noun ambience, atmosphere, air, character, tone, suggestion, emanation, vibrations; *inf.* vibes.

**auspices** plural noun patronage, guidance, influence, responsibility, control, protection.

**auspicious** adjective propitious, favorable, promising, bright, optimistic, encouraging, opportune, timely, fortunate, providential.

**austere** adjective **1** *an austere manner* harsh, stern, severe, strict, unfeeling, hard, rigorous, stringent, grim, formal, stiff, aloof, forbidding. **2** *monks lead an austere life* strict, self-denying, self-abnegating, ascetic, Spartan, abstemious, abstinent, celibate, chaste, puritanical. **3** *an austere style* plain, simple, severe, unadorned, unornamented, stark, somber.

**authentic** adjective **1** *an authentic painting* genuine, bona fide, rightful, legitimate, valid; *inf.* the real McCoy, kosher. **2** *an authentic statement* reliable, dependable, trustworthy, truthful, honest, credible.

**authenticate** verb **1** *authenticate an agreement* validate, ratify, confirm, certify, seal, endorse, guarantee, warrant, underwrite. **2** *authenticate the work as being Shakespeare's* verify, substantiate, support, prove, evidence.

**author** noun writer, composer, novelist, dramatist, playwright, screenwriter, poet, essayist, biographer, librettist, lyricist, songwriter, journalist, columnist, reporter.

**authoritative** adjective **1** *an authoritative biography* official, approved, authorized, sanctioned, validated. **2** *authoritative information* sound, dependable, reliable, trustworthy, valid, certified, attested, definitive, accurate. **3** *an authoritative manner* self-assured, confident, assertive, imposing, masterful, arrogant, commanding, domineering.

**authorities** plural noun administration, the establishment, government, officialdom, management, legislation, the police, the powers that be.

**authority** noun **1** *have the authority to decide* authorization, right, power, might, sanction, influence, force, control, prerogative, jurisdiction, rule, command, sovereignty; *inf.* say-so. **2** *an authority on ecology* expert, specialist, professional, master, scholar, pundit; *inf.* walking encyclopedia. **3** *have his authority to act* permission, authorization, sanction. **4** *have the news on their authority* testimony, evidence, witness, attestation, word, avowal, deposition.

**authorize** verb **1** *authorize them to represent us* commission, empower, entitle, enable, accredit, license, certify, validate. **2** *authorize the sale* permit, allow, approve, assent to, agree to, sanction, ratify, warrant; *inf.* give the green light to, give the go-ahead for.

**autocratic** adjective despotic, dictatorial, tyrannical, authoritarian, domineering, imperious, omnipotent, all-powerful, absolute, draconian, oppressive, high-handed; *inf.* bossy.

**automatic** adjective **1** *an automatic washing machine* automated, mechanized, mechanical, push-button, robotic, self-activating, self-regulating. **2** *an automatic reaction* instinctive, spontaneous, involuntary, unconscious, reflex, natural.

**available** adjective accessible, obtainable, at hand, convenient.

**avarice** noun greed, acquisitiveness, covetousness, miserliness.

**average** noun mean, median, midpoint, center; norm, standard, yardstick, rule.

**average** adjective **1** *the team played an average game* ordinary, normal, typical, everyday. **2** *his ability was only average* mediocre, moderate, unexceptional; second-rate, banal, pedestrian.

**aversion** noun dislike, distaste, hatred, repugnance.

**avid** adjective keen, eager, enthusiastic, fervent, zealous, passionate.

**avoid** verb shun, eschew, steer clear of, evade, elude, shirk, dodge, abstain from, refrain from.

**aware** adjective awake, watchful, vigilant, alert, cautious. **aware of** *aware of the problem* conscious of, informed of, familiar with, sensitive to; *inf.* clued in on, in the know about.

**awe** noun amazement, wonder, astonishment, stupefaction; reverence, honor, veneration; dread, fear.

**awful** adjective **1** *an awful cough* nasty, unpleasant, distressing, horrible, ugly, unattractive, foul, disgusting. **2** *the awful power of the gods* awesome, venerable, impressive, daunting.

**awkward** adjective **1** *they arrived at an awkward time* inconvenient, difficult, problematic, annoying, vexatious. **2** *an awkward child* clumsy, ungainly, inelegant, inept, gauche.

**awry** adjective lopsided, uneven, unequal, asymmetrical, askew, crooked.

# *Bb*

**babble** verb **1** *babble away unintelligibly* jabber, chatter, mutter, mumble, prate, drivel, cackle; *inf.* run on. **2** *the stream babbled quietly* murmur, whisper, gurgle.

**baby** noun infant, newborn, child, babe, tiny tot.

**baby** verb pamper, spoil, indulge, pet, humor, coddle, mollycoddle, overindulge, spoonfeed.

**back** noun **1** *hurt one's back* spine, backbone, spinal column; *Med.* dorsum. **2** *the back of the building* rear, rear end, far end, end, reverse side, other side; hind part, posterior, tail end, backside, hindquarters. **behind one's back** secretly, deceitfully, slyly, sneakily, surreptitiously, covertly.

**back** adjective **1** *back garden/teeth* rear, hind, end, hindmost, posterior. **2** *back copies* past, previous, earlier, former, bygone.

**back** verb **1** *back the proposal* support, endorse, approve, favor, advocate, help, aid, promote, champion, encourage, second. **2** *back the theatrical venture* sponsor, finance, subsidize, underwrite. **3** *back her statement* support, confirm, corroborate, substantiate, endorse, second, vouch for, attest to, sanction. **back away** withdraw, retire, retreat, fall back, turn tail. **back down** yield, submit, surrender, give in, concede, backtrack, back-pedal, retract. **back out** go backwards, reverse; go back

on, withdraw from, cancel, renege on, get cold feet, recant; *inf.* chicken out.

**backbiting** noun slander, libel, defamation, abuse, scandalmongering, disparagement, denigration, detraction, malice, spite, spitefulness, cattiness, vilification, vituperation, calumny.

**backbone** noun **1** *an injured backbone* spinal/vertebral column. *See* BACK noun 1. **2** *the backbone of the organization* framework, mainstay, support, foundation, structure. **3** *lacking backbone* strength of character, firmness, determination, resolve, courage, grit, nerve, mettle, pluck, fortitude.

**backer** noun **1** *the theater's backers* sponsor, patron, benefactor, subsidizer, underwriter; *inf.* angel. **2** *backers of the candidate* supporter, advocate, promoter, champion.

**backfire** verb *the plan backfired* miscarry, rebound, recoil, boomerang, fail, disappoint; *inf.* flop.

**background** noun **1** *in the background of the painting* distance, rear, horizon. **2** *posing against a white background* setting, backcloth, backdrop, scene, stage. **3** *check the employee's background* upbringing, rearing, education, history, class, culture, experience, family, circumstances, qualifications, credentials. **4** *the political background* conditions, circumstances, environment, factors, influences.

**backing** noun support, approval, help, assistance, aid, encouragement, cooperation, endorsement, sponsorship, financing, grant, subsidy, funds.

**backlash** noun reaction, counteraction, repercussion, recoil, kickback, boomerang, retaliation.

**backlog** noun accumulation, stockpile, heap, stock, supply; arrears, reserves; *inf.* mountain.

**backpedal** verb retract, take back, withdraw, retreat, backtrack, back down, renege, do an about-face.

**backslide** verb relapse, lapse, regress, retrogress, revert, fall back, stray, degenerate, deteriorate.

**backward** adjective **1** *a backward area* slow, behind, behindhand, underdeveloped, undeveloped, retarded, unprogressive, unsophisticated. **2** *rather backward in a crowd* bashful, shy, retiring, hesitant, shrinking, timid.

**bad** adjective **1** *bad workmanship* poor, unsatisfactory, inadequate, deficient, imperfect, defective, inferior, substandard, faulty, unacceptable, worthless; *inf.* lousy, crummy. **2** *smoking is a bad habit* harmful, hurtful, damaging, injurious, detrimental, destructive, ruinous, deleterious, unhealthy, unwholesome. **3** *a bad man* immoral, wicked, wrong, evil, sinful, corrupt, base, reprobate, depraved, dishonest, dishonorable, crooked. **4** *a bad child* naughty, mischievous, disobedient, unruly, refractory. **5** *bad weather* disagreeable, unpleasant, unwelcome, uncomfortable, nasty, terrible, dreadful, grim, gloomy, unfortunate, unfavorable, distressing. **6** *a bad time for house-buying* adverse, difficult, unfavorable, unsuitable, inappropriate. **7** *a bad mistake/accident* serious, severe, grave, disastrous, terrible, critical, acute. **8** *bad eggs* rotten, decayed, moldy, putrid, tainted, spoiled, contaminated. **9** *an invalid feeling bad* ill, unwell, sick, poorly, indisposed, ailing, weak, feeble, diseased; *inf.* under the weather, below par. **10** *feeling bad about their actions* sorry, apologetic, regretful, conscience-stricken, contrite, remorseful, guilty, penitent, rueful, sad, upset. **11** *a bad check* worthless, invalid, counterfeit, false, spurious, fraudulent, fake; *inf.* bogus, phony. **not bad** all right, quite good, passable, tolerable, fair, average; *inf.* OK, so-so.

**badge** noun **1** *badge on a uniform* crest, emblem, insignia, device, shield, escutcheon. **2** *badge of honor* mark, sign, symbol, indication, indicator, signal, characteristic, trademark.

**badger** verb pester, harass, plague, torment, bother, provoke, hound, nag, goad, bully; *inf.* bug, hassle.

**badly** adverb **1** *do the job badly* poorly, wrongly, incorrectly, unsatisfactorily, inadequately, imperfectly, defectively, faultily, ineptly, inefficiently, shoddily, carelessly. **2** *work out badly* unsuccessfully, unfortunately, unhappily, unfavorably. **3** *badly hurt/defeated* greatly, deeply, severely, seriously, extremely, intensely, exceedingly, acutely. **4** *behave badly* naughtily, wrongly, immorally, wickedly, improperly, criminally. **5** *want something badly* greatly, exceedingly, extremely, enormously, tremendously, considerably.

**baffle** verb **1** *baffled by the problem* puzzle, perplex, mystify, nonplus, stump, flummox, confound, bewilder, confuse. **2** *baffle their plans* thwart, frustrate, foil, check, block, hinder, obstruct.

**bag** noun receptacle; handbag, pocketbook, purse, shoulder bag; suitcase, grip, flight bag, backpack, rucksack, haversack, satchel, duffel bag.

**bag** verb **1** *bag three pheasants* catch, capture, shoot, kill, trap, snare, land. **2** *the pants bagged* sag, hang loosely.

**baggage** noun luggage, gear, equipment, pack; belongings, things, suitcases, bags, effects, paraphernalia, trappings, accoutrements.

**baggy** adjective loose, slack, roomy, oversize, oversized, shapeless, ill-fitting, sagging.

**bail** noun surety, security, bond, guarantee, warranty, pledge, collateral.

**bail** verb **bail out 1** *bail him out* help, assist, aid, rescue, relieve. **2** *bailed out before the crash* escape, get out, withdraw, retreat.

**bait** noun *low prices as bait for the consumer* attraction, lure, incentive, snare, temptation; allurement, enticement, incitement, inducement.

**bait** verb torment, persecute, badger, plague, harry, harass, tease, annoy, irritate; *inf.* hassle, needle.

**bake** verb *earth baked by the sun* scorch, burn, sear, parch, dry, desiccate, fire.

**balance** noun **1** *the balance of power* equilibrium, evenness, symmetry, parity, equity, equipoise, correspondence, uniformity, equivalence. **2** *I tripped and lost my balance* steadiness, stability. **3** *people of ability and balance* composure, poise, equanimity, aplomb, stability, coolness, levelheadedness, sang-froid. **4** *her practicality acts as a balance to his genius* counterbalance, countercheck, counterweight, stabilizer, compensation, recompense, ballast. **5** *pay the balance of the account* remainder, rest, residue, difference. **in the balance** uncertain, at a turning point, critical, at a crisis.

**balance** verb **1** *balance the book on her head* steady, stabilize, poise. **2** *advantages balance the disadvantages* counterbalance, counteract, offset, neutralize, compensate for, make up for, counterpoise. **3** *the profit and loss columns must balance* correspond, match, be level/parallel. **4** *balance the advantages and disadvantages* weigh, compare, evaluate, consider, assess, appraise.

**bald** adjective **1** *a bald man* hairless, bald-headed, depilated. **2** *a bald landscape* barren, treeless, bare, stark, exposed, bleak. **3** *a bald statement* blunt, direct, forthright, straightforward, downright, outright, plain, simple, unadorned, stark, severe.

**balderdash** noun nonsense, rubbish, twaddle, drivel, foolishness, gibberish, bunkum, claptrap; *inf.* bunk, hot air, bilge, poppycock, rot.

**balk** verb refuse, hesitate over, draw back from, flinch/recoil/shrink/shy from, evade, dodge, resist, eschew.

**ball** noun sphere, globe, orb, globule, spheroid.

**balloon** verb swell out, puff out, fill out, billow, blow up, inflate.

**ballyhoo** noun fuss, commotion, to-do, hullabaloo, racket; publicity, propaganda, promotion, buildup; *inf.* hype.

**balm** noun **1** *apply balm to the burns* ointment, lotion, cream, salve, emollient, embrocation, liniment, unguent. **2** *balm for a troubled mind* remedy, curative, cure, restorative, palliative, solace, consolation, comfort.

**balmy** adjective **1** *balmy breezes* mild, gentle, temperate, calm, soothing, soft, fragrant, perfumed. **2** *you're balmy* silly, eccentric, peculiar, weird; *inf.* daft, batty, nutty, loony, loopy.

**bamboozle** verb trick, cheat, deceive, delude, hoodwink, mislead, hoax, fool, dupe, defraud, swindle; *inf.* gull, con.

**ban** verb prohibit, forbid, veto, disallow, bar, debar, outlaw, proscribe, suppress, reject, restrict, banish.

**ban** noun prohibition, veto, bar, embargo, boycott, proscription, interdict, interdiction, suppression, stoppage, restriction, taboo.

**banal** adjective hackneyed, trite, clichéd, commonplace, platitudinous, stock, stereotyped, pedestrian, unoriginal, unimaginative, stale, uninspired, tired, inane, jejune.

**band**[1] noun **1** *iron/rubber band* bond, binding, cord, strap, tie, link, chain, fetter, manacle, ligature, ring, hoop. **2** *a band round the waist/hair* belt, cord, braid, sash, girdle, ribbon, fillet, cincture. **3** *a band of white on the black* strip, stripe, streak, line, bar, striation.

**band**[2] noun **1** *a band of robbers* group, troop, company, gang, mob, pack, bunch, assembly, assemblage, association, club, set, coterie. **2** *a brass/jazz band* combo, ensemble, orchestra.

**band**[3] verb join, group, unite, merge, combine, team up, gather, ally, affiliate, associate.

**bandage** verb bind, bind up, dress, cover, plaster.

**bandit** noun robber, brigand, outlaw, desperado, hijacker, plunderer, marauder, gangster, criminal, gunman, highwayman, pirate, racketeer.

**bane** noun ruin, death, ruination, scourge, torment, plague, affliction, calamity, misery, woe, nuisance, trial, burden, blight, curse, bête noir.

**bang** noun **1** *a loud bang* report, burst, boom, clash, peal, clap, pop, thud, thump. **2** *a bang on the head* blow, bump, hit, slap, punch, smack, whack, rap, cuff; *inf.* wallop, sock.

**bang** verb hit, strike, beat, thump, hammer, knock, rap, pound, thud, pummel, whack, slam, crash; *inf.* bash.

**banish** verb exile, deport, expel, eject, drive away, expatriate, cast out, outlaw, transport, oust, evict, throw out, exclude, dismiss, send away, dispel, get rid of, ban, bar, eliminate, dislodge.

**banishment** noun exile, deportation, expulsion, expatriation, transportation, proscription.

**bank**[1] noun **1** *a grassy bank* slope, rise, incline, gradient, mound, hillock, knoll. **2** *the bank of a river* edge, side, shore, brink, margin, embankment.

**bank**[2] noun **1** *empty the child's bank* piggy bank, cashbox, safe, strongbox, coffer. **2** *a bank of information* store, reserve, accumulation, stock, stockpile, reservoir, supply, fund, hoard, storehouse, repository, depository.

**bankrupt** adjective insolvent, failed, ruined, financially embarrassed, distressed, in the red; *inf.* on the rocks, broke, hard up.
**bankrupt of** *bankrupt of ideas* wanting, without, deprived of, bereft of.

**bankruptcy** noun insolvency, liquidation, indebtedness, failure, ruin, ruination, penury.

**banner** noun flag, standard, colors, pennant, pennon.

**banner** adjective *a banner year* excellent, red-letter, outstanding, notable, exceptional.

**banquet** noun dinner, dinner party, feast, meal, party, repast, treat, revel.

**banter** noun repartee, badinage, teasing, joking, jesting, raillery; *inf.* kidding, ribbing, joshing.

**banter** verb tease, joke, jest, mock; *inf.* kid, rib, rag, josh.

**baptize** verb christen, name, immerse, sprinkle; initiate, introduce, inaugurate, launch.

**bar** noun **1** *an iron bar* rod, pole, stake, stick, shaft, rail, spar, crosspiece. **2** *a bar of soap* block, brick, cake, wedge, lump. **3** *no bar to promotion* obstacle, hindrance. *See* BARRIER 2. **4** *bar of light* band, strip, line, belt, streak, stripe. **5** *a ship stuck on a bar* sandbar, shoal, shallow, reef, sandbank, ridge, ledge, shelf. **6** *drinking in a bar* tavern, saloon, pub, lounge.

**bar** verb **1** *bar the door* bolt, lock, fasten, padlock, secure, latch. **2** *bar from entering* prohibit, preclude, forbid, ban, exclude, keep out, block, impede; obstruct, hinder, restrain, check, stop, defer.

**barb** noun insult, sneer, gibe, affront; scoffing, scorn, sarcasm; *inf.* dig.

**barbarian** noun savage, brute, wild man/woman, troglodyte, ruffian, lout, vandal, hooligan, boor, ignoramus, philistine, yahoo.

**barbarian** adjective savage, uncivilized, primitive, brutish, wild, loutish, hooligan, boorish, uncivilized, wild, rough, coarse, uncouth, vulgar, philistine.

**barbaric** adjective **1** *barbaric tribes* savage, uncivilized. **2** *barbaric customs* brutal, savage, cruel, vicious, fierce, ferocious, bestial, barbarous, murderous, inhuman, ruthless.

**barbarity** noun brutality, savagery, cruelty, viciousness, bestiality, inhumanity, ruthlessness; atrocity, outrage, enormity.

**bare** adjective **1** *sunbathing bare* naked, stark naked, nude, exposed, unclothed, undressed, unclad, stripped, denuded. **2** *a bare room* empty, vacant, unfurnished, unadorned, stark, austere, unembellished. **3** *a bare landscape* bleak, unsheltered, unprotected, unshielded, desolate, barren. **4** *the bare facts* simple, plain, bald, basic, essential, straightforward, stark, unembellished, cold, literal. **5** *the bare minimum* mere, basic, meager, scanty, inadequate.

**bare** verb reveal, uncover, expose, lay bare, unveil, disclose, show, divulge, unmask, bring to light.

**barefaced** adjective blatant, flagrant, glaring, arrant, shameless, brazen, bold, impudent, insolent, audacious, brash, open, undisguised, unconcealed, transparent, patent, manifest, palpable.

**barely** adverb hardly, scarcely, only just, just, by the skin of one's teeth.

**bargain** noun **1** *make a bargain* agreement, pact, transaction, deal, treaty, negotiation, arrangement, compact, promise, engagement. **2** *get a bargain* discount, reduction, good buy; *inf.* steal, giveaway.

**bargain** verb haggle, barter, deal, trade, traffic. **bargain for** expect, anticipate, be prepared for, allow for. **bargain on** rely on, depend on, count on.

**barge** verb barge in *barge in during prayers* burst in, break in, intrude, interrupt; *inf.* butt in, horn in. **barge into** *people barging into each other* bump into, crash into, collide with, plow into, smash into.

**bark** verb **1** *the dog barked* howl, woof, yelp, yap, bay, growl, snarl. **2** *the teacher barked at the students* shout, yell, bawl, thunder, scream, screech, shriek, snap, snarl, bluster.

**baron** noun noble, nobleman, aristocrat, peer, lord; tycoon, magnate, executive, industrialist, financier, captain of industry.

**baroque** adjective ornate, elaborate, embellished, ostentatious, showy, florid, convoluted, rococo.

**barrage** noun bombardment, shelling, volley, salvo; deluge, stream, torrent, onslaught, avalanche, burst, abundance, superabundance, plethora, profusion.

**barrel** noun cask, keg, butt, vat, tun, tub, tank, hogshead.

**barren** adjective **1** *a barren woman | barren land* infertile, sterile, childless, unproductive, unfruitful, arid, desert, waste. **2** *barren discussion* uninteresting, boring, dull, uninspiring, prosaic, futile, worthless, useless, vapid, lackluster.

**barricade** noun obstacle, obstruction. *See* BARRIER 1.

**barricade** verb block, blockade, obstruct, bar, shut off/in, fence in, defend, fortify.

**barrier** noun **1** *the barrier in the parking lot* barricade, bar, fence, railing, obstacle, blockade, roadblock. **2** *a barrier to success* obstacle, hindrance, impediment, drawback, check, hurdle, restriction, stumbling block, difficulty.

**barter** verb **1** *barter his horse for food* trade, exchange, swap. **2** *barter for a better price* bargain, haggle.

**base** noun **1** *the base of a column* foundation, support, prop, stand, pedestal, rest, bottom, bed, foot, substructure, plinth. **2** *paints with an oil base* basis, core, essence, component, essential, fundamental, root, heart. **3** *mountaineers setting up a base* headquarters, center, camp, site, station, settlement, post.

**base** verb **1** *based on historical facts* found, build, construct, form, establish, ground, rest, root, derive. **2** *based in Chicago* locate, station, situate, post, place, install.

**base** adjective **1** *base motives* low, mean, sordid, immoral, dishonorable, evil, wicked, nefarious, debased, sinful, disreputable, corrupt, depraved, vile, ignoble, vulgar, foul, despicable, contemptible. **2** *base servitude* menial, subservient, servile, lowly, slavish, groveling, sniveling, cowering.

**baseless** adjective groundless, unfounded, unsubstantiated, uncorroborated, unjustifiable.

**bashful** adjective shy, reserved, diffident, retiring, modest, coy, demure, reticent, hesitant, shrinking, timid, blushing.

**basic** adjective fundamental, elementary, rudimentary, primary, radical, key, central, essential, indispensable, intrinsic, underlying.

**basically** adverb fundamentally, at heart, intrinsically, inherently, mostly.

**basics** plural noun fundamentals, (bare) essentials, rudiments, principles, practicalities, realities, ABCs; *inf.* brass tacks, nuts and bolts.

**basis** noun **1** *no basis for the statement* support, foundation, base, footing, reasoning, grounds. **2** *the basis of the discussion* starting point, premise, fundamental point/principle, main ingredient, core, essence. **3** *on a part-time basis* footing, procedure, condition, status, position.

**bask** verb **1** *bask in the sunshine* lie, laze, lounge, relax, loll, sunbathe. **2** *bask in their admiration* luxuriate, revel, wallow, enjoy, relish, savor.

**bastard** noun **1** *born a bastard* illegitimate child, love child. **2** *a rotten bastard* scoundrel, cad, blackguard, villain, rascal.

**bastard** adjective *a bastard language* adulterated, impure, hybrid, alloyed, inferior, imperfect, spurious, counterfeit.

**bastardize** verb debase, degrade, devalue, depreciate, corrupt, adulterate, defile, contaminate.

**bastion** noun bulwark, rampart, fortress, citadel, keep, stronghold, protection, protector, defense.

**batch** noun group, quantity, lot, bunch, cluster, set, collection, assemblage, pack, crowd, aggregate, conglomeration.

**bathe** verb **1** *bathe every day* have/take a bath, wash, soak, shower. **2** *bathe the wound* clean, cleanse, wash, steep, immerse, wet, moisten, rinse, suffuse.

**bathroom** noun toilet, men's/ladies' room, facilities, lavatory, washroom; *inf.* john.

**baton** noun stick, bar, wand, rod, staff, club, truncheon, mace.

**batter** verb **1** *battering their prisoners* hit, strike, beat, bash, assault, wallop, thump, thrash, lash, pound, pummel. **2** *countries battered by war* damage, injure, hurt, harm, bruise, wound, crush, shatter, destroy, demolish, ruin.

**battery** noun **1** *a battery of tests* series, sequence, set, cycle, chain, string. **2** *convicted of assault and battery* attack, mugging, beating, striking, thumping, thrashing, bashing.

**battle** noun **1** *battle between enemy forces* war, armed conflict, conflict, fight, skirmish, engagement, encounter, confrontation, collision, campaign, crusade, tussle, scuffle, scrap, melee. **2** *a battle of wills* clash, contest, competition, tournament, struggle, disagreement, argument, dispute, controversy, debate, dissension, altercation, strife.

**battle** verb **1** *battle for fair wages* fight, struggle, strive, combat, contend, labor, push. **2** *neighbors constantly battling* fight, war, feud, argue, quarrel, bicker, wrangle.

**battle cry** noun war cry, rallying call, slogan, motto, watchword, catchword, shibboleth.

**battlefield** noun battleground, front, battlefront, field of operations, combat zone, theater/arena of war, war zone.

**batty** adjective foolish, silly, eccentric; *inf.* daft, bonkers, loony.

**bauble** noun trinket, knickknack, trifle, ornament, toy, gewgaw, gimcrack, bagatelle.

**bawdy** adjective obscene, vulgar, blue, racy, titillating, crude, coarse, ribald, lewd, dirty, smutty, off-color, suggestive, salacious, erotic, prurient, lascivious, licentious, risqué, pornographic; *inf.* raunchy.

**bawl** verb **1** *a child bawling* cry, sob, weep, wail, blubber, snivel, squall. **2** *he bawled a reply* shout, call/cry out, yell, roar, bellow, screech, scream, howl. **bawl out** *bawled me out for being late* rebuke, chastise, yell at, scold.

**bay**¹ noun *ships moored in the bay* cove, inlet, indentation, gulf, basin, sound, arm.

**bay**² noun *a table in the bay* alcove, recess, niche, opening, nook.

**bay**³ verb *hounds baying* howl, bark, yelp, cry, growl.

**bazaar** noun market, marketplace, mart, exchange, fair, sale.

**beach** noun seaside, coast, seashore, shore, water's edge, coastline, sands, sand, strand.

**beacon** noun signal fire/light, flare, beam, lighthouse.

**bead** noun **1** *glass beads* ball, pellet, pill, globule, spheroid, oval. **2** *beads of sweat* drop, droplet, bubble, blob, dot, glob, dewdrop, teardrop.

**beam** noun 1 *the roof beams* board, timber, plank, joist, rafter, girder, spar, support, lath. 2 *a beam of light* ray, shaft, stream, streak, flash, gleam, glow, glimmer, glint.

**beam** verb 1 *light beamed from the window* emit, radiate, shine. 2 *beam radio/television programs* broadcast, transmit, direct, aim. 3 *beam from ear to ear* smile, grin.

**bear** verb 1 *bear gifts* carry, bring, transport, move, convey, take, fetch, haul; *inf.* tote. 2 *bear tales* spread, transmit, carry. 3 *bear a signature/inscription* carry, display, exhibit, show, be marked with. 4 *bear a crop* yield, produce, give forth, give, provide, supply, generate. 5 *bear a son* give birth to, breed, bring forth, beget, engender. 6 *bear the cost* carry, sustain, support, shoulder, uphold. 7 *cannot bear his attitude* stand, endorse, tolerate, abide, stomach, brook. 8 *much pain to bear* suffer, endure, undergo, experience, go through, support, weather. 9 *bear a grudge* have, hold, harbor, possess, entertain, cherish. 10 *bear left* veer, curve, go, move, turn, fork, diverge, deviate, bend. **bear out** *bear out the facts* confirm, corroborate, substantiate, endorse, vindicate, give credence to, support, ratify, warrant, uphold, justify, prove, authenticate, verify. **bear up** cope, persevere, manage, endure. **bear with** tolerate, put up with, endure, make allowances for, be patient with.

**beard** noun whiskers, bristle, stubble, five o'clock shadow; goatee, Vandyke, sideburns, muttonchops.

**bearing** noun 1 *a distinguished bearing* deportment, posture, carriage, gait. 2 *her bearing throughout the trial* attitude, behavior, manner, demeanor. 3 *have a bearing on the case* relevance, pertinence, connection. 4 *lose one's bearings* orientation, location, position, situation, track, way.

**beast** noun 1 *a beast of the jungle* animal, creature, mammal, quadruped. 2 *a cruel beast to his family* brute, monster, savage, swine, pig, ogre.

**beastly** adjective 1 *a beastly apparition* beastlike, bestial, animal-like, brutal. 2 *a beastly cold* awful, terrible, horrible, rotten, nasty, foul, vile.

**beat** verb 1 *he would never beat the dog* hit, strike, batter, thump, wallop, hammer, punch, knock, thrash, pound, pummel, slap, smack, flay, whip, lash, chastise, thwack, cuff, bruise, buffet, box, cudgel; *inf.* belt, bash, whack, clout, slug, lay into, knock about, rough up. 2 *their hearts beating* throb, pound, thump, pulsate, pulse, palpitate, vibrate. 3 *the bird's wings beat* flap, flutter, quiver, tremble, vibrate. 4 *beat the eggs* mix, blend, whip, whisk, stir. 5 *waves beating against the shore* strike, dash, break against, lap, wash. 6 *beat metal into rods* hammer, forge, form, shape, work, stamp, fashion, model. 7 *beat a path* tread, tramp, trample, wear, track, groove. 8 *beat the opposition* defeat, conquer, vanquish, trounce, rout, quash; *inf.* lick. 9 *beat the record* outdo, surpass, exceed, eclipse. **beat up** assault, attack, mug, batter, thrash; *inf.* work over, clobber, rough up.

**beat** noun 1 *the beat of the drum* bang, banging, stroke, striking, blow, hit. 2 *the beat of his heart* throb, throbbing, pounding, pulsating, thumping, palpitating, vibrating, vibration. 3 *musical beat* rhythm, stress, meter, time, measure, accent, cadence. 4 *policeman's beat* round, circuit, course, route, way, path, orbit.

**beat** adjective exhausted, tired, worn out, fatigued, weary, spent.

**beatific** adjective blessed, blissful, heavenly, celestial, paradisiacal; rapturous, joyful, ecstatic, blissful.

**beautiful** adjective ravishing, gorgeous, stunning, alluring, lovely, attractive, pretty, handsome, good-looking, pleasing, comely, charming, delightful, glamorous, appealing, fair, fine, becoming, seemly, winsome, graceful, elegant, exquisite.

**beautify** verb adorn, embellish, enhance, decorate, ornament, garnish, gild, smarten, prettify, glamorize, primp, preen; *inf.* do/doll oneself up.

**beauty** noun 1 *the beauty of the surroundings* loveliness, attractiveness, prettiness, handsomeness, allure, allurement, charm, glamour, grace, artistry, symmetry; *fml.* pulchritude. 2 *the sisters were all great beauties* belle, charmer, enchantress, seductress, femme fatale, Venus, goddess; *inf.* good-looker, lovely, stunner, knockout, dish. 3 *the beauty of the scheme* attraction, good thing, advantage, benefit, asset, strong point, boon, blessing.

**beckon** verb 1 *beckon to the waiter* signal, gesture, gesticulate, motion, wave, nod, call, summon, bid. 2 *the sea beckons him* draw, pull, call, attract, tempt, entice, allure.

**become** verb 1 *she became rich* come to be, turn out to be, grow, grow into, mature into, evolve into, pass into, change into, turn into. 2 *the dress becomes her* suit, flatter, look good on, set off, enhance. 3 *it ill becomes you to behave like that* befit, behoove, suit, be suitable/fitting to.

**becoming** adjective 1 *a becoming hat* flattering, comely, attractive, lovely, pretty, handsome, stylish, elegant, chic, tasteful. 2 *hardly becoming behavior* suitable, fitting, appropriate, apt, proper, right, decent, seemly, decorous, graceful.

**bed** noun **1** *she liked to sleep in her own bed* bunk, cot, couch; *inf.* sack. **2** *a flower bed* plot, area, lot, patch, space, border, strip, row. **3** *a bed of concrete* base, basis, foundation, bottom, support, substructure.

**bed** verb **1** *stones bedded in concrete* embed, set, fix into, insert, inlay, implant, bury. **2** *desiring to bed her* go to bed with, have sex with, sleep with, spend the night with. **bed down** go to bed/sleep, retire, settle down, have a nap; *inf.* turn in, hit the sack/hay.

**bedeck** verb deck, decorate, adorn, ornament, trim, festoon, array, embellish.

**bedevil** verb afflict, torment, beset, plague, harass, distress, annoy, vex, irritate, irk, pester.

**bedlam** noun uproar, pandemonium, commotion, confusion, furor, hubbub, clamor, disorder, chaos, tumult.

**bedraggled** adjective muddy, muddied, wet, dirty, messy, sodden, soaking, soaking wet, soaked, drenched, saturated, dripping, soiled, stained, disheveled, untidy.

**beefy** adjective **1** *beefy wrestler* brawny, muscular, hefty, burly, thickset, solid, strong, powerful, heavy, robust, sturdy, stocky. **2** *a beefy youngster* heavy, solid, fat, chubby, plump, overweight, stout, obese, fleshy, portly, corpulent, paunchy, dumpy.

**beer** noun ale, stout, lager, malt liquor, porter; *inf.* brew, suds.

**befall** verb happen, occur, take place, chance, arise, come about, come to pass, transpire.

**befitting** adjective fitting, suitable. *See* APPROPRIATE.

**before** adverb **1** *we've met before* previously, earlier, formerly, hitherto, in the past. **2** *they went on before* ahead, in front, in advance, in the lead.

**beforehand** adverb in advance, in readiness, ahead of time.

**befriend** verb make friends with, help, assist, aid, stand by, succor, advise.

**befuddled** adjective **1** *befuddled from the anesthetic* confused, dazed, groggy, muddled, numbed; *inf.* woozy. **2** *befuddled partygoers* drunk, drunken, intoxicated, inebriated, stupefied; *inf.* blotto, bombed, out of it, smashed, wasted, wrecked, zonked.

**beg** verb **1** *beg in order to live* solicit money, seek charity/alms, cadge, scrounge; *inf.* sponge, bum, mooch. **2** *beg for money/mercy* ask for, request, seek, look for, plead for, beseech, entreat, importune.

**beggar** noun tramp, vagrant, mendicant, cadger, vagabond, pauper, down-and-out, derelict; *inf.* scrounger, sponger, bum, moocher, bag lady, hobo.

**begin** verb **1** *begin work* start, commence, set about, embark on, initiate, set in motion, institute, inaugurate. **2** *trouble began immediately* arise, come into existence/being, happen, occur, spring up, crop up, emerge, dawn, appear, originate.

**beginner** noun novice, trainee, learner, apprentice, student, recruit, tyro, fledgling, neophyte, initiate, tenderfoot; *inf.* greenhorn, rookie.

**beginning** noun **1** *from the beginning of time* start, starting point, commencement, onset, outset, dawn, birth, inception, conception, emergence, rise; *inf.* kickoff. **2** *the beginning of the book* first part, opening, prelude, preface, introduction. **3** *philosophy has its beginnings in religion* origin, source, fountainhead, spring, mainspring, embryo, germ, roots, seeds.

**begrudge** verb *begrudge him his success* grudge, envy, resent, hold against, be jealous of.

**beguile** verb **1** *the comedian beguiling the audience* delight, please, enchant, bewitch, seduce, occupy, engage, distract. **2** *beguile the hours* pass, while away, spend.

**beguiling** adjective charming, enchanting, bewitching, seductive.

**behalf** noun **on behalf of 1** *acting on behalf of his client* for, representing, in the interests of, in the name of, in support of. **2** *collecting on behalf of the blind* for, for the benefit/good/sake of, to the advantage of, on account of, in support of.

**behave** verb **1** *they behaved well/badly* act, perform, conduct oneself, acquit oneself, comport oneself. **2** *she behaves like a dictator* act, perform, function, operate. **behave oneself** *the children must behave themselves* act correctly/properly, conduct oneself well, act in a polite way, show good manners, mind one's manners.

**behavior** noun conduct, comportment, deportment, bearing; actions, manners, ways; performance, functioning, operation, reaction, response.

**behead** verb decapitate, guillotine, decollate.

**behest** noun order, command, decree, edict, directive, instruction, request, charge, bidding, wish.

**behind** preposition **1** *behind the woodshed* at the rear of, beyond, on the other side of, in back of. **2** *running behind us* after, to the rear of, following, in the wake of, close upon, hard on the heels of. **3** *behind the others in English* less advanced than, slower than, weaker than, inferior to. **4** *he's behind the trouble* at the bottom of, responsible for, causing, giving rise to, instigating. **5** *we're behind you all the way* backing, supporting, in agreement with, financing.

**behold** verb look at, see, observe, view, gaze at, stare at, regard, contemplate, take note of, mark, consider.

**beholden** adjective indebted, under obligation, obligated, bound, owing, thankful, grateful.

**behoove** verb 1 *it behooves him to reconsider* be necessary for, be expected of, be advisable for, be wise for, be fitting, be suitable for, be seemly, be proper.

**beige** adjective fawn, mushroom, neutral, buff, sand, oatmeal, ecru, coffee.

**being** noun 1 *the purpose of our being* existence, living, life, vital force, entity. 2 *shocked to the depths of her being* spirit, soul, nature, essence. 3 *a sentient being* creature, person, human being, human, individual, mortal, living thing.

**belabor** verb 1 *belabor the actor* criticize, attack, berate, censure, castigate, lay into, flay. 2 *belabor the point* overelaborate, discuss at length, harp on.

**belated** adjective late, overdue, behind time, delayed, tardy, unpunctual.

**beleaguered** adjective 1 *a beleaguered city* besieged, under siege, surrounded, blockaded, encircled, hemmed in, under attack. 2 *a movie star beleaguered by fans* harassed, bothered, beset, pestered, plagued, tormented.

**belie** verb 1 *her smile belied her anger* contradict, deny, disprove, refute, gainsay, confute. 2 *the official report belies the situation* misrepresent, falsify, distort, conceal, disguise.

**belief** noun 1 *it is my belief that she is dead* opinion, feeling, impression, view, conviction, judgment, thinking, theory, notion. 2 *no belief in his powers* faith, credence, trust, reliance, confidence. 3 *political beliefs* doctrine, teaching, creed, dogma, ideology, principles, tenet, canon, credence, credo.

**believable** adjective credible, plausible, likely, creditable, probable, conceivable, imaginable.

**believe** verb 1 *don't believe his story* accept, credit, be convinced by, trust; *inf.* swallow, fall for, buy. 2 *I believe he's retired* think, be of the opinion that, understand, suppose, assume, presume, surmise, reckon, guess. **believe in** *believe in alternative medicine* have faith in, trust, set store by, value, swear by.

**belittle** verb disparage, decry, deprecate, undervalue, underrate, underestimate, minimize, make light of, slight, detract from, downgrade, play down, scoff at, sneer at.

**belligerent** adjective 1 *in a belligerent mood* aggressive, antagonistic, pugnacious, quarrelsome, argumentative, disputatious, combative, quick-tempered, hot-tempered, irascible. 2 *belligerent nations* warring, battling, militant, martial, warlike, warmongering.

**bellow** verb roar, shout, yell, shriek, howl, screech, cry out, whoop, ululate; *inf.* holler.

**belly** noun 1 *a stabbing pain in the belly* stomach, abdomen, paunch; intestines, innards; *inf.* tummy, insides, guts, pot, bread basket, potbelly, beer belly. 2 *the belly of the plane* underside, underpart, underbelly.

**belong** verb fit in, be suited to, have a rightful place, be part of; *inf.* go, click.

**belong to** 1 *the house belongs to them* be owned by, be the property of, be held by, be at the disposal of. 2 *she belongs to the sailing club* be a member of, be affiliated to/with, be allied to, be associated with, be included in, be an adherent of. 3 *this lid belongs to that box* be part of, be an adjunct of, go with, relate to.

**belongings** plural noun possessions, effects, goods, accoutrements, appurtenances; property, paraphernalia; *inf.* gear, things, stuff, junk.

**beloved** adjective adored, much loved, precious, cherished, treasured, prized, worshiped, idolized; admired, respected, valued, esteemed, revered.

**beloved** noun sweetheart, fiancé, fiancée, boyfriend, girlfriend, love, lover, betrothed; paramour, inamorato, inamorata.

**belt** noun 1 *a leather belt* girdle, sash, cummerbund, waistband, band. 2 *America's corn belt* zone, region, area, district, tract, stretch, extent.

**belt** verb 1 *with her waist belted* encircle, gird, encompass, bind, tie, fasten. 2 *belt prisoners on their backs* strap, flog, whip, lash, cane, thrash, scourge, flail.

**bemused** adjective confused, bewildered, puzzled, perplexed, dazed, stupefied, preoccupied, absentminded, engrossed.

**benchmark** noun standard, point of reference, gauge, criterion, test, norm, guideline, specification, model, pattern, touchstone, yardstick.

**bend** verb 1 *bend the little finger* curve, crook, flex, twist, bow, arch, warp, contort. 2 *the road bends to the right* curve, turn, twist, swerve, veer, incline, diverge. 3 *bend down over the sink* stoop, crouch, lean down/over, bow, hunch. 4 *bend them to our will* mold, shape, direct, force, influence, persuade, sway, subjugate. 5 *bend our minds to the task* direct, point, aim, turn, train.

**bend** noun curve, turn, corner, twist, angle, arc, swerve, incline, divergence, crook, deviation, deflection, coiling, spiral, loop, hook; dogleg, hairpin turn, zigzag.

**beneath** preposition **1** *sank beneath the waves* below, under, underneath, lower than. **2** *people beneath her socially* inferior to, secondary to, subservient to. **3** *beneath him to behave like that* unworthy of, undignified for, unbefitting, unbecoming.

**benefactor** noun helper, patron, backer, sponsor, supporter, promoter, contributor, subsidizer, donor, philanthropist, sympathizer, well-wisher.

**beneficial** adjective advantageous, favorable, propitious, promising, helpful, accommodating, obliging, useful, serviceable, valuable, profitable, rewarding, gainful.

**beneficiary** noun heir, inheritor, recipient, receiver, legatee, payee, assignee.

**benefit** noun advantage, good, gain, profit, help, aid, assistance, interest, welfare, well-being, betterment, asset, avail, use, service.

**benefit** verb **1** *discoveries benefiting society* do good to, be of service to, serve, be of advantage to, help, aid, assist, better, improve, advance, further. **2** *criminals benefiting from their deeds* profit, gain, reap benefits, make money; *inf.* cash in, make a killing.

**benevolence** noun kindness, kindheartedness, goodness, generosity, altruism, goodwill, compassion, humanitarianism.

**benevolent** adjective kindhearted, friendly, generous, magnanimous, considerate, thoughtful, altruistic, humane, compassionate, caring, sympathetic, humanitarian, philanthropic.

**benign** adjective **1** *a benign attitude* kindly, gracious, benevolent, gentle. **2** *a benign climate* health-giving, wholesome, salubrious, temperate, pleasant, mild, agreeable, refreshing. **3** *benign circumstances* favorable, advantageous, propitious, auspicious, opportune.

**bent** adjective **bent on** *bent on winning* determined to, set on, insistent on, resolved to, fixed on, inclined to, disposed to.

**bent** noun inclination, predisposition, disposition, leaning, tendency, penchant, bias, predilection, proclivity, propensity, aptitude, facility.

**bequeath** verb leave, will, cede, endow on, bestow on, consign, commit, entrust, grant, transfer, hand down, pass down/on, impart, transmit.

**bequest** noun legacy, inheritance, endowment, estate, heritage, bestowal, bequeathal, gift, settlement.

**berate** verb scold, rebuke, reprimand, chide, reprove, upbraid, castigate, censure, criticize, rail at, harangue, lambaste, fulminate against, vituperate; *inf.* tell off, bawl out.

**bereavement** noun loss, deprivation, dispossession, death, passing, demise.

**bereft** adjective **bereft of** deprived of, robbed of, cut off from, parted from, devoid of, wanting, lacking, minus.

**berserk** adjective frenzied, mad, insane, crazed, hysterical, maniacal, manic, raving, wild, enraged, raging, uncontrollable, amok, unrestrainable, out of one's mind.

**berth** noun **1** *book a berth in the ship* bed, bunk, billet, hammock, cot. **2** *ships at their berths* anchorage, mooring, docking site. **3** *a well-paid berth* job, post, position, employment, appointment. **give a wide berth to** avoid, keep a careful distance from, stay away from.

**beseech** verb beg, implore, entreat, plead with, pray, petition, appeal to, supplicate.

**beset** verb **1** *beset with fears* attack, worry, plague, trouble, torment, pester, bedevil, harry. **2** *beset by enemy forces* surround, besiege, encircle, enclose, encompass, hem in.

**beside** preposition **1** *walking beside him* alongside, abreast of, next to, with, by, adjacent to, close to, near, neighboring. **2** *beside her work, his is poor* compared with, next to, against, in contrast to/with. **beside oneself** frantic, crazed, distraught, hysterical, uncontrolled, unrestrained. **beside the point** irrelevant, not applicable, immaterial.

**besiege** verb **1** *the castle was besieged by the enemy* lay siege to, beleaguer, blockade, surround, encircle, encompass. **2** *movie stars besieged by reporters* surround, enclose, beleaguer, beset. **3** *besieged with doubts* harass, assail. *See* BESET 1.

**best** adjective **1** *the best player* foremost, finest, leading, top, chief, principal, highest, worthiest, supreme, superlative, unsurpassed, unexcelled, excellent, first-class, first-rate, outstanding, preeminent; *inf.* ace. **2** *the best way to get there* most fitting, most suitable, most desirable.

**best** noun **1** *only the best may enter* finest, first class, top, cream, pick, flower, choice, elite. **2** *do your best* utmost, hardest; *inf.* damnedest. **3** *at his best in the morning* peak, prime, top form, height, apex. **4** *dressed in her best* best clothes, finery, finest clothes; *inf.* Sunday best, best bib and tucker. **5** *give him my best* best wishes, regards, kindest regards, greetings, love.

**best** verb *best the opposition* defeat, beat, conquer, get the better of, triumph over, get the upper hand of, prevail over, outdo, surpass, outwit.

**bestial** adjective **1** *bestial treatment of prisoners* brutish, savage, brutal, inhuman, barbarous, abominable, cruel, primitive,

2 *bestial sexual practices* depraved, vile, sordid, degenerate, carnal, lustful, lecherous, prurient.

**bestow** verb give, present, confer on, grant, donate, endow with, hand over, allot, assign, consign, apportion, distribute, bequeath, impart, accord, award, honor with.

**bet** verb 1 *bet $100 that he wins* wager, gamble, stake, pledge, risk, venture, hazard, chance. 2 *he never bets* gamble, wager, speculate. 3 *you can bet they've gone* be certain/sure, state confidently, predict.

**bet** noun 1 *enter into a bet* wager, gamble, speculation, venture, game of chance, lottery, sweepstake. 2 *place a bet of $100* wager, stake, ante, pledge. 3 *my bet is that they'll go* prediction, forecast, opinion, belief, feeling, view, theory. 4 *that's our best bet* choice, option, alternative, selection, course of action.

**betray** verb 1 *betray one's friends/wife* be disloyal/unfaithful to, treat treacherously, break faith with, break one's promise to, abandon, desert, forsake; *inf.* tell on, double-cross, stab in the back, sell down the river, walk out on, jilt. 2 *betray a secret* reveal, disclose, divulge, give away, let slip, blurt out, blab, lay bare, bring to light, uncover, expose.

**betrayal** noun 1 *betrayal of friends* informing on/against, being disloyal to, breaking faith with, breach of faith, bad faith, disloyalty, perfidy, treachery, duplicity, double-dealing; *inf.* double-crossing. 2 *betrayal of a secret* revelation, disclosure, divulgence, giving away.

**betrothal** noun engagement, marriage contract, espousal, pledge, promise, compact, covenant.

**better** adjective 1 *better players* finer, greater, superior, worthier, fitter. 2 *better course of action* more fitting, more suitable, more appropriate, more desirable, more advantageous, more useful. 3 *feeling better* healthier, fitter, less ill, stronger, well, cured, recovered; *inf.* mending, on the mend.

**better** verb 1 *better the conditions of the poor* raise, improve, ameliorate, advance, amend, rectify, relieve, reform, enhance. 2 *better the previous record* improve on, beat, surpass, exceed, top, outstrip, outdo.

**bevel** noun slope, slant, oblique, tilt, angle, cant, bezel.

**beverage** noun drink, potation, potable; refreshment, liquid, liquor; *inf.* libation.

**beware** verb be careful/wary, be cautious, be on one's guard, take heed, watch out, look out, be on the lookout/alert for.

**bewilder** verb confuse, mix up, muddle, puzzle, perplex, baffle, mystify, nonplus, disconcert, confound, bemuse, daze, stupefy.

**bewitched** adjective charmed, enchanted, beguiled, captivated, entranced, fascinated, spellbound, mesmerized.

**bias** noun 1 *cut on the bias* slant, cross, diagonal. 2 *a bias in favor of socialism | a musical bias* tendency, inclination, leaning, bent, partiality, penchant, predisposition, propensity, proclivity, predilection, prejudice, bigotry, intolerance.

**bias** verb prejudice, influence, sway, predispose, distort, bend, twist, warp, weight.

**bicker** verb wrangle, quarrel, argue, squabble, fight, disagree, dispute, spar; *inf.* scrap.

**bid** verb 1 *bid $100* offer, tender, proffer, propose. 2 *they bade him go* command, order, ask, direct, demand, require, invite.

**bid** noun 1 *put in a bid* offer, proposition, proffer, proposal, submission, price, sum, amount. 2 *a bid for power* attempt, effort.

**bidding** noun 1 *at his father's bidding* command, order, direction, demand, request, call, behest, invitation. 2 *present at the bidding* auction; offers, tenders, proposals.

**big** adjective 1 *a big garden/car* large, sizable, great, huge, enormous, immense, vast, massive, extensive, substantial, spacious, colossal, gigantic, mammoth, prodigious. 2 *a big man* large, tall, bulky, burly, hulking, huge, enormous, muscular, beefy, brawny, strapping, thickset, heavy, solid, corpulent, fat, obese, stout, gargantuan. 3 *a big boy now | a big sister* grown-up, adult, grown, mature, elder. 4 *a big decision* important, significant, serious, momentous. 5 *a big figure in the movement* influential, powerful, prominent, eminent, outstanding, leading, well-known, principal, foremost, noteworthy, notable, eminent, distinguished. 6 *big ideas/talk* arrogant, pretentious, ambitious, inflated, pompous, proud, haughty, conceited, boastful, bragging, bombastic. 7 *a big heart* generous, kindly, kindhearted, benevolent, magnanimous, unselfish.

**bigot** noun fanatic, zealot, sectarian, dogmatist, chauvinist, jingoist, racist, sexist.

**bigoted** adjective prejudiced, intolerant, fanatical, narrow-minded, biased, partial, one-sided, dogmatic, chauvinistic, jingoistic, racist, sexist.

**bigotry** noun prejudice, intolerance, fanaticism, narrow-mindedness, bias, partiality, dogmatism, discrimination, unfairness, injustice, chauvinism, jingoism, racism, sexism, provincialism.

**bigwig** noun VIP, dignitary, notable, personage, celebrity; *inf.* somebody, heavyweight, big shot, big gun.

**bilge** noun *don't talk bilge* rubbish, nonsense, drivel, gibberish, balderdash, hogwash; *inf.* rot.

**bilious** adjective **1** *feeling bilious* out of sorts, queasy, nauseated, sick. **2** *a bilious temperament* bad-tempered, ill-tempered, ill-humored, cross, irritable, crotchety, grumpy, peevish, crabby, testy, nasty; *inf.* grouchy.

**bilk** verb swindle, cheat, defraud, fleece, deceive, trick, bamboozle, gull; *inf.* con, do.

**bill** noun **1** *pay the bill* account, invoice, statement, reckoning, check; *inf.* tab. **2** *post no bills* poster, advertisement, flyer, notice, announcement, leaflet, circular, handout, handbill, brochure, placard, bulletin; *inf.* ad. **3** *top of the bill* program, playbill, list, listing, agenda, card, schedule, timetable. **4** *a congressional bill* proposal, measure, piece of legislation.

**bill** verb **1** *bill them for the goods* invoice, charge, debit, send a statement to. **2** *billed as the year's best musical* advertise, announce, post, give notice of, put up in lights.

**billet** verb accommodate, put up, house, quarter, station, shelter.

**billow** verb puff up, swell, fill out, balloon, belly, surge, roll.

**bin** noun container, receptacle, box, can, crate.

**bind** verb **1** *bind the twigs together* tie, tie up, fasten, secure, attach, rope, strap, truss, lash, tether, fetter, chain, hitch, wrap. **2** *bind the wound* bandage, dress, tape, wrap, cover, swathe. **3** *bind the surfaces together* stick, glue, cement, paste. **4** *bind the seams with gold* edge, trim, hem, border, finish. **5** *bind to secrecy* compel, obligate, oblige, constrain, force, impel, engage, require, prescribe. **6** *bound by family ties* constrain, restrain, restrict, hinder.

**bind** noun quandary, dilemma, predicament, difficulty, spot, tight spot.

**binding** adjective irrevocable, unalterable, compulsory, obligatory, imperative, mandatory.

**binge** noun spree, orgy, drinking bout, fling; *inf.* bender, jag.

**biography** noun life history, life, life story, memoir, profile, account; *inf.* bio.

**birth** noun **1** *present at the child's birth* childbirth, delivery, parturition, nativity. **2** *the birth of jazz* origin, beginnings, start, source, emergence, commencement, fountainhead, genesis. **3** *of noble birth* origin, descent, ancestry, lineage, line, extraction, derivation, family, parentage, house, blood, breeding, heritage, stock, strain, background.

**birthright** noun right, due, privilege, heritage, patrimony, legacy.

**bisect** verb halve, cleave, bifurcate, dichotomize.

**bisexual** adjective hermaphrodite, androgynous, epicene; *inf.* AC/DC, swinging both ways, switch-hitting, bi.

**bit** noun **1** *bits of bread* small piece, piece, section, part, segment, portion, particle, fragment, atom, flake, sliver, chip, crumb, grain, speck, scrap, shred, trace, morsel, iota, jot, whit, modicum, shard, hint, tinge, suggestion. **2** *see you in a bit* little, little while, short time, moment, minute, second, instant, short spell, flash, blink of an eye; *inf.* jiffy.

**bitch** noun **1** *the boss is a bitch* shrew, vixen, virago, harpy. **2** *this job's a real bitch* problem, difficulty, predicament, dilemma.

**bitch** verb complain, grumble, moan, carp, grouse, whine; *inf.* gripe, beef, bellyache.

**bitchy** adjective nasty, mean, spiteful, malicious, catty, vindictive, rancorous, venomous, snide, shrewish.

**bite** verb **1** *bite one's nails* chew, nibble at, gnaw at. **2** *dogs biting people* sink one's teeth into, nip, snap at, tear at. **3** *insects are biting* sting, prick, wound. **4** *biting on his pipe* clamp, grip, hold on to. **5** *measures beginning to bite* take effect, work, have results. **6** *fish/new clients not biting* take the bait, be lured, be enticed, be tempted. **7** *what's biting you?* annoy, irritate, bother, peeve, provoke, vex; *inf.* bug. **bite into 1** *bite into the food* eat, masticate, chew, munch, crunch, nibble. **2** *acids biting into the metal* eat into, corrode, burn, eat away at, erode, wear away.

**bite** noun **1** *the dog's playful bite* nip, snap. **2** *insect bites* sting, prick, puncture, wound, itch, smarting. **3** *a bite of the food* mouthful, piece, morsel, bit. **4** *a bite to eat* snack, refreshment. **5** *the sauce had bite* sharpness, spiciness, piquancy, pungency, edge; *inf.* kick, punch.

**biting** adjective **1** *biting winds* sharp, freezing, bitterly cold, harsh, nipping, stinging, piercing, penetrating. **2** *biting words* sharp, bitter, cutting, caustic, sarcastic, scathing, trenchant, mordant, stinging.

**bitter** adjective **1** *bitter substance* acid, pungent, acrid, tart, sour, biting, harsh. **2** *bitter old woman* resentful, embittered, rancorous, acrimonious, sullen, crabbed, sour, morose, begrudging. **3** *bitter experience* painful, distressing, distressful, harrowing, heartbreaking, heart-rending, agonizing, poignant, grievous, tragic, galling, vexatious. **4** *bitter winds* biting, sharp, harsh, stinging, piercing, penetrating, fierce. **5** *bitter quarrels* virulent, acrimonious, hostile, antagonistic, spiteful, vicious, rancorous, vindictive, malicious.

**bitterness** noun **1** *the bitterness of the medicine* acidity, pungency, acridity, tartness, sourness. **2** *the bitterness of the old woman* resentment, rancor, animosity, acrimony, sullenness, sourness. **3** *the bitterness of the memories* pain, painfulness, distress, agony, sadness, poignancy. **4** *the bitterness of the wind* sharpness, harshness, coldness, intensity. **5** *the bitterness of the quarrel* acrimony, hostility, spitefulness, rancor, malice, venom.

**bizarre** adjective strange, weird, peculiar, odd, unusual, uncommon, curious, abnormal, extraordinary, queer, freakish, offbeat, outlandish, unconventional, fantastic, *outré*, eccentric, grotesque, ludicrous, comical, ridiculous, droll, deviant, aberrant; *inf.* oddball, wacky, way-out, off-the-wall.

**blab** verb **1** *blab a secret* blurt out, let slip, reveal, disclose, divulge, tell, inform, report, let the cat out of the bag, tattle; *inf.* squeal, sing. **2** *blabbing on the phone* gossip, chat, chatter, blabber.

**black** adjective **1** *black horses* dark, pitch-black, pitch-dark, pitch, jet-black, jet, ebony, raven, sable, inky, coal-black. **2** *the black race* African-American, Negro, Negroid, colored, dark-skinned. **3** *black skies* dark, starless, moonless, unlit, unlighted, unilluminated, gloomy. **4** *children with black hands* dirty, grubby, filthy, grimy, unclean, muddy, sooty, soiled, stained, dingy. **5** *a black day* sad, melancholy, depressing, dismal, distressing, gloomy, somber, doleful, mournful, lugubrious, funereal. **6** *a black mood* angry, threatening, menacing, hostile, belligerent, resentful, sullen. **7** *black hearts* evil, wicked, sinful, bad. **8** *black humor* cynical, sick, macabre.

**black** noun **in the black** solvent, without debt. **in black and white** in print, written down, clearly/plainly/explicitly defined; in absolute terms, unequivocally, categorically, uncompromisingly.

**blackball** verb blacklist, bar, ban, exclude, shut out, expel, drum out, oust, cashier, ostracize, reject, repudiate, boycott, snub, shun.

**blacken** verb **1** *smoke blackening the walls* make black, darken, make dirty/sooty/smoky, besmudge. **2** *the sky blackened* darken, grow dim. **3** *they blackened his character* defame, speak ill/evil of, slander, libel, denigrate, disparage, slur, sully, vilify, defile, smear, besmirch, tarnish, stain.

**blacklist** verb debar, ban. *See* BLACKBALL.

**blackmail** noun extortion, exaction, extraction, intimidation, bribery, wresting, wringing, milking, bleeding, bloodsucking.

**blackmail** verb extort, exact, extract, bribe, wrest, force, hold to ransom, threaten, coerce, compel.

**blame** verb **1** *blame him for the accident* hold responsible/accountable, condemn, assign fault/liability/guilt. **2** *they're always blaming the child* find fault with, criticize, censure, reprimand, reproach, reprove, upbraid, scold, chide, berate, take to task. **blame on** ascribe to, attribute to, lay at the door of; *inf.* pin on, stick on.

**blame** noun **1** *put the blame on him* responsibility, guilt, accountability, liability, onus, culpability, fault; *inf.* rap. **2** *incur much blame for his behavior* censure, criticism, incrimination, accusation, condemnation.

**blameless** adjective innocent, guiltless, above reproach/suspicion, in the clear, without fault, virtuous, irreproachable, unimpeachable, unoffending, sinless.

**bland** adjective **1** *bland food* tasteless, flavorless, mild, insipid. **2** *a bland speech* dull, middle-of-the-road, mediocre, nondescript, humdrum, boring, uninteresting, monotonous, unexciting. **3** *a bland manner* smooth, affable, amiable, agreeable, gentle. **4** *bland breezes* mild, soft, calm, temperate, balmy, soothing.

**blank** adjective **1** *a blank paper/expression* void, empty, vacant, deadpan, impassive, poker-faced, vacuous. **2** *my mind went blank* uncomprehending, without ideas, at a loss, confused, puzzled. **3** *a blank refusal* outright, absolute, unqualified, utter, complete.

**blank** noun space, gap, emptiness, void, vacuum.

**blanket** noun **1** *cover with a blanket* coverlet, bedcover, spread, afghan; *inf.* throw. **2** *a blanket of snow* covering, mass, layer, coat, coating, film, sheet, carpet, cloak, mantle.

**blanket** adjective across the board, overall, inclusive, all-inclusive, comprehensive, general, wide-ranging, sweeping.

**blanket** verb *snow/mist blanketing the hills* cover, overlay, coat, carpet, conceal, hide, mask, cloud, cloak, veil, shroud, envelop, surround. **blanket out** *the storm blanketed out the broadcast* obscure, suppress, extinguish, stifle, smother.

**blare** verb trumpet, blast, clamor, boom, roar, bellow, resound, honk, toot, peal, clang, screech.

**blasé** adjective indifferent, apathetic, uninterested, unexcited, nonchalant, uncaring, unmoved, emotionless, phlegmatic, lukewarm, unconcerned, offhand, bored, weary, world-weary, jaded.

**blaspheme** verb profane, desecrate, swear, curse, revile, abuse, utter profanities.

**blasphemous** adjective profane, sacrilegious, irreligious, irreverent, impious, ungodly, godless, unholy.

**blasphemy** noun profanity, sacrilege, irreverence, impiety, impiousness, profaneness, ungodliness, unholiness, desecration, execration, cursing, swearing; curses, oaths, profanities.

**blast** noun 1 *a blast of cold air* gust, rush, draft, blow, gale, squall, storm. 2 *heard a blast of noise* blare, blaring, trumpeting, clamor, bellowing, boom, roar, clang, screech, wail, toot, honk, peal. 3 *killed by the blast* explosion, detonation, discharge, blow-up, blowing-up, eruption. 4 *receive a blast from the teacher* reprimand, rebuke, reproof.

**blast** verb 1 *car horns blasting away* boom, roar. See BLARE 1. 2 *blast the building to bits* blow, demolish, shatter, explode, break up. 3 *poverty blasted their hopes* blight, kill, destroy, wither, shrivel, crush, dash, blight, wreck, ruin, spoil, annihilate. 4 *blast the pupils for being late* reprimand, rebuke, criticize, upbraid, berate, castigate.

**blatant** adjective flagrant, glaring, obtrusive, obvious, overt, manifest, conspicuous, prominent, pronounced, bare-faced, naked, sheer, outright, out-and-out, unmitigated, brazen, shameless.

**blaze** noun 1 *destroyed in the blaze* fire, conflagration, holocaust, flames. 2 *a blaze of light* flash, flare, glare, streak, glitter; brightness, radiance, brilliance. 3 *a blaze of anger* outburst, burst, eruption, flare-up, explosion.

**blaze** verb 1 *the logs blazed* burn, be ablaze, flame. 2 *lights blazed in the street* shine, beam, flash, flare, glare, glitter. 3 *blaze with fury* flare up, blow up, explode, seethe, boil, smolder; *inf.* see red.

**bleach** verb make white/whiter, make pale/paler, lighten, blanch, fade, wash out.

**bleak** adjective 1 *a bleak landscape* bare, barren, desolate, exposed, unsheltered, open, windswept, windy, chilly, cold, waste, arid, desert. 2 *bleak surroundings/prospects* dreary, dismal, dark, gloomy, depressing, grim, miserable, cheerless, joyless, disheartening, unpromising, hopeless.

**bleary** adjective 1 *bleary eyes* blurred, blurry, tired, watery. 2 *bleary view* indistinct, hazy, foggy, fuzzy.

**bleed** verb 1 *the wounded were bleeding* shed/lose blood, emit blood. 2 *sap bleeding from a cut in the trunk* flow, run, ooze, seep, exude, trickle, weep, gush, spurt. 3 *bleeding money from the old man* extort, extract, squeeze, fleece. 4 *bleeding their resources* drain, exhaust, sap, deplete. 5 *hearts are bleeding for*

*them* ache, grieve, mourn, sorrow, suffer, agonize, feel.

**blemish** noun defect, flaw, blot, taint, stain, smirch, dishonor, disgrace; mark, blotch, spot, patch, bruise, scar, speck, imperfection, discoloration, disfigurement, birthmark, nevus, pimple; *inf.* zit.

**blemish** verb damage, mar, spoil, flaw, mark, spot, speckle, blotch, disfigure, discolor, deface, sully, tarnish, blot, taint, stain, besmirch, injure, damage, impair, flaw.

**blend** verb 1 *blend the ingredients* mix, combine, intermix, admix, mingle, commingle, unite, merge, compound, alloy, homogenize. 2 *colors blending with each other* harmonize, go with, complement, fit, suit.

**blend** noun mixture, mix, combination, amalgamation, amalgam, union, merging, compound, alloy, composite.

**bless** verb 1 *bless the altar* consecrate, sanctify, hallow, dedicate. 2 *bless God's name* glorify, praise, laud, extol. 3 *bless you for helping* give thanks for/to, thank. 4 *blessed with good looks* endow, bestow, favor, provide, grace. 5 *bless the enterprise* sanction, approve, endorse, support.

**blessed** adjective 1 *a blessed place* consecrated, sanctified, hallowed, sacred, holy, revered. 2 *blessed with talent* favored, endowed. 3 *blessed time* happy, joyful, joyous, blissful.

**blessing** noun 1 *utter a blessing* benediction, dedication, thanksgiving, consecration, invocation, grace. 2 *give the plan his blessing* approval, approbation, sanction, endorsement, support, good wishes. 3 *the blessing of good health* advantage, benefit, help, boon, godsend, favor, gift, luck, good fortune.

**blight** noun 1 *plants killed by blight* disease, canker, infestation, pestilence, fungus, mildew. 2 *the blight that destroyed the city* affliction, plague, scourge, bane, woe, curse, misfortune, calamity, trouble, tribulation.

**blight** verb kill, destroy, crush, ruin. See BLAST verb 3.

**blind** adjective 1 *blind people* unsighted, sightless, visually impaired, visionless, unseeing, stone-blind. 2 *he must be blind not to know* imperceptive, slow, slow-witted, dim-witted, obtuse, dense, thick. 3 *blind loyalty* unreasoned, uncritical, unthinking, mindless, injudicious, undiscerning, indiscriminate. 4 *a blind rage* rash, impetuous, hasty, reckless, uncontrolled, unrestrained, violent, furious, irrational. 5 *a blind entrance* concealed, hidden, obscured, out of sight. **blind to** unmindful of, heedless of, oblivious to, indifferent to, unaware of, ignorant of, insensitive to.

**blind** verb **1** *blinded in the accident | blinding the driver* deprive of sight/vision, render unsighted/sightless, obscure/block (one's) vision, get in (one's) line of vision, dazzle. **2** *blinded by love* deprive of judgment/reason, deceive, delude, beguile, hoodwink.

**blind** noun **1** *a window blind* screen, shade, curtain, shutter; venetian blind. **2** *the duck hunters' blind* camouflage, screen, façade, cover.

**blindly** adverb **1** *feeling his way blindly* without sight, sightlessly. **2** *rushing on blindly* unmindfully, carelessly, heedlessly, rashly, impetuously, recklessly, irrationally. **3** *loving him blindly* uncritically, injudiciously, undiscerningly, indiscriminately.

**blink** verb **1** *eyes blinking in the light* flutter, flicker, wink, bat, peer, squint. **2** *city lights blinking* flicker, twinkle, waver, wink, glimmer, glitter, sparkle, shimmer, gleam, shine. **3** *blink at corruption* turn a blind eye to, take no notice of, disregard, overlook, ignore, condone.

**bliss** noun ecstasy, joy, elation, rapture, euphoria, happiness, delight, heaven, paradise, seventh heaven, blessedness, beatitude.

**blister** noun **1** *blisters on the skin* pustule, pimple, boil, cyst, abscess, carbuncle, ulcer. **2** *blisters on the painted surface* bubble, swelling, bulge, protuberance.

**blithe** adjective **1** *a blithe mood* happy, cheerful, cheery, lighthearted, jolly, merry, carefree, buoyant, jaunty, sprightly. **2** *blithe disregard for others* casual, indifferent, careless, nonchalant, uncaring, unconcerned.

**blitz** noun bombardment, attack, assault, raid, offensive, onslaught, strike, all-out effort, endeavor.

**bloat** verb swell, puff up/out, blow up, distend, inflate, balloon, enlarge, expand, dilate.

**blob** noun **1** *a blob of whipped cream* globule, glob, bubble, pellet, dollop, lump. **2** *a blob of paint* spot, dab, splash, daub, blotch, blot, smudge.

**bloc** noun alliance, coalition, union, federation, league, ring, group, syndicate, combine, entente, party, wing, faction, cabal, clique, coterie.

**block** noun **1** *block of chocolate/soap* bar, cake, brick, chunk, hunk, lump, cube, ingot, wedge. **2** *building a new science block* building, complex. **3** *block of seats/shares* group, batch, band, cluster, set, section, quantity. **4** *a block in the pipe* blockage, obstruction, stoppage. **5** *a block to progress* deterrent, stumbling block. *See* BARRIER 2.

**block** verb **1** *block the pipe* clog, stop up, choke, plug, close, obstruct. **2** *block progress* hinder, impede, halt, stop, bar, check, arrest, deter, thwart, frustrate.

**blockade** noun *a blockade at the border* barrier, obstacle, obstruction, hindrance.

**blockhead** noun dunce, numskull, dolt, fool, simpleton, oaf, ass, dullard, idiot, ignoramus, bonehead, nincompoop; *inf.* chump, dingbat.

**blond, blonde** adjective fair, fair-haired, golden-haired, flaxen, tow-headed; fair-skinned, fair-complexioned, light.

**blood** noun **1** *blood was flowing* lifeblood, vital fluid. **2** *of noble blood* ancestry, kinship. *See* BIRTH 3. **3** *own flesh and blood* relations, kin, kindred.

**bloodshed** noun killing, slaughter, slaying, carnage, butchery, massacre, murder, blood-letting, blood bath, gore.

**bloodthirsty** adjective murderous, homicidal, savage, vicious, ruthless, barbarous, barbaric, brutal, bloody, sadistic, slaughterous, warlike, bellicose, sanguinary.

**bloody** adjective **1** *a bloody cloth* blood-stained, blood-soaked, blood-marked, blood-spattered. **2** *bloody actions/thoughts* savage, vicious. *See* BLOODTHIRSTY.

**bloom** noun **1** *perfect blooms* flower, blossom, floweret; flowering, blossoming, efflorescence. **2** *beauty losing its bloom* freshness, glow, luster, sheen, radiance.

**bloom** verb **1** *plants blooming* flower, blossom, open, open out, bud, burgeon. **2** *they've bloomed since moving to the country* flourish, thrive, prosper, succeed.

**blossom** noun flowers, flowerets. *See* BLOOM noun 1.

**blossom** verb **1** *trees blossoming* flower, burgeon. *See* BLOOM verb 1. **2** *she blossomed in her new environment* flourish, thrive. *See* BLOOM verb 2.

**blot** noun **1** *blots of ink/grease* spot, blotch, smudge, patch, dot, mark, speck, smear. **2** *a blot on his character* fault, imperfection. *See* BLEMISH noun.

**blot** verb **1** *paper blotted with ink-spots* spot, blotch, smudge, dot, smear, bespatter. **2** *the event blotted his reputation* besmirch, blacken. *See* BLEMISH verb. **blot out 1** *blot out the typist's mistake* erase, obliterate, delete, rub out. **2** *blot out the view* hide, conceal, obscure, obliterate. **3** *blot out memories* wipe out, erase, efface, obliterate, expunge. **blot up** *blot up the grease* soak up, absorb, dry up, take up.

**blotch** noun **1** *blotch of ink* smudge, dot, spot, speck, blot, stain, smear. **2** *blotch on the skin* patch, blemish, eruption, birthmark, nevus.

**blow** verb **1** *the wind was blowing* puff, flurry, bluster, blast, gust. **2** *hair blowing in the breeze* wave, flap, flutter, waft, stream, drift, whirl. **3** *wind blowing the leaves/boats* toss, sweep, whisk, drive, buffet, whirl, transport, convey. **4** *blow cigarette smoke* exhale, emit, expel. **5** *he was blowing a bit* puff, pant, wheeze, gasp, huff and puff. **6** *blow the trumpet* sound, play, toot, blare, blast. **7** *blow $100 on a meal* squander, fritter away, spend freely. **8** *blow one's chances* spoil, ruin, bungle, muff; *inf.* botch. **blow out 1** *blow out the candle* put out, extinguish, snuff, douse. **2** *the walls suddenly blew out* break open, burst, shatter, rupture, crack. **blow over** *their anger had blown over by morning* pass, die down, be forgotten, disappear, cease, subside. **blow up 1** *the bombed building blew up* explode, burst open, shatter, rupture. **2** *the bomb blew up* explode, go off, detonate, erupt. **3** *blow up the building* bomb, detonate, explode, blast. **4** *blow up the tire* inflate, pump up, swell, enlarge, distend. **5** *blow up the story* exaggerate, overstate, embroider, expand on. **6** *he blew up at the news* lose one's temper, go wild, rage; *inf.* hit the roof, fly off the handle.

**blow** noun **1** *a blow on the head* hit, knock, bang, punch, thump, smack, whack, thwack; *inf.* sock, wallop. **2** *her death was a blow* shock, upset, calamity, setback, jolt, reversal.

**blowzy** adjective **1** *a blowzy young woman* disheveled, slovenly, unkempt, untidy, sloppy, bedraggled. **2** *a blowzy drunk* coarse-looking, florid, ruddy-complexioned, red-faced.

**bludgeon** verb **1** *bludgeoned to death* club, cudgel, strike, hit, beat, beat up; *inf.* clobber. **2** *bludgeoned into agreeing* coerce, force, compel, browbeat, bully, railroad, steamroll, pressure; *inf.* strong-arm.

**blue** adjective **1** *a blue dress* azure, sky-blue, powder-blue, deep blue, royal blue, sapphire, ultramarine, navy, indigo, cyan, cobalt, cerulean. **2** *feeling blue* depressed, gloomy, dejected, downcast, unhappy, sad, melancholy; *inf.* down in the dumps. **3** *blue jokes* obscene, indecent, coarse, vulgar, bawdy, lewd, risqué, smutty, offensive.

**blueprint** noun plan, design, prototype, draft, outline, sketch, pattern, layout.

**blues** plural noun *a case of the blues* depression, dejection, despondency, unhappiness, sadness, melancholy, glumness, moroseness.

**bluff¹** verb **1** *he's only bluffing* pretend, fake, feign, put on, lie. **2** *he's bluffing you* deceive, delude, mislead, trick, hoodwink, bamboozle; *inf.* put one over on.

**bluff²** noun deception, deceit, pretense, sham, subterfuge, feint, delusion, hoax, fraud.

**bluff³** noun cliff, headland, ridge, promontory, peak, crag, bank, slope, escarpment.

**blunder** noun mistake, error, fault, slip, oversight, *faux pas*, gaffe; *inf.* slipup, booboo.

**blunder** verb **1** *management blundered badly* make a mistake, err; *inf.* slip up, screw up, blow it. **2** *blunder about in the dark* stumble, flounder, lurch, stagger, falter.

**blunt** adjective **1** *a blunt knife* unsharpened, dull, dulled. **2** *a blunt remark/person* frank, candid, outspoken, plainspoken, direct, bluff, to the point, brusque, curt.

**blunt** verb dull, take the edge off, deaden, dampen, numb, weaken.

**blur** verb **1** *blur the view* make indistinct/vague/hazy, obscure, dim, bedim, befog, fog, cloud, mask, veil. **2** *blur the windshield* smear, smudge, spot, blotch. **3** *blur one's judgment/memory* dull, numb, dim.

**blur** noun **1** *just a blur on the landscape* haze, haziness, indistinctness, dimness. **2** *a blur on the windshield* smear, smudge, spot, blotch.

**blurt** verb **blurt out** call out, cry out, exclaim, ejaculate, blab, disclose, divulge, let slip, let the cat out of the bag; *inf.* spill the beans.

**blush** verb redden, turn red/crimson/scarlet, flush, be red-faced.

**bluster** verb **1** *wind blustering* blast, gust, storm, roar. **2** *bullies blustering* rant, bully, domineer, harangue, threaten, boast, brag, swagger.

**bluster** noun **1** *the bluster of the wind* noise, roar, tumult. **2** *the bullies' bluster* ranting, bravado, bombast, boasting, bragging, swaggering, braggadocio; empty threats.

**board** noun **1** *a wooden board* plank, beam, panel, slat. **2** *pay for one's board* food, sustenance, meals, provisions, victuals; *inf.* grub, nosh. **3** *the board met to discuss policy* committee, council, panel, directorate, advisory group.

**board** verb **1** *they board with her* lodge, live, room. **2** *she boards three people* take in, put up, accommodate, house, feed. **3** *board the plane/train* get on, enter, embark. **board up** cover up/over, close up, shut up, seal.

**boast** verb **1** *boasting about his achievements* brag, crow, exaggerate, swagger, blow one's own trumpet, sing one's own praises, congratulate oneself, pat oneself on the back. **2** *the town boasts two museums* possess, own, enjoy, pride oneself/itself on.

**boat** noun vessel, craft; yacht, dinghy, sloop, sailboat, motorboat, speedboat, rowboat, punt, canoe, kayak.

**bob** verb move up and down, float, bounce, nod, jerk.

**bode** verb augur, presage, portend, betoken, foretell, prophesy, predict, forebode, foreshadow, indicate, signify, purport.

**bodily** adjective physical, corporeal, corporal, carnal, fleshly.

**body** noun 1 *well-formed bodies* frame, form, figure, shape, build, physique, framework, skeleton, trunk, torso. 2 *a body in the morgue* corpse, cadaver, carcass, remains; *inf.* stiff. 3 *more bodies than the room could hold* person, individual, being, human, creature. 4 *the body of the plane* main part, hub, core. 5 *a body of water* mass, expanse, extent, aggregate. 6 *the body of opinion* majority, preponderance, bulk, mass. 7 *the ruling body* group, party, band, association, company, confederation, bloc. 8 *material with little body* substance, firmness, solidity, density, shape, structure.

**bog** noun marsh, marshland, swamp, mire, quagmire, morass, slough, fen.

**bogged** verb **bogged down** stuck, impeded, halted, stopped, delayed, slowed down; trapped, entangled.

**bogeyman** noun monster, evil spirit, ghost, apparition, specter, phantom, goblin, hobgoblin; *inf.* spook.

**bogus** adjective fraudulent, counterfeit, fake, spurious, false, forged, sham, artificial, mock, make-believe, quasi, pseudo; *inf.* phony.

**bohemian** adjective unconventional, unorthodox, nonconformist, offbeat, avant-garde, eccentric, alternative, artistic; *inf.* arty, way-out.

**bohemian** noun nonconformist, hippie, beatnik, dropout.

**boil** verb 1 *the soup is boiling | boil the soup* bubble, simmer, cook, seethe, heat. 2 *the sea was boiling* seethe, bubble, churn, froth, foam. 3 *the teacher boiled with impatience* rage, fume, seethe, rant, rave, flare up.

**boil** noun carbuncle, furuncle, abscess, pustule, pimple.

**boiling** adjective 1 *boiling hot | boiling weather* scorching, roasting, baking, blistering, sweltering, searing, torrid. 2 *she was boiling at his insults* furious, angry, incensed, fuming, in a rage, enraged, infuriated, seething, irate.

**boisterous** adjective 1 *boisterous children/parties* noisy, loud, rowdy, unruly, wild, unrestrained, romping, disorderly, rambunctious. 2 *boisterous winds* blustery, gusty, stormy, rough, turbulent.

**bold** adjective 1 *a bold explorer | bold deeds* daring, intrepid, audacious, courageous, brave, valiant, fearless, adventurous, undaunted, valorous. 2 *a bold youth* brazen, shameless, forward, brash, impudent, saucy, immodest. 3 *bold colors* striking, vivid, showy, flashy, eye-catching, conspicuous, prominent.

**bolster** verb strengthen, reinforce, support, boost, prop up, buoy up, shore up, buttress, aid, invigorate.

**bolt** noun 1 *window bolts* bar, catch, latch, lock, fastener, hasp. 2 *bolt of lightning* flash, shaft, streak, burst, discharge, flare. 3 *make a bolt for it* dash, dart, run, bound, spring, jump.

**bolt** verb 1 *bolt the door* bar, lock, fasten, latch. 2 *bolt the pieces together* rivet, pin, clamp, fasten, batten. 3 *bolt from the room* dash, dart, run, sprint, hurtle, rush, flee, fly, spring, leap. 4 *bolting his food* gulp, gobble, devour, wolf, guzzle.

**bolt** adverb **bolt upright** straight up, very straight, rigid, stiff, completely upright.

**bomb** noun 1 *dropped a bomb on the target* explosive, incendiary, blockbuster, grenade, shell, missile, torpedo, letter bomb, nuclear bomb. 2 *the movie was a bomb* flop, failure, fiasco; *inf.* washout, turkey.

**bomb** verb 1 *bomb the target* bombard, blow up; shell, torpedo, blitz, strafe, cannonade. 2 *the movie bombed at the box office* flop, fail, fall flat, founder; *inf.* go up in smoke, go belly up.

**bombard** verb 1 *bombard military establishments* bomb, shell, torpedo, pound, blitz, strafe, pepper, fire at, attack, assault, raid. 2 *bombard with questions* assail, attack, besiege, beset, bother, hound.

**bombardment** noun bombing, shelling, strafing, blitz, blitzkrieg, air raid, strafe, cannonade, fusillade, attack, assault.

**bombast** noun pomposity, rant, bluster, turgidity, pretentiousness, ostentation, rodomontade.

**bona fide** adjective genuine, authentic, real, true, actual, sterling, sound, legal, legitimate.

**bonanza** noun windfall, godsend, stroke/run of luck, boon, bonus.

**bond** noun 1 *the bond/bonds of friendship* tie, link, binding, connection, attachment, union. 2 *sign a bond* agreement, contract, pact, covenant, compact, pledge, promise. **bonds** *freed from his bonds* chains, fetters, shackles, manacles.

**bond** verb join, connect, fasten, stick, unite, attach, bind; glue, gum, fuse, weld.

**bondage** noun slavery, enslavement, captivity, servitude, serfdom, oppression.

**bonus** noun 1 *the pleasant company was a bonus* extra, plus, gain, benefit, boon, perquisite, dividend, premium. 2 *a Christmas bonus* gratuity, tip, gift, perk, honorarium, reward.

**bony** adjective angular, rawboned, gaunt, scraggy, scrawny, skinny, skeletal.

**book** noun volume, tome, work, publication, title, opus, treatise, manual; booklet, pad, notebook, ledger, log.

**book** verb 1 *book a room/speaker* reserve, engage, charter. 2 *book the meeting* arrange, program, schedule, line up.

**bookish** adjective studious, scholarly, academic, literary, intellectual, brainy, highbrow, erudite, learned.

**boom** verb 1 *guns booming | the teacher boomed* resound, bang, blast, blare, roar, rumble, thunder, shout. 2 *the housing market boomed* burgeon, flourish, thrive, prosper, succeed, grow, expand, increase.

**boom** noun 1 *the boom of the guns/orator's voice* explosion, blast, blare, roar, bellow, rumble, reverberation, thundering. 2 *the boom in low-income housing* increase, upturn, upsurge, upswing, advance, growth, spurt, expansion, improvement, boost.

**boomerang** verb rebound, come back, spring back, return, recoil, reverse, ricochet, backfire.

**boon** noun benefit, advantage, gain, blessing, godsend, windfall.

**boor** noun lout, oaf, philistine, vulgarian, yahoo, barbarian; *inf.* clodhopper, clod, peasant.

**boorish** adjective rough, rude, coarse, ill-bred, ill-mannered, uncouth, churlish, gruff, uncivilized, unsophisticated, unrefined, crude, vulgar.

**boost** verb 1 *boost him up the tree* lift, raise, hoist, push, thrust, shove, heave, elevate. 2 *boost morale* raise, increase, improve, encourage, heighten, help, promote, foster. 3 *boost sales* increase, expand, improve, amplify, enlarge, inflate, develop, further, foster. 4 *boost their products* promote, advertise, publicize; *inf.* plug.

**boost** noun 1 *give him a boost into the tree* lift (up), push, thrust, shove, heave. 2 *a boost to morale* uplift, shot in the arm, help, inspiration, stimulus. 3 *a boost in sales* increase, expansion, rise, improvement, advance.

**boot** verb *boot the ball* kick, punt. **boot out** *boot him out* throw out, kick out, dismiss, sack, expel, eject, oust.

**booth** noun stall, stand, kiosk; cubicle, compartment, enclosure.

**booty** noun spoil, loot, plunder, pillage, prize, haul; spoils, profits, pickings, takings, winnings; *inf.* swag, boodle, the goods.

**border** noun 1 *the border of the lawn* edge, verge, perimeter, boundary, margin, skirt; fringes, bounds, limits, confines. 2 *passport checks at the border* frontier, boundary, divide.

**border** verb 1 *woods border the fields* edge, skirt, bound. 2 *Portugal borders Spain* adjoin, abut (on), be adjacent to, be next to, neighbor, touch. **border on** *his reply borders on rudeness* verge on, approach, come close to, near/similar to, resemble.

**bore**¹ verb pierce, perforate, puncture, penetrate, drill, tap, tunnel, burrow, mine, dig out, gouge out, sink.

**bore**² verb weary, tire, fatigue, send to sleep, exhaust, wear out; bore to tears, bore to death, bore out of one's mind.

**bore**³ noun tiresome person/thing, tedious person/thing, nuisance, bother, pest; *inf.* drag.

**boredom** noun tedium, tediousness, dullness, monotony, flatness, sameness, dreariness, weariness, ennui, world-weariness, malaise.

**boring** adjective tedious, dull, monotonous, humdrum, repetitious, unvaried, uninteresting, unexciting, flat, dry as dust, weary, wearisome, tiring, tiresome.

**borrow** verb 1 *borrow money* ask for the loan of; *inf.* cadge, mooch, scrounge, sponge, beg, bum. 2 *borrow another's ideas* appropriate, commandeer, copy, plagiarize, pirate, take, adopt, steal, filch; abstract, imitate, simulate.

**bosom** noun 1 *woman with a large bosom* breasts, bust, chest. 2 *bosom of the family* heart, center, core, midst, circle, protection, shelter. 3 *nurturing warm feelings in their bosoms* heart, soul, being; emotions, affections.

**bosom** adjective close, intimate, boon, confidential, dear, inseparable, faithful.

**boss** noun head, chief, manager, director, chief executive, administrator, leader, superintendent, supervisor, foreman, overseer, employer, master, owner; *inf.* honcho, top dog.

**boss** verb. **boss around** order about/around, bully, push around, domineer, dominate, ride roughshod over, control.

**bossy** adjective domineering, dominating, overbearing, dictatorial, authoritarian, despotic, imperious, high-handed, autocratic.

**botch** verb *botch (up) the situation/repair* bungle, make a mess of, spoil, mar, muff, mismanage, mangle, fumble; *inf.* mess up, foul up, screw up, blow, louse up.

**bother** verb 1 *don't bother your father* disturb, trouble, worry, pester, harass, annoy, upset, irritate, vex, inconvenience, provoke, plague, torment, nag. **2** *don't bother yourself with that* concern oneself, trouble oneself, inconvenience oneself, worry oneself. **3** *it bothers me that I lost it* upset, trouble, worry, concern, distress.

**bother** noun **1** *don't go to any bother* trouble, effort, inconvenience, exertion, strain; pains. **2** *what a bother we've missed it* nuisance, pest, annoyance, irritation, inconvenience, difficulty.

**bottle** noun flask, carafe, decanter, pitcher, flagon, demijohn, magnum.

**bottle** verb **bottle up** keep back, suppress, restrain, curb, contain, shut in, conceal.

**bottleneck** noun constriction, narrowing, obstruction, congestion, blockage, jam, gridlock.

**bottom** noun **1** *the bottom of the hill/pile* foot, lowest part/point, base. **2** *the bottom of the pillar* base, foundation, support, pedestal, substructure, underpinning. **3** *the bottom of the car* underside, underneath, undersurface, belly. **4** *the bottom of the sea* floor, bed, depths. **5** *the bottom of the class* lowest level, least important part, least honorable/valuable part. **6** *sitting on his bottom* hindquarters, buttocks, rear end, rear, rump; *inf.* backside, behind. **7** *his jealousy was at the bottom of it* origin, cause, root, source, starting point. **8** *get to the bottom of it* core, center, heart, base, basis, foundation, reality, essence, nitty-gritty, essentials.

**bottomless** adjective **1** *bottomless pit* deep, immeasurable, fathomless, unfathomable. **2** *bottomless reserves of energy* boundless, inexhaustible, infinite, unlimited, immeasurable, endless, limitless.

**bough** noun branch, limb, twig.

**boulevard** noun avenue, drive, road, thoroughfare, promenade.

**bounce** verb **1** *the ball bounced* rebound, spring back, bob, recoil, ricochet. **2** *children bouncing about* leap, skip, caper. See BOUND verb. **3** *bounce the troublemakers* throw out, eject, remove, expel, oust, evict; *inf.* kick out, boot out.

**bounce** noun **1** *ball without much bounce* spring, springiness, rebound, recoil, resilience, elasticity, give. **2** *losing bounce over the years* vitality, vigor, energy, vivacity, liveliness, spirit, dynamism; *inf.* go, getup-and-go, pep, oomph. **3** *with a run and a bounce* leap, spring. See BOUND².

**bound¹** verb leap, jump, spring, bounce, hop, vault, hurdle, prance, romp, caper, frolic, gambol.

**bound²** noun leap, jump, spring, bounce, hop, vault, hurdle; skip, bob, dance, prance, romp, caper, frolic, gambol.

**bound³** verb **1** *views bounded by prejudice* limit, confine, restrict, cramp, straiten,

restrain, demarcate, define. **2** *estates bounded by walls* enclose, surround, wall in, encircle, hem in. **3** *Germany is bounded on the west by France* border, adjoin, abut.

**boundary** noun **1** *the boundary between the countries* border, frontier, partition, dividing/bounding line. **2** *the boundary of the forest* border, periphery. See BOUNDS. **3** *the boundary between sentiment and sentimentality* dividing line, borderline, demarcation line. **4** *push back the boundaries of knowledge* bounds, limits, outer limits, confines, extremities, barriers.

**boundless** adjective limitless, without limit, unlimited, unbounded, endless, unending, inexhaustible, infinite, interminable, unceasing, untold, immeasurable, immense, vast.

**bounds** plural noun limits, boundaries, confines, restrictions, borders, margins, edges, fringes; periphery, perimeter, precinct, pale.

**bountiful** adjective **1** *a bountiful hostess* generous, magnanimous, liberal, giving, openhanded, unstinting, unsparing, munificent. **2** *a bountiful supply of food* ample, abundant, bumper, plentiful, copious, lavish, prolific, profuse, bounteous.

**bounty** noun *a bounty for finding the treasure* reward, recompense, remuneration, gratuity, tip, premium, bonus.

**bouquet** noun **1** *the bride's bouquet* bunch/spray of flowers, spray, posy, wreath, garland, nosegay, boutonnière, chaplet, corsage. **2** *the wine's bouquet* aroma, smell, fragrance, perfume, scent, redolence, savor, odor. **3** *bouquets from the management* compliment, commendation, tribute, praise, congratulations.

**bourgeois** adjective **1** *bourgeois values* materialistic, capitalistic, money-oriented. **2** *bourgeois way of life* conventional, ordinary, uncultured, philistine, uncreative, unimaginative.

**bout** noun **1** *bouts of inactivity* spell, period, time, stretch, stint, turn, fit, run, session. **2** *a bout of flu* attack, fit, paroxysm. **3** *defeated in the last bout* match, contest, round, competition, encounter, fight.

**bovine** adjective cowlike, sluggish, stolid, phlegmatic, dull, dense, doltish.

**bow** verb **1** *bow to the queen* make obeisance, nod, curtsy, genuflect, bend the knee, salaam, kowtow, prostrate oneself. **2** *age had bowed his back* bend, stoop, curve, arch, crook. **3** *bow to the inevitable* give in, yield, submit, capitulate, acquiesce. **bow out** leave, resign, withdraw, step down, give up, get out, quit, pull out.

**bowels** plural noun **1** *an infection affecting the bowels* intestines, entrails, viscera, guts; *inf.* insides, innards. **2** *the bowels of the earth/machine* interior, inside, core, belly, cavity, depths.

**bowl** noun **1** *a bowl of fruit* dish, basin, vessel. **2** *dust bowl* hollow, crater, hole, depression, valley.

**bowl** verb **bowl over** overwhelm, astound, amaze, dumbfound, stun, surprise; *inf.* floor.

**box**[1] noun **1** *a box of cigars | a box shipped from Hawaii* crate, case, carton, pack, package, chest, trunk, bin, casket. **2** *a theater/jury box* compartment, cubicle, enclosure.

**box**[2] verb **box in/up** enclose, shut in, hem in, confine, restrain, constrain, cage in, coop up.

**box**[3] verb **1** *he boxes professionally* fight, spar, grapple. **2** *box him on the ears* strike, hit, thump, cuff, slap, punch, knock, wallop, batter, pummel, thwack, buffet; *inf.* belt, sock, clout, whack, slug, slam, whop.

**boxer** noun fighter, pugilist, prizefighter, sparring partner.

**boy** noun youth, lad, youngster, kid, junior, stripling.

**boy** interjection *boy, what a great book* wow, gosh, gee, god, Lord, holy cow, jeepers, goodness.

**boycott** verb spurn, avoid, eschew, shun, reject, blackball, blacklist, ban, bar, embargo, prohibit, outlaw.

**boyfriend** noun sweetheart, young man, lover, man, suitor, beau, admirer; *inf.* steady, date.

**boyish** adjective youthful, young, childlike, immature, adolescent, juvenile, childish, callow, green, puerile.

**brace** noun **1** *hold in a brace* clamp, vice, fastener, coupling. **2** *the wall's brace* support, prop, beam, strut, stay, truss, buttress.

**brace** verb **1** *beams firmly braced* support, strengthen, reinforce, fortify, shore up, prop up, hold up, buttress. **2** *brace oneself for the results* prepare, steady, strengthen, fortify, tense.

**bracing** adjective invigorating, refreshing, stimulating, energizing, exhilarating, reviving, fortifying, strengthening, restorative.

**bracket** noun **1** *a wall bracket* support, prop, buttress. **2** *in a different financial bracket* group, grouping, category, grade, classification, class, set, section, division.

**brag** verb boast, crow, show off, bluster, blow one's own trumpet, sing one's own praises, pat oneself on the back.

**braggart** noun boaster, brag, show-off, trumpeter, braggadocio.

**braid** verb weave, interweave, plait, entwine, twine, intertwine, interlace, twist.

**braid** noun **1** *trim it with braid* cord, thread, tape, twine, yarn, edging, rickrack. **2** *hair in braids* plait, pigtail.

**brain** noun **1** *studying the brain* cerebral matter, encephalon. **2** *a good brain* mind, intellect, brainpower, intelligence, wit, head; *inf.* gray matter. **3** *one of the brains of our group* genius, intellectual, intellect, thinker, mind, scholar, mastermind; *inf.* highbrow, egghead.

**brains** plural noun intellect, intelligence, wit, head, sense, cleverness, brightness, understanding, shrewdness, sagacity, acumen, capacity, capability; *inf.* savvy.

**brainwashing** noun indoctrination, inculcation, persuasion, conditioning.

**brainy** adjective clever, intelligent, bright, brilliant, smart, gifted.

**brake** noun curb, check, damper, restraint, constraint, rein, control.

**brake** verb reduce speed, slow, slow down, decelerate.

**branch** noun **1** *the branch of a tree* bough, limb, stem, twig, shoot, sprig, arm. **2** *the branch of the deer's antlers* offshoot, prong. **3** *the local branch of the bank* division, subdivision, section, subsection, department, part, wing, office.

**branch** verb *the road branches before the village* fork, divide, furcate, bifurcate, divaricate; separate, diverge. **branch off** diverge, deviate, depart, turn aside. **branch out** extend, spread out, widen, broaden, diversify, expand, enlarge.

**brand** noun **1** *a brand of soup/comedy* make, line, label, trade name, trademark; kind, type, sort, variety, style, stamp, cast. **2** *recognize the cow by its brand* tag, marker, earmark. **3** *a brand on him for life* stigma, stain, blot, taint, slur.

**brand** verb **1** *identifying marks branded on cattle* burn, burn in, scorch, sear. **2** *experiences branded on his mind* stamp, imprint, print, engrave, impress, fix. **3** *branded as a thief* stigmatize, mark, disgrace, discredit, denounce.

**brandish** verb wave, flourish, wield, raise, swing, display, flaunt.

**brash** adjective **1** *a loud, brash young man* bold, self-assertive, audacious, aggressive, brazen, forward, cocky, impudent, insolent. **2** *brash actions* hasty, rash, impetuous, impulsive, reckless, heedless. **3** *brash colors* loud, showy, garish, gaudy, vulgar, tasteless.

**brassy** adjective **1** *a brassy teenager* loud, self-assertive, flashy, vulgar, showy, garish. *See* BRAZEN. **2** *brassy music* blaring, noisy, thundering, deafening, harsh.

**brat** noun imp, rascal, little devil, urchin, minx, whippersnapper.

**bravado** noun swagger, swaggering, blustering, boasting, boastfulness, bragging, bombast, braggadocio.

**brave** adjective **1** *brave soldiers* courageous, valiant, intrepid, fearless, plucky, gallant, bold, daring, undaunted, dauntless, lion-hearted, valorous; *inf.* gutsy, spunky. **2** *a brave show* splendid, fine, grand.

**brave** verb face, stand up to, endure, put up with, bear, suffer, withstand, defy, challenge, confront.

**bravery** noun courage, courageousness, valor, fearlessness, pluck, pluckiness, gallantry, boldness, daring, grit, mettle, spirit, dauntlessness; *inf.* guts, spunk.

**brawl** noun fight, fracas, wrangle, melee, rumpus, scuffle, altercation, squabble, free-for-all, tussle, brouhaha, commotion, uproar, donnybrook.

**brawl** verb fight, wrangle, wrestle, scuffle, tussle, clash, battle, quarrel, argue; *inf.* scrap.

**brawn** noun muscle, muscularity, burliness, heftiness, huskiness, strength, might; *inf.* beefiness, beef.

**brawny** adjective muscular, burly, hefty, strong, powerful, strapping, husky, sinewy.

**brazen** adjective bold, audacious, defiant, forward, brash, presumptuous, impudent, insolent, impertinent, brassy, pert, saucy, shameless, immodest, unashamed, unabashed; *inf.* pushy.

**breach** noun **1** *a breach in the seawall* break, rupture, split, crack, fissure, fracture, rent, rift, cleft. **2** *a breach of confidence* breaking, violation, infringement, transgression. **3** *a breach between the two families* breaking-off, estrangement, separation, severance, rift, schism, disunion, alienation, dissension, falling-out, quarrel, discord.

**breach** verb **1** *breach the enemy defenses* break/burst through, rupture, split. **2** *breach the contract* break, violate, infringe, defy, disobey.

**breadth** noun **1** *the breadth of the room* width, broadness, wideness, thickness, span. **2** *the breadth of her knowledge* extent, extensiveness, scope, range, scale, degree, spread, vastness, expanse, magnitude, measure. **3** *breadth of spirit* liberality, broad-mindedness, freedom, latitude, magnanimity.

**break** verb **1** *break the cup/rope* smash, shatter, crack, fracture, split, burst, fragment, splinter, shiver, crash, snap, rend, tear, divide, sever, separate, part, demolish, disintegrate. **2** *break the law* contravene, violate, infringe, breach, defy, disobey. **3** *break for lunch* stop, pause, discontinue, rest; *inf.* knock off, take five. **4** *break one's concentration/journey* interrupt, suspend, discontinue, disturb, interfere with. **5** *break his resolve* overcome, crush, subdue, defeat, weaken, impair, undermine, cripple, enfeeble. **6** *he broke under questioning* crack, collapse, give in, yield, cave in. **7** *the recession broke him* ruin, crush, humble, degrade, bankrupt. **8** *break the news gently* tell, announce, impart, reveal, disclose. **9** *break the record* beat, surpass, outdo, better, exceed, top; *inf.* cap. **10** *break the code* decipher, decode, unravel, solve, figure out. **11** *the day/scandal broke* begin, emerge, erupt, appear. **12** *the weather broke* change, alter, vary, shift. **13** *break one's fall* cushion, soften, lessen, diminish. **break away** make a break for it, flee, make off, escape, decamp; detach oneself, secede, part company, leave. **break down 1** *the talks broke down* fail, collapse, founder, fall through. **2** *he broke down and cried* lose control, collapse, cave in, crumble, be overcome, go to pieces, come apart at the seams; *inf.* crack up. **3** *break down the figures in the budget* separate out, analyze, dissect, itemize. **break in 1** *break in hurriedly* burst in, barge in. **2** *he broke in with his own comments* interrupt, butt in, intervene, cut in, intrude. **3** *he broke in last night* break and enter, burgle, rob. **4** *break in the horse* train, tame, condition, prepare, initiate, show the ropes to. **break into** *break into song* commence, launch into, burst into, give way to. **break off 1** *break off a branch* pull off, snap off, detach, separate, sever. **2** *break off diplomatic relations* end, terminate, stop, cease, finish, discontinue, call a halt to. **break out** *war/fighting broke out* start/commence/occur suddenly, erupt, burst out, set in, arise. **break out of** *break out of prison* escape from, make one's escape from, break loose of/from, burst out of, get free of/from, free oneself of/from. **break up 1** *the meeting broke up at midnight* adjourn, end, come to an end, stop, discontinue, terminate. **2** *the crowd broke up* disperse, go their separate ways, part company. **3** *the police broke up the crowd* disperse, scatter, disband, separate, put to rout, send off. **4** *the couple have broken up* separate, part, divorce, split up, come to a parting of the ways. **5** *jealousy broke up their marriage* bring to an end, end, terminate, bring to a halt, kill, destroy. **6** *break up at his jokes* laugh, guffaw, double up, split one's sides, hold one's sides; *inf.* in stitches.

**break** noun **1** *a break in the seawall* crack, hole, gap, opening, gash, chink, fracture, split, fissure, tear, rent, rupture, rift, chasm, cleft. **2** *a break for lunch* interval, stop, pause, halt, rest, respite, lull, interlude, intermission, recess; coffee break; *inf.* breather, breathing spell, letup, time out, down time, vacation, time off, recess. **3** *a break in their education* interruption, discontinuation, suspension, hiatus. **4** *a break in the weather* change, alteration, variation. **5** *a break in diplomatic relations* rift, breach, split, rupture, schism, chasm. **7** *although losing, we got a break* lucky break, stroke of luck, advantage, chance, opening.

**breakable** adjective fragile, frangible, frail, delicate, flimsy, insubstantial, brittle, crumbly, friable, destructible.

**breakdown** noun **1** *the car's breakdown* failure, malfunctioning; *inf.* conking out. **2** *the breakdown of the talks* failure, collapse, foundering, falling through; *inf.* fizzling out. **3** *suffer a breakdown* collapse, nervous breakdown, loss of control, going to pieces, disintegration; *inf.* crack-up. **4** *a breakdown of the figures* itemization, analysis, dissection, categorization, classification.

**breakneck** adjective fast, rapid, speedy, swift, reckless, dangerous.

**breakup** noun end, termination, cessation, dissolution, disintegration, splitting up, breakdown, failure, collapse, foundering.

**breath** noun **1** *take a deep breath* inhalation, inspiration, exhalation, expiration, pant, gasp, wheeze; breathing, respiration. **2** *no breath left in him* breath of life, life, life force, vital force. **3** *hardly a breath of air* breeze, puff, gust, waft, zephyr. **4** *a breath of spring* hint, suggestion, whiff, trace, touch, whisper. **5** *stop for breath* pause, lull, rest, respite; *inf.* breather.

**breathe** verb **1** *she breathed deeply* respire, inhale, inspire, exhale, expire, puff, pant, gasp, wheeze, gulp. **2** *the wind breathing through the trees* blow, whisper, murmur, sigh.

**breather** noun stop, pause. *See* BREAK noun 2.

**breathless** adjective **1** *find myself breathless when climbing stairs* out of breath, wheezing, panting, puffing, gasping, choking, gulping, winded. **2** *breathless with excitement* agog, avid, eager, excited, on edge.

**breathtaking** adjective spectacular, impressive, magnificent, awesome, awe-inspiring.

**breed** verb **1** *lions breeding in captivity* reproduce, procreate, multiply, give birth, beget, propagate. **2** *breed horses* raise, rear, nurture. **3** *born and bred in the town* bring up, rear, raise, develop, educate, train, nurture. **4** *breed discontent* cause, bring about, give rise to, create, produce, generate, arouse, stir up, induce, occasion, make for.

**breed** noun **1** *a breed of cows* family, variety, strain, stock, line, race, lineage, extraction, pedigree. **2** *a new breed of doctor* kind, type, variety, class, brand, strain.

**breeding** noun **1** *the season for breeding* reproduction, generation, propagation. **2** *a lady by breeding* upbringing, rearing, education, training, nurture. **3** *people of breeding* refinement, cultivation, culture, polish, civility, gentility, courtesy, manners.

**breeze** noun zephyr, flurry, waft, draft.

**breezy** adjective **1** *a breezy day* windy, blustery, gusty. **2** *a breezy manner/individual* jaunty, cheerful, lighthearted, carefree, blithe, free and easy, easygoing, casual, airy, sprightly, lively, spirited, animated.

**brevity** noun **1** *the brevity of the report* shortness, briefness, conciseness, succinctness, compactness, terseness, pithiness. **2** *the brevity of summer* shortness, transitoriness, transience, impermanence, ephemerality.

**brew** verb **1** *brew beer* make, ferment. **2** *brew tea* infuse, steep, prepare. **3** *trouble is brewing* gather, gather force, form, loom, threaten, impend. **4** *brewing something evil* plot, scheme, hatch, plan, devise, invent, concoct, stir up, foment; *inf.* cook up.

**bribe** noun inducement, enticement, lure, subornation, carrot; *inf.* graft, hush money, protection money, boodle, kickback, payola.

**bribe** verb buy off, corrupt, suborn; *inf.* grease/oil the palm of, get at, pay off.

**bridal** adjective nuptial, marital, matrimonial, connubial, conjugal.

**bride** noun wife; newlywed, honeymooner, blushing bride; war bride.

**bridge** noun **1** *a bridge over the river* arch, span, overpass, viaduct. **2** *a bridge between the two families* bond, link, tie, connection, cord, binding.

**bridge** verb span, cross, cross over, go over, pass over, traverse, extend across, reach across, arch over.

**bridle** verb **1** *bridle your tongue/anger* curb, restrain, hold back, keep control of, keep in check, put a check on, govern, master, subdue. **2** *she bridled at his insults* bristle, become indignant, rear up, draw oneself up, feel one's hackles rise.

**brief** adjective **1** *a brief report* short, concise, succinct, to the point, terse, pithy, crisp, condensed, compressed, thumbnail, epigrammatic, sparing, compendious. **2** *a brief life* short, short-lived, fleeting, momentary, passing, transitory, transient, temporary, impermanent, ephemeral, evanescent. **3** *the boss was rather brief with him* short, abrupt, curt, brusque.

**brief** verb instruct, inform, direct, guide, advise, prepare, prime; *inf.* give someone the rundown/low-down, fill in.

**briefly** adverb concisely, succinctly, to the point, tersely, economically, sparingly.

**brigand** noun robber, ruffian, freebooter. *See* BANDIT.

**bright** adjective **1** *a bright light* shining, brilliant, vivid, intense, blazing, dazzling, beaming, sparkling, flashing, glittering, scintillating, gleaming, glowing, twinkling, glistening, shimmering; illuminated, luminous, lustrous, radiant, effulgent, incandescent, phosphorescent. **2** *bright colors* vivid, brilliant, intense, glowing, bold, rich. **3** *bright children/minds* clever, intelligent, sharp, quick-witted, quick, smart. **4** *a bright smile/personality* happy, genial, cheerful, jolly, joyful, vivacious, lively, buoyant. **5** *a bright future* promising, optimistic, favorable, auspicious, providential, fortunate, golden.

**brighten** verb **1** *lights brighten the room* light up, lighten, illuminate, illumine, irradiate. **2** *brighten her day/mood* cheer up, gladden, enliven, buoy up, animate; *inf.* buck up, pep up.

**brilliant** adjective **1** *a brilliant light* blinding, resplendent, coruscating. *See* BRIGHT 1. **2** *brilliant children* brainy, intellectual, gifted, talented, accomplished, learned, erudite, cerebral. **3** *a brilliant course of action* clever, intelligent, smart, astute, masterly. **4** *a brilliant display* magnificent, splendid, superb, impressive, remarkable, exceptional, glorious, illustrious.

**brim** noun **1** *the brim of the cup* rim, lip, brink, edge. **2** *the brim of the hat* visor, shield, shade.

**bring** verb **1** *bring books/water* carry, bear, take, fetch, convey, transport, deliver, lead, guide, conduct, usher, escort. **2** *war brought hardship* cause, create, produce, result in, wreak, effect, contribute to, engender, occasion. **3** *his job brings good wages* make, fetch, yield, net, gross, return. **bring about** cause, create, produce, give rise to, achieve, result in, effect, occasion. **bring down 1** *bring down prices/the government* cause to fall, lower, reduce, overthrow, pull down, lay low. **2** *the bad news brought her down* depress, sadden, cast down, make desolate, weigh down. **bring forward** raise, put forward, propose, suggest, bring to/put on the table. **bring in 1** *his son brings in $3000* earn, yield, gross, net, return, realize. **2** *bring in a new bill* introduce, launch, inaugurate, initiate, institute. **bring off** pull off, carry off, achieve, succeed in,

accomplish. **bring up 1** *bring up the children* rear, raise, train, educate, nurture, foster, develop. **2** *bring up the subject* raise, broach, introduce, mention, touch upon.

**brink** noun **1** *the brink of the cliff* edge, verge, margin, rim, extremity, limit, border, boundary, fringe, skirt. **2** *the brink of disaster* verge, threshold, point.

**brisk** adjective **1** *at a brisk pace* quick, rapid, fast, swift, speedy, energetic, lively, vigorous, agile, sprightly, spirited. **2** *brisk weather* bracing, crisp, keen, biting, invigorating, refreshing. **3** *a brisk manner* nononsense, brusque, abrupt, sharp, curt, snappy. **4** *business was brisk* rapid, busy, bustling, active, hectic.

**bristle** noun stubble, whiskers; prickle, spine, quill, thorn, barb.

**bristle** verb **1** *the dog's hair bristled* stiffen, rise, stand up, stand on end. **2** *she bristled at the insults* bridle, become indignant, rear up, draw oneself up.

**brittle** adjective **1** *a brittle substance/relationship* breakable, splintery, shatterable, crisp, fragile, frail, delicate, frangible, weak, unstable. **2** *a brittle laugh* harsh, hard, sharp, strident, grating, rasping.

**broach** verb introduce, bring up, raise, mention, open, put forward, propound, propose, suggest, submit.

**broad** adjective **1** *a broad street* wide, large. **2** *broad plains* extensive, vast, spacious, expansive, sweeping, boundless. **3** *a broad range of subjects* wide-ranging, broad-ranging, general, comprehensive, inclusive, encyclopedic. **4** *the broad outline of the plan* general, nonspecific, vague, loose. **5** *a broad hint* open, obvious, direct, plain, explicit, unmistakable. **6** *broad daylight* full, complete, total, clear, open. **7** *a woman of broad views* liberal, tolerant. *See* BROAD-MINDED. **8** *broad humor* coarse, vulgar, gross, unrefined, indelicate.

**broadcast** verb **1** *broadcast a program* transmit, relay, beam, send out, put on the air, radio, televise, telecast. **2** *broadcast the news of his downfall* make public, announce, report, publicize, publish, advertise, proclaim, air, spread, circulate, pass around, disseminate. **3** *broadcast seed* scatter, sow, disperse, strew.

**broadcast** noun program, show, transmission, telecast.

**broaden** verb widen, expand, enlarge, extend, increase, augment, amplify, fill out, develop.

**broad-minded** adjective open-minded, liberal, tolerant, forbearing, indulgent, impartial, unprejudiced, unbiased, unbigoted, undogmatic, catholic, flexible, dispassionate, just, fair, progressive, free-thinking.

**brochure** noun booklet, leaflet, pamphlet, folder, handbill, handout, circular, notice, advertisement, flyer.

**broke** adjective penniless, bankrupt, insolvent, poverty-stricken, impoverished, impecunious, penurious, indigent, destitute, stone-broke, flat broke; *inf.* cleaned out, strapped for cash.

**broken** adjective **1** *a broken cup* smashed, shattered, cracked, fractured, split, burst, fragmented, splintered, shivered, crushed, snapped, rent, torn, severed, destroyed. **2** *the machine is broken* damaged, faulty. *See* BROKEN-DOWN 1. **3** *broken laws* contravened, violated, infringed, disobeyed, ignored, transgressed. **4** *a broken sleep/chain of thought* interrupted, disconnected, disrupted, discontinuous, intermittent, spasmodic. **5** *a broken man* beaten, defeated, subdued, crushed, humbled, ruined, demoralized, dispirited. **6** *broken businesses* ruined, crushed, bankrupt. **7** *broken English* halting, hesitating, disjointed, faltering, imperfect.

**broken-down** adjective **1** *a broken-down machine* broken, damaged, faulty, defective, out of order/commission, nonfunctioning, inoperative; *inf.* on the blink, kaput, bust, busted. **2** *a broken-down old shack* dilapidated, in disrepair, ramshackle.

**brokenhearted** adjective heartbroken, grief-stricken, desolate, devastated, inconsolable, miserable, overwhelmed, wretched, sorrowing, mourning, forlorn, woeful, crestfallen.

**broker** noun agent, negotiator, middleman, intermediary, factor, dealer.

**brood** noun young, offspring, progeny, family, hatch, clutch, nest, litter, children.

**brood** verb *brood about the problem* worry, fret, agonize, think, ponder, meditate, muse, mull, dwell (on/upon), ruminate.

**brook** noun stream, streamlet, creek, rivulet, rill, brooklet, runnel.

**brook** verb tolerate, stand, bear, allow.

**brothel** noun bordello, house of ill repute, bawdy house, whorehouse.

**brother** noun **1** *she has two brothers* sibling, blood-brother; kinsman; *inf.* sib, bro. **2** *brothers in crime* associate, colleague, companion, partner, comrade; *inf.* pal, chum.

**brotherhood** noun **1** *feelings of brotherhood* comradeship, fellowship, companionship, camaraderie, friendship, esprit de corps. **2** *a brotherhood of merchants* association, alliance, society, union, league, fraternity, lodge.

**brotherly** adjective fraternal; friendly, affectionate, amicable, cordial, benevolent, neighborly, philanthropic.

**browbeat** verb intimidate, terrorize. *See* BULLY verb.

**brown** adjective **1** *brown hair* chocolate, cocoa, umber, reddish-brown, auburn, copper, copper-colored, bronze, henna, mahogany, walnut, rust, brick, terra-cotta, tan, tawny, ginger, cinnamon, hazel, fawn, beige. **2** *brown bodies on the beach* tanned, sunburned, bronze, bronzed.

**browse** verb **1** *not reading/buying, just browsing* scan, skim, glance/look through, thumb/leaf/flip through, look around, have a look, window-shop. **2** *cows browsing* graze, feed, eat, nibble, pasture.

**bruise** verb **1** *bruise the skin/fruit* discolor, mark, blemish, contuse, injure, damage. **2** *her feelings are easily bruised* hurt, upset, offend, insult, wound, displease, distress.

**bruise** noun black-and-blue mark, mark, blemish, contusion, injury, swelling.

**brunt** noun full force, force, impact, shock, burden, thrust, violence, pressure, strain, stress; repercussions, consequences.

**brush** noun **1** *sweep/paint with a brush* broom, besom, whisk. **2** *with a brush of his arm* touch, stroke; *inf.* swipe. **3** *a brush with the law/enemy* encounter, clash, conflict, confrontation, fight, battle.

**brush** verb **1** *brush one's clothes/teeth* sweep, groom, clean, buff. **2** *breeze brushing her cheek* touch, caress, glance, contact, stroke. **brush aside** dismiss, shrug off, disregard, ignore, forget about, have no time for. **brush off** cold-shoulder, give the cold shoulder to, rebuff, snub, spurn, disregard, reject, scorn, disdain. **brush up/brush up on** refresh one's memory of, relearn; *inf.* bone up.

**brusque** adjective abrupt, curt, blunt, sharp, caustic, gruff, bluff, hasty, discourteous, rude.

**brutal** adjective **1** *a brutal attack* savage, cruel, bloodthirsty, vicious, ruthless, merciless, pitiless, uncivilized, inhuman, barbarous. **2** *brutal instincts* bestial, brutish, beastly, animal, coarse, carnal, sensual.

**brute** noun **1** *the howling brutes of the jungle* beast, wild beast, wild animal, animal, creature. **2** *a murderous brute* monster, savage, sadist, barbarian, devil, fiend, ogre, lout, oaf, boor, churl, dolt.

**bubble** noun **1** *blowing soap bubbles* globule, glob, bead, blister, drop, droplet. **2** *misled by the real-estate bubble* illusion, delusion, fantasy, dream, chimera.

**bubble** verb **1** *champagne bubbling* fizz, effervesce, sparkle, foam, froth, spume. **2** *stew bubbling on the stove* boil, simmer, seethe, percolate. **3** *bubble with happiness* overflow, brim over, be filled.

**bubbly** adjective **1** *bubbly soda* fizzy, effervescent, carbonated, sparkling, foamy, frothy, sudsy. **2** *a bubbly personality* vivacious, effervescent, animated, ebullient, bouncy, buoyant, lively.

**buccaneer** noun pirate, corsair, sea rover, freebooter, Viking.

**buck** verb **buck up** cheer up, perk up, take heart; *inf.* shake it off.

**bucket** noun pail, scuttle, can.

**buckle** noun **1** *the belt buckle* clasp, clip, catch, fastener, fastening, hasp. **2** *a buckle in the floorboards* kink, warp, curve, distortion, wrinkle, bulge.

**buckle** verb **1** *buckling his belt* fasten, hook, secure, clasp, catch, clip. **2** *the floorboards buckled* warp, bulge, crumple, cave in.

**bucolic** adjective rural, rustic, pastoral, country, agricultural.

**bud** noun shoot, sprout, flowerlet, floret.

**budding** adjective promising, developing, beginning, fledgling, incipient, embryonic.

**budge** verb **1** *the car won't budge* move, shift, stir, go, proceed. **2** *he's obstinate so he won't budge* change one's mind, give way, give in, yield, acquiesce. **3** *you won't budge him as he's determined* influence, sway, convince, persuade, bend.

**budget** verb **1** *budget money/time* plan, schedule, allocate, ration, apportion. **2** *budget for a new car* allow, save, set aside.

**buff** verb polish, burnish, rub, smooth, polish, shine.

**buff** noun *a theater buff* fan, enthusiast, devotee, aficionado, addict, admirer, expert; *inf.* freak. **in the buff** naked, nude, bare, in the raw, buck naked, au naturel, undressed; *inf.* in one's birthday suit.

**buffer** noun cushion, bulwark, guard, safeguard, shield, screen, intermediary.

**buffet** verb **1** *winds buffeting the trees* batter, beat/knock against, strike, hit, bang, push against. **2** *the fighter buffeted his opponent* slap, smack, thump, wallop, clout, whack, thwack.

**buffoon** noun **1** *the buffoons in Shakespeare's plays* clown, jester, comic, comedian, wit, wag, merry andrew. **2** *he's just a buffoon* fool, dolt, idiot, nincompoop.

**bug** noun **1** *bitten by bugs* insect, beetle, fly, flea, mite; *inf.* creepy-crawly. **2** *an illness caused by a bug* bacterium, germ, virus, microorganism; infection. **3** *he's caught the dancing bug* craze, fad, mania, obsession, passion, fixation. **4** *get rid of all the bugs in the machine* fault, flaw, defect, imperfection; *inf.* glitch, gremlin.

**bug** verb **1** *bug a phone/conversation* tap, wiretap, listen in on, eavesdrop on. **2** *he really bugs me* annoy, irritate, exasperate, anger, irk, vex, try one's patience; *inf.* get on one's nerves.

**bugbear** noun bane, abomination, pet hate, nightmare, dread, bête noire; goblin, bogeyman, hobgoblin.

**build** verb **1** *build a house/road* construct, erect, put up, assemble, set up, raise, make, manufacture, fabricate, form. **2** *hopes built on false premises* found, base, establish. **3** *build a new career* start, begin, inaugurate, initiate, develop. **build up 1** *build up a business* establish, develop, expand. **2** *build up her morale/strength* boost, strengthen, increase, improve, develop. **3** *build up the product* advertise, promote, publicize; *inf.* plug, hype.

**build** noun body, frame, physique, figure, form, structure, shape.

**building** noun structure, construction, edifice, erection.

**buildup** noun **1** *the buildup of resources* expansion, increase, growth, enlargement, escalation, development. **2** *the buildup of paperwork* accumulation, stockpile, accretion, mass, heap, stack, pile. **3** *the product's buildup* promotion, publicity, advertising; *inf.* hype, ballyhoo.

**bulge** noun **1** *a bulge in her pocket* swelling, bump, lump, protuberance, protrusion, prominence, projection. **2** *a population bulge* boost, increase, rise, surge, intensification.

**bulge** verb swell, swell out, puff up/out, stick out, bag, balloon, balloon up/out, protrude, distend, expand, dilate, bloat.

**bulk** noun **1** *the sheer bulk of the packages/work* size, volume, bulkiness, quantity, weight, extent, mass, substance, massiveness, hugeness, amplitude; dimensions. **2** *the bulk of the applicants are women* majority, preponderance, lion's share.

**bulky** adjective large, substantial, huge, enormous, massive, immense, voluminous, hulking, heavy, weighty, stout, thickset, awkward-shaped, awkward, unwieldy, cumbersome.

**bulldoze** verb **1** *bulldoze the area/buildings* demolish, flatten, level, raze. **2** *bulldoze his way through* force, push, drive, shove, propel. **3** *they bulldozed him into going* coerce, steamroll, railroad; *inf.* strong-arm. *See* BULLY *verb.*

**bullet** noun pellet, ball, slug, shot, missile, projectile. **bullets** ammunition *inf.* ammo, lead.

**bulletin** noun **1** *a television bulletin* report, statement, announcement, flash, account, message, communiqué, dispatch. **2** *an in-house bulletin* newspaper, newsletter, pamphlet, leaflet.

**bully** noun browbeater, intimidator, oppressor, tyrant, tormentor, tough, ruffian, thug, hooligan, rowdy; *inf.* hood.

**bully** verb browbeat, intimidate, coerce, oppress, dominere, persecute, cow, tyrannize, pressurize, pressure, bulldoze; *inf.* push around, strong-arm.

**bulwark** noun **1** *a bulwark against flooding* rampart, fortification, buttress, bastion, embankment. **2** *a bulwark of classical education* support, mainstay, defense, safeguard; defender, protector.

**bum** noun **1** *a bum begging for money* tramp, vagrant, beggar, derelict, mendicant; bag lady, hobo. **2** *just a lazy bum* loafer, idler, good-for-nothing, ne'er-do-well.

**bum** verb *bum money* borrow, scrounge, sponge; *inf.* mooch. **bum around** loaf, lounge, idle, laze, wander; *inf.* hang out.

**bum** adjective **1** *a bum stereo | gave me a bum deal* useless, worthless, inferior, unsatisfactory, low-grade, poor, bad. **2** *a bum leg* lame, game, bad.

**bumbling** adjective clumsy, blundering, awkward, bungling, incompetent, inept, lumbering, foolish.

**bump** verb **1** *bump his head on the bar* hit, bang, strike, knock, slam, injure, damage. **2** *the wagon bumping along the road* bounce, jolt, jerk, rattle, shake. **3** *bumped from their seats* displace, supplant, remove, eject. **bump into 1** *the cars bumped into each other* collide with, crash/smash into, run into. **2** *we bumped into old friends* run into, come across, meet, meet up with, encounter. **bump off** kill, murder, do away with, assassinate, eliminate, liquidate.

**bump** noun **1** *hear a bump* thud, thump, bang, crash. **2** *land with a bump* jolt, crash, smash, bang, thud, thump, impact. **3** *a bump on his head* lump, swelling, injury, contusion, protuberance. **4** *a bump in the road* bulge, hump, lump, knob, knot, protuberance.

**bumper** adjective *a bumper crop* large, big, abundant, bountiful, exceptional.

**bumptious** adjective self-assertive, overbearing, puffed up, cocky, presumptuous, pompous, forward; *inf.* pushy.

**bumpy** adjective **1** *a bumpy road* uneven, rough, potholed, rutted, pitted, lumpy, knobby. **2** *a bumpy flight* choppy, jolting, jerky, jarring, bouncy, rough.

**bunch** noun cluster, assemblage, collection, batch, pile, bundle, mass, quantity, accumulation, agglomeration, group, collection, gathering, band, crowd, multitude.

**bundle** noun **1** *a bundle of papers* collection, quantity. *See* BUNCH. **2** *send bundles of clothes* package, pack, bale, parcel, packet.

**bundle** verb **1** *bundle them up* tie, tie up, tie together, package, wrap, bind, fasten together, bale, truss. **2** *bundle people*

*inside/outside* hurry, hustle, rush, push, shove, thrust, throw. **3** *bundle children up in warm clothes* clothe, wrap, cover.

**bungle** verb botch, muff, spoil, make a mess of, mess up, mishandle, mismanage, fudge, mar, ruin; *inf.* louse up, screw up, foul up.

**bungling** adjective clumsy, incompetent, inept, unskillful, inexpert, maladroit; *inf.* ham-handed.

**bunk** noun nonsense, rubbish. *See* BUNKUM.

**bunkum** noun nonsense, rubbish, balderdash, twaddle, claptrap, humbug, tomfoolery; *inf.* rot, poppycock, baloney, piffle, bilge, bosh, hogwash, hooey.

**buoy** verb **buoy up** cheer, cheer up, hearten, encourage, support, sustain, raise, boost, uplift, lift.

**buoyant** adjective **1** *a buoyant mood/personality* cheerful, cheery, lighthearted, bouncy, carefree, vivacious, animated, lively, sprightly, jaunty, breezy.

**burden** noun **1** *the donkey's burden* load, cargo, weight, freight. **2** *the burden of parenthood* responsibility, onus, charge, duty, obligation, tax, trouble, care, worry, anxiety, tribulation, difficulty, strain, stress, weight, encumbrance, millstone.

**burden** verb **1** *donkeys were burdened with heavy loads* load, lade, weight, charge, weigh down, encumber, hamper. **2** *burdened with sorrow* oppress, trouble, worry, distress, bother, afflict, torment, strain, stress, tax, overwhelm.

**bureau** noun **1** *a travel bureau* agency, office, service. **2** *a government bureau* department, division, branch. **3** *polish the bureau* dresser, chest of drawers, highboy.

**bureaucracy** noun **1** *rule by bureaucracy* civil service, central administration, directorate; government officials. **2** *cut through the bureaucracy to get a passport* red tape, officialdom, formalities, rules and regulations.

**burgeon** verb **1** *flowers burgeoning* bud, sprout, put forth shoots, shoot, germinate. **2** *the population burgeoned* grow, develop, flourish, thrive, mushroom, proliferate, snowball.

**burglar** noun housebreaker, cat burglar, thief, robber, picklock; *inf.* second-story man.

**burial** noun interment, entombment, inhumation, sepulture; funeral, obsequies, exequies. **burial ground** cemetery, graveyard, churchyard; *inf.* potter's field.

**burlesque** noun parody, caricature, travesty, farce, mockery, imitation, satire, lampoon; *inf.* send-up, takeoff, spoof.

**burly** adjective thickset, brawny, muscular, strapping, hulking, hefty, beefy, bulky, sturdy, stocky, stout.

**burn** verb **1** *watching the house burn* be on fire, be afire, be ablaze, blaze, go up, smoke, flame, flare, flash, flicker, glow. **2** *he burned the papers* set on fire, ignite, put a match to, light, kindle, incinerate, reduce to ashes. **3** *burn the shirt with the iron* scorch, singe, sear, char. **4** *burn with fever* be hot, be warm, feel hot, be feverish; *inf.* be on fire. **5** *burn with pain* smart, sting, tingle. **6** *liquid burning his throat* sting, bite, prickle, irritate. **7** *burn with excitement* be aroused, simmer, smolder, seethe. **8** *burn to get the prize* long, yearn, desire, hunger after, lust, itch. **9** *burn energy* use, use up, consume, expend, eat up.

**burning** adjective **1** *a burning house* blazing, flaming, flaring, raging, ignited, glowing, flickering, smoldering, scorching. **2** *a burning sensation* smarting, stinging, biting, prickling, caustic, searing, corrosive. **3** *a burning desire* intense, fervent, ardent, eager. **4** *the burning issues of the day* crucial, significant, urgent, pressing.

**burnish** verb polish, shine, brighten, rub, buff, buff up, smooth.

**burrow** noun *rabbit burrows* tunnel, hole, hollow, excavation, lair, den, retreat.

**burrow** verb **1** *burrow holes* dig, tunnel, excavate, hollow out, gouge out, scoop out. **2** *burrow under the blankets* go under, hide, shelter, conceal oneself.

**burst** verb **1** *the pipe has burst* split, split open, break open, rupture, crack, fracture, fragment, shatter, fly open. **2** *the grenade burst* blow up, explode, detonate, fulminate. **3** *the water burst through the dam* break out, pour forth, gush out, surge out, rush out. **4** *burst into tears/laughter* break out, erupt. **burst out** *"coward!" she burst out* exclaim, cry out, call out, shout, yell. **2** *burst out crying* begin/start suddenly.

**bury** verb **1** *bury the corpse* inter, lay to rest, consign to the grave, entomb. **2** *bury her head in her hands* conceal, hide, put out of sight, sink, secrete, enshroud. **3** *bury the nail in the wood* drive in, embed, implant, sink, submerge. **4** *bury yourself in your work* absorb oneself, immerse oneself, engross oneself, engage oneself.

**bushy** adjective thick, shaggy, fuzzy, fluffy, luxuriant, unruly, rough.

**business** noun **1** *what business is he in?* occupation, line, profession, career, trade, work, employment, job. **2** *do business with the French* trade, commerce, trafficking, buying and selling, merchandizing, bargaining; dealings, transactions. **3** *running her own business* firm, company, concern, enterprise, organization, store, shop, venture. **4** *that's none of your business* concern, affair, responsibility, duty, function,

task, problem. **5** *the main business of the meeting* matter, subject, topic, point of discussion, theme, issue, question. **6** *it was a peculiar business* affair, matter, thing, case.

**businesslike** adjective **1** *businesslike behavior* professional, efficient, orderly, organized, practical, pragmatic, thorough, painstaking, meticulous, correct. **2** *the businesslike performance of the play* workaday, routine, prosaic, conventional, unimaginative.

**bust** verb **1** *the crash will bust him* bankrupt, ruin, impoverish, pauperize, break. **2** *the police busted him* arrest, capture, catch, seize; *inf.* collar, nab.

**bustle** verb hurry, rush, dash, scuttle, scurry, hasten, scamper, scramble, flutter, fuss; *inf.* tear.

**bustle** noun activity, flurry, stir, commotion, tumult, excitement, agitation, fuss; *inf.* to-do.

**bustling** adjective active, full of activity, energetic, lively, busy, brisk, animated.

**busy** adjective **1** *the doctor's busy* occupied, engaged, working, at work, on duty, in a meeting, otherwise engaged. **2** *a busy day/person* active, energetic, strenuous, full, hectic, exacting, bustling, industrious, lively; *inf.* on the go. **3** *busy patterns* ornate, overelaborate, overdetailed, overdecorated, cluttered, fussy.

**busy** verb *busy himself in the garden* occupy, engage, employ, absorb, immerse, engross, involve, interest.

**busybody** noun meddler, interferer, snooper, snoop, gossip, scandalmonger.

**butcher** verb **1** *butcher cattle* slaughter, cut up, carve up, slice up, prepare, dress. **2** *butcher the enemy* slay, massacre, murder, kill, exterminate, liquidate. **3** *butcher the piano concerto* botch, make a mess of, wreck, ruin, spoil, bungle; *inf.* louse up, screw up, foul up.

**butchery** noun slaughter, massacre, slaying, murder, mass murder, homicide, bloodshed.

**butt**[1] noun **1** *the butt of a gun* handle, shaft, hilt, haft. **2** *the butt of a cigarette* stub, end, remnant; *inf.* roach. **3** *sitting on his butt* bottom, rump. *See* BUTTOCKS.

**butt**[2] noun *the butt of his jokes* scapegoat, dupe, target, victim, laughingstock, object, subject.

**butt**[3] verb push, thrust, shove, ram, bump, prod, poke, jab. **butt into** *butt into a conversation* interrupt, intrude/interfere in, put one's oar into; *inf.* stick one's nose into.

**buttocks** noun bottom, posterior, rump; hindquarters; *inf.* behind, backside, butt, can, ass.

**buttonhole** verb accost, waylay, take aside, importune, detain, grab, catch, talk at.

**buttress** noun **1** *a stone buttress* prop, support, abutment, strut, reinforcement. **2** *a buttress to the family* mainstay, upholder, sustainer, cornerstone, pillar.

**buttress** verb strengthen, reinforce, prop up, support, shore up, underpin, brace, uphold, defend, back up.

**buxom** adjective plump, large-bosomed, big-bosomed, full-bosomed, shapely; *inf.* busty.

**buy** verb **1** *buy a house* purchase, pay for, invest in, procure. **2** *he bought his way in* bribe, suborn, corrupt; *inf.* fix, rig.

**buy** noun purchase, acquisition, deal, bargain.

**buzz** noun **1** *the buzz of the bees* hum, murmur, drone, whirr, hiss, sibilation, whisper. **2** *the buzz is he's gone* rumor, gossip, talk, scuttlebutt, report, whisper, scandal, hearsay.

**buzz** verb **1** *bees buzzing* hum, murmur, drone, whirr, hiss, whisper, sibilate. **2** *tongues buzzing* gossip, chatter, tattle. **3** *people buzzing about* rush, dash. *See* BUSTLE verb.

**buzzing** adjective active, alive. *See* BUS-TLING.

**bygone** adjective past, departed, former, one-time, previous, forgotten, olden, ancient, obsolete, out-of-date, outmoded.

**bypass** verb *bypass the city/difficulty/boss* go around, pass around, get around, circumvent, avoid, evade, ignore, pass over, go over the head of.

**bystander** noun onlooker, looker-on, observer, eyewitness, witness, spectator, gaper, passerby; *inf.* rubberneck.

**byword** noun proverb, maxim, adage, aphorism, apothegm. **byword for** *a byword for reliability* slogan for, catchword for, example of, personification of, embodiment of.

# Cc

**cab** noun **1** *order a cab* taxi, taxicab, hackney carriage, hackney, *inf.* hack. **2** *the driver's cab* cabin, compartment, quarters, cubicle.

**cabin** noun **1** *a cabin by the lake* log cabin, hut, chalet, cottage, shack, shanty, shed. **2** *a first-class cabin in the ship* stateroom, room, sleeping quarters, berth, compartment.

**cabinet** noun **1** *a china cabinet | a filing cabinet* cupboard, chest, locker, dresser, closet, chiffonier, case, container. **2** *the president's cabinet* advisers, council, committee, board, administration.

**cable** noun **1** *tied with cable* rope, cord, wire, line, cordage. **2** *send a cable* cablegram, telegram, telegraph, wire.

**cache** noun **1** *hide the treasure in a cache* hiding place, hide-out, secret place, hole. **2** *find the cache of jewels* hoard, store, collection, fund, supply, hidden treasure, treasure, loot; *inf.* stash.

**cackle** verb **1** *hens cackling* cluck, clack, squawk. **2** *the audience cackling at his jokes* chuckle, chortle, laugh, giggle, titter, snigger, tee-hee. **3** *people cackling at the bus stop* chatter, jabber, prattle, babble, gibber, blather, blab; *inf.* spout away.

**cad** noun scoundrel, rat, rogue, rascal, double-crosser; *inf.* bounder, heel.

**cadence** noun **1** *musical/metrical cadence* rhythm, beat, pulse, rhythmical flow/pattern, measure, meter, tempo, swing, lilt. **2** *the cadence of her speech* intonation, inflection, accent, modulation.

**café** noun coffee shop, snack bar, tearoom, restaurant, cafeteria, bar, bistro; *inf.* greasy spoon.

**cage** noun enclosure, pen, corral, pound, lockup, coop; birdcage, aviary.

**cage** verb confine, shut in, impound, pen, corral, lock up, incarcerate, imprison, coop, coop up, hem in, restrict, restrain.

**cagey, cagy** adjective guarded, secretive, noncommittal, cautious, chary, wary, careful, shrewd, wily.

**cajole** verb wheedle, coax, beguile, seduce, entice, tempt, inveigle, maneuver, humor; *inf.* sweet-talk, soft-soap, butter up.

**calamitous** adjective disastrous, catastrophic, cataclysmic, devastating, ruinous, dire, tragic.

**calamity** noun disaster, catastrophe, tragedy, misfortune, cataclysm, devastation, scourge, mishap, ruin, tribulation, woe.

**calculate** verb **1** *calculate the sum* work out, compute, estimate, count up, figure out, evaluate, enumerate, determine.

**2** *calculate the chances* estimate, gauge, judge, measure, weigh, reckon, rate. **3** *a proposal calculated to appeal to investors* design, plan, aim, intend.

**calculated** adjective *a calculated risk* considered, planned, premeditated, deliberate, intentional, intended, purposeful.

**calculating** adjective scheming, designing, devious, shrewd, manipulative, sharp, sly, crafty, Machiavellian.

**calculation** noun **1** *by their calculations it will cost $3000* computation, estimation, estimate, reckoning, figuring, forecast, gauging, judgment. **2** *the calculation is wrong* result, answer. **3** *got the job by sheer calculation* scheming, designing, deviousness, shrewdness.

**caliber** noun *statesmen of his caliber* quality, worth, distinction, stature, excellence, merit, ability, competence, endowments, scope.

**call** verb **1** *call out in pain* cry, cry out, shout, exclaim, yell, scream, shriek, roar. **2** *call him in the morning* awaken, waken, arouse, rouse. **3** *call her tomorrow* call up, phone, telephone, give one a ring; *inf.* give one a buzz. **4** *call at the house* pay a call, pay a visit, pay a brief visit, stop by; *inf.* drop in, pop in. **5** *call a meeting* call together, convene, summon, order, convoke, assemble, announce, declare, proclaim, decree. **6** *call a doctor/taxi* send for, ask for, summon, contact, order, bid, fetch. **7** *they called the baby Jane* name, christen, designate, dub, entitle, denominate, label, term. **8** *I call it disgraceful* consider, think, regard, judge, estimate. **9** *called to the bar | he was called to the church* appoint, elect, ordain. **call for 1** *this calls for a celebration* need, require, be grounds for, justify, necessitate, demand, entail. **2** *call for the packages* collect, pick up, fetch, go for. **call off 1** *call off the dogs* order off, order away, stop, hold back, check, rein in. **2** *call off the date* cancel, postpone, countermand, rescind, revoke. **call on/upon 1** *call on his aunt* visit, pay a visit to, go and see; *inf.* look up, look in on, drop in on. **2** *call on them to help* appeal to, ask, request, entreat, urge, supplicate, invoke. **call up 1** *call me up* phone, telephone. *See* CALL verb 3. **2** *call up painful memories* recall, bring/call to mind, summon up, evoke. **3** *call up all the young men* enlist, recruit, sign up; draft.

**call** noun **1** *a call of pain* cry, shout, exclamation, yell, scream, shriek, roar. **2** *the call of the bird* cry, song, chirp, chirping, tweet. **3** *have a prearranged call* signal, hail, whoop. **4** *give me a call* ring; *inf.* buzz. **5** *paid her a call* visit, brief visit. **6** *a call for unity* summons, invitation,

request, plea, bidding, order, command, appeal, notice. **7** *there's no call to be rude* need, occasion, reason, cause, justification, grounds, excuse. **8** *there's no call for expensive wine here* demand, request, want, requisition. **9** *the call of the wild* attraction, lure, allurement, fascination, appeal.

**calling** noun vocation, occupation, career, profession, business, work, employment, job, trade, craft, line, line of work, pursuit, métier, walk of life, province, field.

**callous** adjective **1** *a callous jail warden* hardened, tough, cold, insensitive, unfeeling, hard-hearted, heartless, hard-bitten, cruel, obdurate, inured, uncaring, unsympathetic. **2** *callous skin* hard, hardened, thickened, leathery.

**callow** adjective immature, inexperienced, uninitiated, naive, unsophisticated, innocent, undeveloped, adolescent.

**calm** adjective **1** *a calm day* still, windless, mild, tranquil, balmy, halcyon, peaceful, restful. **2** *a calm sea* still, smooth, motionless, placid, waveless, unagitated, storm-free. **3** *be/remain calm during the trouble* composed, collected, cool, coolheaded, controlled, self-controlled, self-possessed, unruffled, relaxed, serene, unflappable, undisturbed, imperturbable, unemotional, unmoved, equable, stoical; *inf.* together.

**calm** noun **1** *the calm before the storm* stillness, tranquillity, serenity, quietude, peace, restfulness, repose. **2** *nothing disturbs her calm* composure, coolness, self-control, tranquillity, serenity, equanimity, imperturbability, poise, sang-froid; *inf.* cool.

**calm** verb *calm the child* soothe, quieten, pacify, hush, lull, mollify, appease, still, settle, settle down, relax.

**camp**[1] noun *soldier's/Scout camp* encampment, camping ground, campsite, tents, bivouac, cantonment. **2** *the right-wing camp* faction, party, group, clique, coterie, set, sect, cabal.

**camp**[2] verb *we camped in a field* pitch tents, pitch camp, set up camp, encamp, tent. **camp out 1** *we camped out in that field* sleep out, camp. **2** *we're camping out here till the house is rebuilt* live simply; *inf.* rough it, slum it.

**camp**[3] verb **camp it up** overdo it, overact, behave theatrically/affectedly, posture, ham it up, lay it on.

**campaign** noun **1** *Grant's Vicksburg Campaign* war, battle, expedition, offensive, attack, crusade. **2** *a campaign against litter* operation, promotion, strategy, set of tactics, drive, push, crusade, movement.

**campaign** verb fight, battle, work, push, crusade, strive, struggle, agitate.

**cancel** verb **1** *cancel a vacation/date/contract* call off, stop, discontinue, give up, withdraw from, revoke, rescind, annul, declare void, nullify, quash, invalidate, set aside, retract, negate, repudiate, repeal, abolish. **2** *cancel that last paragraph* delete, cross out, erase, strike out, rub out, blot out, expunge, eliminate. **3** *his friendliness cancels out her hostility* counterbalance, balance, offset, compensate, make up for, neutralize, redeem.

**candid** adjective **1** *candid remarks* frank, open, honest, truthful, sincere, forthright, direct, outspoken, blunt, unequivocal, bluff; *inf.* straight from the shoulder. **2** *candid snapshots* unposed, spontaneous, impromptu, uncontrived, informal, unstudied.

**candidate** noun applicant, job applicant, office seeker, contender, nominee, contestant, aspirant, possibility; *inf.* runner.

**candor** noun frankness, openness, honesty, truthfulness, sincerity, forthrightness, directness, outspokenness, bluntness, bluffness, brusqueness.

**candy** noun sweet, sweets, confectionery, confection, bonbon.

**cane** noun **1** *a walking cane* stick, staff, rod, stave; walking stick, shepherd's crook. **2** *pruning the raspberry canes* stem, stalk, shoot, reed.

**canon** noun **1** *the canons of good taste* principle, standard, criterion, test, measure, yardstick, benchmark, precept, norm, convention. **2** *a Church canon* law, rule, regulation, statute, decree, edict, dictate. **3** *the canon of Shakespeare's plays* official list, list, catalog, enumeration, litany, roll.

**canopy** noun awning, shade, sunshade, cover, covering, tarpaulin.

**cant**[1] noun **1** *thieves' cant* slang, jargon, patter, lingo, terminology, argot. **2** *religious cant* hypocrisy, insincerity, sanctimony, sanctimoniousness, humbug, pretense.

**cant**[2] noun *the table is on a cant* slant, slope, tilt, angle, inclination.

**cantankerous** adjective bad-tempered, crabby, surly, irascible, grumpy, difficult, disagreeable, quarrelsome, touchy, testy, peevish, crusty; *inf.* grouchy, crotchety, cranky.

**canter** noun amble, saunter, trot, jog, lope, gallop.

**canvass** verb **1** *canvassing during the general election* solicit votes, campaign, electioneer, drum up support, persuade, convince. **2** *canvass buying habits* survey, scan, poll.

**canyon** noun ravine, gully, valley, gorge, chasm, gulf, abyss.

**cap** noun **1** *doffing his cap* hat, bonnet, headgear. **2** *the cap on the bottle* top, lid, stopper, cork, plug. **3** *mountain caps* top, crest, peak, summit, apex, pinnacle.

**cap** verb **1** *mountains capped with snow* cover, top, crown, overlie, overspread, coat, blanket. **2** *cap the high-jump record* beat, better, surpass, excel, outshine, transcend, eclipse, outdo, outstrip, exceed. **3** *cap the price* limit, set a limit to, restrict, curb.

**capability** noun **1** *the capability to do well* ability, capacity, potential, aptitude, faculty, facility, power, competence, efficiency, effectiveness, proficiency, accomplishment, talent, adeptness, skill, skillfulness, experience, cleverness, intelligence, smartness. **2** *offer capabilities* talent, gifts, skill, aptitude, flair, knack.

**capable** adjective able, competent, adequate, efficient, effective, proficient, accomplished, talented, gifted, adept, skillful, masterly, experienced, practiced, qualified, clever, intelligent, smart. **capable of 1** *capable of murder/lying* tending to, inclined to, predisposed to, prone to, liable to, likely to do. **2** *capable of improvement* requiring, wanting, susceptible to, admitting of, receptive of.

**capacity** noun **1** *the capacity to seat twenty* space, room, size, largeness, ampleness, amplitude, scope, magnitude, dimensions, proportions, extent. **2** *the capacity to do the job* ability, intelligence. *See* CAPABILITY. **3** *in his capacity as a teacher* position, post, job, office, function, role, appointment.

**cape**[1] noun cloak, mantle, shawl, wrap, poncho, pelisse.

**cape**[2] noun headland, head, point, promontory, neck, peninsula.

**caper** verb frolic, frisk, romp, skip, gambol, cavort, prance, dance, leap, hop, jump, bound, spring, bounce.

**caper** noun **1** *the energetic capers of the children* frolics, romping, skipping, gambols, cavorting, prancing, leap. **2** *tired of their mischievous capers* prank, trick, practical joke, antic, high jinks, mischief, escapade, stunt; *inf.* shenanigans.

**capital** adjective **1** *our capital concern* principal, chief, main, major, prime, paramount, foremost, predominant, overruling, leading, cardinal, central, key. **2** *a capital error* grave, vital, important, serious, crucial, fatal. **3** *a capital piece of work* splendid, excellent, first-rate, outstanding.

**capital** noun *enough capital to buy the firm* money, finance, finances, funds, cash, hard cash, wherewithal, means, assets, liquid assets, wealth, resources, reserves, principal.

**capitalize** verb *capitalize the firm* finance, back, provide backing for, fund, sponsor. **capitalize on** *capitalize on her rival's mistakes* take advantage of, put to advantage, profit from, cash in on, make the most of, exploit.

**capitulate** verb surrender, yield, submit, give in, give up, come to terms, succumb, accede, back down, cave in, relent, acquiesce; *inf.* throw in the towel.

**caprice** noun whim, whimsy, vagary, fancy, notion, fad, freak, humor, impulse, quirk; changeableness, fickleness, volatility, inconstancy.

**capricious** adjective changeable, unpredictable, fickle, variable, inconstant, unstable, mercurial, volatile, impulsive, erratic, fanciful, whimsical, wayward, quirky.

**capsize** verb overturn, turn over, upset, upend, knock over, tip over, invert, keel over.

**capsule** noun *pain-relieving capsules* pill, tablet, lozenge.

**captain** noun *the captain of the ship/team* commander, master, leader, head, skipper; *inf.* honcho.

**caption** noun heading, title, wording, head, legend, inscription.

**captivate** verb charm, delight, enchant, bewitch, fascinate, beguile, enthrall, entrance, enrapture, attract, allure, lure, infatuate, seduce, ensnare, dazzle, hypnotize, mesmerize.

**captive** noun prisoner, prisoner of war, hostage, slave, bondsman, convict, jailbird, detainee; *inf.* con.

**captivity** noun imprisonment, custody, detention, confinement, internment, incarceration, restraint, constraint, committal, bondage, slavery, servitude, enslavement, subjection.

**capture** verb catch, arrest, apprehend, take prisoner, take captive, take into custody, seize, take, lay hold of, trap; *inf.* nab, collar, pinch, nail, bag.

**car** noun vehicle, motor vehicle, automobile, motorcar; sedan, station wagon, hatchback, coupe; *inf.* wheels, heap, crate, jalopy, limo, auto.

**caravan** noun *caravan of pilgrims* convoy, troop, band, company, group, cavalcade, procession.

**carcass** noun **1** *vultures searching for carcasses* corpse, dead body, body; remains, cadaver; *inf.* stiff. **2** *move your carcass* body, person, self.

**card** noun *in the cards* likely, possible, probable; most likely, certain.

**cardinal** adjective *cardinal sins/errors* main, chief, principal, greatest, vital, key, central, foremost, leading, prime, paramount, fundamental, basic.

**care** noun **1** *free from care* worry, anxiety, disquiet, unease, distress, sorrow, anguish,

grief, sadness, hardship, tribulation, responsibility, stress, pressure, strain; burdens. **2** *no care for others* concern, regard, interest, solicitude. **3** *arrange the flowers with care* carefulness, attention, thought, regard, mindfulness, conscientiousness, painstakingness, pains, precision, meticulousness, fastidiousness. **4** *cross the road with care* caution, heedfulness, alertness, vigilance, wariness, circumspection, prudence. **5** *in the care of her uncle* charge, protection, custody, keeping, safekeeping, control, management, supervision.

**care** verb *she cared about her work* be concerned, be interested, have regard, worry, trouble, bother, mind; *inf.* give a damn, give a hoot. **care for 1** *he cares for his colleagues* be fond of, like, find congenial. **2** *would you care for tea?* wish, want, desire, fancy, hanker after, long for; *inf.* have a yen for. **3** *care for the children* take care of, look after, mind, watch, tend, attend to, minister to, nurse, provide for.

**career** noun **1** *choose a career* occupation, profession, vocation, calling, employment, job, métier. **2** *watch the career of the political party* course, progress, progression, procedure, passage, path. **3** *stop the horse in mid-career* rush, onrush, run, race, bolt, dash, gallop, impetus.

**carefree** adjective lighthearted, happy-go-lucky, cheerful, cheery, happy, merry, jolly, buoyant, breezy, easygoing, blithe, airy, nonchalant, unworried, untroubled, insouciant.

**careful** adjective **1** *be careful crossing the road* cautious, heedful, alert, aware, attentive, watchful, vigilant, wary, on guard, chary, circumspect, prudent, mindful. **2** *be careful of your reputation | be careful about what you say* mindful, heedful, protective; solicitous, thoughtful, attentive, concerned. **3** *a careful worker* attentive, conscientious, painstaking, meticulous, accurate, precise, scrupulous, punctilious, fastidious.

**careless** adjective **1** *a careless driver* inattentive, negligent, remiss, irresponsible, lax, slack. **2** *a careless piece of work* hasty, cursory, perfunctory, inaccurate, disorganized, slapdash, slipshod; *inf.* sloppy. **3** *a careless remark* unthinking, thoughtless, insensitive, indiscreet, unguarded. **4** *careless elegance* unstudied, artless, casual.

**caress** noun touch, stroke, fondling, pat, embrace, cuddle, hug, nuzzle, kiss.

**caress** verb cuddle, fondle, pet, pat, embrace, hug, nuzzle, kiss.

**cargo** noun freight, freightage, load, lading, haul, consignment, contents, goods, merchandise, baggage; shipment, shipload, boatload, truckload.

**caricature** noun cartoon, parody, burlesque, mimicry, travesty, distortion, satire, farce, lampoon; *inf.* send-up, takeoff, spoof.

**carnage** noun slaughter, butchery, massacre, bloodshed, blood bath.

**carnal** adjective sexual, sensual, fleshly, erotic, lustful, lascivious, lecherous, lewd, prurient, salacious, lubricious.

**carouse** verb binge, party, paint the town red, overindulge, live it up, go on a bender.

**carp** verb complain, faultfind, find fault, criticize, cavil, pick on, quibble, censure, reproach, nag; *inf.* nitpick.

**carriage** noun 1 *an elegant carriage* posture, bearing, stance, comportment, manner, presence, air, demeanor. 2 *free carriage* transport, freight, conveyance, delivery.

**carry** verb 1 *carry a package* transport, convey, move, take, bring, bear, lug, haul, fetch; conduct, pass on, transmit, relay. 2 *carry responsibilities* support, sustain, bear, shoulder. 3 *carry the day* win, capture, gain, secure, accomplish. 4 *a store carrying a brand* sell, stock, offer, retail. 5 *carry the latest news* communicate, give, release, publish, broadcast. 6 *carry the audience* influence, affect, motivate, stimulate. 7 *carry themselves well* bear oneself, hold oneself, comport oneself. **carry on** 1 *carry on talking* go on, continue, keep on, persist in, persevere in. 2 *carry on a business* run, operate, conduct, manage, administer. 3 *he's carrying on with his secretary* have an affair, commit adultery; *inf.* fool around. 4 *children carrying on* cause a fuss/commotion; cry, create a scene. **carry out** 1 *carry out a promise/threat* fulfill, carry through, implement, realize, execute. 2 *carry out an experiment* conduct, perform.

**cart** noun handcart, wheelbarrow, pushcart.

**cart** verb 1 *cart away the trash* transport, convey, haul, transfer, move, shift. 2 *cart the luggage* lug, tote, carry.

**carton** noun box, package, cardboard box, container, case.

**cartridge** noun case, container, cylinder, capsule, cassette, magazine.

**carve** verb 1 *carve a figure out of stone* sculpt, sculpture, cut, chisel, hew, whittle, chip, form, shape, fashion. 2 *carve initials on a tree* engrave, etch, notch, incise. 3 *carve meat* slice, cut up. **carve up** divide, partition, parcel out, apportion.

**cascade** noun waterfall, falls, fountain, shower, cataract, torrent, flood, deluge, outpouring.

**cascade** verb tumble, descend, pour, gush, surge, spill, overflow.

**case**[1] noun 1 *a cigarette case* container, box, receptacle, holder, canister. 2 *a case of wine* crate, box, carton; coffer, casket. 3 *bullet case|tape case* casing, covering, sheath, sheathing, wrapper, cover, envelope, housing.

**case**[2] noun 1 *as has been the case* position, situation, circumstances, occurrence, happening, occasion, conditions, plight, predicament. 2 *a case of cheating* instance, occurrence, example, illustration, specimen. 3 *the case comes up next week* lawsuit, suit, action, trial, proceedings. 4 *his case was that he was elsewhere* statement, plea, claim, alibi, explanation, exposition, thesis.

**cash** noun 1 *no cash with me* money, ready money, coinage, notes, bank notes, currency; specie, legal tender. 2 *he has no cash of any kind* money, finance, wherewithal, resources, funds, capital; *inf.* dough, bread, cabbage.

**cash** verb exchange, change, turn into cash/money.

**cask** noun barrel, keg, tun, vat, vessel, hogshead.

**casket** noun 1 *funeral casket* coffin, pall, sarcophagus; *inf.* box. 2 *a jewel casket* chest, coffer. See CASE 1.

**cast** verb 1 *cast a stone in the lake* throw, toss, fling, pitch, hurl, sling, let fly. 2 *cast their skins/coats* shed, discard, slough off, peel off, throw off. 3 *cast a glance* shoot, direct, turn, send out. 4 *cast a soft light* emit, give off, send out, shed, radiate. 5 *cast doubt* throw, bestow, impart, confer, give, grant. 6 *cast figures in bronze* shape, fashion, form, mold, sculpt.

**cast** noun 1 *the cast of the dice* throw, toss, fling, pitch, hurl, lob. 2 *cast of features/mind* sort, kind, style, type, stamp, nature. 3 *plaster cast* figure, shape, mold, form.

**caste** noun class, social class, order, social order, grade, station, place, standing, position, status.

**castigate** verb punish, discipline, chastise, rebuke, scold, reprimand, upbraid, berate, chide, admonish, criticize, chasten, take to task, dress down, rake over the coals.

**castle** noun stronghold, fortress, keep, hold, citadel, palace, chateau.

**casual** adjective 1 *a casual meeting* chance, accidental, unintentional, unexpected, unforeseen, fortuitous, serendipitous. 2 *a casual remark* offhand, random, impromptu, spontaneous. 3 *a casual read* cursory, perfunctory, superficial, desultory, hasty. 4 *a casual attitude* indifferent, apathetic, uncaring, uninterested, unconcerned, lackadaisical, blasé. 5 *casual clothes* informal, relaxed, leisure; *inf.* sporty. 6 *a casual acquaintance* slight, superficial, shallow.

**casualties** plural noun *the casualties of the war* dead, fatalities, losses, dead and wounded, wounded, injured, missing in action, missing.

**casualty** noun **1** *a war casualty* fatality, dead/wounded/injured person, victim. **2** *the firm was a casualty of the recession* victim, sufferer, loser, loss.

**cat** noun feline; *inf.* pussy, pussy cat, puss; tabby, tomcat, tom, tortoiseshell, kitten, mouser, alley cat.

**catalog** noun list, record, register, inventory, directory, index, roll, table, calendar, classification, guide, brochure.

**catalog** verb list, classify, categorize, index, inventory, record, register, file, alphabetize.

**catapult** verb launch/propel rapidly, hurtle, shoot, fling.

**catastrophe** noun disaster, calamity, tragedy, blow, adversity, trouble, trials, mishap, misfortune, mischance, misadventure, failure, reverses, affliction, distress.

**catch** verb **1** *catch the ball* grasp, snatch, grab, seize, grip, clutch, clench, pluck, receive, acquire, come into the possession of, intercept. **2** *catch the prisoner* take captive, arrest, snare. *See* CAPTURE. **3** *catch what he said* understand, follow, comprehend, take in; *inf.* get the drift of. **4** *catch him unawares* surprise, discover, come across, startle, detect. **5** *catch pneumonia* contract, get, become infected with, develop, succumb to, come down with. **6** *catch his attention* capture, attract, draw, captivate, bewitch. **7** *catch a likeness* reproduce, represent, photograph, draw, paint. **catch on 1** *sports catching on* become popular/fashionable, come into fashion/vogue; *inf.* become trendy. **2** *did not understand at first, but eventually caught on* grasp, understand, comprehend, see the light; *inf.* get the picture.

**catch** noun **1** *the catch of the door/suitcase* bolt, lock, fastener, fastening, clasp, hasp, hook, clip, latch. **2** *what's the catch?* snag, disadvantage, drawback, hitch, fly in the ointment, trap, trick.

**catching** adjective **1** *is the disease catching?* contagious, infectious, communicable, transmittable, transmissible. **2** *a catching manner* attractive, winning, captivating, charming, fetching, enchanting.

**catchword** noun slogan, motto, password, watchword, byword, shibboleth, formula, refrain.

**catchy** adjective memorable, popular, appealing, captivating.

**categorical** adjective unqualified, unconditional, unequivocal, explicit, unambiguous, absolute, direct, downright, emphatic.

**categorize** verb classify, class, group, grade, order, arrange, sort, rank, break down, catalog, list, tabulate.

**category** noun class, classification, group, grouping, head, heading, list, listing, designation, type, sort, kind, variety, grade, grading, order, rank, status, division.

**cater** verb provide food, feed, provision. **cater to** provide, furnish, supply, purvey.

**cathartic** adjective purgative, purifying, cleansing, release-bringing.

**catholic** adjective **1** *of catholic interest* universal, widespread, global, comprehensive, all-encompassing. **2** *catholic tastes/views* wide, broad, eclectic, liberal, tolerant.

**cattle** plural noun bovines, steer, oxen; stock, livestock.

**cause** noun **1** *the cause of the fire* origin, root, source, beginning, genesis, occasion, mainspring, originator, author, creator, producer, agent, prime mover, maker. **2** *no cause for alarm* reason, grounds, justification, call, basis, motive, motivation. **3** *the cause of human rights* principle, ideal, belief, conviction, tenet. **4** *plead his cause* case, point of view, contention.

**cause** verb make happen, bring about, give rise to, begin, create, produce, originate, occasion, generate, effect, engender, lead to, result in, precipitate, provoke.

**caustic** adjective **1** *caustic chemical substances* corrosive, corroding, burning, destructive. **2** *caustic wit* sarcastic, cutting, biting, mordant, stinging, trenchant.

**caution** noun carefulness, attention, attentiveness, watchfulness, guardedness, discretion, forethought. *See* CARE noun 4.

**caution** verb warn, advise, counsel, urge, admonish.

**cautious** adjective wary, shrewd, discreet, guarded; *inf.* cagey. *See* CAREFUL 1.

**cavalier** adjective condescending, haughty, arrogant, disdainful, patronizing, contemptuous.

**cavalry** noun mounted troops, horse soldiers, horsemen, horse, troopers, dragoons, lancers; reinforcements.

**cave** noun cavern, grotto, hollow, tunnel, cellar, dugout, den.

**caveat** noun warning, caution, admonition, monition; *inf.* red flag.

**cavern** noun grotto, hollow. *See* CAVE.

**cavernous** adjective large, huge, deep, hollow, sunken, yawning, unfathomable, dark.

**cavity** noun hole, hollow, crater, pit, orifice, aperture, gap, dent.

**cease** verb **1** *cease working* stop, discontinue, desist, desist from, end, finish, leave off, quit, conclude, terminate, suspend, break off. **2** *the rain ceased* come to a stop, come to an end, let up, die away, abate, terminate.

**cede** verb yield, surrender, concede; relinquish, renounce, forsake, abandon, turn over, transfer, deliver up, grant, bequeath.

**celebrate** verb **1** *celebrate their anniversary | celebrate after the exams* commemorate, observe, honor, mark, keep, drink to, toast, rejoice, party, paint the town; *inf.* go on a spree, go out on the town, whoop it up. **2** *celebrate his achievement* proclaim, make known, herald, announce, publicize, broadcast, advertise. **3** *a poem celebrating the joys of love* praise, laud, extol, glorify, exalt, eulogize. **4** *celebrate a religious ceremony* perform, solemnize, ceremonialize.

**celebrated** adjective famous, famed, noted, renowned, well-known, prominent, distinguished, great, eminent, preeminent, illustrious, acclaimed, legendary, lionized.

**celebration** noun commemoration, observance, honoring, keeping, remembrance; party, carousal, festival, fête, carnival, gala; festivity, merrymaking, revelry; *inf.* spree, binge, bash.

**celebrity** noun **1** *celebrities at a charity ball* VIP, dignitary, big name, name, personality, star, superstar, lion, notable, luminary, personage; *inf.* bigwig, big shot, big wheel. **2** *his celebrity spread far* fame, renown, notability, popularity, reputation, honor, prominence, prestige, distinction, eminence, preeminence.

**celestial** adjective **1** *celestial beings* heavenly, divine, godly, godlike, ethereal, sublime, paradisiacal, elysian, spiritual, angelic. **2** *celestial bodies/navigation* heavenly, astronomical, extraterrestrial, stellar.

**celibacy** noun chastity, singleness, abstinence, self-denial, self-restraint, continence, asceticism, virginity, bachelorhood.

**cell** noun **1** *a prison/monastic cell* cubicle, room, apartment, compartment, chamber, stall, enclosure, dungeon, lockup. **2** *a political cell* faction, nucleus, clique, coterie, group, unit.

**cement** noun adhesive, bonding, binder, glue, superglue, gum, paste.

**cement** verb bind, bond, stick, join, unite, attach, cohere, combine, affix, glue, gum, paste, solder, weld.

**cemetery** noun graveyard, burial ground, burial place, churchyard.

**censor** verb expurgate, bowdlerize, cut, delete, make cuts/changes to, blue-pencil.

**censure** verb criticize, condemn, blame, castigate, denounce, disapprove of, berate, upbraid, reproach, rebuke, scold, chide.

**censure** noun criticism, condemnation, blame, castigation, denunciation, disapproval, berating, upbraiding, reproach, rebuke, reprimand.

**center** noun middle, middle point, midpoint, nucleus, heart, core, hub, focus, focal point.

**center** verb *her interests center on basketball* concentrate, focus, pivot, converge, close in.

**central** adjective **1** *a central position* middle, mid, median, mean; inner, interior. **2** *a central issue* fundamental, basic, key, essential, pivotal, focal, core.

**ceramics** plural noun pottery, earthenware, clay pots, crocks.

**ceremonious** adjective **1** *a ceremonious occasion* ceremonial, formal, ritual. **2** *behave in a ceremonious manner* punctilious, precise, scrupulous, stately, courtly, courteous, civil, deferential, stiff, rigid; *inf.* just-so.

**ceremony** noun **1** *a wedding ceremony* rite, service, formality, observance, function, custom, sacrament, show. **2** *conducted with ceremony* formalities, niceties, pomp, protocol, decorum, etiquette, propriety.

**certain** adjective **1** *I'm certain he's guilty* sure, positive, confident, convinced, assured, satisfied, persuaded. **2** *her success/failure is certain* destined, fated, inevitable, reliable, inescapable, bound to happen, inexorable; *inf.* in the bag. **3** *it is certain that he will go* definite, unquestionable, beyond question, indubitable, undeniable, irrefutable, obvious, evident, clear. **4** *no certain cure | a certain sign* unfailing, unquestionable, undisputed, dependable, reliable, trustworthy, sound, foolproof; *inf.* sure-fire. **5** *there is no certain date yet* definite, decided, settled, fixed, established, determined. **6** *a certain lady/place that will remain anonymous* particular, specific, individual, special, precise. **7** *to a certain extent* indeterminate, moderate, minimum.

**certainly** adverb surely, definitely, assuredly, undoubtedly, undeniably, obviously, plainly, clearly.

**certainty** noun **1** *I cannot say with certainty* sureness, assuredness, positiveness, confidence, conviction, reliability, validity, conclusiveness, authoritativeness, truth, fact, factualness. **2** *it's a certainty that they will lose* inevitability, indubitability, inescapability, fact; *inf.* sure thing, cinch.

**certificate** noun document, authorization, credentials, testimonial, warrant, license, voucher, diploma.

**certify** verb **1** *a document certifying their marriage* testify to, attest, corroborate, substantiate, verify, confirm, endorse, validate, vouch for, guarantee, authenticate, document, bear witness to, ratify. **2** *she has been certified to teach* accredit, license, authorize, qualify.

**cessation** noun end, termination, finish, conclusion, pause, break, respite, letup.

**chafe** verb **1** *his shirt chafed his neck* rub, abrade, graze, excoriate, scrape, scratch, rasp. **2** *fabric chafed by the rock* wear, wear away/down, wear out, wear to shreds, fray, tatter, erode. **3** *the passengers were chafed by the delay* annoy, anger, irritate, exasperate, vex, worry, peeve, irk, ruffle.

**chaff** noun **1** *chaff from the grain* husks, hulls, pods, shells, cases, casing. **2** *chaff for the cattle* straw, hay, fodder, silage. **3** *throw away the chaff* rubbish, refuse, waste, garbage, trash, dregs, remains, debris, junk, dross, detritus.

**chagrin** noun annoyance, irritation, vexation, displeasure, dissatisfaction, resentment, rankling, smarting, disquiet, embarrassment, mortification, humiliation, shame.

**chain** noun *a chain of events* series, succession, string, sequence, train, progression, course, set, cycle, line, row, concatenation.

**chain** verb fasten, secure, tie, bind, tether, shackle, fetter, manacle; handcuff, confine, restrain, trammel, gird, imprison.

**chains** plural noun bonds, fetters, shackles, manacles, trammels.

**chair** noun seat; stool, bench, pew, stall, throne.

**chair** verb *chair the meeting* preside over, lead, direct, manage, control, oversee, supervise.

**chalk** verb *chalk up* chalk it up to experi-ence put down, ascribe, attribute, accredit, impute, charge.

**challenge** noun **1** *accept a sporting challenge* summons, call, invitation, bidding. **2** *a new challenge in his life* difficult task/venture, hazard, risk, obstacle. **challenge to** *a challenge to tradition* questioning of, opposition to, defiance of, confrontation with.

**challenge** verb **1** *challenge someone to a competition* dare, summon, invite, bid, throw down the gauntlet to. **2** *challenge their authority* question, call into question, dispute, protest against. **3** *the job really challenges him* test, tax, stimulate, arouse, inspire, excite, spur on.

**chamber** noun **1** *the judge's chambers* room, apartment, compartment, cubicle. **2** *the princess retiring to her chamber* bedroom, bedchamber, boudoir. **3** *the chambers in the caves* compartment, cavity, hollow, cell.

**champion** noun **1** *the champion of the com-petition* winner, title-holder, victor, con-queror, hero. **2** *the champion of the cause* defender, protector, upholder, supporter, advocate, backer.

**champion** verb defend, protect, uphold, support, fight for, advocate, promote.

**chance** noun **1** *meet by chance* accident, coincidence, serendipity, fate, luck. **2** *a good chance that he'll win* prospect, pos-sibility, probability, likelihood. **3** *a second chance* opportunity, opening, occasion; *inf.* shot. **4** *take a chance and run* risk, gamble, hazard, venture, speculation.

**chance** verb **1** *it chanced that they ar-rived last* happen, occur, take place, come about. **2** *have to chance it* risk, hazard, gamble, venture, speculate, try one's luck, take a leap in the dark. **chance on/upon** come across, stumble on, come upon, encounter; *inf.* bump into, run into.

**chance** adjective accidental, unexpected, unanticipated, unforeseen, unintended, unpremeditated, fortuitous, serendipitous.

**chancy** adjective risky, uncertain, hazard-ous, speculative, dangerous; *inf.* dicey, iffy.

**change** verb **1** *change one's attitude* al-ter, modify, transform, convert, vary, re-model, recast, reconstruct, reorganize, metamorphose, transmute, permutate. **2** *she's changed* move on, evolve, fluctuate; *inf.* do an about-face. **3** *change a pair of pants* exchange, interchange, substitute, switch, replace, trade, barter; *inf.* swap.

**change** noun **1** *a change in plan* difference, alteration, modification, transformation, conversion, variation, reconstruction, re-organization, innovation, metamorpho-sis, vicissitude, mutation, permutation. **2** *a change of jobs* exchange, interchange, substitution, switch. **3** *he needs a change* diversion, variation; *inf.* break. **4** *have no change* coins, coinage, cash, silver, petty cash.

**changeable** adjective **1** *changeable weather* variable, chameleonlike, protean, shifting, vacillating, volatile, mercurial, capricious, fluctuating, fluid, kaleidoscopic, fitful, wavering, unstable, unsettled, irregular, erratic, unreliable, inconstant, fickle, mu-table, unpredictable. **2** *changeable laws* alterable, modifiable, convertible, mutable.

**channel** noun **1** *the channel connecting the seas* passage, sea passage, strait, neck, narrows, waterway, watercourse, fiord. **2** *rainwater running through the channels* gutter, groove, furrow, conduit, duct, cul-vert, ditch. **3** *new channels for their en-ergy* course, way, direction, path, route, approach. **4** *channels of communication* means, medium, agency, vehicle, route.

**chant** verb sing, recite, intone, cantillate.

**chaos** noun disorder, confusion, pandemo-nium, bedlam, tumult, uproar, disarray, anarchy, lawlessness.

**chaotic** adjective disordered, confused, tumultuous, disorganized, jumbled, topsy-turvy, in disarray, anarchic, lawless.

**chaperon, chaperone** verb accompany, escort, watch over, keep an eye on, protect, guard, safeguard.

**chapter** noun 1 *the next chapter in the book* division, section, part. 2 *a tragic chapter in our history* period, time, phase, stage, episode. 3 *a chapter of the society* branch, division, wing, offshoot.

**char** verb scorch, singe, sear, toast, carbonize, cauterize.

**character** noun 1 *her character has changed* personality, nature, disposition, temperament; ethos, individuality, constitution, makeup, attributes, bent, genius. 2 *a person of character* moral strength/fiber, strength, honor, integrity, rectitude, uprightness. 3 *damage his character* reputation, name, standing, position, status. 4 *a local character* eccentric, oddity, original, individual; *inf.* oddball. 5 *they're all friendly characters* person, individual, human being, fellow; *inf.* guy, sort, type, customer.

**characteristic** noun quality, attribute, feature, trait, property, mannerism, mark, trademark, idiosyncrasy, peculiarity, quirk.

**characteristic** adjective typical, distinguishing, distinctive, particular, special, individual, specific, peculiar, idiosyncratic, singular.

**characterize** verb 1 *the landscape is characterized by hills and rivers* typify, distinguish, identify, denote, designate, mark, stamp, brand. 2 *the witness characterized the scene as shocking* portray, depict, present, represent, describe.

**charade** noun pretense, travesty, fake, farce, pantomime.

**charge** verb 1 *what do you charge for a room?* ask, expect, impose, levy. 2 *charge it to my account* debit, put down to, bill. 3 *charge the murder suspect* accuse, indict, arraign, impeach. 4 *charge the enemy* attack, storm, assault, rush, open fire on, fall on. 5 *charged with the guardianship of the child* entrust, tax, weigh, weigh down, load, burden, encumber, hamper, saddle. 6 *charged with emotion* fill, load, imbue, suffuse, infuse, instill.

**charge** noun 1 *what is the charge for a room?* cost, price, fee, amount, rate, expense, levy, toll. 2 *murder charge* accusation, allegation, indictment, arraignment, citation, imputation. 3 *a cavalry charge* attack, storming, assault, onrush, onslaught. 4 *have charge of the children* responsibility, care, custody, guardianship, trust. 5 *your charge is to drive the car* duty, task, job, responsibility,

office, obligation, assignment. 6 *pay for his charge's education* ward, protégé, dependent, minor.

**charitable** adjective 1 *be charitable toward the poor* philanthropic, giving, benevolent, generous, liberal, openhanded, kind, magnanimous, beneficent, munificent. 2 *a charitable interpretation* tolerant, broad-minded, understanding, sympathetic, compassionate, lenient, indulgent.

**charity** noun 1 *rely on charity for survival* financial assistance, donations, contributions, handouts, endowments, financial relief. 2 *behave with charity toward others* goodwill, compassion, humanity, humanitarianism, kindliness, love, sympathy, tolerance, indulgence, liberality, benevolence.

**charlatan** noun quack, sham, fraud, fake, impostor, pretender, cheat, deceiver, swindler; *inf.* con man.

**charm** noun 1 *the charm of the resort/hostess* attractiveness, attraction, appeal, allure, fascination, captivation, desirability, delightfulness; beauty, wiles, blandishments. 2 *the sorcerer's charm* spell, magic formula, magic word, abracadabra, sorcery, magic. 3 *the charms on her bracelet* trinket, ornament, bauble, souvenir. 4 *a lucky charm* amulet, talisman, fetish.

**charm** verb delight, please, attract, win, win over, captivate, allure, lure, draw, fascinate, bewitch, beguile, enchant, enrapture, seduce, cajole.

**charming** adjective delightful, pleasing, pleasant, appealing, attractive, winning, fetching, taking, captivating, winsome, engaging, lovely, agreeable, alluring, fascinating, bewitching, beguiling, enchanting, irresistible, seductive.

**chart** noun graph, table, map, diagram, plan, blueprint, guide, scheme.

**chart** verb tabulate, map, map out, plot, graph, delineate, diagram, sketch.

**charter** noun 1 *privileges granted by royal charter* authority, authorization, sanction, warrant, document, covenant, deed, bond, permit, prerogative, privilege, right. 2 *the charter of the United Nations* constitution, code, canon, body of laws; principles, rules, laws.

**chase** verb pursue, run after, follow, hunt, hound, track, trail, tail. **chase away** *chase away the blues* put to flight, drive away, send away, send packing.

**chasm** noun 1 *a landscape full of chasms* gorge, abyss, canyon, ravine, pit, crater, crevasse, gap, fissure, crevice, cleft, rift. 2 *a chasm between their points of view* schism, breach, gulf.

**chaste** adjective 1 *nuns leading a chaste life* virgin, virginal, vestal, celibate, abstinent, unmarried. 2 *chaste conduct/speech* virtuous, pure, decent, moral, decorous, modest, wholesome, righteous, upright. **3** *a chaste style* simple, plain, unadorned.

**chasten** verb **1** *chastened by the experience* subdue, restrain, tame, curb, check, humble, cow, tone down. **2** *chasten the students* discipline, punish. *See* CHASTISE 2.

**chastise** verb **1** *mutineers chastised the harsh captain* punish, discipline, castigate, beat, thrash, smack, flog, whip, strap, cane, lash, scourge; *inf.* wallop, thump, tan one's hide. **2** *the staff were chastised for tardiness* scold, upbraid, reprimand, reprove, chide, take to task, haul over the coals, chasten, castigate.

**chastity** noun **1** *nuns take vows of chastity* virginity, celibacy, abstinence, singleness. **2** *chastity of conduct/speech* virtue, goodness, innocence, purity, decency, morality, decorum, modesty, wholesomeness, righteousness.

**chat** verb talk, gossip, chatter, converse, prattle, jabber, prate; *inf.* have a confab, jaw, chew the fat, rap.

**chat** noun talk, conversation, chatter, heart-to-heart, tête-à-tête; *inf.* confab.

**chatty** adjective **1** *a chatty person* talkative, gossipy, garrulous, loquacious, voluble, glib, effusive. **2** *a chatty style* informal, conversational, colloquial, familiar, friendly, lively.

**cheap** adjective **1** *cheap prices/housing* inexpensive, low-priced, low-cost, economical, reasonable, moderately priced, bargain, economy, sale, reduced, marked-down, slashed, discounted; *inf.* bargain-basement. **2** *cheap and gaudy jewelry* poor-quality, inferior, shoddy, common, trashy, tawdry, paltry, worthless, second-rate, gimcrack; *inf.* tacky. **3** *he felt cheap after what he had done* ashamed, shameful, embarrassed, humiliated, mortified, debased, degraded, abashed, discomfited, disconcerted. **4** *he's too cheap to buy a raffle ticket* stingy, parsimonious, tight-fisted, niggardly, penny-pinching, frugal.

**cheapen** verb **1** *cheapen the cost of travel* lower, reduce, cut, mark down, slash, discount, depreciate. **2** *cheapening herself by working in that club* degrade, debase, demean, devalue, lower, belittle, denigrate, discredit.

**cheat** verb **1** *cheat his partner* deceive, trick, swindle, defraud, dupe, hoodwink, double-cross, gull; exploit, take advantage of, victimize; *inf.* con, bamboozle, finagle, bilk; rip off, fleece, take for a ride. **2** *cheat death* avoid, elude, evade, dodge, escape.

**cheat** noun cheater, swindler, fraud, confidence man/woman, trickster, deceiver, double-crosser, crook, rogue, shark, charlatan; *inf.* con man.

**check** verb **1** *check the roof for holes* examine, inspect, look at, look over, scrutinize, test, monitor, investigate, probe, study; *inf.* give the once-over to. **2** *check that the door's locked* confirm, make sure, verify, corroborate, validate, substantiate. **3** *check the disease* stop, arrest, halt, bring to a standstill, slow down, brake, bar, obstruct, impede, block, retard, curb, delay. **4** *check one's laughter/tears* restrain, suppress, repress, contain, control, bridle, inhibit. **5** *their stories don't check* correspond, agree, tally, dovetail, harmonize. **check up on** investigate, examine, inspect, research, scrutinize, probe.

**check** noun **1** *a security check* examination, inspection, scrutiny, scrutinization, test, monitoring, investigation, probe, inquiry, study; *inf.* once-over. **2** *a check in the production rate* stop, stopping, stoppage, arrest, halt, slowing-down, retardation, delay. **3** *act as a check to the celebration* restraint, constraint, control, deterrent, impediment, obstruction, limitation, curb. **4** *the customer asked for his check* bill, account, invoice, reckoning, tally; *inf.* tab.

**checkered** adjective *a checkered career* mixed, varied, diverse, diversified, eventful; full of ups and downs.

**checkup** noun examination, inspection, appraisal, assessment, analysis, scrutinization, scrutiny, exploration, probe.

**cheek** noun **1** jowl, chop, gill. **2** *have the cheek to appear* impudence, audacity, temerity, brazenness, effrontery, nerve; *inf.* gall.

**cheeky** adjective impudent, audacious, impertinent, insolent, forward, pert, disrespectful, fresh, insulting; *inf.* saucy, sassy.

**cheer** verb **1** *crowds cheered the president* hail, acclaim, hurrah, hurray, applaud, shout at, clap for. **2** *his arrival cheered her* raise the spirits of, brighten, buoy up, perk up, enliven, animate, elate, exhilarate, hearten, uplift, give a lift to, gladden, encourage, incite, stimulate, arouse, comfort, solace, console, inspirit; *inf.* buck up.

**cheer** noun **1** *the cheers of the crowd* acclaim, acclamation, hurrah, hurray, applause, ovation, plaudit, hailing, shouting, clapping. **2** *a time of cheer* cheerfulness, gladness, happiness, merriment, mirth, gaiety, joy, pleasure, high spirits, lightheartedness, glee, merrymaking, rejoicing, revelry, festivity. **3** *tables laden with seasonal cheer* fare, food, provisions, foodstuffs, drink; *inf.* eats.

**cheerful** adjective **1** *a cheerful disposition* happy, bright, merry, glad, gladsome, gay, sunny, joyful, jolly, blithe, buoyant,

**cheerless** · **chivalrous**

60

lighthearted, sparkling, carefree, happy-go-lucky, breezy, cheery, sprightly, jaunty, smiling, laughing, bright-eyed and bushy-tailed, optimistic, hopeful, positive. **2** *a cheerful room* pleasant, agreeable, friendly, happy. **3** *his cheerful acceptance of the situation* willing, obliging, cooperative, compliant.

**cheerless** adjective gloomy, dreary, miserable, dull, depressing, dismal, bleak, drab, grim, austere, desolate, dark, dingy, somber, uninviting.

**cheers** interjection here's to you, good luck, to your health, *skol, prosit; inf.* here's mud in your eye, bottoms up, down the hatch.

**cheery** adjective happy, merry. *See* CHEERFUL 1.

**cherish** verb **1** *cherish a friendship* treasure, prize, hold dear, adore, revere, indulge; care for, look after, tend, protect, preserve, shelter, support, nurture, foster. **2** *cherish hopes* entertain, harbor, cling to.

**chest** noun **1** *injured her chest* thorax, breast, sternum. **2** *pack belongings in chests* box, crate, case, trunk, container, coffer, casket.

**chew** verb masticate, munch, champ, crunch, bite, gnaw, grind. **chew over** meditate on, ruminate on, mull over, consider, deliberate upon, reflect upon.

**chic** adjective stylish, fashionable, smart, elegant, modish, voguish; *inf.* trendy.

**chicanery** noun deception, deceitfulness, duplicity, guile, cheating, duping, hoodwinking, dishonesty, subterfuge, craftiness, wiles, sophistry.

**chide** verb scold, reproach, lecture, call to account. *See* CASTIGATE.

**chief** noun head, headman, leader, chieftain, ruler, overlord, lord and master, commander, sachem; principal, director, chairman, chairperson, chief executive, manager, superintendent, master, foreman; *inf.* boss, boss man, kingpin, top dog.

**chief** adjective **1** *chief priest* supreme, head, foremost, highest, leading, superior, premier, directing, governing. **2** *the chief point* main, principal, most important, uppermost, primary, central, key, vital, essential, predominant, preeminent.

**chiefly** adverb mainly, in the main, principally, primarily, predominantly, especially, particularly, essentially, mostly, for the most part, on the whole, above all.

**child** noun **1** *two adults and a child* youngster, young person, young one, little one, boy, girl, baby, babe, infant, toddler, tot, tiny tot, adolescent, youth, juvenile, minor; *derog.* brat; *inf.* kid, shaver. **2** *parents and their children* offspring, progeny, issue; descendant, scion; son, daughter.

**childhood** noun youth, infancy, babyhood, preteens, minority, immaturity; boyhood, girlhood.

**childish** adjective **1** *the childish behavior of the adults* immature, infantile, juvenile, puerile, silly, foolish, irresponsible, jejune. **2** *childish laughter* children's, childlike, youthful.

**childlike** adjective **1** *childlike activities* children's, youthful. **2** *childlike reactions* ingenuous, innocent, artless, guileless, simple, naive, trusting, trustful.

**chill** noun **1** *a chill in the air* chilliness, coldness, iciness, crispness, rawness, sharpness, nip, bite. **2** *a chill in her manner* aloofness, distance, coolness, unresponsiveness, lack of sympathy, frigidity, hostility, unfriendliness. **3** *cast a chill over the proceedings* cloud, depression, damper.

**chill** verb *chill the enthusiasm* lessen, reduce, dampen, depress, dispirit, discourage, dishearten.

**chilly** adjective **1** *a chilly breeze* cold, cool, icy, crisp, brisk, fresh, raw, sharp, biting, penetrating, freezing, frigid; *inf.* nippy. **2** *a chilly manner* cold, cool, aloof, distant, unresponsive, unsympathetic, frigid, unwelcoming, hostile, unfriendly.

**chime** verb ring, peal, toll, sound, ding, ding-dong, clang, boom, tinkle, resound, reverberate. **chime in** *he's always chiming in when we're talking* interrupt, cut in, interpose; *inf.* butt in; jump in.

**chimes** plural noun bells, carillon, wind chimes.

**china** noun porcelain, faience, ceramics, pottery; dishes, tableware, dinner/tea service.

**chip** noun **1** *chips on the sawmill's floor* shaving, paring, shard, flake, shred, sliver, splinter, fragment, snippet, scrap. **2** *the cup with a chip in it* nick, crack, notch, flaw. **3** *gambling chips* counter, token, disk.

**chip** verb **1** *chip a glass* nick, crack, damage. **2** *the paint chips easily* break off, crack, fragment, crumble. **3** *chipping away at a chunk of wood* whittle, chisel, hew. **chip in 1** *he's always chipping in with suggestions* interrupt, cut in, interpose; *inf.* chime in, butt in. **2** *chip in to buy a present* contribute, make a contribution, donate.

**chirp** verb chirrup, cheep, twitter, tweet, warble, trill, chatter.

**chitchat** noun small talk, idle gossip, gossip, chatter.

**chivalrous** adjective **1** *behaving in a chivalrous way toward women* gallant, gentlemanly, courteous, gracious, mannerly, well-mannered, polite, thoughtful, protective, courtly. **2** *chivalrous followers of King Arthur* knightly, courtly, bold, courageous,

61

**chivalry · circulate**

brave, valiant, heroic, daring, intrepid, honorable, high-minded, just, fair, loyal, constant, true, gallant, magnanimous.

**chivalry** noun **1** *chivalry toward women* gallantry, gentlemanliness, courtesy, courteousness, graciousness, mannerliness, politeness, thoughtfulness, protectiveness, courtliness. **2** *the chivalry of King Arthur's followers* courtliness, boldness, valor, honor, high-mindedness, integrity, justness, fairness, loyalty, constancy.

**choice** noun **1** *the choice of candidates* selection, picking, preference, election, adoption. **2** *no choice but to resign* alternative, option, possibility, solution, answer, way out. **3** *a wide choice of candy* range, variety, supply, store. **4** *he was considered the right choice* selection, appointment, appointee, nominee, candidate.

**choice** adjective **1** *choice fruit* best, select, superior, first-class, first-rate, excellent, prime, prize. **2** *a few choice phrases* well-chosen, select, handpicked, appropriate, apt.

**choke** verb **1** *choked to death* strangle, strangulate, throttle. **2** *smoke choking him* asphyxiate, suffocate, smother, stifle. **3** *he choked on a bone* gag, gasp, retch, asphyxiate, suffocate. **4** *the storm drains are choked with leaves* clog, block, obstruct, occlude, plug, dam up. **choke back** *choke back tears* contain, suppress, control, repress, curb, bridle.

**choose** verb **1** *choose a book/career* select, pick, pick out, handpick, take, opt for, settle on, decide on, fix on, single out, adopt, designate, elect, espouse. **2** *do as you choose* prefer, like, wish, want, desire, fancy, favor.

**choosy** adjective fussy, finicky, persnickety, fastidious, particular, exacting, discriminating.

**chop** verb cut up, cube, dice, fragment, crumble. **chop down** cut down, fell, hew, bring down, saw down. **chop off** *chop off branches* cut off, lop, sever, hack off.

**choppy** adjective rough, bumpy, turbulent, blustery, stormy, tempestuous.

**chore** noun task, job, duty, errand, burden.

**chortle** verb chuckle, cackle, guffaw, laugh uproariously, roar/shake with laughter.

**chorus** noun **1** *sing in a chorus* choir, ensemble, choral group; choristers, singers, vocalists. **2** *the chorus of the song* refrain, strain, response. **in chorus** *give a reply in chorus* in unison, in concert, in harmony.

**christen** verb baptize, sprinkle, immerse; give a name to, name, call, dub, style, term, designate, denominate.

**chronic** adjective *a chronic illness/habit* persistent, long-lasting, long-standing, constant, continual, continuous, incessant, lingering, deep-rooted, deep-seated, ingrained, inveterate, confirmed, habitual, hardened.

**chronicle** noun register, record, annals, calendar, diary, journal, log, account, archive, history, story.

**chronicle** verb record, put on record, set down, document, register, report, enter, note, relate, tell about.

**chronological** adjective sequential, consecutive, progressive, serial, historical.

**chubby** adjective plump, tubby, rotund, stout, portly, round, dumpy, fat, fleshy, flabby, paunchy.

**chuck** verb **1** *chuck it in the bucket* toss, fling, throw, cast, pitch, hurl, shy, heave, sling, let fly. **2** *chuck his job/girlfriend* abandon, give up, relinquish, quit, forsake; *inf.* drop.

**chuckle** verb laugh quietly, laugh to oneself, chortle, giggle, titter, cackle.

**chum** noun friend, bosom friend, companion, comrade, crony, alter ego; *inf.* pal, buddy.

**chunk** noun lump, hunk, block, slab, mass, square, wedge, dollop, piece, portion, part.

**church** noun place of worship, the house of God, the Lord's house; cathedral, minster, chapel, temple, tabernacle, mosque, synagogue.

**churn** verb beat, whip up, agitate, disturb, stir up, shake up.

**cinema** noun films, pictures, movies, motion pictures; *inf.* big screen, silver screen.

**circle** noun **1** *draw a circle* ring, disk, loop, circumference, ball, globe, sphere, orb. **2** *move in different circles* sphere, domain, province, realm, region, circuit, orbit, compass. **3** *her circle of friends* group, set, company, crowd, ring, coterie, clique.

**circle** verb **1** *vultures circling above* rotate, revolve, circulate, whirl, gyrate, pivot, swivel. **2** *circle the estate/world* surround, encircle, ring, enclose, envelop, hem in, gird, belt, circumscribe; orbit, circumnavigate.

**circuit** noun **1** *run a circuit of the track* lap, turn, beat, cycle, loop. **2** *the circuit of the estate/field* border, boundary, bounds, compass, limits, circumference.

**circuitous** adjective roundabout, winding, meandering, tortuous, twisting, rambling, indirect, maze-like, labyrinthine.

**circular** adjective round, ring-shaped, annular, spherical, spheroid, globular.

**circulate** verb **1** *circulate the news* spread, disseminate, propagate, distribute, transmit, give out, make known, make public, broadcast, publicize, advertise. **2** *blood/air* *circulating* flow, move round, go round, rotate, revolve, whirl, gyrate.

**circumference** noun perimeter, periphery, border, boundary, bounds, limits, confines, outline, circuit, compass, extremity, edge, rim.

**circumlocution** noun periphrasis, tautology, redundancy, discursiveness, verbosity, wordiness, prolixity, long-windedness.

**circumscribe** verb 1 *circumscribe the area* enclose, encircle, bound, encompass, gird; define, delineate, outline, demarcate, delimit, mark off. 2 *activities circumscribed by poverty* restrict, limit, curb, confine, restrain.

**circumspect** adjective wary, cautious, careful; prudent, judicious, politic.

**circumstances** plural noun 1 *I know nothing of the circumstances* situation, state of affairs, conditions, position, event, occurrence, background. 2 *living in poor circumstances* financial plight, predicament, means, resources, lifestyle, station.

**circumstantial** adjective 1 *circumstantial evidence* indirect, incidental, evidential, deduced, presumed, inferential, conjectural. 2 *a circumstantial account* detailed, precise, particular, exact, accurate, minute.

**citation** noun 1 *citations from the classics* quotation, quote, extract, excerpt, reference, illustration, allusion, passage, source. 2 *a citation for heroism* commendation, award, honor, mention. 3 *a citation from the courts* summons, subpoena, arraignment.

**cite** verb 1 *cite the statistics as evidence* quote, mention, name, enumerate, refer to, allude to, exemplify, excerpt, extract. 2 *cited for heroism* commend, recommend, pay tribute to, mention.

**citizen** noun resident, inhabitant, dweller, denizen, townsman, townswoman, taxpayer, voter, constituent, subject.

**city** noun metropolitan area, conurbation, metropolis, municipality, town.

**civic** adjective municipal, public, community, local, civil, communal, urban, metropolitan.

**civil** adjective 1 *civil responsibilities* municipal, public. *See* CIVIC. 2 *civil government/rulers* civilian, lay, nonmilitary, nonreligious, secular. 3 *in a civil manner* polite, courteous, well-mannered, mannerly, well-bred, gentlemanly, ladylike, refined, urbane, polished, civilized.

**civility** noun 1 *treat even his opponents with civility* courtesy, courteousness, politeness, good manners, mannerliness, graciousness, cordiality, geniality, pleasantness, gallantry. 2 *exchange civilities* courtesy, etiquette, protocol, propriety, decorum.

**civilization** noun 1 *a threat to modern civilization* development, advancement, progress, enlightenment, culture, cultivation, edification, refinement, sophistication. 2 *ancient civilizations* society, community, nation, country, people, way of life.

**civilized** adjective developed, modern, socialized, educated, cultured, cultivated, sophisticated, enlightened, urbane.

**claim** verb 1 *claim the prize* lay claim to, ask as one's right, demand, request, requisition. 2 *claim that he's innocent* profess, maintain, assert, declare, protest, avow, aver, allege.

**claim** noun 1 *a claim for damages* demand, request, application, petition, call. 2 *his claim to the crown* right, rights, title, prerogative, privilege, heritage, inheritance, legacy. 3 *dispute his claims of innocence* profession, assertion, declaration, protestation, avowal, allegation.

**claimant** noun applicant, candidate, petitioner, supplicant, suppliant, suitor, postulant, pretender, plaintiff.

**clairvoyance** noun second sight, psychic powers, extrasensory perception, ESP, telepathy, sixth sense.

**clamor** noun 1 *the clamor of children's voices* uproar, noise, din, racket, shout, shouting, yelling, blaring, commotion, hubbub, hullabaloo, outcry, vociferation. 2 *answer their clamors for more money* demand, call, petition, request, urging, protest, complaint, insistence.

**clamp** noun vice, press, brace, clasp, fastener, hasp.

**clamp** verb 1 *a pipe clamped between his teeth* grip, hold, fix, clench, press, squeeze, secure, make fast, brace. 2 *clamp a curfew on the city* impose, inflict, lay on, set, charge, burden. **clamp down on** hold in check, crack down on, be severe with, suppress, prevent.

**clan** noun 1 *tired of the clan of socialites* set, circle, crowd, in-crowd, gang, band, group, faction, clique, coterie. 2 *our clan gathers for every holiday* family, kin, kinfolk, relatives, kith and kin.

**clandestine** adjective secret, undercover, surreptitious, cloak-and-dagger, back-alley, furtive, concealed, hidden, underhand.

**clang** noun ring, clank, clash, clangor, bong, chime, toll, clink, clunk, jangle.

**clang** verb ring, resound, reverberate, clank, clash, bong, clink, chime, toll, peal.

**clarify** verb clear up, resolve, make plain, explain, elucidate, illuminate, throw light on, make simple, simplify.

**clarity** noun 1 *the clarity of his prose* clearness, lucidity, lucidness, plainness, simplicity, intelligibility, comprehensibility, unambiguity, precision. **2** *the clarity of the water* clearness, transparency, limpidity, translucence, pellucidity, glassiness.

**clash** verb **1** *clash the cymbals* strike, bang, clang, crash, clatter, clank, clink, rattle, jangle. **2** *the two sides clashed* be in conflict, war, fight, contend, do battle, come to blows, feud, grapple, wrangle, quarrel, cross swords, lock horns. **3** *the appointments clash* coincide, conflict. **4** *the colors clash* be discordant, jar, be incompatible.

**clash** noun **1** *the clash of cymbals* striking, bang, clang, crash, clatter, clank. **2** *the clash of the opposing sides* conflict, collision, confrontation, brush, warring, fighting, contending, feud, grappling, wrangling, quarreling. **3** *the clash of the colors* discordance, discord, lack of harmony, incompatibility, jarring.

**clasp** noun **1** *the clasp of the necklace* catch, fastener, fastening, clip; hook, hook and eye, clamp, buckle, hasp. **2** *engage in a loving clasp* embrace, hug, cuddle, hold, grip, grasp.

**class** noun **1** *professional class* social order/division, stratum, rank, level, status, sphere, grade, group, grouping, set, caste. **2** *degrees divided into three classes* category, classification, division, section, group. **3** *a class of objects* kind, sort, type, collection, denomination, order, species, genre, genus. **4** *a woman of class* quality, excellence, distinction, stylishness, elegance.

**classic** adjective **1** *a classic performance* first-rate, first-class, excellent, brilliant, finest, outstanding, exemplary, masterly, consummate. **2** *a classic case/example* typical, standard, model, guiding, archetypal, stock, true-to-form, paradigmatic, prototypical. **3** *classic styles* simple, traditional, timeless, ageless, long-lasting, enduring, abiding, long-standing.

**classic** noun great work, established work, masterpiece.

**classical** adjective **1** *a classical scholar/classical architecture* Greek, Grecian, Hellenic, Attic, Greco-Roman, Roman, Latin. **2** *classical music* orchestral, symphonic. **3** *a classical style of design* simple, plain, restrained, pure, understated, harmonious, well-proportioned, balanced, symmetrical, elegant.

**classification** noun categorizing, categorization, grouping, grading, arrangement, codification, taxonomy.

**classify** verb categorize, class, group, grade, arrange, order, sort, type, rank, rate, designate, codify, catalog.

**clause** noun section, paragraph, article, note, item, point, passage, part, heading.

**claw** noun nail, talon, pincer, nipper, chela.

**claw** verb scratch, tear, lacerate, scrape, graze, rip, dig into, maul.

**clean** adjective **1** *clean hands/clothes* unsoiled, unstained, unspotted, unsullied, unblemished, spotless, immaculate, speckless, hygienic, sanitary, washed, cleansed, laundered, scrubbed. **2** *clean air* pure, clear, natural, unpolluted, unadulterated, uncontaminated, untainted. **3** *clean lives* good, upright, honorable, respectable, virtuous, righteous, moral, reputable, upstanding. **4** *a clean piece of paper* unused, unmarked, blank, vacant, void. **5** *the clean lines of the airplane* streamlined, smooth, well-defined, definite, clean-cut, regular, simple, elegant, graceful, uncluttered. **6** *a clean break* complete, thorough, total, conclusive, decisive, final.

**clean** verb **1** *clean one's hands/walls* wash, cleanse, wipe, sponge, scrub, scour, swab. **2** *clean one's clothes* dry-clean, launder. **3** *clean the room* tidy, pick up; vacuum, dust, mop, sweep.

**cleanse** verb **1** *cleanse the wound* clean, wash, bathe, rinse, disinfect. **2** *cleanse of sin* purify, purge, absolve.

**clear** adjective **1** *a clear day* bright, cloudless, unclouded, fair, fine, light, undimmed, sunny, sunshiny. **2** *clear glass* transparent, limpid, translucent, crystalline. **3** *it was clear that he was guilty* obvious, evident, plain, apparent, sure, definite, unmistakable, indisputable, patent. **4** *a clear account of the incident* understandable, comprehensible, intelligible, plain, explicit, lucid, coherent. **5** *a clear thinker* astute, keen, sharp, quick, perceptive, discerning, perspicacious. **6** *a clear view* open, empty, free, unobstructed, unimpeded, unhindered, unlimited. **7** *a clear conscience* untroubled, undisturbed, innocent, guiltless, guilt-free.

**clear** verb **1** *the weather cleared* clear up, brighten, lighten, break. **2** *clear the plates* remove, take away, tidy up/away. **3** *clear the drains* unblock, unclog, unstop. **4** *clear the room of objects* empty, vacate, evacuate, void, free, rid. **5** *clear the accused of charges* absolve, acquit, discharge, let go, exonerate, vindicate. **6** *clear the fence* jump, vault, leap, hop, pass over. **7** *clear $500* net, make a profit of, realize a profit of, gain, earn, make, bring, reap. **8** *the ship was cleared* authorize, sanction, pass, approve, permit/allow to pass. **clear out 1** *clear out the cupboard* empty, evacuate, tidy, tidy up. **2** *clear out the trash* get rid of, throw out, throw away, eject, eliminate. **3** *boys told to clear out* go away, get out, leave, depart, make oneself scarce, decamp. **clear up 1** *clear up the mystery* solve, resolve, straighten out, find an answer to, unravel, untangle, explain, elucidate; *inf.* crack. **2** *the weather cleared up* improve, brighten. *See* CLEAR *verb* 1.

**clearance** *noun* **1** *slum clearance* clearing, removal, evacuation, eviction, emptying. **2** *the clearance under the bridge* clearing, space, gap, allowance, margin, headroom, leeway. **3** *clearance for the plans* authorization, consent, permission, sanction, go-ahead, leave; *inf.* green light.

**clear-cut** *adjective* definite, specific, precise, explicit, unambiguous, unequivocal.

**clearly** *adverb* obviously, undoubtedly, without doubt, indubitably, plainly, undeniably, decidedly, surely, certainly, irrefutably, incontestably, patently.

**cleave** *verb* **cleave to** cling to, stick to, hold to, stand by, abide by, adhere to, be loyal/faithful to.

**cleft** *noun* split, crack, gap, fissure, crevice, rift, break, fracture.

**clemency** *noun* mercy, leniency, compassion, humanity, pity, sympathy, kindness, magnanimity, fairness.

**clench** *verb* **1** *clench the teeth* close, shut, seal, fasten. **2** *clench the table edge* grip, grasp, clutch, hold, seize.

**clergy** *noun* priests, clerics, ecclesiastics; ministry, priesthood, the cloth, first estate.

**clergyman, clergywoman** *noun* churchman, churchwoman, man/woman of the cloth, man/woman of God, cleric, ecclesiastic, divine; vicar, parson, pastor, priest, father, padre, reverend, rector, rabbi, chaplain.

**clerical** *adjective* **1** *clerical duties* secretarial, office, writing, typing, filing, bookkeeping. **2** *clerical clothes* ecclesiastical, churchly, priestly, pastoral, sacerdotal, apostolic, canonical.

**clever** *adjective* **1** *clever people* intelligent, bright, sharp-witted, quick-witted, talented, gifted, smart, capable, able, competent, knowledgeable, educated; *inf.* brainy. **2** *a clever move* shrewd, astute, adroit, canny, cunning, ingenious, artful, wily, inventive. **3** *clever with their hands* dexterous, skillful, adroit, nimble, deft, handy.

**cliché** *noun* hackneyed phrase, platitude, banality, truism, saw, bromide; *inf.* chestnut.

**click** *verb* **1** *the key clicked in the lock* clink, clack, chink, snap, tick. **2** *it suddenly clicked* become clear, fall into place, come home to one, make sense. **3** *the two girls clicked immediately* get on, take to each other, hit it off, be compatible, be on the same wavelength, feel a rapport. **4** *the new toys clicked with the children* make a

hit, prove popular, be successful, succeed, go down well.

**client** *noun* customer, patron, regular, habitué, buyer, purchaser, shopper; patient.

**cliff** *noun* precipice, rock face, face, crag, bluff, escarpment, scarp, overhang, tor.

**climate** *noun* **1** *temperate climate* weather, temperature. **2** *visit various climates* clime, country, place, region, area, zone. **3** *the political climate* atmosphere, mood, temper, spirit, feeling, feel, ambience, aura, ethos.

**climax** *noun* culmination, height, peak, pinnacle, high point, summit, top, highlight, acme, zenith, apex, apogee, crowning point; orgasm.

**climb** *verb* **1** *climb up the ladder | climb to the top* go, ascend, mount, scale, clamber. **2** *prices are climbing* go up, rise, increase, shoot up, soar. **3** *the road climbs steeply* slope upward, incline, bank.

**clinch** *verb* **1** *clinch the deal* settle, secure, seal, set the seal on, complete, assure, cap, close, wind up; *inf.* sew up. **2** *clinch a nail* fasten, make fast, secure, fix, clamp, bolt, rivet. **3** *boxers/lovers clinching* hug, embrace, squeeze, clutch, grasp, grapple.

**cling** *verb* *the surfaces clung together* stick, adhere, hold, grip, clasp, clutch. **cling to 1** *cling to the rope* hold on to, hang on to, clutch, grip, grasp, clasp, cleave to. **2** *cling to one's beliefs* stick to, hold to, stand by, abide by, adhere to, be loyal/faithful to, remain true to, remain attached to; *inf.* stick with.

**clinical** *adjective* **1** *a clinical attitude* objective, dispassionate, detached, uninvolved, cold, unsympathetic, unfeeling. **2** *clinical designs* plain, simple, unadorned, stark, austere, severe.

**clip** *verb* **1** *clip hair/hedges* cut, crop, snip, trim, shear, prune. **2** *clip him across the jaw* hit, strike, box, cuff, smack, wallop, thump, punch, knock; *inf.* clout, whack. **3** *the train was clipping along* speed, race, gallop, rush, dash, zoom.

**clique** *noun* coterie, circle, crowd, incrowd, set, gang, group, clan, faction, pack, band, ring, fraternity.

**cloak** *noun* **1** *wearing a black cloak* cape, mantle, wrap, shawl, pelisse, coat. **2** *a cloak of secrecy* cover, screen, blind, mask, mantle, veil, shroud, shield, front, camouflage, pretext.

**cloak** *verb* hide, conceal, cover, cover up, screen, mask, veil, shroud, shield, cloud, camouflage, obscure, disguise.

**clock** *noun* timekeeper, timepiece, timer; chronometer, chronograph.

**clog** *verb* **1** *leaves clogging the drains* block, obstruct, dam, congest, jam, occlude, stop up, dam up. **2** *clog the system with red tape* hinder, impede, hamper.

**cloister** noun *walking in the cloisters* covered walk, walkway, corridor, aisle, arcade, gallery, piazza.

**cloistered** adjective secluded, sheltered, sequestered, confined, restricted, reclusive, hermitic.

**close** verb **1** *close the door* shut, slam, fasten, secure, lock, bolt, bar, latch, padlock. **2** *close the bottle* stop up, plug, seal, clog, choke, obstruct, occlude. **3** *close the meeting* bring to an end, end, conclude, finish, terminate, wind up. **4** *close the bargain* complete, settle, clinch, seal. **5** *the gap closed* narrow, lessen, grow smaller, dwindle, reduce. **6** *his arms closed around her* come together, join, connect, come into contact, unite.

**close** noun end, finish, conclusion, termination, cessation, completion, culmination, finale, wind-up.

**close** adjective **1** *our two houses are close* near, adjacent, in close proximity, adjoining, neighboring, abutting. **2** *a close resemblance* near, similar, like, alike, comparable, parallel, corresponding, akin. **3** *a close friend* intimate, dear, bosom, close-knit, inseparable. **4** *close formation* dense, condensed, compact, crowded, packed, solid, tight, cramped, congested. **5** *a close game* evenly matched, well-matched, hard-fought, sharply contested, neck-and-neck, nose-to-nose; *inf.* fifty-fifty. **6** *a close description* accurate, true, faithful, literal, exact, precise. **7** *close attention* intense, keen, thorough, rigorous, searching. **8** *under close arrest* strict, stringent, rigorous, thorough, tight. **9** *close weather* humid, muggy, stuffy, heavy, oppressive, stifling, suffocating. **10** *he's very close about his affairs* uncommunicative, reserved, private, unforthcoming, secretive. **11** *close with money* miserly, stingy, niggardly, parsimonious, tight-fisted, tight.

**closure** noun termination, finish, conclusion.

**clot** verb coagulate, set, congeal, jell, thicken, cake, curdle.

**cloth** noun *silk cloth* fabric, material, stuff; textiles, dry goods, soft goods.

**clothe** verb **1** *clothed in pure wool* dress, attire, rig, rig out, turn out, apparel, fit out, outfit, robe, garb, array, deck out, drape; *inf.* doll up. **2** *hills clothed in clouds* cover, wrap, cloak, envelop, swathe.

**clothing** noun clothes, garments; dress, attire, apparel, outfit, costume, garb, ensemble, vestments, raiment; *inf.* gear, togs, get-up.

**cloud** noun **1** *clouds in the sky* rain cloud, storm cloud, thundercloud, billow; haze, cloudbank. **2** *a cloud of smoke* pall, shroud, mantle, cloak, screen, cover. **3** *a cloud on their happiness* shadow, threat; gloom, darkness. **4** *a cloud of insects* swarm, flock, mass, multitude, host, horde, throng.

**cloudy** adjective **1** *a cloudy sky* overcast, hazy, dark, gray, somber, leaden, heavy, gloomy, dim, lowering, sunless, starless. **2** *cloudy recollections* blurred, vague, indistinct, hazy, indefinite, nebulous, obscure, confused, muddled. **3** *cloudy liquids* opaque, murky, muddy, milky, emulsified, opalescent, turbid.

**clout** noun **1** *give him a clout* smack, slap, thump. **2** *because of your clout in the firm* influence, power, pull, weight, authority, prestige, standing.

**clown** noun **1** *circus clowns* jester, fool, buffoon, zany, harlequin. **2** *he's a real clown* joker, comedian, comic, humorist, funnyman, wag, wit, prankster.

**club** noun **1** *hit him with a club* cudgel, bludgeon, stick, staff, truncheon, bat, baton, blackjack. **2** *a swimming/bridge club* society, group, association, organization, affiliation, league, union, federation.

**clue** noun hint, indication, sign, intimation, pointer, guide, lead, tip, tip-off, inkling.

**clump** noun group, cluster, bunch, collection, assembly, assemblage; mass, lump, clod, glob, agglutination.

**clump** verb **1** *houses clumped together* group, cluster, bunch, collect, assemble, congregate, mass, lump, bundle, pack. **2** *clump around in heavy boots* clomp, stamp, stomp, thump, thud, tramp, lumber, plod, trudge.

**clumsy** adjective **1** *clumsy and always breaking things* awkward, uncoordinated, ungainly, bumbling, inept, maladroit, unhandy, unskillful, like a bull in a china shop; *inf.* ham-handed, butter-fingered. **2** *a clumsy piece of furniture* unwieldy, hulking, heavy, solid, unmaneuverable. **3** *a clumsy apology* awkward, gauche, graceless, tactless, unpolished, crude.

**cluster** noun bunch, clump, collection, knot, group; gathering, band, company, body, assemblage, congregation.

**cluster** verb gather, collect, assemble, congregate, group, flock together.

**clutch** verb **1** *clutching her purse* grip, grasp, clasp, cling to, hang on to, clench. **2** *clutch at the branch* reach for, snatch at, grab, make a grab for, seize.

**clutches** plural noun hands, power, control, hold, grip, grasp, claws.

**clutter** noun mess, muddle, disorder, chaos, disarray, state of confusion/untidiness; heap, litter; *inf.* junk, stuff.

**clutter** verb litter, make a mess of, mess up, be strewn about, be scattered about.

**coach** noun instructor, trainer, teacher, tutor, mentor.

**coach** verb instruct, train, teach, tutor, drill, put one through one's paces.

**coagulate** verb congeal, gel. *See* CLOT.

**coalesce** verb unite, combine, merge, amalgamate, integrate, affiliate, blend, fuse.

**coalition** noun union, alliance, affiliation, league, association, federation, confederacy, bloc.

**coarse** adjective **1** *coarse material* rough, bristly, scratchy, prickly, hairy, shaggy. **2** *coarse features* heavy, rugged, craggy, unrefined. **3** *coarse flour* crude, unrefined, unprocessed, unpurified. **4** *coarse manners* rude, ill-mannered, uncivil, rough, boorish, loutish, churlish, crass. **5** *coarse humor* bawdy, earthy, blue, ribald, vulgar, smutty, obscene, lewd, pornographic, prurient; *inf.* raunchy.

**coast** noun coastline, shore, seashore, shoreline, seacoast, beach, strand, seaboard, water's edge.

**coast** verb freewheel, cruise, taxi, drift, glide, sail.

**coat** noun **1** *a winter coat* overcoat, topcoat, jacket. **2** *animals' coats* fur, hair, wool; fleece, hide, pelt, skin. **3** *a coat of paint/dust* layer, covering, overlay. *See* COATING.

**coating** noun covering, layer, film, coat, dusting, blanket, sheet, glaze, skin, veneer, finish, lamination, patina, membrane.

**coax** verb wheedle, cajole, talk into, beguile, flatter, inveigle, entice, induce, persuade, prevail upon, win over; *inf.* sweet-talk, soft-soap.

**cocky** adjective arrogant, conceited, egotistical, swellheaded, cocksure, swaggering, brash.

**coddle** verb pamper, mollycoddle, indulge, spoil, baby, humor.

**code** noun **1** *a message in code* cipher, secret writing, cryptograph. **2** *code of honor|legal code* laws, rules, regulations, system, canon.

**coerce** verb compel, force, pressure, drive, impel, constrain, oblige; *inf.* twist one's arm, lean on, put the screws on, strongarm.

**coffin** noun casket, box, sarcophagus.

**cogent** adjective convincing, forceful, effective, persuasive, compelling, powerful, strong, potent, authoritative.

**cogitate** verb think, ponder, contemplate, consider, deliberate, meditate, reflect, mull over, muse, ruminate.

**cognate** adjective **1** *cognate words* related, kindred, akin, allied, consanguine. **2** *cognate sciences* allied, affiliated, associated, similar, alike, connected, corresponding, correlated, analogous.

**cognizant** adjective aware, conscious, knowing, alive to, sensible of, familiar with, acquainted with, conversant with; *inf.* wise to.

**coherent** adjective logical, rational, reasoned, lucid, articulate, systematic, orderly, organized, comprehensible, intelligible.

**cohort** noun troop, brigade, legion, squad, squadron, column, group, company, body, band.

**coil** verb wind, spiral, loop, curl, twist, twine, entwine, snake, wreathe, convolute.

**coin** noun coins, coinage, change, specie, silver, copper, gold.

**coin** verb *coin a word* invent, create, make up, devise, conceive, originate, formulate, fabricate.

**coincide** verb **1** *dates coinciding* be concurrent, occur simultaneously, happen together, coexist, concur, synchronize. **2** *stories coinciding* accord, agree, correspond, concur, match, square, tally, harmonize.

**coincidence** noun accident, chance, a fluke, luck, fortuity, serendipity.

**coincidental** adjective **1** *a coincidental meeting* accidental, chance, unplanned, unintentional, casual, lucky, fortuitous, serendipitous; *inf.* fluky. **2** *coincidental concerts* simultaneous, concurrent, synchronous.

**cold** adjective **1** *a cold day* chilly, freezing, bitter, raw, icy, frigid, wintry, frosty, arctic, windy, glacial, polar; *inf.* nippy. **2** *feeling cold* chilly, chilled, cool, freezing, frozen, frozen stiff, frozen/chilled to the bone/marrow. **3** *a cold person/attitude* unresponsive, unfeeling, unemotional, unmoved, indifferent, apathetic, aloof, distant, reserved, standoffish, unsympathetic, heartless, callous, cold-hearted. **4** *the story is cold* dead, gone, extinguished, finished, defunct.

**cold-blooded** adjective savage, inhuman, barbaric, heartless, pitiless, merciless.

**collaborate** verb cooperate, work together/jointly, join forces, join, unite, combine; conspire, fraternize, collude.

**collaborator** noun coworker, associate, colleague, partner, confederate; conspirator, traitor, quisling, turncoat.

**collapse** verb **1** *the roof collapsed* fall in, cave in, give way, come apart, fall to pieces, crumple. **2** *the onlooker collapsed* faint, pass out, lose consciousness, keel over, swoon. **3** *the business/talks collapsed* break down, fall through, fail, disintegrate, fold, founder, miscarry; *inf.* flop.

**collapse** noun **1** *the collapse of the roof* cave-in, giving way. **2** *the collapse of the onlooker* fainting, passing out, swooning, swoon. **3** *the collapse of the talks/firm* breakdown, failure, disintegration, foundering. **4** *suffer a collapse* breakdown, nervous breakdown, attack, seizure, prostration; *inf.* crack-up.

**collate** verb *collate pages/information* arrange, put in order, order, sort, categorize.

**collateral** noun security, surety, guarantee, pledge.

**colleague** noun associate, partner, teammate, workmate, fellow worker, coworker, collaborator, confederate, comrade.

**collect** verb **1** *collect all sorts of stuff* gather, accumulate, assemble, amass, pile up, stockpile, save, store, hoard, heap up, aggregate. **2** *a crowd collected* congregate, converge, cluster, convene. **3** *collect money* gather, solicit, raise, secure, obtain, acquire. **4** *collect one's wits* get together, muster, summon.

**collection** noun **1** *a collection of junk* accumulation, pile, stockpile, store, supply, stock, hoard, heap, mass, aggregation. **2** *a collection of people* gathering, assembly, assemblage, crowd, body, group, cluster, company, number, throng, congregation, flock, convocation. **3** *a collection of stamps* set, series, array, assortment. **4** *a collection of essays* anthology, corpus, compilation, miscellanea. **5** *the amount of the collection* subscription, donation, contribution, gift, alms; offering, offertory, tithe.

**collective** adjective joint, united, combined, shared, common, concerted, cooperative, corporate, collaborative.

**college** noun **1** *she went to college* school, technical college, community college, university. **2** *the college of thespians* association, fellowship, society, academy.

**collide** verb **1** *cars colliding* crash, crash head on, smash, bump, bang. **2** *views collide* conflict, be in conflict, clash, differ, disagree, be at variance.

**collision** noun **1** *a highway collision* crash, accident, smash, pileup, impact. **2** *a collision of views* conflict, clash, difference, disagreement, variance, opposition.

**colloquial** adjective conversational, informal, everyday, casual, familiar, chatty, idiomatic, vernacular.

**collusion** noun connivance, complicity, collaboration, intrigue, plotting; *inf.* cahoots.

**colony** noun **1** *the king visited the colony* settlement, territory, province, dominion, protectorate, dependency, possession, satellite state. **2** *the Chinese colony in San Francisco* community, section, ghetto, district, quarter. **3** *a colony of artists* community, group, association, commune, settlement.

**color** noun **1** *a red color* hue, shade, tint, tone, tinge. **2** *add color to her cheeks* pinkness, rosiness, redness, ruddiness, blush, flush, glow, bloom. **3** *nations of different colors* skin color, complexion, coloring, pigmentation. **4** *add color to the description* vividness, life, animation, richness. **5** *under the color of friendship* guise, show, semblance, pretense, pretext.

**color** verb **1** *color the fabric yellow* tint, paint, dye, stain, tinge. **2** *she colored with embarrassment* blush, flush, redden, go red, burn. **3** *attitude colored by childhood experiences* influence, affect, prejudice, distort, slant, taint, pervert, warp. **4** *color the facts* exaggerate, overstate, embroider, varnish, misrepresent, falsify.

**colorful** adjective **1** bright-colored, deep-colored, bright, brilliant, intense, vivid, rich, vibrant, multicolored, many-colored, variegated, psychedelic; *inf.* jazzy. **2** *a colorful description* vivid, graphic, interesting, lively.

**colorless** adjective **1** *colorless fabric* uncolored, achromatic, white, bleached, faded. **2** *colorless city people* pale, wan, anemic, washed-out, ashen, sickly. **3** *colorless accounts* uninteresting, dull, lifeless, dreary, lackluster, insipid, vapid.

**colors** plural noun **1** *raised the colors* flag, standard, banner, ensign. **2** *a club's colors* badge, uniform, insignia, ribbon, rosette. **3** *saw his true colors* nature, character, identity, aspect.

**colossal** adjective huge, gigantic, immense, enormous, massive, vast, gargantuan, mammoth, prodigious, mountainous, elephantine, monumental.

**column** noun **1** *marble columns* pillar, support, upright, post, shaft; pilaster, obelisk. **2** *a column of people* line, file, row, rank, string, procession, train.

**coma** noun unconsciousness, insensibility, stupor, oblivion, blackout.

**comatose** adjective **1** *comatose after the accident* in a coma, unconscious, insensible, out cold, blacked-out. **2** *feeling comatose after the night shift* sluggish, lethargic, somnolent, torpid.

**comb** verb **1** *comb one's hair* groom, untangle, curry, arrange. **2** *comb the area for clues* search, scour, ransack, go over with a fine-tooth comb.

**combat** noun battle, fight, conflict, clash, skirmish, single combat, hand-to-hand combat; fighting, hostilities.

**combat** verb fight, do battle, wage war, clash, take up arms (against), grapple, oppose, strive against, make a stand against, resist, withstand, defy.

**combatant** noun fighter, soldier, serviceman, servicewoman, warrior, battler; adversary, antagonist, contender, opponent, enemy, foe, rival.

**combative** adjective pugnacious, belligerent, aggressive, militant, bellicose, warlike, quarrelsome, argumentative, contentious.

**combination** noun **1** *in combination with others* cooperation, association, union, alliance, partnership, coalition, league, consortium, syndication, federation. **2** *a combination of guilt and grief* mixture, mix, blend, amalgam, amalgamation, compound, alloy, composite.

**combine** verb **1** *combine to finish their work* join forces, unite, team up, cooperate, associate, ally, pool resources. **2** *combine their efforts* join, put together, unite, pool, merge, integrate, fuse, marry, unify. **3** *combine ingredients* mix, blend, admix, amalgamate, bind, bond, compound, alloy, homogenize.

**combustible** adjective inflammable, flammable, incendiary, explosive, conflagratory.

**combustion** noun burning, firing, fire, kindling, igniting, ignition.

**come** verb **1** *they came last night* arrive, appear, put in an appearance, turn up, enter, materialize; *inf.* show up, blow in. **2** *Easter came in March* occur, fall, take place, happen, transpire, come about, come to pass. **3** *the dress comes to her ankles* reach, extend, stretch. **4** *the car comes in red* be available, be made, be produced, be offered. **come about** arise, come to pass, transpire, result, befall. **come across 1** *come across an old friend* meet, encounter, run into, run across, chance upon, happen upon, find, discover, unearth; *inf.* bump into. **2** *his message came across* be communicated, be understood, be clear, be perceived. **come across with** *come across with the money* hand over, deliver, produce, pay up; *inf.* come up with, fork over, cough up. **come along 1** *patients coming along well* progress, make progress, develop, improve, show improvement, make headway, get better, pick up. **2** *come along!* hurry, hurry up, make haste, speed up; *inf.* get a move on, move it, step on it, make it snappy. **come apart** break up, fall to pieces, disintegrate, come unstuck, crumble, separate, split, tear. **come around 1** *coming around annually* occur, take place, happen. **2** *come around after fainting* come to, regain consciousness, revive, wake up, recover. **3** *come around in the evening* come round, visit, call; *inf.*

drop in, drop by, stop by, pop in. **come around to** *come around to one's way of thinking* be converted to, be persuaded by, give way to, yield to. **come by** get, obtain, acquire, procure, get possession of, get/lay hold of, get one's hands on, secure, win. **come clean** own up, confess. **come down** *the report came down against punishment* decide, reach a decision, recommend, choose, opt. **come down on** rebuke, reprimand, criticize, berate. **come down to** amount to, boil down to, end up as, result in. **come down with** fall ill with, become sick with, catch, contract, fall victim to, be stricken with. **come forward** volunteer, offer one's services. **come into** *come into money* inherit, be left, be willed, acquire, obtain. **come off** *the attempt did not come off* succeed, be successful, be accomplished, work out, transpire, take place. **come out 1** *the newspaper comes out daily* be published, appear. **2** *the full story came out* become known, become common knowledge, be revealed, be disclosed, be released. **3** *come out all right* end, finish, conclude, terminate. **come out with 1** *coming out with a new movie* release, bring out, circulate, publish. **2** *come out with a surprise confession* reveal, let out, blurt out. **come through** *come through the war* get through, survive, outlast, outlive. **come to 1** *the bill comes to $5* total, add up to, amount to. **2** *come to after fainting* regain consciousness, awaken. See COME AROUND 2. **come up** *something came up* arise, crop up, turn up, spring up. **come up to 1** *she came up to his shoulder* come to, reach, extend to. **2** *come up to standards* reach, measure up to, match up to, compare with, bear comparison with, hold a candle to. **come up with** *come up with a plan* suggest, propose, submit, put forward, present, offer.

**comeback** noun **1** *the actor making a comeback* return, rally, resurgence, recovery, revival, rebound. **2** *making witty comebacks* retort, reply, rejoinder, response, retaliation, riposte.

**comedian** noun **1** *television comedian* comic, funny man, funny woman, comedienne, humorist. **2** *he's a real comedian* joker, wit, wag, jester, clown; *inf.* card, laugh.

**comedown** noun loss of status, loss of face, demotion, downgrading, degradation, humiliation, deflation, decline, reversal, anticlimax.

**comedy** noun **1** *theaters staging both comedy and tragedy* farce, burlesque, pantomime, slapstick, satire, vaudeville, comic opera; *inf.* sitcom. **2** *the comedy of the situation* humor, funniness, hilarity, levity, facetiousness.

**comely** adjective **1** *a comely young woman* attractive, good-looking, pretty, beautiful, handsome, lovely, fair, winsome, pleasing. **2** *not comely behavior* fit, fitting, suitable, proper, seemly, decent, decorous.

**come-on** noun inducement, lure, enticement, allurement, temptation.

**comeuppance** noun just deserts, deserts, retribution, punishment, recompense, requital.

**comfort** noun **1** *live in comfort* contentment, well-being, coziness, plenty, sufficiency, luxury, opulence. **2** *bring comfort to the bereaved* consolation, solace, condolence, sympathy, commiseration, help, support, succor, relief.

**comfort** verb **1** *comfort the bereaved* console, solace, give sympathy to, succor, reassure, soothe, assuage, cheer. **2** *comforted by the fire* ease, soothe, refresh, revive, hearten, cheer.

**comfortable** adjective **1** *a comfortable room* homey, cozy, snug. **2** *comfortable clothes/shoes* well-fitting, loose-fitting, roomy. **3** *a comfortable lifestyle* pleasant, adequate, free from hardship, well-off, well-to-do, affluent, opulent. **4** *feeling comfortable* at ease, relaxed, serene, tranquil, contented, cozy.

**comforting** adjective consoling, soothing, reassuring, encouraging.

**comic** adjective funny, humorous, amusing, entertaining, diverting, droll, jocular, joking, facetious, comical, witty, farcical, hilarious, zany, sidesplitting, priceless, waggish, whimsical.

**comic** noun **1** *worked as a comic* stand-up comic, humorist. *See* COMEDIAN 1. **2** *he's a real comic* joker, wag. *See* COMEDIAN 2. **comics** comic strips, comic books; *inf.* funnies.

**comical** adjective **1** *a comical performance* funny, amusing. *See* COMIC adjective. **2** *a comical hat* absurd, ridiculous, silly, laughable, ludicrous.

**command** verb **1** *command you to go* order, give orders to, direct, charge, instruct, bid, enjoin, adjure, summon, prescribe, require. **2** *he commands the unit* have charge of, control, rule, govern, direct, preside over, head, lead, manage, supervise.

**command** noun **1** *follow the commands* order, decree, dictate, edict, instruction, directive, direction, bidding, injunction, behest, mandate, fiat, precept, commandment. **2** *under the command of the French* charge, control, authority, power, government, direction, management, administration, supervision, dominion, sway, domination.

**commandeer** verb seize, take possession of, requisition, expropriate, appropriate, hijack.

**commander** noun leader, head, director, chief, boss; officer, captain; commander in chief, commanding officer; *inf.* top dog, kingpin, big cheese.

**commanding** adjective controlling, directing, dominating, dominant, superior, advantageous; authoritative, autocratic, masterful, assertive, peremptory, imposing, impressive, august.

**commemorate** verb celebrate, pay tribute to, remember, honor, salute, memorialize.

**commemorative** adjective memorial, remembering, in memory of, in remembrance of.

**commence** verb **1** *ready to commence* begin, start, go ahead, be off, embark, set sail, set the ball rolling, get something off the ground; *inf.* get the show on the road. **2** *commence the proceedings* open, enter/embark upon, inaugurate, initiate, originate.

**commend** verb **1** *commend his work* praise, applaud, speak highly of, approve, acclaim, extol, laud, eulogize. **2** *commend action* recommend, approve, endorse, advocate. **3** *commend her to your care* entrust, trust, deliver, commit, hand over, give, consign, assign.

**commendable** adjective praiseworthy, admirable, laudable, estimable, worthy, deserving.

**commendation** noun praise, applause, acclaim, acclamation, approval, approbation, credit, eulogies, laudation, encomium, panegyric.

**commensurate** adjective **1** *a commensurate amount of water to wine* equivalent, equal, corresponding, comparable, proportionate. **2** *a salary commensurate with experience* in accordance with, proportionate to, appropriate to, consistent with.

**comment** verb **1** *he commented unfavorably on her actions* remark, speak, express an opinion on. **2** *"Good," he commented* say, remark, state, observe, interpose. **3** *comment on the text* annotate, explain, interpret, elucidate, clarify, shed light on.

**comment** noun remark, opinion, observation, view, statement, criticism; annotation, note, footnote, gloss, marginalia, interpretation, elucidation.

**commentary** noun account, review, analysis, interpretation, exegesis, critique.

**commentator** noun reporter, broadcaster, correspondent; interpreter, critic.

**commerce** noun **1** *work in commerce* business, trade, buying and selling, merchandising, dealing, finance, marketing, traffic. **2** *everyday (social) commerce* social relations, socializing, communication, dealings.

**commercial** adjective **1** *commercial training* business, trade, marketing, merchandising, sales, mercantile. **2** *a commercial proposition* profitable, profit-making, profit-oriented, money-oriented, mercantile, materialistic, mercenary.

**commission** noun **1** *a commission on the sale* percentage, brokerage, share, fee, compensation; *inf.* cut. **2** *the commission of designing the building* task, employment, duty, charge, mission, responsibility. **3** *a commission of inquiry* committee, board, council, advisory body, delegation. **4** *the commission of a crime* execution, perpetration, performance.

**commission** verb **1** *commission an artist* employ, engage, contract, appoint, book, authorize. **2** *commission a portrait* order, put in an order for, place an order for, contract for, pay for, authorize.

**commit** verb **1** *commit a crime* perform, carry out, execute, enact, perpetrate, effect, do. **2** *commit to one's care* entrust, trust, deliver, hand over, give, consign, assign. **3** *commit oneself to take part* pledge, promise, engage, bind, covenant, obligate, dedicate. **4** *commit the thief/patient* imprison, jail, confine, lock up, put into custody, put away; hospitalize, institutionalize, confine.

**commitment** noun **1** *too many commitments* undertaking, obligation, responsibility, duty, liability, tie, task, engagement. **2** *have no commitment to the job* dedication, devotion, loyalty, allegiance, adherence. **3** *make a commitment* pledge, promise, vow, assurance, covenant.

**commodity** noun thing, item, article, product, article of merchandise.

**common** adjective **1** *the common people* ordinary, average, normal, typical, unexceptional, run-of-the-mill, plain, simple. **2** *a common style* unexceptional, undistinguished, workaday, mediocre, pedestrian, humdrum. **3** *a common occurrence* usual, ordinary, everyday, frequent, customary, habitual, routine, standard, repeated, commonplace. **4** *a common response* familiar, routine, stock, standard, conventional, traditional. **5** *a common belief* widespread, general, universal, popular, accepted, prevalent, prevailing. **6** *for the common good* communal, collective, community, public, popular. **7** *a common young woman* low, vulgar, coarse, uncouth, inferior.

**commonplace** adjective **1** *a commonplace novel/youngster* ordinary, unexceptional. *See* COMMON 2. **2** *air travel is now commonplace | commonplace events* ordinary, routine. *See* COMMON 3.

**common sense** noun good sense, sense, practicality, judgment, levelheadedness, prudence, discernment, astuteness, shrewdness, judiciousness, wisdom; *inf.* horse sense.

**commotion** noun disturbance, racket, uproar, rumpus, tumult, clamor, riot, hubbub, hullabaloo, brouhaha, furor, disorder, confusion, upheaval, agitation, excitement, fuss, disquiet, to-do.

**communal** adjective common, collective, shared, joint, general, public, community.

**commune** verb communicate, speak, have a tête-à-tête, confer, confide; feel in close touch, feel at one, empathize, identify.

**communicable** adjective infectious, contagious, catching, transmittable, transferable.

**communicate** verb **1** *communicate information* transmit, pass on, transfer, impart, convey, relay, spread, disseminate, make known, publish, broadcast, announce, report, divulge, disclose. **2** *not to communicate with him* be in touch, be in contact, have dealings, interface. **3** *you must be able to communicate* get one's ideas/message across, be articulate, be fluent, be eloquent.

**communication** noun **1** *communication is difficult* information transmission/transfer, dissemination, contact, getting in touch, radio/telephone link, connection, interface. **2** *received the communication* message, letter, report, statement, dispatch.

**communicative** adjective expansive, forthcoming, talkative, loquacious, voluble, chatty.

**communion** noun rapport, empathy, sympathy, accord, affinity, fellowship, togetherness, harmony, closeness, agreement, sharing, concord.

**communism** noun collectivism, Sovietism, Bolshevism, Marxism, Leninism.

**community** noun **1** *move to a new community* locality, district, neighborhood. **2** *the community condemned her* residents, inhabitants; population, populace. **3** *work for the community* society, public, general public, body politic, nation, state. **4** *the Jewish community in New York* group, section, body, company, set, ghetto. **5** *community of interests* similarity, likeness, agreement, affinity.

**commute** verb **1** *commute from the suburbs* travel to and from, travel back and forth, shuttle. **2** *commute a sentence/penalty* lessen, reduce, shorten, curtail, mitigate, modify. **3** *commute an annuity to a lump sum* exchange, change, interchange, substitute, trade, barter, switch.

**compact** adjective **1** *a compact parcel* dense, packed close, pressed together, close, firm, solid, compressed, condensed. **2** *a compact style* concise, succinct, terse, brief, condensed, pithy, to the point, epigrammatic, compendious.

**compact** verb pack down, press down, compress, press together, condense, tamp.

**compact** noun contract, agreement, covenant, pact, indenture, bond, treaty, alliance, bargain, deal.

**companion** noun **1** *the girl and her companions* partner, escort, consort, friend, crony, comrade, colleague, associate, ally, confederate; *inf.* buddy, pal. **2** *the princess and her companion* attendant, aide, chaperon, duenna, squire. **3** *the companion of this bookend* fellow, mate, twin, match, counterpart, complement. **4** *the Reader's Companion* guide, handbook, manual.

**companionship** noun friendship, fellowship, company, society, togetherness, social intercourse, comradeship, camaraderie, intimacy, rapport.

**company** noun **1** *enjoy their company* friendship, fellowship. *See* COMPANIONSHIP. **2** *address the company* assembly, assemblage, gathering, meeting, audience, group, crowd, throng, congregation, convention. **3** *a company of actors* group, band, party, body, association, society, fellowship, troupe, collection, circle, league, crew, guild. **4** *a retail company* business, firm, concern, corporation, house, establishment, conglomerate; *inf.* outfit. **5** *expecting company* guest(s), visitor(s), caller(s).

**comparable** adjective equivalent, commensurable, corresponding, proportional, proportionate, similar, like, parallel, analogous, related. **comparable to** as good as, equal to, on a par with, in the same class/league as/with.

**compare** verb **1** *compare the two styles* contrast, juxtapose, weigh/balance/measure the differences between, collate, differentiate. **2** *the island has been compared to heaven* liken, equate, analogize. **compare with** *his work does not compare with hers* bear comparison to, be comparable to, be on a par with, be in the same class with, compete with, approach, come up to, hold a candle to.

**comparison** noun **1** *make a comparison* contrast, juxtaposition, collation, differentiation. **2** *no comparison between their works* resemblance, likeness, similarity, correlation.

**compartment** noun **1** *luggage compartment* section, part, partition, bay, chamber, niche. **2** *compartments of one's life* part, section, division, department, area.

**compassion** noun tender-heartedness, pity, softheartedness, tenderness, gentleness, mercy, leniency, understanding, sympathy, concern, humanity, kindness.

**compassionate** adjective softhearted, tender, gentle, merciful, lenient, understanding, sympathetic, pitying, humanitarian, humane, kindly, kindhearted.

**compatible** adjective **1** *compatible couples* well-suited, suited, like-minded, of the same mind, in agreement, in tune, in harmony. **2** *views not compatible with actions* consistent, in keeping, reconcilable, consonant, congruous, congruent.

**compel** verb **1** *compel them to leave* force, make, coerce, drive, pressure, dragoon, constrain, impel, oblige, necessitate, urge; *inf.* bulldoze, railroad, twist one's arm, strong-arm, put the screws on. **2** *compel obedience* force, enforce, exact, insist upon, necessitate, extort.

**compelling** adjective **1** *a compelling story* fascinating, gripping, enthralling, irresistible, hypnotic, mesmeric. **2** *compelling reasons* cogent, convincing, forceful, powerful, weighty, telling, conclusive, irrefutable.

**compensate** verb **1** *compensate for his evil deed* make amends, make restitution, make reparation, make up for, atone, expiate. **2** *compensate for her loss* recompense, repay, reimburse, requite, indemnify. **compensate for** counterbalance, counterpoise, counteract, balance, cancel out, neutralize, nullify.

**compensation** noun **1** *receive compensation for her loss* recompense, repayment, reimbursement, requital, indemnification, indemnity, damages. **2** *make compensation for his deed* amends, restitution, redress, atonement, expiation.

**compete** verb contend, vie, strive, struggle, fight, pit oneself (against); *inf.* throw one's hat in the ring, be in the running.

**competence** noun capability, ability, capacity, proficiency, adeptness, expertise, skill.

**competent** adjective capable, able, proficient, qualified, efficient, adept, accomplished, skillful; adequate, appropriate, suitable.

**competition** noun **1** *a chess competition* contest, match, game, tournament, event, meet, quiz. **2** *the competition between opponents* rivalry, vying, contest, opposition, struggle, contention, strife. **3** *the competition is poor* field, opposition, challengers, opponents, rivals.

**competitive** adjective ambitious, combative, aggressive, dog-eat-dog, cutthroat.

**competitor** noun rival, opponent, adversary, antagonist; contestant, contender, challenger, participant.

**compilation** noun collection, anthology, album, corpus, ana.

**compile** verb gather, collect, accumulate, amass, assemble, put together, collate, marshal.

**complacent** adjective smug, self-satisfied, pleased with oneself, satisfied, contented, self-contented, pleased, placid.

**complain** verb 1 *complain about the service* lodge a complaint, criticize, find fault, carp, make a fuss. 2 *always complaining* grumble, grouse, gripe, moan, grouch, whine; *inf.* bellyache, beef, bitch.

**complaint** noun 1 *manager attending to complaints* criticism, grievance, charge, accusation, protest, remonstrance. 2 *a painful complaint* illness, disease, ailment, disorder, sickness, affliction, malady.

**complement** noun 1 *the perfect complement to the food* companion, addition, supplement, accessory, final/finishing touch. 2 *the school's full complement* amount, allowance, total, capacity, quota.

**complementary** adjective complemental, completing, finishing, perfecting, culminative, consummative.

**complete** adjective 1 *the complete collection* entire, whole, full, total, intact, unbroken, undivided, uncut, unabridged, plenary. 2 *the task is complete* finished, ended, concluded, accomplished, finalized. 3 *a complete fool* absolute, out-and-out, thoroughgoing, thorough, utter, total, perfect, consummate, unqualified, dyed-in-the-wool.

**complete** verb 1 *complete the task* finish, end, conclude, finalize, realize, accomplish, achieve, fulfill, execute, effect, discharge, settle, clinch, do; *inf.* wrap up, polish off. 2 *complete the outfit* finish off, round off, perfect, crown, cap, add the finishing touch to.

**completely** adverb totally, utterly, absolutely, thoroughly, quite, wholly, altogether.

**completion** noun finish, ending, conclusion, close, finalization, realization, accomplishment, achievement, fulfillment, execution, consummation.

**complex** adjective 1 *a complex subject* complicated, difficult, involved, intricate, convoluted, knotty, perplexing. 2 *a complex structure* composite, compound, compounded, multiple, manifold, multiplex, heterogeneous.

**complex** noun 1 *building complex | complex of regulations* structure, scheme, composite, conglomerate, aggregation, network, system. 2 *a complex about her nose* obsession, phobia, fixation, preoccupation, *idée fixe.*

**complexion** noun 1 *ruddy complexion* skin color, skin tone, coloring, pigmentation. 2 *put a new complexion on it* aspect, appearance, guise, look, angle. 3 *his brother is of a different complexion* character, nature, disposition, cast, stamp.

**complexity** noun complication, difficulty, intricacy, convolution.

**compliance** noun yielding, submissiveness, deference, passivity, subservience, servility. **compliance with** obedience to, observance of, abiding by, conforming to.

**complicate** verb make difficult, make involved/intricate, confuse, muddle, jumble, snarl up, entangle.

**complicated** adjective difficult, entangled, Byzantine. *See* COMPLEX adjective 1.

**complication** noun 1 *meet complications* difficulty, problem, drawback, snag, obstacle. 2 *a great deal of complication* difficulty, intricacy, complexity, confusion.

**complicity** noun collusion, conspiracy, collaboration, connivance, abetment.

**compliment** noun *compliments* praise, tribute, homage, admiration, flattery, commendation, laudation, eulogy.

**compliment** verb congratulate, felicitate, speak highly of, praise, sing the praises of, pay tribute/homage to, salute, admire, flatter, commend, honor, acclaim, laud, eulogize.

**complimentary** adjective 1 *complimentary remarks* congratulatory, admiring, appreciative, approving, flattering, commendatory, laudatory. 2 *complimentary tickets* free, gratis; *inf.* on the house.

**comply** verb **comply with** obey, observe, abide by, adhere to, conform to, acquiesce to, assent to, consent to, follow, respect, yield, submit.

**component** noun part, piece, section, constituent, element, unit, module.

**compose** verb 1 *compose a poem* write, make up, create, think up, devise, concoct, invent, compile, contrive, formulate, fashion, produce. 2 *compose one's dress/plans* put together, arrange, put in order, align, organize, assemble, collate, systematize. 3 *peoples composing a nation* make up, form, constitute, comprise. 4 *compose oneself* calm, calm down, quiet, collect, control, soothe.

**composed** adjective calm, cool, collected, serene, tranquil, relaxed, poised, at ease, unruffled, untroubled, confident, self-possessed; *inf.* together.

**composite** adjective compound, complex, combined, blended, mixed.

**composite** noun compound, amalgam, blend, mixture, complex, combination, fusion, conglomerate, synthesis.

# composition · concentrate

**composition** noun **1** *the composition of the soil* structure, constitution, makeup, conformation, configuration, organization, arrangement, layout, character. **2** *the composition of a poem* writing, creation, concoction, invention, compilation. **3** *a brilliant composition* work of art, creation, literary/musical/artistic work. **4** *students writing a composition* essay, theme. **5** *admire the painting's composition* arrangement, proportions, harmony, balance, symmetry.

**composure** noun aplomb, poise, self-possession, presence of mind, sang-froid, equanimity, equilibrium, self-control, calm, calmness, coolness, serenity, tranquillity.

**compound** noun alloy, conglomerate, synthesis, medley, hybrid. *See* COMPOSITE noun.

**compound** verb **1** *compound the two substances* mix, blend, combine, put together, amalgamate, unite, coalesce, alloy, fuse, mingle, intermingle, synthesize. **2** *compound the problem* worsen, add to, augment, exacerbate, magnify, aggravate, intensify, heighten.

**comprehend** verb understand, grasp, take in, assimilate, fathom, perceive, discern, apprehend, conceive, imagine.

**comprehensible** adjective intelligible, understandable, graspable, fathomable, discernible.

**comprehension** noun understanding, grasp, perception, ken, discernment, conception.

**comprehensive** adjective inclusive, all-inclusive, all-embracing, complete, full, encyclopedic, exhaustive, thorough, extensive, broad, widespread, far-reaching, blanket.

**compress** verb **1** *compress the pile of sand* squeeze together, squash, crush, cram, constrict. *See* COMPACT verb. **2** *compress the text* abbreviate, shorten, abridge, contract, reduce.

**comprise** verb consist of, contain, include, be composed of, take in, embrace, encompass.

**compromise** verb **1** *compromise on the wording* come to terms, come to an understanding, make a deal, make concessions, find a happy medium, find the middle ground, strike a balance, meet halfway. **2** *compromise his reputation/chances* endanger, jeopardize, imperil, prejudice, damage, injure, weaken.

**compromise** noun understanding, deal, happy medium, middle course, balance, trade-off.

**compulsion** noun **1** *under no compulsion to go* obligation, force, duress, constraint, coercion, pressure. **2** *feel a compulsion to travel* urge, need, desire, preoccupation, obsession.

**compulsive** adjective **1** *compulsive viewing* fascinating, gripping. *See* COMPELLING 1. **2** *a compulsive desire to wash/eat/drink* obsessive, uncontrollable, irresistible, driving, overwhelming, addictive, obsessional, out of control, ungovernable.

**compulsory** adjective obligatory, mandatory, required, forced, necessary, de rigueur.

**compunction** noun remorse, regret, guilt, contrition, penitence, repentance; scruples.

**compute** verb calculate, reckon, count, add up, total, figure out, enumerate, sum, tally.

**comrade** noun companion, friend, colleague, partner, associate, coworker, fellow worker, mate, teammate, ally, confederate, compatriot; *inf.* pal, buddy.

**con** verb swindle, deceive, cheat, hoodwink, mislead, delude, bamboozle.

**con** noun con man, confidence man, swindler, deceiver, cheater.

**concave** adjective curved in, hollowed out, depressed, sunken, indented.

**conceal** verb hide, cover, keep out of sight, keep hidden, screen, obscure, disguise, camouflage, mask; keep secret, keep dark, hush up, cover up, dissemble; *inf.* keep the lid on.

**concede** verb **1** *concede defeat* acknowledge, admit, accept, own, allow, grant. **2** *concede territory* give up, yield, surrender, relinquish, cede, hand over.

**conceit** noun **1** *the winner full of conceit* pride, arrogance, vanity, self-admiration, self-love, self-importance, self-adulation, narcissism, egotism, vainglory. **2** *exchanging clever conceits* witticism, quip, bon mot. **3** *a mind occupied with conceits* fancy, notion, whim; fantasy, imagination, whimsy, vagary.

**conceited** adjective proud, arrogant, vain, self-important, cocky, haughty, supercilious, narcissistic, egotistical, puffed up, self-satisfied, complacent, boastful, vainglorious; *inf.* bigheaded, swellheaded, stuck-up.

**conceivable** adjective credible, believable, imaginable, thinkable, possible, comprehensible.

**conceive** verb **1** *conceive a plan* think up, draw up, form, formulate, produce, develop, devise, contrive, conjure up. **2** *cannot conceive that/how he lost* imagine, think, believe, realize, understand, comprehend, perceive, grasp.

**concentrate** verb **1** *concentrate one's efforts on* focus, center, converge, centralize, consolidate, bring to bear, congregate, cluster, amass. **2** *concentrate the liquid* condense, boil down, reduce, compress, distill. **concentrate on** be absorbed in, focus attention on, be engrossed in.

**concentrated** adjective intensive, intense, consolidated, rigorous, vigorous; *inf.* all-out.

**concentration** noun close attention, absorption, application, engrossment, single-mindedness, heed.

**concept** noun idea, notion, abstraction, conceptualization, conception, hypothesis, theory.

**conception** noun **1** *when conception took place* fertilization, impregnation, fecundation. **2** *at the conception of the project* inception, beginning, origin, birth, initiation, formation, launching, outset. **3** *a brilliant conception* plan, design, invention, creation, project, scheme, proposal. **4** *no conception of how to behave* idea, notion, appreciation, understanding, clue, inkling.

**concern** verb **1** *affairs that concern you* be the business of, affect, be relevant to, involve, apply to, pertain to, have a bearing on, touch. **2** *a report concerning cancer* be about, deal with, relate to. **3** *you should not concern yourself (in/with)* interest/involve oneself (in), take/have a hand (in), busy oneself (with), devote one's time (to), be busy (with). **4** *their behavior concerned us* worry, disturb, trouble, bother, perturb, distress.

**concern** noun **1** *none of your concern* business, affair, interest, involvement, responsibility, charge, duty, job, task, department, field. **2** *news of concern to all* interest, importance, relevance, bearing, applicability. **3** *parents full of concern* worry, anxiety, disquiet, distress, apprehension. **4** *parents demonstrating their concern* care, solicitude, attentiveness, attention, consideration, regard. **5** *start a publishing concern* business, firm. *See* COMPANY 4.

**concerned** adjective **1** *concerned parties* interested, involved, implicated. **2** *concerned citizens* caring, responsible, solicitous; worried, disturbed, anxious, apprehensive.

**concerning** preposition about, on the subject of, relating to, regarding, with reference to, with respect to, in the matter of, re.

**concert** noun **in concert** act in concert together, jointly, in combination, co-operatively, in unison.

**concerted** adjective combined, cooperative, joint, coordinated, united, collaborative, synchronized.

**concession** noun **1** *the concession of defeat* acknowledgment, admission, acceptance, recognition. **2** *the concession of territory* yielding, surrender, relinquishment, ceding, giving up. **3** *as a concession to their youth* allowance, adjustment, modification, indulgence, exception. **4** *price concessions* reduction, cut, discount, decrease. **5** *grant the concession* franchise, license, permit, authorization.

**conciliate** verb placate, appease, pacify, propitiate, mollify, assuage, calm down, soothe, humor, reconcile.

**conciliatory** adjective appeasing, pacifying, propitiative, mollifying, assuaging, reconciliatory, peacemaking.

**concise** adjective succinct, short, crisp, summary, synoptic. *See* COMPACT adjective 2.

**conclude** verb **1** *we concluded the meeting* end, finish, close, halt, cease, terminate, discontinue; *inf.* wind up. **2** *conclude an agreement* negotiate, come to terms on, bring about, pull off, work out, accomplish, effect, establish, engineer. **3** *conclude that he had won* deduce, infer, decide, gather, reckon, judge, assume, surmise.

**conclusion** noun **1** *the conclusion of the meeting* end, discontinuance. *See* CLOSE noun. **2** *a predictable conclusion* outcome, result, upshot, issue, culmination, consequence. **3** *reach the conclusion that he was guilty* deduction, inference, decision, opinion, judgment, verdict, conviction. **in conclusion** in closing, to sum up, finally, lastly.

**conclusive** adjective decisive, clinching, definitive, final, categorical, incontestable, convincing.

**concoct** verb **1** *concoct a meal/stew* prepare, put together, cook, mix, blend, brew; *inf.* rustle up. **2** *concoct an excuse* devise, invent, make up, think up, dream up, fabricate, hatch; *inf.* cook up.

**concoction** noun **1** *a tasty concoction* preparation, mixture, blend, combination, brew, creation. **2** *don't believe that concoction* invention, fabrication, plot, scheme.

**concrete** adjective **1** *concrete evidence* actual, real, factual, definite, genuine, substantial, material, tangible, specific. **2** *a concrete substance* solid, solidified, firm, compact, dense, compressed, coalesced, calcified.

**concur** verb **1** *they concur on/over the verdict* agree, be in accord/harmony, be of the same mind, be in concord. **2** *the two events concurred* coincide, be simultaneous, coexist, synchronize. **3** *they concurred in the attempt* cooperate, combine, unite, collaborate, join forces.

**concurrent** adjective **1** *concurrent sentences* simultaneous, parallel, coincident, contemporaneous, synchronous, side-by-side. **2** *concurrent lines* converging, convergent, meeting, intersecting. **3** *concurrent attitudes* agreeing, in accord, in harmony, harmonious, assenting, of the same mind, like-minded, compatible. **4** *concurrent action* cooperative, combined, united, joint, collaborative.

**condemn** verb **1** *condemn all violence* censure, denounce, deprecate, disapprove of, criticize, berate, upbraid, reprove, reproach, blame. **2** *condemn him to death/poverty* sentence, pass sentence on, convict; doom, damn, force, compel, coerce, impel.

**condensation** noun **1** *the condensation of the sauce* concentration, reduction. **2** *the condensation of steam* liquefaction, liquidization, deliquescence, precipitation, distillation. **3** *the condensation of the report* abridgment, summarization, summary, précis, digest, abstract, synopsis.

**condense** verb **1** *condense the sauce by boiling* concentrate, thicken, boil down, reduce, solidify, coagulate. **2** *steam condensing on the mirror* liquefy, liquidize, deliquesce, precipitate. **3** *condense the report* shorten, abridge, abbreviate, cut, compress, contract, compact, encapsulate.

**condescend** verb **1** *condescend to speak to him* lower oneself, deign, stoop, descend, vouchsafe; *inf.* come down from one's high horse. **2** *condescend to younger people* patronize, talk down to, look down one's nose at.

**condescending** adjective patronizing, disdainful, supercilious, superior, snobbish, lofty, lordly; *inf.* snooty, snotty, uppity.

**condition** noun **1** *the human condition* state, circumstance, situation. **2** *in a miserable condition* position, plight, predicament, quandary. **3** *athletes in good/poor condition* shape, form, order, fitness, health, fettle, kilter, trim, working order. **4** *a condition of the job* qualification, requirement, necessity, essential, demand, prerequisite, stipulation. **5** *the conditions of the agreement* restriction, rule, provision, proviso, contingency, stipulation. **6** *a heart condition* disease, disorder, illness, complaint, problem, ailment.

**condition** verb **1** *lotions conditioning the skin/leather* improve, tone up, prepare, make ready. **2** *cats conditioned to live in apartments* accustom, adapt, habituate, inure. **3** *childhood experiences conditioning later responses* influence, affect, govern, determine.

**conditional** adjective *a conditional offer* qualified, with reservations, restrictive, provisional, provisory, stipulatory.

**conditions** plural noun circumstances, surroundings, environment, situation.

**condolence** noun commiseration, sympathy, compassion, pity, solace, comfort.

**condone** verb overlook, disregard, let pass, turn a blind eye to, wink at, excuse, pardon, forgive.

**conducive** adjective contributing, helpful, instrumental, favorable.

**conduct** noun **1** *guilty of evil conduct* behavior, comportment, bearing, deportment; actions, ways, habits, practices, manners. **2** *the conduct of the war* direction, running, management, administration, control, guidance, supervision.

**conduct** verb **1** *conduct oneself well/badly* behave, act, comport, deport, acquit. **2** *conduct the proceedings* direct, run, be in charge of, manage, administer, handle, control, supervise, lead, preside over. **3** *conduct us to our seats* show, guide, lead, escort, accompany.

**conduit** noun duct, pipe, tube, channel, canal, trough, passageway.

**confederacy** noun alliance, federation, partnership, union, collaboration, association, league, coalition.

**confederate** noun accomplice, abettor, accessory, ally, associate, collaborator, colleague, partner.

**confer** verb **1** *confer a title/favor* bestow, present, grant, award, give, give out, hand out, accord. **2** *confer with her colleagues* discuss, talk, consult, converse.

**conference** noun meeting, congress, convention, seminar, symposium, colloquium, forum, convocation.

**confess** verb **1** *confess her guilt* admit, acknowledge, make a clean breast of, own up to, declare, make known, disclose, reveal, divulge, blurt out, expose. **2** *I must confess I don't know* admit, concede, grant, allow, own.

**confidant, confidante** noun friend, crony, intimate, familiar, alter ego; *inf.* chum, pal, mate, bosom buddy.

**confide** verb **1** *confide a secret to | confide in a friend* disclose, reveal, divulge, impart, tell, open one's heart to, unburden oneself to, tell one's all to. **2** *confide a task* entrust, consign, hand over, commit, commend, assign.

**confidence** noun **1** *candidates full of confidence* self-confidence, self-assurance, assurance, self-reliance, self-possession, aplomb, poise. **2** *have no confidence in them* trust, reliance, faith, dependence, belief, credence. **3** *exchange confidences* secret, confidentiality, intimacy.

**confidential** adjective **1** *confidential information* secret, private, classified, off-the-record, restricted, personal, intimate, privy; *inf.* hush-hush. **2** *a confidential friend* close, bosom, intimate, trusted, trustworthy, reliable, dependable.

**confidentially** adverb in confidence, in secret, in private, privately, behind closed doors, sub rosa.

**confine** verb **1** *birds confined in a cage* enclose, shut up, shut, cage, keep, coop up, pen, box up, lock up, imprison, incarcerate, impound. **2** *remarks confined to the discussion* restrict, limit.

**confinement** noun custody, imprisonment, detention, captivity, internment, incarceration.

**confirm** verb **1** *evidence confirms her statement* bear out, verify, corroborate, prove, endorse, validate, authenticate, substantiate, give credence to. **2** *confirm that he would appear* reassert, give assurance, affirm, pledge, promise, guarantee. **3** *confirm his appointment* ratify, endorse, approve, sanction, underwrite. **4** *confirm my doubts* strengthen, reinforce, fortify.

**confirmation** noun **1** *confirmation of her statement/booking* verification, corroboration, proof, evidence, endorsement, validation, authentication. **2** *confirmation of the appointment* ratification, endorsement, approval, sanction, authorization.

**confiscate** verb seize, impound, take possession of, appropriate, commandeer, expropriate, sequester, arrogate.

**conflict** noun **1** *the military conflict* battle, fight, war, warfare, clash, engagement, encounter, hostilities, contest, combat, collision, struggle, strife, tussle, scuffle; *inf.* set-to. **2** *bitter conflict between the families* dissension, hostility, feud, discord, antagonism, antipathy, ill will, bad blood, contention. **3** *the conflict between love and duty* clash, variance, opposition, friction.

**conflict** verb clash, differ, disagree, be at variance, be in opposition, be at odds, be incompatible, collide.

**conflicting** adjective clashing, differing, disagreeing, contradictory, contrary, opposing, incompatible, inconsistent, discordant, at odds.

**conform** verb follow convention, comply, adapt, adjust, follow the crowd, run with the pack. **conform to** *conform to accepted standards* comply with, fall in with, follow, obey, adapt to, accommodate to, adjust to, observe.

**conformist** noun conventionalist, traditionalist, conservative; *inf.* yes-man, stick-in-the-mud, square.

**conformity** noun **1** *noted for their conformity* conventionality, traditionalism, orthodoxy. **2** *their conformity to accepted standards* compliance, obedience, observance, adaptation, adjustment, accommodation. **3** *having a certain conformity*

likeness, similarity, resemblance, correspondence, agreement, compatibility, congruity, consonance.

**confound** verb **1** *confounded at the news* dumbfound, astound, amaze, astonish, stun, flabbergast, disconcert, perplex, puzzle, mystify, baffle, nonplus, confuse, bewilder, dismay. **2** *confound the argument* refute, contradict, demolish, annihilate, explode.

**confront** verb **1** *confronting the enemy* defy, oppose, challenge, attack, assault, accost, waylay. **2** *confront one's problems* face, tackle, come to grips with, meet head on. **3** *confront them with the proof* bring face to face, show, present. **4** *problems confront us* threat, trouble, harass, annoy, molest.

**confrontation** noun conflict, clash, contest, collision, encounter; *inf.* set-to, showdown.

**confuse** verb **1** *confused by all the questions* bewilder, bemuse, perplex, baffle, puzzle, confound, mystify. **2** *confuse the issue* muddle, mix up, throw into disorder, disorder, disarrange, tangle up; *inf.* snarl up. **3** *confuse the twins with each other* mistake, mix up.

**confused** adjective **1** *a confused recollection* unclear, blurred, indistinct, hazy, foggy. **2** *a confused mess* muddled, jumbled, untidy, disorderly, chaotic, disorganized, upset, topsy-turvy. **3** *a confused old woman* muddled, addled, dazed, disoriented, at sea, unbalanced, unhinged, demented; *inf.* discombobulated.

**confusing** adjective unclear, puzzling, baffling, ambiguous, misleading, inconsistent.

**confusion** noun **1** *people in a state of confusion* bewilderment, perplexity, bafflement, puzzlement, mystification, disorientation, befuddlement. **2** *the room in a state of confusion* untidiness, disorder, chaos, shambles, disarrangement, disorganization. **3** *frightened by the confusion at the airport* bustle, commotion, upheaval, turmoil.

**congeal** verb solidify, harden, coagulate, thicken, set, concentrate, cake.

**congenial** adjective **1** *a congenial companion* sympathetic, compatible, like-minded, kindred. **2** *congenial work/places* agreeable, pleasant, pleasing, nice, suitable, well-suited, fit, favorable.

**congenital** adjective inborn, inbred, innate, inherent, constitutional, inherited, hereditary.

**conglomerate** noun corporation, multinational, joint concern, cartel.

**congregate** verb gather, assemble, group, flock together, convene, meet, amass, crowd, cluster, throng, rendezvous.

**congregation** noun gathering, assembly, group, convention, congress, mass, throng,

**congress · conservative**

conclave, convocation; flock, parishioners, parish.

**congress** noun *an international congress* assembly, meeting, gathering, conference, convention, convocation, council, synod.

**conjecture** noun guess, inference, fancy, notion, suspicion, presumption, theory, hypothesis; guessing, surmise, surmising, speculation, theorizing; *inf.* guesstimate.

**conjugal** adjective connubial, matrimonial, nuptial, marital, married, wedded, spousal.

**conjunction** noun *the conjunction of events* coincidence, co-occurrence, simultaneousness, coexistence, contemporaneousness, concomitance.

**conjure** verb summon, call up, invoke, rouse, raise up. **conjure up** recall, bring/call to mind, evoke, re-create.

**connect** verb **1** *connect the hose to the faucet* join, attach, fasten, affix, couple, clamp, secure, rivet, fuse, solder, weld. **2** *a road connecting the towns* join, link, unite, bridge. **connect with** *she connects him with sadness* associate with, link with/to, relate to, identify with, equate with.

**connection** noun **1** *the connection has come loose* attachment, fastening, coupling, clamp, clasp, joint. **2** *the connection between the events* link, relationship, relatedness, association, bond, tie-in, correspondence, parallel, analogy. **3** *in that connection* context, reference, frame of reference, relation. **4** *get a job through a connection* contact, friend, acquaintance, ally, associate, sponsor.

**connive** verb conspire, collaborate, collude, be in collusion, intrigue, plot, scheme, be a party to, be an accessory to.

**connoisseur** noun expert, authority, specialist, pundit, cognoscenti (pl.), savant.

**connotation** noun undertone, nuance, hint, intimation, suggestion, implication, allusion, insinuation.

**conquer** verb **1** *conquer the enemy* defeat, beat, overpower, overthrow, vanquish, subdue, rout, trounce, subjugate, crush, quell. **2** *conquer the territory* seize, occupy, invade, annex, appropriate. **3** *conquer one's fears* overcome, get the better of, master, surmount, rise above, prevail over.

**conqueror** noun victor, winner, champion, hero, lord, master, conquistador.

**conquest** noun **1** *the conquest of/over the enemy* victory, defeat, overpowering, overthrow, vanquishment, rout, triumph. **2** *the conquest of the territory* seizing, possession, occupation, invasion, annexation, appropriation. **3** *the conquest of the audience* captivation, enchantment, bewitching, seduction, enticement, enthrallment.

**4** *yet another of her conquests* admirer, fan, adherent, follower, supporter, worshiper.

**conscience** noun morals, scruples, principles, ethics.

**conscience-stricken** adjective contrite, penitent, repentant, remorseful, sorry, regretful, guilty, guilt-ridden, troubled, ashamed.

**conscientious** adjective diligent, careful, attentive, thorough, meticulous, punctilious, painstaking, hard-working, dedicated; precise, accurate, detailed.

**conscious** adjective **1** *a conscious attempt at humor* deliberate, calculated, premeditated, on purpose, reasoned, willed, volitional. **2** *in a conscious state* awake, aware, sentient, responsive, alert. **conscious of** *conscious of the problem* aware of, alert to, cognizant of.

**consciousness** noun **1** *regain consciousness* awareness, sentience, responsiveness, alertness. **2** *lack consciousness of the situation* realization, cognizance, perception, apprehension, recognition.

**consecrate** verb **1** *consecrate the building* sanctify, bless, make holy, hallow, dedicate to God. **2** *a life consecrated to science* dedicate, devote, pledge, commit.

**consecutive** adjective successive, succeeding, following, in sequence, sequential, serial, continuous, uninterrupted, unbroken.

**consensus** noun agreement, consent, common consent, unanimity, unity, concurrence.

**consent** verb **consent to** agree to, accept, approve, go along with, acquiesce in/to, accede to, concede to, yield to, give in to, submit to, comply with.

**consent** noun acceptance, approval, permission, sanction, acquiescence, compliance, concurrence.

**consequence** noun **1** *the consequence of the decision* result, effect, upshot, outcome, issue, aftermath, repercussion. **2** *a matter of consequence* importance, note, significance, import, moment, weight. **3** *a person of consequence* distinction, standing, status, prominence, prestige, eminence, rank.

**consequent** adjective resulting, resultant, ensuing, following, subsequent, successive, sequential.

**consequently** adverb as a result, therefore, thus, hence, subsequently, accordingly, ergo.

**conservation** noun preservation, protection, safeguarding, safekeeping, care, custody, upkeep, maintenance.

**conservative** adjective **1** *politically conservative* right-wing, reactionary, traditionalist. **2** *a conservative hairstyle* conventional, traditional, cautious, prudent, moderate, middle-of-the-road, temperate, stable, unchanging, old-fashioned, unprogressive.

**conserve** verb preserve, save, keep, protect, take care of, hoard, store up, husband, reserve.

**consider** verb 1 *consider your application* think about, give thought to, examine, ponder, contemplate, deliberate over, cogitate about, chew over. 2 *consider the feelings of others* take into consideration, take into account, make allowances for, respect, bear in mind, have regard to. 3 *consider you suitable* think, believe, regard as, deem, hold to be, judge. 4 *consider the horizon* contemplate, observe, regard, survey, scrutinize, scan.

**considerable** adjective 1 *a considerable amount* sizable, substantial, appreciable, goodly, tolerable, fair, ample, plentiful, noticeable, decent, great, large. 2 *a considerable artist* noteworthy, important, significant, influential, illustrious.

**considerate** adjective thoughtful, attentive, concerned, solicitous, mindful, heedful, kind, kindly, unselfish, compassionate, sympathetic.

**consideration** noun 1 *give consideration to the proposal* thought, attention, heed, notice, regard, deliberation, reflection, contemplation, examination, inspection, scrutiny, analysis, review. 2 *show consideration to their parents* thoughtfulness, attentiveness, concern, solicitousness, kindness, compassion, sympathy, patience, charity. 3 *money a major consideration* issue, factor, point, concern. 4 *for a small consideration* payment, fee, remuneration, compensation, recompense. 5 *take age into consideration* account, reckoning, allowance.

**consign** verb 1 *consign her to his care* hand over, give over, entrust, commend, remit, bequeath. 2 *consign to the junk pile* assign, deliver, commit.

**consist** verb consist of *consist of flour and water* comprise, contain, include, incorporate, embody, involve.

**consistency** noun 1 *mix to the right consistency* thickness, density, firmness, solidity, viscosity, cohesion. 2 *attitudes lacking consistency* dependability, constancy, uniformity.

**consistent** adjective 1 *consistent attitudes* steady, dependable, constant, uniform, unchanging, undeviating. 2 *testimony consistent with the facts* compatible, congruous, agreeing, accordant, consonant.

**consolation** noun 1 *words of consolation* compassion, pity, encouragement, soothing. See COMFORT noun 2. 2 *the baby is a consolation to her* comfort, solace, support.

**console** verb commiserate with, cheer, encourage. See COMFORT verb 1.

**consolidate** verb 1 *consolidate his position* strengthen, make secure, stabilize, reinforce, fortify, cement. 2 *consolidate the territories* combine, unite, merge, amalgamate, join.

**conspicuous** adjective 1 *conspicuous changes* obvious, evident, apparent, noticeable, observable, recognizable, discernible, manifest, vivid. 2 *conspicuous colors* obtrusive, blatant, flagrant, showy, garish, bold, ostentatious.

**conspiracy** noun 1 *a conspiracy to overthrow the government* plot, scheme, stratagem, plan, machination; collusion, connivance, collaboration.

**conspirator** noun conspirer, plotter, schemer, intriguer, colluder, collaborator, confederate.

**conspire** verb 1 *conspire against the leader* plot, scheme, intrigue, collude, collaborate, cabal, machinate; *inf.* be in cahoots with. 2 *events conspire against us* act together, work together, combine, unite, join forces, gang up (on).

**constancy** noun 1 *her lover's constancy* faithfulness, fidelity, devotion, loyalty, staunchness, dependability, adherence. 2 *constancy of purpose* firmness, steadfastness, resoluteness, fixedness, determination, perseverance, tenacity, doggedness. 3 *constancy of temperature* uniformity, evenness, regularity, stability, immutability.

**constant** adjective 1 *at a constant speed/temperature* uniform, even, regular, stable, steady, fixed, unvarying, unchanging, immutable. 2 *a constant stream of people/chatter* continuous, unbroken, uninterrupted; continual, never-ending, endless, unending, nonstop, incessant, unceasing, persistent, interminable, unremitting, relentless, unrelenting. 3 *a constant lover* faithful, devoted, loyal, staunch, dependable, true, trustworthy, trusty. 4 *constant in his purpose* firm, steadfast, steady, resolute, determined, persevering, tenacious, dogged, unwavering.

**constantly** adverb always, all the time, continually, continuously, endlessly, nonstop, incessantly, persistently, interminably, relentlessly.

**consternation** noun astonishment, dismay, bewilderment, confusion, anxiety, distress, alarm, panic, dread.

**constitute** verb 1 *the countries that constitute the alliance* form, make up, compose, comprise. 2 *his suggestion constitutes a warning* be tantamount to, be the equivalent of, be, be regarded as, act as. 3 *constitute a committee* appoint, establish, authorize, commission, charter.

**constitution** noun **1** *the society's constitution* system of laws/rules, code, charter, canon; laws, rules, fundamental principles; bill of rights. **2** *the constitution of the committees varies* composition, makeup, structure, organization. **3** *people having a strong constitution* state of health, physique, physical condition. **4** *people of a nervous constitution* disposition, temperament, temper, nature, character, mood.

**constrain** verb **1** *feel constrained to co-operate* force, compel, coerce, drive, impel, oblige, press, pressure. **2** *research constrained by lack of resources* hold back, restrict, hinder, impede, hamper, limit, curb, check, restrain. **3** *constrain political opponents* confine, chain, shut in, lock up, imprison, incarcerate.

**constraint** noun **1** *act under constraint* force, compulsion, coercion, obligation, pressure, impulsion. **2** *no constraints on their activities* restriction, hindrance, impediment, limitation, curb, check, restraint, damper. **3** *subject political opponents to constraint* confinement, imprisonment, incarceration. **4** *constraint of manner* forcedness, unnaturalness, inhibition, reservedness.

**constrict** verb **1** *a medication that constricts the blood vessels* narrow, compress, contract, squeeze, strangle, strangulate. **2** *constrict the flow of traffic* impede, obstruct, hinder, hamper, limit, restrict, check, curb, inhibit.

**construct** verb **1** *construct a bridge* build, erect, put up, set up, assemble, manufacture, fabricate, make. **2** *construct a plan/theory* form, formulate, devise, design, invent, compose, fashion, shape, frame, forge, engineer.

**construction** noun **1** *a bridge under construction* building, erection, establishment, assembly, manufacture, fabrication. **2** *an impressive construction* structure, building, edifice, assembly, framework. **3** *put a different construction on her words* interpretation, reading, meaning, explanation, inference.

**constructive** adjective useful, helpful, productive, practical, positive, valuable.

**consult** verb **1** *consult an expert* | *consult a reference book* ask, seek advice/information from, call in, turn to, take counsel from, look up in, check (in), refer to, turn to. **2** *consult with his colleagues* confer, discuss, talk over, exchange views, deliberate, parley.

**consultant** noun adviser, expert, authority, specialist.

**consultation** noun **1** *have a consultation with one's adviser* meeting, talk, discussion, interview, session, audience, tête-à-tête, parley. **2** *international consultations* conference, convention, symposium, forum, session, seminar.

**consume** verb **1** *consume dinner/lemonade* eat, drink, devour, ingest, swallow, gobble, guzzle, snack on; *inf.* tuck into, scoff down, put away, polish off; chug. **2** *consumed by a desire* absorb, engross, obsess, grip. **3** *buildings consumed by fire* destroy, demolish, lay waste, wipe out, annihilate, devastate, raze, gut, ravage. **4** *cars consuming too much gasoline* use up, expend, deplete, exhaust; waste, squander, dissipate, fritter away.

**consumer** noun user, buyer, purchaser, customer, shopper, client, patron.

**consuming** adjective absorbing, compelling, preoccupying, engrossing, devouring, obsessive, gripping, overwhelming.

**consummate** adjective complete, total, utter, absolute, perfect; accomplished, expert, proficient, masterly, talented, gifted.

**consumption** noun **1** *unfit for human consumption* eating, drinking, ingestion. **2** *consumption by fire* destruction, demolition, annihilation, devastation, razing, gutting, ravaging. **3** *the consumption of fuel* utilization, expenditure, depletion, exhaustion, waste, draining, dissipation.

**contact** noun **1** *following contact with chemicals* touch, touching, proximity, exposure, contiguity, junction, union, tangency. **2** *be in contact with* touch, communication, connection, correspondence, association. **3** *get a job through contacts* connection, acquaintance.

**contact** verb get/be in touch with, get hold/ahold of, communicate with; write to, write, notify, phone, call, speak to, reach.

**contagious** adjective catching, communicable, transmittable, spreadable, infectious, epidemic, pandemic.

**contain** verb **1** *the cabin contained four people* hold, have capacity for, carry, accommodate. **2** *the committee contains six members* include, comprise, embrace, take in, incorporate, involve. **3** *contain your laughter* hold in, restrain, control, keep in check, suppress, repress, curb, stifle.

**contaminate** verb pollute, adulterate, defile, debase, corrupt, taint, infect, foul, spoil, soil, sully, tarnish, stain, befoul, vitiate.

**contemplate** verb **1** *contemplate the Portrait* look at, view, regard, examine, survey, scrutinize, scan, stare at, gaze at. **2** *contemplate the future* think about, ponder over, ponder, reflect over, mull over, muse on, deliberate over, cogitate over, ruminate over, turn over in one's mind. **3** *he is contemplating going* consider, intend, plan, propose.

**contemplation** noun **1** *his contemplation of the painting* viewing, examination, inspection, observation, scrutiny, regard. **2**

*contemplation of the future* pondering, reflection, rumination, deliberation, cogitation. **3** *lost in contemplation* thought, meditation, reflection; *inf.* brown study.

**contemplative** adjective thoughtful, pensive, reflective, meditative, musing, ruminative, introspective.

**contemporary** adjective **1** *contemporary writers* contemporaneous, coexisting, coexistent, concurrent, synchronous. **2** *contemporary fashion* modern, present-day, current, up-to-date, up-to-the-minute, latest, recent, ultramodern, newfangled; *inf.* with it.

**contemporary** noun *Shakespeare and his contemporaries* peer, compeer, fellow.

**contempt** noun scorn, disdain, disrespect, condescension, derision, mockery, disgust, loathing, abhorrence.

**contemptible** adjective despicable, detestable, ignominious, lamentable, pitiful, low, mean, shameful, base, vile, sordid, degenerate.

**contemptuous** adjective scornful, disdainful, disrespectful, insulting, insolent, derisory, derisive, mocking.

**contend** verb **1** *armies contending with each other* compete, oppose, vie, contest, clash, strive, struggle, grapple, scuffle, skirmish, battle, combat, fight, war. **2** *contend that he's mad* assert, maintain, hold, claim, profess, allege. **contend with** cope with, face, grapple with, take on, pit oneself against.

**content** noun **1** *the content of the mixture* component parts/elements. *See* CONTENTS 1. **2** *the content of the essay* subject matter, subject, material, substance, theme, ideas, gist. **3** *foods with a low sodium content* amount, proportion, quantity.

**content** adjective *content with life* contented, satisfied, pleased, happy, cheerful, glad, gratified, fulfilled, at ease, at peace, comfortable, serene, tranquil, unworried, untroubled, complacent.

**contented** adjective satisfied, pleased. *See* CONTENT adjective.

**contention** noun **1** *two groups in contention for the title* competition, contest, rivalry, opposition, striving, struggle, combat, battle. **2** *much contention between the families* discord, feuding, hostility, enmity, strife, dissension. **3** *it was her contention that she won* assertion, claim, stand, position, opinion, view, belief.

**contentious** adjective **1** *contentious people* argumentative, quarrelsome, bickering, wrangling, disputatious, factious, litigious, combative, pugnacious. **2** *a contentious subject* controversial, disputable, debatable, controvertible.

**contentment** noun content, contentedness, satisfaction, pleasure, happiness, cheerfulness, gladness, gratification, fulfillment, ease, comfort, peace, equanimity, serenity, tranquillity.

**contents** plural noun **1** *the contents of the mixture/box* constituents, components, ingredients, elements, items; content, load. **2** *the contents of the book* text, subject matter, theme.

**contest** noun **1** *a sport/dancing contest* competition, match, game, event, tournament, meet, trial. **2** *a leadership contest* struggle, conflict, battle, fight, combat, tussle.

**contest** verb *contest the decision/point* challenge, question, call into question, oppose, doubt, dispute, argue, debate, quarrel over.

**contestant** noun competitor, entrant, candidate, participant, player, contender, rival, opponent, adversary, antagonist, aspirant.

**context** noun **1** *in the present financial context* circumstances, conditions, situation, state of affairs, background, environment. **2** *take a statement out of context* text, frame of reference, subject.

**contiguous** adjective touching, in contact, meeting, joining, connecting, abutting, bordering, neighboring, adjacent.

**contingent** adjective chance, accidental, fortuitous, random, haphazard; uncertain, possible. **contingent on/upon** dependent on, subject to, hinging on.

**continual** adjective **1** *continual complaints* frequent, repeated, constant, regular, persistent, habitual, recurrent, repetitive, oft-repeated. **2** *continual noise* perpetual, endless. *See* CONTINUOUS.

**continue** verb **1** *the desert continues for miles* go on, extend, keep on, carry on, maintain course, drag on. **2** *the firm may continue* last, remain, stay, endure, survive, live on, persist, abide. **3** *continue the session as long as possible* maintain, sustain, retain, prolong, protract, perpetuate, preserve. **4** *continue trying* keep on, keep at, persist in, persevere in; *inf.* stick with/at. **5** *continue the search after a break* resume, renew, recommence, start again, carry on with, return to, take up, proceed, pick up where one has left off.

**continuity** noun **1** *continuity of supplies* continuousness, uninterruptedness, flow, regular flow, progression. **2** *continuity in the prose* cohesion, coherence, connection, interrelatedness, linkage, sequence.

**continuous** adjective uninterrupted, unbroken, consecutive, constant, nonstop, perpetual, ceaseless, incessant, unceasing, unremitting, endless, everlasting, interminable.

**contort** verb twist, wrench/bend out of shape, warp, deform, misshape.

**contour** noun outline, silhouette, profile, figure, shape, form; lines, curves.

**contraband** noun smuggling, trafficking, black marketing, black marketeering, bootlegging.

**contract** noun agreement, compact, covenant, pact, settlement, arrangement, transaction, bargain, deal.

**contract** verb 1 *metals contracting | contracting metals* get/make smaller, become/make shorter, shrink, reduce, shrivel. 2 *blood vessels contracting | muscles contracting* constrict, become narrower, narrow, tighten, become tighter, tense, draw in. 3 *contract a word/text* shorten, abbreviate, abridge, compress, condense. 4 *contract (with) them to do the work* arrange, agree, come to terms, negotiate, bargain, strike a bargain, close/clinch a deal, close, engage. 5 *contract a disease* catch, get, come down with, develop. 6 *contract a debt* incur, acquire, fall into.

**contraction** noun shrinking, narrowing, tightening, constricting, tensing.

**contradict** verb 1 *contradict his father* say the opposite of, oppose, challenge, counter, be at variance with; deny, dispute, refute, rebut, controvert, impugn, confute. 2 *the statements contradict each other* disagree with, be in conflict with, clash with, contravene, run counter to, be inconsistent with, negate.

**contradiction** noun 1 *the contradiction of his statement* disputing, countering, refuting, rebuttal, controverting, impugning, confutation. 2 *the contradiction between the two statements* disagreement, conflict, clash, inconsistency, dissension, contravention, negation.

**contradictory** adjective 1 *hold a contradictory view* opposing, opposite, dissenting, contrary, dissident; at variance, at odds. 2 *contradictory statements* conflicting, clashing, contrasting, incompatible, irreconcilable, inconsistent, antithetical.

**contraption** noun device, machine, mechanism, gadget, contrivance, apparatus, invention, appliance; *inf.* thingamajig, thingamabob, whatsit, doodad, gizmo.

**contrary** adjective 1 *holding contrary views* opposite, opposing, incongruous. See CONTRADICTORY 2. 2 *a contrary young woman* willful, obstinate, stubborn, headstrong, pigheaded, intractable, recalcitrant, intransigent, refractory.

**contrast** noun 1 *a marked contrast between them* difference, dissimilarity, distinction, disparity, dissimilitude, differentiation, distinguishment. 2 *he is a complete contrast to his brother* opposite, antithesis.

**contrast** verb 1 *contrast the two writers* compare, juxtapose, set side by side, distinguish, differentiate, discriminate. 2 *theories and actions contrast sharply* contradict, be at variance, be contrary, diverge, differ.

**contravene** verb 1 *contravene a law* disobey, break, infringe, violate, transgress. 2 *evidence contravenes that theory* contradict, be in conflict with, be in opposition to, clash with, be at variance with, run counter to, refute, rebut.

**contribute** verb 1 *contribute money/time to the charity | happy to contribute* give, donate, hand out, present, grant, endow, bestow, accord, confer, provide, supply, furnish; *inf.* chip in, pitch in. 2 *sensible eating contributes to good health* be conducive to, lead to, be instrumental in, promote, advance.

**contribution** noun 1 *contributions to the fund* donation, gift, offering, present, grant, bestowal, allowance, subsidy, endowment. 2 *appreciated your contribution during the discussion* input, participation; *inf.* two cents' worth.

**contributor** noun giver, donor, patron, supporter, backer, benefactor, subsidizer.

**contrite** adjective penitent, repentant, remorseful, regretful, sorry, chastened, conscience-stricken, guilt-ridden, in sackcloth and ashes.

**contrivance** noun 1 *a contrivance for plowing* device, invention, gadget, contraption, appliance, apparatus, implement, tool, machine, mechanism, equipment, gear, tackle. 2 *fooled by a clever contrivance* stratagem, scheme, ruse, trick, plot, machination, fabrication, artifice. 3 *the contrivance of the schemer* inventiveness, ingenuity, creativity, originality.

**contrive** verb 1 *contrive a brilliant scheme* devise, concoct, engineer, invent, originate, create, construct, design, plan, work out, think/dream up, plot, fabricate. 2 *contrive to win* manage, find a way, engineer, maneuver, scheme.

**contrived** adjective unnatural, artificial, forced, strained, labored, nonspontaneous.

**control** verb 1 *control the organization* be in charge of, head, manage, direct, preside over, conduct, command, rule, govern, lead, supervise, superintend, oversee, dominate, master, reign over, be in the driver's seat of, be in the saddle of. 2 *control prices* keep in check, restrain, curb, contain, hold back, restrict, limit, regulate, constrain, subdue, bridle.

**control** noun 1 *have control over the organization* charge, management, authority,

**power**, command, direction, rule, government, jurisdiction, supervision, dominance, mastery, reign, supremacy. **2** *get control of oneself* self-control, self-restraint, restraint, hold. **3** *arms control | import controls* limitation, restriction, regulation, check, curb.

**controversial** adjective disputed, disputable, debatable, under discussion, at issue, contentious, contended, controvertible.

**controversy** noun dispute, argument, polemic, debate, disagreement, dissension, altercation, wrangling, quarreling, squabbling, bickering.

**contusion** noun bruise, discoloration, blemish, injury, bump, lump.

**conundrum** noun riddle, puzzle, word game; problem, enigma, mystery; *inf.* brainteaser.

**convalescence** noun recovery, recuperation, improvement, rehabilitation, mending, restoration.

**convene** verb **1** *convene a meeting* call, call together, summon, convoke, round up, rally. **2** *the meeting convened* assemble, gather, collect, congregate, meet, muster.

**convenience** noun **1** *the convenience of the time/arrangement* accessibility, availability, suitability, appropriateness, fitness, fittingness, favorableness, favorability, advantageousness, opportuneness, propitiousness, expedience, usefulness, utility, serviceability. **2** *do it at your convenience* suitable opportunity, leisure, spare moment, free time. **3** *for the convenience of all* service, use, benefit, advantage, accommodation, enjoyment, comfort, ease. **4** *few conveniences in the kitchen* gadget, laborsaving device, appliance, appurtenance, amenity.

**convenient** adjective **1** *stores convenient to the highway* accessible, handy, at hand, close at hand, within reach, nearby, just around the corner, at one's fingertips, available. **2** *choose a convenient time/setting* suitable, suited, appropriate, fit, fitting, favorable, advantageous, opportune, expedient, useful, serviceable.

**convention** noun **1** *a medical/political convention* conference, congress, gathering, meeting, assembly, convocation, synod, conclave. **2** *follow convention* protocol, propriety, code, custom, tradition, usage, practice. **3** *a convention between countries* agreement, contract, pact, treaty.

**conventional** adjective **1** *conventional behavior/attitudes* accepted, customary, usual, standard, normal, ordinary, decorous, proper, orthodox, traditional, prevailing, prevalent, conformist, conservative; *inf.* square, straight, straitlaced. **2** *conventional works of art* run-of-the-mill, commonplace,

ordinary, everyday, garden-variety, prosaic, routine, pedestrian, hackneyed, unoriginal.

**converge** verb meet, intersect, join, merge, unite, come together, become one.

**conversant** adjective acquainted with, familiar with, knowledgeable about, well-versed in, informed about; *inf.* (well) up on.

**conversation** noun discussion, dialogue, discourse, communication, conference, colloquy; talk, chat, exchange, gossip, tête-à-tête; *inf.* confab, rap session.

**converse** verb talk, speak, discuss, chat, communicate.

**converse** noun opposite, contrary, reverse, antithesis, obverse.

**conversion** noun **1** *the conversion of liquid to gas* transformation, metamorphosis, transfiguration, transmutation; *inf.* transmogrification. **2** *the conversion of the building* alteration, adaptation, modification, reshaping, refashioning, remodeling. **3** *religious conversion* reformation, regeneration, proselytization. **4** *conversion of pounds to dollars* change, exchange, substitution, switch.

**convert** verb **1** *convert liquid to gas* change, transform, metamorphose, transfigure, transmute; *inf.* transmogrify. **2** *the sofa converts to a bed* change (into), make (into), adapt, transform (into). **3** *convert the building* alter, adapt, modify, reshape, refashion, remodel, restyle. **4** *convert the heathens* reform, regenerate, bring to God, baptize, proselytize. **5** *convert yards to meters* change, turn into; exchange for, substitute by.

**convey** verb **1** *convey the goods* transport, carry, bring, fetch, bear, move, shift, transfer, cart, lug. **2** *convey information* transmit, pass on, send, dispatch, communicate, make known, impart. **3** *convey property* transfer, transmit, devolve, lease, bequeath, will.

**conveyance** noun **1** *by public conveyance* transport, transportation, carriage, transfer, transference, transmission, haulage, portage, cartage, shipment, freightage. **2** *the conveyance of information* transmission, passing on, communication, imparting. **3** *conveyance of property* transfer, granting, ceding, cession.

**convict** noun prisoner, criminal, offender, lawbreaker, felon; *inf.* crook, con, jailbird.

**conviction** noun **1** *she spoke with conviction* confidence, assurance, certainty, certitude, firmness, earnestness. **2** *my conviction is that he is dead* belief, opinion, view, persuasion. **3** *a person of conviction* principle, belief, faith, creed.

**convince** verb **1** *she convinced me that I was wrong* prove to, satisfy, assure, reassure.

**2** *convince him to vote for them* persuade, prevail upon, sway, bring around.

**convincing** adjective cogent, powerful, persuasive, plausible, incontrovertible, conclusive; plausible, credible.

**convivial** adjective genial, cordial, sociable, friendly, affable, amiable, congenial, agreeable.

**convoy** noun **1** *the convoy set off* assemblage, line, fleet, cortege, caravan. **2** *a fleet/company under convoy* escort, protection, guard, bodyguard, defense.

**convulse** verb **1** *convulsed with laughter* shake, churn up, discompose, unsettle. **2** *a city convulsed with rioting* agitate, disturb, upset, disorder, unsettle, wrack.

**convulsion** noun **1** *the child went into convulsions* fit, seizure, paroxysm, spasm, contractions. **2** *political convulsions in the city* turmoil, tumult, commotion, upheaval, agitation, unrest, upset, disorder, chaos.

**cook** verb **1** *cook a dish/meal* prepare, put together, concoct. **2** *cook the books* falsify, forge, alter. **3** *what's cooking?* happen, occur, take place. **cook up** concoct, contrive, fabricate, improvise.

**cool** adjective **1** *cool weather* coldish, chilly, chilled, nippy, unheated, sunless, windy, breezy, drafty. **2** *keep cool in an emergency* calm, composed, collected, self-possessed, self-controlled, levelheaded, unexcited, unperturbed, unmoved, unruffled, unemotional; *inf.* together. **3** *a cool welcome* chilly, impassive, undemonstrative, unresponsive, unenthusiastic, indifferent. **4** *the cool method of the killer* calculated, premeditated, planned, deliberate, dispassionate, cold, cold-blooded. **5** *thinks he's really cool* sophisticated, suave, stylish, urbane, cosmopolitan. **6** *what a cool idea* great, superb, excellent, splendid; *inf.* awesome, far-out.

**cool** verb **1** *cool the milk* cool down, chill, refrigerate, freeze. **2** *the milk cooled* become cold/colder, lose heat. **3** *cool his passion* lessen, abate, moderate, temper, diminish, reduce, dampen.

**cool** noun **1** *lose one's cool* self-control, control, calmness, composure, poise. **2** *the cool of the evening* coolness, freshness, crispness, coldness, chill.

**coop** noun cage, pen, enclosure, hutch, pound, lockup.

**coop** verb **coop up** cage, cage/pen in, confine, enclose, hem in, shut/lock up, imprison.

**cooperate** verb **1** *cooperate in the venture* work together, act/pull together, join forces, unite, combine, collaborate, pool resources. **2** *he'll be released if he cooperates* assist, help, contribute, participate, go along; *inf.* pitch in, play ball.

**cooperation** noun **1** *cooperation between the departments* collaboration, coordination, teamwork, give and take, synergy. **2** *thank you for your cooperation* assistance, help, aid, contribution, helping hand, participation.

**cooperative** adjective **1** *a cooperative venture* joint, united, shared, unified, combined, concerted, coordinated, collaborative. **2** *the public's being cooperative* helpful, obliging, accommodating, participating, responsive.

**coordinate** verb **1** *coordinate the effort* organize, order, integrate, synchronize, correlate. **2** *coordinating for the common good* unite, combine, collaborate, interrelate.

**cope** verb manage, succeed, survive, carry on, get through, get on, get along, get by, subsist. **cope with** handle, deal with, weather, contend with, grapple with, wrestle with.

**copious** adjective abundant, superabundant, plentiful, ample, profuse, full, extensive, generous, lavish, rich, liberal, bounteous, bountiful.

**copy** noun **1** *a copy of the document* transcript, facsimile, duplicate, duplication, carbon, carbon copy, photocopy; *TM* Xerox, Photostat. **2** *a clever copy of the vase* imitation, reproduction, replica, likeness, counterfeit, forgery, fake. **3** *three copies of the book* specimen, example, sample, issue.

**copy** verb **1** *copy the document* duplicate, photocopy, Xerox (*trademark*), Photostat (*trademark*), transcribe. **2** *copy the vase/painting* reproduce, replicate, forge, counterfeit; imitate, mimic, emulate, follow, echo, mirror, simulate, ape, parrot.

**cordial** adjective **1** *a cordial welcome* warm, friendly, genial, affable, amiable, pleasant, gracious, warmhearted, sincere, hearty, wholehearted, heartfelt. **2** *cordial dislike* intense, acute, strong, fierce, keen.

**cordon** verb **cordon off** close off, fence off, shut off, enclose, encircle, surround.

**core** noun center, heart, nucleus, nub, kernel, crux, heart of the matter, essence, quintessence, substance, gist, pith; *inf.* nitty-gritty.

**corner** noun **1** *the corner of the road* angle, bend, curve, crook, turn; intersection, junction, fork, convergence, juncture. **2** *hidden in secret corners* nook, cranny, niche, recess, hideaway, hide-out. **3** *in a remote corner of Maine* part, region, area, district, section, quarter. **4** *in a difficult corner* predicament, plight, tight spot; *inf.* pickle. **5** *a corner of the property market* dominance, monopoly.

**corner** verb **1** *corner the enemy* block off, trap, bring to bay. **2** *corner the market* gain control, dominate, monopolize.

**corny** adjective banal, trite, hackneyed, stale, commonplace, platitudinous, inane, fatuous, jejune, sentimental, mawkish; *inf.* old hat.

**coronation** noun crowning, enthronement, enthroning, accession to the throne, investiture, anointing, inauguration.

**coronet** noun crown, circlet, garland, wreath, chaplet.

**corporal** adjective bodily, fleshly, physical, corporeal, material, carnal.

**corporate** adjective **1** *review corporate finances* company, organization, business. **2** *for the corporate good* communal, collective, shared, collaborative.

**corporation** noun company, firm, trust, partnership, combine, conglomerate.

**corps** noun **1** *an army corps* unit, division, detachment, company, troop, contingent, squad, squadron. **2** *diplomatic/press corps* group, body, band, contingent, pack, crew.

**corpse** noun cadaver, carcass, skeleton; remains; *inf.* stiff.

**corpulent** adjective fat, obese, plump, portly, stout, overweight, beefy, thickset, heavy, heavyset, well-padded, fleshy, rotund, roly-poly.

**correct** adjective **1** *the correct answer* right, accurate, true, actual, exact, precise, unerring, close, faithful, strict, faultless, flawless; *inf.* OK, on the mark, on the beam. **2** *correct behavior* proper, suitable, fit, fitting, befitting, appropriate, apt, seemly, conventional, approved, accepted, standard, usual, customary.

**correct** verb **1** *correct the errors* rectify, right, amend, remedy, redress, cure, improve, better, ameliorate, repair. **2** *correct a defect* counteract, offset, counterbalance, compensate for, make up for, neutralize. **3** *correct an instrument* adjust, regulate, fix, set, standardize. **4** *correct the children* scold, rebuke, chide, reprimand, reprove, admonish, discipline, punish, chastise.

**correction** noun **1** *the correction of the text* amendment, emendation, rectification, improvement, modification, alteration, amelioration, repair. **2** *a house of correction* punishment, discipline, castigation, reformation.

**corrective** adjective **1** *corrective surgery* remedial, therapeutic, restorative, curative, reparative, rehabilitative. **2** *corrective training* punitive, penal, reformatory.

**correctly** adverb **1** *answer correctly* accurately, unerringly, precisely, faultlessly. **2** *dressed correctly* properly, suitably, fittingly, appropriately, aptly.

**correlate** verb **1** *subjects correlating with each other* correspond, tie in, equate, interact, relate, agree, coordinate. **2** *correlate the facts* bring together, compare, show a connection/relationship, connect.

**correlation** noun correspondence, equivalence, reciprocity, interrelationship, interdependence, connection, relationship.

**correspond** verb **1** *the accounts do not correspond* agree, be in agreement, accord, concur, coincide, conform, match, fit together, square, tally, dovetail, correlate. **2** *Congress corresponds to Parliament* be analogous, be similar, be comparable.

**correspondence** noun **1** *lack of correspondence between the accounts* agreement, accordance, accord, concurrence, conformity, harmony. **2** *a backlog of correspondence* mail, communication; letters, notes, messages, E-mail.

**correspondent** noun **1** *her brothers are regular correspondents* letter writer, pen pal. **2** *newspaper correspondent* reporter, journalist; *inf.* stringer.

**corridor** noun passage, passageway, aisle, hallway.

**corroborate** verb back up, support. *See* CONFIRM 1.

**corrode** verb eat away, wear away, erode, gnaw, abrade, destroy, consume, rust, oxidize, oxidate; waste away, disintegrate, crumble, fragment, be destroyed.

**corrosive** adjective corroding, eroding, erosive, abrasive, biting, caustic, acrid, destructive.

**corrugated** adjective furrowed, grooved, ridged, fluted, crinkled, wrinkled, crumpled, striate.

**corrupt** adjective **1** *corrupt officials* dishonest, bribable, crooked, fraudulent, dishonorable, unscrupulous, untrustworthy, venal; *inf.* bent, shady. **2** *a corrupt young man* immoral, depraved, wicked, evil, sinful, degenerate. **3** *a corrupt substance* adulterated, impure, alloyed, contaminated, tainted.

**corrupt** verb **1** *corrupt the official* bribe, suborn, buy, buy off; *inf.* pay off, grease the palm of. **2** *corrupt the young boy* deprave, pervert, warp, debauch. **3** *corrupt the atmosphere* pollute, putrefy, taint, infect, contaminate. **4** *corrupt the substance* adulterate, alloy, contaminate, taint, defile, debase. **5** *corrupt the text* alter, tamper with, falsify, doctor.

**corruption** noun **1** *officials involved in corruption* bribery, subornation, extortion, dishonesty, crookedness, fraud, fraudulence, unscrupulousness, shadiness, profiteering, criminality, venality; *inf.* graft. **2** *guilty of moral corruption* immorality, depravity, vice, wickedness, evil, sin, iniquity, turpitude, degeneracy. **3** *corruption of the atmosphere* pollution, contamination.

**cortege** noun **1** *a funeral cortege* procession, column, file, line, parade, cavalcade. **2** *the bride and her cortege* retinue, entourage, train; attendants.

**cosmetic** adjective **1** *a cosmetic improvement* superficial, surface. **2** *cosmetic surgery* beautifying, nonessential, nonmedical.

**cosmic** adjective **1** *cosmic laws* universal, worldwide. **2** *disasters of cosmic proportion* vast, huge, immense, enormous, immeasurable, measureless, infinite, limitless.

**cosmopolitan** adjective **1** *a cosmopolitan city* international, multiethnic, universal, global, worldwide. **2** *a cosmopolitan attitude* sophisticated, urbane, worldly, worldly-wise, well-traveled, jet-setting, globe-trotting, unprovincial, cultivated.

**cost** verb **1** *the book costs $30* be priced at, sell for, fetch, come to, amount to; *inf.* set one back. **2** *tragedy costing lives | work costing effort* involve, result in, lead to, involve the loss/expense/sacrifice of, necessitate.

**cost** noun **1** *the cost of the house* price, asking price, selling price, charge, amount, value, valuation, quotation, rate, worth, payment, expenditure, expense, outlay; *inf.* damage. **2** *work done at great cost* sacrifice, expense, loss, penalty, suffering, harm, damage, deprivation.

**costly** adjective **1** *a costly house* expensive, high-cost, high-priced, valuable, exorbitant, extortionate, extravagant; *inf.* steep. **2** *a costly victory* ruinous, catastrophic, disastrous, damaging, harmful.

**costume** noun **1** *dressed in national costume* style of dress, fashion, clothing, attire, apparel, garb, uniform, livery, habit; *inf.* get-up, gear, togs. **2** *a woman in a green costume* suit, outfit, ensemble.

**coterie** noun clique, set, crowd, circle, gang, club, league, faction.

**cottage** noun cabin, chalet, hut, bungalow, shack.

**couch** noun sofa, settee; ottoman, *chaise longue*, chesterfield, davenport, divan, day bed, love seat.

**council** noun **1** *the governor's council* advisory body, board, board of directors, committee, assembly, panel, trustees. **2** *the council of committee members* conference, conclave, assembly, convocation; meeting, gathering.

**counsel** noun **1** *seek expert counsel* advice, guidance, direction, recommendation, information; opinion, suggestion. **2** *hold counsel with a friend* consultation, discussion, conference, deliberation, dialogue. **3** *counsel handling his case* lawyer, attorney, advocate.

**counsel** verb advise, give guidance/direction, guide, direct, recommend, give one's opinion/suggestions.

**counselor** noun adviser, guidance counselor, director, mentor, confidant, guide.

**count** verb **1** *count the numbers* add up, total, sum up, calculate, compute, enumerate, tally. **2** *counting everyone* include, take into account, embrace. **3** *count himself lucky* consider, regard, hold, judge, rate, deem. **4** *his presence does not count* matter, enter into consideration, be of account, be of consequence, have effect, signify, carry weight, mean anything, amount to anything, make a difference, rate; *inf.* carry (any) weight/clout. **count on** rely on, depend on, lean on, bank on, trust. **count out** exclude, disregard, ignore, pass over.

**count** noun **1** *after the ballot count* counting, enumeration, calculation, computation, tally. **2** *know the calorie count* total, sum total, amount, aggregate, whole.

**countenance** noun **1** *angry countenance* face, features, facial expression, expression, look, appearance, aspect, air, complexion, visage, physiognomy, mien. **2** *not give countenance to the plan* support, backing, encouragement, endorsement, assistance, aid, approval. **3** *lose countenance* composure, calmness, coolness, poise, self-possession, self-control, equanimity.

**counter** verb oppose, resist, rebut, combat, dispute, contradict, retaliate, ward off.

**counteract** verb thwart, frustrate, foil, impede, check, counterbalance, offset, neutralize, annul, negate.

**counterfeit** adjective fake, faked, copied, forged, imitation, feigned, simulated, fraudulent, sham, spurious, bogus, ersatz; *inf.* phony, pseudo.

**counterfeit** noun fake, copy, forgery, reproduction, imitation, fraud, sham; *inf.* phony.

**counterfeit** verb fake, copy, reproduce, imitate, simulate, feign, falsify, sham.

**countermand** verb cancel, annul, revoke, rescind, reverse, repeal, retract.

**counterpart** noun equivalent, equal, opposite number, match, twin, mate, fellow, analog, correlative.

**countless** adjective innumerable, incalculable, immeasurable, endless, limitless, boundless, infinite, inexhaustible, untold, legion, myriad.

**country** noun **1** *countries at war* nation, state, sovereign state, kingdom, realm, people, community, commonwealth. **2** *love for one's country* native land, homeland, fatherland, motherland, mother country. **3** *driving through rough country* terrain, land, territory; region, area, district, part, neighborhood; parts; *inf.* neck of the woods. **4** *the will of the country* people, nation, public, population, populace, citizenry; inhabitants, residents, citizens, electors, voters. **5** *live in the country, not the city* countryside, rural area, farmland, great outdoors; *derog.* backwoods, sticks, wilds, wilderness, middle of nowhere; *inf.* boondocks, boonies.

**coup** noun **1** *pull off quite a coup* feat, masterstroke, deed, accomplishment, stroke, stroke of genius, maneuver, stratagem, stunt. **2** *a military coup* overthrow, seizure of power, coup d'état, revolt, revolution, rebellion, mutiny, insurgence.

**couple** noun pair, duo, twosome, dyad; partners, lovers, husband and wife, cohabitees.

**couple** verb connect, unite, hitch together, join, link, associate, ally.

**courage** noun bravery, valor, gallantry, heroism, fearlessness, intrepidity, lionheartedness, stouteheartedness, pluck, nerve, boldness, daring, mettle; *inf.* spunk, guts, grit, moxie.

**courageous** adjective brave, valiant, valorous, gallant, heroic, fearless, intrepid, lionhearted, plucky, bold, daring, audacious, dauntless.

**courier** noun messenger, carrier, bearer, runner, conveyor, envoy, emissary, harbinger, herald.

**course** noun **1** *the course of history* progression, advance, march, furtherance, unfolding, flow, movement, continuity. **2** *go a bit off course* route, way, track, direction, tack, path, line. **3** *pursue a different course (of action)* method, way, process, procedure, manner, mode of behavior/conduct. **4** *in the course of an hour* duration, passage, lapse, period, term, span. **5** *an English course* course of study, curriculum, program, schedule; classes, lectures, studies. **6** *a course of treatment* sequence, series, system, regimen. **7** *a waterlogged course* racecourse, track, circuit, ground. **in due course** in time, sooner or later, eventually. **of course** naturally, obviously, certainly, definitely, undoubtedly.

**course** verb flow, move, run, rush, surge, gush, race, hurry, speed, charge, dash.

**court** noun **1** *appear before the court* court of law, bench, bar, court of justice, justiciary, tribunal. **2** *the queen's court* royal household, retinue, entourage, train, suite, cortege; attendants. **3** *situated near the queen's court* royal residence, palace, castle, manor, hall, chateau. **4** *paying court to the young lady* attention, homage, deference, suit, wooing, courtship. **5** *walking in the campus court* atrium, esplanade, patio, piazza.

**court** verb **1** *he's courting her sister* woo, pursue, chase, run after, set one's cap for, pay suit to. **2** *the couple are courting* go

out, go steady, date, keep company. **3** *court the manager* curry favor with, pander to, fawn over; *inf.* soft-soap, butter up. **4** *court fame* seek, solicit, ask for, crave. **5** *court disaster* invite, risk, provoke, bring on, elicit.

**courteous** adjective polite, well-mannered, mannerly, civil, chivalrous, gallant, gracious, diplomatic, politic, well-bred, polished, refined, urbane.

**courtesy** noun **1** *have the courtesy to wait* politeness, civility, chivalry, gallantry, good breeding, gentility, graciousness, kindness, consideration, respect, deference, decorum, refinement, elegance; good manners, manners. **2** *your tickets are by courtesy of the management* generosity, benevolence, indulgence, favor.

**courtyard** noun quadrangle, square, cloister, esplanade, court.

**covenant** noun contract, agreement, pledge, promise, commitment, compact, pact, arrangement, treaty, concordat.

**cover** verb **1** *cover the potatoes* place under cover, protect, shield, shelter, conceal, hide, house, secrete, bury. **2** *snow covering the fields* overlay, overspread, blanket, carpet, coat. **3** *girls covered in silk* clothe, attire, outfit, garb, robe, wrap. **4** *cover all the entrances* protect, defend, guard, shield, safeguard. **5** *cover several issues* include, deal with, involve, provide for, embrace, incorporate, refer to, consider, examine. **6** *money to cover expenses* offset, balance, counterbalance. **7** *cover against fire* insure, indemnify, protect. **8** *cover 30 miles* travel, travel/pass over, traverse, cross. **cover for 1** *doctors covering for each other* relieve, substitute for, take over for/from, fill in for. **2** *the thief's sister covering for him* give an alibi, provide an alibi, shield, protect. **cover up** conceal, hide, keep secret, hush up, keep dark, suppress, stonewall; *inf.* whitewash.

**cover** noun **1** *take cover from the storm* protection, shield, shelter, concealment, housing, refuge, sanctuary, haven, hiding place. **2** *the cover for the pot/box* lid, top, cap, covering. **3** *a cover of dust/snow* layer, coating, film, blanket, overlay, carpet. **4** *the business is a cover for spying* front, pretense, façade, pretext, false front, screen, smokescreen, mask, cloak. **5** *under plain cover* envelope, wrapper, package. **6** *protecting the cover for wildlife* undergrowth, woods, shrubbery, thicket, copse.

**coverage** noun **1** *news coverage* reporting, reportage; reports, accounts, articles, pieces, stories. **2** *coverage against fire* insurance, protection, compensation, indemnification, indemnity.

**covering** noun **1** *provide covering for the children* protection, shelter. *See* COVER noun 1. **2** *a covering of dust/snow* layer, coating. *See* COVER noun 3. **3** *the boiler covering* casing, case, sheath, sheathing, jacket, housing.

**covers** noun bedclothes, sheets, blankets; bedcovers, quilts, comforters, duvets, bedspreads.

**covert** adjective secret, concealed, hidden, surreptitious, furtive, stealthy, underground.

**covet** verb desire, want, yearn for, crave, hanker/lust after, thirst for, hunger after, set one's heart on.

**coward** noun poltroon, craven, dastard, recreant, renegade; *inf.* chicken, scaredy-cat, yellowbelly, sissy, big baby.

**cowardly** adjective lily-livered, faint-hearted, chickenhearted, craven, spineless, timorous, timid, shrinking, pusillanimous, dastardly, afraid of one's (own) shadow; *inf.* chicken, yellow, gutless, yellow-bellied.

**cowboy** noun cowhand, cattleman, cowherd, herdsman, drover, stockman, rancher, ranchero; *inf.* cowpuncher, cowpoke, broncobuster, gaucho.

**cower** verb cringe, shrink, flinch, draw back, recoil, crouch, wince, blench, quail, quake, tremble, quiver, grovel.

**coy** adjective coquettish, flirtatious, kittenish, shy, modest, bashful, reticent, shrinking, timid, demure.

**cozen** verb cheat, deceive, beguile, trick, double-cross, swindle, take advantage of, dupe, defraud, fleece, hoodwink.

**cozy** adjective snug, comfortable, warm, homelike, homey, sheltered, secure, safe, at ease; *inf.* comfy, snug as a bug.

**crabby** adjective crabbed, bad-tempered, ill-tempered, ill-natured, ill-humored, cross, cantankerous, crotchety, irritable, touchy, testy, grouchy, snappy, peevish, churlish, surly, sour, morose.

**crack** verb **1** *crack the cup* chip, fracture, fragment, break, split, splinter, snap, cleave. **2** *the rifle cracked* ring out, go bang, pop, snap, crackle, boom, explode, detonate. **3** *crack his head on a beam* hit, bang, bump, strike, knock, smack, whack, thump; *inf.* wallop, clout, clip. **4** *crack under questioning* give way, break down, collapse, go to pieces, lose control, yield, succumb, founder; *inf.* fall/come apart at the seams. **5** *crack the problem* solve, work out, get the answer to, find the solution to, fathom, decipher. **crack up** break down, have a breakdown, go out of one's mind, go mad; *inf.* freak out.

**crack** noun **1** *a crack in the cup/wall* chip, fracture, break. *See* CREVICE. **2** *the crack of the gun* bang, report, pop, snap, crackle, boom, explosion, detonation. **3** *a crack*

*on the head* blow, hit, bang, bump, strike, knock, smack, whack, thump; *inf.* wallop, clout, clip. **4** *another crack at the competition* attempt, try, shot, opportunity; *inf.* go, stab. **5** *laugh at his cracks* wisecrack, joke, quip.

**cradle** verb hold, rock, nestle, shelter, support.

**craft** noun **1** *admire the artist's craft* skill, skillfulness, expertise, expertness, ability, mastery, artistry, art, technique, workmanship, aptitude, dexterity, talent, flair, knack. **2** *use craft to get his way* craftiness, cunning, artifice, guile, subterfuge, stratagem, slyness, wiliness, shrewdness, trickery, duplicity, deceit; wiles, ruses. **3** *take up a new craft* occupation, trade, vocation, pursuit, line. **4** *pilot a craft* vessel, ship, boat, aircraft, plane, spacecraft.

**crafty** adjective cunning, artful, scheming, designing, calculating, wily, sly, devious, guileful, tricky, duplicitous, deceitful, crooked, fraudulent, underhanded.

**crag** noun cliff, bluff, escarpment, scarp, ridge, peak, pinnacle, tor.

**cram** verb **1** *cram clothes into the suitcase* stuff, push, shove, force, pack in, ram down, press, squeeze, jam, crush, compress, compact, condense. **2** *a bus crammed with people* stuff, fill, fill to overflowing, stuff to the gills, fill to the brim, overcrowd.

**cramped** adjective **1** *cramped accommodations* narrow, small, restricted, limited, confined, closed in, hemmed in, tight, crowded, packed, squeezed, jammed in. **2** *cramped handwriting* small, squeezed, crabbed, illegible, unreadable, indecipherable.

**cranky** adjective **1** *a cranky old man | a cranky diet* eccentric, unconventional, odd, peculiar, queer, strange, bizarre, idiosyncratic, quirky; *inf.* funny, wacky. **2** *a cranky teacher* bad-tempered, cross. *See* CRABBY.

**crash** verb **1** *the glass crashed on the floor* smash, batter, dash, shatter, break, disintegrate, shiver, splinter, fracture, fragment. **2** *the cymbals crashed* clash, clang, clank, clatter, bang, boom, thunder, explode. **3** *the business crashed* collapse, fail, fold, fold up, go under, founder, be ruined, cave in; *inf.* go broke/bust. **4** *crash the party* gatecrash, intrude, sneak/slip into.

**crash** noun **1** *the crash of cymbals* clash, clank, clang, clatter, bang, smash, clangor, racket, din, boom, thunder, explosion. **2** *involved in a crash* accident, smash, smash-up, collision, pileup. **3** *the market crash* collapse, failure, bankruptcy, fold, smash, fall, ruin, ruination, downfall, depression, debacle.

88

**crass** adjective boorish, coarse, gross, vulgar, crude, rude, uncouth, unsophisticated, unrefined; insensitive, stupid, dense.

**crave** verb 1 *crave a chocolate bar* long/yearn for, desire, hanker after, need, hunger/thirst for, be dying for, cry out for, lust after, pant for. 2 *crave pardon* plead/beg for, entreat, beseech, petition.

**craven** adjective chickenhearted, lily-livered. See COWARDLY.

**craving** noun longing, yearning, desire, hankering, need, urge, hunger, thirst, lust, appetite, addiction; *inf.* yen.

**crawl** verb creep, go on all fours, move on hands and knees, inch, drag/pull oneself along, drag, slither, squirm, wriggle, writhe, worm one's way, advance slowly/stealthily, sneak.

**craze** noun fad, vogue, trend, fashion, obsession, mania, fixation, fancy, novelty, whim, rage; *inf.* thing, the latest.

**crazy** adjective 1 *a crazy person* crazed, of unsound mind, insane, mad, mad as a hatter, mad as a March hare, lunatic, wild, unbalanced, demented, deranged, berserk, unhinged, touched, maniacal, delirious, out of one's mind/head; *inf.* cracked, daft, bats, batty, loony, loopy, screwy, flaky, nuts, nutty, nutty as a fruit cake, cuckoo, bonkers, mental, not all there, out to lunch, off one's nut/rocker, around/round the bend. 2 *a crazy idea* absurd, idiotic, stupid, silly, ridiculous, foolish, peculiar, odd, strange, queer, weird, eccentric, bizarre, fantastic, outrageous, wild, ludicrous, inane, puerile, impracticable, senseless, unworkable, foolhardy, unrealistic, unwise, imprudent, ill-conceived, preposterous; *inf.* screwy, screwball, harebrained, cockeyed, half-baked. **crazy about** *crazy about opera* enthusiastic about, mad about, wild about, avid about, keen about, infatuated with, passionate about, smitten with/by, fanatical about, devoted to, fond/enamored of, zealous about/for, fervent, fervid about, excited about; *inf.* nuts about/on.

**creak** verb squeak, screech, squeal, groan, grate, grind, jar, rasp, scrape, scratch.

**cream** noun 1 *beauty/antiseptic cream* lotion, emulsion, emollient, paste; cosmetic, ointment, salve, unguent, liniment. 2 *the cream of the college* best/choice part, flower, elite, pick, prime, crème de la crème.

**create** verb 1 *create a new environment* generate, originate, invent, initiate, engender, produce, design, devise, make, frame, fabricate, build, construct, erect, develop, shape, form, mold, forge, concoct, hatch. 2 *create a good impression* produce, make, result in, cause.

**creation** noun 1 *the creation of a new environment* generation, origination, invention, initiation, inception, design, devising, formation, production, fabrication, building, shaping, hatching. 2 *everything in creation* the world, the living/natural world, the universe, the cosmos, nature, life; all living things. 3 *the poet's creation* work, work of art, achievement, production, opus, invention, handiwork.

**creative** adjective inventive, imaginative, original, artistic, inspired, visionary, talented, gifted, resourceful, ingenious, clever, productive, fertile.

**creator** noun *the creator of the series* author, inventor, originator, initiator, maker, designer, producer, architect, prime mover, begetter, generator.

**creature** noun living thing/entity, being; animal, beast; person, human being, human, individual, character, fellow, soul, mortal; *inf.* critter, body.

**credentials** plural noun testimonial, proof of identity/qualifications, evidence, documentation, references.

**credibility** noun 1 *the credibility of the story* plausibility, tenability. 2 *the government lacks credibility* trustworthiness, reliability, dependability, integrity.

**credible** adjective 1 *a scarcely credible story* believable, conceivable, imaginable, plausible, tenable. 2 *the more credible party* acceptable, trustworthy, reliable, dependable.

**credit** noun 1 *receive credit for his performance* acknowledgment, tribute, kudos, glory, recognition, regard, respect, merit; thanks. 2 *he gained credit in the city* reputation, prestige, influence, standing, status, regard, esteem; *inf.* clout. 3 *a credit to the town* source of honor/pride, feather in the cap, asset, boast, glory. 4 *the story gaining credit* belief, believability, credence, faith, trust, reliability, reliance, confidence. **on credit** in installments, by deferred payment, on account.

**credulous** adjective gullible, naïve, green, dupable, deceivable, unsuspicious, unskeptical, uncritical; *inf.* wet behind the ears.

**creed** noun beliefs, principles, rules, articles of faith, maxims.

**creek** noun stream, brook, rivulet, small river, channel; *inf.* crick.

**creep** verb 1 *creeping along the ground* go on all fours, move on hands and knees. See CRAWL. 2 *creep up on them* move stealthily, steal, sneak, tiptoe, approach unnoticed, slink, skulk.

**creepy** adjective horrifying, horrific, frightening, terrifying, hair-raising, disturbing, eerie, sinister, weird, nightmarish, macabre, menacing, ominous, threatening, disgusting, repellent, repulsive, revolting; *inf.* scary.

**crest** noun **1** *a cock's crest* | *the helmet crest* cockscomb, comb, tuft, plume, topknot, tassel, mane, panache. **2** *the crest of the hill* summit, top, pinnacle, peak, crown, apex, ridge. **3** *the club crest* regalia, insignia, badge, emblem, device, coat of arms.

**crestfallen** adjective downcast, dejected, depressed, glum, downhearted, disheartened, discouraged, dispirited, disappointed, disconsolate, in the doldrums, down in the dumps.

**crevice** noun fissure, cleft, chink, crack, cranny, split, rift, slit, gash, rent, fracture, opening, gap, hole, interstice.

**crew** noun **1** *the camera crew* team, company, party, working party, gang, squad, force, corps. **2** *that crew over there* crowd, lot, gang, troop, band, group, bunch, set.

**crime** noun **1** *convicted of the crime* offense, misdemeanor, misdeed, wrong, felony, violation, transgression, trespass. **2** *a crime against humanity* sin, evil, evil action, wrong, wrongdoing, vice, iniquity. **3** *crime is on the increase* lawbreaking, delinquency, wrongdoing, villainy, malefaction, illegality, misconduct, corruption.

**criminal** adjective **1** *a criminal act* unlawful, illegal, lawbreaking, illicit, lawless, felonious, indictable, delinquent, culpable, wrong, villainous, corrupt, evil, wicked, iniquitous, nefarious; *inf.* crooked. **2** *a criminal waste of resources* deplorable, scandalous, shameful, reprehensible, senseless, foolish, ridiculous, sinful, immoral.

**criminal** noun lawbreaker, offender, wrongdoer, felon, delinquent, miscreant, malefactor, culprit, villain, gangster, bandit, transgressor, sinner, trespasser; *inf.* crook, con, jailbird, perp.

**cringe** verb cower, shrink, draw back, quail, flinch, recoil, start, shy, blench, dodge, duck, crouch, wince, tremble, quiver, shake.

**cripple** verb **1** *the accident crippled him* make lame, disable, incapacitate, debilitate, impair, maim, enfeeble, paralyze. **2** *businesses crippled by the recession* injure, ruin, destroy, weaken, impair, hamstring, hamper, impede, cramp, spoil.

**crippled** adjective lame, disabled, incapacitated, physically impaired/handicapped, deformed; paralyzed, immobilized.

**crisis** noun **1** *the crisis of the fever* | *reach a crisis* turning point, critical/decisive point, crux, climax, culmination, height, moment of truth, zero hour; *inf.* crunch. **2** *a financial crisis* extremity, predicament, plight, mess, trouble, difficulty, dilemma, quandary, exigency; dire straits; *inf.* fix, pickle, scrape.

**crisp** adjective **1** *crisp toast* brittle, crispy, crumbly, crunchy, breakable. **2** *crisp lettuce* firm, fresh, unwilted, unwithered. **3** *crisp weather* brisk, bracing, fresh, refreshing, invigorating, dry, cool, chilly. **4** *a crisp account* brief, terse, succinct, concise, short, incisive, clear, pithy. **5** *a crisp manner* brisk, vigorous, decisive. **6** *a crisp appearance* clean-cut, neat, smart, spruce, trim, well-groomed; *inf.* snappy.

**criterion** noun measure, gauge, scale, yardstick, standard, norm, benchmark, touchstone, barometer, model, exemplar.

**critic** noun **1** *theater critics* reviewer, commentator, pundit, arbiter, evaluator, analyst, judge. **2** *answer his critics* faultfinder, attacker, detractor, backbiter; *inf.* nitpicker.

**critical** adjective **1** *a critical point in history* crucial, deciding, decisive, climacteric, pivotal, important, momentous, high-priority, urgent, pressing, compelling. **2** *in a critical condition* dangerous, grave, serious, risky, perilous, hazardous, touch-and-go, uncertain, precarious; *inf.* chancy. **3** *a critical attitude* faultfinding, captious, censorious, carping, quibbling, judgmental, hypercritical; *inf.* nitpicking. **4** *a critical essay* evaluative, analytic, interpretative, expository, commentative, explanatory.

**criticism** noun **1** *actions receiving criticism* faultfinding, censure, reproof, condemnation, disapproval, disparagement, captiousness, carping; *inf.* nitpicking, flak, bad press, bad notices, knocking, panning, slamming. **2** *studying literary criticism* evaluation, comment, assessment, appreciation, appraisal, interpretation, explanation, explication, elucidation, annotation. **3** *read the criticism* review, notice, commentary, critique, analysis, appraisal.

**criticize** verb find fault with, censure, denounce, blame, condemn, pick holes in, disapprove of, disparage, carp at, cavil at, excoriate; *inf.* nitpick, hand out brickbats, give flak to, knock, pan, slam.

**critique** noun evaluation, commentary. See CRITICISM 2, 3.

**crony** noun friend, companion, chum, comrade, associate, confederate; *inf.* pal, buddy.

**crook** noun **1** *crooks imprisoned* thief, robber, swindler, cheat, racketeer; *inf.* shark, con man. **2** *the crook of one's arm* bend, curve, curvature, angle, bow.

**crooked** adjective **1** *a crooked branch/road* bent, curved, twisted, contorted, warped, irregular, angled, bowed, hooked, flexed, winding, twisting. **2** *a crooked back* deformed, misshapen, disfigured, crippled. **3** *the picture is crooked* tilted, angled, slanted, aslant, slanting, sloping, askew, awry, to one side, off-center, lopsided, uneven, asymmetrical. **4** *a crooked politician/deal* criminal, dishonest, corrupt, dishonorable, unscrupulous, unprincipled, fraudulent, illegal, unlawful, underhanded; *inf.* shady.

**crop** noun **1** *the apple crop* harvest, yield, produce, vintage, gathering, reaping, gleaning, garnering. **2** *the year's crop of students* batch, lot, collection, assortment, selection, supply.

**crop** verb cut short, lop. *See* CUT verb 4.
**crop up** happen, occur, arise, turn up, spring up, emerge, appear, come to pass.

**cross** noun **1** *the sign of the cross* crucifix, rood. **2** *a cross to bear* trouble, worry, burden, trial, disaster; tribulation, affliction, misfortune, adversity, misery, woe, pain, suffering. **3** *a cross between two breeds/types* crossbreed, hybrid, mixture, amalgam, blend, combination, mongrel, cur.

**cross** verb **1** *the bridge crossing the river* span, extend/stretch across, pass over, bridge, ford. **2** *cross the road* go/travel across, cut across, traverse. **3** *the roads/lines crossed there* intersect, meet, join, converge, crisscross, interweave, intertwine. **4** *hates being crossed* oppose, resist, thwart, frustrate, deny, contradict. **5** *cross two species* crossbreed, interbreed, cross-fertilize, cross-pollinate, hybridize, mix, blend. **cross out** delete, strike out, blue-pencil, cancel, eliminate, obliterate.

**cross** adjective **1** *she was cross at/with the children* angry, annoyed, irritated, in a bad mood, peeved, vexed, upset, piqued, out of humor. **2** *a cross old woman* irritable, short-tempered, bad-tempered, ill-humored, surly, churlish, disagreeable, irascible, touchy, snappish, peevish, petulant, fractious, crotchety, grouchy, grumpy, querulous, cantankerous, testy, captious, splenetic, waspish. **3** *cross purposes* contrary, opposing, opposite, adverse, unfavorable.

**crouch** verb squat, bend, bend down, hunker, stoop, hunch over, cower, cringe.

**crow** verb boast, brag, trumpet, gloat, show off, swagger, bluster, strut; *inf.* blow one's own horn.

**crowd** noun **1** *a crowd of people* throng, horde, mob, rabble, mass, multitude, host, army, herd, flock, drove, swarm, pack, flood, collection, company, gathering, assembly, assemblage. **2** *nonconformists don't follow the crowd* majority, multitude, common people, populace, general public, mob, rank and file, hoi polloi, proletariat; riff-raff; masses. **3** *the late-night crowd* group, set, lot, gang, bunch, clique. **4** *the show played to a capacity crowd* gate, house, turnout, audience, attendance; spectators, listeners, viewers.

**crowd** verb **1** *crowd around the teacher* gather, cluster, congregate, flock, swarm, throng, huddle. **2** *people crowding into the*

hall push, shove, thrust forward, elbow, squeeze. **3** *tourists crowding the streets* throng, pack, fill, overfill, congest. **4** *crowd people into the trains* pack, squeeze, cram, jam, stuff, pile.

**crowded** adjective full, overfull, busy, overflowing, packed, jam-packed, crushed, cramped, congested, teeming, swarming, thronged, populous, mobbed.

**crown** noun **1** *the king's crown* diadem, coronet, coronal, tiara. **2** *the champion wins the crown* prize, trophy; honor, distinction, glory, kudos; laurels. **3** *the power of the Crown* monarchy, monarch, sovereignty, sovereign, king, queen, emperor, empress. **4** *the crown of the hill* top, crest, summit, apex, head, tip, pinnacle. **5** *the crown of his achievements* height, culmination, pinnacle, zenith, acme.

**crown** verb **1** *crown the queen* invest, inaugurate, induct, install. **2** *crown his career* cap, round off, be the culmination/climax of, consummate, top off, complete, perfect. **3** *the steeple crowning the church* top, surmount, overtop.

**crucial** adjective determining, central, essential, vital. *See* CRITICAL 1.

**crude** adjective **1** *crude oil/flour* raw, unrefined, natural, coarse, unprocessed. **2** *a crude sculpture/dwelling* rudimentary, primitive, rough, rough-hewn, makeshift, unfinished, unpolished, unformed, undeveloped, rude. **3** *a crude manner* coarse, vulgar, rude, uncouth, indelicate, boorish, crass, tasteless.

**cruel** adjective **1** *a cruel dictator* savage, brutal, inhuman, barbarous, vicious, ferocious, fierce, evil, fiendish, callous, cold-blooded, sadistic, ruthless, merciless, pitiless, unfeeling, heartless, inhumane, severe, harsh, stern. **2** *a cruel stroke of fate* unkind, painful, distressing, harrowing, harsh, grim, heartless.

**cruelty** noun **1** *the cruelty of the dictator* savageness, savagery, brutality, inhumanity, viciousness, ferocity, fierceness, evil, callousness, sadism, ruthlessness, pitilessness, severity, harshness. **2** *the cruelty of the blow* unkindness, painfulness, grimness, heartlessness.

**crumb** noun bit, fragment, morsel, particle, grain, atom, speck, scrap, shred, sliver, mite.

**crumble** verb **1** *crumble the crackers* break up, crush, pulverize, pound, grind, powder. **2** *the empire was crumbling* disintegrate, fall to pieces, fall apart, collapse, decay, deteriorate, degenerate, go to rack and ruin, rot, rot away, molder, perish, vanish, fade away.

**crunch** verb **1** *crunching carrots* munch, champ, chomp, gnaw, masticate. **2** *crunch* *the snow* crush, grind, pulverize, pound, smash.

**crusade** noun campaign, war, drive, push, struggle, cause, movement.

**crusade** verb campaign, fight, work, do battle, take up arms.

**crusader** noun campaigner, fighter, battler, champion, advocate, reformer.

**crush** verb 1 *crush the grapes* squash, squeeze, mash, press, press down, compress, bruise. 2 *crush the material* crease, crumple, rumple, wrinkle, crinkle. 3 *crush the stones* smash, shatter, pound, pulverize, grind, crumble, crunch. 4 *crush the rebellion* put down, quell, quash, suppress, subdue, overcome, overwhelm, defeat, conquer. 5 *crushed by his criticism* mortify, humiliate, abash, quash, shame, chagrin; *inf.* put down. 6 *crush her in his arms* embrace, enfold, hug.

**cry** verb 1 *babies crying* weep, sob, wail, snivel, blubber, whimper, whine, bawl, howl. 2 *he cried out her name* call out, exclaim, yell, scream, screech, bawl, shout, bellow, howl.

**cry** noun call, exclamation, scream, screech, yell, shout, bellow, howl. **cries** weeping, sobbing, sniveling, blubbering, wailing, lamenting, lamentation; sobs, wails, howls.

**cuddle** verb 1 *cuddling his wife* hug, embrace, enfold, clasp. 2 *cuddling by the fire* embrace, pet, fondle; *inf.* neck, smooch. 3 *cuddle (up) in bed* snuggle, nestle, curl up.

**cuddly** adjective cuddlesome, huggable, warm, soft.

**cue** noun 1 *"away" is your cue* catchword, keyword, prompt, reminder. 2 *your cue to begin* signal, sign, indication, hint, suggestion, intimation.

**cuff** noun **off the cuff** impromptu, ad lib, extempore, extemporaneous, extemporaneously, off the top of one's head, unrehearsed, improvised, offhand.

**culmination** noun high point, consummation, completion, close. *See* CLIMAX.

**culpable** adjective at fault, in the wrong, guilty, answerable, blameworthy, blamable, to blame, censurable, reproachable, reprovable.

**culprit** noun guilty party, wrongdoer, evildoer, lawbreaker, criminal, miscreant, delinquent, reprobate, transgressor, felon, sinner, malefactor; *inf.* bad guy.

**cult** noun 1 *belong to a secretive cult* sect, religion, faith, belief, persuasion, faction, clique. 2 *the rap music cult* craze, fashion, fad; admiration, devotion, obsession, homage, worship, idolization.

**cultivate** verb 1 *cultivate the fields* till, farm, work, plow, dig, prepare, fertilize. 2 *cultivate a crop* plant, raise, tend, bring

on, produce. 3 *cultivate the mind* culture, educate, train, civilize, enlighten, enrich, improve, better, develop, refine, polish. 4 *cultivate a friendship* pursue, foster, promote, encourage, support.

**cultivated** adjective cultured, educated, civilized, enlightened, refined, polished, sophisticated, discerning, discriminating, urbane.

**cultural** adjective 1 *cultural interests* artistic, enlightening, enriching, broadening, edifying, civilizing, elevating. 2 *cultural differences* lifestyle, ethnic, folk, racial.

**culture** noun 1 *a woman of culture* cultivation, education, enlightenment, accomplishment, edification, erudition, refinement, polish, sophistication, urbanity, discernment, discrimination, good taste, taste, breeding, politeness, gentility, *savoir faire*. 2 *belong to a different culture* civilization, way of life, lifestyle; customs, habits, ways, mores.

**cultured** adjective cultivated, artistic, educated, enlightened, learned, knowledgeable, intellectual, highbrow, scholarly, well-informed, well-read, erudite, accomplished, well-versed, refined, genteel, polished, sophisticated, urbane.

**cumbersome** adjective 1 *cumbersome packages* awkward, unwieldy, bulky, hefty, clumsy, unmanageable, burdensome, inconvenient. 2 *cumbersome procedures* slow, slow-moving, inefficient, unwieldy.

**cumulative** adjective accumulative, increasing, growing, enlarging, accruing, snowballing.

**cunning** adjective 1 *a cunning thief* crafty, devious, deceitful, wily, sly, shifty, artful, foxy, tricky, guileful, shrewd, astute, sharp, knowing, subtle, Machiavellian. 2 *a cunning device/artist* clever, ingenious, resourceful, inventive, imaginative.

**cunning** noun 1 *the cunning of the thief* craftiness, deviousness, deceitfulness, deceit, wiliness, slyness, artfulness, foxiness, trickery, guile, shrewdness, astuteness. 2 *admire the cunning of the process/artist* cleverness, ingenuity, resourcefulness, inventiveness, imaginativeness, skill, dexterity, ability, capability.

**curb** verb restrain, check, control, constrain, contain, hold back, bite back, repress, suppress, moderate, dampen, impede, retard, subdue, bridle.

**curb** noun *curbs on expenditure* restraint, check, control, constraint, limitation, limit, damper, brake, rein.

**cure** noun remedy, curative, medicine, cure-all, panacea, restorative, corrective, antidote, nostrum; treatment, therapy.

**cure** verb 1 *cure the patient* heal, restore to health, rehabilitate, treat. 2 *cure*

# curiosity · cut

92

the disease remedy, doctor, fix, repair.
**3** *cure meat* preserve, smoke, salt, dry,
pickle.

**curiosity** noun **1** *curiosity about the past*
inquisitiveness, interest, questioning, prying, snooping; *inf.* nosiness. **2** *the curiosities
on display* novelty, oddity, phenomenon,
rarity, wonder, marvel, sight, spectacle.

**curious** adjective **1** *curious to know the facts*
inquisitive, inquiring, interested, investigating, searching, questioning. **2** *curious about others' affairs* prying, snooping,
meddling, meddlesome, interfering, intrusive; *inf.* nosy, snoopy. **3** *a curious
site* strange, unusual, rare, odd, peculiar, extraordinary, remarkable, singular,
novel, queer, bizarre, unconventional,
unorthodox, weird, freakish, marvelous,
prodigious, exotic, mysterious.

**curl** verb **1** *the smoke curled upward* spiral,
coil, twist, twist and turn, wind, curve,
bend, loop, twirl, wreathe, meander, snake,
corkscrew. **2** *curl the hair* crimp, crinkle,
kink, frizz, wave.

**curl** noun **1** *put curls in one's hair* kink,
ringlet, coil, wave, curlicue, corkscrew.
**2** *curls of smoke* spiral, coil, twist, whorl,
helix.

**currency** noun **1** *foreign currency* money,
legal tender, cash, coinage, coin, specie, paper money; coins, bank notes,
notes, bills. **2** *story gaining currency* prevalence, acceptance, popularity, vogue, circulation.

**current** adjective **1** *current fashions* present, present-day, contemporary, ongoing,
extant, existing, popular, modern, up-to-
date, up-to-the-minute. **2** *ideas no longer
current* prevalent, accepted, in circulation, going around, common, popular,
widespread.

**current** noun **1** *current of air* steady flow,
draft, updraft, downdraft, wind, thermal.
**2** *swimmers swept away by the current* stream,
tide, channel. **3** *disturb the even current
of their life* course, flow, progression. **4**
*currents of opinion* trend, drift, tendency,
tenor.

**curse** noun **1** *a voodoo curse* malediction, evil eye, execration, imprecation,
anathema, damnation, excommunication;
*inf.* jinx. **2** *angrily uttering curses* oath,
swearword, expletive, profanity, obscenity; swearing, blasphemy; *inf.* cussword.
**3** *the curse of poverty* evil, affliction, burden, cross, bane, scourge, plague, torment.

**curse** verb **1** *the sorcerer cursed them* accurse,
put the evil eye on, execrate, imprecate,
anathematize, damn, excommunicate; *inf.*
put a jinx on, jinx. **2** *curse at the policeman*
swear, blaspheme; *inf.* cuss. **3** *poverty*

*cursed his childhood* blight, afflict, trouble,
beset, plague, torment.

**curt** adjective abrupt, brusque, blunt, short-
spoken, short, snappy, snappish, sharp,
crisp, tart, rude, impolite, unceremonious,
brief, concise.

**curtail** verb reduce, cut short, truncate,
shorten, abbreviate. *See* CUT verb 6.

**curtain** noun **1** *hang curtains* drape, dra-
pery, window hanging; screen, blind. **2**
*a curtain of secrecy* screen, cover, shield,
cloak, veil.

**curve** noun arc, bend, arch, turn, bow,
loop, hook, half moon, crescent.

**curve** verb bend, arc, arch, bow, turn,
inflect, swerve, twist, wind, hook, loop,
spiral, coil.

**cushion** noun pillow, throw pillow, bolster,
pad; hassock, mat, beanbag.

**cushion** verb **1** *cushion her head* pillow,
bolster, cradle, support, prop up. **2**
*cushion the blow* soften, lessen, diminish,
mitigate, allay, deaden, muffle, stifle. **3**
*cushion the child from reality* protect, shield,
buttress.

**custody** noun **1** *in the custody of his mother*
guardianship, wardship, trusteeship,
charge, care, keeping, keep, safekeeping,
protection, guidance, supervision. **2** *sus-
pects in custody* imprisonment, detention,
confinement, incarceration.

**custom** noun **1** *it was their custom to leave
early* habit, practice, routine, way, wont,
policy, rule. **2** *local customs* practice,
convention, ritual, procedure, ceremony,
form, usage, observance, way, fashion,
mode, style.

**customary** adjective accustomed, usual,
regular, common, habitual, traditional,
routine, fixed, set, established, everyday.

**customer** noun patron, client, buyer, purchaser, shopper, consumer; clientele; *inf.*
regular.

**cut** verb **1** *cut his finger/throat* gash, slash,
lacerate, slit, nick, notch, pierce, penetrate, wound, lance, incise, score. **2** *cut
the logs/meat* chop, sever, divide, cleave,
carve, slice. **3** *cut a key/gem* shape, fashion,
form, mold, chisel, carve, sculpt, sculpture, chip away, whittle, engrave, incise,
score. **4** *cut their hair | cut the hedge/grass*
trim, clip, snip, crop, prune, dock, shear,
shave, pare, mow. **5** *cut some flowers* detach, gather, harvest, reap. **6** *cut expendi-
tures* reduce, curtail, curb, retrench, cut
back/down on, decrease, lessen, lower,
diminish, contract, ease up on, prune,
slash, slim down, slenderize, economize
on. **7** *cut the text* shorten, abridge, condense, abbreviate, summarize, epitomize.
**8** *cut the unsuitable parts* delete, edit out,

blue-pencil, excise. **9** *his behavior cut me* hurt, offend, wound, distress, grieve, pain, sting. **10** *his old friend cut him* shun, ignore, snub, spurn, give the cold shoulder to. **11** *cut the engine* stop, halt, turn off, switch off. **12** *cut a record/tape* record, put on disk/tape, make a tape of, tape-record. **cut across** *cut across national prejudices* transcend, go beyond, rise above. **cut down 1** *cut down a tree* fell, saw down, hew, chop/hack down. **2** *cut down in his prime* kill, slay, slaughter, massacre, mow down, dispatch. **cut in** *cut in on a conversation* interrupt, interpose, break in, intervene, intrude; *inf.* butt in. **cut off 1** *cut off supplies/communication* break off, disconnect, interrupt, suspend, discontinue, halt, stop. **2** *cut off from the town by snow* isolate, separate, sever. **3** *cut off without a penny* disinherit, disown, renounce. **cut out 1** *cut out eating chocolate* give up, refrain from, stop, cease. **2** *cut out the middleman* leave out, omit, eliminate, exclude, do away with. **3** *the engine cut out* stop, malfunction. **4** *not cut out for teaching* suit, equip/design for. **cut short** *cut short a vacation* interrupt, break off, leave unfinished, truncate, abort. **cut up** verb **1** *cut up in a street fight* slash, knife, stab, lacerate, wound, injure. **2** *the teacher really cut up his essay/friend* criticize, ridicule, find fault with, tear to pieces/shreds, take apart.

**cut** noun **1** *a cut on his finger* gash, slash, laceration, incision, slit. **2** *a cut in expenditure/salary* cutback, decrease, reduction, lessening, curtailment, retrenchment, contraction. **3** *I want my cut* share, portion, proportion.

**cutthroat** adjective **1** *a cutthroat attack* murderous, death-dealing, homicidal, savage, violent, bloody, bloodthirsty, fierce, ferocious, barbarous, cruel. **2** *a cutthroat business* ruthless, merciless, pitiless, unfeeling, relentless, dog-eat-dog, fiercely competitive.

**cutting** adjective **1** *a cutting wind* biting, bitter, piercing, raw, keen, penetrating, stinging, sharp, chill, chilling, icy. **2** *a cutting remark* hurtful, wounding, caustic, acid, barbed, acrimonious, trenchant, mordant, scathing.

**cycle** noun **1** *occur in cycles* rotation, round, revolution. **2** *compare the completed cycles* series, sequence, succession, run.

**cynic** noun pessimist, skeptic, scoffer, doubter, doubting Thomas, misanthrope.

**cynical** adjective pessimistic, skeptical, scoffing, doubting, unbelieving, disbelieving, distrustful, suspicious, misanthropic, critical, sardonic.

**cynicism** noun pessimism, skepticism, scoffing, doubt, unbelief, disbelief, distrust, suspicion, misanthropy.

# *Dd*

**dab** verb pat, press, touch, blot, smudge.

**dab** noun *add a dab of paint/butter* touch, bit, spot, drop, dash, tinge, suggestion, hint, modicum.

**dabble** verb **dabble in** *dabble in politics* toy with, dip into, flirt with, trifle with, play with, fiddle with.

**daft** adjective silly, absurd, stupid, foolish, idiotic, fatuous, ridiculous, ludicrous, asinine, simple, simpleminded, feebleminded, slow-witted; crazy, insane, mad.

**dagger** noun stiletto, dirk, bayonet, knife, blade.

**dainty** adjective **1** *dainty china figures* petite, neat, delicate, exquisite, refined, tasteful, fine, elegant, graceful, pretty. **2** *a dainty morsel* tasty, delicious, appetizing, choice, delectable, luscious. **3** *a dainty eater* particular, discriminating, fastidious, fussy, choosy, finicky, refined.

**dam** noun barricade, barrier, embankment, obstruction, hindrance.

**damage** verb harm, injure, hurt, impair, abuse, spoil, mar, deface, defile, vandalize.

**damage** noun harm, injury, hurt, impairment, abuse, defacement, detriment, vandalism, destruction, ruin, loss.

**damages** plural noun *receive damages from the court* compensation, indemnity, reparation, restitution.

**damn** verb **1** *damned for his blasphemy* curse, doom, execrate, imprecate, excommunicate, anathematize. **2** *damned by the neighbors/critics* condemn, censure, criticize, castigate, denounce, attack, flay; *inf.* pan, slam.

**damn** interjection *inf.* darn, rats, shoot.

**damned** adjective **1** *damned souls* cursed, accursed, doomed, lost, condemned, exe-

crated, excommunicated, anathematized.
**2** *this damned machine/weather* annoying,
confounded, nasty, hateful, detestable,
odious.

**damp** adjective wettish, moist, dank, soggy,
rainy, drizzly, humid, clammy, muggy,
misty, foggy.

**dampen** verb **1** *dampen the clothes/atmos-
phere* wet, moisten, humidify. **2** *dampen
their enthusiasm* discourage, dull, dash,
check, curb, restrain, stifle, inhibit, deter.

**dampness** noun damp, wetness, moisture,
dankness.

**dance** verb move/sway to music, twirl,
pirouette; caper, skip, prance, hop, frolic,
gambol, jump, jig, romp, bounce, whirl,
spin.

**danger** noun risk, peril, hazard, jeopardy,
precariousness, menace, threat.

**dangerous** adjective risky, perilous, hazardous, chancy, precarious, insecure, unsound, unsafe; menacing, threatening,
alarming, ominous, treacherous.

**dangle** verb **1** *keys dangling from her waist*
hang, hang down, swing. **2** *dangle the keys*
swing, wave, brandish, flourish, flaunt.

**dare** verb **1** *dare to go* have the courage, be
brave enough, have the nerve, risk, haz-
ard, venture. **2** *dare him to go* challenge,
provoke, goad, taunt.

**daredevil** adjective daring, adventurous,
bold, audacious, courageous, intrepid, fearless, rash, heedless, foolhardy, impetuous,
incautious.

**daredevil** noun adventurer, stunt man,
exhibitionist; *inf.* show-off.

**daring** adjective bold, adventurous, brave,
courageous, audacious, intrepid, fearless,
rash, reckless.

**daring** noun *the daring of the explorers* bravery, courage, valor, audacity, nerve, pluck,
temerity; *inf.* guts.

**dark** adjective **1** *a dark night* black, pitch-
black, inky, unlit, unlighted, dim, indistinct, shadowy, shady, murky, overcast,
sunless. **2** *dark thoughts* dismal, gloomy,
somber, bleak, drab, dreary, depressed, dejected, melancholy, grave, morose, mournful, doleful. **3** *a dark mood* angry, moody,
brooding, sullen, dour, glum, morose,
sulky, frowning, scowling, glowering, forbidding, threatening, ominous. **4** *dark
deeds* evil, wicked, sinful, villainous, vile,
base, foul, horrible, atrocious, abominable, nefarious, sinister. **5** *a dark secret*
concealed, hidden, veiled, mysterious.

**dark** noun **1** *sitting in the dark* darkness,
blackness, gloom, murkiness, shade. **2**
*when dark comes* night, nighttime, dead of
night, evening, twilight.

**darken** verb **1** *the sky darkened* grow
dark/darker, blacken, cloud over, dim,
grow dim. **2** *darken the room* make dim,
shade. **3** *darken one's skin* tan, blacken.
**4** *his mood/face darkened* blacken, grow
angry, become gloomy, sadden.

**darkness** noun blackness, gloom; night.
*See* DARK noun.

**darling** noun dear, dearest, dear one, love,
sweetheart, beloved, honey, charmer,
favorite, pet; *inf.* sweetie.

**darling** adjective **1** *his darling wife* dear, beloved, adored, cherished, treasured, precious. **2** *a darling little girl* adorable, sweet,
lovely, charming, enchanting; *inf.* cute.

**dart** noun **1** *throwing a poisoned dart* arrow,
barb. **2** *make a sudden dart* dash, rush,
run, bolt, bound, spring, leap, start.

**dart** verb **1** *dart into the bushes* dash, rush,
bolt, sprint, tear, run, bound, spring,
leap, start; *inf.* scoot. **2** *dart an angry
look* throw, cast, shoot, send, fling, toss,
flash, hurl.

**dash** noun **1** *make a dash for freedom* rush,
bolt, run, race, flight, dart, sprint, spurt.
**2** *a dash of salt* bit, drop, pinch, sprinkling,
splash, grain, trace, suggestion.

**dash** verb **1** *dash into the road* rush, hurry,
hasten, bolt, run, race, fly, dart, sprint,
tear. **2** *waves dashing against the shore*
strike, beat, break, crash, smash, batter.
**3** *dash the plate to the floor* smash, crash,
throw, hurl, fling, slam, cast. **4** *dash her
hopes* shatter, destroy, ruin, spoil, frustrate,
thwart.

**dashing** adjective debonair, stylish, smart,
jaunty, sporty, elegant, fashionable, showy,
flamboyant; gallant, bold, daring.

**data** plural noun facts, figures, statistics,
details; information, material, input.

**date** noun **1** *a lunch date* appointment, engagement, meeting, rendezvous, tryst. **2**
*who is his date?* partner, escort, girlfriend,
boyfriend, beau; *inf.* steady. **to date** so
far, as of now, up to now.

**date** verb *dating the girl next door* go out
with, go with, take out; *inf.* go steady with.

**dated** adjective out-of-date, outdated, old-
fashioned, outmoded, passé.

**daub** verb smear, plaster, smudge, spatter, slap.

**daunt** verb intimidate, frighten, scare,
alarm, dismay, disconcert, unnerve, discourage, dishearten, dispirit, deter, put off.

**dawdle** verb go slowly, loiter, dally, linger,
delay, idle; *inf.* dilly-dally.

**dawn** noun **1** *get up at dawn* daybreak,
break of day, sunrise, first light, sunup.

**2** *the dawn of civilization* dawning, beginning, birth, start, rise, emergence, origin, inception, genesis, outset, onset, advent, unfolding.

**dawn** verb *day dawned* begin, break, lighten, brighten. **dawn on** *the truth suddenly dawned on them* occur to, strike, hit.

**day** noun **1** *when day dawns* daytime, daylight hours, broad daylight. **2** *in this modern day* period, time, age, era, epoch, generation. **3** *the steam train has had its day* prime, heyday, peak, zenith, ascendancy. **day after day** *raining day after day* continuously, relentlessly, persistently, ceaselessly, regularly. **day by day** *grow bigger day by day* daily, gradually, steadily, progressively.

**daybreak** noun break of day, sunrise. *See* DAWN noun 1.

**daydream** noun reverie, fantasy, fancy, hallucination; dream, wishful thinking; castles in the air.

**daydream** verb dream, muse, fantasize, hallucinate; *inf.* space.

**daylight** noun light of day, natural light, sunlight, daytime, broad daylight; dawn, daybreak, sunrise. **see daylight** understand, comprehend, see the light; *inf.* catch on, get the picture.

**daze** verb stun, stupefy, shock, confuse, bewilder, numb, paralyze; amaze, astonish, astound, dumbfound.

**daze** noun stupor, state of shock; confusion, bewilderment, distraction, numbness.

**dazzle** verb daze, overpower, overwhelm, awe, hypnotize, amaze, astonish; *inf.* bowl over, take one's breath away.

**dead** adjective **1** *the dead man/flower* deceased, late, departed, lifeless, expired, extinct. **2** *dead matter* inanimate, lifeless. **3** *a dead language* obsolete, outmoded, outdated, extinct, passé, discontinued. **4** *dead fingers* numb, unfeeling, paralyzed. **5** *a dead time of day* dull, boring, tedious, tiresome, uneventful, humdrum. **6** *feeling dead* tired, exhausted, worn out, fatigued, spent; *inf.* pooped.

**dead** adverb *dead right/serious/tired* completely, absolutely, totally, entirely, utterly, thoroughly, categorically.

**deaden** verb blunt, dull, muffle, weaken, diminish, reduce, suppress, moderate, abate, mitigate, alleviate, smother, stifle, numb, mute, desensitize, anesthetize.

**deadlock** noun stalemate, impasse, standstill, stand-off, tie, draw.

**deadly** adjective fatal, lethal, mortal, dangerous, destructive, harmful, pernicious, noxious, malignant, venomous, toxic, poisonous, virulent.

**deaf** adjective unhearing, hard of hearing, stone deaf. **deaf to** *deaf to their pleas* unmoved by, indifferent to, oblivious to, heedless of, unmindful of.

**deafening** adjective earsplitting, earpiercing, overpowering, booming, thunderous, resounding, reverberating, ringing.

**deal** verb **1** *deal with a problem* attend to, see to, take care of, cope with, handle, manage, sort out. **2** *the book deals with Mozart* be about, have to do with, concern, discuss, consider. **3** *deal in stocks and bonds* trade, traffic, buy and sell, negotiate. **4** *deal cards* distribute, hand out, dole out, mete out, allocate, dispense.

**deal** noun arrangement, transaction, agreement, negotiation, bargain, contract, pact.

**dealer** noun trader, salesman, saleswoman, salesperson, retailer, wholesaler, vendor, trafficker.

**dealings** plural noun *have dealings with the firm* business, trade, commerce; transactions, relations, negotiations.

**dear** adjective **1** *his dear wife* beloved, loved, darling, adored, cherished, intimate. **2** *her dearest possessions* precious, treasured, valued, prized, cherished, favorite. **3** *what a dear child* sweet, darling, endearing, lovable, enchanting. **4** *the car was too dear for me* expensive, costly, high-priced, overpriced; *inf.* pricey, steep.

**dear** noun love, beloved, darling, sweetheart, honey, precious, angel.

**dearth** noun lack, scarcity, want, deficiency, shortage, insufficiency, paucity, sparseness, meagerness.

**death** noun **1** *death by drowning* dying, demise, end, passing, eternal rest. **2** *the death of his hopes* end, termination, cessation, extinction, destruction, eradication, obliteration. **3** *the death on the battlefield* killing, slaying, murder, slaughter, fatality; bloodshed, massacre, carnage.

**debacle** noun fiasco, failure, downfall, collapse, disintegration, disaster, catastrophe, ruin, devastation, defeat, rout.

**debatable** adjective arguable, disputable, questionable, controversial, contentious, doubtful, dubious, undecided.

**debate** noun **1** *a formal debate* discussion, argument, dispute, altercation, controversy, contention. **2** *after some debate* consideration, deliberation, reflection, contemplation.

**debate** verb **1** *debate the issue* discuss, argue, dispute, contend, contest. **2** *debated in his mind* consider, think over, deliberate, reflect, contemplate.

**debauchery** noun dissipation, dissoluteness, corruption, immorality, profligacy, licentiousness, promiscuity, wantonness.

**debonair** adjective suave, urbane, elegant, refined, well-bred, genteel, dashing, dapper, gallant, chivalrous; carefree, jaunty, lighthearted, cheerful, vivacious, buoyant.

**debris** noun rubble, wreckage, detritus, rubbish, litter; remains, ruins, fragments.

**debt** noun indebtedness, obligation, liability; arrears.

**debut** noun premiere, beginning, introduction, coming-out, entrance.

**decadence** noun 1 *the decadence of the empire* decay, degeneration, deterioration, decline, retrogression. 2 *the decadence of the wealthy set* dissipation, debauchery, immorality, self-indulgence, licentiousness, hedonism, epicureanism, corruption, depravity.

**decadent** adjective 1 *a decadent empire* decaying, degenerating, deteriorating, declining. 2 *decadent behavior* dissolute, debauched, degenerate, immoral, self-indulgent, licentious, hedonistic, epicurean, corrupt, depraved.

**decay** verb 1 *food decaying* rot, go bad, decompose, putrefy, spoil, perish, corrode. 2 *an empire decaying* degenerate, deteriorate, decline, dwindle, crumble, disintegrate, collapse, wither, die, atrophy.

**decay** noun 1 *the decay of the food* rotting, decomposition, putrefaction, putrescence, spoilage, corrosion. 2 *spot the decay in the teeth* rot, decomposition; caries, gangrene. 3 *the decay of the empire* degeneration, deterioration, decline, failure, disintegration, collapse.

**deceased** adjective late, departed. *See* DEAD adjective 1.

**deceit** noun deception, duplicity, fraud, fraudulence, cheating, trickery, chicanery, underhandedness, pretense, artifice, treachery; trick, stratagem, ruse, subterfuge, swindle, sham, hoax, misrepresentation; *inf.* hanky-panky.

**deceitful** adjective lying, untruthful, dishonest, mendacious, insincere, false, untrustworthy; deceptive, duplicitous, misleading, fraudulent, crooked.

**deceive** verb take in, mislead, delude, fool, misguide, trick, hoodwink, dupe, swindle, bamboozle, seduce; betray; *inf.* con.

**decency** noun propriety, decorum, seemliness, modesty, good taste, respectability, etiquette, delicacy, dignity, appropriateness, fitness, suitability.

**decent** adjective 1 *a scarcely decent exhibition* decorous, seemly, modest, proper, nice, tasteful, polite, respectable, dignified, appropriate, fitting, fit, suitable, becoming. 2 *a decent person* obliging, helpful,

accommodating, generous, kind, thoughtful, courteous, civil, honorable, worthy, respectable. 3 *a decent salary* acceptable, adequate, sufficient, ample, competent.

**deception** noun duplicity, fraud. *See* DECEIT.

**deceptive** adjective 1 *appearances can be deceptive* deceiving, misleading, false, illusory, fallacious, ambiguous, specious, spurious. 2 *deceptive practices* deceitful, duplicitous, fraudulent, crooked; *inf.* sneaky, tricky.

**decide** verb 1 *decide to go* reach/make a decision, resolve, choose. 2 *decided the matter* settle, resolve, determine, clinch. 3 *the judge decided the case* judge, adjudicate, arbitrate, referee, pass/pronounce judgment.

**decided** adjective 1 *a decided difference* distinct, clear, clear-cut, definite, marked, pronounced, obvious, unmistakable, undeniable, unequivocal, indisputable, unquestionable. 2 *a decided effort* determined, resolute, firm, dogged, purposeful, unswerving, emphatic.

**decision** noun 1 *come to a decision* resolution, conclusion, determination, settlement. 2 *the judge announced his decision* judgment, ruling, pronouncement, verdict, adjudication, arbitration; findings. 3 *a man of decision* decisiveness, determination, resoluteness, resolve, purpose, purposefulness.

**decisive** adjective 1 *a decisive person* determined, resolute. *See* DECIDED adjective 2. 2 *a decisive factor* deciding, determining, definitive, conclusive, final, settling, critical, crucial, significant, influential, important.

**declaration** noun 1 *declaration of war* announcement, statement, proclamation, notification, pronouncement, edict, manifesto. 2 *his declaration that he was innocent* statement, assertion, insistence, protestation, affirmation, contention, claim, avowal.

**declare** verb 1 *declare war* announce, proclaim, pronounce, publish, broadcast, promulgate, trumpet, blazon. 2 *he declared that he was innocent* state, assert, maintain, aver, affirm, profess, claim, allege, swear.

**decline** verb 1 *decline an invitation* turn down, rebuff, refuse. 2 *his influence declined* lessen, decrease, diminish, wane, dwindle, fade, ebb. 3 *the empire is declining* deteriorate, degenerate, decay, fail, fall, wither, weaken, ebb. 4 *the terrain declines here* descend, slope/slant down.

**decline** noun 1 *the decline of his influence* decrease, downturn, downswing, ebb, slump, plunge. 2 *the decline of the empire* deterioration, degeneration, decay, failure, fall, wane. **3** *hikers sighting a decline* slope, declivity, dip.

**decompose** verb decay, rot, putrefy, fester; break up, fall apart, disintegrate, crumble.

**decorate** verb trim, embellish, garnish, festoon, beautify, enhance; renovate, refurbish; *inf.* spruce up.

**decoration** noun **1** *holiday decorations* adornment, ornamentation, beautification, enhancement; furnishing; ornament, trinket, bauble; trimming. **2** *a decoration for bravery* award, medal, badge, star, ribbon; colors, insignia.

**decorum** noun propriety, decency, good taste, correctness, politeness, courtesy, refinement, dignity, respectability; etiquette, protocol.

**decoy** noun lure, bait, enticement, entrapment, snare, trap.

**decrease** verb lessen, grow less, diminish, reduce, drop, fall off, decline, dwindle; abate, subside, taper off, peter out.

**decrease** noun **1** *the decrease in numbers/amount* lessening, reduction, reduction, drop, decline, falling off, downturn, cutback, curtailment, shrinkage. **2** *the decrease in the wind* dying down, abatement, subsidence, letting up, letup, slackening.

**decree** noun edict, order, law, statute, act, ordinance, regulation, rule, injunction, mandate, proclamation, dictum.

**decree** verb ordain, rule, order, command, dictate, lay down, prescribe, pronounce, proclaim.

**decrepit** adjective **1** *decrepit old men* doddering, tottering, aged, old, elderly, feeble, enfeebled, infirm, weak, weakened, weakly, frail, wasted, debilitated. **2** *decrepit houses* dilapidated, rickety, brokendown, tumbledown, ramshackle, rundown, worn-out, battered, decayed, deteriorated.

**decry** verb disparage, criticize, carp at, cavil at, censure, blame, condemn, denounce, run down, rail against.

**dedicate** verb **1** *dedicate her life to the poor* devote, commit, pledge. **2** *dedicate a church* bless, consecrate, sanctify, hallow.

**dedicated** adjective devoted, committed, wholehearted, single-minded, enthusiastic, zealous.

**dedication** noun devotion, devotedness, commitment, wholeheartedness, singlemindedness, enthusiasm, zeal.

**deduce** verb conclude, infer, reason, gather, glean.

**deduct** verb subtract, take away, take off, withdraw, discount; *inf.* knock off.

**deduction** noun **1** *the detectives' sound deduction* conclusion, inference, reasoning, assumption, presumption. **2** *the deduction of tax* subtraction, withdrawal, removal.

**deed** noun *brave deeds* act, action, feat, exploit, performance, achievement, accomplishment, undertaking, enterprise.

**deem** verb think, believe, consider, judge, feel, imagine, conceive, regard, see, hold.

**deep** adjective **1** *a deep hole/wound* cavernous, yawning, profound, bottomless, immeasurable, fathomless, unfathomable. **2** *a deep voice* low, low-pitched, full-toned, bass, resonant, sonorous. **3** *a deep red* dark, intense, vivid, rich, strong. **4** *deep distrust* profound, extreme, intense, great, grave, deep-seated, deep-rooted. **5** *a deep thinker/person* learned, wise, sagacious, sage, discerning, penetrating, perspicacious. **6** *deep affection* intense, heartfelt, fervent, ardent, impassioned. **7** *a deep mystery/secret* obscure, abstruse, unfathomable, recondite, esoteric, enigmatic, arcane.

**deepen** verb grow, increase, intensify, magnify, strengthen, heighten, reinforce.

**deeply** adverb greatly, extremely, profoundly, intensely, keenly, acutely, sharply.

**deface** verb spoil, disfigure, mar, blemish, deform, ruin, sully, tarnish, damage, vandalize, injure.

**defamation** noun slander, libel, character assassination, aspersion, calumny, vilification, defilement, obloquy, contumely, denigration, detraction, derogation; smear, slur, insult; *inf.* mudslinging.

**defame** verb slander, libel, cast aspersions on, asperse, blacken the name/character of, malign, smear, vilify, traduce, besmirch, disparage, denigrate; *inf.* do a hatchet job on, drag through the mud; bad-mouth.

**defeat** verb **1** *defeat their team/army* beat, conquer, vanquish, rout, trounce, thrash, overcome, overpower, overthrow, overwhelm, crush, quash, quell, subjugate, subdue, repulse; *inf.* clobber, zap. **2** *defeat your own purpose* hinder, prevent, ruin, thwart, frustrate, foil.

**defeat** noun **1** *suffer defeat by the enemy* conquest, vanquishment, rout, beating. **2** *the defeat of their plans* failure, ruin, abortion, miscarriage; undoing, reverse, disappointment, setback.

**defect** noun **1** *a defect in the machine/writing* fault, flaw, imperfection, weak spot/point, snag, kink, blemish, mistake, error; *inf.* bug. **2** *defects in the educational system* deficiency, inadequacy, insufficiency, shortcoming, lack, want, omission, weakness, failing.

**defect** verb **1** *soldiers defected* desert, turn traitor, change sides/allegiances, shift ground, break faith, apostatize. **2** *defect from one's party* abandon, forsake, renounce, repudiate, secede from.

**defective** adjective **1** *a defective machine* faulty, flawed, imperfect, weak, deficient. **2** *defective in character* lacking, wanting, deficient, inadequate, insufficient. **3** *mentally defective* impaired, retarded, abnormal, subnormal.

**defector** noun deserter, turncoat, traitor, renegade, apostate, recreant; *inf.* rat, Benedict Arnold.

**defend** verb **1** *defend the city* protect, guard, safeguard, watch over, keep from harm, preserve, secure, shield, fortify, garrison, fight for. **2** *defend one's ideas* vindicate, justify, argue/speak for, make a case for, plead for, explain, give reasons for. **3** *the newspaper defended its journalist* support, back, stand by, stand/stick up for.

**defendant** noun accused, appellant, litigant, respondent.

**defender** noun protector, guard, bodyguard, guardian, preserver; supporter, backer, champion.

**defense** noun **1** *a defense against the enemy* protection, shield, safeguard, guard, security, cover, shelter, screen, fortification; barricade, rampart, bulwark, buttress, fortress. **2** *published a defense of his ideas* vindication, justification, apologia, apology, argument, explanation, explication. **3** *the accused gave his defense* denial, rebuttal, plea, declaration, case, excuse, alibi.

**defenseless** adjective undefended, unprotected, unguarded, unfortified, unarmed, helpless, vulnerable, weak, powerless, impotent, wide open, exposed, endangered.

**defer**[1] verb *defer the meeting* postpone, put off, adjourn, delay, hold over, shelve, put on ice, put on the back burner, pigeonhole, suspend, table, stay, hold in abeyance, prorogue.

**defer**[2] verb *defer to the expert* yield, submit, bow, give way, give in, surrender, accede, capitulate, acquiesce.

**deference** noun **1** *deference for the old* respect, regard, consideration, thoughtfulness, courteousness, courtesy, dutifulness, reverence, veneration. **2** *deference to the expert* submission, capitulation, accession, acquiescence, complaisance, obeisance.

**defiance** noun **1** *treat the enemy with defiance* resistance, opposition, confrontation, noncompliance, disobedience, recalcitrance, rebelliousness, insubordination, contempt, scorn, insolence. **2** *a spirit of defiance* challenge, provocation, daring, boldness, audacity, bravado, aggression, truculence.

**defiant** adjective **1** *defiant opposition* resistant, rebellious, insubordinate, mutinous, refractory, contemptuous, scornful, insolent. **2** *a defiant air* challenging, provocative, bold, audacious, aggressive, truculent.

**deficiency** noun **1** *vitamin deficiency* lack, want, shortage, dearth, insufficiency, inadequacy, scarcity, deficit, scantiness, paucity, absence. **2** *a deficiency in the system* weakness, failing, shortcoming. *See* DEFECT noun 1.

**deficient** adjective **1** *deficient in vitamins* lacking, wanting, short of, low on. **2** *deficient quantities* insufficient, inadequate, scanty, meager, skimpy, sketchy. **3** *a deficient system* defective, faulty, flawed, imperfect.

**deficit** noun shortfall, deficiency, shortage.

**defile** verb **1** *streets defiled by filth* pollute, foul, befoul, dirty, soil. **2** *defile young minds* corrupt, contaminate, taint, infect, tarnish, sully, pervert, vitiate. **3** *defile reputations* defame, blacken, denigrate, besmirch, stigmatize. **4** *defile young girls* ravish, rape, deflower, violate, dishonor.

**define** verb **1** *define one's terms/position* spell out, describe, explain, expound, elucidate, clarify, set out, outline, detail, specify, designate. **2** *define the boundary* mark out, fix, establish, settle, demarcate, bound, delimit, delineate, circumscribe.

**definite** adjective **1** *definite plans* specific, particular, precise, exact, defined, well-defined, clear, clear-cut, explicit, express, determined, fixed, established, confirmed. **2** *it's definite that he's going* certain, sure, positive, guaranteed, settled, decided, assured, conclusive, final. **3** *definite boundaries* fixed, marked, demarcated, delimited, circumscribed.

**definitely** adverb certainly, surely, for sure, without doubt/question, undoubtedly, indubitably, positively, absolutely, undeniably, unmistakably, plainly, clearly, obviously.

**definition** noun **1** *the definition of terms* meaning, description, explanation, exposition, expounding, interpretation, elucidation, clarification. **2** *the definition of boundaries* fixing, settling, establishment, determination, demarcation, delineation, circumscribing. **3** *the definition of the image* precision, sharpness, distinctness, clearness, clarity, contrast, visibility, focus.

**definitive** adjective **1** *the definitive answer* conclusive, final, ultimate, decisive, unconditional, unqualified, absolute, categorical. **2** *the definitive edition* authoritative, most reliable, most complete, exhaustive.

**deflate** verb **1** *deflate the air mattress* let down, collapse, flatten, void, puncture. **2** *deflate the pompous man* humble, humiliate, mortify, chasten, subdue, dispirit; *inf.* put down, debunk. **3** *deflate a currency* devalue, depreciate, depress, diminish, reduce.

**deflect** verb turn aside/away, turn, alter course, change course/direction, diverge, deviate, veer, swerve, slew, drift, bend.

**deformed** adjective **1** *deformed bodies* misshapen, malformed, distorted, contorted, twisted, crooked, curved, gnarled, crippled, maimed, disfigured, damaged, marred, mutilated, mangled. **2** *deformed minds* twisted, warped, perverted, corrupted, depraved, vile, gross.

**defraud** verb cheat, swindle, rob, fleece, sting, dupe, rook, bilk; *inf.* gyp, con, rip off.

**deft** adjective dexterous, adroit, handy, nimble, nimble-fingered, agile, skillful, skilled, proficient, adept, able, clever, expert.

**defunct** adjective **1** *defunct ancestors* dead, deceased, departed, extinct, gone. **2** *defunct organizations* obsolete, expired, nonexistent, inoperative.

**defy** verb **1** *defied their parents* disobey, disregard, ignore, slight, flout, fly in the face of, thumb one's nose at, spurn, scoff at, deride, scorn. **2** *defy the enemy forces* resist, withstand, brave, stand up to, confront, face, meet head-on, square up to, repulse, repel, thwart. **3** *I defy you to stay* challenge, dare, throw down the gauntlet to.

**degeneracy** noun corruption, decadence, immorality, depravity, dissoluteness, debauchery, profligacy, wickedness, vileness, sinfulness, baseness, turpitude.

**degenerate** verb deteriorate, decline, worsen, decay, rot, fail, fall off, sink, slip, slide, go downhill, regress, retrogress, lapse; *inf.* go to pot, go to the dogs, hit the skids.

**degradation** noun **1** *the degradation of his family* debasement, discrediting, demeaning, deprecation, shaming, disgracing, dishonoring, humiliation, mortification. **2** *a scene of degradation* degeneracy, corruption, decadence, depravity, squalor.

**degrade** verb **1** *his family was degraded by his behavior* discredit, belittle, demean, deprecate, deflate, devalue, lower, reduce, shame, disgrace, humble, humiliate, abase. **2** *officers were degraded* downgrade, demote, cashier, depose, unseat, dethrone; *inf.* drum out. **3** *degraded by her immoral associates* debase, corrupt, pervert, defile, sully, debauch.

**degrading** adjective debasing, discrediting, cheapening, belittling, demeaning, lowering, shaming, shameful, humiliating, mortifying, disgraceful.

**degree** noun **1** *a high degree of competence* stage, level, grade, step, gradation, rung, point, mark, measure, notch, limit. **2** *to a marked degree* extent, measure, magnitude, level, amount, quality, intensity, strength, proportion, ratio. **3** *people of higher degree* rank, class, standing, status, station, position, grade, level, order, condition, estate. **by degrees** gradually, slowly, step by step, little by little, bit by bit.

**dehydrate** verb dry, dry up/out, sun-dry, desiccate, parch, sear.

**deify** verb idolize, exalt, worship, adore, venerate, revere, pay homage to.

**deign** verb condescend, stoop, lower oneself, think/see fit, deem worthy, consent.

**deity** noun god, goddess, divine being, celestial being, supreme being, divinity; godhead.

**dejected** adjective depressed, dispirited, disheartened, downhearted, crestfallen, cast down, downcast, down, disappointed, unhappy, sad, miserable, blue.

**delay** verb **1** *delay our meeting* postpone, put off. See DEFER[1]. **2** *visitors delayed by the traffic* hold up/back, detain, slow up, set back, hinder, obstruct, hamper, impede, bog down, check, hold in check, restrain. **3** *don't delay!* linger, loiter, dawdle, dally, dilly-dally, lag/fall behind, tarry.

**delay** noun **1** *the delay to the meeting* postponement, adjournment, deferment, suspension, tabling, stay. **2** *holiday traffic delays* holdup, wait, setback, detainment, detention, hindrance, obstruction, impediment, check, stoppage, halt, interruption. **3** *the delay between trains* wait, interval, lull, interlude, intermission.

**delectable** adjective **1** *delectable food* appetizing, tasty. See DELICIOUS 1. **2** *delectable manner/appearance* delightful, charming, enchanting, captivating, winning, engaging, winsome, pleasing, agreeable.

**delegate** noun representative, deputy, agent, spokesman, spokeswoman, spokesperson, ambassador, envoy, legate, messenger, go-between, proxy, emissary, commissary.

**delegate** verb **1** *delegate tasks* pass on, hand over, transfer, give, commit, entrust, assign, relegate, consign. **2** *delegate him leader* authorize, deputize, commission, empower.

**delete** verb cross/strike out, cut out, erase, blue-pencil, edit out, remove, take out, expunge, eradicate; *inf.* scratch, kill.

**deleterious** adjective harmful, injurious, hurtful, damaging, destructive, ruinous, bad, disadvantageous, noxious.

**deliberate** adjective **1** *a deliberate act* intentional, planned, considered, calculated, designed, studied, studious, painstaking, conscious, purposeful, willful, premeditated, preplanned, prearranged, preconceived, predetermined, aforethought. **2** *deliberate speech/steps* careful, unhurried, cautious, thoughtful, steady, regular, measured, determined, resolute, ponderous, laborious.

**deliberate** verb **1** *looking out of the window deliberating* ponder, think, muse, meditate, reflect, cogitate, ruminate, brood, excogitate. **2** *deliberate the advantages* think over, consider, reflect on, mull over, evaluate. **3** *deliberate with colleagues* discuss, debate, confer, consult.

**delicate** adjective **1** *delicate china/material* fine, exquisite, fragile, slender, slight, elegant, graceful, dainty, flimsy, silky, gauzy, gossamer, wispy. **2** *his wife is delicate* frail, sickly, weak, debilitated, infirm. **3** *delicate colors* pastel, pale, muted, subtle, soft, subdued, understated, faint. **4** *a delicate matter/situation* difficult, tricky, sensitive, ticklish, critical, precarious, touchy; *inf.* sticky, dicey. **5** *require delicate handling* careful, considerate, tactful, discreet, diplomatic, politic, kid-glove. **6** *a delicate palate* discriminating, discerning, refined, perceptive, critical, fastidious, finicky, persnickety, squeamish. **7** *a delicate mechanism* sensitive, precise, accurate, exact. **8** *a delicate touch* deft, skilled, skillful, expert.

**delicious** adjective **1** *delicious food* tasty, appetizing, mouthwatering, delectable, choice, savory, flavorsome, flavorful, luscious, palatable, toothsome, ambrosial, ambrosian; *inf.* scrumptious, yummy. **2** *a delicious evening* delightful, exquisite, enjoyable, pleasurable.

**delight** noun pleasure, joy, happiness, gladness, gratification, bliss, rapture, ecstasy, elation, jubilation; excitement, entertainment, amusement; transports.

**delight** verb **1** *delighted by the news* please, gladden, cheer, gratify, thrill, excite, transport, enchant, captivate, entrance, charm, entertain, amuse, divert. **2** *delight in reading* take/find pleasure, indulge, glory.

**delighted** adjective pleased, joyful, happy, glad, gratified, overjoyed, blissful, enraptured, ecstatic, jubilant, thrilled, transported, excited, enchanted, captivated, entertained, amused, diverted.

**delightful** adjective pleasant, pleasing, agreeable, enjoyable, amusing, entertaining, diverting, pleasurable, gratifying, delectable, joyful, exciting, thrilling, rapturous, enchanting.

**delinquent** noun *damage done by delinquents* offender, wrongdoer, culprit, lawbreaker, criminal, hooligan, vandal, ruffian, hoodlum, miscreant, malefactor, transgressor.

**delirious** adjective **1** *delirious patients* raving, incoherent, babbling, light-headed,

irrational, unhinged. **2** *delirious at the good news* ecstatic, euphoric, beside oneself, carried away, transported, hysterical, frenzied.

**deliver** verb **1** *deliver the mail/groceries* distribute, carry, bring, take, transport, convey. **2** *deliver the prisoners to the enemy* hand over, turn over, transfer, commit, grant, make over, give up, yield, surrender, relinquish. **3** *deliver them from enemies* free, liberate, release, save, rescue, set loose, loose, extricate, discharge, ransom, emancipate, redeem. **4** *deliver a speech* utter, speak, express, pronounce, enunciate, proclaim, announce, declare. **5** *deliver a blow* direct, aim, administer, launch, inflict, throw, strike, hurl, pitch, discharge. **6** *deliver better sales figures* come up with, achieve, attain, provide, supply.

**deliverance** noun **1** *deliverance from prison/evil* liberation, release, rescue, escape, discharge, ransom, emancipation, salvation, redemption, manumission. **2** *deliverances from the pulpit* pronouncement, declaration, announcement, proclamation, report, lecture, sermon, speech.

**delivery** noun **1** *delivery is extra* distribution, carriage, transporting, transport, conveyance, dispatch. **2** *receive a delivery* consignment, load, batch. **3** *admire his clear delivery* enunciation, articulation, intonation, elocution, utterance, presentation. **4** *the pitcher's delivery* directing, aiming, launching, throwing, pitching.

**delude** verb mislead, deceive, fool, take in, trick, dupe, cheat, hoodwink, beguile, outwit, misguide, lead on, bamboozle, defraud, swindle, double-cross, cozen; *inf.* con, pull a fast one on, take for a ride, put one over on, two-time.

**deluge** noun **1** *houses swept away by the deluge* flood, spate, inundation, overflowing, flash flood, cataclysm; downpour, torrent, torrential rain, cloudburst. **2** *a deluge of correspondence* flood, rush, spate, torrent, avalanche, barrage, outpouring.

**deluge** verb **1** *towns deluged with polluted water* flood, inundate, swamp, engulf, submerge, drown, soak, drench, douse. **2** *deluged by correspondence* inundate, flood, overrun, overwhelm, engulf, swamp, overload.

**delusion** noun **1** *delusions of grandeur* false impression, false belief, misconception, misapprehension, misbelief, self-deception, illusion, fancy, phantasm, fool's paradise. **2** *victims of their own delusion* deluding, misleading, deception, fooling, tricking, duping.

**deluxe** adjective luxurious, sumptuous, palatial, opulent, lavish, superior, exclusive, choice, select, elegant, splendid, costly, expensive; *inf.* plush, upscale, upmarket.

**demand** verb 1 *workers demanding a raise* press for, insist on, urge, clamor for. 2 *"What's that?" he demanded* ask, inquire, question, interrogate, challenge. 3 *work demanding care* require, need, necessitate, call for, take, involve, want, cry out for. 4 *demand payment* expect, insist on, exact, order, requisition.

**demand** noun 1 *give in to demands* request, entreaty, claim, requisition; insistence, pressure, clamor. 2 *answer his demand* inquiry, question, interrogation, challenge. 3 *the demands of the job* requirement, need, necessity, want, claim, imposition, exigency. **in demand** sought-after, popular, in vogue, fashionable; *inf.* trendy.

**demanding** adjective 1 *demanding children* nagging, harassing, clamorous, importunate, insistent, imperious. 2 *demanding jobs* challenging, taxing, exacting, exigent, tough, hard, difficult, tiring, wearing, exhausting.

**demean** verb debase, demote. *See* DE-GRADE 1.

**demeanor** noun behavior, conduct, bearing, air, appearance, mien, deportment, carriage, comportment.

**demented** adjective insane, mad, crazy, crazed, deranged, of unsound mind, out of one's mind, unhinged, unbalanced, touched, *non compos mentis*, maniacal, manic, frenzied, distraught, foolish, idiotic, crackbrained, lunatic; *inf.* daft, balmy, loopy, batty, dippy, wacky.

**demolish** verb 1 *demolish the building* knock down, pull/tear down, bring down, flatten, raze, level, bulldoze, dismantle, break up, pulverize. 2 *demolish his self-confidence* destroy, put an end to, ruin, wreck, undo. 3 *demolish the opposition* defeat, conquer, vanquish, overthrow, overturn, quell, quash, annihilate.

**demolition** noun 1 *the demolition of the buildings* razing, leveling, bulldozing. 2 *the demolition of the argument/opposition* destruction, ruin, ruination, undoing, defeat, conquest, overthrow, destruction, annihilation.

**demon** noun 1 *demons from hell* devil, fiend. 2 *a demon for work* hard worker, powerhouse, dynamo, workaholic; *inf.* whiz kid, eager beaver, busy bee. 3 *a demon at sailing* master, wizard; *inf.* ace, wiz.

**demonic, demoniac, demoniacal** adjective 1 *demonic spirits* diabolic, diabolical, devilish, fiendish, satanic, hellish, infernal, evil, wicked, Mephistophelian. 2 *demonic eyes/laughter* maniacal, manic, mad, crazed, frenzied, frantic, feverish, hysterical.

**demonstrate** verb 1 *demonstrate the proof of the proposition* determine, prove, validate, confirm, verify, establish. 2 *blushes demonstrating embarrassment* show, indicate, display, exhibit, express, manifest, evince, evidence. 3 *demonstrate putting on a bandage* illustrate, teach (about), describe, explain (about), expound on. 4 *demonstrate against war* protest, march, parade, rally, sit in, picket.

**demonstration** noun 1 *demonstration of the proof of the proposition* substantiation, confirmation, affirmation, verification, validation. 2 *a gymnastics demonstration* illustration, description, explanation, presentation, exhibition; *inf.* expo. 3 *an anti-war demonstration* protest, march, parade, rally, sit-in, picket.

**demonstrative** adjective *a demonstrative person* emotional, unreserved, unrestrained, expressive, open, effusive, expansive, gushing, nonreticent, affectionate, loving, warm.

**demur** verb object, take exception, express reluctance/reservations/doubts, be unwilling, protest, dispute, dissent, balk at, hesitate, cavil.

**demure** adjective 1 *demure young girls* modest, unassuming, decorous, meek, reserved, quiet, shy, bashful, retiring, diffident, reticent, timid, shrinking. 2 *demure young ladies* overmodest, coy, prim, priggish, prissy, prudish, goody-goody, straitlaced.

**den** noun 1 *the fox's den* lair, hole, hollow, shelter, hide-out. 2 *den of thieves* site, haunt; *inf.* dive, joint. 3 *writing in his den* study, retreat, sanctum, *sanctum sanctorum*, sanctuary, hideaway.

**denial** noun 1 *a denial of the statement* contradiction, repudiation, disclaimer, retraction, abjuration, disaffirmation; negation, dissent. 2 *the denial of the request* refusal, rejection, dismissal, rebuff, repulse, veto, turndown; *inf.* thumbs down. 3 *denial of beliefs* renunciation, renouncement, disowning, repudiation, disavowal.

**denote** verb 1 *a smile denoting delight | the color yellow denoting happiness* indicate, signify, betoken, symbolize, represent, stand for, typify. 2 *the word bankruptcy denotes financial ruin* mean, convey, designate.

**denounce** verb 1 *denounce the council's policies* condemn, criticize, attack, censure, castigate, decry, rail/inveigh/fulminate against, declaim against. 2 *denounce his partner* accuse, inform against, incriminate, implicate, inculpate, charge.

**dense** adjective 1 *a dense forest/crowd* close-packed, tightly packed, crowded, thickset, closely set, jammed together, crammed, compressed, compacted. 2 *dense fog/smoke* thick, concentrated, opaque, impenetrable. **3** *too dense to understand* thick, slow, dull-witted, blockish, obtuse; *inf.* dim.

**deny** verb **1** *deny the charge/statement* contradict, negate, nullify, dissent from, disagree with, repudiate, refute, controvert, disclaim. **2** *deny the request* refuse, reject, turn down, dismiss, repulse, decline, veto; *inf.* give the thumbs down to, give the red light to. **3** *to deny one's citizenship* renounce, disown, turn one's back on, repudiate, discard, disavow.

**depart** verb **1** *they departed at noon* leave, go, go away/off, take one's leave, withdraw, set off/out, start out, get going, get under way, quit, make an exit, exit, break camp, decamp, retreat, retire; *inf.* make tracks, shove off, split, cut out, vamoose, hightail it. **2** *depart from the norm* deviate, diverge, differ, vary, digress, veer, branch off, fork, swerve, turn aside.

**departure** noun **1** *the hour of their departure* leaving, leave-taking, going, going away/off, withdrawal, setting off/out, starting out, exit, exodus, decamping, retreat. **2** *a departure from the norm* deviation, divergence, variation, digression, veering, branching off, swerving. **3** *a new departure for the firm* change of direction, change, difference of emphasis, shift, innovation, branching out, novelty.

**depend** verb **1** *success depends on hard work* turn/hinge on, hang on, rest on, be contingent upon, be subject to, be controlled/determined by, be based on, revolve around, be influenced by. **2** *depend on him for help* rely on, count/bank on, lean on, cling to, trust in, put one's faith in, have confidence in, swear by, be sure of.

**dependable** adjective reliable, trustworthy, faithful, responsible, steady, stable, sure, unfailing, true, steadfast.

**dependence** noun **1** *pity the children's dependence* helplessness, weakness, defenselessness, vulnerability, exposure. **2** *alcohol dependence* addiction, overuse, abuse.

**dependent** adjective **1** *dependent on circumstances* depending on, conditional on, contingent on, determined by, subject to. **2** *dependent children* helpless, weak, defenseless, vulnerable, immature. **3** *dependent countries* subsidiary, subject, subservient. **dependent on/upon** *dependent on their mother* relying on, reliant on, counting on, leaning on, supported by, sustained by.

**depict** verb **1** *the painting depicts him sitting* portray, represent, draw, paint, sketch, illustrate, delineate, outline, reproduce, render, limn, chart, map out. **2** *the account depicts his faults* describe, set forth/out, detail, relate, narrate, recount, record, chronicle.

**deplete** verb exhaust, use up, consume, expend, spend, drain, empty, milk, evacuate, bankrupt, impoverish, reduce, decrease, diminish.

**depletion** noun exhaustion, consumption, expenditure, draining, emptying, reduction, decrease, dwindling, diminution, lessening.

**deplorable** adjective **1** *deplorable behavior* disgraceful, shameful, dishonorable, blameworthy, disreputable, scandalous, reprehensible, despicable, abominable. **2** *in deplorable circumstances* lamentable, regrettable, unfortunate, wretched, dire, miserable, pitiable, pathetic, distressing, grievous.

**deplore** verb **1** *deplore his behavior* be scandalized/shocked by, disapprove of, condemn, censure, deprecate, denounce, decry. **2** *deplore the passing of steam trains* regret, lament, mourn, rue, bemoan, bewail, pine for.

**deploy** verb arrange, position, dispose, spread out, extend, redistribute, station, utilize, set out/up, bring into play.

**deport** verb **1** *deport the refugees* banish, expel, exile, evict, transport, oust, expatriate, extradite. **2** *deport oneself badly* behave, conduct oneself, act, acquit oneself, comport oneself.

**depose** verb *depose the ruler* remove, unseat, dethrone, oust, displace, dismiss, discharge, cashier, demote.

**deposit** verb **1** *deposit the package on the floor* put, lay, set, set/put/lay down, drop, let fall. **2** *deposit money/jewels in the safe* bank, entrust, consign, save, store, hoard, stow, put away, lay in, squirrel away.

**deposit** noun **1** *a chemical deposit* precipitation, sediment, sublimate, accumulation, deposition; dregs, lees; silt, alluvium. **2** *coal/iron deposits* bed, vein, lode, layer. **3** *put a deposit on the goods* down/part payment, installment, security, retainer.

**depot** noun **1** *buses/trains returning to the depot* terminal, terminus; bus/railroad station, garage. **2** *stored in the depot* storehouse, warehouse, repository, depository, magazine, cache, arsenal.

**depraved** adjective corrupt, corrupted, immoral, unprincipled, dissolute, perverted, degenerate, profligate, debased, degraded, wicked, sinful, vile, base, iniquitous, lewd, licentious, lascivious, lecherous, prurient.

**depravity** noun corruption, immorality, debauchery, dissoluteness, perversion, degradation, degeneracy, profligacy, contamination, wickedness, sinfulness, vileness, baseness, iniquity, criminality, viciousness, brutality, brutishness, lewdness, licentiousness, lasciviousness, lechery, prurience.

**deprecate** verb **1** *deprecate the commit-*

*tee's actions* disapprove of, deplore, frown upon, censure, condemn, protest against, inveigh/rail against, denounce; *inf.* knock. **2** *deprecate his achievement* belittle, disparage, denigrate, decry, discredit, deflate, diminish, depreciate.

**depreciate** verb **1** *depreciate the value | depreciate the furniture* devalue, reduce, lower in value/price, mark down, cheapen, cut, slash. **2** *depreciate efforts to help* belittle, make light of, discredit, underrate, undervalue, underestimate, deflate, detract from, diminish, minimize, run down.

**depress** verb **1** *news that depressed her* sadden, deject, cast down, dispirit, dishearten, discourage, dampen the spirits of, weigh down, oppress. **2** *depress economic activity* slow down/up, weaken, lower, reduce, sap, impair, enfeeble, exhaust, drain. **3** *depress prices* reduce, lower, cut, cheapen, slash, depreciate, devalue, diminish, downgrade.

**depressed** adjective **1** *depressed spirits* sad, gloomy, blue, glum, dejected, downhearted, cast down, downcast, down, crestfallen, despondent, dispirited, low, melancholy, disheartened, discouraged, desolate, moody, morose, pessimistic, weighed down, oppressed; *inf.* down in the dumps. **2** *a depressed section of land* sunken, hollow, concave, indented, dented, pushed in, recessed, set back. **3** *a depressed economy* weak, weakened, slow, enervated, debilitated, devitalized, impaired. **4** *depressed prices* reduced, lowered, cut, cheapened, slashed, devalued, markeddown, discounted. **5** *a depressed area* poverty-stricken, poor, destitute, disadvantaged, deprived, needy, distressed, rundown.

**depressing** adjective *depressing news* saddening, sad, unhappy, gloomy, dismal, bleak, somber, grave, melancholy, dispiriting, disheartening, discouraging, distressing, painful.

**depression** noun **1** *bad news caused her depression* sadness, unhappiness, despair, gloom, glumness, dejection, downheartedness, despondency, dispiritedness, melancholy, discouragement, desolation, dolefulness, moodiness, moroseness, pessimism, hopelessness; melancholia; low spirits, blues; *inf.* the dumps. **2** *a depression in the landscape* hollow, indentation, dent, cavity, concavity, dip, valley, pit, hole, bowl, sink, sinkhole, excavation. **3** *an economic depression* slump, recession, decline, slowdown, standstill; paralysis, inactivity, stagnation.

**deprivation** noun **1** *the deprivation of their rights* withholding, denial, withdrawal, removal, dispossession, stripping, expropriation, seizure, confiscation, robbing,

appropriation, divestment, divestiture, wresting. **2** *areas of social deprivation* poverty, hardship, privation, destitution, disadvantage, need, neediness, want.

**deprive** verb dispossess, strip, expropriate, divest, wrest, rob.

**depth** noun **1** *measure the depth of the hole* deepness, drop, vertical extent, profundity. **2** *a person of depth* profundity, wisdom, understanding, sagacity, discernment, insight, awareness, intuition, penetration, astuteness, acumen, shrewdness, acuity. **3** *an issue of great depth* gravity, seriousness, weight, importance, complexity, intricacy, obtuseness, abstruseness, obscurity, reconditeness. **4** *the depth of the color* intensity, richness, darkness, vividness, strength, brilliance. **5** *the depths of the sea* remotest area, bottom, floor, bed, abyss, back, pit; bowels. **in depth** thoroughly, extensively, comprehensively, intensively.

**deputy** noun substitute, stand-in, representative, second in command, assistant, surrogate, proxy.

**deputy** adjective assistant, substitute, stand-in, representative, surrogate, proxy, subordinate.

**deranged** adjective unbalanced, unhinged, insane, mad, crazy, crazed, demented, disturbed, irrational, of unsound mind, *non compos mentis*, berserk, frenzied.

**derelict** adjective **1** *derelict factories/ships* abandoned, forsaken, deserted, discarded, rejected, cast off, relinquished, ownerless. **2** *derelict properties* dilapidated, ramshackle, tumbledown, rundown, broken-down, in disrepair, crumbling, falling to pieces, rickety, neglected. **3** *derelict officers* negligent, neglectful, remiss, lax, careless, sloppy, slipshod, slack, irresponsible, delinquent.

**derelict** noun vagrant, tramp, beggar, bum, hobo, outcast, pariah, ne'er-do-well, good-for-nothing, wastrel.

**deride** verb mock, ridicule, jeer at, scoff at, sneer at, make fun of, poke fun at, laugh at, scorn, pooh-pooh, lampoon, satirize.

**derision** noun mockery, ridicule, jeering, scoffing, sneering, scorn, contempt, taunting, ragging, teasing, raillery, disdain; jeers, sneers, taunts, insults; satire, lampoon.

**derivative** adjective *derivative research* imitative, unoriginal, uninventive, noninnovative, copied, plagiaristic, plagiarized, secondhand, secondary, rehashed.

**derive** verb **1** *happiness deriving from marriage* originate, stem, proceed, flow, emanate, issue. **2** *derive satisfaction* acquire, obtain, get, gain, procure, extract. **3** *derive sufficient facts* draw out, elicit, educe, deduce, infer.

**derogatory** adjective disparaging, denigratory, belittling, slighting, deprecatory, depreciatory, detracting, deflating, discrediting, dishonoring, unfavorable, disapproving, uncomplimentary, unflattering, insulting, offensive.

**descend** verb **1** *descend the hill/stairs* go down, come down, move down, climb down, pass down; drop, fall, sink, subside, plummet, plunge, tumble, slump. **2** *the hill descended to the valley* go down, slope, incline, dip, slant. **3** *will not descend to talk to servants* condescend, stoop, lower/abase oneself. **4** *descend in quality/values* degenerate, deteriorate, decline, sink, go downhill; *inf.* go to pot, go to the dogs. **5** *enemies/visitors descending on us* pounce, raid, swoop, charge, come in force, arrive in hordes. **6** *houses descending from father to son* be handed/passed down, pass by heredity.

**descendants** plural noun offspring, progeny, issue, family; scions.

**descent** noun **1** *the descent of the balloon* going down, drop, fall, sinking, subsiding, plummeting, plunge. **2** *walk down the descent* slope, incline, dip, drop, gradient, declivity, declination, slant. **3** *descent in quality/values* deterioration, decline, debasement, degradation, sinking, decadence. **4** *of German descent* ancestry, parentage, lineage, extraction, genealogy, heredity, succession, stock, line, blood, strain; origins.

**describe** verb **1** *describe the incident* narrate, put into words, detail, tell, express, recount, relate, report, set out, chronicle, define, explain, elucidate, illustrate. **2** *he was described as brilliant* characterize, portray, depict, style, label. **3** *describe a circle* draw, delineate, mark out, outline, trace, sketch.

**description** noun **1** *a description of the incident* account, detailed statement, report, setting out, chronicle, narration, recounting, relation, commentary, explanation, elucidation, illustration; details. **2** *the description of him as dishonest* characterization, portrayal, depiction. **3** *the description of a circle* drawing, delineation, outline, tracing. **4** *vegetables of every description* kind, sort, variety, type, brand, breed, category, class, designation, genre, ilk, mold.

**descriptive** adjective graphic, vivid, striking, expressive, detailed, explanatory, elucidatory, illustrative, pictorial, depictive, picturesque.

**desecrate** verb violate, defile, profane, treat sacrilegiously, blaspheme, debase, degrade, dishonor.

**desert** verb **1** *desert one's wife/post* abandon, forsake, give up, cast off, leave, turn one's back on, leave high and dry, leave in the lurch, throw over, betray, jilt, strand, leave stranded, maroon, neglect, shun, relinquish, renounce; *inf.* walk/run out on. **2** *the soldier has deserted* abscond, defect, run away, make off, decamp, flee, fly, bolt, turn tail, go AWOL, depart, quit, escape.

**desert** noun wasteland, waste, wilderness, barrenness, solitude; wilds.

**desert** adjective arid, dry, moistureless, parched, scorched, dried up, burnt, hot, burning, torrid; desolate, barren, bare, wild, empty, uninhabited, solitary, lonely, uncultivable, infertile, unproductive, sterile, uncultivated, untilled.

**deserter** noun **1** *army deserters* defector, runaway, fugitive, truant, escapee, derelict. **2** *deserters from the cause* defector, renegade, turncoat, traitor, betrayer, apostate, derelict; *inf.* rat.

**deserve** verb merit, be worthy of, warrant, rate, justify, earn, be entitled to, have a right to, have a claim on, be qualified for.

**deserved** adjective well-earned, merited, warranted, justified, justifiable, earned, rightful, due.

**deserving** adjective worthy, meritorious, commendable, praiseworthy, laudable, admirable, estimable.

**design** verb **1** *architects designing the structure* plan, draw, sketch, outline, map out, plot, block out, delineate, draft. **2** *design clothes/schemes* create, invent, originate, think up, conceive, fashion, fabricate, hatch, innovate; *inf.* dream up. **3** *a course designed for beginners* intend, aim, devise, contrive, tailor.

**design** noun **1** *the design was inadequate* plan, blueprint, drawing, sketch, outline, map, plot, diagram, delineation, draft, depiction, scheme, model. **2** *admire the fabric designs* pattern, motif, style, arrangement, composition, makeup, constitution, configuration, organization, construction, shape, figure. **3** *a clever design to defeat the enemy* scheme, plot, intrigue, expedient, stratagem, device, artifice. **4** *with the design of entering* intention, aim, purpose, objective, goal, end, target.

**designate** verb **1** *a new atomic particle designated "quark"* call, name, entitle, term, christen, dub, style, label, denominate, nickname. **2** *designated ambassador* appoint, nominate, depute, delegate, select, choose, elect, ordain, induct. **3** *at designated times* state, appoint, specify, define, stipulate, particularize, earmark, set aside, pinpoint. **4** *arrows designating direction* show, indicate, point out, mark, denote.

**designing** adjective scheming, plotting,

intriguing, conspiring, conniving, calculating, Machiavellian, cunning, crafty, artful, wily, devious, shrewd, sly, underhand, deceitful, tricky; *inf.* crooked.

**desirable** adjective **1** *a desirable job* attractive, sought-after, in demand, popular, covetable, enviable, agreeable, appealing, pleasant, admirable, worthwhile, profitable, good, excellent. **2** *it is desirable that no one knows* preferable, advisable, advantageous, beneficial, expedient. **3** *a desirable young woman* seductive, alluring, erotic, fetching, fascinating, beguiling; *inf.* sexy.

**desire** verb **1** *desire happiness* wish for, want, long/yearn for, crave, set one's heart on, hanker after, have a fancy for, fancy, be bent on, covet, lust after, burn for; *inf.* have a yen for; lech after, have the hots for. **2** *desire a cup of tea* request, ask for, want.

**desire** noun **1** *her desire for success* wish, want, fancy, inclination, preference; wanting, longing, yearning, craving, eagerness, enthusiasm, hankering, predilection, aspiration, proclivity, predisposition. **2** *overcome by desire* lust, lustfulness, sexual appetite, passion, carnal passion, concupiscence, libido, sensuality, sexuality, lasciviousness, lechery, libidinousness; *inf.* the hots.

**desired** adjective **1** *fitted to the desired length* required, necessary, proper, right, correct, appropriate, fitting, suitable, preferred, expected. **2** *the desired prize* wished for, longed for, craved, coveted.

**desirous** adjective **desirous of** *desirous of success* desiring, wishing (for), wishful of, hopeful of, avid/eager/anxious for, craving, ambitious for.

**desist** verb stop, cease, discontinue, abstain, give up, forbear/refrain from, break/leave off.

**desolate** adjective **1** *desolate plains* bare, barren, bleak, dismal, desert, waste, wild. **2** *desolate farms* deserted, uninhabited, unoccupied, depopulated, forsaken, abandoned, unpeopled, untenanted, unfrequented, unvisited, solitary, lonely, isolated. **3** *desolate at the news* sad, unhappy, wretched, downcast, disconsolate, forlorn, cheerless, distressed, grieving, bereft.

**despair** noun **1** *unemployed and full of despair* hopelessness, dejection, depression, desperation, disheartenment, discouragement, despondency, disconsolateness, defeatism, pessimism, melancholy, gloom, melancholia, misery. **2** *the boy is the despair of the teacher* hopeless case, bane, burden, bother, scourge.

**despair** verb lose hope, give up hope, give up, lose heart, be discouraged, be despondent, be pessimistic, resign oneself, throw in the towel.

**desperado** noun outlaw, bandit, gunman, criminal, lawbreaker, gangster, terrorist, thug, ruffian, hooligan, villain, hoodlum, mugger.

**desperate** adjective **1** *a desperate criminal/act* reckless, rash, hasty, impetuous, foolhardy, bold, madcap, wild, violent, frantic, mad, frenzied; risky, hazardous, precipitate, harebrained, imprudent, incautious, injudicious, indiscreet, ill-conceived. **2** *in desperate need* urgent, pressing, compelling, acute, critical, crucial, drastic, serious, grave, dire, extreme, great. **3** *the desperate state of the country* grave, appalling, outrageous, intolerable, deplorable, lamentable. **4** *trying to help desperate people* despairing, hopeless, wretched. **5** *desperate measures* last-ditch, last-resort, do-or-die.

**despicable** adjective contemptible, beyond contempt, reprehensible, vile, base, low, mean, scurvy, abominable, loathsome, hateful, detestable, odious, disreputable, ignoble, shameful, ignominious.

**despise** verb scorn, look down on, spurn, shun, disdain, slight, undervalue, deride, scoff/jeer at, sneer at, mock, revile, hate, detest, loathe, abhor, abominate, execrate, contemn.

**despite** preposition in spite of, notwithstanding, regardless of, in defiance of, in the face of.

**despondent** adjective hopeless, in despair, despairing, downcast, down, low, disheartened, discouraged, disconsolate, low-spirited, dispirited, downhearted, melancholy, gloomy, glum, morose, doleful, woebegone, miserable, wretched, distressed.

**despot** noun absolute ruler, autocrat, dictator, tyrant, oppressor.

**despotic** adjective absolute, autocratic, dictatorial, tyrannical, oppressive, totalitarian, domineering, imperious, arrogant, high-handed, authoritarian, arbitrary.

**destined** adjective **1** *a plane destined for Chicago* bound for, en route for, heading for/toward, directed/routed to, scheduled for. **2** *destined for the state* designed, intended, meant, set, set apart, designated, appointed, allotted. **3** *destined to die young* fated, ordained, preordained, foreordained, predestined, predetermined, doomed, foredoomed, certain, sure, bound, written in the cards.

**destiny** noun **1** *couldn't escape his destiny* fate, fortune, lot, portion, cup, due, future, doom. **2** *destiny drew them together* fate, divine decree, predestination, luck, fortune, chance, karma, kismet; the stars.

**destitute** adjective **1** *destitute refugees* poverty-stricken, indigent, impoverished, penurious, impecunious, penniless, insolvent, beggarly, down-and-out, poor, needy, hard up, badly off, on the breadline, pauperized; *inf.* up against it. **2** *destitute of ideas* devoid of, without, bereft of, deficient in, lacking, wanting, deprived of, empty, drained.

**destroy** verb **1** *destroy the bridge* demolish, knock down, pull down, tear down, level, raze, fell, dismantle, wreck, smash, shatter, crash, blow up, blow to bits, explode, annihilate, wipe out, bomb, torpedo. **2** *destroy the countryside* ruin, spoil, devastate, lay waste, ravage, wreak havoc on, ransack. **3** *destroy their confidence* terminate, quash, quell, crush, stifle, subdue, squash, extinguish, extirpate. **4** *destroy the herd/tribe* kill, kill off, slaughter, put to sleep, exterminate; slay, murder, assassinate, wipe out, massacre, liquidate, decimate. **5** *destroy the enemy/opponents* defeat, beat, conquer, vanquish, trounce, rout, drub; *inf.* lick, thrash.

**destruction** noun **1** *the destruction of the building* demolition, knocking down, pulling down, tearing down, leveling, razing, dismantling, wrecking, smashing, blowing up, wiping out, annihilation. **2** *the destruction of the countryside* ruination, ruin, spoiling, devastation, laying waste, desolation, ransacking, ravaging. **3** *the destruction of their confidence* termination, quashing, quelling, crushing, stifling, squashing, extinguishing, extirpation, extinction. **4** *the destruction of the herd/tribe* killing, slaughter, slaying, murder, assassination, massacre. **5** *the destruction of the enemy/opponents* defeat, beating, conquest, vanquishing, trouncing, rout.

**destructive** adjective **1** *destructive winds/wars* ruinous, devastating, disastrous, catastrophic, calamitous, cataclysmic, ravaging, fatal, deadly, dangerous, lethal, damaging, pernicious, noxious, injurious, harmful, detrimental, deleterious, hurtful. **2** *destructive comments* discrediting, invalidating, derogatory, denigrating, disparaging, disapproving, discouraging, undermining, negative, adverse.

**desultory** adjective haphazard, random, aimless, rambling, erratic, irregular, unmethodical, unsystematic, chaotic, inconsistent, inconstant, fitful, capricious.

**detach** verb **1** *detach the collar* unfasten, disconnect, unhitch, remove, separate, uncouple, loosen, free, sever, tear off, disengage, disjoin, disunite. **2** *detach oneself from the group* separate, move off, dissociate, segregate, isolate, cut off, disconnect, divide.

**detached** adjective **1** *a detached collar* unfastened, disconnected, unhitched, sep-

arate, loosened, free, severed. **2** *observing in a detached way* dispassionate, aloof, indifferent, unconcerned, reserved, unemotional, impersonal, cool, remote. **3** *detached commentators* objective, disinterested, unbiased, unprejudiced, impartial, nonpartisan, neutral, fair.

**detail** noun item, particular, fact, point, factor, element, circumstance, aspect, feature, respect, attribute, part, unit, component, member, accessory; unimportant point, insignificant item, trivial fact. **details** *fill in the details* particulars, fine points, niceties, minutiae, trivia. **in detail** comprehensively, fully, thoroughly, exhaustively.

**detail** verb specify, set forth, set out, list, enumerate, tabulate, catalog, spell out, delineate, relate, recount, narrate, recite, rehearse, describe, cite, point out, indicate, portray, depict, itemize, particularize, individualize.

**detailed** adjective **1** *a detailed bill/description* itemized, particularized, full, comprehensive, thorough, exhaustive, all-inclusive, circumstantial, precise, exact, specific, particular, meticulous. **2** *a detailed picture/story* complex, involved, elaborate, complicated, intricate, convoluted, entangled.

**detain** verb **1** *detained by business* hold/keep back, hold up, delay, keep, slow up/down, hinder, impede, check, retard, inhibit, stay. **2** *detain the accused* put/keep in custody, confine, imprison, lock up, incarcerate, impound, intern, restrain, hold.

**detect** verb **1** *detect hostility/smoke* notice, note, discern, perceive, make out, observe, spot, become aware of, recognize, distinguish, identify, catch, decry, sense, see, smell. **2** *accountants detected the error* discover, find out, turn up, uncover, bring to light, expose, unearth, reveal, unmask, unveil.

**detective** noun investigator; private investigator, FBI agent, police officer; *inf.* sleuth, tec, dick, private eye, tail, shadow, cop, gumshoe, G-man.

**deter** verb put off, prevent, stop, discourage, dissuade, talk out of, check, restrain, caution, frighten, intimidate, daunt, scare off, warn against, hold back, prohibit, hinder, impede, obstruct, block, inhibit.

**deteriorate** verb **1** *moral values deteriorating* get worse, worsen, decline, degenerate, sink, slip, go downhill, slide, lapse, fail, fall, drop, ebb, wane, retrograde, retrogress, slump, depreciate; *inf.* go to pot, go to hell, go to the dogs. **2** *buildings/food deteriorating* decay, decompose, disintegrate, become dilapidated, decline, degenerate, crumble, fall apart, fall to pieces, fall down, break up.

**determination** noun **1** *behave with determination* firmness, firmness of purpose, resoluteness, steadfastness, tenacity, single-mindedness, resolve, drive, push, thrust, fortitude, dedication, backbone, stamina, mettle, strong will, persistence, perseverance, conviction, doggedness, stubbornness, obduracy, intransigence. **2** *the committee's determination | the legal determination* decision, conclusion, judgment, verdict, opinion, diagnosis, prognosis.

**determine** verb **1** *determine the place of meeting* settle, fix, decide, agree on, establish, judge, arbitrate, decree, ordain. **2** *determine the argument* resolve, conclude, end, terminate, finish. **3** *determine the room dimensions* find out, discover, learn, establish, ascertain, check, verify, certify. **4** *determine to go alone* decide, resolve, choose, elect. **5** *conditions determining the nature of the soil* affect, influence, act/work on, decide, control, direct, rule, dictate, govern.

**determined** adjective **1** *a determined person/attitude* firm, resolute, steadfast, tenacious, purposeful, single-minded, dedicated, strong-willed, mettlesome, plucky, persistent, persevering, dogged, unflinching, unwavering, stubborn, obdurate, intransigent, indomitable, inflexible. **2** *determined on going* bent, intent, set.

**deterrent** noun disincentive, discouragement, curb, check, restraint, obstacle, hindrance, impediment, obstruction, block, barrier, inhibition.

**detest** verb loathe, abhor, hate, despise, abominate, execrate, feel aversion/hostility/animosity toward, feel disgust/distaste for, recoil/shrink from, feel repugnance toward.

**detract** verb **detract from** *their conduct detracts from their achievement* diminish, lower, devalue, devaluate, depreciate.

**detriment** noun injury, harm, damage, impairment, hurt, loss, disadvantage, disservice, ill, wrong, mischief.

**detrimental** adjective injurious, harmful, damaging, hurtful, deleterious, destructive, pernicious, disadvantageous, adverse, unfavorable, inimical, prejudicial.

**devastate** verb **1** *fire devastated the warehouse* lay waste, leave desolate, destroy, ruin, demolish, wreck, raze, level, annihilate, ravage, ransack, sack, despoil, spoil. **2** *devastated by the news* overcome, overwhelm, shock, traumatize, disconcert, discompose, discomfit, perturb.

**devastation** noun **1** *a scene of devastation* desolation, destruction, waste, ruin, wreckage, demolition, razing, annihilation. **2** *her complete devastation* shock, traumatization,

bewilderment, discomposure, discomfiture, perturbation.

**develop** verb **1** *cities developing rapidly* grow, evolve, mature, expand, enlarge, spread, advance, progress, prosper, flourish, make headway. **2** *develop a plan* begin, commence, start, set in motion, originate, invent, form, establish, institute, fashion, generate. **3** *develop a cough* begin to have, acquire, contract, pick up. **4** *develop a theme* elaborate (on), unfold, work out, enlarge on, expand (on), broaden, amplify, add to, augment, magnify, supplement, reinforce. **5** *an argument developed* come about, follow, happen, result, ensue, break out.

**development** noun **1** *the development of cities* growth, evolution, maturing, expansion, spread, progress, headway. **2** *the development of a plan* originating, invention, forming, establishment, institution; generation, propagation, rearing, cultivation. **3** *the development of themes* elaboration, unfolding, enlarging, expansion, augmentation. **4** *new developments in the affair* event, turn of events, occurrence, happening, circumstance, incident, situation, issue, outcome, upshot. **5** *a housing development* complex, estate, structure, conglomeration.

**deviant** adjective deviating, aberrant, divergent, abnormal, irregular, nonstandard, anomalous, peculiar, curious, queer, bizarre, eccentric, idiosyncratic, unorthodox, offbeat, wayward, perverse, warped, twisted, perverted; *inf.* bent, kinky, quirky.

**deviate** verb diverge, turn aside, step aside, depart from, digress, deflect, differ, vary, change, veer, swerve, bend, drift, stray, tack.

**deviation** noun divergence, departure, digression, deflection, variation, veering, straying, fluctuation, aberration, abnormality, irregularity, anomaly, inconsistency, discrepancy; change, shift, veer, swerve, bend, drift.

**device** noun **1** *a handy device* appliance, gadget, implement, utensil, tool, piece of equipment/apparatus, apparatus, instrument, machine, contrivance, contraption, invention; *inf.* gizmo. **2** *win by a cunning device* design, plot, scheme, ploy, project, stratagem, trick, artifice, ruse, dodge, gambit, maneuver, machination, strategy, intrigue, wile. **3** *the club device* emblem, symbol, insignia, crest, coat of arms, seal, badge, token, motif, design, mark, figure, motto, slogan, legend, logo, colophon, trademark.

**devil** noun **1** *the Devil defeated by God* Satan, Lucifer, Prince of Darkness, the Evil One, the Archfiend, Beelzebub, Lord of the Flies, *inf.* Old Nick. **2** *tempted by devils* demon, fiend, evil spirit. **3** *the master was* *a devil* brute, savage, beast, monster, ogre, demon, fiend, barbarian, rogue, scoundrel, villain, bully, knave. **4** *the child's a little devil* imp, scamp, rascal, rogue, mischief-maker, troublemaker. **5** *feel pity for the poor devils* wretch, unfortunate, beggar, creature, thing, sad case.

**devilish** adjective **1** *devilish practices* diabolic, diabolical, demonic, demoniacal, fiendish, satanic, infernal, hellish. **2** *a devilish creature* wicked, evil, abominable, atrocious, detestable, villainous, sinister, accursed, damnable.

**devious** adjective **1** *a devious merchant* underhand, underhanded, cunning, crafty, sly, wily, artful, guileful, scheming, designing, calculating, dishonest, deceitful, double-dealing; *inf.* crooked. **2** *go by a devious route* indirect, roundabout, deviating, circuitous, tortuous, rambling, wandering, erratic, digressive, excursive.

**devise** verb concoct, contrive, work out, plan, form, formulate, plot, scheme, project, invent, originate, create, compose, construct, frame, think/dream up, conceive, imagine, fabricate, hatch, put together, arrange.

**devote** verb assign, allot, allocate, set aside, set apart, reserve, commit, apply, consign, pledge, give, offer, dedicate, surrender.

**devoted** adjective **1** *a devoted follower* loyal, faithful, true, true blue, staunch, steadfast, constant, committed, dedicated, devout, fond, loving, admiring, affectionate, caring, attentive, warm, ardent. **2** *time devoted to reading* assigned, allotted, set aside, dedicated. **3** *buildings devoted to God* dedicated, consecrated, blessed, sanctified, hallowed.

**devotee** noun enthusiast, fan, admirer, addict, follower, adherent, disciple, supporter, champion, advocate, votary, fanatic, zealot; *inf.* buff, freak.

**devotion** noun **1** *the devotion of his followers* loyalty, faithfulness, fidelity, steadfastness, constancy, commitment, adherence, allegiance, dedication; fondness, love, admiration, affection, attentiveness, caring, warmness, closeness. **2** *men full of devotion* devoutness, piety, religiousness, spirituality, godliness, holiness, sanctity, saintliness.

**devour** verb **1** *devour the feast* eat greedily/hungrily, eat up, consume, swallow up, gulp down, gobble up, bolt, wolf down, guzzle, stuff down, cram in, gorge oneself on, feast on; *inf.* tuck into, pack away, polish off, stuff one's face with, pig out on. **2** *flames devoured the house* consume, engulf, envelop, destroy, devastate, lay waste, demolish, wipe out, ruin, wreck, annihilate. **3** *children devouring books* feast on, revel in, delight in, enjoy, relish, appreciate.

**4** *devoured by anxiety/jealousy* consume, swallow up, engulf, swamp, overcome, overwhelm.

**devout** adjective **1** *a devout Christian* pious, religious, reverent, churchgoing, godly, saintly, holy, prayerful, orthodox, pure, righteous. **2** *devout hope* sincere, genuine, deep, profound, heartfelt, earnest, fervent, fervid, intense, ardent, vehement, passionate, zealous.

**dexterity** noun **1** *craftsmen showing dexterity* deftness, adroitness, nimbleness, agility, skillfulness, skill, knack, adeptness, handiness, facility, proficiency. **2** *crisis management requires dexterity* cleverness, shrewdness, smartness, astuteness, cunning, craft, sagacity, sharp-wittedness, acuteness, ingenuity, resourcefulness, inventiveness.

**dexterous** adjective **1** *dexterous craftsmen* deft, adroit, nimble, agile, skillful, skilled, adept, handy, proficient, expert, talented, accomplished, artistic. **2** *a dexterous businessman* clever, shrewd, smart, astute, cunning, crafty, wily, artful, sagacious, sharp-witted, acute, ingenious, resourceful, inventive.

**diabolic, diabolical** adjective **1** *diabolic forces* devilish, fiendish, demonic, demoniacal, satanic, infernal, hellish. **2** *a diabolic slave master* fiendish, wicked, evil, sinful, savage, brutish, cruel, malevolent, malicious, black-hearted, nasty, abominable, hateful, damnable. **3** *a diabolic task* difficult, complicated, complex, tricky, nasty, unpleasant, dreadful, vile.

**diagnose** verb identify, determine, distinguish, recognize, detect, pinpoint, pronounce.

**diagram** noun drawing, sketch, draft, illustration, picture, representation, outline, delineation.

**dialogue** noun conversation, talk, tête-à-tête, chat, chitchat, gossip, communication, debate, argument, exchange of views, discourse, discussion, conference, converse, colloquy, interlocution, duologue, confabulation, parley, palaver; *inf.* powwow, confab, rap session.

**diaphanous** adjective sheer, fine, delicate, light, thin, silken, chiffony, gossamer, gauzy, cobwebby, translucent, transparent, see-through.

**diary** noun day-by-day account, daily record, journal, chronicle, log, logbook; blog, weblog.

**diatribe** noun tirade, harangue, denunciation, philippic, reproof, reprimand, rebuke, upbraiding; invective, vituperation, abuse, castigation, criticism, stricture; *inf.* tongue-lashing, knocking.

**dicey** adjective uncertain, risky, chancy,

difficult, tricky, dangerous, ticklish; *inf.* hairy.

**dictate** verb **1** *dictate the letter* read aloud, speak, say, utter, recite. **2** *dictate terms* prescribe, lay down, impose, set down, order, command, decree, ordain, direct, pronounce, enjoin, promulgate. **3** *always dictating to others* give orders, order about, lay down the law, impose one's will, boss about, domineer; *inf.* call the shots, throw one's weight around.

**dictator** noun absolute ruler, despot, autocrat, tyrant, oppressor.

**dictatorial** adjective **1** *dictatorial government* absolute, unlimited, unrestricted, arbitrary, omnipotent, all-powerful, autocratic, totalitarian, authoritarian, despotic, tyrannical, autarchic. **2** *dictatorial bosses* tyrannical, despotic, oppressive, iron-handed, imperious, overbearing, domineering, peremptory, high-handed, authoritarian, dogmatic, high and mighty; *inf.* bossy.

**dictatorship** noun autarchy, totalitarian state, absolute monarchy, absolute rule; despotism, autocracy, tyranny, authoritarianism, totalitarianism, absolutism.

**diction** noun **1** *learn diction through elocution lessons* enunciation, articulation, elocution, pronunciation, speech, intonation, inflection, delivery. **2** *impressed by the writer's diction* style, language, phraseology phrasing, wording, expression, idiom.

**didactic** adjective *didactic prose* instructive, instructional, edifying, preceptive, pedagogic, pedantic, moralistic.

**die** verb **1** *she died last night* pass away, pass on, lose one's life, depart this life, expire, decease, breathe one's last, meet one's end, lay down one's life, be no more perish, go to one's last resting place; *inf.* give up the ghost, kick the bucket, push up the daisies, bite the dust, snuff it, croak, turn up one's toes, cash in one's chips. **2** *hope died* come to an end, end, vanish, disappear, pass, fade, fall away, dwindle, melt away, dissolve, subside, decline, sink, lapse, ebb, wane, wilt, wither, evanesce. **3** *the engine died* stop, halt, fail, break down, peter out, fizzle out, run down, fade away, lose power. **4** *I nearly died laughing* collapse with, be overcome with, be overwhelmed/overpowered by, succumb to. **5** *dying to see you* be eager, be desperate, long.

**differ** verb **1** *tastes differ* be different, be unlike, be dissimilar, be distinguishable, vary, diverge. **2** *parties agreeing to differ* disagree, fail to agree, dissent, be at variance, be in dispute/opposition, oppose, take issue, conflict, clash, quarrel, argue, wrangle, quibble, squabble, altercate, **differ from** *results differing from the norm* vary from,

diverge from, deviate from, depart from, run counter to, contravene, contradict, contrast with.

**difference** noun **1** *the difference between/in their lifestyles* dissimilarity, unlikeness, dissimilitude, contrast, distinction, distinctness, differentiation, variance, variation, divergence, deviation, disparity, incongruity. **2** *spot the difference* distinction, peculiarity, oddity, idiosyncrasy, singularity, eccentricity, individuality. **3** *the two had a difference* disagreement, dispute, disputation, argument, debate, misunderstanding, quarrel, row. **4** *pay the difference* balance, remainder, rest, residue, residuum, excess.

**different** adjective **1** *tastes different from ours* unlike, dissimilar, contrasting, diverse, divergent, deviating, disparate, incompatible, inconsistent, opposed, at variance, at odds, clashing, conflicting, discrepant. **2** *a different dress every day* separate, other, nonidentical, distinct, individual, discrete. **3** *available in different colors* various, several, many, numerous, assorted, varied, miscellaneous, diverse. **4** *looking for something different* unusual, out of the ordinary, uncommon, distinctive, rare, unique, novel, special, singular, unconventional, atypical, odd, strange, bizarre.

**differentiate** verb distinguish, discriminate, make a distinction, contrast, see/discern a difference; tell apart, set apart, separate, mark off.

**difficult** adjective **1** *digging in this soil is difficult* hard, strenuous, arduous, laborious, demanding, formidable, tough, onerous, burdensome, exhausting, tiring, wearisome, backbreaking, painful, oppressive; *inf.* no picnic. **2** *a difficult problem* complicated, complex, involved, intricate, puzzling, problematic, baffling, perplexing, knotty, thorny, ticklish, delicate, obscure, abstract, abstruse, recondite, enigmatic, profound, deep. **3** *a difficult child* troublesome, tiresome, demanding, unmanageable, intractable, perverse, recalcitrant, obstreperous, refractory, fractious, unaccommodating, uncooperative, uncompliant, unamenable. **4** *difficult people to choose presents for* hard to please, fussy, particular, fastidious, perfectionist, critical, hypercritical, finicky. **5** *arrive at a difficult time* inconvenient, ill-timed, disadvantageous, unfavorable. **6** *go through difficult times* hard, straitened, hard-pressed, bad, tough, grim, dark.

**difficulty** noun **1** *dig with difficulty* difficultness, strenuousness, arduousness, laboriousness, toughness, struggling, awkwardness; labor, strain, struggle. **2** *the difficulty of the problem* complexity, intricacy, perplexity, knottiness, delicacy, prescribe for, attend to, minister· to, care for, cure, heal. **2** *doctor the machinery* patch up, repair, fix, mend, botch. **3** *doctor the drinks* adulterate, contaminate, dilute, water down, weaken, mix, cut, lace; *inf.* spike. **4** *doctor the evidence* tamper with, in-obscurity, abstruseness. **3** *encounter a difficulty* complication, problem, snag, hitch, hindrance, obstacle, pitfall, hurdle, impediment, obstruction, barrier. **4** *raise difficulties* protest, objection, complaint, gripe, demur, cavil. **5** *in difficulty|in financial difficulties* predicament, quandary, dilemma, plight, distress, embarrassment, trouble, hot/deep water; straits; *inf.* fix, jam, spot, scrape. **6** *the difficulty of the times* hardship, trial, tribulation, ordeal, exigency.

**diffident** adjective shy, bashful, modest, sheepish, unconfident, unassertive, timid, timorous, apprehensive, fearful, shrinking, reserved, withdrawn, hesitant, reluctant, doubtful, unsure, insecure.

**diffuse** adjective **1** *diffuse light* diffused, spread out, scattered, dispersed, not concentrated. **2** *a diffuse style* verbose, wordy, prolix, long-winded, copious, profuse, discursive, rambling, wandering, meandering, digressive, circuitous.

**diffuse** verb spread around, scatter, disperse, disseminate, dissipate, dispel.

**dig** verb **1** *enjoy digging|dig the earth* break up soil/ground; work, break up, loosen up, turn over, spade, delve, till, cultivate, harrow, plow. **2** *dig a tunnel/hole* dig out, excavate, quarry, hollow out, scoop out, gouge, tunnel, burrow, mine, channel. **3** *dig someone in the ribs* poke, prod, jab, thrust, drive, push, punch. **4** *dig into the history* delve, search, probe, investigate, research. **5** *dig potatoes* unearth, dig up. **6** *dig the music* like, love, enjoy, appreciate. **7** *I dig what you're saying* understand, comprehend, follow, grasp, make out; *inf.* get. **dig up** *dig up new information* uncover, root out, extricate, bring to light, come up with, discover, find, come across.

**dig** noun **1** *a dig in the ribs* poke, prod, jab, thrust, push, punch. **2** *tired of digs at/about his baldness* gibe, jeer, taunt, sneer, insult, slur, quip; *inf.* wisecrack, crack.

**digest** verb **1** *digest food* assimilate, absorb, break down, dissolve, macerate. **2** *digest the facts* take in, understand, comprehend, grasp, master, consider, think about, contemplate, mull over, weigh up, reflect on, ponder, meditate on, study. **3** *digest the information* shorten, reduce, condense, abridge, compress, compact, summarize, précis.

**digest** noun summary, synopsis, abstract, précis, résumé, outline, abridgment, epitome, review, compendium.

**dignified** adjective stately, noble, solemn, grave, formal, decorous, reserved, ceremonious, courtly, majestic, august, lofty, exalted, regal, lordly, imposing, impressive, grand.

**dignify** verb add dignity/distinction to, distinguish, honor, grace, adorn, exalt, enhance, ennoble, glorify, elevate, make lofty, aggrandize, upgrade.

**dignitary** noun public figure, notable, notability, worthy, personage, luminary, VIP, pillar of society, leading light, celebrity, big name, somebody, star, lion; *inf.* bigwig, top brass, big gun, big shot, big wheel, celeb.

**dignity** noun **1** *the dignity of the occasion* stateliness, nobleness, nobility, solemnity, gravity, formality, decorum, propriety, reserve, ceremoniousness, courtliness, majesty, augustness, loftiness, exaltedness, regalness, regality, lordliness, impressiveness, grandeur. **2** *the dignity of work* worthiness, honorability, nobility, excellence, respectability; worth, merit, virtue. **3** *achieve dignity in social affairs* high rank, high standing, high station, status, elevation, eminence, honor, glory, greatness, importance.

**digress** verb get off the subject, stray from the point, deviate/deflect from the topic, go off at a tangent, diverge, turn aside, depart, drift, ramble, wander, meander.

**dilapidated** adjective rundown, broken-down, tumbledown, ramshackle, in ruins, ruined, falling to pieces, falling apart, in disrepair, shabby, battered, rickety, shaky, crumbling, decayed, decaying, decrepit, worn-out, neglected, uncared-for.

**dilatory** adjective delaying, dallying, dilly-dallying, procrastinating, postponing, deferring, putting off, stalling, time-wasting.

**dilemma** noun devil and the deep blue sea, Catch-22, vicious circle, quandary, predicament, plight, difficulty, tight corner/spot, problem, puzzle.

**diligent** adjective assiduous, industrious, conscientious, hardworking, painstaking, meticulous, thorough, careful, attentive, heedful, intent, earnest, studious, constant, persevering, sedulous, persistent, dogged, plodding, slogging, laborious.

**dim** adjective **1** *a dim light* faint, weak, feeble, pale, dull, dingy, lackluster, muted. **2** *dim skies* dark, darkish, gray, overcast, leaden, gloomy, somber, dusky, lowering, cloudy, hazy, misty, foggy, crepuscular, tenebrous. **3** *dim corridors* dark, darkened, gloomy, badly lit, poorly lit, dingy, dismal. **4** *a dim shape/recollection* vague, ill-defined, indistinct, unclear, shadowy, blurred, blurry, fuzzy, imperceptible, nebulous, obscured, bleared, bleary, hazy, confused, imperfect. **5** *prospects are rather dim* unpromising, unfavorable, discouraging, disheartening, depressing.

**dim** verb **1** *dim the stage lights* turn down, lower. **2** *the light dimmed* grow dim, fade, grow faint/feeble, dull, pale, blur. **3** *the skies dimmed* grow dark, darken, cloud over, grow leaden. **4** *memories/recollections dimming* grow dim, fade, blur, become blurred/confused.

**dimension** noun **1** *of huge dimension | the dimensions of the tank* extent; length, width, breadth, depth, area, size, volume, capacity, bulk; proportions. **2** *add another dimension to entertainment* aspect, side, feature, facet, element. **dimensions** *the dimensions of the problem* size, extent, scope, measure, scale, range, magnitude, greatness, importance.

**diminish** verb **1** *their power diminished | time diminished their power* lessen, grow less, decrease, reduce, shrink, contract, abate, grow weak/weaker; lower, curtail, cut, contract, narrow. **2** *diminish his reputation* belittle, disparage, denigrate, depreciate, deprecate, derogate, devalue, demean, detract from.

**diminutive** adjective small, little, tiny, petite, slight, elfin, minute, miniature, mini, small-scale, compact, microscopic, midget, undersized, dwarfish, pygmy, Lilliputian; *inf.* wee, baby.

**din** noun uproar, row, racket, commotion, hullabaloo, hubbub, tumult, clangor, outcry, brouhaha, crash, clatter, clash, shouting, yelling; clamor, noise, pandemonium, bedlam, babel.

**dine** verb eat, sup, feed, feast, banquet. **dine on** eat, consume, feed on.

**dingy** adjective dark, dull, dim, gloomy, drab, dismal, dreary, cheerless, dusky, somber, murky, hazy, smoggy, smoky, sooty, dirty, discolored, grimy, soiled, faded, shabby, worn, seedy, rundown.

**dip** verb **1** *dip the garment in dye* immerse, submerge, plunge, duck, dunk, lower, sink, souse, douse, soak, drench, steep, bathe, rinse. **2** *the sun dipping behind the horizon* sink, set, descend, fade, disappear, subside. **3** *profits dipping* fall, go down, drop, drop/fall off, decrease, decline, slump. **4** *the road dips* slope, descend, fall, slant down, droop, sag. **5** *dip water* scoop up, scoop, spoon, ladle. **dip into 1** *dip into a book* skim, browse, glance at. **2** *dip into art* dabble in, scratch the surface of, play at, sample. **3** *dip into one's savings* draw on, take out of, use/spend part of.

**dip** noun **1** *give the garment a dip | take a dip* immersion, plunge, ducking, dunking, sousing, dousing, soaking, drenching; swim, dive, plunge. **2** *a dip in profits* fall, falling-off, drop, dropping-off, decrease, decline, lowering, slump. **3** *a dip in the terrain* slope, incline, decline, slant, descent, hollow, concavity, depression, basin.

**diplomacy** noun **1** *ministers skilled in di-* plomacy statesmanship, statecraft, international relations/politics; negotiations. **2** *treating her objections with diplomacy* tactfulness, tact, subtlety, discretion, judiciousness, prudence, delicacy, sensitivity, finesse, *savoir faire*, politeness, cleverness, artfulness, cunning, skill.

**diplomat** noun **1** *an international meeting of diplomats* ambassador, foreign minister, envoy, emissary, legate, consul, attaché. **2** *the diplomat of the firm* conciliator, reconciler, peacemaker, mediator, negotiator, tactician, arbitrator.

**diplomatic** adjective **1** *a diplomatic post* ambassadorial, consular. **2** *diplomatic handling* tactful, discreet, judicious, prudent, careful, delicate, sensitive, politic, clever, skillful, artful.

**dire** adjective **1** *in dire straits | dire poverty* terrible, dreadful, appalling, frightful, awful, horrible, atrocious, grim, cruel, grievous, disastrous, ruinous, miserable, wretched, woeful, calamitous, catastrophic, cataclysmic, distressing, harrowing, shocking. **2** *dire warnings* ominous, sinister, portentous, gloomy, gloom-and-doom, grim, dreadful, dismal, unpropitious, inauspicious, unfavorable, pessimistic. **3** *in dire need of money* urgent, desperate, drastic, pressing, crying, vital, grave, critical, crucial, extreme, compelling, exigent.

**direct** verb **1** *direct the operation* administer, manage, be in charge/control/command of, lead, run, command, control, govern, conduct, handle, preside over, rule, supervise, superintend, oversee, guide, mastermind, regulate, orchestrate, engineer; *inf.* be the boss of, run the show, call the shots. **2** *directed to work late* command, order, instruct, charge, bid, dictate, adjure, enjoin. **3** *direct them to the station* give directions to, guide, steer, lead, conduct, accompany, usher, escort, navigate, pilot. **direct at** aim at, address to, intend/mean for, destine for, focus on, train at, turn on, fix on.

**direct** adjective **1** *a direct road* straight, undeviating, unswerving, uncircuitous, shortest. **2** *a direct approach* immediate, firsthand, personal, face-to-face, head-on, noninterventional. **3** *a direct statement/manner* frank, blunt, straightforward, straight, straight to the point, explicit, clear, plain, unequivocal, unambiguous, honest, candid, open, sincere, plainspoken, outspoken, forthright, downright, point blank, matter-of-fact, categorical. **4** *the direct opposite* exact, absolute, complete, downright, thorough, diametrical. **5** *a direct quotation* exact, precise, word for word, verbatim, accurate, correct.

**direction** noun **1** *his direction of the project* administration, management, government, supervision, superintendence, regulation, orchestration; control, command, conduct, handling, running, overseeing, masterminding, disposal; leadership, guidance. **2** *ignore the teacher's direction* command, order, instruction, bidding, charge, dictate, enjoinment, prescription. **3** *which direction did they take?* way, route, course, path, track, road, line, run, bearing, orientation. **4** *the direction of their policy/statement* drift, aim, tack, scope, bent, bias, tendency.

**directive** noun ruling, regulation, decree, edict, notice, ordinance, mandate, fiat. *See* DIRECTION 2.

**directly** adverb **1** *travel directly* straight, in a straight line, as the crow flies, by the shortest route, without deviation. **2** *leave directly* immediately, at once, instantly, right/straight away, without delay/hesitation, quickly, speedily, promptly; *inf.* pronto. **3** *speak directly* frankly, bluntly, straightforwardly, explicitly, clearly, plainly, unequivocally, unambiguously, sincerely, truthfully, outspokenly, forthrightly, point-blank, matter-of-factly. **4** *talk directly to the manager* at first hand, firsthand, personally, face to face, head on. **5** *it's directly opposite* exactly, immediately, diametrically.

**director** noun administrator, controller, manager, executive, chairman, chairwoman, chairperson, chair, head, chief, principal, leader, governor, president, superintendent, supervisor, overseer, organizer, producer; *inf.* boss, kingpin, top dog, honcho.

**dirge** noun elegy, lament, funeral song/chant, burial hymn, dead march, requiem, keen, threnody.

**dirt** noun **1** *clean the dirt from the room* grime, dust, soot, smut, muck, mud, filth, mire, sludge, slime, ooze, waste, dross, pollution; smudge, stain, tarnish; *inf.* crud, yuck, grunge. **2** *piles of dirt by the roadside* earth, soil, loam, clay, silt. **3** *disapprove of the dirt in modern novels* obscenity, indecency, smut, sordidness, coarseness, bawdiness, ribaldry, salaciousness, lewdness, pornography; *inf.* sleaze, sleaziness. **4** *spreading dirt about the neighbors* scandal, gossip, talk, rumor.

**dirty** adjective **1** *dirty rooms/clothes* unclean, soiled, grimy, begrimed, grubby, messy, dusty, sooty, mucky, muddy, filthy, bedraggled, slimy, polluted, sullied, foul, stained, spotted, smudged, tarnished, defiled, nasty; *inf.* cruddy, yucky, grungy. **2** *dirty jokes* blue, obscene, indecent, vulgar, smutty, coarse, bawdy, suggestive, ribald, salacious, risqué, prurient, lewd, lascivious, licentious, pornographic, off color; *inf.* sleazy. **3** *a dirty cheat* nasty, mean, base, low, vile, contemptible, des-

picable, cowardly, ignominious, sordid, beggarly, squalid. **4** *a dirty trick | dirty play* unsporting, unfair, dishonorable, unscrupulous, dishonest, crooked, illegal, deceitful, double-dealing, corrupt. **5** *a dirty look* malevolent, smoldering, resentful, bitter, angry, indignant, annoyed, peeved, offended. **6** *a dirty rumor* nasty, unkind, scandalous, defamatory, slanderous, libelous.

**dirty** verb soil, stain, muddy, begrime, blacken, mess up, spatter, smudge, smear, spot, splash, spoil, sully, pollute, foul, defile, besmirch.

**disability** noun impairment, disablement, infirmity, defect, handicap, disorder, affliction, ailment, complaint, illness, malady; incapacity, unfitness, weakness, incapability, inability, incompetence, ineptitude, disqualification.

**disable** verb incapacitate, impair, damage, put out of action, debilitate, indispose, weaken, enfeeble, cripple, lame, handicap, immobilize, hamstring, paralyze, prostrate.

**disabled** adjective incapacitated, impaired, handicapped, debilitated, unfit, out of action, infirm, weak, weakened, enfeebled, crippled, lame, immobilized, bedridden, paralyzed.

**disadvantage** noun **1** *the disadvantages of the situation* drawback, snag, downside, weak spot/point, weakness, flaw, defect, fault, handicap, trouble, liability; *inf.* minus, fly in the ointment. **2** *people suffering from financial disadvantage* deprivation, privation, hardship, lack, burden. **3** *to their disadvantage* disservice, detriment, prejudice, harm, damage; loss, injury, hurt, mischief.

**disagree** verb **1** *the two sides disagreed* differ, fail to agree, dissent, stand opposed, be at variance/odds, diverge, disaccord. **2** *the stories disagreed* differ, vary, conflict, clash, contrast, diverge, be discordant. **3** *children constantly disagreeing* quarrel, argue, bicker, wrangle, squabble, spar, dispute; *inf.* fall out, have words.

**disagreeable** adjective **1** *a disagreeable experience* unpleasant, displeasing, nasty, horrible, dreadful, hateful, detestable, abominable, odious, objectionable, offensive, obnoxious, repugnant, repulsive, repellent, revolting, disgusting, distasteful, nauseating, unsavory, unpalatable. **2** *a disagreeable old man* bad-tempered, ill-natured, nasty, cross, irritable, rude, surly, discourteous, impolite, churlish, peevish, contrary.

**disagreement** noun **1** *the disagreement of the two sides* difference of opinion, dissent, dispute, contention, disaccord, discord. **2** *the disagreement of/between the* *accounts* difference, dissimilarity, variation, variance, discrepancy, disparity, dissimilitude, incompatibility, incongruity, contradiction, conflict, clash, contrast, divergence, deviation. **3** *the disagreement between the children* quarrel, argument, wrangle, squabble, altercation, dispute, debate, disputation, discord, strife, conflict, war of words; bickering, sparring, contention, dissension, disharmony; *inf.* falling out.

**disappear** verb **1** *the sun disappearing below the horizon* pass from sight, vanish, be lost to view/sight, recede, recede from view, fade, fade/melt away, withdraw, depart, retreat, ebb, wane, dematerialize, evanesce, evaporate; *inf.* vamoose. **2** *customs that have disappeared* die out, die, cease to be/exist, end, pass away, expire, perish, become extinct.

**disappoint** verb **1** *sorry to disappoint you* let down, fail, dishearten, depress, dispirit, upset, sadden, dash the hopes of, chagrin, dismay, disgruntle, disenchant, disillusion, dissatisfy, vex. **2** *disappoint their plans* thwart, frustrate, foil, defeat, baffle, hinder, obstruct, hamper, impede, interfere with.

**disappointed** adjective upset, saddened, let down, disheartened, downhearted, cast down, downcast, depressed, dispirited, chagrined, disenchanted, disillusioned, discontented, dissatisfied; thwarted, frustrated, foiled, defeated, failed, baffled.

**disappointment** noun **1** *hide one's disappointment* sadness, regret, distress, chagrin, disgruntlement, displeasure, disenchantment, disillusionment, discontent, dissatisfaction, vexation. **2** *the disappointment of their plans* thwarting, frustration, foiling; defeat, failure, unfulfillment. **3** *the event was a disappointment* letdown, failure, fiasco, setback, blow, misfortune, disaster; *inf.* washout.

**disapprove** verb **1** *disapprove of their behavior* find unacceptable, be against, deplore, criticize, frown on, take a dim view of, look askance at, censure, blame, condemn, denounce, object to, take exception to, reproach, rebuke, reprove. **2** *disapprove the plans* turn down, reject, veto, disallow, set aside; *inf.* give the thumbs down to.

**disarray** noun disorder, untidiness, confusion, chaos, dishevelment; mess, muddle, clutter, jumble, mix-up, tangle; shambles.

**disaster** noun **1** *natural disasters* catastrophe, calamity, cataclysm, tragedy, act of God, accident, mishap, misadventure, mischance, stroke of ill-luck, setback, reverse/reversal of fortune, reversal, heavy blow, shock, buffet; adversity, trouble, misfortune, ruin, ruination. **2** *the play was*

*a disaster* failure, fiasco; *inf.* flop, bomb, dud, washout.

**disastrous** adjective catastrophic, calamitous, cataclysmic, tragic, devastating, ravaging, dire, terrible, shocking, appalling, dreadful, black, harmful, injurious, detrimental, ruinous, unfortunate.

**disbelief** noun unbelief, lack of belief, skepticism, incredulity, doubt, discredit, distrust, mistrust, questioning, agnosticism, atheism, nihilism.

**discard** verb throw away/out, get rid of, dispose of, toss out, jettison, scrap, dispense with, cast aside, reject, repudiate, abandon, relinquish, forsake, drop, have done with, shed; *inf.* dump, ditch.

**discern** verb see, notice, observe, perceive, make out, distinguish, detect, descry, recognize, determine, differentiate.

**discernible** adjective visible, noticeable, observable, perceptible, perceivable, distinguishable, detectable, recognizable, apparent, obvious, clear.

**discerning** adjective discriminating, astute, shrewd, ingenious, clever, intelligent, perceptive, sharp, quick, perspicacious, penetrating, critical, percipient, judicious, subtle, prudent, sound, wise, knowing, sagacious, sapient.

**discharge** verb **1** *discharge the patient/soldier* set free, free, let go, release, liberate. **2** *discharge from employment* dismiss, remove, get rid of, oust, expel, cashier; *inf.* sack, fire, ax, send packing, give the ax/sack/boot to, boot out. **3** *discharge a weapon* fire, shoot, let/set off, explode, detonate. **4** *discharge pus/fumes* exude, ooze, excrete, give off, leak, dispense, emit, send out, send/pour forth, eject, release, gush, void. **5** *discharge a duty* carry out, perform, do, accomplish, achieve, fulfill, execute, observe, abide by. **6** *discharge a load* unload, disburden, remove, unburden, off-load, relieve. **7** *discharge a debt/obligation* pay, settle, clear, honor, meet, liquidate, satisfy; *inf.* square.

**discharge** noun **1** *soldiers receiving a discharge* release, liberation, clearance. **2** *his discharge from the firm* dismissal, removal, ejection, ousting, expulsion, cashiering, *inf.* firing, axing, sacking. **3** *the discharge from a weapon* firing, shooting, explosion, detonation, blast, burst, pop, report, volley, salvo, fusillade. **4** *the discharge of pus/fumes* excretion, emission, ejection, release, voidance. **5** *a watery discharge* excretion, exudate, emission, flow, secretion, ooze, suppuration, pus, seepage. **6** *discharge of duty* carrying out, performing, accomplishment, achievement, fulfillment, execution, observance, performance. **7** *discharge of a debt* payment, settlement, clearance, honoring, meeting.

**disciple** noun apostle, follower, pupil, student, believer, adherent, devotee, votary, upholder, supporter, advocate, proponent, satellite, partisan.

**discipline** noun **1** *yoga is a useful discipline* training, drilling, exercise, regimen, routine, method; instruction, coaching, teaching, indoctrination, inculcation. **2** *discipline required for the exercise* control, self-control, self-restraint, strictness, orderliness, regulation, direction, government, restriction, limitation; restraint, check, curb. **3** *students in need of discipline* punishment, chastisement, castigation, correction; penalty, reprimand, rebuke, reproof. **4** *literature and other disciplines* field of study, field, branch of knowledge, course of study, course, area, subject, specialty.

**discipline** verb **1** *discipline the troops* train, drill, break in, exercise, instruct, coach, teach, educate, tutor, prepare, ground, indoctrinate, inculcate, inure, toughen. **2** *discipline oneself* control, restrain, regulate, govern, restrict, limit, check, curb. **3** *discipline the children* punish, chastise, castigate, correct, penalize, reprimand, rebuke, reprove.

**disclose** verb **1** *disclose confidential details* reveal, divulge, tell, impart, communicate, make public, broadcast, publish, release, unveil, leak, let slip, blurt out, blab, admit, confess, avow; *inf.* spill the beans about, let the cat out of the bag about, blow the lid off, squeal about. **2** *disclose the contents of the box* uncover, show, exhibit, expose, lay bare, unveil, bring to light.

**discomfit** verb **1** *discomfited by personal questions* embarrass, disconcert, make uncomfortable, take aback, nonplus, abash, confuse, ruffle, fluster, upset, disturb, perturb, discompose, discomfort; *inf.* faze, rattle, discombobulate. **2** *discomfit the enemy's plans* thwart, frustrate, foil, obstruct, hinder, hamper, check, upset.

**disconcert** verb **1** *disconcerted by the silence in the room* unsettle, shake, disturb, perturb, daunt, bewilder, upset, agitate, worry, perplex, confound, distract, throw off balance; *inf.* throw, faze, rattle. *See* DISCOMFIT 1. **2** *disconcerting their plans* thwart, upset, undo. *See* DISCOMFIT 2.

**disconnect** verb sever, uncouple, disengage, detach, unhook, unhitch, unlink, disjoin, disunite, separate, part, split up, interrupt.

**disconsolate** adjective despondent, wretched, miserable, heartbroken, forlorn, grief-stricken, inconsolable, woebegone, dejected, low, low-spirited, dispirited, down, depressed, downcast, gloomy, melancholy, blue; *inf.* down in the mouth/dumps.

**discontent** noun discontentment, dissatisfaction, restlessness, impatience, fretfulness, displeasure, unhappiness, envy, regret, umbrage, disaffection, disquiet.

**discontented** adjective dissatisfied, fed up, restless, impatient, fretful, complaining, displeased, disgruntled, querulous, unhappy, envious, regretful, disaffected, exasperated.

**discontinue** verb stop, end, put an end/stop to, finish, bring to a halt, terminate, cease, abandon, give up, break off, cancel, drop, refrain from, quit, suspend, interrupt; *inf.* cut out.

**discord** noun **1** *bitter discord between the leaders* dissension, conflict, friction, contention, strife, opposition, hostility, wrangling, clashing, incompatibility, variance, disunity, rupture. **2** *the discord of the instruments* disharmony, dissonance, cacophony, harshness, jarring, jangling, din, racket.

**discount** verb **1** *discount what he says* disregard, ignore, pass over, overlook, pay no attention to, take no notice of, brush off, gloss over. **2** *discount $5 from the price* deduct, take off, rebate; *inf.* knock off. **3** *discount the regular price* reduce, lower, lessen, mark down; *inf.* knock down.

**discount** noun markdown, deduction, price cut, cut, rebate, price concession, reduction.

**discourage** verb **1** *the outcome discouraged him* dishearten, dispirit, deject, cast down, depress, demoralize, disappoint, daunt, intimidate, cow, unnerve. **2** *discourage them from applying* put off, dissuade, deter, talk out of, advise against, urge against, caution against, restrain, inhibit. **3** *discourage the idea* oppose, disapprove of, repress, deprecate, put a damper on, throw cold water on. **4** *a preparation discouraging mildew* prevent, check, curb, hinder, obstruct, suppress, inhibit.

**discourse** noun **1** *engage in discourse* conversation, talk, dialogue, communication, discussion, conference, colloquy, converse, chat, chitchat, confabulation; *inf.* confab. **2** *a discourse on art* address, speech, lecture, oration, homily, essay, treatise, dissertation, paper, study.

**discourteous** adjective rude, impolite, ill-mannered, bad-mannered, unmannerly, uncivil, curt, abrupt, brusque, short, gruff, boorish, churlish, ungracious, ungentlemanly, unladylike, ill-bred, uncouth, disrespectful, ungallant, insolent, impertinent, impudent.

**discover** verb **1** *discover new talent* find, come across/upon, stumble upon, chance upon, light upon, locate, bring to light, uncover, unearth, turn up; *inf.* dig up. **2**

*discover that he was lying* find out, come to know, learn, realize, detect, determine, ascertain, recognize, see, spot, notice, perceive, reveal, disclose; *inf.* get wise to the fact. **3** *discover a new drug* invent, originate, devise, pioneer, design, contrive, conceive of.

**discovery** noun **1** *the discovery of a quiet village* finding, locating, location, uncovering. **2** *the discovery that they lied* realization, detection, determination, recognition, revelation, disclosure. **3** *discovery of new drugs* invention, origination, devising, pioneering, introduction. **4** *recent discoveries* find, invention, breakthrough, innovation, findings.

**discredit** verb **1** *discredit their rivals* detract from, bring into disrepute, defame, slur, slander, cast aspersions on, vilify, disparage, deprecate, denigrate, devalue, devaluate, degrade, belittle, decry, dishonor, disgrace, censure. **2** *evidence to discredit the research* disprove, invalidate, refute, dispute, challenge, destroy the credibility of, shake one's faith in, reject, deny. **3** *the jury discredited the witness* disbelieve, give no credence to, discount, doubt, distrust, mistrust.

**discredit** noun **1** *bring discredit on the neighborhood* disrepute, ill repute, infamy, disgrace, dishonor, shame, humiliation, ignominy, stigma, harm, damage, censure, blame, reproach, scandal, odium. **2** *regard the story with discredit* disbelief, lack of credence, incredulity, question, doubt, distrust, mistrust, skepticism, suspicion.

**discreet** adjective prudent, judicious, careful, cautious, circumspect, wary, guarded, chary, tactful, reserved, diplomatic, considerate, politic, strategic, wise, sensible.

**discrepancy** noun inconsistency, variance, variation, disparity, deviation, divergence, incongruity, difference, disagreement, dissimilarity, contrariety, conflict, discordance, gap.

**discrete** adjective separate, distinct, individual, detached, unattached, disconnected.

**discretion** noun **1** *act with discretion* prudence, judiciousness, care, carefulness, caution, circumspection, wariness, guardedness, chariness, tactfulness, tact, reserve, diplomacy, consideration, discrimination, wisdom, sense, good sense, discernment, sagacity, acumen, forethought. **2** *at the discretion of the manager* choice, option, volition, will, preference, inclination, pleasure, liking, wish, desire.

**discrimination** noun **1** *wine lovers of discrimination* discernment, perception, perspicacity, acumen, astuteness, shrewdness, selectivity, fastidiousness, judgment, taste, refinement, sensitivity, cultivation, culture. **2** *guilty of discrimination* prejudice, bias, unfairness, inequity, intolerance, bigotry, narrow-mindedness, favoritism.

**discuss** verb talk over, talk/chat about, converse about, confer about, debate, exchange views on/about, deliberate, consider, go into, thrash out, examine, review, study, scrutinize, analyze; *inf.* kick around.

**discussion** noun talk, conversation, dialogue, chat, conference, debate, discourse, exchange of views, symposium, seminar, consultation, deliberation, parley; *inf.* confab.

**disdain** noun scorn, scornfulness, contempt, contemptuousness, derision, sneering, deprecation, disparagement, denigration, arrogance, superciliousness, haughtiness, hauteur, snobbishness, aloofness, indifference.

**disdain** verb scorn, show contempt for, spurn, reject, refuse, rebuff, disregard, sneer at, deride, belittle, undervalue, slight, despise, look down on; *inf.* pooh-pooh, look down one's nose at.

**disdainful** adjective scornful, contemptuous, sneering, derisive, slighting, disparaging, arrogant, proud, supercilious, haughty, superior, snobbish, aloof, indifferent; *inf.* high and mighty, hoity-toity.

**disease** noun illness, sickness; disorder, complaint, malady, ailment, affliction, condition, indisposition, infirmity, disability, abnormality; infection, contagion, pestilence, plague, canker, blight.

**disenchanted** adjective disillusioned, disabused, undeceived, set straight, disappointed, let down, blasé, cynical, soured.

**disentangle** verb **1** *disentangle the knotted yarn* unravel, unwind, untwist, undo, unknot, untie, unsnarl, unkink, smooth out, straighten, comb, card. **2** *disentangle oneself* extricate, disentwine, release, loosen, detach, unfasten, unclasp, free, set free, liberate, disconnect.

**disfavor** noun **1** *look upon with disfavor* disapproval, disapprobation, dislike, displeasure, dissatisfaction, disregard, low opinion, low esteem. **2** *fall into disfavor* disapproval, unpopularity, discredit, disrepute, ill repute, ignominy, disgrace, shame.

**disfigure** verb deface, deform, mutilate, blemish, flaw, scar, uglify, spoil, mar, damage, injure, maim, vandalize, ruin.

**disgorge** verb **1** *volcanoes disgorging lava/disgorging phlegm* spit out, spew out, belch, discharge, spout, vomit, regurgitate, throw up, eject, emit, expel, empty. **2** *disgorging their booty* give up, surrender, yield, cede, relinquish, hand over.

**disgrace** noun **1** *the disgrace of being in*

*prison* shame, humiliation, dishonor, scandal, degradation, ignominy, infamy, discredit, debasement. **2** *brought him disgrace* disfavor, discredit, disrepute, loss of face, disrespect, disapproval, disapprobation, disesteem.

**disgrace** verb **1** *disgrace the family* shame, humiliate, dishonor, discredit, degrade, debase, sully, besmirch, taint, stigmatize, brand, drag through the mud. **2** *the soldier was publicly disgraced* discredit, disfavor, humiliate, mortify, disparage, demean, denigrate, belittle.

**disgraceful** adjective shameful, shameless, dishonorable, disreputable, degrading, ignominious, blameworthy, culpable, contemptible, despicable, reprehensible, appalling, dreadful, terrible, shocking, improper, unseemly, unworthy.

**disgruntled** adjective discontented, dissatisfied, displeased, annoyed, exasperated, vexed, irritated, peeved, put out, resentful, sulky, sullen, petulant, grumpy, churlish, testy; *inf.* ticked off, fed up.

**disguise** verb **1** *disguised as a policeman* camouflage, conceal, hide, mask, screen, shroud, veil, cloak, dress up, be under cover, be incognito. **2** *disguise the truth* cover up, misrepresent, falsify, fake, fudge, feign, dissemble, gloss over, varnish.

**disgust** verb **1** *the slimy food disgusted me* sicken, nauseate, turn one's stomach, revolt, repel; *inf.* turn off. **2** *her behavior disgusted me* offend, outrage, shock, appall, scandalize, displease, dissatisfy, annoy, anger.

**disgust** noun **1** *look with disgust at the food* revulsion, repugnance, repulsion, aversion, nausea, distaste, abhorrence, loathing, detestation. **2** *disgust at her behavior* outrage, shock, disapproval, displeasure, dissatisfaction, annoyance, anger.

**disgusting** adjective **1** *disgusting odor* sickening, nauseating, nauseous, revolting, repellent, unpalatable, foul, nasty, unappetizing, distasteful, abhorrent, loathsome, detestable, obnoxious, odious. **2** *disgusting behavior* offensive, objectionable, outrageous, shocking, shameless, shameful, appalling, scandalous, vulgar, gross, vile, displeasing, annoying.

**dishearten** verb discourage, cast down, dispirit, depress, crush, make crestfallen/downhearted, dash, dampen, put a damper on, daunt, disappoint, deter, sadden, weigh down.

**disheveled** adjective untidy, tousled, rumpled, bedraggled, disordered, disarranged, messy, in a mess, unkempt, uncombed, slovenly, slatternly, blowzy, frowzy; *inf.* mussed.

**dishonest** adjective fraudulent, cheating,

untrustworthy, false, untruthful, dishonorable, unscrupulous, unprincipled, corrupt, swindling, deceitful, deceiving, deceptive, lying, crafty, cunning, designing, mendacious, double-dealing, underhand, underhanded, treacherous, perfidious; *inf.* crooked, shady.

**dishonesty** noun fraud, fraudulence, cheating, chicanery, untrustworthiness, falseness, falsity, falsehood, untruthfulness, dishonor, unscrupulousness, corruption, criminality, deceit, deception, duplicity, lying, craft, cunning, trickery, wiliness, guile, double-dealing, underhandedness, treachery, perfidy, graft, improbity, rascality, knavishness; *inf.* crookedness, shadiness.

**dishonor** noun **1** *bring dishonor to the regiment* disgrace, shame, humiliation, scandal, discredit, degradation, ignominy, infamy, disrepute, ill repute, loss of face, disfavor, debasement, abasement, odium. **2** *do him a dishonor* indignity, insult, affront, offense, abuse, outrage, slight, discourtesy. **3** *a dishonor to his profession* disgrace, blot, blemish, stigma.

**dishonor** verb **1** *dishonor the flag* disgrace, bring dishonor/shame to, shame, humiliate, discredit, degrade, debase, sully, stain, stigmatize. **2** *dishonor their hosts* insult, affront, abuse, slight, offend.

**dishonorable** adjective **1** *a dishonorable act* disgraceful, shameful, shameless, shaming, disreputable, degrading, debasing, ignominious, ignoble, blameworthy, contemptible, despicable, reprehensible, base. **2** *a dishonorable man* unprincipled, blackguardly, unscrupulous, corrupt, untrustworthy, treacherous, perfidious, traitorous, disreputable, discreditable; *inf.* shady.

**disillusion** verb disabuse, disenchant, open the eyes of, shatter the illusions of, undeceive, set straight, enlighten, disappoint, make sadder and wiser.

**disinclined** adjective reluctant, unenthusiastic, not in the mood, hesitant, unwilling, loath, averse, antipathetic, resistant, opposed, recalcitrant.

**disinfect** verb sterilize, sanitize, clean, cleanse, purify, fumigate, decontaminate.

**disingenuous** adjective insincere, duplicitous, false, lying, untruthful, artful, cunning, crafty, wily, sly, shifty, scheming, calculating, designing, insidious.

**disintegrate** verb fall apart, fall to pieces, break up, break apart, shatter, splinter, crumble, decompose, decay, rot, molder, erode, dissolve, go to wrack and ruin.

**disinterested** adjective **1** *disinterested judges* unbiased, unprejudiced, impartial, detached, objective, uninvolved, dispassionate, impersonal, open-minded, neutral, outside, fair, just, equitable, evenhanded, unselfish. **2** *disinterested in the lecture* uninterested, unconcerned, uninvolved, unresponsive, indifferent, bored, apathetic, blasé.

**disjointed** noun **1** *a disjointed talk* incoherent, unconnected, disconnected, ununified, discontinuous, disorganized, disordered, fitful, spasmodic, aimless, directionless. **2** *disjointed limbs* dislocated, displaced, severed, separated, disarticulated.

**disloyal** adjective unfaithful, faithless, false, false-hearted, untrue, inconstant, untrustworthy, treacherous, perfidious, traitorous, disaffected, subversive, seditious, unpatriotic, renegade, apostate, dissident, two-faced, double-dealing, deceitful.

**dismal** adjective **1** *dismal weather/surroundings* gloomy, miserable, wretched, forlorn, lugubrious, dreary, bleak, drab, dingy, cheerless, desolate, depressing, grim, funereal, comfortless, inhospitable, uninviting. **2** *a dismal piece of work* bad, poor, inept, bungling, disgraceful.

**dismay** verb disconcert, upset, jolt, unsettle, unnerve, alarm, frighten, scare, dishearten, dispirit, daunt.

**dismiss** verb **1** *dismissed from the firm for theft* discharge, expel, cashier, remove, oust, eject, lay off; *inf.* sack, fire, give one one's marching orders, send packing, give the boot/heave-ho to, boot out. **2** *dismiss an assembly/army* disband, disperse, dissolve, discharge, send away, let go, release, free. **3** *dismiss foolish thoughts* put away, banish, think no more of, put out of one's mind, set/lay aside, abandon, have done with, reject, drop, disregard.

**dismissal** noun **1** *his dismissal from the firm* notice, discharge, expulsion, removal, ejection; *inf.* sacking, firing. **2** *the dismissal of the assembly* dispersal, dissolution, discharge, permission to go/depart/leave, release.

**disobedient** adjective insubordinate, unruly, wayward, undisciplined, rebellious, defiant, mutinous, recalcitrant, intractable, willful, refractory, disorderly, delinquent, noncompliant, perverse, naughty, mischievous, contrary.

**disobey** verb defy, disregard, flout, contravene, infringe, overstep, resist, rebel against, fly in the face of, transgress, violate.

**disorder** noun **1** *tidy up the disorder* untidiness, mess, chaos, muddle, clutter, jumble, confusion, disorderliness, disarray, disorganization; *inf.* shambles. **2** *police quelling the disorder* disturbance, disruption, tumult, riot, breach of the peace, fracas, rumpus, brouhaha, melee, unrest.

**3** *a disorder of the kidneys* disease, ailment, complaint, affliction, malady, sickness, illness.

**disorderly** adjective **1** *disorderly rooms* untidy, messy, chaotic, cluttered, jumbled, muddled, out of order, out of place, in disarray, confused, deranged, upside-down, at sixes and sevens. **2** *disorderly crowds* unruly, boisterous, rough, rowdy, disobedient, undisciplined, lawless, wild, unmanageable, uncontrollable, ungovernable, refractory, rebellious, mutinous, turbulent, tumultuous, rioting.

**disorganized** adjective random, unorganized, unmethodical, unsystematic, haphazard, disorderly, chaotic, out of order, in disarray, confused; *inf.* hit-or-miss.

**disown** verb repudiate, renounce, reject, cast off, abandon, forsake, turn one's back on, disclaim, deny, disallow, abnegate, disavow, disinherit.

**disparage** verb **1** *disparage their efforts* belittle, slight, depreciate, devalue, devaluate, downgrade, demean, detract from, discredit, deprecate, denigrate, derogate, deflate, minimize, undervalue, underestimate, underrate, make light of, play down. **2** *disparage their competitors* defame, run down, slander, libel, malign, cast aspersions on, impugn, calumniate, vilify, traduce; *inf.* do a hatchet job on, bad-mouth, trash.

**disparity** noun discrepancy, inequality, unevenness, inconsistency, imbalance, incongruity, difference, dissimilarity, contrast, gap.

**dispassionate** adjective **1** *a dispassionate demeanor* unemotional, emotionless, unmoved, unexcited, unexcitable, unflappable, unperturbed, nonchalant, unruffled, cool, collected, cool and collected, calm, composed, self-possessed, level-headed, self-controlled, temperate, sober, placid, equable, tranquil, serene; *inf.* laid-back, together. **2** *dispassionate judges* indifferent, uninvolved, impersonal. *See* DISINTERESTED 1.

**dispatch** verb **1** *dispatch a letter* send, send off, post, mail, forward, transmit, consign, remit, convey. **2** *dispatch the task in an hour* finish, dispose of, discharge, execute, perform, expedite, push through, accelerate, hasten, speed up, hurry on; *inf.* make short work of. **3** *a flurry of bullets dispatched the terrorists* kill, put to death, slay, finish off, slaughter, murder, assassinate, execute; *inf.* bump off, do in, knock off, eliminate, erase.

**dispatch** noun **1** *carried out with dispatch* promptness, promptitude, speed, alacrity, quickness, haste, hurry, swiftness, rapidity, expedition, expeditiousness. **2** *military dispatches | a journalist's dispatch* communication, communiqué, bulletin, report, account, document, missive, letter, epistle, message, item, piece, article, news, instruction.

**dispel** verb drive away, drive off, chase away, banish, rout, expel, disperse, scatter, dissipate, disseminate, dismiss.

**dispensable** adjective expendable, disposable, unnecessary, unessential, nonessential, needless, superfluous, uncalled-for.

**dispense** verb **1** *dispense supplies* distribute, hand out, deal out, dole out, share out, divide out, parcel out, allocate, allot, apportion, assign, bestow, confer, supply, disburse. **2** *dispense justice* administer, discharge, carry out, execute, implement, apply, enforce, effectuate, operate, direct. **3** *dispense medicines* make up, prepare, mix, supply. **4** *dispense him from that obligation* exempt, excuse, except, release, relieve, reprieve, absolve; *inf.* let off. **dispense with 1** *dispense with the formalities* waive, do without, omit, forgo, give up, relinquish, renounce, ignore, disregard, pass over, brush aside. **2** *dispense with their services* do away with, get rid of, dispose of, abolish, revoke, rescind, cancel, shake off, manage without.

**disperse** verb **1** *the crowd dispersed* break up, disband, separate, scatter, dissolve, leave, vanish; dissipate, dispel, drive away, banish. **2** *disperse seeds* scatter, disseminate, distribute, sow, sprinkle, spread, diffuse, strew, bestrew. **3** *disperse information* circulate, broadcast, publish, publicize, spread, diffuse.

**dispirit** verb dishearten, discourage, cast down, make dejected, depress, crush, dash, dampen the spirits of, daunt, disappoint, deter, sadden; *inf.* throw cold water on.

**displace** verb **1** *displace the tribe* move, shift, relocate, transfer, resettle. **2** *displace from office* remove, depose. *See* DISMISS 1. **3** *displaced the aging chairman* replace, take the place of, take over from, supplant, oust, supersede, succeed; *inf.* crowd out.

**displaced** adjective **displaced person** refugee, DP, exile, émigré, fugitive.

**display** verb **1** *display the goods* show, exhibit, put on view, present, unveil, set forth, arrange, dispose, array, demonstrate, advertise, publicize. **2** *display their military power* show off, flaunt, parade, flourish, boast, vaunt; *inf.* flash. **3** *display emotion* evince, manifest, reveal, disclose.

**display** noun **1** *a display of sculpture* show, exhibition, exhibit, presentation, demonstration, spectacle, array. **2** *military display* show, spectacle, parade, pageant; pomp, flourish, ostentation.

**displease** verb put out, annoy, irritate, anger, irk, vex, provoke, offend, pique,

peeve, gall, nettle, exasperate, perturb, aggravate.

**displeasure** noun dissatisfaction, discontentment, disgruntlement, disapproval, distaste, annoyance, irritation, anger, pique, chagrin, indignation, exasperation, perturbation.

**disposable** adjective **1** *disposable plates* throwaway, nonreturnable, paper, plastic, biodegradable. **2** *disposable assets* available, usable, accessible, obtainable.

**dispose** verb **1** *troops disposed in rows* arrange, order, place, put, position, array. **2** *behavior not disposing me to believe him* incline, predispose, prompt, lead, induce, motivate, bias, influence, condition. **dispose of 1** *dispose of the trash* get rid of, throw away/out, clear out, discard, eject, unload, scrap, destroy, dump. **2** *dispose of the business* deal with, settle, determine, decide, finish, conclude, end. **3** *dispose of his estate* distribute, allot, allocate, assign, part with, transfer, give away, bestow. **4** *dispose of his enemy* kill, do away with, put to death, slay, murder, slaughter; *inf.* bump off, knock off.

**disposition** noun **1** *people of a calm disposition* nature, character, temperament, humor, makeup, constitution, spirit, temper, mood. **2** *a disposition to/for moodiness* inclination, tendency, proneness, propensity, leaning, proclivity, bias, bent, predilection, weakness, habit, readiness. **3** *the disposition of the troops* disposal, arrangement, positioning, placement, lining-up, marshaling, grouping. **4** *disposition of property* disposal, distribution, allocation, transfer, transference, bestowal.

**dispossess** verb **1** *dispossess them of their property* deprive, divest, strip, bereave. **2** *dispossess the tenants* dislodge, oust, eject, drive out, evict, turn out, dismiss.

**disprove** verb prove false, invalidate, refute, negate, rebut, confute, contradict, discredit.

**dispute** verb **1** *dispute with colleagues* debate, discuss, argue, disagree, clash, quarrel, wrangle, bicker, squabble. **2** *dispute his right to go* question, call into question, challenge, contest, deny, doubt, contradict, oppose, controvert, impugn, gainsay.

**dispute** noun **1** *open to dispute* debate, discussion, argument, controversy, contention, disagreement, dissension, conflict, friction, discord, litigation. **2** *a dispute over boundaries* argument, row, altercation, clash, quarrel, wrangle, squabble, feud, disturbance, fracas, brawl.

**disqualify** verb declare ineligible, rule out, preclude, debar, reject, prohibit, disentitle.

**disregard** verb **1** *disregard the consequences* ignore, take no notice/account of, pay no attention/heed to, discount, set aside, neglect, forget, never mind, overlook, turn a blind eye to, pass over, gloss over, brush aside, laugh off, make light of; *inf.* play down. **2** *disregard their achievement* slight, disparage, denigrate, disdain.

**disregard** noun **1** *treat danger with disregard* inattention, heedlessness, carelessness, neglect, negligence, indifference. **2** *treat staff/achievements with disregard* scorn, contempt, disparagement, denigration, disdain, disrespect, disesteem.

**disrepair** noun dilapidation, deterioration, decay, collapse, shabbiness, ruin, ruination, decrepitude.

**disreputable** adjective dishonorable, dishonest, unprincipled, villainous, notorious, ignominious, corrupt, unworthy, base, low, mean, questionable, unsavory, unscrupulous, rascally, contemptible, reprehensible, despicable, discreditable, disgraceful, shameful, shocking, outrageous, scandalous; *inf.* crooked, shady.

**disrepute** noun notoriety, discredit, ill repute, disfavor, ill favor, disesteem, disgrace, shame, dishonor, infamy, ignominy, degradation, odium.

**disrespect** noun discourtesy, incivility, impoliteness, unmannerliness, rudeness, ungraciousness, irreverence, lack of consideration, disregard, insolence, impudence, scorn, contempt; ill manners.

**disrespectful** adjective discourteous, uncivil, impolite, unmannerly, ill-mannered, rude, irreverent, inconsiderate, insolent, impudent, impertinent, scornful, contemptuous, insulting.

**disrupt** verb throw into disorder/disarray, disorder, disorganize, cause confusion/turmoil in, disarrange, disturb, upset; interrupt, suspend, discontinue, interfere with, obstruct, impede, hamper; *inf.* throw a monkey wrench in/into (the works of).

**disruptive** adjective *disruptive children* troublemaking, troublesome, divisive, unruly, disorderly, undisciplined, upsetting, disturbing, distracting, noisy.

**dissatisfaction** noun discontent, discontentment, disapproval, disappointment, frustration, unhappiness, dismay, vexation, annoyance, irritation.

**dissatisfied** adjective discontented, displeased, disgruntled, disapproving, unsatisfied, disappointed, unfulfilled, frustrated, unhappy, regretful, vexed, angry, resentful, restless.

**dissect** verb *dissect the information* analyze, break down, examine, study, inspect, scrutinize, probe, explore, investigate.

**disseminate** verb spread, circulate, broadcast, publish, publicize, proclaim, prom-

ulgate, propagate, dissipate, scatter, distribute, disperse, diffuse.

**dissension** noun disagreement, dispute, argument, dissent, nonconformity, variance, conflict, friction, strife, discord, contention, quarreling, wrangling, bickering.

**dissent** verb **dissent from 1** *dissent from official policy* disagree with, differ from, be at variance with, decline/refuse to support, protest against, object to, dispute. **2** *dissent from established practice* reject, repudiate, renounce, abjure, secede from, apostatize.

**dissenter** noun dissident, objector, protester, protestant, disputant, rebel, revolutionary, nonconformist, apostate, sectarian, heretic.

**dissertation** noun treatise, thesis, discourse, essay, critique, exposition, disquisition.

**disservice** noun bad/ill turn, dirty trick, disfavor, unkindness, injury, harm, hurt, damage, wrong, injustice; *inf.* kick in the teeth.

**dissident** noun protester, nonconformist. *See* DISSENTER.

**dissimilar** adjective unlike, unalike, different, varying, variant, disparate, unrelated, divergent, deviating, diverse, various, contrasting, mismatched, distinct.

**dissipate** verb **1** *dissipate one's fears | the crowd dissipated* dispel, dissolve. *See* DISPERSE 1. **2** *dissipate their resources* squander, fritter, misspend, lavish, waste, exhaust, drain, deplete, spend, expend, burn up, use up, consume, run through.

**dissipated** adjective **1** *a dissipated young man* dissolute, debauched, intemperate, profligate, abandoned, rakish, licentious, promiscuous, drunken, self-indulgent, wild, unrestrained, wanton, depraved, degenerate, corrupt. **2** *dissipated resources* squandered, frittered away, wasted, exhausted, depleted, consumed.

**dissolute** adjective debauched, intemperate. *See* DISSIPATED.

**dissolve** verb **1** *salt dissolves in water* liquefy, melt, deliquesce. **2** *his hopes dissolved* disappear, vanish, melt away, evaporate, dissipate, disintegrate, crumble, decompose, perish, die, evanesce. **3** *dissolve a partnership* end, terminate, break up, discontinue, wind up, disband, dismiss, suspend, ruin. **4** *the crowds dissolved* separate, sever, disunite, disjoin, disperse, scatter, go their separate ways. **5** *dissolve in tears/mirth* break into, collapse into, be overcome with.

**distance** noun **1** *the distance between the fields* space, interval, span, gap, separation, stretch, extent; length, width, depth.

**2** *the distance of the farm from the highway* remoteness, farness. **3** *upset by her colleague's distance* aloofness, reserve, remoteness, reticence, coolness, coldness, frigidity, stiffness, formality, restraint, unresponsiveness. **in the distance** far away, far off, on the horizon, afar, yonder.

**distant** adjective **1** *a distant place* far, faraway, far off, remote, out of the way, outlying, abroad, far-flung. **2** *a distant time* far-off, long ago. **3** *three miles distant from each other* away, off, apart, separated. **4** *a distant relative/likeness* not close, remote, indirect, slight. **5** *a distant memory* vague, faint, indistinct, obscure, uncertain. **6** *a distant smile* aloof, reserved, remote, uncommunicative, unapproachable, standoffish, restrained, cool, unresponsive, unfriendly.

**distasteful** adjective unpleasant, disagreeable, displeasing, undesirable, uninviting, objectionable, offensive, obnoxious, revolting, repugnant, abhorrent, loathsome, detestable; unpalatable, unsavory, unappetizing, disgusting, sickening, nauseating, nauseous.

**distinct** adjective **1** *a distinct resemblance* clear, clear-cut, well-defined, sharp, marked, decided, definite, unmistakable, recognizable, obvious, plain, plain as day, evident, apparent, manifest, patent, palpable, unambiguous, unequivocal. **2** *two distinct jobs* separate, individual, different, unconnected, unassociated, detached, discrete, dissimilar, unlike, disparate.

**distinction** noun **1** *make the distinction between right and wrong* differentiation, contradistinction, discrimination, division, separation, dividing line, contrast. **2** *fail to notice the identifying distinctions* difference, dissimilarity, dissimilitude, contrast, differential, subtlety, nicety, nuance. **3** *the distinctions of wealth and rank* feature, characteristic, mark, individuality, peculiarity. **4** *pass the exam with distinction* honor, credit, excellence, merit. **5** *people of distinction* note, consequence, importance, account, significance, prestige, prominence, eminence, repute, reputation, renown, fame, honor, excellence, glory.

**distinctive** adjective distinguishing, characteristic, typical, individual, particular, peculiar, special, different, uncommon, unusual, remarkable, singular, extraordinary, noteworthy, original, idiosyncratic.

**distinctly** adverb **1** *distinctly annoyed* obviously, plainly, evidently, manifestly. **2** *speak distinctly* clearly, plainly, intelligibly, precisely.

**distinguish** verb **1** *distinguish one color from another* tell apart, differentiate, discriminate, determine; tell the difference between, decide between. **2** *his hair distinguishes him from the others* make distinctive, set apart, separate, single out, mark off, characterize, individualize, designate, categorize, classify. **3** *distinguish a black shape* make out, see, discern, perceive, observe, notice, detect, recognize, identify, pick out. **4** *distinguish himself in battle* bring fame/honor to, ennoble, dignify, glorify, win acclaim for, lionize, immortalize.

**distinguished** adjective *a distinguished scientist* famous, famed, eminent, renowned, prominent, well-known, noted, notable, esteemed, acclaimed, illustrious, celebrated, legendary.

**distinguishing** adjective *a distinguishing mark* distinctive, determining, individualistic, peculiar, singular, characteristic, typical.

**distort** verb **1** *distort their features* twist, warp, contort, bend, buckle, deform, misshape, disfigure, mangle, wrench, wring, wrest. **2** *distort the facts* misrepresent, pervert, twist, falsify, garble, slant, bias, color, tamper with, alter, change.

**distortion** noun **1** *a distortion in the metal* twist, warp, contortion, bend, buckle, curvature, deformation, deformity, malformation, gnarl, knot. **2** *a distortion of the truth* misrepresentation, perversion, twisting, falsification, garbling, coloring, alteration.

**distract** verb **1** *distract them from work* deflect, divert, sidetrack, turn aside, draw away. **2** *distract the children* amuse, entertain, divert, beguile, absorb, engage, occupy. **3** *bright lights distracting her* confuse, bewilder, fluster, agitate, disconcert, discompose, confound. **4** *grief distracting her* make frantic, drive/make mad, madden, derange, throw into a frenzy.

**distracted** adjective **1** *rushing around in a distracted way* confused, bewildered, agitated, flustered, harassed, worried; *inf.* hassled. **2** *distracted women mourning their sons* grief-stricken, distraught, frantic, frenzied, raving, wild, hysterical, overwrought, mad, maddened, crazed, deranged.

**distraction** noun **1** *distraction from their work* diversion, interruption, disturbance, interference, obstruction. **2** *distractions for the children* amusement, entertainment, diversion, pastime, recreation, hobby, game, occupation. **3** *a look of distraction amid the crowds* confusion, bewilderment, befuddlement, perplexity, disturbance, agitation, perturbation, harassment. **4** *pity the distraction of the widow* frenzy, hysteria, distress, madness, insanity, derangement, delirium.

**distress** noun **1** *the lost child's distress* anguish, suffering, pain, agony, ache, affliction, discomfort, heartache, heartbreak, sorrow, grief, woe, sadness, desolation, trouble, worry, anxiety, perturbation, uneasiness, angst; tribulations, cries, wails. **2** *old people in distress* hardship, adversity, misfortune, need, want, poverty, lack, privation, destitution, indigence, impoverishment, penury; difficulties, dire straits.

**distress** verb **1** *the news distressed her* pain, upset, make miserable/wretched, grieve, sadden, trouble, worry, bother, perturb, disturb, vex, harrow, torment. **2** *distress the furniture* dent, scratch, antique, simulate age/wear in.

**distribute** verb **1** *distribute rations to the crowd* give out, hand out, allocate, allot, issue, dispense, administer, apportion, assign, deal out, dole out, measure out, mete out, parcel out, dispose. **2** *distribute advertising leaflets* circulate, pass out/around, hand out, deliver, convey, transmit. **3** *distribute seeds evenly* disseminate, disperse, diffuse, scatter, spread, strew, sow. **4** *luggage distributed by size* arrange, organize, group, class, classify, categorize, file, assort.

**distribution** noun **1** *distribution of rations* allocation, allotment, dispensation, administering, assignment, dealing out, division. **2** *distribution of seeds* dissemination, dispersal, diffusion, scattering. **3** *the distribution of luggage by size* organization, grouping, classification. **4** *in charge of sales and distribution* handling, delivery, transport, transportation, conveyance, mailing.

**district** noun area, region, place, locality, neighborhood, quarter, sector, vicinity, community, territory, domain; county, ward, parish, constituency, department, canton.

**distrust** verb mistrust, be suspicious of, be wary/chary of, be skeptical of, have doubts about, doubt, have misgivings about, be leery of, wonder about, question, suspect, disbelieve, discredit.

**distrust** noun mistrust, lack of faith, suspicion, wariness, chariness, skepticism, doubt, doubtfulness, dubiety, misgiving, questioning, qualms, leeriness.

**disturb** verb **1** *disturb them while they are working* interrupt, butt in on, distract, bother, trouble, pester, intrude on, interfere with, hinder, plague, harass, molest; *inf.* hassle. **2** *disturb papers on a desk* disarrange, muddle, disorganize, disorder, confuse. **3** *the news disturbed them* trouble, worry, upset, agitate, fluster, discomfit, disconcert, alarm, frighten, startle, dismay, distress, ruffle, shake.

**disturbance** noun **1** *please excuse the disturbance* interruption, distraction, intrusion, interference, hindrance, harassment. **2** *police called to a disturbance* uproar, commotion, row, rumpus, hullabaloo, tumult, turmoil, fracas, affray, brawl, riot; *inf.* ruckus.

**disturbed** adjective *emotionally disturbed* unbalanced, disordered, maladjusted, neurotic, psychotic; *inf.* screwed up.

**disturbing** adjective troubling, worrying, upsetting, disconcerting, alarming, disquieting, startling, dismaying, frightening, distressing, unsettling, bewildering.

**ditch** noun trench, channel, watercourse, dike, canal, drain, gutter, gully, moat, furrow, rut.

**ditch** verb **1** *ditch the plan* abandon, throw out, discard, drop, scrap, jettison, get rid of, dispose of, dump. **2** *ditch the police* evade, escape, elude, shake off.

**dive** verb **1** *dive from the springboard* plunge/descend into water, plummet, nosedive, fall, descend, submerge, drop, swoop, dip, bellyflop. **2** *dive out of sight* jump, lunge, rush, dart, dash, duck, dodge.

**diverge** verb **1** *the roads diverged* separate, divide, subdivide, split, part, disunite, fork, branch off, radiate, spread out, bifurcate, divaricate. **2** *opinions diverge* differ, disagree, be at variance/odds, conflict, clash. **3** *diverge from the norm* deviate, digress, depart, veer, stray, drift, turn aside, wander.

**diverse** adjective various, miscellaneous, assorted, mixed, diversified, variegated, varied, varying, heterogeneous, different, differing, distinct, unlike, dissimilar, distinctive, contrasting.

**diversify** verb vary, variegate, modify, assort, mix, alter, change, transform.

**diversion** noun **1** *the diversion of the stream* redirection, deflection, digression, deviation, divergence. **2** *diversions for the children* amusement, entertainment, pastime, distraction, recreation, fun, relaxation.

**diversity** noun diverseness, variety, miscellany, assortment, mixture, range, medley, multiplicity, variegation, heterogeneity, difference, unlikeness, dissimilarity, contrast.

**divert** verb **1** *divert the stream* turn aside, deflect, draw away, avert, redirect. **2** *divert him from his work* distract, detract, sidetrack, lead away, turn aside. **3** *clowns diverted the children* amuse, entertain, distract, delight, beguile, enchant, interest, occupy, absorb.

**diverting** adjective amusing, entertaining, humorous, fun, enjoyable, pleasurable, recreational, beguiling, interesting, absorbing.

**divest** verb **1** *trees divested of their leaves* unclothe, undress, disrobe, strip, denude.

**2** *divest them of property* deprive, strip, dispossess, relieve, bereave.

**divide** verb **1** *divide the apple in two* cut up, sever, split, shear, bisect, halve, quarter, cleave, rend, sunder, rive; separate, part, segregate, partition, detach, disconnect, disjoin. **2** *the road divides here* diverge, branch, fork, split in two, divaricate. **3** *divide the food* share, allocate, allot, apportion, portion out, distribute, dispense, deal out, hand out, dole out, measure out, parcel out, *inf.* divvy (up/out). **4** *politics divided them* estrange, alienate, separate, split up, disunite, disaffect, set/pit against one another, cause disagreement between, sow dissension between. **5** *divide into types* classify, sort, arrange, order, group, grade, rank, categorize.

**divine** adjective **1** *a divine being* godly, godlike, heavenly, celestial, holy, angelic, seraphic, spiritual, saintly. **2** *divine worship* religious, holy, sacred, sanctified, consecrated, spiritual. **3** *divine music* supernatural, superhuman, mystical, exalted, beatific, blissful, ethereal, transcendental, transcendent. **4** *looking divine | a divine evening* lovely, beautiful, charming, perfect, excellent, superlative, wonderful, glorious, marvelous, admirable; *inf.* super, stunning.

**divine** verb **1** *divine their plans* guess, surmise, conjecture, speculate, suspect, deduce, infer, theorize, hypothesize. **2** *divine their need* intuit, discern, perceive, understand, grasp, apprehend, comprehend. **3** *divine the future* foretell, predict, foresee, forecast, presage, augur, portend, prognosticate, forebode.

**division** noun **1** *the division of the groups* parting, separation, segregation, partitioning, disconnection, detachment. **2** *the division of rations* allocation, allotment, apportionment, distribution. **3** *cross the division* dividing line, divide, boundary, border, partition. **4** *divisions of equal size* section, part, portion, piece, bit, segment; compartment, category, class, group, grade, family. **5** *divisions of the firm* branch, department, section, sector, arm. **6** *a bitter division between the families* disagreement, feud, breach, rupture, split; dissension, conflict, discord, variance, disunion, estrangement, alienation.

**divorce** verb split up, break up, separate, part, disconnect, divide, dissociate, detach, disunite, sever, disjoin, split.

**divulge** verb disclose, reveal, make known, expose, uncover, bring into the open, let slip, leak, let the cat out of the bag about, confess, betray; *inf.* spill the beans about.

**dizzy** adjective **1** *get dizzy on top of the ladder* light-headed, faint, vertiginous, weak at/in the knees, shaky, wobbly, off-balance, reeling, staggering; *inf.* woozy. **2** *feeling dizzy at the amount of information* dazed, bewildered, confused, muddled, bemused, befuddled, puzzled, perplexed. **3** *dizzy young girls* giddy, scatterbrained, featherbrained, flighty, foolish, silly, capricious, inconstant.

**do** verb **1** *do as you know you should* act, behave, conduct oneself, comport oneself. **2** *do the job* perform, carry out, undertake, discharge, execute, accomplish, implement, achieve, complete, finish, conclude, bring about, effect, effectuate, realize, produce, engineer. **3** *this amount will do* be enough, be sufficient, be adequate, suffice, be satisfactory, be of use, fill/fit the bill, answer/serve the purpose, meet the needs, pass muster, measure up. **4** *do the meals* make, prepare, get ready, fix, produce, see to, arrange, organize, be responsible for, be in charge of, look after, take on. **5** *do a large picture* create, make, produce, originate, form, fashion, design, fabricate, manufacture. **6** *they're doing three plays* put on, perform, act, present, produce, give. **7** *do me a favor* render, afford, give, bestow, grant, pay. **8** *can't do this math problem* solve, resolve, work out, figure out, decipher. **9** *what does he do?* work at, be employed at, earn a living at. **10** *how are you doing?* get on/along, progress, fare, make out, manage, continue. **11** *the play was done in Russian* translate, put, render, adapt, transform. **12** *the car was doing 90 mph* travel at, go/proceed at, be driven at. **13** *we did 50 miles* travel, journey, cover, traverse. **14** *they're doing the museums today* sightsee, look at, visit, tour. **do away with 1** *do away with the penalty* abolish, get rid of, discard, remove, discontinue, eliminate, repeal, revoke, rescind, cancel, annul, nullify. **2** *do away with his enemy* kill, put to death, slay, murder, slaughter, liquidate, assassinate, execute, destroy; *inf.* do in, bump off, knock off, eliminate. **do in 1** *do in his business* ruin, reduce to nothing, wreck, destroy, smash, crush, wreak havoc on. **2** *the walk did me in* tire out, exhaust, wear out, fatigue, weary. **do out of** prevent from having, deprive of, swindle/cheat/trick out of; *inf.* con out of. **do without** forgo, dispense with, abstain from, give up, refrain from, eschew.

**docile** adjective manageable, controllable, tractable, malleable, amenable, accommodating, compliant, pliant, obedient, biddable, dutiful, submissive, yielding, ductile.

**dock** noun pier, quay, wharf, jetty, marina, waterfront.

**docket** noun agenda, roster, schedule, slate, program.

**doctor** verb **1** *doctor the patients* treat,

terfere with, alter, change, falsify, disguise, fudge, pervert, misrepresent.

**doctrine** noun creed, credo, dogma, belief, conviction, teaching; tenet, principle, precept, maxim; articles of faith, canons.

**document** noun paper, form, certificate, record, report, deed, voucher, instrument, charter; paperwork, documentation.

**document** verb **1** *document their statement* prove, back up, support, corroborate, substantiate, authenticate, verify, validate, certify. **2** *the war was well documented in the press* report, record, detail, tabulate, chart, register, cite, instance.

**doddering** adjective tottering, staggering, shuffling, faltering, shaky, unsteady, trembling, trembly, quivering, infirm, decrepit, aged, in one's dotage, senile.

**dodge** verb **1** *dodge behind the door* dart, duck, dive, swerve, sidestep, veer; jump away, move aside. **2** *dodge the police* evade, elude, escape, fend off, avoid, stay/steer clear of, deceive, trick; *inf.* give the slip to. **3** *dodge the question/work* evade, get out of, parry, fend off, fudge, shirk, shun, stay/steer clear of.

**dodge** noun **1** *a dodge to the right* dart, duck, dive, swerve, jump. **2** *a tax dodge* ruse, ploy, scheme, stratagem, subterfuge, trick, wile, deception, maneuver, device, machination, contrivance, artifice, expedient.

**dog** verb pursue, follow, track, trail, shadow, hound, plague, trouble, haunt; *inf* tail.

**dogged** adjective determined, resolute, obstinate, stubborn, tenacious, relentless, intent, single-minded, unshakable, unflagging, indefatigable, tireless, unfaltering, unwavering, persistent, persevering, pertinacious, unyielding, obdurate, firm, steadfast, steady, staunch.

**dogma** noun creed, credo, conviction, teaching; belief, tenet, principle, precept, maxim; articles of faith, canons.

**dogmatic** adjective **1** *dogmatic religious tenets* doctrinal, canonical, authoritative, *ex cathedra.* **2** *dogmatic statement/manner* assertive, insistent, doctrinaire, emphatic, categorical, authoritarian, opinionated, peremptory, domineering, imperious, arrogant, overbearing, dictatorial, intolerant.

**doldrums** plural noun **1** *a fit of the doldrums* downheartedness, dejection, depression, melancholy, gloom, inertia, apathy, listlessness, malaise, boredom, tedium, ennui; blues, low spirits. **2** *a business in the doldrums* inactivity, inertia, flatness, stagnation, dullness, sluggishness, torpor.

**dole** verb dole out deal out, allocate, allot, apportion, share (out), mete out, distribute, divide up, dispense, hand out, give out, issue, assign, administer.

**doleful** adjective mournful, sorrowful, sad, dejected, disconsolate, depressed, gloomy, melancholy, blue, miserable, wretched; *inf.* down in the mouth/dumps.

**dolt** noun blockhead, dunderhead, thickhead, numskull, nitwit, dunce, fool, idiot, ass, simpleton, nincompoop, ignoramus, dullard; *inf.* dope, chump, clod, boob, jerk, dimwit, nerd, airhead.

**domain** noun **1** *the king's domain* realm, kingdom. See DOMINION 2. **2** *the scientific domain* area, field, region, province, sphere, section, discipline.

**dome** noun cupola, rotunda; hemisphere.

**domestic** adjective **1** *an unhappy domestic life* home, family, household, domiciliary, residential, private. **2** *preferring domestic people* housewifely, stay-at-home, home-loving. **3** *a domestic animal* domesticated, tame, pet, house-trained, housebroken, trained. **4** *domestic markets/plants* home, internal; native, indigenous, homegrown, home-bred.

**domesticate** verb **1** *domesticate an animal* tame, house-train, housebreak, train, break in, gentle. **2** *domesticate a foreign tree* naturalize, acclimatize, habituate, accustom, familiarize, assimilate.

**domicile** noun home, house, residence, residency, dwelling, dwelling place, abode, habitation, lodging, accommodation.

**domicile** verb settle, make one's home, take up one's abode, ensconce oneself.

**dominant** adjective **1** *the dominant member of the team* ruling, governing, controlling, commanding, ascendant, presiding, supreme, authoritative, most influential, superior, most assertive, domineering, alpha. **2** *the dominant issue* predominant, most important, chief, main, principal, leading, primary, paramount, preeminent, outstanding, prominent, prevailing.

**dominate** verb **1** *dominate the council* rule, govern, control, command, direct, preside over, have ascendancy/mastery over, master, domineer, tyrannize, intimidate, have the upper hand over, ride roughshod over; have under one's thumb, be in the driver's seat, be in the saddle, wear the pants; *inf.* boss, call the shots. **2** *the hill dominates the town* overlook, tower above, stand over, project/jut over, hang/loom over, bestride.

**domineering** adjective overbearing, imperious, authoritarian, high-handed, auto-the-mill, prosaic, commonplace, unvaried, repetitive. **3** *in a dreary frame of mind* gloomy, glum, sad, miserable, wretched, downcast, dejected, depressed, despondent, doleful, mournful, melancholic.

cratic, peremptory, arrogant, haughty, dictatorial, coercive, tyrannical, despotic, oppressive, subjugating, iron-fisted, iron-handed; *inf.* bossy, pushy.

**dominion** noun **1** *have dominion over smaller states* supremacy, ascendancy, sway, mastery, sovereignty, jurisdiction, control, command, direction, authority, power, domination, suzerainty. **2** *the king's dominions* realm, kingdom, empire, domain, country, province, territory, region, estate.

**donate** verb give, contribute, make a contribution of, subscribe, make a gift of, gift, present, pledge, put oneself down for, bestow; *inf.* chip in, kick in.

**donation** noun contribution, subscription, gift, present, grant, offering, gratuity, alms; charity, benefaction, largesse.

**done** adjective **1** *the job is done* accomplished, complete, completed, executed, perfected, finished, ended, concluded, terminated, realized, consummated. **2** *such behavior is not done* acceptable, proper, seemly, decorous, conventional, de rigueur. **done for** finished, ruined, destroyed, broken, wrecked, undone, doomed, lost, defeated, beaten, foiled; *inf.* washed-up. **done in** worn out, exhausted, tired out, weary, fatigued, played out, on one's last legs; *inf.* dog-tired, all in, dead beat, bushed, pooped.

**donor** noun contributor, donator, grantor, benefactor, benefactress, supporter, backer, philanthropist; *inf.* angel.

**doom** noun **1** *companies facing doom* ruin, ruination, rack and ruin, downfall, destruction, catastrophe, disaster, extinction, annihilation, death, termination. **2** *the prisoner hearing his doom* condemnation, sentence, judgment, pronouncement, decree, damnation. **3** *predicting doom* the Last Judgment, Judgment Day, doomsday, Armageddon, end of the world.

**doom** verb **1** *children doomed to be poor* fate, destine, predestine, ordain, preordain, foreordain, consign, condemn. **2** *prisoners doomed to die* condemn, sentence, judge, pronounce, decree, damn.

**doomed** adjective *doomed plans/lovers* ill-fated, star-crossed, foredoomed, unlucky, damned, bedeviled, ruined, crushed.

**door** noun **1** *wooden doors* doorway, portal, entrance, entry, exit, barrier. **2** *doors to academic success* access, opening, entrée, gateway, way, path, road, ingress. **out of doors** outside, outdoors, out, in/into the open air, alfresco.

**dormant** adjective sleeping, asleep, inactive, inert, latent, fallow, quiescent, inoperative, hibernating, comatose, stagnant.

**dot** noun spot, speck, fleck, point, mark, dab, particle, atom, iota, jot, mote, mite;

period, decimal point. **on the dot** *arrive on the dot* to the minute, on time, punctually, promptly; *inf.* on the button.

**dot** verb spot, fleck, bespeckle, mark, dab, stud, bestud, stipple, pock, freckle, sprinkle, scatter, pepper.

**dote** verb *dote on/upon* idolize, adore, hold dear, love dearly, treasure, prize, make much of, lavish affection on, indulge, spoil, pamper.

**doting** adjective adoring, devoted, loving, fond, indulgent, pampering.

**double** noun *the double of his cousin* look-alike, twin, clone, doppelgänger, duplicate, replica, copy, facsimile, counterpart, match, mate, fellow; *inf.* spitting image, dead ringer, ringer. **on the double** at full speed, as fast as possible, with haste, in double time, post-haste, right away, immediately, without delay, straight away; *inf.* p.d.q.

**double-cross** verb betray, cheat, defraud, trick, hoodwink, mislead, deceive, swindle; *inf.* two-time, take for a ride.

**double-dealing** noun duplicity, treachery, betrayal, double-crossing, bad faith, perfidy, breach of trust, fraud, fraudulence, underhandedness, cheating, dishonesty, untrustworthiness, mendacity, deception, trickery, deceit, two-facedness, hypocrisy; *inf.* crookedness.

**doubt** verb **1** *doubt his motives* suspect, distrust, mistrust, lack confidence in, have misgivings about, feel uneasy/apprehensive about, call in question, query, question. **2** *doubt that it is genuine* be dubious, hesitate to believe, feel uncertain, be undecided, lack conviction.

**doubt** noun **1** *have doubts about his motives* distrust, mistrust, skepticism, uneasiness, apprehension; reservations, misgivings, suspicions, qualms. **2** *express doubt that it is genuine* dubiousness, lack of certainty/conviction, incredulity; queries, questions. **3** *full of doubts* uncertainty, indecision, hesitation; hesitancy, wavering, vacillation, irresolution, lack of conviction. **in doubt** *the issue is still in doubt* undecided, unsettled, unresolved, confused, open to question. **no doubt** *no doubt he will win* doubtless, certainly, of course, surely.

**doubter** noun skeptic, questioner, disbeliever, doubting Thomas, unbeliever, agnostic, scoffer, dissenter, pessimist.

**doubtful** adjective **1** *it is doubtful that he will come* in doubt, uncertain, unsure, unconfirmed, improbable, unlikely. **2** *doubtful of/about his motives* suspicious, distrustful, mistrustful, skeptical, apprehensive, uneasy, unsure. **3** *its genuineness is doubtful* dubious, open to question, questionable, debatable, disputable, not definite, inconclusive. **4** *doubtful about his religious convictions* uncertain, indecisive, hesitating, irresolute, wavering, vacillating.

**dour** adjective unsmiling, sullen, morose, sour, gruff, churlish, forbidding, grim, stern, severe, austere, harsh, dismal, dreary, gloomy.

**douse, dowse** verb **1** *douse the walls with soapy water* drench, saturate, soak, souse, flood, deluge, wet, splash, hose down. **2** *douse the clothes in the tub* plunge, immerse, submerge, dip, dunk. **3** *douse the light/candle* extinguish, put out, blow out, quench, snuff.

**dowdy** adjective frumpish, frumpy, unfashionable, inelegant, shabby, untidy, dingy, frowzy.

**down** adjective **1** *feeling down* downhearted, dejected. *See* DOWNCAST. **2** *prices are down* lower, reduced, of lower/less value. **down on** *wish I hadn't been so down on school* against, prejudiced against, set against, antagonistic to/toward, hostile to/toward, negative toward/about.

**down** verb **1** *down three of the enemy* knock/throw/bring down, floor, fell, tackle, trip up, overthrow, defeat, conquer, subdue. **2** *down three glassfuls* drink, gulp down, swallow; *inf.* put away, chug (down), chug-a-lug, swill.

**downbeat** adjective *too many downbeat stories in the news* depressing, sad, gloomy, disheartening, dreary, dispiriting, bleak.

**downcast** adjective *downcast at the news* disheartened, dispirited, downhearted, dejected, depressed, discouraged, daunted, dismayed, disappointed, disconsolate, crestfallen, despondent, sad, unhappy, miserable, wretched, down, low, blue, gloomy, glum, melancholy, sorrowful, doleful, mournful.

**downfall** noun fall, collapse, undoing, ruin, ruination, crash, destruction, debasement, degradation, disgrace, overthrow, defeat.

**downgrade** verb **1** *downgrade the officers* demote, degrade, humble, debase; *inf.* take down a peg or two. **2** *downgrade their achievement* disparage, denigrate, detract from, run down, decry, belittle, make light of, minimize.

**downhearted** adjective disheartened, dispirited. *See* DOWNCAST.

**downpour** noun rainstorm, snowstorm, deluge, torrential/pouring rain, cloudburst, downfall; torrents of rain.

**downright** adjective **1** *a downright lie* complete, total, absolute, out and out, outright, utter, sheer, thorough, thoroughgoing, categorical, unmitigated, unqualified, unconditional, positive, simple, wholesale, all out, arrant, rank. **2** *a downright person* frank,

forthright, straightforward, open, candid, plainspoken, matter-of-fact, outspoken, blunt, brusque.

**downright** adverb *downright rude* completely, totally, absolutely, utterly, thoroughly, profoundly, categorically, positively.

**down-to-earth** adjective practical, sensible, realistic, matter-of-fact, no-nonsense, hardheaded, sane, mundane, unromantic, unidealistic.

**downtrodden** adjective oppressed, burdened, weighed down, overwhelmed, tyrannized, ground down, helpless, powerless, prostrate, poor, miserable, wretched, distressed.

**doze** verb nap, take a nap, catnap, slumber, take a siesta; *inf.* nod off, drift off, snooze, have a snooze, catch forty winks, get some shut-eye, catch/grab some Z's.

**drab** adjective **1** *drab clothes/surroundings* dull, dull-colored, colorless, mousy, gray, grayish, dingy, dreary, dismal, cheerless, gloomy, somber, depressing. **2** *a drab talk* uninteresting, boring, tedious, dry, dreary, lifeless, lackluster, uninspired.

**draft** verb **1** *draft a proposal* outline, plan, draw (up), frame, sketch (out), design, delineate. **2** *drafted by/into the army* recruit, conscript, call up, induct.

**drag** verb **1** *drag the body from the sea* haul, pull, draw, tug, yank, trail, tow, lug. **2** *time dragged* go/move slowly, creep/limp along, crawl, go at a snail's pace. **3** *the movie dragged* go on too long, go on and on, become tedious. **drag out** *drag out the lecture* protract, prolong, draw out, spin out, stretch out, lengthen, extend.

**drain** verb **1** *drain the water from the tank* draw off, extract, withdraw, remove, pump off, milk, bleed, tap, filter. **2** *drain the tank* empty, void, evacuate. **3** *the liquid drained (away)* flow out, ooze, trickle, seep out, leak, discharge, exude, effuse. **4** *legal costs draining resources* use up, exhaust, deplete, consume, expend, empty, sap, strain, tax, bleed.

**drain** noun **1** *a sewage drain* channel, conduit, culvert, duct, gutter, sewer, trench, ditch, dike, pipe, outlet. **2** *a drain on resources* exhaustion, depletion, consumption, expenditure, outflow, sapping, strain, tax.

**drama** noun **1** *studying drama* dramatic art, stagecraft, theater, acting, dramatics. **2** *a Chekhov drama* play, show; stage play, screenplay, radio play, television play, stage show, theatrical work, theatrical piece. **3** *the drama at the police station* exciting/emotional scene, thrilling/tense spectacle, excitement, crisis; dramatics, theatrics, histrionics.

**dramatic** adjective **1** *dramatic art* theatrical, stage, thespian. **2** *dramatic scenes in court* exciting, sensational, spectacular, startling, unexpected, thrilling, tense, suspenseful, electrifying, stirring, affecting. **3** *a dramatic view/description* striking, impressive, vivid, spectacular, breathtaking, moving, affecting, emotive, graphic, effective, powerful. **4** *a dramatic gesture* theatrical, artificial, exaggerated, overdone, stagy, histrionic.

**dramatist** noun playwright, scriptwriter, screenwriter, tragedy writer, comedy writer, dramaturgist, dramaturge.

**drape** verb **1** *drape the walls in tapestry* cover, envelope, blanket, overlay, cloak, veil, shroud, decorate, adorn, array, deck, festoon. **2** *drape a shawl around her* hang, arrange, let fall in folds. **3** *drape an arm on the chair* hang, let fall, place loosely, lean, dangle, droop.

**drastic** adjective extreme, severe, desperate, dire, radical, harsh, sharp, forceful, rigorous, draconian.

**draw** verb **1** *draw a chair up | draw the table away* pull, haul, tow, trail, tug, yank. **2** *draw alongside | drew to a close* move, go, come, proceed, approach. **3** *draw a sword/gun* pull out, take out, bring out, extract, withdraw, produce, unsheathe. **4** *draw the curtains* shut, close, pull together. **5** *draw attention* attract, allure, lure, entice, invite, engage, interest, win, catch the eye of, capture, captivate, fascinate, tempt, seduce. **6** *draw a breath* breathe in, inhale, suck in, inspire, respire. **7** *draw a salary* take, take in, receive, be in receipt of, get, procure, obtain, earn. **8** *draw a conclusion* deduce, infer, conclude, derive, gather, glean. **9** *draw liquid* drain, siphon off, pump off, tap, milk, bleed, filtrate. **10** *draw lots/straws* choose, pick, select, opt for, make a choice of, decide on, single out. **11** *draw a house* sketch, portray, depict, delineate, represent, trace, map out, mark out, chart, paint, design. **draw on** *draw on experience* make use of, use, have recourse to, exploit, employ, rely on. **draw out 1** *draw out the talk* prolong, protract. See DRAG. **2** *draw the child out* induce to talk, persuade to speak, put at ease. **draw up** *draw up a document* compose, formulate, frame, write out, put in writing, put down on paper, draft, prepare.

**draw** noun **1** *the draw of the circus* attraction, lure, allure, pull, enticement, magnetism. **2** *the match ended in a draw* tie, dead heat, stalemate.

**drawback** noun disadvantage, snag, catch, problem, difficulty, trouble, flaw, stumbling block, hitch, handicap, hindrance, obstacle, impediment, hurdle, obstruction, barrier, curb, check, deterrent, damper,

inconvenience, nuisance, detriment, fault, weak spot, weakness, imperfection, defect; *inf.* fly in the ointment.

**drawing** noun sketch, picture, illustration, representation, portrayal, delineation, depiction, composition, study, diagram, outline.

**drawn** adjective *pale and drawn* pinched, haggard, hollow-cheeked, strained, stressed, fatigued, tired, worn, drained, wan, sapped.

**dread** verb fear, be afraid of, be terrified by, tremble/shudder about, cringe/shrink from, quail/cower/flinch from; worry about, be anxious about, have forebodings about.

**dread** noun fear, fright, alarm, terror, apprehension, trepidation, horror, anxiety, concern, foreboding, dismay, perturbation, trembling, shuddering, flinching; *inf.* blue funk, heebie-jeebies.

**dreadful** adjective **1** *a dreadful sight/accident* terrible, frightful, horrible, grim, awful, dire, frightening, terrifying, alarming, distressing, shocking, appalling, harrowing, ghastly, fearful, hideous, horrendous, gruesome, tragic, calamitous, grievous. **2** *dreadful weather* nasty, unpleasant, disagreeable, frightful, shocking, very bad, distasteful, repugnant, odious. **3** *a dreadful waste of time* shocking, outrageous, inordinate, great, tremendous.

**dream** noun **1** *saw his mother in a dream* nightmare; vision, fantasy, hallucination. **2** *his dream to become rich* ambition, aspiration, goal, design, plan, aim, hope, yearning, desire, wish, notion, daydream, fantasy. **3** *the car was a dream* beauty, vision, delight, pleasure to behold, joy, marvel. **4** *go around in a dream* daydream, reverie, trance, daze, fog, stupor.

**dream** verb **1** *he thought he saw a ghost but he was dreaming* hallucinate, have a vision, imagine things, fantasize. **2** *she was dreaming instead of working* daydream, be in a trance/reverie, be lost in thought, muse, be preoccupied. **3** *never dream that they would go* think, consider, visualize, conceive, suppose. **dream up** *dream up new schemes* conjure up, think up, invent, concoct, devise, create, hatch, fabricate; *inf.* cook up.

**dreamer** noun daydreamer, visionary, fantasist, fantasizer, romantic, romancer, idealist, theorizer, Utopian, Don Quixote.

**dreamland** noun land of make-believe, never-never land, fairyland, fantasy world.

**dreary** adjective **1** *a dreary day* gloomy, dismal, bleak, somber, dull, dark, overcast, depressing. **2** *lead a dreary life* dull, drab, uninteresting, flat, dry, colorless, lifeless, tedious, wearisome, boring, humdrum, routine, monotonous, uneventful, run-of-

**dregs** plural noun **1** *the dregs of the wine* sediment, deposit, residue, precipitate, sublimate, scum, debris, dross, detritus, refuse, draff; lees, grounds. **2** *the dregs of society* scum, riff-raff, rabble, refuse; down-and-outs, good-for-nothings, outcasts, deadbeats, tramps, vagrants.

**drench** verb soak, saturate, permeate, drown, inundate, flood, steep, douse, souse, wet, slosh.

**dress** noun **1** *wearing a black dress* gown, garment, robe. **2** *with her dress in disarray* clothes, garments; clothing, attire, apparel, costume, outfit, ensemble, garb; *inf.* gear, get-up, togs, duds. **3** *birds/trees in their winter dress* covering, outer covering, plumage, feathers, pelt.

**dress** verb **1** *she was dressed in black* clothe, attire, garb, fit out, turn out, array, apparel, robe. **2** *dress poultry* prepare, get ready, clean; stuff. **3** *dress a wound* cover, bandage, bind up, put a plaster on. **dress down** reprimand, scold, upbraid, rebuke, reprove, berate, castigate, rake over the coals; *inf.* tell off. **dress up 1** *dress up for the occasion* dress formally/smartly, wear evening dress; *inf.* doll oneself up, dress to the nines, put on one's glad rags. **2** *dress the room up* decorate, adorn, ornament, trim, embellish, beautify, prettify.

**dressing** noun **1** *a dressing for the salad* relish, sauce, condiment. **2** *a dressing on the wound* covering, bandage, gauze.

**drift** verb **1** *boats/leaves drifting along* be carried along/away, be borne, be wafted, float, go with the current, coast. **2** *people drifting about* wander, roam, rove, meander, stray. **3** *snow drifting* pile up, bank up, accumulate, gather, amass.

**drift** noun **1** *a drift to the right* movement, deviation, digression, variation. **2** *the drift of his argument* gist, essence, meaning, substance, core, significance, import, purport, tenor, vein, direction, course, tendency, trend.

**drill** noun **1** *military drill* training, instruction, coaching, teaching, grounding, indoctrination. **2** *early morning drill* exercises, workout. **3** *not know the drill* procedure, routine, practice.

**drink** verb **1** *drink the water* swallow, gulp down, drain, quaff, imbibe, partake of, swill, guzzle, sip; *inf.* chug, swig. **2** *her son drinks* tipple, indulge; *inf.* hit the bottle, bend one's elbow, booze, **drink in** be absorbed/rapt/lost in, be fascinated by. **drink to** toast, propose a toast to, salute.

**drink** noun **1** *food and drink* beverage, drinkable/potable liquid, liquid refreshment; thirst-quencher. **2** *no drink at the dance* alcohol, liquor, spirits; *inf.* booze, hard stuff, hooch. **3** *take a drink from the cup* swallow,

**drink** noun **1** *food and drink* beverage, drinkable/potable liquid, liquid refreshment; thirst-quencher. **2** *no drink at the dance* alcohol, liquor, spirits; *inf.* booze, hard stuff, hooch. **3** *take a drink from the cup* swallow, gulp, sip, swill; *inf.* swig, slug.

**drinker** noun social drinker, heavy/hard drinker, serious drinker, alcoholic, problem drinker, alcohol abuser, drunk, drunkard, dipsomaniac, tippler, toper, sot, inebriate, imbiber; *inf.* boozer, soak, lush, wino, alky, elbow-bender.

**drip** verb drop, dribble, trickle, splash, sprinkle, plop, leak, ooze, exude, filter, percolate.

**drive** verb **1** *drive a car* operate, steer, handle, guide, direct, manage. **2** *he drove us here* chauffeur, run, give one a lift. **3** *drive cattle to the barn* urge, press, push, impel, propel, herd, round up. **4** *driven to steal/despair* force, compel, constrain, impel, oblige, coerce, make, pressure, goad, spur, prod. **5** *drove himself too hard* work, overwork, tax, overtax, overburden. **6** *drive the stake into the ground* hammer, ram, bang, sink, plunge, thrust, stab, **drive at** *what are you driving at?* mean, suggest, imply, hint at, refer to, allude to, intimate; *inf.* get at.

**drive** noun **1** *go for a drive* run, trip, jaunt, outing, journey, excursion, tour, turn; *inf.* spin, joyride. **2** *the tree-lined drive* driveway, road, roadway, avenue. **3** *a sales drive* effort, push, campaign, publicity campaign, crusade, surge. **4** *a young man with drive* energy, vigor, verve, ambition, push, enterprise, motivation, initiative, action, aggressiveness; *inf.* get-up-and-go, zip.

**drivel** noun **1** *speak drivel* nonsense, twaddle, gibberish, balderdash, rubbish, mumbo jumbo; *inf.* rot, poppycock, garbage, tripe, bunk, hogwash, crap. **2** *wipe away the drivel* saliva, drool, drooling, dribble, slaver, slobber.

**droll** adjective amusing, comical, waggish, witty, whimsical.

**drone**[1] noun *the drone of aircraft* hum, buzz, whirr, whirring, purr.

**drone**[2] noun *the workers and the drones in the firm* idler, loafer, layabout, lounger, do-nothing, sluggard, parasite, leech; *inf.* lazybones, scrounger, sponger.

**droop** verb **1** *flowers drooping* hang, hang down, bend, bow, stoop, sag, sink, slump, fall down, drop. **2** *drooping at the news | spirits drooping* flag, fade, languish, falter, weaken, wilt, shrivel, wither.

**drop** noun **1** *a drop of water* droplet, globule, bead, bubble, blob, spheroid, oval. **2** *add just a drop* little, bit, dash, spot, dribble, splash, sprinkle, trickle, taste, trace, pinch, dab, speck, particle, modicum; *inf.* smidgen, smidge, tad. **3** *a drop in prices* decline, decrease, reduction, cut, cutback, lowering, falling-off, downturn, depreciation, devaluation, slump. **4** *the path ended in a sudden drop* descent, incline, declivity, slope, plunge; abyss, chasm, precipice, cliff.

**drop** verb **1** *water dropping from the trees* fall, drip, dribble, trickle, plop, leak. **2** *the plane dropped out of the sky* drop down, descend, plunge, plummet, dive, tumble. **3** *she dropped from exhaustion* fall/sink down, collapse, faint, swoon, drop/fall dead. **4** *prices dropped* fall, decrease, lessen, diminish, depreciate, go into decline, dwindle, sink, slacken off, plunge, plummet. **5** *drop singing lessons* give up, discontinue, end, stop, cease, terminate, finish with, withdraw/retire from, quit, abandon, forgo, relinquish, dispense with. **6** *drop his girlfriend* desert, abandon, forsake, leave, throw over, jilt, discard, reject, repudiate, renounce, disown; *inf.* ditch, chuck, run out on, leave flat. **7** *drop half the workforce* dismiss, discharge, let go; *inf.* sack, fire, boot out. **8** *drops the second syllable in "mathematics"* omit, leave out, eliminate, elide, contract, slur. **drop off 1** *drop the goods/passengers off* deliver, deposit, set down, unload, leave. **2** *people dropping off* fall asleep, doze, doze off, have a nap, catnap, drowse; *inf.* nod off, snooze, take forty winks, get some shut-eye.

**drove** noun **1** *a drove of cattle/sheep* herd, flock, pack. **2** *droves of people going shopping* crowd, horde, swarm, multitude, mob, throng, host, collection, gathering, assembly, company, herd.

**drown** verb **1** *the cornfields were drowned when the dam burst* flood, submerge, immerse, inundate, deluge, swamp, engulf, drench. **2** *outside noise drowning her speech* drown out, muffle, deaden, stifle, overpower, overwhelm, overcome, engulf, swallow up. **3** *drowning his grief in work* suppress, quash, quench, extinguish, obliterate, wipe out, get rid of.

**drowsy** adjective **1** *feeling drowsy* sleepy, half asleep, tired, weary, heavy-eyed, yawning, lethargic, sluggish, somnolent, dazed, drugged; *inf.* dopey. **2** *drowsy weather* sleepy, sleep-inducing, soporific, somniferous, lulling, soothing, dreamy.

**drubbing** noun beating, thrashing, walloping, thumping, battering, trouncing, whipping, flogging, pounding, pummeling, bludgeoning; *inf.* hammering, licking, clobbering, working-over.

**drudgery** noun menial/hard work, toiling, toil, labor, hard labor, chores; *inf.* grind.

**drug** noun **1** *a new cancer drug* medicine, medication, medicament, remedy, cure,

cure-all, panacea, physic. **2** *addicted to drugs* narcotic, opiate; *inf.* dope.

**drug** verb anesthetize, knock out, make/render unconscious, make/render insensible, stupefy, befuddle; *inf.* dope (up).

**drugged** adjective anesthetized, knocked out, comatose, stupefied, insensible, befuddled; *inf.* doped, stoned, dopey, on a trip, spaced out, zonked, high, high as a kite, turned on, flying, charged up.

**drum** verb **1** *drum one's fingers* tap, beat, rap, knock, strike. **2** *drum information into the students* drive home, instill, hammer, inculcate. **drum out** expel from, dismiss/discharge from, throw out, oust from. **drum up** obtain, get, attract, canvass, solicit, petition, bid for.

**drunk** adjective drunken, blind drunk, dead drunk, intoxicated, inebriated, inebriate, under the influence, tipsy, soused; *inf.* tight, tiddly, woozy, pie-eyed, three sheets to the wind, under the table, out of it, legless, plastered, smashed, sloshed, stoned, well-oiled, blotto, blitzed, lit up, stewed, pickled, tanked up, bombed.

**drunk** noun drunkard, inebriate, heavy/hard drinker, sot, toper, tippler, alcoholic, dipsomaniac, serious/problem drinker; *inf.* boozer, lush, alky, wino, elbow-bender.

**dry** adjective **1** *dry ground/regions* arid, parched, scorched, waterless, unwatered, moistureless, rainless, torrid, thirsty, droughty, barren, unproductive, sterile. **2** *dry leaves* withered, shriveled, wilted, dehydrated, desiccated, wizened, sapless, juiceless. **3** *a dry talk* dull, uninteresting, boring, tedious, tiresome, wearisome, dreary, monotonous, flat, unimaginative, commonplace, prosaic, run-of-the-mill, humdrum, vapid. **4** *a dry wit* subtle, low-key, deadpan, laconic, sly, sharp, ironic, droll, waggish. **5** *a dry response/greeting* unemotional, indifferent, cool, cold, aloof, remote, impersonal.

**dry** verb **1** *the sun drying the earth/leaves* dry out/up, parch, scorch, dehydrate, desiccate, dehumidify, sear, wither, shrivel, wilt, wizen, mummify. **2** *dry the wet patch* dry off, mop up, blot up, towel, drain. **dry up** *inspiration dried up* fail, become unproductive, grow barren/sterile, cease to yield.

**dual** adjective double, twofold, duplicate, duplex, binary, twin, matched, paired, coupled.

**dub** verb call, name, christen, designate, term, entitle, style, label, denominate, nominate, tag, nickname.

**dubious** adjective **1** *dubious about going* doubtful, uncertain, hesitant, undecided, wavering, vacillating; *inf.* iffy. **2** *the outcome is dubious* unsure, unsettled, undetermined, indefinite, unresolved, up in the air, open.

**3** *a dubious reply* equivocal, ambiguous, indeterminate, indefinite, unclear, vague, imprecise, enigmatic, cryptic. **4** *a dubious character* questionable, suspicious, suspect; *inf.* shady, fishy.

**duck** verb **1** *duck behind the wall* bend, bow down, bob down, stoop, crouch, squat, hunch down, hunker down. **2** *duck one's head* bow, lower, drop. **3** *duck him in the pond* immerse, submerge, plunge, dip, souse, douse, dunk. **4** *duck the police/work* dodge, evade, sidestep, avoid, steer clear of, elude, escape, shirk, shun.

**duct** noun pipe, tube, conduit, channel, passage, canal, culvert.

**dud** noun failure, flop; *inf.* washout, lemon, loser.

**dudgeon** noun **in high dudgeon** angry, annoyed, furious, in a temper, indignant, enraged, fuming, vexed, offended.

**due** adjective **1** *money/thanks due (to) them* owing, owed, payable, outstanding. **2** *recognition due (to) a hero* deserved by, merited by, earned by, justified by, appropriate to, fit for, fitting to, suitable for, right for. **3** *treat with due respect* proper, right and proper, correct, rightful, fitting, appropriate, apt, adequate, sufficient, enough, ample, satisfactory, requisite, apposite. **4** *the essay is due tomorrow* scheduled, expected, required, awaited, anticipated.

**due to** *due to uncertainty* attributable to, ascribed to, ascribable to, caused by, assignable to, because of, owing to.

**due** noun *receive only his due* right, just deserts, deserts; *inf.* comeuppance.

**dull** adjective **1** *dull of wit* dull-witted, slow, slow-witted, unintelligent, stupid, dense, doltish, stolid, vacuous; *inf.* dim, dim-witted, thick, dumb, birdbrained. **2** *a dull reaction* insensitive, unfeeling, unemotional, indifferent, unresponsive, apathetic. **3** *feeling dull in the winter* inactive, inert, slow, slow-moving, sleepy, drowsy, idle, sluggish, stagnant, lethargic, listless, languid, heavy, apathetic, torpid, phlegmatic, vegetative. **4** *a dull speech* uninteresting, boring, tedious, tiresome, wearisome, dry, monotonous, flat, bland, unimaginative, humdrum, uneventful, vapid. **5** *dull weather* overcast, cloudy, gloomy, dark, dim, dismal, dreary, bleak, somber, leaden, murky, sunless. **6** *dull colors* drab, dreary, somber, dark, subdued, muted, toned-down, lackluster, lusterless, colorless, faded, washed-out. **7** *a dull sound* muffled, muted, indistinct, feeble. **8** *a dull edge* blunt, blunted, unsharpened, dulled, edgeless.

**dull** verb **1** *dull the appetite* take the edge off, blunt, lessen, decrease, diminish, reduce, deaden, mute, tone down, allay, ease, soothe, assuage, alleviate, palliate.

**2** *drugs dull the senses* numb, benumb, stupefy, drug, sedate, tranquilize. **3** *time dulling the colors* fade, bleach, wash out. **4** *the sky dulled by clouds* darken, dim, bedim, obscure. **5** *spirits dulled by the bad news* dispirit, dishearten, depress, deject, sadden, discourage, cast down, dampen, put a damper on, cast a pall over.

**dumb** adjective **1** *struck dumb at the sight* speechless, wordless, silent, mute, at a loss for words, voiceless, soundless, inarticulate, taciturn, uncommunicative, tongue-tied; *inf.* mum. **2** *dumb people and clever people* stupid, dull, dull-witted, slow, slow-witted, unintelligent, dense, foolish, doltish; *inf.* dim, dim-witted, thick.

**dumbfound** verb astound, astonish, amaze, startle, surprise, stun, take aback, stagger, overwhelm, confound, shock, confuse, bewilder, baffle, nonplus, perplex, disconcert; *inf.* flabbergast, throw, shake, throw for a loop.

**dump** verb **1** *dump the goods on the floor* drop, let fall, throw down, fling down. **2** *dump the unwanted goods* dispose of, get rid of, throw away/out, scrap, jettison. **3** *the tanker dumped its load* discharge, empty out, pour out, tip out, unload, jettison. **4** *dump his wife* abandon, desert, leave, leave in the lurch, forsake, walk out on.

**dump** noun **1** *take the debris to the dump* refuse/rubbish dump, rubbish heap, junkyard, scrapyard; transfer station. **2** *what a dump!* hovel, shack, slum, shanty, pigsty; *inf.* hole, joint.

**dunce** noun dolt, blockhead, dunderhead, thickhead, numskull, nincompoop, ninny, simpleton, halfwit, idiot, moron, ass, ignoramus, dullard; *inf.* dimwit, dummy.

**dungeon** noun cell, lockup, black hole, oubliette; keep.

**duplicate** noun **1** *a duplicate of the chair* copy, replica, facsimile, reproduction, twin, double, clone, match, mate, fellow, counterpart, look-alike, spitting image; *inf.* ringer, dead ringer. **2** *make a duplicate of the document* copy, carbon copy, carbon, photocopy, facsimile, fax; Photostat (*trademark*), Xerox (*trademark*).

**duplicate** verb **1** *duplicate the documents* copy, make a carbon/facsimile of, photocopy, fax, reproduce, make a replica of, replicate, clone; Photostat (*trademark*), Xerox (*trademark*). **2** *duplicate the task* repeat, do over again, perform again, replicate.

**duplicity** noun deceitfulness, double-dealing, trickery, guile, chicanery, artifice, dishonesty, knavery.

**durable** adjective **1** *durable affection* lasting, enduring, abiding, continuing, constant, stable, fast, firm, fixed, permanent, unfading, changeless, unchanging, invariable, dependable, reliable. **2** *durable clothing/goods* long-lasting, hard-wearing, strong, sturdy, sound, tough, resistant, substantial, imperishable.

**duress** noun force, compulsion, coercion, pressure, pressurization, constraint, arm-twisting, enforcement, exaction.

**dutiful** adjective respectful, filial, deferential, obedient, compliant, pliant, docile, submissive.

**duty** noun **1** *a sense of duty to one's country/parents* responsibility, obligation, allegiance, loyalty, faithfulness, fidelity, respect, deference, reverence, homage. **2** *share the duties* task, job, chore, assignment, commission, mission, function, office, charge, part, role, requirement, work, burden. **3** *pay duty* tax, levy, tariff, excise, toll, fee, impost; customs, dues.

**dwarf** verb **1** *dwarfed by the effects of a drug* stunt, arrest/check growth, atrophy. **2** *a novelist who dwarfs his contemporaries* tower above/over, overshadow, stand head and shoulders over, dominate, diminish, minimize.

**dwell** verb reside, live, be domiciled, lodge, stay, abide. **dwell on/upon** spend time on, linger over, harp on, discuss at length, expatiate on, elaborate on, expound on, be preoccupied with/by, be obsessed with/by.

**dwelling** noun residence, home, house, abode, domicile, establishment.

**dwindle** verb **1** *savings/hope dwindling* decrease, lessen, diminish, shrink, contract, fade, wane. **2** *the Roman empire dwindling* decline, fail, sink, ebb, degenerate, deteriorate, decay, wither, rot, disappear, vanish, die out; *inf.* peter out.

**dyed-in-the-wool** adjective entrenched, inveterate, established, deep-rooted, confirmed, complete, absolute, through and through, utter, thoroughgoing.

**dying** adjective **1** *a dying woman* terminally ill, breathing one's last, on one's deathbed, passing away, sinking fast, expiring, moribund, *in extremis*; *inf.* in the jaws of death, having one foot in the grave, on one's/its last legs, at death's door. **2** *dying customs* passing, fading, vanishing, failing, ebbing, waning. **3** *dying words* final, last.

**dynamic** adjective energetic, active, lively, alive, spirited, vital, vigorous, strong, forceful, powerful, potent, effective, effectual, high-powered, magnetic, aggressive, go-ahead, driving, electric; *inf.* zippy, peppy.

**dynasty** noun line, succession, house, regime, rule, reign, dominion, empire; sovereignty, ascendancy, government, authority, administration, jurisdiction.

# *Ee*

**eager** adjective **1** *eager students* keen, enthusiastic, impatient, avid, fervent, earnest, diligent, zealous, passionate, wholehearted, ambitious, enterprising; *inf.* bright-eyed and bushy-tailed. **2** *eager for news* agog, anxious, intent, longing, yearning, itching, wishing, desirous, hopeful, thirsty, hungry, greedy; *inf.* hot.

**ear** noun *have the ear of the president* attention, attentiveness, notice, heed, regard, consideration.

**early** adjective **1** *an early crop/birth* advanced, premature, untimely. **2** *an early reply* prompt, quick, speedy, rapid, fast, expeditious, timely. **3** *early man* primitive, primeval, primordial, prehistoric.

**earmark** verb *earmark the money for a vacation* set/lay aside, keep back, allocate, reserve, designate, label, tag.

**earn** verb **1** *earn a good salary* make, get, receive, obtain, draw, clear, collect. **2**

*earn their admiration* gain, win, rate, merit, achieve, secure, deserve.

**earnest** adjective **1** *an earnest young man* serious, solemn, grave, intense, staid, studious, thoughtful, dedicated, assiduous. **2** *her earnest request* sincere, fervent, ardent, passionate, heartfelt, wholehearted, zealous.

**earnest** noun **in earnest 1** *in earnest about the punishment* serious, not joking, sincere. **2** *working in earnest* zealously, ardently, fervently, fervidly, passionately, wholeheartedly, resolutely.

**earnings** plural noun income, salary, wage, pay, take-home pay, remuneration, revenue, yield, profit, gain, return; wages.

**earth** noun **1** *earth, moon, and stars* globe, world, planet, sphere, orb. **2** *dig up the earth* soil, loam, clay, dirt, sod, turf, ground. **3** *between the earth and the sky* ground, dry ground, land.

**earthly** adjective *earthly joys* worldly, temporal, secular, mortal, human, material, materialistic, corporeal.

**earthy** adjective **1** *earthy people* down-to-earth, unsophisticated, simple, plain, unpretentious, rough, robust. **2** *an earthy sense of humor* bawdy, crude, coarse, ribald.

**ease** noun **1** *succeed with ease* facility, simplicity, effortlessness, deftness, adroitness, proficiency, mastery. **2** *his ease of manner* naturalness, informality, amiability, affability, composure, aplomb, nonchalance, insouciance, urbanity, suaveness. **3** *a life of ease* comfort, affluence, wealth, prosperity, luxury, opulence; bed of roses.

**ease** verb **1** *ease the pain* mitigate, lessen, reduce, lighten, moderate, abate, ameliorate, relieve, assuage, allay. **2** *ease her mind* comfort, console, soothe, calm, pacify. **3** *ease his promotion* facilitate, expedite, assist, help, aid, advance, further. **4** *ease it into position* guide, maneuver, steer, slide, slip.

**easy** adjective **1** *an easy task* simple, effortless, uncomplicated, straightforward, undemanding, painless, facile. **2** *easy prey* compliant, susceptible, docile, gullible, tractable, trusting, acquiescent. **3** *an easy manner* natural, casual, informal, easygoing, amiable, affable, composed, carefree, nonchalant; *inf.* laid-back. **4** *an easy pace* even, steady, regular, comfortable, moderate, unhurried.

**easygoing** adjective happy-go-lucky, relaxed, carefree, nonchalant, amiable; *inf.* laid-back.

**eat** verb **1** *eat chocolate* consume, devour, munch, gulp down, bolt, wolf; dine; *inf.* snack, graze. **2** *eating the rock away* erode, corrode, wear, dissolve, rot, decay, destroy.

**ebb** verb **1** *the tide ebbed* go out, retreat, fall back, recede, abate, subside. **2** *its popularity ebbed* decline, fade away, die out, lessen, wane, decrease, diminish, flag, dwindle, deteriorate, decay.

**ebullient** adjective exuberant, buoyant, exhilarated, elated, euphoric, animated, vivacious.

**eccentric** adjective odd, queer, strange, peculiar, weird, anomalous, unconventional, singular, idiosyncratic, capricious, quirky.

**echo** verb **1** *echo around the room* reverberate, resound, reflect, ring. **2** *echo a statement* copy, imitate, reproduce, repeat, reiterate, parrot.

**economical** adjective **1** *economical with resources* thrifty, sparing, careful, prudent, frugal, scrimping, stingy, parsimonious. **2** *an economical vacation* cheap, inexpensive, reasonable, low-cost, low-budget, budget.

**economize** verb cut back, retrench, budget, scrimp, save; *inf.* cut corners, tighten one's belt, pinch pennies.

**ecstasy** noun bliss, rapture, elation, euphoria, joy.

**ecstatic** adjective blissful, joyful, joyous, jubilant, elated, on cloud nine, in seventh heaven.

**edge** noun **1** *the edge of the lake* border, side, boundary, rim, margin, fringe, verge, brink, lip, perimeter, periphery. **2** *a voice with an edge* sting, bite; sharpness, severity, pointedness, acidity, acrimony. **3** *have the edge on her* advantage, upper hand, dominance, superiority. **on edge** nervous, tense.

**edge** verb **1** *edge with lace* trim, hem, border, fringe. **2** *edge one's way through the crowd* inch, elbow, worm, work, sidle, creep, steal.

**edgy** adjective nervous, tense, ill at ease, anxious, on tenterhooks, restive, uneasy, irritable, touchy; *inf.* uptight, wired.

**edict** noun decree, order, command, ruling, statute, injunction, mandate, manifesto, proclamation, dictate, dictum, fiat.

**edifice** noun building, structure, construction.

**educate** verb instruct, teach, school, tutor, train, inform, enlighten.

**educated** adjective literate, schooled, well-read, informed, knowledgeable, enlightened, lettered, erudite, cultivated, cultured, refined; *inf.* highbrow.

**education** noun schooling, teaching, instruction, tuition, tutelage, enlightenment; edification, cultivation, development.

**eerie** adjective uncanny, mysterious, strange, unnatural, frightening, spine-chilling, blood-curdling; *inf.* spooky, scary, creepy.

**effect** noun **1** *the effect of the changes* result, outcome, consequence, conclusion; results, fruits. **2** *the law goes into effect tomorrow* force, implementation, execution, action. **3** *speak to great effect* effectiveness, success, influence, efficacy, weight, power, cogency. **4** *or words to that effect* sense, meaning, drift, significance, essence. **in effect** effectively, actually, really, in reality, in essence.

**effect** verb *effect a plan* carry out, cause, make, produce, create, achieve, accomplish, complete, fulfill, implement, execute.

**effective** adjective **1** *effective administration* successful, productive, competent, capable, able, efficient, adequate. **2** *effective lighting* striking, impressive, exciting, attractive. **3** *effective arguments* powerful, forceful, cogent, compelling, persuasive, convincing, moving. **4** *rules become effective tomorrow* valid, operative, active.

**effects** plural noun belongings, (personal) possessions, goods, accoutrements, paraphernalia; property, gear, equipment; *inf.* things, stuff.

**efficient** adjective **1** *an efficient person* capable, able, competent, effective, productive, adept, organized, businesslike. **2** *an efficient office* organized, well-run, streamlined.

**effort** noun **1** *put effort into it* exertion, force, energy, work, muscle, labor, toil, struggle, strain; *lit.* travail; *inf.* elbow grease. **2** *admire his artistic efforts* achievement, accomplishment, attainment, creation, production, opus, feat.

**effortless** adjective easy, simple, uncomplicated, undemanding, painless, facile.

**egg** verb **egg on** encourage, urge, push, drive, goad, prod, prompt.

**egghead** noun intellectual, academic, scholar, brain, genius, bookworm; *inf.* Einstein.

**egoism** noun self-interest, self-centeredness, selfishness, egocentricity, egomania, narcissism, vanity, conceit, pride, self-importance.

**egotistic** adjective egocentric, narcissistic, conceited, vain, proud, arrogant, boastful.

**eject** verb **1** *eject sewage* emit, discharge, excrete, release, spew out, disgorge. **2** *ejected from the vehicle* propel, thrust out, throw out. **3** *eject him from the stadium* throw out, remove, evict, expel, oust, banish, deport; *inf.* kick out, bounce.

**elaborate** adjective complicated, detailed, complex, involved, intricate, painstaking; ornate, fancy, showy, ostentatious, extravagant.

**elaborate** verb expand on, amplify, flesh out; develop, work out, refine, polish, embellish, enhance; ornament, embroider.

**elastic** adjective stretchy, springy, flexible, pliant, supple, rubbery, resilient.

**elated** adjective overjoyed, euphoric. *See* ECSTATIC.

**elation** noun ecstasy, bliss, euphoria, rapture, joy, jubilation, exhilaration, delight.

**elderly** adjective aged, old, gray-haired, ancient; *inf.* over the hill.

**elderly** plural noun **the elderly** senior citizens, seniors.

**elect** verb vote for, choose, pick, select, designate, determine.

**electric** adjective **1** *electric power* galvanic, voltaic. **2** *an electric moment* tense, charged, exciting, thrilling.

**elegance** noun style, grace, tastefulness, polish, refinement, finesse, propriety, haute couture.

**elegant** adjective stylish, graceful, tasteful, fashionable, beautiful, lovely, exquisite, polished, cultivated, refined, dignified, luxurious, sumptuous, opulent.

**element** noun **1** *an element of truth* basis, ingredient, factor, feature, component, part, segment, member. **2** *in his natural element* environment, habitat, medium, milieu, field, domain.

**elementary** adjective easy, simple, straightforward, facile, simplistic; basic, fundamental, rudimentary, primary, preparatory, introductory.

**elevate** verb **1** *elevate the load* raise, lift, hoist. **2** *elevate to management* promote, upgrade, advance; *inf.* kick upstairs. **3** *elevate her spirits* cheer, gladden, brighten, perk up, lighten.

**elf** noun fairy, pixie, sprite, dwarf, gnome, goblin, imp, leprechaun, troll.

**elfin** adjective pixielike, little, diminutive, wee, Lilliputian; mischievous, impish, puckish.

**elicit** verb obtain, draw out, extract, exact, wrest, evoke, derive.

**elite** noun pick, cream, elect; aristocracy, nobility, gentry, upper crust.

**elongate** verb lengthen, extend, prolong, protract.

**eloquent** adjective expressive, well-spoken, articulate, fluent, pithy, persuasive.

**elude** verb *the fox eluded the hunter* avoid, dodge, evade, escape, lose, duck; *inf.* ditch.

**elusive** adjective **1** *an elusive person* evasive, slippery, shifty, cagey. **2** *an elusive perfume* indefinable, subtle, intangible, impalpable, fleeting. **3** *an elusive answer* ambiguous, baffling, puzzling, equivocal.

**emaciated** adjective wasted, gaunt, skeletal, cadaverous, shriveled, shrunken, withered, pinched, wizened.

**emanate** verb arise, originate, stem, derive, emerge; discharge, emit, exhale, radiate.

**emancipate** verb free, set free, liberate, release, let loose, deliver; unchain, unfetter, untie.

**embargo** noun ban, prohibition, interdiction, proscription; restriction, restraint, check, barrier, impediment, obstruction.

**embark** verb **embark on** *embark on an adventure* begin, start, commence, undertake, initiate.

**embarrass** verb disconcert, discomfit, fluster, agitate, distress, shame, humiliate.

**embassy** noun **1** *the British embassy* conbroider, enrich, deck, festoon; elaborate, exaggerate, fabricate.

**embezzle** verb steal, rob, thieve, pilfer, appropriate, misappropriate, purloin, filch; *inf.* rip off. age

**emblem** noun crest, badge, symbol, token, mark, sign; insignia.

**embody** verb incorporate, comprise, include, contain, constitute, encompass, assimilate, integrate, concentrate; personify, represent, symbolize, exemplify.

**embrace** verb 1 *embrace his wife* hold, hug, cuddle, clasp, squeeze, clutch. 2 *embrace the new philosophy* welcome, accept, take up, adopt; *fml* espouse.

**embrace** noun hug, cuddle, squeeze, clasp, hold, clutch.

**embroider** verb 1 *embroider a tablecloth* sew, decorate. 2 *embroider the truth* embellish, elaborate, exaggerate, invent, fabricate.

**emend** verb edit, correct, revise, alter, rewrite, improve, polish, refine.

**emerge** verb come out, appear, surface, materialize, arise, proceed, issue, emanate; become known.

**emergency** noun crisis, danger, accident, difficulty, plight, predicament.

**emigration** noun migration, departure, relocation, expatriation, exodus, defection.

**eminence** noun importance, greatness, prestige, reputation, fame, distinction, renown, preeminence, celebrity, rank.

**eminent** adjective important, great, distinguished, celebrated, famous, renowned, noted, prominent, esteemed, outstanding, high-ranking, revered, august.

**emission** noun *the emission of fumes* discharge, issue, excretion, secretion, ejection, emanation, radiation, exhalation, effusion.

**emit** verb *emit fumes/light* discharge, issue, ooze, leak, excrete, secrete, eject, emanate, radiate, exude.

**emotion** noun feeling, sentiment, passion, sensation; warmth, ardor, fervor, vehemence.

**emotional** adjective 1 *emotional person* feeling, passionate, hot-blooded, demonstrative, sentimental, ardent, fervent, sensitive. 2 *an emotional farewell* moving, touching, poignant, heart-rending, soul-stirring, impassioned.

**emphasis** noun stress, accent, accentuation, weight; importance, attention, priority, significance, intensity, import.

**emphasize** verb stress, accentuate, underline, call attention to, highlight, point up, spotlight, play up, foreground, underscore.

**emphatic** adjective marked, pronounced, decided, positive, definite, unmistakable, strong, striking, resounding, certain, determined, forceful, earnest, vigorous, unequivocal.

**empire** noun kingdom, realm, domain, territory, jurisdiction, province, commonwealth; sovereignty, dominion.

**employ** verb 1 *employ three people* hire, engage, take on, enroll, commission, enlist, retain. 2 *employ cunning* use, apply, exercise, utilize.

**employee** noun worker, wage earner, hand, hired hand, assistant, laborer, hireling.

**employer** noun boss, manager, owner, proprietor, contractor, director; firm, organization.

**employment** noun 1 *the employment of new staff* hiring, engagement, enrollment. 2 *employment as a teacher* job, work, business, line, occupation, profession, trade, vocation, craft, métier, pursuit.

**empower** verb authorize, license, certify, accredit, qualify, sanction; allow, enable, equip.

**emptiness** noun 1 *an emptiness in her life* vacuum, void, hollowness. 2 *the emptiness of the house* vacantness, desolation, bareness, barrenness, blankness, clearness. 3 *the emptiness of the threats* meaninglessness, futility, ineffectiveness, uselessness, worthlessness, fruitlessness. 4 *the emptiness of her existence* aimlessness, meaninglessness, worthlessness, barrenness, senselessness, banality, triviality.

**empty** adjective 1 *empty house* vacant, hollow, void, unoccupied, uninhabited, desolate, bare, blank, clear. 2 *empty threats* meaningless, futile, ineffective, ineffectual, worthless, idle. 3 *empty stare* blank, expressionless, vacant, vacuous, absent.

**empty** verb 1 *empty the room* vacate, clear, evacuate, unload. 2 *empty the liquid* drain, exhaust, use up, deplete.

**enable** verb authorize, entitle, qualify, license, sanction, accredit, validate, empower; allow, permit, equip, prepare.

**enact** verb *a bill enacted by Congress* legislate, rule, pass, approve, ratify, sanction; order, decree, pronounce.

**enchant** verb bewitch, fascinate, charm, captivate, entrance, enthrall, mesmerize, enrapture.

**enchanting** adjective bewitching, charming, delightful, captivating, irresistible, fascinating, engaging, entrancing, alluring.

*problem* difficult, complex, complicated, intricate.

**fierce** adjective 1 *a fierce animal/enemy* ferocious, savage, wild, vicious, feral, untamed, bloodthirsty, dangerous, cruel,

**enclose** verb **1** *enclosing the garden* surround, circle, ring, confine, circumscribe. **2** *enclose a check* include, insert.

**encounter** verb meet, run into, run across, confront, accost; *inf.* bump into.

**encounter** noun meeting; fight, battle, clash, conflict, contest, collision, confrontation, engagement, skirmish, scuffle; *inf.* run-in, brush.

**encourage** verb **1** *encouraging the runners to press on* cheer, motivate, inspire, stir, incite, animate, hearten, invigorate; urge, prompt, exhort, spur, goad. **2** *exercise encourages good health* help, assist, aid, support, boost, promote, further, foster, advance.

**encouragement** noun stimulation, motivation, inspiration, incitement; persuasion, exhortation; help, assistance, support, promotion, advocacy, backing.

**encumbrance** noun **1** *the encumbrance of heavy luggage* hindrance, obstruction, impediment, inconvenience, handicap, constraint. **2** *debts are an encumbrance* burden, weight, load, responsibility, obligation, strain.

**end** noun **1** *the end of the table* edge, border, boundary, extremity, limit, margin. **2** *the end of the affair* finish, close, conclusion, termination, completion, resolution, finale, epilogue. **3** *the commercial end of the business* side, section, area, field, part, portion, segment. **4** *the end was that he got the promotion* result, consequence, outcome, upshot.

**end** verb **1** *the show ended | to end a relationship* finish, close, stop, cease, conclude, terminate, complete, dissolve, discontinue, break off. **2** *end his hopes* destroy, annihilate, extinguish.

**endanger** verb threaten, expose, risk, jeopardize, imperil, compromise.

**endearing** adjective charming, attractive, adorable, lovable, sweet, engaging, winning, winsome.

**endeavor** verb try, attempt, strive, venture, aspire, undertake, struggle, labor, essay.

**endeavor** noun *his best endeavor* try, attempt, trial, effort, venture, struggle, essay; *inf.* crack, shot.

**ending** noun end, finish, close, conclusion, cessation, termination, expiration, resolution, completion.

**endless** adjective **1** *endless patience* unending, unlimited, infinite, limitless, boundless, constant, unfading, everlasting, unceasing, untold. **2** *an endless loop* continuous, uninterrupted, unbroken, never-ending. **3** *endless traveling* nonstop, interminable, monotonous, incessant, unremitting, boring.

**endorse** verb **1** *endorse a check* countersign, sign, autograph, underwrite, validate. **2** *endorse the course of action* approve, support, back, favor, recommend, advocate, champion, authorize, ratify, sanction, warrant.

**endow** verb **1** *endow with talent* provide, give, present, gift, confer, bestow, supply, furnish. **2** *endow a foundation* bestow, will, finance, fund.

**endowment** noun **1** *offer an endowment to the school* gift, present, grant, donation, legacy, largesse, funding, revenue, income. **2** *natural endowments* ability, gift, talent, flair, aptitude, capacity, facility, faculty, characteristic, quality.

**endurance** noun **1** *endurance of his love* durability, stability, permanence, continuance, continuity. **2** *beyond endurance* toleration, sufferance, fortitude, forbearance, perseverance, patience. **3** *a test of endurance* stamina, staying power, fortitude, tenacity; *inf.* guts.

**endure** verb **1** *love endures* last, continue, persist, remain, stay, survive. **2** *endure the difficult situation* stand, bear, tolerate, suffer, abide; *inf.* stomach, swallow. **3** *endure pain* experience, undergo, bear, tolerate, suffer, brave, withstand, weather.

**enduring** adjective lasting, durable, permanent, steady, steadfast, eternal, perennial, unwavering, unfaltering.

**enemy** noun foe, opponent, rival, adversary, antagonist, opposition.

**energetic** adjective **1** *energetic exercises* active, lively, vigorous, strenuous, brisk, dynamic, spirited, animated, indefatigable, peppy. **2** *energetic approach* forceful, determined, emphatic, aggressive, high-powered.

**energize** verb activate, stimulate, arouse, rouse, motivate, stir, goad, prompt; enliven, animate, invigorate, electrify, vitalize.

**energy** noun vigor, strength, stamina, power, drive; enthusiasm, animation, life, liveliness, pep, vivacity, vitality, spirit, exuberance.

**enervate** verb weaken, exhaust, tire, fatigue, debilitate, sap, incapacitate.

**enforce** verb **1** *enforce the law* apply, carry out, administer, implement, impose, discharge. **2** *enforce silence* force, compel, require, necessitate, oblige, exact, coerce.

**engage** verb **1** *engage a housekeeper* employ, hire, take on, appoint, commission. **2** *engaged in a book* occupy, fill, hold; preoccupy, absorb, engross. **3** *engage to marry* contract, promise, agree, guarantee, undertake, pledge, vouch, vow, covenant. **4** *armies engaging at dawn* do battle, fight, wage war, attack, clash, skirmish. **engage in** participate, join, undertake, tackle.

**engaged** adjective **1** *the conference room is engaged* busy, occupied, unavailable, in use, reserved, booked; *inf.* tied up. **2** *engaged couples* betrothed, affianced, espoused.

**engagement** noun **1** *a previous engagement* appointment, date, commitment. **2** *an engagement at sea* fight, battle, clash, conflict, attack, assault, confrontation, encounter, offensive.

**engaging** adjective attractive, charming, appealing, pleasing, pleasant, agreeable, delightful, winning, captivating, winsome.

**engineer** verb cause, plan, plot, scheme, contrive, devise, manipulate, orchestrate, originate, manage, control, direct, conduct.

**engrave** verb carve, etch, inscribe, chisel, print; fix, set, imprint, stamp.

**engrossed** adjective preoccupied, absorbed, engaged, riveted, captivated, immersed, rapt.

**engulf** verb consume, overwhelm, flood, submerge, immerse, inundate.

**enhance** verb increase, heighten, strengthen, improve, augment, boost, intensify, magnify, amplify, complement; raise, lift, escalate, elevate.

**enigma** noun mystery, puzzle, riddle, conundrum, paradox, problem, quandary, dilemma, labyrinth, maze.

**enigmatic** adjective mysterious, puzzling, baffling, obscure, perplexing, mystifying, cryptic, unfathomable, Sphinxlike; ambiguous, equivocal, paradoxical.

**enjoy** verb like, love, delight in, appreciate, relish, savor; have, possess, own.

**enjoyable** adjective entertaining, amusing, nice, pleasant, lovely, fine, agreeable, pleasurable, delicious, delectable, satisfying, gratifying.

**enjoyment** noun amusement, entertainment, diversion, recreation, pleasure, delight, happiness, gladness, fun, gaiety, satisfaction, gratification, relish, gusto; benefit, advantage, blessing.

**enlarge** verb **1** *enlarge the living area* expand, extend, amplify, augment, supplement, magnify; widen, broaden, lengthen, elongate, deepen, thicken. **2** *his spleen is enlarged* distend, dilate, swell, inflate, bloat, bulge.

**enlighten** verb inform, instruct, teach, educate, illuminate, cultivate.

**enlightened** adjective informed, aware, educated, knowledgeable, learned, wise, literate, intellectual, illuminated, apprised; civilized, refined, cultured, cultivated, sophisticated, open-minded, broad-minded.

**enlist** verb **1** *enlist staff* recruit, hire, employ, register, take on, engage, muster. **2** *enlist in the army* join, join up, enroll, sign up for.

**enliven** verb excite, stimulate, rouse, refresh, exhilarate, invigorate, revitalize, vitalize, light a fire under; *inf.* perk up, spice up, jazz up.

**enormity** noun outrageousness, wickedness, evilness, vileness, monstrousness, hideousness, dreadfulness.

**enormous** adjective huge, immense, massive, vast, gigantic, colossal, astronomic, mammoth, mountainous, gargantuan, tremendous, titanic.

**enough** adjective sufficient, adequate, ample, abundant.

**enough** noun sufficiency, adequacy, abundance, plenty.

**enrage** verb anger, infuriate, madden, exasperate, provoke, incense, irk, agitate, inflame, incite.

**enraged** adjective angry, furious, irate, livid, fuming, incensed, provoked, agitated, inflamed.

**enroll** verb **1** *enroll three new students* register, sign on/up, enlist, recruit, enter, admit, accept. **2** *he enrolled for military service* sign on, volunteer, register, matriculate.

**ensemble** noun **1** *the parts formed a pleasing ensemble* whole, collection, set, accumulation, sum, entirety, assemblage, aggregate, composite. **2** *a green ensemble* outfit, costume, suit. **3** *a jazz ensemble* group, band, company, troupe, cast, chorus; trio, quartet, quintet.

**ensue** verb follow, result, occur, happen, transpire, proceed, succeed, issue, derive, stem.

**ensure** verb guarantee, secure, effect, warrant, certify, confirm; protect, guard, safeguard.

**entail** verb involve, require, necessitate, demand, impose; cause, produce, occasion.

**entangle** verb **1** *entangle the cords* tangle, twist, knot, intertwine, snarl. **2** *entangle in a net* catch, trap, snare, entrap.

**entanglement** noun **1** *the entanglement of his business affairs* complication, confusion, mix-up, mess. **2** *his entanglement with his secretary* affair, liaison, amour, intrigue.

**enter** verb **1** *a river entering the sea* pass into, move into, flow into, penetrate, pierce, puncture. **2** *enter the teaching profession* join, enroll in, enlist in, take up. **3** *enter the date of birth* record, register, note, catalog, document, list, log, file, index. **4** *enter a protest* put forward, offer, present, proffer, submit, register, tender. **5** *enter into negotiations* begin, start, commence, engage in, undertake.

**enterprise** noun **1** *a challenging enterprise* venture, undertaking, project, operation, endeavor, effort, task, plan, scheme, campaign. **2** *private enterprise* business, industry, firm, corporation, establishment.

**enterprising** adjective resourceful, entrepreneurial, imaginative, spirited, enthusiastic, eager, keen, zealous, ambitious, energetic, bold, adventurous, audacious.

**entertain** verb **1** *entertain the guests* amuse, divert, delight, please, charm, cheer, beguile, interest, engage, occupy; treat, welcome, fête. **2** *entertain the idea* consider, contemplate, weigh, ponder.

**entertaining** adjective amusing, diverting, delightful, pleasurable, engaging, interesting, funny, humorous.

**entertainment** noun amusement, fun, enjoyment, diversion, recreation, distraction; pastime, hobby.

**enthrall** verb captivate, enchant, entrance, fascinate, bewitch, rivet, intrigue.

**enthusiasm** noun eagerness, keenness, ardor, fervor, warmth, passion, zeal, zest, excitement, exuberance, wholeheartedness.

**enthusiastic** adjective eager, keen, ardent, fervent, warm, passionate, zealous, excited, exuberant, wholehearted.

**entice** verb lure, tempt, seduce, inveigle, coax, cajole, bait.

**entire** adjective **1** *one's entire life* whole, complete, total, full, continuous, unbroken. **2** *not an entire success* absolute, total, outright, unqualified. **3** *surprised to find an entire vase in the rubble* sound, intact, undamaged, unharmed, unbroken.

**entitle** verb *entitle you to claim the estate* qualify, authorize, sanction, allow, permit, enable, empower, warrant, accredit.

**entity** noun **1** *a living entity* body, being, person, creature, individual, organism, object, article, thing. **2** *the organization's very entity* being, existence, life, substance, essence.

**entourage** noun retinue, escort, attendant, company, cortege, train, suite, bodyguard; companions, followers; *inf.* groupies.

**entrance** noun **1** *the entrance to the building* approach, door, doorway, gate, driveway, foyer, lobby, portal, threshold. **2** *the entrance of the gladiators* entry, appearance, arrival, introduction. **3** *refused entrance to the club* entry, admission, admittance, access, entrée.

**entreat** verb beg, implore, beseech, petition, solicit, pray, exhort, supplicate.

**entreaty** noun appeal, plea, petition, solicitation, prayer, supplication, suit.

**entrust** verb commit, assign, consign, deliver; charge, invest, delegate, commend.

**entry** noun **1** *the main entry to the building* way in, entrance, access, approach, doorway, gate, gateway, driveway, foyer, lobby, portal, threshold. **2** *the entry of the soldiers* entrance, appearance, arrival, introduction. **3** *refuse entry to the protesters* entrance, admission, admittance, access. **4** *an entry in his diary* item, line item, statement, listing, record, note, jotting, memo, account. **5** *fifty entries in the competition* entrant, competitor, contestant, participant, player, candidate. **6** *you can submit four entries* submission, attempt, try, effort.

**enumerate** verb list, itemize, specify, spell out, name, cite, detail; count, calculate, total, compute, tally.

**envelop** verb *the fog enveloped him* cover, wrap, cloak, blanket, surround, engulf, conceal, hide, obscure.

**envious** adjective jealous, covetous, desirous, green-eyed, grudging, begrudging, resentful.

**environment** noun surroundings, conditions, circumstances; habitat, territory, domain, milieu, element, location, locale, background, setting, scene, context, ambience.

**envoy** noun **1** *envoys living in the embassy* legate, consul, attaché, chargé d'affaires. **2** *the president's envoy* emissary, courier, representative, intermediary, delegate, deputy, agent.

**envy** noun covetousness, jealousy, desire; resentment, resentfulness, discontent, spite.

**envy** verb covet, begrudge, grudge.

**epic** adjective **1** *an epic poem* heroic, grand, long. **2** *of epic proportions* huge, long, grand, extraordinary, ambitious.

**epicure** noun gourmet, gastronome, connoisseur.

**epidemic** noun **1** *a typhoid epidemic* outbreak, plague, scourge. **2** *an epidemic of burglaries* wave, upsurge, upswing, increase.

**epidemic** adjective *reaching epidemic proportions* rampant, wide-ranging, extensive, widespread, rife, sweeping.

**episode** noun **1** *the second episode of the story* installment, part, section, chapter, passage, scene. **2** *an episode in his life* incident, occurrence, experience, adventure, occasion, matter, affair.

**epitome** noun *the epitome of politeness* personification, embodiment, essence, quintessence, archetype, representation, model, type, example, exemplar, prototype.

**equal** adjective **1** *of equal height* the same, identical, alike, comparable, commensurate. **2** *a sum equal to the previous sum* identical to, equivalent to, commensurate with. **3** *an equal contest* even, balanced, level. **4** *receive equal treatment* like, uniform, unbiased, impartial, nonpartisan, fair, just, evenhanded, egalitarian. **5** *keep it at an equal temperature* even, constant, uniform, steady, stable, level. **equal to** *equal to the task* capable of, fit for, up to, adequate for, sufficient for.

**equal** verb **1** *four plus five equals nine* be equal to, be equivalent to, come to, amount to, make, total. **2** *she equals him in strength* match, parallel, correspond to, rival. **3** *equal the previous record* match, reach, parallel, achieve.

**equip** verb *equipped for the sea crossing* fit, rig out, prepare, supply, stock, array, outfit; suit, endow.

**equipment** noun gear, tools, tackle, apparatus, outfit, matériel; supplies, paraphernalia, accoutrements.

**equitable** adjective fair, fair-minded, just, evenhanded, proper, reasonable, honest, impartial, unbiased.

**equity** noun fairness, fair-mindedness, justice, evenhandedness, rightfulness, rectitude, reasonableness, honesty, integrity, uprightness, impartiality.

**equivalent** adjective *a job with equivalent status* similar, like, alike, comparable, corresponding, commensurate, equal, the same, matching.

**era** noun age, epoch, eon, period, time, generation, stage.

**erase** verb remove, rub out, obliterate, efface, expunge, excise, cross out, strike out, delete, cancel.

**erect** verb build, construct, put up, assemble, set up, raise, elevate.

**erect** adjective **1** *stand erect* upright, straight, vertical. **2** *an erect penis* hard, rigid, stiff, firm.

**erode** verb *wind eroded the rocks* wear, eat away at, corrode, abrade, gnaw, consume, disintegrate, deteriorate.

**erotic** adjective titillating, erogenous, aphrodisiac, seductive, sensual, salacious, suggestive; *inf.* sexy.

**errand** noun message, task, job, commission, chore, assignment, charge, mission.

**erratic** adjective inconsistent, variable, irregular, unstable, unreliable, unpredictable, capricious, eccentric, wandering, meandering, wavering, directionless.

**erroneous** adjective wrong, incorrect, inaccurate, untrue, false, mistaken, fallacious, spurious, invalid, faulty, flawed, unsound, specious.

**error** noun **1** *detect an error in the arith-* metic mistake, inaccuracy, miscalculation, fault, flaw, fallacy. **2** *see the error of his ways* wrongdoing, mischief, misconduct, delinquency, sinfulness, evil.

**erudite** adjective learned, educated, well-read, scholarly, intellectual, knowledgeable, literate, cultured; *inf.* highbrow.

**erupt** verb **1** *the volcano erupted* belch, gush, vent, spew, boil over. **2** *violence erupted* break out, flare up, explode, pop up, emerge, become visible.

**escalate** verb **1** *the war escalated* mushroom, increase, heighten, intensify, accelerate. **2** *prices will escalate* go up, mount, soar, climb, spiral.

**escapade** noun adventure, stunt, prank, caper, romp, frolic, fling, spree; *inf.* lark, shenanigans.

**escape** verb **1** *the prisoners escaped* get away, break out, flee, bolt, abscond, fly. **2** *escape punishment* avoid, evade, dodge, elude, sidestep, circumvent; *inf.* duck. **3** *gas escaping* leak, seep, gush, spurt, issue, flow, discharge, drain.

**escape** noun **1** *the escape from jail* breakout, flight, getaway. **2** *an escape from punishment* avoidance, evasion, circumvention. **3** *an escape of gas* leak, leakage, seepage, flow, discharge.

**escort** noun **1** *the bridal party and its escort* entourage, retinue, train, cortege, protection, defense, convoy; attendant, guide, chaperon, guard, protector. **2** *her escort for the evening* partner, companion, beau; *inf.* date.

**escort** verb **1** *escort the ambulance* accompany, guide, conduct, lead, usher, shepherd, guard, protect, safeguard, defend. **2** *escort her to the dance* accompany, take out.

**esoteric** adjective abstruse, obscure, cryptic, recondite, arcane, mysterious, hidden, secret, private, mystic.

**especially** adverb **1** *especially talented* exceptionally, extraordinarily, uncommonly, unusually, remarkably, notably, eminently. **2** *especially in the summer* particularly, mainly, chiefly, principally. **3** *bought especially for you* specifically, exclusively, expressly, particularly, uniquely.

**essence** noun **1** *the essence of truth* substance, nature, crux, heart, soul, life, lifeblood, kernel, reality. **2** *essence of peppermint* extract, concentrate, distillate; scent, perfume. **in essence** basically, fundamentally, in effect, substantially, virtually. **of the essence** essential, necessary, indispensable, vital, crucial.

**essential** adjective **1** *cost-cutting is essential* necessary, indispensable, vital, crucial, requisite. **2** *the essential theme of the* *play* basic, fundamental, inherent, intrinsic, elemental, characteristic, principal. **3** *the essential gentleman* absolute, complete, perfect, ideal, quintessential.

**essential** noun *experience is an essential* necessity, prerequisite, requisite, sine qua non; *inf.* must.

**establish** verb **1** *establish a new colony* set up, form, found, institute, start, begin, create, inaugurate, organize, build, construct, install, plant. **2** *establish his guilt* prove, show, demonstrate, certify, confirm, verify, substantiate, corroborate, validate, authenticate.

**esteem** noun estimation, regard, respect, admiration, honor, deference, veneration, appreciation.

**esteem** verb regard, respect, value, admire, honor, revere, venerate, appreciate, cherish, prize, treasure.

**estimate** verb *estimate the cost* assess, compute, gauge, reckon, evaluate, judge, rate, appraise, guess; consider, believe, conjecture, surmise.

**estimate** noun *the plumber's estimate* price, valuation, evaluation, assessment, appraisal, estimation.

**estimation** noun opinion, judgment, consideration, mind; view, esteem, regard, respect, admiration.

**etch** verb engrave, carve, cut, furrow, imprint, inscribe, ingrain.

**eternal** adjective **1** *life eternal* everlasting, endless, never-ending, immortal, infinite, enduring, deathless, permanent, immutable. **2** *stop that eternal racket* ceaseless, incessant, constant, interminable, tedious, unremitting, relentless.

**eternity** noun **1** *believe in eternity* immortality, everlasting life, afterlife, heaven, paradise, nirvana. **2** *on the phone for an eternity* age, ages, forever.

**ethical** adjective moral, honorable, upright, righteous, good, virtuous, decent, principled, honest, just.

**ethics** plural noun moral code, morality; morals, principles, virtues.

**etiquette** noun manners; code of conduct, protocol, form, courtesy, propriety, decorum.

**eulogy** noun panegyric, praise, tribute, accolade, acclamation, paean, panegyric, encomium.

**evacuate** verb **1** *people evacuated the flooded town* leave, vacate, abandon, quit, flee, desert, forsake. **2** *firemen evacuated the room* empty, clear. **3** *evacuate waste matter* excrete, expel, eject, discharge, eliminate, void, purge, drain.

**evacuation** noun **1** *the people's evacuation*

*of the town* abandonment, withdrawal, retreat, exodus, departure, flight, desertion. **2** *evacuation of waste products* excretion, expulsion, ejection, discharge, elimination, purging, emptying.

**evade** verb avoid, dodge, elude, sidestep, circumvent, shun, shirk; hedge, parry; *inf.* duck.

**evaluate** verb assess, appraise, size, gauge, judge, rate, rank, estimate, measure.

**evaporate** verb **1** *water evaporates in heat* vaporize. **2** *the hot sun evaporated the puddles* vaporize, dry, dry up, dehydrate, desiccate, sear, parch. **3** *the vision evaporated* vanish, fade, disappear, dissolve, dissipate.

**evasion** noun avoidance, dodging, eluding, elusion, sidestepping, circumvention; subterfuge, deception, trickery, cunning, hedging; *inf.* ducking.

**evasive** adjective **1** *evasive tactics* avoiding, dodging, escaping, eluding, sidestepping, shunning, shirking. **2** *evasive replies* equivocal, indirect, roundabout, circuitous, oblique; *inf.* cagey.

**even** adjective **1** *an even surface* level, flat, plane, smooth, uniform, flush, true. **2** *an even temperature* uniform, constant, steady, stable, consistent, unchanging. **3** *even chances of success* equal, identical, like, similar, comparable, commensurate. **4** *an even disposition* even-tempered, placid, serene, composed, calm, tranquil. **get even** take one's revenge, reciprocate.

**even** adverb **1** *even colder* yet, still, more so. **2** *even the teacher laughed* unexpectedly, paradoxically, surprisingly. **even so** *even so I shall attend* nevertheless, nonetheless, still, yet, notwithstanding.

**evening** noun **1** *go out in the evening* close of day, twilight, dusk, nightfall, sunset, sundown; *lit.* eve, eventide.

**event** noun **1** *the party was a successful event* occasion, affair, business, matter, happening, occurrence, episode, experience, circumstance. **2** *the javelin event* competition, contest, game, tournament, heat, match, round, bout, race. **in any event** at any rate, in any case, anyhow, anyway, regardless.

**eventful** adjective busy, full, lively, active, important, noteworthy, memorable, notable, remarkable, fateful, significant, historic, consequential, decisive.

**eventual** adjective final, end, concluding, ultimate, resulting, ensuing, consequent, subsequent.

**ever** adverb **1** *'twas ever thus* always, forever, eternally. **2** *grew ever larger* always, constantly, continually, endlessly, unendingly, incessantly, unceasingly, perpetually.

**everlasting** adjective **1** *everlasting life* never-ending, endless, eternal, perpetual, undying, immortal, abiding, enduring, infinite, boundless, timeless. **2** *their everlasting complaints* interminable, incessant. *See* ETERNAL adjective 2.

**everyday** adjective daily, diurnal; ordinary, common, usual, regular, customary, habitual, familiar, routine, plain, workaday, mundane.

**evict** verb turn out, put out, throw out, eject, expel, oust, remove, dispossess, dislodge.

**evidence** noun **1** *produce evidence of guilt* proof, confirmation, verification, substantiation, corroboration, support; grounds. **2** *give evidence in court* testimony, deposition, declaration, allegation, affidavit. **3** *evidence of a struggle* sign, indication, mark, manifestation. **in evidence** *with police in evidence* obvious, noticeable, conspicuous, visible.

**evident** adjective obvious, clear, apparent, plain, unmistakable, noticeable, conspicuous, perceptible, visible, discernible, manifest.

**evil** adjective **1** *evil deeds* wicked, bad, immoral, sinful, vile, base, corrupt, depraved, heinous, villainous, nefarious, reprobate, sinister, atrocious, malicious, malevolent, demonic, devilish, diabolic. **2** *evil influence* bad, harmful, hurtful, injurious, destructive, detrimental, deleterious, pernicious, malignant. **3** *evil temper* unpleasant, nasty, disagreeable, horrible, foul, vile.

**evil** noun **1** *more evil in the world than good* wickedness, badness, sin, sinfulness, immorality, vice, iniquity, baseness, corruption, depravity, villainy, atrocity, malevolence. **2** *the evils of war* harm, pain, hurt, misery, sorrow, suffering, misfortune.

**evoke** verb *evoke a response* cause, bring about, induce, arouse, excite, awaken, kindle, stimulate, elicit; summon, raise, recall.

**evolve** verb develop, unfold, unroll, grow, progress, mature, expand.

**exact** adjective precise, accurate, correct, unerring, faithful, true, just, literal, strict.

**exaggerate** verb overstate, overemphasize, overestimate, magnify, amplify, aggrandize, embellish, amplify, embroider.

**exalt** verb **1** *exalt to the highest rank* elevate, promote, raise, advance, ennoble. **2** *exalt the composer* praise, extol, glorify, acclaim, laud, worship, revere.

**exalted** adjective **1** *his exalted position in the firm* high, high-ranking, lofty, grand, eminent, prestigious, elevated, august. **2** *exalted aims* high-minded, lofty, elevated, noble, sublime, inflated.

**examination** noun **1** *examination of the facts* study, inspection, scrutiny, investigation, analysis, review, exploration, consideration, appraisal. **2** *a medical examination* checkup, observation. **3** *examination of witnesses* questioning, interrogation, cross-examination, third degree. **4** *college examinations* exam, test, midterm, final.

**examine** verb **1** *examine the facts* study, inspect, survey, scrutinize, investigate, analyze, review, probe, consider, appraise. **2** *examine a patient* inspect, check over, observe. **3** *examine the witnesses* question, test, quiz, interrogate, cross-examine; *inf.* grill.

**example** noun **1** *an example of cave painting* sample, specimen, instance, illustration. **2** *follow her example* model, pattern, precedent, paradigm, standard, criterion; ideal, paragon. **3** *punished him as an example to others* warning, caution, lesson, admonition.

**exasperate** verb *exasperate the teacher* anger, annoy, irritate, provoke, irk, vex, gall, pique; *inf.* bug, needle.

**excavate** verb **1** *excavate a trench* dig, dig out, gouge, cut out, quarry, mine. **2** *excavate an ancient city* unearth, dig up, uncover, disinter, exhume.

**exceed** verb pass, top, surpass, better, outdo, outstrip, outshine, transcend, overshadow, eclipse; overstep.

**exceedingly** adverb extremely, exceptionally, extraordinarily, tremendously, enormously, vastly, greatly, highly, hugely, supremely, inordinately.

**excel** verb stand out, shine; surpass, outshine, eclipse, overshadow, outdo, outclass, top, pass, transcend.

**excellence** noun merit, eminence, preeminence, distinction, quality, superiority, supremacy.

**excellent** adjective first-rate, first-class, great, fine, distinguished, superior, superb, outstanding, marvelous, brilliant, notable, eminent, preeminent, admirable, prime, select.

**except** preposition excluding, but, besides, barring, bar, other than, omitting, saving, save.

**exceptional** adjective **1** *an exceptional flavor* unusual, uncommon, atypical, odd, anomalous, singular, peculiar. **2** *exceptional ability* excellent, extraordinary, remarkable, outstanding, special, phenomenal, prodigious.

**excerpt** noun extract, citation, quotation, quote, passage, selection, part, section, fragment, piece, portion.

**excess** noun **1** *an excess of energy* surplus,

surfeit, overabundance, plethora, glut. **2** *throw out the excess* remainder, residue; leftovers. **3** *a life of excess* overindulgence, prodigality, debauchery, dissipation, dissoluteness.

**excess** adjective extra, additional, surplus, superfluous, spare.

**excessive** adjective too much, superfluous, immoderate, extravagant, lavish, superabundant, unreasonable, undue, uncalled-for, extreme, inordinate, unwarranted, unnecessary, needless, disproportionate, exorbitant.

**exchange** verb trade, swap, barter, reciprocate.

**exchange** noun **1** *the exchange of information* interchange, trade, barter, traffic, reciprocity. **2** *the floor of the exchange* stock exchange, stock market, market.

**excite** verb **1** *excite the children too much* stimulate, rouse, animate, move, thrill; *inf.* wind up. **2** *excite feelings of love* arouse, awaken, incite, stimulate, kindle, elicit. **3** *excite a rebellion* cause, incite, stir up, instigate, foment, provoke.

**exciting** adjective *an exciting event* thrilling, stirring, stimulating, exhilarating, rousing, electrifying, invigorating, moving, inspiring, titillating, provocative, sensational.

**exclamation** noun call, cry, shout, yell, ejaculation, interjection; expletive.

**exclude** verb **1** *exclude women from membership* bar, prohibit, forbid, prevent, disallow, refuse, ban, blackball, veto, proscribe, interdict. **2** *exclude the possibility* eliminate, rule out, preclude, reject, except, repudiate, omit, ignore.

**exclusion** noun **1** *the exclusion of women* prevention, refusal, proscription. **2** *the exclusion of robbery as a motive* elimination, precluding, rejection, omission.

**exclusive** adjective **1** *an exclusive club* select, selective, restrictive, private, cliquish, snobbish, fashionable, chic, elegant, luxurious; *inf.* posh, classy. **2** *my exclusive attention* complete, undivided, full, absolute, entire, whole, total. **3** *the exclusive means of travel* sole, only, unique, single. **4** *exclusive of drinks* excluding, omitting, excepting, barring. **5** *mutually exclusive* incompatible, antithetical.

**excruciating** adjective *an excruciating pain* agonizing, racking, torturous, insufferable, unbearable, severe, intense, extreme, searing, piercing, acute; *fml.* exquisite.

**excursion** noun **1** *a shopping excursion* trip, day trip, expedition, jaunt, outing, journey, tour. **2** *an excursion from the main topic* digression, deviation, detour.

**excusable** adjective forgivable, pardonable, defensible, justifiable, understandable, condonable.

**excuse** verb **1** *excuse the wrongdoer* forgive, pardon, exonerate, absolve, acquit, indulge. **2** *excuse their behavior* forgive, tolerate, condone, justify. **3** *excuse them from heavy work* exempt, spare, release, relieve.

**excuse** noun defense, justification, reason, explanation, apology, vindication, mitigation, grounds; pretext, pretense, fabrication; *inf.* cop-out.

**execute** verb **1** *execute a murderer* put to death, kill; hang, behead, guillotine, decapitate, electrocute, shoot, crucify; *inf.* string up, fry. **2** *execute a plan of action* carry out, accomplish, perform, implement, achieve, complete, fulfill, enact, enforce, administer, attain, realize.

**execution** noun **1** *the execution of a murderer* capital punishment; death sentence; killing, hanging, decapitation, electrocution, crucifixion. **2** *the execution of a plan* implementation, accomplishment, performance, achievement, completion, fulfillment, enactment, enforcement, discharge, realization. **3** *execution of a piece of music | her superb execution of the dance* performance, presentation, staging, rendition, delivery.

**exemplary** adjective **1** *exhibiting exemplary behavior* ideal, model, perfect, excellent, admirable, commendable, faultless, laudable, praiseworthy, meritorious. **2** *exemplary member of the species* typical, representative, illustrative, characteristic, epitomic.

**exemplify** verb typify, epitomize, represent, personify, embody, illustrate.

**exempt** adjective *exempt from taxation* free from, excused from, immune to, excepted from, spared, released from.

**exercise** noun *physical exercise* activity, exertion, effort, action, work, drill; workout, warm-up, aerobics, calisthenics.

**exercise** verb **1** *exercise in order to lose weight* work out, train, drill. **2** *exercise patience* employ, use, utilize, apply, implement, practice, exert.

**exert** verb **1** *exert pressure* exercise, employ, use, utilize, apply, wield, expend. **2** *exert (yourself) and succeed* strive, endeavor, struggle, labor, toil, strain, work, push, drive.

**exertion** noun **1** *physical exertion* effort, exercise, work, struggle, strain, stress, toil, labor; pains. **2** *the exertion of pressure* exercise, employment, use, utilization, expenditure, application.

**exhaust** verb **1** *the climb exhausted them* tire, tire out, wear out, fatigue, weary, enervate, tax, overtax, debilitate. **2** *ex-*

*haust the supply of fuel* use up, consume, finish, deplete, expend, spend; empty, drain, void.

**exhausted** adjective **1** *cold and exhausted* tired out, worn out, fatigued, weary, sapped, enervated, weak, faint, debilitated, spent; *inf.* all in, done in, dead tired, dog-tired, pooped. **2** *exhausted supplies* used up, consumed, finished, depleted.

**exhausting** adjective tiring, fatiguing, wearying, wearing, grueling, punishing, strenuous, arduous, backbreaking, taxing, laborious, enervating.

**exhaustive** adjective comprehensive, intensive, in-depth, total, encyclopedic, thorough, complete, full, extensive, sweeping.

**exhibit** verb **1** *exhibit products* display, show, demonstrate, present, model, expose, air, unveil, array, flaunt, parade. **2** *exhibit signs of sadness* show, express, indicate, reveal, display, demonstrate, betray.

**exhibit** noun *a furniture exhibit* display, show, demonstration, presentation, exhibition.

**exhibition** noun **1** *a book exhibition* display, show, fair, demonstration, presentation, exhibit, exposition. **2** *an exhibition of bad temper* display, show, expression, indication, revelation, demonstration, manifestation.

**exile** verb *be exiled from one's country* banish, expatriate, deport, expel, eject, bar, ban.

**exile** noun **1** *sent into exile* banishment, expatriation, deportation, expulsion. **2** *exiles from their homeland* expatriate, refugee, outlaw, outcast, pariah.

**exist** verb **1** *doubting that ghosts exist* be, live, subsist, breathe. **2** *cannot exist in a cold climate* live, survive, subsist, remain, continue, last, endure, prevail. **3** *enough money to exist on* survive, live, stay alive, subsist.

**exonerate** verb absolve, acquit, clear, discharge, vindicate, exculpate, excuse, pardon.

**exorbitant** adjective excessive, extreme, unreasonable, immoderate, inordinate, outrageous, preposterous.

**exotic** adjective foreign, nonnative, tropical, novel, alien; striking, outrageous, colorful, extraordinary, extravagant, sensational, unusual, remarkable, outlandish, bizarre, peculiar, curious, unfamiliar.

**expand** verb **1** *metals expand when heated* enlarge, increase, swell, inflate, distend, stretch. **2** *expand the business* increase, magnify, amplify, extend, multiply. **3** *expand one's account of the accident* elaborate, amplify, embellish, flesh out, develop.

**expanse** noun *an expanse of water* area, stretch, region, tract, breadth, extent, sweep, plain, field.

**expect** verb **1** *don't expect that he will come* think, believe, assume, suppose, imagine, presume, conjecture. **2** *expect a large crowd* anticipate, await, envisage, predict, forecast. **3** *teachers expect your complete attention* require, demand, exact, want.

**expectant** adjective anticipating, anticipatory, expecting, awaiting, eager, hopeful, ready, watchful, anxious, on tenterhooks.

**expedient** adjective *expedient to tell a white lie* convenient, advantageous, useful, beneficial, profitable, practical, pragmatic, politic, judicious, opportune.

**expedite** verb accelerate, speed, hurry, hasten, precipitate, quicken, advance, facilitate, further, promote; dispatch.

**expedition** noun **1** *an expedition into the jungle* undertaking, enterprise, mission, quest, safari. **2** *a shopping expedition* trip, excursion, outing, journey, jaunt. **3** *members of the expedition* group, team, party, company, crew, band, troop. **4** *carry out orders with expedition* speed, haste, promptness, swiftness, alacrity, quickness, dispatch.

**expel** verb banish, exile, evict, oust, cast out, deport, proscribe, outlaw; bar, ban, throw out, dismiss.

**expend** verb **1** *expend time and money on luxuries* spend, disburse, lavish, squander. **2** *expend all one's ammunition* use up, consume, exhaust, deplete, drain, sap, empty.

**expendable** adjective dispensable, replaceable, nonessential, unimportant.

**expense** noun **1** *the expense of college* cost, price, charge, fee. **2** *the expense of time and money* outlay, disbursement. **3** *victory at the expense of lives* cost, sacrifice.

**expensive** adjective costly, high-priced, exorbitant, overpriced, lavish, extravagant; *inf.* steep.

**experience** noun **1** *a frightening experience* event, incident, occurrence, happening, affair, episode, circumstance, ordeal. **2** *practical experience* skill, knowledge, practice, training, understanding, wisdom, maturity; *inf.* know-how.

**experience** verb *experience hardship* undergo, encounter, meet, feel, know, face, sustain, suffer.

**experienced** adjective practiced, accomplished, skillful, proficient, seasoned, trained, expert, veteran.

**experiment** noun **1** *medical experiments with rats* test, investigation, trial, examination, observation, inquiry, pilot study. **2** *results obtained by experiment* research, experimentation, observation, analysis, testing.

**experiment** verb test, investigate, examine, explore, observe.

**expert** noun authority, master, specialist, professional, pundit, maestro, virtuoso, wizard, connoisseur.

**expert** adjective skillful, experienced, practiced, knowledgeable, professional, proficient, adept, brilliant, accomplished, adroit; *inf.* crack, top-notch.

**expertise** noun skill, skillfulness, mastery, proficiency, knowledge, command, facility, ability, capability, competence; *inf.* know-how.

**expire** verb *your license has expired* run out, finish, end, terminate, conclude, discontinue, stop, cease, lapse.

**explain** verb **1** *explain the procedure* describe, define, spell out, interpret, clarify, decipher, decode, elucidate, expound, explicate, delineate, demonstrate, teach, illustrate. **2** *explain their actions* justify, defend, vindicate, mitigate.

**explanation** noun **1** *the explanation of the procedure* description, definition, interpretation, clarification, elucidation, explication, demonstration, illustration. **2** *an explanation of their motives* account, justification, reason, excuse, defense, vindication, mitigation, apologia.

**explicit** adjective **1** *explicit instructions* detailed, clear, crystal-clear, direct, plain, obvious, precise, exact, straightforward, definite, specific, unequivocal, unambiguous. **2** *explicit sexual description* outspoken, unrestrained, unreserved, uninhibited, open, candid, frank, forthright.

**explode** verb **1** *the boiler exploded* blow up, detonate, burst, erupt. **2** *explode in anger* blow up, rage, rant and rave; *inf.* fly off the handle, hit the roof, flip one's lid. **3** *world population exploding* mushroom, escalate, burgeon, rocket, accelerate.

**exploit** noun feat, deed, adventure, stunt, achievement, accomplishment, attainment.

**exploit** verb **1** *exploit natural resources* utilize, use, profit from, capitalize on; *inf.* cash in on. **2** *exploit the workers* take advantage of, abuse, impose upon, misuse.

**exploration** noun investigation, study, survey, research, inspection, probe, examination, scrutiny, observation, search, inquiry, analysis.

**explore** verb **1** *explore the Antarctic* travel, traverse, tour, survey, inspect, scout. **2** *explore possibilities* investigate, consider, examine, research, survey, scrutinize, study, review.

**explosion** noun **1** *a loud explosion* bang, blast, boom, rumble, crash, crack, report,

thunder, detonation, discharge, eruption. **2** *an explosion of anger* outburst, flare-up, fit, outbreak, eruption. **3** *an explosion of population* mushrooming, escalation, burgeoning, rocketing, acceleration.

**explosive** adjective **1** *explosive substance* inflammable, volatile, eruptive, unstable. **2** *explosive temperament* fiery, angry, touchy, stormy, violent, volatile. **3** *an explosive situation* tense, charged, critical, inflammable, volcanic, dangerous, perilous, hazardous.

**expose** verb **1** *expose the skin to sunlight* uncover, bare, strip, reveal. **2** *expose to danger* endanger, risk, hazard. **3** *expose one's ignorance* reveal, show, display, exhibit, disclose, manifest, unveil. **4** *expose a criminal* uncover, reveal, divulge, unearth, unmask, detect.

**exposition** noun **1** *the exposition of modern educational theories* explanation, interpretation, description, elucidation, explication, illustration; commentary, study, treatise, discourse; *fml.* exegesis. **2** *an art exposition* exhibition, fair, display, show, presentation.

**exposure** noun **1** *the exposure of the skin to sunlight* uncovering, baring, denudation. **2** *exposure of one's ignorance* revelation, display, exhibition, disclosure, manifestation. **3** *exposure of a criminal* disclosure, revelation, divulgence, detection, betrayal. **4** *resent the exposure given to the affair* publicity, advertising, broadcasting, air time.

**expound** verb **1** *expound one's views on education* explain, detail, spell out, set forth, describe, discuss. **2** *expound (on) the Scriptures* interpret, explain, annotate, illustrate, explicate.

**express** verb **1** *express one's feelings* state, voice, enunciate, communicate, utter, pronounce, articulate, verbalize, assert, say. **2** *express appreciation* show, indicate, demonstrate, convey, manifest.

**express** adjective **1** *express service* rapid, swift, fast, quick, speedy, prompt, highspeed, expeditious, direct, nonstop. **2** *express instructions* explicit, clear, plain, distinct, precise, specific, unequivocal.

**expression** noun **1** *public expression of grievances* statement, voicing, utterance, articulation, verbalization, assertion; indication, demonstration, conveyance, illustration, manifestation. **2** *a particularly apt expression* word, phrase, term, wording, language, phrasing, speech, diction, idiom, style, delivery, intonation, execution; *fml.* locution. **4** *a sad expression on her face* look, appearance, air, countenance; *fml.* mien. **5** *playing the piano with expression* feeling, emotion, passion, intensity, poignancy, depth, ardor.

**expressive** adjective **1** *an expressive gesture* emotional, eloquent, demonstrative, vivid. **2** *an expressive piece of music* emotional, eloquent, passionate, intense, poignant, moving, evocative, ardent. **3** *expressive of their contempt* indicative, demonstrative, revealing.

**expressly** adverb **1** *expressly forbidden* absolutely, explicitly, clearly, plainly, distinctly, specifically, unequivocally. **2** *laws expressly made to stop vandalism* purposefully, particularly, specially, especially, specifically.

**expulsion** noun *expulsion from school* dismissal, removal, eviction, ejection, banishment, discharge.

**exquisite** adjective **1** *exquisite earrings* beautiful, lovely, delicate, fragile, elegant, fine. **2** *exquisite taste* discriminating, discerning, selective, refined, cultivated, cultured, impeccable, polished.

**extemporaneous, extemporary** adjective *an extemporaneous vote of thanks* extempore, impromptu, spontaneous, ad lib, improvised, unrehearsed, unplanned, unprepared; *fml.* improvisatory.

**extend** verb **1** *extend the ladder* expand, lengthen, stretch, elongate. **2** *extend the scope of the law* widen, increase, expand, broaden, enlarge, augment, amplify. **3** *extend the period of credit* prolong, lengthen, protract. **4** *extend a welcome* offer, give, grant, proffer, present, confer, impart. **5** *the road extends for many miles* continue, stretch out, last, unfold, range.

**extension** noun **1** *the extension of the ladder* expansion, increase, enlargement; elongation. **2** *the extension of a period of credit* prolongation, lengthening, protraction. **3** *an extension to the house* annex, wing, addition.

**extensive** adjective **1** *extensive grounds around the house* large, sizable, substantial, spacious, considerable, capacious, commodious. **2** *extensive knowledge* comprehensive, thorough, complete, broad, wide, wide-ranging.

**extent** noun **1** *the full extent of the park* length, area, expanse, stretch, range. **2** *the extent of her knowledge* coverage, breadth, range, scope, degree.

**exterior** noun *the exterior of the building* outside, façade, covering, shell.

**exterior** adjective *the exterior layer* outer, outside, outermost, outward, external, surface.

**exterminate** verb kill, destroy, eradicate, annihilate, eliminate, extirpate.

**external** adjective **1** *an external wall* outer, outside, outward, exterior, surface, extrinsic. **2** *external affairs* foreign, international, alien.

**extinct** adjective **1** *an extinct species* dead, defunct, vanished, wiped-out, gone, lost. **2** *an extinct volcano* inactive, extinguished, quenched, doused.

**extinguish** verb **1** *extinguish the fire* put out, quench, smother, douse, snuff out. **2** *extinguish passion* destroy, kill, end, remove, eliminate, eradicate, erase, expunge.

**extol** verb praise, applaud, acclaim, laud, eulogize, exalt, commend, congratulate, celebrate, compliment.

**extort** verb *extort money* extract, force, exact, coerce, wring, wrest, squeeze.

**extra** adjective **1** *extra money required* more, additional, further, supplementary, supplemental, added, auxiliary. **2** *have extra food* spare, surplus, leftover, excess, superfluous, redundant, reserve, unused.

**extract** verb **1** *extract a tooth* draw out, pull out, remove, take out, uproot, withdraw, extirpate. **2** *extract money* extort, force, exact, elicit, coerce, wrest, wring, squeeze. **3** *extract juice* squeeze, press, express, distill. **4** *extract a section from a chapter* select, reproduce, copy, quote, cite, cull.

**extract** noun **1** *vanilla extract* concentrate, essence, distillate, juice. **2** *extracts from newspapers* excerpt, passage, citation, selection, quotation, clipping.

**extraneous** adjective **1** *extraneous forces* external, outside, exterior, extrinsic, alien, foreign. **2** *extraneous material* irrelevant, immaterial, inapplicable, inappropriate, unrelated, unconnected, peripheral.

**extraordinary** adjective **1** *extraordinary talent* exceptional, unusual, uncommon, rare, unique, singular, signal, unprecedented, outstanding, striking, remarkable, phenomenal, marvelous, wonderful; *inf.* fabulous. **2** *how extraordinary that we met* amazing, surprising, strange, astounding, curious.

**extravagant** adjective **1** *extravagant way of life* spendthrift, profligate, prodigal, wasteful, lavish, reckless, imprudent, excessive. **2** *extravagant prices* exorbitant, outrageous, excessive, extortionate, unreasonable, inordinate; expensive, costly, overpriced; *inf.* steep.

**extravaganza** noun spectacle, pageant, spectacular/impressive show/display.

**extreme** adjective **1** *extreme cold* utmost, maximum, supreme, greatest, acute, intense, severe, ultimate. **2** *extreme punitive measures* harsh, severe, drastic, radical. **3** *an extreme radical* immoderate, intemperate, fanatical, excessive, overzealous, unreasonable.

**exuberant** adjective *exuberant with joy* elated, exhilarated, high-spirited, buoyant, cheerful, effervescent, excited, unreserved, ebullient, enthusiastic, irrepressible.

**exude** verb 1 *sweat exuding through the pores* ooze, seep, filter, leak, trickle, drip, issue; excrete, emit, emanate. 2 *exuding confidence* ooze, emit, emanate, display.

**exult** verb rejoice, revel; triumph, gloat; be overjoyed, be in ecstasy, be on cloud nine, be in seventh heaven.

**eyesore** noun blemish, blot, scar, blight, defacement, monstrosity, carbuncle, ugliness; *inf.* sight.

**eyewitness** noun witness, observer, onlooker, bystander, spectator, watcher, viewer, beholder, passerby.

*Ff*

**fable** noun 1 *a fable about a fox* | *Norse fables* tale, fairy tale, moral tale, parable; story, legend, myth, saga, epic, lay. 2 *children telling fables* lie, untruth, falsehood, white lie, fib, fabrication, invention, story, fairy tale, cock-and-bull story, fantasy; *inf.* tall story, yarn.

**fabric** noun 1 *a silky fabric* cloth, material, textile, stuff, web. 2 *the fabric of the building* | *the fabric of society* framework, frame, structure, makeup, constitution, essence.

**fabricate** verb 1 *fabricate the furniture from components* assemble, construct, build, erect, put together, make, form, frame, fashion, shape, manufacture, produce. 2 *fabricate a reason for lateness* make up, invent, think up, concoct, hatch, trump up, devise, formulate. 3 *fabricate a document* forge, falsify, fake, counterfeit.

**fabulous** adjective 1 *fabulous wealth* incredible, unbelievable, inconceivable, unimaginable, astounding, amazing, astonishing. 2 *a fabulous time at the party* marvelous, wonderful, great, superb, spectacular; *inf.* fab, fantastic, super. 3 *fabulous creatures* mythical, legendary, imaginary, fantastical, fictitious, fictional, made-up, invented, unreal.

**façade** noun 1 *the façade of the building* front, frontage, face, exterior, outside. 2 *a façade of friendliness* show, appearance, guise, semblance, mask, veneer, masquerade, camouflage, pretense, illusion.

**face** noun 1 *a beautiful face* countenance, visage, physiognomy; features; *inf.* mug, kisser. 2 *with a furious face* expression, look, air, demeanor, aspect. 3 *make a face* scowl, grimace, frown, pout, moue. 4 *the face of the building* front, frontage. *See* FAÇADE 1. 5 *put a brave/bold face on it* appearance, façade, display, show, exterior, guise. 6 *lose face* prestige, standing, status, dignity, honor, respect, image. 7 *have*

*the face to turn up* audacity, effrontery, impudence, impertinence, cheek, boldness, presumption, temerity; *inf.* nerve, gall.

**face** verb 1 *face rejection/reality* encounter, meet, come across, be confronted by, come up against, experience; face up to, come to terms with, accept, confront, meet head-on, cope with, deal with, come to grips with. 2 *face criticism/danger* dare, brave, defy, oppose, resist, withstand.

**facet** noun 1 *one facet of the problem* aspect, angle, side, slant, feature, characteristic, factor, element, point, part, phase. 2 *facet of a gem* side, plane, surface, face.

**facetious** adjective jocular, playful, frivolous, lighthearted, funny, amusing, humorous, comical, comic, joking, jesting, witty, droll, whimsical, tongue-in-cheek, waggish, jocose.

**facilitate** verb smooth, assist, help, aid, expedite, speed up, accelerate.

**facility** noun 1 *perform the task with facility* ease, effortlessness. 2 *facility of expression* ease, smoothness, fluency, eloquence, articulateness, slickness, glibness. 3 *a facility for wood carving* skill, aptitude, ability, gift, talent, knack, proficiency, bent. 4 *a research facility* establishment, structure, building, buildings, complex, system, plant.

**facsimile** noun copy, replica, reproduction, duplicate, carbon, carbon copy, photocopy, transcript, reprint, clone, image; fax; Xerox (*trademark*), Photostat (*trademark*).

**fact** noun 1 *fact, not rumor* actuality, reality, certainty, factuality, certitude; truth, naked truth, gospel. 2 *do not omit a single fact* detail, particular, point, item, piece of information/data, factor, element, circumstance. *See* FACTS. **in fact** actually, in point of fact, indeed.

**faction** noun 1 *a more radical faction* sector, section, group, side, party, band, set, ring, division, contingent, lobby, camp, bloc, clique, coalition, caucus, cabal, junta, splinter group, pressure group, minority (group). **2** *a club full of faction* infighting, dissension, discord, strife, contention, conflict, friction, argument, division, divisiveness, disharmony, disunity, variance, dissidence, rebellion, insurrection, sedition, mutiny, schism.

**factious** adjective dissenting, contentious, discordant, conflicting, divisive, clashing, warring, at variance, at loggerheads, at odds, dissident, rebellious, insurrectionary, seditious, mutinous.

**factor** noun element, part, component, ingredient, constituent, point, detail, item, facet, aspect, feature, characteristic, consideration, influence, circumstance, thing, determinant.

**facts** plural noun *the police just want the facts* information, whole story; details, data; *inf.* info, low-down, poop, word, score, dope.

**factual** adjective fact-based, real, true to life, true, truthful, accurate, authentic, genuine, exact, precise, strict, honest, faithful, literal, unbiased, objective, unvarnished, unadorned, unadulterated, unexaggerated.

**faculties** plural noun powers, capabilities, senses, wits; reason, intelligence.

**faculty** noun **1** *the faculty of speech* power, capability, capacity, attribute, property. **2** *a faculty for learning languages* aptitude, ability, facility, flair, gift, talent, bent, knack, disposition, proficiency, readiness, skill, dexterity, adroitness.

**fad** noun craze, mania, rage, enthusiasm, fancy, passing fancy, whim, vogue, fashion, trend.

**fade** verb **1** *the curtains/color faded* become washed out, grow dull/dim, lose luster. **2** *time had faded the colors* pale, bleach, whiten, wash out, dull, discolor, decolorize, dim. **3** *flowers fading* wither, wilt, die, droop, shrivel, decay. **4** *light/hope fading* grow less, dim, die away, dwindle, grow faint, fail, wane, disappear, vanish, die, decline, diminish, dissolve, peter out, melt away, evanesce.

**fail** verb **1** *their attempt failed* fall through, fall flat, miscarry, founder, misfire, fizzle out, miss the mark, run aground, go astray; *inf.* flop, come a cropper, bite the dust. **2** *fail the exam | failed twice* be found wanting/deficient/defective, not make the grade, not pass muster, be rejected; *inf.* flunk. **3** *words fail me* let down, desert, forsake, abandon, disappoint. **4** *the crops failed* be insufficient, be inadequate, be deficient, fall short. **5** *the light/hope failing* grow less, dim. *See* FADE 4. **6** *the engine failed* break down; *inf.* conk out. **7** *the old*

*man is failing* grow weak/weaker, become feeble, lose strength, flag, sink. **8** *her health failed* decline, fade, diminish, dwindle, wane, ebb, deteriorate, sink, degenerate. **9** *his business failed* collapse, crash, go under, go to the wall, go bankrupt, close down; *inf.* fold.

**failing** noun fault, shortcoming, weakness, weak spot, imperfection, defect, flaw, blemish, frailty, foible, drawback.

**failure** noun **1** *the failure of their attempt* abortion, miscarriage, defeat, frustration, collapse, foundering, misfiring, coming to nothing, fizzling out. **2** *their plan was a failure* vain attempt, fiasco, debacle, botch, blunder; *inf.* flop, washout. **3** *he sees himself as a failure* incompetent, loser, nonachiever, ne'er-do-well, disappointment; *inf.* flop, dud, washout. **4** *failure in the line of duty* omission, neglect; negligence, remissness, nonobservance, dereliction, delinquency. **5** *the failure of the crops* insufficiency, inadequacy, deficiency, lack, dearth, scarcity, shortfall. **6** *the failure of his health* failing, decline, fading, dwindling, waning, sinking, deterioration, collapse, breakdown, loss, decay, crumbling, degeneration. **7** *The failure of his business* collapse, bankruptcy, ruin, ruination; *inf.* folding, flop.

**faint** adjective **1** *a faint mark/noise* indistinct, unclear, dim, obscure, vague, low, soft, muted, weak, feeble. **2** *a faint chance* slight, small, remote, minimal. **3** *feeling faint* giddy, dizzy, light-headed, weak-headed, weak; *inf.* woozy.

**faint** verb lose consciousness, black out, pass out, collapse; *inf.* keel over, conk out; *lit.* swoon.

**faint-hearted** adjective timid, timorous, fearful, spiritless, weak, cowardly, unmanly, lily-livered; *inf.* chickenhearted, yellow.

**faintly** adverb **1** *not faintly amusing* slightly, remotely, vaguely, somewhat, a little, in the least. **2** *call faintly* indistinctly, softly, weakly, feebly, in a whisper, in subdued tones.

**fair** adjective **1** *a fair decision* just, impartial, unbiased, unprejudiced, objective, disinterested, detached, equitable, aboveboard, lawful, legal, legitimate, proper, square; *inf.* on the level. **2** *a fair person* fair-minded, just, impartial, unbiased, unprejudiced, open-minded, honest, upright, honorable, trustworthy. **3** *fair winds* favorable, advantageous, helpful, beneficial. **4** *fair hair* blond/blonde, yellow, flaxen, strawberry blond, tow-headed. **5** *fair skin* pale, white, creamy, chalky. **6** *fair maidens* beautiful, pretty, lovely, attractive, good-looking, comely; *lit.* beauteous. **7** *a fair number of people | a fair* *chance of winning* ample, adequate, sufficient; decent, pretty good, moderate, so-so, average, fair-to-middling.

**fair** noun exhibition, display, show, exhibit, exposition; *inf.* expo.

**fairly** adverb **1** *treated fairly* justly, equitably, impartially, evenhandedly. **2** *fairly good* quite, reasonably, passably, tolerably, moderately, rather.

**fair-minded** adjective just, impartial. *See* FAIR adjective 2.

**fairness** noun **1** *treat everyone with fairness* justness, impartiality, objectivity, evenhandedness, disinterest, equitability. **2** *the fairness of the judge* fair-mindedness, justness, impartiality, open-mindedness, honesty, integrity, probity, rectitude, trustworthiness. **3** *the fairness of the maidens* beauty, prettiness, loveliness, attractiveness, comeliness.

**fairy** noun pixie, elf, sprite, imp, brownie, leprechaun, dwarf, gnome, goblin, hobgoblin.

**faith** noun **1** *have faith in the doctor* trust, belief, confidence, conviction. **2** *of what faith are they?* religion, church, persuasion, belief, creed, sect, denomination. **3** *keep/break faith* loyalty, allegiance, faithfulness, fidelity, fealty.

**faithful** adjective **1** *faithful followers* loyal, constant, devoted, dependable, reliable, true, true-blue, trusty, trustworthy, staunch, unswerving, unwavering, steadfast, obedient, dutiful, dedicated, committed. **2** *a faithful copy* accurate, true, exact, precise, close, strict.

**faithless** adjective **1** *faithless followers* unfaithful, disloyal, false, false-hearted, untrue, untrustworthy, traitorous, treacherous, perfidious, inconstant, fickle, unreliable. **2** *the missionary appealed to the faithless crowd* unbelieving, disbelieving, doubting, skeptical, agnostic, atheistic.

**fake** adjective **1** *a fake license* counterfeit, forged, sham, imitation, fraudulent, false, bogus, spurious, pseudo; *inf.* phony. **2** *fake furs/pearls* artificial, synthetic, mock, simulated, ersatz. **3** *a fake accent* affected, put-on, assumed, feigned.

**fake** noun **1** *the document is a fake* counterfeit, forgery, copy, sham, imitation, fraud, reproduction, hoax; *inf.* phony. **2** *the doctor is a fake* charlatan, impostor, mountebank, quack; *inf.* phony.

**fall** verb **1** *leaves/rain falling* descend, drop, drop down, sink, gravitate, cascade, plop, plummet. **2** *the child fell* fall down, fall over, trip, stumble, slip, slide, tumble, topple over, keel over, go head over heels, collapse, take a spill. **3** *demand/prices fell* fall off, drop off, go down, decline, decrease, grow less, diminish, dwindle,

depreciate, plummet, slump. **4** *empires falling* die, fade, fail, decline, deteriorate, flag, wane, ebb, degenerate, go downhill; *inf.* go to the dogs. **5** *towns falling to the enemy* surrender, yield, submit, give in, give up, give way, capitulate, succumb, resign oneself; be overthrown by, be taken by, be defeated by, be conquered by, lose one's position to, pass into the hands of. **6** *it so fell that she died* occur, happen, take place, come about, come to pass, befall, chance, arise, result. **7** *God punishing angels for falling* sin, do wrong, transgress, err, go astray, yield to temptation. **fall apart** fall to pieces, disintegrate, break up, crumble, dissolve. **fall back** retreat, withdraw, draw back, retire. **fall back on** resort to, call upon, have recourse to, rely on, depend on. **fall behind 1** *fall behind in the race* lose one's place, lag, trail, not keep up. **2** *fall behind with the rent* get into arrears/debt, not keep up with. **fall down** *fall down on the task* fail, not make the grade, not come up to expectations, fall short, disappoint. **fall for 1** *fall for his friend's sister* fall in love with, become infatuated with, be attracted/smitten by. **2** *fall for an old trick* be taken in by, be fooled/deceived/duped by; *inf.* swallow. **fall in** cave in, collapse, sink inward, come down about one's ears, crash in, crumble. **fall in with 1** *fall in with bad company* meet, encounter, get involved with, take up with. **2** *fall in with their plans* agree to/with, go along with, support, back, cooperate with. **fall out** quarrel, argue, squabble, fight, bicker, differ, disagree, clash, wrangle. **fall short (of)** fail to meet/reach, fail to live up to, miss. **fall through** come to nothing, fail, fail to happen, miscarry, abort, go awry; *inf.* fizzle out.

**fall** noun **1** *the child had a fall* trip, tumble, spill, stumble, topple, nosedive. **2** *a fall in prices* drop, dropping off, decline, decrease, cut, lessening, lowering, dip, diminishing, dwindling, reduction, depreciation, plummeting, slump. **3** *the fall of the Roman empire* death, demise, downfall, ruin, collapse, failure, decline, deterioration, wane, ebb, degeneration, destruction, overthrow. **4** *the fall of the city to the enemy* surrender, yielding, submission, capitulation. **5** *the fall of the land* slope, declivity, descent, downgrade.

**fallacy** noun misconception, false notion, misapprehension, misjudgment, miscalculation, error, untruth, inconsistency, illusion, delusion, sophism; sophistry.

**fallible** adjective liable/prone/open to error, erring, errant, imperfect, flawed.

**false** adjective **1** *a false interpretation/account* incorrect, wrong, erroneous, faulty, invalid, unfounded; untruthful, fictitious, concocted, fabricated, invented, inaccurate, inexact, imprecise, flawed, unreal, counterfeit, forged, fraudulent, spurious, misleading. **2** *a false friend* false-hearted, unfaithful, faithless, treacherous, disloyal, traitorous, perfidious, two-faced, double-dealing, untrustworthy, untrue, deceitful, deceiving, deceptive, dishonorable, dishonest, duplicitous, hypocritical, unreliable, unsound, untruthful, lying, mendacious. **3** *false furs/pearls* artificial, imitation. *See* FAKE *adjective* 1, 2.

**falsehood** noun lie, fib, untruth, false statement, falsification, perjury, fabrication, invention; prevarication, equivocation, mendacity.

**falsify** verb **1** *falsify a document* alter, counterfeit, forge, fake, doctor, tamper with, distort, adulterate, pervert. **2** *falsify their statement* disprove, refute, rebut, contradict, oppose.

**falter** verb **1** *falter before proceeding* hesitate, waver, oscillate, fluctuate, delay, vacillate, blow hot and cold, shilly-shally, hem and haw, sit on the fence. **2** *falter over her words* stammer, stutter, stumble.

**fame** noun renown, celebrity, eminence, notability, note, distinction, mark, prominence, esteem, preeminence, glory, honor, illustriousness, stardom, reputation, repute; notoriety, infamy.

**familiar** adjective **1** *familiar face/task/excuse* well-known, known, recognized, customary, accustomed, common, everyday, ordinary, commonplace, frequent, habitual, usual, repeated, routine, stock, conventional, household. **2** *a familiar atmosphere* informal, casual, relaxed, comfortable, easy, unceremonious, open, natural, simple. **3** *familiar acquaintances* close, intimate, confidential, bosom. **4** *object to him being familiar with the staff* overfamiliar, presumptuous, disrespectful, forward, bold. **familiar with** acquainted with, conversant with, versed in, knowledgeable about, instructed in, no stranger to.

**familiarity** noun **1** *the familiarity of the atmosphere* informality, casualness, ease, comfortableness, friendliness, lack of ceremony, naturalness, simplicity. **2** *the familiarity of their relationship* closeness, intimacy, nearness, friendliness. **3** *object to his familiarity* overfamiliarity, presumption, presumptuousness, disrespect, forwardness, intrusiveness; liberties. **familiarity with** knowledge of, mastery of, understanding of, experience of, skill with.

**family** noun **1** *two families living together* household, clan, tribe. **2** *she wants a family* children, offspring, progeny, descendants, issue, scions; brood; *inf.* kids. **3** *the man had no family* relatives, relations, people, kin, kinfolk, kinsmen, one's own flesh and blood. **4** *a noble family* ancestry, extraction, parentage, birth, pedigree, descent, lineage, line, bloodline, blood, race, strain, stock, breed; dynasty, house. **5** *a family of plants* class, genus, species, kind, type, group.

**famine** noun scarcity, lack, dearth, want, deficiency, shortage, insufficiency, paucity; starvation, hunger.

**famished** adjective starving, starving to death, starved, ravenous, hungry, undernourished.

**famous** adjective well-known, renowned, celebrated, famed, prominent, noted, notable, great, eminent, preeminent, distinguished, esteemed, illustrious, acclaimed, popular, legendary.

**fan** verb **1** *fan the atmosphere* cool, ventilate, air, aerate, blow, freshen, refresh. **2** *fan the flames* stir up, work up, whip up, incite, instigate, provoke. **fan out** spread, spread out, open out/up, unfurl, unfold, outspread, stretch out.

**fan** noun admirer, lover, enthusiast, devotee, addict, aficionado, zealot, follower, disciple, adherent, supporter, backer, champion, votary; *inf.* buff, fiend, freak, nut, groupie.

**fanatic** noun zealot, extremist, radical, activist, militant, sectarian, bigot, partisan.

**fanatical** adjective **1** *a fanatical sect* extremist, extreme, zealous, radical, activist, militant, sectarian, rabid. **2** *a fanatical moviegoer* enthusiastic, eager, fervent, passionate, obsessive, immoderate; *inf.* wild, gung-ho.

**fanciful** adjective **1** *fanciful notions* imaginary, fancied, fantastic, romantic, mythical, fabulous, legendary, unreal, illusory, visionary, made-up, make-believe, fairytale. **2** *a fanciful child* imaginative, inventive, whimsical, capricious, visionary, chimerical. **3** *fanciful decoration* imaginative, creative, curious, extravagant, fantastic, bizarre.

**fancy** noun **1** *a child subject to fancy* caprice, whimsy, vagary, eccentricity, peculiarity; quirk, notion, kink. **2** *have a fancy for ice cream* desire, urge, wish, want, yearning, longing, hankering; fondness, liking, partiality, preference; *inf.* yen, itch. **3** *the poet's fancy* imagination, creativity, conception; images, visualizations. **4** *I have a fancy it will rain* idea, guess, thought, notion.

**fancy** adjective **1** *fancy decorations* ornate, elaborate, ornamented, ornamental, decorated, decorative, adorned, embellished, intricate, lavish, ostentatious, showy, luxurious, sumptuous, baroque, rococo; *inf.* jazzy, ritzy, snazzy, posh, classy. **2** *fancy notions* imaginary, far-fetched, flighty. *See* FANCIFUL 1, 2.

**fanfare** noun **1** *the queen greeted by a fanfare* flourish, trumpet call, blast of trumpets, fanfaronade. **2** *the store opened with much fanfare* show, showiness, display, ostentation, commotion, fuss, publicity, ballyhoo; *inf.* to-do, hype.

**fantastic** adjective **1** *fantastic notions* fanciful, imaginary, romantic, unreal, illusory, make-believe, irrational, extravagant, wild, mad, absurd, incredible, strange, eccentric. **2** *fantastic shapes* bizarre, grotesque, freakish, strange, weird, queer, peculiar, outlandish, unreal, extravagant, elaborate, ornate, intricate, rococo, baroque, phantasmagoric. **3** *a fantastic amount of work* tremendous, enormous, huge, impressive, overwhelming. **4** *the movie was fantastic* marvelous, wonderful, sensational, superb, top-notch; *inf.* cool, awesome.

**fantasy** noun **1** *novels full of fantasy* fancy, imagination, creativity, invention, originality, vision, myth. **2** *indulge in fantasy* fancy, speculation, daydreaming, reverie; flight of fancy, daydream, pipedream. **3** *see* fantasies apparition, phantom, specter, ghost, hallucination, vision, illusion, mirage.

**farce** noun **1** *starring in a bedroom farce* slapstick, slapstick comedy, burlesque, burlesque show/routine, satire, parody, travesty, buffoonery, absurdity, ridiculousness. **2** *the interviews were just a farce* mockery, absurdity, sham, pretense, joke.

**farcical** adjective **1** *a farcical situation* ridiculous, ludicrous, absurd, laughable, risible, preposterous, facetious, silly, foolish, nonsensical, asinine. **2** *a farcical play* comic, slapstick, humorous, amusing.

**farewell** interjection good-bye, so long, adieu, ciao, adios, *auf Wiedersehen, au revoir; inf.* see you, see you later, toodle-oo.

**farewell** noun good-bye, adieu, leave-taking, parting, send-off, departure.

**far-fetched** adjective improbable, unlikely, remote, implausible, incredible, unbelievable, dubious, doubtful, unconvincing, strained, labored, fanciful, unrealistic; *inf.* hard to swallow/take.

**farm** verb *farm the land* cultivate, till, work, plow, plant. **farm out** contract out, subcontract, delegate; rent, rent out, lease, let.

**farsighted** adjective *farsighted in his choice* prescient, prudent, discerning, judicious, shrewd, provident, wise, sagacious.

**fascinate** verb captivate, enchant, beguile, bewitch, enthrall, infatuate, enrapture, entrance, hold spellbound, transfix, rivet, mesmerize, hypnotize, allure, lure, tempt, entice, draw, tantalize, charm, attract, intrigue, delight, absorb, engross.

**fascinating** adjective captivating, enchanting, beguiling, bewitching, enthralling, ravishing, entrancing, compelling, spellbinding, riveting, gripping, alluring, charming, intriguing, absorbing.

**fascination** noun enchantment, allure, lure, attraction, appeal, charm, magnetism, pull, draw, spell, sorcery, magic, glamour.

**fashion** noun **1** *the fashion in clothes* style, vogue, trend, latest thing, mode, craze, rage, fad, convention, custom, practice. **2** *she works in fashion* clothes, clothes industry/design, couture; *inf.* rag trade. **3** *working in an untidy fashion* manner, way, style, method, mode, system, approach. **4** *a boat of some fashion* kind, type, sort, make, design, description. **after a fashion** somehow or other, in a rough way, to a certain extent, in a manner of speaking.

**fashion** verb make, construct, build, manufacture, create, devise, shape, form, mold, forge.

**fashionable** adjective **1** *fashionable clothes* in fashion, stylish, up-to-date, up-to-the-minute, modern, voguish, in vogue, modish, popular, all the rage, trendsetting, latest, smart, chic, elegant, natty; *inf.* trendy, with it. **2** *fashionable areas* high-class; *inf.* classy, swank.

**fast** adjective **1** *at a fast pace* quick, rapid, swift, speedy, brisk, fleet-footed, hasty, hurried, accelerated, express, flying. **2** *fast friends* loyal, devoted, faithful, firm, steadfast, staunch, constant, lasting, unchanging, unwavering, enduring. **3** *held fast by a rope* fastened, closed, shut, secured, secure, firmly fixed. **4** *fast women* promiscuous, licentious, dissolute, loose, wanton. **5** *lead fast lives* wild, dissipated, dissolute, debauched, promiscuous, intemperate, immoderate, rakish, unrestrained, reckless, profligate, self-indulgent, extravagant.

**fast** adverb **1** *run fast* quickly, rapidly, swiftly, speedily, briskly, hastily, hurriedly, post-haste, expeditiously, with dispatch, like the wind, like a shot/flash, hell-bent, hell-bent for leather, like a bat out of hell; *inf.* lickety-split. **2** *stuck fast* firmly, tightly, securely, immovably, fixedly. **3** *live fast* wildly, dissipatedly, intemperately, rakishly, recklessly.

**fasten** verb **1** *fasten a brooch to the dress* attach, fix, affix, clip, pin, tack. **2** *fasten the door* bolt, lock, secure, make secure/fast, chain, seal. **3** *fasten his gaze on her* direct, aim, point, focus, fix, rivet, concentrate, zero in. **4** *the lions fastening on their prey* take hold of, seize, catch/grab hold of, grab, snatch.

**fastidious** adjective hard to please, critical, overcritical, hypercritical, fussy, finicky, overparticular; *inf.* choosy, picky, persnickety.

**fat** adjective **1** *fat people* plump, stout, overweight, obese, heavy, large, solid, corpulent, chubby, tubby, portly, rotund, pudgy, flabby, gross, potbellied, paunchy; *inf.* beefy, roly-poly, elephantine. **2** *fat substances* fatty, greasy, oily, oleaginous, adipose, unctuous, sebaceous. **3** *fat land* fertile, productive, fruitful, rich, lush, flourishing, thriving. **4** *a fat part in a play* substantial, large, sizable, major, important, significant, considerable.

**fatal** adjective **1** *a fatal blow/illness* mortal, deadly, lethal, death-dealing, killing, terminal, final, incurable. **2** *fatal to our plans* ruinous, destructive, disastrous, catastrophic, calamitous, cataclysmic. **3** *the fatal moment* fateful, critical, crucial, decisive, determining, pivotal, momentous, important.

**fatality** noun **1** *three fatalities in the accident* dead person, death, casualty, mortality, loss; dead. **2** *the fatality of the blow* deadliness, lethalness.

**fate** noun **1** *fate meant them to meet* destiny, providence, God's will, kismet, predestination, predetermination, chance, one's lot in life; the stars. **2** *courts deciding our fate* future; outcome, upshot, end. **3** *met his fate in battle* death, end, destruction, ruin, doom.

**fated** adjective predestined, preordained, foreordained, destined, inevitable, inescapable, sure, ineluctable, doomed.

**fateful** adjective **1** *a fateful meeting* critical, crucial, decisive, determining, pivotal, momentous, important, fated. **2** *a fateful course of action* disastrous, ruinous, destructive, fatal, lethal, deadly.

**father** noun **1** begetter, paterfamilias, patriarch; *inf.* dad, daddy, pop, pops, poppa, pa, old man. **2** *investigate the history of his fathers* forefather, ancestor, forebear, progenitor, primogenitor, predecessor, forerunner, precursor. **3** *the father of modern history* founder, originator, initiator, prime mover, architect, inventor, creator, maker, author. **4** *the city fathers* leader, elder, patriarch, senator.

**fatherly** adjective paternal, kindly, kind, affectionate, tender, caring, protective, supportive, patriarchal.

**fathom** verb **1** *fathom the depth of the water* sound, plumb, measure, estimate, gauge, probe. **2** *fathom their motives* understand, comprehend, grasp, perceive, penetrate, divine, search out, get to the bottom of, ferret out.

**fatigue** verb tire, tire out, overtire, make weary, weary, exhaust, wear out, drain, prostrate, enervate; *inf.* take it out of, do in, poop out.

**fatigue** noun tiredness, overtiredness, weariness, exhaustion, prostration, lassitude, debility, enervation, lethargy, listlessness.

**fatuous** adjective silly, foolish, stupid, inane, pointless, senseless, nonsensical, childish, puerile, idiotic, brainless, mindless, vacuous, asinine, moronic, witless.

**fault** noun **1** *a fault in the material* defect, flaw, imperfection, blemish, snag. **2** *a fault in her character* defect, flaw, failing, shortcoming, weakness, weak point, infirmity, lack, deficiency. **3** *a fault in the calculation* error, mistake, inaccuracy, blunder, oversight; *inf.* slipup, booboo. **4** *blame one child for another's faults* misdeed, wrongdoing, offense, misdemeanor, misconduct, sin, vice, lapse, indiscretion, peccadillo, transgression, trespass. **5** *whose fault was it?* culpability, blameworthiness, responsibility, accountability, answerability. **at fault** blameworthy, blamable, in the wrong, culpable, responsible, accountable, answerable. **to a fault** excessively, unduly, in the extreme, needlessly, overly.

**faultfinding** adjective critical, overcritical, hypercritical, censorious, carping, captious, caviling, quibbling, niggling, hairsplitting; *inf.* nitpicking.

**faultless** adjective **1** *a faultless piece of work* perfect, flawless, unblemished, impeccable, accurate, correct, exemplary, model. **2** *the wife of the prisoner was faultless* innocent, guiltless, blameless, above reproach, irreproachable, sinless, pure, unsullied.

**faulty** adjective **1** *a faulty lock* broken, malfunctioning, out of order, damaged, defective, unsound; *inf.* on the blink, kaput. **2** *faulty reasoning* defective, flawed, unsound, wrong, inaccurate, incorrect, erroneous, imprecise, fallacious, impaired, weak, invalid.

**faux pas** noun blunder, gaffe, mistake, slipup, indiscretion, impropriety, lapse of etiquette, peccadillo; *inf.* booboo.

**favor** noun **1** *do me a favor* good turn, service, good deed, kindness, courtesy, benefit. **2** *look on him with favor* approval, approbation, esteem, goodwill, kindness, benevolence, friendliness. **3** *owe his job to favor rather than merit* favoritism, bias, partiality, prejudice, partisanship.

**favor** verb **1** *he favors returning* advocate, approve of, recommend, support, back, endorse, sanction. **2** *the young man favored blondes* prefer, go in for, go for, choose, opt for, select, fancy, like, incline toward. **3** *the wind favored the other team* be advantageous to, benefit, help, assist, aid, advance, abet. **4** *favor us with a smile* oblige, serve, accommodate, satisfy, please.

**favorable** adjective **1** *a favorable report*

good, approving, commendatory, praising, well-disposed. **2** *the circumstances are favorable* advantageous, beneficial, hopeful, promising, auspicious, propitious, opportune, timely, encouraging, conducive, convenient. **3** *a favorable impression* pleasing, agreeable, successful, positive.

**favorite** adjective best-loved, most-liked, pet, favored, dearest, preferred, ideal.

**favorite** noun preference, first choice, choice, pick, pet, beloved, darling, idol, jewel, jewel in the crown; blue-eyed boy, apple of one's eye, teacher's pet.

**favoritism** noun bias, partiality, prejudice, unfair preference, partisanship, nepotism, unfairness, inequity.

**fawn** verb **fawn on** kowtow to, bow and scrape to, grovel before, curry favor with, ingratiate oneself with, lick the boots of; *inf.* butter up.

**fear** noun **1** *filled with fear at the danger* fright, fearfulness, terror, alarm, panic, trepidation, apprehensiveness, dread, fear and trembling, timidity, trembling, quaking, quivering, consternation, dismay; shivers, butterflies, tremors. **2** *all her fears were removed* phobia, aversion, dread, bugbear, nightmare, horror, terror. **3** *express fear that he would die* anxiety, worry, unease, uneasiness, apprehension, nervousness, agitation, concern, disquiet, angst. **4** *fear of the Lord* awe, wonder, amazement, reverence, veneration.

**fear** verb **1** *she fears spiders* be afraid of, dread, have a horror/dread of, have a phobia about. **2** *they fear God* stand in awe of, revere, reverence, venerate. **3** *I fear you may be right* suspect, have a suspicion, expect, anticipate, have a foreboding. **fear for** worry about, feel anxious/concerned about, have anxieties/qualms about.

**fearful** adjective **1** *fearful of making a noise* afraid, frightened, scared, terrified, alarmed, apprehensive, uneasy, nervous, tense, panicky, timid, timorous, fainthearted, intimidated, hesitant, disquieted, trembling, quaking, quivering, shrinking, cowering, cowardly, pusillanimous; *inf.* jittery, jumpy. **2** *a fearful accident* terrible, dreadful, appalling, frightful, ghastly, horrific, horrible, horrendous, shocking, awful, atrocious, hideous, monstrous, dire, grim, unspeakable, gruesome, distressing, harrowing, alarming.

**fearless** adjective unafraid, brave, courageous, valiant, intrepid, valorous, gallant, plucky, lionhearted, stouthearted, heroic, bold, daring, confident, audacious, indomitable, undaunted, unflinching, unshrinking; *inf.* game, gutsy, spunky.

**feasible** adjective practicable, possible, likely, workable, doable, achievable, attainable, accomplishable, realizable, reasonable, viable, realistic.

**feast** noun **1** banquet, repast; orgy; revels, festivities; *inf.* blowout, spread, bash. **2** *the feast of St. Stephen* celebration, festival, feast day, saint's day, holy day, holiday, fête, festivity. **3** *a feast for the eyes* pleasure, gratification, delight, treat, joy.

**feast** verb wine and dine, regale, entertain, treat. **feast on** *feast on a holiday dinner* wine and dine, gorge oneself on, eat one's fill of, partake of, indulge in, overindulge in, gormandize, stuff one's face with, stuff oneself with.

**feat** noun deed, act, action, exploit, accomplishment, achievement, attainment, move, stunt.

**feature** noun **1** *one feature of life in the country* aspect, characteristic, facet, side, point, attribute, quality, property, trait, mark, hallmark, trademark, peculiarity, idiosyncrasy. **2** *the tractor pull is a popular feature of the fair* special attraction, attraction, highlight, focal point, focus, draw.

**feature** verb present, give prominence to, promote, star, spotlight, highlight, emphasize, play up, accentuate.

**federal** adjective national, civil, nationwide, governmental.

**federation** noun confederation, confederacy, federacy, league, alliance, coalition, union, syndicate, association, amalgamation, combination, combine, entente, society, fraternity.

**fee** noun charge, price, cost, payment, remuneration, emolument.

**feeble** adjective **1** *grow feeble with age* weak, weakly, weakened, frail, infirm, delicate, slight, sickly, puny, failing, ailing, helpless, powerless, debilitated, decrepit, doddering, tottering, enervated, enfeebled, effete. **2** *a feeble attempt at humor* ineffective, ineffectual, unsuccessful, inadequate, unconvincing, futile, poor, weak, tame, paltry, slight. **3** *a feeble light/voice* dim, indistinct, faint, unclear, vague, inaudible.

**feebleminded** adjective stupid, idiotic, foolish, halfwitted, slow on the uptake; *inf.* boneheaded, dumb, soft in the head, out to lunch.

**feed** verb **1** *feed the family* nurture, nourish, sustain, cater for, provide for, wine and dine. **2** *feed his self-esteem* gratify, bolster up, strengthen, augment, add to, encourage, minister to, add fuel to. **3** *feed logs to the fire* supply, provide, give, furnish.

**feed** noun **1** *cattle feed* food, fodder, provender, forage, pasturage, silage. **2** *a good feed* feast, meal, dinner, repast, banquet; *inf.* spread.

**feel** verb **1** *feel her face* touch, stroke, caress, fondle, finger, thumb; handle, manipulate; paw, maul. **2** *feel the ship's motion* notice, observe, perceive, have a sensation of. **3** *feel pain* experience, know, have, undergo, go through, bear. **4** *feel one's way* grope, fumble, poke, explore. **5** *he feels that he should go* think, believe, consider it right, be of the opinion, hold, judge, deem. **6** *I feel that he's hiding something* sense, get the impression, have a hunch, just know. **7** *the air feels damp* seem, appear, strike one as. **feel for** sympathize with, commiserate with, empathize with. **feel like** wish, desire, fancy; *inf.* have a yen for.

**feel** noun **1** *the material has a nice feel* texture, surface, finish. **2** *I don't like the feel of the place* atmosphere, ambience, aura, mood, air, impression; *inf.* vibrations, vibes. **3** *a feel for that kind of work* knack, aptitude, flair, talent, gift, art, faculty.

**feeling** noun **1** *tell what it is by feeling* feel, touch. **2** *a feeling of pain* awareness, consciousness, sensation, sense, perception. **3** *I had a feeling that you would be there* suspicion, notion, inkling, hunch, presentiment, premonition, foreboding. **4** *look at him with feeling* emotion, affection, fondness, warmth, love, sentiment, passion, ardor, fervor. **5** *show feeling for others* sympathy, pity, compassion, understanding, concern, sensitivity, tender-heartedness, empathy. **6** *my feeling is that he will go* instinct, opinion, intuition, impression, point of view, thought, way of thinking, theory, hunch. **7** *a feeling of neglect about the place* atmosphere, ambience. *See* FEEL noun 2.

**feeling** adjective *a feeling person* sensitive, warm, tender, caring, softhearted, sympathetic, compassionate, responsive, demonstrative.

**feign** verb fake, simulate, sham, affect, pretend, make believe, act, play-act.

**felicitous** adjective **1** *a felicitous expression* apt, well-chosen, well-expressed, well-put, fitting, suitable, appropriate, apposite, pertinent, germane, to the point. **2** *a felicitous event* happy, joyful, harmonious, fortunate, lucky, successful, prosperous.

**fell** verb cut down, hew, level, raze, raze to the ground, demolish, knock down/over, strike down, flatten, ground, floor, prostrate, overthrow, kill.

**fellowship** noun **1** *a need for fellowship* companionship, companionability, sociability, comradeship, fraternization, camaraderie, friendship, amiability, amity, affability, geniality, kindliness, cordiality, intimacy, social intercourse; *inf.* chumminess. **2** *the church fellowship* association, society, club, league, union, guild, affiliation, order, fraternity, brotherhood.

**feminine** adjective **1** *a very feminine young woman* delicate, gentle, tender, graceful, womanly, ladylike, girlish, refined, modest. **2** *a man with a feminine manner* effeminate, womanish, effete, unmanly, unmasculine, weak.

**fence** noun enclosure, barrier, railing, rail, wall, hedge; barricade, rampart, stockade, palisade. **on the fence** uncommitted, uncertain, undecided, vacillating, irresolute, neutral, impartial.

**fence** verb **1** *fence the garden* enclose, surround, circumscribe, encircle, encompass. **2** *fence when asked questions* hedge, be evasive, beat around/about the bush, dodge the issue, prevaricate, equivocate, fudge the issue, shilly-shally, vacillate. **fence in** shut in, confine, pen, separate off, secure, imprison.

**fend** verb **fend off** ward off, keep off, turn aside, stave off, divert, deflect, avert, defend oneself against, guard against. **fend for oneself** provide/shift for oneself, take care of oneself, get by.

**ferocious** adjective **1** *a ferocious animal/criminal* fierce, savage, wild, feral, untamed, predatory, rapacious; ruthless, brutal, brutish, cruel, pitiless, merciless, vicious, violent, inexorable, barbarous, barbaric, inhuman, bloodthirsty, murderous. **2** *ferocious heat* fierce, intense, extreme, acute.

**ferret** verb **ferret out** unearth, discover, disclose, elicit, bring to light, search out, get at, run to earth, track down, dig up, root out, hunt out, drive out, fish out, nose out, sniff out, smell out.

**fertile** adjective **1** *fertile soil* fruitful, productive, fecund, rich. **2** *reach the age of being fertile* potent, virile, child-producing, fecund, reproductive, propagative. **3** *fertile imaginations* inventive, creative, original, ingenious, resourceful, visionary, constructive, productive.

**fervent** adjective passionate, ardent, impassioned, intense, vehement, heartfelt, fervid, emotional, emotive, warm, devout, sincere, eager, earnest.

**fervid** adjective ardent, intense. *See* FERVENT.

**fervor** noun fervency, passion, ardor, intensity, vehemency, fervidness, emotion, warmth, devoutness, sincerity, eagerness, earnestness, zeal, enthusiasm.

**fester** verb **1** *a wound festering* suppurate, matter, come to a head, gather, maturate, run, discharge. **2** *animal corpses festering* rot, decay, go bad, go off, decompose, disintegrate. **3** *resentment festering in their minds* rankle, chafe, gnaw.

**festival** noun **1** *a church festival* saint's day,

holy day. *See* FEAST noun 2. **2** *the town's annual festival* fair, gala, fête, carnival; celebrations, festivities.

**festive** adjective joyous, joyful, happy, jolly, merry, gay, jovial, lighthearted, cheerful, cheery, jubilant, convivial, good-time, gleeful, mirthful, celebratory, gala.

**festivity** noun **1** *the festivity of the occasion* joyfulness, jollity, merriment, pleasure, gaiety, cheerfulness, jubilance, convivialness, cheeriness, gleefulness, glee, mirthfulness, mirth, revelry. **2** *enjoy the festivities* celebration, festival, entertainment, party, revelry, carousal, sport; fun and games.

**festoon** verb garland, wreathe, hang, drape, decorate, adorn, ornament, array, deck, bedeck, swathe, beribbon.

**fetch** verb **1** *fetch the doctor* go and get, get, go for, bring, carry, deliver, convey, transport, escort, conduct, lead, usher in. **2** *the vase fetched $40* sell for, go for, bring in, realize, yield, earn, cost.

**fetching** adjective attractive, charming, enchanting, sweet, winsome, taking, captivating, fascinating, alluring.

**fête** noun gala, fair, garden party, festival, celebration.

**fetish** noun **1** *a leather fetish* fixation, compulsion, obsession, mania, *idée fixe*; *inf.* thing. **2** *carry a fetish* talisman, charm, amulet.

**fetter** verb **1** *fetter the prisoners* chain, chain up, shackle, bind, tie, tie up, hobble. **2** *fettered by petty restrictions* restrict, hinder, impede, obstruct, constrain, confine, restrain.

**fetters** plural noun chains, shackles, irons, manacles, trammels; restraint, tether, check.

**feud** noun vendetta, rivalry, hostility, enmity, conflict, strife, discord, bad blood, animosity, antagonism, unfriendliness, grudge, estrangement, schism; quarrel, conflict, argument, bickering, falling-out.

**fever** noun **1** *the child's fever subsided* feverishness; *inf.* temperature, temp. **2** *a fever of excitement* ferment, frenzy, furor; turmoil, agitation, excitement, restlessness, unrest, passion, intensity.

**feverish** adjective **1** *the child is feverish* fevered, febrile, burning, hot, flushed. **2** *feverish excitement* frenzied, frenetic, agitated, worked up, overwrought, frantic.

**fiasco** noun failure, disaster, catastrophe, mess, ruination, debacle; *inf.* flop, washout.

**fib** noun lie, white lie, untruth, falsehood, fabrication, piece of fiction, fiction, fairy story/tale.

**fiber** noun **1** *the fibers of the carpet* thread, strand, tendril, filament, fibril; material,

substance, cloth, stuff. **2** *a person of a different fiber* character, nature, makeup, spirit, disposition, temperament.

**fickle** adjective capricious, changeable, variable, unpredictable, volatile, mercurial, inconstant, unstable, vacillating, unsteady, unfaithful, faithless, irresolute, flighty, giddy, erratic, fitful, irregular, mutable.

**fiction** noun storytelling, romance, fable, fantasy, legend; fabrication, invention, concoction, lie, fib, untruth, falsehood, fairy tale/story, tall story, prevarication; *inf.* cock-and-bull story, whopper, fish story.

**fictional** adjective fictitious, made up, invented, imaginary, unreal, nonexistent.

**fictitious** adjective **1** *a fictitious character* made up, imaginary. *See* FICTIONAL. **2** *a fictitious address/account* false, untrue, bogus, sham, counterfeit, fake, fabricated, assumed, invented, made up, concocted, spurious, imagined, imaginary, apocryphal.

**fiddle** verb **1** *fiddling with a pencil* fidget, play, fuss, toy, mess about, fool around; waste time, act aimlessly. **2** *fiddle with the engine* tinker, tamper, interfere; *inf.* monkey around.

**fidelity** noun **1** *his fidelity to his country* faithfulness, loyalty, devotedness, devotion, allegiance, commitment, constancy, true-heartedness, trustworthiness, dependability, reliability, staunchness, obedience. **2** *the fidelity of the copy* accuracy, exactness, exactitude, precision, preciseness, strictness, closeness, faithfulness, correspondence, conformity, authenticity.

**fidget** verb wriggle, squirm, twitch, jiggle; *inf.* have ants in one's pants.

**fidgety** adjective restless, restive, on edge, jumpy, uneasy, nervous, twitchy; *inf.* jittery, like a cat on a hot tin roof.

**field** noun **1** *cows in the field* pasture, meadow; grassland; *lit.* lea, greensward. **2** *the field of electronics* area, sphere, regime, discipline, province, department, line, specialty, métier. **3** *field of vision* range, scope, purview; limits, confines. **4** *the field for the race is high quality* applicants, candidates, entrants, competitors; competition.

**fiend** noun **1** *fiends of hell* devil, demon, evil spirit. **2** *the slave driver was a fiend* brute, savage, beast, barbarian, monster, ogre, sadist. **3** *a drug fiend* addict, abuser, user.

**fiendish** adjective **1** *a fiendish stepfather* wicked, cruel, brutal, brutish, savage, barbaric, ferocious, ruthless, heartless, pitiless, merciless, black-hearted, unfeeling, malevolent, malicious, devilish, diabolical, hellish, demonic, satanic. **2** *a fiendish*

153

**fierce · filter**

brutal, murderous, slaughterous, menacing, threatening, terrible, grim. **2** *a fierce love* intense, ardent, passionate, impassioned, fervent, fervid, uncontrolled, violent, strong, tempestuous, raging, furious. **3** *suffer from fierce headaches* severe, intense, grave, awful, dreadful. **4** *fierce competition* keen, intense, strong, relentless.

**fight** verb **1** *the armies fought* battle, do battle, war, wage war, take up arms, combat, engage, clash, skirmish, struggle, contend, grapple, wrestle, scuffle, tussle, collide, spar, joust, tilt. **2** *the two men fought* come to blows, exchange blows, attack/assault each other, hit/punch each other, box, brawl; *inf.* scrap. **3** *the two families have been fighting for years* feud, quarrel, argue, bicker, squabble, wrangle, dispute, be at odds, disagree, battle, altercate; *inf.* fall out. **4** *fight the council's decision* contest, take a stand against, oppose, dispute, object to, withstand, resist, defy, strive/struggle against, take issue with, **fight back 1** *children fight to fight back* defend oneself, retaliate, counterattack, give tit for tat. **2** *fight back tears* suppress, repress, check, curb, restrain, contain, bottle up. **fight off** ward off, beat off, stave off, repel, repulse, hold at bay.

**fight** noun **1** *the army lost the last fight* battle, engagement, action, clash, conflict, combat, contest, encounter, skirmish, scuffle, tussle. **2** *a fight outside the bar* brawl, affray, fracas, melee, sparring match, free-for-all, disturbance; fisticuffs; *inf.* set-to, scrap. **3** *the two families had a fight* quarrel, disagreement, difference of opinion, dispute, argument, altercation, feud. **4** *lose all the fight in him* spirit, will to win, gameness, pluck, aggression, belligerence, militancy, resistance.

**figurative** adjective nonliteral, metaphorical, allegorical, representative, emblematic,. symbolic.

**figure** noun **1** *add up a column of figures* number, whole number, numeral, digit, integer, cipher. **2** *put a figure on the work involved* cost, price, amount, value, total, sum, aggregate. **3** *figures unrecognizable in the mist* shape, form, outline, silhouette. **4** *a well-developed figure* body, physique, build, frame, torso; proportions; *inf.* vital statistics. **5** *see figure 20* diagram, illustration, picture, drawing, sketch, chart, plan, map. **6** *the lily is a figure of purity* symbol, emblem, sign, representative. **7** *the figures on the wood* pattern, design, motif, device, depiction. **8** *a noted historical figure* dignitary, notable, personage, somebody, worthy, celebrity, leader, force, personality, presence, character; *inf.* big shot, bigwig.

**figure** verb **1** *figure a total* calculate, work out, compute, tally, reckon. **2** *she figures in*

*his autobiography* appear, be featured/mentioned, play a part/role. **3** *we figure that they'll go* think, consider, conclude, **figure out 1** *figure out the cost* work out, calculate, compute, reckon, assess. **2** *figure out why they came* understand, comprehend, fathom, decipher, resolve; *inf.* make heads or tails of.

**file**[1] noun **1** *put documents/data in a file* folder, box, portfolio, document case, filing cabinet. **2** *get out your file* dossier, folder, information; documents, records, data, particulars, case notes. **3** *a file of people* line, column, row, string, chain, queue.

**file**[2] verb **1** *file the information* categorize, classify, organize, put in place, put in order, pigeon-hole, record, enter, store, archive. **2** *file for divorce* apply, put in, register, sign up. **3** *people filing in* march, parade, troop.

**file**[3] verb *file one's nails* smooth, shape, buff, rub, rub down, polish, burnish, furbish, refine, scrape, abrade, rasp, sandpaper, pumice.

**fill** verb **1** *people filled the room* occupy all of, crowd, overcrowd, congest, cram, pervade. **2** *fill the shelves* stock, pack, load, supply, furnish, provide, replenish, restock, refill. **3** *fill the children* feed fully, satisfy, stuff, cram, satiate, sate; surfeit, glut. **4** *perfume/hostility filled the air* permeate, suffuse, imbue, charge, saturate. **5** *fill the hole* stop, stop up, block up, plug (up), seal, close, clog. **6** *he filled the post of manager* occupy, hold, take up. **fill in 1** *fill in for the manager* substitute, stand in, take over. **2** *fill me in on the events* inform, advise, tell, notify, acquaint, apprise, update; *inf.* put wise, bring up to speed.

**film** noun **1** *a film of dust* layer, coat, coating, covering, cover, dusting, sheet, blanket, skin, tissue, membrane. **2** *peering through a film* haze, mist, cloud, blur, veil; murkiness. **3** *see a recent film* movie, motion picture, picture; DVD; *inf.* video, flick.

**film** verb **1** *film the wedding* photograph, shoot, videotape. **2** *her eyes filmed (over)* blur, cloud over, mist over, dull, blear.

**filmy** adjective diaphanous, transparent, see-through, translucent, sheer, gauzelike, gauzy, gossamer, cobwebby, delicate, fine, light, thin, airy, fragile, flimsy, unsubstantial.

**filter** noun strainer, purifier, cleaner, gauze, netting, cheesecloth.

**fit** verb **1** *facts fitting our theory* agree with, concur with, correspond with, match, dovetail with, tally with, suit, go with. **2** *fit the parts together* join, connect, put together. **3** *fit the carpet* position, lay, fix, insert,

**filter** verb **1** *filter the liquid* strain, sieve, sift, filtrate; clarify, purify, clear, refine. **2** *light filtering through* trickle, ooze, seep, leak, dribble, percolate, drain, escape, leach.

**filth** noun **1** *the floors covered in filth* dirt, muck, grime, mud, mire, sludge, slime, squalor, excrement, dung, manure, sewage, rubbish, refuse, garbage, trash; filthiness, uncleanness, foulness, nastiness; *inf.* crud. **2** *objecting to filth in magazines* pornography, obscenity, indecency, smut; *inf.* porn, hard porn, raunchiness.

**filthy** adjective **1** *filthy water* dirty, mucky, muddy, murky, slimy, squalid, unclean, foul, nasty, feculent, polluted, contaminated, rotten, decaying, smelly, fetid, putrid. **2** *filthy clothes* unwashed, dirty, dirt-encrusted, grubby, muddy, mucky, black, blackened. **3** *a filthy liar* low-down, despicable, contemptible, base, mean, vile, nasty, sordid. **4** *filthy magazines* pornographic, obscene, indecent, smutty, coarse, bawdy, vulgar, lewd, licentious, dirty, impure; *inf.* blue, raunchy.

**final** adjective **1** *the final act* last, closing, concluding, finishing, end, ending, terminating, terminal, ultimate, eventual, endmost. **2** *their decision is final* absolute, conclusive, irrevocable, unalterable, irrefutable, incontrovertible, indisputable, unappealable, decisive, definitive, definite, settled.

**finale** noun end, finish, close, conclusion, climax, culmination, denouement, last act, final scene, final curtain, epilogue; *inf.* wind-up.

**finality** noun conclusiveness, decisiveness, definiteness, definitiveness, completeness, absoluteness, irrevocableness.

**finalize** verb complete, conclude, settle, tie up, wrap up, put the finishing touches to; *inf.* sew up, clinch.

**finally** adverb at last, at long last, ultimately, eventually, at the last minute, in the long run, when all was said and done.

**finance** noun **1** *she works in finance* money management, commerce, business, investment, banking, accounting. **2** *finances are low* funds, assets, resources; money, capital, cash, wealth, wherewithal, revenue, stock.

**finance** verb pay for, fund, back, subsidize, underwrite, capitalize.

**financial** adjective money, monetary, pecuniary, fiscal, economic, budgetary.

**find** verb **1** *find a gold watch* come across, chance upon, light upon, happen upon, stumble on. **2** *find a cure/answer/hotel* discover, come up with, hit upon, turn up,

bring to light, uncover, unearth, ferret out, locate. **3** *find the missing glove* recover, retrieve, regain, repossess, recoup. **4** *find happiness* get, obtain, acquire, procure, gain, earn, achieve, attain, win. **5** *find it pays to be honest* discover, become aware, realize, learn, conclude, detect, observe, notice, note, perceive. **6** *find the cheese too strong* consider, regard as, think, judge, deem, gauge, rate. **7** *the arrow found its mark* reach, attain, arrive at, gain, achieve.

**find out 1** *we found out they were lying* realize, learn. See FIND verb 5. **2** *find out the truth* discover, detect, bring to light, reveal, expose, unearth, disclose, unmask, ferret out, lay bare.

**find** noun asset, acquisition, lucky discovery, catch, bargain, good buy, godsend, boon, windfall.

**finding** noun decision, verdict, conclusion, pronouncement, judgment, decree, order, recommendation.

**fine** adjective **1** *that's fine with me* all right, satisfactory, acceptable, agreeable, convenient, suitable, good; *inf.* OK. **2** *a fine painting/wine* excellent, first-class, first-rate, great, exceptional, outstanding, admirable, quality, superior, splendid, magnificent, beautiful, exquisite, choice, select, prime, supreme, rare; *inf.* A-1, splendiferous, top-notch. **3** *fine china/bones* fragile, delicate, frail, dainty, slight, sheer, light, thin, flimsy. **4** *a fine sand/powder* fine-grained, powdery, powdered, ground, crushed, pulverized. **5** *a fine distinction* subtle, fine-drawn, tenuous, hairsplitting, precise, minute, elusive, abstruse. **6** *a fine taste in art* discriminating, discerning, tasteful, fastidious, critical, sensitive, refined, intelligent. **7** *a fine mind* keen, acute, sharp, quick, clever.

**finesse** noun tact, discretion, diplomacy, delicacy, refinement, grace, elegance, sophistication, subtlety, polish, *savoir faire*, skill, expertise, craft; tactfulness, adroitness, adeptness, skillfulness, cleverness, artfulness.

**finicky** adjective fussy, overparticular, fastidious, persnickety, hard to please, overcritical, difficult; *inf.* picky, choosy.

**finish** verb **1** *finish the task* complete, accomplish, execute, discharge, carry out, do, get done, fulfill, achieve, attain, end, conclude, close, finalize; *inf.* wind up, wrap up, sew up, polish off, knock off. **2** *finish working* stop, cease, discontinue, give up, have done with, suspend. **3** *finish up/off the supply* use, use up, consume, exhaust, empty, deplete, drain, expend, dispatch, dispose of. **4** *the job finished her | finish off the enemy* overcome, defeat, overpower, conquer, overwhelm, get the better of, best, worst, rout, bring down, annihilate, kill, exterminate; *inf.* wipe out, do in. **5** *finish the surface of the table* varnish, lacquer, stain, coat, veneer, wax, gild, glaze.

**finish** noun **1** *at the finish of the task/race* completion, accomplishment, execution, fulfillment, achievement, consummation, end, conclusion, close, closing, cessation, finale, denouement; last stages; *inf.* winding up. **2** *the finish of the enemy* defeat, overpowering, destruction, rout, end, annihilation, ruination; *inf.* ruin, curtains. **3** *a table with a beautiful finish* surface, texture, grain, veneer, coating, lacquer, glaze, luster, gloss, polish, shine, patina.

**finished** adjective **1** *finished tasks* completed, accomplished, executed, over and done with, over, in the past; *inf.* wrapped up, sewn up. **2** *the finished carton of milk* empty, drained, used up, exhausted, spent. **3** *a finished performance* accomplished, expert, proficient, masterly, polished, impeccable, consummate, flawless, skillful, elegant, graceful. **4** *the business was finished* over with, doomed, lost, ruined, bankrupt, wrecked; *inf.* washed up.

**finite** adjective bounded, limited, restricted, delimited, demarcated, terminable.

**fire** noun **1** *killed in a fire* blaze, conflagration, inferno, holocaust; flames. **2** *enemy fire* gunfire, sniping, flak, bombardment, shelling; volley, barrage, fusillade, salvo. **3** *people of fire* energy, spirit, life, liveliness, animation, vigor, verve, vivacity, sparkle, scintillation, dash, vim, gusto, élan, enthusiasm, fervor, force, potency, vehemence, ardor, passion, intensity, zeal; *inf.* pep. **4** *writings with fire* passion, ardor, intensity, inspiration, imagination, creativity, inventiveness, flair. **on fire 1** *houses on fire* burning, ablaze, blazing, aflame, in flames, flaming, alight, fiery. **2** *on fire with passion* passionate, ardent, fervent, intense, excited, eager, enthusiastic.

**fire** verb **1** *fire the haystacks* set fire to, set on fire, set ablaze, put a match to, light, ignite, kindle. **2** *fire the guns* shoot, let off, discharge, trigger, set off. **3** *fire a missile* launch, hurl, discharge, eject. **4** *fire the explosives* explode, detonate, touch off. **5** *fired with enthusiasm* arouse, rouse, stir up, excite, enliven, inflame, animate, inspire, motivate, stimulate, incite, galvanize, electrify, impassion. **6** *fire the assistant* dismiss, discharge, give someone his/her marching orders, get rid of, show someone the door, oust, depose, cashier; *inf.* sack, ax.

**fireworks** plural noun *there were fireworks when she heard the news* tantrums, hysterics, paroxysms, pyrotechnics; outburst, fit, frenzy, uproar.

**firm** adjective **1** *a firm surface* hard, hardened, stiff, rigid, inflexible, inelastic, unyielding, resistant, solid. **2** *the poles were firm in the ground* fixed, fast, secure, secured, stable, set, established, tight, immovable, anchored, rooted, embedded; riveted, braced, cemented, nailed, tied. **3** *firm plans* fixed, settled, decided, definite, established, unalterable, unchangeable. **4** *a firm handshake* strong, vigorous, sturdy. **5** *a firm friendship* constant, unchanging, enduring, abiding, durable, deep-rooted, long-standing, long-lasting, steady, stable, staunch. **6** *firm about not going* resolute, determined, decided, resolved, unfaltering, unwavering, unflinching, unswerving, unyielding, unbending, inflexible, obdurate, obstinate, stubborn, intransigent, unmalleable.

**firm** noun company, business, concern, house, establishment, organization, corporation, conglomerate, partnership, cooperative; *inf.* outfit.

**firmament** noun sky, heaven, the blue, vault of heaven; heavens, skies.

**firmness** noun **1** *the firmness of the surface* hardness, stiffness, rigidity, inflexibility, inelasticity, resistance, solidity. **2** *the firmness of the handshake* strength, vigor, sturdiness. **3** *the firmness of the friendship* constancy, endurance, durability, steadiness, stability, staunchness. **4** *the firmness of the refusal/teacher* resolution, determination, resolve, obduracy, inflexibility, stubbornness, strictness, intransigence.

**first** adjective **1** *the first stages of life* earliest, initial, opening, introductory, original, premier, primitive, primeval, primordial, pristine. **2** *first principles* basic, fundamental, key, rudimentary, cardinal. **3** *the first people in the land* leading, foremost, principal, highest, ruling, chief, head, main, major, greatest, preeminent, supreme.

**first-rate** adjective first-class, second to none, top, premier, superlative, prime, excellent, superb, outstanding, exceptional, tip-top, admirable; *inf.* top-notch, ace, A-1, crack.

**fishy** adjective *something fishy about it* questionable, dubious, doubtful, suspect, suspicious, odd, queer, peculiar, strange, not quite right; *inf.* funny, shady, not kosher.

**fissure** noun crack, crevice, cleft, groove, slit, gash, fracture, fault, rift, split, rent.

**fit** adjective **1** *feeling fit* well, healthy, in good shape, strong, robust, hale and hearty, sturdy, hardy, stalwart, vigorous. **2** *fit to drive* able, capable, competent, adequate, good enough, satisfactory, ready, prepared, qualified, trained, equipped. **3** *a fit occasion* | *fit behavior* fitting, proper, due, seemly, decorous, decent, right, correct, apt, appropriate, suitable, convenient, apposite, relevant, pertinent.

arrange, adjust, shape. **4** *the training will fit him for many jobs* make suitable, qualify, prepare, make ready, prime, condition, train. **5** *fit the kitchen with units* fit out, equip, provide, supply, furnish.

**fit** noun **1** *an epileptic fit* convulsion, spasm, paroxysm, seizure, attack. **2** *a fit of coughing* attack, bout, spell, burst, outburst, outbreak. **3** *she'll have a fit* tantrum, outburst of anger/rage; *inf.* hissy fit. **by fits and starts** on and off, spasmodically, intermittently, sporadically, erratically, fitfully.

**fitful** adjective broken, disturbed, irregular, uneven, intermittent, sporadic, spasmodic.

**fitness** noun **1** *improve your fitness* physical fitness, condition, shape, strength, robustness, sturdiness, vigor. **2** *his fitness to drive* ability, capability, competency, preparedness, qualification, eligibility, worthiness. **3** *the fitness of the occasion* properness, propriety, seemliness, correctness, aptness, suitability, convenience, relevance, pertinence.

**fitting** adjective proper, due. *See* FIT adjective 3.

**fix** verb **1** *fix the shelf to the wall* fasten, secure, make fast, attach, connect, join, couple; stick, glue, cement, pin, nail, screw, bolt, clamp, bind, tie, pinion. **2** *fix the post in the ground* plant, implant, install, anchor, embed. **3** *fix a date/price* decide on, settle, set, agree on, arrange, determine, establish, name. **4** *fix the car* repair, mend, patch up, put right, put to rights, restore, remedy, rectify, adjust. **5** *fix her gaze on them* direct, focus, level at, rivet. **6** *fix something to eat* prepare, make, make ready, put together, cook. **7** *I'll fix him for that* get even with, wreak vengeance on, take retribution on, punish; *inf.* get back at, pay someone back. **8** *fix the outcome of the race* rig, manipulate, maneuver, arrange fraudulently; *inf.* fiddle with, **fix up** *fix you up with a bed* provide, supply, furnish, accommodate.

**fix** noun *in a bit of a fix* predicament, plight, quandary, dilemma, difficulty, muddle, mess, corner, ticklish/tricky situation, tight spot; *inf.* pickle, jam, hole, spot, scrape, bind.

**fixation** noun obsession, preoccupation, complex, compulsion, mania, *idée fixe*, phobia; *inf.* hang-up, thing.

**fizz** verb bubble, effervesce, sparkle, froth, foam; hiss, sputter, fizzle, sibilate.

**fizzle** verb **fizzle out** peter out, come to nothing, fall through, come to grief, end in failure, fail, miscarry, abort, collapse; *inf.* flop, fold.

**flabbergast** verb astound, amaze, dumbfound, strike dumb, render speechless,

stun, stagger, confound, daze, overcome, overwhelm, nonplus, disconcert; *inf.* bowl over.

**flabby** adjective flaccid, unfirm, out of tone, drooping, pendulous, limp; *inf.* out of shape.

**flaccid** adjective unfirm, limp. *See* FLABBY.

**flag** noun standard, ensign, banner, pennant, burgee, streamer; bunting; colors.

**flagrant** adjective glaring, obvious, blatant, egregious, outrageous, scandalous, shocking, disgraceful, shameless; notorious, heinous, atrocious, monstrous, wicked, iniquitous, villainous.

**flair** noun **1** *a flair for languages* ability, aptitude, capability, facility, skill, talent, gift, knack, bent, feel, genius. **2** *all the women had flair* style, panache, elegance, dash, élan, taste.

**flake** verb chip, peel, peel off, scale off, blister, exfoliate.

**flamboyant** adjective **1** *flamboyant gestures* extravagant, theatrical, showy, ostentatious, dashing, swashbuckling. **2** *flamboyant clothes/colors* colorful, bright, exciting, dazzling, glamorous, splendid, resplendent, showy, gaudy, flashy.

**flame** noun **1** *flames burst from the ashes* fire, blaze, conflagration. **2** *burn with a flame* brilliant light, brightness, glow, gleam. **3** *the flame of love* passion, warmth, ardor, fervor, fire, excitement, enthusiasm. **4** *an old flame* boyfriend, girlfriend, sweetheart, lover, partner, beloved, beau.

**flame** verb **1** *the wood flamed* burn, blaze, burst into flame, catch fire. **2** *the light flamed* glow, shine, flash, beam, glare, sparkle.

**flaming** adjective **1** *a flaming bonfire* blazing, ablaze, burning, on fire, afire, in flames, aflame, ignited, fiery, red-hot, raging, glowing. **2** *flaming colors* bright, brilliant, vivid, flamboyant, red, reddish-orange, scarlet. **3** *a flaming idiot* utter, absolute.

**flap** verb flutter, sway, wave, agitate, vibrate, wag, waggle, shake, swing, oscillate, flail.

**flare** verb **1** *the fire flared* flare up, blaze, flame, burn unsteadily. **2** *lights flared on the shore* flash, gleam, glow, sparkle, glitter, flicker. **3** *his nostrils flared* broaden, widen, splay, **flare up 1** *trouble/disease flared up* broke out, burst out, recur. **2** *the two women flared up* lose one's temper, lose control, explode, boil over; *inf.* blow one's top, fly off the handle, boil one's cool.

**flash** verb **1** *lights flashed* light up, shine out, flare, blaze, glare, beam, gleam, glint, sparkle, flicker, shimmer, twinkle, glimmer, glisten, scintillate, coruscate. **2** *the* *runners flashed past* dart, dash, tear, shoot, zoom, streak, fly, rush, bolt, race, bound, speed; *inf.* scoot. **3** *flask her new ring* show off, flaunt, flourish, display, exhibit.

**flash** noun **1** *a flash of light* blaze, burst, glare, flare, shaft, ray, streak, gleam, glint, sparkle, flicker, shimmer, twinkle, glimmer. **2** *he came in a flash* instant, moment, second, split second, minute, trice, twinkling, twinkling of an eye, two shakes of a lamb's tail; *inf.* jiffy, bat of an eye. **3** *a flash of enthusiasm/wit* outburst, burst, outbreak.

**flashy** adjective ostentatious, showy, tasteless, pretentious, cheap, tawdry, garish, loud, flamboyant, gaudy; *inf.* tacky, snazzy, jazzy, glitzy, ritzy, bling, bling-bling.

**flat** adjective **1** *a flat surface* level, horizontal, leveled, even, smooth, unbroken, plane. **2** *lying flat on the ground* stretched out, spread-eagle, prone, supine, prostrate, recumbent. **3** *a flat tire* deflated, collapsed, blown out, burst, punctured, ruptured. **4** *a flat denial* outright, direct, out-and-out, explicit, absolute, definite, positive, utter, categorical, unqualified, unconditional, unquestionable, unequivocal. **5** *a flat voice | flat jokes* monotonous, boring, dull, tedious, uninteresting, lifeless, lackluster, dead, vapid, bland, insipid, prosaic. **6** *the market is flat* slow, inactive, sluggish, slack.

**flat** adverb **flat out 1** *asked flat out for a raise* directly, bluntly, openly; *inf.* without batting an eye. **2** *the boat passed us flat out* at full speed, at full tilt, full steam ahead; *inf.* hell-bent for leather.

**flatten** verb **1** *flatten the surface* make flat, level, level out/off, make even, even out, smooth, smooth out/off, plane; compress, press down, crush, squash, compact. **2** *flatten the old buildings* demolish, tear down, raze, raze to the ground. **3** *flatten his opponent* knock down, knock to the ground, floor, knock off one's feet, fell, prostrate; crush, quash, squash, deflate, snub, humiliate; *inf.* put down.

**flatter** verb **1** *salesmen flattering the customers* compliment, praise, sing the praises of, praise to excess, praise to the skies, eulogize, puff up, blandish, fawn upon, cajole, humor; *inf.* sweet-talk, soft-soap, butter up, lay it on thick to/for, play up to. **2** *that dress flatters her coloring* suit, become, set off, show to advantage, enhance; *inf.* do something for.

**flattery** noun praise, adulation, false praise, eulogy, puffery, fawning, cajolery; compliments, blandishments; *inf.* sweet talk, soft soap, buttering-up,

**flaunt** verb show off, parade, exhibit, draw attention to, make a show of, wave, brandish.

**flavor** noun **1** *dislike the flavor of the herb* taste, savor, tang, relish. **2** *add some flavor to the sauce* flavoring, seasoning, tastiness, piquancy, spiciness, zest; *inf.* zing. **3** *capture the flavor of the place* spirit, essence, soul, nature, character, quality, feel, ambience, tone, style, stamp.

**flavor** verb season, spice, lace, imbue, infuse.

**flaw** noun fault, defect, imperfection, blemish, failing, foible, shortcoming, weakness, weak spot; crack, fracture, fissure, tear.

**flawless** adjective faultless, perfect, impeccable, blemish-free, unimpaired, unmarred, undamaged.

**fleck** noun spot, mark, speck, speckle, freckle.

**flee** verb **1** *she fled from the blaze* run, run away, run off, bolt, take flight, make off, fly, abscond, retreat, beat a retreat, beat a hasty retreat, make a quick exit, run for it, make a run for it, take off, take to one's heels, decamp, escape, make one's escape/getaway, do a disappearing act, vanish; *inf.* cut and run, make oneself scarce, beat it, skedaddle, split, scram. **2** *they fled the country* run away from, escape from; *inf.* skip.

**fleece** verb **1** *fleece the sheep* shear, clip. **2** *a con man fleeced the elderly woman* swindle, defraud, cheat, rob, strip, bilk, overcharge; *inf.* con, take for a ride, rip off, sting, bleed, take to the cleaners, soak.

**fleet** noun flotilla, naval force, navy, convoy, squadron, armada, argosy.

**fleet** adjective swift, fast, rapid, quick, speedy, expeditious, nimble, fleet of foot, nimble-footed, swift-footed, like the wind.

**fleeting** adjective brief, short-lived, momentary, transient, transitory, ephemeral, evanescent, fugacious, vanishing, flying, passing.

**flesh** noun **1** *flesh and bones* muscle, tissue, brawn. **2** *carry too much flesh* fat; fatness, obesity, corpulence. **3** *not much flesh in the essay* substance, pith, matter, body. **4** *the pleasure of the flesh* body, physical nature, physicality, corporeality, carnality, animality, sensuality, sensualism. **5** *all flesh would perish in such conditions* mankind, man, humankind, people, humanity, *Homo sapiens;* animate life, the living; human beings, living creatures, **flesh and blood** family, kin, kinfolk, relatives, relations, **in the flesh** in person, before one's eyes.

**flexible** adjective **1** *flexible materials* bend-

**high-Class** adjective superior, luxurious, deluxe, select, choice, elite, top-flight, first-rate, elegant, posh, upper-class, upscale, upmarket; *inf.* tip-top, A-l, super, super-duper, classy.

able, pliant, pliable, elastic, springy, plastic, moldable. **2** *my arrangements are flexible* adaptable, adjustable, open, open to change, changeable, variable. **3** *the young man is too flexible* tractable, malleable, compliant, manageable, docile, submissive.

**flicker** verb **1** *lights flickering* twinkle, sparkle, blink, flash, shimmer, glitter, glimmer, glint, flare. **2** *with eyelids flickering* flutter, quiver, vibrate, bat.

**flight** noun *the flight of the beaten army* retreat, departure, exit, exodus, decamping, escape, getaway, disappearance, vanishing. **put to flight** chase, chase off, drive off, scare off, rout, scatter, disperse, stampede. **take flight** run away, make off. *See* FLEE 1.

**flighty** adjective frivolous, giddy, scatterbrained, harebrained, fickle, changeable, inconstant, unsteady, whimsical, capricious, skittish.

**flimsy** adjective **1** *a flimsy box* insubstantial, slight, makeshift, jerry-built, gimcrack, rickety, ramshackle, shaky, fragile, frail. **2** *made of a flimsy material* thin, light, lightweight, delicate, sheer, filmy, diaphanous, gossamer, gauzy. **3** *a flimsy excuse* feeble, weak, poor, inadequate, unconvincing, implausible, unsatisfactory, paltry, trifling, trivial, shallow.

**flinch** verb draw back, pull back, recoil, withdraw, shrink back, shy away, cringe, cower, crouch, quail, wince, blench. **flinch from** *flinch from his duty* dodge, avoid, duck, balk at.

**fling** verb throw, toss, hurl, cast, pitch, sling, heave, fire, shy, launch, propel, catapult, send flying, let fly; *inf.* lob, chuck.

**fling** noun **1** *with one fling of the javelin* throw, toss, hurl, cast, pitch, shot, heave; *inf.* lob, chuck. **2** *a last fling before marriage* binge, spree, good time, bit of fun, night on the town. **3** *have a fling at winning the match* try, attempt, go, shot, stab, venture; *inf.* crack, whirl.

**flip** verb **1** *flip a coin* flick, toss, throw, pitch, cast, spin, twist. **2** *flip a switch* flick, click, tap. **flip through** skim (through), flick through, glance over/through, browse through, thumb through, skip over.

**flippant** adjective frivolous, glib, thoughtless, offhand, disrespectful, impertinent, impudent, irreverent, saucy; *inf.* flip.

**flirt** verb **flirt with 1** *she's always flirting with the boys* toy with, trifle with, make eyes at, ogle, lead on; philander with, dally with. **2** *flirt with the idea of going* play with, entertain, consider, give thought to, dabble in.

**flirt** noun coquette, tease, vamp, heartbreaker, trifler, philanderer.

**flirtatious** adjective coquettish, provocative, teasing, amorous, philandering, dallying.

**float** verb **1** *craft floating along* bob, glide, sail, drift. **2** *not working, just floating about* drift, wander, meander; *inf.* bum (around).

**flock** noun **1** *a flock of sheep* fold, drove, herd. **2** *a flock of birds/geese* flight, bevy, skein, gaggle. **3** *a flock of people* crowd, gathering, assembly, company, collection, congregation, group, throng, mass, host, multitude, troop, herd, convoy.

**flood** noun **1** *houses damaged in the flood* deluge, inundation, torrent, spate, overflow, flash flood. **2** *a flood of mail* profusion, overabundance, superabundance, plethora, superfluity, glut; *inf.* tons, heaps.

**flood** verb **1** *rivers flooding | flood the town* overflow, break the banks, brim over, swell, surge, inundate, deluge, immerse, submerge, swamp, drown, engulf. **2** *flood the market with fruit* overfill, oversupply, saturate, glut, overwhelm.

**flop** verb **1** *flop into a chair* collapse, slump, drop, fall, tumble. **2** *the dog's ears flopped* dangle, droop, sag. **3** *the play flopped* fail, fall flat, founder, close, go over like a lead balloon; *inf.* bomb.

**flop** noun *the play was a flop* failure, fiasco, loser, disaster, debacle; *inf.* no-go, washout, dud, lemon, bomb, bust.

**florid** adjective **1** *a florid complexion* ruddy, red-faced, red, reddish, flushed, blushing, rubicund. **2** *florid decorations* ornate, flamboyant, overelaborate, embellished, busy, baroque. *See* FLOWERY 2.

**flounder** verb thrash, struggle, stumble, blunder, fumble, grope, falter, muddle, bungle.

**flourish** verb **1** *flourish the sword/prize* brandish, wave, twirl, wield, swing, hold aloft, display, exhibit, flaunt, parade, vaunt; *inf.* show off. **2** *the plants are flourishing* thrive, burgeon, bloom, blossom, bear fruit, burst forth. **3** *we are all flourishing* be well, be in good health, get on well, prosper, succeed; *inf.* be in the pink, be fine and dandy, go great guns.

**flout** verb defy, scorn, disdain, show contempt for, spurn, scoff at, mock, laugh at, deride, ridicule.

**flow** verb *blood/rivers flowing* course, run, circulate, glide, stream, ripple, swirl, surge, sweep, roll, rush, whirl, drift, slide, trickle, gurgle, babble. **2** *blood flowing from the wound* gush, stream, well, spurt, spout, squirt, spew, jet, spill, leak, seep, ooze, drip. **3** *ideas flowing from her pen* arise, issue, spring, originate, derive, emanate, emerge, pour, proceed. **flow with** overflow with, be abundant in, abound in, teem with, be rich in, be full of.

**flow** noun **1** *the flow of the water* course, current, drift, stream, spate, tide. **2** *stem the flow of blood* gush, stream, welling, spurting, spouting, outflow. **3** *a flow of complaints* flood, deluge, outpouring, abundance, plethora, excess, effusion, succession, train.

**flower** noun **1** *pick/plant several flowers* bloom, blossom, floweret, floret; annual, perennial. **2** *in the flower of their youth* prime, peak, zenith, acme, height, heyday, springtime; salad days. **3** *the flower of the nation died in battle* finest, best, pick, choice, elite, cream, crème de la crème.

**flowery** adjective **1** *flowery patterns* floral, flower-covered, flower-patterned. **2** *flowery language* high-flown, ornate, fancy, elaborate, overelaborate, grandiloquent, purple, bombastic.

**fluctuate** verb **1** *prices fluctuating* seesaw, yo-yo, vary, shift, change, alter, swing, oscillate, undulate, ebb and flow. **2** *she fluctuates between going and not going* waver, vacillate, shilly-shally, hem and haw, teeter, blow hot and cold.

**fluent** adjective **1** *a fluent speaker* articulate, eloquent, smooth-spoken, silver-tongued, voluble. **2** *fluent prose* smooth, flowing, fluid, graceful, effortless, natural, easy, elegant, mellifluous, euphonious.

**fluffy** adjective **1** *a fluffy blanket* soft, downy, cottony, puffy, airy, light. **2** *a fluffy movie* frivolous, superficial, meaningless, thin, insubstantial, nonintellectual.

**fluid** noun liquid, gas, solution.

**fluid** adjective **1** *a fluid substance moving along the pipe* gaseous, gassy, liquid, liquefied, melted, molten, uncongealed, running, flowing. **2** *a fluid prose style* smooth, graceful. See FLUENT 2. **3** *our plans are fluid* flexible, open to change, adaptable, adjustable, not fixed, not settled, variable, mutable. **4** *the situation is fluid* subject/likely to change, unstable, unsteady, ever-shifting, fluctuating, mobile, mercurial.

**flurry** noun **1** *a flurry of snow/rain* squall, gust, shower; burst, spurt, outbreak, spell, bout. **2** *the hostess in a flurry of excitement* fluster, fuss, bustle, whirl, stir, ferment, hubbub, commotion, hustle.

**fluster** verb ruffle, unsettle, upset, bother, put on edge, discompose, agitate, panic, perturb, disconcert, confuse, throw off balance, confound, nonplus; *inf.* rattle, faze, throw into a tizzy.

**flutter** verb **1** *a bird fluttering its wings* flap, beat, quiver, agitate, vibrate, ruffle. **2** *flags fluttering in the breeze* flap, wave, flop, ripple, quiver, shiver, tremble. **3** *with hearts fluttering* pulsate, palpitate.

**fly** verb **1** *birds flying overhead* flutter, flit, hover, soar, wing, wing its way, take wing, take to the air, mount. **2** *flags flying* flap, wave, flutter, toss. **3** *the runners flew by* race, dash, shoot, rush, tear, bolt, zoom, scoot, dart, speed, hasten, hurry, scamper, career, go like the wind. **4** *watched their beaten opponents fly* run, run away. See FLEE.

**foam** noun froth, bubbles, fizz, effervescence, head, spume, lather, suds.

**foam** verb froth, froth up, cream, bubble, fizz, effervesce, spume, lather.

**foe** noun enemy, opponent, adversary, rival, antagonist, combatant.

**fog** noun **1** *fog decreasing visibility* mist, mistiness, smog, murk, murkiness, haze; *inf.* pea soup. **2** *a mental fog* haze, daze, stupor, trance; bewilderment, confusion, perplexity, bafflement, vagueness, stupefaction, disorientation.

**fog** verb **1** *windshields fogging over/up* mist over, become misty, cloud over, steam up. **2** *alcohol fogging their minds* befuddle, becloud, bedim, bewilder, confuse, muddle, perplex, baffle, blind, darken, obscure, daze, stupefy, obfuscate.

**foggy** adjective **1** *a foggy day* misty, smoggy, dark, dim, gray, overcast, murky, hazy, gloomy; *inf.* soupy. **2** *a foggy recollection of the event* vague, indistinct, dim, hazy, shadowy, cloudy, clouded, dark, obscure, unclear, befuddled, confused, bewildered, muddled.

**foible** noun weakness, weak point, failing, shortcoming, flaw, blemish, defect, frailty, infirmity, quirk, idiosyncrasy.

**foil** verb thwart, frustrate, baffle, defeat, check, checkmate, circumvent, counter, impede, obstruct, hamper, hinder, cripple, nip in the bud.

**fold** noun overlap, layer, pleat, turn, gather, crease, dog-ear; wrinkle, pucker, furrow, crinkle.

**fold** verb **1** *fold the paper* double, double over, double up, crease, turn under, turn up, bend, overlap, tuck, gather, pleat, crimp, crumple, dog-ear. **2** *fold her in his arms* enfold, wrap, enclose, envelop, clasp, embrace, hug, squeeze. **3** *the firm folded* fail, collapse, go out of business, close, shut down, go bankrupt, crash; *inf.* go bust, go under, flop.

**folklore** noun legend, myth, mythology, lore, oral history, tradition, folk tradition; legends, fables, myths, old wives' tales.

**follow** verb **1** *children following after each other* go behind/after, come behind/after, walk behind, tread on the heels of. **2** *dogs following rabbits* chase, pursue, run after, trail, shadow, hunt, stalk, track, dog, hound, course; *inf.* tail. **3** *follow the rules* obey, observe, comply with, conform to, heed, pay attention to, note, have regard to, mind, be guided by, accept, yield to. **4** *the conclusion follows logically* result, arise, develop, ensue, emanate, issue, proceed, spring, flow. **5** *follow an argument* understand, comprehend, take in, grasp, fathom, get, catch on to, keep up with, see; *inf.* latch on to. **6** *he followed the style of Dickinson* copy, imitate, emulate; pattern oneself on, adopt the style of, style oneself on. **7** *he follows science fiction* be a fan/admirer/devotee of, cultivate an interest in, support, keep abreast of, keep up to date with. **follow through (on)** complete, bring to completion, bring to a finish. **follow up (on)** look into, check out, pursue.

**follower** noun **1** *the gang leader and his followers* companion, escort, attendant, henchman, minion, lackey, toady; servant, page, squire; *inf.* hanger-on, sidekick. **2** *Picasso and his followers* imitator, emulator, copier; *inf.* copycat. **3** *followers of Christ* apostle, disciple, adherent, supporter, believer, worshiper, votary, student, pupil. **4** *followers of the Yankees* supporter, enthusiast, fan, admirer, devotee; *inf.* groupie, camp follower, rooter.

**following** noun backing, clientele, public, audience, circle, coterie, retinue, train; supporters, backers, admirers, fans, adherents, devotees, advocates, patrons.

**folly** noun foolishness, absurdity, absurdness, stupidity, silliness, nonsense, senselessness, illogicality, inanity, madness, craziness, idiocy, imbecility, lunacy, ridiculousness, ludicrousness, fatuousness, fatuity, rashness, recklessness, imprudence, indiscretion, irrationality.

**foment** verb instigate, incite, provoke, agitate, excite, stir up, arouse, encourage, urge, actuate, initiate.

**fond** adjective **1** *a fond look* adoring, devoted, loving, affectionate, caring, warm, tender, amorous, doting, indulgent, overindulgent. **2** *fond hopes of success* deep, cherished, heartfelt. **fond of** partial to, keen on, attached to, enamored of, having a soft spot for, addicted to; *inf.* hooked on.

**fondle** verb caress, stroke, touch, pat, pet, cuddle, hug, nuzzle.

**fondness** noun **1** *look upon his brother with fondness* affection, love, warmth, tenderness, kindness, devotion, care, attachment. **2** *a fondness for chocolate* liking, love, taste, partiality, preference, weakness, soft spot, penchant, predilection, fancy, susceptibility.

**food** noun **1** *give food to the children* nourishment, sustenance, nutriment, subsistence, aliment, fare, diet, menu, table, bread,

daily bread, board, provender, cooking, cuisine; foodstuffs, refreshments, edibles, meals, provisions, rations, stores, viands, victuals/vittles, commons, comestibles; solids; *inf.* eats, eatables, nosh, grub, chow. **2** *food for the cattle* fodder, feed, provender, forage.

**fool** noun **1** *don't try to explain—he's a fool* idiot, ass, nitwit, halfwit, numskull, nincompoop, ninny, blockhead, dunce, dunderhead, dolt, ignoramus, dullard, moron, simpleton, jackass, loon; *inf.* dope, clod, chump, bonehead, fathead, birdbrain, twit, twerp, nerd, airhead. **2** *make a fool of him* dupe, butt, laughingstock, pushover, easy mark; *inf.* stooge, sucker, sap, fall guy. **3** *the fools of Shakespeare's day* jester, clown, buffoon, comic, jokester, zany, merry andrew, harlequin.

**fool** verb **1** *they certainly fooled the teacher* deceive, trick, play a trick on, hoax, make a fool of, dupe, take in, mislead, hoodwink, bluff, delude, beguile, bamboozle, cozen, gull; *inf.* con, kid, put one over on. **2** *we thought he was sick but he was only fooling* pretend, make believe, feign, put on an act, act, fake, counterfeit; *inf.* kid. **fool around 1** *the boys are always fooling around* jest, joke, clown, caper, cavort. **2** *fool around with the controls* fiddle, play, toy, trifle, meddle, tamper, monkey. **3** *fool around with someone else's wife* have an affair, philander, flirt.

**foolhardy** adjective reckless, rash, daredevil, devil-may-care, impulsive, hotheaded, impetuous, madcap, heedless, precipitate, incautious, imprudent, irresponsible, injudicious, desperate.

**foolish** adjective **1** *a foolish plan/idea* silly, absurd, senseless, nonsensical, unintelligent, inane, pointless, fatuous, ridiculous, laughable, derisible, risible, imprudent, incautious, irresponsible, injudicious, indiscreet, unwise, unreasonable, ill-advised, ill-considered, impolitic; *inf.* damfool, crackbrained, nutty, for the birds. **2** *a foolish fellow* stupid, silly, idiotic, simple, unintelligent, halfwitted, brainless, doltish, dull, dull-witted, dense, ignorant, moronic, witless, weak-minded, mad, crazy; *inf.* dumb, dopey, daft, balmy, batty, dippy, cuckoo, screwy, wacky.

**foolishness** noun **1** *the foolishness of their actions* stupidity, silliness. See FOLLY. **2** *talk foolishness* nonsense, rubbish, bunkum, gobbledegook, humbug, balderdash, claptrap, hogwash, rigmarole; *inf.* rot, bunk, poppycock, piffle, hooey, garbage, crap.

**foolproof** adjective infallible, never-failing, unfailing, certain, sure, guaranteed, safe, dependable, trustworthy.

**footing** noun **1** *lose one's footing* foothold, grip, toehold, support. **2** *his business* *was on a secure footing* basis, foundation, groundwork, establishment. **3** *on a friendly footing* relationship, standing, state, condition, position, basis, foundation; relations, terms.

**forage** verb search, look around, hunt, rummage around, scour; *inf.* scrounge around.

**forbear** verb refrain from, abstain from, desist from, keep from, restrain oneself from, hold back from, cease, give up, leave off, break off.

**forbearance** noun tolerance, toleration, patience, resignation, endurance, long-suffering, self-control, restraint, leniency, clemency, indulgence.

**forbid** verb prohibit, ban, bar, debar, outlaw, veto, proscribe, disallow, interdict, preclude, exclude, rule out, stop.

**forbidden** adjective prohibited, out of bounds, banned, debarred, outlawed, vetoed, proscribed, interdicted, taboo, verboten.

**forbidding** adjective **1** *a forbidding manner* stern, harsh, grim, hard, tough, hostile, unfriendly, disagreeable, nasty, mean, abhorrent, repellent. **2** *a forbidding landscape* frightening, threatening, ominous, menacing, sinister, daunting, foreboding.

**force** noun **1** *requiring a lot of force* strength, power, potency, vigor, energy, might, muscle, stamina, effort, exertion, impact, pressure, life, vitality, stimulus, dynamism; *inf.* punch. **2** *use force to persuade them* compulsion, coercion, duress, pressure, constraint, enforcement, violence; *inf.* arm twisting. **3** *arguments with force* persuasiveness, cogency, validity, weight, effectiveness, efficacy, efficaciousness, influence, power, strength, vehemence, significance; *inf.* bite, punch. **4** *speaking with great force* vehemence, intensity, vigor, drive, fierceness, feeling, passion, vividness. **in force 1** *rules no longer in force* in operation, operative, valid, current, effective, binding. **2** *the fans were out in force* in full strength, in great numbers, in great quantities, in hordes.

**force** verb **1** *force them to go* compel, coerce, make, pressure, constrain, impel, drive, oblige; *inf.* put the squeeze/bite on, use strong-arm tactics on. **2** *force the door/safe* force open, break open, burst open, blast, prize open, crack. **3** *the wind forced them back* drive, propel, push, thrust, shove, press. **4** *force a confession* wrest, extract, wring, extort, drag.

**forced** adjective **1** *a forced march* enforced, compulsory, compelled, obligatory, mandatory, involuntary, unwilling. **2** *a forced laugh* strained, unnatural, artificial, feigned, affected, stilted, labored, wooden, self-conscious.

**forceful** adjective vigorous, powerful, potent, strong, weighty, dynamic, energetic, assertive, effective, cogent, telling, persuasive, convincing, compelling.

**forebear** noun forefather, ancestor, forerunner, progenitor, primogenitor, predecessor, father.

**forebode** verb augur, presage, portend, foreshadow, foreshow, foretoken, betoken, prefigure, signify, mean, indicate, point to, foretell, forecast, predict, prophesy, forewarn.

**foreboding** noun **1** *a foreboding that the car would crash* presentiment, premonition, intuition, sixth sense, feeling, vague feeling, misgiving, suspicion. **2** *the forebodings of the soothsayer* augury, prophecy, prediction, prognostication, forecast, warning, omen, portent.

**forecast** verb predict, foretell, foresee, prophesy, prognosticate, augur, divine, guess, conjecture, speculate, estimate, calculate.

**forecast** noun prediction, prophecy, prognostication, augury, guess, conjecture, speculation, prognosis, projection; *inf.* guesstimate.

**forefather** noun ancestor, forerunner. *See* FOREBEAR.

**forefront** noun front, fore, foreground, lead, head, van, vanguard, spearhead.

**foregoing** adjective preceding, precedent, prior, previous, former, above, aforesaid, aforementioned.

**foreign** adjective **1** *from foreign parts* overseas, alien, distant, remote. **2** *foreign objects* strange, unfamiliar, unknown, exotic, outlandish, odd, peculiar, curious. **3** *matters foreign to the discussion* irrelevant, not pertinent, unrelated, unconnected, inappropriate, extraneous.

**foreigner** noun nonnative, alien, immigrant, newcomer, stranger, outsider.

**foreman** noun overseer, supervisor, manager, superintendent; *inf.* boss.

**foremost** adjective leading, principal, premier, prime, top, first, primary, paramount, chief, main, supreme, highest, preeminent.

**forerunner** noun predecessor, precursor, ancestor, antecedent, forefather, herald, harbinger, usher, advance guard.

**foresee** verb anticipate, envisage, predict. *See* FORECAST verb.

**foreshadow** verb bode, presage. *See* FOREBODE.

**foresight** noun forethought, discernment, farsightedness, circumspection, prudence,

**forest** noun woods, wood, woodland, plantation; trees.

**forestall** verb preempt, intercept, anticipate, thwart, frustrate, stave off, ward off, fend off, avert, prevent, hinder, impede.

**foretell** verb **1** *she foretold his death* predict, foresee. See FORECAST. verb. **2** *the first match foretold the final result* augur, presage. See FOREBODE.

**forever** adverb **1** *loving each other forever* always, evermore, for all time, till the end of time, till the cows come home, till hell freezes over, till doomsday, eternally, undyingly, perpetually, in perpetuity; *inf.* for keeps, for good. **2** *he's forever playing loud music* incessantly, continually, constantly, perpetually, endlessly, unremittingly, interminably, everlastingly.

**forewarn** verb prewarn, warn, give fair warning to, put on one's guard, tip off, put on the qui vive, alert, caution, advise, apprise, precaution.

**foreword** noun introduction, preface, preamble, preliminary/front matter, prologue.

**forfeit** verb relinquish, hand over, give up, surrender, renounce, be stripped/deprived of.

**forge** verb **1** *blacksmiths forging horseshoes* / *forge a treaty* hammer out, beat into shape, shape, form, fashion, mold, found, cast, make, manufacture, frame, construct, create. **2** *forge an excuse* invent, make up, devise, coin, fabricate. **3** *forge handwriting/checks* copy, imitate, fake, falsify, counterfeit.

**forget** verb **1** *forget her phone number* be unable to think of, let slip; *inf.* draw a blank on. **2** *it's best to forget unhappy times* put out of one's mind, disregard, ignore. **3** *I forgot my gloves* overlook, miss. **forget oneself** misbehave, behave improperly.

**forgetful** adjective **1** *growing forgetful* absentminded, amnesic, amnesiac, abstracted, vague. **2** *forgetful of one's duties* neglectful, negligent, heedless, careless, unmindful, inattentive, oblivious, lax, remiss, disregardful.

**forgive** verb pardon, excuse, exonerate, absolve, acquit, let off, let bygones be bygones, bear no malice, harbor no grudge, bury the hatchet; *inf.* let someone off the hook.

**forgiveness** noun pardon, amnesty, exoneration, absolution, acquittal, remission, absence of malice/grudges, mercy.

**forgiving** adjective lenient, merciful, compassionate, magnanimous, humane, clement, mild, softhearted, forbearing, tolerant, placable.

**forgo, forego** verb do/go without, waive, renounce, relinquish, sacrifice, surrender, abstain from, refrain from, eschew.

**forgotten** adjective unremembered, out of mind, beyond/past recall/recollection, consigned to oblivion, obliterated, blotted out, buried, left behind.

**forlorn** adjective **1** *looking forlorn* unhappy, sad, miserable, wretched, pathetic, woebegone, lonely, disconsolate, desolate, cheerless, pitiable. **2** *a forlorn farmhouse* abandoned, forsaken, deserted, forgotten, neglected. **3** *a forlorn attempt* hopeless, desperate.

**form** verb **1** *form shapes* make, fashion, shape, model, mold, forge, found, construct, build, assemble, put together, set up, erect, create, produce, concoct, devise. **2** *form plans* formulate, devise, think up, plan, draw up, frame, forge, hatch, develop, organize; *inf.* dream up. **3** *shapes began to form* take shape, materialize, appear, show up. **4** *form bad habits* acquire, develop, get, pick up, contract, grow into; *inf.* get into. **5** *form the children into lines* arrange, draw up, line up, assemble, organize, order, rank. **6** *these books form the complete series* make, make up, comprise, constitute, compose. **7** *forming young children's minds* develop, train, teach, instruct, educate, school, drill, discipline.

**form** noun **1** *observe the form of the crystals* shape, configuration, formation, conformation, structure, construction, arrangement, disposition, appearance, exterior. **2** *a well-built form* body, physique, figure, shape, build, frame, anatomy, silhouette, contour. **3** *help came to the farmers in the form of rain* shape, appearance, manifestation, semblance, guise, character. **4** *a form of punishment* type, kind, sort, variety, species, genus, genre, stamp. **5** *his literary work lacks form* structure, framework, format, organization, planning, order, orderliness, symmetry, proportion. **6** *put the mixture into a form* mold, cast, shape, matrix, pattern. **7** *not good form to yawn* manners; behavior, conduct, etiquette, convention, protocol. **8** *the ceremony has followed the same form for years* manner, method, mode, style, system, formula, set formula, procedure, convention, custom, ritual, protocol, etiquette; rules.

**formal** adjective **1** *formal documents/procedures* official, set, fixed, conventional, standard, regular, customary, prescribed, pro forma. **2** *a formal dinner* ceremonial, ceremonious, ritualistic, elaborate, ritual. **3** *a formal manner* reserved, aloof, remote, correct, proper, conventional, precise, exact, punctilious, stiff, unbending. **4** *a formal garden* symmetrical, regular, orderly, arranged, methodical.

**formality** noun **1** *dislike the formality of the occasion* conventionality, ceremoniousness, ritual, decorum, etiquette, protocol. **2** *obey the formalities* rule, convention, custom, procedure; form, punctilio.

**formation** noun **1** *planes flying in formation* configuration, format, structure, organization, order, arrangement, pattern, design, disposition, grouping, layout. **2** *the formation of the new buildings/government* construction, building, erecting, fashioning, shaping, setting up, establishment, institution, creation.

**former** adjective **1** *the former ruler* ex-, previous, prior, preceding, precedent, foregoing, earlier, one-time, erstwhile, sometime. **2** *in former times* earlier, past, bygone, ancient, of yore.

**formidable** adjective **1** *a formidable appearance* intimidating, redoubtable, daunting, alarming, frightening, terrifying, dreadful, awesome, fearsome, menacing, dangerous. **2** *a formidable task* arduous, onerous, difficult, tough, challenging, overwhelming, staggering; *inf.* mind-boggling, mind-blowing. **3** *a formidable opponent* strong, powerful, mighty, impressive, redoubtable.

**formula** noun recipe, prescription, rubric, blueprint, method, procedure, convention, ritual, modus operandi; principles, rules, precepts.

**formulate** verb **1** *formulate one's thoughts in plain English* define, articulate, set down, frame, specify, particularize, itemize, detail, designate, systematize, indicate. **2** *formulate our plans* work out, map out, conceive, create, invent, originate, coin, design. *See* FORM *verb* 2.

**forsake** verb **1** *forsake his wife and children* desert, abandon, leave, leave in the lurch, quit, throw over, jilt, cast off, discard, repudiate, reject, disown; *inf.* leave flat, give someone the air. **2** *forsake her life of luxury* give up, renounce, relinquish, forgo, turn one's back on, repudiate, have done with, discard, set aside.

**fort** noun fortress, stronghold, citadel, garrison, castle, tower, keep, turret, fortification, redoubt, battlement.

**forte** noun strong point, strength, métier, specialty, talent, skill, gift, bent; *inf.* bag, thing.

**forth** adverb **1** *from that day forth* onward, forward. **2** *go forth from the tent* out, outside, away, off.

**forthcoming** adjective **1** *forthcoming events* future, coming, approaching, expected, prospective, imminent, impending. **2** *no reply was forthcoming* available, ready, at hand, accessible; *inf.* on tap. **3** *the children are not very forthcoming* communicative, talkative, expansive, voluble, chatty, conversational, loquacious, open, unreserved.

**forthright** adjective direct, frank, candid, blunt, outspoken, plain-speaking, plain-spoken, straightforward, open, honest.

**forthwith** adverb right away, immediately, at once, this instant, straightaway.

**fortification** noun **1** *the fortification of the walls* strengthening, reinforcement, bracing. **2** *soldiers manning the fortifications* battlement, rampart, bastion, bulwark, parapet, blockhouse, stronghold, stockade, outwork.

**fortify** verb **1** *fortify the town* garrison, embattle, guard, cover, protect, secure. **2** *fortify the walls* strengthen, reinforce, shore up, brace, buttress. **3** *fortify himself with a drink* invigorate, energize, revive, embolden, encourage, cheer, hearten, buoy up.

**fortitude** noun strength, firmness of purpose, backbone, grit, mettle, courage, nerve, pluck, bravery, fearlessness, valor, intrepidity, stoutheartedness, endurance, tenacity, perseverance, resoluteness.

**fortress** noun stronghold, citadel. *See* FORT.

**fortuitous** adjective chance, unexpected, unanticipated, unforeseen, serendipitous, random, accidental, unintentional, unplanned; lucky, fortunate, felicitous; *inf.* fluky.

**fortunate** adjective **1** *a fortunate person* lucky, in luck, favored, blessed, born under a lucky star, having a charmed life, prosperous, well-off, successful, flourishing; *inf.* sitting pretty. **2** *a fortunate position* advantageous, favorable, helpful, auspicious, propitious, opportune, felicitous, profitable.

**fortune** noun **1** *a merchant of great fortune* wealth, treasure, affluence, opulence, prosperity, substance, property; riches, assets, means, possessions, estates. **2** *the ring cost a fortune* mint, king's ransom; *inf.* packet, bundle, bomb, pile. **3** *by good fortune he won* chance, accident, coincidence, fortuity, serendipity, luck, providence. **4** *tell one's fortune* destiny, fate, lot, cup, portion, kismet; stars. **5** *fortune smiled on him* Lady Luck, Dame Fortune, fate.

**fortune-teller** noun seer, soothsayer, prophet, prophetess, augur, diviner, sibyl, oracle, clairvoyant, psychic, prognosticator; astrologer, palm reader, phrenologist; *inf.* stargazer.

**forum** noun meeting, assembly, symposium, round-table conference, debate, discussion place, discussion medium.

**forward** adjective **1** *a forward movement* onward, advancing, progressing, progressive. **2** *forward for her age* advanced, well-advanced, early, premature, precocious. **3** *a forward young woman* bold, brash, brazen, audacious, presumptuous, overassertive, overweening, aggressive, impudent; *inf.* pushy, cocky, fresh.

**forward** adverb **1** *move forward* frontward, onward, on, ahead, forth. **2** *step forward for the prize* out, forth, into view, into the open.

**foster** verb **1** *foster freedom of thought* encourage, promote, further, stimulate, boost, advance, forward, cultivate, foment, help, aid, assist, support, uphold, back, give backing to, facilitate. **2** *foster a child* bring up, rear, raise, care for, take care of, mother, parent. **3** *foster hopes of being rich* cherish, harbor, entertain, nurse, nourish, nurture, hold, sustain.

**foul** adjective **1** *that drink looks foul* disgusting, revolting, repulsive, nauseating, sickening, loathsome, abominable, odious, offensive, nasty. **2** *that cheese smells foul* evil-smelling, ill-smelling, stinking, fetid, rank, mephitic. **3** *foul water* contaminated, polluted, adulterated, infected, tainted, defiled, impure, filthy, dirty, unclean. **4** *foul carcasses* rotten, rotting, decayed, decomposed, putrid, putrescent, putrefactive. **5** *foul language* foul-mouthed, blasphemous, profane, obscene, vulgar, gross, coarse, filthy, dirty, indecent, indelicate, suggestive, smutty, blue, off-color, low, lewd, ribald, salacious, scatological. **6** *he's a foul creature* horrible, detestable, abhorrent, loathsome, hateful, despicable, contemptible, abominable, offensive, odious, disgusting, revolting, dishonorable, disgraceful, base, low, mean, sordid, vile, wicked, vicious, heinous, execrable, iniquitous, nefarious, notorious, infamous, scandalous, egregious. **7** *foul play by their competitors* unfair, unjust, dishonorable, dishonest, underhand, underhanded, unsportsmanlike, unsporting, unscrupulous, unprincipled, immoral, crooked, fraudulent, dirty; *inf.* shady. **8** *foul clothes* dirty, filthy, unwashed, soiled, grimy, grubby, stained, dirt-encrusted, muddied. **9** *foul weather* nasty, disagreeable, bad, rough, wild, stormy, rainy, wet, blustery, foggy, murky, gloomy.

**foul** verb dirty, soil, stain, blacken, defile, pollute, contaminate, taint, sully. **foul up** ruin, spoil, bungle, mismanage, mishandle, botch (up), mess up, make a mess of; *inf.* blow, screw up, louse up.

**found** verb **1** *found a new company* establish, set up, institute, originate, initiate, create, start, inaugurate, constitute, endow, organize, develop. **2** *his story was founded on rumors* base, ground, construct, build, rest.

**foundation** noun **1** *the foundation of the building* base, bottom, bedrock, substruc-

ture, substratum, understructure, underpinning. **2** *lay the foundations of mathematics* basis, groundwork; principles, fundamentals, rudiments. **3** *the foundation of the company* founding, establishing, setting up, institution, initiation, inauguration, constitution, endowment.

**founder** noun builder, constructor, maker, establisher, institutor, initiator, beginner, inventor, discoverer, framer, designer, architect, creator, author, originator, organizer, developer, generator, prime mover, father, patriarch.

**founder** verb **1** *ships foundered* sink, submerge, go down, be lost at sea, capsize, run aground, be swamped; *inf.* go to Davy Jones's locker. **2** *plans foundered* fail, fall through, break down, go awry, misfire, come to nothing, miscarry, abort, flounder, collapse; *inf.* come a cropper. **3** *the horse foundered* stumble, trip, stagger, lurch, fall, topple, sprawl, go lame, collapse.

**fracas** noun disturbance, quarrel, altercation, fight, brawl, affray, row, rumpus, scuffle, tussle, skirmish, free-for-all, brouhaha, melee, donnybrook, riot, uproar, commotion; trouble, tumult, turmoil, pandemonium.

**fractious** adjective **1** *fractious children* cross, irritable, peevish, petulant, ill-humored, querulous, testy, snappish, touchy. **2** *the fractious element on the committee* unruly, rebellious, insubordinate, contrary, refractory, unmanageable, intractable.

**fracture** noun **1** *a bone fracture* breaking, breakage, splitting, cleavage, rupture; break, crack, split. **2** *a fracture in the rock* fissure, cleft, rift, slit, rent, chink, crevice, gap, opening, aperture.

**fracture** verb break, crack, split, splinter, rupture.

**fragile** adjective breakable, brittle, frangible, splintery, frail, insubstantial, delicate, dainty.

**fragment** noun **1** *fragments of glass from the bowl* piece, part, particle, chip, chink, shard, sliver, splinter, smithereen. **2** *a fragment of cloth* scrap, bit, snip, snippet, wisp, tatter. **3** *the fragments of a book* remnant, remainder, fraction; remains, shreds.

**fragmentary** adjective incomplete, disconnected, disjointed, broken, discontinuous, incoherent, sketchy, unsystematic.

**fragrance** noun **1** *the fragrance of the roses* scent, perfume, bouquet, aroma, smell, redolence. **2** *a bottle of fragrance* scent, perfume, toilet water; cologne, eau de cologne.

**fragrant** adjective scented, perfumed, aromatic, sweet-smelling, redolent, balmy, odoriferous.

**frail** adjective **1** *frail china* fragile, breakable, frangible, delicate. **2** *frail old ladies* infirm, weak, slight, slender, puny, unsound, ill, ailing. **3** *frail creatures* easily led/tempted, susceptible, impressionable, vulnerable, fallible.

**frailty** noun **1** *the frailty of the china* fragility, brittleness, frangibility, flimsiness, insubstantiality, delicacy, daintiness, fineness. **2** *the frailty of the old* infirmity, weakness, delicacy, slightness, puniness, illness. **3** *the frailty of human nature* weakness, susceptibility, impressionability, vulnerability, fallibility; foible, weak point, flaw, blemish, defect, failing, fault, shortcoming, deficiency, peccadillo.

**frame** noun **1** *a frame of steel* framework, substructure, structure, shell, casing, support, skeleton, scaffolding, foundation, body, chassis. **2** *the man had a huge frame* body, physique, build, figure, shape, size, skeleton, carcass. **3** *alter the frame of society* order, organization, scheme, system, plan, fabric, form, constitution. **4** *a sad frame of mind* state, condition; mood, humor, temper, spirit, attitude.

**frame** verb **1** *frame the structure* assemble, build, construct, erect, elevate, fashion, mold, shape, forge. **2** *frame a policy* put together, formulate, draw up, plan, draft, map/plot/sketch out, shape, compose, form, devise, create, establish, conceive, think up, hatch; *inf.* dream up, cook up. **3** *frame a picture | hair framing his face* enclose, encase, surround.

**framework** noun **1** *the framework of the building* shell, skeleton. *See* FRAME noun 1. **2** *the framework of society* order, organization. *See* FRAME noun 3.

**frank** adjective **1** *a frank person/reply* candid, direct, forthright, plain, plainspoken, straight, straight from the shoulder, downright, explicit, outspoken, blunt, bluff, open, sincere, honest, guileless, artless. **2** *show frank admiration* open, obvious, transparent, patent, manifest, undisguised, unconcealed, unmistakable, evident.

**frantic** adjective frenzied, wild, hysterical, frenetic, distraught, overwrought, panicky, beside oneself, at one's wits' end, worked up, distracted, agitated, distressed, out of control.

**fraternity** noun brotherhood, kinship; club, society, association, guild, set, circle.

**fraud** noun **1** *found guilty of fraud* fraudulence, cheating, swindling, trickery, deceit, double-dealing, duplicity, treachery, chicanery, skulduggery, imposture, embezzlement, crookedness; *inf.* monkey business. **2** *perpetrate a fraud* ruse, trick, hoax, deception, subterfuge, stratagem, wile, artifice, swindle; *inf.* con, rip-off. **3** *the man is a fraud* impostor, fake, sham,

trickster, pretender, charlatan; *inf.* phony, quack, con man. **4** *the vase is a fraud* fake, sham, counterfeit, forgery; *inf.* phony.

**fraudulent** adjective dishonest, cheating, swindling, criminal, deceitful, double-dealing, duplicitous, dishonorable, unscrupulous; *inf.* crooked, shady.

**freak** noun **1** *that animal is a freak* freak of nature, aberration, abnormality, irregularity, oddity, monster, monstrosity, malformation, mutant. **2** *the neighbors think he's a bit of a freak* oddity; *inf.* queer fish, oddball, weirdo, nutcase. **3** *sci-fi freaks* enthusiast, fan, fanatic, addict, aficionado, devotee; *inf.* buff, fiend, nut. **4** *the storm was a freak* anomaly, quirk; *inf.* fluke.

**freak** adjective abnormal, unusual, atypical, aberrant, exceptional, bizarre, queer, odd; *inf.* fluky.

**free** adjective **1** *a free booklet* free of charge, for nothing, complimentary, gratis, without charge, at no cost; *inf.* for free, on the house. **2** *he is free today* unoccupied, available, not busy, not tied up, idle, at leisure, with time on one's hands. **3** *is this seat free?* empty, vacant, available, spare, unoccupied, untaken, uninhabited, tenantless. **4** *a free nation* independent, self-governing, self-governed, self-ruling, self-directing, sovereign, autonomous, democratic, emancipated, enfranchised, manumitted. **5** *the animals are free* at liberty, at large, loose, on the loose, unconfined, unbound, untied, unchained, unshackled, unfettered, unrestrained, wild. **6** *free to choose* able, allowed, permitted, unrestricted. **7** *a free flow of water* unobstructed, unimpeded, unhampered, clear, unblocked. **8** *the free end of the rope* not fixed, unattached, unfastened, loose. **9** *free with their money* generous, lavish, liberal, openhanded, unstinting, giving, munificent, bountiful, bounteous, charitable, extravagant, prodigal. **10** *a free manner* free and easy, easygoing, natural, open, frank, relaxed, casual, informal, unceremonious, unforced, spontaneous, uninhibited, artless, ingenuous; *inf.* laid-back. **free of** without, devoid of, sans, exempt from, clear of, unencumbered by.

**free** verb **1** *free the prisoners/animals* set free, release, let go, set at liberty, liberate, set/let/turn loose, untie, unchain, unfetter, unshackle, unmanacle, uncage, unleash, deliver. **2** *free the accident victims from the car* extricate, disentangle, disengage, disencumber. **3** *freed from paying tax* exempt, make exempt, except, excuse, relieve.

**freedom** noun **1** *colonies seeking their freedom* independence, self-government, sovereignty, autonomy, democracy, emancipation, manumission, enfranchisement, home rule. **2** *prisoners enjoying their freedom* liberty, release, deliverance, nonconfinement. **3** *freedom from tax* exemption, immunity, impunity. **4** *freedom of speech* right, privilege, prerogative. **5** *freedom to move around* scope, latitude, elbowroom, wide margin, flexibility, facility, free rein, license. **6** *admire her freedom of manner* naturalness, openness, casualness, informality, spontaneity, ingenuousness.

**freely** adverb **1** *I speak freely* frankly, openly, candidly, plainly, bluntly, unreservedly. **2** *prisoners not allowed to speak freely* of one's own volition/accord, voluntarily.

**freight** noun transportation, conveyance, freightage, carriage, portage, haulage; cargo, load, lading, consignment, merchandise; goods.

**frenzy** noun **1** *go into a frenzy at the news* wildness, hysteria, distraction, agitation; madness, mania, insanity; fit. **2** *a frenzy of activity* bout, outburst, fit.

**frequent** adjective recurrent, repeated, persistent, continuing, many, numerous; regular, habitual, customary, common, usual, familiar, everyday.

**frequent** verb visit, attend, haunt, patronize; *inf.* hang out at.

**fresh** adjective **1** *is the fruit fresh?* garden-fresh, newly harvested, crisp, unwilted, unfaded. **2** *fresh fruit, not canned* raw, natural, unprocessed, unpreserved, undried, uncured, crude. **3** *fresh ideas* new, innovative, original, novel, unusual, unconventional, unorthodox. **4** *feeling fresh and alive* energetic, vigorous, invigorated, refreshed, rested, restored, revived, like a new person, fresh as a daisy; *inf.* full of vim/beans, raring to go, bright-eyed and bushy-tailed, chipper. **5** *a fresh complexion* healthy-looking, healthy, clear, bright, youthful-looking, wholesome, glowing, fair, rosy, pink, reddish, ruddy. **6** *curtains looking fresh* bright, clean, spick-and-span, unfaded. **7** *fresh supplies* more, other, additional, further, extra, supplementary, auxiliary. **8** *fresh air* pure, unpolluted, clean, refreshing. **9** *fresh winds* cool, chilly, brisk, bracing, invigorating. **10** *fresh recruits* untrained, inexperienced, untried, raw, callow, green, immature, artless, ingenuous, naïve; *inf.* wet behind the ears. **11** *a fresh young man* familiar, overfamiliar, presumptuous, forward, bold, audacious, brazen, impudent, impertinent, insolent, disrespectful; *inf.* cocky.

**freshen** verb **1** *a walk will freshen you | the swim freshened her up* refresh, rouse, stimulate, revitalize, restore, revive, liven up. **2** *freshen the room* air, ventilate, deodorize, purify. **freshen up** wash, wash up, tidy/spruce oneself up.

**fret** verb worry, agonize, anguish, be distressed, be upset, be anxious, pine, brood, mope.

**fretful** adjective peevish, petulant, out of sorts, irritable, bad-tempered, ill-natured, grumpy, crotchety, touchy, captious, testy, querulous, cranky.

**friction** noun **1** *ropes worn by friction* rubbing, abrading, abrasion, attrition, chafing, gnawing, grating, rasping, scraping, excoriation. **2** *cause friction in the family* dissension, dissent, disagreement, discord, strife, conflict, clashing, contention, quarreling, bickering, squabbling, wrangling, hostility, animosity, antagonism, bad feeling, ill feeling, bad blood, disharmony.

**friend** noun companion, crony, comrade, playmate, soul mate, intimate, confidante, confidant, familiar, alter ego, ally, associate; *inf.* pal, chum, buddy.

**friendly** adjective **1** *a friendly person* affable, amiable, warm, genial, agreeable, companionable, cordial, convivial, sociable, hospitable, comradely, neighborly, outgoing, approachable, accessible, communicative, kindly, amenable, sympathetic; *inf.* chummy, buddy-buddy. **2** *on friendly terms* amicable, congenial, cordial, familiar, peaceable, peaceful, conciliatory. **3** *a friendly wind* helpful, favorable, advantageous.

**friendship** noun **1** *their friendship lasted years* companionship, intimacy, amity, affinity, rapport, harmony, comradeship, fellowship, attachment, alliance. **2** *she always shows friendship to new people* friendliness, affability, amiability, warmth, geniality, cordiality, neighborliness, good-naturedness, kindliness.

**fright** noun **1** *start back in fright* fear, fear and trembling, terror, alarm, horror, dread, fearfulness, apprehension, trepidation, consternation, dismay, perturbation, disquiet, panic, nervousness, jitteriness; scare, shock; shivers; *inf.* jitters, the heebie-jeebies. **2** *you look a fright* eyesore; *inf.* mess, sight.

**frighten** verb scare, alarm, startle, terrify, terrorize, petrify, shock, appall, panic, throw into panic, unnerve, intimidate, cow, daunt, dismay, make one's blood run cold; *inf.* scare the living daylights out of, scare stiff, scare out of one's wits, make one's hair stand on end, make one's hair curl, make someone jump out of his/her skin, spook.

**frightful** adjective **1** *the corpse was a frightful sight* dreadful, terrible, horrible, horrid, hideous, ghastly, grim, dire, abhorrent, revolting, repulsive, loathsome, odious, fearful, fearsome, terrifying, alarming, shocking, harrowing. **2** *a frightful woman* unpleasant, disagreeable, appalling, insufferable, unbearable, annoying, irritating. **3** *a frightful cold* terrible, dreadful, awful, ghastly, nasty.

**frigid** adjective **1** *frigid conditions* bitter, freezing, frozen, icy, frosty, chilly, wintry, arctic, glacial, Siberian, polar. **2** *a frigid welcome* cold, austere, distant, aloof, remote, stiff, formal, cool, unfeeling, unfriendly, hostile.

**frills** plural noun ornamentation, decoration, embellishment, fanciness, ostentation, fuss; trimmings, falderals, affectations, extras, additions, superfluities; *inf.* jazz, flash.

**fringe** noun *on the fringe of the forest* outer edge, edge, borderline, perimeter, periphery, margin, rim; limits, borders, outskirts, verges.

**frisky** adjective lively, bouncy, active, frolicsome, coltish, playful, romping, rollicking, spirited.

**fritter** verb **fritter away** squander, waste, overspend, misspend, spend like water, dissipate, run through, go through, misuse.

**frivolous** adjective **1** *frivolous young girls* giddy, flighty, dizzy, silly, foolish, facetious, zany, lighthearted, merry, superficial, shallow, inane, empty-headed, featherbrained; *inf.* flip. **2** *frivolous details* trivial, trifling, minor, petty, insignificant, unimportant, paltry, niggling, peripheral.

**frolic** verb frisk, gambol, cavort, caper, skip, leap, romp, skylark, prance, rollick.

**frolic** noun **1** *enjoy a frolic in the garden* game, romp, lark, antic, caper, escapade, prank, revel, spree. **2** *the children's frolic* fun, fun and games, gaiety, merriment, mirth, amusement, laughter, jollity; *inf.* high jinks.

**front** noun **1** *the front of the building* fore, forepart, forefront, anterior; frontage, face, facing, façade. **2** *at the front of the line* beginning, head, top, lead. **3** *put on a brave front* look, appearance, face, exterior, air, manner, expression, show, countenance, demeanor, bearing, mien, aspect. **4** *the pawnshop is a front for drug dealing* cover, cover-up, blind, façade, disguise, pretext, mask.

**front** verb *the house fronts on the lake* face toward, look out on, overlook.

**frontier** noun border, boundary, bound, limit, edge, rim.

**frown** verb **1** *frowning at each other* scowl, glower, glare, look daggers at; *inf.* give a dirty look to. **2** *frown at/on sloppy clothes* disapprove of, dislike, discourage, look askance at, not take kindly to, not think much of, take a dim view of.

**frugal** adjective **1** *a frugal old man* thrifty, sparing, economical, saving, provident, unwasteful, abstemious, scrimping, niggardly, penny-pinching, miserly, parsimonious, stingy. **2** *a frugal meal* meager, scanty, paltry, insufficient.

**fruitful** adjective *fruitful discussions* productive, profitable, beneficial, rewarding, gainful, useful, worthwhile, successful, effective.

**fruition** noun fulfillment, realization, materialization, actualization, achievement, attainment, success, completion, consummation, perfection, maturity, maturation, ripening.

**fruitless** adjective futile, vain, in vain, useless, abortive, to no avail, worthless, pointless, to no effect, idle, ineffectual, ineffective, inefficacious, unproductive, unsuccessful, unavailing.

**frustrate** verb **1** *frustrate their attempts* defeat, thwart, check, block, counter, foil, balk, disappoint, forestall, baffle, stymie, stop, spoil, cripple, nullify, obstruct, impede, hamper, hinder, circumvent. **2** *lack of success frustrated him* discourage, dishearten, dispirit, depress, dissatisfy, anger, annoy, vex, irk, irritate, embitter.

**frustration** noun **1** *the frustration of their plans* defeat, thwarting, foiling, balking, forestalling, hampering, circumvention. **2** *full of frustration at their failure* dissatisfaction, disappointment, discontentment, anger, annoyance, irritation, vexation, resentment, bitterness.

**fudge** verb **1** *fudge the issue* evade, dodge, skirt, avoid. **2** *fudge the accounts* falsify, fake; *inf.* cook. **3** *fudge his way through the speech* equivocate, hedge, hem and haw, shuffle.

**fuel** noun **1** *fuel for the furnace/car* coal, wood, oil, gasoline, gas, kerosene. **2** *his answer was fuel to her anger* incitement, provocation, goading, stimulus, incentive, encouragement, ammunition.

**fuel** verb **1** *fuel the steam engine* fire, stoke up, charge, power. **2** *fuel her anger* fan, inflame, incite, provoke, goad, stimulate, encourage.

**fugitive** noun escapee, runaway, deserter, refugee.

**fulfill** verb **1** *fulfill his task* carry out, accomplish, achieve, execute, perform, discharge, implement, complete, bring to completion, finish, conclude, effect, effectuate, perfect. **2** *fulfill his desire* satisfy, realize, attain, consummate. **3** *fulfill the job requirements* fill, answer, meet, obey, comply with, satisfy, conform to, observe.

**full** adjective **1** *the cup is full* filled, filled up, filled to the brim, brimful, brimming, filled to capacity. **2** *the theater was full* crowded, packed, crammed, chock-full; *inf.* jam-packed, wall-to-wall. **3** *dinner guests feeling full* replete, satisfied, sated, gorged, glutted, cloyed. **4** *a full list of names* complete, entire, whole, comprehensive, thorough, exhaustive, detailed, all-inclusive, all-encompassing, extensive, unabridged. **5** *a full program of events* abundant, plentiful, copious, ample, sufficient, broad-ranging, satisfying, complete. **6** *a full figure* well-rounded, rounded, plump, buxom, shapely, curvaceous, voluptuous; *inf.* busty. **7** *a full skirt* loose-fitting, baggy, voluminous, capacious. **8** *a full voice* rich, deep, resonant, loud, strong. **full of** filled with, abounding in, replete with; *inf.* loaded with.

**full-fledged** adjective mature, complete; qualified, official.

**full-scale** adjective thorough, comprehensive, extensive, exhaustive, all-out, all-encompassing, all-inclusive, thoroughgoing, wide-ranging, sweeping, major, in-depth.

**fulsome** adjective excessive, extravagant, overdone, immoderate, inordinate, overappreciative, insincere, ingratiating, fawning, sycophantic, adulatory, cloying, nauseating, sickening, saccharine, unctuous; *inf.* smarmy.

**fumble** verb **1** *fumble for his keys | fumble in the dark* grope, feel about/around, fish (around), search blindly, stumble, blunder, flounder. **2** *fumble her speech* bungle, botch, mismanage, mishandle, muff, spoil; *inf.* make a mess/hash of, fluff, screw up, foul up, flub.

**fume** verb be enraged, seethe, boil, be livid, rage, be furious, be incensed, flare up; *inf.* be up in arms, get hot under the collar, be at boiling point, get all steamed up, blow one's top.

**fumes** plural noun vapor, gas, smoke, exhalation, exhaust, pollution.

**fun** noun amusement, entertainment, relaxation, recreation, enjoyment, pleasure, diversion, distraction, play, good time, merrymaking; merriment, gaiety, mirth, laughter, hilarity, glee, gladness, cheerfulness, joy; zest; high spirits. **in fun** jokingly, as a joke, in jest, for a laugh. **make fun of** ridicule, rag, deride, mock, scoff at, sneer at, taunt, jeer at, parody, lampoon.

**fun** adjective **1** *a fun time* amusing, entertaining, enjoyable, diverting, pleasurable. **2** *a fun person* amusing, witty, entertaining, lively, convivial.

**function** noun **1** *his function in the firm* role, capacity, responsibility, duty, task, chore, job, post, situation, office, occupation,

employment, business, charge, concern, province, part, activity, operation, line, mission. **2** *what is that machine's function?* use, purpose, task. **3** *invited to a function* occasion, affair, gathering, reception, party; *inf.* do.

**function** verb work, go, run, be in working/running order, operate. **function as** serve as, act as, perform, operate as, officiate as, do (the) duty of, have/do the job of, play the role of, act the part of.

**fund** noun **1** *the church preservation fund* reserve, pool, collection, kitty, endowment, foundation, grant, investment, capital; savings. **2** *a fund of knowledge* stock, store, accumulation, mass, mine, reservoir, supply, storehouse, treasury, treasure-house, hoard, repository.

**fund** verb finance, back, pay for, capitalize, subsidize, stake, endow, support, float.

**fundamental** adjective basic, rudimentary, elemental, underlying, primary, cardinal, prime, first, principal, chief, key, central, structural, inherent, intrinsic, vital, essential, important, indispensable, necessary.

**fundamentals** plural noun basics, first/basic principles, essentials, rudiments; crux, crux of the matter, sine qua non; *inf.* nuts and bolts, nitty-gritty.

**funds** plural noun money, ready money, cash, hard cash, capital, the wherewithal; means, assets, resources, savings; *inf.* dough, bread, the ready.

**funny** adjective **1** *a funny story/person* amusing, comic, comical, humorous, hilarious, entertaining, diverting, laughable, hysterical, riotous, sidesplitting, droll, absurd, rich, ridiculous, ludicrous, risible, witty, waggish, jocular, farcical, silly, slapstick. **2** *what a funny hat* strange, peculiar, odd, queer, weird, bizarre, curious. **3** *there's something funny going on* mysterious, suspicious, dubious; *inf.* shady.

**furious** adjective **1** *furious parents* enraged, raging, infuriated, fuming, boiling, incensed, inflamed, indignant, mad, raving mad, maddened, wrathful, beside oneself, in high dudgeon; *inf.* livid, hot under the collar, up in arms. **2** *a furious struggle* violent, fierce, intense, vehement, tumultuous, turbulent.

**furnish** verb fit out, outfit, supply, equip, provide, provision, give, grant, present, offer, bestow on, endow.

**furor** noun **1** *a furor when they found out* commotion, uproar, disturbance, hullabaloo, turmoil, tempest, tumult, brouhaha, stir, excitement, to-do, outburst, outcry. **2** *in a furor* rage, madness, frenzy, fit.

**furrow** noun **1** groove, trench, channel, rut, trough, hollow, ditch, seam. **2** *furrows on her brow/skin* crease, line, wrinkle, corrugation, crinkle, crow's foot.

**further** verb advance, forward, promote, back, contribute to, encourage, foster, champion.

**furthermore** adverb moreover, what's more, additionally, on top of that, over and above that.

**furtive** adjective secret, secretive, stealthy, surreptitious, sneaky, sneaking, skulking, slinking, clandestine, hidden, covert, cloaked, under the table.

**fury** noun **1** *the fury of the parents* rage, ire, wrath, furor. **2** *the fury of the storm* fierceness, ferocity, violence, turbulence, tempestuousness, intensity, vehemence, force, power, potency. **3** *she is a real fury* virago, hellcat, termagant, spitfire, vixen, shrew, hag.

**fuse** verb **1** *fuse the ingredients* blend, intermix, intermingle, merge, meld, coalesce, compound, join, integrate, weld, solder. **2** *fuse the solid* melt, melt down, smelt, dissolve, liquefy.

**fuss** noun **1** *the fuss over the preparations* fluster, flurry, bustle, to-do, ado, agitation, excitement, bother, stir, commotion, confusion, tumult, uproar, upset, worry, overanxiety; *inf.* tempest in a teacup, much ado about nothing, flap, tizzy, stew. **2** *a fuss in the bar last night* row, altercation, squabble, quarrel, dispute, upset; trouble, bother, unrest.

**fuss** verb **1** *tell the organizers to stop fussing* | *fuss over details* bustle, bustle about, dash about, rush about, tear around, buzz around; worry, be agitated/worried, make a big thing out of nothing, make a mountain out of a molehill; *inf.* get worked up over nothing, be in a tizzy, be in a stew. **2** *fuss about the service* kick up a fuss, complain, raise an objection; *inf.* grouse, gripe.

**fussy** adjective particular, overparticular, finicky, persnickety, fastidious, hard to please, difficult, exacting, demanding, discriminating, selective, dainty; *inf.* choosy, picky, nitpicking.

**futile** adjective **1** *a futile search* vain, in vain, to no avail, unavailing, useless, ineffectual, ineffective, inefficacious, unsuccessful, fruitless, unproductive, unprofitable. **2** *a futile statement* trivial, unimportant, petty, trifling, valueless, worthless, inconsequential, idle.

**fuzzy** adjective **1** *fuzzy hair* | *a fuzzy peach* frizzy, downy, down-covered, woolly, linty. **2** *everything's gone all fuzzy* out of focus, blurred, blurry, bleary, misty, indistinct, unclear, distorted. **3** *fuzzy recollection* confused, muddled, befuddled, foggy, misty, shadowy.

# Gg

**gadget** noun appliance, apparatus, instrument, implement, tool, contrivance, device, mechanism, invention; *inf.* contraption, widget, gizmo.

**gag** noun *his gags amused her* joke, jest, witticism, quip; *inf.* wisecrack, crack.

**gag** verb **1** *gag his mouth* stop up, block, plug, clog, stifle, smother, muffle. **2** *the press have been gagged* silence, muzzle, curb, check, restrain, suppress, repress. **3** *he gagged when he saw the corpse* choke, retch, gasp, vomit.

**gaiety** noun **1** *the gaiety of the children* merriment, glee, blitheness, gladness, happiness, high spirits, good spirits, delight, joy, joyousness, exuberance, elation, mirth, joviality, liveliness, vivacity, animation, effervescence, buoyancy, *joie de vivre*. **2** *join in the gaiety of the fair* fun, festivity, merrymaking, revelry, revels, celebration. **3** *the gaiety of the dresses* colorfulness, brightness, brilliance, sparkle, glitter, showiness.

**gain** verb **1** *gain an advantage* obtain, get, acquire, procure, secure, attain, build up, achieve, arrive at, come to have, win, capture, net, pick up, reap, gather. **2** *gain a wage* earn, bring in, make, get, clear, gross, net, realize. **gain on 1** *the police were gaining on the escaped prisoner* catch up with, close in on, overtake. **2** *the escaped prisoner was gaining on the police* leave behind, draw away from, outdistance, do better than. **gain time** stall, procrastinate, delay, temporize.

**gain** noun **1** *his gain from the deal was negligible* profit, earnings, income, advantage, benefit, reward, emolument, yield, return, winnings, proceeds, dividend, interest. **2** *a gain in experience/weight* increase, augmentation, addition, rise, increment, accretion, accumulation. **3** *their gain against the enemy* advance, advancement, progress, forward movement, headway, improvement, step forward.

**gait** noun walk, step, stride, pace, tread, bearing, carriage.

**gala** noun festival, fête, festivities, carnival, pageant, jamboree, party, celebration.

**gala** adjective *a gala occasion* festive, celebratory, merry, gay, joyous, joyful, jovial, entertaining, spectacular, showy, ceremonial, ceremonious.

**gall** noun **1** *have the gall to answer back* impudence, insolence, impertinence, nerve, audacity, brashness, effrontery, temerity; *inf.* brass, chutzpah. **2** *words full of gall* bitterness, resentment, rancor, acrimony, malice, spite, venom, sourness, acerbity, animus, bile, spleen.

**gall** verb **1** *gall the skin* abrade, chafe, rub, rub raw, scrape, excoriate, bark. **2** *her attitude galls him* vex, irritate, irk, annoy, rub the wrong way, exasperate, rile, bother, rankle; *inf.* aggravate, peeve.

**gallant** adjective **1** *gallant soldiers* brave, courageous, valiant, valorous, bold, plucky, daring, fearless, intrepid, manly, manful, dashing, heroic, lionhearted, stouthearted, doughty, mettlesome. **2** *gallant to the ladies* chivalrous, gentlemanly, courtly, courteous, mannerly, polite, attentive, gracious. **3** *a gallant ship* dignified, stately, noble, elegant, majestic, imposing, glorious, regal, august.

**gallop** verb canter, lope, run, race, rush, dash, tear, sprint, bolt, fly, shoot, dart, hurry, hasten, speed, career, scamper, scurry, zoom.

**gamble** verb **1** *he loves to gamble* bet, wager, place a bet, lay a wager/bet, game, try one's luck; *inf.* play the ponies. **2** *he gambled when he invested in that firm* take a chance, take a risk, speculate, venture, buy a pig in a poke; *inf.* stick one's neck out, go out on a limb.

**gamble** noun risk, hazard, chance, lottery, speculation, venture, pig in a poke.

**gambol** verb frolic, frisk, cavort, caper, skip, dance, leap, romp, hop, jump, rollick.

**game** noun **1** *children's games* pastime, diversion, entertainment, amusement, recreation, play, sport, distraction. **2** *we were only playing a game on him* joke, practical joke, prank, jest, trick, hoax. **3** *there's a game tomorrow* match, contest, tournament, meet, round, bout. **4** *he's in the oil game* business, line, occupation, trade, profession, industry, enterprise, activity, calling. **5** *what's his game?* scheme, trick, plot, ploy, stratagem. **6** *they went shooting game* wild animals, wild fowl, quarry, prey,

big game. **make game of** make fun of, ridicule, deride, mock, make sport of.

**game** adjective **1** *who's game enough to knock at her door?* plucky, brave, courageous, unafraid, fearless, bold, daring. **2** *I'm game to go if you are* willing, ready, prepared, disposed.

**gamut** noun entire range, whole spectrum, complete scale, whole series, full sweep, full compass, entire scope.

**gang** noun **1** *a gang of people gathered* group, band, crowd, company, gathering, pack, horde, mob, herd. **2** *the young man and his gang* clique, circle, social set, coterie, lot, ring, club; fraternity, sorority; *inf.* crew. **3** *gang of workers* crew, squad, team, troop, shift, detachment, posse, troupe.

**gangster** noun racketeer, bandit, brigand, robber, ruffian, thug, hoodlum, tough, desperado, Mafioso, terrorist; *inf.* crook, mobster, hood.

**gap** noun **1** *a gap in the wall* opening, cavity, hole, aperture, space, breach, orifice, break, fracture, rift, rent, fissure, cleft, chink, crack, crevice, cranny, divide, interstice. **2** *gaps in the program* pause, intermission, interval, interlude, break, recess. **3** *gaps in his account* omission, blank, hole, void. **4** *the gap between the old and the young* breach, difference, divergence, disparity.

**gape** verb **1** *gape at the procession* stare, stare in wonder, gaze, ogle; *inf.* gawk, rubberneck. **2** *the chasm gaped before them* open wide, yawn, part, crack, split.

**garb** noun **1** *admire the fine garb | the garb of a soldier* clothes, clothing, garments, dress, attire, apparel, costume, outfit, wear, habit, uniform, array, habiliment, vestments, livery, trappings; style, fashion, look; *inf.* gear, get-up, togs, duds. **2** *wearing the garb of sanity* appearance, guise, exterior, aspect, semblance, look.

**garbage** noun **1** *put the garbage out* trash, waste, rubbish, refuse, debris, detritus, litter, junk; swill, scraps, leftovers, remains, slops. **2** *talk a lot of garbage* nonsense, rubbish, twaddle, drivel, foolishness, balderdash; *inf.* hogwash, poppycock, rot.

**garble** verb mix up, jumble, confuse, distort, twist, warp, slant, mutilate, tamper with, doctor, falsify, pervert, corrupt, adulterate, misstate, misquote.

**gargantuan** adjective gigantic, giant, enormous, monstrous, huge, colossal, vast, immense, tremendous, massive, hulking, towering, mammoth, prodigious, elephantine, mountainous, monumental, titanic; *inf.* jumbo, humongous, whopping.

**garish** adjective flashy, loud, showy, gaudy, glaring, flaunting, bold-colored, glittering, tinselly, brassy, tawdry, raffish, tasteless, in bad taste, vulgar, cheap, flashy.

**garland** noun wreath, festoon, lei, laurel, laurels, coronet, crown, circlet, chaplet, fillet, headband.

**garment** noun clothes, clothing. See GARB 1.

**garner** verb gather, collect, accumulate, heap, pile up, amass, assemble, stack up, store, lay by, put/stow away, hoard, stockpile.

**garnish** verb decorate, adorn, trim, ornament, embellish, deck, deck out, bedeck, festoon, enhance, grace, beautify, prettify, set off, add the finishing touch to.

**garrison** noun 1 *the garrison arrived at the fort* platoon, brigade, squadron; troops, militia, soldiers. 2 *the garrison was under siege* fort, fortress, fortification, stronghold, blockhouse, citadel, camp, encampment, command post, base, station; barracks.

**garrulous** adjective 1 *a garrulous old man* talkative, chatty, chattering, gossiping, loquacious, voluble, verbose, long-winded, babbling, prattling, prating, blathering, jabbering, gushing, effusive; *inf.* mouthy, gabby. 2 *a garrulous account* long-winded, wordy, verbose, rambling, prolix, diffuse.

**gash** noun cut, slash, wound, tear, laceration, gouge, incision, slit, split, nick, cleft.

**gasp** verb pant, puff, blow, catch one's breath, gulp, choke, fight for breath, wheeze, huff and puff.

**gather** verb 1 *people gathered in the church | gather the children* come together, collect, assemble, congregate, meet, group, cluster together, crowd, mass, flock together, convene, converge; call together, summon, round up, muster, marshal. 2 *gather cans of food* get/put together, accumulate, amass, garner, store, stockpile, heap up, pile up, stack up, hoard; *inf.* stash away. 3 *the event gathered a huge audience* attract, draw, pull, pull in. 4 *we gather that he is dead* infer, deduce, conclude, assume, surmise. 5 *gather to one's bosom* embrace, clasp, enfold, hold, hug, cuddle. 6 *gather the harvest* harvest, collect, pick, pluck, cull, garner, crop, reap, glean. 7 *gather in strength* increase, grow, rise, build, expand, enlarge, swell, extend, wax, intensify. 8 *gather the waist of the dress* ruffle, shirr, pleat, pucker, tuck, fold.

**gathering** noun 1 *a gathering of people* assembly, assemblage, collection, company, congregation, group, party, band, knot, crowd, flock, throng, mass, mob, horde, meeting, meet, convention, conclave, rally. 2 *his gathering of coins* collection, accumulation, assemblage, aggregation, aggregate, mass, store, stock, stockpile, heap, pile, cluster, conglomeration, concentration.

**gauche** adjective awkward, socially inept, lacking in social graces, inelegant, unpolished, unsophisticated.

**gaudy** adjective garish, loud, glaring, flashy, showy, ostentatious, tawdry, raffish, tasteless, vulgar, cheap.

**gauge** verb 1 *gauge the thickness of the metal* measure, calculate, compute, count, weigh. 2 *you must gauge his aptitude* evaluate, appraise, assess, judge, rate, reckon, determine.

**gauge** noun 1 *find a gauge of his abilities* measure, basis, standard, guide, guideline, touchstone, yardstick, benchmark, criterion, rule, norm, example. 2 *the gauge of a barrel/railroad* area, size, measure, capacity, magnitude, depth, height, width, thickness, span, bore.

**gaunt** adjective 1 *illness had left her gaunt* haggard, drawn, cadaverous, skeletal, emaciated, bony, angular, rawboned, hollow-cheeked, starved-looking, scrawny, scraggy, shriveled, wasted, withered. 2 *gaunt landscape* bleak, barren, bare, desolate, dreary, dismal, forlorn, grim, stern, harsh, forbidding.

**gawky** adjective ungainly, ungraceful, uncoordinated, lanky, clumsy, lumbering, maladroit, oafish, loutish.

**gay** adjective 1 *feeling gay* lighthearted, cheerful, mirthful, jovial, glad, happy, bright, in good spirits, in high spirits, joyful, elated, exuberant. 2 *have a gay time* merry, festive, amusing, enjoyable, entertaining, convivial, hilarious. 3 *gay colors* bright, vivid, brilliant, multicolored, flamboyant, gaudy. 4 *gay men/women* homosexual, lesbian; *derog. inf.* queer, limp-wristed, butch.

**gaze** verb stare, stand agog, watch in wonder, ogle, eye, take a good look, contemplate; *inf.* gawk, rubberneck, give the once-over.

**gear** noun 1 *the steering gear of a boat* gears, mechanism, machinery, works. 2 *the workman's gear* equipment, tools, implements, tackle, appliances, contrivances, utensils, supplies, accoutrements, trappings, accessories, paraphernalia; *inf.* stuff. 3 *wearing modern gear* clothes, dress. See GARB 1. 4 *their daughter and all her gear* belongings, things, luggage, baggage, effects, paraphernalia, accoutrements, possessions, trappings; *inf.* stuff.

**general** adjective 1 *the general practice* usual, customary, common, ordinary, normal, standard, regular, typical, conventional, everyday, habitual, run-of-the-mill. 2 *in general use* common, extensive, widespread, broad, wide, accepted, prevalent, prevailing, universal, popular, public, generic. 3 *a general tax hike/rule* across-the-board, blanket, universal, sweeping, broad, broad-ranging, comprehensive, all-inclusive, encyclopedic, indiscriminate, catholic. **4** *his general knowledge* mixed, assorted, miscellaneous, variegated, diversified, composite, heterogeneous. **5** *a general account* loose, approximate, unspecific, vague, indefinite, imprecise, rough.

**generally** adverb **1** *it generally rains there in the spring* usually, as a rule, normally, ordinarily, customarily, habitually, typically, for the most part, on the whole, in most cases. **2** *not generally known* commonly, widely, extensively, comprehensively, universally. **3** *speaking generally* loosely, approximately, broadly. **4** *they are generally liked* mostly, mainly, in the main, largely, chiefly.

**generate** verb **1** *generate children* beget, procreate, engender, sire, father, breed, spawn, produce, propagate. **2** *generate an argument* cause, give rise to, create, produce, initiate, originate, occasion, sow the seeds of.

**generic** adjective general, common, collective, inclusive, all-inclusive, all-encompassing, comprehensive, blanket, sweeping, universal.

**generosity** noun **1** *the generosity of our host* liberalness, liberality, kindness, magnanimity, benevolence, beneficence, bounteousness, bounty, munificence, hospitality, charitableness, charity, openhandedness, lavishness. **2** *the generosity of his spirit* nobility, nobleness, magnanimity, loftiness, high-mindedness, honorableness, honor, goodness, unselfishness.

**generous** adjective **1** *generous with money | a generous host* liberal, kind, benevolent, beneficent, bountiful, bounteous, munificent, hospitable, charitable, openhanded, lavish, ungrudging, unstinting. **2** *a generous spirit* noble, magnanimous, lofty, high-minded, honorable, good, unselfish, altruistic, unprejudiced, disinterested. **3** *a generous supply of caviar* abundant, plentiful, lavish, ample, copious, overflowing.

**genesis** noun beginning, commencement, start, outset, birth, origin, source, root, creation, engendering, inception, generation, propagation.

**genial** adjective amiable, affable, good-humored, good-natured, warm, cordial, amenable, friendly, congenial, amicable, sociable, convivial, kind, kindly.

**genius** noun **1** *the boy is a genius* virtuoso, prodigy, master, mastermind, maestro, intellectual, intellect, expert; *inf.* brains, mental giant, Einstein. **2** *a person of genius* brilliance, intellect, cleverness, brains. **3** *a genius for cooking* gift, talent, flair, bent, knack, aptitude, faculty, ability, capability.

**genteel** adjective **1** *living in genteel surroundings* well-born, aristocratic, noble, blue-blooded, patrician, well-bred, respectable, refined, stylish, elegant, ladylike, gentlemanly. **2** *genteel behavior* polite, well-mannered, mannerly, courteous, civil, decorous, gracious, courtly, polished, cultivated. **3** *the king's servants were very genteel* overpolite, mannered, affected, ultrarefined.

**gentle** adjective **1** *a gentle person* kind, kindly, tender, benign, humane, lenient, merciful, clement, compassionate, tenderhearted, sweet-tempered, placid, mild, soft, quiet, tranquil, meek, dovelike. **2** *a gentle wind* mild, moderate, light, temperate, soft, smooth, soothing. **3** *a gentle child* docile, manageable, tractable, meek. **4** *a gentle slope* gradual, slight, easy, imperceptible. **5** *of gentle birth* upper-class, high-born. *See* GENTEEL 1.

**genuine** adjective **1** *a genuine diamond* real, authentic, true, pure, actual, bona fide, veritable, sound, sterling, legitimate, lawful, legal, valid, original, unadulterated, unalloyed; *inf.* the real McCoy, honest-to-goodness, kosher. **2** *a genuine person* sincere, truthful, honest, frank, candid, open, natural, unaffected, artless, ingenuous; *inf.* up-front.

**germane** adjective relevant, pertinent, material, applicable, related, connected, akin, apropos, apposite, appropriate, apt, fitting, suited, to the point/purpose.

**gesture** noun sign, signal, motion, motioning, wave, indication, gesticulation.

**gesture** verb gesticulate, sign, signal, motion, wave, indicate.

**get** verb **1** *where did you get that hat?* acquire, obtain, come by, procure, secure, buy, purchase. **2** *go and get that book* go for, fetch, bring, collect, carry, transport, convey. **3** *get what you want* gain, acquire, achieve, attain, reach, win, find; *inf.* bag. **4** *get $400 per week* earn, bring in, make, clear, gross, net, pocket; *inf.* pull in, take home. **5** *the police got the thief* capture, seize, grab, lay hold of, grasp, collar, take captive, arrest, apprehend, take, trap, entrap; *inf.* nab, bag. **6** *get flu/measles* catch, contract, come down with, be afflicted by. **7** *try to get that station* reach, communicate with, contact, get in touch with. **8** *I didn't get what he said* hear, catch, take in, perceive. **9** *don't you get what he means?* understand, grasp, comprehend, see, fathom, follow, make head or tail of; *inf.* catch on to, get the hang of. **10** *we got home early* arrive, reach, come; *inf.* make it. **11** *we got her to go* persuade, induce, coax, wheedle into, talk into, prevail upon. **12** *get to see the new movie* manage, succeed, arrange, contrive. **13** *get fat/wet/old* become, grow, come to be, turn, turn into, wax. **14** *that music gets me* affect, move, touch, stir, arouse, stimulate, impress, leave an impression on; *inf.* send, turn on. **15** *I'll get him for that* avenge oneself on, take vengeance on, get even with, pay someone back, give tit for tat to, settle the score with; *inf.* get back at. **16** *you've really got me there* baffle, puzzle, stump, mystify, confound, nonplus. **get across** communicate, make understood/clear, impart, convey, transmit. **get ahead** make good, do well, succeed, prosper, flourish, rise in the world; *inf.* go places, get somewhere. **get along 1** *I don't get along with his mother* get on, agree, see eye to eye; *inf.* hit it off. **2** *how are you getting along?* get on, fare, manage, cope; *inf.* get by, make out. **get around 1** *get around his objections* circumvent, bypass, outmaneuver, outwit, outsmart. **2** *get around his father* prevail upon, wheedle, coax, win over, convert, sway. **3** *she certainly gets around* travel, visit, circulate, socialize. **get at** suggest, hint, imply, intend, lead up to, mean. **get away** escape, flee, break free, break out, decamp, depart. **get back 1** *get back at dawn* return, come home, come back. **2** *get back her gloves* recover, retrieve, regain, repossess, recoup. **3** *get back at his torturer* avenge oneself on, get even with. *See* GET 15. **get by** cope, manage, subsist, survive, exist, fare, get along, contrive to get along, make both ends meet, keep the wolf from the door; *inf.* keep one's head above water, make out. **get off** *get off the bus* alight from, climb off, dismount from, leave; descend from, disembark, exit. **get on 1** *get on the bus* board, climb on; mount, ascend, embark. **2** *how are you getting on?* get along, fare, manage, cope; *inf.* get by, make out. **3** *husband and wife do not get on* be on friendly terms, be in harmony. *See* GET ALONG 1. **get out 1** *let's get out now* leave, depart, go away, be off, withdraw; *inf.* vamoose, clear out. **2** *the news has got out* be made public, become known, be revealed, be publicized, be disclosed, leak, be leaked, spread, circulate. **get out of** avoid, dodge, evade, escape, shirk. **get over 1** *get over the flu* recover from, recuperate from, get better after, pull through, survive. **2** *get over one's fear of dogs* overcome, master, get the better of, shake off, defeat. **get to** irritate, get on someone's nerves, annoy, vex, rile, rub someone the wrong way, upset, bother, nettle; *inf.* bug, get someone's goat. **get together 1** *get together the evidence* collect, gather, assemble, accumulate, compile, amass. **2** *we must get together soon* meet, meet up, socialize, congregate.

**getaway** noun escape, flight, breakout, break, decampment.

**get-together** noun meeting, party, social gathering, gathering; *inf.* do, bash.

**get-up** noun outfit, clothes, clothing, dress, garb, apparel, garments.

**get-up-and-go** noun go, energy, vigor, vitality, vim, enthusiasm, eagerness, drive, push, initiative, ambition; *inf.* bounce.

**ghastly** adjective **1** *a ghastly murder/accident* terrible, horrible, frightful, dreadful, awful, horrid, horrendous, hideous, shocking, grim, grisly, gruesome, gory, terrifying, frightening. **2** *a ghastly mistake* serious, grave, critical, unforgivable. **3** *what a ghastly man* odious, loathsome, nasty, foul, contemptible, appalling. **4** *her ghastly appearance* deathlike, deathly pale, pale, pallid, wan, ashen, colorless, white, white as a sheet, ghostlike, ghostly, spectral, cadaverous.

**ghost** noun **1** *haunted by a ghost* specter, apparition, phantom, spirit, phantasm; *inf.* spook. **2** *the ghost of a smile* suggestion, hint, trace, glimmer, semblance, shadow, impression.

**ghostly** adjective ghostlike, spectral, phantomlike, phantom, phantasmal, unearthly, supernatural, otherworldly, insubstantial, shadowy, eerie, weird, uncanny; *inf.* spooky.

**giant** noun colossus, Titan, Goliath, behemoth, leviathan; superhuman.

**giant** adjective gigantic, enormous, colossal, huge, immense, vast, mammoth, monumental, monstrous, gargantuan, titanic, elephantine, prodigious, stupendous; *inf.* jumbo, humongous, industrial-size.

**gibberish** noun babble, jabbering, nonsense, rubbish, twaddle, drivel, balderdash, mumbo jumbo, blather, double-talk, prattle; *inf.* poppycock, gobbledegook, rot, piffle.

**gibe, jibe** verb jeer, mock, sneer at, scoff at, taunt, scorn, deride, ridicule, hold up to ridicule, laugh at, poke fun at, make fun of, tease, twit; *inf.* rib, rag.

**giddy** adjective **1** *get giddy climbing ladders* dizzy, light-headed, faint, reeling, unsteady; *inf.* woozy. **2** *a giddy girl* flighty, silly, frivolous, skittish, capricious, featherbrained, scatterbrained, fickle, changeable, inconstant, mercurial, volatile, unsteady, thoughtless, heedless, carefree, insouciant.

**gift** noun **1** *receive a birthday gift* present, offering, bounty, largesse, donation, contribution, boon, grant, bonus, gratuity, benefaction, bequest, legacy, inheritance, endowment. **2** *a gift for foreign languages* talent, flair, aptitude, facility, knack, ability, faculty, genius, mind for.

**gifted** adjective talented, brilliant, intelligent, clever, bright, smart, sharp, ingenious, able, accomplished, capable, masterly, skilled, adroit, proficient, expert.

**gigantic** adjective enormous, colossal. *See* GIANT adjective.

**giggle** verb titter, snigger, snicker, chuckle, chortle, laugh, cackle; *inf.* tee-hee, ha-ha.

**gimmick** noun contrivance, stunt, scheme, trick, dodge, ploy, stratagem.

**gingerly** adverb cautiously, with caution, warily, charily, cannily, carefully, attentively, heedfully, vigilantly, watchfully, judiciously, hesitantly, reluctantly, timidly.

**gird** verb 1 *gird on his sword* belt, bind, fasten. 2 *trees girded the lake* surround, circle, encircle, ring, enclose, encompass, compass, confine, hem in, pen, enfold, engird, girdle. 3 *gird oneself for battle* prepare, make ready, ready, brace, fortify, steel, buttress.

**gist** noun essence, quintessence, drift, sense, core, nucleus, nub, kernel, pith, marrow, burden, crux.

**give** verb 1 *gave him the book* hand, present, donate, bestow, contribute, confer, hand over, turn over, award, grant, accord, leave, will, bequeath, make over, entrust, consign, vouchsafe. 2 *give the impression* show, display, demonstrate, set forth, indicate, manifest, evidence. 3 *give them time* allow, permit, grant, accord, offer. 4 *give a reprimand* administer, deliver, deal. 5 *give advice* provide, supply, furnish, proffer, offer. 6 *give no trouble* cause, be a source of, make, create. 7 *give news of the battle* impart, communicate, announce, transmit, convey, transfer, send, purvey. 8 *land giving a good crop* produce, yield, afford, result in. 9 *the car gave a jolt* perform, execute, make, do. 10 *give a shout/yell* let out, utter, issue, emit. 11 *give his life for his country* give up, sacrifice, relinquish, devote. 12 *gave his seat to the new senator* surrender, concede, yield, give up, cede. 13 *she gave me to believe* lead, make, cause, force. 14 *the chair gave* give way, collapse, break, break down, fall apart, come apart; bend, buckle. **give away** 1 *give away secrets* reveal, disclose, divulge, let slip, leak, let out, expose, uncover. 2 *give his friend away* betray, inform on; *inf.* rat on, blow the whistle on. **give in** give up, surrender, admit/concede defeat, concede, yield, capitulate, submit, comply, succumb, quit, retreat; *inf.* throw in the towel. **give off** emit, send out, give out, pour out, throw out, discharge, exude, exhale, release, vent, produce. **give out** 1 *give out fumes* emit, send out. *See* GIVE OFF. 2 *give out the prizes* distribute, allocate, allot, mete out, hand out, disperse, apportion, dole out, assign; *inf.* dish out. 3 *give out that he is leaving* announce, declare, make known, communicate, impart, broadcast, publish, disseminate. 4 *supplies were giving out* run out, be used up, be consumed, be exhausted, be depleted, come to an end, fail. **give up** 1 *give up smoking* stop, cease, quit, desist from, leave off, swear off, renounce, forswear, abandon, discontinue; *inf.* cut out. 2 *give up in the face of the enemy* surrender, yield. *See* GIVE IN. 3 *she's just given up* despair, lose heart, abandon hope, give up hope.

**giver** noun donor, contributor, granter, benefactor, backer, fairy godmother; *inf.* angel.

**glad** adjective 1 *glad you're here* happy, pleased, pleased as Punch, well-pleased, delighted, gratified, thrilled, overjoyed, elated, satisfied, contented, grateful; *inf.* tickled pink. 2 *glad to help* willing, more than willing, eager, ready, prepared, happy, pleased, delighted. 3 *hear the glad news* happy, joyful, delightful, welcome, cheering, cheerful, pleasing, gratifying.

**glamorous** adjective 1 *a glamorous woman* alluring, dazzling, glittering, well-dressed, smart, elegant, attractive, charming, fascinating, beguiling, bewitching, enchanting, entrancing, irresistible, tantalizing; *inf.* glitzy, ritzy. 2 *a glamorous career* exciting, stimulating, thrilling, high-profile, dazzling, glossy, glittering; *inf.* ritzy, glitzy.

**glamour** noun 1 *women with glamour* beauty, loveliness, attractiveness, allure, attraction, elegance, charm, fascination; *inf.* glitz, pizzazz. 2 *the glamour of foreign travel* excitement, enchantment, captivation, magic, spell.

**glance** verb 1 *glance at the stranger* glimpse, peek, peep; *inf.* sneak a look. 2 *glance through the paper* skim, leaf, flip, thumb, scan. 3 *lights glancing on water* flash, gleam, glitter, glisten, glint, glimmer, shimmer, flicker, sparkle, twinkle, reflect. 4 *the arrow glanced off the tree | the car glanced the wall* ricochet, rebound, bounce; graze, skim, touch, brush. **glance at/over** touch upon, mention in passing, mention, skim over.

**glance** noun 1 *take a glance at* glimpse, peek, peep; *inf.* gander, once-over. 2 *the glance of the sun on the water* flash, gleam, glitter, glint, glimmer, shimmer, flicker, sparkle, twinkle, reflection.

**glare** verb 1 *glare at the trespassers* glower, scowl, frown, give someone dirty looks, look daggers. 2 *lights glaring* blaze, flare, flame, beam, dazzle.

**glare** noun 1 *give a glare at his enemy* glower, scowl, frown, dirty look. 2 *the glare of lights* blaze, flare, flame, harsh beam, dazzle.

**glaring** adjective *a glaring error* conspicuous, obvious, overt, manifest, patent, visible, unconcealed, flagrant, blatant, egregious, outrageous, gross.

**glasses** plural noun *put on his glasses* eyeglasses, spectacles, bifocals, sunglasses, lorgnette, pince-nez.

**glassy** adjective **1** *a glassy surface on the table* glasslike, shiny, glossy, smooth, mirrorlike, clear, crystal-clear, transparent, translucent, limpid. **2** *a glassy stare* expressionless, glazed, blank, empty, vacant, vacuous, deadpan, fixed, unmoving, motionless, lifeless.

**gleam** noun **1** *a gleam of light* beam, flash, glow, shaft, ray, flare, glint. **2** *the gleam of the polished brass* glow, luster, gloss, shine, sheen, brightness, brilliance, flash. **3** *a gleam of hope* glimmer, flicker, ray, trace, suggestion, hint, inkling, grain.

**gleam** verb shine, radiate, flash, glow, flare, glint, glisten, glitter, beam, shimmer, glimmer, glance, sparkle, twinkle, scintillate.

**glee** noun exaltation, elation, exuberance, merriment, gaiety, mirth, mirthfulness, delight, joy, joyousness, exhilaration, high spirits, blitheness, cheerfulness.

**gleeful** adjective elated, exuberant, joyful, overjoyed, joyous, jovial, exhilarated, high-spirited, blithe, cheerful.

**glib** adjective slick, smooth, smooth-talking, smooth-spoken, fast-talking, plausible, fluent, suave; talkative, voluble, loquacious, unctuous.

**glide** verb slide, slip, skim, sail, skate, float, drift, flow, coast.

**glimmer** noun **1** *a glimmer of light* gleam, flash, flicker, glint, shimmer, blink, twinkle, sparkle, glow, ray. **2** *a glimmer of hope* flicker, ray. *See* GLEAM noun 3.

**glimmer** verb gleam, flash, flicker, shimmer, blink, twinkle, sparkle, glow.

**glimpse** noun glance, quick look, peek, peep.

**glisten** verb shine, shimmer, sparkle, twinkle, flicker, blink, wink, glint, glance, gleam, flash, scintillate.

**glitter** verb sparkle, twinkle, flicker, blink, wink, shimmer, glimmer, glint, gleam, flash, scintillate, coruscate.

**glitter** noun *the glitter of show business* showiness, flashiness, ostentation, glamour, pageantry, fanfare, splendor; *inf.* razzle-dazzle, glitz, ritziness, pizzazz.

**gloat** verb relish, take pleasure in, delight in, revel in, rejoice in, glory in, exult in, triumph over, crow about; *inf.* rub it in.

**global** adjective **1** *global recession* worldwide, world, universal, international, planetary. **2** *a global rule* general, comprehensive, all-inclusive, all-encompassing, all-out, encyclopedic, exhaustive, thorough, total, across-the-board, with no exceptions.

**globe** noun world, universe, earth, planet; sphere, spheroid, orb, ball.

**gloom** noun **1** *the gloom of the night* gloominess, dimness, darkness, dark, blackness, murkiness, murk, shadowiness, shadow, shade, obscurity, dusk, twilight. **2** *a state of gloom* low spirits, melancholy, despondency, misery, dejection, glumness, depression, the blues, despair, pessimism, hopelessness.

**gloomy** adjective **1** *a gloomy day/room* dark, sunless, dull, dim, shadowy, dismal, dreary, black, murky, somber. **2** *a gloomy outlook* distressing, somber, melancholy, depressing, dispiriting, disheartening, disappointing, pessimistic, hopeless. **3** *feeling gloomy* in low spirits, melancholy, woebegone, despondent, disconsolate, miserable, dejected, downcast, downhearted, dispirited, glum, depressed, blue.

**glorify** verb **1** *glorify God* worship, adore, exalt, extol, pay homage to, pay tribute to, honor, revere, reverence, venerate. **2** *the reports glorified the war* add luster to, aggrandize, ennoble, elevate, raise, lift up, magnify, dignify, advance, boost, promote. **3** *glorify the conqueror* praise, sing/sound the praises of, extol, laud, eulogize, magnify, acclaim, applaud, cheer, hail, celebrate, lionize.

**glorious** adjective **1** *our glorious history* illustrious, noble, celebrated, famous, famed, renowned, magnificent, majestic. **2** *a glorious day* beautiful, bright, brilliant, sunny, perfect. **3** *have a glorious time* splendid, marvelous, wonderful, delightful, terrific.

**glory** noun **1** *to the glory of God* worship, adoration, exaltation, extolment, honor, reverence, veneration. **2** *win glory in battle* renown, fame, prestige, honor, distinction, illustriousness, acclaim, credit, accolade, recognition. **3** *the glory of Versailles* splendor, resplendence, magnificence, grandeur, majesty, pomp, pageantry.

**gloss** noun **1** *the gloss on the furniture* shine, sheen, luster, gleam, brightness, brilliance, sparkle, shimmer, polish, burnish. **2** *a gloss of respectability* façade, front, camouflage, disguise, mask, semblance, show, veneer, surface.

**glossy** adjective shining, shiny, glassy, gleaming, bright, brilliant, sparkling, shimmering, polished, burnished, glazed.

**glow** noun **1** *the glow from the light* gleam, glimmer, incandescence, luminosity, phosphorescence. **2** *the glow of the garden flowers* brightness, vividness, brilliance, colorfulness, richness, radiance, splendor. **3** *the glow of her complexion* blush, flush, rosiness, pinkness, redness, crimson, scarlet, reddening, bloom. **4** *induce a warm glow* warmth, happiness, contentment, satisfaction. **5** *the glow of his love* passion, ardor, fervor, vehemence, intensity.

**glow** verb **1** *the light/fire glowed* shed a glow, gleam, glimmer, shine, smolder. **2** *glow with pleasure* blush, flush, redden, color. **3** *glow with pride* radiate, thrill, tingle.

**glower** verb scowl, stare angrily, glare, frown, give someone dirty looks, look daggers.

**glowing** adjective **1** *glowing coals* aglow, smoldering, incandescent, candescent, luminous, phosphorescent. **2** *a glowing complexion* rosy, pink, reddish, red, ruddy, florid. **3** *glowing colors* bright, vivid, brilliant, colorful, rich, radiant. **4** *a glowing report* complimentary, ecstatic, rhapsodic, eulogistic, laudatory, adulatory; *inf.* rave.

**glue** noun adhesive, fixative, gum, paste, cement, mucilage, epoxy.

**glum** adjective in low spirits, melancholy. *See* GLOOMY 3.

**glut** noun surplus, excess, surfeit, superfluity, overabundance, superabundance, oversupply, saturation.

**gluttony** noun gourmandism, gormandizing, insatiability, voraciousness, voracity, greed, greediness; *inf.* piggishness, hoggishness.

**gnaw** verb chew, munch, crunch, masticate, bite. **gnaw at** prey on someone's mind, torment, plague, fret, distress, trouble, worry. **gnaw away** erode, corrode, wear away, wear down, eat away, fret, consume, devour.

**go** verb **1** *go forward/backward/up* move, proceed, progress, pass, walk, travel, journey, repair. **2** *time to go* go away, leave, depart, withdraw, set off, set out, decamp; *inf.* beat it, scram. **3** *does the machine go?* work, function, operate, run, perform. **4** *go pale/bad* become, grow, get, come to be, wax. **5** *this road goes all the way to the sea* extend, stretch, reach, spread, give access, lead. **6** *where does this book go?* belong, fit in, be located, be situated, be found, lie, stand. **7** *her headache has gone* stop, cease, disappear, vanish, be no more, fade away, melt away. **8** *all my money has gone* be finished, be spent, be used up, be exhausted, be consumed. **9** *the elderly patient has gone* die, pass away, decease, expire, perish; *inf.* give up the ghost, kick the bucket. **10** *these clothes will have to go* be discarded, be thrown away, be disposed of. **11** *some of the staff will have to go* be dismissed, be laid off; *inf.* fired, be axed, get the ax. **12** *the money will go to charity* be assigned, be allotted, be applied, be devoted, be awarded, be granted/given, be ceded. **13** *how did your interview go?* turn out, work out,

fare, progress, develop, result, end, end up, eventuate. **14** *the carpet and curtains don't go* go together, go with each other, match, harmonize, blend, suit each other, be suited, complement each other, be in accord, accord, be compatible. **15** *this goes to prove his theory* serve, contribute, help, incline, tend. **16** *the bridge went* break, give way, collapse, fall down, cave in, crumble, disintegrate, fall to pieces. **go about** *how do you go about buying a house?* set about, begin, approach, tackle, undertake. **go along with** *I'll go along with your plans* comply with, cooperate with, acquiesce in, follow, agree with, assent to, concur with. **go around** *a rumor going around* circulate, pass around; be passed around, be spread, be broadcast. **go back on** *go back on one's word* renege on, repudiate, retract. **go by 1** *as time goes by* pass, pass by, elapse, move on, proceed, flow, lapse, slip away, tick away, fly. **2** *go by the rules* follow, obey, observe, be guided by, heed. **go down 1** *the ship went down in a storm* sink, be submerged, founder, go under. **2** *prices are going down* decrease, drop, fall, be reduced, decline, plummet. **3** *the champion went down* be beaten, be defeated, suffer defeat, lose, fail, collapse. **4** *his name will go down in history* be commemorated, be remembered, be recalled, be immortalized. **go far** *a young man bound to go far* do well, do well for oneself, be successful, succeed, get on, get on in the world, get ahead, make a name for oneself, advance oneself, set the world on fire. **go for 1** *the dog went for him* attack, assault, assail, launch oneself at, set upon, spring at/upon, rush at. **2** *he doesn't go for quiet women* be attracted to, be fond of, admire, favor, like, prefer, choose, hold with. **go in for** *go in for tennis* engage in, take part in, participate in, practice, pursue, take up, espouse, adopt, embrace. **go into** *the police are going into the evidence thoroughly* investigate, research, inquire into, look into, examine, study, review, check, scrutinize, analyze, delve into, dig into, pursue, probe. **go off 1** *the bomb went off* explode, detonate, blow up, burst, erupt; *inf.* go bang. **2** *we went off at dawn* leave, go away, depart, set out, set off, decamp, move out. **go on 1** *how long did the talk go on?* last, continue, proceed, endure, persist, stay, remain, happen, occur. **2** *she did go on too long* ramble on, talk on and on, chatter, prattle. **go out 1** *he has gone out of the office* leave, exit, depart from. **2** *the lights/passion went out* be extinguished, be turned off, be doused, be quenched, fade, die out. **3** *a boy and girl going out* go with each other, go together, see each other, court; *inf.* go steady, date. **go over** *go over the accounts* read over, look over, inspect, examine, study, scan, run over; *inf.* give the once-over. **go through 1** *go through torture* undergo, suffer, experience, bear, stand, tolerate, endure, weather, brook, brave. **2** *go through money* spend, use up, run through, consume, exhaust. **3** *go through someone's pockets* look through, search, hunt through, check, inspect, examine; *inf.* frisk. **4** *the carpets and curtains do not go together* match, harmonize. *See* GO *verb* 14. **2** *they have been going together for months* see each other, court, keep company. *See* GO OUT 3. **go under 1** *the ship went under* sink, founder. *See* GO DOWN 1. **2** *the firm has gone under* fail, founder, go bankrupt, go into receivership, go to the wall; *inf.* go bust, fold, flop. **go with 1** *the carpets do not go with the curtains* match, complement. *See* GO *verb* 14. **2** *his sister is going with her brother* see; *inf.* go steady with. *See* GO OUT 3.

**go** noun **1** *have a go at hang gliding* try, attempt, effort, bid, essay, endeavor; *inf.* shot, stab, crack, whirl, whack. **2** *people with a lot of go* energy, vigor, dynamism, force, verve, vim, vitality, vivacity, drive, push, enterprise; *inf.* get-up-and-go, pep, oomph.

**go-ahead** noun permission, assent, consent, authorization, sanction, leave, warranty, confirmation; *inf.* green light, OK, thumbs up.

**goal** noun aim, objective, object, end, purpose, target, ambition, design, intention, intent, aspiration, ideal.

**go-between** noun intermediary, mediator, middleman, medium, agent, broker, dealer, factor, liaison, contact, contact person; pander, panderer.

**God** noun God Almighty, the Almighty, the Godhead, the Supreme/Divine Being, the Deity, the Holy One, God the Father, Our Father, the Creator, Our Maker, the Lord, Jehovah, Allah.

**god** noun **1** *tribal gods* deity, divine being, divinity, spirit. **2** *false gods* idol, graven image, icon, golden calf.

**godforsaken** adjective desolate, dismal, dreary, bleak, wretched, miserable, gloomy, deserted, abandoned, forlorn, remote, backward.

**godless** adjective **1** *godless intellectuals* atheistic, agnostic, skeptical, faithless. **2** *preaching to the godless convicts* heathen, pagan, ungodly, impious, irreligious, unrighteous, unprincipled, sinful, wicked, evil, depraved.

**godlike** adjective godly, divine, celestial, heavenly, sacred, holy, saintly, deific, deiform, transcendent, superhuman.

**godly** adjective God-fearing, devout, pious, religious, pietistic, believing, righteous, moral, virtuous, good, holy, saintly.

**goings-on** plural noun misconduct, misbehavior, conduct, behavior, mischief, pranks; *inf.* funny business, monkey business, hanky-panky.

**golden** adjective **1** *golden hair* gold-colored, blond, blonde, yellow, yellowish, fair, flaxen, tow-colored, bright, gleaming, resplendent, brilliant, shining. **2** *a golden future* successful, prosperous, flourishing, thriving, rosy, bright, brilliant, rich. **3** *golden times* happy, joyful, delightful, glorious, precious, treasured. **4** *golden opportunities* fine, superb, excellent, favorable, opportune, promising, rosy, advantageous. **5** *the golden boy of the track team* talented, gifted, special, favorite, favored, cherished, beloved, pet, acclaimed, applauded, praised, lauded.

**good** adjective **1** *a good person* virtuous, moral, ethical, righteous, right-minded, right-thinking, honorable, honest, upright, high-minded, noble, worthy, admirable, estimable, exemplary. **2** *a good child* well-behaved, obedient, well-mannered, manageable, tractable. **3** *that's good* satisfactory, acceptable, adequate, fine, excellent; *inf.* great, OK, hunky-dory. **4** *a good thing to do* right, correct, proper, fitting, suitable, appropriate, decorous, seemly. **5** *a good driver* competent, capable, able, accomplished, efficient, skillful, adept, proficient, dexterous, expert, excellent, first-class, first-rate; *inf.* A-1, tip-top, topnotch. **6** *good brakes/friends* reliable, dependable, trustworthy. **7** *in good condition* fine, healthy, sound, robust, strong, vigorous. **8** *a good party* enjoyable, pleasant, agreeable, pleasing, pleasurable, amusing, cheerful, convivial, congenial. **9** *good of you to come* kind, kindly, kindhearted, good-hearted, friendly, charitable, gracious, benevolent, benign, altruistic. **10** *come at a good time* convenient, fitting, suitable, favorable, advantageous, fortunate, lucky, propitious, auspicious. **11** *broccoli is good for you* wholesome, healthful, nutritional, beneficial, salubrious, salutary. **12** *is this cheese still good?* eatable, edible, untainted, fresh. **13** *the food here is good* delicious, tasty, appetizing; *inf.* scrumptious, yummy. **14** *a good reason for going* valid, genuine, authentic, legitimate, sound, bona fide. **15** *wait a good hour* full, entire, whole, complete, solid. **16** *a good number came* considerable, substantial, goodly, sizable, large, sufficient, ample. **17** *good friends* close, intimate, bosom, fast, dear, valued, treasured. **18** *wear her good clothes* best, finest, newest, nicest, smartest, special, party, Sunday. **19** *good weather* fine, fair, mild, clear, bright, cloudless, sunshiny, sunny, calm, balmy, tranquil, clement, halcyon. **make good 1** *make good the damage* compensate for, make recompense for, make amends for, make restitution for, pay for, reimburse for. **2** *make good a promise* fulfill, carry out, effect, discharge, live up to. **3** *make good a statement* substantiate, back up, confirm, prove, validate, authenticate. **4** *he made good in America* succeed, do well, get ahead, reach the top.

**good** noun **1** *for your own good* benefit, advantage, behalf, gain, profit, interest, well-being, welfare, usefulness, avail, service. **2** *tell good from bad* virtue, goodness, morality, ethics, righteousness, rightness, rectitude, honor, honesty, uprightness, integrity, probity, worth, merit. **for good** for always, for ever, permanently.

**good-bye** interjection farewell, au revoir, adieu; *inf.* bye, cheers, see you later, see you, so long, toodle-oo, ciao; *inf.* bye-bye, ta-ta.

**good-for-nothing** adjective useless, of no use, no-good, lazy, idle, slothful, feckless.

**good-for-nothing** noun ne'er-do-well, wastrel, black sheep, layabout, idler, loafer, sluggard.

**good-humored** adjective amiable, affable, easygoing, genial, cheerful, cheery, happy, pleasant, good-tempered.

**good-looking** adjective attractive, handsome, pretty, lovely, beautiful, personable, comely, fair.

**good-natured** adjective kind, kindly, kind-hearted, warmhearted, generous, benevolent, charitable, friendly, helpful, accommodating, amiable, tolerant.

**goodness** noun **1** *the goodness of the saint* virtue, virtuousness, morality, righteousness, rectitude, honor, honesty, uprightness, integrity, probity, nobility, worthiness, merit. **2** *she had the goodness to stay* kindness, kindliness, kindheartedness, warmheartedness, generosity, obligingness, benevolence, beneficence, friendliness, goodwill, graciousness, charitableness, unselfishness. **3** *the goodness in the food* nourishment, nutrition, wholesomeness.

**goods** plural noun belongings, possessions, property, effects, gear, things, paraphernalia, chattels, appurtenances, trappings, accoutrements; *inf.* stuff.

**goodwill** noun friendliness, kindness, kindliness, benevolence, compassion, amity.

**gorge** noun chasm, canyon, ravine, abyss, defile, pass, cleft, crevice, rift, fissure.

**gorge** verb bolt, gobble, wolf (down), devour, stuff down, gormandize; *inf.* shovel in. **gorge on** stuff with, cram with, fill with, fill up on, glut with, satiate with, surfeit with, overeat.

**gorgeous** adjective **1** *a gorgeous sight* magnificent, splendid, superb, grand, resplendent, stately, impressive, imposing, sumptuous, luxurious, elegant, opulent, dazzling, brilliant, glittering, breathtaking, stunning. **2** *we had a gorgeous time* wonderful, marvelous, first-rate, delightful, enjoyable, entertaining, excellent.

**gory** adjective bloody, bloodthirsty, violent, murderous, brutal, savage, horror-filled, horrific; *inf.* blood-and-guts.

**gossamer** adjective cobwebby, silky, gauzy, chiffony, feathery, light, fine, delicate, frail, flimsy, insubstantial, airy, diaphanous, sheer, transparent, see-through.

**gossip** noun **1** *have you heard the gossip?* rumors, scandal, hearsay, smear campaign, mudslinging, dirt, low-down. **2** *he's just a gossip* gossipmonger, scandalmonger, busybody, tattletale.

**gossip** verb spread rumors/stories; talk, blab, tattle.

**govern** verb **1** *govern the country* rule, reign over, hold sway over, preside over, administer, lead, be in charge of, control, command, direct, manage, oversee, supervise, superintend, steer, pilot. **2** *govern one's passions* control, restrain, keep in check, check, curb, hold back, bridle, rein in. **3** *the weather will govern our decision* determine, decide, sway, rule, influence.

**government** noun **1** *the country's government* administration, regime, congress, parliament, ministry, council, executive, (the) powers that be. **2** *their government of the country* rule, administration, leadership, command, direction, control, guidance, management, conduct, supervision, superintendence.

**gown** noun dress, evening gown, ball gown.

**grab** verb grasp, clutch, grip, clasp, lay hold of, catch hold of, take hold of, fasten upon; seize, snatch, pluck, snap up, appropriate, capture; *inf.* bag, nab.

**grab** noun **up for grabs** available, accessible, obtainable, to be had, up for sale, for the taking.

**grace** noun **1** *the grace of the ballerina* gracefulness, suppleness, fluidity of movement, smoothness, ease, agility; *inf.* poetry in motion. **2** *the grace of the women* elegance, refinement, finesse, cultivation, polish, suaveness, good taste, taste, tastefulness, charm, loveliness. **3** *have the grace to apologize* manners, mannerliness, courtesy, courteousness, decency, consideration, tact, tactfulness, breeding, decorum, propriety, etiquette. **4** *fall from grace* favor, goodwill, preferment. **5** *by the grace of our benefactors* goodwill, generosity, kindness, kindliness, benefaction, beneficence, indulgence. **6** *beg for grace from the jury* mercy, leniency, clemency, indulgence, charity, quarter. **7** *ask for a year's grace* delay, postponement, deferment, deferral. **8** *say grace* blessing, benediction, thanks, thanksgiving.

**grace** verb **1** *paintings gracing the room* adorn, decorate, ornament, embellish, enhance, beautify, prettify, set off, deck, enrich, garnish. **2** *grace the gathering with his presence* dignify, distinguish, honor, favor, glorify, elevate.

**graceful** adjective **1** *graceful ballerinas* supple, fluid, flowing, smooth, easy, agile, nimble. **2** *graceful women* elegant, refined, cultured, cultivated, polished, suave, charming, lovely.

**gracious** adjective **1** *a gracious lady* kind, kindly, kindhearted, warmhearted, benevolent, friendly, amiable, affable, cordial, courteous, considerate, polite, chivalrous, well-mannered, beneficent, benign. **2** *a gracious room* elegant, tasteful, comfortable, luxurious. **3** *gracious God* merciful, compassionate, clement.

**grade** noun **1** *what grade did he reach?* level, stage, echelon, rank, standing, station, position, order, class. **2** *all belonging to the same grade* category, class, classification, type, brand. **3** *a steep grade* gradient, slope, incline, hill, rise, bank, acclivity, declivity. **make the grade** pass, pass muster, measure up, come up to standard, come up to scratch/snuff, qualify, get through.

**grade** verb classify, class, categorize, sort, group, order, brand, size, rank, evaluate, rate, value, range, graduate.

**gradual** adjective step-by-step, degree-by-degree, progressive, successive, continuous, systematic, regular, steady, even, moderate, slow, measured, unhurried.

**graft** noun *get ahead in business by graft* bribery, payola; *inf.* palm-greasing.

**grand** adjective **1** *grand houses* impressive, magnificent, imposing, splendid, striking, superb, stately, large, monumental, majestic. **2** *a grand feast* luxurious, sumptuous, lavish, opulent, princely. **3** *in the company of grand people* great, noble, aristocratic, distinguished, august, illustrious, eminent, esteemed, prominent, renowned. **4** *make a grand gesture* ostentatious, showy, pretentious, lordly, ambitious, imperious. **5** *the grand total* complete, comprehensive, all-inclusive, inclusive, exhaustive. **6** *the grand hall* principal, main, chief, leading, head, supreme. **7** *have a grand time* wonderful, marvelous, first-rate, outstanding.

**grandeur** noun **1** *the grandeur of the houses/feast* impressiveness, magnificence, splendor, splendidness, superbness, stateliness, largeness, majesty, luxuriousness, luxury, sumptuousness, lavishness, opulence. **2** *the grandeur of the ruling classes* greatness, nobility, illustriousness, eminence.

**grandiose** adjective **1** *grandiose plans* ambitious, overambitious, extravagant, high-flown, high-sounding, pompous, pretentious, flamboyant. **2** *grandiose buildings* impressive, magnificent. *See* GRAND 1.

**grant** verb **1** *grant them an interview* agree/consent/assent/accede to give, permit, allow, accord. **2** *grant them an award* bestow on, confer on, give to, impart to, award with, present with, donate to, contribute to, provide with, endow with, furnish with. **3** *I grant you that you may be right* admit to, acknowledge to, concede to, go along with, yield to. **4** *grant property to his heirs* transfer, convey, transmit, pass on, hand over, assign, bequeath.

**grant** noun award, endowment, donation, contribution, allowance, subsidy, allocation, allotment.

**graphic** adjective **1** *a graphic description* vivid, striking, expressive, descriptive, lively, forcible, detailed, well-drawn, telling, effective, cogent, clear, lucid, explicit. **2** *a graphic representation* diagrammatic, representational, pictorial, illustrative, drawn, delineative.

**grapple** verb *grapple (with) the enemy* wrestle, fight, struggle, tussle, clash. **grapple with** tackle, face, cope with, come to grips with.

**grasp** verb **1** *grasp his hand* grip, clutch, clasp, hold, clench, catch, seize, grab, snatch. **2** *grasp the point* understand, comprehend, perceive, apprehend, get, get the picture, catch on.

**grasp** noun **1** *take a firm grasp of the rail* grip, hold, clutch, clasp, clench. **2** *beyond the grasp of her enemy* clutches, power, control, command, mastery, dominion, rule. **3** *well within your grasp* capacity, reach, scope, limits, range, compass. **4** *a good grasp of the subject* understanding, comprehension, perception, apprehension, knowledge.

**grate** verb **1** *grate cheese/onions* shred, pulverize, mince, grind, granulate. **2** *the knife grated against the metal* rasp, scrape, jar, scratch, grind, creak, rub. **grate on** irritate, set someone's teeth on edge, rub someone the wrong way, irk, annoy, vex, gall, nettle, peeve, rile, exasperate, chafe; get on someone's nerves.

**grateful** adjective **1** *grateful to you* thankful, indebted, obliged, obligated, beholden, appreciative. **2** *a grateful rest* pleasant, agreeable, refreshing, welcome, acceptable.

**gratify** verb **1** *their appreciation gratified her* please, delight, gladden, satisfy, warm the cockles of the heart. **2** *gratify their desires* fulfill, indulge, humor, comply with, pander to, cater to, give in to.

**grating** adjective **1** *a grating noise/voice* rasping, scraping, scratching, harsh, raucous, strident, screeching, piercing, shrill, squawking, squawky, hoarse, croaky. **2** *a grating personality* irritating, annoying, vexatious, irksome, galling, exasperating, offensive, disagreeable, unpleasant.

**gratitude** noun gratefulness, thankfulness, thanks, thanksgiving, appreciation, indebtedness.

**gratuitous** adjective **1** *gratuitous work* free, gratis, complimentary, voluntary, unasked-for, free of charge, for nothing, on the house. **2** *gratuitous insults* unjustified, unprovoked, groundless, without cause, without reason, uncalled-for, unwarranted, unmerited, needless, unnecessary, superfluous.

**gratuity** noun tip, perquisite, fringe benefit, bonus, gift, present, donation, reward, recompense, largesse; *inf.* perk.

**grave** adjective **1** *a grave expression/mood* solemn, earnest, serious, sober, somber, severe, unsmiling, long-faced, pensive, sedate, dignified, staid, dour. **2** *grave matters* serious, momentous, weighty, urgent, pressing, of great consequence, critical, acute, pivotal, life-and-death

**graveyard** noun cemetery, burial ground, churchyard, memorial park; *inf.* boneyard, potter's field.

**gravitate** verb **1** *gravitate to the bottom* sink, fall, drop, descend, settle. **2** *gravitate toward the arts* be drawn to, be pulled toward, be attracted to, incline toward.

**gravity** noun **1** *the gravity of her expression* solemnity, earnestness, seriousness, somberness, severity, pensiveness, sedateness, dignity. **2** *the gravity of the situation* seriousness, significance, weightiness, consequence, criticalness, acuteness.

**graze** verb **1** *the car grazed the wall* brush, brush against, touch, shave, glance off, skim, kiss. **2** *graze his knee* scrape, abrade, skin, scratch, chafe, bark, bruise.

**gray** adjective **1** *a gray dress* grayish, silvery, pearly, smoke-colored. **2** *complexion looking gray* ashen, wan, pale, pallid, colorless, bloodless, anemic. **3** *a gray day* cloudy, overcast, dull, dark, sunless, gloomy, dim, dreary, dismal, drab, cheerless. **4** *a gray area* doubtful, unclear, uncertain, indistinct, mixed.

**great** adjective **1** *a great expanse of forest* large, big, extensive, vast, immense, unlimited, boundless, spacious, huge, enormous, gigantic, colossal, mammoth, monstrous, prodigious. **2** *describe in great detail* considerable, substantial, pronounced, exceptional, sizable. **3** *the great cities of the world* major, main, leading, chief, principal, capital, paramount, primary. **4** *a great occasion* grand, impressive, magnificent, imposing, splendid, majestic. **5** *the great people of the land* prominent, eminent, preeminent, illustrious, celebrated, famous, renowned, leading, top, high-ranking, noble. **6** *a great thinker/athlete* gifted, talented, outstanding, remarkable, exceptional, first-rate, incomparable, expert, skillful, masterly, adept, adroit, proficient; *inf.* crack, ace, A-1. **7** *a great moviegoer* enthusiastic, eager, keen, zealous. **8** *we had a great time* enjoyable, excellent, marvelous, wonderful. **9** *he's a great friend* thoroughgoing, total, complete, perfect, unqualified, consummate.

**greatness** noun **1** *the greatness of the forest* largeness, bigness, boundlessness, extensiveness, vastness, immensity, hugeness, enormity, prodigiousness. **2** *the greatness of the occasion* grandeur, impressiveness, magnificence, pomp, splendor, majesty. **3** *the greatness of the leaders* eminence, distinction, luster, illustriousness, renown, nobility. **4** *the greatness of the players* talent, expertise, skill, adeptness, proficiency.

**greed** noun greediness, avarice, acquisitiveness, rapacity, covetousness, cupidity, miserliness, tight-fistedness, parsimony; avidity, eagerness, hunger, craving, longing.

**greedy** adjective **1** *a greedy miser* avaricious, acquisitive, grasping, rapacious, grabbing, covetous, hoarding, miserly, niggardly, tight-fisted, close-fisted, parsimonious; *inf.* money-grubbing. **2** *greedy for knowledge* avid, eager, hungry, desirous, craving, longing.

**green** adjective **1** *green clothes* greenish, aquamarine, aqua, olive, emerald, sage, chartreuse. **2** *green land* verdant, grass-covered, grassy, leafy. **3** *a green apprentice* inexperienced, untrained, raw, immature, unsophisticated, unpolished, naïve, innocent, ingenuous, callow, gullible, wet behind the ears. **4** *look/go green* ashen, sickly, unhealthy, nauseous. **5** *green issues* environmentalist, conservationist, preservationist; environmentally sound/friendly, ecologically sound.

**greet** verb address, salute, hail, nod to, wave to; receive, meet, welcome.

**gregarious** adjective sociable, social, company-loving, companionable, convivial, outgoing, friendly, affable.

**grief** noun sorrow, mourning, mournfulness, bereavement, lamentation, misery, sadness, anguish, pain, distress, agony, heartache, heartbreak, heaviness of heart, trouble, woe, tribulation, trial, remorse, regret. **come to grief** fail, miscarry, meet with failure, meet with disaster; *inf.* come a cropper.

**grievance** noun **1** *answer the workers' grievances* complaint, charge, protest, ax to grind, bone to pick; *lit.* plaint; *inf.* grouse, gripe, beef. **2** *workers claiming a grievance* wrong, injustice, unfairness, injury, damage, hardship, offense, affront, insult.

**grieve** verb **1** *the widow is still grieving* mourn, lament, sorrow, weep and wail, cry, sob, suffer, ache, be in anguish, be distressed, eat one's heart out; bewail, bemoan, regret, rue, deplore. **2** *his behavior grieved her* hurt, wound, pain, sadden, break someone's heart, upset, distress.

**grievous** adjective **1** *a grievous injury* painful, agonizing, hurtful, afflicting, wounding, damaging, injurious. **2** *grievous news* calamitous, disastrous, distressing, dire. **3** *grievous sins/crimes* heinous, flagrant, glaring, outrageous, shocking, appalling, atrocious, dreadful, egregious. **4** *a grievous sound* grief-stricken, anguished, agonized, mournful, sorrowful, tragic, pitiful, heart-rending.

**grim** adjective **1** *a grim look* stern, forbidding, formidable, fierce, ferocious, threatening, menacing, harsh, somber. **2** *grim determination* resolute, determined, firm, unyielding, obdurate, inflexible, unrelenting, relentless. **3** *a grim sight/accident* dreadful, dire, ghastly, horrendous, appalling, frightful, shocking, harrowing, grisly, gruesome, hideous, macabre.

**grimace** verb scowl, frown, mouth, sneer, pout.

**grimace** noun scowl, frown, sneer, face, pout, mouth, moue.

**grind** verb **1** *grind coffee beans/nuts* crush, pound, pulverize, mill, powder, granulate, grate, crumble, mash, smash. **2** *grind knives* sharpen, file, whet, smooth, polish, sand. **3** *grind one's teeth* gnash, grit, grate, scrape, rasp. **4** *grind away at the task* labor, toil, slog, slave, drudge, plod, sweat; *inf.* plug. **grind down** oppress, torture, torment, molest, harass, harry.

**grind** noun *his job is a grind* drudgery, chore, slog, travail, mill, hard work, labor, slavery, forced labor, exertion; *inf.* drag, sweat.

**grip** noun **1** *lose his grip of the railing* hold, grasp, clutch, clasp, clench, hug, embrace; *inf.* clinch. **2** *have a grip of the problem* understanding, apprehension. See GRASP noun 4. **3** *in the grip of an addiction* clutches, control. See GRASP noun 2. **4** *pack a grip* bag, carryall, overnight bag, valise. **come to grips with** face up to,

meet head on, confront, encounter, deal with, cope with, handle, tackle, grapple with, contend with.

**grip** verb **1** *grip the railing* grasp, clutch, clasp, clench, hold, latch on to, grab, seize, catch, catch at. **2** *the speech gripped the audience* absorb, engross, rivet, spellbind, hold spellbound, entrance, fascinate, hold.

**gripe** verb complain, grumble, moan, groan, protest, whine; *inf.* grouse, bellyache, beef, bitch.

**gripe** noun complaint, grumble, moan, groan, grievance, objection, protest; *inf.* grouse, beef.

**gripping** adjective riveting, spellbinding, compelling, absorbing, engrossing.

**grisly** adjective gruesome, ghastly, frightful, horrid, horrifying, horrible, horrendous, grim, hideous, repulsive, repugnant, revolting, repellent, macabre, spine-chilling, sickening, shocking, appalling, loathsome, abhorrent, odious.

**grit** noun **1** *boots tracking grit into the carpet* granules, sand, gravel, pebbles, dust, dirt. **2** *he has no grit* pluck, mettle, backbone, spirit, nerve, gameness, courage, bravery, toughness; *inf.* gumption, guts, spunk.

**gritty** adjective **1** *a gritty substance* sandy, grainy, granular, gravelly, pebbly, powdery, dusty. **2** *a gritty fighter* plucky, mettlesome, spirited, game, courageous, brave, hardy, tough, determined, resolute, dogged; *inf.* gutsy, spunky.

**groan** verb **1** *groan in pain* moan, cry, call out, sigh, murmur, whimper. **2** *groan about working conditions* complain, object. See GRIPE verb. **3** *the gate groaned* creak, grate, squeak, screech.

**groggy** adjective dazed, in a stupor, dizzy, faint, befuddled, muddled, confused, punch-drunk, shaky, staggering, reeling, unsteady, wobbly; *inf.* woozy.

**groom** verb **1** *groom one's hair | groom oneself* dress, tidy, brush, comb, smooth, spruce up, smarten up, preen, primp, freshen up. **2** *groom the horses* curry, brush, rub, rub down, clean. **3** *groom the students for college* prepare, prime, make ready, ready, instruct, tutor, drill, train, coach, school.

**groove** noun **1** *a groove in the ground* furrow, channel, trench, trough, canal, gouge, hollow, indentation, rut, gutter, cutting, cut, score, rabbet. **2** *the same old groove* rut, routine, habit, treadmill; *inf.* daily grind.

**grope** verb feel, fumble, fish, search, hunt, look, feel.

**gross** adjective **1** *gross in size* obese, massive, immense, huge, corpulent, overweight, bloated, bulky, cumbersome, unwieldy. **2** *gross jokes* coarse, crude, vulgar, obscene, rude, indecent, indelicate, improper, offensive. **3** *her brother is gross* boorish, loutish, oafish, coarse, crass, vulgar, ignorant, unrefined. **4** *a gross error* flagrant, blatant, glaring, egregious, manifest, obvious, plain, apparent. **5** *gross income* total, whole, entire, aggregate.

**grotesque** adjective bizarre, weird, outlandish, freakish, odd, peculiar, unnatural, incongruous, misshapen, distorted, twisted, deformed, malformed, misproportioned.

**ground** noun **1** *fall to the ground* earth, terra firma, floor; *inf.* deck. **2** *the ground is wet* earth, soil, dirt, land, terrain, clay, loam, turf, sod.

**groundless** adjective baseless, unfounded, unsupported, unsubstantiated, unwarranted, unjustified, uncalled-for, unreasonable, irrational, illogical, empty, idle, chimerical.

**grounds** plural noun **1** *take a walk around the grounds* surroundings, land, property, estate, lawns, gardens, park, area, domain, holding, territory. **2** *grounds for concern* reason, cause, basis, base, foundation, call, justification, rationale, argument, premise. **3** *coffee grounds* dregs, lees, deposit, sediment, precipitate, settlings, grouts.

**groundwork** noun foundation, base, basis, cornerstone, footing, underpinning, fundamentals, basics, ABCs, elements, essentials, preliminaries, preparations, spadework.

**group** noun **1** *divide the books into groups* category, classification, class, set, lot, batch, family, species, genus, bracket. **2** *a group of people/things* band, company, party, body, gathering, congregation, assembly, collection, clump, cluster, crowd, flock, pack, troop, gang, batch; clique, coterie, faction, circle, set; society, association, league, guild, club; *inf.* bunch.

**group** verb **1** *group students according to ability* classify, class, categorize, sort, grade, rank, bracket. **2** *group the children for a photograph* assemble, collect, gather together, arrange, organize, marshal, line up. **3** *they grouped (together) to form a club* get together, band together, associate, consort.

**grovel** verb abase oneself, kowtow, bow and scrape, crawl, fawn, curry favor, bootlick, flatter; *inf.* butter someone up, suck up to, throw oneself at someone's feet.

**grow** verb **1** *the child/pile grew* stretch, heighten, lengthen, enlarge, extend, expand, spread, thicken, widen, fill out, swell, increase, multiply. **2** *the plants are growing* shoot up, spring up, develop, sprout, burgeon, bud, germinate. **3** *her fear grows from her insecurity* arise, originate, stem, spring, issue. **4** *the business*

*is growing* flourish, thrive, prosper, succeed, progress, make headway, advance, improve, expand. **5** *grow prettier* become, get, turn, wax. **6** *grow corn* cultivate, produce, farm, propagate, raise.

**growl** verb snarl, howl, yelp, bark.

**growth** noun **1** *the growth in population* augmentation, increase, proliferation, multiplication, enlargement, expansion, extension, aggrandizement, magnification, amplification. **2** *the growth of the plants* development, maturation, germination, burgeoning, sprouting, blooming. **3** *the growth of the industry* expansion, rise, progress, success, advance, advancement, improvement. **4** *a growth on her body* tumor, lump, excrescence.

**grubby** adjective dirty, unwashed, grimy, filthy, messy, soiled, smutty, scruffy, shabby, untidy, unkempt, slovenly, squalid; *inf.* grungy, cruddy.

**grudge** noun resentment, spite, ill-will, pique, umbrage, grievance, hard feelings, rancor.

**grueling** adjective exhausting, tiring, fatiguing, wearying, taxing, demanding, trying, arduous, laborious, backbreaking, strenuous, punishing, crushing, draining, stiff, grinding, brutal.

**gruesome** adjective ghastly, frightful. *See* GRISLY.

**gruff** adjective **1** *a gruff voice* hoarse, harsh, rough, throaty, husky, croaking, rasping, guttural. **2** *a gruff old man* surly, churlish, brusque, curt, blunt, abrupt, grumpy, crotchety, crabby, crusty, bearish, sullen, sour; *inf.* grouchy.

**grumble** verb **1** *always grumbling about the weather* complain, moan, groan, protest, object, find fault with, carp, whine; *inf.* grouse, gripe, bellyache, beef, bitch, grouch. **2** *stomach was grumbling* rumble, gurgle, murmur, growl, mutter, roar.

**grumpy** adjective surly, churlish, crotchety, crabby, crusty, bearish, bad-tempered, ill-natured; *inf.* grouchy.

**guarantee** noun **1** *get a guarantee for the product* warranty, warrant, contract, covenant, bond, guaranty. **2** *give his guarantee that he will return* pledge, promise, assurance, word, word of honor, oath, bond. **3** *the house acts as a guarantee for a loan* collateral, security, surety, earnest, guaranty.

**guarantee** verb **1** *guarantee a loan* underwrite, sponsor, vouch for, support, back. **2** *I guarantee that I shall return* promise, pledge, give one's word, swear.

**guard** verb **1** *guard the town* stand guard over, protect, watch over, cover, patrol, police, defend, shield, safeguard, preserve,

save, conserve, secure, screen, shelter.
**2** *guard the prisoners* keep under surveillance, keep watch over, mind, supervise.
**guard against** beware of, keep an eye out for, be on the alert against/for, be on the lookout against/for; *inf.* keep one's eyes peeled for.

**guard** noun **1** *volunteer as guards* protector, defender, guardian, guarder, bodyguard, custodian, sentinel, sentry, watchman, scout, lookout, watch, picket. **2** *prison guards* jailer, keeper; *inf.* screw. **3** *kept under guard* watch, close watch, watchfulness, vigilance, care, wariness. **4** *a guard for a machine* safeguard, shield, screen, fence, fender, bumper, buffer, cushion, pad. **off one's guard, off guard** unprepared, unready, unalert, unwatchful, napping. **on one's guard** on the alert, vigilant, wary, watchful, on the lookout, on the qui vive, prepared, ready.

**guarded** adjective careful, cautious, circumspect, wary, chary, reluctant, noncommittal, reticent, restrained, reserved, discreet, prudent; *inf.* cagey.

**guardian** noun guard, protector, defender, preserver, champion, custodian, warden, keeper, curator, caretaker, steward, trustee.

**guess** verb **1** *guess the answer* conjecture, surmise, estimate, reckon, fathom, hypothesize, postulate, predict, speculate; *inf.* guesstimate. **2** *I guess that you're right* suppose, believe, think, imagine.

**guess** noun conjecture, surmise, estimate, guesswork, hypothesis, theory, supposition, feeling, assumption, inference, prediction, speculation; *inf.* guesstimate.

**guest** noun visitor, caller, company; boarder, lodger, roomer, patron, customer.

**guidance** noun **1** *under the guidance of the president* direction, leadership, auspices, management, control, handling, charge, rule, teaching, instruction. **2** *career guidance* counseling, counsel, advice, direction, recommendation, suggestion, tip, pointer, instruction.

**guide** verb **1** *guide them to their seats* lead, conduct, show, usher, shepherd, direct, pilot, steer, escort, accompany, attend. **2** *guide the firm through its problems* control, direct, steer, manage, command, govern, rule, preside over, superintend, supervise, handle, manipulate, maneuver. **3** *guide the young graduates* counsel, advise, give direction to.

**guide** noun **1** *a tourist guide* leader, conductor, director, courier, pilot, usher, escort, attendant, convoy, chaperon. **2** *act as a career guide* counselor, adviser, mentor, confidant, tutor, teacher, guru, therapist. **3** *the lighthouse was the captain's guide* marker, indicator, pointer, mark, landmark, guiding light, sign, signal, beacon, lodestar,

signpost, key, clue. **4** *use that essay as a guide* model, pattern, example, exemplar, norm, archetype, prototype, paradigm, ideal, precedent. *See* GUIDELINE. **5** *read a guide to Paris* guidebook, tourist guide, travelogue, directory, handbook, manual, instructions, key, catalog.

**guideline** noun criterion, measure, standard, gauge, yardstick, benchmark, touchstone, rule, regulation.

**guild** noun association, society, club, union, league, federation, organization, company, fellowship, order, lodge, brotherhood, fraternity, sisterhood, sorority, alliance.

**guile** noun cunning, duplicity, craftiness, craft, artfulness, art, artifice, wiliness, wiles, foxiness, slyness, deception, deceit, underhandedness, double-dealing, trickery, trickiness.

**guileless** adjective ingenuous, artless, open, sincere, genuine, naïve, simple, innocent, unsophisticated, unworldly, trustful, trusting.

**guilt** noun **1** *prove/admitted his guilt* guiltiness, culpability, blame, blameworthiness, wrongdoing, criminality, misconduct, delinquency, sin, sinfulness, iniquity. **2** *haunted by guilt* remorse, regret, contrition, contriteness, repentance, penitence, compunction, conscience, self-accusation, self-reproach.

**guiltless** adjective innocent, blameless, unimpeachable, irreproachable, above reproach, clear, pure, sinless, faultless.

**guilty** adjective **1** *found guilty of the crime* blameworthy, blamable, culpable, at fault, responsible, censurable, criminal, convicted; reproachable, condemnable, erring, errant, wrong, delinquent, offending, sinful, wicked, evil, unlawful, illegal, illicit, reprehensible, felonious, iniquitous. **2** *feel guilty* conscience-stricken, remorseful, ashamed, shamefaced, regretful, contrite, compunctious, repentant, penitent, rueful, sheepish.

**guise** noun **1** *in the guise of a witch* appearance, likeness, costume, clothes, outfit, dress, habit, style. **2** *under the guise of friendship* pretense, disguise, show, screen, cover, blind.

**gulf** noun **1** *ships sailing into the gulf* bay, cove, inlet, bight, creek. **2** *a gulf opened up by an earthquake* chasm, abyss, hollow, pit, hole, opening, rift, cleft, fissure, split, crevice, gully, canyon, gorge, ravine. **3** *the gulf between disputing parties* chasm, abyss, split, division, gap.

**gullible** adjective credulous, trustful, overtrustful, unsuspecting, ingenuous, naïve, green, foolish, wet behind the ears.

**gully** noun ravine, valley, gulch. *See* GULF 2.

**gumption** noun initiative, resourcefulness, enterprise, cleverness, astuteness, shrewdness, acumen, common sense, spirit, forcefulness, backbone, pluck, mettle, nerve, courage; *inf.* get-up-and-go, grit, spunk, savvy, horse sense.

**gun** noun firearm, pistol, revolver, automatic, repeater, six-shooter, handgun; *inf.* gat, piece, rod, heater, Saturday-night special.

**gunman** noun armed robber, bandit, sniper, gunfighter, assassin, murderer; *inf.* gunslinger, hitman, hired gun, hood, mobster.

**guru** noun teacher, tutor, sage, swami, maharishi, mentor, leader, master, authority.

**gush** verb 1 *water gushing from the pipe* stream, rush forth, spout, spurt, surge, jet, well out, pour forth, burst forth, cascade, flood, flow, run, issue, emanate. 2 *she gushed about the beautiful room* effuse, enthuse, wax enthusiastic, wax lyrical, effervesce, bubble over, get carried away, fuss, babble, make too much, overstate the case.

**gush** noun outpouring, spurt, jet, spout, burst, rush, surge, cascade, flood, torrent, spate, freshet, stream.

**gust** noun 1 *a gust of wind* blast, flurry, puff, blow, rush, squall, breeze, gale. 2 *a gust of laughter* outburst, burst, outbreak, eruption, explosion, gale, fit, paroxysm, storm, surge.

**gusto** noun relish, zest, enthusiasm, zeal, fervor, verve, enjoyment, delight, exhilaration, pleasure, appreciation, liking, fondness, appetite.

**guts** plural noun courage, bravery, valor, backbone, nerve, fortitude, pluck, mettle, gameness, spirit, boldness, audacity, daring, hardiness, toughness, forcefulness, stamina, willpower, tenacity; *inf.* grit, gumption, spunk.

**gutter** noun drain, sewer, sluice, culvert, conduit, pipe, duct, channel, trough, trench, ditch, furrow.

**guzzle** verb gulp, gobble, bolt, down, quaff, swill; *inf.* chug, chug-a-lug.

**gypsy** noun traveler, migrant, rover, roamer, wanderer, rambler; transient, vagrant, vagabond.

**gyrate** verb rotate, revolve, circle, whirl, pirouette, twirl, swirl, spin, swivel.

# *Hh*

**habit** noun 1 *it was his habit to take a daily walk* custom, practice, procedure, wont, way, routine, style, pattern, convention, policy, mode, rule. 2 *smoking is a bad habit* addiction, dependence, weakness, fixation, obsession. **habit of** *he had a habit of staring* tendency for, propensity for, predisposition for, proclivity for, penchant for, inclination for.

**habitat** noun 1 *the animal's natural habitat* environment, setting, element. 2 *the habitat of students* home, abode. *See* HABITATION 2.

**habitation** noun 1 *fit for habitation* occupancy, occupation, tenancy, living, dwelling, housing, inhabitance, lodging. 2 *settled into a new habitation* home, house, residence, residency, dwelling, dwelling place, abode, domicile, lodging, quarters, living quarters, rooms, apartment, flat, accommodation, housing, roof over one's head; *inf.* pad, digs.

**habitual** adjective 1 *taking his habitual route* customary, accustomed, regular, usual, normal, set, fixed, established, routine, wonted, common, ordinary, familiar, traditional. 2 *a habitual smoker* persistent, constant, repeated, confirmed, chronic, inveterate.

**hackneyed** adjective hack, banal, trite, overused, overworked, tired, worn-out, time-worn, stale, stereotyped, clichéd, commonplace, pedestrian, prosaic, run-of-the-mill, stock, conventional; *inf.* played-out, corny, old-hat.

**hag** noun crone, witch, gorgon, harridan, harpy, shrew, virago; *inf.* battleax, old bat/bag.

**haggard** adjective drawn, gaunt, pinched, hollow-cheeked, hollow-eyed, peaked, drained, careworn, emaciated, wasted.

**haggle** verb 1 *haggle over the price* bargain, drive a hard bargain, argue, dicker. 2 *children haggling* squabble, bicker, quarrel, argue, dispute.

**hail**[1] verb 1 *hail a friend* salute, greet, nod to, wave to, lift one's hat to, acknowledge. 2 *hail a taxi* signal, flag, flag down, call, shout to. 3 *hail the king* acclaim, applaud, cheer, praise, laud, extol.

**hail from** come from, be a native of, originate in.

**hail²** noun *a hail of bullets* shower, rain, storm, volley, barrage, bombardment, pelting.

**hail³** verb **hail down on** shower, rain down on/upon, pelt, pepper, batter, bombard.

**hair** noun **1** *brushed her hair* locks, tresses; *inf.* mane, mop. **2** *animal's hair* coat, fur, pelt, hide, wool, fleece, mane. **by a hair, by a hair's breadth** by a narrow margin, by the skin of one's teeth, by a split second, by a whisker. **let one's hair down** relax; *inf.* hang loose, let it all hang out, chill out. **split hairs** quibble, niggle, cavil; *inf.* nitpick.

**hair-raising** adjective spine-chilling, spine-tingling, bloodcurdling, terrifying, horrifying, frightening; *inf.* scary, creepy.

**hairy** adjective hair-covered, hirsute, pilose, pileous, woolly, furry, fleecy, fuzzy; bearded, unshaven, bewhiskered, stubbly.

**hale** adjective well, fit. See HEALTH 1.

**half-baked** adjective *half-baked notions* ill-conceived, unplanned, not thought through, premature, undeveloped, unformed, shortsighted, injudicious, impractical; *inf.* crackpot.

**halfhearted** adjective lukewarm, unenthusiastic, apathetic, indifferent, uninterested, unconcerned, cool, cursory, perfunctory, superficial.

**halfwit** noun simpleton, idiot, dolt, blockhead, dunderhead, dullard, dunce, fool, numskull, nitwit; *inf.* moron, dimwit, imbecile, crackpot, nut.

**halfwitted** adjective simpleminded, feebleminded, simple, stupid, idiotic, doltish, dull-witted, foolish, silly.

**hall** noun **1** *concerts held in the main hall* auditorium, assembly room, chamber. **2** *guests were greeted in the hall* vestibule, hallway, entry, lobby, foyer, passageway, passage.

**hallmark** noun *good craftsmanship is his hallmark* mark, trademark, stamp, sign, sure sign, telltale sign, badge, device, symbol.

**hallucinate** verb fantasize, imagine things, dream, be delirious; *inf.* see things, trip.

**hallucination** noun illusion, figment of the imagination, imagining, vision, mirage, fantasy, apparition, dream, delirium, phantasmagoria.

**halo** noun nimbus, aureole, aureola, aura, ring of light, crown of light, corona.

**halt¹** verb **1** *halt at the traffic lights* stop, come to a standstill, pull up, draw up, wait. **2** *halt for the day* finish, cease, break off, call it a day, desist, discontinue, rest; *inf.* knock off. **3** *halt progress* arrest, check,

block, curb, stem, terminate, end, put an end to, put a stop to, frustrate, obstruct, impede.

**halt²** noun stop, stoppage, cessation, close, end, desistance, discontinuation, discontinuance, standstill, pause, interval, interlude, intermission, break, hiatus, rest, respite, breathing space, time out; *inf.* breather.

**halt³** verb **1** *halt when speaking* falter, hesitate, stammer, stutter, stumble, flounder. **2** *halting between going and staying* hesitate, waver, vacillate, dither.

**hammer** verb **1** *hammer it on the anvil* beat, shape, form, mold, forge, fashion, make, fabricate. **2** *hammer the punching bag/opposition* beat, batter, pound, pummel, hit, strike; trounce, thrash, worst, drub; *inf.* murder, clobber, wallop. **3** *hammer facts into their heads* drum, drive, drub. **hammer away at** persevere at, persist at; *inf.* stick to/with, plug away at. **hammer out** thrash out, work out, resolve, sort out, settle, negotiate, bring about, produce, carry through, effect.

**hamper** verb hinder, obstruct, impede, hold back, inhibit, retard, slow down, hold up, restrain, curb, interfere with, cramp, restrict, bridle, handicap, hamstring.

**hamstring** verb *hamstring the opposition plans* frustrate, thwart, balk, foil, check, curb, hamper, ruin, prevent, stop.

**hand** noun **1** *large hands* palm, fist; *inf.* paw, mitt, duke. **2** *the hand of a clock* pointer, indicator, needle. **3** *give me a hand* helping hand, help, assistance, aid, support, succor, relief. **4** *hired a number of hands* worker, workman, employee, operative, hired hand, laborer, artisan, crewman. **5** *have a neat hand* writing, handwriting, penmanship, script, calligraphy. **6** *try your hand at baking* ability, skill, art, artistry, craftsmanship. **7** *give the singer a big hand* applause, round of applause, clap, ovation. **at hand 1** *help is at hand* available, accessible. See HANDY 1. **2** *your big moment is at hand* close at hand, imminent, approaching, impending. **from hand to mouth** precariously, uncertainly, insecurely, improvidently. **hand in glove** in partnership, in league, in collusion; *inf.* in cahoots. **hand in hand** *work hand in hand together*, closely, side by side, in partnership. **in hand 1** *have the matter in hand* under control, under way. **2** *have money in hand* ready, available, in reserve, put by. **try one's hand** attempt, essay; *inf.* have/take a shot, have a go.

**hand** verb give, pass, pass over, hand over, deliver, present. **hand down** transfer, transmit, bequeath, will. **hand out** distribute, give out, pass out, deal out, dole out, mete out, dispense, apportion, disburse; *inf.* dish out. **hand over** turn over, deliver, surrender, yield, release; *inf.* fork out/over.

**handbag** noun purse, bag, shoulder bag, clutch, pocketbook.

**handbook** noun guide, guidebook, travel guide, manual, instruction manual, instructions.

**handful** noun **1** *not many, just a handful* few, small number/amount, sprinkling. **2** *the child is a handful* nuisance, pest, bother, irritant; *inf.* pain, pain in the neck.

**handicap** noun **1** *born with a handicap* disability, disadvantage, abnormality, impairment. **2** *her poverty was a handicap* disadvantage, impediment, hindrance, obstruction, obstacle, encumbrance, barrier, stumbling block, drawback, shortcoming.

**handicap** verb put at a disadvantage, impede, hinder, impair, hamper, obstruct, check, block, encumber, curb, trammel, bridle, hold back, constrain, restrict, limit.

**handle** noun shaft, grip, handgrip, hilt, haft, knob, stock.

**handle** verb **1** *handle the goods* touch, feel, finger, hold, grasp, grip, pick up, caress, stroke, fondle, poke, maul; *inf.* paw. **2** *handle difficult problems/people* cope with, deal with, treat, manage, be in charge of, control, administer, direct, guide, conduct, supervise, take care of. **3** *dealers handling grain* deal in, traffic in, trade in, market, sell, stock, carry.

**handout** noun **1** *not accepting handouts* alms, charity; gift, sample, free sample; *inf.* freebie. **2** *read the handout* press release, circular, flyer, leaflet, brochure, pamphlet, bulletin.

**hands** plural noun *in the hands of the enemy* possession, keeping, charge, care, power, authority, command, management, control, custody, guardianship, supervision, jurisdiction. **hands down** *win hands down* easily, with no trouble, effortlessly; *inf.* no sweat.

**handsome** adjective **1** *a handsome man/woman* good-looking, attractive, elegant, fine, well-formed, well-proportioned, stately, dignified; *inf.* gorgeous, easy on the eyes, foxy. **2** *a handsome gift* generous, magnanimous, liberal, lavish, bounteous, considerable, sizable, large.

**handy** adjective **1** *is the book handy?* at hand, available, within reach, accessible, near, nearby, close, at one's fingertips, convenient; *inf.* on tap. **2** *a handy instrument* useful, helpful, practicable, practical, serviceable, functional, easy-to-use, convenient. **3** *a handy person* dexterous, deft, nimble-fingered, adroit, adept, proficient, skillful, good with one's hands.

**hang** verb **1** *mobiles hanging from the ceiling* hang down, be suspended, dangle, swing, sway, be pendent. **2** *hang the picture* suspend, put up, put on a hook. **3** *hang the convicted killer* send to the gallows, put the noose on, send to the gibbet, gibbet, execute; lynch; *inf.* string up. **4** *hang wallpaper* stick on, attach, fix, fasten on, append, paste, glue, cement. **5** *walls hung with tapestries* decorate, adorn, ornament, deck, drape, cover, furnish. **6** *hawks hanging in the air* hover, float, be poised, flutter, flit, drift, remain static. **hang around/about 1** *hang around, he won't be long* linger, loiter, tarry, dally, waste time; *inf.* hang on. **2** *hang around bars* frequent, be a regular at, haunt; *inf.* hang out in. **3** *hang around with thugs* associate, keep company; *inf.* hang out. **hang back** hold back, stay back, stay in the background, be reluctant, hesitate, demur, recoil, shrink back. **hang fire** delay, procrastinate, stall. **hang on 1** *everything hangs on the budget* depend, turn on, hinge on, rest on, be contingent upon, be determined by, be conditioned by. **2** *hang on till things improve* persevere, persist, go on, carry on, continue, remain, endure. **hang on to** cling to, grip, clutch, grasp, cleave to. **hang over** *the threat of layoffs is hanging over them* loom over, menace, threaten.

**hang** noun **get the hang of** get the knack of, catch on, grasp, comprehend, understand.

**hanger-on** noun parasite, minion, lackey, vassal, flunky, camp follower, sycophant, fawner, sponger, leech; *inf.* groupie, freeloader.

**hang-up** noun preoccupation, fixation, obsession, bee in one's bonnet, *idée fixe*; psychological block, block, inhibition, difficulty, problem; *inf.* thing.

**hanker** verb **hanker after/for** long for, yearn for, crave, desire, hunger for, thirst for, set one's heart on, pine for, lust after; *inf.* be dying for, have a yen for.

**hankering** noun longing, yearning, craving, desire, hunger, thirst, want, lust; *inf.* yen.

**haphazard** adjective random, unsystematic, unorganized, unmethodical, orderless, aimless, indiscriminate, slapdash, thrown together, careless, casual, hit-or-miss.

**hapless** adjective unlucky, luckless, unfortunate, ill-starred, forlorn, wretched, woebegone; *inf.* down on one's luck.

**happen** verb take place, occur, come about, come to pass, present itself, arise, materialize, appear, come into being, chance, arrive, transpire, crop up, develop; *inf.* come off.

**happening** noun occurrence, event, incident, occasion, affair, circumstance, action.

187

# happily · hard-hitting

**happily** adverb **1** *I shall happily go* with pleasure, gladly, delightedly, willingly, freely, contentedly, enthusiastically, with all one's heart and soul. **2** *children playing happily* cheerfully, merrily, gaily, lightheartedly, joyfully, blithely. **3** *happily, it turned out all right* luckily, fortunately, as luck would have it, providentially.

**happiness** noun cheerfulness, cheeriness, merriness, gaiety, good spirits, high spirits, lightheartedness, joy, joyfulness, joviality, glee, blitheness, gladness, delight, exuberance, elation, ecstasy, bliss, blissfulness, euphoria.

**happy** adjective **1** *a happy mood* cheerful, cheery, merry, gay, lighthearted, joyful, joyous, jovial, gleeful, buoyant, blithe, blithesome, carefree, untroubled, exuberant, elated, ecstatic, blissful, euphoric, in seventh heaven, floating/walking on air; *inf.* on cloud nine, on top of the world. **2** *happy to see you* glad, pleased, delighted, contented, satisfied, gratified, thrilled. **3** *a happy chance* lucky, fortunate, favorable, advantageous, beneficial, helpful, opportune, timely, convenient, propitious, auspicious. **4** *a happy choice* apt, appropriate, fitting, fit, proper, seemly.

**happy-go-lucky** adjective carefree, lighthearted, devil-may-care, blithe, free and easy, easygoing, nonchalant, casual, untroubled, unworried, unconcerned, insouciant.

**harangue** noun lecture, tirade, diatribe, sermon, exhortation, declamation; *inf.* spiel.

**harass** verb **1** *children harassing their mother* bother, pester, annoy, exasperate, worry, fret, disturb, agitate, provoke, badger, hound, torment, plague, persecute, harry, tease, bait, nag, molest, bedevil; *inf.* hassle, give someone a hard time, drive someone up the wall. **2** *troops harassing the enemy* harry, raid, beleaguer, press hard.

**harbinger** noun herald, forerunner, precursor, sign, portent, omen, augury.

**harbor** noun port, anchorage, dock, marina; refuge, shelter. *See* HAVEN 1, 2.

**harbor** verb **1** *harbor criminals* shelter, house, lodge, put up, take in, billet, provide refuge for, shield, protect, conceal, hide, secrete. **2** *harbor resentment* nurture, maintain, hold on to, cherish, cling to, retain, entertain, brood over.

**hard** adjective **1** *hard ground* firm, solid, solidified, compact, compacted, compressed, dense, rigid, stiff, unyielding, resistant, unmalleable, inflexible, unpliable, tough, strong, stony, rocklike. **2** *hard physical work* arduous, strenuous, heavy, tiring, fatiguing, exhausting, backbreaking, laborious, rigorous, exacting,

tough, uphill, toilsome, Herculean. **3** *a hard problem* difficult, complicated, complex, involved, intricate, puzzling, perplexing, knotty, thorny. **4** *a hard master* harsh, severe, stern, cold, grim, ruthless, oppressive, tyrannical, implacable, obdurate. **5** *hard living conditions* unpleasant, disagreeable, uncomfortable, intolerable, unendurable, unbearable, insupportable, distressing, painful. **6** *a hard blow/knock* forceful, violent, heavy, strong, powerful, sharp, fierce. **7** *a hard worker* industrious, diligent. *See* HARDWORKING. **8** *hard words/feelings* angry, acrimonious, bitter, antagonistic, hostile, resentful, rancorous. **9** *the hard facts* actual, definite, undeniable, indisputable, verifiable, plain, cold, bare, unvarnished, unembellished.

**hard** adverb **1** *push hard* strenuously, energetically, powerfully, heavily, with all one's might, with might and main, vigorously, forcefully, forcibly, fiercely, intensely. **2** *work hard* industriously, diligently, assiduously, conscientiously, enthusiastically, sedulously. **3** *our victory was hard won* with effort, laboriously, after a struggle, painfully. **4** *her death hit him hard* intensely, violently, forcefully, distressingly, painfully, agonizingly. **5** *it was raining hard* heavily, steadily; *inf.* cats and dogs, buckets. **6** *look hard at* keenly, sharply, carefully, closely, painstakingly. **hard by** right by, beside, near, nearby, close to, within a stone's throw of. **hard up** poor, short of money/cash, in financial difficulties, impoverished, destitute, bankrupt, in the red.

**hard-and-fast** adjective binding, set, strict, stringent, inflexible, rigorous, immutable, unalterable, uncompromising.

**hard-boiled** adjective cynical, unsentimental, tough.

**hard-core** adjective **1** *hard-core socialists* diehard, dyed-in-the-wool, staunch, steadfast, dedicated. **2** *hard-core pornography* explicit, blatant.

**harden** verb **1** *the cement hardened* solidify, set, stiffen, bake, anneal, cake, freeze, congeal, clot, coagulate. **2** *harden one's heart* toughen, deaden, numb, benumb. **3** *harden to cold* accustom, habituate, acclimatize, inure.

**hardened** adjective chronic, inured, seasoned, inveterate, incorrigible.

**hardheaded** adjective shrewd, astute, sharp, practical, pragmatic, realistic.

**hard-hearted** adjective heartless, unfeeling, unsympathetic, uncompassionate, cold, cold-hearted, uncaring, unconcerned, cruel, callous, merciless, pitiless, stony-hearted, stony.

**hard-hitting** adjective vigorous, tough, uncompromising, unsparing, blunt, frank, critical.

**hard-line** adjective extreme, uncompromising, inflexible, unyielding, intransigent.

**hardly** adverb scarcely, barely, only just, just.

**hard-pressed** adjective overloaded, overburdened, overworked, overtaxed, under pressure, harassed, harried, hounded; *inf.* pushed, up against it.

**hardship** noun adversity, privation, want, need, destitution, poverty, austerity, desolation, misfortune, distress, suffering, affliction, pain, misery, wretchedness, tribulation.

**hardworking** adjective diligent, industrious, conscientious, assiduous, sedulous, energetic, keen, enthusiastic, zealous, busy, with one's shoulder to the wheel.

**hardy** adjective 1 *hardy children* robust, sturdy. *See* HEALTHY 1. 2 *hardy men defying death* brave, courageous, valiant, bold, valorous, intrepid, stouthearted, daring, plucky, mettlesome.

**harebrained** adjective foolish, foolhardy, rash, reckless, madcap, wild, ridiculous, brainless, giddy, dizzy, whimsical, capricious, flighty. *See* HALF-BAKED.

**hark** verb harken, listen, pay attention, pay heed, give ear. **hark back to** go back to, turn back to, revert to, regress to, remember, recall, recollect.

**harlot** noun whore, prostitute, call girl, streetwalker, loose woman, fallen woman, lady of the evening, madam, procuress; *inf.* tramp, hooker.

**harm** noun 1 *inflict harm* hurt, injury, pain, suffering, trauma, adversity, disservice, abuse, damage, mischief, detriment, destruction, loss, ruin. 2 *full of harm* badness, evil, wrongdoing, wrong, wickedness, vice, iniquity, sin, sinfulness, immorality, nefariousness.

**harm** verb hurt, injure, wound, abuse, maltreat, ill-treat, ill-use, molest, do violence to, damage, do mischief to, deface, defile, impair, spoil, mar, blemish, destroy.

**harmful** adjective hurtful, injurious, detrimental, deleterious, disadvantageous, destructive, pernicious, noxious, baneful, toxic.

**harmless** adjective innocuous, safe, nontoxic, nonirritant, mild, inoffensive, unoffending.

**harmonious** adjective 1 *a harmonious musical piece* melodious, tuneful, musical, harmonizing, sweet-sounding, mellifluous, dulcet, euphonious, symphonious. 2 *a harmonious relationship* peaceful, peaceable, friendly, amicable, cordial, amiable, agreeable, congenial, in tune, attuned. 3 *a harmonious collection of buildings* compatible, congruous, coordinated, concordant, well-matched, matching.

**harmonize** verb 1 *the colors/stories harmonize* go together, fit together, be compatible, match, agree, correspond, coincide, be congruent. 2 *harmonize relations* settle differences, reconcile, patch up, negotiate peace between, heal the breach.

**harmony** noun 1 *working in harmony* agreement, accord, cooperation, unanimity, unity, amity, goodwill, affinity, rapport, fellowship, peace, peacefulness. 2 *the harmony of the colors* compatibility, congruity, consonance, concord, coordination, blending, balance, symmetry, suitability.

**harness** verb 1 *harness the horses* saddle, yoke, bridle, hitch up, couple. 2 *harness the sun's rays* control, utilize, apply, exploit, channel, mobilize, capitalize on.

**harp** noun **harp on** dwell on, persist in talking about, nag about, belabor the point about; *inf.* go on and on about.

**harridan** noun shrew, harpy, virago, termagant, vixen, scold, nag, fishwife, hellcat, spitfire, fury. *See* HAG.

**harrowing** adjective distressing, agonizing, excruciating, traumatic, painful, racking, chilling, horrifying.

**harry** verb 1 *invaders harrying the villagers* plunder, rob, raid, sack, pillage, devastate, ravage, despoil, lay waste to. 2 *children harrying their mother* annoy, bother. *See* HARASS 1.

**harsh** adjective 1 *a harsh noise* grating, jarring, grinding, rasping, strident, raucous, discordant, dissonant, unharmonious. 2 *harsh colors* gaudy, garish, glaring, bold, loud, flashy, showy, crass, crude, vulgar. 3 *harsh conditions/countryside* grim, severe, desolate, stark, austere, barren, bleak, inhospitable, comfortless, spartan. 4 *a harsh reply* abrupt, brusque, blunt, curt, gruff, short, surly, concise, impolite, discourteous, uncivil, ungracious. 5 *a harsh ruler* cruel, brutal, savage, barbarous, hard-hearted, despotic, tyrannical, ruthless, uncompassionate, unfeeling, merciless. 6 *a harsh measure* stern, severe, grim, stringent, austere, uncompromising, inflexible, punitive, draconian.

**harvest** noun 1 *a good harvest of apples* crop, yield, vintage. 2 *the squirrels have a harvest of nuts* store, supply, stock, stockpile, hoard, cache, accumulation. 3 *the harvest of hard work* product, fruits, return, effect, result, consequence.

**harvest** verb 1 *harvest the crop* gather in, gather, reap, glean, pick, pluck, collect. 2 *harvest benefits from his experience* acquire, gain, obtain, get, derive, procure, secure, net.

**hassle** noun 1 *tired of all the hassle* inconvenience, trouble, bother, annoyance, nuisance, harassment, badgering, difficulty, problem, struggle. **2** *a hassle at the bar last night* fight, quarrel, squabble, argument, disagreement, dispute, altercation, tussle.

**hassle** verb annoy, badger. *See* HARASS 1.

**haste** noun **1** *fulfill the order with haste* speed, swiftness, rapidity, quickness, alacrity, promptness, dispatch, expeditiousness, celerity, fleetness, briskness. **2** *haste causes carelessness* hastiness, hurriedness, hurry, rushing, hustling, impetuosity, recklessness, rashness, impulsiveness.

**hasten** verb **1** *you must hasten to get there on time* make haste, hurry, hurry up, dash, rush, race, sprint, fly, tear along, bolt, scurry, scamper, scuttle; *inf.* get a move on, step on it, hotfoot it, hightail it. **2** *hasten the growth* speed up, accelerate, quicken, advance, precipitate, boost, increase, step up.

**hasty** adjective **1** *with hasty steps* swift, rapid, quick, fast, speedy, hurried, prompt, expeditious, fleet, brisk. **2** *a hasty visit/glance* brief, short-lived, fleeting, transitory, cursory, perfunctory. **3** *a hasty decision* rushed, impetuous, reckless, rash, foolhardy, precipitate, impulsive, headlong, heedless, ill-conceived. **4** *a hasty nature* hotheaded, quick-tempered, irascible, fiery, excitable, volatile, choleric.

**hat** noun cap, bonnet, beret, tam-o'-shanter, hard hat, bowler, top hat, deerstalker, Homburg, Stetson, boater, panama, toque, cloche, pillbox, helmet, turban, fez, skullcap, yarmulke.

**hatch** verb **1** *hatch eggs* incubate, brood, sit on, cover. **2** *hatch a scheme* devise, concoct, contrive, plan, scheme, design, conceive, dream up, think up; *inf.* cook up.

**hate** verb **1** *hate his job* loathe, detest, abhor, abominate, despise, be unable to abide/bear/stand, be repelled by, recoil from. **2** *I hate to upset her* be reluctant, be loath, be unwilling, feel disinclined, be sorry, dislike, not have the heart.

**hateful** adjective loathsome, detestable, abhorrent, abominable, despicable, odious, revolting, repugnant, repellent, disgusting, obnoxious, offensive, insufferable, foul, vile, heinous.

**hatred** noun hate, loathing, detestation, abhorrence, abomination, aversion, hostility, ill will, enmity, animosity, antagonism, antipathy, revulsion, repugnance, odium, rancor.

**haughty** adjective proud, arrogant, conceited, self-important, egotistical, vain, supercilious, condescending, lofty, patronizing, snobbish, imperious; *inf.* on one's high horse, snooty, high and mighty, stuck-up, hoity-toity, uppity.

**haul** verb drag, draw, pull, tug, heave, trail, lug, tow; transport, convey, move, cart, carry, convoy, ship.

**haunt** verb **1** *haunt bars* frequent, be a regular at; *inf.* hang out in, hang around/about. **2** *thoughts of guilt haunted him* obsess, prey on, torment, plague, beset, burden, weigh on, recur to, come back to.

**haunt** noun stamping ground, favorite spot, resort, rendezvous; *inf.* hangout.

**haunting** adjective persistent, recurring, recurrent, indelible, unforgettable.

**have** verb **1** *we have two cars* own, possess, keep, use, hold, retain. **2** *we had news of him* get, receive, obtain, acquire, procure, secure, gain. **3** *the apartment has five rooms* contain, include, comprise, embrace, embody, incorporate. **4** *she had a lot of trouble* experience, undergo, go through, encounter, meet, find, suffer from, endure, tolerate, put up with. **5** *have doubts* feel, entertain, harbor, foster, nurse, cherish. **6** *have the impudence to answer back* show, display, exhibit, demonstrate, manifest, express. **7** *they had her do all their work* make, force to, coerce to, induce to, prevail upon to, talk into, persuade to. **8** *I'll have the technician repair the telephone* ask to, request that, bid to, tell to, order to, command to, direct to. **9** *she won't have such behavior* permit, allow, put up with, tolerate, stand, brook, endure, abide. **10** *she had a daughter* bear, deliver, be delivered of, bring into the world, beget. **11** *they certainly had you* fool, trick, take in, dupe, outwit, deceive, cheat, swindle. **12** *he boasted that he had had all the women there* have sex with, make love to/with, copulate with; *inf.* bed, lay. **have had it** be finished, be out, be defeated, have lost.

**have on 1** *I have something on today* have planned, have arranged, be committed to, have on the agenda. **2** *the police have something on him* have information about, have evidence against, know something bad/incriminating about. **have to** must, have got to, be bound to, be obliged to, be under an obligation to, be forced to, be compelled to.

**haven** noun **1** *ships entering a haven* harbor, port, anchorage, moorage, dock, cove, bay. **2** *refugees seeking a safe haven* refuge, shelter, sanctuary, asylum, retreat, sanctum, sanctum sanctorum, covert.

**havoc** noun **1** *forest fires wreaking havoc* devastation, destruction, damage, ruination, ruin, rack and ruin, waste, wreckage, desolation. **2** *the havoc in the room after the party* chaos, disorder, confusion, disruption, disorganization, mayhem; *inf.* shambles.

**hazard** noun danger, peril, risk, jeopardy, threat, menace.

**hazard** verb **1** *hazard a guess* venture, put forward, proffer, offer, submit, advance, volunteer. **2** *hazard his life* risk, endanger, imperil, jeopardize.

**hazardous** adjective **1** *a hazardous journey* dangerous, danger-filled, risky, perilous, fraught with danger/risk/peril, precarious; *inf.* dicey, hairy. **2** *a hazardous venture* chancy, uncertain, unpredictable, speculative.

**haze** noun **1** *haze covered the town* mist, mistiness, fog, cloud, cloudiness, smog, vapor. **2** *her mind is in a haze* vagueness, confusion, befuddlement, bewilderment, obscurity, dimness.

**hazy** adjective **1** *a hazy day* misty, foggy, cloudy, smoggy. **2** *hazy memories* vague, indefinite, blurred, fuzzy, unclear, obscure, dim, indistinct, ill-defined.

**head** noun **1** *hurt his head* skull, cranium; *inf.* pate, nut, noodle, noggin, bean. **2** *use your head* mind, intellect, intelligence, brain, brains, mentality, wit, wits, wisdom, sense, reasoning, rationality, understanding; *inf.* gray matter. **3** *a head for business* aptitude, ability, capacity, flair, talent, faculty. **4** *the head of the organization* leader, chief, commander, director, chairman, chair, chairperson, manager, superintendent, controller, administrator, supervisor. **5** *(at) the head of the firm* top, command, control, controls, charge, leadership, directorship. **6** *at the head of the line* front, fore, forefront, van, vanguard. **7** *matters coming to a head* climax, culmination, crisis, critical point, turning point, crossroads. **8** *at the head of the stream* origin, source, fountainhead, fount, wellhead, wellspring, headwater. **9** *the material is listed under various heads* category, classification. *See* HEADING 1. **go to one's head 1** *the wine has gone to my head* make someone intoxicated/dizzy, make someone's head spin; *inf.* make someone woozy. **2** *their praise went to her head* make someone conceited/arrogant/boastful, puff someone up. **head first 1** *fall head first down the stairs* on one's head, head foremost. *See* HEADLONG 1. **2** *rush into things head first* rashly, recklessly. *See* HEADLONG 2. **head over heels** utterly, completely, thoroughly, fully, wholeheartedly, intensely. **keep one's head** keep calm, keep cool, remain unruffled, maintain one's equilibrium. **lose one's head** panic, lose control of oneself, lose control of the situation, get flustered/confused, get angry, get excited, get hysterical; *inf.* lose one's cool, blow one's top, freak out, fly off the handle.

**head** adjective chief, leading, main, principal, premier, foremost, topmost, supreme, cardinal.

**head** verb **1** *head the expedition/firm* lead, be the leader of, be at the head of, be in charge of, be in command of, command, control, run, manage, direct, administer, supervise. **2** *a tower headed by a spire* crown, top, surmount, cap, tip. **3** *head for town* make for, aim for, set out for, start out for, go/turn toward, steer toward. **head off** intercept, deflect, turn aside, block off, cut off, ward off, fend off, forestall, avert.

**headache** noun *her nephew is nothing but a headache to her* nuisance, bother, pest, trouble, vexation, bane, bugbear, worry, inconvenience; *inf.* pain, pain in the neck.

**heading** noun **1** *materials listed under various headings* head, category, class, classification, subject, topic, division, section. **2** *put headings on the illustrations* title, caption, headline, name, rubric.

**headlong** adverb **1** *fall headlong into the bushes* head first, on one's head, head foremost, head on, diving, plunging. **2** *rush headlong into a decision* hastily, in haste, hurriedly, impetuously, impulsively, without thinking, rashly, prematurely, precipitately, carelessly, heedlessly.

**headstrong** adjective stubborn, obstinate, obdurate, mulish, intransigent, intractable, pigheaded, refractory, recalcitrant, ungovernable, wayward, contrary, willful, perverse.

**headway** noun **make headway** make progress, progress, advance, gain ground.

**heady** adjective **1** *a heady drink* intoxicating, inebriating, potent, strong. **2** *heady with success* exhilarated, excited, overjoyed, thrilled, overwhelmed, euphoric, ecstatic; *inf.* in seventh heaven, on cloud nine. **3** *the heady days of youth* stimulating, rousing, arousing, invigorating, thrilling, electrifying. **4** *a heady action* impetuous, rash, reckless, wild, foolhardy.

**heal** verb **1** *heal the wound* cure, make well, make better, remedy, treat, mend, restore, regenerate. **2** *heal the breach* reconcile, patch up, settle, set right, put right.

**health** noun **1** *full of health* healthiness, fitness, well-being, good condition, good shape, soundness, robustness, strength, vigor, salubrity. **2** *his health is poor* constitution, condition, form, tone.

**healthy** adjective **1** *a healthy young man* in good health, fit, physically fit, able-bodied, in good condition/trim/shape, in fine fettle, in fine/top form, robust, strong, vigorous, hardy, flourishing, hale and hearty, hale, hearty, bursting with health; *inf.* in the pink, fit as a fiddle. **2** *a healthy climate* health-giving, salubrious, invigorating, bracing, stimulating, refreshing, tonic. **3** *a healthy diet* healthful, nutritious, nourishing, wholesome, beneficial.

**heap** noun pile, stack, mass, mound, mountain, stockpile, accumulation, collection, hoard, store, stock, supply. **heaps, a heap** a lot, lots, a great deal, an abundance, plenty, considerable, a mint; *inf.* oodles, loads, tons.

**heap** verb **heap on** bestow on, confer on, shower on, load on. **heap up** pile up, stack, stack up, amass, stockpile, accumulate, collect, assemble, hoard, store, stock up, set aside, lay by.

**hear** verb **1** *I didn't hear what he said* catch, take in, overhear; *inf.* get. **2** *we heard that he was ill* be informed, be told, be made aware, find out, discover, learn, gather, pick up, be given to understand, hear tell, get wind.

**hearing** noun *present at the hearing* inquiry, trial, inquest, investigation, inquisition, review, examination.

**hearsay** noun rumor, gossip, idle talk, mere talk, talk of the town, word of mouth; *inf.* buzz, grapevine.

**heart** noun **1** *love her with all his heart* passion, love, affection, emotions, feelings. **2** *he has no heart* tenderness, compassion, sympathy, empathy, humanity, fellow feeling, benevolence, kindness, kindliness, brotherly love. **3** *I don't have the heart to tell him the truth* courage, bravery, valor, intrepidity, fearlessness, mettle, backbone, nerve, fortitude, purpose, resolution, determination; *inf.* guts, spunk, gumption. **4** *the heart of the matter/universe* center, core, nucleus, middle, kernel, hub, quintessence, essence, crux, marrow, pith, substance, sum and substance. **at heart** basically, fundamentally, in essence, essentially, in reality, really, in fact. **by heart** by rote, word for word, pat, by memory. **do one's heart good** please, gladden, cheer, delight, gratify, satisfy. **eat one's heart out** sorrow, grieve, mourn, agonize, pine, mope, fret, brood, repine. **from the bottom of one's heart** profoundly, deeply, sincerely, devoutly, heartily, fervently, passionately. **have a heart** be kind, be merciful, be lenient, be compassionate, be sympathetic, be considerate. **have one's heart set on** long for, yearn for, desire, be desirous of, crave. **heart and soul** enthusiastically, eagerly, zealously, wholeheartedly, gladly, with open arms, thoroughly, completely. **take heart** cheer up, brighten up, perk up, revive; *inf.* buck up. **with one's heart in one's mouth** fearfully, apprehensively, with fear and trembling, with trepidation, with bated breath.

**heartache** noun sorrow, grief, sadness, anguish, pain, hurt, agony, suffering, misery, woe, dolor.

**heartbreaking** adjective sad, pitiful, poignant, tragic, painful, agonizing, distressing, heart-rending, grievous, harrowing, tear-jerking, excruciating.

**heartbroken** adjective brokenhearted, heartsick, miserable, sorrowful, sad, anguished, grieving, dejected, dispirited, downcast, crestfallen, crushed, despondent, in low spirits.

**hearten** verb cheer, cheer up, raise the spirits of, invigorate, revitalize, energize, animate, revivify, exhilarate, uplift, elate, comfort, encourage, buoy up, pep up; *inf.* buck up, give a shot in the arm to.

**heartfelt** adjective deep, profound, sincere, genuine, earnest, ardent, fervent, warm, cordial, enthusiastic, eager.

**heartless** adjective unfeeling, unsympathetic, uncompassionate, unkind, uncaring, cold, cold-hearted, hard-hearted, cruel, harsh, hard, merciless, pitiless, ruthless.

**heart-rending** adjective sad, distressing. *See* HEARTBREAKING.

**heartsick** adjective sick at heart, heavy-hearted, dejected, depressed, despondent, disappointed, heartsore.

**heartwarming** adjective **1** *a heartwarming story* touching, moving, affecting, cheering, gladdening, encouraging, uplifting. **2** *a heartwarming job* gratifying, satisfying, rewarding.

**hearty** adjective **1** *a hearty welcome* enthusiastic, eager, warmhearted, warm, cordial, jovial, friendly, affable, unreserved, uninhibited, ebullient, exuberant, effusive. **2** *a hearty dislike* wholehearted, complete, total, absolute, thorough. **3** *a hearty young/old man* strong, robust. *See* HEALTHY. **4** *a hearty meal* substantial, solid, abundant, ample, sizable, filling, nutritious, nourishing.

**heat** noun **1** *the heat of summer* hotness, warmth, sultriness, torridness, swelter, heatwave, hot spell; *inf.* dog days. **2** *caught up in the heat of his speech* warmth, passion, vehemence, intensity, ardor, fervor, zeal, eagerness, enthusiasm, animation, earnestness, excitement, agitation.

**heat** verb **heat up 1** *heat up the milk* warm, warm up, reheat, cook. **2** *the day heated up* grow hot, grow warm, get hotter/warmer. **3** *the argument heated up* grow passionate/vehement/fierce/angry.

**heated** adjective passionate, vehement, fierce, angry, furious, stormy, tempestuous, intense, impassioned, violent, excited, inflamed.

**heathen** noun *missionaries converting heathens* unbeliever, infidel, pagan, idolater, atheist, heretic.

**heathen** adjective **1** *converting a heathen tribe* infidel, pagan, godless, irreligious, idolatrous. **2** *invaded by heathen tribes* barbarian, barbarous, savage, uncivilized, brutish.

**heave** verb **1** *heaving heavy weights* lift, haul, pull, tug, raise, hoist, upheave. **2** *heave the hammer in the games* throw, cast, toss, fling, hurl, let fly, pitch, send; *inf.* sling, chuck. **3** *heave a sigh* give, utter, let out, pant, gasp, sigh, sob. **4** *people heaving as the ship sailed* vomit, be sick, spew, retch, gag; *inf.* throw up.

**heaven** noun **1** *departed souls abiding in heaven* Kingdom of God, paradise, next life, life to come, next world, the hereafter, Zion, nirvana, Valhalla, Elysium, Elysian Fields, empyrean, happy hunting ground. **2** *she was in heaven at the news* ecstasy, bliss, sheer bliss, rapture, supreme happiness, seventh heaven, paradise, Eden, Utopia, dreamland. **3** *the heavens opened* sky, skies, firmament, ether, empyrean, aerosphere, vault of heaven; *inf.* (wild) blue yonder.

**heavenly** adjective **1** *heavenly concerns* cosmic, extraterrestrial, unearthly, not of this world, otherworldly. **2** *heavenly beings* celestial, divine, angelic, seraphic, cherubic, blessed, beatific, beatified, immortal, superhuman, paradisiacal. **3** *a heavenly party/dress* delightful, pleasurable, enjoyable, marvelous, exquisite, perfect, superb, enchanting, sublime; *inf.* glorious, divine.

**heavy** adjective **1** *a heavy log/load* weighty, bulky, hefty, substantial, massive, enormous, mighty, colossal, ponderous, unwieldy, cumbersome. **2** *a heavy responsibility* onerous, burdensome, oppressive, unbearable. **3** *a heavy blow* hard, forceful, strong, severe, grievous, harsh, intense, sharp. **4** *a heavy man* stout, overweight, fat, obese, corpulent, portly, tubby, paunchy, lumbering. **5** *heavy traffic/losses* great, large, considerable, abundant, copious, profuse, superabundant. **6** *heavy fighting* severe, intense, serious, grave. **7** *heavy reading* difficult, deep, profound, dull, tedious, boring, uninteresting, dry, wearisome, dry as dust. **8** *feeling heavy after dinner* sluggish, inactive, indolent, listless, torpid. **9** *heavy of heart* sad, sorrowful, dejected, disheartened, despondent, downhearted, depressed. **10** *heavy seas/waves* rough, wild, stormy, tempestuous, turbulent, squally, boisterous, violent. **11** *heavy day/skies* cloudy, overcast, gray, dark, dull, gloomy, dreary, leaden. **12** *heavy pastries* filling, indigestible, dense; sickening.

**heavy-handed** adjective **1** *heavy-handed and always breaking things* clumsy, awkward, maladroit, bungling, blundering, unhandy, ham-handed, ham-fisted, inept, like a bull in a china shop. **2** *too heavy-handed to deal with the bereaved* insensitive, tactless, thoughtless. **3** *a heavy-handed father* harsh, hard, stern, severe, oppressive, domineering, overbearing, autocratic.

**heckle** verb shout down, interrupt, disrupt, jeer, taunt, badger, bait, harass.

**hectic** adjective frantic, frenetic, frenzied, bustling, flustering, flurried, fast and furious, turbulent, tumultuous, confused, exciting, excited, wild.

**hedge** verb **1** *she hedged when questioned* equivocate, prevaricate, dodge/duck the question/issue, sidestep the issue, hem and haw, beat around the bush, pussyfoot around, temporize, quibble. **2** *hedge yourself against inflation* safeguard, guard, protect, cover, shield, insure. **hedge in** **1** *the trees hedge in the garden* surround, enclose, encircle, border, edge, skirt. **2** *hedged in by petty restrictions* hem in, confine, restrict, hinder, obstruct.

**heed** noun heedfulness, attention, attentiveness, notice, note, regard, mindfulness, consideration, thought, care, caution.

**heed** verb pay heed to, be heedful of, pay attention to, attend to, take notice of, take note of, notice, note, bear in mind, be mindful of, mind, mark, consider.

**heedful** adjective attentive, careful, mindful, cautious, prudent, circumspect, wary, chary, observant, watchful, vigilant.

**heedless** adjective unheeding, inattentive, careless, incautious, unmindful, unthinking, thoughtless, unwary, oblivious, unobservant, negligent, neglectful, rash, reckless.

**heel** noun **1** *the heel of the loaf* crust, end, remnant, remainder, tail-end, stump, butt, rump. **2** *he's an utter heel* scoundrel, cad, blackguard; *inf.* rat, swine, bounder. **down at (the) heel(s)** shabby, out at the elbows, seedy, rundown, slovenly, slipshod. **take to one's heels** run away, run off, take flight, flee, escape; *inf.* skedaddle, hightail it, hotfoot it, split, vamoose.

**hefty** adjective **1** *hefty young man* heavy, bulky, hulking, stout, massive, muscular, brawny, strapping, sturdy, rugged, beefy. **2** *a hefty blow* hard, forceful, powerful, vigorous, mighty. **3** *a hefty load* heavy, weighty, big, large, tremendous, immense, bulky, awkward, unwieldy. **4** *a hefty sum* substantial, sizable, expensive, huge, colossal, overpriced.

**height** noun **1** *measure the height* highness, altitude, loftiness, elevation, tallness, stature. **2** *the height overlooking the valley* top, mountaintop, hilltop, summit, crest, crown, pinnacle, peak, vertex. **3** *at the height of his powers* culmination, crowning point, high point, peak, zenith, apogee, climax, consummation, perfection, apex. **4** *the height of fashion* utmost, uttermost, ultimate, acme, ne plus ultra, limit, extremity, maximum, ceiling.

**heighten** verb **1** *heighten the ceiling* raise, lift, elevate. **2** *heighten the tension* intensify, raise, increase, augment, build up, boost, strengthen, amplify, magnify, aggravate, enhance, improve.

**heinous** adjective atrocious, abominable, abhorrent, odious, detestable, loathsome, hateful, execrable, wicked, contemptible, reprehensible, despicable.

**heir, heiress** noun beneficiary, legatee, inheritor, successor, next in line, scion.

**hell** noun **1** *wicked spirits in hell* infernal regions, inferno, hellfire, eternal fire, fire and brimstone, nether world, lower world, abode of the damned, perdition, abyss, bottomless pit, Hades. **2** *it was hell in the battle* torment, torture, misery, suffering, affliction, anguish, agony, ordeal, wretchedness, nightmare, woe. **3** *get hell from the teacher* upbraiding, scolding, castigation, vituperation, reprimand, censure, criticism, disapprobation; *inf.* what for. **hell for leather** pell-mell, post-haste, at the double, headlong, full tilt; *inf.* like a bat out of hell. **raise hell 1** *partygoers raising hell* party, carouse, revel. **2** *his father raised hell* be furious, be enraged, protest, complain, object, remonstrate, raise the roof, raise Cain.

**helm** noun **at the helm** in charge, in command, in control, in authority, at the wheel, in the driver's seat, in the saddle.

**help** verb **1** *help the neighbors* assist, aid, lend a helping hand to, lend a hand to, be of service to, succor, befriend. **2** *help the charity* contribute to, support, back, promote, boost. **3** *help the pain/situation* soothe, relieve, ameliorate, alleviate, mitigate, assuage, remedy, cure, heal, improve, ease. **help oneself to** *he helped himself to my books* appropriate, commandeer, steal, make free with; *inf.* pinch, walk off with.

**help** noun **1** *give the woman some help* assistance, aid, helping hand, service, use, guidance, benefit, advantage, avail, support, backing, succor. **2** *no help for the condition* relief, remedy, cure, restorative, corrective, balm, salve. **3** *ask the help for assistance* helper, assistant, employee, worker, hired help, maid, servant.

**helper** noun assistant, aide, auxiliary, right-hand man/woman, girl/man Friday, helpmate, partner, ally, collaborator.

**helpful** adjective useful, of use, of service, beneficial, advantageous, valuable, profitable, instrumental, constructive, practical, productive.

**helpless** adjective **1** *a helpless invalid* weak, feeble, impotent, incapable, infirm, debilitated, powerless, dependent. **2** *left helpless in the wilderness* defenseless, unprotected, vulnerable, exposed.

**helter-skelter** adverb hastily, hurriedly, pell-mell, headlong.

**henceforth** adverb from now on, from this day forward, hereafter, in the future, hence, in time to come.

**henchman** noun follower, right-hand man/woman, subordinate, underling, lackey, flunky, toady, hired killer/assassin; *inf.* hit man, hatchet man.

**henpecked** adjective *henpecked husbands* bullied, dominated, browbeaten, led by the nose, cringing, cowering, meek, timid, docile; *inf.* under the thumb.

**herald** verb **1** *companies heralding their new products* announce, make public, make known, proclaim, broadcast, publicize, advertise, promote, promulgate, trumpet, beat the drum about. **2** *prototypes heralding major new inventions* usher in, pave the way for, show in, precede, be the forerunner/precursor of, portend, indicate, augur, presage, promise.

**herd** noun **1** *a herd of cattle* drove, collection, assemblage, flock, pack, cluster. **2** *a herd of people* crowd, horde, multitude, mob, mass, host, throng, swarm, press. **3** *ignore the tastes of the herd* masses, mob, populace, rabble, riff-raff, hoi polloi, peasants; *inf.* great unwashed.

**herd** verb **1** *herd the sheep into the pens* drive, round up, shepherd, guide, lead, force, urge, goad. **2** *people herding (together) in the hall* assemble, gather, collect, congregate, flock, rally, muster, huddle. **3** *shepherds herding the sheep* look after, take care of, watch, stand guard over, guard, tend.

**hereafter** adverb after this, from now on. *See* HENCEFORTH.

**hereafter** noun **the hereafter** life after death, the afterlife, the afterworld, the next world, the beyond, eternity, immortality. *See* HEAVEN 1.

**hereditary** adjective genetic, congenital, innate, inborn, inherent, inbred, family, transmissible, transferable, inherited, handed down.

**heredity** noun genetics, genetic makeup, genes, congenital characteristics/traits.

**heresy** noun apostasy, dissent, dissension, dissidence, unbelief, skepticism, agnosticism, atheism, nonconformity, unorthodoxy, separatism, sectarianism, free-thinking, heterodoxy, revisionism, idolatry, paganism.

**heretic** noun apostate, dissenter, dissident, unbeliever, skeptic, agnostic, atheist, nonconformist, separatist, sectarian, freethinker, renegade, revisionist, idolater, pagan, heathen.

**heritage** noun history, tradition, background; ancestry, lineage, descent, extraction, family, dynasty, bloodline, heredity, birth.

**hermit** noun recluse, solitary, anchorite/anchoress, eremite, ascetic.

**hero** noun champion, conquering hero, victor, conqueror; man of the hour, celebrity, lion, cavalier; paragon, shining example, exemplar, idol, ideal.

**heroic** adjective **1** *heroic deeds* brave, courageous, valiant, valorous, intrepid, fearless, gallant, stouthearted, lionhearted, bold, daring, undaunted, dauntless, doughty, manly, virile, chivalrous. **2** *heroic ambitious* epic, epical, high-flown, high-sounding, extravagant, grandiose, pretentious, elevated.

**heroism** noun bravery, courage, valor, fearlessness, gallantry, stoutheartedness, boldness, daring, dauntlessness, doughtiness, manliness, virility, mettle, spirit, fortitude, chivalry.

**hesitant** adjective uncertain, unsure, doubtful, dubious, skeptical, irresolute, indecisive, vacillating, wavering, oscillating, shilly-shallying, hanging back, stalling, delaying, disinclined, reluctant, unwilling, halfhearted, diffident, timid, shy.

**hesitate** verb **1** *he always hesitates before deciding* pause, delay, hang back, wait, be uncertain, be unsure, be doubtful, be indecisive, vacillate, oscillate, waver, shilly-shally, dally, stall, temporize; *inf.* dilly-dally. **2** *she hesitates to interfere* be reluctant, be unwilling, be disinclined, shrink (from), hang back (from), think twice (about), balk (at), have misgivings/qualms (about), be diffident (about). **3** *he hesitates a lot when speaking* stammer, stumble, stutter, falter, hem and haw, fumble for words.

**hew** verb carve, sculpt, sculpture, shape, fashion, form, model, whittle, chip, chisel, rough-hew. **hew down** chop, chop down, hack, hack down, ax, cut/saw down, fell. **hew off** lop, cut off, chop off, sever, trim, prune.

**heyday** noun prime, prime of life, bloom, full flowering, flowering, peak, peak of perfection, pinnacle, culmination, crowning point, salad days.

**hiatus** noun gap, break, lacuna, blank, discontinuity, interruption; interval, intermission, pause, lull, rest, break, suspension, abeyance.

**hidden** adjective concealed, unrevealed, secret, unseen, out of sight, covered, masked, shrouded, obscure, cryptic, mysterious, covert, under wraps, clandestine.

**hide** verb **1** *prisoners hiding from the police* go into hiding, conceal oneself, take cover, lie low, keep out of sight, secrete oneself, go underground, cover one's tracks; *inf.* hole up. **2** *hide the jewels* secrete, conceal, store away, stow away, stash, lock up. **3** *clouds hiding the sun* obscure, cloud, darken, block, eclipse, obstruct. **4** *hide one's motives* conceal, withhold, suppress, hush up, mask, veil, shroud, camouflage, disguise; *inf.* keep mum, keep under one's hat.

**hide** noun skin, pelt, coat, fur, fleece.

**hideaway** noun hiding place, den, lair, retreat, shelter, refuge, hermitage, hide-out.

**hideous** adjective **1** *a hideous sight* ugly, unsightly, grotesque, monstrous, repulsive, repellent, revolting, gruesome, disgusting, grim, ghastly, macabre. **2** *a hideous crime* horrible, horrific, horrendous, horrifying, frightful, shocking, dreadful, outrageous, monstrous, appalling, heinous, abominable, foul, vile, odious, loathsome, contemptible, execrable.

**hide-out** noun hiding place, shelter. *See* HIDEAWAY.

**high** adjective **1** *a high building* tall, lofty, elevated, soaring, towering, steep. **2** *a high official* high-ranking, leading, top, ruling, powerful, important, principal, chief, main, prominent, eminent, influential, distinguished, notable, exalted, illustrious. **3** *high ideals* noble, virtuous. *See* HIGH-MINDED. **4** *a high wind* intense, extreme, strong, forceful, vigorous, powerful, potent, sharp, violent. **5** *high prices* dear, top, excessive, stiff, inflated, exorbitant, extortionate, high-priced, expensive, costly; *inf.* pricey, steep. **6** *a high lifestyle* high-living, extravagant, luxurious, lavish, rich, grand, prodigal. **7** *a high opinion* favorable, approving, admiring, flattering. **8** *feeling high before the holidays* excited, in high spirits, high-spirited, ebullient, bouncy, elated, ecstatic, euphoric, exhilarated, joyful, merry, happy, cheerful, jolly. **9** *high on drugs* drugged, intoxicated, inebriated, delirious, hallucinating; *inf.* stoned, turned on, tripping, hyped up, freaked out, spaced out. **10** *high voice/notes* high-pitched, acute, high-frequency, soprano, treble, piping, shrill, sharp-toned, piercing, penetrating. **high and dry** stranded, marooned, abandoned, helpless, destitute, bereft. **high and mighty** haughty, arrogant, self-important, proud, conceited, egotistic, overweening, overbearing, snobbish, condescending, disdainful, supercilious, imperious; *inf.* stuck-up, uppity, highfalutin.

**high** adverb high up, far up, way up, aloft. **high and low** everywhere, all over, far and near, far and wide, in every nook and cranny, exhaustively.

**highbrow** adjective intellectual, scholarly, bookish, cultured, cultivated, educated, sophisticated; *inf.* brainy.

**high-flown** adjective extravagant, pretentious, overblown, overdone, overdrawn, exaggerated, elaborate.

**high-handed** adjective arbitrary, autocratic, dictatorial, domineering, peremptory, imperious, overbearing; *inf.* bossy.

**highlight** noun main feature, feature, high point, high spot, best part, climax, peak, memorable part, focal point, focus, center of interest, cynosure.

**highlight** verb call attention to, focus attention on, feature, emphasize, accentuate, accent, stress, underline, spotlight, foreground.

**highly** adverb **1** *highly entertaining* greatly, extremely, decidedly, certainly, exceptionally, tremendously, vastly, immensely, eminently, supremely, extraordinarily. **2** *speak highly of* approvingly, favorably, well, warmly, appreciatively, admiringly.

**high-minded** adjective noble-minded, moral, virtuous, ethical, upright, righteous, principled, honorable, good, fair, pure, lofty, elevated, high.

**high-powered** adjective dynamic, aggressive, assertive, energetic, driving, ambitious, effective, enterprising, vigorous, forceful.

**high-pressure** adjective aggressive, insistent, persistent, intensive, forceful, high-powered, importunate, bludgeoning, coercive; *inf.* pushy.

**high-priced** adjective expensive, costly. *See* HIGH 5.

**high-spirited** adjective spirited, lively, full of life, animated, active, energetic, vigorous, boisterous, bouncy, frolicsome, effervescent, buoyant, ebullient, exhilarated, vivacious, full of fun.

**high-strung** adjective nervous, on edge, edgy, excitable, tense, taut, stressed, temperamental, neurotic, overwrought, restless, wound up.

**hijack** verb commandeer, seize, expropriate, take over, skyjack.

**hike** verb walk, march, tramp, trek, trudge, plod, ramble, wander, backpack; *inf.* hoof it. **hike up 1** *he hiked up his pants/load* hitch up, pull up, jack up, lift, raise. **2** *they've hiked up the prices* raise, increase, add to; *inf.* jack up.

**hike** noun walk, march, tramp, trek, ramble, trudge.

**hilarious** adjective uproarious, sidesplitting, humorous, entertaining, comical, amusing, merry, jolly, mirthful, animated, vivacious, sparkling, exuberant, boisterous.

**hilarity** noun mirth, laughter, merriment, levity, glee, high spirits, amusement, comedy.

**hill** noun **1** *the hills behind the town* elevation, heights, hillock, hilltop, knoll, hummock, mound, tor, mount, ridge. **2** *cars going slowly up the hill* slope, rise, incline, gradient, acclivity. **3** *a hill of garbage* mountain, heap, pile, mound, stack, drift.

**hilt** noun handle, haft, handgrip, grip, shaft, hold. **to the hilt** completely, fully, wholly, entirely, totally, all the way.

**hind** adjective rear, back, hinder, posterior, caudal.

**hinder** verb hamper, impede, hold back, interfere with, delay, hold up, slow down, retard, obstruct, inhibit, handicap, hamstring, block, interrupt, check, trammel, forestall, curb, balk, thwart, frustrate, foil.

**hindrance** noun impediment, obstacle, interference, obstruction, handicap, block, restraint, check, bar, barrier, drawback, snag, stumbling block, encumbrance, curb, trammel, deterrent.

**hinge** verb **hinge on** depend on, turn on, be contingent on, hang on, pivot on, revolve around, rest on, center on.

**hint** noun **1** *give a hint that he was leaving* inkling, clue, suggestion, innuendo, tip-off, insinuation, implication, indication, mention, allusion, intimation, whisper. **2** *write gardening hints* tip, pointer, advice, help. **3** *just a hint of garlic* suspicion, suggestion, trace, touch, dash, soupçon, speck, sprinkling, tinge.

**hint** verb suggest, insinuate, imply, indicate, intimate, signal.

**hire** verb appoint, sign on, take on, engage, employ, secure the services of, enlist.

**hiss** verb sibilate, buzz, whistle, wheeze; boo, jeer, deride, catcall, hoot, taunt, ridicule.

**historian** noun chronicler, annalist, archivist, recorder, historiographer, antiquarian.

**historic** adjective notable, celebrated, renowned, momentous, significant, important, consequential, red-letter, memorable, remarkable, outstanding, extraordinary.

**historical** adjective **1** *a historical account* factual, recorded, documented, chronicled, archival, authentic, actual, attested, verified, confirmed. **2** *historical times* past, former, bygone, ancient.

**history** noun **1** *the history of the times* annals, chronicles, records, public records, account, study, story, tale, saga, narrative, recital, reports, memoirs, biography, autobiography. **2** *that is history now* the past, the old days, days of yore, antiquity, yesteryear.

**jingoism** noun patriotism, excessive patriotism, blind patriotism, nationalism, chauvinism, flag-waving.

**hit** verb **1** *hit him in anger* strike, slap, smack, buffet, punch, box, cuff, beat, thump, batter, pound, pummel, thrash, hammer, bang, knock, swat; *inf.* whack, wallop, bash, belt, clout, clip, clobber, sock, swipe. **2** *the car hit the truck* run into, bang into, smash into, crash into, knock into, bump into, collide with, meet head-on. **3** *her death really hit him* affect, have an effect on, leave a mark on, move, touch, overwhelm, devastate, damage, hurt. **4** *hit the right tone in his speech* achieve, accomplish, reach, attain, arrive at, gain, secure, touch, strike. **hit it off** get on well, be/get on good terms, take to each other; *inf.* be on the same wavelength. **hit on/upon** stumble on, chance on, light on, come upon, blunder on, discover, arrive at.

**hit** noun blow, slap, smack, punch, thump; *inf.* whack, wallop, clout, swipe.

**hitch** verb **1** *hitch the trailer to the car* fasten, connect, attach, join, couple, unite, tie, tether, bind, harness, yoke. **2** *hitching up their skirts* pull up, hike up, jerk up; *inf.* yank up.

**hitch** noun *what's the hitch?* holdup, delay, catch, difficulty, problem. *See* HINDRANCE.

**hit-or-miss** adjective haphazard, random, aimless, undirected, disorganized, indiscriminate, careless, casual, offhand, cursory.

**hoard** noun store, stockpile, supply, reserve, cache, accumulation, heap, pile, mass, aggregation, treasure trove; *inf.* stash.

**hoard** verb store, store up, stock up, stockpile, pile up, stack up, stow away, accumulate, amass, heap up, collect, gather, squirrel away; *inf.* stash away.

**hoarse** adjective croaking, croaky, throaty, harsh, rough, gruff, husky, gravelly, grating, rasping, guttural, raucous.

**hoary** adjective **1** *hoary hair/head* gray, gray-haired, white, white-haired, silvery, silvery-haired, grizzled, grizzly. **2** *hoary gentleman* old, elderly, aged, venerable, time-honored.

**hoax** noun practical joke, joke, jest, prank, trick, ruse, deception, fraud, imposture, cheat, spoof, swindle; *inf.* con, fast one, scam.

**hoax** verb trick, fool, deceive, bluff, hoodwink, cozen, delude, dupe, take in, spoof, cheat, swindle; *inf.* con, take someone for a ride, put one over on someone.

**hobble** verb limp, falter, shuffle, totter, stagger, reel.

**hobby** noun pastime, diversion, recreation, relaxation, divertissement, sideline.

**hobnob** verb fraternize, associate, socialize, mingle, mix, keep company, go around, consort; *inf.* hang around, hang out.

**hodgepodge** noun jumble, mishmash, miscellany, medley, mélange, mess, clutter, odds and ends, potpourri, olio, olla podrida.

**hogwash** noun nonsense, rubbish, gibberish, gobbledygook, drivel, balderdash, humbug, bunkum; *inf.* piffle, bunk, bosh, tosh, bilge, tripe, rot, tommyrot, crap, hooey.

**hoist** verb lift, raise, upraise, heave, jack up, hike up, elevate.

**hoist** noun crane, winch, pulley, jack, elevator, lift.

**hold** verb **1** *hold his hand* hold on to, clasp, clutch, grasp, grip, seize, clench, cling to. **2** *hold his sweetheart* embrace, hug, enfold, cradle, fondle. **3** *hold the relevant documents* have, possess, own, retain, keep. **4** *will it hold his weight?* bear, carry, take, support, hold up, keep up, sustain, prop up, buttress, brace. **5** *police are holding the suspect* detain, confine, hold in custody, impound, lock up, imprison, put behind bars, incarcerate. **6** *you cannot hold him from going* hold back, restrain, impede, check, bar, curb, stop, retard, delay, prevent. **7** *hold the interest of the audience* keep, maintain, occupy, engage, involve, absorb, engross, immerse, monopolize, arrest, catch, spellbind, fascinate, rivet. **8** *he holds a well-paid post* hold down, be in, occupy, fill, maintain, continue in, enjoy, boast. **9** *the hall holds 400 people* contain, accommodate, take, comprise. **10** *we hold that he is guilty* maintain, think, believe, consider, regard, deem, judge, assume, presume, reckon. **11** *will the good weather hold?* go on, carry on, remain, continue, stay, persist, last, endure, keep up. **12** *the old rule still holds* hold good, stand, apply, be in force, remain valid, exist. **13** *hold a meeting* call, convene, assemble, conduct, run, preside over, officiate at. **hold back 1** *hold back a laugh* keep back, suppress, repress, stifle, smother. **2** *hold back progress* prevent, impede, obstruct, hinder, check, curb, inhibit, restrain, control. **3** *hold back from hitting him* keep, desist, forbear, stop oneself, restrain oneself. **4** *hold back information* withhold, suppress. **hold down 1** *hold down prices* keep low, keep down. **2** *hold down a job* be in, occupy. *See* HOLD verb 8. **hold forth 1** *hold forth about politics* declaim, discourse, lecture, harangue, preach, orate, speechify, sermonize; *inf.* spout, spiel. **2** *hold forth the hand of friendship* hold out, extend, present, proffer, offer. **hold off 1** *hold off the attack* keep off, keep at bay, fend off, stave off, ward off, repel, repulse. **2** *hold off making a decision* delay, postpone, put off, defer, keep from, refrain from, avoid. **hold on** *if the survivors can hold on* survive, last, carry on, keep going, continue; *inf.* hang on. **hold on to** *hold on to the house* keep, retain possession of, retain ownership of. **hold out** *as long as supplies hold out* last, continue, remain. **hold over** put off, postpone, defer, delay, adjourn, suspend, waive. **hold up 1** *hold up traffic* delay, hinder, impede, obstruct, retard, slow, slow down, set back, stop, bring to a halt. **2** *hold up his weight* bear, carry. *See* HOLD *verb* 4. **3** *she held up her father as an example* display, exhibit, show, present, flaunt, brandish. **4** *hold up a bank* rob, waylay, mug; *inf.* stick up. **5** *will his story hold up?* bear examination, be verifiable, hold water. **hold with** approve of, agree with, be in favor of, support, subscribe to, countenance, take kindly to.

**hold** noun **1** *keep a firm hold of the child's hand* grasp, grip, clutch, clasp. **2** *the government tightened its hold on the country* grip, power, control, dominion, authority, ascendancy, influence, mastery, dominance, sway. **3** *put it on hold* pause, delay, postponement, deferment.

**holdup** noun **1** *a holdup on the highway* delay, wait, stoppage, obstruction, bottleneck, traffic jam, hitch, snag. **2** *a bank holdup* robbery, theft, burglary, mugging; *inf.* stick-up.

**hole** noun **1** *a hole in the material* opening, aperture, orifice, gap, space, breach, break, fissure, crack, rift, puncture, perforation, cut, incision, split, gash, rent, slit, vent, notch. **2** *a hole in the ground* excavation, pit, crater, shaft, mine, dugout, cave, cavern, pothole, cavity, chamber, hollow, scoop, pocket, depression, dent, dint, dip. **3** *an animal's hole* burrow, lair, den, covert, nest. **4** *they took us to a real hole for dinner* slum, hovel; *inf.* dump, dive, joint. **5** *the captives were thrown into the hole* dungeon, prison, cell. **6** *spot the hole in their argument* flaw, fault, defect, loophole, inconsistency, discrepancy, error, fallacy. **7** *they are in a financial hole* predicament, mess, plight, difficulty, trouble, corner, spot, tight spot; *inf.* fix, jam, scrape, pickle, hot water. **pick holes in** find fault with, criticize, pull to pieces, run down, cavil at, carp at, disparage, denigrate.

**hole** verb **hole up** hide, hide out, lie low, go underground, hibernate.

**holier-than-thou** adjective sanctimonious, self-righteous, pietistic, religiose, priggish, smug; *inf.* goody-goody.

**holiness** noun sanctity, saintliness, godliness, blessedness, spirituality, religiousness, piety, righteousness, goodness, virtue, virtuousness, purity.

**hollow** adjective **1** *a hollow vessel* empty, unfilled, vacant, void, hollowed out.

**2** *hollow cheeks/marks* sunken, dented, indented, depressed, concave, caved-in, incurvate, cavernous. **3** *a hollow sound* muffled, muted, dull, flat, toneless, dead, sepulchral. **4** *a hollow victory/triumph* valueless, worthless, useless, of no avail, fruitless, profitless, pointless, meaningless, pyrrhic. **5** *hollow compliments* insincere, hypocritical, spurious, unsound, flimsy.

**hollow** noun **1** *hollows in the ground* depression, indentation, concavity, dent, dint, dip, dimple, hole, crater, cavern, pit, cavity, well, trough, basin, cup, bowl, niche, nook, cranny, recess. **2** *picnic in the hollow* valley, dell, dale, glen, gorge, ravine.

**hollow** verb **hollow out** scoop out, gouge out, dig out, excavate, furrow, groove.

**holocaust** noun fire, inferno, conflagration, destruction, devastation, annihilation; massacre, mass murder, extermination, genocide, ethnic cleansing.

**holy** adjective **1** *a holy person* God-fearing, godly, pious, pietistic, devout, spiritual, religious, righteous, good, virtuous, moral, saintly, saintlike, sinless. **2** *a holy place* blessed, blest, sanctified, consecrated, hallowed, sacred, dedicated, venerated, divine, religious.

**home** noun **1** *where is his home?* house, abode, domicile, residence, dwelling, dwelling place, habitation. **2** *live a long way from one's home* home town, birthplace. *See* HOMELAND. **3** *agents advertising homes* house, apartment, condominium, bungalow, cottage; *inf.* condo, digs, pad. **4** *couldn't bear to put her mother in a home* institution, shelter, refuge, hostel, hospice, retirement home, nursing home, rest home, convalescent home/hospital, children's home; *inf.* old folk's home. **5** *the home of the buffalo* abode, habitat, natural habitat, environment, stamping ground, haunt, domain. **at home in** familiar with, used to, comfortable in, at ease in, relaxed in, in one's element in, on familiar territory in, on home ground in. **at home with** familiar with, proficient in, conversant with, skilled in, competent at, well-versed in; *inf.* up on. **bring home** emphasize, stress, impress upon someone, underline, highlight. **nothing to write home about** nothing important, nothing worth mentioning, nothing out of the ordinary.

**home** verb **home in on** aim at, focus on, pinpoint, zero in on, zoom in on.

**homeland** noun native land, fatherland, motherland, mother country.

**homeless** adjective down-and-out, destitute, derelict, dispossessed, on the streets, without a roof over one's head, vagrant.

**homely** adjective **1** *a homely girl* plain, plain-featured, plain-looking, unattractive, ugly; *inf.* not much to look at, short on looks. **2** *homely atmosphere* homelike, homey, comfortable, cozy, snug, welcoming, informal, relaxed, downhome; *inf.* comfy. **3** *a homely but friendly place* plain, simple, modest, unsophisticated, natural, everyday, ordinary, unpretentious.

**homespun** adjective plain, simple, homely, artless, unpolished, unrefined, coarse, rustic. *See* HOMELY 3.

**homicidal** adjective murderous, death-dealing, mortal, deadly, lethal, violent, maniacal.

**homicide** noun **1** *found guilty of homicide* murder, manslaughter, killing, slaying, slaughter, assassination, patricide, matricide, fratricide, infanticide. **2** *a convicted homicide* murderer, killer, slayer, assassin, patricide, matricide, fratricide, infanticide; *inf.* hit man.

**homily** noun sermon, preaching, lecture, discourse, lesson, talk, speech, address, oration.

**homogeneous** adjective identical, alike, the same, uniform, unvaried, unvarying, similar, kindred, comparable, analogous.

**homogenize** verb make uniform, combine, coalesce, fuse, merge, blend, emulsify.

**honest** adjective **1** *honest people* upright, honorable, moral, ethical, principled, righteous, right-minded, virtuous, good, worthy, decent, law-abiding, high-minded, upstanding, just, fair, incorruptible, trustworthy, scrupulous, reputable. **2** *an honest reply* truthful, sincere, candid, frank, direct, forthright, straightforward, open, plain-speaking, matter-of-fact, outspoken, blunt, unfeigned, unequivocal. **3** *an honest mistake* real, true, genuine, authentic, actual, aboveboard, bona fide, proper; *inf.* on the level, honest-to-goodness.

**honesty** noun **1** *honesty is its own reward* uprightness, honorableness, honor, integrity, morals, morality, ethics, principle, high principles, righteousness, rectitude, virtue, goodness, probity, worthiness, justness, fairness, incorruptibility, truthfulness, truth, veracity, trustworthiness, reliability, conscientiousness, reputability. **2** *the honesty of his reply* truthfulness, truth, sincerity, candor, frankness, forthrightness, openness, genuineness, bluntness.

**honor** noun **1** *a man of honor* uprightness, integrity. *See* HONESTY 1. **2** *the honor of winning the battle* fame, renown, glory, prestige, illustriousness, esteem, distinction, notability, credit. **3** *his honor is at stake* reputation, good name, name. **4** *protecting a lady's honor* chastity, virginity, virtue, purity, innocence, modesty. **5** *treat the hero with honor* homage, praise, reverence, veneration, adulation, exaltation.

**6** *it was an honor to serve him* privilege, pleasure, joy.

**honor** verb **1** *all his pupils honor him* esteem, respect, admire, defer to, reverence, revere, venerate, worship, idolize, value, prize. **2** *the crowd honored the victor* acclaim, applaud, pay homage to, pay tribute to, lionize, praise, cheer, compliment, laud, eulogize. **3** *honor the agreement* fulfill, discharge, carry out, observe, keep, be true to, be faithful to, live up to. **4** *honor the check* cash, clear, accept, take, pass.

**honorable** adjective **1** *honorable men* upright, moral. *See* HONEST 1. **2** *an honorable victory* renowned, prestigious, distinguished, esteemed, notable, noted, great, eminent, noble, illustrious, creditable. **3** *an honorable member of the community* worthy, respected, respectable, reputable, decent, venerable.

**honors** plural noun rewards, awards, prizes, decorations, commendations, recognition, titles, distinctions, laurels.

**honorary** adjective nominal, in name only, titular, unofficial, ex officio, complimentary, unpaid.

**hoodlum** noun **1** *hoodlums vandalizing telephone booths* ruffian, hooligan, thug, rowdy, delinquent, vandal, mugger; *inf.* tough, rough, hood. **2** *hoodlums killing policemen* gangster, mobster, gunman, murderer, assassin, terrorist; *inf.* hit man, hatchet man; hood.

**hoodwink** verb deceive, delude, dupe, outwit, fool, trick, get the better of, cheat, take in, hoax, cozen, mislead, defraud, swindle, gull, pull the wool over someone's eyes; *inf.* con, bamboozle, pull a fast one on, put one over on, take for a ride, make a sucker of.

**hook** noun **1** *the hook of the dress is broken* fastener, catch, clasp, clip, link, hook and eye. **2** *a hook in the river* crook, angle, loop, curve, bend, bow, arc, dogleg, horseshoe bend, oxbow, hairpin turn. **by hook or by crook** by fair means or foul, no matter how, somehow or other. **hook, line, and sinker** completely, entirely, thoroughly, wholly, totally. **off the hook** acquitted, cleared, exonerated, let off, vindicated.

**hook** verb **1** *hook the necklace* fasten, secure, fix, clasp. **2** *finally hooked a marriage partner* snare, ensnare, trap, entrap.

**hooked** adjective hook-shaped, hooklike, aquiline, curved, bent, bowed, angular. **hooked on** addicted to, devoted to, given to.

**hooligan** noun ruffian, thug. *See* HOODLUM 1.

**hoop** noun ring, band, circle, circlet, loop, wheel, girdle.

**hoot** noun **1** *the owl's hoot* call, screech, whoop, cry. **2** *the hoots of the audience* boo, hiss, jeer, catcall; *inf.* raspberry, Bronx cheer.

**hoot** verb **1** *the owls hooted* call, screech, whoop, cry. **2** *hooted off the stage* boo, hiss, jeer, deride, mock, taunt, ridicule.

**hop** verb jump, leap, bound, spring, vault, bounce, skip, caper, dance, frisk.

**hop** noun jump, leap, bound, spring, vault, bounce, skip.

**hope** noun hopefulness, expectation, expectancy, anticipation, desire, longing, wish, wishing, craving, yearning, aspiration, ambition, dream, confidence, conviction, faith, trust, optimism.

**hope** verb expect, anticipate, look forward to, await, contemplate, foresee, desire, long, wish, crave, yearn, dream, believe, rely on, count on, trust in.

**hopeful** adjective **1** *hopeful candidates* expectant, optimistic, confident, assured, buoyant, sanguine. **2** *hopeful news/signs* promising, encouraging, heartening, gladdening, optimistic, reassuring, auspicious, favorable, propitious.

**hopeless** adjective **1** *feeling hopeless* despairing, in despair, desperate, pessimistic, defeatist, dejected, downhearted, despondent, demoralized, disconsolate, suicidal. **2** *a hopeless case* lost, beyond remedy, irremediable, beyond recovery, past cure, incurable, beyond repair, irreparable, irreversible, serious, grave. **3** *a hopeless task* impossible, impracticable, futile, useless, vain, pointless, worthless, no-win, unattainable, unachievable. **4** *she's hopeless at math* poor, incompetent, inadequate, inferior; *inf.* no good.

**horde** noun crowd, mob, throng, mass, multitude, host, army, pack, gang, troop, drove, crew, band, flock, swarm, gathering, assemblage.

**horizon** noun *broaden the child's horizon* scope, range of experience/knowledge, perspective, perception, prospect, outlook, compass, sphere, purview.

**horizontal** adjective flat, flat as a pancake, plumb, level, supine, prone.

**horrendous** adjective **1** *a horrendous sight* dreadful, awful. *See* HORRIBLE 1. **2** *a horrendous child* nasty, disagreeable. *See* HORRIBLE 2.

**horrible** adjective **1** *a horrible sight/accident* dreadful, awful, horrid, terrible, horrifying, terrifying, frightful, fearful, horrendous, shocking, appalling, hideous, grim, ghastly, harrowing, gruesome, disgusting, revolting, repulsive, loathsome, abhorrent, detestable, hateful, abominable. **2** *horrible child/weather/food/picture/mess* nasty,

disagreeable, unpleasant, mean, unkind, obnoxious, odious, horrid, awful, dreadful, terrible, beastly, ghastly, frightful, horrendous, shocking, appalling, hideous, revolting, abominable.

**horrid** adjective **1** *a horrid sight* dreadful, awful. *See* HORRIBLE 1. **2** *a horrid child* nasty, disagreeable. *See* HORRIBLE 2.

**horrify** verb **1** *the apparition horrified the children* terrify, terrorize, intimidate, frighten, frighten out of one's wits, alarm, scare, scare to death, startle, panic, throw into a panic, make someone's blood run cold; *inf.* make someone's hair stand on end, scare stiff, scare the living daylights out of. **2** *his attitude horrifies me* shock, appall, outrage, scandalize, disgust, revolt, repel, nauseate, sicken, offend.

**horror** noun **1** *full of horror at the sight* terror, fear, fear and trembling, fearfulness, fright, alarm, dread, awe, panic, trepidation. **2** *view his attitude with horror* abhorrence, abomination, loathing, hate, detestation, repulsion, revulsion, disgust, distaste, aversion, antipathy.

**horse** noun mount, steed, pony, racehorse, draft horse, packhorse, bay, sorrel, pinto, piebald; foal, colt, stallion, mare; *inf.* nag, dobbin, filly.

**horseplay** noun clowning, fooling, fooling around, antics, capers, high jinks, rough-and-tumble, roughhouse.

**horse sense** noun common sense, sense one is born with, mother wit, practicality; *inf.* gumption, savvy.

**hosiery** noun hose, socks, stockings, tights, knee socks, ankle socks, leggings.

**hospitable** adjective welcoming, sociable, convivial, generous, liberal, bountiful, openhanded, congenial, friendly, neighborly, warm, warmhearted, cordial, kindly, amicable.

**hospital** noun medical center, clinic, infirmary, sanatorium.

**hospitality** noun welcome, sociability, conviviality, generosity, liberality, friendliness, neighborliness, warmth, warmheartedness, cordiality, kindness, kindheartedness, amicability.

**host**¹ noun **1** *the host of the lodge* proprietor, proprietress, landlord, landlady, manager, innkeeper, hotelkeeper, hotelier. **2** *the host of the show* presenter, master of ceremonies, MC, emcee.

**host**² noun multitude, crowd, throng, horde, mob, army, legion, herd, pack, flock, swarm, troop, band, mass, assemblage, assembly, array, myriad.

**hostile** adjective **1** *hostile to the idea* antagonistic, opposed, averse, opposite, ill-disposed, against, inimical; *inf.* anti. **2**

*hostile weather conditions* adverse, unfavorable, unpropitious, disadvantageous, inauspicious. **3** *a hostile crowd* belligerent, bellicose, aggressive, warlike, warring, militant, antagonistic, unfriendly, unsympathetic, spiteful, wrathful, angry.

**hostilities** plural noun war, warfare, fighting, conflict, militancy, strife, action, battles.

**hostility** noun antagonism, opposition, aversion, animosity, ill will, enmity, belligerence, bellicosity, militancy, malevolence, malice, spite, wrath, anger.

**hot** adjective **1** *hot food/weather* boiling, boiling hot, piping, piping hot, scalding, red-hot, sizzling, steaming, scorching, roasting, searing, blazing hot, sweltering, parching, blistering, baking, torrid, sultry. **2** *the curry is very hot* peppery, spicy, pungent, piquant, fiery, sharp, biting. **3** *the child is hot* feverish, fevered, febrile, flushed. **4** *hot on/about the idea of free speech* ardent, eager, enthusiastic, keen, fervent, fervid, zealous, vehement, passionate, animated, excited. **5** *hot with anger* inflamed, furious, infuriated, seething, raging, fuming. **6** *hot young lovers* passionate, impassioned. *See* HOT-BLOODED. **7** *a hot temper/argument* heated, violent, furious, fierce, ferocious, stormy, tempestuous, savage. **8** *fresh from the presses/warehouses* new, fresh, recent, late, brand-new, just out, just released, just issued. **9** *these cameras are not this year* popular, in vogue, in demand, sought-after. **10** *hot on their heels* close, following closely, near. **11** *hot goods* stolen, illegally obtained, smuggled, wanted. **hot air** empty talk, nonsense, bombast, verbiage, wind, blather, claptrap; *inf.* gas, bunkum, guff.

**hot-blooded** adjective **1** *hot-blooded young lovers* hot, passionate, impassioned, ardent, sensual, sex-hungry, lustful, libidinous; *inf.* horny. **2** *hot-blooded people* quarreling excitable, temperamental, fiery, spirited, impulsive, rash, wild, quixotic.

**hotel** noun inn, hostelry, motel, boarding-house, guesthouse.

**hotheaded** adjective hot-tempered, short-tempered, quick-tempered, fiery, hasty, excitable, volatile, rash, impetuous, impulsive, reckless, foolhardy, wild, unruly.

**hound** verb **1** *police hounding the criminal* chase, give chase to, pursue, follow, hunt, hunt down, stalk, track, trail, shadow; *inf.* tail. **2** *hound him to do as they wished* nag, bully, browbeat, pester, harass, harry, keep after, urge, badger, goad, prod, pressure.

**house** noun **1** *his house is over there* abode, residence, domicile, home, habitation; condominium, cottage; *inf.* condo. **2** *descended from a royal house* family, clan, family tree, line, lineage, dynasty, ancestry, ancestors, kindred, blood, race, strain, tribe. **3** *a publishing house* firm, business, company, concern, corporation, enterprise, organization; *inf.* outfit. **4** *a large house for the event* audience, gathering, assembly, congregation, listeners, spectators.

**house** verb **1** *the building houses 20 people* accommodate, lodge, put up, take in, have room for, have space/capacity for, sleep, shelter, harbor. **2** *the box houses the machinery* cover, sheathe, protect, shelter, guard, contain, keep.

**household** noun family, family circle, house, home, ménage.

**household** adjective domestic, family, ordinary, everyday, common, usual, run-of-the-mill.

**housing** noun **1** *a shortage of housing* accommodations, houses, dwellings, homes, shelter, habitations. **2** *housing for machinery* case, casing, cover, covering, sheath, container, enclosure, jacket, capsule, holder.

**hovel** noun shack, shanty, hut; *inf.* dump, hole.

**hover** verb **1** *kites hovering in the air* hang, flutter, float, drift, be wafted. **2** *hover between going and staying* waver, vacillate, fluctuate, oscillate, alternate, seesaw. **hover by/around/near** linger around/by/near, hang around/about, wait near, stay near.

**however** adverb nevertheless, be that as it may, nonetheless, notwithstanding, anyway, anyhow, regardless, despite that, still, yet, just the same.

**howl** verb bay, yowl, yelp, wail, yell, bawl, scream, shriek, bellow, caterwaul, cry, weep, ululate; *inf.* holler.

**howl** noun bay, yowl, yelp, wail, yell, bawl, bellow, roar.

**hub** noun **1** *the hub of a wheel* pivot, axis, nave. **2** *the hub of the firm* center, core, heart, nerve center, focus, focal point.

**huddle** verb crowd, press, throng, flock, pack, cram, herd, squeeze, bunch up, cluster, gather, congregate.

**hue** noun **1** *a blue hue* color, tone, shade, tint, tinge, dye. **2** *political opinions of every hue* complexion, cast, aspect, light.

**hug** verb **1** *hug his wife* embrace, cuddle, take in one's arms, hold close, enfold in one's arms, clasp/press to one's bosom, squeeze. **2** *hug the shore* keep close to, stay near to, follow closely. **3** *hug his memories* cling to, hold onto, cherish, harbor, nurse.

**hug** noun embrace, cuddle, squeeze, hold, clasp, bear hug; *inf.* clinch.

**huge** adjective enormous, immense, great, massive, colossal, vast, prodigious, gigantic, giant, gargantuan, mammoth, monumental, monstrous, elephantine, extensive, bulky, mountainous, titanic, Herculean; *inf.* jumbo.

**hullabaloo** noun uproar, commotion, roar, racket, din, clamor, disturbance, hubbub, outcry, furor, brouhaha, hue and cry, pandemonium, tumult, turmoil, fuss, to-do, bedlam, babel; *inf.* ruckus.

**hum** verb **1** *bees/machines humming* drone, murmur, vibrate, throb, thrum, buzz, whirr, purr. **2** *things are humming* be busy, be active, bustle, move quickly, vibrate, pulsate, buzz.

**hum** noun drone, murmur, vibration, throb, thrum, buzz, whirr, purr.

**human** adjective **1** *human frailty* mortal, physical, bodily, fleshly, carnal, corporal. **2** *a very human person* kind, kindly. *See* HUMANE. **3** *they're only human* mortal, flesh and blood, fallible, weak, frail, vulnerable, erring.

**humane** adjective kind, kindly, kindhearted, good, good-natured, compassionate, considerate, understanding, sympathetic, forgiving, merciful, lenient, forbearing, gentle, tender, mild, clement, benign, benevolent, charitable, generous, magnanimous, approachable, accessible.

**humanitarian** adjective **1** *humanitarian enemy soldiers* kind, compassionate. *See* HUMANE. **2** *humanitarian issues* philanthropic, altruistic, welfare, charitable.

**humanitarian** noun philanthropist, altruist, benefactor, good Samaritan, social reformer, do-gooder.

**humble** adjective **1** *brilliant but humble* modest, unassuming, self-effacing, unassertive, unpretentious, unostentatious, meek. **2** *born of humble people* plain, common, ordinary, simple, poor, lowranking, low, lowly, inferior, plebeian, proletarian, unrefined, unimportant, insignificant, inconsequential, undistinguished. **3** *a humble apology* servile, submissive, obsequious, subservient, deferential, slavish, sycophantic.

**humble** verb **1** *humble them by his criticism* mortify, shame. *See* HUMILIATE. **2** *feel humbled in the king's presence* belittle, demean, deflate, depreciate, disparage.

**humdrum** adjective *humdrum life* routine, unvaried, unvarying, mundane, monotonous, repetitious, dull, uninteresting, banal, boring, tedious, tiresome, wearisome.

**humid** adjective muggy, sticky, steamy, clammy, close, sultry, damp, moist, dank, wet, soggy, misty.

**humiliate** verb mortify, humble, shame, bring low, put to shame, make ashamed, disgrace, embarrass, discomfit, chasten, subdue, abash, abase, debase, degrade, crush, make someone eat humble pie, take down a peg or two; *inf.* put down; make someone eat crow.

**humiliation** noun mortification, humbling, shame, disgrace, loss of face, dishonor, indignity, embarrassment, discomfiture, abasement, debasement, degradation, submission, humble pie; *inf.* put-down.

**humility** noun humbleness, modesty, modestness, meekness, self-effacement, unpretentiousness, unobtrusiveness, diffidence; servility, submissiveness, obsequiousness, subservience, deference, sycophancy.

**humor** noun **1** *see the humor of the situation* funny side, funniness, comic side, comical aspect, comedy, laughableness, facetiousness, farcicalness, farce, jocularity, hilarity, ludicrousness, absurdness, absurdity, drollness. **2** *entertain them with his humor* comedy, jokes, joking, jests, jesting, gags, wit, wittiness, witticisms, waggishness, pleasantries, buffoonery; *inf.* wisecracks. **3** *what humor is she in today?* mood, temper, temperament, frame of mind, disposition, spirits.

**humor** verb **1** *humor the child* indulge, pamper, spoil, coddle, mollycoddle. **2** *humor their idiosyncrasies* adapt to, make provision for, give in to, yield to, pander to, go along with, accommodate, acquiesce in, tolerate, permit, allow, suffer.

**humorous** adjective **1** *a humorous story* funny, comic, comical, witty, jocular, amusing, laughable, hilarious, sidesplitting, rib-tickling, facetious, farcical, ridiculous, ludicrous, absurd, droll, waggish, whimsical.

**hump** noun protuberance, protrusion, projection, bulge, swelling, lump, bump, knob, hunch, mass, nodule, node, intumescence, tumefaction. **over the hump** out of the woods, in the clear, getting better, making progress.

**hunch** noun **1** *a hunch on his back* protrusion, bulge. *See* HUMP. **2** *have a hunch that she will win* feeling, presentiment, premonition, intuition, sixth sense, suspicion, inkling.

**hunch** verb hump, arch, curve, crook, curl up. **hunch up** crouch over, stoop over, bend over, huddle over.

**hunger** noun **1** *suffering from hunger* hungriness, ravenousness, starvation, famine, voracity; greed, greediness. **2** *a hunger for knowledge* craving, longing, yearning, desire, want, need, thirst, appetite, pining, itch, lust, hankering; *inf.* yen.

**hunger** verb **hunger for/after** crave, have a craving for, long for, yearn for, have a yearning for, desire, want, need, thirst for, have an appetite for, pine for, lust after, itch for, hanker after; *inf.* have a yen for.

**hungry** adjective **1** ravenous, famished, famishing, starving, starved, half-starved; greedy, voracious; *inf.* peckish.

**hunt** verb **1** *hunt deer/criminals* chase, pursue. *See* HOUND 1. **2** *hunt for her keys* search, look, look high and low, forage, fish, rummage.

**hunt** noun **1** *the hunt for game* chase, pursuit, course, coursing, stalking, tracking, trailing, shadowing; *inf.* tailing. **2** *the hunt for eggs* search, quest, rummage; foraging, ransacking.

**hurdle** noun bar, barrier, barricade, obstacle, hindrance, impediment, obstruction, stumbling block, snag, complication, difficulty, handicap.

**hurl** verb throw, fling, pitch, cast, toss, heave, fire, launch, let fly, propel, project, dart, catapult; *inf.* sling, chuck.

**hurried** adjective **1** *with hurried steps* quick, fast, swift, rapid, speedy, hasty, breakneck. **2** *a hurried glance* rushed, cursory, superficial, perfunctory, offhand, passing, fleeting, transitory.

**hurry** verb hurry up, make haste, hasten, speed, speed up, lose no time, press on, push on, run, dash, rush, go hell for leather; *inf.* get a move on, step on it, get cracking, shake a leg, fly, race, scurry, scamper, go like a bat out of hell, hightail it, hotfoot it.

**hurry** noun haste, urgency, rush, flurry, bustle, hubbub, turmoil, agitation, confusion, commotion.

**hurt** verb **1** *my foot hurts* ache, smart, nip, sting, throb, tingle, burn. **2** *he has hurt his leg* injure, wound, bruise, cut, scratch, lacerate, maim, mutilate, damage, disable, incapacitate, debilitate, impair. **3** *his cruel words hurt her* upset, sadden, grieve, wound, distress, pain, cut to the quick, sting, offend, give offense. **4** *hurt his reputation* harm, damage, spoil, mar, blight, blemish, impair.

**hurt** noun **1** *the hurt in his hand* pain, soreness, ache, smarting, stinging, throbbing, suffering, pangs, discomfort. **2** *a hurt on his leg* sore, wound, injury, bruise, cut, scratch, laceration. **3** *the hurt he caused her* upset, sadness, sorrow, suffering, grief, distress, pain, misery, anguish, affliction. **4** *the hurt caused to his reputation* harm, damage, injury, detriment, blight, loss, disadvantage, mischief.

**hurt** adjective **1** *a hurt leg* wounded, injured, bruised, cut, lacerated, sore, painful, aching, smarting, throbbing. **2** *a hurt expression* upset, aggrieved, distressed, anguished, offended, piqued.

**hurtful** adjective **1** *hurtful remarks* upsetting, wounding, distressing, unkind, nasty, mean, malicious, spiteful, cutting, cruel, mischievous, offensive. **2** *actions hurtful to his career* harmful, damaging, injurious, detrimental, disadvantageous, deleterious.

**hush** verb **1** *hush the children* silence, shush; *inf.* shut up. **2** *they suddenly hushed* fall silent, become silent; *inf.* pipe down, shut up. **3** *hush their fears* still, quieten, calm, soothe, allay, assuage, pacify, mollify, compose. **hush up** suppress, conceal, cover up, keep secret, keep dark, smother, stifle, squash.

**hush** noun quiet, quietness, silence, stillness, still, soundlessness, peacefulness, peace, calm, tranquillity.

**hush-hush** adjective top secret, secret, confidential, classified, restricted.

**husky** adjective **1** *a husky voice* throaty, gruff, deep, gravelly, hoarse, coarse, croaking, croaky, rough, thick, guttural, harsh, rasping. **2** *a husky young man* brawny, well-built, strapping, muscular, rugged, burly, sturdy, thickset; *inf.* beefy.

**hussy** noun minx, seductress, trollop, slut, loose woman; *inf.* vamp, tramp, bimbo, floozy.

**hustle** verb **1** *hustle them out of the way* push, shove, thrust, crowd, jostle, elbow, nudge, shoulder. **2** *hustle them into making a decision* coerce, pressure, prompt, urge, goad, prod, spur, propel, egg on. **3** *hustle to get there on time* hurry, hasten, dash, rush, fly; *inf.* get a move on, step on it.

**hut** noun shed, lean-to, shack, cabin, shanty, hovel.

**hybrid** noun crossbreed, cross, mixedbreed, half-blood, mixture, conglomerate, composite, compound, amalgam; *derog.* half-breed.

**hygienic** adjective sanitary, clean, germfree, disinfected, sterilized, aseptic, sterile, unpolluted, uncontaminated, healthy, pure.

**hymn** noun psalm, anthem, carol, religious song, paean, chant, plainsong, spiritual.

**hype** noun publicity, promotion, advertising, ballyhoo; *inf.* plugging.

**hypnotic** adjective mesmerizing, sleepinducing, sleep-producing, soporific, somniferous, somnific, numbing, sedative, stupefactive.

**hypnotize** verb **1** *hypnotize the patient* put under, put out, send into a trance, mesmerize, put to sleep. **2** *they were hypnotized by her beauty* fascinate, bewitch, entrance, beguile, spellbind, magnetize.

**hypocrisy** noun sanctimoniousness, sanctimony, pietism, insincerity, deceptiveness, deceit, deceitfulness, deception, dishonesty, duplicity, imposture, two-facedness, double-dealing, pretense; *inf.* phoniness.

**hypocrite** noun pharisee, deceiver, impostor, pretender; *inf.* phony.

**hypocritical** adjective sanctimonious, pietistic, unctuous, insincere, false, deceitful, deceptive, dishonest, duplicitous, two-faced, double-dealing; *inf.* phony.

**hypothesis** noun theorem, thesis, proposition, theory, postulate, axiom, premise; supposition, assumption, presumption, conjecture, speculation.

**hypothetical** adjective supposed, assumed, presumed, theoretical, conjectured, imagined, speculative, academic.

**hysteria** noun hysterics, frenzy, outburst/fit of agitation/panic, madness, delirium.

**hysterical** adjective **1** *hysterical at the news of his death* frenzied, frantic, out of control, berserk, beside oneself, distracted, distraught, overwrought, agitated, mad, crazed, out of one's mind/wits. **2** *hysterical play/game* hilarious, uproarious, sidesplitting, amusing, comical, farcical, funny.

# *Ii*

**icon** noun image, idol, likeness, representation, figure, statue.

**icy** adjective **1** *icy winds/weather* freezing, frigid, chill, chilly, chilling, frosty, biting, bitter, raw, arctic, glacial, Siberian, polar, gelid. **2** *icy roads* frozen over, ice-bound, frosty, rimy, glassy, like a sheet of glass, slippery. **3** *an icy welcome* cold, cool, frigid, frosty, stiff, aloof, distant, unfriendly.

**idea** noun **1** *the idea of death scares her* concept, conception, conceptualization, image, abstraction, perception. **2** *tell him your ideas on the subject* thought, theory, view, viewpoint, opinion, feeling, outlook, belief. **3** *I had an idea that he would win* feeling, notion, suspicion, fancy, inkling. **4** *could you give me some idea of the cost?* estimation, approximation, guess, surmise; *inf.* guesstimate. **5** *our idea is to open a new store* plan, design, scheme, aim, intention, objective, object, purpose, end, goal, target. **6** *she's not my idea of a good mother* notion, vision, archetype, ideal example, exemplar, pattern.

**ideal** noun epitome, peak of perfection, paragon, nonpareil; archetype, model, exemplar, paradigm.

**ideal** adjective **1** *ideal beauty* perfect, consummate, supreme, absolute, complete, flawless, exemplary, classic, archetypal, model, quintessential. **2** *confusing ideal and concrete matters* abstract, conceptual, theoretical, hypothetical. **3** *she dreams of an ideal world* unattainable, Utopian, unreal, impractical, ivory-towered, visionary, fanciful.

**idealistic** adjective Utopian, perfectionist, visionary, romantic, quixotic, unrealistic.

**ideally** adverb in a perfect world, all things being equal, theoretically, hypothetically, in theory.

**ideals** plural noun principles, standards, morals, morality, ethics.

**identical** adjective same, very same, one and the same, selfsame; alike, very much the same, indistinguishable.

**identification** noun **1** *identification of the criminal* recognition, singling out, spotting, pinpointing, naming; *inf.* fingering. **2** *the identification of the best method* establishment, finding out, ascertainment, diagnosis, selection, choice. **3** *show his identification* ID card, ID, badge; papers, credentials. **4** *her identification with her patient* empathy, rapport, bond, sympathy.

**identify** verb **1** *identify the criminal* recognize, single out, pick out, spot, point out, pinpoint, discern, distinguish, name; *inf.* put the finger on, finger. **2** *identify the problem* establish, find out, ascertain, diagnose, select, choose. **3** *I identify her with my youth* associate, connect. **identify with** empathize with, sympathize with, relate to, respond to.

**identity** noun **1** *the identity of the criminal* name, specification. **2** *he lost his identity on emigrating* personality, self, selfhood, ego, individuality, distinctiveness, singularity, uniqueness, differentness. **3** *a case of mistaken identity* identification, recognition, naming. **4** *the identity of their interests* identicalness, sameness, indistinguishability, interchangeability.

**ideology** noun doctrine, creed, credo, teaching, dogma, theory, thesis; tenets, beliefs.

**idiocy** noun stupidity, stupidness, foolishness, senselessness, inanity, absurdity, fatuity, fatuousness, asininity, lunacy, craziness, insanity; *inf.* dumbness.

**idiosyncrasy** noun peculiarity, singularity, oddity, eccentricity, mannerism, quirk, habit, characteristic, specialty, quality, feature.

**idiot** noun blockhead, nitwit, dunderhead, dolt, dunce, halfwit, fool, ass, boob, nincompoop, ninny, ignoramus, cretin, moron; *inf.* numskull, dimwit.

**idiotic** adjective stupid, foolish, senseless, inane, absurd, fatuous, asinine, unintelligent, halfwitted, harebrained, lunatic, crazy, insane, moronic; *inf.* dumb.

**idle** adjective **1** *an idle fellow* lazy, indolent, slothful, shiftless, loafing, dronish. **2** *idle machines/workers* not in operation, inoperative, inactive, unused, mothballed; unemployed, out of work, jobless, out of a job, laid off; *inf.* on the dole. **3** *idle hours* unoccupied, empty, vacant, unfilled. **4** *idle rumors* groundless, baseless, lacking foundation. **5** *idle remarks/pleasures* unimportant, trivial, trifling, shallow, foolish, insignificant, superficial, inane, meaningless. **6** *idle threats* useless, vain, worthless, futile, ineffective, ineffectual, inefficacious, unproductive, fruitless.

**idle** verb **1** *idle away the hours* while, laze, loaf, lounge, loiter, dawdle, dally, fritter, waste. **2** *stop idling and work* laze, loaf, mark time, shirk, slack, vegetate; *inf.* rest on one's oars.

**idol** noun **1** *pagans worshiping idols* icon, god, false god, effigy, image, graven image, fetish. **2** *the singer is a teenage idol* hero, heroine, favorite, darling, beloved, pet, superstar; *inf.* pinup.

**idolatry** noun **1** *religion based on idolatry* idolization, idol-worship, fetishism, icon-worship, paganism, heathenism. **2** *the fans' idolatry of Elvis* idolizing, worshiping, hero-worship, adulation, adoration, blind adoration, admiration, doting, lionizing, reverence, glorification.

**idolize** verb **1** *idolize false gods* worship, bow down before, glorify, exalt, revere, adore, deify. **2** *idolize the singer* adulate, love, look up to, admire, dote upon, lionize, venerate.

**iffy** adjective doubtful, uncertain, unsure, undecided, unsettled, indeterminate, unresolved; *inf.* up in the air.

**ignite** verb **1** *ignite the fire* light, set fire to, set on fire, fire, kindle, inflame, touch off, put a match to. **2** *the fire ignited* catch/take fire, catch, burst into flames, burn up, burn, flame up.

**ignominious** adjective shameful, dishonorable, disgraceful, discreditable, disreputable, ignoble, inglorious, scandalous, abject, sorry, base, contemptible, despicable, wicked, vile.

**ignominy** noun shame, dishonor, disgrace, humiliation, discredit, disrepute, infamy, opprobrium, contemptibleness, wickedness, baseness, vileness, dishonesty, treachery.

**ignorance** noun **1** *ignorance of the law* unawareness, unfamiliarity, inexperience, greenness, innocence. **2** *appalled at the ignorance of the pupils* illiteracy, unintelligence, stupidity, thickness, denseness, unenlightenment, benightedness.

**ignorant** adjective **1** *ignorant of legal procedure* unaware of, unfamiliar with, unconversant with, unacquainted with, unconscious of, uninformed about, unenlightened about, inexperienced in, blind to, uninitiated in, unschooled in, naïve about, innocent about; *inf.* in the dark about. **2** *ignorant pupils* unscholarly, uneducated, untaught, unschooled, untutored, untrained, illiterate, unlettered, unlearned, unread, uninformed, unknowledgeable, unintelligent, stupid, unenlightened, benighted; *inf.* thick, dense, dumb.

**ignore** verb disregard, pay no attention/heed to, take no notice of, brush aside, pass over, shrug off, push aside, shut one's eyes to, be oblivious to, turn a blind eye to, turn a deaf ear to, spurn, cold-shoulder, look right through.

**ill** adjective **1** *feeling rather ill* unwell, ailing, poorly, sick, sickly, on the sick list, infirm, off-color, afflicted, indisposed, out of sorts, diseased, bedridden, weak, feeble; *inf.* under the weather, laid up, queasy. **2** *the ill feeling in the firm* hostile, antagonistic, acrimonious, belligerent, bellicose, unfriendly, unkind, spiteful, rancorous, resentful, malicious, malevolent, bitter. **3** *his ill temper* fractious, irritable, irascible, cross, cantankerous, crabbed, surly, snappish, gruff, sullen. **4** *an ill wind* adverse, unfavorable, unadvantageous, unlucky, unfortunate, unpropitious, inauspicious, unpromising, ominous, infelicitous. **5** *the ill effects of the medicine* harmful, detrimental, deleterious, hurtful, damaging, pernicious, destructive, ruinous. **6** *a person of ill repute* bad, infamous, wicked, nefarious, vile, evil, foul, sinful, iniquitous, sinister, corrupt, depraved, degenerate. **7** *ill management* unsatisfactory, unacceptable, inadequate, deficient, faulty, poor, unskillful, inexpert. **ill at ease** adjective uncomfortable, uneasy, awkward, self-conscious, out of place, unquiet, disturbed, discomfited, anxious, on edge, nervous.

**ill-advised** adjective unwise, ill-considered, imprudent, incautious, injudicious, impolitic, misguided, foolish, foolhardy, shortsighted.

**ill-bred** adjective ill-mannered, bad-mannered, unmannerly, rude, impolite, discourteous, uncivil, ungentlemanly, unladylike, boorish, churlish, loutish, vulgar, coarse, crass, uncouth.

**illegal** adjective unlawful, illegitimate, illicit, lawless, criminal, actionable, felonious, unauthorized, unsanctioned, unofficial, outlawed, banned, forbidden, barred, prohibited, proscribed, contraband, black-market, under the counter, bootleg.

**illegible** adjective unreadable, indecipherable, unintelligible, scrawled, scribbled, squiggly, crabbed, faint.

**illegitimate** adjective 1 *illegitimate use of property* unlawful, illicit. See ILLEGAL. 2 *an illegitimate child* natural, love, born out of wedlock, fatherless, bastard.

**ill-fated** adjective unlucky, luckless, unfortunate, hapless, unhappy, doomed, blighted, star-crossed, ill-starred, ill-omened.

**ill feeling** noun ill will, bad blood, hostility, enmity, hatred, no love lost, antipathy, aversion, dislike, antagonism, acrimony, animus, unfriendliness, spite, rancor, grudge, resentment, bitterness, malice, hard feelings.

**ill-founded** adjective baseless, groundless, without foundation, unjustified, unsupported, unsubstantiated, unproven, unverified, unauthenticated, unreliable.

**illicit** adjective unlawful, illegitimate. See ILLEGAL.

**illiterate** adjective unlettered, uneducated, untaught, unschooled, untutored, uninstructed, unlearned, ignorant.

**ill-mannered** adjective unmannerly, rude. See ILL-BRED.

**ill-natured** adjective ill-tempered, bad-tempered, ill-humored, moody, irritable, irascible, surly, peevish, petulant, cross, crabbed, testy, grouchy, disagreeable, spiteful, malicious.

**illness** noun ailment, sickness, disorder, complaint, malady, disease, affliction, attack, disability, indisposition, infection, contagion; ill health, poor health.

**illogical** adjective unsound, unreasonable, irrational, faulty, spurious, fallacious, fallible, unproved, untenable, specious, unscientific, sophistic, casuistic, inconsistent, invalid.

**ill-tempered** adjective choleric, cantankerous, grumpy, splenetic. See ILL-NATURED.

**ill-timed** adjective inopportune, inconvenient, awkward, inappropriate, untimely, mistimed, badly timed, unwelcome, unfavorable, unfortunate.

**ill-treat** verb abuse, harm, injure, damage, mishandle, ill-use, maltreat, misuse; *inf.* knock about.

**illuminate** verb 1 *lights illuminating the hall* light, light up, throw/cast light upon, brighten, shine on, irradiate, illumine. 2 *illuminate the problem* clarify, make clear, clear up, shed/cast light on, elucidate, explain, explicate, expound. 3 *illuminate a manuscript* adorn, decorate, ornament, embellish, enhance, illustrate.

**illusion** noun 1 *the illusion of depth* false/deceptive appearance, deception, faulty perception, misperception. 2 *under the illusion that he was her first love* delusion, misapprehension, misconception, false/mistaken impression, fallacy, error, misjudgment, fancy. 3 *see an illusion* hallucination, figment of the imagination, phantom, specter, mirage, phantasm, fantasy, will-o'-the-wisp, ignis fatuus.

**illusive, illusory** adjective deceptive, delusory, false, fallacious, mistaken, erroneous, misleading, untrue, specious; unreal, imagined, imaginary, fancied, nonexistent, fanciful, notional, chimerical, dreamlike.

**illustrate** verb 1 *illustrate the story* adorn, decorate, ornament, embellish. 2 *illustrate his point* exemplify, demonstrate, point up, clarify, bring home, emphasize.

**illustration** noun 1 *the illustration in the child's book* picture, drawing, sketch, plate, figure; artwork, adornment, decoration, ornamentation, embellishment. 2 *interesting illustrations explaining his theory* example, typical case, case in point, instance, specimen, sample, exemplar.

**illustrative** adjective exemplifying, explanatory, elucidative, explicative, interpretive.

**illustrious** adjective renowned, famous, famed, well-known, celebrated, acclaimed, noted, notable, distinguished, esteemed, honored, prominent, preeminent.

**ill will** noun bad blood, hostility. See ILL FEELING.

**image** noun 1 *images of the saints* likeness, representation, resemblance, effigy, figure, figurine, doll, statue, statuette, sculpture, bust, idol, icon, fetish, graven image, painting, picture, portrait. 2 *the image formed by the camera* reproduction, representation, reflection; picture, facsimile, photograph, snapshot, photo. 3 *an image of what the new country would be like* vision, concept, conception, idea, perception, impression, fancy, thought. 4 *he is the image of his father* double, living image, replica, clone, copy, reproduction, counterpart, similitude, doppelgänger; *inf.* spitting image, ringer, dead ringer. 5 *he* *is the image of goodness* emblem, symbol, archetype, embodiment, incarnation.

**imaginable** adjective thinkable, conceivable, supposable, believable, credible, comprehensible, possible, within the bounds of possibility, probable, likely, plausible, feasible.

**imaginary** adjective fanciful, fancied, unreal, nonexistent, illusory, visionary, dreamy, dreamlike, shadowy, unsubstantial, chimerical, fictitious, fictional, legendary, mythical, mythological, made-up, invented, hallucinatory, phantasmal, phantasmic, spectral, ghostly, ideal.

**imagination** noun **1** *the project requires imagination* creativity, vision, inventiveness, originality, innovation, resourcefulness, ingenuity, enterprise, cleverness. **2** *it's only your imagination* illusion, fancy, figment of the imagination, vision, dream, chimera, shadow, phantom.

**imaginative** adjective creative, fanciful, inventive, original, innovative, resourceful, ingenious, enterprising, clever, whimsical.

**imagine** verb **1** *he imagines a bright future for himself* picture, see in the mind's eye, visualize, envisage, envision, conjure up, dream about, dream up, fantasize about, conceptualize, think up, conceive, think of, plan, project, scheme. **2** *I imagine he will be late* assume, presume, suppose, think, believe, gather, fancy, judge, deem, infer, deduce, conjecture, surmise, guess, reckon, suspect.

**imbecile** noun fool, idiot, dolt, halfwit, nitwit, dunce, simpleton; *inf.* dimwit, dope.

**imbecilic** adjective stupid, foolish, idiotic, halfwitted, witless, dull; silly, senseless, absurd, crazy, mad, fatuous, inane, asinine; *inf.* dim-witted, dopey.

**imitate** verb **1** *imitate the language of Shakespeare* copy, emulate, follow, follow suit, take a page from someone's book, tread in the steps of, walk in the footsteps of, echo. **2** *comics imitating celebrities* mimic, ape, impersonate, do an impression of, parody, mock, caricature, burlesque, travesty; *inf.* send up, take off, spoof, do, make like. **3** *the stage set imitated a city street* look like, simulate, echo, mirror. **4** *imitate the portrait* copy, reproduce, replicate, duplicate, counterfeit, forge, fake.

**imitation** noun **1** *a house built in imitation of Frank Lloyd Wright* emulation, resemblance. **2** *the comic's imitations of celebrities* impersonation, impression, parody, caricature, burlesque, travesty; *inf.* send-up, takeoff, spoof. **3** *a bad imitation of the portrait* copy, reproduction, counterfeit, forgery, fake.

**imitation** adjective artificial, synthetic, simulated, man-made, ersatz, mock, sham, fake, reproduction, repro; *inf.* pseudo, phony.

**imitator** noun copier, copyist, emulator, follower, mimic, echo, impersonator, epigone, plagiarist, counterfeiter, forger, ape, parrot.

**immaculate** adjective **1** *immaculate rooms* clean, spotless, unsoiled, unstained, spick-and-span, neat, neat as a pin, spruce, trim. **2** *of immaculate character* flawless, faultless, stainless, unblemished, spotless, pure, incorrupt, guiltless, sinless, unsullied, undefiled, untarnished, uncontaminated, unpolluted.

**immaterial** adjective **1** *it's immaterial what he thinks* unimportant, inconsequential, of little account, irrelevant, insignificant, trivial, petty, slight, inappreciable. **2** *as immaterial as ghosts* incorporeal, bodiless, unembodied, disembodied, intangible, impalpable, ethereal, unsubstantial, airy, ghostly, unearthly, supernatural.

**immature** adjective **1** *immature fruit/plans* unripe, undeveloped, unformed, imperfect, unfinished, incomplete, half-grown, crude, raw, green, unmellowed, unfledged, untimely. **2** *an immature young man* adolescent, childish, babyish, infantile, juvenile, puerile, jejune, callow, inexperienced, green, unsophisticated; *inf.* wet behind the ears.

**immaturity** noun **1** *the immaturity of the fruit/plans* unripeness, imperfection, crudeness, rawness, greenness. **2** *the immaturity of the men* childishness, babyishness, juvenility, puerility, inexperience.

**immeasurable** adjective measureless, limitless, boundless, unbounded, illimitable, infinite, incalculable, unfathomable, fathomless, undeterminable, indeterminate, inestimable, extensive, vast.

**immediate** adjective **1** *an immediate reaction* instant, instantaneous, on the spot, prompt, swift, speedy. **2** *his immediate neighbor* near, nearest, close, closest, adjacent, adjoining, abutting, contiguous. **3** *our immediate plans* present, current, existing. **4** *get immediate experience* direct, firsthand, hands on, in the field, on the job.

**immediately** adverb right away, right now, straight away, at once, instantly, this instant, directly, promptly, forthwith, posthaste, *tout de suite*; *inf.* before you can say Jack Robinson, in the twinkling of an eye, lickety-split, pronto.

**immense** adjective huge, vast, massive, enormous, gigantic, colossal, giant, great, extensive, infinite, immeasurable, illimitable, monumental, tremendous, prodigious, elephantine, monstrous, titanic; *inf.* mega.

**immerse** verb **1** *immerse the cloth in the dye* submerge, plunge, dip, dunk, duck, sink, douse, souse, soak, drench, imbue, saturate. **2** *immerse oneself in one's work* absorb, engross, occupy, engage, preoccupy, involve, engulf, lose.

**immigrant** noun nonnative, settler, newcomer, new arrival, naturalized citizen, expatriate.

**imminent** adjective impending, at hand, fast-approaching, close, near, upon us, in the offing, on the horizon, in the air, brewing, threatening, menacing, looming.

**immobile** adjective immobilized, unmoving, motionless, immovable, still, static, at rest, stationary, at a standstill, stock-still, dormant, rooted, fixed to the spot, riveted.

**immobilize** verb bring to a standstill, halt, stop, put out of action, inactivate, paralyze, freeze, transfix, disable, cripple.

**immoderate** adjective excessive, extreme, intemperate, lavish, undue, inordinate, extravagant, unreasonable, unjustified, unwarranted, uncalled-for, outrageous, egregious.

**immoral** adjective bad, wrong, unprincipled, dishonest, unethical, wicked, evil, sinful, impure, iniquitous, corrupt, depraved, vile, base, degenerate, debauched, abandoned, dissolute, villainous, nefarious, perverted, indecent.

**immortal** adjective **1** *immortal beings/love* undying, deathless, eternal, everlasting, never-ending, endless, imperishable, perdurable, timeless, indestructible, unfading, undecaying, perennial, evergreen, perpetual, lasting, enduring, constant, abiding, sempiternal. **2** *immortal poets* famous, celebrated, remembered, commemorated, honored, lauded, glorified.

**immortalize** verb commemorate, memorialize, eternalize, eternize, perpetuate, exalt, laud, glorify.

**immovable** adjective **1** *immovable pillars* fast, firm, fixed, secure, stable, rooted, riveted, moored, anchored, stuck, jammed, unbudgeable. **2** *the spectators stood immovable* motionless, unmoving, stationary, still, stock-still. **3** *the court was immovable in its ruling* adamant, firm, steadfast, unwavering, resolute, tenacious, obdurate, inflexible, uncompromising, unshakeable.

**immune** adjective not subject to, not liable to, protected from, safe from, unsusceptible to, secure against, exempt from, clear of, free from, absolved from, released from, excused from, relieved of, spared from, excepted from, unaffected by, resistant to, protected from/against.

**immunity** noun indemnity, privilege, prerogative, liberty, license, permission. **immunity from 1** *immunity from the disease* nonsusceptibility to, resistance to, protection from. **2** *immunity from tax* exemption from, exception from, freedom from, release from, dispensation from, absolution from, exoneration from, excusal from.

**imp** noun **1** *devils and imps* demon, hobgoblin, goblin, elf, sprite, puck, gnome, dwarf. **2** *the child's a little imp* scamp, rogue, rascal, mischief-maker, troublemaker, prankster.

**impact** noun **1** *the impact of the two cars* collision, contact, crash, striking, clash, bumping, banging. **2** *the impact of his talk* influence, effect, impression; results, consequences, repercussions. **3** *he took the full impact of the blow* force, full force, shock, brunt, impetus, pressure.

**impair** verb weaken, lessen, decrease, reduce, blunt, diminish, enfeeble, debilitate, enervate, damage, mar, spoil, injure, harm, hinder, disable, cripple, impede, undermine, vitiate.

**impale** verb transfix, pierce, stab, prick, stick, spear, spike, run through, disembowel.

**impart** verb **1** *impart the news* pass on, convey, communicate, transmit, relate, tell, make known, report, disclose, reveal, divulge, proclaim, broadcast. **2** *age imparts wisdom* bestow, confer, give, grant, lend, accord, afford, assign, offer.

**impartial** adjective unbiased, unprejudiced, disinterested, detached, objective, neutral, equitable, evenhanded, fair, fairminded, just, open-minded, nonpartisan, with no ax to grind, without fear or favor.

**impasse** noun deadlock, dead end, stalemate, checkmate, standstill, full/dead stop, stand-off.

**impassioned** adjective passionate, ardent, fervent, fervid, vehement, intense, violent, fiery, burning, inflamed, emotional, emotive, zealous, eager, enthusiastic, aroused.

**impatience** noun **1** *wait with impatience* restlessness, restiveness, excitability, anxiety, agitation, nervousness, edginess, fretfulness, jitteriness, fluster, disquiet, disquietude. **2** *answer with impatience* abruptness, brusqueness, shortness, curtness, irascibility, irritability, testiness, snappiness, querulousness, peevishness.

**impatient** adjective **1** *an impatient crowd* restless, restive, excitable, agitated, nervous, edgy. **2** *an impatient answer* abrupt, brusque, terse, short, short-tempered, quick-tempered, curt, irritated, angry, testy, snappy, querulous, peevish. **3** *impatient to see her boyfriend* anxious, eager, keen, avid, desirous.

**impeccable** adjective **1** *impeccable behavior* perfect, faultless, flawless, unblemished, exemplary, correct, exact, precise, ideal. **2** *an impeccable young woman* virtuous, innocent, chaste, pure, sinless, irreproachable, unimpeachable, above suspicion, incorrupt.

**impede** verb hinder, obstruct, hamper, handicap, block, check, bar, curb, hold back, hold up, delay, interfere with, disrupt, retard, slow, slow down, brake, restrain, thwart, frustrate, balk, stop; *inf.* throw a monkey wrench in the works.

**impediment** noun **1** *an impediment to our plans* hindrance, obstruction, obstacle, handicap, block, stumbling block, check, encumbrance, bar, barrier, curb, brake, restraint, drawback, difficulty, snag, setback. **2** *a speech impediment* stammer, stutter, speech defect, hesitancy, faltering.

**impel** verb urge, press, exhort, force, oblige, constrain, necessitate, require, demand, make, pressure, spur, prod, goad, incite, prompt, persuade, inspire.

**impending** adjective approaching, coming. *See* IMMINENT.

**impenetrable** adjective **1** *impenetrable containers* impervious, impermeable, solid, dense, thick, hard, closed, sealed, tight, unpierceable. **2** *impenetrable forests* impassable, unpassable, inaccessible, thick, dense, overgrown, jungly. **3** *impenetrable jargon* incomprehensible, unintelligible, baffling, puzzling, abstruse, obscure, hidden, inexplicable, unfathomable, recondite, inscrutable, enigmatic.

**imperative** adjective **1** *it is imperative that you stay* vital, crucial, critical, necessary, required, mandatory, pressing, urgent. **2** *an imperative tone of voice* imperious, authoritative, peremptory, commanding, lordly, masterful, autocratic, dictatorial, domineering, overbearing.

**imperceptible** adjective unnoticeable, unobtrusive, unapparent, slight, small, gradual, subtle, faint, fine, inappreciable, inconsequential, undetectable, indistinguishable, indiscernible, invisible, indistinct, obscure, vague, indefinite.

**imperfect** adjective faulty, flawed, defective, blemished, impaired; incomplete, deficient, partial, inadequate, insufficient, lacking.

**imperfection** noun **1** *an imperfection in the finish* fault, flaw, defect, deformity, blemish; crack, break, scratch, cut, tear, stain, spot. **2** *an imperfection in his character* failing, flaw, foible, deficiency, weakness, weak point, shortcoming, fallibility, frailty, infirmity, peccadillo.

**imperial** adjective **1** *his/her imperial majesty* royal, sovereign, regal, monarchal, kingly, queenly, princely. **2** *an imperial bearing* majestic, magnificent, grand, great, lofty, imposing, august, stately. **3** *the imperial ruler of the region* supreme, absolute, dominant, predominant, paramount, chief. **4** *an imperial tone of voice* commanding, lordly, masterful, authoritative, imperious, peremptory, domineering.

**imperil** verb endanger, put in danger/jeopardy, put at risk, risk, jeopardize, hazard, gamble with, take a chance with.

**impersonal** adjective **1** *an impersonal assessment of the candidates* detached, objective, dispassionate, neutral. *See* IMPARTIAL. **2** *an impersonal manner* cool, aloof, formal, stiff, rigid, wooden, starchy, stilted, stuffy, matter-of-fact, businesslike, bureaucratic.

**impersonate** verb masquerade as, pose as, pass oneself off as. *See* IMITATE 2.

**impertinence** noun insolence, impudence, cheek, rudeness, impoliteness, unmannerliness, lack of civility, discourtesy, boldness, brazenness, audacity, effrontery, gall, presumptuousness, brashness; *inf.* nerve, lip.

**impertinent** adjective **1** *an impertinent youth/act* insolent, impudent, cheeky, rude, impolite, unmannerly, ill-mannered, uncivil, discourteous, disrespectful, bold, brazen, audacious, presumptuous, forward, pert, brash, shameless; *inf.* fresh, flip. **2** *this document is impertinent to the case* irrelevant, inapplicable, inapposite, unrelated, unconnected, not germane.

**impervious** adjective *impervious containers* impermeable, sealed. *See* IMPENETRABLE 1. **impervious to** *impervious to arguments* unmoved by, unaffected by, proof against, immune to, invulnerable to, unreceptive to, untouched by, closed to.

**impetuous** adjective **1** *an impetuous action/person* hasty, precipitate, headlong, impulsive, spontaneous, spur-of-the-moment, unthinking, unplanned, unthought out, ill-conceived, ill-considered, unreasoned, reckless, rash, foolhardy, heedless, eager, enthusiastic, impatient, excitable, ardent, passionate, zealous, wild, uncontrolled. **2** *an impetuous wind* violent, forceful, powerful, vigorous, vehement, raging, rampant, unrestrained, uncontrolled, unbridled.

**impetus** noun **1** *the car lost impetus on the hill* momentum, propulsion, energy, force, power. **2** *the student needs some impetus to start studying* stimulus, instigation, actuation, motivation, inspiration, encouragement, push, urging, pressing, spur, goad.

**impish** adjective **1** *impish little boys* mischievous, mischief-making, full of mischief, rascally, roguish, prankish, unruly, trouble-making, devilish, sportive. **2** *an impish* *smile* elfin, pixieish, puckish, mischievous, roguish.

**implacable** adjective unappeasable, unpacifiable, unmollifiable, inexorable, unrelenting, relentless, ruthless, unsympathetic, remorseless, merciless, pitiless.

**implausible** adjective unlikely, improbable, incredible, unbelievable, hard to swallow, unimaginable, inconceivable.

**implement** noun **1** *garden/kitchen implements* tool, utensil, appliance, instrument, device, apparatus, contrivance, gadget; *inf.* gizmo. **2** *an implement of peace* agent, medium, channel, expedient, means.

**implement** verb fulfill, carry out, execute, perform, discharge, accomplish, achieve, realize, put into effect/action, bring about, effect, enforce.

**implicate** verb involve, concern, include, associate, connect, embroil, entangle; incriminate, compromise, inculpate, accuse, charge, blame.

**implication** noun **1** *resent the implication that he was lying* suggestion, inference, insinuation, innuendo, hint, allusion, reference, assumption, presumption. **2** *their implication in the events* involvement, concern, association, connection, entanglement.

**implicit** adjective **1** *implicit criticism* implied, indirect, inferred, deducible, unspoken, unexpressed, undeclared, unstated, tacit, understood, hinted, suggested. **2** *implicit trust* absolute, complete, utter, unconditional, unquestioning.

**implied** adjective indirect, unspoken. *See* IMPLICIT 1.

**implore** verb appeal to, beg, entreat, plead with, beseech, pray, ask, request, solicit, supplicate, importune, press; crave, plead for, appeal for.

**imply** verb **1** *he implied that all was not well* hint, suggest, intimate, give to understand, signal, indicate, insinuate. **2** *being a civil servant implies discretion* involve, entail, presuppose, presume, assume. **3** *war implies bloodshed* signify, mean, indicate, denote, connote, betoken, point to.

**impolite** adjective unmannerly, ill-mannered, ungracious, ungallant, disrespectful, inconsiderate, rough, crude, unrefined, indelicate, indecorous. *See* ILL-BRED.

**importance** noun **1** *the importance of the talks* significance, momentousness, seriousness, graveness, urgency, gravity, weightiness, value. **2** *people of importance* prominence, eminence, preeminence, note, notability, noteworthiness, influence, power, high rank, status, prestige, standing, mark.

**important** adjective **1** *important talks* of import, consequential, significant, critical, crucial, pivotal, momentous, of great moment, serious, grave, urgent, substantial, weighty, valuable. **2** *the important points to remember* salient, chief, main, principal, major. **3** *the important people in the town* prominent, eminent, preeminent, leading, foremost, outstanding, distinguished, esteemed, notable, influential, powerful, high-ranking, high-level, top-level.

**impose** verb **1** *impose a tax* apply, exact, levy, charge, put on, lay on, set, establish, fix, decree, ordain, institute, introduce, promulgate; require, demand, dictate; *inf.* saddle with. **2** *impose her views on the group* force, foist, inflict, thrust, obtrude. **3** *impose fake antiques on the public* palm off, foist, pass off. **impose on** *impose on her good nature* take advantage of, abuse, exploit, play on. **impose oneself** *impose herself on the company* intrude, break in; *inf.* gatecrash, crash, butt in, horn in.

**imposing** adjective impressive, striking, splendid, grand, majestic, august, lofty, stately, dignified.

**imposition** noun **1** *the imposition of new taxes* application, exacting, levying, decreeing, institution. **2** *unfair impositions on the poor* burden, load, charge, onus, encumbrance.

**impossible** adjective **1** *an impossible task* beyond the realm/bounds of possibility, out of the question, unthinkable, unimaginable, inconceivable, impracticable, unattainable, unachievable, unobtainable, beyond one, hopeless. **2** *an impossible story* unbelievable, incredible, absurd, ludicrous, ridiculous, preposterous, outlandish, outrageous. **3** *impossible behavior* objectionable, unacceptable, intolerable, unbearable, unendurable.

**impostor, imposter** noun masquerader, pretender, deceiver, fake, fraud, sham, charlatan, quack, mountebank, bluffer, trickster, deluder, duper, cheat, cheater, swindler, defrauder, exploiter, confidence man/woman, rogue; *inf.* phony, con man, con artist.

**impotent** adjective powerless, helpless, unable, incapable, incapacitated, incompetent; enfeebled, weak, feeble, frail, worn out, exhausted, spent, enervated, debilitated, prostrate, crippled, paralyzed, infirm; ineffective, ineffectual, inefficient, inadequate, inept, useless, worthless, vain, futile, unavailing, unsuccessful, profitless.

**impound** verb **1** *impound stray animals* pen in/in, fence in, coop up, hem in, tie up, cage, enclose, confine, imprison, incarcerate, immure. **2** *impound legal documents* appropriate, take possession of, seize, commandeer, expropriate.

**impoverished** adjective **1** *impoverished homeless people* poverty-stricken, destitute, penurious, beggared, indigent, impecunious, penniless, poor, needy, in distressed/reduced/straitened circumstances, down-and-out, bankrupt, insolvent, ruined; *inf.* broke, flat-broke, stone-broke, strapped. **2** *impoverished soil* exhausted, depleted, diminished, weakened, drained, used up, spent, played out.

**impractical** adjective **1** *an impractical solution* unworkable, useless, ineffective, ineffectual, inefficacious, unrealistic, impossible, nonviable, inoperable, inoperative, unserviceable. **2** *his ideas are too impractical to implement* theoretical, abstract, academic, speculative. **3** *an impractical young woman* unrealistic, unbusinesslike, starry-eyed, visionary, quixotic.

**impregnable** adjective **1** *an impregnable castle* impenetrable, unattackable, unassailable, inviolable, secure, strong, stout, invulnerable, invincible, unconquerable, unbeatable, indestructible. **2** *an impregnable argument* irrefutable, indisputable, incontestable, unquestionable, flawless, faultless.

**impress** verb **1** *impress the crowd with his speech* move, sway, bend, influence, affect, affect deeply, stir, rouse, excite, inspire, galvanize; *inf.* grab. **2** *impress upon them the need for action* emphasize, stress, bring home, establish, instill, inculcate, urge. **3** *impress one's name on a metal strip* stamp, imprint, print, mark, engrave, emboss.

**impression** noun **1** *make an impression on the crowd* effect, influence, sway, impact, hold, power, control. **2** *the impression made by the ring* mark, indentation, dent, hollow, outline, stamp, stamping, imprint, impress. **3** *I have the impression that he is bored* feeling, sense, awareness, perception, notion, idea, thought, belief, opinion, conviction, fancy, suspicion, inkling, intuition, hunch. **4** *his impression of the politician* impersonation, mimicry. *See* IMITATION noun 2.

**impressionable** adjective susceptible, suggestible, persuadable, receptive, responsive, sensitive, open, gullible, ingenuous, pliable, malleable.

**impressive** adjective imposing, magnificent, splendid; moving, affecting, touching, stirring, rousing, exciting, powerful, inspiring.

**imprint** noun print, mark. *See* IMPRESSION 2.

**imprison** verb put in prison, send to prison, jail, lock up, shut away, take into custody, put under lock and key, put away, incarcerate, intern, confine, detain, constrain, impound, coop up, immure; *inf.* send up, send up the river.

**imprisonment** noun custody, incarceration, internment, confinement, detention.

**improbable** adjective unlikely, highly unlikely, doubtful, dubious, questionable, implausible, far-fetched, unconvincing, unbelievable, incredible, ridiculous.

**impromptu** adjective ad lib, unrehearsed, unprepared, extempore, extemporized, extemporaneous, spontaneous, improvised, unscripted, unstudied, unpremeditated; *inf.* off the cuff.

**impromptu** adverb ad lib, extempore, spontaneously, on the spur of the moment; *inf.* off the cuff, off the top of one's head.

**improper** adjective **1** *improper behavior* unseemly, indecorous, unbecoming, unfitting, unladylike, ungentlemanly, impolite, indiscreet, injudicious. **2** *an improper remark* indecent, risqué, off-color, indelicate, suggestive, blue, smutty, obscene, lewd, pornographic. **3** *draw an improper inference* inaccurate, incorrect, wrong, erroneous, false. **4** *an improper tool for the job* inappropriate, unsuitable, unsuited, unfitting, inapt, inapplicable, incongruous.

**impropriety** noun incorrectness, indecorum, indecorousness, unseemliness, indiscretion, bad taste, immodesty, indecency.

**improve** verb **1** *improve conditions* make better, better, ameliorate, amend, mend, reform, rehabilitate, set/put right, correct, rectify, help, advance, upgrade, revamp, modernize, gentrify; *inf.* give a face-lift to. **2** *things are improving* get/grow better, advance, come along, develop, progress, pick up, rally, perk up; *inf.* look up, take a turn for the better, get a new lease on life.

**improvement** noun **1** *the improvement of conditions* betterment, amelioration, reform, rehabilitation, rectifying, rectification, advance, upgrading, gentrification; *inf.* face-lift. **2** *an improvement in the economy* betterment, advance, development, rally, recovery, upswing, comeback; progress, growth.

**improvise** verb **1** *if you aren't prepared, you will have to improvise* ad lib, extemporize; *inf.* speak off the cuff, play it by ear, wing it. **2** *improvise a shelter* throw/put together, devise, contrive, concoct, rig, jury-rig.

**imprudent** adjective indiscreet, ill-considered, thoughtless, unthinking, injudicious, unwise, ill-advised, impolitic, careless, hasty.

**impudence** noun insolence, pertness, sauciness, presumption, bumptiousness. *See* IMPERTINENCE.

**impudent** adjective insolent, brazen-faced, saucy, bumptious, impolite, rude, ill-mannered, ill-bred, immodest; *inf.* cocky. *See* IMPERTINENT 1.

**impugn** verb challenge, call into question, question, dispute, cast aspersions on, attack, assail, berate, criticize, denounce, censure.

**impulse** noun **1** *the impulse driving the machine* impetus, propulsion, impulsion, momentum, force, thrust, push, surge. **2** *the literary impulse* stimulus, inspiration, stimulation, incitement, incentive, inducement, motivation; urge, drive, instinct, appetite, proclivity. **3** *buy the coat on impulse* sudden desire/fancy, (the) spur of the moment, notion, whim, caprice.

**impulsive** adjective hasty, impromptu, snap, spontaneous, extemporaneous, sudden, quick, precipitate, impetuous, ill-considered, unplanned, unpremeditated, thoughtless, rash, reckless, instinctive, intuitive, passionate, emotional.

**impunity** noun immunity, indemnity, excusal, nonliability, license, dispensation.

**impure** adjective **1** *impure chemicals* adulterated, alloyed, mixed, admixed, combined, blended, debased. **2** *impure water* contaminated, polluted, tainted, infected, foul, dirty, filthy, unclean, feculent, sullied, defiled, unwholesome, poisoned. **3** *impure persons/thoughts* unchaste, immoral, loose, promiscuous, wanton, immodest, dissolute, licentious, lascivious, prurient, lustful, lecherous, lewd, obscene, dirty, indecent, ribald, risqué, smutty, pornographic.

**impurity** noun **1** *the impurity of the chemical* adulteration, admixture, debasement. **2** *the impurity of the water* contamination, pollution, foulness, filthiness, unwholesomeness. **3** *impurities in the chemicals/water* foreign body, contaminant, pollutant, adulterant; dross, dirt, filth, grime, scum. **4** *regretted the impurity of their past/thoughts* immorality, looseness, promiscuity, wantonness, immodesty, lasciviousness, lust, lechery, lewdness, lustfulness, obscenity, ribaldry, smut, smuttiness, impropriety, crudity, vulgarity.

**inability** noun incapability, incapacity, incompetence, ineptitude, unfitness, powerlessness, uselessness, inefficacy.

**inaccessible** adjective unreachable, out of reach, beyond reach, unapproachable, impenetrable, unattainable, out of the way, remote, godforsaken.

**inaccuracy** noun **1** *the inaccuracy of the results* incorrectness, erroneousness, wrongness, mistakenness, fallaciousness, faultiness, inexactness, inexactitude, imprecision. **2** *the accounts were full of inaccuracies* error, mistake, miscalculation, erratum, corrigendum, slip, slip of the pen, fault, blunder, defect; *inf.* slipup, typo, booboo.

**inaccurate** adjective incorrect, wrong, erroneous, faulty, inexact, imprecise, fallacious, false, imperfect, flawed, defective,

unsound, unreliable, wide of the mark; *inf.* full of holes.

**inactive** adjective **1** *all the machines lying inactive* idle, inoperative, nonfunctioning, unused, not in use, unoccupied, unemployed, inert, mothballed. **2** *a former athlete now completely inactive* idle, inert, slow, sluggish, indolent, lazy, lifeless, slothful, lethargic, stagnant, vegetating, sedentary. **3** *an inactive volcano* dormant, quiescent, latent, passive.

**inadequacy** noun **1** *the inadequacy of the supply* inadequateness, insufficiency, dearth, deficiency, meagerness, scantness, scarcity, paucity, shortage, deficit, lack. **2** *the inadequacy of the staff* incompetence, incapability, unfitness, ineffectiveness, ineffectuality, ineptness. **3** *his inadequacies as a manager* shortcoming, fault, failing, flaw, defect, imperfection, weakness, foible.

**inadequate** adjective **1** *inadequate supplies* insufficient, meager, scanty, scant, niggardly, scarce, sparse, skimpy, sketchy, incomplete. **2** *an inadequate teacher* incompetent, incapable, unfit, ineffective, ineffectual, unskillful, unadept, inexpert, inproficient, inept; *inf.* not up to scratch/snuff.

**inadvertent** adjective **1** *an inadvertent omission* accidental, unintentional, chance, unpremeditated, unplanned, uncalculated, unconscious, unwitting, involuntary. **2** *an inadvertent driver* inattentive, careless, negligent, heedless, unheeding, unmindful, unobservant.

**inadvisable** adjective ill-advised, unwise, injudicious, ill-judged, imprudent, impolitic, inexpedient, foolish.

**inane** adjective silly, foolish, stupid, idiotic, absurd, ridiculous, ludicrous, fatuous, frivolous, senseless, mindless, puerile, asinine, futile, worthless, vacuous, vapid; *inf.* daft.

**inanimate** adjective **1** *inanimate objects* lifeless, exanimate, dead, inert, insentient, insensate. **2** *inanimate people* spiritless, apathetic, lazy, inactive, phlegmatic, listless, lethargic, sluggish, torpid.

**inappropriate** adjective unsuitable, unfitting, inapt, unseemly, unbecoming, indecorous, improper, inapposite, incongruous, out of place/keeping, untimely.

**inapt** adjective **1** *an inapt remark* unsuitable, unsuited, unfitting. *See* INAPPROPRIATE. **2** *an inapt plumber* inept, incompetent, unadept, incapable, unskillful, inexpert, clumsy, awkward, maladroit, undexterous, heavy-handed.

**inarticulate** adjective **1** *inarticulate cries/sounds* unintelligible, incomprehensible, incoherent, unclear, indistinct, blurred, muffled, mumbled, muttered. **2**

*inarticulate speakers* nonfluent, faltering, hesitating, halting, stumbling, stuttering, stammering. **3** *inarticulate emotion* unspoken, unuttered, unexpressed, unvoiced, wordless, silent, mute, dumb, speechless, voiceless.

**inattentive** adjective distracted, preoccupied, absentminded, daydreaming, woolgathering, lost in thought, with one's head in the clouds, neglectful, negligent, remiss, careless, heedless; *inf.* miles away.

**inaudible** adjective out of earshot, faint, muted, soft, low, muffled, stifled, hard to make out, indistinct, imperceptible, whispered, murmured.

**inaugural** adjective first, initial, introductory, opening, maiden, dedicatory.

**inaugurate** verb **1** *inaugurate the conference proceedings* initiate, begin, start, commence, launch, start off, set in motion, get going, get under way, raise the curtain on, get off the ground. **2** *inaugurate the new president* install, instate, induct, invest, ordain.

**inauspicious** adjective unpropitious, unpromising, unlucky, unfortunate, infelicitous, unfavorable, ill-omened, ominous, ill-fated, ill-starred, untoward, untimely.

**inborn** adjective innate, inherent, inherited, congenital, hereditary, in the family, in the blood/genes, inbred, connate, ingrained.

**incalculable** adjective **1** *the number is incalculable* immeasurable, measureless, inestimable, uncountable, incomputable, infinite, boundless, limitless, fathomless, bottomless, countless, without number, numberless, multitudinous, enormous, immense, vast. **2** *an incalculable risk* unpredictable, indeterminable, unforeseeable.

**incantation** noun chant, chanting, invocation, conjuration, spell; abracadabra, open sesame.

**incapable** adjective incompetent, ineffective, ineffectual, inadequate, unfit, unqualified, inept, useless, feeble; *inf.* not up to scratch/snuff. **incapable of** *problems incapable of solution* not open to, impervious to, resistant to, not susceptible to.

**incapacitated** adjective disabled, debilitated, unfit, immobilized, crippled, indisposed; *inf.* laid up, out of action.

**incapacity** noun inability, incapability, incompetence, incompetency, inadequacy, unfitness, ineffectiveness, ineffectuality, inefficiency, powerlessness, impotence.

**incarcerate** verb jail, throw in prison/jail. *See* IMPRISON.

**incarceration** noun captivity, bondage. *See* IMPRISONMENT.

**incendiary** adjective **1** *an incendiary bomb* combustible, flammable, fire-producing.

**2** *an incendiary speech* inflammatory, incensing, inciting, instigating, arousing, stirring, provocative, rabble-rousing, seditious, subversive.

**incendiary** noun **1** *buildings set on fire by incendiaries* arsonist, fire-setter, pyromaniac; *inf.* firebug. **2** *crowds driven to rioting by incendiaries* demagogue, agitator, agent provocateur, rabble-rouser, instigator, inciter, insurgent, firebrand, revolutionary.

**incense** verb anger, enrage, infuriate, exasperate, irritate, madden, provoke, rile, inflame, agitate, nettle, vex, irk, get one's hackles up; *inf.* make one's blood boil, make one see red, ruffle one's feathers, get one's dander up.

**incentive** noun inducement, incitement, stimulus, stimulant, impetus, encouragement, motivation, inspiration, impulse, goad, spur, lure, bait; *inf.* carrot.

**inception** noun beginning, commencement, start, starting point, outset, opening, debut, inauguration, initiation, institution, birth, dawn, origin, rise; *inf.* kickoff.

**incessant** adjective ceaseless, unceasing, nonstop, endless, unending, never-ending, everlasting, eternal, constant, continual, perpetual, continuous, uninterrupted, unbroken, ongoing, unremitting, persistent, recurrent.

**incidence** noun rate, frequency, prevalence, occurrence, amount, degree, extent.

**incident** noun **1** *unhappy incidents in her life* event, happening, occurrence, episode, adventure, experience, proceeding, occasion, circumstance, fact, matter. **2** *the police were called to an incident in the bar* disturbance, commotion, scene, fracas, contretemps, skirmish, clash, conflict, confrontation.

**incidental** adjective **1** *her part in the event was incidental* accidental, by chance, chance, fortuitous, random. **2** *incidental expenses* minor, trivial, trifling, petty, small, meager. **incidental to** *travel incidental to her job* related to, connected with, associated with, accompanying, attendant to, concomitant to, contingent to/on.

**incidentally** adverb by the way, by the by, in passing, speaking of which, while we're on the subject, apropos.

**incision** noun cut, opening, slit, gash, slash, notch, nick.

**incisive** adjective **1** *an incisive mind* keen, acute, sharp, penetrating, astute, shrewd, perspicacious, clever, smart, quick. **2** *an incisive remark* caustic, acid, sharp, biting, cutting, stinging, tart, trenchant, mordant, sarcastic, sardonic.

**incite** verb instigate, provoke, foment, whip up, stir up, prompt, egg on, encourage, urge, goad, spur on, prod, stimulate, drive on, excite, arouse, agitate, inflame.

**inclination** noun **1** *an inclination to over-eat* tendency, leaning, propensity, proclivity, proneness, liableness, disposition, predisposition, subjectivity, weakness. **2** *an inclination for books* penchant, predilection, partiality, preference, affinity, attraction, fancy, liking, fondness, affection, love. **3** *an inclination of the head* bow, bowing, bend, bending, nod, lowering, stooping. **4** *an inclination in the terrain* incline, slope, slant, gradient, bank, ramp, lift, tilt, acclivity, rise, ascent, declivity, descent.

**incline** verb **1** *the land inclines toward the shore* curve, bend, slope, slant, bank, cant, bevel, tilt, lean, tip, list, deviate. **2** *I'm inclined to believe you* predispose, dispose, influence, bias, prejudice, sway, persuade, bend. **3** *incline the head* bow, bend, nod, lower, stoop, cast down. **incline to/toward** tend to/toward, lean to/toward, swing to/toward, veer to/toward, have a preference/penchant for, be attracted to.

**include** verb **1** *the group includes all the representatives* contain, hold, take in, admit, incorporate, embrace, encompass, comprise, embody, comprehend, subsume. **2** *include them on the list* allow for, add, insert, put in, enter, count in, take account of, build in, number, incorporate.

**incognito** adjective/adverb in disguise, disguised, in masquerade, camouflaged, unrecognized, unidentified, sailing under false colors.

**incognizant** adjective unaware, unconscious, ignorant, unknowing, unsuspecting, unknowledgeable, unenlightened.

**incoherent** adjective unconnected, disconnected, disjointed, disordered, confused, mixed-up, muddled, jumbled, scrambled, rambling, wandering, discursive, illogical, unintelligible, inarticulate, mumbled, muttered, stuttered, stammered.

**income** noun salary, pay, remuneration, revenue; earnings, wages, receipts, takings, profits, gains, proceeds, means.

**incoming** adjective approaching, entering, arriving; new, succeeding.

**incomparable** adjective beyond compare, inimitable, unequaled, without equal, matchless, nonpareil, unrivaled, peerless, unparalleled, unsurpassed, superlative, supreme.

**incompatible** adjective *incompatible views/siblings* inharmonious, uncongenial, incongruous, uncomplementary, conflicting, antagonistic, antipathetic, disagreeing, discordant, like oil and water, clashing, jarring. **incompatible with** differing from, contrary to.

*See* INCONGRUOUS WITH (INCONGRUOUS).

**incompetent** adjective **1** *incompetent to do the task* unable, incapable, unqualified, inadequate, deficient. **2** *an incompetent performance* unskillful, inexpert, inept, bungling, maladroit, clumsy.

**incomplete** adjective unfinished, unaccomplished, partial, undone, deficient, lacking, wanting, defective, imperfect.

**incomprehensible** adjective unintelligible, inapprehensible, beyond comprehension, unfathomable, impenetrable, profound, deep, inexplicable, puzzling, enigmatic, mysterious, abstruse, recondite.

**inconceivable** adjective unimaginable, unthinkable,,incomprehensible, incredible, unbelievable, implausible, impossible, out of the question, preposterous, ridiculous, ludicrous.

**inconclusive** adjective indefinite, indecisive, indeterminate, undetermined, still open to question, open to doubt, vague, unestablished, unsettled, ambiguous; *inf.* up in the air.

**incongruous** adjective out of place/keeping, strange, odd, absurd, unsuitable, inappropriate, incompatible, inharmonious, discordant, clashing, jarring. **incongruous with** *behavior incongruous with his principles* incompatible with, inconsistent with, out of keeping/place with, differing from, contrary to, inappropriate to, unsuited to, at odds with, in opposition to, diametrically opposed to, conflicting with, irreconcilable with.

**inconsequential** adjective insignificant, negligible, inappreciable, unimportant, of minor importance, of little/no account, trivial, trifling, petty; *inf.* piddling.

**inconsiderate** adjective thoughtless, unthinking, unthoughtful, uncaring, heedless, unmindful, insensitive, tactless, uncharitable, unkind, ungracious, selfish, self-centered, egotistic.

**inconsistent** adjective changeable, variable, erratic, irregular, inconstant, unstable, unsteady, unpredictable, capricious, fickle, whimsical, mercurial, volatile. **inconsistent with** incompatible with, out of keeping with. *See* INCONGRUOUS WITH (INCONGRUOUS).

**inconsolable** adjective grief-stricken, brokenhearted, heartbroken, sick at heart, bowed down, miserable, wretched, woebegone, disconsolate, desolate, despairing.

**inconspicuous** adjective unnoticeable, unobtrusive, indistinct, ordinary, plain, run-of-the-mill, unremarkable, undistinguished, unostentatious, unimposing, hidden, camouflaged, quiet, retiring, in the background; *inf.* low-key.

**inconvenience** noun trouble, bother, disruption, disturbance, vexation, worry, annoyance, difficulty, nuisance, burden, hindrance; *inf.* pain, drag, bore.

**inconvenience** verb disturb, bother, trouble, worry, disrupt, put out, impose upon, burden, distract, annoy.

**inconvenient** adjective awkward, unsuitable, inappropriate, inopportune, disadvantageous, disturbing, troublesome, bothersome, annoying, ill-timed, untimely, unhandy, difficult.

**incorporate** verb **1** *incorporate the ingredients to form a whole* merge, coalesce, fuse, blend, mix, amalgamate, combine, unite, integrate, unify, compact. **2** *the document incorporates all our thoughts* embody, include, comprise, embrace, absorb, subsume, assimilate.

**incorrect** adjective **1** *an incorrect answer/account* wrong, inaccurate, erroneous, wide of the mark, mistaken, faulty, inexact, untrue, fallacious, flawed; *inf.* full of holes. **2** *incorrect behavior* improper, unbecoming, unseemly, indecorous, unsuitable, inappropriate, unladylike, ungentlemanly.

**incorrigible** adjective *an incorrigible criminal* hardened, incurable, inveterate, unreformable, irredeemable, hopeless, beyond hope/redemption, impenitent, uncontrite, unrepentant.

**incorruptible** adjective **1** *incorruptible members of society* virtuous, upright, high-principled, honorable, honest, moral, ethical, trustworthy, straight, unbribable. **2** *incorruptible materials* imperishable, indestructible, nonbiodegradable, indissoluble, indissolvable, everlasting.

**increase** verb **1** *demand has increased* grow, expand, extend, multiply, intensify, heighten, mount, escalate, snowball, mushroom, proliferate, swell, wax. **2** *increase the demand* add to, boost, enhance, build up, augment, enlarge, spread, raise, strengthen, magnify, inflate; *inf.* step up.

**increase** noun growth, rise, enlargement, expansion, extension, increment, addition, development, intensification, heightening, escalation, snowballing, mushrooming, boost, augmentation, strengthening, magnification, inflation.

**incredible** adjective **1** *find his story incredible* unbelievable, hard to believe, beyond belief, far-fetched, inconceivable, unimaginable, unthinkable, impossible, implausible, highly unlikely, absurd, preposterous, questionable, dubious, doubtful. **2** *an incredible performance* extraordinary, supreme, great, wonderful, marvelous, tremendous, prodigious, astounding, amazing, astonishing, awe-inspiring, awesome, superhuman, fabulous, fantastic.

**incredulous** adjective disbelieving, unbelieving, skeptical, cynical, distrusting, distrustful, mistrusting, mistrustful, doubtful, doubting, dubious, unconvinced, suspicious.

**incriminate** verb charge, accuse, indict, impeach, arraign, blame, implicate, inculpate, involve, inform against, blacken the name of, stigmatize; *inf.* finger, point the finger at, stick/pin the blame on, rat on.

**incur** verb bring upon oneself, expose oneself to, lay oneself open to, provoke, be liable/subject to, contract, meet with, experience.

**incurable** adjective **1** *an incurable illness* cureless, unhealable, terminal, fatal, untreatable, inoperable, irremediable. **2** *an incurable romantic* inveterate, dyed-in-the-wool, incorrigible, hopeless, beyond hope.

**indebted** adjective beholden, obliged, obligated; grateful, thankful, appreciative.

**indecency** noun **1** *the indecency of the remark* suggestiveness, indelicacy, improperness, impurity, ribaldry, bawdiness, foulness, vulgarity, grossness, crudity, dirtiness, smuttiness, smut, coarseness, obscenity, lewdness. **2** *the indecency of the abrupt departure* impropriety, unseemliness, indecorum, indecorousness, inappropriateness, bad taste, tastelessness, unacceptability, offensiveness.

**indecent** adjective **1** *an indecent suggestion/joke* suggestive, indelicate, improper, impure, risqué, off-color, ribald, bawdy, foul, vulgar, gross, crude, dirty, smutty, coarse, obscene, blue, lewd, lascivious, licentious, salacious, pornographic, scatological; *inf.* raunchy. **2** *marry with indecent haste after the funeral* improper, unseemly, indecorous, unbecoming, unsuitable, inappropriate, unfitting, unbefitting, in bad taste, tasteless, unacceptable, offensive, outrageous.

**indecision** noun indecisiveness, irresolution, irresoluteness, vacillation, fluctuation, hesitancy, hesitation, tentativeness, ambivalence, doubt, shilly-shallying, uncertainty.

**indecisive** adjective **1** *an indecisive person* irresolute, vacillating, wavering, fluctuating, hesitant, tentative, faltering, ambivalent, doubtful, of two minds, shilly-shallying, undecided, indefinite, uncertain, unresolved, undetermined, on the fence; *inf.* blowing hot and cold. **2** *an indecisive ballot* inconclusive, open, indeterminate, unsettled, unclear; *inf.* up in the air.

**indeed** adverb in fact, in point of fact, in truth, truly, actually, really, in reality, certainly, surely, for sure, to be sure, positively, absolutely, doubtlessly, undoubtedly, without doubt, undeniably, veritably.

**indefinite** adjective **1** *the time of the meeting is still indefinite* undecided, unfixed, undetermined, unsettled, inconclusive, undefined, unknown, uncertain, unspecific, unexplicit, imprecise, inexact, vague, doubtful. **2** *an indefinite shape in the distance* ill-defined, indistinct, blurred, fuzzy, hazy, dim, vague, obscure. **3** *an indefinite answer* vague, unclear, imprecise, inexact, ambiguous, ambivalent, equivocal, confused, evasive, abstruse. **4** *she's a bit indefinite about her plans* undecided, irresolute. *See* INDECISIVE 1. **5** *an indefinite number/amount* indeterminate, unspecified, unlimited, limitless, infinite, immeasurable, boundless.

**indelible** adjective inerasable, ineradicable, ineffaceable, unexpungeable, indestructible, permanent, lasting, enduring, inextirpable, ingrained, unfading, imperishable.

**indelicate** adjective **1** *indelicate manners/behavior* vulgar, coarse, rough, unrefined, uncultivated, tasteless, immodest, boorish, churlish, loutish, offensive. **2** *indelicate jokes* risqué, ribald. *See* INDECENT 1.

**indemnify** verb **1** *indemnify them for their loss* reimburse, compensate, make restitution/amends to, recompense, repay, pay, pay back, remunerate. **2** *indemnify against travel risks* insure, underwrite, guarantee, protect, secure, make secure, give security to, endorse.

**indemnity** noun **1** *receive indemnity for losses sustained* reimbursement, compensation, restitution, reparation, redress, requital, atonement, payment, repayment, remuneration, recompense; amends. **2** *take out indemnity against lost luggage* insurance, assurance, protection, security, endorsement; guarantee, safeguard. **3** *receive diplomatic indemnity for his crimes* immunity, exemption, privilege, prerogative, impunity.

**indentation** noun indent, notch, cut, nick, groove, furrow, gouge, score; recess, niche, concavity, hollow, impression, depression, dimple, cranny.

**independence** noun **1** *states seeking independence* self-government, self-rule, home rule, self-determination, sovereignty, autonomy, nonalignment, freedom, separation, autarchy. **2** *financial independence* self-sufficiency, self-reliance. **3** *independence of spirit* individualism, boldness, liberation, unconstraint, unrestraint, lack of constraint/restraint.

**independent** adjective **1** *an independent state* self-governing, self-ruling, self-legislating, self-determining, sovereign, autonomous, autonomic, free, absolute, nonaligned, autarchic. **2** *the two firms are independent of/from each other* separate,

unconnected, unrelated, unattached, distinct, individual. **3** *an independent person* self-sufficient, self-supporting, self-reliant, individualistic, unconventional, bold, liberated, unconstrained, unrestrained; *inf.* standing on one's own feet.

**indescribable** adjective undescribable, inexpressible, undefinable, beyond words/description, surpassing description, incommunicable, ineffable, unutterable, incredible, extraordinary, remarkable, prodigious.

**indestructible** adjective durable, enduring, unbreakable, infrangible, imperishable, inextinguishable, undecaying, perennial, deathless, undying, immortal, endless, everlasting.

**index** noun **1** *an index to the information* guide, key, directory, catalog, table of contents. **2** *appearance can be an index of character* mark, token, sign, symptom, indication, clue, hint. **3** *the index on the compass* pointer, indicator, needle, hand.

**indicate** verb **1** *his visage indicates his distress* reveal, be a sign/symptom of, be symptomatic of, mark, signal, denote, bespeak, betoken, connote, suggest, imply. **2** *he indicated the right direction* point to/out, designate, specify. **3** *he indicated his displeasure* show, demonstrate, exhibit, display, manifest, evince, express, make known, tell, state, reveal, disclose, register, record.

**indication** noun **1** *his tiredness is an indication of his overwork* sign, symptom, mark, manifestation, signal, omen, augury, portent, warning, hint. **2** *he frowned as an indication of his displeasure* show, demonstration, exhibition, display, manifestation, revelation, disclosure, register, record.

**indicative** adjective suggestive, symptomatic, typical, characteristic, symbolic, emblematic.

**indicator** noun **1** *the indicator on the dial* pointer, needle, marker. **2** *a temperature indicator* gauge, meter, display. **3** *an economic indicator* index, guide, mark, sign, signal, signpost.

**indict** verb accuse, charge, arraign, impeach, prosecute, bring to trial, put on trial, cite, summons, incriminate, inculpate.

**indictment** noun accusation, charge, arraignment, impeachment, prosecution, citation, summons, incrimination, inculpation.

**indifference** noun **1** *the indifference of the spectators* apathy, disregard, lack of interest, aloofness, detachment, coldness, coolness, impassivity. **2** *the indifference of the players* mediocrity, adequacy, ordinariness, lack of distinction. **3** *the indifference of the issues* unimportance, insignificance, inconsequence, triviality, slightness, pettiness, irrelevance. **4** *the indifference of the judges* impartiality, disinterest, nonpartisanship, neutrality, objectivity, detachment, equitability, evenhandedness, fairness, fair-mindedness.

**indifferent** adjective **1** *totally indifferent spectators* apathetic, unconcerned, uncaring, uninterested, unimpressed, aloof, detached, distant, cold, cool, impassive, dispassionate, unresponsive, passionless, unemotional, emotionless, unmoved, unexcited, unfeeling, unsympathetic, uncompassionate, callous. **2** *an indifferent player* mediocre, middling, moderate, medium, fair, not bad, passable, adequate, average, ordinary, commonplace, undistinguished, uninspired; *inf.* OK, so-so. **3** *an indifferent issue* unimportant, insignificant, inconsequential, minor, trivial, trifling, petty. **4** *an indifferent judge* disinterested, unbiased. *See* IMPARTIAL.

**indigenous** adjective native, original, local, endemic, aboriginal.

**indigent** adjective poverty-stricken, penniless. *See* IMPOVERISHED 1.

**indigestion** noun dyspepsia, hyperacidity, acidity, heartburn, pyrosis.

**indignant** adjective angry, irate, incensed, furious, infuriated, annoyed, wrathful, enraged, exasperated, heated, riled, in a temper, in high dudgeon, provoked, piqued, disgruntled, in a huff, huffy, miffed, fuming, livid, aggravated, mad; *inf.* seeing red, up in arms.

**indignation** noun anger, fury, rage, wrath, exasperation, pique, disgruntlement, umbrage, offense, resentment, ire.

**indirect** adjective **1** *an indirect route* roundabout, circuitous, deviant, divergent, wandering, meandering, winding, curving, tortuous, zigzag. **2** *an indirect way of giving the news* oblique, discursive, digressive, long-drawn-out, rambling, circumlocutory, periphrastic, allusive. **3** *an indirect insult* backhanded, left-handed, devious, insidious, deceitful, underhand, surreptitious; *inf.* sneaky. **4** *an indirect result of the talks* incidental, accidental, unintended, secondary, subordinate, ancillary, collateral, contingent.

**indirectly** adverb **1** *hear the information indirectly* secondhand, in a roundabout way. **2** *tell them the news indirectly* by implication, obliquely, periphrastically.

**indiscreet** adjective unwise, imprudent, injudicious, impolitic, ill-advised, ill-considered, incautious, careless, tactless, untactful, insensitive, undiplomatic.

**indiscretion** noun **1** *guilty of indiscretion* imprudence, injudiciousness, foolishness, folly, carelessness, tactlessness, lack of diplomacy. **2** *embarrassed by her indiscretions* gaffe, faux pas, breach of etiquette, slip, blunder, lapse, mistake, error; *inf.* slipup.

**indiscriminate** adjective **1** *indiscriminate reading habits* undiscriminating, unselective, uncritical, undifferentiating, aimless, haphazard, random, unsystematic, unmethodical, broad-based, wholesale, general, sweeping; *inf.* hit-or-miss. **2** *an indiscriminate collection of furniture* jumbled, mixed, motley, miscellaneous, diverse, varied, mongrel, confused, chaotic, thrown together; *inf.* higgledy-piggledy.

**indispensable** adjective essential, of the essence, vital, crucial, imperative, key, necessary, requisite, required, needed, important, of the utmost importance, urgent, pressing, high-priority, fundamental.

**indisputable** adjective incontestable, incontrovertible, undeniable, irrefutable, unquestionable, indubitable, beyond dispute/question/doubt, beyond the shadow of a doubt, unassailable, certain, sure, positive, definite, absolute, final, conclusive.

**indistinct** adjective blurred, fuzzy, out of focus, bleary, hazy, misty, shadowy, dim, obscure, indefinite, indistinguishable, barely perceptible, undefined.

**indistinguishable** adjective **1** *the twins are indistinguishable* identical, alike, very similar; *inf.* as like as two peas in a pod. **2** *his identity was indistinguishable in the dark* indiscernible, imperceptible, hard to make out, indefinite, obscure.

**individual** adjective **1** *each individual flower/house* single, separate, sole, lone, solitary, distinct, distinctive, particular, specific, peculiar, detached, isolated. **2** *an individual style* characteristic, distinctive, peculiar, typical, personal, personalized, own, private, special, especial, singular, original, unique, exclusive, idiosyncratic.

**individual** noun **1** *a most unpleasant individual* person, personage, human being, creature, mortal, living soul, body, character, type. **2** *she's very much an individual* individualist, free spirit, nonconformist, original, eccentric, bohemian, maverick, rara avis, rare bird, rarity, loner, lone wolf.

**individualist** noun free spirit, nonconformist. *See* INDIVIDUAL noun 2.

**individualistic** adjective freethinking, independent, nonconformist, unorthodox, unconventional, original, eccentric, bohemian, maverick.

**individuality** noun distinctiveness, distinction, originality, uniqueness, singularity, peculiarity, personality, character.

**individually** adverb one at a time, one by one, singly, separately, independently, apart; personally.

**indoctrinate** verb instruct, teach, drill, ground, initiate, inculcate, impress (on), instill (in), imbue, impregnate, brainwash, propagandize, proselytize.

**indolent** adjective lazy, idle, slothful, do-nothing, sluggish, lethargic, slow, slow-moving, slack, shiftless, languid, lackadaisical, apathetic, listless, impassive, inactive, inert, torpid.

**induce** verb **1** *induce them to go* persuade, talk into, get, prevail upon, prompt, move, inspire, instigate, influence, exert influence on, press, urge, incite, encourage, impel, actuate, motivate, inveigle, coax, wheedle. **2** *induce a reaction* bring about, bring on, cause, produce, effect, create, give rise to, generate, originate, engender, occasion, set in motion.

**inducement** noun **1** *offer a salary increase as an inducement* incentive, attraction, encouragement, bait, lure, reward, inducement, stimulus, influence, spur, goad, impetus, motive, provocation; *inf.* carrot, come-on. **2** *gave in to their inducement to go* persuasion, prompting, urging, incitement, encouragement, inveigling.

**indulge** verb **1** *indulge one's appetites* give way to, yield to, pander to, cater to, satisfy, gratify, fulfill, satiate, appease. **2** *indulge in a bout of self-pity* give oneself up to, give rein to, give free rein to, wallow in, luxuriate in, revel in. **3** *indulge the child* pamper, spoil, coddle, mollycoddle, pander to, humor, go along with, baby, pet. **indulge oneself** treat oneself, give oneself a treat, splurge; *inf.* have a spree.

**indulgence** noun **1** *the indulgence of one's appetites* satisfaction, gratification, fulfillment, satiation, appeasement. **2** *lead a life of indulgence* self-gratification, dissipation, dissoluteness, intemperance, immoderation, immoderateness, debauchery, excess, lack of restraint, unrestraint, prodigality, extravagance. **3** *traveling is his only indulgence* extravagance, luxury, treat. **4** *I was allowed the indulgence of going on board ship* privilege, courtesy, favor, treat. **5** *treat the prisoners with indulgence* tolerance, forbearance, compassion, humanity, sympathy, forgiveness, leniency, mercy, clemency. **6** *too much indulgence was bad for the children* pampering, spoiling, coddling, mollycoddling, cosseting, humoring.

**indulgent** adjective tolerant, forbearing, forgiving, lenient, merciful, clement; permissive, compliant, pampering, spoiling, mollycoddling, cosseting, humoring.

**industrious** adjective hardworking, diligent, assiduous, sedulous, conscientious, steady, laborious, busy, busy as a bee, active, bustling, energetic, on the go, vigorous, determined, indefatigable, tireless.

**industry** noun **1** *involved in heavy industry* manufacturing, production, fabrication, construction. **2** *the publishing industry* business, trade, commercial enterprise, field, line, craft, métier. **3** *work with industry* industriousness, diligence, assiduity, application, sedulousness, sedulity, conscientiousness, concentration, intentness, steadiness, laboriousness, busyness, tirelessness, persistence.

**inebriated** adjective intoxicated, drunk, drunken, blind drunk, tipsy; *inf.* tight, under the influence, three sheets to the wind, plastered, stoned, loaded, blotto, pickled, out of it, smashed, sloshed, soused, well-oiled, well-lubricated, stewed to the gills, tanked (up).

**inedible** adjective unedible, uneatable, not fit to eat, unconsumable, unwholesome, off, rotten, bad, putrid, poisonous.

**ineffective** adjective **1** *ineffective attempts to stem the revolt* ineffectual, vain, to no avail, unavailing, useless, worthless, unsuccessful, futile, fruitless, unproductive, profitless, abortive, inefficacious, idle, feeble, inept, lame, barren, sterile. **2** *ineffective people* ineffectual, powerless, impotent, incompetent, inept, feeble, weak.

**ineffectual** adjective **1** *ineffectual efforts* vain, unavailing. See INEFFECTIVE 1. **2** *ineffectual people* powerless, inept. See INEFFECTIVE 2.

**inefficient** adjective ineffective, disorganized, wasteful, uneconomical, lax, slipshod, sloppy, slack.

**ineligible** adjective unqualified, unfit, unequipped, unsuitable, unacceptable, undesirable, ruled out, disqualified.

**inept** adjective **1** *an inept mechanic* unadept, unskillful, unskilled, clumsy, awkward, maladroit, undexterous, heavy-handed, ham-handed, incompetent, inadequate, bungling. **2** *an inept remark* out of place, badly timed, inapt, inappropriate, unsuitable, infelicitous. **3** *always doing inept things* absurd, foolish, silly, stupid, inane, nonsensical, senseless, farcical, ridiculous.

**inequality** noun **1** *inequality of opportunity* unequalness, disparity, imparity, imbalance, unevenness, disproportion, discrepancy, nonconformity, difference, dissimilarity, contrast. **2** *treat women with inequality* bias, prejudice, discrimination, preferentiality.

**inequitable** adjective unjust, unfair, partial, prejudiced, biased, partisan, discriminatory, preferential, one-sided, intolerant, bigoted.

**inequity** noun unfairness, injustice, partisanship, partiality, bias, discrimination.

**inert** adjective **1** *inert bodies* unmoving, motionless, immobile, still, stock-still, stationary, static, lifeless, inanimate, unconscious, passive, out cold, comatose, dormant, dead. **2** *inert members of the company* inactive, dull, sluggish, lethargic, stagnant, listless, torpid.

**inertia** noun inertness, inactivity, inaction, immobility, stagnation, stasis, passivity, indolence, sloth, dullness, sluggishness, lethargy, languor, listlessness, torpor.

**inescapable** adjective unavoidable, unpreventable. *See* INEVITABLE.

**inestimable** adjective immeasurable, measureless, incalculable; priceless, beyond price, precious, invaluable, worth its weight in gold, worth a king's ransom.

**inevitable** adjective unavoidable, unpreventable, inexorable, inescapable, fixed, settled, irrevocable, fated, destined, predestined, ordained, decreed, out of one's hands, assured, certain, sure, bound/sure to happen, for sure, necessary, ineluctable.

**inexact** adjective imprecise, approximate; inaccurate, incorrect.

**inexcusable** adjective unpardonable, unforgivable, unatonable, inexpiable, unjustifiable, unwarrantable, indefensible.

**inexhaustible** adjective **1** *an inexhaustible supply* unlimited, limitless, infinite, boundless, endless, never-ending, bottomless, measureless. **2** *inexhaustible workers* indefatigable, tireless, untiring, unwearying, weariless, unfaltering, unfailing, unflagging.

**inexorable** adjective **1** *the inexorable march of progress* relentless, unavoidable, inescapable. *See* INEVITABLE. **2** *inexorable tyrants* adamant, obdurate, unbending, unyielding, immovable, intransigent, implacable, inflexible.

**inexpensive** adjective low-cost, low-price, low-priced, reasonable, economical, cheap, budget, reduced, sale-price, half-price, marked-down, discount, discounted, cutrate, bargain, bargain-basement.

**inexperienced** adjective untrained, untutored, unpracticed, amateur, unskilled, uninitiated, unversed, naïve, unsophisticated, untried, unseasoned, new, callow, immature, fresh, green, raw; *inf.* wet behind the ears.

**inexplicable** adjective unexplainable, unaccountable, incomprehensible, beyond comprehension/understanding, unfathomable, baffling, puzzling, inscrutable.

**infallible** adjective **1** *an infallible remedy* unfailing, foolproof, dependable, reliable, certain; *inf.* sure-fire. **2** *an infallible memory* unerring, faultless, flawless, impeccable, unimpeachable, perfect.

**infamous** adjective **1** *an infamous robber* notorious, disreputable, ill-famed, of ill-repute. **2** *guilty of infamous conduct* iniquitous, ignominious, dishonorable, discreditable, villainous, bad, wicked, vile, odious, nefarious, abominable, outrageous, shocking, monstrous, disgraceful, shameful, atrocious, heinous.

**infant** noun baby, babe, newborn, little child, tot, little one; neonate.

**infantile** adjective babyish, childish, puerile, immature, juvenile.

**infatuated** adjective in love, head over heels in love, hopelessly in love; enamored, besotted, captivated, bewitched, beguiled, taken with, under the spell of, obsessed, swept off one's feet; *; inf.* smitten, sweet on, keen on, mad about, wild about, crazy about, nuts about, stuck on, turned on by.

**infatuation** noun passing fancy, fancy, passion, obsession, fixation, craze, mania; *inf.* puppy love, crush, thing.

**infect** verb **1** *infect the air/water* contaminate, pollute, taint, make foul, blight, spoil, mar, impair. **2** *infect others with his wickedness* influence, corrupt, pervert, debauch, debase, degrade, vitiate. **3** *infect others with his enthusiasm* imbue, infuse, excite, inspire, stimulate, animate.

**infectious** adjective **1** *an infectious disease | infectious laughter* infective, communicable, transmittable, transmissible, catching, spreading, contagious. **2** *infectious material* germ-laden, contaminating, polluting, septic, toxic, noxious, virulent, poisonous.

**infer** verb **1** *from the evidence they inferred that he was guilty* deduce, reason, conclude, gather, conjecture, surmise, theorize, hypothesize. **2** *his conduct inferred a guilty conscience* indicate, point to, signal, signify, bespeak, evidence. **3** *her speech inferred that he was a coward* imply, insinuate, hint, suggest, intimate.

**inference** noun **1** *dispute the inference from the evidence* deduction, conclusion, ratiocination, conjecture, surmise. **2** *resent her inference that he was a coward* implication, insinuation, suggestion, intimation.

**inferior** adjective **1** *in an inferior position* lower, lesser, subordinate, junior, secondary, subsidiary, second-class, second-fiddle, minor, subservient, menial. **2** *inferior goods* substandard, low-quality, low-grade, shoddy, reject. **3** *an inferior teacher* second-rate, indifferent, mediocre, incompetent, poor, bad, awful.

**inferior** noun *despise his inferiors* subordinate, junior, underling, menial.

**infernal** adjective hellish, diabolical, devilish, demonic, demoniac, fiendish, satanic, malevolent, malicious, heinous, vile, atrocious, execrable, unspeakable, outrageous.

**infertile** adjective barren, unfruitful, unfructuous, sterile, infecund, childless.

**infest** verb overrun, spread through, take over, overspread, pervade, permeate, penetrate, infiltrate, invade, swarm over, crawl over, beset, pester, plague.

**infidel** noun unbeliever, disbeliever, heathen, heretic, pagan, agnostic, atheist, irreligionist.

**infidelity** noun 1 *discovering the spouse's infidelity* unfaithfulness, adultery, cuckoldry; affair, liaison, intrigue, amour; *inf.* fooling/playing around, cheating, hanky-panky. 2 *the servant's infidelity to his master* breach of trust, faithlessness, unfaithfulness, treachery, perfidy, perfidiousness, disloyalty, falseness, traitorousness, treason.

**infiltrate** verb pervade, penetrate, filter through, percolate through, seep into/through, soak into; sneak into, invade, intrude on.

**infinite** adjective 1 *infinite space/numbers* boundless, unbounded, unlimited, limitless, without limit/end, extensive, vast, countless, numberless, innumerable, immeasurable, incalculable, indeterminable, enormous. 2 *infinite patience* inexhaustible, interminable, absolute, total.

**infinitesimal** adjective minute, tiny, microscopic, minuscule, teeny, wee, Lilliputian.

**infirm** adjective 1 *infirm people* feeble, enfeebled, weak, frail, debilitated, decrepit, disabled, failing, ailing, doddering, tottering, lame. 2 *infirm judgment* indecisive, irresolute, wavering, vacillating, fluctuating, faltering. 3 *infirm furniture* rickety, unsteady, shaky, wobbly, unsound, flimsy, tumbledown, jerry-built.

**inflame** verb 1 *inflame the passions of the crowd* incite, excite, arouse, rouse, stir up, work up, whip up, agitate, fire, ignite, kindle, foment, impassion, provoke, stimulate, actuate. 2 *inflame the onlookers with his cruelty* enrage, incense, infuriate, exasperate, anger, madden, provoke, rile. 3 *inflame the feud* aggravate, intensify, make worse, exacerbate, fan, fuel.

**inflamed** adjective 1 *an inflamed arm* swollen, sore, infected, festered, septic. 2 *inflamed passions* excited, aroused, roused, stirred, kindled, impassioned.

**inflammation** noun swelling, soreness, sore, infection, festering, suppuration.

**inflammatory** adjective *an inflammatory speech* stirring, fiery, passionate, impassioned, provocative, fomenting, rabble-rousing, demagogic, rebellious, revolutionary, insurgent, seditious.

**inflate** verb 1 *inflate the air mattress* blow up, pump up, aerate, puff up, puff out, dilate, distend, swell. 2 *he always inflates his stories* amplify, augment, expand, intensify, exaggerate, add to, boost, magnify, escalate, aggrandize.

**inflated** adjective 1 *inflated prices* increased, raised, escalated, stepped up. 2 *an inflated sense of his own importance* exaggerated, magnified, aggrandized. 3 *inflated prose* high-flown, extravagant, pretentious, pompous, grandiloquent, bombastic.

**inflexible** adjective 1 *an inflexible substance* rigid, stiff, unbendable, unyielding, taut, hard, firm, inelastic, unmalleable. 2 *inflexible rules* unalterable, unchangeable, immutable, unvarying, fixed, hard and fast. 3 *inflexible people/attitudes* adamant, immovable, unadaptable, dyed-in-the-wool, unaccommodating, uncompliant, stubborn, obdurate, obstinate, unbending, uncompromising.

**inflict** verb lay on, impose, levy, exact, wreak.

**influence** noun 1 *have a good/bad influence on them* effect, impact; control, sway, ascendancy, power, mastery, agency, guidance, domination, rule, supremacy, leadership, direction, pressure. 2 *he has influence on the board* prestige, standing, footing; *inf.* clout, pull.

**influence** verb 1 *his illness influenced his behavior* affect, have an effect on, impact on, sway, bias, incline, motivate, actuate, determine, guide, control, change, alter, transform. 2 *he tried to influence the jury* affect, sway, bias, bring pressure to bear on; *inf.* pull strings with, pull rank on. 3 *he influenced her not to go* persuade, induce, impel, incite, prompt.

**influential** adjective powerful, important, leading, authoritative, controlling, dominant, guiding, significant, persuasive.

**inform** verb 1 *inform him of/about the facts* tell, let know, apprise, advise, notify, announce to, impart to, relate to, communicate to, acquaint, brief, instruct, enlighten; *inf.* fill in, clue in/up, put wise, spill the beans to, tip off, give the low-down to, give the inside story to. 2 *optimism informs her writing* characterize, typify, pervade, permeate, suffuse, infuse, imbue. **inform on** betray, denounce, incriminate, inculpate; *inf.* rat on, squeal on, tell on, blow the whistle on, put the finger on, sell down the river, snitch on.

**informal** adjective 1 *an informal party | informal dress* casual, unceremonious, unofficial, simple, unpretentious, everyday, relaxed, easy. 2 *informal language* colloquial, vernacular, nonliterary, natural; *inf.* slangy.

**informality** noun casualness, lack of ceremony, simplicity, naturalness, ease.

**information** noun data, facts; knowledge, intelligence, news, notice, word, tidings, message, report, communiqué, communication; *inf.* info, low-down, dope, poop, inside story, dirt.

**informative** adjective instructive, illuminating, enlightening, revealing, telling, newsy.

**informed** adjective knowledgeable, abreast of the facts, well-posted, primed, well-versed, up-to-date, au courant, *au fait*.

**informer** noun informant, betrayer, traitor, Judas; *inf.* rat, squealer, stool pigeon, tattletale, whistleblower, canary, snitch.

**infraction** noun breach, violation, transgression, infringement.

**infrequent** adjective few and far between, rare, occasional, uncommon, unusual, exceptional.

**infuriate** verb enrage, incense, inflame, madden, exasperate, anger, provoke, rile, make one's blood boil, make one's hackles rise; *inf.* make one see red.

**ingenious** adjective clever, shrewd, astute, sharp, resourceful, inventive, creative, original, crafty, wily.

**ingenuous** adjective open, sincere, honest, frank, candid, artless, guileless, simple, naïve, innocent, genuine, undeceitful, undeceptive, undissembling, aboveboard, trustful, unsuspicious.

**ingrained** adjective fixed, rooted, deep-rooted, deep-seated, permanent, built-in.

**ingratiate** verb **ingratiate oneself with** curry favor with, toady to, crawl to, grovel to, fawn over, play up to, be a yes-man to; *inf.* suck up to, lick the boots of.

**ingratiating** adjective sycophantic, toadying, fawning, unctuous, obsequious, servile, overhumble, crawling, flattering, wheedling, cajoling; *inf.* bootlicking.

**ingredient** adjective constituent, component, element, part, unit, item, feature.

**inhabit** verb live in, dwell in, reside in, occupy, lodge in, make one's home in, settle in; settle, people, populate.

**inhabitant** noun resident, resider, dweller, occupant, occupier, habitant, settler.

**inherent** adjective intrinsic, innate, built-in, inseparable, essential, basic, fundamental, ingrained.

**inherit** verb **1** *inherit a fortune/estate* become/fall heir to, be bequeathed, be left, be willed, come into/by. **2** *inherit the title* succeed to, accede to, assume, take over, be elevated to.

**inheritance** noun legacy, bequest, endowment, birthright, heritage, patrimony.

**inhibit** verb **1** *inhibit progress* hold back, impede, hinder, hamper, interfere with, obstruct, curb, check, restrict, restrain, constrain, bridle, rein in, balk, frustrate, arrest, prevent, stop. **2** *inhibit them from going* forbid, prohibit, ban, bar, debar, interdict, proscribe.

**inhibited** adjective *feel inhibited in the presence of parents* self-conscious, reserved, constrained, repressed, subdued, withdrawn; *inf.* uptight.

**inhospitable** adjective **1** *an inhospitable host* unwelcoming, unsociable, unfriendly, ungracious, uncongenial, ungenerous, aloof. **2** *an inhospitable landscape* uninviting, barren, bleak, desolate, forbidding, hostile.

**inhuman** adjective **1** *an inhuman cry* nonhuman, animal, ghostly. **2** *inhuman people* unkind, inconsiderate. *See* INHUMANE.

**inhumane** adjective unkind, unkindly, inconsiderate, uncompassionate, unfeeling, unsympathetic, unforgiving, cold-blooded, heartless, hard-hearted, pitiless, merciless, ruthless, remorseless, brutal, cruel, harsh, savage, vicious, barbaric, barbarous.

**inimitable** adjective matchless, unmatched, incomparable, unparalleled, unrivaled, unsurpassed, unsurpassable, unique, supreme, perfect, consummate, ideal, nonpareil, peerless.

**iniquitous** adjective wicked, sinful, evil, immoral, villainous, criminal, heinous, vile, foul, base, odious, abominable, execrable, atrocious, malicious, outrageous, monstrous, shocking, scandalous, reprehensible.

**iniquity** noun **1** *his falling into iniquity* wickedness, sin, sinfulness, vice, evil, ungodliness, godlessness, wrong, wrongdoing, badness, villainy, knavery, lawlessness, crime, baseness, heinousness. **2** *appalled at his iniquities* sin, vice, offense, crime, transgression, injury, violation, atrocity, outrage.

**initial** adjective first, beginning, opening, early, introductory, inaugural, inceptive, incipient.

**initiate** verb **1** *initiate the proceedings* begin, start off, commence, open, institute, inaugurate, get under way, set in motion, lay the foundations of, lay the first stone of, launch, actuate, instigate, trigger, originate, pioneer, sow the seeds of; start the ball rolling for. **2** *initiate the students in science* teach, instruct, coach, tutor, school, train, drill, prime, familiarize, indoctrinate, inculcate. **3** *initiate the new member into the organization* induct, install, instate, ordain, invest.

**initiation** noun **1** *the initiation of the proceedings* beginning, commencement, opening, institution, inauguration, launch. **2** *rites of initiation* admission, admittance, introduction; induction, installation, ordination, investment, baptism.

**initiative** noun **1** *take the initiative* first step, first move, first blow, lead, gambit, opening move/gambit. **2** *promotion for those with initiative* enterprise, inventiveness, resourcefulness, originality, creativity, drive, dynamism, ambition, leadership; *inf.* get-up-and-go, zing, push, pep, zip.

**injure** verb **1** *injure his foot* hurt, harm, damage, wound, maim, cripple, disable, mutilate, deform, mangle. **2** *guilty of injuring his fellow citizens* do an injury to, wrong, do an injustice to, offend against, abuse, maltreat, defame, vilify, malign.

**injured** adjective **1** *his injured leg* hurt, wounded, broken, fractured, damaged, sore, maimed, crippled, disabled, lame. **2** *the injured party* wronged, offended, abused, maltreated, ill-treated, defamed, vilified, maligned. **3** *an injured look* reproachful, hurt, wounded, upset, disgruntled, displeased.

**injurious** adjective harmful, hurtful, damaging, deleterious, detrimental, disadvantageous, unfavorable, destructive, pernicious, ruinous, disastrous, calamitous, malignant.

**injury** noun **1** *machines bound to cause injury* harm, hurt, wounding, damage, impairment, affliction. **2** *injuries taking long to heal* wound, sore, bruise, cut, gash, laceration, abrasion, lesion, contusion, trauma. **3** *do an injury to his neighbors* injustice, wrong, ill, offense, disservice, grievance, evil.

**injustice** noun **1** *the injustice of the verdict* unjustness, unfairness, inequitableness, inequity, bias, prejudice, favoritism, partiality, one-sidedness, discrimination, partisanship. **2** *injustices done to others* wrong, injury, offense, evil.

**inkling** noun **1** *he gave no inkling of his intention* hint, clue, intimation, suggestion, indication, whisper, suspicion, insinuation. **2** *no inkling of how to proceed* idea, (the) vaguest idea, notion, glimmering; *inf.* (the) foggiest.

**inlet** noun cove, bay, arm of the sea, bight, creek, fjord, sound.

**inmate** noun prisoner, convict, captive, jailbird.

**inn** noun hotel, lodge, bed and breakfast, hostelry; public house, tavern, bar, pub.

**innate** adjective **1** *an innate tendency* inborn, inbred, connate, congenital, hereditary, inherited, in the blood/family. **2** *an innate part of the plan* inherent, intrinsic, essential, basic, fundamental, quintessential, organic, radical. **3** *an innate capacity* instinctive, intuitive, unlearned, untaught.

**inner** adjective **1** *the inner rooms* interior, inside, central, middle, further in. **2** *the inner circle* confidential, intimate, private,

exclusive, secret. **3** *the inner meaning* unapparent, veiled, obscure, esoteric, hidden, secret, unrevealed, deep. **4** *the inner life* spiritual, emotional, mental, psychological, psychic, subconscious, unconscious, innermost.

**innermost, inmost** adjective **1** *the innermost section* furthest in, deepest within, central. **2** *innermost beliefs* intimate, private, personal, deep, deepest, profound, secret, hidden.

**innkeeper** noun host, proprietor, manager, landlady, landlord, hotelier; barkeeper, barkeep.

**innocence** noun **1** *the innocence of the prisoners* guiltlessness, blamelessness, inculpability, unimpeachability, irreproachability, clean hands. **2** *the innocence of their play* harmlessness, innocuousness, inoffensiveness. **3** *the innocence of youth* virtuousness, virtue, purity, sinlessness, decency, righteousness, chastity, virginity, spotlessness. **4** *the innocence of the new recruits* ingenuousness, naïveté, artlessness, guilelessness, frankness, openness, credulity, gullibility.

**innocent** adjective **1** *innocent prisoners* not guilty, guiltless, blameless, clear, in the clear, above suspicion, unblameworthy, inculpable, unimpeachable, irreproachable, clean-handed. **2** *innocent fun* harmless, innocuous, safe, noninjurious, unmalicious, unobjectionable, inoffensive, playful. **3** *innocent youth* virtuous, pure, sinless, moral, decent, righteous, upright, chaste, virginal, pristine, spotless, stainless, unblemished, unsullied, incorrupt, uncorrupted. **4** *too innocent for the world* ingenuous, naïve, unsophisticated, artless, guileless, childlike, frank, open, unsuspicious, trustful, trusting, credulous, inexperienced, unworldly, green, gullible; *inf.* wet behind the ears.

**innocent of** *innocent of guile* free from, without, lacking, devoid of, unacquainted with, ignorant of, unaware of, unfamiliar with.

**innocuous** adjective **1** *an innocuous substance* harmless, unhurtful, uninjurious, safe, danger-free, nonpoisonous. **2** *an innocuous person* inoffensive, unobjectionable, bland, commonplace, run-of-the-mill, insipid.

**innuendo** noun insinuation, implication, suggestion, hint, overtone, imputation, aspersion.

**innumerable** adjective numerous, countless, untold, incalculable, numberless, beyond number, infinite, myriad; *inf.* umpteen, masses, oodles.

**inoperative** adjective **1** *inoperative machines* not operative, not in operation, not working, out of order, out of service/commission/action, inactive, idle, broken, broken-down, defective, faulty; *inf.*

down, kaput. **2** *an inoperative system* useless, ineffectual, ineffective, inefficient, worthless, unproductive.

**inopportune** adjective inconvenient, ill-timed, badly timed, mistimed, untimely, unseasonable, inappropriate, unsuitable, inapt, ill-chosen.

**inordinate** adjective excessive, immoderate, extravagant, unrestrained, unrestricted, unlimited, unwarranted, uncalled-for, undue, unreasonable, disproportionate, exorbitant, extreme, outrageous, preposterous, unconscionable.

**inquire** verb ask, quiz, interrogate; *inf.* grill. **inquire into** investigate, research, look into, examine, explore, probe.

**inquiring** adjective questioning, investigative, curious, interested, probing, exploring, searching, scrutinizing, inquisitive.

**inquiry** noun investigation, examination, exploration, probe, search, scrutiny, study, inspection, interrogation.

**inquisition** noun interrogation, cross-examination, quizzing, questioning; *inf.* grilling, third degree.

**inquisitive** adjective inquiring, questioning, probing, scrutinizing, curious; over-interested, intrusive, meddlesome, prying, snooping, snoopy, peering, spying; *inf.* nosy.

**insane** adjective **1** *driven insane by isolation* mad, of unsound mind, deranged, demented, *non compos mentis*, out of one's mind; *inf.* unhinged, crazed, crazy, non compos. **2** *he's insane to take that job* foolish, out of one's mind, unhinged, not all there, crazy; *inf.* bonkers, cracked, crackers, balmy, batty, bats, cuckoo, loony, loopy, nuts, nutty, screwy, bananas, out of one's head, around/round the bend. **3** *an insane idea* idiotic, stupid, senseless, nonsensical, irrational, impracticable, pointless, absurd, ridiculous, ludicrous, bizarre, fatuous; *inf.* daft.

**insanity** noun **1** *patients suffering from insanity* madness, mental derangement, dementia, frenzy, delirium. **2** *the insanity of the idea* folly, foolishness, craziness, idiocy, stupidity, senselessness, irrationality, absurdity.

**insatiable** adjective insatiate, unappeasable, unquenchable, greedy, voracious, ravening, gluttonous, omnivorous.

**inscribe** verb **1** *inscribe one's name on the book/stone* imprint, write, stamp, impress, mark, brand, engrave, etch, carve, cut. **2** *inscribe the candidates in the book* enter, register, record, write, list, enroll.

**inscription** noun engraving, writing, etching, lettering, legend, epitaph, epigraph.

**inscrutable** adjective enigmatic, unreadable, impenetrable, cryptic, sphinxlike, mysterious, inexplicable, unexplainable, unfathomable, arcane.

**insecure** adjective **1** *insecure children* diffident, timid, uncertain, hesitant, anxious, fearful, apprehensive, worried. **2** *insecure fortresses* vulnerable, defenseless, unprotected, unguarded, exposed. **3** *insecure bookshelves* loose, weak, unsubstantial, jerry-built, rickety, wobbly, shaky, unsteady, unstable, unsound.

**insecurity** noun **1** *the insecurity of the children* diffidence, timidity, uncertainty, anxiety, apprehension, worry. **2** *the insecurity of the fortresses* vulnerability, defenselessness, lack of protection, peril, perilousness. **3** *the insecurity of the bookshelves* looseness, flimsiness, ricketiness, instability.

**insensitive** adjective unfeeling, callous, thick-skinned, uncaring, unconcerned, uncompassionate, unsympathetic. **insensitive to** unresponsive to, impervious to, indifferent to, unaffected by, unmoved by, oblivious to, unappreciative of.

**insert** verb **1** *insert a coin into the slot* put in/into, place in, press in, push in, stick in, thrust in, drive in, work in, slide in, slip in, tuck in; *inf.* pop in. **2** *insert a sentence if the paragraph is too short* put in, introduce, enter, interpolate, inset, interpose, interject, implant, infix.

**inside** adjective **1** *the inside part* interior, inner, internal, inward, on/in the inside, inmost, innermost, intramural. **2** *inside information* confidential, classified, restricted, privileged, private, internal, privy, secret, exclusive, esoteric.

**insidious** adjective sneaky, cunning, crafty, designing, intriguing, Machiavellian, artful, guileful, sly, wily, tricky, slick, deceitful, deceptive, underhanded, double-dealing, duplicitous, dishonest, insincere, disingenuous, treacherous.

**insight** noun intuition, perception, awareness, discernment, understanding, penetration, acumen, perspicacity, discrimination, judgment, shrewdness, sharpness, acuteness, vision.

**insignia** noun/plural noun **1** *insignia of office* badge, decoration, medallion, ribbon, crest, emblem, symbol, sign, mark, seal, signet. **2** *the insignia of the firm* trademark, label, trait, characteristic.

**insignificant** adjective unimportant, of little import, trivial, trifling, negligible, inconsequential, inconsiderable, not worth mentioning, nugatory, meager, paltry, scanty, petty, insubstantial, unsubstantial, flimsy, irrelevant, immaterial; *inf.* dinky.

**insincere** adjective disingenuous, dissembling, pretended, devious, hypocritical, deceitful, deceptive, dishonest, underhand, double-dealing, false, two-faced.

**insinuate** verb **1** *he insinuated that she was dishonest* imply, hint, whisper, suggest, indicate, convey the impression, intimate. **2** *insinuate doubts into their minds* implant, instill, introduce, inculcate, infuse, inject. **insinuate oneself into** worm oneself into, work one's way into.

**insinuation** noun **1** *resent the insinuation* implication, suggestion, hint, innuendo, intimation, allusion. **2** *the insinuation of doubts* infiltration, implanting, instilling, instillation, introduction.

**insipid** adjective **1** *an insipid person/book* colorless, anemic, drab, vapid, dull, uninteresting, boring, unentertaining, unimaginative, flat, bland, prosaic. **2** *insipid food* tasteless, flavorless, savorless, bland, unappetizing, unpalatable.

**insist** verb **1** *if they refuse you must insist* stand firm, be firm, stand one's ground, be resolute, be emphatic, not take no for an answer, brook no refusal. **2** *insist that they go* demand, require, command, importune, entreat, urge, exhort. **3** *she insists that she is innocent* maintain, assert, declare, hold, contend, aver, avow, vow, swear, emphasize, stress, repeat, reiterate.

**insistent** adjective **1** *she is insistent that you go* emphatic, determined, resolute, tenacious, importunate, persistent, unyielding, obstinate, dogged, unrelenting. **2** *insistent demands for payment* persistent, dogged, incessant, urgent, pressing, compelling, high-pressure, coercive, demanding. **3** *the insistent caw of the crow* constant, incessant, iterative, repeated.

**insolence** noun impertinence, impudence, cheek, rudeness, disrespect, incivility, insubordination, contempt, contumely, audacity, nerve, boldness, brazenness, brashness, pertness, forwardness, effrontery, gall; *inf.* lip, chutzpah.

**insolent** adjective impertinent, impudent, cheeky, rude, disrespectful, insubordinate, contemptuous, audacious, bold, brazen, brash, pert, forward; *inf.* fresh.

**insoluble** adjective insolvable, unsolvable, baffling, unfathomable, complicated, intricate, involved, impenetrable, inscrutable, enigmatic, obscure, mystifying, inexplicable, incomprehensible, mysterious.

**insolvent** adjective bankrupt, indebted, in debt, liquidated, ruined, in the hands of the receivers; *inf.* gone bust, gone to the wall, on the rocks, in the red.

**inspect** verb examine, check, go over, look over, survey, scrutinize, audit, study, pore over, view, scan, observe, investigate, assess, appraise; *inf.* give the once-over.

**inspection** noun examination, check, checkup, survey, scrutiny, view, scan, observation, investigation, probe, assessment, appraisal; *inf.* once-over, going-over, look-see.

**inspector** noun examiner, checker, auditor, surveyor, investigator, assessor, appraiser.

**inspiration** noun **1** *acts as an inspiration to his work* stimulus, stimulation, motivation, encouragement, influence, muse, goad, spur, incitement, arousal, rousing, stirring. **2** *his pictures lack inspiration* creativity, originality, inventiveness, genius, insight, vision.

**inspire** verb stimulate, motivate, encourage, influence, inspirit, animate, fire the imagination of, rouse, stir, spur, goad, energize, galvanize, quicken, inflame, touch off, spark off, ignite, kindle, give rise to, prompt, instigate.

**inspired** adjective **1** *an inspired operatic performance* brilliant, outstanding, supreme, superlative, dazzling, exciting, thrilling, enthralling, wonderful, marvelous, memorable; *inf.* out of this world. **2** *an inspired guess* intuitive, instinctive.

**instability** noun **1** *instability of human relationships* impermanence, unendurability, temporariness, transience, inconstancy, unsteadiness, uncertainty, precariousness, shakiness, frailty, insecurity, unpredictability, unreliability; *inf.* chanciness. **2** *upset by her instability* changeableness, variability, capriciousness, volatility, flightiness, vacillation, wavering, fitfulness, oscillation.

**install** verb **1** *install microwave ovens* put in place, position, place, emplace, fix, locate, situate, station, lodge. **2** *install her as president* induct, instate, institute, inaugurate, invest, ordain, introduce, initiate. **3** *install themselves in the best seats* ensconce, position, settle.

**instance** noun case, case in point, example, illustration, exemplification, occasion, occurrence.

**instant** noun **1** *gone in an instant* moment, minute, second, split second, trice, twinkling, twinkling of an eye, flash; *inf.* jiffy, jif, sec, two shakes of a lamb's tail. **2** *at this instant I am not sure* time, present time, juncture, point.

**instant** adjective **1** *instant recognition* instantaneous, immediate, on-the-spot, prompt, rapid, sudden, abrupt. **2** *at his instant request* urgent, pressing, earnest, importunate, exigent, imperative.

**instantaneous** adjective immediate, on the spot. *See* INSTANT adjective 1.

**instantaneously** adverb right away, straight away, immediately, at once, instantly, forthwith, quick as lightning, in a trice, in less than no time, in the twinkling of an eye, before you can say Jack Robinson; *inf.* in a jiffy.

**instigate** verb 1 *instigate a rebellion* bring about, start, initiate, actuate, generate, incite, provoke, inspire, foment, kindle, stir up, whip up. 2 *instigate them to rebel* encourage, egg on, urge, prompt, goad, prod, induce, impel, constrain, press, persuade, prevail upon, sway.

**instigator** noun prime mover, inciter, motivator, agitator, fomenter, troublemaker, agent provocateur, ringleader, leader.

**instill** verb infuse, implant, teach, drill, imbue, permeate, inculcate.

**instinct** noun 1 *birds migrate by instinct* innate inclination, intuition, sixth sense, inner prompting. 2 *an instinct for poetry* talent, gift, ability, capacity, faculty, aptitude, knack, bent.

**instinctive** adjective 1 *instinctive behavior* inborn, inherent, innate, inbred, natural, intuitive, intuitional, involuntary, untaught, unlearned. 2 *an instinctive reaction* automatic, reflex, mechanical, spontaneous, involuntary, impulsive, intuitive, unthinking, unpremeditated.

**institute** verb 1 *institute legal proceedings* begin, start, commence, set in motion, put into operation, initiate. 2 *institute reforms* found, establish, start, launch, bring about, set up, organize, develop, create, originate, pioneer.

**institute** noun institution, organization, foundation, society, association, league, guild, consortium, academy, school, college, conservatory, seminary.

**institution** noun 1 *educational/research institutions* organization, society. *See* INSTITUTE. 2 *an institution for life* hospital, mental hospital, asylum, prison, reformatory. 3 *local institutions* law, rule, custom, tradition, convention, practice. 4 *the traffic cop was an institution in the neighborhood* familiar sight, fixture, habitué; *inf.* part of the furniture.

**institutional** adjective 1 *institutional food/furniture* uniform, monotonous, bland, dull, insipid. 2 *an institutional atmosphere in the building* cold, clinical, unwelcoming, uninviting, impersonal, formal, forbidding.

**instruct** verb 1 *instruct the messenger to take a reply* tell, direct, order, command, bid, charge, enjoin, demand, require. 2 *instruct the students in science* teach, educate, tutor, coach, train, school, drill, ground, prime, prepare, guide, inform, enlighten, edify, discipline. 3 *instruct them that I shall be late* inform, tell, notify, acquaint, make known to, advise, apprise, brief.

**instruction** noun 1 *get good instruction in the arts* teaching, education, tutoring, tutelage, coaching, training, schooling, drilling, grounding, preparation, guidance, information, enlightenment, edification, discipline; lessons, classes, lectures. 2 *his instruction was to leave at once* direction, directive, briefing, order, command, charge, injunction, ruling, mandate.

**instructive** adjective instructional, informative, informational, educational, enlightening, useful, helpful, edifying.

**instructor** noun teacher, schoolteacher, schoolmaster, schoolmistress, educator, lecturer, professor, pedagogue, tutor, coach, trainer, adviser, counselor, guide, mentor.

**instrument** noun 1 *surgical instruments* implement, tool, appliance, apparatus, mechanism, utensil, gadget, contrivance, device, aid; *inf.* contraption. 2 *the instrument of his downfall* agency, agent, prime mover, catalyst, cause, factor, channel, medium, force, mechanism, instrumentality, vehicle, organ; means. 3 *he was just the ringleader's instrument* pawn, puppet, tool, dupe, minion, flunky; *inf.* stooge.

**instrumental** adjective helpful, useful, contributory, active, involved, influential.

**insubordinate** adjective rebellious, mutinous, insurgent, seditious, insurrectional, riotous, disobedient, defiant, refractory, recalcitrant, ungovernable, uncontrollable, unmanageable.

**insubstantial** adjective 1 *insubstantial buildings/arguments* flimsy, fragile, frail, weak, feeble, jerry-built, slight, tenuous. 2 *insubstantial shapes* unsubstantial, unreal, illusory, hallucinatory, phantom, spectral, ghostlike, incorporeal, visionary, imaginary, imagined, fanciful, chimerical, airy, vaporous.

**insufferable** adjective intolerable, unbearable, unendurable, insupportable, too much to bear, impossible, too much, more than one can stand, more than flesh and blood can put up with, enough to try the patience of Job, enough to test the patience of a saint.

**insufficient** adjective inadequate, deficient, in short supply, scarce, meager, scant, scanty, not enough, lacking, wanting, at a premium.

**insulate** verb *cloistered monks are insulated from the world* segregate, separate, isolate, detach, cut off, keep/set apart, sequester, exclude, protect, shield.

**insult** verb offend, give/cause offense to, affront, slight, hurt the feelings of, hurt, abuse, injure, wound, mortify, humiliate, disparage, discredit, depreciate, impugn, slur, revile.

**insult** noun affront, slight, gibe, snub, barb, slur; abuse, disparagement, depreciation, impugnment, revilement, insolence, rudeness, contumely; aspersions; *inf.* dig.

**insulting** adjective offensive, slighting, abusive, injurious, wounding, mortifying, humiliating, disparaging, snubbing, insolent, rude, contumacious.

**insurance** noun **1** *take out travel insurance* financial protection, indemnity, indemnification, surety, security, coverage, guarantee, warranty, warrant. **2** *he took an umbrella as (an) insurance against the rain* safeguard, precaution, protection, provision.

**insurgent** noun rebel, revolutionary, mutineer, rioter, insurrectionist, insurrectionary, seditionist, malcontent.

**insurgent** adjective rebellious, revolutionary, mutinous, rioting, lawless, insurrectionist, insurrectionary, seditious, factious, subversive, insubordinate, disobedient.

**insurmountable** adjective insuperable, invincible, unconquerable, impassable, overwhelming, unassailable, hopeless, impossible.

**insurrection** noun rebellion, revolt, revolution, uprising, rising, riot, mutiny, sedition, coup, coup d'état, putsch; insurgency, insurgence.

**intact** adjective whole, complete, entire, perfect, all in one piece, sound, unbroken, unsevered, undamaged, unscathed, uninjured, unharmed, inviolate, undefiled.

**intangible** adjective **1** *intangible things* impalpable, untouchable, incorporeal, phantom, spectral, ghostly. **2** *an intangible air of sadness* indefinable, indescribable, vague, subtle, unclear.

**integral** adjective **1** *an integral part of the organization* essential, necessary, indispensable, requisite, basic, fundamental, intrinsic; constituent, component, integrant. **2** *an integral design* entire, complete, whole, total, full, intact, unified, integrated, undivided.

**integrate** verb unite, join, combine, amalgamate, consolidate, blend, incorporate.

**integrated** adjective **1** *integrated parts* united, joined, amalgamated, consolidated, assimilated. **2** *integrated schools* desegregated, nonsegregated, unsegregated, racially mixed, racially balanced.

**integrity** noun **1** *doubt the integrity of the council* uprightness, honesty, rectitude, righteousness, virtue, probity, morality, honor; principles, ethics. **2** *challenge the*

*integrity of the nation* unity, wholeness, entirety, completeness, totality, cohesion.

**intellect** noun **1** *a person of little intellect* reason, understanding. *See* INTELLIGENCE 1. **2** *leave the decisions to the intellects* intellectual, genius, thinker, mastermind; *inf.* brain, mind, egghead, Einstein.

**intellectual** adjective **1** *an intellectual family* intelligent, academic, well-educated, well-read, erudite, learned, bookish, highbrow, scholarly, studious. **2** *an intellectual approach* mental, cerebral, rational, logical, clinical, unemotional, nonemotional, academic.

**intellectual** noun **1** *one of the great intellectuals* genius, thinker. *See* INTELLECT 2. **2** *sought the company of other intellectuals* academic, academician, man/woman of letters, bluestocking, pundit, highbrow, bookworm, pedant; *inf.* egghead, walking encyclopedia.

**intelligence** noun **1** *people of great intelligence* intellect, mind, brain, brainpower, mental capacity/aptitude, reason, understanding, comprehension, acumen, wit, cleverness, brightness, brilliance, sharpness, quickness of mind, alertness, discernment, perception, perspicacity, penetration, sense, sagacity; brains; *inf.* gray matter. **2** *the intelligence came too late* news, notification, knowledge. *See* INFORMATION. **3** *he's in military intelligence* information collection, surveillance, observation, spying.

**intelligent** adjective **1** *intelligent children* clever, bright, brilliant, sharp, quick, smart, apt, discerning, thinking, perceptive, perspicacious, sensible, sagacious, enlightened, knowledgeable; *inf.* brainy. **2** *is there intelligent life on the planet?* rational, reasoning, higher-order.

**intemperate** adjective immoderate, self-indulgent, excessive, inordinate, extreme, extravagant, unreasonable, unrestrained, uncurbed, unbridled, ungoverned; drunken, drunk, intoxicated, inebriated, dissolute, dissipated, debauched, loose, wild, wanton.

**intend** verb **1** *he intends to go* mean, plan, have in mind, propose, aim, resolve, expect, contemplate, think of. **2** *they intended the bullet for the leader* destine, purpose, plan, scheme, devise.

**intense** adjective acute, fierce, severe, extreme, harsh, strong, powerful, potent, vigorous, great, profound, deep, concentrated, consuming, impassioned, passionate, fervent, fervid, burning.

**intensify** verb heighten, deepen, strengthen, increase, reinforce, magnify, enhance, fan, whet; aggravate, exacerbate, worsen, inflame; extend, augment, boost, escalate, step up.

**intensity** noun acuteness, fierceness, severity, strength, power, potency, vigor, concentration, fervor, vehemence.

**intensive** adjective in-depth, concentrated, exhaustive, all-out, thorough, thoroughgoing, total, all-absorbing.

**intent** adjective **1** *an intent expression* concentrated, fixed, steady, steadfast, absorbed, attentive, engrossed, occupied, wrapped up, focused, earnest, committed, intense. **2** *intent on getting their own way* set on, bent on, committed to, firm about, determined to, resolved to.

**intent** noun purpose, aim. *See* INTENTION. **to/for all intents and purposes** virtually, practically, as good as.

**intention** noun aim, purpose, intent, goal, objective, end, end in view, target, ambition, wish, plan, design, resolve, resolution, determination; premeditation, preconception.

**intentional** adjective intended, deliberate, meant, done on purpose, willful, purposeful, purposed, planned, calculated, designed, premeditated, preconceived, predetermined.

**intentionally** adverb deliberately, on purpose, purposefully, by design, willfully.

**inter** verb bury, consign to the grave, entomb, lay to rest, inhume, inearth, sepulcher.

**intercede** verb mediate, negotiate, arbitrate, intervene, interpose, step in, plead for, petition for.

**intercept** verb stop, cut off, deflect, head off, seize, expropriate, commandeer; check, arrest, block, obstruct, impede.

**intercession** noun mediation, negotiation, arbitration, intervention, interposition, pleading, petition, entreaty, supplication; good offices.

**interchangeable** adjective exchangeable, transposable, equivalent, corresponding, correlative, reciprocal, comparable.

**interest** noun **1** *look with interest at the game* attentiveness, attention, absorption, engrossment, heed, regard, notice, scrutiny, curiosity, attraction, appeal, fascination, charm, allure. **2** *a matter of interest to all of us* concern, importance, import, consequence, moment, significance, note, relevance, seriousness. **3** *his interests include reading and music* pastime, hobby, diversion, amusement, pursuit, relaxation; *inf.* thing. **4** *have an interest in the business* share, stake, portion, claim, investment; stock, equity. **5** *you must declare your interest in the case* involvement, partiality, attraction, preference, onesidedness, favoritism, bias, prejudice. **6** *his commercial interests are in trouble* concern, business, matter, care; affairs. **7**

*earn interest on investments* dividend, profit, return, percentage, gain. **8** *it is in their interests to go* benefit, advantage, good, profit, gain. **in the interests of** for the sake/benefit of, to the advantage of, in the furtherance of.

**interest** verb **1** *the book interests her* attract/hold/engage the attention of, attract, absorb, engross, fascinate, rivet, grip, captivate, amuse, intrigue, arouse curiosity in. **2** *the outcome of the war interests us all* affect, have an effect/bearing on, concern, involve.

**interested** adjective **1** *the interested children* attentive, intent, absorbed, engrossed, curious, fascinated, riveted, gripped, captivated, intrigued. **2** *interested parties waiting in the lawyer's office* concerned, involved, implicated. **3** *no interested person can judge the contest* partial, partisan, one-sided, biased, prejudiced.

**interesting** adjective absorbing, engrossing, fascinating, riveting, gripping, compelling, compulsive, spellbinding, captivating, appealing, engaging, amusing, entertaining, stimulating, thought-provoking, diverting, exciting, intriguing.

**interfere** verb **interfere in** meddle with, butt into, pry into, tamper with, intrude into, intervene in, get involved in, intercede in; *inf.* poke one's nose in, horn in on. **interfere with** hinder, inhibit, impede, obstruct, get in the way of, check, block, hamper, handicap, cramp, trammel, frustrate, thwart, balk.

**interference** noun *resent her interference in their affairs* meddling, meddlesomeness, prying, intrusion, intervention.

**interim** noun meantime, meanwhile, interval, interregnum.

**interior** adjective **1** *the interior part of the building* inner, inside, internal, inward. **2** *the interior parts of the country* inland, noncoastal, central, midland, up-country, remote. **3** *his interior self* inner, spiritual, mental, psychological, emotional, private, personal, intimate, secret, hidden.

**interior** noun *the interior of the country* center, midland, heartland, hinterland.

**interject** verb throw in, insert, introduce, interpolate, interpose, insinuate, add, mingle, intersperse.

**interloper** noun trespasser, invader, intruder, encroacher, gatecrasher.

**interlude** noun interval, intermission, break, recess, pause, respite, rest, breathing space.

**intermediary** noun mediator, go-between, broker, agent, middleman, negotiator, arbitrator.

**interment** noun burial, burying, entombment, inhumation, sepulture, funeral.

**interminable** adjective **1** *an interminable road* (seemingly) endless, never-ending, without end, everlasting, ceaseless, incessant. **2** *an interminable talk* tedious, wearisome, boring, long-winded, rambling.

**intermingle** verb mingle, mix, commingle, intermix, blend, fuse, merge, combine.

**intermission** noun interval, interlude, interim, entr'acte, break, half-time, recess, rest, pause, respite, lull, stop, stoppage, halt, cessation, suspension; *inf.* letup, breather, time out.

**intermittent** adjective fitful, spasmodic, irregular, sporadic, occasional, periodic, cyclic, recurrent, recurring, broken, discontinuous, on again and off again, on and off.

**internal** adjective **1** *internal wall* interior, inside, inner, inward. **2** *the country's/firm's internal affairs* home, domestic, civil, interior, in-house, in-company. **3** *his internal opinion* mental, psychological, emotional, subjective, private, intimate.

**international** adjective cosmopolitan, global, universal, worldwide, intercontinental.

**interpret** verb **1** *interpret the text* explain, elucidate, expound, explicate, clarify, illuminate, shed light on, gloss, simplify, spell out. **2** *interpret her silence as consent* understand, understand by, construe, take, take to mean, read. **3** *interpret for the foreign ambassador* translate, transcribe, transliterate, paraphrase, decode, decipher. **4** *dancers interpreting the ballet* portray, depict, present, perform, execute, enact.

**interpretation** noun **1** *the interpretation of the text* explanation, elucidation, expounding, explication, clarification, exegesis. **2** *his interpretation of her silence as consent* understanding, construal, reading. **3** *the scientist's interpretation of the results* analysis, reading, diagnosis. **4** *her interpretation of the foreign ambassador's speech* translation, transcription, transliteration; paraphrase. **5** *the dancer's interpretation of the ballet* portrayal, depiction, presentation, performance, execution, rendering, rendition, enactment.

**interrogate** verb question, put/pose questions to, inquire of, examine, cross-examine, cross-question, quiz, pump, grill, give the third degree to, probe, catechize.

**interrogation** noun **1** *give way under interrogation* questioning, quizzing, examination, cross-examination, cross-questioning, pumping, grilling, third degree, probing, inquisition. **2** *complain about the policeman's interrogations* question, query, inquiry, poser.

**interrupt** verb **1** *interrupt his speech* cut in (on), break in (on), barge in (on), intrude (on), disturb, interfere (with); *inf.* butt in (on), chime in (on), horn in (on), muscle in (on). **2** *interrupt the talks for a time* suspend, discontinue, break, break off, hold up, delay, lay aside, leave off, postpone, stop, halt, cease, end, cancel. **3** *only a few trees interrupted the flatness of the landscape* break, break up, punctuate. **4** *the building interrupts our view* obstruct, impede, block, interfere with, cut off.

**interruption** noun **1** *resent his interruption* cutting in, interference, disturbance, intrusion, obtrusion; *inf.* butting in. **2** *the interruption of/in the talks* suspension, discontinuance, breaking off, delay, postponement, stopping, halt, cessation; intermission, interval, interlude, break, pause, recess, gap, hiatus.

**intersect** verb cut across/through, halve, divide, bisect; cross, crisscross, meet, connect.

**interval** noun **1** *in the interval before the next meeting* interim, interlude, period, meantime, meanwhile, wait, space. **2** *drinks served in the theater during the interval* break, pause. *See* INTERMISSION.

**intervene** verb *intervene in the dispute* mediate, involve oneself, interpose, interfere, intrude. *See* INTERCEDE.

**intervention** noun intercession, mediation, arbitration, negotiation, agency, involvement, interference, intrusion.

**interview** noun **1** *candidates nervous at the interview* conference, discussion, meeting, talk, dialogue, evaluation. **2** *give an interview to the press* audience, question and answer session, exchange, colloquy, interlocution.

**interview** verb talk to, have a discussion/dialogue with, hold a meeting with, confer with, question, put questions to, sound out, examine, interrogate, cross-examine, evaluate.

**interweave** verb **1** *interweave strands of various fabrics* weave, intertwine, twine, twist, interlace, braid, plait. **2** *their financial affairs are interwoven* intermingle, mingle, interlink, intermix, mix, blend, fuse, interlock, knit, connect, associate.

**intimate** adjective **1** *intimate friends* close, near, dear, nearest and dearest, cherished, bosom, familiar, confidential; *inf.* thick, buddy-buddy. **2** *in an intimate atmosphere* informal, warm, cozy, friendly, comfortable, snug; *inf.* comfy. **3** *a diary giving intimate details* personal, private, confidential, secret, privy. **4** *his intimate views* private, innermost, inmost, inner, inward, intrinsic, deep-seated, inherent. **5** *an intimate knowledge of the law* experienced, deep, in-depth, profound, detailed, thorough, exhaustive, personal, firsthand, direct, immediate. **6** *the intimate relations of lovers* sexual, carnal.

**intimate** verb imply, suggest, let it be known, hint, insinuate, give an inkling that, indicate, signal.

**intimation** noun implication, suggestion, hint, insinuation, inkling, indication, signal, reference, allusion.

**intimidate** verb frighten, terrify, scare, alarm, terrorize, cow, daunt, domineer, browbeat, bully, tyrannize, coerce, compel, bulldoze, pressure, threaten; *inf.* push around, lean on, twist someone's arm.

**intimidation** noun **1** *the intimidation of residents by gangs* frightening, terrorization, bullying, coercion, threatening; *inf.* arm-twisting. **2** *leave his premises out of intimidation* fear, terror, alarm, trepidation.

**intolerable** adjective unbearable, unendurable, beyond endurance. *See* INSUFFERABLE.

**intolerance** noun bigotry, illiberalism, narrow-mindedness, parochialism, provincialism, insularity, prejudice, bias, partisanship, one-sidedness.

**intolerant** adjective bigoted, illiberal, narrow-minded, narrow, parochial, provincial, insular, small-minded, prejudiced, biased, partial, partisan, one-sided.

**intonation** noun pitch, tone, timbre, cadence, lilt, inflection, accentuation, emphasis, stress.

**intoxicated** adjective inebriated, inebriate, drunk, drunken, dead drunk, under the influence, tipsy, befuddled, stupefied, staggering; *inf.* drunk as a skunk, three sheets to the wind, tight, pickled, soused, under the table, sloshed, plastered, stewed, well-oiled, loaded, stoned, bombed out of one's mind, lit up, tanked up, smashed.

**intoxicating** adjective **1** *intoxicating drinks* intoxicant, alcoholic, strong, spirituous, inebriant. **2** *intoxicating news* exhilarating, heady, elating, thrilling, animating, exciting.

**intoxication** noun **1** *suffering from the effects of intoxication* drunkenness, inebriation, inebriety, insobriety, alcoholism, dipsomania, tipsiness, befuddlement, stupefaction. **2** *intoxication following the good news* exhilaration, elation, ecstasy, euphoria, thrill, invigoration, animation, excitement, rapture, delirium.

**intrepid** adjective fearless, unafraid, undaunted, dauntless, undismayed, unalarmed, unflinching, bold, daring, adventurous, reckless, brave, courageous, gallant, stalwart; *inf.* gutsy, spunky.

**intricate** adjective **1** *intricate patterns* tangled, entangled, raveled, twisted, knotty,

convoluted, mazelike, labyrinthine, serpentine, sinuous, fancy, elaborate, ornate, Byzantine, rococo. **2** *intricate problems* complex, complicated, difficult, involved, thorny, mystifying, enigmatic.

**intrigue** verb **1** *your behavior intrigues me* interest, absorb, arouse one's curiosity, attract, draw, pull, rivet, fascinate, charm, captivate. **2** *they are intriguing to overthrow the dictator* plot, conspire, scheme, connive, maneuver, machinate, devise.

**intrigue** noun **1** *an intrigue to overthrow the dictator* plot, conspiracy, collusion, conniving, cabal, scheme, ruse, stratagem, wile, dodge, artifice, maneuver, machination, trickery, double-dealing. **2** *her husband found out about the intrigue* love affair, affair, liaison, amour; adultery; *inf.* carrying on.

**intriguing** adjective interesting, absorbing, compelling, attractive, appealing, riveting, fascinating, captivating, diverting, titillating, tantalizing.

**intrinsic** adjective inborn, inbred, natural, native, elemental, true, genuine, real, authentic. *See* INHERENT.

**introduce** verb **1** *introduce his friends to each other* present, acquaint, make acquainted. **2** *introduce his talk with a joke* preface, precede, lead into, commence, start off, begin. **3** *introduce a new method* bring in, bring into being, originate, launch, inaugurate, institute, initiate, establish, found, set in motion, organize, develop, start, begin, commence, usher in, pioneer. **4** *introduce his ideas* propose, put forward, suggest, broach, advance, bring up, set forth, submit. **5** *introduce a note of solemnity to the party* insert, inject, interject, interpose, add, bring, infuse, instill.

**introduction** noun **1** *an introduction to the book* foreword, preface, front matter, preamble, prologue, prelude, lead-in; *inf.* intro, prelims. **2** *the introduction of new methods* origination, launch, inauguration, institution, establishment, development, start, commencement, pioneering. **3** *his introduction to a new way of life* baptism, initiation, inauguration, debut. **4** *the course provides an introduction to the subject* basics, rudiments, fundamentals; groundwork. **5** *the introduction of a serious note to the party* insertion, injection, interjection, infusion.

**introductory** adjective **1** *the speaker's introductory remarks* prefatory, preliminary, lead-in, opening, initial, starting, commencing. **2** *an introductory course* preparatory, elementary, basic, basal, rudimentary, fundamental.

**introspective** adjective self-analyzing, self-examining, contemplative, reflective, meditative, musing, pensive, brooding, preoccupied.

**introverted** adjective inward-looking, self-absorbed; withdrawn, shy, reserved.

**intrude** verb interrupt, push/thrust oneself in, gatecrash, barge in, encroach, butt in, interfere, obtrude; invade, impinge on, infringe on, trespass on, violate.

**intruder** noun invader, prowler, trespasser; interloper, infiltrator, gatecrasher.

**intrusion** noun interruption, encroachment, invasion, infringement, trespass, obtrusion, violation.

**intrusive** adjective interfering, invasive, obtrusive, trespassing, meddlesome, inquisitive; *inf.* pushy, nosy.

**intuition** noun instinct, sixth sense, divination, presentiment, clairvoyance, second sight, extrasensory perception, ESP, feeling, feeling in one's bones, hunch, inkling, presentiment.

**intuitive** adjective instinctive, instinctual, innate, unlearned, spontaneous, automatic.

**inundate** verb 1 *the river inundating the town* flood, deluge, overflow, overrun, swamp, submerge, engulf, drown, cover, saturate, soak. 2 *inundated with correspondence* overwhelm, overpower, overburden, swamp, bog down, glut.

**inure** verb harden, toughen, season, temper, habituate, familiarize, accustom, acclimatize.

**invade** verb 1 *the enemy invaded the city* march into, overrun, occupy, storm, take over, descend upon, make inroads on, attack, assail, assault, raid, plunder. 2 *invade their privacy* intrude on, obtrude on, encroach on, infringe on, trespass on, burst in on, violate. 3 *doubts invaded his mind* assail, permeate, pervade, fill, spread over.

**invader** noun 1 *enemy invaders* attacker, assailant, assaulter, raider, plunderer. 2 *invaders of their privacy* intruder, encroacher, infringer, trespasser, violator.

**invalid** adjective 1 *the contract is now invalid* inoperative, null, null and void, void, not binding, nullified, revoked, rescinded, abolished. 2 *an invalid assumption* untenable, illogical, irrational, unscientific, false, faulty, fallacious, spurious, ineffectual, unsound, weak.

**invalidate** verb 1 *invalidate the contract* void, nullify, annul, cancel, quash, veto, negate, revoke, rescind, abolish, terminate, repeal, repudiate. 2 *invalidate the argument* disprove, refute, rebut, negate, discredit.

**invaluable** adjective priceless, beyond price, inestimable, precious, costly, worth its weight in gold, worth a king's ransom.

**invariable** adjective unchanging, changeless, unchangeable, constant, unvarying, unalterable, immutable, fixed, stable, set, steady, unwavering, consistent.

**invariably** adverb always, each and every time, without fail/exception, regularly, consistently, habitually, unfailingly.

**invasion** noun 1 *the invasion of the city* overrunning, occupation, incursion, offensive, attack, assailing, assault, raid, foray, onslaught, plundering. 2 *the invasion of privacy* interruption, intrusion, obtrusion, encroachment, infringement, breach, infraction, violation.

**invent** verb 1 *invent a new machine* originate, create, innovate, discover, design, devise, contrive, formulate, think up, conceive, come up with, hit upon, compose, frame, coin. 2 *he invented that story* make up, fabricate, concoct, hatch, trump up, forge; *inf.* cook up.

**invention** noun 1 *the invention of the zipper | his most famous invention* origination, creation, innovation, discovery, design, contrivance, construction, coinage; *inf.* brainchild. 2 *an artist of great invention* inventiveness, originality, creativity, creativeness, imagination, artistry, inspiration, ingenuity, resourcefulness, genius, skill. 3 *his account of the event was pure invention* fabrication, concoction, fiction, falsification, forgery, fake, deceit, myth, fantasy, romance, illusion, sham, lie, untruth, falsehood, fib, figment of one's imagination, yarn, story; *inf.* tall story.

**inventive** adjective original, creative, innovative, imaginative, artistic, inspired, ingenious, resourceful.

**inventor** noun originator, creator, innovator, discoverer, author, architect, designer, deviser, developer, initiator, coiner, father, prime mover, maker, framer, producer.

**inventory** noun list, listing, checklist, catalog, record, register, tally, account.

**invert** verb turn inside out, turn upside down, overturn, upturn, turn turtle.

**invest** verb 1 *the priest will be invested tomorrow* install, induct, inaugurate, instate, ordain, initiate, swear in, consecrate, crown, enthrone. 2 *the bride was invested in silk* clothe, attire, dress, garb, robe, gown, drape, swathe, adorn, deck. **invest in** 1 *invest in the business* put/sink money into, lay out money on/for, provide capital for, fund, subsidize. 2 *invest energy in the venture* spend on, expend on/for, devote to, contribute to, give to. 3 *invest power in his heirs* vest in, confer to, bestow to, grant to, entrust to.

**investigate** verb research, probe, explore, inquire into, make inquiries about, go/look into, search, scrutinize, study, examine, inspect, consider, sift, analyze; *inf.* check out.

**investigation** noun research, probe, exploration, inquiry, fact-finding, search, scrutiny, study, survey, review, examination, inspection, analysis, inquest, hearing, inquisition.

**investigator** noun researcher, prober, explorer, inquirer, fact finder, searcher, scrutinizer, reviewer, examiner, inspector, analyzer, questioner, inquisitor. **private investigator** (private) detective; *inf.* private eye, dick, sleuth, Sherlock, gumshoe.

**inveterate** adjective **1** *an inveterate conservative/drinker* confirmed, habitual, inured, hardened, chronic, diehard, dyed-in-the-wool, long-standing, addicted, hard-core, incorrigible. **2** *an inveterate habit* ingrained, deep-seated, deep-rooted, deep-set, entrenched, long-established, ineradicable, incurable.

**invigorate** verb revitalize, energize, fortify, strengthen, put new strength/life/heart in, brace, refresh, rejuvenate, enliven, liven up, animate, exhilarate, pep up, perk up, stimulate, motivate, rouse, excite, wake up.

**invincible** adjective **1** *an invincible opponent* unconquerable, undefeatable, unbeatable, unassailable, invulnerable, indestructible, impregnable, indomitable. **2** *an invincible hurdle* insuperable, insurmountable, overwhelming, overpowering.

**inviolate** adjective intact, unbroken, whole, entire, untouched, undamaged, unscathed, unmarred, unspoiled, unsullied, unstained, undefiled, unpolluted, pure, virgin.

**invisible** adjective **1** *invisible to the passersby* undetectable, imperceivable, indiscernible, indistinguishable, unseen, unnoticed, unobserved, hidden, concealed. **2** *invisible hairnets* inconspicuous, unnoticeable, imperceptible.

**invitation** noun **1** *reject their invitation to lunch* asking, bidding, call; *inf.* invite. **2** *accept their invitation to apply for the post* request, call, appeal, petition, solicitation, supplication, summons. **3** *the rebate was an invitation to buy the car* encouragement, overture, attraction, draw, allurement, lure, bait; *inf.* come-on.

**invite** verb **1** *they invited him to dinner* ask, bid, summon. **2** *invite applications* ask for, request, call for, solicit, look for, seek, appeal for, petition. **3** *invite disaster* cause, bring on, bring upon oneself, draw, make happen, induce, provoke. **4** *they invite trouble by leaving the doors unlocked* welcome, encourage, foster, attract, draw, allure, entice, tempt, court.

**inviting** adjective attractive, appealing, tempting, enticing, alluring, winning, beguiling, fascinating, captivating, intriguing, irresistible.

**invoke** verb **1** *invoke God's help* call for, request, supplicate, entreat, solicit, beseech, beg, implore, importune, petition, appeal to. **2** *invoke the constitutional amendment* apply, implement, put into effect/use, resort to, use, have recourse to.

**involuntary** adjective **1** *an involuntary reaction* reflexive, reflex, automatic, mechanical, unconditioned, spontaneous, instinctive, instinctual, unconscious, unthinking, unintentional, uncontrolled. **2** *their cooperation was involuntary* unwilling, against one's will/wishes, reluctant, unconsenting, grudging, forced, coerced, compelled, compulsory, obligatory.

**involve** verb **1** *his new job involves total discretion* entail, imply, require, necessitate, presuppose. **2** *try to involve everyone in the party* include, count in, cover, embrace, take in, number, incorporate, encompass, comprise, contain. **3** *the suspect tried to involve others in the crime* implicate, incriminate, inculpate, associate, connect, concern. **4** *introduce the students to something that involves them* interest, be of interest to, absorb, engage, rivet, grip, occupy, preoccupy, engross.

**involved** adjective **1** *an involved situation* complicated, difficult. *See* INTRICATE. **2** *involved parties should speak up* associated, concerned, participating.

**invulnerable** adjective impenetrable, secure, safe. *See* INVINCIBLE. **invulnerable to/against** insensitive to, insusceptible to.

**inwardly** adverb at heart, deep down/within, in one's heart, inside, privately, secretly.

**irascible** adjective quick-tempered, short-tempered, snappish, testy, irritable, touchy, edgy, surly, cross, crotchety, cantankerous.

**irate** adjective incensed, enraged, raging, fuming, infuriated, furious, indignant, ireful, ranting, raving, angry, mad, in a frenzy; *inf.* foaming at the mouth.

**ire** noun anger, wrath, rage, fury, indignation, annoyance, exasperation, resentment, choler, spleen.

**iridescent** adjective shimmering, glittering, sparkling, dazzling, kaleidoscopic, multicolored, rainbowlike.

**irk** verb irritate, annoy, provoke, vex, pique, peeve, nettle, exasperate, ruffle, discountenance, anger, infuriate, incense, try one's patience; *inf.* get one's goat, get one's back up.

**irksome** adjective irritating, annoying, vexing, vexatious, exasperating, infuriating, tiresome, wearisome, tedious, trying, troublesome.

**iron** verb **iron out 1** *iron out the problems* straighten out, sort out, clear up, settle, solve, resolve, unravel. **2** *iron out their differences* get rid of, eliminate, eradicate, erase, harmonize, reconcile, smooth over.

**ironic** adjective **1** *an ironic remark/wit* satirical, mocking, scoffing, ridiculing, derisory, derisive, scornful, sneering, sardonic, wry, double-edged, sarcastic. **2** *ironic that Beethoven became deaf* paradoxical, incongruous.

**irony** noun **1** *use irony in your story* satire, mockery, ridicule, derision, scorn, wryness, sarcasm. **2** *it was a sad irony that the millionaire died a pauper* paradox, incongruity, incongruousness.

**irrational** adjective **1** *irrational fears* illogical, unreasonable, groundless, implausible, absurd, foolish, senseless, nonsensical, ludicrous, preposterous. **2** *an irrational person* demented, insane, crazy, unstable.

**irreconcilable** adjective **1** *irreconcilable points of view* incompatible, at odds, at variance, opposite, contrary, incongruous, opposing, conflicting, clashing, discordant. **2** *irreconcilable enemies* implacable, unappeasable, uncompromising, intransigent, hard-line, inflexible.

**irregular** adjective **1** *an irregular coastline* asymmetric, unsymmetric, nonuniform, uneven, broken, jagged, ragged, serrated, crooked, curving, craggy. **2** *an irregular churchgoer* inconsistent, erratic, sporadic, variable, inconstant, desultory, haphazard, intermittent, occasional, unsystematic, capricious, unmethodical. **3** *his appointment was most irregular* out of order, contrary, perverse, against the rules, unofficial, unorthodox, unconventional, abnormal. **4** *an irregular result* anomalous, aberrant, deviant, abnormal, unusual, uncommon, freak, extraordinary, exceptional, odd, peculiar, strange. **5** *an irregular army* guerrilla, underground, resistance, mercenary.

**irregularity** noun **1** *the irregularity of the coastline* lack of symmetry, asymmetry, unsymmetricalness, nonuniformity, unevenness, jaggedness. **2** *the irregularity of the pulse* unevenness, unsteadiness, shakiness, fitfulness, fluctuation. **3** *the irregularity of their attendance* inconsistency, inconstancy, desultoriness, haphazardness, intermittence, patchiness. **4** *the irregularity of his appointment* unorthodoxy, unconventionality. **5** *the irregularity of the result* anomaly, anomalousness, aberrance, aberrancy, deviation, abnormality, unusualness, freakishness. **6** *spot the irregularities in the result* anomaly, aberration, deviation, abnormality.

**irrelevant** adjective nongermane, immaterial, unrelated, unconnected, inappropriate, extraneous, beside the point, not to the point, out of place, nothing to do with it, neither here nor there.

**irreparable** adjective beyond repair, past mending, irreversible, irrevocable, irretrievable, irrecoverable, irremediable, incurable.

**irreplaceable** adjective priceless, invaluable, inestimably precious, unique, worth its weight in gold, rare.

**irrepressible** adjective unrestrainable, uncontainable, insuppressible, uncontrollable, unstoppable, unquenchable, unreserved, unchecked, unbridled.

**irresistible** adjective **1** *an irresistible impulse* overwhelming, overpowering, compelling, insuppressible, irrepressible, forceful, potent, imperative, urgent. **2** *an irresistible beauty/dessert* fascinating, alluring, enticing, seductive, captivating, enchanting, ravishing, tempting, tantalizing.

**irresponsible** adjective **1** *irresponsible people* undependable, unreliable, untrustworthy, careless, reckless, rash, flighty, giddy, scatterbrained, erratic, harebrained, featherbrained, immature; *inf.* harumscarum. **2** *irresponsible actions* thoughtless, ill-considered, unwise, injudicious.

**irreverent** adjective disrespectful, unrespectful, impertinent, insolent, impudent; impious, irreligious, heretical, sacrilegious, blasphemous.

**irreversible** adjective unalterable, irreparable, unrectifiable, irrevocable, unrepealable, final, fixed, settled.

**irrevocable** adjective unalterable, unchangeable. *See* IRREVERSIBLE.

**irritable** adjective bad-tempered, ill-tempered, ill-humored, irascible, cross, snappish, snappy, edgy, testy, touchy, crabbed, peevish, petulant, cantankerous, grumpy, grouchy.

**irritate** verb **1** *the barking dogs irritate the neighbors* annoy, vex, provoke, irk, aggravate, nettle, peeve, get on one's nerves, exasperate, infuriate, anger, make one's hackles rise, ruffle, disturb, put out, bother, pester, try one's patience; *inf.* rub the wrong way, get one's goat, get one's back up, drive up the wall, drive one bananas. **2** *the rough cloth irritated her skin* chafe, fret, rub, pain, hurt, inflame, aggravate.

**irritating** adjective annoying, vexing, provoking, irksome, exasperating, infuriating, maddening, disturbing, bothersome, troublesome, pestering, aggravating.

**island** noun isle, islet, key, cay, atoll.

**isolate** verb set apart, segregate, cut off, separate, detach, quarantine, sequester, insulate.

**isolated** adjective **1** *feeling isolated far from her friends* alone, solitary, lonely, separated, segregated, exiled, forsaken, forlorn. **2** *an isolated place* remote, out of the way, off the beaten track, outlying, secluded, hidden, unfrequented, desolate, godforsaken. **3** *an isolated example* single, solitary, unique, uncommon, exceptional, atypical.

**isolation** noun **1** *the isolation of the patients was necessary* segregation, separation, detachment, abstraction, quarantine, sequestration, insulation. **2** *the prisoner's feeling of isolation* exile, forlornness, aloneness, solitariness, loneliness. **3** *the isolation of the village* remoteness, seclusion, loneliness, desolation.

**issue** noun **1** *debate the issue for hours* matter, matter in question, point at issue, question, subject, topic, affair, problem, bone of contention, controversy, argument. **2** *the issue is still in doubt* result, outcome, decision, upshot, end, conclusion, consequence, effect. **3** *the next issue of the magazine* edition, number, printing, print run, impression, copy, installment, version. **4** *the issue of the new stamps/paper/shares* issuance, publication, circulation, distribution, dissemination, sending out, delivery. **5** *Abraham and his issue* offspring, progeny, children; heirs, scions, descendants; *inf.* brood. **6** *the issue of the stream* outflow, effusion, discharge, debouchment, emanation. **at issue** to be

discussed, under discussion, for debate, in dispute, to be decided. **take issue with** disagree with, dispute with, challenge, oppose.

**issue** verb **1** *issue new stamps | issue a statement* put out, give out, deal out, send out, distribute, circulate, release; disseminate, announce, proclaim, broadcast. **2** *smoke issuing from the chimney* emit, exude, discharge, emanate, gush, pour forth, seep, ooze. **3** *people issued from the building* emerge, come out, come forth, appear; leave. **4** *his knowledge issues from a love of books* derive, arise, stem, proceed, spring, originate, result.

**itching** adjective **1** *an itching scalp* itchy, tingling, prickling. **2** *itching to go/know* longing, yearning, craving, aching, burning, avid, agog, keen, eager, impatient, raring, dying.

**item** noun **1** *three items for sale* article, thing, piece of merchandise; goods. **2** *several items to be discussed* point, detail, matter, consideration, particular, feature, circumstance, aspect, component, element, ingredient. **3** *a news item* piece, story, bulletin, article, account, report, feature, dispatch.

**itemize** verb list, inventory, tabulate, detail, particularize, specify, instance, enumerate, number.

**itinerant** adjective traveling, peripatetic, journeying, wandering, roaming, roving, rambling, wayfaring, unsettled, nomadic, migratory, vagabond, vagrant, gypsy.

# Jj

**jab** verb *jab him in the ribs* poke, prod, dig, nudge, elbow, stab, tap, punch, box; *inf.* sock.

**jab** noun *a jab in the ribs* poke, prod, dig, nudge, stab, punch.

**jabber** verb chatter, gibber, prattle, babble, prate, blather, rattle, ramble.

**jacket** noun *a jacket and matching pants* sport(s) coat, blazer, windbreaker, parka, anorak.

**jagged** adjective serrated, toothed, notched, spiked, barbed, uneven, rough, ragged, craggy, broken, cleft.

**jail** noun *sent to jail* prison, lockup, jailhouse, penitentiary; *inf.* pen, clink, inside, stir, slammer, cooler, jug, can, big house.

**jail** verb *they jailed him for life* imprison, incarcerate, send up, lock up, put away, confine, detain, intern, impound, immure.

**jailer** noun prison warden, warden, guard, keeper, captor.

**jam** verb **1** *jam something in the door* wedge, insert, force, ram, stick, press, cram, sandwich, stuff. **2** *the ushers jammed too many people into the hall* cram, pack, crowd, squeeze, crush. **3** *the broken-down vehicles jammed the roads* obstruct, block, clog, congest. **4** *the machine has jammed* stick, stall, halt, stop.

**jam** noun **1** *caught in a jam on the highway* obstruction, congestion, bottleneck, stoppage, gridlock, traffic jam, holdup. **2** *in a financial jam* predicament, plight, straits, trouble, quandary; *inf.* fix, tight spot, scrape.

**jangle** verb **1** *the chains jangled* clank, clink, clang, clash, clatter, rattle. **2** *the noise jangled his nerves* irritate, disturb, jar on, grate on.

**jangle** noun *the jangle of chains* clank, clink, clang, clash, clatter, rattle, cacophony, din, dissonance.

**jar** verb *the sound jarred his nerves* grate (on), jangle, irritate, disturb, upset, irk, annoy, nettle, vex.

**jargon** noun **1** *the jargon of the neighborhood kids* cant, slang, argot, idiom, vernacular, dialect, patois; *inf.* lingo. **2** *technical jargon* computerese, legalese, bureaucratese, journalese, buzzword, gobbledegook, psychobabble.

**jaundiced** adjective **1** *jaundiced skin* yellow, yellowish, sallow. **2** *a jaundiced view of life* cynical, pessimistic, skeptical, distrustful, suspicious, misanthropic, bitter.

**jaunt** noun outing, drive, excursion, expedition, stroll.

**jaunty** adjective **1** *in a jaunty mood* sprightly, bouncy, buoyant, lively, breezy, perky, blithe. **2** *a jaunty outfit* smart, stylish, trim, dapper; *inf.* natty.

**jealous** adjective **1** *jealous of her beauty* grudging, resentful, envious, green-eyed, covetous, desirous. **2** *a jealous lover* suspicious, distrustful, mistrustful, doubting, insecure, possessive.

**jealousy** noun **1** *show jealousy at her rival's success* resentment, resentfulness, ill-will, bitterness, spite, envy, covetousness. **2** *the jealousy of her husband* suspicion, suspiciousness, distrust, mistrust, doubt, insecurity, possessiveness.

**jeer** verb *crowds jeering the politician* mock, ridicule, deride, taunt, gibe, scorn, contemn, flout, cry down, tease, boo, hiss; scoff at, laugh at, sneer at; *inf.* knock.

**jeer** noun *the jeers of the crowd* mockery, ridicule, derision; banter, scoffing, teasing, sneer, taunt, gibe, boo, hiss, catcall, abuse.

**jell** verb **1** *let the dessert jell* set, stiffen, solidify, harden, thicken, congeal, coagulate. **2** *ideas beginning to jell* take shape, take form, form, crystallize, come together.

**jeopardize** verb endanger, imperil, put in jeopardy, put at risk, expose to danger, threaten, menace, take a chance with, gamble with.

**jeopardy** noun risk, danger, endangerment, peril, hazard, precariousness, insecurity, vulnerability, threat, menace.

**jerk** verb **1** *jerk him by the arm* pull, yank, tug, wrench, tweak, pluck. **2** *the car jerked* along jolt, lurch, bump, jump, bounce, jounce. **3** *his arm was jerking* twitch, shake, tremble, convulse.

**jerk** noun **1** *pull it out with a jerk* pull, yank, tug, wrench, tweak. **2** *the car stopped with a jerk* jolt, lurch, bump, start, jar. **3** *he's a complete jerk* fool, idiot, rogue, scoundrel; *inf.* twit, creep.

**jest** noun **1** *tell jests* joke, witticism, gag, quip, bon mot; *inf.* crack, wisecrack. **2** *play a jest on someone* prank, hoax, practical joke, trick, jape. **3** *they did it in jest* fun, sport, play.

**jest** verb **1** *they joked and jested all evening* joke, crack jokes, quip, banter; *inf.* wisecrack. **2** *but they were only jesting* fool, fool around, tease, play a prank, play a practical joke, play a hoax, pull someone's leg; *inf.* kid.

**jester** noun **1** *her uncle's a jester* joker, comic, comedian, humorist, wag, wit, quipster, prankster. **2** *the jesters in Shakespeare's plays* fool, court fool, clown, buffoon, merry-andrew, harlequin.

**jet** noun **1** *a jet of water* stream, gush, spurt, spout, spray, rush, fountain, spring. **2** *put a jet on the hose* nozzle, spout, sprinkler, rose, atomizer.

**jet** verb *water jetted out of the hose* shoot, gush, spurt, spout, well, rush, spray, squirt, spew, stream, surge, flow, issue.

**jettison** verb **1** *jettison heavy goods from a ship* eject, throw overboard, throw over the side, unload. **2** *jettison unwanted clothes* discard, get rid of, toss out, scrap, dump, throw out, throw away.

**jetty** noun *tie the boat to the jetty* pier, wharf, quay, breakwater.

**jewel** noun **1** *a crown set with priceless jewels* gem, gemstone, precious stone, bijou; *inf.* rock. **2** *the jewel of his collection* pearl, flower, pride, pride and joy, cream, crème de la crème, plum, boast.

**jeweler** noun lapidary, gemologist.

**jewelry** noun jewels, gems, precious stones, treasure, regalia, trinkets, ornaments; costume jewelry.

**jiffy** noun moment, second, split second, minute, instant, flash, trice, twinkling of an eye; *inf.* two shakes of a lamb's tail.

**jilt** verb reject, cast aside, discard, throw over, drop, leave, forsake; *inf.* ditch, dump.

**jingle** verb **1** *money jingling* clink, chink, jangle, rattle, clank. **2** *the bell jingled* tinkle, ding, ring, chime, tintinnabulate.

**jingle** noun **1** *the jingle of money* clink, chink, jangle, rattle, clank. **2** *the jingle of the bell* tinkle, tinkling, ding, ding-dong, ting-a-ling, ringing, tintinnabulation, chime. **3** *sing a little jingle* ditty, melody, tune, chorus, refrain, catchy tune.

**jinx** noun malediction, curse, spell, plague, affliction; black magic, voodoo, evil eye, bad luck, evil fortune, hex.

**jinx** verb curse, cast a spell on, put a voodoo spell on, bewitch, hex.

**jittery** adjective nervous, nervy, uneasy, anxious, agitated, shaky, fidgety, jumpy.

**job** noun **1** *this job will take hours* task, undertaking, chore, assignment, venture, enterprise, activity, business, affair. **2** *what is his job?* occupation, profession, trade, employment, vocation, calling, career, field of work, métier, position, post, situation, appointment. **3** *it is his job to open the mail* duty, task, chore, errand, responsibility, concern, function, role, charge, office, commission, capacity, contribution. **4** *we must get this job off to the distributors* product, batch, lot, consignment.

**jockey** verb *jockey for position* maneuver, manipulate, engineer, elbow, insinuate; *inf.* finagle.

**jocular** adjective humorous, funny, witty, comic, comical, joking, jesting, playful, roguish, waggish, whimsical, droll, jocose, teasing, sportive, amusing, entertaining, diverting.

**jog** verb **1** *she jogs for exercise* dogtrot, trot, canter, lope. **2** *the sight jogged her memory* stimulate, activate, stir, arouse, prompt. **3** *his backpack jogged up and down on his back* bounce, bob, joggle, jiggle, jounce, jolt, jerk, shake.

**join** verb **1** *join the pieces of string/metal together* fasten, attach, tie, bind, couple, connect, unite, link, splice, knit, glue, cement, fuse, weld, solder. **2** *the two clubs have joined together* amalgamate, merge, combine, unify, ally, join forces. **3** *we joined them in their venture* join forces with, team up with, band together with, cooperate with, collaborate with, affiliate with. **4** *join the army/club* enlist, sign up, enroll; become a member of, sign up for. **5** *join the search party* join in, participate in, take part in, partake in, contribute to, lend a hand with.

**joint** noun **1** *reinforce the pipes at the joint* junction, juncture, intersection, nexus, knot, seam, coupling. **2** *drinking in some joint* club, nightclub, bar, place, establishment. **3** *smoke a joint* marijuana cigarette; *inf.* reefer.

**joint** adjective *a joint interest* common, shared, joined, mutual, combined, collective, cooperative, allied, united.

**joke** noun **1** *tell a joke* jest, witticism, quip, gag, yarn, pun; *inf.* wisecrack. **2** *play a joke on him* prank, trick, hoax, practical joke.

**3** *he is the joke of the class* laughingstock, butt, target.

**3** *he is the joke of the class* laughingstock, butt, target.

**joke** verb **1** *they joked all evening* jest, banter, quip, tell jokes, crack jokes; *inf.* wisecrack. **2** *they were only joking* fool, fool around, tease, pull someone's leg; *inf.* kid.

**joker** noun comic, comedian, humorist, funny man/woman, jester, wag, wit, quipster, prankster, practical joker, trickster; *inf.* kidder, wisecracker.

**jolly** adjective merry, gay, jovial, mirthful, gleeful, cheerful, cheery, lively, bright, lighthearted, jocund, exuberant.

**jolt** verb **1** *the car jolted along* bump, bounce, jounce, start, jerk, lurch. **2** *the accident jolted him* upset, disturb, perturb, shake, shake up, shock, stun, disconcert, disquiet, startle, surprise.

**jolt** noun **1** *the car moved with a jolt* bump, bounce, jounce, shake, jerk, lurch, start. **2** *her death came as a jolt* shock, bombshell, blow, setback, surprise, thunderbolt.

**jostle** verb **1** *people jostling each other* bump, knock against, bump into, bang into, collide with, jolt, push, shove, elbow. **2** *jostle her way through* push, thrust, shove, press, squeeze, elbow.

**jot** noun *not care a jot* iota, whit, bit, scrap, atom, grain, particle, morsel, mite, speck, trace, trifle, smidgen, *inf.* smidge, tad.

**journal** noun **1** *keep a journal on his travels* diary, daybook, notebook, log, logbook, chronicle, record, register; blog, weblog. **2** *publish medical journals* periodical, magazine, trade magazine, review, professional publication. **3** *the proprietor of several national journals* newspaper, paper, daily newspaper, daily, weekly newspaper, weekly, gazette.

**journalist** noun reporter, newsman/newswoman, newshound, feature writer, columnist, correspondent, contributor, commentator, reviewer, editor; broadcaster; *inf.* stringer. **journalists** the press.

**journey** noun trip, expedition, excursion, tour, trek, voyage, cruise, safari, peregrination, globe-trotting, odyssey, pilgrimage, outing, jaunt. **journey** verb travel, tour, voyage, sail, cruise, fly, hike, trek, roam, rove, ramble, wander, meander, peregrinate, globe-trot.

**jovial** adjective jolly, jocular, jocose, jocund, happy, cheerful, cheery, glad, merry, gay, mirthful, blithe, buoyant, convivial.

**joy** noun **1** *receive the gift with joy* delight, pleasure, gladness, enjoyment, gratification, happiness, rapture, glee, bliss, ecstasy, elation, rejoicing, exultation, jubilation. **2** *their daughter is a joy* treasure, prize, gem, jewel, delight. **3** *it is a joy to see you* pleasure, delight, treat, thrill.

**joyful** adjective **1** *joyful at the news* overjoyed, elated, thrilled, delighted, pleased, gratified, happy, glad, blithe, gleeful, jubilant, exultant; *inf.* tickled pink. **2** *we heard the joyful news* glad, happy, good, pleasing, cheering, gratifying, heartwarming. **3** *a joyful occasion* joyous, happy, cheerful, merry, gay, festive, celebratory.

**joyless** adjective **1** *a joyless place* gloomy, dreary, drab, dismal, bleak, depressing, cheerless, grim, desolate, comfortless. **2** *joyless people* unhappy, sad, miserable, wretched, downcast, dejected, depressed, despondent, melancholy, mournful.

**jubilant** adjective rejoicing, overjoyed, exultant, triumphant, elated, thrilled, euphoric, ecstatic, on cloud nine.

**jubilation** noun exultation, triumph, elation, joy, euphoria, ecstasy, rapture.

**jubilee** noun celebration, commemoration, anniversary, holiday, feast day, festival, gala, carnival, fête, festivity, revelry.

**judge** verb **1** *judge the murder case* try, hear evidence in, sit in judgment on/of, give a verdict in, pass sentence in, decree. **2** *judge the contest* adjudicate, adjudge, umpire, referee, arbitrate, mediate. **3** *judge his conduct for yourself* assess, appraise, evaluate, size up, gauge, examine, review, criticize.

**judge** noun **1** *the judge pronounced sentence* justice, reviewer, magistrate, his/her honor. **2** *The contest judge* appraiser, assessor, evaluator, critic, expert, adjudicator, umpire, referee, arbiter, arbitrator, mediator.

**judgment** noun **1** *he has no judgment* discernment, acumen, shrewdness, common sense, sense, perception, perspicacity, discrimination, wisdom, judiciousness, prudence, sagacity, understanding, intelligence, powers of reasoning. **2** *the judge gave his judgment* verdict, decision, adjudication, ruling, finding, opinion, conclusion, decree, sentence. **3** *in my judgment he is dishonest* opinion, view, belief, conviction, estimation, evaluation, assessment, appraisal.

**judicial** adjective **1** *judicial process* judiciary, juridical, judicatory, legal. **2** *a judicial mind* judgelike, impartial, unbiased, critical, analytical, discriminating, discerning, perceptive.

**judicious** adjective wise, prudent, politic, sagacious, shrewd, astute, sensible, sound, well-advised, well-considered, considered, thoughtful, expedient, practical, discerning, discriminating, informed, intelligent, enlightened, rational, discreet, careful, cautious, circumspect.

**jug** noun pitcher, ewer, crock, carafe, decanter, jar, urn, vessel, receptacle, container.

**juicy** adjective **1** *juicy fruit* succulent, moist, lush, watery, wet, flowing. **2** *a juicy tale* racy, risqué, spicy, sensational, thrilling, fascinating, colorful, exciting, vivid.

**jumble** verb disarrange, disorganize, disorder, muddle, confuse, shuffle, mix, mix up, mingle, put in disarray, make a shambles of, throw into chaos.

**jumble** noun clutter, muddle, confusion, litter, mess, hodgepodge, mishmash, miscellany, motley collection, mixture, medley, gallimaufry.

**jumbo** adjective giant, gigantic, immense, huge, extra large, oversized.

**jump** verb **1** *jump around* spring, leap, bound, hop, bounce, skip, caper, gambol, frolic, frisk, cavort. **2** *jump over the rope* high-jump, leap over, vault, pole-vault, hurdle, clear, sail over. **3** *she jumped when she heard the noise* start, flinch, jerk, recoil, twitch, quiver, shake, wince. **4** *jump (over) a piece of text* skip, miss, omit, leave out, cut out, pass over, overlook, disregard, ignore. **5** *prices jumped* rise, go up, leap up, increase, mount, escalate, surge, soar. **6** *the cat jumped the mouse* pounce on, set upon, fall on, attack, assault; *inf.* mug. **jump at** *jump at the opportunity* grab, snatch. **jump the gun** anticipate, act prematurely.

**jump** noun **1** *with one jump* spring, leap, vault, bound, hop, bounce, skip. **2** *the jumps in the race* hurdle, fence, rail, hedge, obstacle, barrier, gate. **3** *a jump in the sequence* gap, break, hiatus, interruption, space, lacuna, breach, interval. **4** *she gave a jump at the sight* start, flinch, jerk, twitch, quiver, shake, wince. **5** *a jump in prices* rise, increase, upturn, upsurge, escalation, hike, boost, elevation.

**jumpy** adjective nervous, edgy, on edge, jittery, agitated, fidgety, anxious, uneasy, restive, tense, apprehensive.

**junction** noun **1** *reinforcement at the junction of the pipes* joint, juncture, link, connection, seam; joining, coupling, linking, welding, union. **2** *cars stop at the junction* crossroads, crossing, intersection, interchange.

**juncture** noun point, point in time, time, stage, period, critical point, crucial moment.

**jungle** noun **1** *wild animals in the jungle* forest, tropical forest, rain forest, wilderness, wilds, the bush. **2** *a jungle of paperwork* jumble, tangle, disarray, confusion, hodgepodge, heap, mass, mess, mishmash, gallimaufry.

**junior** adjective **1** *the junior member* younger. **2** *the junior position* subordinate, lesser, lower, minor, secondary, inferior.

**junk** noun rubbish, refuse, litter, scrap, waste, garbage, trash, debris, remnants, castoffs, rejects, odds and ends.

**junk** verb discard, get rid of, dispose of, throw out, throw away, scrap; *inf.* dump.

**jurisdiction** noun **1** *under the governor's jurisdiction* authority, control, administration, command, leadership, power, dominion, sovereignty, rule, mastery, sway, say, influence. **2** *living in adjoining jurisdictions* territory, district, province, domain, principality, realm, area, zone. **3** *the jurisdiction of his authority* extent, range, scope, bounds, compass, sphere, area, field, orbit.

**just** adjective **1** *a just judge* fair, fair-minded, equitable, evenhanded, impartial, unbiased, objective, neutral, unprejudiced, openminded. **2** *a just man* upright, honorable, honest, ethical, moral, virtuous, principled, good, decent, truthful. **3** *just criticism* valid, sound, well-founded, well-grounded, justified, reasonable. **4** *just deserts* deserved, well-deserved, merited, rightful, due, proper, fitting, appropriate, apt, suitable, condign. **5** *the just heir* lawful, legitimate, legal, licit, rightful, genuine.

**just** adverb **1** *I just saw him* recently, lately, not long ago, only now, a moment ago. **2** *the house is just right* exactly, precisely, absolutely, completely, totally, entirely, perfectly. **3** *we just made it* barely, scarcely, hardly, by a hair's breadth. **4** *she's just a child* only, merely, simply, but, nothing but, no more than.

**justice** noun **1** *expect justice from the courts* fairness, fair-mindedness, justness, equity, evenhandedness, impartiality, objectivity, neutrality, lack of prejudice, openmindedness. **2** *a man of justice* integrity, honor, honesty, ethics, morals, justness, uprightness, virtue, principle, decency,
propriety. **3** *see the justice of his criticism* validity, justification, soundness, reasonableness. **4** *the justice of his heirdom* lawfulness, legitimacy, legality, licitness. **5** *demand justice* amends, recompense, redress, compensation, reparation, requital, retribution, penalty, punishment. **6** *the justice passed sentence* judge, magistrate, sheriff.

**justifiable** adjective valid, sound, well-founded, lawful, legitimate, legal, tenable, defensible, supportable, sustainable, warrantable, reasonable, acceptable, plausible.

**justification** noun **1** *give as the justification of his behavior* grounds, reason, just cause, basis, explanation, rationalization, defense. **2** *outline the justification of our fears* warranty, substantiation, verification, reasonableness, confirmation. **3** *the justification of the accused* acquittal, absolution, exoneration, exculpation, pardon.

**justify** verb **1** *justify his behavior* give grounds for, give reasons for, show just cause for, explain, rationalize, defend, stand up for, uphold. **2** *he had to justify his claim* substantiate, prove, establish, verify, certify, legitimize. **3** *his conduct justified our worries* warrant, substantiate, bear out, confirm. **4** *the accused was finally justified* acquit, clear, absolve, exculpate, exonerate, pardon, excuse.

**jut** verb stick out, project, protrude, overhang, beetle.

**juvenile** adjective **1** *juvenile entrants* young, junior, minor. **2** *a juvenile attitude* childish, puerile, infantile, jejune, immature, unsophisticated, naive; *inf.* wet behind the ears.

# *Kk*

**keen** adjective **1** *a keen edge to the blade* sharp, sharp-edged, fine-edged, razor-sharp. **2** *a keen sense of smell* sharp, acute, discerning, perceptive, sensitive, discriminating. **3** *a keen mind* sharp, astute, quick-witted, sharp-witted, shrewd, perceptive, penetrating, perspicacious, clever. **4** *be the butt of her keen wit* acerbic, acid, biting, caustic, tart, pointed, razorlike, razor-sharp, cutting, stinging, scathing, sardonic. **5** *keen students* willing, eager, enthusiastic, avid, earnest, zealous, fervent. **6** *keen to learn* eager, longing, yearning, impatient, itching.

**keenness** noun **1** *the keenness of the blade* sharpness, razor-sharpness. **2** *the keenness of her sense of smell* sharpness, acuteness, perceptiveness, sensitivity. **3** *the keenness of his mind* sharpness, astuteness, quick-wittedness, sharp-wittedness, perspicacity, shrewdness, cleverness, intelligence. **4** *the keenness of her wit* acerbity, acidity, causticity, tartness. **5** *the keenness of the students* willingness, eagerness, enthusiasm, avidity, zeal, fervor, devotion, impatience.

**keep** verb **1** *keep going* carry on, continue, maintain, persist, persevere. **2** *he keeps* *the ring that she gave him* retain, hold on to, keep hold of; preserve, conserve; *inf.* hang on to. **3** *he keeps all his old newspapers* save, accumulate, store, hoard, collect. **4** *the druggist keeps (a supply of) insulin* sell, stock, have in stock, carry. **5** *he is responsible for keeping the estate* look after, tend, mind, maintain, manage, superintend. **6** *the boy keeps the sheep | keep him from harm* tend, care for, look after, mind, guard, safeguard, protect, watch over, shield, shelter, preserve, protect. **7** *he could not keep a family on his salary* provide for, support, maintain, sustain, subsidize, feed, nurture. **8** *keep it from her* hide, conceal, withhold, hush, suppress. **9** *keep one's promise* abide by, fulfill, carry out, effectuate, stand by, honor, obey, observe. **10** *keep the Sabbath* observe, hold, celebrate, commemorate, respect, ritualize, solemnize, ceremonialize. **11** *what kept you?* delay, detain, hold back, hold up, retard, hinder, obstruct, impede, hamper, prevent. **12** *keep myself from falling* prevent, stop, restrain, check, halt. **keep at** *the teacher kept at us to work* badger, nag, harass. **keep at it** *we'll finish in time if we keep at it* persist, persevere, carry on, continue. **keep off 1** *keep off his property* stay away from, stay off, remain at a distance from, not approach, not trespass on. **2** *keep off the subject* avoid, steer clear of, not mention, evade, dodge, shun, eschew. **3** *keep off cigarettes* refrain from, abstain from, give up, quit. **4** *the rain kept off* stay away, not start, not begin. **keep on 1** *keep on going* go on, carry on, continue, persist, persevere. **2** *the boss decided to keep the man on* continue to employ, retain the services of, not dismiss. **keep to 1** *keep to his word* abide by, stand by, honor. *See* KEEP *verb* 9. **2** *keep to the subject* not stray from, not wander from, stay with; *inf.* stick with. **keep up 1** *keep up the payments* maintain, continue with, carry on with. **2** *try to keep up in the race* keep pace, keep abreast, not lag behind. **keep up with 1** *keep up with the competitors/developments* keep pace with, keep abreast of, compete with, vie with, rival; keep informed about, retain an interest in. **2** *keep up with old friends* stay in touch with, keep in contact with, remain in correspondence with.

**keep** noun **1** *pay for their keep* maintenance, support, board, room and board, subsistence, sustenance, food, livelihood, upkeep. **2** *enemies storming the keep* donjon, dungeon, tower, stronghold, citadel, fortress, fort, castle.

**keeper** noun **1** *prisoners escaping their keeper* jailer, warden, guard, custodian, sentry. **2** *a lighthouse keeper* curator, conservator, attendant, caretaker, steward, superintendent, overseer, administrator. **3** *his brother's keeper* guardian, escort, bodyguard, chaperon, nursemaid, nurse.

**keeping** noun **1** *children/property in the keeping of the grandfather* guardianship, protection, trusteeship, trust, safekeeping, care, charge, custody. **2** *behavior in keeping with their beliefs* agreement, harmony, accordance, accord, concurrence, conformity, consistency.

**keepsake** noun memento, souvenir, remembrance, reminder, token of remembrance.

**keg** noun barrel, cask, vat, tun, butt, drum, hogshead, firkin.

**kernel** noun **1** *grown from a kernel* grain, seed, germ, stone, nut. **2** *the kernel of the problem* nub, nucleus, core, center, heart, marrow, pith, substance, essence.

**key** noun **1** *key in the lock* latchkey, passkey, master key, skeleton key. **2** *the key to the problem* answer, solution, explanation, clue, cue, pointer, interpretation, clarification, exposition, translation. **3** *musical key* tone, pitch, tonality.

**keystone** noun **1** *the keystone of the pillar* cornerstone, central stone, quoin. **2** *the keystone of the theory* principle, basis, foundation, linchpin.

**kick** verb **1** *kick the ball* boot, punt. **2** *the gun kicked* recoil, spring back. **3** *always kicking about something* protest, resist, oppose, rebel, spurn, object, complain, grumble; *inf.* gripe, grouse, beef, bitch. **4** *kick the habit* give up, stop, abandon, quit. **kick around 1** *kick around the poor people* abuse, mistreat, maltreat. **2** *kick around ideas* discuss, talk over, debate. **kick off** *kick off the proceedings* start, begin, commence, open, get under way, initiate. **kick out** eject, expel, force out, turn out, oust, evict, dismiss, discharge; *inf.* send packing, sack, fire.

**kick** noun **1** *gave the ball a kick* boot, punt. **2** *she steals for kicks* thrill, excitement, stimulation, fun, pleasure, enjoyment, amusement, gratification; *inf.* buzz. **3** *the drink has quite a kick* strength, potency, tang, zip; *inf.* punch, zing. **4** *there's no kick left in the campaign* vigor, force, forcefulness, energy, vitality, verve, animation, enthusiasm, zest, zip.

**kid** noun child, young one, youngster, toddler, tot, adolescent, juvenile, teenager, youth.

**kid** verb **1** *he was only kidding* tease, joke, jest, fool around. **2** *don't kid yourself* deceive, delude, fool, trick, cozen, gull, hoodwink, bamboozle.

**kill** verb **1** *he killed three people* slay, murder, do away with, slaughter, butcher, massacre, assassinate, liquidate, take someone's life, wipe out, destroy, erase, eradicate, exterminate, eliminate, dispatch, put to death, execute; *inf.* bump off, do in, knock off, rub out. **2** *kill all his hopes* destroy, ruin, extinguish, scotch, quell. **3** *kill time* pass, spend, expend, while away. **4** *the walk will kill you* exhaust, overtire, fatigue, wear out, overtax, strain. **5** *kill the congressional bill* defeat, veto, vote down, reject, overrule.

**killing** noun **1** *guilty of killing* murder, slaying, manslaughter, homicide, slaughter, butchery, massacre, bloodshed, carnage, liquidation, destruction, extermination, execution. **2** *make a killing on the stock market* bonanza, fortune, windfall, gain, profit, coup.

**killing** adjective **1** *a killing blow* deadly, fatal, lethal, mortal, death-dealing, murderous, homicidal. **2** *a killing task* exhausting, tiring, fatiguing, debilitating, taxing, punishing.

**killjoy** noun spoilsport; *inf.* wet blanket, party pooper.

**kin** noun *no kin living in the area* relatives, relations, family, connections, folks, people, kindred, kinfolk, kinsfolk.

**kind** adjective kindhearted, generous, charitable, benevolent, magnanimous, bighearted, warmhearted, altruistic, philanthropic, humanitarian, humane, tenderhearted, softhearted, gentle, mild, lenient, merciful, clement, pitying, forbearing, patient, tolerant, sympathetic, compassionate, understanding, considerate, helpful, thoughtful, good, nice, decent, pleasant, benign, friendly, genial, congenial, amiable, amicable, cordial, courteous, gracious, good-natured, warm, affectionate, loving, indulgent, obliging, accommodating, neighborly.

**kind** noun **1** *different kinds of creatures* sort, type, variety, brand, class, category; genus, species, family, strain. **2** *a difference in kind rather than degree* nature, character, manner, aspect, disposition, type, stamp, mold.

**kindle** verb **1** *kindle a fire* light, set fire to, ignite, start, torch. **2** *kindle interest* stimulate, rouse, arouse, excite, stir, awaken, inspire, inflame, touch off.

**kindly** adjective kindhearted, warmhearted. *See* KIND adjective.

**kindness** noun **1** *the kindness of the people* kindheartedness, generosity, charitableness, charity, goodwill, benevolence, magnanimity, hospitality, philanthropy, warmheartedness, altruism, humanitarianism, humaneness, tender-heartedness, gentleness, mildness, leniency, clemency, patience, tolerance, sympathy, compassion, understanding, consideration, helpfulness, thoughtfulness, goodness, niceness, decency, pleasantness, friendliness, geniality, congeniality, amiability, cordiality, graciousness, warmth, affection, loving-

ness, love, indulgence, neighborliness. **2** *do the neighbors a kindness* kind act, good deed, good turn, favor, help, service, aid.

**kindred** adjective **1** *kindred members of the wedding party* related, connected, of the same blood, consanguineous. **2** *kindred spirits* like, similar, corresponding, matching, congenial, allied.

**king** noun **1** *king of Sweden* monarch, sovereign, ruler, crowned head, majesty, royal personage, emperor, sultan, overlord, prince. **2** *king of jazz* luminary, star, superstar, kingpin.

**kingdom** noun **1** *the ruler's kingdom* realm, empire, domain, country, land, nation, state, province, territory; monarchy, sovereignty. **2** *the plant kingdom* division, grouping, group, classification, class, category, family, genus, kind.

**kink** noun **1** *a kink in the rope* twist, bend, coil, corkscrew, knot, tangle, entanglement. **2** *a kink in one's hair* curl, wave, crimp, frizz, crinkle. **3** *a kink in the neck* crick, spasm, twinge. **4** *a few kinks in the plan* flaw, defect, imperfection, hitch, snag, difficulty, complication. **5** *a person full of kinks* quirk, whimsy, caprice, vagary, eccentricity, foible, idiosyncrasy.

**kinky** adjective **1** *a kinky rope* twisted, bent, coiled, curled. **2** *kinky hair* curly, crimped, frizzy. **3** *kinky ideas* quirky, peculiar, odd, strange, queer, bizarre, eccentric, idiosyncratic, weird, outlandish, unconventional, unorthodox, whimsical, capricious, fanciful. **4** *kinky sexual behavior* deviant, abnormal, degenerate, perverted, warped, lascivious, licentious.

**kinship** noun **1** *kinship was thought more of than friendship* blood relationship, blood ties, family ties, consanguinity, common ancestry, common lineage, kindred. **2** *kinship between their interests* affinity, similarity, likeness, correspondence, concordance, alliance, association.

**kismet** noun destiny, fate, fortune, providence, portion, lot, predestination, preordination, predetermination.

**kit** noun **1** *bicycle repair kit* equipment, apparatus, tools, implements, instruments, utensils, gear, tackle, supplies, paraphernalia, accoutrements, effects, stuff, trappings, appurtenances; *inf.* things. **2** *build furniture from a kit* set of parts, set of components; do-it-yourself kit.

**knack** noun talent, aptitude, gift, flair, bent, forte, ability, capacity, expertise, skill, genius, facility, propensity, adroitness, readiness, quickness, ingenuity, proficiency, handiness.

**knave** noun scoundrel, blackguard, villain, rogue, reprobate, miscreant, rascal, cur, louse.

**knickknack** noun trifle, trinket, bauble, gewgaw, gimcrack, bagatelle, bibelot, piece of bric-à-brac.

**knife** noun blade, cutting tool, dagger, dirk; machete, sword; stiletto, scalpel; Swiss Army (*trademark*) knife; cleaver, paring knife, table knife, steak knife, penknife, pocket knife, bowie knife, jackknife, switchblade.

**knife** verb stab, pierce, run through, impale, bayonet, cut, slash, lacerate.

**knight** noun horseman, equestrian, cavalryman, gallant, protector, knight errant, Sir Lancelot, Sir Galahad; dragon slayer.

**knit** verb 1 *knit wool into a sweater* loop, weave, interweave, crochet. 2 *knit one's brows* wrinkle, crease, furrow, gather, draw in, contract. 3 *the tragedy knitted the community together* join, link, bind, unite, draw (together), ally. 4 *the wound is knitting* heal, mend, become whole, draw together.

**knob** noun 1 *the knob on the door/machine* doorknob, handle, switch. 2 *iron knobs on the saddle* stud, boss, protuberance, knop.

**knock** verb 1 *knock on the door* tap, rap, bang, pound, hammer. 2 *knock his head on the low doorframe* strike, hit, slap, smack, box, pound, cuff, buffet, thump, thwack, batter, pummel; *inf.* clip, wallop. 3 *knock the play* criticize, run down, shoot down, carp at, cavil at, deprecate, belittle, disparage, censure, condemn; *inf.* slam, lambaste, pan. **knock about/around** 1 *fighters knocking each other around* strike, hit, beat, beat up, batter, maul, punch, abuse, manhandle, hurt, injure, bruise, wound, damage. 2 *knock about the countryside* travel, wander, roam, ramble, rove, range, saunter, stroll, gallivant, traipse through/about, gad about. **knock down** 1 *knock down the buildings* demolish, pull down, level, raze. 2 *knock down the trees* fell, cut down, hew. **knock off** 1 *they knock off at 5 o'clock* stop work, finish working, close shop, shut down; *inf.* call it a day. 2 *knock off his rival* kill, slay, murder, assassinate, eliminate, do away with, dispose of; *inf.* do in, bump off, rub out. **knock out** 1 *knock him out with the blow* render unconscious, floor, prostrate; *inf.* KO. 2 *knock out his opponent in the first round* eliminate, defeat, beat, vanquish, overthrow. 3 *the storm knocked out the electrical supply* destroy, damage, make inoperative, put out of order. 4 *knocked out by her performance* overwhelm, dazzle, amaze, astound, impress; *inf.* bowl over. **knock up** make pregnant, impregnate, inseminate.

**knock** noun 1 *a knock at the door* tap, rap, rat-tat, bang. 2 *a knock on the head* slap, smack, blow, punch, cuff, buffet, thump; *inf.* clip, clout, wallop. 3 *the knocks of*

*the reviewers* criticism, strictures, faultfinding, carping, caviling, deprecation, disparagement, censure, condemnation.

**knot** noun 1 *a knot in the string/tie* loop, twist, bend, ligature, joint. 2 *a knot in the wood* lump, knob, node, nodule, protuberance, knurl, gnarl. 3 *a knot of people/trees* group, cluster, bunch, clump, band, circle, ring, gathering.

**knot** verb tie, loop, bind, secure, tether, lash.

**knotty** adjective 1 *a knotty problem* difficult, complicated, intricate, complex, Byzantine, thorny, perplexing, baffling, mystifying, obscure, unfathomable. 2 *a knotty piece of wood* knotted, gnarled, knurled, lumpy, bumpy, nodular, rough, coarse.

**know** verb 1 *know what they are saying* notice, perceive, realize, be aware of, sense, recognize. 2 *know the rules* understand, comprehend, apprehend, be familiar with. 3 *know tragedy* experience, undergo, go through, be acquainted with. 4 *get to know one's neighbors* be acquainted with, associate with, be friends with, socialize with, fraternize with. 5 *know one brand from another* distinguish, differentiate, tell, identify, discern.

**know-how** noun knowledge, savoir faire, expertise, skill, skillfulness, proficiency, adeptness, aptitude, ability, capability, competence.

**knowing** adjective 1 *give a knowing look* astute, shrewd, perceptive, meaningful, significant, eloquent, expressive. 2 *a knowing child* aware, astute, shrewd, perceptive, sophisticated, worldly-wise. 3 *a knowing infringement of rules* conscious, intentional, intended, deliberate, willful, purposeful, calculated, on purpose, by design.

**knowledge** noun 1 *be taught by people of knowledge* learning, erudition, scholarship, letters, education, enlightenment, wisdom. 2 *his knowledge of the subject* understanding, grasp, comprehension, apprehension, cognition, expertise, proficiency, know-how. 3 *his knowledge of the area* acquaintanceship, familiarity, conversance. 4 *where do you acquire the knowledge?* information, facts, intelligence, data; news, reports, rumors.

**knowledgeable** adjective *knowledgeable people* well-informed, informed, educated, learned, erudite, scholarly, well-read, cultivated, enlightened.

**known** adjective recognized, acknowledged, admitted, declared, avowed, confessed, published, revealed.

**kudos** noun prestige, glory, acclaim, acclamation, praise, tribute, honor.

# *Ll*

**label** noun **1** *put a label on the luggage* identification tag, ID tag, tag, sticker, marker. **2** *his friends gave him the label "Lefty"* epithet, name, nickname, title, sobriquet, designation, characterization; *inf.* moniker. **3** *goods sold under a famous label* brand, brand name, trade name, trademark, proprietary name, logo.

**label** verb **1** *label the specimens* tag, ticket, stamp, mark, put stickers on. **2** *label him a liar* describe, designate, identify, classify, categorize, brand, call, name, term, dub.

**labor** noun **1** *paid well for his labor* work, toil, exertion, effort, industry, industriousness, travail, drudgery. **2** *the labors of Hercules* task, job, chore, undertaking, commission, assignment, charge, venture. **3** *a lack of available labor* employees, workers, workforce, hands. **4** *in labor* childbirth, parturition, delivery, contractions, labor pains.

**labor** verb **1** *labor for little reward* toil, drudge, sweat, struggle, strive, work, endeavor, exert oneself, travail; *inf.* plug away. **2** *labor the point* belabor, overemphasize, overdo, strain, dwell on. **labor under** *laboring under a delusion* suffer from, be a victim of, be burdened by, be disadvantaged by.

**labored** adjective **1** *labored breathing* difficult, strained, forced, heavy, awkward. **2** *a labored style of writing* contrived, affected, studied, stiff, strained, stilted, forced, unnatural, artificial, overdone, overworked, heavy, ponderous, ornate, elaborate, convoluted, complex, laborious.

**laborer** noun worker, workman, hand, manual worker, unskilled worker, blue-collar worker, drudge, menial.

**laborious** adjective **1** *a laborious task* hard, heavy, difficult, arduous, strenuous, fatiguing, tiring, wearying, wearisome, tedious. **2** *the laborious style of the writer* strained, forced. *See* LABORED 2.

**labyrinth** noun maze, warren, network, convolution, entanglement, jungle, snarl, puzzle, riddle, enigma.

**lace** verb **1** *lace the shoes* fasten, secure, close, bind, tie, thread, string. **2** *lace the coffee with brandy* mix, blend, flavor, fortify, strengthen, stiffen; *inf.* spike.

**lacerate** verb tear, gash, slash, cut, mangle, hurt, wound, injure.

**lack** noun absence, want, need, deprivation, deficiency, privation, dearth, insufficiency, shortage, scarcity, paucity.

**lack** verb have need of, need, require, want, be short of, be deficient in, miss.

**lackadaisical** adjective indifferent, half-hearted, lukewarm, apathetic, listless, languid, lethargic, limp, sluggish, spiritless, unanimated, uninterested, unenthusiastic, idle, lazy.

**lackey** noun toady, sycophant, flatterer, flunky, minion, stooge, hanger-on, parasite, tool, puppet, instrument, pawn, creature; *inf.* yes-man.

**lackluster** adjective **1** *lackluster prose* bland, insipid, vapid, dull, flat, dry, prosaic, run-of-the-mill, commonplace, unimaginative, uninspired, boring, tedious, wearisome. **2** *lackluster people* dull, uninteresting, spiritless, unanimated, dull-witted.

**laconic** adjective **1** *a laconic reply* brief, concise, terse, succinct, short, economical, pithy, to the point, incisive. **2** *a laconic person* of few words, reticent, reserved, taciturn, quiet.

**lad** noun boy, youth, juvenile, youngster, stripling, young man; *inf.* kid.

**lady** noun **1** *give that lady your seat* woman, female. **2** *the lady and her servants* noblewoman, gentlewoman, duchess, countess, peeress, viscountess, baroness.

**ladylike** adjective genteel, refined, well-bred, cultivated, polished, decorous, proper, correct, respectable, well-mannered, courteous, polite, civil, gracious.

**lag** verb **1** *stop lagging and keep up* loiter, linger, dally, straggle, dawdle, hang back, delay, drag one's feet; *inf.* dilly-dally. **2** *their efforts were lagging* flag, wane, ebb, fall off, diminish, decrease, ease up, let up, slacken, abate, fail, falter.

**laggard** noun loiterer, lingerer, dawdler, straggler, sluggard, snail, slowpoke, loafer, lounger; *inf.* lazybones.

**laid-back** adjective relaxed, at ease, easy, leisurely, unhurried, casual, easygoing, informal, nonchalant, unexcitable, imperturbable; *inf.* unflappable.

**lair** noun **1** *the animal's lair* den, hole, covert, burrow, nest, tunnel, dugout, hollow, cave, haunt. **2** *retreat to his lair* retreat, hideaway, refuge, sanctuary, sanctum, sanctum sanctorum, study, den; *inf.* hide-out.

**laissez-faire** noun free enterprise, private enterprise, individualism, free trade, nonintervention, noninterference.

**lambaste** verb scold, reprimand, rebuke, chide, reprove, admonish, berate, upbraid, rail at, rant at; *inf.* lace into.

**lame** adjective **1** *a lame leg* limping, hobbling, halting, crippled, game, disabled, incapacitated, defective. **2** *a lame excuse* weak, feeble, thin, flimsy, unconvincing, unsatisfactory, inadequate, insufficient, deficient, defective, ineffectual.

**lament** verb **1** *widows lamenting* mourn, grieve, sorrow, wail, moan, groan, weep, cry, sob, complain, keen, ululate, howl, beat one's breast. **2** *lamenting the lack of sports facilities* bemoan, bewail, deplore, complain about.

**lament** noun **1** *the laments of the bereaved* wail, wailing, lamentation, moan, moaning, groan, weeping, crying, sob, sobbing, complaint, keening, ululation, howl. **2** *recite a lament* dirge, requiem, elegy, threnody.

**lamentable** adjective **1** *a lamentable state of affairs* deplorable, regrettable, tragic, terrible, wretched, woeful, sorrowful, distressing, grievous. **2** *a lamentable salary* miserable, pitiful, poor, meager, low, unsatisfactory, inadequate; *inf.* measly.

**lampoon** noun satire, burlesque, travesty, parody, caricature, pasquinade, takeoff; *inf.* send-up.

**lampoon** verb satirize, parody, caricature, ridicule, mock, make fun of, burlesque, pasquinade, do a takeoff of; *inf.* send up.

**land** noun **1** *glad to be back on land* ground, solid ground, earth, terra firma. **2** *the land is fertile there* soil, earth, loam, dirt. **3** *houses with plenty of land around them* grounds, fields, open space, open area, expanse, stretch, tract, property, acres, real estate, realty. **4** *born in a far land* country, nation, fatherland, motherland, state, realm, province, territory, district, region, area, domain.

**land** verb **1** *the plane landed* touch down, alight, make a landing. **2** *we landed at Boston* berth, dock, reach the shore, go ashore, disembark, debark. **3** *how did we land here?* arrive, get, reach, find oneself, end up, turn up; *inf.* wind up. **4** *land a good job* get, acquire, obtain, procure, secure, gain.

**landlady, landlord** noun owner, proprietor, lessor, householder; innkeeper, hotelkeeper, hotelier, host.

**landmark** noun **1** *one of the landmarks of the town* feature, monument, distinctive feature, prominent feature. **2** *a landmark in the town's history* milestone, watershed, turning point, critical point, historic

event. **3** *landmarks indicating the distance* milepost, milestone, guidepost, marker.

**lane** noun **1** *travel through the lanes* narrow road, narrow way, passageway, passage, alley, path, pathway, footpath, track. **2** *traffic lanes* track, course, road division.

**language** noun **1** *children acquiring language* speech, speaking, talking, words, vocabulary, utterance, verbal expression, verbalization, vocalization, communication, conversation, discourse. **2** *the French language* tongue, speech, parlance, native tongue; *inf.* lingo. **3** *various forms of language throughout the country* speech, dialect, vernacular, patois, lingua franca, colloquialism, slang, idiom, jargon, patter, cant; *inf.* lingo. **4** *admire the language of the speaker/writer* vocabulary, terminology, wording, phrasing, phraseology, style, diction, expression, rhetoric.

**languid** adjective **1** *languid people* languishing, listless, lackadaisical, spiritless, vigorless, lethargic, torpid, idle, inactive, indolent, lazy, sluggish, slow-moving, indifferent. **2** *feeling languid after her illness* weak, sickly, faint, feeble, frail, limp, flagging, drooping, fatigued. **3** *a languid response* apathetic, lukewarm, halfhearted, unenthusiastic.

**languish** verb **1** *she languished after the tragedy* droop, flag, wilt, wither, fade, fail, weaken, decline, waste away. **2** *people languishing in institutions* waste away, decay, wither away, be abandoned, be neglected. **languish for** *languish for her lover* pine for, yearn for, long for, sigh for, hunger for, desire, want, grieve for, mourn for.

**languor** noun **1** *feeling full of languor* listlessness, lethargy, torpor, idleness, indolence, laziness, sluggishness, sleepiness, drowsiness, somnolence. **2** *disturb the languor of the atmosphere* stillness, tranquillity, calm, calmness, lull, silence.

**lank** adjective **1** *lank hair* lifeless, lusterless, limp, straggling, straight. **2** *lank youths* tall, thin, lean, lanky, skinny, spindly, gangling, gangly, angular, bony, rawboned, gawky, rangy.

**lap** noun **1** *three laps of the stadium* circuit, circle, loop, orbit, round, compass, ambit. **2** *the last lap of the journey* section, stage, leg.

**lap** verb **1** *water lapping against the shore* wash, splash, swish, slap, slosh. **2** *cats lapping milk* drink, lick up, sip.

**lapse** noun **1** *forgive his occasional lapse* slip, error, mistake, blunder, fault, omission, oversight; *inf.* slipup. **2** *after a lapse of time* interval, gap, pause, intermission, interlude, lull, hiatus, break, passage. **3** *a lapse in standards* decline, downturn, fall, drop, deterioration, worsening, degeneration, backsliding. **4** *the lapse of her* *season ticket* expiry, expiration, invalidity, termination. **5** *lapse of faith* abandonment, forsaking, relinquishment, defection, renunciation, repudiation, rejection, disavowal, denial, abjuration, apostasy.

**lapse** verb **1** *standards have lapsed* decline, fall, fall off, drop, deteriorate, worsen, degenerate; *inf.* go downhill. **2** *our friendship lapsed when we left school* cease, end, stop, terminate. **3** *the season ticket has lapsed* become void, become invalid, expire, run out, terminate. **4** *lapse into sleep* slide, slip, drift, sink, subside, submerge. **5** *time has lapsed* elapse, pass, go by, glide by, run its course.

**larceny** noun theft, grand larceny, petty larceny, stealing, robbery, pilfering, purloining, burglary, misappropriation.

**large** adjective **1** *large buildings* big, great, sizable, substantial, goodly, tall, high, huge, immense, enormous, colossal, massive, mammoth, vast, prodigious, gigantic, giant, monumental, stupendous, gargantuan, considerable; *inf.* jumbo, whopping. **2** *a large man* big, burly, heavy, bulky, thickset, powerfully built, heavyset, chunky, strapping, hulking, hefty, ample, fat, obese, corpulent. **3** *a large supply* abundant, copious, plentiful, ample, liberal, generous. **at large 1** *wild animals at large* at liberty, free, unconfined, unrestrained, roaming, on the loose, on the run, fugitive. **2** *society at large* as a whole, as a body, generally, in general, in the main. **by and large** on the whole, generally, in general, all things considered, for the most part, in the main, as a rule.

**largely** adverb *he is largely to blame* to a large extent, to a great degree, chiefly, for the most part, mostly, mainly, in the main, principally, in great measure.

**large-scale** adjective extensive, widereaching, wide-ranging, sweeping, wholesale, global.

**largesse** noun **1** *known for her largesse* generosity, kindness, liberality, openhandedness, munificence, bounty, bountifulness, beneficence, charity, philanthropy. **2** *distributing largesse* gifts, presents, contributions, donations, handouts, endowments, grants, aid, alms.

**lark** noun prank, horseplay, trick, fooling, antic, mischief, escapade, fun, cavorting, caper, play, game, romp, frolic, sport, rollicking, gambol.

**lascivious** adjective **1** *lascivious men* lewd, lecherous, lustful, licentious, promiscuous, libidinous, prurient, salacious, lubricious, concupiscent, debauched, depraved, degenerate, dissolute, dissipated. **2** *lascivious magazines* lewd, blue, obscene, pornographic, smutty, bawdy, risqué, suggestive, dirty, salacious; *inf.* raunchy.

**lash** noun **1** *a lash to beat the horses* whip, horsewhip, bullwhip, scourge, flagellum, cat-o'-nine-tails. **2** *six lashes with a whip* stroke, stripe, blow, hit, strike, thwack, thump; *inf.* swipe, wallop, whack.

**lash** verb **1** *the driver lashed the horses* whip, horsewhip, scourge, birch, switch, flog, flail, flagellate, thrash, beat, strike; *inf.* wallop, whack. **2** *waves lashing the ship* buffet, pound, batter, strike. **3** *lions lashing their tails* flick, wag, wave, whip, switch. **4** *lash the boat to the side of the ship* fasten, bind, tie, tether, hitch, attach, join, rope, strap, leash, make fast, secure. **lash out at** *lash out at his critics* speak out against, shout at, lose one's temper at, attack verbally, denounce, harangue, rant at, fulminate against, criticize, condemn, censure; *inf.* lace into.

**lass** noun girl, young woman, young lady, schoolgirl, maid, maiden, miss; *inf.* lassie.

**last** adjective **1** *the last runner arrived* hindmost, rearmost, final, aftermost. **2** *his last words* final, closing, concluding, ending, finishing, terminating, ultimate, terminal. **3** *the last thing she would want* least likely, most unlikely, least suitable, least wanted, least favorite. **4** *last Thursday* latest, most recent.

**last** adverb *come last* at the end, at/in the rear, behind, after.

**last** verb **1** *how long will the symptoms last?* continue, go on, carry on, remain, persist, keep on. **2** *how long will the climbers last in the snow?* survive, exist, live, subsist, hold on, hold out. **3** *those shoes won't last* last long, wear well, stand up to wear, keep, endure.

**last-ditch** adjective *a last-ditch attempt* desperate, frantic, frenzied, wild, struggling, final, last-chance, last-minute, last-gasp, all-out.

**lasting** adjective enduring, long-lived, lifelong, abiding, continuing, long-term, persisting, permanent, deep-rooted, durable, constant, eternal, undying, everlasting, perennial, perpetual, unending, never-ending, immortal, ceaseless, unceasing, interminable, imperishable, indestructible.

**lastly** adverb finally, in conclusion, to conclude, to sum up.

**latch** noun catch, fastening, hasp, hook, bar, bolt, lock.

**latch** verb fasten, secure, make fast, bar, bolt, lock.

**late** adjective **1** *she's always late* tardy, overdue, delayed, behind schedule, behind, not on time, dilatory, slow. **2** *her late husband* deceased, dead, departed. **3** *some* *late news* recent, fresh, new, last-minute, up-to-date, up-to-the-minute.

**late** adverb **1** *he arrived late* belatedly, tardily, behind time, at the last minute, dilatorily. **2** *we worked late yesterday* past the usual finishing/stopping/closing time, after hours.

**lately** adverb of late, recently, in the past few days, in recent times.

**latent** adjective dormant, quiescent, inactive, passive, hidden, unrevealed, concealed, imperceptible, invisible, covert, undeveloped, unrealized, potential.

**later** adjective *the later bus* subsequent, next, following, succeeding, successive, sequential.

**later** adverb **1** *I'll come later* later on, at a future time/date, at some point in the future, in time to come. **2** *he arrived first, and she came later* later on, after, afterward, subsequently, by and by, in a while, after a bit.

**lateral** adjective sidewise, sideways, sidelong, sideward, edgewise, edgeways, indirect, oblique, slanting, askance.

**lather** noun **1** *soap producing lather* suds, soapsuds, foam, froth, bubbles. **2** *horses covered in lather* sweat, perspiration.

**latitude** noun **1** *on the same latitude as Moscow* parallel, meridian, grid line. **2** *give his staff latitude in decision-making* scope, freedom of action, freedom, liberty, free play, carte blanche, leeway, elbowroom, license, indulgence, laxity.

**latter** adjective **1** *the latter is the better* second, second-mentioned, last-mentioned, second of the two. **2** *the latter part of the year* later, hindmost, closing, end, concluding, final. **3** *the technology of latter times* recent, latest, modern.

**laudable** adjective praiseworthy, commendable, admirable, meritorious, deserving, creditable, worthy, estimable, exemplary.

**laudatory** adjective acclamatory, commendatory, praising, extolling, admiring, approving, approbatory, complimentary, adulatory, celebratory, eulogizing, eulogistic, panegyric, panegyrical, encomiastical.

**laugh** verb chuckle, chortle, guffaw, giggle, titter, snigger, ha-ha, tee-hee, burst out laughing, split one's sides, be rolling in the aisles; *inf.* be in stitches, crack up. **laugh at 1** *laugh at the fortune-tellers* mock, ridicule, deride, scoff at, jeer at, sneer at, make fun of, poke fun at, lampoon, satirize, taunt, tease; *inf.* send up. **2** *laugh at danger* laugh off, belittle, make light of, discount, ignore, dismiss, disregard, shrug off, brush aside, scoff at, pooh-pooh.

**laugh** noun chuckle, chortle, guffaw, giggle, titter, snigger, roar/hoot of laughter, peal of laughter, belly laugh.

**laughable** adjective **1** *a laughable business proposition* ludicrous, ridiculous, absurd, risible, preposterous, outrageous. **2** *children finding the entertainment laughable* amusing, funny, humorous, hilarious, comical, comic, entertaining, diverting, droll, mirthful, sidesplitting.

**laughter** noun laughing, chuckling, chortling, guffawing, giggling, tittering, sniggering.

**launch** verb **1** *launch the ship* set afloat, float. **2** *launch a missile* fire, discharge, propel, project, send forth, throw, cast, hurl, let fly. **3** *launch a project* initiate, instigate, set in motion, begin, start, commence, embark upon, institute, inaugurate, establish, introduce, usher in.

**laurels** plural noun honors, awards, trophies, prizes, rewards, tributes, praises, acclaim, acclamation, commendation, credit, glory, honor, distinction, fame, renown, prestige, recognition; *inf.* kudos.

**lavish** adjective **1** *a lavish supply* copious, abundant, superabundant, plentiful, profuse. **2** *lavish in her catering* extravagant, excessive, immoderate, profligate, unrestrained. **3** *a lavish hostess* generous, liberal, bountiful, openhanded, unstinting, free, munificent, overgenerous, extravagant. **4** *a lavish display of flowers* luxuriant, lush, gorgeous, sumptuous, costly, opulent, pretentious, showy.

**law** noun **1** *the law of the land* legal code, system of laws, body of laws, constitution, charter, rules and regulations, jurisprudence. **2** *the legislature issuing laws* statute, rule, regulation, enactment, act, decree, edict, ordinance, directive. **3** *moral laws* rule, principle, precept, standard, criterion, formula, tenet, doctrine, canon. **4** *law of nature* generalization, general truth, axiom, maxim, truism. **5** *a career in law* the legal profession, the bar. **6** *the law has arrived* police, authorities, officers of the law; *inf.* fuzz, cops.

**lawful** adjective **1** *lawful actions* legal, legitimate, licit, just, valid, permissible, allowable, rightful, proper, constitutional, sanctioned, authorized, warranted, approved, recognized. **2** *a lawful person* law-abiding, righteous, honorable, orderly, honest, upright, upstanding, peaceable, dutiful.

**lawless** adjective **1** *a lawless country* without law and order, anarchic, disorderly, ungoverned, unruly, insurrectionary, insurgent, revolutionary, rebellious, insubordinate, riotous, mutinous, seditious, terrorist. **2** *lawless actions* unlawful, illegal, illicit, criminal, felonious, miscreant.

**lawsuit** noun legal action, legal proceedings, suit, case, proceedings, litigation, trial.

**lawyer** noun attorney, legal adviser, counsel, criminal lawyer, civil lawyer, advocate, solicitor, legal practitioner.

**lax** adjective **1** *lax about discipline in the school* slack, slipshod, negligent, neglectful, remiss, careless, heedless, unmindful, inattentive, casual, easygoing, lenient, permissive, indulgent, overindulgent, complaisant. **2** *a lax description* loose, inexact, inaccurate, imprecise, unrigorous, vague, indefinite, nonspecific, broad, general.

**lay** verb **1** *lay the groceries on the table* put, place, set, deposit, plant, settle, posit. **2** *lay the carpet* position, set out, arrange, dispose. **3** *lay a case before a judge* put forward, bring forward, advance, submit, present, offer, lodge. **4** *lay the blame* attribute, assign, ascribe, allocate, allot, impute. **5** *lay money on it* wager, bet, gamble, stake, give odds, hazard, risk, chance. **6** *lay plans* devise, arrange, contrive, make, prepare, work out, hatch, concoct, design, plan, plot. **7** *lay the burden on him* impose, inflict, encumber, saddle, tax, charge, burden, apply. **8** *lay eggs* deposit, produce, bear, oviposit. **lay bare** *lay bare one's secret thoughts* reveal, make known, disclose, divulge, show, expose, exhibit, uncover, unveil, unmask. **lay down 1** *lay down their weapons* surrender, relinquish, give up, yield, cede, turn over. **2** *lay down the law* set down, stipulate, formulate, prescribe, order, command, ordain, postulate, demand, proclaim, assert, maintain. **lay (one's) hands on 1** *if I ever lay (my) hands on the thief* get (a) hold of, catch, seize, grab, snatch, grasp. **2** *I just can't lay (my) hands on that book* find, locate, unearth, bring to light, discover, acquire, turn up. **3** *priests laying hands on members of the congregation* bless, consecrate, confirm, ordain. **lay in** *lay in a supply of logs* stockpile, store, accumulate, amass, hoard, collect. **lay into 1** *lay into their attackers* set upon, assail, attack, strike out at. **2** *lay into the child for being late* scold, rebuke, chide, berate, upbraid, reproach, reprove, castigate, criticize, censure, condemn, rant at, rave at, harangue; *inf.* lace into, lambaste. **lay it on** *he's laying it on to charm his mother-in-law* exaggerate, overdo it, flatter, soft-soap; *inf.* pile it on, lay it on thick, sweet-talk. **lay off 1** *lay off half of the workforce* let go, dismiss, discharge; *inf.* sack, fire. **2** *lay off alcohol* quit, stop, cease, desist from, refrain from, give up. **lay out 1** *lay out the plans* spread out, set out, arrange, display, exhibit. **2** *lay out a garden* set out, arrange, plan, design. **3** *lay out refreshments* provide, supply, furnish, give. **4** *lay out a lot of money* spend,

expend, pay, disburse, contribute, give, invest; *inf.* shell out, fork out.

**lay** adjective **1** *a lay preacher* laic, laical, secular, nonclerical, nonordained. **2** *a lay member of the club* nonprofessional, amateur, nonspecialist, dilettante.

**layoff** noun *many layoffs at the factory* dismissal, discharge; *inf.* sacking, firing.

**layout** noun **1** *the layout of the house* arrangement, geography, plan. **2** *the magazine's layout* arrangement, design, format, formation.

**lazy** adjective idle, indolent, slothful, sluggish, lethargic, languorous, listless, torpid, slow-moving, remiss, negligent, lax.

**lead** verb **1** *lead him to the right spot* guide, conduct, show the way, usher, escort, steer, pilot. **2** *the evidence led her to believe he was guilty* cause, induce, prompt, move, incline, dispose, predispose, persuade, sway, influence, prevail on. **3** *lead the procession* head, be at the head of, be at the front of. **4** *lead the discussion* command, direct, govern, rule, manage, be in charge of, regulate, preside over, head, supervise, superintend, oversee; *inf.* head up. **5** *leading the field* be in the lead, be in front (of), be ahead (of), be first, come first, precede, outdistance, outrun, outstrip, leave behind, outdo, excel, exceed, surpass, outrival, outshine, eclipse, transcend. **6** *lead a happy life* live, pass, spend, experience, undergo. **lead off** begin, start, start off, commence, open; *inf.* kick off. **lead on** *they are just leading her on* deceive, mislead, delude, hoodwink, dupe, trick, beguile, tempt, entice, lure, tantalize, inveigle, seduce; *inf.* string along. **lead the way 1** *he led the way to the spot* guide one, conduct one, show (one) the way. **2** *the scientist led the way in space development* break ground, blaze a trail, lay the foundation, lay the first stone, initiate things, take the first step. **lead to** *his action led to disaster* cause, result in, bring on, call forth, provoke, contribute to.

**lead** noun **1** *the runner in the lead* first place, advance position, van, vanguard. **2** *take the lead in the market* first position, head place, forefront, primacy, pre-eminence, supremacy, advantage, edge, precedence. **3** *a lead of half a lap* margin, gap, interval. **4** *she's the lead in the new play* star, principal character, leading role, star/starring role, title role, principal part, leading man, leading lady, hero, heroine. **5** *a dog's lead* leash, tether, rein, cord, rope, chain. **6** *we have no leads in the investigation* clue, pointer, hint, tip, suggestion, indication, tip-off.

**leader** noun **1** *the leader of the country/committee* ruler, head, chief, commander, director, governor, principal, captain, skipper, manager, superintendent, supervisor, overseer, foreman, kingpin; *inf.* boss, head honcho. **2** *a leader of fashion* pacesetter, trendsetter, front runner. **3** *a leader in the field of genetics* innovator, pioneer, trailblazer, pathfinder, groundbreaker, originator, front runner.

**leadership** noun rule, command, directorship, direction, governorship, administration, captaincy, management, supervision, control, guidance, authority, superintendency, initiative, influence.

**leading** adjective **1** *play the leading role* chief, main, principal, foremost, supreme, paramount, dominant, superior, ruling, directing, guiding, controlling; *inf.* number-one. **2** *one of the leading writers* foremost, greatest, best, outstanding, preeminent, supreme, principal, top-rank, top-ranking, first-rate. **3** *the leading runner* front, first, in first place.

**leaf** noun **1** *a leaf from the tree* frond, flag, needle, pine needle, pad, lily pad; *Tech* cotyledon. **2** *a leaf missing from the book* page, sheet, folio, flyleaf. **turn over a new leaf** reform, mend/change one's ways, make a fresh start, start with a clean slate.

**leaflet** noun pamphlet, flyer, booklet, brochure, handbill, circular.

**league** noun **1** *a league of nations* alliance, confederation, confederacy, federation, union, association, coalition, combine, consortium, affiliation, guild, corporation, conglomerate, cooperative, partnership, fellowship, syndicate. **2** *a football league* group, band, association. **3** *he is not in the same league as his brother* level, class, category. **in league** in alliance, allied, cooperating, collaborating, linked, hand in glove, in collusion; *inf.* in cahoots.

**leak** noun **1** *a leak in the bucket* hole, opening, crack, crevice, chink, fissure, puncture, cut, gash, slit, rent, break, rift. **2** *a water/gas leak* drip, leakage, escape, seepage, oozing, discharge. **3** *a leak of secret information* disclosure, divulgence, revelation.

**leak** verb **1** *water/gas leaking* escape, drip, seep out/through, ooze out, exude, discharge, issue, gush out. **2** *leak information* disclose, divulge, reveal, tell, impart, pass on, relate, give away, let slip; *inf.* spill the beans about.

**lean** verb **1** *his wife leaning on his arm* rest, be supported, be propped up, recline, repose. **2** *the pole is leaning* incline, bend, slant, tilt, be at an angle, slope, bank, list, heel, careen. **lean on** *they lean on each other* depend on, be dependent on, rely on, count on, have faith in, trust. **lean toward** *she leans toward anarchy* incline toward, tend toward, have a tendency toward, have a propensity for, have

a proclivity for, gravitate toward, have an affinity with.

**lean** adjective **1** *lean people* thin, slender, slim, spare, lank, skinny, scrawny, bony, rawboned, rangy, gangling. **2** *lean meat* nonfat, low-fat. **3** *a lean harvest* meager, scanty, sparse, poor, inadequate, insufficient. **4** *lean years for art* unproductive, unfruitful, arid, barren, bare, nonfertile.

**leap** verb **1** *children leaping around* jump, bound, bounce, hop, skip, romp, caper, spring, frolic, frisk, cavort, gambol, dance. **2** *leap to one's feet* jump, jump up, spring. **3** *leap the obstacle* jump, jump over, high-jump, vault over, vault, spring over, bound over, hurdle, clear, sail over. **4** *leap to help* jump, hurry, hasten, rush. **5** *prices have leapt* soar, rocket, skyrocket, shoot up, escalate, mount. **leap at** *leap at the chance* accept eagerly, grasp, grab, take advantage of. **leap to** *leap to conclusions* arrive at hastily, reach hurriedly, form hastily.

**leap** noun **1** *clear the obstacle at the first leap* jump, vault, spring, bound, hop, skip. **2** *a leap in the number of unemployed* escalation, soaring, surge, upsurge, upswing, rapid increase, sudden rise. **by leaps and bounds** *progress by leaps and bounds* rapidly, swiftly, quickly, speedily, at an amazing rate.

**learn** verb **1** *learn French* acquire a knowledge of, become competent in, grasp, master, absorb, assimilate, pick up. **2** *learn the poem* memorize, commit to memory. **3** *we learned that he had gone* discover, find out, detect, become aware, gather, hear, be informed, understand, ascertain, discern, perceive.

**learned** adjective erudite, scholarly, well-educated, knowledgeable, well-read, well-versed, well-informed, lettered, cultured, intellectual, academic, literary, bookish, studious, pedantic, sage, wise; *inf.* highbrow.

**learning** noun **1** *a woman of learning* erudition, scholarship, knowledge, education, letters, culture, intellect, pedantry, sageness, wisdom. **2** *an opportunity for learning* study, studying, education, schooling, instruction.

**lease** verb **1** *lease a house/car from an agency* rent, hire, charter. **2** *lease their house to visitors* rent, rent out, let, hire, hire out, sublet, sublease.

**leash** noun **1** *a dog's leash* lead, rein, tether, rope, cord, chain. **2** *keep a tight leash on his anger* rein, curb, control, check, restraint, hold.

**leash** verb **1** *leash the dog* tether, tie up, fasten, secure. **2** *leash one's anger* curb, control, keep under control, check, restrain, hold back, suppress.

**leather** noun skin, hide, kid, doeskin, pigskin, suede.

**leave** verb 1 *leave hurriedly* depart, go away, go, withdraw, retire, take off, exit, take one's leave, make off, pull out, quit, decamp, disappear; *inf.* push off, shove off, split. 2 *leave for Bermuda* set off, set sail. 3 *leave his wife* abandon, desert, forsake, discard, turn one's back on, leave in the lurch. 4 *has left his job* give up, quit, abandon. 5 *leave his gloves at the hotel* forget, mislay, leave behind. 6 *leave the job to them* assign, allot, consign, hand over, give over, refer, commit, entrust. 7 *he left the estate to his nephew* bequeath, will, endow, hand down, transfer, convey; *fml.* devise. 8 *the quarrel left feelings of resentment* cause, produce, generate, result in. **leave in the lurch** let down, leave stranded, leave high and dry, abandon, desert, forsake. **leave out** *leave out a sentence* omit, fail to include, overlook. **leave out** *please leave him out of it* exclude from, omit from, except from, eliminate from, count out of, disregard from.

**leave** noun 1 *get leave to be absent* permission, consent, authorization, sanction, warrant, dispensation, concession, indulgence. 2 *going on (a) leave for three weeks* vacation, break, time off, furlough, sabbatical, leave of absence. 3 *they took their leave* departure, parting, withdrawal, exit, farewell, good-bye, adieu.

**lecherous** adjective lustful, promiscuous, carnal, sensual, licentious, lascivious, lewd, salacious, libertine, libidinous, lubricious, concupiscent, debauched, dissolute, wanton, intemperate, dissipated, degenerate, depraved; *inf.* horny, raunchy.

**lechery** noun lust, carnality, sensuality, licentiousness, lasciviousness, lewdness, salaciousness, salacity, libertinism, libidinousness, lubricity, concupiscence, debauchery, dissoluteness, wantonness, intemperance, dissipation, degeneracy, depravity; *inf.* horniness, raunchiness.

**lecture** noun 1 *attend a lecture on the environment* talk, speech, address, discourse, disquisition, lesson, sermon, homily, harangue. 2 *given a lecture for being late* scolding, chiding, reprimand, rebuke, reproof, reproach, remonstration, upbraiding, berating, tirade, diatribe; *inf.* dressing-down, talking-to.

**lecture** verb 1 *lectured on local politics* give a lecture, give a talk, talk, make a speech, speak, give an address, discourse, expound, hold forth, give a sermon, sermonize, harangue; *inf.* spout, jaw. 2 *lecture the children for being late* scold, chide, reprimand, rebuke, reprove, reproach, remonstrate with, upbraid, berate, castigate; *inf.* lambaste, tell off.

**ledge** noun shelf, sill, mantel, mantelpiece, projection, protrusion, overhang, ridge, step.

**leech** noun hanger-on, parasite, barnacle, sycophant, toady, bloodsucker, extortioner, sponger; *inf.* scrounger, freeloader.

**leer** verb leer at ogle, eye, wink at, watch, stare at, sneer at, smirk at; *inf.* give someone the once-over.

**leer** noun lascivious look, lecherous glance, wink, stare, sneer, smirk, grin; *inf.* the once-over.

**leery** adjective wary, chary, cautious, careful, guarded, on one's guard, suspicious, distrustful.

**leeway** noun room to maneuver, room to operate, latitude, elbowroom, slack, space, margin, play.

**left** adjective 1 *the left side* left-hand, sinistral, sinister, sinistrous; port. 2 *a left politician* left-wing, leftist, socialist, radical, progressive, liberal, communist.

**leftover** adjective remaining, excess, surplus, extra, uneaten, unused, unwanted.

**leftovers** plural noun remainder, excess, surplus, leavings, uneaten food, unused supplies, scraps, odds and ends.

**leg** noun 1 *her injured leg* lower limb, limb, member, appendage, shank; *inf.* drumstick. 2 *the legs of the tripod* support, upright, prop, brace, underpinning. 3 *the final leg of the journey* part, portion, segment, section, bit, stretch, stage, lap.

**legacy** noun 1 *a legacy of several million dollars* bequest, inheritance, heritage, bequeathal, endowment, gift, patrimony, heirloom; *fml.* devise. 2 *a legacy of Navajo culture | the legacy of unemployment* inheritance, heritage, tradition, hand-me-down, residue.

**legal** adjective 1 *legal behavior* lawful, legitimate, licit, valid, permissible, permitted, allowable, allowed, aboveboard, admissible, acceptable, authorized, sanctioned, warranted, licensed; *inf.* legit. 2 *legal processes* judicial, jurisdictive, forensic.

**legate** noun envoy, emissary, agent, ambassador, representative, commissioner, nuncio, messenger.

**legation** noun 1 *part of the American legation in Britain* mission, diplomatic mission, embassy, consulate, ministry, delegation, deputation, representation, envoys. 2 *the address of the American legation* embassy, consulate, diplomatic establishment, ministry.

**legend** noun 1 *a book of Scandinavian legends* myth, saga, epic, folk tale, folk story, tale, story, narrative, fable, romance. **2** *Greta Garbo became a legend* celebrity, star, superstar, luminary. **3** *the legends under the photographs* caption, inscription, dedication, motto, device. **4** *the legends accompanying the tables* key, code, cipher, explanation, table of symbols.

**legendary** adjective **1** *legendary figures in Icelandic saga* mythical, heroic, traditional, fabled, fictitious, fictional, storybook, romantic, fanciful. **2** *a legendary actor* celebrated, acclaimed, illustrious, famous, famed, renowned, immortal.

**legerdemain** noun **1** *magicians practicing legerdemain* sleight of hand, juggling, conjuring, prestidigitation, trickery, hocuspocus, thaumaturgy. **2** *a politician noted for his legerdemain* trickery, cunning, artfulness, craftiness, craft, wiles, deceit, deception, double-dealing, sophistry.

**legible** adjective readable, decipherable, clear, distinct, plain, neat.

**legion** noun **1** *legions of soldiers* army, brigade, regiment, battalion, company, troop, division, unit, force. **2** *legions of people arrived for the festival* horde, host, throng, multitude, crowd, drove, mass, mob, gang, swarm, flock, herd.

**legislation** noun **1** *his office is in charge of legislation* lawmaking, law enactment, law formulation, codification. **2** *dislike the new legislation* law, body of laws, constitution, rule(s), regulation(s), act(s), bill(s), statute(s), enactment(s), charter(s), ordinance(s), measure(s), canon, code.

**legislator** noun lawmaker, lawgiver, congressman, congresswoman, senator, parliamentarian, politician.

**legitimate** adjective **1** *legitimate actions* legal, lawful, licit; *inf.* legit. **2** *the legitimate heir* lawful, rightful, genuine, authentic, real, true, proper, correct, authorized, sanctioned, warranted, acknowledged, recognized, approved. **3** *a legitimate reason for being late* valid, sound, admissible, acceptable, well-founded, justifiable, reasonable, plausible, credible, believable, reliable, logical, rational; *inf.* legit, kosher.

**leisure** noun free time, spare time, idle hours, inactivity, time off, relaxation, recreation, freedom, holiday, vacation, respite; *inf.* time to kill. **at one's leisure** at one's convenience, when it suits one, without haste, unhurriedly, when one gets around to it.

**leisurely** adjective unhurried, relaxed, easy, easygoing, gentle, comfortable, restful, slow, lazy, lingering; *inf.* laid-back.

**lend** verb **1** *lend him a book* loan, advance. **2** *the flowers lend beauty to the room* impart, add, give, bestow, confer, provide, supply, furnish. **3** *lend his professional skill to the venture* contribute, donate, grant.

**lend a hand** help, help out, assist, give assistance, aid, make a contribution; *inf.* pitch in. **lend itself to** *the house does not lend itself to being divided* be suitable for, be suited to, be appropriate for, be adaptable to.

**length** noun **1** *what length is the yarn?* distance, extent, linear measure, span, reach. **2** *a length of time* period, stretch, duration, term, span. **3** *a length of cloth* piece, portion, section, measure, segment, swatch. **4** *a speech noted for its length* lengthiness, extensiveness, protractedness, prolixity, wordiness, verbosity, verboseness, long-windedness, tediousness, tedium. **at length 1** *speak at length* for a long time, on and on, interminably, endlessly. **2** *deal at length with the problem* fully, to the fullest extent, in detail, in depth, thoroughly, exhaustively, completely. **3** *at length he agreed to accept* finally, at last, eventually, in the end, ultimately, in time.

**lengthen** verb **1** *lengthen a skirt* make longer, elongate, let down. **2** *the days are lengthening* grow longer, get longer, draw out, stretch. **3** *lengthen the time taken* prolong, increase, extend, expand, protract, stretch out, draw out.

**lengthy** adjective **1** *a lengthy affair* long, long-lasting, prolonged, extended, protracted, long-drawn-out. **2** *a lengthy speech* long, protracted, long-drawn-out, diffuse, discursive, verbose, wordy, prolix, long-winded, tedious.

**lenient** adjective **1** *a lenient judge* merciful, clement, sparing, moderate, compassionate, humane, forbearing, tolerant, liberal, magnanimous, indulgent. **2** *a lenient jail sentence* mild, merciful, moderate.

**less** adjective *of less importance* smaller, slighter, not so much.

**lessen** verb **1** *the pain lessened* abate, decrease, diminish, subside, moderate, slacken, die down, let up, ease off, ebb, wane. **2** *the massage lessened the pain* relieve, soothe, allay, assuage, alleviate, palliate, ease, dull, deaden, blunt, take the edge off. **3** *his behavior lessened him in their eyes* diminish, lower, reduce, minimize, degrade, discredit, devalue, belittle.

**lesser** adjective less important, minor, slighter, secondary, inferior, subordinate.

**lesson** noun **1** *have a music lesson* class, period of instruction/teaching/coaching/tutoring/schooling. **2** *children doing lessons* exercise, schoolwork, homework, assignment. **3** *reading the lesson in church* Bible passage, Bible reading, scripture, text. **4** *punished as a lesson to others* example, warning, deterrent, message, moral, precept. **5** *hardship taught him valuable lessons* knowledge, wisdom, enlightenment, experience.

**let** verb **1** *let them play there* allow to, permit to, give permission to, give leave to, authorize to, sanction to, grant to, warrant to, license to; *inf.* give the green light to. **2** *let the people through* allow to go, permit to pass. **3** *let it be known* cause, make, enable. **let down 1** *he let them down* fail, disappoint, disillusion, forsake, leave stranded, betray. **2** *let down the skirt* lengthen, make longer. **let in** allow to enter, admit, open the door to, give access to, receive, welcome, greet. **let in on** *let them in on the deal* include in, count in on, admit. **let off 1** *let off the firework* explode, detonate. **2** *letting off fumes* give off, discharge, emit, release, exude, leak. **3** *let the guilty man off* acquit, release, discharge, reprieve, absolve, exonerate, pardon, forgive, exempt, spare. **let on 1** *don't let on that you know him* reveal, make known, tell, disclose, divulge, give away, leak. **2** *he let on that he was deaf* pretend, feign, affect, make believe, simulate, fake. **let out 1** *let the caged animals out* release, liberate, allow to leave, open the door for, let go, free, set free. **2** *she let out a scream* emit, utter, give vent to, produce. **let up 1** *the storm finally let up* lessen, abate, decrease, diminish, subside, moderate, slacken, die down, ease off, ebb, wane. **2** *please let up on the child* treat less severely, be more lenient with, be kinder to; *inf.* go easy on.

**letdown** noun disappointment, disillusionment, fiasco, anticlimax; *inf.* washout.

**lethal** adjective fatal, deadly, mortal, death-dealing, murderous, poisonous, toxic, dangerous, virulent, noxious, destructive, disastrous, calamitous, ruinous.

**lethargic** adjective sluggish, inactive, slow, slothful, torpid, phlegmatic, listless, languid, apathetic, passive.

**lethargy** noun sluggishness, inertia, inactivity, sloth, idleness, torpor, torpidity, lifelessness, dullness, listlessness, languor, languidness, apathy, passivity, lassitude.

**letter** noun **1** *written in bold letters* character, alphabetical character, sign, symbol. **2** *send a letter* written message, communication, note, line, missive, epistle, dispatch, billet-doux, fan mail, reply, acknowledgment. **to the letter** *follow our instructions to the letter* strictly, precisely, exactly, accurately, literally, word for word, verbatim.

**letup** noun lessening, abatement, decrease, diminishing, diminution, moderation, slackening, dying down, easing off, ebbing, waning.

**level** adjective **1** *a level surface* flat, smooth, even, uniform, plane, flush, horizontal. **2** *keep the temperature level* even, uniform, regular, consistent, constant, stable, steady, unchanging, unvarying, unfluctuating. **3** *hang the pictures level with each other* at the same height, aligned, in line, balanced. **4** *have a level temper* even, equable, steady, stable, calm, serene, tranquil, composed, unruffled.

**level** noun **1** *at eye level* height, altitude, elevation. **2** *what level is he in the firm?* position, rank, standing, status, station, degree, grade, stage, standard. **3** *levels of rock* layer, stratum, bed. **4** *what level do you live on?* floor, story. **on the level** honest, aboveboard, straight, fair, genuine, true, sincere, open, straightforward; *inf.* upfront.

**level** verb **1** *level the surface* even off, even out, make flat, flatten, smooth, smooth out, plane. **2** *level the buildings* raze, demolish, flatten, bulldoze, pull down, knock down, tear down, lay waste, destroy. **3** *level his opponent* knock down, knock to the ground, lay out, flatten, floor, fell, knock out; *inf.* KO. **4** *level his gun at the target* aim, point, direct, train, sight, focus, beam, zero in on, draw a bead on. **level with** be honest with, be aboveboard with, tell the truth to, be frank with, be open with, hide nothing from, be straightforward with; *inf.* be upfront with.

**levelheaded** adjective sensible, prudent, circumspect, reasonable, rational, sane, composed, calm, cool, collected, coolheaded, balanced, self-possessed, unruffled, even-tempered, imperturbable; *inf.* unflappable, together.

**leverage** noun **1** *not enough leverage to move the load* purchase, force, strength. **2** *not have the leverage to win over the committee* power, influence, authority, weight, ascendancy, rank; *inf.* pull, clout.

**levity** noun lightheartedness, humor, facetiousness, fun, jocularity, hilarity, frivolity, flippancy, triviality, silliness, giddiness.

**levy** noun **1** *the levy of taxes* collection, gathering, raising, imposition, exaction, assessment. **2** *unable to pay the levy* tax, taxation, tariff, toll, excise, customs, duty, dues, imposition, impost, assessment.

**levy** verb **1** *levy taxes* collect, gather, raise, impose, exact, demand, charge, tax. **2** *levy troops* conscript, call up, draft, enlist, muster, mobilize, rally, press.

**lewd** adjective **1** *lewd behavior* lecherous, lustful, licentious, lascivious, promiscuous, carnal, sensual, prurient, salacious, lubricious, libidinous, concupiscent, debauched, dissipated, dissolute, profligate, unchaste, wanton. **2** *lewd literature* obscene, pornographic, blue, bawdy, salacious, suggestive, ribald, indecent, vulgar, crude, smutty, dirty, coarse; *inf.* raunchy.

**liability** noun **1** *admit liability for the lost*

*goods* responsibility, accountability, blame, culpability. **2** *meet his financial liabilities* obligation, debt, indebtedness, debit, arrears, dues. **3** *the extra suitcase proved to be a liability* hindrance, encumbrance, burden, impediment, handicap, nuisance, inconvenience, drawback, drag, disadvantage, millstone around one's neck. **4** *he has a liability to cheat* aptness, likelihood, inclination, tendency, disposition, predisposition.

**liable** adjective *not liable for customers' lost property* responsible, accountable, answerable, chargeable, at fault. **liable to 1** *liable to injury* exposed to, open to, subject to, susceptible to, vulnerable to, in danger of, at risk of. **2** *liable to burst into tears* apt to, likely to, inclined to, tending to, disposed to, predisposed to, prone to.

**liaison** noun **1** *no liaison between the offices* communication, contact, connection, interchange, link, linkage. **2** *he acts as liaison between the departments* intermediary, contact person, go-between. **3** *his wife found out about his liaison* affair, adulterous affair, love affair, relationship, romance, intrigue, amour, flirtation; *inf.* hanky-panky.

**liar** noun fibber, perjurer, falsifier, false witness, fabricator, equivocator, prevaricator, deceiver.

**libel** noun defamation of character, defamation, slander, false report, denigration, vilification, disparagement, derogation, aspersions, calumny, traducement, obloquy, abuse, slur, smear, smear campaign.

**liberal** adjective **1** *a liberal supply of food* abundant, copious, ample, plentiful, lavish, profuse, munificent, bountiful, rich, handsome, generous. **2** *hosts liberal with their hospitality* generous, magnanimous, openhanded, unsparing, unstinting, lavish, beneficent, bighearted, kindhearted, kind, philanthropic, charitable, altruistic, unselfish. **3** *too liberal to abide such discrimination* tolerant, unprejudiced, unbiased, unbigoted, impartial, nonpartisan, broad-minded, enlightened, catholic. **4** *a liberal interpretation of the law* broad, loose, flexible, nonrestrictive, free, general, nonliteral, inexact, imprecise. **5** *liberal in his politics* advanced, forward-looking, progressive, reformist, radical, latitudinarian. **6** *a liberal education* wide-ranging, broad-based, general, humanistic.

**liberate** verb emancipate, set free, free, release, let go, discharge, set loose, unshackle, unfetter, unchain, deliver, rescue, manumit.

**libertine** adjective licentious, lustful, lecherous, lascivious, dissolute, dissipated, debauched, immoral, wanton, decadent, depraved, profligate, rakish, sensual, promiscuous, unchaste, impure, sinful, intemperate, corrupt.

**libertine** noun lecher, seducer, profligate, rake, roué, wanton, sensualist, reprobate, womanizer, adulterer, Don Juan, Lothario, Casanova; *inf.* lech.

**liberty** noun **1** *countries that have liberty* freedom, independence, autonomy, sovereignty, self-government, self-rule. **2** *prisoners gaining their liberty* freedom, liberation, release, discharge, deliverance, emancipation, manumission. **3** *have the liberty to choose* freedom, free will, volition, latitude, option, choice. **4** *given the liberty to leave the grounds* right, prerogative, privilege, permission, sanction, authorization, license, dispensation, exemption. **at liberty 1** *the thief/animal is still at liberty* free, loose, on the loose, at large, unconfined. **2** *you are at liberty to do as you wish* free, permitted, allowed, entitled. **take liberties** *taking liberties with the staff* be overfamiliar, be familiar, be disrespectful, breach etiquette, be impertinent, be insolent, be impudent, be presumptuous, be forward, be audacious.

**license** noun **1** *license to sell their wares* permission, leave, consent, authority, authorization, sanction, approval, warranty, certification, accreditation, entitlement, privilege, prerogative, right, dispensation, exemption. **2** *they have the license to do as they please* freedom, liberty, latitude, choice, option, independence, self-determination. **3** *a driver's license* permit, certificate, credential, document, documentation, pass.

**license** verb authorize, permit, allow, entitle, sanction, empower, warrant, certify, accredit, charter, franchise.

**licentious** adjective dissolute, lustful, lecherous, lascivious, dissipated, debauched, immoral, wanton, decadent, depraved, profligate, sensual, promiscuous, unchaste, impure, intemperate.

**lick** verb **1** *lick the ice cream* tongue, taste, lap. **2** *flames licking the walls* touch, play over, flick over, dart over, ripple over. **3** *lick the opponents* defeat, beat, conquer, trounce, thrash, rout, vanquish, overcome, overwhelm, overpower, drub; *inf.* wipe the floor with. **4** *lick the problem* get the better of, overcome, solve.

**lid** noun cover, top, cap, cork, stopper, plug.

**lie**[1] noun untruth, falsehood, fib, fabrication, invention, piece of fiction, falsification, falsity, prevarication; *inf.* tall tale, whopper.

**lie**[2] verb *the witness was lying* perjure oneself, fib, invent/make up a story, prevaricate, depart from the truth.

**lie**[3] verb **1** *he was lying, not sitting* recline,

sprawl, rest, repose, relax, lounge, loll, be recumbent, be prostrate, be supine, be prone, be stretched out. **2** *the town lies on the other side of the hill* be situated, be located, be placed, be positioned, be found. **3** *two poets lie there* be buried, be interred. **4** *lie dormant* remain, continue, stay. **5** *their strength lies in their faith* consist, exist, reside, be inherent. **lie low** *they lay low during the police search* hide, go into hiding, hide out, conceal oneself, keep out of sight, keep a low profile, take cover, go underground; *inf.* hole up.

**life** noun **1** *as long as there is life in my body* existence, being, animation, viability. **2** *is there life on Mars?* living things, living beings, living creatures, human/animal/plant life, fauna, flora. **3** *many lives were lost in the war* person, human being, individual, mortal, soul. **4** *worked hard all her life* lifetime, days, course of life, life span, time on earth, existence, career. **5** *the life of a battery* duration, active life, period of usefulness. **6** *that's life* the human condition, the way of the world, the way it is, the way things go. **7** *an affluent life* way of living, manner of living, lifestyle, situation, position. **8** *he wrote a life of the poet* biography, autobiography, life story, memoirs, history, career, diary, journal, confessions. **9** *put some life in the party* animation, vivacity, liveliness, vitality, verve, high spirits, sparkle, exuberance, buoyancy, effervescence, enthusiasm, energy, vigor, dynamism; *inf.* pizazz, pep, zing. **10** *he was the life of the firm* life force, vital spirit, spirit, moving force, lifeblood, very essence, essence, heart, core, soul. **give one's life 1** *he gave his life for his friend* die, sacrifice oneself. **2** *give one's life to teaching* dedicate oneself, devote oneself, give oneself, pledge oneself, surrender oneself.

**lifeblood** noun life force, animating spirit, moving force, driving force, vital spark, inspiration, animus, essence, heart, core, élan vital.

**lifeless** adjective **1** *lifeless bodies* dead, deceased, cold, defunct; motionless, limp. **2** *lifeless statues lined the corridor* inanimate, inorganic, abiotic. **3** *lifeless stretches of country* barren, sterile, bare, desolate, stark, arid, unproductive, uncultivated, empty, uninhabited, unoccupied. **4** *a lifeless performance* spiritless, lacking vitality, unspirited, lackluster, apathetic, uninspired, colorless, dull, flat, stiff, wooden, tedious, uninspiring.

**lift** verb **1** *lift the furniture* pick up, uplift, hoist, upheave, raise, raise up, heft. **2** *your visit lifted his spirits* raise, buoy up, boost, elevate. **3** *the mist lifted* rise,

disperse, dissipate, disappear, vanish, be dispelled. **4** *lift the ban* raise, remove, withdraw, revoke, rescind, cancel, annul, void, countermand, relax, end, stop, terminate. **5** *lift one's voice* raise, make louder, amplify. **6** *lift a passage from the book* plagiarize, pirate, copy, abstract. **7** *someone lifted my purse* steal, thieve, rob, pilfer, purloin, filch, pocket, take, appropriate; *inf.* pinch, swipe.

**lift** noun **1** *give the child a lift up* hoist, heave, push, thrust, shove, help, a helping hand. **2** *the visitors gave the patient a lift* boost, pick-me-up, stimulus; *inf.* shot in the arm. **3** *the new player gave their game a lift* boost, improvement, enhancement, upgrading. **4** *give the children a lift to school* ride, car ride, transportation.

**light**[1] noun **1** *see by the light of the fire* illumination, luminescence, luminosity, gleaming, brightness, brilliance, glowing, blaze, glare, incandescence, effulgence, refulgence, radiance, luster. **2** *bring the light over here* lamp, flashlight, lantern, beacon, candle, taper, torch. **3** *we like to travel in the light, not the dark* daylight, daylight hours, daytime, day, hours of sunlight. **4** *see things in a different light* aspect, angle, slant, approach, viewpoint, point of view. **5** *light finally dawned on me* enlightenment, illumination, understanding, comprehension, awareness, knowledge, elucidation, explanation. **bring to light** *the search brought to light new evidence* reveal, disclose, expose, uncover, show up, unearth, bring to notice. **come to light** *new evidence came to light* appear, come out, turn up, be discovered, be uncovered, be unearthed, be brought to light. **in the light of** *in the light of his previous convictions* considering, taking into consideration, taking into account, bearing in mind, keeping in mind, mindful of, taking note of, in view of. **shed/throw (any) light on** *can you shed (any) light on this matter?* elucidate, clarify, clear up, explain, offer an/any explanation for.

**light**[2] adjective **1** *a light room* full of light, bright, well-lit, well-lighted, well-illuminated, sunny. **2** *wearing light clothes* light-colored, light-toned, pale-colored, pastel, pastel-colored, faded, bleached. **3** *she had light hair* light-colored, fair, blond.

**light**[3] verb **1** *light the kindling* ignite, kindle, set burning, set fire to, set a match to. **2** *fireworks lit up the sky* illuminate, brighten, lighten, irradiate; *lit.* illumine. **3** *a smile lit up her face* irradiate, brighten, animate, make cheerful, enliven.

**light**[4] adjective **1** *the suitcases are light* easy to carry, portable; slight, underweight, small, tiny. **2** *wearing light clothes* lightweight, thin, flimsy, insubstantial, delicate, floaty, gossamer. **3** *a light tap on the shoulder* gentle, slight, delicate, soft, weak, faint, indistinct. **4** *light tasks* moderate, easy, simple, undemanding, untaxing, unexacting, effortless, facile; *inf.* cushy. **5** *light entertainment* nonserious, readily understood, lighthearted, entertaining, diverting, recreative, pleasing, amusing, humorous, funny, frivolous, superficial, trivial, trifling. **6** *a light jail sentence* nonsevere, mild, moderate, slight. **7** *this is no light matter* unimportant, insignificant, trivial, trifling, petty, inconsequential. **8** *a light meal* small, modest, scanty, skimpy, frugal, easily digested. **9** *with (a) light heart* carefree, cheerful, cheery, happy, lighthearted, gay, merry, blithe, sunny, untroubled. **10** *was light of foot* nimble, deft, agile, supple, lithe, spry, sprightly, graceful. **11** *feeling light in the head* giddy, dizzy, light-headed, vertiginous, faint, unsteady; *inf.* woozy. **12** *light soil* porous, crumbly, friable.

**lighten**[1] verb **1** *the sky lightened* become lighter, grow brighter, brighten. **2** *the larger windows lightened the room* brighten, light up, illuminate, shed light on, cast light on, irradiate. **3** *the sun had lightened the colors* whiten, bleach, pale.

**lighten**[2] verb **1** *lighten the horse's load* lessen, reduce, ease. **2** *lighten his burden of pain* lessen, ease, alleviate, mitigate, allay, relieve, assuage, ameliorate. **3** *the good news lightened his mood* brighten, cheer up, gladden, hearten, buoy up, perk up, lift, uplift.

**light-headed** adjective giddy, dizzy, vertiginous, faint, unsteady; *inf.* woozy.

**lighthearted** adjective carefree, cheerful, cheery, happy, glad, gay, merry, playful, jolly, joyful, jovial, gleeful, frolicsome, effervescent, in good spirits, blithe, sunny, untroubled; *inf.* upbeat.

**lightly** adverb **1** *snow falling lightly* slightly, thinly, softly, gently. **2** *salt the food lightly* sparingly, sparsely, slightly. **3** *get off lightly* easily, without severe punishment, leniently. **4** *jump lightly over the fence* easily, nimbly, agilely, lithely, spryly, gracefully. **5** *dismiss the subject lightly* airily, carelessly, heedlessly, uncaringly, indifferently, thoughtlessly, flippantly, frivolously; *inf.* breezily.

**likable, likeable** adjective pleasant, nice, friendly, agreeable, amiable, genial, charming, engaging, appealing, winsome.

**like** adjective *houses of like design* similar, comparable, corresponding, resembling, analogous, parallel, equivalent, of a kind, identical, matching, akin.

**like** verb **1** *they like each other* be fond of, have a liking/fondness for, be attracted to. **2** *he likes swimming* enjoy, find/take pleasure in, delight in, relish, revel in; *inf.* get a kick from. **3** *would like a piece of cake* wish, want, desire, prefer. **4** *how would you like it if it happened to you?* feel about, regard, think about, appreciate.

**likeable** adjective. *See* LIKABLE.

**likelihood** noun probability, chance, good chance, prospect, reasonable prospect, possibility, distinct possibility, strong possibility.

**likely** adjective **1** *it is likely that he will go* probable, distinctly possible, to be expected, odds-on. **2** *it is likely to rain* apt, inclined, tending, disposed, liable, prone. **3** *he gave a likely enough reason* reasonable, plausible, feasible, acceptable, believable, credible, tenable, conceivable. **4** *a likely place for a picnic* suitable, appropriate, fit, fitting, acceptable, proper, right, qualified, relevant, reasonable.

**likeness** noun **1** *there is a distinct likeness in the faces of the two friends* resemblance, similarity, sameness, similitude, correspondence, alikeness. **2** *appear in the likeness of Santa Claus* guise, semblance, appearance, outward form, form, shape, character. **3** *he will draw a likeness of your child* picture, drawing, sketch, painting, portrait, photograph, study, representation, image, sculpture.

**likewise** adverb **1** *she left early and he did likewise* in like manner, in the same way, similarly, in similar fashion, the same. **2** *we enjoyed the food and likewise the company* in addition, also, too, besides, moreover, furthermore, into the bargain, as well.

**liking** noun fondness, love, affection, desire, preference, partiality, penchant, bias, weakness, soft spot, appreciation, taste, predilection, fancy, inclination, bent, leaning, affinity.

**limb** noun **1** *injure a limb* arm, leg, wing, member, extremity, appendage. **2** *cut down limbs from the tree* branch, bough. **3** *the society is a limb of an international organization* branch, section, member, offshoot.

**limelight** noun focus of attention, public eye, publicity, fame, renown, celebrity, stardom, notability, eminence, prominence, spotlight.

**limit** noun **1** *the 200-mile fishing limit* boundary, boundary line, partition line, demarcation line, endpoint, cutoff point, termination. **2** *push his patience to the limit* extremity, utmost, ultimate, breaking point, endpoint. **3** *cross the limits of his land* boundary, border, bound, frontier, edge, perimeter, confines, periphery. **4** *a speed/spending limit* maximum, ceiling, limitation, restriction, curb, check, restraint.

**limit** verb **1** *limit their expenditure* place a limit on, restrict, curb, check, keep within bounds, restrain, confine, control, ration. **2** *the bulky jacket limited her movement* restrict, restrain, constrain, hinder, impede, hamper, trammel.

**limited** adjective **1** *committees having only limited powers* restricted, curbed, checked, controlled, restrained, constrained. **2** *provide limited accommodation* scanty, sparse, cramped, basic, minimal, inadequate. **3** *of limited experience* little, narrow, scanty, basic, minimal, inadequate, insufficient. **4** *he's a hard worker but he's a bit limited* slow, slow-witted, dull-witted, dense, unimaginative, stolid.

**limitless** adjective **1** *a limitless expanse of forest* infinite, endless, never-ending, interminable, immense, vast, extensive, measureless. **2** *limitless optimism/enthusiasm* boundless, unbounded, illimitable, infinite, endless, never-ending, unceasing, interminable, inexhaustible, constant, perpetual.

**limp** verb **1** *he still limps after the injury* hobble, shuffle, walk with a limp. **2** *the damaged ship limped into harbor* move slowly, crawl, drag.

**limp** noun *walk with a pronounced limp* lameness, hobble, jerk, uneven gait, shuffle.

**limp** adjective **1** *limp leaves* lacking firmness, floppy, drooping, droopy, soft, flaccid, flabby, loose, slack. **2** *feeling limp after the long illness* without energy, tired, fatigued, weary, exhausted, worn-out, lethargic, enervated, feeble, frail, debilitated.

**line** noun **1** *draw lines* bar, score, stroke, slash, underline, underscore. **2** *lines of white through the black material* band, stripe, strip, belt, seam. **3** *lines on her face* furrow, wrinkle, crease, crow's-foot, groove. **4** *admire the lines of the sculpture* outline, contour, configuration, shape, figure, delineation, silhouette, profile. **5** *the ball went over the line | the state line* boundary, boundary line, limit, border, borderline, frontier, demarcation line, edge, margin, perimeter, periphery. **6** *our line of flight* course, route, track, channel, path, way, road, lane, trajectory. **7** *his line of thought* direction, course, drift, tack, tendency, trend. **8** *what line is he in?* line of work, business, field, area, trade, occupation, employment, profession, work, job, calling, career, pursuit, specialty; *inf.* game. **9** *stocking a new line of cosmetics* brand, kind, sort, type, variety. **10** *a line of figures/people* row, column, series, sequence, succession, queue,

procession, file, string, chain, array. **11** *behind enemy lines* formation, position, disposition, front, front line, firing line. **12** *he comes from a noble line* lineage, descent, ancestry, parentage, family, extraction, heritage, stock, strain, race, breed. **13** *hang the wash on the line | fishing line* rope, string, cord, cable, wire, thread, twine, strand, filament. **14** *drop her mother a line* note, letter, card, postcard, message, word, communication. **15** *give his usual line about having no money* spiel, story, patter, piece of fiction. **draw the line at** *draw the line at lending him money* stop short of, bar, proscribe, set a limit at; *inf.* put one's foot down about. **in line 1** *stand in line to be served* in a row, in a column, in single file, in a queue. **2** *are the two pipes in line?* in alignment, aligned, straight, plumb, true. **3** *their views are very much in line* in agreement, in accord, in harmony, in step, in conformity, in rapport. **4** *keep the junior staff in line* under control, in order, in check, obedient. **in line for** *in line for the promotion* a candidate for, in the running for, on the short list for, being considered for, next in succession for. **lay it on the line** *lay it on the line to him about his drinking* speak frankly, state openly, be direct, pull no punches; *inf.* give it to someone straight. **lay/put on the line** *put his job on the line* risk, put at risk, put in danger, endanger, imperil. **toe the line** *those who do not toe the line are asked to leave* conform, obey the rules, abide by the rules, submit, yield.

**line** verb **1** *grief had lined her face* mark with lines, furrow, wrinkle, crease. **2** *trees lined the driveway* border, edge, fringe, bound, skirt, hem, rim. **line up 1** *line up the toy soldiers* arrange in a line, arrange in lines, put in rows/columns, group, marshal. **2** *the children lined up* form a line, form lines, get into rows/columns, file, form a queue, group together, fall in. **3** *line up entertainment for the party* get together, organize, prepare, assemble, obtain, procure, secure, produce, come up with.

**lineage** noun line, descent, ancestry, family, extraction. *See* LINE noun 12.

**lineup** noun **1** *the lineup for tonight's show/game* list, roster, team, selection, array. **2** *the lineup for inspection* line, row, queue.

**linger** verb **1** *linger after the others went* stay, remain, hang around, delay, dawdle, loiter, dally, tarry; *inf.* dilly-dally. **2** *the infection lingered* persist, continue, be protracted, endure. **3** *dying man is lingering (on)* stay alive, cling to life, survive, last, continue, hang on.

**link** noun **1** *a link in the metal chain* ring, loop, connection, coupling, joint, knot. **2** *one of the links in the organization* component, constituent, element, part, piece, member. **3** *a link between smoking and cancer* connection, relationship, association, tie. **4** *strong family links* bond, tie, attachment, connection, relationship, association, affiliation.

**link** verb **1** *the joint linking the two pieces* join, connect, fasten together, attach, bind, unite, couple. **2** *the press linking their names* join, connect, associate, relate, bracket.

**lionhearted** adjective brave, courageous, valiant, gallant, intrepid, valorous, fearless, bold, daring, dauntless, stouthearted, stalwart, heroic.

**lionize** verb glorify, exalt, magnify, acclaim, praise, extol, laud, eulogize, fête, pay tribute to, put on a pedestal, hero-worship, worship, idolize, adulate, aggrandize.

**lip** noun **1** *the lip of a cup/crater* edge, rim, brim, border, verge, brink. **2** *no one wants to listen to your lip* impertinence, impudence, insolence, rudeness, audacity, effrontery, cheek; *inf.* back talk, sass.

**liquid** adjective **1** *liquid substances* fluid, flowing, running, runny, watery, aqueous, liquefied, melted, molten, dissolved, hydrous. **2** *liquid eyes* clear, transparent, limpid, unclouded, bright, shining, glowing, gleaming. **3** *liquid assets* convertible, negotiable.

**liquidate** verb **1** *liquidate debts* pay, pay in full, pay off, settle, clear, discharge, square, make good, honor. **2** *liquidate a business/partnership* close down, dissolve, break up, disband, terminate, annul. **3** *liquidate assets* convert to cash, convert, cash in, sell off, realize. **4** *liquidate an enemy* kill, murder, put to death, do away with, assassinate, eliminate, dispatch, finish off, destroy, annihilate, obliterate; *inf.* bump off, rub out, wipe out.

**liquor** noun alcohol, alcoholic drink, spirits, drink, intoxicant, inebriant; *inf.* booze, hard stuff, grog, the sauce, hooch, rotgut.

**list**[1] noun *a list of purchases/films* catalog, inventory, record, register, roll, file, index, directory, listing, enumeration, table, tabulation, schedule, syllabus, calendar, program.

**list**[2] verb *list the purchases* make a list of, write down, record, register, enter, itemize, enumerate, catalog, file, tabulate, schedule, chronicle, classify.

**list**[3] verb *vessels listing* lean, tilt, tip, heel, careen, cant, incline, slant, slope.

**listen** verb *listen to the speaker* pay attention, be attentive, give ear, lend an ear; hang on someone's words, keep one's ears open, prick up one's ears; *inf.* be all ears. **2** *if you had listened in the classroom, you would have passed* take heed, heed, take notice, mind, obey. **listen in on** *listen in on someone's conversation* eavesdrop on, overhear, tap (into), wiretap; *inf.* bug.

**listless** adjective languid, lethargic, enervated, lackadaisical, spiritless, lifeless, inactive, inert, indolent, apathetic, passive, dull, sluggish, slothful, limp, languorous, torpid, supine, indifferent, uninterested, impassive.

**litany** noun **1** *church litany* prayer, invocation, petition, supplication, devotion; *lit.* orison. **2** *a litany of complaints* recital, recitation, catalog, list, listing, enumeration.

**literacy** noun reading ability, reading proficiency, learning, education, culture, knowledge, scholarship, erudition, learnedness, enlightenment, articulateness.

**literal** adjective **1** *a literal translation* word-for-word, verbatim, line-for-line, exact, precise, faithful, close, strict, accurate. **2** *a literal account* true, accurate, genuine, authentic, veritable, plain, unexaggerated, unvarnished, unembellished, undistorted. **3** *rather a literal person* literal-minded, down-to-earth, prosaic, factual, matter-of-fact, unimaginative, colorless, commonplace, tedious, uninspiring.

**literally** adverb **1** *translated literally* word for word, verbatim, line for line, exactly, precisely, faithfully, closely, strictly, accurately. **2** *literally thousands of people* actually, really, truly, honestly, certainly, surely, positively, absolutely.

**literary** adjective **1** *literary works* written, published, printed, in print. **2** *a literary man* well-read, widely read, educated, well-educated, scholarly, learned, intellectual, cultured, erudite, bookish, studious, lettered; *inf.* highbrow. **3** *a literary word* formal, poetic.

**literate** adjective **1** *scarcely literate* able to read and write, educated, schooled. **2** *the most literate people of his family* educated, well-educated, well-read, scholarly, learned, intellectual, erudite, cultured, cultivated, knowledgeable, well-informed. **3** *literate prose* well-written, stylish, polished, articulate, lucid, eloquent.

**literature** noun **1** *study English literature* writings, printed works, published works, belles lettres. **2** *receive literature about the course* printed matter, brochure, leaflet, pamphlet, flyer, circular, information, data, facts; *inf.* info.

**lithe** adjective agile, flexible, supple, limber, loose-limbed, pliant, pliable, lissome.

**litigation** noun lawsuit, legal case, case, legal dispute, legal action, legal proceedings, suit.

**litter** noun **1** *litter lying on the grass* trash, rubbish, debris, refuse, junk, detritus, flotsam. **2** *a litter of books everywhere* disorder, untidiness, clutter, jumble, confusion, mess, disarray, disorganization; *inf.* shambles. **3** *a litter of pups* brood, young, offspring, progeny, family, issue. **4** *invalids carried on litters* stretcher, cot.

**little** adjective **1** *a little person/dog/insect/car* small, short, slight, petite, tiny, wee, miniature, diminutive, minute, minuscule, dwarf, midget, pygmy, bantam; *inf.* teeny, teeny-weeny, pint-sized. **2** *he began painting when he was little* small, young, junior. **3** *after a little period* short, brief, fleeting, short-lived, momentary, transitory. **4** *exaggerate little difficulties* unimportant, insignificant, minor, trivial, trifling, petty, paltry, inconsequential, negligible, nugatory. **5** *gain little advantage* scant, meager, skimpy, sparse, insufficient, exiguous; *inf.* piddling. **6** *nasty little minds* mean, narrow, narrow-minded, small-minded, base, cheap, shallow, petty, illiberal, provincial, parochial, insular.

**little** adverb **1** *little known as an artist* hardly, barely, scarcely, not much, only slightly, only just. **2** *snow is little seen around here* hardly, scarcely, rarely, seldom, infrequently. **little by little** gradually, slowly, bit by bit, by degrees, step by step, progressively.

**little** noun *add just a little* small amount, bit, touch, trace, hint, soupçon, trifle, dash, taste, pinch, dab, spot, sprinkling, speck, modicum, grain, fragment, snippet, smidgen; *inf.* smidge.

**live** verb **1** *when dinosaurs lived* be alive, breathe, draw breath, exist, walk the earth. **2** *patients not expected to live* remain/stay alive, survive, last, endure, persist, abide, continue, stay around. **3** *live quietly* pass/spend one's life, have a life/lifestyle, conduct oneself, lead one's life, behave, comport oneself. **4** *he lives by begging* survive, make a living, earn one's living, subsist, support oneself, maintain oneself, make ends meet. **5** *live in the city* dwell, reside, have one's home, have one's residence, lodge, be settled; *inf.* hang one's hat. **6** *he really lived when he was young* enjoy life, enjoy oneself, have fun, make the most of life, flourish, prosper, thrive. **live it up** live extravagantly, live in clover; *inf.* go on a spree, paint the town red, have a ball. **live on** *live on vegetables* subsist on, feed on, thrive on, eat nothing but.

**live** adjective **1** *live bodies* alive, living, breathing, animate, vital; *inf.* in the land of the living. **2** *a real live tiger* genuine, authentic, actual, in the flesh, true-to-life. **3** *a live show* nonrecorded, in real time, unedited, with an audience. **4** *live coals* glowing, aglow, burning, alight, flaming, blazing, hot, smoldering. **5** *live electric wires* charged, connected, active, switched on. **6** *live bombs* unexploded, explodable, explosive. **7** *a live issue* current, topical, active, prevalent, important, of interest, lively, vital, pressing, burning, pertinent, controversial, debatable, unsettled. **live wire** person of energy, self-starter, self-motivator; *inf.* ball of fire, human dynamo, go-getter, hustler.

**livelihood** noun **1** *earn a livelihood* living, subsistence, means of support, income, keep, maintenance, sustenance, upkeep. **2** *a poorly paid livelihood* job, work, employment, occupation, trade, profession, career.

**lively** adjective **1** *lively young people* active, animated, energetic, vigorous, spirited, high-spirited, vivacious, enthusiastic, cheerful, buoyant, sparkling, bouncy, perky, sprightly, spry, frisky; *inf.* chipper, peppy. **2** *maintain a lively pace* brisk, quick, rapid, swift, vigorous. **3** *a lively discussion* animated, spirited, stimulating, heated, enthusiastic. **4** *a lively scene at the beach* busy, crowded, bustling, hectic, swarming, teeming, buzzing. **5** *lively writing* vivid, colorful, striking, graphic, stimulating, exciting, effective, imaginative.

**liven** verb **liven up 1** *liven the party up* enliven, animate, vitalize, vivify, put some life into, brighten up, cheer up, perk up; *inf.* pep up. **2** *livened up when they arrived* cheer up, brighten up, perk up.

**livid** adjective **1** *livid with his son* furious, infuriated, fuming, seething, beside oneself, incensed, enraged, angry, wrathful, ireful; *inf.* boiling. **2** *a livid patch on his forehead* discolored, bruised, black-and-blue, purplish, bluish.

**living** adjective **1** *living creatures* animate, vital, alive, live, breathing, existing, existent. **2** *living languages* current, in use, extant, existing, contemporary, operating, active, ongoing, continuing, surviving, persisting.

**living** noun **1** *earn a living* livelihood, subsistence, means of support, income, keep, maintenance, sustenance, upkeep. **2** *lose his living* job, work, employment, occupation, trade, profession, career. **3** *high living* lifestyle, way of life, conduct, behavior.

**load** noun **1** *the truck's load* cargo, freight, charge, burden, lading, contents, consignment, shipment. **2** *the heavy load of negotiating a truce | illness added to his load* burden, onus, weight, responsibility, duty, charge, obligation, strain, trouble, worry, encumbrance, oppression, trial, tribulation, cross, millstone, albatross, incubus.

**load** verb **1** *load the truck* fill, fill up, lade, pack, pile, heap, stack, stuff. **2** *load the staff with responsibility* burden, weigh down, weight, saddle, charge, tax, encumber, oppress, trouble. **3** *load a gun* prime, charge, fill. **4** *load the dice* weight, bias, rig.

**loaded** adjective **1** *a loaded truck* full, filled, laden, freighted, packed. **2** *a loaded gun* primed, charged, filled. **3** *loaded dice* weighted, biased, rigged. **4** *loaded questions* manipulative, cunning, insidious, artful, crafty, tricky. **5** *those people are probably loaded* rich, wealthy, well off, well-to-do, affluent, moneyed; *inf.* well-heeled, flush. **6** *got loaded at the party* drunk, intoxicated, inebriated; *inf.* plastered, smashed.

**loaf** verb *loafing at home* laze, lounge, idle, lie around, hang about, waste time.

**loan** noun advance, credit, mortgage.

**loan** verb lend, advance, give credit, give on loan, let out.

**loathe** verb hate, detest, abhor, despise, abominate, have an aversion to, shrink from, recoil from, execrate.

**loathsome** adjective hateful, detestable, abhorrent, odious, repugnant, disgusting, repulsive, revolting, abominable, vile, nasty, obnoxious, horrible, offensive, disagreeable, despicable, contemptible, reprehensible, execrable; *inf.* horrid.

**lobby** noun **1** *wait for them in the lobby* porch, hall, hallway, entrance hall, entrance, vestibule, foyer, passageway, ante-room, antechamber. **2** *the animal rights lobby* pressure group, interest group, supporters.

**lobby** verb *lobby the legislators* pressure, solicit, seek to influence, urge, press. **lobby for** *lobby for animal rights* campaign for, press/push for, promote.

**local** adjective **1** *local politics* community, district, neighborhood, regional, city, town, municipal, provincial, village, parish. **2** *our local store* nearby, near, at hand, close by, neighborhood. **3** *a local anesthetic* confined, restricted, contained, limited, circumscribed, delimited, specific.

**locale** noun place, site, spot, position, location, venue, area, neighborhood, locality, setting, scene.

**locality** noun **1** *the locality of the crime* vicinity, surrounding area, area, neighborhood, district, region, environs, locale; *fml.* locus. **2** *identify the locality of the car* location, position, place, whereabouts, bearings; *fml.* locus.

**localize** verb confine, restrict, contain, limit, circumscribe, delimit.

**locate** verb **1** *locate the source of infection* find, discover, identify, pinpoint, detect, uncover, track down, unearth, pin down, define. **2** *factories located near the sea* situate, site, position, place, put, build, establish, station, set, fix, settle.

**location** noun **1** *identify the location of the ship* position, place, situation, whereabouts, bearings, site, point; *fml.* locus. **2** *a pleasant location for a house* position, place, situation, site, spot, scene, setting, venue, locale.

**lock** verb **1** *lock the door* bolt, fasten, bar, secure, padlock. **2** *pieces of the puzzle locking together* interlock, engage, mesh, join, link, unite. **3** *wheels locked* jam, become rigid. **4** *locked in each other's arms | locked in combat* clasp, clench, entangle, entwine, embrace. **lock out** *lock out late arrivals* exclude, bar, ban, refuse entrance to, deny admittance to, ostracize. **lock up** *lock up prisoners* confine, imprison, jail, incarcerate, cage, coop up.

**lock**[1] noun *force the lock* bolt, catch, fastener, clasp, bar, hasp, padlock.

**lock**[2] noun *a lock of hair* strand, tuft, tress, curl, ringlet, lovelock.

**lodge** noun **1** *a ski lodge* house, cottage, cabin, chalet. **2** *the Masonic lodge* branch, chapter, section, association, society, club, group, fraternity, sorority. **3** *an animal's lodge* lair, den, hole, retreat, shelter.

**lodge** verb **1** *he's lodging at the Smiths'* stay, reside, dwell, room, sojourn, stop. **2** *the Smiths can lodge all of the children* house, accommodate, put up, billet, shelter, harbor, entertain. **3** *lodge a complaint* register, submit, put forward, place, file, lay, put on record, record. **4** *the bullet lodged in his brain* become fixed, become embedded, stick, come to rest.

**lodger** noun boarder, paying guest, guest, tenant, roomer.

**lodging** noun **1** *gave them lodging for the night* accommodation, shelter, board, housing, a roof over one's head. **2** *move to new lodgings* accommodation, rooms, place, residence, dwelling, abode, habitation; *inf.* digs.

**lofty** adjective **1** *lofty peaks* towering, soaring, tall, high, elevated, sky-high, skyscraping. **2** *lofty contempt* arrogant, haughty, proud, self-important, conceited, overweening, disdainful, supercilious, condescending, patronizing, lordly, snobbish, scornful, contemptuous; *inf.* high-and-mighty, stuck-up, snooty, uppity. **3** *lofty ideals* noble, exalted, grand, sublime. **4** *lofty members of the community* eminent, leading, notable, distinguished, famous, renowned, illustrious, esteemed, celebrated.

**logic** noun **1** *studying logic* science of reasoning, science of deduction, science of thought, dialectics, argumentation, ratiocination. **2** *her logic was flawed* line of reasoning, chain of reasoning, reasoning, argument, argumentation. **3** *no logic in her actions* reason, judgment, wisdom, sense, common sense, rationale, coherence; *inf.* horse sense.

**logical** adjective **1** *a logical argument* reasoned, rational, sound, cogent, coherent, clear, consistent, relevant. **2** *the logical thing to do* rational, reasonable, sensible, intelligent, wise, judicious. **3** *the logical outcome* likeliest, plausible, obvious. **4** *not a logical person* reasoning, thinking, straight-thinking, rational.

**logo** noun trademark, emblem, device, symbol, design, seal, stamp, logotype.

**loiter** verb hang around, linger, wait, skulk, loaf, lounge, idle, dally, waste time; *lit.* tarry.

**loll** verb **1** *lolling on the sofa* slump, flop, sprawl, relax, recline. **2** *loll around the house* lounge, loaf, idle, loiter, hang around, vegetate, languish. **3** *with his tongue lolling* hang down, hang, hang out, dangle, droop, sag, flap, flop.

**lone** adjective by oneself, alone, single, solitary, sole, unaccompanied, without companions, companionless, lonely.

**lonely** adjective **1** *feeling lonely* friendless, companionless, lonesome, forlorn, forsaken, isolated, outcast, despondent. **2** *lead a lonely existence* lone, by oneself, single, solitary, sole, companionless. **3** *a lonely landscape* desolate, barren, isolated, out-of-the-way, remote, secluded, off the beaten track, deserted, uninhabited, unfrequented, unpopulated, godforsaken, lone.

**lonesome** adjective friendless, forlorn, isolated. *See* LONELY 1.

**long** adjective **1** *four feet long* in length, lengthways, lengthwise. **2** *a long way* lengthy, extended, extensive, stretched out, spread out. **3** *ten long years* lengthy, prolonged, protracted, extended, long-drawn-out, interminable, tedious.

**long** verb **long for** wish for, desire, want, yearn for, crave, hunger for, thirst for, itch for, covet, lust after, hope for, dream of, pine for, hanker for/after; *inf.* have a yen for.

**longing** noun wish, desire, yearning, craving, hunger, thirst, itch, lust, hope, dream, aspiration, pining, fancy, urge, hankering; *inf.* yen.

**long-standing** adjective established, fixed, long-established, well-established, time-honored, abiding, enduring.

**long-suffering** adjective patient, forbearing, tolerant, uncomplaining, stoical, resigned, charitable, forgiving.

**long-winded** adjective verbose, wordy, garrulous, prolix, discursive, diffuse, rambling, lengthy, prolonged, protracted, long-drawn-out, tedious.

**look** verb **1** *look over there!* see, glance, fix one's gaze, focus, observe, view, regard, eye, take in, watch, scan, scrutinize, survey, consider, peep, peek, glimpse, gaze, stare, gape, ogle; *inf.* take a gander, rubberneck, eyeball. **2** *she looks ill* seem, seem to be, appear, appear to be, look to be, strike someone as being. **3** *the room looks east* face, front, front on. **look after** take care of, care for, attend to, tend, mind, keep an eye on, watch, supervise, protect, guard. **look at** observe, view, eye, watch, examine, study, inspect, scan, scrutinize, survey, check, consider, run one's eyes over. **look down on** scorn, disdain, regard with contempt, hold in disdain, sneer at, spurn, disparage, pooh-pooh, despise; *inf.* turn up one's nose at. **look for 1** *look for the lost glove* search for, hunt for, seek. **2** *look for some improvement* anticipate, expect, await, count on, hope for, look forward to. **look forward to** anticipate, await with pleasure, count the days until. **look into** investigate, explore, research, probe, inquire about, make inquiries about, examine, study, scrutinize, check, follow up on, check up on, check out. **look like** resemble, bear a resemblance to, put someone in mind of, take after; *inf.* be the spitting image of, be a dead ringer for, favor. **look on** *with a crowd looking on* watch, observe, spectate, be a spectator, view, witness. **look on/upon** *look on it as a favor* | *look upon him as a brother* regard, consider, think of, deem, judge, see, take, reckon. **look out** *you'll drop it if you don't look out* watch out, beware, be on guard, be alert, be wary, be vigilant, be careful, pay attention, take heed, keep an eye out, be on the qui vive. **look over** inspect, examine, check, monitor, scan, run through, give something/someone the once-over, check out, peruse; *inf.* eyeball. **look to 1** *look to the future* consider, give thought to, think about, turn one's thoughts to. **2** *look to the family for support* turn to, have recourse to, fall back on, avail oneself of. **look up 1** *look up the information* search for, seek out, research, find, locate. **2** *look them up in San Diego* visit, pay a visit to, call on; *inf.* drop in on. **look up to** *look up to his brother* admire, think highly of, hold in high regard, respect, hold in esteem, esteem, revere, idolize, worship, hero-worship, put on a pedestal, lionize.

**look** noun **1** *one look at the evidence* sight, glance, observation, view, examination, study, inspection, scan, survey, peep, peek, glimpse, gaze; *inf.* eyeful, gander, looksee, once-over. **2** *an angry look* expression, face, countenance, features, mien. **3** *houses having a Colonial look* appearance, air, aspect, bearing, cast, demeanor, features, semblance, guise, façade, impression, effect. **4** *miniskirts are the look this year* fashion, style, vogue, trend, fad, craze, rage.

**lookout** noun **1** *on the lookout for danger* watch, guard, vigil, alertness, qui vive. **2** *lookouts located along the coast* observation post, lookout station, lookout tower, watchtower, tower. **3** *the lookout kept watch until dawn* guard, sentry, sentinel, watchman.

**loom** verb **1** *a shape loomed out of the darkness* appear, emerge, become visible, take shape, materialize. **2** *cliffs loomed above them* tower, soar, rise, rise up, overhang, hang over. **3** *exams are looming* be imminent, impend, be close, threaten, menace.

**loop** noun coil, hoop, noose, circle, ring, oval, spiral, curl, twirl, whorl, twist, convolution, bend, curve, kink, arc.

**loop** verb **1** *loop the string* coil, form hoops with, bend into spirals. **2** *loop the sections together* fasten, tie, join, connect. **loop around** *the road loops around the lake* encircle, surround, encompass.

**loophole** noun escape clause, escape route, ambiguity, omission.

**loose** adjective **1** *cows loose in the street* at large, at liberty, free, on the loose, unconfined, untied, unchained, untethered, unsecured, unfastened, unrestricted, unbound, freed, liberated, released. **2** *the handle is loose* wobbly, insecure, rickety, unsteady, movable. **3** *loose hair* untied, unpinned, unbound, hanging free, flowing. **4** *loose clothes* loose-fitting, slack, baggy, sagging, sloppy. **5** *a loose translation* inexact, imprecise, vague, indefinite, broad, general. **6** *loose morals* immoral, disreputable, dissolute, corrupt, fast, promiscuous, debauched, dissipated, degenerate, wanton, unchaste, licentious, lascivious, libertine, reprobate. **7** *hang loose* relaxed, informal, uninhibited, unreserved, frank, open, unceremonious, unconstrained. **at loose ends** unsettled, restless, undecided, unemployed, unoccupied, idle, twiddling one's thumbs. **break loose** escape, make one's escape, run away, flee, take to one's heels. **let loose 1** *let the cows loose* set free, unloose, turn loose, loose, untie, unchain, untether, unfasten, detach, unleash, let go, release, free, liberate. **2** *let loose a cry of pain* give, emit, burst out with, shout, yell, bellow. **on the loose** *cows on the loose* at liberty, free, at large, unconfined.

**loose** verb **1** *loose the dogs* set free, turn

loose. *See* LET LOOSE (LOOSE adj.). **2** *loose her grip* loosen, relax, slacken, weaken, lessen, reduce, diminish, moderate, soften. **3** *loose a missile* discharge, shoot, fire off, eject, catapult.

**loosen** verb **1** *loosen a nut/belt* slacken, slack, unstick, let out, undo, unfasten, unhook. **2** *the nut loosened* become loose, work loose, work free. **3** *loosen her grip* relax, slacken, lessen. *See* LOOSE verb 2. **loosen up** relax, calm down, take it easy, ease up; *inf.* hang loose, lighten up, chill, chill out.

**loot** noun booty, spoils, spoil, plunder, haul, pillage, prize; *inf.* the goods, boodle.

**loot** verb plunder, pillage, rob, burgle, steal from, ransack, sack, maraud, ravage, despoil, spoliate.

**lopsided** adjective asymmetrical, unsymmetrical, uneven, unbalanced, off-balance, unequal, askew, squint, tilting, crooked, out of line, awry.

**loquacious** adjective talkative, garrulous, voluble, long-winded, wordy, verbose, effusive, chattering; *inf.* having the gift of the gab, bigmouthed, gabby.

**lord** noun **1** *lord of all he surveys* master, lord and master, ruler, leader, chief, monarch, sovereign, king, emperor, prince, governor, commander, captain, overlord, suzerain, baron, potentate, liege. **2** *the lords and ladies* noble, nobleman, peer, aristocrat, landowner, lord of the manor; duke, earl, viscount. **3** *believe in the Lord* God, Jesus, Jesus Christ, Christ, Christ the Lord, the Redeemer, the Savior.

**lordly** adjective **1** *a lordly disregard for others* imperious, arrogant, haughty, highhanded, overbearing, overweening, overconfident, dictatorial, authoritarian, peremptory, autocratic, tyrannical, supercilious, disdainful, condescending, patronizing; *inf.* high-and-mighty, bossy, stuck-up, snooty, uppity, hoity-toity. **2** *lordly splendor* noble, aristocratic, lofty, exalted, majestic, grand, regal, princely, kingly, imperial, stately, dignified, magnificent, grandiose.

**lore** noun **1** *researching Cherokee lore* traditions, folklore, beliefs, superstitions, legends. **2** *bird lore* knowledge, learning, wisdom, know-how, skill.

**lose** verb **1** *has lost his keys* mislay, misplace, drop, forget. **2** *losing a lot of blood* be deprived of, suffer the loss of. **3** *trying to lose the police* outdistance, outstrip, outrun; escape from, evade, elude, dodge, shake off, throw off, duck. **4** *lose the way* stray from, wander from. **5** *lose the opportunity* fail to grasp/take, let pass, miss, forfeit, neglect; *inf.* pass up, lose out on. **6** *lost the battle* suffer defeat, be defeated, be worsted, be beaten, be conquered, be vanquished, be trounced, fail, meet one's Waterloo. **7** *lose time* waste, squander, dissipate, spend, expend, consume, deplete, exhaust, use up.

**loss** noun **1** *report the loss of the keys* misplacement, mislaying, dropping, forgetting. **2** *loss of prestige* deprivation, privation, forfeiture, bereavement, disappearance, waste, losing, dissipation. **3** *families/firms suffering loss* deprivation, privation, detriment, disadvantage, damage, injury, impairment, harm, hurt, ruin, destruction. **4** *regret the civilian losses* casualty, fatality, dead, death toll. **5** *the company has made significant losses* deficit, debit, debt, deficiency, depletion. **at a loss** *we are at a loss to understand his motives* baffled, nonplussed, mystified, stumped, puzzled, perplexed, bewildered, ignorant, confused; *inf.* clueless.

**lost** adjective **1** *lost books* missing, gone astray, mislaid, misplaced, vanished, disappeared, forgotten. **2** *lost travelers* stray, astray, off-course, off-track, disorientated, adrift, going around in circles, at sea. **3** *lost opportunities* missed, passed, forfeited, neglected, wasted, squandered, dissipated, frittered; *inf.* down the drain. **4** *lost tribes* extinct, dead, bygone, past, vanished, forgotten. **5** *lost ships* destroyed, ruined, wiped out, wrecked, finished, perished, demolished, obliterated, effaced, exterminated, eradicated, annihilated, extirpated. **6** *lost souls* damned, fallen, irredeemable, hopeless. **lost in** *she was lost in a book* engrossed in, absorbed in, preoccupied by, spellbound by, distracted by, entranced by.

**lot** noun **1** *draw lots* slip of paper, number, straw, counter. **2** *decided by lot* chance, luck, lottery, drawing lots, accident, serendipity, fortuity. **3** *his lot in life* fate, destiny, fortune, situation, circumstances, portion, plight. **4** *the brothers' lots* share, portion, quota, ration, allowance, percentage, piece; *inf.* cut. **5** *sold as a lot* set, batch, collection, group, bundle, consignment, parcel. **6** *parking lots* plot, patch of ground, tract of land, building lot. **a lot** *smile a lot* much, a good/great deal, often, frequently, many times. **a lot of** *a lot of people* many, a good/great deal of, a great quantity of, numerous, an abundance of, plenty of, masses of, scores of; *inf.* loads of, heaps of, piles of, oodles of, scads of, wads of, oceans of, gobs of. **throw in one's lot** *threw in his lot with thieves* join forces, form an alliance, ally, link up, combine.

**lotion** noun cream, salve, ointment, moisturizer, balm, emollient, lubricant, unguent, liniment, embrocation, pomade.

**lottery** noun draw, raffle, sweepstake, game of chance, gamble, lotto, bingo; risk, hazard, venture.

**loud** adjective **1** *loud noises* blaring,

booming, noisy, deafening, resounding, reverberant, stentorian, roaring, thunderous, tumultuous, clamorous, ear-splitting, ear-piercing, piercing, strident, harsh, raucous. **2** *loud young women* brash, brazen, bold, loudmouthed, vociferous, raucous, aggressive, coarse, crude, rough, crass, vulgar, brassy; *inf.* pushy. **3** *loud demands* vociferous, clamorous, insistent, vehement, emphatic, urgent, importunate, demanding. **4** *loud colors* garish, gaudy, flashy, bold, flamboyant, lurid, glaring, showy, obtrusive.

**loudmouth** noun **1** *loudmouths showing off* braggart, brag, boaster, blusterer, swaggerer, braggadocio; *inf.* bigmouth. **2** *loudmouths discussing neighbors' affairs* blabbermouth, gossip, gossipmonger, scandalmonger, busybody.

**lounge** verb laze, lie, lie around, recline, relax, take it easy, sprawl, loaf, idle, loll, repose.

**lousy** adjective **1** *lousy workmanship* poor, incompetent, inadequate, unsatisfactory, inferior, careless, second-rate, terrible, miserable; *inf.* rotten, no-good. **2** *a lousy trick to play* dirty, low, mean, base, despicable, contemptible, low-down, hateful, detestable, loathsome, vile; *inf.* rotten. **lousy with** *places lousy with tourists* full of, covered in, crowded with, overrun by, swarming with, teeming with, crawling with.

**lout** noun boor, oaf, dolt, churl, bumpkin, yahoo; brute, rowdy, barbarian; *inf.* slob, clodhopper, clod, lummox.

**lovable** adjective adorable, dear, sweet, cute, charming, delightful, captivating, enchanting, engaging, pleasing, appealing, winsome, winning, endearing, affectionate, warmhearted, cuddly.

**love** verb **1** *he loves her* prize, cherish, care for, be fond of, be attracted to, be attached to, hold dear, adore, dote on, worship, idolize, treasure, be devoted to, desire, want, be infatuated with, lust after, long for, yearn for, adulate; *inf.* fancy, have a crush on. **2** *she loves chocolate* like, have a liking for, have a weakness for, be partial to, relish, savor, appreciate, take pleasure in, delight in; *inf.* get a kick out of.

**love** noun **1** *the couple's love for/of each other* affection, fondness, care, concern, attachment, regard, warmth, intimacy, devotion, adoration, passion, ardor, desire, lust, yearning, infatuation, adulation. **2** *her love of/for chocolate* liking, weakness, partiality, enjoyment, appreciation, relish, passion. **3** *love for/toward one's neighbor* care, caring, regard, solicitude, sympathy, warmth, friendliness, friendship, rapport, brotherhood, kindness, charity. **4** *be brave, my love* beloved, loved one, true love, dear, dearest, darling, sweetheart, angel, lover, inamorato/inamorata. **5** *their love was short-lived* romance, relationship, love affair, affair, liaison. **love affair** affair, romance, relationship, liaison, amour, intrigue, *affaire de coeur.* **in love with** attracted to, infatuated with, enamored of, smitten by, besotted with, devoted to, having a passion for, lusting after; *inf.* having the hots for.

**lovely** adjective **1** *a lovely face* beautiful, pretty, attractive, good-looking, comely, handsome, sweet, fair, charming, adorable, enchanting, engaging, winsome. **2** *a lovely surprise* delightful, pleasant, nice, agreeable, marvelous, wonderful.

**lover** noun **1** *send flowers to his/her lover* boyfriend, girlfriend, mistress, ladylove, paramour, beau, loved one, beloved, sweetheart, inamorato/inamorata. **2** *a lover of antiques* admirer, devotee, fan, enthusiast, aficionado; *inf.* buff, freak.

**loving** adjective affectionate, fond, devoted, caring, adoring, doting, solicitous, demonstrative, tender, warm, warmhearted, friendly, kind, sympathetic, charitable, cordial, amiable, amorous, ardent, passionate.

**low** adjective **1** *a low table* short, small, little, squat, stubby, stunted, truncated, dwarfish. **2** *low land* low-lying, ground-level, sea-level, flat, sunken, depressed, nether. **3** *of low birth* lowly, humble, low-ranking, plebeian, peasant, poor, common, ordinary, simple, plain, unpretentious, inferior, subordinate. **4** *supplies are low* sparse, meager, scarce, scanty, scant, few, little, deficient, inadequate, paltry, measly, depleted, diminished. **5** *a low hum* soft, quiet, muted, subdued, muffled, hushed, whispered, murmured, gentle, dulcet, indistinct, inaudible. **6** *feeling low* low-spirited, down, depressed, dejected, despondent, disheartened, downhearted, downcast, gloomy, glum, unhappy, sad, miserable, blue, morose, moody, heavy-hearted, forlorn; *inf.* down in the mouth, down in the dumps. **7** *of low intelligence* low-grade, inferior, substandard, below par, second-rate, deficient, defective, wanting, lacking, inadequate, mediocre. **8** *low expectations* modest, unambitious, unpretentious, unaspiring, simple, plain, ordinary, commonplace, run-of-the-mill. **9** *have a low opinion of them* unfavorable, poor, bad, adverse, hostile, negative. **10** *a low thing to do* mean, nasty, foul, bad, wicked, evil, vile, despicable, contemptible, base, dishonorable, unprincipled, dastardly, ignoble, sordid. **11** *low comedy* vulgar, crude, coarse, obscene, indecent, gross, ribald, smutty, bawdy, pornographic, blue, rude, rough, unrefined, offensive. **12** *low prices* cheap, inexpensive, moderate, reasonable, modest, bargain-basement.

**lower** adjective **1** *of lower status* lesser, subordinate, junior, inferior, minor, secondary. **2** *lower bunk* under, underneath, nether. **3** *lower prices* cheaper, reduced, decreased, cut, slashed.

**lower** verb **1** *lower the flag/weight* let down, take down, drop, let fall, let sink. **2** *lower the volume* modulate, soften, quieten, hush, tone down, muffle, turn down, mute. **3** *will only lower him in her eyes* degrade, debase, demean, downgrade, discredit, devalue, dishonor, disgrace, belittle. **4** *lower the temperature/prices* reduce, bring down, decrease, lessen, cut, slash. **5** *the winds lowered* abate, die down, subside, let up, moderate, slacken, dwindle, lessen, ebb, wane, taper off.

**low-key** adjective restrained, muted, subtle, quiet, understated, relaxed, easygoing, modulated, softened; *inf.* laid-back.

**lowly** adjective **1** *of lowly birth* humble, poor, common. *See* LOW adjective 3. **2** *feeling lowly before God* humble, meek, submissive, modest, unassuming. **3** *lowly ambitions* low, simple, ordinary, commonplace, run-of-the-mill, modest, unambitious, unpretentious, unaspiring.

**loyal** adjective faithful, true, true-hearted, trusted, trustworthy, steadfast, staunch, dependable, reliable, devoted, dutiful, patriotic, constant, unwavering, unswerving.

**loyalty** noun faithfulness, fidelity, fealty, allegiance, trueness, trustworthiness, steadfastness, staunchness, dependability, reliability, devotion, patriotism, constancy.

**lubricant** noun lubricator, oil, grease, emollient, lard, fat, moisturizer, lotion, unguent.

**lucid** adjective **1** *a lucid description* clear, clear-cut, comprehensible, intelligible, understandable, plain, simple, direct, straightforward, transparent, cogent. **2** *he is scarcely lucid* sane, rational, in one's right mind, of sound mind, *compos mentis*, sensible, clearheaded; *inf.* all there, with all one's marbles.

**luck** noun **1** *as luck would have it* serendipity, fate, fortune, destiny, chance, fortuity, accident, hazard. **2** *wishing you luck* good luck, good fortune, success, prosperity, advantage, advantageousness, felicity. **in luck** lucky, fortunate, favored, advantaged, successful. **out of luck** unlucky, unfortunate, luckless, cursed with ill/bad luck, unsuccessful, disadvantaged.

**lucky** adjective **1** *lucky people* fortunate, favored, born under a lucky star, charmed; successful, prosperous, advantaged. **2** *a lucky guess* fortunate, fortuitous, providential, advantageous, timely, opportune, expedient, auspicious, propitious.

**lucrative** adjective profitable, profit-making, moneymaking, high-income, well-paid, high-paying, gainful, remunerative, productive, fat, fruitful, rewarding, worthwhile.

**ludicrous** adjective absurd, ridiculous, laughable, risible, derisible, comical, farcical, silly, funny, amusing, hilarious, crazy, outlandish, preposterous.

**luggage** noun bags, baggage, suitcases, trunks, things, gear, belongings, effects, impedimenta, paraphernalia, accoutrements.

**lugubrious** adjective mournful, doleful, melancholy, dismal, gloomy, somber, funereal, sorrowful, morose, miserable, joyless, woebegone, woeful, dirgelike, elegiac.

**lukewarm** adjective **1** *lukewarm water* tepid, warm, warmish, at room temperature. **2** *lukewarm response* indifferent, cool, halfhearted, apathetic, unenthusiastic, impassive, dispassionate, sluggish, phlegmatic.

**lull** verb **1** *lull the child to sleep* rock (gently), soothe, quiet, hush, silence, calm. **2** *the storm lulled* abate, die down, subside, let up, moderate, slacken, lessen, dwindle, decrease, diminish, ebb, fade away, wane, taper off.

**lull** noun **1** *a lull in the proceedings* pause, respite, interval, break, hiatus; *inf.* letup. **2** *the lull before the storm* calm, stillness, quiet, tranquillity, silence, hush.

**lumber** noun timber, wood, boards, planks, planking, beams.

**lumber** verb *heard him lumbering around upstairs* clump, stump, plod, trudge, stamp, shuffle, stumble.

**luminary** noun leading light, star, superstar, notable, dignitary, VIP, celebrity, big name, household name; *inf.* bigwig, big shot.

**luminous** adjective lighted, lit, illuminated, shining, bright, brilliant, radiant, dazzling, glowing, effulgent, luminescent, phosphorescent, vivid, resplendent.

**lump** noun **1** *a lump of putty/coal* chunk, wedge, hunk, piece, mass, cake, nugget, ball, dab, pat, clod, gob, wad, clump, mound. **2** *a lump on his head* bump, swelling, bruise, bulge, protuberance, protrusion, growth, carbuncle, hump, tumor, tumescence, node.

**lump** verb *lump all the expenses together* combine, group, unite, pool, blend, merge, mass, fuse, conglomerate, consolidate.

**lumpy** adjective **1** *a lumpy mattress* bumpy, knobby, bulging, uneven. **2** *lumpy custard* curdled, clotted, granular, grainy.

**lunacy** noun **1** *suffering from lunacy* insanity, madness, mental illness/derangement, dementia, dementedness, loss of reason, mania, frenzy, psychosis; *inf.* craziness. **2** *the sheer lunacy of the decision* madness, insanity, foolishness, folly, foolhardiness,

stupidity, idiocy, irrationality, illogicality, senselessness, absurdity, ludicrousness; *inf.* craziness, daftness.

**lunatic** noun maniac, madman, madwoman, imbecile, idiot, psychopath; *inf.* loony, nut, nutcase, basket case, psycho.

**lunatic** adjective mad, insane, foolish, foolhardy, idiotic, crackbrained, irrational, illogical, senseless, nonsensical, absurd, silly, asinine, ludicrous, preposterous; *inf.* crazy, daft.

**lunge** noun **1** *make a lunge toward the open door* spring, jump, leap, bound, dash, charge, pounce, dive. **2** *take a lunge at his attacker* stab, jab, poke, thrust, swing, pass, cut, feint; *inf.* swipe.

**lunge** verb *lunge toward the door* spring, jump, leap, bound, dash, charge, pounce, dive. **lunge at** *lunge at his attacker* charge, rush, jump, attack, pounce on, lash out at, take a swing at; *inf.* take a swipe at.

**lurch** verb **1** *drunks lurching home* stagger, sway, reel, weave, stumble, totter. **2** *ships lurching in the storm* list, roll, pitch, toss, sway, veer, swerve.

**lure** verb entice, attract, induce, inveigle, decoy, draw, lead, allure, tempt, seduce, beguile, ensnare, cajole.

**lure** noun enticement, attraction, inducement, decoy, draw, temptation, bait, magnet, drawing card, carrot; *inf.* come-on.

**lurid** adjective **1** *lurid colors/sunsets* overbright, brilliant, glaring, flaming, dazzling, glowing, intense, vivid, showy, gaudy, fiery, blood-red, burning. **2** *lurid descriptions of their affair* sensational, melodramatic, exaggerated, extravagant, graphic, explicit, unrestrained, shocking, startling; *inf.* full-frontal. **3** *lurid details of the murder* gruesome, gory, grisly, macabre, repugnant, revolting, disgusting, ghastly.

**lurk** verb skulk, lie in wait, hide, crouch, sneak, slink, prowl, steal, tiptoe.

**luscious** adjective delicious, juicy, sweet, succulent, mouthwatering, tasty, appetizing, delectable, palatable, toothsome; *inf.* scrumptious, yummy.

**lush** adjective **1** *lush vegetation* luxuriant, abundant, profuse, exuberant, dense, thick, riotous, overgrown, prolific, rank, teeming, junglelike, flourishing, verdant, green. **2** *lush fruits* juicy, succulent, fleshy, pulpy, ripe, soft, tender, fresh. **3** *lush penthouse* luxurious, sumptuous, grand, palatial, opulent, lavish, elaborate, extravagant; *inf.* plush, ritzy.

**lust** noun **1** *physical lust* sexual desire, sexual appetite, libido, sex drive, sexuality; lechery, lasciviousness, lewdness, carnality, licentiousness, salaciousness, salacity, prurience, concupiscence, wantonness; *inf.* horniness. **2** *a lust for power* greed, greediness, desire, craving, covetousness, avidness, avidity, cupidity, longing, yearning, hunger, thirst, appetite, passion.

**lust** verb desire, crave, covet, want, need, long for, yearn for, hunger for, thirst for, ache for; *inf.* have the hots for.

**luster** noun **1** *admire the luster of the table* sheen, gloss, shine, burnish, glow, gleam, sparkle, shimmer. **2** *bring luster to the school* honor, glory, credit, merit, prestige, renown, fame, distinction, notability. **3** *the luster of the stars* brilliance, brightness, radiance, luminousness.

**lustrous** adjective shiny, shining, glossy, gleaming, glowing, bright, burnished, polished, dazzling, sparkling, glistening, twinkling, shimmering, luminous.

**lusty** adjective **1** *lusty young men* healthy, strong, vigorous, robust, hale and hearty, hearty, energetic, lively, rugged, sturdy, tough, stalwart, brawny, hefty, husky, burly, powerful, virile, red-blooded. **2** *a lusty cry* loud, vigorous, hearty, powerful, forceful.

**luxuriant** adjective **1** *luxuriant vegetation* lush, abundant, prolific, verdant. *See* LUSH adjective 1. **2** *luxuriant prose* florid, flowery, ornate, elaborate, fancy, adorned, decorated, embellished, embroidered, extravagant, flamboyant, ostentatious, showy, high-flown, baroque, rococo.

**luxurious** adjective **1** *luxurious surroundings* opulent, affluent, sumptuous, expensive, rich, costly, deluxe, lush, grand, splendid, magnificent, lavish, well-appointed, comfortable, extravagant, ornate, fancy; *inf.* plush, posh, ritzy, swanky. **2** *luxurious habits* self-indulgent, sensual, epicurean, hedonistic, sybaritic.

**luxury** noun **1** *live in luxury* opulence, affluence, sumptuousness, richness, grandeur, splendor, magnificence, lavishness, luxuriousness, lap of luxury, bed of roses. **2** *the luxury of independence* boon, benefit, advantage, delight, bliss, comfort. **3** *one of life's luxuries* extra, nonessential, frill, extravagance, indulgence, treat, refinement.

**lying** noun untruthfulness, fabrication, fibbing, perjury, falseness, falsity, dishonesty, mendacity, storytelling, dissimulation, dissembling, prevarication, deceit, guile, crookedness, double-dealing.

**lyric** adjective **1** *lyric poetry* songlike, musical, melodic, melodious, expressive, personal, subjective, emotional, passionate, lyrical. **2** *lyric voices* light, silvery, clear, lilting, flowing, dulcet, sweet, mellifluous, mellow, lyrical.

**lyrics** plural noun words, libretto, book, text.

# *Mm*

**macabre** adjective gruesome, grisly, grim, gory, morbid, ghastly, hideous, horrific, horrible, horrifying, dreadful, appalling, loathsome, repugnant, repulsive.

**mace** noun staff, club, cudgel, bludgeon.

**machinations** plural noun schemes, plot, intrigues, conspiracies, complots, designs, plans, devices, ploys, ruses, trick, wiles, stratagems, tactics, maneuvers, contrivances, expedients.

**machine** noun **1** *the washing machine broke down* appliance, apparatus, instrument, tool, device, contraption, gadget, mechanism, engine, motor. **2** *the party machine* organization, system, structure, agency, machinery, council, cabal, clique; *inf.* setup.

**machinery** noun **1** *factory machinery* equipment, apparatus, mechanism, gear, tackle, instruments, gadgetry. **2** *the machinery of government* workings, organization, system, structure, agency, channel, vehicle;

*inf.* setup, nuts and bolts, brass tacks, nitty-gritty.

**machismo** noun masculinity, manliness, virility, toughness, chauvinism, male chauvinism, sexism.

**mad** adjective **1** *mad with grief* stark (raving) mad, insane, deranged, demented, of unsound mind, crazed, lunatic, *non compos mentis*, unbalanced, unhinged, unstable, distracted, manic, frenzied, raving, distraught, frantic, hysterical, delirious, psychotic, not quite right, mad as a hatter, mad as a March hare, foaming at the mouth; *inf.* crazy, out of one's mind, nuts, nutty, off one's rocker, round/around the bend, balmy, batty, bonkers, crackers, cuckoo, loopy, loony, bananas, loco, dippy, screwy, with a screw loose, out of one's tree, off one's trolley, off the wall, not all there, not right. **2** *the vandalism made them mad* angry, furious, infuriated, irate, raging, enraged, fuming, in a towering rage, incensed, wrathful, indignant, exasperated, irritated, berserk, out of control, beside oneself, livid. **3** *a mad scheme/idea* insane, foolish, stupid, lunatic, idiotic, crackbrained, irrational, illogical, senseless, absurd, impractical, silly, inane, imprudent, preposterous. **4** *mad, passionate love* wild, unrestrained, uncontrolled, abandoned, excited, frenzied, frantic, frenetic, ebullient, energetic, boisterous. **like mad 1** *run like mad* furiously, energetically; *inf.* like crazy, like a house on fire. **2** *love her like mad* madly, enthusiastically, wildly, passionately, intensely, ardently, fervently, to distraction, devotedly. **mad about** *mad about jazz* keen on, fanatical about, devoted to, infatuated with, in love with; *inf.* crazy about, nuts about, hooked on, wild about.

**madcap** adjective daredevil, impulsive, wild, reckless, rash, hotheaded, daring, adventurous, heedless, imprudent, ill-advised, foolhardy, impractical, harebrained.

**madden** verb *her behavior maddened them* anger, infuriate, send into a rage, enrage, incense, exasperate, irritate, inflame, annoy, provoke, upset, agitate, vex, irk, pique, gall, make one's blood boil, make one see red.

**maddening** adjective infuriating, exasperating, irritating, annoying, provoking, upsetting, vexing, irksome, unsettling, disturbing.

**made-up** adjective **1** *a made-up story* invented, fabricated, trumped-up, concocted, devised, manufactured, fictional, false, untrue, unreal, sham, specious, spurious, imaginary, mythical. **2** *made-up faces* painted, done up, powdered, rouged.

**madhouse** noun **1** *confined to a madhouse* mental hospital, psychiatric hospital, asylum; *inf.* nuthouse, funny farm, loony bin. **2** *the place is a madhouse!* bedlam, babel, chaos, pandemonium, uproar, turmoil, disarray, disorder, three-ring circus.

**madly** adverb **1** *behaving madly* insanely, distractedly, frenziedly, maniacally, frantically, hysterically, deliriously, wildly. **2** *rush around madly* furiously, hastily, energetically. **3** *love her madly* enthusiastically, wildly, intensely.

**madman** noun maniac, lunatic, psychopath; *inf.* loony, nut, nutcase, psycho.

**madness** noun **1** *madness caused by grief* insanity, insaneness, dementia, mental illness/derangement, dementedness, lunacy, mania, frenzy, psychosis, craziness. **2** *with madness in her voice* anger, fury, rage, wrath, ire, indignation, exasperation, irritation. **3** *the madness of the decision* insanity, folly, foolishness, stupidity, lunacy, idiocy, senselessness, absurdity, silliness, inanity.

**maelstrom** noun **1** *ships destroyed in a maelstrom* whirlpool, vortex, eddy, swirl, Charybdis. **2** *the maelstrom of war* turbulence, tumult, uproar, commotion, chaos, confusion, upheaval, pandemonium, bedlam.

**magazine** noun periodical, journal, publication, supplement, color supplement; *inf.* glossy.

**magic** noun **1** *believers in magic* sorcery, witchcraft, wizardry, enchantment, necromancy, occultism, the occult, black magic, voodoo, thaumaturgy. **2** *skills of magic* sleight of hand, legerdemain, conjuring, illusion, prestidigitation; *inf.* hocus-pocus. **3** *the magic of the stage* allure, enchantment, fascination, charm.

**magic** adjective magical, enchanting, entrancing, spellbinding, fascinating, captivating, charming, glamorous, magnetic, irresistible, hypnotic.

**magician** noun **1** *frightened by the magician* sorcerer, sorceress, witch, wizard, warlock, enchanter, enchantress, necromancer. **2** *the magician at the party* illusionist, conjuror, legerdemainist, prestidigitator. **3** *a magician at the piano* genius, master, virtuoso, expert, marvel, wizard, maestro; *inf.* ace, whiz.

**magnanimity** noun generosity, charitableness, benevolence, bigheartedness, munificence, bountifulness, largesse, unselfishness, selflessness, self-sacrifice, mercy, leniency.

**magnanimous** adjective generous, benevolent, beneficent, bighearted, greathearted, munificent, bountiful, noble, unselfish, ungrudging, forgiving, merciful, lenient, indulgent.

**magnate** noun tycoon, captain of industry, baron, industrialist, entrepreneur, financier, VIP, notable, nabob, grandee; *inf.* big shot, bigwig, big wheel, fat cat, mogul.

**magnet** noun **1** *a magnet attracting iron filings* lodestone, magnetite. **2** *the ad worked as a magnet* lure, attraction, fascination, enticement, draw, temptation, come-on.

**magnetic** adjective alluring, attractive, captivating, entrancing, enchanting, enthralling, engaging, seductive, inviting, bewitching, charismatic, hypnotic, mesmeric.

**magnetism** noun allure, attraction, appeal, draw, drawing power, pull, charm, charisma.

**magnification** noun increase, augmentation, enlargement, extension, expansion, intensification, heightening, enhancement, aggrandizement.

**magnificence** noun splendor, grandeur, glory, sumptuousness, opulence, luxuriousness, luxury, lavishness, richness, brilliance, radiance, elegance.

**magnificent** adjective **1** *a magnificent procession/apartments* splendid, resplendent, grand, grandiose, impressive, majestic, august, noble, stately, sumptuous, opulent, luxurious; *inf.* splendiferous, ritzy, posh. **2** *a magnificent performance* masterly, virtuoso, impressive, marvelous, wonderful; *inf.* terrific, brilliant, out of this world.

**magnify** verb **1** *bacteria visible when magnified* increase, augment, enlarge, expand, amplify, intensify, boost, enhance, aggrandize. **2** *magnify their troubles* exaggerate, overstate, overemphasize, overplay, color, embroider, embellish, enhance, inflate; *inf.* blow up, blow up out of all proportion.

**magnitude** noun **1** *the magnitude of the explosion/epidemic* size, extent, measure, proportions, dimensions, volume, weight, quantity, mass, bulk, amplitude; greatness, largeness, bigness, immensity, vastness, hugeness, enormity, enormousness, expanse. **2** *the magnitude of his rank* importance, significance, weight, moment, consequence, mark, notability, note, greatness, distinction, eminence, fame, renown. **of the first magnitude** of the utmost importance, of the greatest significance.

**maid** noun maidservant, housemaid, chambermaid, servant, domestic, girl, au pair.

**maiden** adjective **1** *maiden aunt* unmarried, spinster, unwed, unwedded, single, celibate. **2** *maiden voyage* first, initial, inaugural, introductory, initiatory. **3** *maiden territory* virgin, intact, undefiled, untrodden, untapped, unused, fresh, new.

**mail** noun letters, packages, parcels, correspondence, communications, airmail, registered mail; electronic mail, E-mail.

**maim** verb cripple, disable, put out of action, lame, incapacitate, impair, mar, mutilate, disfigure, mangle, wound, injure, hurt.

**main** adjective **1** *the main office* head, chief, principal, leading, foremost, central, prime, premier, primary, supreme, predominant, preeminent, paramount, cardinal, pivotal. **2** *by main force* sheer, pure, utter, downright, mere, plain, brute, stark, absolute, out-and-out, direct.

**mainly** adverb for the most part, mostly, in the main, on the whole, largely, by and large, predominantly, chiefly, overall, in general, generally.

**mainstay** noun chief support, prop, linchpin, pillar, bulwark, buttress, backbone, anchor.

**maintain** verb **1** *maintain friendly relations* continue, keep up, carry on, preserve, conserve, prolong, perpetuate, sustain. **2** *maintain the roads* keep in repair, keep up, keep intact, take care for, take good care of, look after. **3** *maintain a family* support, provide for, keep, finance, feed, nurture, nourish, sustain. **4** *maintain his innocence* declare, assert, state, affirm, aver, avow, profess, claim, allege, contend, asseverate. **5** *maintain a position* uphold, defend, fight for, stand by, support, back, advocate.

**maintenance** noun **1** *the maintenance of friendly relations* continuation, continuance, preservation, perpetuation. **2** *the maintenance of the property* upkeep, repairs, preservation, conservation, care.

**majestic** adjective regal, royal, kingly, queenly, princely, noble, lordly, august, exalted, lofty, stately, dignified, magnificent, grand, splendid, resplendent, glorious, impressive, imposing.

**majesty** noun **1** *the majesty of the procession* nobility, augustness, loftiness, stateliness, dignity, magnificence, grandeur, grandness, splendor, resplendence, glory. **2** *the majesty invested in him* sovereignty, authority, power, dominion, supremacy.

**major** adjective **1** *the major part is complete* larger, bigger, greater, main. **2** *one of our major poets* greatest, best, most important, leading, foremost, chief, main, outstanding, first-rate, notable, eminent, preeminent, supreme. **3** *a major issue* important, significant, crucial, vital, great, weighty, serious.

**make** verb **1** *make furniture* build, construct, assemble, put together, put up, erect, manufacture, produce, fabricate, create, form, fashion, model, mold, shape, forge. **2** *make them pay* force (to), compel (to), coerce (into), press (into), drive (into), pressure (into), oblige (to), require (to), prevail upon (to), impel (to); *inf.* railroad (into), put the heat on, put the screws on, strong-arm. **3** *make a noise/scene* cause, create, give rise to, produce, bring about, generate, engender, occasion, effect. **4** *make a bow* perform, execute, do, accomplish, carry out, practice, engage in. **5** *make him chairman* appoint, designate, name, nominate, select, elect, vote in, install, invest, ordain, assign. **6** *make a will/movie* compose, put together, frame, formulate, prepare, write, direct. **7** *make money* gain, acquire, obtain, get, realize, secure, win, earn, net, gross, clear, bring in, take home, pocket. **8** *make tea/dinner* prepare, get ready, put together, concoct, cook; *inf.* whip up, fix. **9** *make laws* draw up, frame, form, formulate, enact, lay down, establish, institute, found, originate. **10** *that makes $100* come to, add up to, total, amount to. **11** *what do you make the total to be?* estimate, calculate, compute, gauge, reckon. **12** *make a decision* come to, settle on, determine on, conclude, establish, seal. **13** *make a speech* give, deliver, utter, give voice to, enunciate, recite, pronounce. **14** *the sofa makes a good bed* act as, serve as, constitute, play the part of, represent, embody. **15** *made the team* achieve, attain, get into, gain access to, gain a place in. **16** *make the bus/party* catch, arrive at, reach, get to. **make as if/though** act as if/though, pretend, feign, give the impression, make a show of, affect, feint; *inf.* put it on. **make believe** pretend, fantasize, indulge in fantasy, daydream, build castles in the air, build castles in Spain, dream, imagine, romance, playact, act, enact. **make do** get by, get along, scrape by, manage, cope, survive, muddle through. **make for 1** *make for a safe place* go toward, head for, aim for, make one's way toward, proceed toward. **2** *this will make for a good relationship* contribute to, be conducive to, promote, facilitate, further, advance, forward, favor. **make off** run away/off, take to one's heels, beat a hasty retreat, flee, bolt, fly, make a getaway, make a quick exit, abscond, decamp; *inf.* clear off, beat it, make tracks, split, cut and run, skedaddle, vamoose, hightail it. **make off with** steal, purloin, appropriate, kidnap, abduct; *inf.* swipe, nab, waltz off with, filch. **make out 1** *make out a figure in the distance* discern, see, distinguish, espy, behold, perceive, descry, notice, observe, recognize, pick out, detect, discover. **2** *unable to make out what she says* understand, comprehend, follow, grasp, fathom, work out, figure out, interpret. **3** *unable to make out the handwriting* decipher, work out, figure out, understand, interpret. **4** *they made out that he was violent* allege, claim, suggest, imply, pretend. **5** *how did you make out?* get on, get along, fare, do, get by, proceed, go, progress, manage, survive. **make over** renovate, remodel, redo, restore, redecorate, brighten up, improve, upgrade; *inf.* do up. **make up 1** *their statements make up the argument* comprise, form, compose, constitute. **2** *make up the balance* supply, furnish, provide. **3** *make up for previous rudeness* make amends, atone, compensate, make recompense, make reparation, make redress. **4** *kiss and make up* be friends again, bury the hatchet, declare a truce, make peace, forgive and forget, shake hands, become reconciled, settle differences, mend fences. **5** *make up a prescription* prepare, mix, concoct, put together. **6** *make up an excuse* invent, fabricate, concoct, hatch, coin, trump up, dream up, think up, devise, manufacture, formulate, frame, construct; *inf.* cook up. **7** *make up a short story* compose, write, create, originate, devise. **8** *make up her face* apply cosmetics to, powder,

rouge; *inf.* put on, do, paint, do up, apply warpaint to.

**make** noun **1** *different makes of car* brand, label, trademark, sort, type, variety, style, mark, marque. **2** *a clumsy make of machine* build, form, frame, structure, construction, shape. **3** *a different make from his brother* character, nature. *See* MAKEUP 3.

**make-believe** noun pretense, fantasy, daydreaming, dreaming, imagination, romancing, fabrication, playacting, charade, masquerade.

**make-believe** adjective pretended, feigned, made-up, fantasy, dream, imaginary, unreal, fictitious, mock, sham; *inf.* pretend.

**maker** noun manufacturer, builder, constructor, producer, creator, fabricator, author, architect, framer.

**makeshift** adjective stopgap, make-do, provisional, temporary, rough-and-ready, substitute, improvised, standby, jerry-built, thrown-together.

**makeup** noun **1** *putting on their makeup* cosmetics, greasepaint, foundation; *inf.* warpaint, face paint. **2** *the makeup of the machines* structure, composition, constitution, configuration, construction, assembly, arrangement, organization. **3** *the makeup of a criminal* character, nature, temperament, temper, personality, disposition, humor, make, stamp, mold.

**makings** plural noun qualities, characteristics, ingredients, materials, essentials, beginnings, basics.

**maladjusted** adjective disturbed, unstable, neurotic; *inf.* mixed-up, screwed-up.

**malady** noun disease, disorder, illness, sickness, ailment, affliction, complaint, infection, indisposition, infirmity.

**malaise** noun lassitude, listlessness, languor, enervation, weakness, feebleness, infirmity, illness, sickness, unease, discomfort, anxiety, angst, disquiet, melancholy, depression, weariness, ennui.

**malcontent** noun grumbler, complainer, moaner, faultfinder, carper, agitator, troublemaker, mischief-maker, rebel; *inf.* grouser, griper, nitpicker, bellyacher.

**male** adjective masculine, manlike, manly, virile.

**male** noun **1** *clothing for males* man, gentleman, boy, lad; *inf.* fellow, guy. **2** *The male has brighter plumage* tomcat, bull, ram, stallion, buck, stag, boar, billy goat, cock, gander, drake.

**malevolent** adjective malign, malignant, malicious, maleficent, evil-intentioned, evil-minded, ill-natured, hostile, unfriendly, spiteful, baleful, vindictive, revengeful, rancorous, vicious, pernicious, cruel.

**malfunction** verb go wrong, break down, break, fail; *inf.* conk out, go kaput.

**malfunction** noun fault, defect, flaw, impairment, glitch; breakdown, failure, collapse.

**malice** noun malevolence, maliciousness, malignity, evil intentions, ill will, ill feeling, animosity, animus, hostility, enmity, bad blood, hatred, hate, spite, spitefulness, vindictiveness, rancor, bitterness, grudge, venom, spleen.

**malicious** adjective malevolent, malign, malignant, evil, evil-intentioned, ill-natured, hostile, spiteful, baleful, vindictive, rancorous, bitter, venomous, pernicious, harmful, hurtful, destructive, defamatory; *inf.* bitchy, catty.

**malign** verb slander, libel, defame, smear, calumniate, vilify, speak ill of, spread lies about, cast aspersions on, misrepresent, traduce, denigrate, disparage, slur, derogate; *inf.* bad-mouth, run down, drag through the mud.

**malignant** adjective 1 *malignant intentions* malevolent, evil. See MALICIOUS. 2 *a malignant growth/disease* cancerous, dangerous, virulent, uncontrollable, deadly, fatal, life-threatening, lethal.

**malleable** adjective 1 *malleable substances* workable, shapable, moldable, plastic, pliant, ductile, tractile. 2 *malleable people* pliable, compliant, accommodating, adaptable, amenable, biddable, tractable, manageable, governable.

**malnutrition** noun undernourishment, starvation, famine, anorexia.

**malpractice** noun unprofessional conduct, dereliction, negligence, carelessness, unethical behavior, misconduct, wrongdoing.

**maltreat** verb ill-treat, ill-use. See MISTREAT.

**maltreatment** noun ill treatment, ill use, mistreatment, abuse, rough handling, manhandling, bullying, injury, harm.

**mammoth** adjective huge, enormous. See MASSIVE.

**man** noun 1 *a fine man* male, gentleman; *inf.* fellow, guy. 2 *no man is perfect* human being, human, mortal, person, individual, one. 3 *the evolution of man* mankind, the human race, the human species, *Homo sapiens*, humankind, human beings, humans, people. 4 *employ a man to do the garden* workman, worker, laborer, helper, hand. 5 *the ambassador and his man* valet, manservant, gentleman's gentleman; page, footman; flunky. 6 *his sister and her man* husband, spouse, boyfriend, partner, lover, escort, beau, significant other. **to a man** with no ex-

ceptions, without exception, bar none, unanimously, as one.

**manacles** plural noun handcuffs, chains, irons, hand shackles/fetters; *inf.* cuffs, bracelets.

**manage** verb 1 *manage the team/organization* run, head, direct, control, preside over, lead, govern, rule, command, superintend, supervise, oversee, administer, organize, conduct, handle, guide, be at the helm of; *inf.* head up. 2 *manage to survive* succeed (in), contrive, engineer, bring about/off, achieve, accomplish, effect; cope, get along, carry on, survive, make do; *inf.* make out, get by. 3 *can you manage the dog?* deal with, handle, control, master, influence. 4 *manage a weapon* wield, use, operate, work, ply, handle, manipulate.

**manageable** adjective doable, practicable, possible, feasible; controllable, governable, tamable, tractable, docile, accommodating, amenable.

**management** noun 1 *the dispute with management* managers, employers, owners, proprietors, directors, executives; *inf.* bosses, top brass. 2 *the management of the firm* administration, running, charge, care, direction, command, supervision.

**manager** noun employer, director, executive, department head, administrator, superintendent, supervisor; *inf.* boss.

**mandate** noun direction, instruction, order, command, directive, ruling, decree, edict, dictate.

**mandatory** adjective obligatory, compulsory, binding, required, requisite, essential, imperative, necessary.

**maneuver** noun 1 *maneuver of troops* movement, deployment, operation, exercise. 2 *with one deft maneuver* move, stroke; trick, stratagem, tactic, machination, artifice, dodge, ploy, ruse, scheme.

**maneuver** verb 1 *maneuver the car* move, work, negotiate, steer, guide, direct, manipulate. 2 *maneuvers things to suit himself* manage, manipulate, contrive, engineer, devise, plan, plot; *inf.* wangle. 3 *maneuver for the leadership* scheme, intrigue, plot.

**mangle** verb 1 *the mower mangled the hose* mutilate, hack, cut up, lacerate, maul, tear at, rend, butcher, disfigure, deform. 2 *mangle the piece of music* spoil, ruin, bungle, make a mess of; *inf.* murder.

**mangy** adjective 1 *mangy animals* scabby, scabious, scaly. 2 *mangy carpets* shabby, scruffy, shoddy, squalid, seedy. 3 *a mangy individual* contemptible, despicable, nasty, mean, base, low.

**manhandle** verb shove, maul, mistreat, ill-treat, abuse, injure, damage, beat, batter; *inf.* paw, knock about, beat up, rough up.

**manhood** noun **1** *reach manhood* adulthood, maturity, sexual maturity, puberty. **2** *insult his manhood* maleness, masculinity, virility, machismo. **3** *soldiers demonstrating their manhood* bravery, courage. *See* MANLINESS 1.

**mania** noun *a mania for collecting china* passion, enthusiasm, desire, urge, craving, craze, obsession, compulsion, fixation, fetish, fascination, preoccupation; *inf.* thing.

**maniac** noun madman, madwoman, psychopath, lunatic; *inf.* loony, nutcase, nut, psycho.

**manifest** verb **1** *manifest strange symptoms* display, show, exhibit, demonstrate, present, evince, express, reveal, indicate, make plain, declare. **2** *manifest his guilt* prove, evidence, substantiate, corroborate, verify.

**manifest** adjective obvious, clear, plain, apparent, patent, conspicuous, unmistakable, distinct, blatant, glaring.

**manifestation** noun **1** *a manifestation of solidarity* display, show, exhibition, demonstration, presentation, exposition, illustration, exemplification, indication, declaration. **2** *manifestations of their presence* evidence, proof, testimony, substantiation, sign, indication.

**manifesto** noun proclamation, pronouncement, declaration, announcement.

**manipulate** verb **1** *manipulate the tool/weapon* handle, wield, ply, work, operate, use, employ, utilize, exercise. **2** *manipulate his colleagues* influence, control, use to one's advantage, exploit, maneuver, engineer, steer, direct, guide, pull the strings. **3** *manipulate the figures* juggle, massage, falsify, doctor, tamper with, fiddle with, tinker with; *inf.* cook.

**manipulator** noun exploiter, maneuverer, conniver, intriguer.

**manliness** noun **1** *show their manliness in battle* manhood, bravery, courage, valor, boldness, fearlessness, stoutheartedness. **2** *cologne said to evoke manliness* masculinity, virility, strength, robustness, muscularity, powerfulness, ruggedness, toughness.

**manly** adjective **1** *manly characteristics* manful, brave, courageous, gallant, valiant, valorous, bold, fearless, stout, stouthearted, dauntless; *inf.* macho, Ramboesque. **2** *a manly figure* masculine, virile, robust, muscular, powerful, well-built, strapping, sturdy, rugged, tough; *inf.* hunky, buff.

**man-made** adjective manufactured, synthetic, artificial, imitation, ersatz, plastic.

**manner** noun **1** *work in an efficient manner* way, means, method, system, approach, technique, procedure, process, methodology, routine, practice, fashion, mode. **2** *an unfriendly manner* look, air, appearance, demeanor, aspect, mien, bearing, cast, deportment. **3** *what manner of person is he?* kind, sort, type, variety, form, nature, breed, class, category.

**mannered** adjective affected, unnatural, artificial, stilted, theatrical, posed, stagy.

**mannerism** noun habit, characteristic gesture, trait, idiosyncrasy, quirk, peculiarity.

**manners** plural noun behavior, conduct; correct behavior, etiquette, good form, protocol, politeness, decorum, propriety, social graces, formalities, politesse.

**mansion** noun manor house, manor, hall, stately home; palace, castle.

**manslaughter** noun killing, slaying, murder, homicide.

**manual** noun handbook, instructions, guidebook, guide; *inf.* how-to book, bible.

**manufacture** verb **1** *manufacture cars* produce, mass-produce, turn out, process. *See* MAKE verb 1. **2** *manufacture an excuse* invent, fabricate. *See* MAKE UP 6 (MAKE verb).

**manufacture** noun making, production, mass production, construction, assembly, creation, fabrication, processing.

**manure** noun dung, excrement, muck, guano, droppings, fertilizer.

**many** adjective numerous, innumerable, countless, scores of, myriad, multitudinous, multiple, copious, abundant, various, sundry, diverse, several, frequent; *inf.* umpteen, lots of, scads of, heaps of, piles of, bags of, tons of, oodles of, an army of, zillions of.

**many** noun scores, a host, a horde, a crowd, a multitude, a mass, an accumulation, an abundance, a profusion, plenty. **the many** *the wishes of the many* majority, the people, the masses, the multitude, the rank and file, the crowd, the hoi polloi.

**map** noun chart, plan, plot, guide, street guide, town plan, road map, atlas, gazetteer.

**map** verb chart, plot, delineate, depict, portray, **map out** lay out, detail, draw up, sketch out, plan, plot out.

**mar** verb spoil, detract from, impair, damage, ruin, wreck, disfigure, blemish, scar, deface, harm, hurt, injure, deform, tarnish, taint, sully, stain, blot.

**maraud** verb raid, plunder, loot, pillage, foray, ransack, forage, ravage, harry, sack, despoil.

**marauder** noun raider, plunderer, pillager, looter, ravager, robber, pirate, freebooter, buccaneer, corsair, rover, bandit, brigand, rusder, highwayman.

**march** verb **1** *armies marching* pace, tread, stride, footslog, tramp, hike, trudge, stalk, strut, parade, file. **2** *time marches on* advance, progress, forge ahead, go on, continue on, roll on, develop, evolve.

**march** noun **1** *scouts on a march* walk, tramp, trek, hike, parade. **2** *a march against the tobacco industry* demonstration, parade, procession, rally. **3** *the march of time* advance, progress, progression, passage, headway, continuance, development, evolution.

**margin** noun **1** *the margin of the lake* edge, side, verge, border, perimeter, boundary, limits, periphery, brink, brim. **2** *the margin between the countries* border, boundary, frontier, demarcation line. **3** *margin for error* leeway, latitude, scope, room, space, allowance, extra, surplus. **4** *win by a narrow margin* difference, amount.

**marginal** adjective *marginal ability* slight, small, tiny, minute, low, minor, insignificant, minimal, negligible.

**marijuana** noun cannabis, hashish, hemp, ganja, sinsemilla; *inf.* dope, hash, grass, pot, mary jane, tea, weed.

**marine** adjective **1** *marine life* sea, aquatic, saltwater, oceanic, pelagic, neritic, thalassic. **2** *marine careers* maritime, nautical, naval, seafaring, seagoing.

**mariner** noun sailor, seaman, seafarer; *inf.* sea dog, (old) salt, bluejacket, tar, gob.

**marital** adjective matrimonial, marriage, wedding, conjugal, connubial, nuptial, spousal, married, wedded.

**mark** noun **1** *marks on the table* stain, blemish, blot, smear, trace, spot, speck, dot, blotch, smudge, splotch, bruise, scratch, scar, dent, pit, pock, chip, notch, nick, line, score, cut, incision, gash. **2** *the marks on a horse/cow* marking, blaze, spot, speckle, stripe, brand, earmark. **3** *marks showing the way* marker, guide, pointer, landmark, direction post, signpost, milestone. **4** *mark of respect* sign, symbol, indication, symptom, feature, token, badge, emblem, evidence, proof, clue, hint. **5** *the corporation's mark* seal, stamp, signet, symbol, emblem, device, badge, motto, monogram, hallmark, trademark, logo, watermark, label, tag, flag. **6** *war left its mark on him* impression, imprint, traces, vestiges, remains, effect, impact, influence. **7** *the mark of an honest man* characteristic, feature, trait, attribute, quality, stamp, peculiarity. **8** *the insult missed its mark* target, goal, aim, bull's-eye, objective, object, end, purpose, intent, intention. **9** *work falling below the mark* standard, norm, par, level, criterion, gauge, yardstick, rule, measure, scale. **10** *a person of mark* dis-

tinction, importance, consequence, eminence, preeminence, prominence, note, notability, fame, repute, greatness, prestige, celebrity, glory, standing, rank. **make one's mark** be successful, succeed, prosper, make good, achieve recognition; *inf.* make it. **wide of the mark** irrelevant, inapplicable, inapposite, inappropriate, not to the point, beside the point; inaccurate, incorrect, wrong, erroneous, inexact, off-target.

**mark** verb **1** *mark the table* stain, smear, smudge, scratch, scar, dent, chip, notch, score, cut, gash. **2** *mark your property* name, initial, put one's seal on, label, tag, stamp, flag, hallmark, watermark, brand, earmark. **3** *mark the places on a map* name, indicate, write down, tag, label, flag. **4** *mark the students' essays* correct, assess, evaluate, appraise, grade. **5** *the children marked his displeasure* see, notice, observe, take note of, discern, spot, recognize. **6** *you should mark his words* heed, take notice of, pay attention to, attend to, note, mind, bear in mind. **7** *a day marked by misfortune* characterize, distinguish, identify, denote, brand, signalize. **8** *mark his birthday* celebrate, commemorate, honor, observe, recognize, acknowledge, solemnize. **mark down** reduce, decrease, lower, cut, slash, put on sale. **mark up** raise, increase, up, hike up, escalate; *inf.* jack up.

**marked** adjective pronounced, decided, striking, clear, glaring, blatant, unmistakable, prominent, conspicuous, noticeable, distinct, salient, obvious, apparent, evident, manifest, patent.

**markedly** adverb decidedly, strikingly, remarkably, unmistakably, conspicuously, noticeably, pointedly, distinctly, recognizably, obviously, clearly, plainly.

**market** noun **1** *shopping at the market* marketplace, mart, shopping center, bazaar. **2** *no market for the product* demand, call, want, desire, need. **3** *the market is sluggish* trade, business, commerce, buying and selling. **in the market for** wishing to buy, in need of, wanting, lacking. **on the market** for sale, purchasable, available, obtainable.

**maroon** verb abandon, forsake, leave behind, leave, desert, strand, leave stranded.

**marriage** noun **1** *join in marriage* matrimony, wedlock, conjugal bond. **2** *invited to their marriage* marriage ceremony, wedding, nuptials. **3** *the marriage of their skills* alliance, union, merger, combination, coupling; *inf.* hookup.

**married** adjective **1** *married couple* wedded, wed, united in wedlock; *inf.* hitched. **2** *married bliss* marital, matrimonial, connubial, conjugal, nuptial, spousal.

**marrow** noun core, kernel, nucleus, pith,

heart, center, soul, spirit, essence, quintessence, gist, substance.

**marry** verb **1** *the couple married last year* wed, become man and wife, become espoused; *inf.* tie the knot, walk down the aisle, take the plunge, get hitched, get yoked. **2** *marry their skills* join, join together, unite, ally, merge, unify, combine, link, connect, fuse, weld, couple.

**marsh** noun marshland, bog, peatbog, swamp, swampland, morass, mire, quagmire, quag, slough, fen, bayou.

**marshal** verb **1** *tried to marshal his thoughts* gather together, assemble, collect, muster, draw up, line up, align, set/put in order, arrange, deploy, dispose, rank. **2** *marshal the guests to their seats* usher, guide, escort, conduct, lead, shepherd, take.

**marshy** adjective boggy, swampy, muddy, miry.

**martial** adjective military, soldierly; militant, warlike, combative, belligerent, bellicose, aggressive, pugnacious.

**martial arts** plural noun judo, jujitsu, aikido, karate, kung fu, t'ai chi (chu'an), tae kwon do.

**martyrdom** noun persecution, ordeal, torture, torment, suffering, agony, anguish.

**marvel** verb be amazed by, be awed by, wonder at, stare at, gape at, goggle at.

**marvel** noun wonder, wonderful thing, amazing thing, prodigy, sensation, spectacle, phenomenon, miracle; *inf.* something else, something to shout about.

**marvelous** adjective **1** *his solo climb was marvelous* amazing, astounding, astonishing, awesome, breathtaking, sensational, remarkable, spectacular, stupendous, phenomenal, wondrous, prodigious, miraculous, extraordinary. **2** *a marvelous singer* excellent, splendid, wonderful, magnificent, superb, glorious, super, great, boffo, smashing, fantastic, terrific, fabulous, awesome; *inf.* mean, bad, wicked.

**masculine** adjective **1** *a masculine physique* virile, robust. See MANLY 2. **2** *joined the army to prove he was masculine* brave, courageous. *see* MANLY 1.

**masculinity** noun **1** *the masculinity of his physique* virility, robustness. *See* MANLINESS 2. **2** *show their masculinity in battle* manhood, bravery. *See* MANLINESS 1.

**mash** verb crush, pulp, purée, smash, squash, pound, beat.

**mash** noun pulp, mush, paste, purée, slush, pap.

**mask** noun *under the mask of being a tourist* disguise, guise, concealment, cover, cover-up, cloak, camouflage, veil, screen, front, false front, façade, blind, semblance, false colors, pretense.

**mask** verb disguise, hide, conceal, cover up, obscure, cloak, camouflage, veil, screen.

**mass** noun **1** *a mass of wood/fibers* concretion, lump, block, chunk, hunk, piece; concentration, conglomeration, aggregation, assemblage, collection. **2** *actors, in the mass, enjoy their work* total, totality, whole, entirety, aggregate. **3** *measure the body's mass* size, magnitude, bulk, dimension, capacity, greatness, bigness. **a mass of** many, a profusion of, numerous, countless. **the mass of** the majority of, the greater part of, the preponderance of, the lion's share of.

**mass** adjective wholesale, universal, widespread, general, large-scale, extensive, pandemic, popular.

**mass** verb amass, accumulate, assemble, gather, collect, draw together, join together; marshal, muster, rally, round up, mobilize.

**massacre** noun mass slaughter, wholesale slaughter, slaughter, mass murder, mass homicide, mass slaying, mass execution, mass destruction, carnage, butchery, blood bath, annihilation, extermination, liquidation, decimation, pogrom, genocide, ethnic cleansing, holocaust.

**massacre** verb slaughter, butcher, slay, murder, kill, annihilate, exterminate, liquidate, decimate, eliminate, kill off, wipe out, mow down, cut down.

**massage** noun rub, rubdown, kneading, pummeling, palpation, manipulation; reflexology, acupressure, shiatsu.

**masses** plural noun common people, populace, proletariat, multitude, commonality, crowd, mob, rabble, hoi polloi; *inf.* great unwashed.

**massive** adjective huge, immense, enormous, vast, mighty, extensive, gigantic, colossal, mammoth, monumental, elephantine, mountainous, gargantuan, king-size, monstrous, prodigious, titanic, hulking, bulky, weighty, hefty, solid, substantial, big, large, great; *inf.* whopping, humongous.

**mast** noun **1** *a ship's mast* spar, boom, yard. **2** *the mast atop the building* flagpole, flagstaff, pole, post, support, upright.

**master** noun **1** *master of the household/hunt* lord and master, lord, overlord, ruler, overseer, superintendent, director, manager, controller, governor, commander, captain, chief, head, headman, principal, owner, employer; *inf.* boss, top dog, big cheese, honcho. **2** *a master of innuendo* expert, adept, professional, authority, pundit, genius, master hand, maestro, virtuoso, prodigy, past master, grand master, wizard; *inf.* ace, pro, maven. **3** *sitting at the feet of the master* guru, teacher, spiritual leader, guide, swami.

**master** adjective **1** *master craftsmen* expert, adept, proficient, skilled, practiced, experienced; *inf.* crack. **2** *master plan* controlling, ruling, directing, commanding, dominating. **3** *master bedroom* chief, main, principal, leading, prime, predominant, foremost.

**master** verb **1** *master one's emotions* conquer, vanquish, defeat, overcome, overpower, triumph over, subdue, subjugate, govern, quell, quash, suppress, control, curb, check, bridle, tame. **2** *master the technique* learn, become proficient in, acquire skill in, grasp; *inf.* get the hang of.

**masterful** adjective **1** *masterful men marrying meek women* dominating, authoritative, powerful, controlling, domineering, tyrannical, despotic, dictatorial, overbearing, overweening, imperious, peremptory, high-handed, arrogant, haughty. **2** *masterful handling of the situation* expert, consummate. *See* MASTERLY.

**masterly** adjective masterful, expert, consummate, adept, skillful, proficient, adroit, deft, dexterous, accomplished, polished, excellent, superlative, first-rate, talented, gifted; *inf.* crack, ace.

**mastermind** verb direct, manage, plan, organize, arrange, engineer, conceive, devise, forge, originate, initiate, think up, come up with; *inf.* be the brains behind.

**mastermind** noun genius, intellect, author, architect, engineer, director, planner, organizer, deviser, originator, manager, prime mover; *inf.* brain, brains.

**masterpiece** noun magnum opus, masterwork, chef-d'oeuvre, work of art, creation.

**mastery** noun **1** *mastery over his emotions* control, domination, command, ascendancy, supremacy, superiority, triumph, victory, power, authority, jurisdiction, dominion, sovereignty. **2** *mastery of the language* command, grasp, knowledge, familiarity with, understanding, comprehension, expertise, skill, prowess, proficiency, ability, capability; *inf.* know-how.

**masturbation** noun autoeroticism, onanism, self-gratification; *inf.* playing with oneself.

**mat** noun **1** *wipe one's feet on the mat* doormat, welcome mat, rug, carpet. **2** *a mat of hair* mass, tangle, knot, mesh.

**match** noun **1** *a tennis match* contest, competition, game, tournament, bout, event, test, trial, meet. **2** *she's no match for the champion* equal, peer, rival, competitor. **3** *this glove is a match for that one* mate, fellow, companion, counterpart,

pair, complement. **4** *the new one is an exact match for the previous one* look-alike, double, twin, duplicate, copy, replica; *inf.* spitting image, ringer, dead ringer. **5** *a good match* pairing, alliance, affiliation, combination.

**match** verb **1** *curtains that match the walls* complement, blend with, harmonize with, go with, coordinate with, correspond to, accord with. **2** *her strength matches his* rival, vie with, compete with, compare with, parallel, keep pace with. **3** *match the socks* pair up, mate, couple, unite, join, combine.

**matching** adjective corresponding, equivalent, complementing, parallel, analogous, complementary, harmonizing, coordinating, the same, paired, twin, coupled, identical, like.

**matchless** adjective unmatched, incomparable, beyond compare, unequaled, without equal, unrivaled, unparalleled, unsurpassed, inimitable, peerless, unique, consummate, perfect.

**mate** noun **1** *she is looking for a mate* husband, wife, spouse, partner, companion, helpmate, lover; *inf.* significant other, other half, better half. **2** *the mate to this sock* twin, match, companion. **3** *they were mates throughout the war* associate, colleague, companion, compeer.

**mate** verb breed, copulate, couple, pair, join.

**material** noun **1** *clothes of strong material* fabric, cloth, stuff, textile. **2** *enough material for a book* data, information, facts, facts and figures, evidence, details, notes; *inf.* info.

**material** adjective **1** *the material world* corporeal, physical, bodily, fleshly, tangible, substantial, concrete, nonspiritual, worldly, earthly, temporal. **2** *a material difference* important, significant, meaningful. **3** *material evidence* relevant, applicable, pertinent, germane.

**materialize** verb **1** *our plans did not materialize* happen, occur, come about, come to pass, take place; *inf.* shape up. **2** *the guests did not materialize* appear, turn up, come to light, emerge.

**mathematical** adjective **1** *mathematical problems* arithmetical, numerical, statistical. **2** *mathematical care* precise, exact, rigorous, strict, meticulous, scrupulous, careful.

**matrimonial** adjective conjugal, connubial, nuptial. *See* MARITAL.

**matrimony** noun holy matrimony, marriage, wedlock, union.

**matted** adjective tangled, entangled, knotted, tousled, disheveled.

**matter** noun **1** *organic matter* material, substance, stuff, medium. **2** *concentrate on the matter, not the style* content, subject matter, text, argument, substance, sense, thesis. **3** *no laughing matter* affair, business, proceeding, situation, circumstance, event, happening, occurrence, incident, episode, occasion, experience. **4** *discuss important matters* subject, topic, issue, question, point, case, concern, theme. **5** *issues of little matter* importance, consequence, significance, note, import, moment, weight. **6** *what is the matter?* trouble, upset, distress, worry, problem, difficulty, complication.

**matter-of-fact** adjective prosaic, down-to-earth, straightforward, plain, unemotional, unsentimental, deadpan, flat, dry.

**mature** adjective adult, grown-up, grown, fully grown, full-grown, of age; ripe, ripened, mellow, ready, seasoned.

**mature** verb grow up, develop fully, reach adulthood, be full-grown, come of age; ripen, mellow, maturate.

**maturity** noun adulthood, manhood/womanhood, puberty, full growth, majority, coming of age; ripeness, mellowness, completion, readiness.

**maudlin** adjective mawkish, sentimental, oversentimental, tearful, lachrymose; *inf.* weepy, mushy, slushy, schmaltzy.

**maul** verb handle roughly, manhandle, paw, molest, beat, batter, claw, lacerate, mutilate, thrash, ill-treat; *inf.* belt, wallop, clobber, rough up, kick about.

**maverick** noun nonconformist, rebel, dissenter, dissident, individualist, bohemian, eccentric.

**maxim** noun aphorism, proverb, adage, saw, saying, axiom, precept, epigram, gnome.

**maximum** noun utmost, uttermost, extremity, upper limit, height, ceiling, top, summit, peak, apogee, acme, zenith.

**maximum** adjective highest, greatest, biggest, largest, topmost, most, utmost, supreme.

**maybe** adverb perhaps, it could be that, possibly; *lit.* peradventure.

**mayhem** noun havoc, disorder, confusion, chaos, bedlam, destruction, violence, trouble, disturbance, commotion, tumult, pandemonium.

**maze** noun labyrinth, network, mesh, web, jungle, tangle, confusion, snarl, imbroglio.

**meadow** noun field, grassland, pasture, paddock, lea.

**meager** adjective **1** *meager supplies* paltry, sparse, scant, scanty, spare, inadequate, insufficient, insubstantial, exiguous, short, little, small, slight, slender, poor, puny, skimpy, scrimpy; *inf.* measly, as scarce as hens' teeth. **2** *meager bodies* thin, lean, emaciated, skinny, spare, scrawny, scraggy, bony, gaunt, starved, underfed.

**meal** noun repast, banquet, feast, picnic, barbecue, buffet.

**mean**[1] verb **1** *what do the words mean?* indicate, signify, betoken, express, convey, denote, designate, spell out, show, stand for, represent, symbolize, portend, connote, imply, purport, suggest, allude to, intimate, hint at, insinuate, drive at. **2** *not mean to break it* intend, have in mind, plan, set out, aim, aspire, desire, want, wish. **3** *not meant for the army* intend, design, destine, predestine, fate. **4** *this will mean war* involve, entail, lead to, result in, give rise to, cause, engender, produce.

**mean**[2] adjective **1** *a mean thing to do* nasty, disagreeable, unpleasant, hurtful, unkind, offensive, obnoxious, cross, ill-natured, bad-tempered, irritable, surly, cantankerous, crotchety, crabbed, crabby, grumpy; *inf.* grouchy. **2** *as mean as Scrooge* niggardly, close-fisted, penny-pinching. See MISERLY. **3** *a mean creature* base, ignoble, disreputable, despicable, contemptible, hateful. **4** *of mean understanding* inferior, poor, limited, restricted, meager, scant. **5** *a mean hovel* shabby, wretched, dismal, squalid, sordid, seedy, mangy, broken-down, rundown. **6** *of mean birth* low, lowly, lowborn, humble, modest, common, ordinary, undistinguished.

**mean**[3] noun midpoint, middle, median, norm, middle course, middle ground, happy medium.

**mean**[4] adjective middle, median, medial, normal, standard, medium.

**meander** verb wander, roam, ramble, rove, stroll, amble, drift; wind, zigzag, snake, curve, turn, bend; *inf.* mosey.

**meaning** noun **1** *the meaning of what he said* sense, message, import, drift, gist, essence, substance, purport, implication, significance, thrust. **2** *what is the meaning of the word?* definition, explanation, connotation, denotation, interpretation, elucidation, explication. **3** *it was not our meaning to delay him* intention, purpose, plan, aim, goal, end, object, objective, aspiration, desire, want, wish. **4** *his life has no meaning* significance, point, value, worth, consequence, account. **5** *a glance full of meaning* significance, implication, allusion, intimation, insinuation, eloquence, expression.

**meaningful** adjective **1** *a meaningful remark* significant, important, relevant, material, valid, worthwhile. **2** *a meaningful glance* pointed, suggestive, eloquent, expressive, pregnant.

**meaningless** adjective senseless, unintelligible, incomprehensible, pointless, purposeless, motiveless, irrational, inane; empty, futile, worthless, trivial, insignificant, inconsequential.

**meanness** noun **1** *an act of such meanness* nastiness, disagreeableness, unpleasantness, unfriendliness, crossness, bad temper, irritability, surliness, cantankerousness. **2** *the meanness of the creature* baseness, vileness, sordidness, foulness, nastiness, contemptibility. **3** *the meanness of his intellect* inferiority, poorness, limitations, meagerness. **4** *the meanness of the hovel* shabbiness, wretchedness, squalor, sordidness, seediness. **5** *the meanness of her birth* lowliness, humbleness, commonness.

**means** plural noun **1** *a means of getting there* way, method, expedient, process, mode, manner, agency, medium, instrument, channel, avenue, course. **2** *a man of means* | *have sufficient means* money, capital, wealth, riches, affluence, substance, fortune, property; resources, funds, wherewithal; *inf.* dough, bread. **by all means** of course, certainly, definitely, surely. **by no means** in no way, not at all, not in the least.

**meanwhile** adverb meantime, in the meantime, for the time being, for now, for the moment, in the interim; at the same time, simultaneously, concurrently.

**measurable** adjective **1** *a measurable quantity* assessable, gaugeable, estimable, appraisable, computable, quantifiable, fathomable. **2** *a measurable improvement* significant, appreciable, noticeable, visible, perceptible, obvious, striking, material.

**measure** noun **1** *find the measure of the material* size, dimension. *See* MEASUREMENT 2. **2** *receive a measure of her father's estate* share, portion, division, allotment, part, piece, quota, lot, ration, percentage. **3** *have a measure of wit* quantity, amount, certain amount, degree. **4** *sales are the measure of the company's success* yardstick, test, standard, touchstone, criterion, benchmark. **5** *take drastic measures* action, act, course, course of action, deed, proceeding, procedure, step, means, expedient, maneuver. **6** *announce measures to control crime* statute, act, bill, law, resolution. **7** *do what you like within measure* moderation, limit, limitation, bounds, control, restraint. **beyond measure** immeasurably, incalculably, infinitely, limitlessly, immensely, extremely. **for good measure** as a bonus, to boot.

**measure** verb **1** *measure the material* calculate, compute, estimate, quantify, weigh, size, evaluate, rate, assess, appraise, gauge, measure out, determine, judge, survey. **2** *measure one's words* choose carefully, select with care, consider, plan, calculate.

**3** *measure his strength against his brother's* pit, set, match, test, put into competition. **measure out** mete out, deal out, dole out, share, divide out, parcel out, allocate, allot, apportion, assign, distribute, administer, dispense, issue. **measure up 1** *he didn't measure up* come up to standard, fulfill expectations, fit/fill the bill, pass muster, be adequate, be suitable; *inf.* make the grade, cut the mustard, be up to snuff. **2** *measure up to the requirements* meet, come up to, match.

**measured** adjective **1** *measured amounts* measured out, calculated, computed, quantified. **2** *measured steps* regular, steady, even, rhythmical, slow, dignified, stately, sedate. **3** *measured words* carefully chosen, well-thought-out, studied, calculated, planned, premeditated, considered, deliberate, reasoned.

**measurement** noun **1** *the measurement of the quantity* calculation, computation, estimation, quantification, evaluation, assessment. **2** *the measurements of the carpet are wrong* size, dimension, proportions, magnitude, amplitude, mass, bulk, volume, capacity, extent, expanse, amount, quantity, area, length, height, depth, weight, width, range.

**meat** noun **1** *meat and drink* flesh, animal flesh, food, nourishment, sustenance, provisions, rations, fare, viands, victuals, comestibles, provender, feed; *inf.* grub, eats, chow, nosh. **2** *the meat of the matter* substance, pith, marrow, heart, kernel, core, nucleus, nub, essence, essentials, gist, fundamentals, basics; *inf.* nitty-gritty, nuts and bolts.

**mechanical** adjective **1** *a mechanical device* automated, automatic, machine-driven, motor-driven, power-driven. **2** *mechanical gestures* automatic, machinelike, unthinking, unconscious, unfeeling, unemotional, cold, routine, habitual, perfunctory, lackluster, lifeless, unanimated, dead.

**mechanism** noun **1** *a mechanism for folding paper* apparatus, appliance. *See* MACHINE 1. **2** *the mechanism of the car* motor, workings, works, gears, components; *inf.* innards, guts. **3** *the mechanism for complaints* process, procedure, system, operation, method, technique, means, medium, agency, channel.

**meddle** verb interfere, butt in, intrude, intervene, interlope, pry, nose; *inf.* stick one's nose in, horn in, snoop.

**meddlesome** adjective meddling, interfering, intrusive, prying; *inf.* snooping, nosy.

**mediate** verb **1** *mediate between the warring factions* arbitrate, negotiate, conciliate, intervene, intercede, interpose, moderate, umpire, referee, bring to terms, step in. **2** *mediate a difference of opinion* settle, reconcile, resolve, mend, clear up, patch up. **3** *mediate a peace settlement* bring about, effect, effectuate, make happen, negotiate.

**mediation** noun arbitration, negotiation, intervention, intercession, good offices.

**mediator** noun arbitrator, arbiter, negotiator, go-between, middleman, intermediary, peacemaker, moderator, umpire, referee, judge, conciliator, reconciler.

**medicinal** adjective medical, therapeutic, curative, healing, remedial, restorative, health-giving, analeptic.

**medicine** noun medication, medicament, drug, remedy, cure, physic. **take one's medicine** accept one's punishment, take the consequences of one's actions.

**mediocre** adjective indifferent, average, middle-of-the-road, middling, ordinary, commonplace, pedestrian, run-of-the-mill, tolerable, passable, adequate, uninspired, undistinguished, unexceptional, inferior, second-rate, second-class, low-grade, poor, shabby, minor; *inf.* so-so, fair-to-middling, nothing to write home about, no great shakes.

**mediocrity** noun ordinariness, commonplaceness, inferiority, poorness, shabbiness.

**meditate** verb *meditating revenge* intend, plan, project, design, devise, scheme, plot. **meditate on/upon** contemplate, think about/over, muse on/about, ponder on/over, concentrate on, reflect on, ruminate about/on/over, brood over.

**meditation** noun contemplation, thought, musing, reflection, deliberation, rumination, brooding, reverie, brown study, concentration.

**medium** noun **1** *the medium between extremes* center point, average, standard. *See* MEAN[3]. **2** *the medium of television* means, agency, channel, avenue, vehicle, organ, instrument, instrumentality. **3** *organisms in their natural medium* habitat, element, environment, surroundings, milieu, setting, conditions, atmosphere. **4** *visit a medium to contact the dead* spiritualist, spiritist, necromancer.

**medium** adjective middle, mean, medial, median, average, midway, midpoint, intermediate.

**medley** noun assortment, miscellany, mixture, mixed bag, mix, mélange, variety, potpourri, conglomeration, patchwork, gallimaufry, olio, salmagundi.

**meek** adjective **1** *meek people/animals* patient, long-suffering, forbearing, resigned, gentle, peaceful, docile, modest, humble, unassuming. **2** *feeling meek among aggressive people* submissive, yielding, unresisting,

compliant, acquiescent, deferential, weak, timid, frightened, spineless, spiritless.

**meet** verb **1** *meet an old friend on the train* encounter, run into, run across, come across, come upon, chance upon, happen upon, light upon; *inf.* bump into, hook up with. **2** *where land and sea meet* come together, abut, adjoin, join, link up, unite, connect, touch, converge, intersect. **3** *the committee met on Saturday* gather, assemble, come together, congregate, convene. **4** *meet the demands of the job* satisfy, fulfill, measure up to, come up to, comply with. **5** *meet one's responsibilities* carry out, perform, execute, discharge, take care of. **6** *meet death bravely* face, encounter, undergo, experience, go through, bear, suffer, endure. **7** *meet the enemy at dawn* confront, engage, engage in battle with, clash with, fight with.

**meeting** noun **1** *the meeting of the friends* encounter, contact, assignation, rendezvous, tryst. **2** *address the meeting* gathering, assembly, conference, congregation, convention, convocation, conclave; *inf.* get-together. **3** *the meeting of land and sea* abutment, junction, conjunction, union, convergence, confluence, concourse, intersection.

**melancholic, melancholy** adjective despondent, dejected, depressed, down, downhearted, downcast, disconsolate, glum, gloomy, miserable, dismal, dispirited, low, in the doldrums, blue, mournful, lugubrious, woeful, woebegone, doleful, sorrowful, unhappy, heavy-hearted, low-spirited, somber, pensive; *inf.* down in the dumps, down in the mouth.

**melancholy** noun despondency, dejection, depression, gloom, gloominess, low spirits, doldrums, blues, woe, sadness, sorrow, unhappiness, pensiveness, melancholia.

**mellow** adjective **1** *mellow fruit* ripe, mature, well-matured, soft, juicy, tender, luscious, sweet, full-flavored, flavorsome. **2** *a mellow voice* dulcet, sweet, sweet-sounding, tuneful, euphonious, melodious, mellifluous, smooth, full, rich, well-rounded. **3** *a mellow person/mood* gentle, easygoing, pleasant, amiable, good-natured, affable, genial, relaxed.

**melodious** adjective melodic, musical, tuneful, harmonious, lyrical, dulcet, sweet, sweet-sounding, sweet-toned, silvery, euphonious.

**melodramatic** adjective theatrical, stagy, overdramatic, histrionic, oversensational, extravagant, overdone, overemotional; *inf.* camp, hammy.

**melody** noun tune, air, strain, music, refrain, theme, song; melodiousness, tunefulness, musicality, harmony, lyricism, sweetness, euphony.

**melt** verb **1** *solids melting* liquefy, dissolve, deliquesce, thaw, defrost, soften. **2** *the crowd melted away* disperse, vanish, vanish into thin air, fade away, disappear, dissolve, evaporate, evanesce. **3** *her story melted the jury* soften, touch, disarm, mollify, assuage, move.

**member** noun **1** *a member of the club* adherent, associate, fellow, participant. **2** *many victims had injured members* organ, limb, appendage, extremity, arm, leg. **3** *a member of the mathematical set* element, constituent, component, part, portion.

**memento** noun souvenir, keepsake, reminder, remembrance, token, memorial, trophy, relic, vestige.

**memorable** adjective unforgettable, signal, momentous, significant, historic, notable, noteworthy, remarkable, outstanding, extraordinary, striking, impressive, distinctive.

**memorandum** noun reminder, note, message, minute, aide-mémoire; *inf.* memo.

**memorial** noun remembrance, reminder, memento, souvenir.

**memory** noun **1** *her memory is excellent* remembrance, recollection, powers of recall, recall, reminiscence, powers of retention, retention. **2** *in memory of him* remembrance, commemoration, honor, tribute.

**menace** noun **1** *an atmosphere full of menace* threat, ominousness, intimidation, warning; danger, peril, risk, hazard. **3** *the child next door is a menace* nuisance, pest, troublemaker, mischief-maker.

**menace** verb **1** *older boys menacing the young ones* threaten, intimidate, frighten, scare, alarm, terrify, bully, browbeat, cow, terrorize. **2** *bad weather menacing* loom, impend, lower, be in the air, be in the offing.

**menacing** adjective **1** *a menacing look/silence* threatening, ominous, intimidating, frightening, terrifying, alarming, forbidding, minatory, minacious. **2** *a menacing storm* looming, lowering, impending.

**mend** verb **1** *mend the furniture* repair, fix, put back together, patch up, restore, rehabilitate, renew, renovate, make whole, make well, cure, heal. **2** *mend socks* sew, stitch, darn, patch. **3** *the patient will soon mend* get better, recover, recuperate, improve. **4** *try to mend matters* put right, set straight, rectify, amend, improve, ameliorate, reform.

**menial** adjective lowly, humble, low-grade, low-status, unskilled, routine, humdrum, boring, dull.

**menstruation** noun period, menses, menstrual cycle, monthly flow; *inf.* the curse.

**mental** adjective **1** *mental work* intellectual, cerebral, brain, thinking. **2** *he's completely mental* mad, insane, deranged, disturbed, unbalanced, mentally ill, unstable.

**mentality** noun **1** *of a slightly twisted mentality* frame of mind, way of thinking, way one's mind works, mind, psychology, mental attitude, outlook, character, disposition, makeup. **2** *of low-grade mentality* intellect, intellectual capabilities, intelligence, IQ (= intelligence quotient), brainpower, brains, understanding, wit; *inf.* gray matter.

**mention** verb allude to, refer to, touch on, speak briefly of, hint at, say, state, name, cite, quote, call attention to, speak about/of, utter, communicate, disclose, divulge, reveal. **don't mention it** no thanks necessary, (it was) a pleasure, any time; don't apologize, don't worry; *inf.* no problem, no sweat, no big deal, forget (about) it. **not to mention** to say nothing of, in addition to.

**mention** noun reference, allusion, observation, remark, statement, announcement, indication, acknowledgment, citation, recognition.

**mentor** noun guide, adviser, counselor, therapist, guru, spiritual leader, confidant, teacher, tutor, coach, instructor.

**mercenary** adjective **1** *mercenary people interested only in money* money-oriented, grasping, greedy, acquisitive, avaricious, covetous; *inf.* money-grubbing. **2** *mercenary soldiers* hired, paid, bought, professional, venal.

**merchandise** noun goods, wares, stock, commodities, produce, vendibles.

**merchandise** verb **1** *merchandise a wide range of goods* market, sell, retail, buy and sell, distribute, deal in, trade in, traffic in, do business in, vend. **2** *merchandise the new cars* promote, advertise, publicize, push; *inf.* hype, plug.

**merchant** noun trader, dealer, trafficker, wholesaler, broker, seller, salesman, saleswoman, salesperson, vendor, retailer, store owner, storekeeper, shopkeeper, distributor.

**merciful** adjective lenient, clement, compassionate, pitying, forgiving, forbearing, sparing, humane, mild, softhearted, tender-hearted, kind, sympathetic, liberal, tolerant.

**merciless** adjective unmerciful, ruthless, relentless, inexorable, harsh, pitiless, uncompassionate, unforgiving, unsparing, unpitying, implacable, barbarous, inhumane, inhuman, hard-hearted, heartless, callous, cruel, unsympathetic, unfeeling.

**mercy** noun **1** *the mercy of the judge* leniency, clemency, compassion, pity, charity, forgiveness, forbearance, quarter, soft-heartedness, tender-heartedness, sympathy. **2** *thankful for small mercies* boon, favor, piece of luck, blessing, godsend. **at the mercy of** in the power of, under/in the control of, threatened by, open to, defenseless against, vulnerable to.

**mere** adjective nothing more than, no better than, no more important than, just a, only a, pure and simple.

**merge** verb **1** *the two companies merged* join together, join forces, amalgamate, unite, combine, incorporate, coalesce, team up. **2** *the colors merged* blend, fuse, mingle, mix, intermix, homogenize, **merge into** run into, melt into, become assimilated into/in, become lost in, be swallowed up by.

**merger** noun amalgamation, combination, union, fusion, coalition, alliance, incorporation.

**merit** noun **1** *the merit of his work* excellence, goodness, quality, high quality, worth, worthiness, value. **2** *the merits of the scheme* good point, strong point, advantage, asset, plus.

**merit** verb deserve, earn, be worthy of, be entitled to, have a right to, warrant.

**meritorious** adjective praiseworthy, laudable, commendable, admirable, estimable, creditable, excellent, exemplary, good, worthy, deserving.

**merriment** noun gaiety, high spirits, jollity, rejoicing, jocundity, conviviality, festivity, merrymaking, revelry, mirth, mirthfulness, glee, gleefulness, laughter, hilarity, amusement, fun.

**merry** adjective cheerful, cheery, gay, high-spirited, blithe, blithesome, lighthearted, buoyant, carefree, joyful, joyous, jolly, jocund, convivial, festive, mirthful, gleeful. **make merry** have fun, have a good time, enjoy oneself, have a party, party, celebrate, carouse, revel, rejoice; *inf.* have a ball.

**mesh** noun **1** *wire mesh* network, netting, net, tracery, web, lattice, latticework, lacework, trellis, reticulation, plexus. **2** *the mesh of political intrigue* net, tangle, entanglement, web, snare, trap.

**mesh** verb connect, interlock, fit together; go together, coordinate, match, harmonize, dovetail.

**mesmerize** verb hypnotize, put into a trance, hold spellbound, spellbind, entrance, enthrall, bewitch, captivate, enchant, fascinate, grip, magnetize.

**mess** noun **1** *clean up the mess in the kitchen* disorder, untidiness, disarray, dirtiness, filthiness, clutter, litter; muddle, chaos, confusion, disorganization, turmoil. **2** *have*

*to get out of this mess* plight, predicament, tight spot, tight corner, difficulty, trouble, quandary, dilemma, muddle, mix-up, confusion, imbroglio; *inf.* jam, fix, pickle, stew. **3** *he made a mess of the project* muddle, botch, bungle; *inf.* hash, foul-up, screw-up. **4** *cat's mess* dirt, excrement, feces, excreta.

**mess** verb *mess with the controls* fiddle, play, tinker, toy. **mess around, mess about** amuse oneself, pass the time, fiddle around/about, play around/about. **mess up 1** *mess up the kitchen* dirty, litter, pollute, clutter up, disarrange, dishevel. **2** *mess up the project* botch, bungle, muff, make a mess of, mar, spoil, ruin; *inf.* make a hash of, foul up, screw up.

**message** noun **1** *send a message* communication, news, word, tidings, note, memorandum, letter, e-mail, missive, bulletin, communiqué, dispatch; *inf.* memo. **2** *the message of the sermon* meaning, import, idea, point, purport, intimation, theme, moral.

**messenger** noun courier, runner, envoy, emissary, agent, go-between, herald, harbinger; *inf.* gofer.

**messy** adjective untidy, disordered, dirty, filthy, grubby, slovenly, cluttered, littered, chaotic, confused, disorganized, in disarray, disarranged, disheveled, unkempt; *inf.* sloppy.

**metamorphosis** noun transformation, transfiguration, change, alteration, conversion, changeover, mutation, transmutation, sea change; *inf.* transmogrification.

**metaphor** noun figure of speech, image, trope, allegory, analogy, symbol, emblem.

**mete** verb **mete out** deal out, dole out. *See* MEASURE OUT (MEASURE verb).

**meteoric** adjective rapid, swift, lightning, rapid, swift, fast, quick, speedy, overnight, sudden, dazzling, brilliant, spectacular, flashing, momentary, fleeting, transient, ephemeral, brief, short-lived.

**method** noun **1** *old-fashioned methods* procedure, technique, system, practice, modus operandi, process, approach, way, course of action, scheme, plan, rule, style, manner, mode. **2** *method in his madness* order, orderliness, organization, arrangement, structure, form, system, plan, design, purpose, pattern, regularity.

**methodical** adjective orderly, well-ordered, organized, systematic, structured, logical, well-regulated, planned, efficient, businesslike.

**meticulous** adjective ultracareful, scrupulous, punctilious, painstaking, demanding, exacting, conscientious, thorough, perfectionist, fastidious, particular, exact, precise, detailed, rigorous

**mettle** noun **1** *it showed us his true mettle* caliber, character, disposition, nature, temperament, temper, personality, makeup, stamp, kind, sort, variety, mold, kidney. **2** *soldiers of mettle* courage, courageousness, bravery, gallantry, valor, intrepidity, fearlessness, boldness, daring, grit, pluck, nerve, backbone, fortitude, indomitability; *inf.* guts, spunk.

**middle** adjective **1** *the middle point between two extremes* mid, mean, medium, medial, median, midway, halfway, central, equidistant. **2** *the middle ranks* intermediate, intermedial.

**middle** noun **1** *the middle of the line* midpoint, halfway point, mean, median, center, dead center. **2** *in the middle of the crowd* heart, center. *See* MIDST. **3** *a thickening middle* midriff, waist, waistline.

**middleman** noun intermediary, go-between, broker, distributor.

**midget** noun dwarf, manikin, pygmy, Tom Thumb; homunculus; *inf.* little person.

**midnight** noun twelve midnight, dead of night, the witching hour.

**midst** noun middle, center, heart, bosom, core, kernel, nucleus, nub, interior, depths, thick.

**mien** noun look, appearance, aspect, aura, expression, countenance, demeanor, air, manner, bearing, carriage, deportment.

**miffed** adjective annoyed, displeased, offended, aggrieved, piqued, nettled, vexed, irked, upset, hurt, put out, resentful, in a huff.

**might** noun force, power, strength, mightiness, powerfulness, forcefulness, potency, toughness, robustness, sturdiness, muscularity, vigor, energy, stamina, stoutness.

**mighty** adjective **1** *a mighty blow* forceful, powerful, strong, lusty, potent, tough, robust, sturdy, muscular, strapping, vigorous, energetic, stout. **2** *a mighty mountain* huge, massive, vast, enormous, colossal, giant, gigantic, prodigious, monumental, mountainous, towering, titanic.

**migrant** adjective traveling, roving. *See* MIGRATORY.

**migrant** noun vagrant, nomad, itinerant, traveler, gypsy, transient, rover, wanderer, drifter.

**migrate** verb emigrate, move, resettle, relocate; travel, voyage, journey, trek, hike, rove, roam, wander, drift.

**migratory** adjective migrant, migrating, traveling, roving, wandering, nomadic, itinerant, vagrant, transient, unsettled.

**mild** adjective **1** *a mild disposition* tender, gentle, soft, softhearted, tenderhearted, sensitive, sympathetic, warm, warmhearted; placid, meek, docile, calm, tranquil, serene, peaceful; amiable, genial, easygoing, mellow. **2** *mild winds* gentle, moderate, warm, balmy. **3** *mild food* bland, spiceless, insipid, tasteless.

**mildness** noun tenderness, gentleness, softness, sensitivity, meekness, docility, calmness, tranquillity, serenity, amiability, mellowness.

**militant** adjective **1** *militant believers* aggressive, assertive, vigorous, active, combative, pugnacious; *inf.* pushy. **2** *militant armies* fighting, warring, contending, clashing, embattled.

**militant** noun **1** *militants in the party* activist, partisan. **2** *militants on the battlefield* fighter, soldier, warrior, combatant, belligerent.

**military** noun armed forces, services, militia, soldiery, army, navy, air force, marines.

**milk** verb **1** *milk sap from a tree* draw, draw off, express, siphon, tap, drain, extract. **2** *milk the poor people* exploit, take advantage of, bleed, suck dry.

**mill** noun factory, plant, foundry, works, workshop, shop.

**mill** verb grind, pulverize, pound, crush, powder, crunch, granulate, comminute, triturate. **mill around/about** wander around/about, amble, meander, crowd.

**millstone** noun burden, weight, onus, misfortune, affliction, cross, albatross.

**mimic** verb **1** *mimic his friend* impersonate, imitate, copy, ape, caricature, parody; *inf.* take off. **2** *the child's actions mimicked his mother's* resemble, echo, mirror, simulate.

**mimic** noun impersonator, impressionist, imitator, parodist, copyist, parrot, ape.

**mince** verb **1** *finely minced beef* chop/cut into tiny pieces, grind, crumble, hash. **2** *I won't mince (my) words* restrain, hold back, moderate, temper, soften, mitigate, refine, weaken.

**mind** noun **1** *all in the mind* brain, head, psyche, ego, subconscious. **2** *have an active mind* brainpower, intellect, mentality, intelligence, powers of reasoning, brain, brains, wits, understanding, comprehension, sense; *inf.* gray matter. **3** *my mind was wandering* thoughts, thinking, concentration, attention; application, absorption. **4** *bring thoughts of him to mind* memory, recollection, remembrance. **5** *be of the same mind* opinion, way of thinking, outlook, view, viewpoint, point of view, belief, judgment, attitude. **6** *have a mind to go* inclination, desire, wish, urge, will, notion, fancy, intention, intent, aim, purpose, design. **7** *of unsound mind* mental balance, sanity, senses, wits, reason, reasoning, judgment. **8** *one of the great minds* genius, intellect, intellectual, thinker; *inf.* brain, egghead. **be of two minds** be undecided, be uncertain, be hesitant, waver, vacillate, dither, shilly-shally. **bear/keep in mind** remember, be mindful of, take into consideration, consider. **put in mind** remind, call up, conjure up, suggest. **to one's mind** in one's opinion, to one's way of thinking, from one's standpoint.

**mind** verb **1** *didn't mind their tardiness* object to, care about, be bothered by, be upset by, resent, dislike, disapprove of, look askance at. **2** *mind what the teacher says* take heed of, heed, pay attention to, attend to, concentrate on, listen to, note, take notice of, mark, observe, respect, obey, follow, comply with, adhere to. **3** *mind your own business* attend to, pay attention to, concentrate on. **4** *mind the step* be careful of, be cautious of, watch out for, look out for, keep one's eyes open for. **5** *mind the store/baby* look after, take care of, attend to, tend, have charge of, keep an eye on, watch.

**mindful** adjective heedful of, watchful of, careful of, wary of, chary of, cognizant of, aware of, conscious of, alert to.

**mindless** adjective **1** *a mindless idiot* stupid, foolish, brainless, senseless, witless, empty-headed, dull, slow-witted, obtuse, weak-minded, featherbrained; *inf.* birdbrained, dumb, dopey, moronic. **2** *mindless violence* unthinking, thoughtless, careless, gratuitous. **3** *mindless tasks* mechanical, automatic, routine.

**mine** noun **1** *work in a mine* colliery, pit, excavation, well, quarry, lode, vein, deposit. **2** *the book is a mine of information* source, reservoir, repository, store, storehouse, wealth, mint; *inf.* gold mine.

**mine** verb excavate, quarry for, dig for, dig up, extract, unearth.

**mingle** verb **1** *mingle the two colors* mix, blend, combine, compound, homogenize, merge, unite, join, intermingle, intermix, coalesce, blend, commingle. **2** *guests mingling at the party* circulate, socialize, hobnob, fraternize.

**miniature** adjective small-scale, scaled-down, mini, midget, baby, toy, pocket, dwarf, Lilliputian, small, tiny, wee, minute, minuscule, microscopic; *inf.* pint-sized.

**minimize** verb **1** *minimize the costs* keep at/to a minimum, reduce, decrease, curtail, cut back on, prune, slash. **2** *minimize the size* reduce, decrease, diminish, abbreviate, attenuate, shrink, miniaturize. **3** *minimize his achievement* belittle, make light of, decry, discount, play

down, deprecate, depreciate, underestimate, underrate.

**minimum** adjective minimal, lowest, smallest, littlest, least, least possible, slightest.

**minion** noun **1** *the general and his minions* lackey, flunky, henchman, toady, sycophant, flatterer, fawner, underling, hireling, servant, dependent, hanger-on, parasite, leech; *inf.* yes-man, bootlicker. **2** *the queen's minion* favorite, pet, darling, jewel, apple of one's eye.

**minister** noun **1** *ministers saying prayers* clergyman, cleric, ecclesiastic, churchman, preacher, priest, parson, pastor, rector, chaplain, padre, curate, vicar. **2** *the British minister in Egypt* ambassador, diplomat, consul, plenipotentiary, envoy, emissary, legate, delegate, representative, chargé d'affaires.

**minister** verb **minister to** administer to, attend to, tend, look after, take care of, see to, cater to, serve, accommodate, be solicitous of, pander to.

**ministry** noun **1** *go in for the ministry* the church, the priesthood, holy orders, the pulpit. **2** *the ministry for foreign affairs* department, office, bureau.

**minor** adjective **1** *a minor poet* little-known, unknown, lesser, insignificant, unimportant, inconsequential, inferior, subordinate. **2** *suffer minor discomfort* slight, small, trivial, negligible, trifling.

**minstrel** noun musician, singer, bard, troubadour, jongleur, goliard.

**mint** noun *earn a mint* fortune, small fortune, millions, king's ransom; *inf.* pile, stack, heap, packet, bundle.

**mint** adjective *in mint condition* brand-new, unblemished, undamaged, unmarred, untarnished, fresh; *inf.* spanking new.

**mint** verb **1** *mint coins* stamp, stamp out, punch, die, cast, strike, coin, monetize, make, manufacture, produce. **2** *mint new words* coin, invent, make up, fabricate, think up, dream up, hatch up, devise, fashion, forge.

**minute** noun **1** *I'll only be a minute* moment, short time, second; *inf.* jiffy, jiff. **2** *the minute he appeared* moment, instant. **in a minute** shortly, very soon, in the twinkling of an eye; *inf.* in a jiffy/jiff, in two shakes of a lamb's tail. **up-to-the-minute** up-to-date, ultramodern, modern, fashionable, in vogue, chic, in, all the rage.

**minute** adjective **1** *a minute creature* tiny, minuscule, microscopic, miniature, diminutive, Lilliputian, little, small; *inf.* knee-high to a grasshopper. **2** *a minute difference* infinitesimal, negligible, trifling, trivial, paltry, petty, insignificant, inconsequential, unimportant, slight, minimal. **3** *in minute detail* detailed, exhaustive, meticulous, punctilious, painstaking, close, strict, exact, precise, accurate.

**minutes** plural noun record, log, proceedings, transactions, notes, transcript, journal, summary.

**miracle** noun wonder, marvel, prodigy, phenomenon.

**miraculous** adjective **1** *Jesus performing miraculous feats* inexplicable, unaccountable, preternatural, superhuman, supernatural, fantastic, magical, thaumaturgic, phenomenal, prodigious, wondrous, remarkable. **2** *a miraculous recovery* amazing, astounding, remarkable, extraordinary, incredible, unbelievable; *inf.* fantastic.

**mirage** noun optical illusion, illusion, hallucination, phantasmagoria, phantasm.

**mire** noun marsh, marshland, bog, peatbog, swamp, swampland, morass, quagmire, quag, slough, fen, bayou; mud, slime, muck, dirt, filth.

**mire** verb **1** *cars mired in the swamp* sink, sink down, bog down, stick in the mud. **2** *mired in financial problems* entangle, catch up, involve, bog down.

**mirror** noun looking glass, glass, reflector, reflecting surface.

**mirror** verb reflect, imitate, emulate, simulate, copy, follow, mimic, echo, ape, parrot, impersonate.

**mirth** noun gaiety, cheerfulness, levity, buoyancy, blitheness, lightheartedness, joviality, enjoyment, amusement, pleasure. *See* MERRIMENT.

**mirthful** adjective gay, high-spirited, laughter-filled, jocular, lighthearted, jovial, fun-filled, amusing, pleasurable, frolicsome, sportive, playful. *See* MERRY.

**misbehave** verb behave badly, be naughty, be disobedient, be bad-mannered, show bad/poor manners, be rude, fool around; *inf.* carry on, act up.

**misbehavior** noun misconduct, bad behavior, disorderly conduct, badness, naughtiness, disobedience, mischief, mischievousness, delinquency, misdeed, rudeness, fooling around; *inf.* carrying on, acting up, shenanigans.

**miscarriage** noun failure, foundering, ruination, nonfulfillment, misfiring, breakdown, thwarting, frustration.

**miscarry** verb *our plan miscarried* go wrong, go awry, go amiss, be unsuccessful, fail, misfire, abort, be abortive, founder, come to nothing, come to grief, meet with disaster, fall through, be ruined, fall flat; *inf.* bite the dust, go up in smoke.

**miscellaneous** adjective varied, assorted, mixed, diverse, sundry, variegated, diversified, motley, multifarious, jumbled, confused, indiscriminate, heterogeneous.

**miscellany** noun assortment, mixture, collection. *See* MEDLEY.

**mischance** noun accident, misfortune, bad luck, ill fortune, ill luck, poor luck, misadventure, mishap, setback, failure, contretemps.

**mischief** noun **1** *involved in mischief* mischievousness, naughtiness, badness, bad behavior, misbehavior, misconduct, pranks, wrongdoing, delinquency; *inf.* monkey tricks, monkey business, shenanigans, goings-on. **2** *with mischief in her eyes* impishness, roguishness, rascality, devilment. **3** *did mischief to their property* harm, hurt, injury, impairment, damage, detriment.

**mischievous** adjective **1** *mischievous child* naughty, misbehaving, disobedient, troublesome, vexatious; playful, frolicsome, rascally, roguish. **2** *a mischievous smile* playful, teasing, impish, roguish, waggish, arch. **3** *mischievous gossip* malicious, spiteful, malignant, vicious, wicked, evil, hurtful, harmful, injurious, damaging, detrimental, deleterious, destructive, pernicious.

**misconception** noun misapprehension, misunderstanding, mistake, error, misinterpretation, the wrong idea, a false impression, delusion.

**misconduct** noun **1** *scolded for their misconduct* bad behavior, naughtiness. *See* MISBEHAVIOR. **2** *doctors guilty of misconduct* unprofessional behavior, unethical behavior, malpractice, impropriety, immorality.

**miscreant** noun villain, wrongdoer, criminal, evildoer, sinner, scoundrel, wretch, reprobate, blackguard, rogue, rascal.

**misdeed** noun wrongdoing, evil deed, crime, misdemeanor, offense, error, peccadillo, transgression, sin.

**miser** noun skinflint, penny-pincher, niggard, Scrooge; *inf.* money-grubber, cheapskate, tightwad.

**miserable** adjective **1** *feeling miserable* unhappy, sorrowful, dejected, depressed, downcast, downhearted, down, despondent, disconsolate, desolate, wretched, glum, gloomy, dismal, blue, melancholy, low-spirited, mournful, woeful, woebegone, sad, doleful, forlorn, crestfallen; *inf.* down in the mouth, down in the dumps. **2** *a miserable hovel* wretched, mean, poor, shabby, squalid, filthy, foul, sordid, seedy, dilapidated. **3** *miserable wretches* poverty-stricken, needy, penniless, impoverished, beggarly, destitute, indigent, down-at-the-heels, out at the elbows. **4** *miserable scoundrels* contemptible, despicable, base, mean, low, vile, sordid. **5** *miserable salaries* meager, paltry, scanty, low, poor, niggardly, pathetic. **6** *miserable weather* unpleasant, disagreeable, displeasing, uncomfortable, wet, rainy, stormy.

**miserly** adjective mean, niggardly, parsimonious, tight-fisted, close-fisted, penny-pinching, penurious, greedy, avaricious, ungenerous, illiberal; *inf.* stingy, tight, money-grubbing, cheap.

**misery** noun **1** *suffer/undergo misery* distress, wretchedness, hardship, suffering, affliction, anguish, torment, torture, agony, pain, discomfort, deprivation, grief, sorrow, despair, depression, woe, sadness, unhappiness. **2** *endure untold miseries* trouble, misfortune, adversity, affliction, ordeal, burden, load, blow, trial, tribulation, woe, catastrophe, calamity, disaster.

**misfire** verb go wrong, go awry, fail. *See* MISCARRY.

**misfit** noun fish out of water, square peg in a round hole, nonconformist, eccentric, maverick; *inf.* oddball, weirdo.

**misfortune** noun **1** *by misfortune we got lost* bad luck, ill fortune, accident, misadventure, mischance. **2** *endure many misfortunes* trouble, setback, reverse, adversity, reverse of fortune, misadventure, mishap, stroke of bad luck, blow, failure, accident, disaster, tragedy, affliction, sorrow, misery, woe, trial, tribulation, catastrophe, calamity.

**misgiving** noun qualm, doubt, reservation, second thoughts, suspicion, distrust, anxiety, apprehension, unease, uncertainty, hesitation.

**misguided** adjective **1** *their action was misguided* mistaken, deluded, erroneous, fallacious, wrong, ill-advised, unwise, injudicious, imprudent, foolish. **2** *misguided people believed him* misled, misdirected, misinformed, deluded.

**mishandle** verb **1** *mishandle the project* mismanage, misdirect, misgovern, misconduct, maladminister, bungle, botch, muff, make a mess of; *inf.* make a hash of, foul up, screw up. **2** *mishandle the prisoners* maltreat, manhandle. *See* MISTREAT.

**mishap** noun **1** *without further mishap* accident, misadventure, mischance. **2** *after a series of mishaps* accident, trouble, setback, reverse, adversity, misfortune, stroke of bad luck.

**mishmash** noun hodgepodge, jumble, tangle, confusion, potpourri, pastiche, gallimaufry, olio, salmagundi, mixed bag.

**mislay** verb lose, misplace, lose track of, miss, be unable to lay one's hands on.

**mislead** verb misinform, misguide, misdirect, delude, take in, deceive, fool, hoodwink, lead astray, throw off the scent, send on a wild-goose chase, pull the wool over someone's eyes; *inf.* lead up the garden path, take for a ride.

**misleading** adjective confusing, deceptive, deceiving, delusive, evasive, equivocal, ambiguous, fallacious, spurious, illusory, casuistic, sophistical.

**mismanage** verb misdirect, misgovern. *See* MISHANDLE 1.

**misogynist** noun woman-hater, antifeminist, male chauvinist, chauvinist; *inf.* male chauvinist pig, MCP.

**misprint** noun printing error, typographical error, typing error, mistake, erratum; *inf.* typo.

**misrepresent** verb misstate, misreport, misquote, misinterpret, falsify, distort, garble.

**miss** verb **1** *miss a shot* let go, bungle, botch, muff, fail to achieve. **2** *miss the meeting* fail to attend, be too late for, absent oneself from, play truant from, take French leave from; *inf.* skip. **3** *miss an opportunity* let slip, let go, pass up, overlook, disregard. **4** *I'm sorry, I missed what you said* fail to hear/catch, fail to take in, mishear, misunderstand. **5** *they miss their father* regret the absence/loss of, feel the loss of, feel nostalgic for, long to see, long for, pine for, yearn for, ache for. **6** *try to miss the traffic* avoid, evade, escape, dodge, sidestep, steer clear of, give a wide berth to.

**miss** noun failure, omission, slip, blunder, error, mistake, fiasco; *inf.* flop.

**misshapen** adjective deformed, malformed, ill-proportioned, misproportioned, twisted, distorted, contorted, warped, curved, crooked, wry, bent, hunchbacked.

**mission** noun **1** *accomplish his mission* assignment, commission, task, job, errand, work, chore, business, undertaking, operation, duty, charge, trust, goal, aim, purpose. **2** *her mission in life is to heal the sick* vocation, calling, pursuit, quest, undertaking. **3** *scientists asked to join the mission* delegation, deputation, committee, commission, task force, legation.

**missionary** noun evangelist, apostle, proselytizer, preacher, minister, priest.

**missive** noun communication, message, letter, note, memorandum, bulletin, communiqué, report, dispatch; *inf.* memo.

**misspent** adjective dissipated, wasted, squandered, thrown away, prodigal.

**mist** noun haze, fog, smog, cloud, vapor, condensation, steam, film.

**mistake** noun error, fault, inaccuracy, slip, blunder, miscalculation, misunderstanding, oversight, gaffe, faux pas, solecism, misapprehension, misreading; *inf.* slipup, booboo.

**mistake** verb get wrong, misunderstand, misapprehend, misinterpret, misconstrue, misread.

**mistaken** adjective wrong, erroneous, inaccurate, incorrect, false, fallacious, unsound, unfounded, misguided, misinformed, wide of the mark.

**mistreat** verb maltreat, treat badly, illtreat, ill-use, misuse, abuse, handle/treat roughly, mishandle, harm, hurt, molest, manhandle, maul, bully; *inf.* beat up, rough up.

**mistress** noun lover, girlfriend, partner, ladylove, paramour, kept woman, concubine, inamorata.

**mistrust** verb **1** *mistrust his motives* distrust, have doubts about, be suspicious of, suspect, have reservations about, have misgivings about, be wary of. **2** *mistrust his ability* have no confidence in, question, doubt, lack faith in.

**mistrustful** adjective distrustful, doubtful, dubious, suspicious, chary, wary, uncertain, cautious, hesitant, skeptical; *inf.* leery.

**misty** adjective hazy, foggy, cloudy; blurred, fuzzy, dim, indistinct, vague, obscure, nebulous.

**misunderstand** verb misapprehend, misinterpret, misconstrue, misread, get the wrong idea, receive a false impression.

**misunderstanding** noun **1** *his misunderstanding of the statement* misapprehension, mistake, error, mix-up, misinterpretation, misconstruction, misreading, misjudgment, miscalculation, misconception, misbelief, wrong idea, delusion, false impression. **2** *the friends have had a misunderstanding* disagreement, difference, difference of opinion, clash of views, dispute, quarrel, argument, tiff, squabble, spat; *inf.* falling-out.

**misuse** verb **1** *misuse their talents* misapply, misemploy, abuse, squander, waste, dissipate. **2** *misuse the furniture* abuse, vandalize. *See* MISTREAT.

**misuse** noun **1** *the misuse of their money* misapplication, misemployment, abuse, squandering, waste, dissipation. **2** *this misuse of the verb* misusage, malapropism, barbarism, catachresis. **3** *misuse of the car* maltreatment, mistreatment, ill use, abuse, rough handling, mishandling, manhandling.

**mitigate** verb alleviate, reduce, diminish, lessen, weaken, attenuate, allay, assuage, palliate, appease, soothe, relieve,

ease, soften, temper, mollify, lighten, still, quieten, quiet, tone down, moderate, modify, extenuate, calm, lull, pacify, placate, tranquilize.

**mitigating** adjective extenuating, exonerative, justificatory, justifying, vindicatory, vindicating, exculpatory, palliative, qualifying, modifying, tempering.

**mix** verb **1** *mix cement* admix, blend, put together, combine, mingle, compound, homogenize, alloy, merge, unite, join, amalgamate, fuse, coalesce, interweave. **2** *he never mixes at parties* socialize, mingle, associate, fraternize, hobnob. **mix up 1** *mix up the dates* confuse, get confused, muddle, muddle up, get muddled up, get jumbled up, scramble, mistake. **2** *don't mix me up* confuse, throw into confusion, fluster, upset. **3** *he is mixed up in the crime* involve, implicate, entangle, embroil, draw into, incriminate.

**mix** noun merger, union, amalgamation, fusion, coalition. *See* MIXTURE 1.

**mixed** adjective **1** *a mixed collection* assorted, varied, miscellaneous, diverse, diversified, motley, heterogeneous. **2** *of mixed breed* hybrid, crossbred, interbred, mongrel. **3** *have mixed reactions* ambivalent, equivocal, unsure, uncertain.

**mixed-up** adjective *a mixed-up kid* maladjusted, ill-adjusted, disturbed, confused; *inf.* screwed-up.

**mixture** noun **1** *pour out the mixture* compound, blend, mix, brew, combination, concoction, alloy. **2** *a mixture of objects* assortment, variety. *See* MEDLEY.

**mix-up** noun confusion, muddle, jumble, misunderstanding, mistake.

**moan** noun groan, lament, lamentation, wail, whimper, whine, sigh, sough, murmur.

**moan** verb **1** *he moans in his sleep* groan, wail, whimper, whine, sigh, sough, murmur. **2** *always moaning about the weather* complain, whine, carp; *inf.* grouse, gripe, grouch, beef.

**mob** noun **1** *the mob of spectators* crowd, horde, multitude, legion, army, throng, host, pack, press, gang, drove, herd, flock, gathering, assemblage. **2** *the cries of the angry mob* masses, populace, commonality, proletariat, rabble, hoi polloi, canaille; *inf.* great unwashed. **3** *those gatecrashers left, but another mob arrived* lot, group, set, troop, company; *inf.* gang.

**mob** verb **1** *fans mobbed the team* crowd around, swarm around, surround, besiege, jostle. **2** *mob the theater* crowd into, cram full, fill to overflowing, fill, pack.

**mobile** adjective **1** *mobile library* movable, transportable, portable, traveling, peripatetic, locomotive. **2** *a mobile face* expressive,

animated, ever-changing, changeable.
**3** *socially mobile* moving, on the move, flexible, adaptable, adjustable.

**mobilize** verb muster, rally, marshal, assemble, organize, make ready, prepare, ready.

**mock** verb **1** *rebels mocking government officials* ridicule, jeer at, sneer at, deride, treat with contempt, scorn, make fun of, poke fun at, laugh at, tease, taunt, insult, flout; *inf.* rag, kid, rib. **2** *mocked their teacher's mannerisms* imitate, mimic, parody, ape, caricature, satirize, lampoon, burlesque. **3** *the wind mocked their progress* defy, challenge, thwart, frustrate, foil, disappoint.

**mock** adjective *mock leather* imitation, artificial, simulated, synthetic, ersatz, so-called, fake, sham, false, spurious, bogus, counterfeit, forged, pseudo, pretended; *inf.* pretend.

**mockery** noun **1** *a note of mockery in his voice* ridicule, jeering, sneer, derision, contempt, scorn, disdain, teasing, taunting, gibe, insult, contumely; *inf.* ribbing. **2** *the trial was a mockery* laughingstock, farce, parody, travesty, caricature, lampoon, burlesque; *inf.* takeoff, send-up, spoof.

**mocking** adjective *a mocking smile* sneering, derisive, derisory, contemptuous, scornful, disdainful, sardonic, insulting, satirical.

**model** noun **1** *a model of a train* replica, representation, mock-up, copy, dummy, imitation, facsimile, image, mannequin. **2** *the model of the commissioned building* prototype, protoplast, archetype, type, mold, original, pattern, design, paradigm, sample, example, exemplar. **3** *the model of car I want* style, design, mode, form, mark, version, type, variety, kind, sort. **4** *a model of tact* ideal, paragon, perfect example, perfect specimen, exemplar, (the) epitome of something, (the) beau ideal, nonpareil, (the) crème de la crème. **5** *he used his wife as a model* sitter, poser, subject.

**model** adjective **1** *the model building* prototypical, prototypal, archetypal, illustrative. **2** *a model teacher* ideal, perfect.

**moderate** adjective **1** *moderate views/demands/behavior* nonextreme, middle-of-the-road, reasonable, within reason, within due limits, restrained, controlled, temperate, sober, steady. **2** *moderate success* average, middling, ordinary, fair, fairish, modest, tolerable, passable, adequate, indifferent, mediocre, run-of-the-mill; *inf.* so-so, fair-to-middling.

**moderate** verb **1** *moderate the force/pain* abate, lessen. *See* MITIGATE. **2** *moderate the debate* arbitrate, mediate, referee, judge, chair, take the chair of, preside over.

**moderately** adverb **1** *moderately expensive* quite, rather, somewhat, fairly, reasonably, to a certain degree, to some extent, within reason, within limits. **2** *the work is moderately good | did moderately well in the test* fairly, tolerably, passably.

**moderation** noun **1** *moderation in all things* moderateness, restraint, self-restraint, control, self-control, temperateness, temperance, nonindulgence. **2** *the moderation of the force/pain* lessening, decrease, mitigation, appeasement, assuagement, soothing, calming. **in moderation** moderately, within reason, within due limits.

**modern** adjective **1** *in modern times* contemporary, present-day, present, current, existing, existent. **2** *her clothes/ideas are very modern* up-to-date, up-to-the-minute, fashionable, in fashion, in style, in vogue, voguish, modish, the latest, new, newfangled, fresh, modernistic, ultramodern, advanced, progressive; *inf.* trendy, with-it.

**modernize** verb update, bring/get up to date, renovate, remodel, remake, redo, refresh, revamp, rejuvenate, move with the times; *inf.* do over, get with it.

**modest** adjective **1** *modest about his achievements* self-effacing, self-deprecating, humble, unpretentious, unassuming. **2** *too modest to speak* shy, bashful, self-conscious, diffident, reserved, retiring, reticent, timid, fearful, meek. **3** *modest behavior/clothes* decorous, decent, seemly, demure, proper, discreet, delicate, chaste, virtuous. **4** *modest improvement* moderate, fair, tolerable, passable, adequate, unexceptional, small, limited. **5** *a modest gift* unpretentious, simple, plain, humble, inexpensive, low-cost.

**modesty** noun **1** *admire his modesty* lack of vanity, humility, self-effacement, lack of pretension, unpretentiousness. **2** *her modesty prevented her speaking* shyness, bashfulness, self-consciousness, reserve, reticence, timidity, meekness. **3** *modesty of her behavior/clothes* decorum, decorousness, seemliness, demureness, propriety, chasteness. **4** *the modesty of their demands* moderation, fairness, adequacy, acceptability, smallness. **5** *the modesty of the house* unpretentiousness, simplicity, plainness, inexpensiveness.

**modicum** noun bit, particle, iota, jot, atom, whit, grain, speck, scrap, crumb, fragment, shred, mite, dash, drop, dab, pinch, ounce, inch, touch, tinge, trifle; *inf.* teeny bit.

**modification** noun **1** *the modification of the punishment* lessening, reduction, decrease, abatement, mitigation, restriction. **2** *the modification of the design* altering, alteration, adjustment, adaptation, refashioning, change, variation, revision, refinement, transformation.

**modify** verb **1** *modify her views* soften, moderate, temper, blunt, dull, tone down, qualify. **2** *modify the design* alter, change, adjust, adapt, vary, revise, recast, reform, reshape, refashion, rework, remold, redo, revamp, reorganize, refine, transform.

**mogul** noun notable, VIP, magnate, tycoon, baron, captain, lord; *inf.* bigwig, big shot, big cheese.

**moist** adjective wet, wettish, damp, dampish, clammy, humid, dank, rainy, dewy, soggy.

**moisten** verb wet, dampen, damp, water, soak, bedew, humidify, irrigate.

**moisture** noun water, liquid, wetness, wet, dampness, damp, humidity, dankness, wateriness, rain, dew, drizzle, perspiration, sweat.

**mold**[1] noun **1** *set the mixture in a mold* cast, die, form, matrix. **2** *the mold of history* shape, form, figure, cast, outline, line, configuration, formation, format, structure, frame, construction, build, cut, style, model, pattern, type, kind, brand, make. **3** *people of heroic mold* character, nature, caliber, kind, sort, ilk, stamp, type, kidney.

**mold**[2] verb **1** *mold the model from clay* shape, form, fashion, model, construct, frame, make, create, design, carve, sculpt, chisel, forge. **2** *mold children's minds* influence, affect, direct, shape, form.

**mold**[3] noun moldiness, fungus, mildew, blight, smut, must, mustiness, dry rot, rot.

**moldy** adjective mildewed, blighted, musty, fusty, decaying, rotting, rotten, bad, spoiled.

**molest** verb **1** *crowds molesting the celebrity* pester, annoy, nag, plague, torment, harass, badger, harry, bother, vex, disturb; *inf.* bug, hassle. **2** *accused of molesting children* abuse, sexually abuse/assault, rape, ravish, assault, attack, injure, hurt, harm, mistreat, maltreat, ill-treat, manhandle.

**mollify** verb calm, calm down, pacify, placate, appease, soothe, still, quiet, tranquilize.

**mollycoddle** verb pamper, coddle, cosset, spoil, overindulge, indulge, baby.

**moment** noun short time, instant. *See* MINUTE noun 1, 2.

**momentary** adjective brief, short, short-lived, fleeting, passing, transient, transitory, ephemeral, evanescent, fugitive, temporary, impermanent.

**momentous** adjective important, significant, consequential, fateful, historic; *inf.* earthshaking, earth-shattering.

**momentum** noun impetus, impulse, propulsion, thrust, push, driving power/force, drive, power, energy, force.

**monarch** noun sovereign, ruler, crowned head, potentate, king, queen, emperor, empress.

**monarchy** noun **1** *abolish the monarchy* absolutism, absolute power, autocracy, monocracy, kingship, royalism, sovereignty, despotism. **2** *the country is a monarchy* kingdom, sovereign state, realm, principality, empire.

**monastery** noun friary, abbey, convent, nunnery, priory.

**monastic** adjective monastical, cloistered, cenobitic, conventual, canonical, ascetic, celibate, contemplative, meditative, sequestered, secluded, reclusive, recluse, eremitic, anchoritic.

**monetary** adjective money, cash, financial, capital, pecuniary, fiscal, budgetary.

**money** noun **1** *not enough money to buy the business* cash, hard cash, ready money, finance, capital, funds, banknotes, currency, coin, coinage, silver, copper, legal tender, specie; *inf.* wherewithal, dough, bread, loot, moolah, filthy lucre, green stuff. **2** *he is a man of money* affluence, wealth, riches, prosperity. **in the money** moneyed, well-to-do, well-off, affluent, rich, wealthy, prosperous, in clover; *inf.* rolling in it, loaded, stinking rich, well-heeled, flush, made of money, on easy street.

**moneymaking** adjective profitable, lucrative, gainful, paying, remunerative, successful, thriving, going.

**mongrel** noun crossbreed, cross, half-breed, mixed breed, hybrid, cur.

**monitor** noun **1** *monitors watching shoppers/workers* detector, scanner, recorder, security system, security camera, observer, watchdog, overseer, supervisor. **2** *computer monitor* screen, cathode-ray tube, CRT.

**monitor** verb observe, scan, record, survey, follow, keep an eye on, keep track of, check, oversee, supervise.

**monk** noun brother, monastic, religious, friar, abbot, prior.

**monkey** noun **1** *monkeys in the jungle* primate, simian. **2** *the child is a little monkey* rascal, scamp, imp, rogue, mischief-maker, devil. **make a monkey of** make a fool of, make a laughingstock of, ridicule, deride, make fun of.

**monkey** verb **monkey around/about** fool around/about, play around/about; *inf.* mess around/about. **monkey with** fiddle with, play with, tinker with, tamper with, interfere with, meddle with, fool with, trifle with, mess with.

**monkey business** noun 1 *children up to monkey business* mischief, naughtiness, pranks, clowning; *inf.* shenanigans. 2 *monkey business in the accounts department* dishonesty, trickery, misconduct, misdemeanor, chicanery, skulduggery; *inf.* funny business, hanky-panky.

**monologue** noun soliloquy, speech, address, lecture, oration, sermon.

**monopolize** verb corner, control, take over, dominate.

**monotonous** adjective 1 *a monotonous job* unvarying, unchanging, repetitious, routine, humdrum, run-of-the-mill, commonplace, mechanical, uninteresting, unexciting, prosaic, wearisome, dull, boring, tedious, tiresome. 2 *a monotonous voice* flat, unvarying, toneless, uninflected, droning, soporific.

**monotony** noun 1 *the monotony of the job* lack of variety, repetition, repetitiveness, sameness, uniformity, routine, routineness, dullness, boredom, tedium, tiresomeness. 2 *the monotony of her voice* flatness, tonelessness, drone.

**monster** noun 1 *frightened by the monster in the myth* fabulous/mythical creature, ogre, giant, dragon, troll, bogeyman, werewolf, sea monster, behemoth. 2 *Hitler was a monster* fiend, beast, brute, barbarian, savage, villain, ogre, devil, demon. 3 *the sideshow monster was a hoax* monstrosity, miscreation, malformation, freak, freak of nature, mutant, lusus naturae. 4 *a monster of a man* giant, mammoth, colossus, titan, behemoth, leviathan.

**monster** adjective *a monster truck* huge, enormous, massive, vast, immense, colossal, gigantic, monstrous, stupendous, prodigious, tremendous, giant, mammoth, gargantuan, titanic; *inf.* jumbo, whopping, humongous.

**monstrous** adjective 1 *Dr. Frankenstein's monstrous creatures* miscreated, malformed, unnatural, abnormal, grotesque, gruesome, repellent, freakish, mutant. 2 *monstrous trucks* huge, enormous. *See* MONSTER adjective. 3 *it was a monstrous thing to do* outrageous, shocking, scandalous, atrocious, heinous, evil, abominable, hideous, loathsome, contemptible, despicable, vicious, cruel, savage, barbaric, inhuman, fiendish, diabolical.

**monument** noun 1 *a monument to the dead soldiers* memorial, statue, shrine, reliquary, sepulcher, mausoleum, cairn, pillar, column, obelisk, dolmen, megalith. 2 *establish a scholarship as a monument to his talent* memorial, commemoration, remembrance, reminder, testament, witness, token.

**monumental** adjective 1 *a monumental effort* great, huge, enormous, immense, vast, exceptional, extraordinary, tremendous, stupendous, prodigious, staggering. 2 *a monumental error* colossal, egregious, catastrophic, staggering, unforgivable, indefensible; *inf.* whopping. 3 *a monumental work of art* massive, impressive, striking, remarkable, magnificent, awe-inspiring, marvelous, majestic, classic, memorable, unforgettable, enduring, permanent, immortal.

**mood** noun humor, temper, disposition, frame of mind, state of mind, spirit, tenor, vein; *bad mood*, bad temper, low spirits, depression.

**moody** adjective 1 *teenagers are often moody* temperamental, changeable, unpredictable, volatile, mercurial, unstable, unsteady, erratic, fitful, impulsive, capricious. 2 *don't say anything—he's moody today* bad-tempered, ill-tempered, ill-humored, irritable, crabby, cross, testy, touchy, petulant, in a pique, sullen, sulky, moping, gloomy, glum, depressed, huffy.

**moor** verb secure, fix firmly, fasten, make fast, tie up, lash, anchor, berth.

**moot** adjective *a moot point* debatable, open to debate, open to discussion, questionable, open to question, open, doubtful, disputable, arguable, contestable, controversial, unresolved, undecided.

**mop** verb clean, wipe, wash, swab, sponge. **mop up** 1 *mop up all the profits* absorb, use up, exhaust, consume, swallow up. 2 *mop up the last bits of work* finish off, make an end of, clear up, eliminate, dispatch.

**mope** verb pine, fret, grieve, brood, sulk, idle, languish, moon.

**moral** adjective 1 *a moral person/act* ethical, good, virtuous, righteous, upright, upstanding, high-minded, principled, honorable, honest, just, decent, chaste, pure, blameless, right, proper, fit, decent, decorous. 3 *moral support* psychological, emotional, mental.

**moral** noun lesson, teaching, message, homily, meaning, significance, point.

**morale** noun self-confidence, confidence, heart, spirit, hope, hopefulness, optimism, determination, zeal.

**morality** noun 1 *a man/woman of morality* ethics, goodness, virtue, righteousness, rectitude, uprightness, integrity, principles, honor, honesty, justness, decency, chasteness, chastity, purity, blamelessness. 2 *discuss morality* moral code, ethics. *See* MORALS.

**morals** plural noun ethics, moral code, principles of right and wrong, principles, moral behavior/conduct, standards/principles of behavior, standards, morality, sense of morality, scruples, mores.

**morbid** adjective **1** *morbid thoughts/details* gruesome, grisly, macabre, hideous, dreadful, horrible, unwholesome; death-orientated, death-obsessed, death-fixated. **2** *don't be so morbid* gloomy, glum, dejected, melancholy, lugubrious, funereal, pessimistic.

**more** adjective additional, supplementary, further, added, extra, increased, spare, fresh, new.

**more** adverb *concentrate more* to a greater extent, further, longer, some more.

**moreover** adverb besides, furthermore, further, what is more, in addition, also, as well, to boot.

**morgue** noun mortuary, funeral parlor, funeral home, charnel house.

**moribund** adjective **1** *moribund patients* dying, on one's deathbed, near death, near the end, breathing one's last, fading fast, failing rapidly, having one foot in the grave, *in extremis*. **2** *moribund customs* dying, declining, on the decline, waning, on the way out, obsolescent, on its last legs.

**morning** noun forenoon, a.m., dawn, daybreak, sunrise; *lit.* morn.

**moron** noun fool, dolt, dunce, dullard, blockhead, dunderhead, ignoramus, numskull, nincompoop, idiot, imbecile, nitwit, halfwit; *inf.* dope, dimwit, dummy, schmuck.

**morose** adjective sullen, gloomy, glum, somber, sober, saturnine, lugubrious, funereal, mournful, depressed, dour, melancholy, melancholic, doleful, blue, down, low, moody; sour, scowling, sulky, crabby, cross.

**morsel** noun bite, nibble, bit, crumb, grain, particle, fragment, scrap, soupçon, taste.

**mortal** adjective **1** *mortal beings* temporal, transient, ephemeral, passing, impermanent, perishable, human, earthly, worldly, corporeal, fleshly. **2** *a mortal blow* death-dealing, deadly, fatal, lethal, killing, murderous, terminal, destructive. **3** *mortal enemies* deadly, to the death, sworn, out-and-out, irreconcilable, bitter, implacable, unrelenting, remorseless. **4** *mortal pain/fear* terrible, awful, intense, extreme, severe, grave, dire. **5** *of no mortal use* conceivable, imaginable, perceivable, possible.

**mortal** noun human being, human, earthling, person, man/woman, being, body, individual.

**mortality** noun **1** *humans subject to mortality* temporality, transience, ephemerality, impermanence, perishability. **2** *appalled at the wartime mortality* bloodshed, death, loss of life, fatalities, killing, slaying, carnage, slaughter.

**mortify** verb **1** *mortified by failure* humiliate, humble, bring low, disgrace, shame, dishonor, abash, fill with shame, put to shame, chasten, degrade, abase, deflate, embarrass. **2** *mortify one's passions* subdue, control, restrain, suppress, discipline, chasten.

**mortuary** noun morgue, funeral parlor, funeral home, charnel house.

**most** noun the majority, the greatest number, nearly all, almost all, the bulk, the mass.

**mostly** adverb **1** *they were mostly young* for the most part, on the whole, largely, mainly, chiefly, predominantly. **2** *mostly we eat at home* usually, generally, as a rule, ordinarily.

**mother** noun materfamilias, matriarch, earth mother; *inf.* mom, mommy, ma, mama, mater, old lady.

**mother** adjective inborn, innate, connate, native, natural.

**mother** verb look after, care for, tend, raise, rear, foster, cherish, fuss over, indulge, spoil.

**motherly** adjective maternal, protective, comforting, caring, loving, affectionate, warm, tender, gentle.

**motion** noun **1** *the motion made her sick* motility, mobility, locomotion, movement, moving. **2** *a motion with her hand* movement, gesture, gesticulation, signal, sign, wave, nod. **set/put in motion** get going, get under way, get in operation, get working/functioning, start, begin, commence.

**motion** verb gesture, gesticulate, signal, sign, wave, nod.

**motionless** adjective unmoving, still, stock-still, at a standstill, stationary, immobile, immovable, static, at rest, halted, stopped, paralyzed, transfixed, frozen, inert, lifeless.

**motivate** verb move, cause, lead, persuade, prompt, actuate, drive, impel, spur, induce, provoke, incite, inspire, give incentive to, stimulate, arouse, stir, goad.

**motivation** noun incentive, stimulus, inspiration, inducement, incitement, motive; ambition, drive, inspiration.

**motive** noun reason, rationale, justification, thinking, grounds, cause, basis, occasion; motivation, incentive, inducement, incitement.

**motley** adjective **1** *motley collection of old clothes* assorted, varied. *See* MISCELLANEOUS. **2** *a motley coat* many-colored, multicolored, parti-colored, many-hued, variegated, kaleidoscopic, prismatic.

**mottled** adjective blotched, blotchy, splotchy, speckled, spotted, streaked, marbled, flecked, freckled, dappled, stippled, variegated, piebald, pied, brindled.

**motto** noun **1** *"waste not, want not" should be your motto* maxim, aphorism, adage, saying, saw, axiom, truism, precept, epigram, proverb, byword, gnome. **2** *the club's motto* slogan, catchword, cry.

**mound** noun **1** *a mound of leaves* heap, pile, stack; *inf.* mountain. **2** *flat country broken by mounds* hillock, hill, knoll, rise, hummock, embankment, bank, dune.

**mound** verb pile, heap (up), stack (up), accumulate, amass, stockpile.

**mount** verb **1** *mount the stairs* ascend, go up, climb up, clamber up, make one's way up, scale. **2** *costs mounting up* accumulate, accrue, pile up, grow, multiply. **3** *prices/fear mounting* increase, grow, escalate, intensify. **4** *mount a campaign/exhibition* stage, put on, install, prepare, organize, arrange, set in motion.

**mount** noun *a plain mount for the gem/picture* setting, fixture, frame, support, stand, base, backing, foil.

**mountain** noun **1** *snowcapped mountains* peak, height, elevation, eminence, pinnacle, alp; *lit.* mount. **2** *mountains of clothes* heap, pile, mound, stack, abundance; *inf.* ton.

**mourn** verb grieve, sorrow, keen, lament, wail.

**mournful** adjective sad, sorrowful, doleful, gloomy, somber, melancholy, lugubrious, funereal, elegiac.

**mourning** noun grief, grieving, sorrowing, lamentation, keening, wailing, weeping, moaning.

**mousy** adjective **1** *a mousy person* timid, fearful, timorous, self-effacing, unobtrusive, unassertive, withdrawn, shy. **2** *mousy hair/colors* brownish-gray, grayish, gray, dun-colored, colorless, neutral, drab, dull, lackluster.

**mouth** noun **1** *open their mouths* lips, jaws, maw, muzzle; *inf.* trap, chops, kisser. **2** *mouth of the cave/trumpet* opening, entrance, entry, inlet, door, doorway, gateway, portal, hatch. **3** *the mouth of the river* estuary, outlet, embouchure. **4** *he's all mouth and no action* empty talk, idle talk, babble, claptrap, boasting, bragging, braggadocio; *inf.* hot air, gas. **5** *don't take any mouth from her* impudence, cheek, insolence, impertinence, rudeness, incivility, effrontery, audacity; *inf.* lip, back talk. **down in the mouth** down, downhearted, dejected, downcast, low in spirits, depressed, dispirited, crestfallen.

**move** verb **1** *men moving slowly* proceed, progress, advance, pass. **2** *move objects* carry, transport, transfer, transpose, change over, shift, switch. **3** *the government must move soon* take action, act, do something, get moving. **4** *our neighbors are moving* relocate, move away, leave, go away. **5** *she was moved by the performance* affect, touch, impress, upset, disturb, disquiet, agitate. **6** *the sight moved her to tears* provoke, incite, actuate, rouse, excite, urge, incline, stimulate, motivate, influence, persuade, lead, prompt, cause, impel, induce. **7** *as the spirit moves him* propel, drive, push, shift, motivate. **8** *nothing can move him on that* change, budge, change someone's mind; *inf.* do an about-face, do a U-turn. **9** *the goods are not moving* sell, be sold, move from the shelf.

**move** noun **1** *birds frightened by the slightest move* motion, action. See MOVEMENT 2. **2** *arrange our move* removal, relocation, transfer. **3** *plan our next move* action, act, deed, measure, step, tack, maneuver, tactic, stratagem, ploy, ruse, trick. **4** *it's your move* turn; opportunity, chance; *inf.* shot. **get a move on** hurry up, get moving; *inf.* get cracking, make it snappy, step on it, shake a leg. **make a move** take action, act, do something. **on the move 1** *she's always on the move* moving, in motion, going, traveling, journeying. **2** *things are on the move* progressing, advancing, moving/going forward.

**movement** noun **1** *the movement of the furniture* moving, carrying, transportation, transferal, shifting. **2** *make a sudden movement* move, motion, action, activity, gesture, gesticulation. **3** *the movement of time* progress, progression, advance, passing, passage. **4** *the clock's movement* mechanism, machinery, works, workings, action, wheels; *inf.* innards, guts. **5** *a peace movement* group, party, organization, faction, wing, coalition, front; campaign, crusade, drive. **6** *a movement toward better government* trend, tendency, drift, swing, current. **7** *no movement in the stock market* rise/fall, change, variation, fluctuation. **8** *some movement has been made in the situation* progress, advance, improvement, step forward, breakthrough.

**moving** adjective **1** *a moving story* affecting, touching, emotive, emotional, poignant, pathetic, stirring, arousing, upsetting, disturbing. **2** *moving parts* movable, mobile, motile, unfixed. **3** *the moving force behind the scheme* driving, dynamic, impelling, motivating, stimulating, inspirational.

**much** adjective a great deal of, plenty of, ample, copious, abundant; *inf.* a lot of, lots of.

**much** adverb **1** *I much regret it* greatly, exceedingly, considerably. **2** *he's not here much* often, frequently; *inf.* a lot.

**muck** noun **1** *clear the muck from the barn* dung, manure, ordure, excrement, guano, droppings, feces. **2** *clean the muck from the* *car* dirt, grime, filth, mud, slime, sludge, scum, mire; *inf.* gunk, grunge.

**mud** noun sludge, clay, silt, mire, dirt, soil.

**muddle** verb **1** *muddle the dates/situation* confuse, mix up, jumble, jumble up, scramble, disarrange, disorganize, throw into disorder, get into a tangle, make a mess of, mess up. **2** *numbers muddle her* confuse, disorient, bewilder, befuddle, daze, perplex, puzzle, baffle.

**muddle** noun **1** *files in a muddle* chaos, disorder, disarray, confusion, disorganization, jumble, mix-up, mess, clutter, tangle. **2** *her mind is in a muddle* state of confusion, disorientation, bewilderment, perplexity, puzzlement, bafflement.

**muddy** adjective **1** *a muddy substance* mucky, miry, oozy, slushy, slimy. **2** *muddy ground* marshy, boggy, swampy. **3** *muddy shoes* mud-caked, dirty, filthy, grubby, grimy. **4** *muddy stream/liquid* cloudy, murky, smoky, dingy, dull, turbid, opaque. **5** *muddy thinking* confused, jumbled, incoherent, unclear, muddied, woolly.

**muffle** verb deaden, dull, dampen, stifle, smother, suppress, soften, hush, mute, silence.

**muggy** adjective close, stuffy, sultry, oppressive, airless, humid, clammy, sticky.

**mull** verb **mull over** think over, think about, consider, ponder, reflect on, contemplate, meditate on, deliberate about/on, muse on, ruminate over/on, examine, study, review.

**multiply** verb increase, grow, accumulate, augment, proliferate, spread, breed, reproduce.

**multitude** noun **1** *multitude of people* crowd, assembly. *See* MOB noun 1. **2** *treat the multitude with disdain* masses, populace. *See* MOB noun 2.

**mundane** adjective **1** *mundane issues/prose* common, ordinary, everyday, workaday, usual, prosaic, pedestrian, routine, customary, regular, normal, typical, commonplace, banal, hackneyed, trite. **2** *mundane, not spiritual, matters* worldly, earthly, terrestrial, secular, temporal, fleshly, carnal, sensual.

**municipal** adjective civic, civil, city, metropolitan, urban, town, borough, community, public.

**munificence** noun liberality, generosity, charity, charitableness, magnanimity, magnanimousness, largesse, bounty, bountifulness, bounteousness.

**munificent** adjective bountiful, bounteous, liberal, generous, free, openhanded, charitable, hospitable, bighearted, beneficent, benevolent, ungrudging, magnanimous, philanthropic.

**murder** noun **1** *guilty of murder* killing, slaying, manslaughter, homicide, slaughter, assassination, butchery, carnage, massacre. **2** *the drive was murder* an ordeal, a trial, a misery, agony; *inf.* hell, hell on earth.

**murder** verb **1** *murder his brother* kill, slay, put to death, take the life of, shed the blood of, slaughter, assassinate, butcher, massacre; *inf.* bump off, do in, eliminate, hit, rub out, blow away. **2** *murder the song* mangle, mutilate, ruin, make a mess of, spoil, mar, destroy. **3** *they murdered our team* trounce, beat soundly, beat decisively, thrash, defeat utterly, give a drubbing to; *inf.* slaughter, hammer, make mincemeat of.

**murderer** noun killer, slayer, homicide, slaughterer, cutthroat, assassin, butcher, patricide, matricide, fratricide.

**murky** adjective **1** *murky streets/shadows* dark, dim, gloomy. **2** *murky weather* foggy, misty, cloudy, lowering, overcast, dull, gray, dismal, dreary, cheerless. **3** *murky pools* dirty, muddy, dingy, dull, cloudy, turbid, opaque. **4** *a murky past* dark, questionable, doubtful, obscure, enigmatic, nebulous, mysterious, hidden, secret.

**murmur** noun **1** *the murmur of the stream* babble, burble, whisper, rustle, buzzing, drone, sigh; *inf.* whoosh. **2** *tell him in a murmur* whisper, undertone, mutter, mumble. **3** *murmurs against his presidency* mutter, grumble, moan, complaint, carping, whisper; *inf.* grouse, gripe, beef.

**murmur** verb **1** *streams murmuring* babble, burble, whisper, rustle, buzz, drone, sigh; *inf.* whoosh. **2** *murmured her desire to leave* whisper, mutter, mumble. **murmur against** grumble, moan, complain, carp; *inf.* grouse, gripe, beef, bitch.

**muscle** noun **1** *strain a muscle* sinew, tendon, ligament, thew. **2** *a man with muscle* muscularity, brawn; *inf.* beef. **3** *the new chairperson has no muscle* power, potency, force, forcefulness, might, strength, weight, influence; *inf.* clout, pull.

**muscular** adjective **1** *muscular men* brawny, strapping, powerfully built, solidly built, hefty, stalwart, sturdy, rugged, burly; *inf.* hunky, buff, beefy, husky. **2** *a muscular attempt* vigorous, potent, powerful, strong, energetic, active, dynamic, aggressive, determined, resolute.

**muse** verb **1** *stand and muse* think, meditate, be lost in contemplation/thought, be in a brown study, reflect, deliberate, daydream, be in a reverie. **2** *muse over the situation* think over, think about. *See* MULL.

**mushroom** verb spring up, shoot up, sprout, burgeon, burst forth, grow/develop rapidly, boom, thrive, flourish, prosper.

**music** noun melody, tune, air, rhythm, harmonization, orchestration.

**musical** adjective tuneful, melodic, melodious, harmonious, lyrical, sweet-sounding, mellifluous, dulcet, euphonious.

**muss** verb disarrange, misarrange, put out of place, make untidy, make a mess of, mess up, rumple, dishevel, tousle.

**muster** verb **1** *muster the soldiers* assemble, bring together, call/gather together, call up, summon, rally, mobilize, round up, marshal, collect, convoke. **2** *we must muster at dawn* meet, congregate, convene. **3** *muster one's courage* call up, gather together, summon, rally, screw up.

**muster** noun **pass muster** measure up, come up to scratch/snuff, be acceptable, qualify; *inf.* make the grade, fill/fit the bill.

**musty** adjective **1** *musty books/food/rooms* moldy, mildewed, mildewy, fusty, decaying, stale, stuffy, airless, damp, dank. **2** *musty ideas* antiquated, obsolete, ancient, antediluvian, out-of-date, outdated, old-fashioned, out-of-fashion, out-of-style, behind the times, passé, moth-eaten, worn-out, threadbare, hackneyed, trite, clichéd.

**mutation** noun change, variation, alteration, modification, transformation, metamorphosis, evolution, transmutation, transfiguration.

**mute** adjective **1** *mute with surprise* silent, speechless, wordless, unspeaking, taciturn, uncommunicative. **2** *animals born mute* dumb, voiceless, speechless, aphasic, aphonic. **3** *a mute appeal* unexpressed, unspoken.

**mutilate** verb **1** *mutilated in the accident* maim, lame, cripple, disable, disfigure, damage, injure, impair; dismember, tear limb from limb, amputate limbs from. **2** *mutilate a text* mar, spoil, ruin, damage, butcher, mangle, distort, cut, hack, censor, bowdlerize, expurgate.

**mutinous** adjective rebellious, insurgent, insurrectionary, revolutionary, anarchistic, subversive, seditious, traitorous, insubordinate, disobedient, riotous.

**mutiny** noun rebellion, revolt, insurrection, insurgence, insurgency, uprising, rising, riot, revolution, resistance, disobedience, defiance, insubordination, protest, strike.

**mutiny** verb rebel, revolt, riot, rise up.

**mutter** verb **1** *going along muttering* talk under one's breath, speak in an undertone, speak sotto voce, mumble, murmur.

**2** *mutter against the government* grumble, moan, complain, carp; *inf.* grouse, gripe, beef, bitch.

**muzzle** verb gag, bridle, silence, censor, suppress, stifle, inhibit, restrain, check, fetter.

**myriad** noun scores, multitude, host, horde, army, legion, mass, throng, swarm, sea; *inf.* millions, thousands, oodles, zillions.

**myriad** adjective innumerable, countless, incalculable, immeasurable, numerous, multitudinous, multifarious, manifold, multiple.

**mysterious** adjective **1** *the ways of nature are mysterious* enigmatic, inscrutable, impenetrable, incomprehensible, inexplicable, unexplainable, unfathomable, unaccountable, insoluble, obscure, arcane, abstruse, cryptic, preternatural, supernatural, uncanny, mystical, peculiar, strange, weird, curious, bizarre, mystifying, baffling, puzzling. **2** *he was mysterious about his whereabouts* secretive, reticent, noncommittal, discreet, evasive, furtive, surreptitious.

**mystery** noun **1** *his death remains a mystery* enigma, puzzle, secret, problem, riddle, conundrum, question, question mark. **2** *his whereabouts are clothed in mystery* secrecy, concealment, obscurity, vagueness, nebulousness, inscrutability, inexplicability.

**mystic, mystical** adjective **1** *a mystic experience* spiritual, paranormal, transcendental, otherworldly, supernatural, preternatural, nonrational, occult, metaphysical. **2** *mystic rites* symbolic, representational, allegorical, metaphorical, emblematic. **3** *mystical events* obscure, cryptic. *See* MYSTERIOUS 1.

**mystify** verb confuse, bewilder, confound, perplex, baffle, puzzle, elude, escape; *inf.* stump, beat.

**myth** noun **1** *read ancient myths* legend, saga, tale, story, fable, folk tale, allegory, parable, fairy tale/story, bestiary. **2** *her having a rich father was just a myth* invention, fabrication, untruth, lie; *inf.* story, fairy tale/story, tall tale.

**mythical** adjective **1** *a mythical creature* legendary, mythological, fabled, chimerical, imaginary, imagined, fabulous, fantastical, fairy-tale, storybook, fictitious, allegorical. **2** *a mythical rich uncle* imaginary, pretended, make-believe, unreal, fictitious, invented, fabricated, made-up, untrue; *inf.* pretend.

# Nn

**nag** verb scold, carp, pick on, harp on at, be on someone's back, henpeck, bully, upbraid, berate, criticize, find fault with, complain to, grumble to, badger, pester, plague, torment, harry, goad, vex, harass, irritate; *inf.* go on (and on) at, hassle, drive up the wall.

**nag** noun shrew, harpy, termagant, faultfinder, carper, caviler, complainer, grumbler.

**nail** noun 1 *drive a nail into the wood* pin, brad, tack, rivet, spike. 2 *the animal's nails* fingernail, toenail, claw, talon, nipper, pincer.

**naïve** adjective 1 *they are still young and naïve* innocent, artless, childlike, simple, ingenuous, guileless, trusting, unsophisticated, unworldly, jejune, natural, unaffected, unpretentious, frank, open, candid. 2 *exploited the naïve employees* gullible, overtrusting, overtrustful, credulous, unsuspicious, unsuspecting, deceivable, dupable, callow, raw, green, immature, inexperienced; *inf.* wet behind the ears.

**naïveté** noun 1 *the young girl's naïveté* innocence, artlessness, simplicity, ingenuousness, guilelessness, lack of guile, unsophistication, lack of sophistication, unworldliness, naturalness, candor. 2 *took advantage of their naïveté* gullibility, credulousness, credulity, overtrustfulness, lack of suspicion, callowness, greenness, immaturity.

**naked** adjective 1 *naked sunbathers* stark naked, nude, in the nude, bare, stripped, exposed, unclothed, undressed, uncovered, undraped, disrobed, au naturel; *inf.* without a stitch on, in one's birthday suit, in the raw, in the altogether, in the buff, naked as the day one was born, buck naked. 2 *naked landscapes/rooms* bare, barren, stark, uncovered, denuded, stripped, treeless, grassless, unfurnished. 3 *the naked truth* undisguised, unqualified, unadorned, stark, bald, unvarnished, unveiled, unmitigated, unexaggerated, plain, simple, open, patent, evident, apparent, obvious, manifest, overt, unmistakable, blatant, glaring, flagrant. 4 *feeling naked in a foreign country* defenseless, unprotected, vulnerable, exposed, helpless, weak, powerless.

**namby-pamby** adjective oversentimental, sentimental, mawkish, maudlin, insipid, colorless, anemic, feeble, weak, vapid, spineless, effeminate, effete, prim, prissy, mincing, simpering; *inf.* wishy-washy, wimpish.

**name** noun 1 *the name of the person/tree* appellation, designation, cognomen, denomination, sobriquet, title, style, label, tag, epithet, first/second name, Christian/given name, surname, family name, maiden name, nickname, pet name, stage name, pseudonym, alias, nom de guerre, nom de plume; *inf.* moniker, handle. 2 *he's a name in the theater* big name, celebrity, luminary, star, dignitary, VIP, lion; *inf.* celeb, megastar, big shot, bigwig. 3 *make his name in motion pictures* reputation, fame, renown, repute, note, distinction, eminence, prominence, prestige.

**name** verb 1 *name the child/plant* baptize, christen, call, entitle, label, style, term, title, dub, denominate. 2 *name the most suitable day* identify, specify, mention, cite, give. 3 *name his successor* appoint, choose, select, pick, nominate, designate.

**nameless** adjective 1 *nameless graves* unnamed, untitled, unlabeled, untagged, innominate. 2 *nameless benefactors* anonymous, unidentified, undesignated, unspecified. 3 *nameless fears* unspeakable, unutterable, inexpressible, unmentionable, indescribable.

**nap** noun catnap, doze, light sleep, rest; *inf.* snooze, forty winks, (some) shut-eye.

**narcissistic** adjective self-admiring, self-loving, in love with oneself, conceited, vain, egotistic.

**narcotic** noun drug, opiate, sleeping pill, anesthetic, painkiller, analgesic, anodyne, tranquilizer, sedative, soporific.

**narrate** verb tell, relate, recount, recite, unfold, give an account of, give a report of, set forth, chronicle, describe, detail, portray, sketch out, rehearse, repeat.

**narration** noun account, story, storytelling, tale, telling, relation, recital, reciting, report, chronicling, chronicle, description, portrayal, sketch, rehearsal, repetition.

**narrative** noun account, statement, report, chronicle, history, story, tale.

**narrow** adjective 1 *narrow roads/waists* narrow-gauged, slender, thin, slim, slight, spare, attenuated, tapering. 2 *narrow spaces* confined, confining, constricted, tight, cramped, close, incommodious, pinched, straitened, squeezed, meager, scant, scanty, spare, scrimped, exiguous. 3 *a narrow range* limited, restricted, select, exclusive. 4 *a* *narrow interpretation* literal, exact, precise, close, faithful. **5** *narrow in her thinking* intolerant, illiberal. *See* NARROW-MINDED.

**narrow-minded** adjective intolerant, illiberal, unliberal, overconservative, conservative, hidebound, reactionary, close-minded, unreasonable, prejudiced, bigoted, biased, discriminatory, jaundiced, parochial, provincial, insular, small-minded, petty-minded, petty, mean-spirited, prudish, straitlaced.

**nasty** adjective **1** *a nasty sight/smell* unpleasant, disagreeable, distasteful, horrible, vile, foul, hateful, loathsome, revolting, disgusting, odious, obnoxious, repellent, repugnant, ugly, offensive, objectionable, noisome, squalid, dirty, filthy, impure, polluted, tainted, unpalatable, unsavory, unappetizing, evil-smelling, foul-smelling, smelly, stinking, rank, fetid, malodorous, mephitic; *inf.* yucky. **2** *a nasty situation* dangerous, serious, critical, crucial, severe, alarming, threatening. **3** *a nasty person* ill-tempered, ill-natured, ill-humored, bad-tempered, cross, surly, unpleasant, disagreeable, vicious, spiteful, malicious, mean; *inf.* grouchy. **4** *nasty jokes/videos* obscene, pornographic, indecent, foul, vile, blue, off-color, smutty, bawdy, vulgar, ribald, risqué, lewd, lascivious, licentious.

**nation** noun country, land, state, kingdom, empire, realm, republic, confederation, commonwealth, people, race, tribe, society, community, population.

**nationalistic** adjective patriotic, chauvinistic, jingoistic, xenophobic.

**native** adjective **1** *native instinct* inborn, inherent, innate, connate, built-in, intrinsic, instinctive, intuitive, natural, natural-born, congenital, hereditary, inherited, in the blood, in the family, inbred, ingrained. **2** *native plants/peoples* indigenous, original, homegrown, homemade, domestic, local, aboriginal, autochthonous.

**native** noun inhabitant, dweller, resident, citizen, national, aborigine, autochthon.

**natural** adjective **1** *in the natural course of events* usual, normal, regular, common, ordinary, everyday, typical, routine, run-of-the-mill. **2** *her natural instincts* inborn, inherent. *See* NATIVE adjective 1. **3** *natural charm* artless, ingenuous, open, frank, genuine, real, authentic, simple, unsophisticated, unaffected, unpretentious, spontaneous, relaxed, unstudied. **4** *natural produce* organic, pure, unrefined, unpolished, unbleached, unmixed, whole, plain, real, chemical-free, additive-free.

**naturalistic** adjective realistic, real-life, true-to-life, lifelike, factual, graphic, representational; *inf.* warts and all.

**naturally** adverb **1** *behave naturally* artlessly, ingenuously, candidly, unaffectedly, unpretentiously, spontaneously. **2** *naturally, he is going* of course, certainly, as might be expected.

**nature** noun **1** *it is in the nature of the species* character, characteristic, essence, constitution, makeup, complexion, stamp, personality, identity. **2** *commune with nature* Mother Nature, natural forces, creation, the environment, the earth, mother earth, the world, the universe, the cosmos; landscape, scenery. **3** *things of this nature* kind, sort, ilk, type, variety, description, category, class, classification, species, style. **4** *he has a pleasant nature* temperament, temper, personality, disposition, humor, mood, outlook.

**naughty** adjective **1** *a naughty child* mischievous, misbehaving, disobedient, defiant, unruly, roguish, wayward, delinquent, undisciplined, unmanageable, ungovernable, fractious, refractory, perverse, errant. **2** *naughty magazines* indecent, improper, vulgar, bawdy, ribald, lewd, licentious.

**nausea** noun **1** *travelers overcome by nausea* sickness, vomiting, retching, gagging, biliousness, queasiness, faintness, seasickness, carsickness, airsickness, motion sickness, morning sickness; *inf.* throwing-up. **2** *horror movies causing feelings of nausea* disgust, revulsion, repugnance, distaste, aversion, loathing, abhorrence, detestation, odium.

**nauseate** verb make sick, sicken, make one's gorge rise, turn one's stomach, revolt, disgust, repel, repulse, offend; *inf.* make someone want to throw up, gross out.

**nauseous** adjective **1** *nauseous food/sights* nauseating, sickening, disgusting, revolting, repulsive, repellent, repugnant, offensive, loathsome, abhorrent, odious. **2** *feeling nauseous* nauseated, sick, sickly, queasy, green, unwell, indisposed, seasick, carsick, airsick; *inf.* green around the gills.

**nautical** adjective maritime, naval, marine, seagoing, seafaring, yachting, boating, sailing.

**navigate** verb **1** *navigate the craft* steer, pilot, maneuver, guide, direct, handle, drive, skipper. **2** *navigate the Atlantic* sail, sail across, cross, traverse, cruise, journey, voyage.

**navigation** noun **1** *the navigation of the craft* steering, pilotage, maneuvering, guidance, directing, handling, driving. **2** *study navigation* sailing, seamanship, pilotage, helmsmanship, chart-reading, map-reading.

**navy** noun naval force(s), fleet, flotilla, armada.

**near** adjective **1** *the store is near* close, close by, nearby, alongside, at close range/quarters, accessible, within reach, close/near at hand, at hand, handy, not far off/away, a stone's throw away, neighboring, adjacent, adjoining, bordering, contiguous, proximate; *inf.* within spitting distance. **2** *the time is near* | *the near future* close/near at hand, approaching, coming, imminent, forthcoming, in the offing, impending, looming, proximate, immediate. **3** *near relatives* closely related, related, connected, akin, allied, close, intimate, familiar, dear. **4** *a near escape* close, narrow, by a hair's breadth; *inf.* by a whisker/hair. **near miss** narrow escape; *inf.* close shave, close call.

**near** adverb close, nearby, within earshot, within sight, not far off/away.

**near** preposition close to, close by, in the neighborhood of, next to, adjacent to, alongside, bordering on, contiguous to.

**near** verb draw near to, get close to, approach, come close to, come toward, move toward, lean toward.

**nearly** adverb almost, all but, as good as, virtually, well-nigh, just about, practically, roughly, approximately, not quite.

**neat** adjective **1** *a neat house* tidy, orderly, well-ordered, straight, in good order, neat and tidy, neat as a pin, in Bristol fashion, shipshape and Bristol fashion, in apple-pie order, spick-and-span. **2** *a neat person* tidy, spruce, trim, smart, dapper, natty; fastidious, organized, well-organized, methodical, systematic. **3** *wearing neat clothes* simple, plain, unadorned, unornamented, unpretentious, unassuming. **4** *a neat solution* elegant, well-put, well-expressed, well-turned, clever, apt. **5** *neat footwork* adroit, skillful, expert, practiced, dexterous, deft, accurate, precise, nimble, agile. **6** *a really neat party* great, terrific, wonderful, excellent, exceptional, first-class, first-rate.

**nebulous** adjective shapeless, unformed, amorphous, shadowy, dim, indistinct, indefinite, vague, unclear, obscure, misty, cloudy, hazy, fuzzy, uncertain, indeterminate, imprecise, muddled, confused, ambiguous.

**necessarily** adverb **1** *plans that are necessarily vague* by force of circumstance, like it or not, perforce. **2** *he will not necessarily have to go* certainly, definitely, undoubtedly, inevitably, unavoidably, inescapably, automatically, incontrovertibly, inexorably.

**necessary** adjective **1** *a necessary reduction in expenditure* needed, needful, essential, required, requisite, vital, indispensable, imperative, mandatory, obligatory, compulsory, de rigueur. **2** *a necessary evil* certain, sure, inevitable, unavoidable, inescapable, inexorable, ineluctable, fated, preordained.

**necessitate** verb require, demand, call for, entail, involve, exact, oblige, compel, impel, force, leave no choice but to.

**necessities** plural noun needs, essentials, requisites, requirements, indispensables, fundamentals, necessaries, exigencies.

**necessity** noun **1** *silence is a necessity* essential, requisite, requirement, prerequisite, necessary, fundamental, sine qua non, desideratum. **2** *she left out of necessity* need, needfulness, force/pressure of circumstance, exigency, obligation. **3** *necessity made them steal* neediness, want, poverty, deprivation, privation, penury, destitution, indigence. **4** *a logical necessity that night follows day* certainty, inevitability, inescapability, inexorability, ineluctability.

**need** verb require, necessitate, demand, call for, have occasion for; want, lack.

**need** noun **1** *their needs are few* requirement, want, wish, demand, prerequisite, requisite, essential, desideratum. **2** *he has need of a coat* want, lack, shortage, requirement. **3** *no need to be frightened* necessity, call, obligation. **4** *people in need* neediness, want, poverty, deprivation, privation, penury, destitution, indigence. **5** *in one's hour of need* crisis, emergency, urgency, distress, trouble, extremity, exigency.

**needle** verb **1** *needle them into action* goad, spur, prod, prick, sting, press, nag, persuade. **2** *deliberately needling the teacher* provoke, bait, harass, annoy, irritate, vex, irk, nettle, taunt, pester; *inf.* aggravate, rile, get to.

**needless** adjective unnecessary, uncalled-for, gratuitous, undesired, unwanted, pointless, useless, dispensable, expendable, inessential.

**needy** adjective necessitous, poor, poverty-stricken, deprived, disadvantaged, penurious, impecunious, impoverished, penniless, destitute, indigent, on the breadline, in straitened circumstances.

**ne'er-do-well** noun good-for-nothing, wastrel, black sheep, loafer, idler, layabout, shirker, sluggard, drone; *inf.* gold brick, lazybones, goof-off.

**nefarious** adjective wicked, evil, sinful, iniquitous, villainous, criminal, heinous, atrocious, vile, foul, base, abominable, odious, horrible, horrendous, dreadful, terrible, detestable, loathsome, execrable, depraved, shameful, scandalous, monstrous, outrageous, flagitious.

**negate** verb **1** *facts negating your theory* nullify, render null and void, annul, void, invalidate, cancel, revoke, rescind, abrogate, repeal, retract, countermand, disestablish, reject, disprove, explode, overrule. **2** *try to negate the existence* *of God* deny, dispute, call in/into question, gainsay, contradict, disprove, refute, discredit, disclaim, repudiate, renounce, oppose.

**negation** noun **1** *the negation of the theory* nullification, voiding, cancellation, revocation, abrogation, repeal, retraction; denial, contradiction, disapproval, repudiation. **2** *anarchy is the negation of government* opposite, reverse, antithesis, contrary, converse. **3** *a life full of negation* nothingness, nothing, nullity, blankness, void, nonexistence, vacuity, nonentity.

**negative** adjective **1** *negative replies* dissenting, contradictory, contradicting, contrary, opposing, opposite, opposed, rejecting, refusing, denying, gainsaying. **2** *a negative person/reaction* pessimistic, defeatist, gloomy, gloom-laden, cynical, jaundiced, critical, faultfinding, complaining, unhelpful, unconstructive, uncooperative.

**neglect** verb **1** *neglect their children* fail to look after, fail to provide for, abandon, forsake, leave alone. **2** *neglect his work* let slide, skimp on, shirk, be remiss about, be lax about, pay little/no attention to, leave undone, procrastinate about. **3** *neglect to lock the door* omit, fail, forget. **4** *neglect his warning* disregard, ignore, pay no attention/heed to, overlook, disdain, scorn, slight, spurn, rebuff.

**neglect** noun **1** *parents/workers guilty of neglect* neglectfulness, dereliction. *See* NEGLIGENCE. **2** *his neglect of her warning* disregard, ignoring, heedlessness, indifference to, disdain, scorn, slight, spurning, rebuff.

**neglected** adjective uncared for, untended, mistreated, abandoned, forsaken, disregarded, ignored, spurned.

**negligence** noun neglect, remissness, laxity, laxness, dereliction, dereliction of duty, carelessness, inattention, inattentiveness, heedlessness, thoughtlessness, unmindfulness, forgetfulness, inadvertence, oversight, omission, failure, disregard, default, shortcoming, indifference, slackness, sloppiness.

**negligent** adjective neglectful, remiss, lax, careless, inattentive, heedless, thoughtless, unmindful, uncaring, forgetful, disregardful, indifferent, offhand, cursory, slack, sloppy, slapdash, slipshod, procrastinating, dilatory.

**negligible** adjective trivial, trifling, insignificant, paltry, petty, tiny, minute, minor, inconsequential, inappreciable, imperceptible.

**negotiable** adjective **1** *pay is negotiable* open to discussion, discussable, debatable, subject to bargaining. **2** *negotiable roads* passable, navigable, crossable, traversable, penetrable, unblocked, unobstructed.

**negotiate** verb **1** *negotiate a deal/settlement* work out, thrash out, arrange, agree on, settle, conclude, pull off, bring off, contract, complete, transact, execute, fulfill, orchestrate, engineer. **2** *union and management negotiate* bargain, drive a bargain, hold talks, confer, debate, discuss, discuss terms, discuss a settlement, parley, haggle, wheel and deal, dicker. **3** *negotiate the hurdles* clear, get over, get through, pass over, make it over, cross, get past, get around, surmount.

**negotiator** noun arbiter, arbitrator, mediator, go-between, moderator; haggler, wheeler-dealer.

**neighborhood** noun district, area, region, locality, part, quarter, precinct, community; vicinity, environs, proximity, purlieus; *inf.* stamping ground, neck of the woods, hood. **in the neighborhood of** around, about, approximately, roughly, nearly, almost, close to, just about.

**neighboring** adjective adjacent, adjoining, bordering, abutting, contiguous, next, nearby.

**neighborly** adjective friendly, cordial, kind, helpful, obliging, generous, hospitable, companionable, sociable, amiable, affable, genial.

**nemesis** noun downfall, undoing, ruin, destruction, Waterloo; retribution, vengeance.

**neophyte** noun novice, beginner, newcomer, initiate, tyro, greenhorn, learner, trainee, apprentice, probationer; *inf.* rookie.

**nerve** noun **1** *rock climbing requires nerve* courage, courageousness, bravery, fearlessness, daring, coolness, coolheadedness, boldness, pluck, gameness, mettle, spirit, backbone, fortitude, endurance, tenacity, steadfastness; *inf.* grit, guts, spunk. **2** *she had the nerve to ask for more* temerity, impudence, impertinence, effrontery, cheek, insolence, audacity, boldness, presumption, gall, brazenness; *inf.* brass, chutzpah.

**nerve-racking** adjective stressful, anxious, tense, harrowing, frightening, distressing, difficult, trying, harassing; *inf.* nail-biting.

**nerves** plural noun strain, anxiety; *inf.* the jitters, the willies. *See* NERVOUSNESS.

**nervous** adjective **1** *a nervous person* easily frightened, timid, timorous, fearful, apprehensive, anxious, edgy, highly strung, tense, strained, excitable, jumpy, hysterical. **2** *feeling nervous about the interview* on edge, tense, anxious, worried, fretful, uneasy, on tenterhooks, fidgety, apprehensive, fearful, scared, with one's heart in one's mouth, quaking, trembling, shaking, shaking in one's shoes, shaky; *inf.*

with butterflies in one's stomach, jittery, in a state, uptight, wired.

**nervousness** noun fearfulness, anxiety, tenseness, edginess, tension, nervous tension, stress, agitation, worry, uneasiness.

**nervy** adjective pushy, presumptuous, impudent, insolent, impertinent, brash, forward, audacious, bold; *inf.* brassy, fresh.

**nest** noun lair, den, lodge, burrow; retreat, hideaway, shelter, refuge, haunt; *inf.* hide-out.

**nestle** verb snuggle, curl up, huddle together, cuddle up, nuzzle.

**net** noun **1** *net curtains* netting, tulle, fishnet, meshwork, mesh, latticework, lattice, openwork, webbing, tracery, reticulum. **2** *fall into the enemy's net* trap, booby trap, snare, mesh, pitfall, stratagem.

**net** verb take home, clear, earn, make, bring in, get, pocket, receive, gain, obtain, realize; *inf.* pull in.

**nether** adjective **1** *the nether part of the store* lower, low, low-level, bottom, under, basement, underground. **2** *the nether regions* infernal, hellish, Hadean, Plutonian, Stygian.

**nettle** verb irritate, provoke, ruffle, try someone's patience, annoy, incense, exasperate, irk, vex, pique, bother, pester, harass, torment, plague, rile, peeve; *inf.* aggravate, rub the wrong way, get under someone's skin, get in someone's hair, get someone's goat, get to.

**network** noun **1** *a pattern consisting of a network of lines* meshwork, latticework, openwork, mesh, lattice, webbing, tracery, filigree, fretwork. **2** *a network of professional women* nexus, system, complex, organization, structure, arrangement, formulation. **3** *a network of roads | electronic network* interconnection, grid, circuitry, plexus.

**neurotic** adjective **1** *treating neurotic patients* mentally disturbed, unstable, maladjusted, obsessive, phobic. **2** *his wife is completely neurotic* overanxious, obsessive, phobic, fixated, compulsive, oversensitive, hysterical, irrational.

**neuter** verb castrate, geld, emasculate; spay; *inf.* fix.

**neutral** adjective **1** *referees must be neutral* impartial, unbiased, unprejudiced, open-minded, nonpartisan, without favoritism, evenhanded, disinterested, nonaligned, dispassionate, objective, detached, uninvolved, uncommitted. **2** *neutral countries during the war* noncombatant, noncombative, nonfighting, nonparticipating, nonaligned, unallied, uninvolved, noninterventionist. **3** *a neutral personality* indefinite, indeterminate, unremarkable, ordinary, common-

place, average, run-of-the-mill, everyday, bland, uninteresting, colorless, insipid, dull. **4** *a neutral color* beige, écru, gray, taupe, stone-colored, stone, pale, colorless, uncolored, achromatic.

**neutralize** verb counteract, cancel, nullify, negate, annul, undo, invalidate, frustrate, be an antidote to, offset, counterbalance, compensate for, make up for, negate.

**never** adverb not ever, at no time, certainly not, under no circumstances; *lit.* ne'er; *inf.* no way, not on your life, not in a million years.

**never-ending** adjective endless, unending, perpetual, everlasting, interminable, ceaseless, unceasing, incessant, nonstop, continuous, continual, uninterrupted, unbroken, unremitting, relentless, persistent, infinite, limitless, boundless, lasting, enduring, abiding.

**nevertheless** adverb nonetheless, even so, however, still, yet, just the same, all the same, regardless.

**new** adjective **1** *new techniques* modern, recent, advanced, state-of-the-art, present-day, contemporary, current, latest, up-to-date, up-to-the-minute, new-fashioned, modish, brand new, ultramodern, avant-garde, futuristic, newfangled; *inf.* way-out, far-out. **2** *in need of new ideas* novel, original, fresh, unhackneyed, imaginative, creative, experimental. **3** *a new book* unused, unworn, pristine, fresh, mint, in mint condition, virgin. **4** *a new job* unfamiliar, unknown, strange, different, unaccustomed, untried. **5** *a new room on the house* additional, added, extra, supplementary, further, another. **6** *feel like a new person* refreshed, renewed, improved, restored, reinvigorated, regenerated, reborn, remodeled.

**newcomer** noun **1** *newcomers to the town* new arrival, immigrant, settler, stranger, outsider, foreigner, alien, intruder, interloper; *inf.* johnny-come-lately. **2** *a newcomer to the game* beginner, trainee. *See* NOVICE.

**newly** adverb just, just recently, lately, of late.

**news** noun information, facts, data, report, story, news item, news flash, account, statement, announcement, press release, communication, communiqué, message, bulletin, dispatch, disclosure, revelation, word, talk, the latest, gossip, rumor, scandal, exposé; *inf.* info, low-down, scuttlebutt, poop, dope.

**newspaper** noun paper, gazette, journal, tabloid, daily, weekly, scandal sheet; *inf.* rag.

**next** adjective **1** *the next day* following, succeeding, successive, subsequent, later, ensuing. **2** *the next house* neighboring, adjacent, adjoining, bordering, contiguous, closest, nearest.

**nibble** verb bite, gnaw, peck at, pick at, pick over, eat, munch; *inf.* snack on.

**nice** adjective **1** *have a nice time* good, pleasant, enjoyable, pleasurable, agreeable, delightful, amusing, satisfying, gratifying, marvelous. **2** *a nice friend* likable, charming, amiable, friendly, kindly, genial, gracious, sympathetic, understanding, compassionate. **3** *nice manners* polite, courteous, civil, refined, cultivated, polished, genteel, elegant, seemly, decorous, proper, fitting, suitable, appropriate, respectable. **4** *a nice distinction* fine, ultrafine, subtle, minute, precise, exact, accurate, strict, close, careful, meticulous, rigorous. **5** *she is too nice to eat with her fingers* fastidious, delicate, refined, dainty, particular, discriminating, overparticular, fussy, finicky; *inf.* persnickety. **6** *landscapers did a nice job* good, acceptable, commendable, admirable.

**nicely** adverb **1** *children behaving nicely* well, politely, courteously, decorously, properly, fittingly, suitably, respectably, virtuously. **2** *did nicely on the exam* well, commendably, admirably.

**nicety** noun finer point, subtlety, nuance, detail; precision, accuracy, exactness, meticulousness, rigor.

**niche** noun **1** *a niche in the wall* alcove, recess, nook, cranny, cubbyhole. **2** *his niche in life* calling, vocation, place, position, job; *inf.* slot.

**nickname** noun pet name, family name, familiar name, diminutive; *inf.* moniker, handle.

**niggardly** adjective **1** *a niggardly person* mean, miserly, stingy, tight-fisted, parsimonious, penny-pinching, avaricious. **2** *a niggardly supply of food* meager, paltry, skimpy, scanty, measly, inadequate, insubstantial, miserable; *inf.* piddling.

**night** noun nighttime, darkness, dark, hours of darkness. **night and day** all the time, around the clock, ceaselessly, incessantly, continuously.

**nightfall** noun sunset, sundown, dusk, evening, twilight; *lit.* eventide, gloaming.

**nightmare** noun **1** *he had nightmares after the accident* bad dream, incubus, phantasmagoria. **2** *the interview was a nightmare* ordeal, horror, torment, torture.

**nihilism** noun **1** *former believers are turning to nihilism* rejection, repudiation, renunciation, denial, abnegation; disbelief, skepticism; negativism, cynicism, pessimism. **2** *political nihilism* anarchy, lawlessness,

disorder, chaos. **3** *in a state of nihilism* nihility, nothingness, nonexistence, void.

**nil** noun zero, nothing, naught, none; *inf.* zilch, goose egg.

**nimble** adjective **1** *nimble movements* agile, lithe, sprightly, spry, lively, quick, graceful, skillful, deft. **2** *nimble of wit* quick-thinking, clever, bright, quick, quick-witted, alert.

**nip** verb **1** *nip his arm* pinch, tweak, squeeze, grip, bite, nibble. **2** *nip (off) the withered shoots* snip, cut, lop, dock. **3** *frost nipping her cheeks* sting, bite, hurt. **nip in the bud** stop, quash, quell, check, thwart, frustrate.

**nirvana** noun enlightenment, paradise, heaven; bliss, joy, peace, serenity, tranquillity.

**nitpicking** adjective captious, hairsplitting, quibbling, faultfinding, hypercritical, caviling.

**nitty-gritty** noun crux, gist, substance, essence, quintessence; core, heart, center, kernel, nucleus; essentials, basics, facts; *inf.* brass tacks, nuts and bolts.

**nitwit** noun fool, ninny, idiot, nincompoop, dolt, dunce, ignoramus; *inf.* dope, dimwit.

**nobility** noun **1** *born to the nobility* lords, peers, plutocracy, aristocracy, high society, elite, upper class; *inf.* upper crust. **2** *the nobility of his deed* magnanimity, generosity, selflessness, honor, integrity, bravery, righteousness, decency.

**noble** adjective **1** *the noble people of the land* aristocratic, patrician, blue-blooded, highborn, titled, landed, born with a silver spoon in one's mouth. **2** *noble deeds* noble-minded, magnanimous, generous, self-sacrificing, honorable, virtuous, brave, righteous, honest, upright, true, loyal, principled, moral, decent, good. **3** *noble thoughts* lofty, grand, exalted, elevated. **4** *of noble appearance* impressive, magnificent, striking, awesome, stately, grand, dignified.

**nod** verb **1** *nod one's head* incline, bob, bow, dip, duck. **2** *nod a greeting* signal, gesture, motion, sign, indicate. **3** *the audience began to nod* doze off, drop off, fall asleep, nap, slumber.

**node** noun protuberance, swelling, lump, growth, excrescence, knob, knot, nodule, bump.

**noise** noun din, hubbub, clamor, racket, row, uproar, tumult, commotion, rumpus, pandemonium.

**noisome** adjective disgusting, repugnant, revolting, repulsive, offensive, nauseating, detestable, loathsome.

**noisy** adjective **1** *noisy neighbors* rowdy, clamorous, boisterous, obstreperous. **2**

*noisy music* loud, blaring, blasting, deafening, earsplitting.

**nomad** noun itinerant, traveler, migrant, wanderer, roamer, rover; transient, vagabond, vagrant, tramp.

**nominal** adjective **1** *the nominal head* in name only, titular, formal; theoretical, self-styled; purported, supposed. **2** *a nominal sum* token, symbolic; minimal, trivial, insignificant.

**nominate** verb **1** *nominate the candidates* name, propose, put forward, submit, present, recommend; *inf.* put up. **2** *nominate his successor* name, designate, appoint, assign, select, choose.

**nonbeliever** noun atheist, agnostic, skeptic, doubter, doubting Thomas, unbeliever, disbeliever, cynic, infidel, pagan, heathen.

**nonchalance** noun coolness, unconcern, indifference, detachment, detachedness, apathy, insouciance; *inf.* cool.

**nonchalant** adjective unexcitable, calm, cool, unconcerned, indifferent, unemotional, blasé, dispassionate, detached, apathetic, casual, offhand, carefree, insouciant.

**noncommittal** adjective cautious, guarded, circumspect, wary, careful, discreet, politic, playing one's cards close to one's chest, giving nothing away, sitting on the fence, temporizing, evasive, equivocal, vague, reserved.

**nonconformist** noun radical, dissenter, protester, maverick, individualist, misfit, eccentric, iconoclast, outsider.

**nondescript** adjective indefinite, indeterminate, unclassifiable, indescribable, indistinguishable, vague, unremarkable, featureless, undistinguished, ordinary, commonplace, unexceptional, unmemorable, uninteresting, dull, colorless, insipid, bland.

**nonentity** noun nobody, person of no account, person of no importance, nonperson; *inf.* nothing, lightweight.

**nonessential** adjective inessential, unessential, unnecessary, needless, unrequired, superfluous, redundant, dispensable, expendable, peripheral, unimportant, insignificant, inconsequential, extraneous.

**nonexistent** adjective unreal, hypothetical, suppositional, fictional, fictitious, imagined, imaginary, fanciful, mythical, legendary, fantasy, illusory, hallucinatory, insubstantial.

**nonplus** verb take aback, stun, dumbfound, confound, astound, astonish, amaze, surprise, disconcert, discomfit, dismay, make one halt in one's tracks, puzzle, perplex, baffle, mystify, stump, confuse, bewilder,

embarrass, fluster; *inf.* faze, flummox, floor.

**nonsense** noun **1** *talk nonsense* rubbish, balderdash, drivel, gibberish, twaddle; *inf.* tripe, gobbledegook, mumbo jumbo, poppycock, claptrap, bilge, bull. **2** *tired of their nonsense* foolishness, folly, silliness, senselessness, stupidity, ridiculousness, ludicrousness, inanity, fatuity, joking, jesting, clowning, buffoonery, drollery.

**nonsensical** adjective **1** *nonsensical remarks* meaningless, incomprehensible, unintelligible, senseless, incongruous. **2** *a nonsensical scheme* foolish, absurd, silly, inane, senseless, stupid, ridiculous, ludicrous, preposterous, harebrained, irrational, idiotic, insane; *inf.* crazy, crackpot, nutty, wacky.

**nonstop** adjective incessant, unceasing, ceaseless, constant, continuous, continual, steady, unremitting, relentless, persistent, endless, never-ending, unending, interminable; *inf.* eternal.

**nonstop** adverb *talk/rain nonstop* incessantly, unceasingly, constantly, continuously, continually, steadily, unremittingly, relentlessly, persistently, endlessly; *inf.* 24/7. See NONSTOP adjective.

**nook** noun **1** *a room full of nooks and crannies* corner, cranny, recess, alcove, niche, opening, cavity, crevice, gap, cubbyhole, inglenook. **2** *find a quiet nook to be alone* hideaway, retreat, refuge, shelter, den, hide-out.

**noon** noun midday, twelve noon, high noon, noontime, noontide, noonday.

**norm** noun **1** *measured against the norm* standard, criterion, measure, gauge, yardstick, benchmark, touchstone, scale, rule, pattern, model, type. **2** *six hours a day is the norm* average, mean, normal rate, the usual, the rule.

**normal** adjective **1** *the normal method* usual, standard, ordinary, conventional, typical, regular, routine, run-of-the-mill, everyday, accustomed, habitual, prevailing, accepted. **2** *of normal size* average, middling, standard, mean. **3** *the patient is not normal* well-adjusted, well-balanced, rational, *compos mentis*, sane.

**normally** adverb **1** *behave normally* as usual, ordinarily, naturally, conventionally, routinely, typically. **2** *normally, we eat late* usually, ordinarily, as a rule.

**north** adjective *north winds* northern, northerly, northwardly, Arctic, arctic, polar, boreal.

**nose** noun **1** *a large nose* proboscis, bill, beak, snout, muzzle, trunk; *inf.* snoot, schnoz. **2** *a nose for a good story* instinct, sixth sense, intuition, insight, perception.

**by a nose** by a hair's breadth, by a narrow margin, narrowly, by the skin of one's teeth; *inf.* by a whisker/hair. **on the nose** exactly, precisely.

**nose** verb **1** *dogs were nosing his arm* nudge, push, nuzzle. **2** *nose around the room* pry, search, peer, prowl, have a good look; *inf.* snoop. **3** *nose the car forward* ease, inch, move, run. **nose into** pry into, interfere in, meddle in, inquire into; *inf.* poke one's nose into. **nose out** smell out, sniff out, follow the scent of, scent out, search for, detect, run to ground.

**nostalgia** noun longing/yearning/pining for the past, regret, recollection, wistfulness, homesickness.

**nostalgic** adjective wistful, sentimental, maudlin, homesick.

**nostrum** noun **1** *prescribing nostrums for patients* patent medicine, medicine, medication, drug, potion, pill, quack remedy, elixir. **2** *claiming to have a nostrum for the country's problems* remedy, cure, cure-all, panacea, solution, answer, magic bullet, magic formula, recipe.

**nosy** adjective prying, inquisitive, quizzing, probing, eavesdropping, curious, interfering, meddlesome, intrusive; *inf.* snooping, snoopy.

**notable** adjective **1** *a notable achievement* noteworthy, remarkable, outstanding, important, significant, momentous, memorable, unforgettable, pronounced, marked, striking, impressive, extraordinary, rare. **2** *notable people in the town* noted, of note, distinguished, eminent, preeminent, well-known, prominent, illustrious, great, famous, famed, renowned, celebrated, acclaimed.

**notable** noun dignitary, celebrity, luminary, star, superstar, lion, VIP; *inf.* celeb, megastar, big shot, somebody.

**notably** adverb *notably successful* remarkably, outstandingly, significantly, markedly, strikingly, impressively, uncommonly, unusually, particularly, especially, extraordinarily, conspicuously, signally.

**notation** noun system of symbols, symbols, signs, code, cipher, hieroglyphics, shorthand, musical notation.

**notch** noun **1** *make a notch in the wood* indentation, dent, nick, groove, gouge, cut, mark, incision, score, scratch, gash, slit, cleft. **2** *several notches above the competition* degree, grade, gradation, level, step, stage, rung.

**note** noun **1** *always kept a note of her purchases* record, account, notation. **2** *write him a note* message, memorandum; letter, epistle, missive; *inf.* memo. **3** *read the notes in the book* footnote, annotation,

commentary, gloss, marginalia, explanation, explication, exposition, exegesis. **4** *worthy of note* notice, attention, attentiveness, heed, observation, consideration, thought, regard, care, mindfulness. **5** *people of note* distinction, eminence, preeminence, illustriousness, greatness, prestige, fame, renown, reputation, acclaim, consequence. **6** *a note of amusement in her voice* tone, intonation, inflection, sound, indication, hint, element.

**note** verb **1** *note the date in your diary* write down, put down, jot down, mark down, enter, mark, record, register. **2** *note his comments in your report* mention, make mention of, refer to, allude to, touch on, indicate, point out, make known, state. **3** *he noted their concern* observe, take in. *See* NOTICE verb.

**noted** adjective of note, eminent. *See* NOTABLE adjective 2.

**notes** plural noun jottings, record, report, observations, impressions, sketch, outline.

**noteworthy** adjective remarkable, outstanding. *See* NOTABLE adjective 1.

**nothing** noun **1** *nothing to declare* naught, nil; *inf.* zilch, zip. **2** *the wound is nothing* trifling matter, piece of trivia, bagatelle; *inf.* no big deal. **3** *they treat her like a nothing* nobody, person of no account, nonentity. **4** *pass into nothing* nothingness, nonexistence, nonbeing. **for nothing 1** *work for nothing* free, for free, gratis, without charge, without payment, gratuitously. **2** *do all that studying for nothing* in vain, to no avail, to no purpose, futilely, needlessly. **nothing but** only, solely.

**notice** noun **1** *escape my notice* attention, cognizance, watchfulness. *See* NOTE noun 4. **2** *the notice on the board* bulletin, poster, handbill, bill, circular, leaflet, pamphlet, advertisement. **3** *receive notice of their arrival* notification, apprisal, announcement, information, intelligence, news, communication, advice, instruction, order, warning. **4** *workers have received/given (their) notice* resignation; dismissal; *inf.* marching orders, walking papers, pink slip, the sack, the boot.

**notice** verb see, note, take note of, observe, perceive, discern, detect, behold, descry, spot, distinguish, make out, heed, pay attention to, mark, regard.

**noticeable** adjective observable, visible, discernible, perceptible, detectable, distinguishable, distinct, evident, obvious, apparent, manifest, patent, plain, clear, conspicuous, unmistakable, pronounced, striking, blatant.

**notify** verb inform, tell, advise, acquaint, apprise, warn, alert, caution.

**notion** noun **1** *have strange notions about religion* idea, belief, opinion, thought, impression, view, concept, theory. **2** *a notion to go to the sea* impulse, inclination, fancy, whim, wish, desire, caprice.

**notoriety** noun infamy, ill/evil repute, bad reputation/name, disrepute, dishonor, scandal, opprobrium, obloquy.

**notorious** adjective **1** *a notorious murderer* infamous, of ill repute, disreputable, dishonorable. **2** *a notorious nightclub* well-known, prominent, legendary, scandalous, opprobrious, obloquial.

**nourish** verb **1** *nourish the children* feed, nurture, provide for, care for, take care of, tend, attend to, bring up, rear. **2** *nourish growth* encourage, promote, foster, stimulate, boost, further, advance, forward, contribute to, be conducive to, assist, help, aid. **3** *nourish hopes of success* cherish, entertain, harbor, foster, hold.

**nourishing** adjective wholesome, healthful. *See* NUTRITIOUS.

**nourishment** noun food, nutriment, nutrition, sustenance, subsistence, aliment, provisions, provender, meat, fare, viands, victuals, daily bread; *inf.* grub, chow, eats.

**novel** adjective new, fresh, different, original, unusual, uncommon, unfamiliar, rare, unique, singular, imaginative, unhackneyed, unconventional, creative, innovative, groundbreaking, trailblazing, modern, ultramodern, advanced, futuristic.

**novelty** noun **1** *the novelty of the idea* newness, freshness, difference, originality, unusualness, uniqueness, rareness, imaginativeness, creativity. **2** *a vendor selling novelties* memento, souvenir, knickknack, trinket, bauble, trifle, gimmick, curiosity, gimcrack.

**novice** noun beginner, newcomer, apprentice, trainee, learner, probationer, student, pupil, (new) recruit, raw recruit, tyro, initiate, neophyte, greenhorn; *inf.* rookie.

**now** adverb **1** *we do not have any now* at present, at this time, currently. **2** *you must go now* right away, immediately, at once, straight away, instantly, promptly, without delay. **now and again/then** occasionally, on occasion, sometimes.

**noxious** adjective nocuous, noisome, harmful, hurtful, injurious, damaging, destructive, ruinous, pernicious, detrimental, deleterious, unwholesome, unhealthy, poisonous, toxic.

**nuance** noun shade, shading, gradation, subtlety, nicety, refinement, degree.

**nucleus** noun core, kernel, center, heart, nub, basis, pith, meat, marrow, focus, pivot.

**nude** adjective in the nude, bare. *See* NAKED 1.

**nudge** noun poke, jab, prod, dig, jog, elbow, bump, touch, push, shove.

**nugget** noun chunk, lump, piece, mass, clump, wad, hunk.

**nuisance** noun pest, bother, plague, irritant, annoyance, vexation, trouble, burden, weight, problem, difficulty, worry, bore, inconvenience, disadvantage, handicap, thorn in the side/flesh; *inf.* drag.

**null** adjective **1** *render the ruling null* null and void, void, invalid, annulled, nullified, canceled, abolished, revoked, rescinded, repealed. **2** *the null effects of the trade embargo* ineffectual, useless, vain, worthless, futile, powerless, unproductive, nonexistent, negative.

**nullify** verb render null and void, declare null and void, annul, void, invalidate, cancel, abolish, set aside, revoke, rescind, repeal, reverse, abrogate, discontinue, retract, withdraw, countermand, veto, negate, terminate, dissolve, do away with.

**numb** adjective benumbed, dead, deadened, insensible, insensate, torpid, dull, anesthetized, drugged, dazed, stunned, stupefied, in shock, paralyzed, immobilized.

**number** noun **1** *add up the numbers* figure, digit, numeral, cipher, character, symbol, unit, integer. **2** *the number of accidents* total, aggregate, score, tally, count, sum, summation. **3** *a large number of people* quantity, amount, group, collection, company, crowd.

**number** verb **1** *number the items* enumerate, count, add up, total, calculate, compute, reckon. **2** *number them among my friends* count, include, reckon. **3** *his days are numbered* limit, restrict, fix.

**numeral** noun figure, digit. *See* NUMBER noun 1.

**numerous** adjective many, very many, innumerable, numberless, countless, myriad, multitudinous, several, quite a few, various, diverse.

**nuptial** adjective matrimonial, marriage, marital, wedding, conjugal, connubial, bridal, spousal, hymeneal.

**nuptials** plural noun wedding, marriage.

**nurse** verb **1** *nurse the patient* take care of, care for, look after, tend, attend to, minister to, treat, doctor. **2** *a mother nursing her baby* suckle, breast-feed, feed, wet-nurse. **3** *nurse her career* nurture, encourage, promote, boost, further, advance, contribute to, assist, help. **4** *nurse* *a grudge* harbor, have, hold, entertain, foster, cherish, nourish.

**nurture** verb **1** *nurture the children* feed, nourish, provide for, care for, take care of, tend, attend to, bring up, rear. **2** *nurture the students* educate, school, train, tutor, coach. **3** *nurture growth* encourage, promote, foster, stimulate, develop, cultivate, boost, further.

**nut** noun **1** *a movie nut* fan, enthusiast, aficionado, devotee, follower; *inf.* buff, freak. **2** *acting like a nut* madman, lunatic; *inf.* nutcase, loony, weirdo, oddball, crackpot, screwball.

**nutrition** noun nutriment, food. *See* NOURISHMENT.

**nutritious** adjective nourishing, nutritive, wholesome, health-giving, healthy, healthful, beneficial.

**nuts** adjective mad, insane, deranged, demented, irrational, *non compos mentis*, lunatic, psychopathic; *inf.* nutty, crazy, bananas, loony, loopy, batty, balmy, out of one's mind, with a screw loose, out to lunch.

**nuzzle** verb **1** *dogs nuzzling their masters* nose, nudge, prod, push. **2** *nuzzle up to her mother* snuggle, cuddle, nestle, curl up.

**nymph** noun sylph, sprite, water sprite, undine, naiad, dryad, oread.

# *Oo*

**oaf** noun **1** *that oaf tripped me up* lout, blunderer, bungler, boor, bumpkin, yokel, gorilla, bull in a china shop: *inf.* clodhopper, lummox, galoot. **2** *the foolishness of an oaf* fool, dolt, blockhead, numskull, dunderhead, dunce, dullard, nincompoop, ninny, simpleton; *inf.* goon, schmuck.

**oasis** noun *an oasis among all the noise* refuge, haven, retreat, sanctuary, sanctum, hiding place, hideaway, hide-out.

**oath** noun **1** *an oath to tell the truth* vow, promise, pledge, avowal, affirmation, attestation, bond, word of honor, word. **2** *spouting oaths* curse, swearword, expletive, blasphemy, profanity, imprecation, malediction, obscenity, four-letter word.

**obedience** noun dutifulness, duteousness, duty, sense of duty, deference, respect, compliance, acquiescence, tractability, amenability, malleability, yielding, submission, docility, meekness.

**obedient** adjective dutiful, duteous, lawabiding, conforming, deferential, respectful, compliant, acquiescent, tractable, amenable, malleable, governable, well-trained, yielding, submissive, docile, meek, subservient, obsequious, servile.

**obeisance** noun **1** *his obeisance to the emperor* bow, curtsy, kneel, genuflection, stoop, salaam, kowtow. **2** *pay obeisance to the emperor* homage, worship, adoration, reverence, respect, veneration, honor, submission.

**obese** adjective overweight, fat, plump, stout, ample, chubby, tubby, portly, rotund, corpulent, pudgy, paunchy, fleshy, big, heavy, on the heavy side, large, bulky, chunky, outsize, massive.

**obesity** noun fatness, corpulence, plumpness, stoutness, rotundness, rotundity, portliness, chubbiness, pudginess, bulk, weight problem, embonpoint.

**obey** verb **1** *obey the rules/orders* abide by, comply with, adhere to, observe, conform to, respect, acquiesce in, consent to, agree to, follow, perform, carry out, execute, fulfill. **2** *obey your mother* be dutiful to, heed, be governed by.

**object** noun **1** *wooden objects* thing, something, anything, body, entity, article, item, device. **2** *the object of our discussion* subject, subject matter, substance, issue, concern. **3** *the object of their affection* focus, target, recipient, butt, victim. **4** *our object is to win* aim, goal. *See* OBJECTIVE noun.

**object** verb raise objections, protest, lodge a protest, demur, beg to differ, remonstrate, expostulate, take exception; oppose, be in opposition to, complain about.

**objection** noun **1** *their objection to the plan* protest, protestation, demurral, opposition, remonstration, remonstrance, expostulation. **2** *lodge/name their objections* argument, counterargument, doubt, complaint, grievance, scruple, qualm.

**objectionable** adjective offensive, obnoxious, unpleasant, disagreeable, unacceptable, nasty, disgusting, repulsive, revolting, loathsome, nauseating, hateful, detestable, insufferable, intolerable, odious, vile, horrid, noxious.

**objective** adjective unbiased, unprejudiced, impartial, neutral, uninvolved, nonpartisan, disinterested, detached, dispassionate, unswayed, evenhanded, equitable, fair, just, open-minded.

**objective** noun object, aim, goal, target, end, ambition, aspiration, intent, intention, purpose, idea, point, desire, hope, design, plan, scheme, plot.

**objectively** adverb with objectivity, without bias, impartially, with detachment, with an open mind, without fear or favor.

**objectivity** noun impartiality, disinterest, detachment, dispassion, dispassionateness, equitability, evenhandedness, open-mindedness.

**obligation** noun **1** *the obligations specified by the contract* requirement, prerequisite, demand, necessity, command, order, constraint. **2** *fulfill/discharge one's obligations* duty, function, chore, task, job, assignment, commission, business, burden, charge, onus, trust, liability, responsibility, accountability, indebtedness, debt. **3** *a sense of obligation* duty, compulsion, necessity, enforcement, duress, pressure. **4** *the obligation is still binding* contract, agreement, deed, covenant, compact, bond, treaty, deal, pact, understanding, transaction.

**obligatory** adjective **1** *the agreement is obligatory* binding, valid, legal, in force, effective. **2** *attendance is obligatory* compulsory, enforced, prescriptive, mandatory, required, requisite, imperative, de rigueur, unavoidable, unescapable.

**oblige** verb **1** *friendship obliges me to go* require, necessitate, obligate, compel, call for, force, constrain, press, pressure, impel. **2** *will you oblige me by going?* do someone a favor/kindness/service, serve, accommodate, put oneself out for, indulge, gratify the wishes of, help, assist.

**obliging** adjective helpful, accommodating, willing, complaisant, indulgent, considerate, cooperative, neighborly.

**oblique** adjective **1** *an oblique line* slanting, slanted, sloping, sloped, inclined, angled, tilted, listing, diagonal, catercornered; *inf.* kitty-corner. **2** *an oblique compliment* indirect, implied, roundabout, circuitous, circumlocutory, ambagious, evasive, backhanded.

**obliterate** verb **1** *obliterate all memories of her* erase, eradicate, efface, blot out, rub out, wipe out, expunge, sponge out, delete, cross out, strike out, blue-pencil, remove, cancel. **2** *the village was obliterated* destroy, exterminate, annihilate, wipe out, eliminate, decimate, liquidate, demolish.

**oblivion** noun obliviousness, heedlessness, unmindfulness, unawareness, unconsciousness, insensibility, inattentiveness, disregard, forgetfulness, absentmindedness, unconcern, abstraction, preoccupation, absorption.

**oblivious** adjective absentminded, abstracted, distrait, preoccupied, absorbed, faraway. **oblivious of/to** heedless of, unmindful of, unaware of, unconscious of, insensible of, ignorant of, blind to, unobservant of, deaf to, inattentive to, disregardful of, neglectful of, forgetful of, careless of, unconcerned with.

**obnoxious** adjective repulsive, repellent, abhorrent, repugnant, despicable, contemptible. *See* OBJECTIONABLE.

**obscene** adjective **1** *obscene jokes* indecent, pornographic, blue, off-color, risqué, lewd, salacious, smutty, lecherous, lascivious, licentious, prurient, lubricious, ribald, scatological, scabrous, bawdy, suggestive, vulgar, dirty, filthy, foul, coarse, gross, vile, nasty, offensive, immoral, impure, immodest, shameless, unchaste, improper, unwholesome, erotic, carnal, sexy; *inf.* raunchy. **2** *the murder was an obscene act* atrocious, heinous, vile, foul, repugnant, revolting, odious.

**obscenity** noun **1** *the obscenity of the publication* indecency, lewdness, salaciousness, smuttiness, lechery, lasciviousness, licentiousness, prurience, lubricity, ribaldry, scatology, scabrousness, bawdiness, suggestiveness, vulgarity, dirt, dirtiness, filth, filthiness, foulness, coarseness, grossness, vileness, nastiness, immorality, impurity, immodesty, shamelessness, unchasteness, impropriety, unwholesomeness, eroticism, carnality, sexiness. **2** *the obscenity of the crime* atrocity, heinousness, vileness, foulness, repugnance. **3** *a stream of obscenities* curse, swearword, dirty word; *inf.* cuss, cussword. *See* OATH 2.

**obscure** adjective **1** *obscure references* unclear, indeterminate, opaque, abstruse, recondite, unexplained, concealed, hidden, arcane, enigmatic, deep, cryptic, mysterious, puzzling, perplexing, confusing, intricate, involved, unfathomable, incomprehensible, impenetrable, indefinite, uncertain, doubtful, dubious, ambiguous, equivocal. **2** *obscure shapes looming out of the mist* indistinct, vague, shadowy, hazy, blurred, fuzzy, cloudy. **3** *obscure parts of the forest* dark, dim, black, unlit, murky, somber, gloomy, shady, shadowy. **4** *obscure villages* unknown, unheard-of, out-of-the-way, off the beaten track, remote, hidden, secluded, godforsaken. **5** *obscure poets* little-known, unknown, unheard-of, undistinguished, insignificant, inconspicuous, minor, unimportant.

**obscure** verb **1** *obscure the main issue* confuse, blur, muddle, complicate, obfuscate, garble, cloud, muddy. **2** *clouds* *obscure the sun* hide, conceal, cover, veil, screen, mask, cloak, shroud, block, block out, eclipse, adumbrate.

**obsequious** adjective servile, slavish, abject, fawning, groveling, cringing, toadying, truckling, sycophantic, ingratiating, unctuous, oily; *inf.* bootlicking.

**observance** noun 1 *observance of laws* obedience to, adherence to, abiding by, compliance with, heeding. 2 *observance of duty* performance, execution, discharge, fulfillment. 3 *religious observances* rite, ritual, ceremony, ceremonial, celebration, festival, practice, tradition, custom.

**observant** adjective 1 *an observant boy spotted the thief* alert, sharp-eyed, eagle-eyed, attentive, vigilant, wide-awake, on the qui vive, on the lookout; *inf.* not missing a thing/trick, on the ball. 2 *observant members of the church* dutiful, obedient, conforming, law-abiding, orthodox, practicing.

**observation** noun 1 *recall our observation of the man* seeing, noticing, watching, viewing, eyeing, witnessing. 2 *keep the thief/patient under observation* scrutiny, scrutinization, watch, monitoring, surveillance, inspection, attention, consideration, study, review, examination. 3 *record your observations on the show* finding, result, remark, comment, note, opinion, thought, reflection. 4 *make a sarcastic observation* remark, comment, statement, utterance, pronouncement, declaration. **observation of** observance of, keeping of. *See* OBSERVANCE 1.

**observe** verb 1 *we observe him go into the bank* see, catch sight of, notice, note, perceive, discern, detect, espy, behold, watch, view, spot, witness; *inf.* get a load of. 2 *police observe the house | doctors observe the patient* keep under observation, keep watch on, keep under surveillance, keep in sight, keep in view, spy upon, monitor; inspect, study, review, examine, check; *inf.* keep an eye on, keep tabs on. 3 *"A good try," he observed* remark, comment, state, utter, announce, declare, pronounce. 4 *observe the rules* keep, adhere to. *See* OBEY 1. 5 *observe Christmas* celebrate, keep, recognize, commemorate, mark, remember, solemnize.

**observer** noun watcher, looker-on, onlooker, witness, eyewitness, spectator, bystander; *inf.* rubberneck.

**obsess** verb preoccupy, haunt, monopolize, have a hold on, possess, consume, engross, have a grip on, grip, dominate, prey on, plague, torment, hound, bedevil.

**obsession** noun preoccupation, fixation, *idée fixe*, ruling/consuming passion, mania, enthusiasm, infatuation, compulsion, phobia, complex, fetish, craze.

**obsessive** adjective excessive, overdone, consuming, compulsive, besetting, gripping, haunting.

**obsolete** adjective outmoded, *démodé*, passé, antiquated, out-of-date, outdated, out, superannuated, out of fashion, out of style, behind the times, old, dated; discontinued, extinct, bygone; *inf.* old hat.

**obstacle** noun bar, barrier, obstruction, impediment, hindrance, hurdle, barricade, blockade, stumbling block, block, blockage, curb, check, stop, stoppage, deterrent, balk, snag, difficulty, catch, drawback, hitch, interference, fly in the ointment.

**obstinate** adjective stubborn, mulish, pigheaded, headstrong, willful, perverse, refractory, recalcitrant, contumacious, unmanageable, inflexible, unbending, immovable, intransigent, intractable, uncompromising, persistent, persevering, pertinacious, tenacious, dogged, single-minded, relentless, unrelenting.

**obstreperous** adjective unruly, disorderly, rowdy, boisterous, rough, riotous, out of hand, wild, rampaging, undisciplined, unrestrained, unbridled, unmanageable, raucous, rambunctious.

**obstruct** verb 1 *logs obstruct the road/river* block, barricade, bar, cut off, shut off, choke, clog (up), dam up. 2 *obstructing our efforts* hinder, impede, hamper, block, interfere with, interrupt, hold up, frustrate, thwart, balk, inhibit, curb, brake, bridle, hamstring, encumber, restrain, slow, retard, delay, arrest, check, stop, halt, restrict, limit.

**obstruction** noun impediment, hindrance, blockage. *See* OBSTACLE.

**obtain** verb 1 *obtain a ticket* get, get hold of, acquire, come by, procure, secure, gain, earn, take possession of, get one's hands on, seize, grab, pick up. 2 *new rules obtain* be in force, exist, stand, prevail, hold, be the case, reign, rule.

**obtrusive** adjective 1 *obtrusive colors/music* conspicuous, blatant, flagrant. 2 *obtrusive behavior* forward, bold, audacious, intrusive, interfering, meddling, officious, importunate; *inf.* pushy.

**obtuse** adjective dull-witted, uncomprehending, imperceptive; *inf.* dense, thick, slow on the uptake.

**obvious** adjective clear, clear-cut, crystal-clear, plain, evident, apparent, manifest, distinct, palpable, patent, conspicuous, overt, pronounced, transparent, unmistakable, indisputable, undeniable, as plain as the nose on one's face, staring someone in the face; *inf.* sticking out like a sore thumb, sticking out a mile.

**obviously** adjective **1** *obviously pregnant* clearly, plainly, visibly, noticeably, unmistakably, undeniably. **2** *obviously, we must go* of course, certainly, undoubtedly.

**occasion** noun **1** *we met on one or two occasions* time, juncture, point, situation, instance, case, circumstance. **2** *a sad occasion* event, incident, occurrence, happening, episode, affair, experience. **3** *we met at a college occasion* function, party, affair, celebration; *inf.* get-together, do. **4** *if the occasion arises* opportunity, golden opportunity, chance, opening, contingency. **5** *have occasion to believe* reason, cause, grounds, justification, call, excuse, inducement.

**occasional** adjective infrequent, intermittent, irregular, sporadic, odd, rare, casual.

**occasionally** adverb now and then, now and again, from time to time, every so often, on occasion, sporadically, infrequently, on and off.

**occult** adjective supernatural, magic, magical, mystical, mystic, preternatural, transcendental, unrevealed, secret, hidden, concealed, invisible, obscure, recondite, arcane, abstruse, esoteric, inexplicable, unfathomable, mysterious, cryptic, enigmatic.

**occult** noun **the occult** the supernatural, magic, black magic, witchcraft, sorcery, wizardry, the black arts, devil worship.

**occupancy** noun occupation, tenancy, tenure, residence, residency, inhabitance, habitation, living, possession, holding.

**occupant** noun occupier, tenant, renter, leaseholder, lessee, inhabitant, resident, dweller, householder, addressee, incumbent, inmate.

**occupation** noun **1** *what is his occupation?* job, work, profession, business, employment, employ, career, calling, métier, vocation, trade, craft, line, field. **2** *occupation of the house* tenancy, tenure. See OCCUPANCY. **3** *the occupation of their land* invasion, seizure, takeover, conquest, capture.

**occupied** adjective **1** *everyone is occupied* busy, engaged, working, at work, employed; *inf.* tied up, hard at it. **2** *the rooms are occupied* full, engaged, taken, in use, unavailable.

**occupy** verb **1** *occupy the apartment* live in, inhabit, reside in, dwell in, stay in. **2** *occupy her time* fill, fill up, take up, use up, utilize. **3** *occupy a top post* hold, fill, have; *inf.* hold down. **4** *occupy oneself* engage, employ, absorb, engross, entertain, divert, amuse, beguile. **5** *the army occupied their country* take possession of, seize, take over, capture, garrison.

**occur** verb **1** *the accident occurred last year* happen, take place, come about, come to pass, materialize, transpire, arise, crop up, turn up, befall. **2** *the disease occurs in the tropics* be found, exist, appear, present itself, show itself, manifest itself. **3** *an idea occurs to me* come to mind, spring to mind, strike one, hit one, dawn on.

**occurrence** noun **1** *an everyday occurrence* happening, event, incident, circumstance, affair, episode, proceeding. **2** *the occurrence of the disease* existence, appearance, manifestation.

**odd** adjective **1** *an odd person/happening* strange, eccentric, queer, peculiar, idiosyncratic, unconventional, outlandish, droll, weird, bizarre, offbeat, freakish, whimsical, unusual, uncommon, irregular, funny, curious, abnormal, atypical, different, out-of-the-ordinary, exceptional, rare, extraordinary, remarkable, singular, deviant, aberrant; *inf.* wacky, freaky, kinky, off-the-wall. **2** *odd jobs/moments* occasional, periodic, irregular, random, chance, fortuitous, various, sundry. **3** *an odd sock* unmatched, unpaired, leftover, spare, remaining, surplus, superfluous. **odd man out** exception, outsider, nonconformist, misfit, maverick.

**oddity** noun **1** *the house is an oddity* curiosity, rarity, anomaly, aberration, irregularity, phenomenon. **2** *he is an oddity* eccentric, crank, original, misfit, fish out of water, rara avis; *inf.* character, oddball, weirdo, odd/queer fish.

**odds** plural noun **1** *the odds are in his favor* advantage, lead, edge, superiority, supremacy, ascendancy. **2** *the odds are that he will win* likelihood, probability, chances, balance. **at odds with** in conflict with, in disagreement with, not in keeping with, in opposition to, at variance with. **odds and ends** bits and pieces, oddments, fragments, remnants, scraps, cuttings, snippets, miscellanea, leftovers, leavings.

**odious** adjective abhorrent, loathsome, detestable, hateful, despicable, contemptible; repugnant, disgusting, repulsive, repellent, unpleasant, disagreeable, objectionable, offensive, abominable.

**odor** noun **1** *the odor of cologne* aroma, smell, scent, perfume, fragrance, bouquet, redolence, essence, stench, stink. **2** *an odor of ill will* atmosphere, air, ambience, aura, spirit, quality, flavor, emanation.

**off** adjective **1** *the game/deal is off* canceled, postponed, shelved. **2** *called on the off chance that you were home* unlikely, doubtful, remote, improbable, implausible. **3** *the food/milk is off* bad, rotten, decomposed, moldy, high, sour, rancid, turned.

**off** adverb **off and on** sporadically, periodically. See OCCASIONALLY.

**offbeat** adjective unconventional, unorthodox, idiosyncratic, unusual, strange, outlandish, outré, Bohemian, hippie; *inf.* way-out, far-out, off-the-wall.

**off-color** adjective risqué, racy. See OBSCENE 1.

**offend** verb **1** *his behavior offended them* wound, affront, upset, displease, annoy, anger, incense, exasperate, vex, pique, put out, gall, irritate, provoke, rile, ruffle, disgruntle, rankle with, outrage, insult, slight, humiliate. **2** *offend her sense of taste* displease, be disagreeable to, be distasteful to, repel, disgust, revolt, nauseate; *inf.* turn someone off. **3** *apologize for having offended* do wrong, sin, go astray, fall from grace, err, transgress.

**offender** noun wrongdoer, culprit, criminal, lawbreaker, miscreant, delinquent, sinner, transgressor, malefactor.

**offense** noun **1** *commit an offense* crime, breach/violation/infraction of the law, wrongdoing, wrong, misdemeanor, misdeed, peccadillo, sin, transgression, shortcoming, fault, lapse. **2** *an offense against society* affront, injury, hurt, outrage, atrocity, insult, injustice, indignity, slight, snub. **3** *her behavior causes offense* annoyance, anger, indignation, exasperation, wrath, ire, displeasure, disapproval, dislike, animosity, resentment, pique, vexation. **4** *the enemy's offense* attack, assault. See OFFENSIVE noun. **take offense at** take umbrage at, get annoyed at, get angry at, resent, get/go into a huff about; *inf.* be miffed at/by.

**offensive** adjective **1** *an offensive remark/person* hurtful, wounding, abusive, displeasing, annoying, exasperating, vexing, galling, irritating, provocative, insulting, humiliating, rude, discourteous, uncivil, impolite, unmannerly, impertinent, insolent, disrespectful. **2** *an offensive smell/sight* disagreeable, unpleasant, foul, repellent, sickening, unsavory, noisome; *inf.* yucky. See OBJECTIONABLE.

**offensive** noun attack, assault, onslaught, drive, invasion, push, thrust, charge, sortie, sally, incursion.

**offer** verb **1** *offer a suggestion* put forward, propose, advance, submit, propound, suggest, recommend, make a motion of. **2** *the job offers good career prospects* afford, provide, supply, give, furnish, make available, present, give an opportunity for.

**offer** noun proposal, proposition, suggestion, submission, approach, overture.

**offering** noun **1** *collect offerings from the members* contribution, donation, subscription, gift, present, alms, charity, handout.

**2** *offerings to the gods* sacrifice, oblation, immolation.

**offhand** adjective casual, unceremonious, cavalier, blasé, curt, abrupt, terse, brusque.

**offhand** adverb **1** *always acts very offhand* casually, unceremoniously, cavalierly, perfunctorily, curtly, abruptly, discourteously, rudely. **2** *I cannot say offhand* extempore, impromptu, ad lib, extemporaneously, spontaneously; *inf.* off the cuff, off the top of one's head, just like that.

**office** noun **1** *his office is near his home* base, workplace, workroom, room. **2** *he has the office of treasurer* post, position, appointment, role, place, situation, station. **3** *to hold high office* work, employment, business, duty, function, responsibility, obligation, charge, tenure.

**officer** noun **1** *the officer in charge of the investigation* policeman/policewoman, officer of the law, detective, constable; *inf.* copper, cop, the law, gumshoe; *inf. derog.* pig, fuzz. **2** *the officers of the club* officeholder, office-bearer, official, committee member, board member, administrator, executive, functionary, bureaucrat.

**official** adjective **1** *official permission | his appointment is now official* authorized, accredited, approved, validated, authenticated, certified, endorsed, sanctioned, licensed, recognized, accepted, legitimate, legal, lawful, bona fide, proper, *ex cathedra*; *inf.* kosher. **2** *an official function* formal, ceremonial, solemn, conventional, ritualistic, pompous; *inf.* stuffed-shirt.

**official** noun **1** *party officials* officeholder, administrator. See OFFICER 2. **2** *officials of the court* officer, representative, agent, deputy.

**officiate** verb be in charge of, be responsible for, chair, preside over, manage, oversee, superintend, conduct, run, operate.

**officious** adjective interfering, intrusive, meddlesome, meddling, importunate, forward, obtrusive, domineering.

**offset** verb counterbalance, counterpoise, counteract, countervail, balance, balance out, cancel out, neutralize, compensate for, make up for.

**offshoot** noun **1** *plant offshoots* sprout, branch, bough, limb, twig, sucker, tendril, runner, scion, spur. **2** *an offshoot of the Hapsburg family* descendant, scion, relation, relative, kin. **3** *his attitude is an offshoot of his war experiences* result, outcome, aftermath, consequence, upshot, product, by-product, spin-off.

**offspring** noun child, children, family, progeny, young, issue, descendant(s), heir(s), successor(s), spawn; *inf.* kid(s), young 'un(s).

**often** adverb frequently, repeatedly, time and time again, time after time, day in (and) day out; *lit.* oft, oft-times.

**ogle** verb stare at, gaze at, eye amorously, leer at, make eyes at, make sheep's eyes at; *inf.* give someone the once-over, undress with one's eyes.

**ogre/ogress** noun **1** *a mythical ogre* monster, giant/giantess, troll, bogeyman, bugbear, demon, devil. **2** *ruled by an ogre* fiend, beast, tyrant, despot, brute, sadist.

**oily** adjective **1** *oily food* greasy, fatty, buttery, swimming in oil/fat, oleaginous. **2** *oily charm* smooth, smooth-talking, unctuous, honey-tongued, flattering, fulsome, glib, suave, urbane.

**ointment** noun emollient, salve, balm, liniment, embrocation, unguent, gel.

**OK** noun *give the OK* agreement, consent, assent, permission, authorization, endorsement, sanction, approval, seal of approval, approbation, thumbs up, go-ahead; *inf.* green light, say-so.

**OK** adjective *an OK job* all right, acceptable, tolerable, passable, satisfactory, adequate, middling; *inf.* not bad, so-so, fair-to-middling.

**OK** verb *OK the project* consent to, say yes to, agree to, approve, pass, authorize, sanction, give something the/a nod, rubber-stamp.

**old** adjective **1** *old people* older, mature, elderly, aged, advanced in years, up in years, getting on, gray-haired, grizzled, hoary, past one's prime, ancient, decrepit, senescent, senile, venerable, senior; *inf.* past it, over the hill, long in the tooth. **2** *old clothes/buildings* worn, worn-out, shabby, torn, tattered, dilapidated, broken-down, rundown, tumbledown, ramshackle, decaying, crumbling, disintegrating. **3** *old ideas* out-of-date, outdated, old-fashioned, outmoded, passé, archaic, obsolete, extinct, antiquated, antediluvian, superannuated; *inf.* old hat. **4** *in the old days* of old, olden, bygone, past, early, earlier, earliest, primeval, primordial, prehistoric. **5** *old customs* age-old, long-standing, long-lived, long-established, time-honored, enduring, lasting. **6** *old for her years* | *he's an old hand* mature, wise, sensible, experienced, knowledgeable, well-versed, practiced, skilled, skillful, adept. **7** *an old girlfriend* ex-, former, previous, one-time, sometime, erstwhile; *lit.* quondam. **old age** elderliness, age, agedness, declining years, advanced years, winter/autumn of one's life, senescence, senility, dotage.

**old-fashioned** adjective old, former, out of fashion, outmoded, démodé, unfashionable, out of style, out-of-date, outdated, dated, behind the times, past, bygone,

passé, archaic, obsolescent, obsolete, ancient, antiquated, superannuated, antediluvian, old-fogyish, old-fangled; *inf.* old hat, not with it.

**old-timer** noun senior citizen, senior; veteran; *inf. derog.* old fogy, old geezer, old codger.

**omen** noun portent, sign, token, foretoken, harbinger, premonition, forewarning, warning, foreshadowing, prediction, forecast, prophecy, augury, straw in the wind, writing on the wall, auspice, presage, presentiment, feeling, foreboding, misgiving; *inf.* funny feeling.

**ominous** adjective threatening, menacing, minatory, sinister, unpromising, unpropitious, inauspicious, unfavorable, unlucky, ill-fated.

**omission** noun **1** *the omission of his name* leaving out, exclusion, exception, noninclusion, deletion, erasure, elimination, expunction. **2** *a sin of omission* neglect, neglectfulness, negligence, dereliction, forgetfulness, oversight, disregard, nonfulfillment, default, failure. **3** *note several omissions from the list* exclusion, oversight, gap, lacuna.

**omit** verb **1** *omit his name from the list* leave out, exclude, except, pass over, drop, delete, erase, eliminate, expunge, rub out, cross out. **2** *omit closing the door* forget, neglect, fail; leave undone, overlook, skip.

**omnipotent** adjective all-powerful, almighty, supreme, preeminent, invincible.

**omniscient** adjective all-knowing, all-wise, all-seeing, all-perceiving.

**once** adverb **1** *they were friends once* at one time, previously, formerly, in the past, long ago. **2** *I saw him only once* on one occasion, one time, one single time. **at once 1** *you must leave at once* immediately, right away, straight away, instantly, forthwith; *inf.* before you can say Jack Robinson. **2** *they both arrived at once* at the same time, together, simultaneously. **once and for all** decisively, conclusively, finally, positively, for good, forever, permanently. **once in a while** occasionally, on the odd occasion, from time to time; *inf.* once in a blue moon.

**oncoming** adjective approaching, advancing, nearing, onrushing, forthcoming, imminent.

**one** adjective **1** *one person* a single, a solitary, a sole, a lone. **2** *they are now one* united, allied, joined, unified, bound, wedded, married.

**onerous** adjective burdensome, heavy, crushing, backbreaking, oppressive, weighty, arduous, demanding, exacting, wearing.

**one-sided** adjective **1** *one-sided opinions* biased, prejudiced, partisan, partial, discriminatory, colored, inequitable, unfair, unjust, narrow-minded, bigoted. **2** *a one-sided game* uneven, unequal, unbalanced, lopsided.

**ongoing** adjective in progress, current, extant, progressing, advancing, successful, developing, evolving, growing, continuous, continual.

**onlooker** noun looker-on, witness. *See* OBSERVER.

**only** adverb **1** *only enough for two* just, at most, not more than, barely, scarcely. **2** *he is only saying that* just, merely, simply, purely.

**only** adjective single, one and only, solitary, sole, lone; individual, unique, exclusive.

**onset** noun start, beginning, commencement, inception, outbreak; *inf.* kickoff.

**onslaught** noun assault, attack, charge, onrush, onset, storming, sortie, sally, raid, foray, push, thrust, drive, blitz.

**onus** noun burden, weight, load, responsibility, liability, obligation, duty, charge, encumbrance, cross to bear, millstone around one's neck, albatross.

**ooze** verb **1** *pus oozing from the wound* flow, discharge, exude, seep, trickle, drip, dribble, filter, filtrate, percolate, excrete, escape, leak, drain, bleed, sweat. **2** *she was positively oozing charm* exude, pour forth, send out, let loose, display, exhibit, manifest.

**opaque** adjective **1** *opaque glass* nontransparent, nontranslucent, cloudy, filmy, blurred, hazy. **2** *opaque prose* unclear, unfathomable, unintelligible, incomprehensible.

**open** adjective **1** *open doors* ajar, wide open, agape, gaping, yawning; unlocked, unbolted, unlatched, unbarred, unfastened, unsecured. **2** *open boxes/drains* uncovered, coverless, unlidded, topless, unsealed. **3** *open spaces* unenclosed, unfenced, exposed, unsheltered, extensive, broad, spacious, sweeping, airy, uncrowded, uncluttered, undeveloped. **4** *open roads* unobstructed, unblocked, clear, passable, navigable. **5** *maps open on the table* spread out, unfolded, unfurled, unrolled, straightened out, extended, stretched out. **6** *quite open about her dislike* frank, candid, honest, forthright, direct, blunt, plainspoken, downright. **7** *an open meeting/competition* public, general, nonexclusive, accessible, nonrestrictive, unrestricted, nondiscriminatory. **8** *the job is still open* vacant, available, unfilled, unoccupied, free. **9** *open hostility* obvious, clear, noticeable, visible, apparent, evident, manifest, overt, conspicuous, patent, unconcealed, unhidden, undis-

guised, blatant, flagrant. **10** *three courses open to us* available, on hand, obtainable, accessible. **11** *the subject is still open* undecided, unresolved, unsettled, arguable, debatable, moot. **12** *keep an open mind* unbiased, unprejudiced. *See* OPENMINDED 1. **open to** *open to abuse* allowing of, permitting, vulnerable to, exposed to, susceptible to, liable to, at the mercy of, an easy target for.

**open** verb **1** *open the door* throw open, unlock, unbolt, unlatch, unbar, unfasten. **2** *open the package* unwrap, undo, untie, unseal. **3** *open the bottle* uncork, broach, crack. **4** *the crack opened* open up, come apart, split, separate, rupture. **5** *we open the campaign tomorrow* start, begin, commence, start the ball rolling; *inf.* kick off. **6** *open his heart* lay bare, bare, uncover, expose, exhibit, disclose, divulge, pour out.

**openhanded** adjective open, generous, liberal, lavish, free, bountiful, bounteous, munificent; benevolent, charitable, magnanimous.

**opening** noun **1** *an opening in the wall* gap, aperture, space, hole, orifice, vent, slot, break, breach, crack, split, fissure, cleft, crevice, chink, interstice, rent, rupture. **2** *an opening in the firm* vacancy, position, job, opportunity, chance. **3** *the opening of the season* beginning, start, commencement, outset, inception, launch, birth, dawn; *inf.* kickoff.

**open-minded** adjective **1** *open-minded judges* unbiased, unprejudiced, prejudicefree, nonpartisan, impartial, nondiscriminatory, objective, disinterested, dispassionate, detached, tolerant, liberal, broadminded, undogmatic. **2** *writers should be open-minded* receptive, open to suggestions, open to new ideas, amenable.

**operate** verb work, function, go, run, perform, act, be in action; make go, use, utilize, employ, handle, manipulate, maneuver, ply, manage, be in charge of.

**operation** noun **1** *operation of the machine* working, functioning, running, performance; using, handling, manipulation. **2** *the operation of radon testing went smoothly* activity, exercise, affair, business, undertaking, enterprise, task, job. **3** *military operations* maneuver, exercise, campaign, assault. **in operation** operational, operative, in force, effective, in use, functioning, working, valid.

**operator** noun **1** *the operator of a car dealership* manager, businessman, businesswoman, business person, administrator, director, supervisor, superintendent. **2** *a smooth operator* maneuverer, manipulator, machinator, mover, wheelerdealer.

**opiate** noun drug, narcotic, sedative, tranquilizer, depressant, bromide, soporific, morphine, opium, laudanum; *inf.* downer.

**opinion** noun point of view, view, viewpoint, belief, thought, thinking, way of thinking, standpoint, theory, judgment, estimation, feeling, sentiment, impression, notion, assumption, conception, conviction, persuasion, creed, dogma.

**opinionated** adjective dogmatic, doctrinaire, cocksure, adamant, obstinate, stubborn, pigheaded, inflexible, uncompromising, bigoted.

**opponent** noun opposer, the opposition, rival, adversary, competitor, enemy, foe, antagonist, contender, dissenter, disputant.

**opportune** adjective advantageous, favorable, auspicious, propitious, timely, well-timed, fortunate, providential, felicitous, convenient, expedient, suitable, apt, fitting, relevant, applicable, pertinent.

**opportunity** noun chance, good time, golden opportunity; *inf.* break.

**oppose** verb 1 *oppose the proposals* disapprove of, be hostile to, contradict, counter, argue against, counterattack, confront, resist, withstand, defy, fight, combat. 2 *oppose memory and imagination* contrast, juxtapose, offset, balance, counterbalance, set against, pit against.

**opposite** adjective 1 *houses opposite each other* facing, face-to-face with; *inf.* eyeball to eyeball with. 2 *opposite opinions* diametrically opposite, opposing, differing, contrary, reverse, contradictory, conflicting, clashing, discordant, dissident, at variance, antipathetical, poles apart. 3 *on opposite sides* opposing, rival, competitive, enemy, warring, fighting, contending, combatant.

**opposition** noun 1 *express their opposition* dislike, disapproval, hostility, resistance, defiance. 2 *back the opposition* opponent, opposing side, other side, rival, adversary, competition, antagonist, enemy, foe.

**oppress** verb 1 *the tyrant oppressed the citizens* tyrannize, crush, suppress, repress, abuse, maltreat, persecute, rule with a rod of iron, trample on, trample underfoot, ride roughshod over. 2 *oppressed by grief* weigh down, lie heavy on, weigh heavy on, burden, crush, depress, dispirit, dishearten, take the heart out of, discourage, sadden, make despondent, deject, desolate.

**oppressed** adjective tyrannized, subjugated, enslaved, crushed, subdued, repressed, persecuted, browbeaten, downtrodden, disadvantaged, underprivileged.

**oppression** noun tyranny, suppression, abuse, persecution, despotism, abuse, maltreatment, cruelty, brutality, injustice, ruthlessness, harshness.

**oppressive** adjective 1 *an oppressive regime* tyrannical, despotic, draconian, iron-fisted, high-handed, repressive, domineering, harsh, crushing, cruel, brutal, ruthless, relentless, merciless, pitiless, inexorable, unjust, undemocratic. 2 *oppressive weather* muggy, close, airless, stuffy, stifling, suffocating, sultry, torrid.

**optimistic** adjective hopeful, full of hope, Pollyannaish, Panglossian, positive, sanguine, confident, bullish, cheerful, buoyant; *inf.* upbeat.

**optimum** adjective 1 *the optimum time to choose* most favorable, best, most advantageous, most appropriate, ideal, perfect. 2 *plants in optimum condition* peak, top, best, perfect, ideal, flawless, superlative, optimal; *inf.* tip-top, A-1.

**option** noun choice, alternative, possibility, preference.

**optional** adjective noncompulsory, voluntary, discretionary, elective.

**opulent** adjective 1 *opulent families* affluent, wealthy, rich, well-off, well-to-do, moneyed, prosperous; *inf.* well-heeled, rolling in it. 2 *opulent houses* luxurious, sumptuous, lavishly appointed; *inf.* plush, plushy, ritzy. 3 *opulent vegetation* abundant, superabundant, copious, plentiful, profuse, prolific, luxuriant.

**oracle** noun 1 *the oracles of classical times* prophet/prophetess, seer, soothsayer, sibyl, augur, sage. 2 *an oracle on architecture* authority, expert, specialist, connoisseur, pundit, guru.

**oral** adjective spoken, verbal, vocal, uttered, said.

**oration** noun speech, lecture, address, homily, sermon, discourse, declamation, harangue, tirade; *inf.* spiel.

**orator** noun speaker, public speaker, speech-maker, lecturer, declaimer, haranguer, rhetorician, Cicero.

**orbit** noun 1 *the planet's orbit* revolution, circle, circuit, cycle, rotation, circumgyration, path, course, track, trajectory. 2 *his orbit of responsibility* sphere, sphere of influence, range, reach, scope, ambit, sweep, domain.

**orbit** verb revolve around, circle around, encircle, circumnavigate.

**orchestrate** verb 1 *orchestrate the music* arrange, score. 2 *orchestrate the event* organize, arrange, put together, set up, manage, stage-manage, mastermind, coordinate, integrate.

**ordain** verb 1 *ordain a priest* appoint, confer holy orders on, frock, induct, install, invest, anoint, consecrate. 2 *his lack of success seems to have been ordained* fate, predestine, predetermine, preordain. 3 *Congress ordained that taxes be increased* decree, legislate, enact, rule, order, command, enjoin, dictate, prescribe, pronounce.

**ordeal** noun trial, test, tribulation, suffering, affliction, distress, agony, anguish, torture, torment, calamity, trouble, nightmare.

**order** noun **1** *restore order to the room* orderliness, neatness, tidiness, trimness, harmony, apple-pie order. **2** *no sense of order in the filing system* method, organization, system, plan, uniformity, regularity, symmetry, pattern. **3** *everything is in working order* condition, state, shape, situation. **4** *in alphabetical/numerical order* arrangement, grouping, system, systemization, organization, form, structure, disposition, classification, categorization, codification, series, sequence, progression, succession, layout, setup. **5** *give orders to fire* command, direction, directive, instruction, behest, decree, edict, injunction, law, rule, regulation, mandate, ordinance, stipulation, dictate, say-so. **6** *lack of order in the land* law, lawfulness, law and order, discipline, control, peace, calm. **7** *place an order for tickets* request, call, requirement, requisition, demand, booking, reservation, commission, notification, application. **8** *the lower orders of society* rank, class, caste, grade, level, degree, position, station. **9** *the social order* grouping, grading, ranking, system, class system, caste system, hierarchy, pecking order. **10** *work of a high order* kind, sort, type, variety, genre, nature. **11** *they all belong to some order* lodge, society, secret society, guild, club, association, league, union, fellowship, fraternity, confraternity, sorority, brotherhood, sisterhood, sodality. **in order 1** *the room is in order* tidy, neat. *See* ORDERLY 1. **2** *is it in order for her to attend?* acceptable, all right, fitting, suitable, appropriate, right, correct. **out of order** *the machine is out of order* broken, broken-down, nonfunctional, inoperative, in disrepair, out of commission; *inf.* down, kaput, on the blink, on the fritz.

**order** verb **1** *order them to fire* give the order to, command, instruct, direct, bid. **2** *the judge ordered that the courtroom be cleared* decree, ordain, rule, legislate, enjoin, prescribe, pronounce. **3** *order dinner* place an order for, request, call for, requisition, book, reserve, contract for, apply for, send away for. **4** *it was time to order his life* put in order, set in order, organize, systematize, arrange, dispose, classify, catalog, codify, tabulate, sort out, tidy up, regulate.

**orderly** adjective **1** *an orderly room* in order, neat, tidy, trim, shipshape, shipshape and Bristol fashion, in Bristol fashion, in apple-pie order. **2** *an orderly person* organized, well-organized,

methodical, systematic, systematized, efficient, businesslike. **3** *an orderly class of students* well-behaved, law-abiding, disciplined, quiet, peaceful, controlled, restrained.

**ordinarily** adverb as a rule, generally, as a general rule, in general, usually, normally.

**ordinary** adjective **1** *our ordinary procedure* usual, normal, standard, typical, stock, common, customary, habitual, accustomed, wonted, everyday, quotidian, regular, routine, established, settled, fixed, prevailing. **2** *we lead very ordinary lives* run-of-the-mill, conventional, standard, typical, average, commonplace, workaday, humdrum, unremarkable, unexceptional, unmemorable, pedestrian, prosaic, unpretentious, modest, plain, simple, humble. **3** *a very ordinary piece of writing* average, run-of-the-mill, pedestrian, prosaic, uninteresting, dull, uninspired, unimaginative, hackneyed, stale, undistinguished, unexceptional, unremarkable, mediocre, indifferent, second-rate.

**organic** adjective **1** *organic ingredients* natural, nonchemical, pesticide-free, chemical-free, additive-free. **2** *organic matter* living, live, animate, biotic, biological. **3** *the music in the play is organic, not incidental* fundamental, basic, structural, integral, inherent, innate, intrinsic, vital, essential, indispensable. **4** *society is an organic whole* structured, organized, systematic, systematized, ordered, methodical, methodized.

**organism** noun **1** *microscopic organisms* being, creature, animal, plant. **2** *the company is a complex organism* structure, system, organization, setup.

**organization** noun **1** *the organization of the firm/files/party* establishment, development, assembly, arrangement, regulation, coordination, systematization, methodization, categorization, administration, running, management. **2** *the human body is a complex organization* whole, unity. *See* ORGANISM 2. **3** *president of the organization* company, firm, concern, operation, corporation, institution, group, consortium, conglomerate, combine, syndicate, federation, confederation, association, body.

**organize** verb establish, set up, form, lay the foundations of, found, institute, create, originate, begin, start, develop, build, frame, construct, assemble, structure, shape, mold, put together, arrange, dispose, regulate, marshal, put in order, put straight, coordinate, systematize, methodize, standardize, collocate, group, sort, sort out, classify, categorize, catalog, codify, tabulate.

**orgy** noun bout, overindulgence, excess, surfeit; carousal, debauch, revel, revels, revelry, bacchanalia, saturnalia; *inf.*

spree, splurge, binge, jag, bender, toot; love-in.

**orient, orientate** verb **1** *orient himself to his new life* adapt, adjust, accommodate, familiarize, acclimatize. **2** *orient the beach chair toward the sun* direct, guide, lead, position something in the direction of, turn. **3** *orient the course for/toward beginners* aim, direct, slant, angle, intend, design. **orient oneself** get/find one's bearings, get the lay of the land, feel one's way.

**orientation** noun **1** *orientation to his new way of life* adaptation, adjustment, accommodation, familiarization, acclimatization. **2** *establish one's orientation* bearings, location, position, direction.

**orifice** noun opening, hole, vent, aperture, gap, space, breach, break, rent, slot, slit.

**origin** noun **1** *the origin of the word* source, derivation, root, roots, provenance, etymology, genesis, etiology. **2** *the origins of life* source, basis, base, wellspring, wellhead, fountainhead, fountain, genesis. **3** *the origin of the age of electronics* birth, dawn, dawning, beginning, start, commencement, emergence, inception, launch, creation, early stages, inauguration, foundation. **4** *explore the family's origin(s)* descent, ancestry, pedigree, lineage, heritage, parentage, extraction, beginnings.

**original** adjective **1** *the original inhabitants* aboriginal, indigenous, early, earliest, first, initial, primary, primordial, primal, primeval, primitive, autochthonal, autochthonous. **2** *his work is original* innovative, inventive, new, novel, fresh, creative, imaginative, resourceful, individual, ingenious, unusual, unconventional, unorthodox, unprecedented, groundbreaking; *inf.* edgy, left-field. **3** *this painting is original* not copied, genuine, authentic, archetypal, prototypical, master.

**original** noun **1** *this is the original, not a copy* original work/painting, archetype, prototype, master. **2** *among architects, he is an original* standout, paragon, nonpareil, exemplar, one of a kind, nonesuch; individualist, eccentric, nonconformist.

**originality** noun inventiveness, newness, novelty, break with tradition, freshness, innovation, creativity, imaginativeness, resourcefulness, individuality, unusualness, unconventionality, unprecedentedness.

**originally** adverb at first, at the start, at the outset, initially.

**originate** verb **1** *the spring originates in/from the mountains* arise, rise, flow, emanate, issue. **2** *the quarrel originated in/from a misunderstanding* stem, spring, result, derive, start, begin, commence. **3** *he originated the idea* give birth to, be the father/mother of, set in motion, set up, invent, dream up,

conceive, discover, initiate, create, formulate, inaugurate, pioneer, introduce, establish, found, evolve, develop, generate.

**originator** noun father/mother, inventor, discoverer, initiator, architect, author, prime mover, founder, pioneer, establisher, developer.

**ornament** noun **1** *shelves of ornaments* knickknack, trinket, bauble, gewgaw, accessory, decoration, frill, whatnot, doodad. **2** *the dress needs little ornament* decoration, adornment, embellishment, trimming, garnish, garnishing. **3** *she's the ornament of the show* jewel, gem, treasure, pride, flower, leading light, crème de la crème.

**ornamental** adjective decorative, decorated, ornate, ornamented, embellished, embroidered, fancy, fanciful.

**ornate** adjective **1** *ornate furnishings* elaborate, overelaborate, decorated, embellished, adorned, ornamented, fancy, fussy, busy, ostentatious, showy, baroque, rococo; *inf.* flashy. **2** *ornate prose* flowery, florid, flamboyant, pretentious, high-flown, high-sounding, grandiose, pompous, bombastic; *inf.* highfalutin.

**orthodox** adjective *orthodox behavior* conventional, accepted, approved, correct, proper, conformist, established, traditional, prevailing, customary, usual, regular, standard, *comme il faut*, de rigueur.

**oscillate** verb swing, sway, fluctuate, seesaw, waver, vacillate, vary, hesitate, yo-yo.

**oscillation** noun swing, swinging, fluctuation, wavering, vacillation, yo-yoing.

**ostensible** adjective outward, apparent, seeming, professed, alleged, claimed, purported, pretended, feigned, specious, supposed.

**ostentatious** adjective showy, conspicuous, obtrusive, loud, extravagant, flamboyant, gaudy, flashy, pretentious, affected, overdone, overelaborate, vulgar, kitsch; *inf.* bling, bling-bling.

**ostracize** verb exclude, shut out, bar, shun, spurn, avoid, boycott, repudiate, cast out, reject, blackball, blacklist, banish, exile, expel, excommunicate, debar, leave out in the cold, give someone the cold shoulder, send to Coventry.

**other** adjective **1** *use other means* different, unlike, variant, dissimilar, disparate, distinct, separate, alternative. **2** *need a few other examples* more, additional, further, extra, supplementary.

**oust** verb drive out, force out, thrust out, expel, eject, put out, evict, throw out, dispossess, dismiss, dislodge, displace, depose, unseat, topple, disinherit; *inf.* fire, sack.

**out** adverb **1** *the manager is out just now* not here, away, elsewhere, absent. **2** *the* *children have gone out* outside, outdoors, out of doors. **3** *tire them out* completely, thoroughly, entirely, wholly. **4** *the fire is out* extinguished, quenched, doused, dead. **5** *the boxer is completely out* cold, unconscious, knocked out, senseless; *inf.* KO'd. **6** *your secret is out* revealed, disclosed, divulged, in the open, out in the open, known, exposed, common knowledge, public knowledge. **7** *the flowers are out* open, in bloom, in full bloom, blooming. **8** *long hair is out this year* unfashionable, out of fashion, dated, out-of-date, not in, behind the times, *démodé*, passé; *inf.* old hat.

**out-and-out** adjective absolute, complete, utter, downright, thorough, thoroughgoing, total, perfect, unmitigated, unqualified, consummate, inveterate, dyed-in-the-wool, true-blue.

**outbreak** noun eruption, flare-up, upsurge, outburst, sudden appearance, start, rash.

**outburst** noun burst, explosion, eruption, outbreak, flare-up, access, attack, fit, spasm, paroxysm.

**outcast** noun pariah, *persona non grata*, leper, untouchable, castaway, exile, displaced person, refugee, evictee, evacuee; *inf.* DP.

**outclass** verb surpass, outshine, eclipse, overshadow, outdistance, outstrip, outdo, outplay, outrank, outrival, trounce, beat, defeat; *inf.* be a cut above, be head and shoulders above, run rings around.

**outcome** noun consequence, result, end result, sequel, upshot, issue, product, conclusion, aftereffect, aftermath, wake; *inf.* payoff.

**outcry** noun clamor, protest, complaints, objections, fuss, outburst, commotion, uproar, tumult, hue and cry, hullabaloo, ballyhoo, racket.

**outdated** adjective out-of-date, out of style, out of fashion, old-fashioned, unfashionable, outmoded, dated, *démodé*, passé, behind the times, antiquated, archaic; *inf.* old hat, not with it.

**outdo** verb surpass, top, exceed, excel, get the better of, transcend, overcome, outsmart, outmaneuver. *See* OUTCLASS.

**outer** adjective **1** *pierce the outer layer* outside, outermost, outward, exterior, external, surface, superficial. **2** *the outer areas of the estate* outlying, distant, remote, faraway, peripheral, fringe.

**outfit** noun **1** *wearing a smart outfit* clothes, dress, ensemble, suit, costume, garb, accoutrements, trappings; *inf.* get-up, gear, togs. **2** *pack the fishing outfit* kit, equipment, tools, tackle, apparatus, paraphernalia. **3** *a publishing outfit | soldiers rejoining their outfit* organization, setup, company, firm,

business, (military) unit, group, team, coterie, clique.

**outfit** verb equip, fit out, rig out, supply, furnish with, provide with, stock with, provision, accoutre, attire.

**outgoing** adjective **1** *outgoing people* extroverted, unreserved, demonstrative, affectionate, warm, friendly, genial, cordial, affable, hail-fellow-well-met, sociable, communicative, open, expansive, talkative, gregarious, approachable, easygoing, easy. **2** *the outgoing president* retiring, departing, leaving, withdrawing.

**outing** noun trip, excursion, jaunt, expedition, pleasure trip, tour, airing; *inf.* spin.

**outlandish** adjective strange, odd, peculiar, queer, curious, singular, eccentric, quaint, bizarre, preposterous, fantastic, outré, weird; *inf.* wacky, far-out, off-the-wall.

**outlaw** noun fugitive, outcast, exile, pariah, bandit, desperado, brigand, criminal, robber.

**outlaw** verb ban, bar, prohibit, forbid, embargo, disallow, proscribe, interdict.

**outlay** noun expenditure, expenses, spending, cost, price, charge, payment, disbursement.

**outlet** noun **1** *water outlets* exit, vent, outfall, valve, safety valve, duct, blowhole, channel, trench, culvert, conduit. **2** *an outlet for her creativity* release, release mechanism, safety valve. **3** *an outlet for their produce* market, marketplace, store, shop.

**outline** noun **1** *an outline of our plans* draft, rough draft, sketch, skeleton, framework, layout, diagram, plan, design, schema. **2** *give an outline of what happened* thumbnail sketch, quick rundown, summary, synopsis, précis, main points, bones, bare bones. **3** *draw an outline of the building* contour, silhouette, profile, lineaments, delineation, configuration, perimeter, circumference.

**outline** verb **1** *outline the shape* sketch, delineate, trace, silhouette. **2** *outline your ideas* give a thumbnail sketch of, give a rough idea of, give a quick rundown on, summarize, précis.

**outlook** noun **1** *a gloomy outlook on life* view, point of view, viewpoint, perspective, attitude, frame of mind, standpoint, slant, angle, interpretation, opinion. **2** *the house has a pleasant outlook* view, vista, prospect, panorama, aspect.

**outlying** adjective outer, outermost, out-of-the-way, remote, distant, faraway, far-flung, peripheral, isolated, inaccessible, off the beaten path/track, backwoods.

**outmoded** adjective old-fashioned, unfashionable, out of fashion, out of style, outdated, out-of-date, dated, passé, *démodé*, behind the times, antiquated, archaic, obsolete; *inf.* old hat.

**out of the way** adjective remote, lonely, obscure, unfrequented. *See* OUTLYING.

**output** noun production, product, productivity, yield, harvest, achievement, accomplishment.

**outrage** noun **1** *outrages committed by the soldiers* atrocity, crime, horror, enormity, brutality, barbarism. **2** *the building is an outrage* offense, affront, insult, injury, abuse, indignity, scandal, desecration, violation. **3** *arouse outrage in the citizens* anger, fury, rage, indignation, wrath, annoyance, shock, resentment, horror, amazement.

**outrage** verb anger, infuriate, enrage, incense, make someone's blood boil, madden, annoy, shock, horrify, amaze, scandalize, offend, insult, affront, vex, distress.

**outrageous** adjective **1** *outrageous behavior* intolerable, insufferable, insupportable, unendurable, unbearable, impossible, exasperating, offensive, provocative, maddening, distressing. **2** *outrageous acts* atrocious, heinous, abominable, wicked, vile, foul, monstrous, horrible, horrid, dreadful, terrible, horrendous, hideous, ghastly, unspeakable, gruesome. **3** *outrageous prices* immoderate, excessive, exorbitant, unreasonable, preposterous, scandalous, shocking; *inf.* steep.

**outright** adjective **1** *an outright fool* absolute, complete. *See* OUT-AND-OUT. **2** *the outright winner* definite, unequivocal, unqualified, incontestable, undeniable, unmistakable.

**outright** adverb **1** *reject the proposal outright* completely, entirely, wholly, totally, categorically, absolutely. **2** *killed outright* instantly, instantaneously, immediately, at once, straight away, then and there, on the spot. **3** *tell her outright* openly, candidly, frankly, honestly, forthrightly, directly, plainly, explicitly, unreservedly.

**outset** noun start, starting point, beginning, commencement, dawn, birth, inception, opening, launch, inauguration; *inf.* kickoff.

**outside** adjective **1** *outside layers* outer, outermost, outward, exterior, external. **2** *outside furniture/plumbing* outdoor, out-of-doors. **3** *an outside chance* unlikely, improbable, slight, slender, slim, small, faint, negligible, marginal, remote, distant, vague.

**outside** noun **1** *brown on the outside* outer side, exterior, surface, outer surface, case, skin, shell, sheath. **2** *the outside of the building* exterior, front, face, façade.

**outsider** noun alien, stranger, foreigner, outlander, immigrant, emigrant, émigré, newcomer, parvenu, arriviste, interloper,

## out of the way · overbearing

intruder, gatecrasher, outcast, misfit, odd man out.

**outsmart** verb get the better of, outwit, outfox, outmaneuver, outperform, outplay, steal a march on, trick, dupe, make a fool of; *inf.* put one over on, pull a fast one on.

**outspoken** adjective candid, frank, forthright, direct, straightforward, straight-from-the-shoulder, plain, plainspoken, explicit, blunt, brusque, unequivocal, unceremonious.

**outstanding** adjective **1** *an outstanding painter* preeminent, eminent, well-known, notable, noteworthy, distinguished, important, famous, famed, renowned, celebrated, great, excellent, remarkable, exceptional, superlative. **2** *the painting is outstanding* striking, impressive, eye-catching, arresting, memorable, remarkable. **3** *outstanding debts* unpaid, unsettled, owing, due, remaining, pending, ongoing.

**outward** adjective *no outward sign of grief* external, superficial, visible, observable, noticeable, perceptible, discernible, apparent, evident, obvious.

**outwardly** adverb **1** *outwardly visible* externally, on the outside. **2** *outwardly he seems all right* on the surface, superficially, on the face of it, to all appearances, to the eye, as far as one can see, to all intents and purposes, apparently, evidently.

**outweigh** verb be greater than, exceed, be superior to, take precedence over, have the edge on/over, preponderate.

**outwit** verb get the better of, outmaneuver. *See* OUTSMART.

**oval** adjective egg-shaped, ovoid, ovate, oviform, elliptical, ellipsoidal.

**ovation** noun applause, handclap, hand-clapping, clapping, cheering, cheers, acclaim, acclamation, praise, plaudits, laurels, tribute, accolade, laudation, extolment; *inf.* bouquets.

**over** adverb **1** *fly over* overhead, above, on high, aloft. **2** *the relationship is over* ended, finished, concluded, terminated, no more, extinct, gone, dead, a thing of the past, ancient history. **over and over** again and again, repeatedly, time and time again, ad nauseam.

**overall** adjective comprehensive, universal, all-embracing, inclusive, all-inclusive, general, sweeping, complete, blanket, umbrella, global.

**overbearing** adjective domineering, autocratic, tyrannical, despotic, oppressive, high-handed, lordly, officious, dogmatic, dictatorial, pompous, peremptory, arrogant, haughty, cocksure, disdainful, contemptuous; *inf.* bossy.

**overblown** adjective extravagant, florid, pompous, overelaborate, pretentious, high-flown, turgid, bombastic, grandiloquent, magniloquent, euphuistic, fustian.

**overcast** adjective cloudy, clouded, clouded over, sunless, darkened, dark, murky, gray, leaden, lowering, threatening, heavy.

**overcome** verb conquer, defeat, vanquish, beat, prevail over, get the better of, triumph over, best, worst, trounce, rout, gain mastery over, master, overpower, overwhelm, overthrow, subdue, subjugate, quell, quash, crush; *inf.* lick, clobber, whip, wipe (up) the floor with, blow out of the water.

**overconfident** adjective cocksure, cocky, swaggering, blustering, brash, overbearing, egotistic, riding/heading for a fall.

**overdo** verb **1** *overdo the sympathy* exaggerate, do to death, go overboard over, carry too far, carry to extremes, belabor, stretch/strain a point over, overstate, overemphasize, hyperbolize, not know when to stop; *inf.* pile on, lay on thick, lay on with a trowel, make a production of, make a big deal out of. **2** *overdo the meat* overcook, overbake, burn, burn to a crisp. **overdo it** overwork, do too much, overtax oneself, overburden oneself, drive oneself too hard, push oneself too far/hard, wear oneself out, burn the candle at both ends, have too many irons in the fire, have too many balls in the air, burn oneself out, bite off more than one can chew; *inf.* knock oneself out, work/run oneself into the ground.

**overdue** adjective **1** *our visit is overdue* late, behind schedule, behindhand, delayed, belated, tardy, unpunctual. **2** *overdue bills* unpaid, owed, owing, outstanding, unsettled, in arrears.

**overeat** verb gorge oneself, stuff oneself, overindulge, surfeit, guzzle, gormandize; *inf.* binge, stuff one's face, eat like a horse, pack it away, make a pig of oneself, pig out.

**overflow** verb **1** *the water was overflowing* flow over, run over, spill over, brim over, well over, pour forth, stream forth, discharge, surge, debouch. **2** *water overflowed the land* flood, deluge, inundate, submerge, cover, swamp, engulf, drown, soak, drench, saturate. **overflowing with** full of, crowded with, thronged with, swarming with, teeming with, abounding in.

**overhaul** verb check out/over, investigate, inspect, examine, service, repair, mend, recondition, renovate, revamp, fix up, patch up.

**overhead** noun expenses, expenditure, outlay, disbursement, running cost(s), operating cost(s).

**overjoyed** adjective elated, jubilant, thrilled, delighted, euphoric, ecstatic, rapturous, enraptured, transported, delirious with happiness, on top of the world; *inf.* tickled pink, on cloud nine, in seventh heaven.

**overlook** verb **1** *he overlooked a mistake on the first page* fail to notice/observe/spot, miss, leave; *inf.* slip up on. **2** *overlook tasks* omit, neglect, forget. **3** *decide to overlook his crime* disregard, take no notice of, ignore, let something pass, turn a blind eye to, wink at, blink at, excuse, pardon, forgive, condone; *inf.* let something ride. **4** *the house overlooks the sea* look over, look onto, front onto, have a view of, afford/command a view of.

**overly** adverb unduly, excessively, inordinately, immoderately.

**overpower** verb **1** *overpower the enemy* get the upper hand over, conquer. *See* OVERCOME. **2** *his charm overpowered her* overwhelm, move, stir, affect, touch, impress, take aback; *inf.* bowl over, knock/hit for a loop, get to.

**overrate** verb overestimate, overvalue, overprize, exaggerate the worth of.

**override** verb **1** *his career overrides all else* take priority/precedence over, supersede, outweigh. **2** *override her objections* trample on, ride roughshod over, set aside, ignore, disregard, discount, pay no heed to, take no account of.

**overriding** adjective most important, predominant, principal, primary, paramount, chief, main, major, foremost, central, focal, pivotal; *inf.* number one.

**overrule** verb rule against, disallow, override, veto, set aside, overturn, cancel, reverse, rescind, repeal, revoke, repudiate, annul, nullify, declare null and void, invalidate, void, abrogate.

**overrun** verb **1** *the enemy was overrunning their country* invade, march into, penetrate, occupy, besiege, storm, attack, assail. **2** *rats overrunning the warehouses* swarm over, surge over, inundate, overwhelm, permeate, infest. **3** *weeds overrunning the garden* spread over, spread like wildfire over, grow over, cover, choke, clog; *inf.* run riot over.

**overseer** noun supervisor, superintendent, foreman, manager, master, boss; *inf.* super, honcho.

**overshadow** verb **1** *that runner overshadows the others* outshine, eclipse, put in the shade, surpass, be superior to, outclass, outstrip, outdo, top, transcend, tower above, dwarf, upstage; *inf.* be head and shoulders above, be a cut above. **2** *his death overshadowed the gathering* cast gloom over, blight, take the pleasure out of, mar, spoil, ruin. **3** *clouds overshadowing the sun* darken, bedim, dim, conceal, obscure, eclipse, screen, shroud, veil.

**oversight** noun **1** *done in oversight* carelessness, inattention, neglect, inadvertence, laxity, dereliction, omission. **2** *an oversight in the article* mistake, error, blunder, gaffe, fault, omission, slip, lapse; *inf.* slipup, goof, booboo. **3** *have oversight of the workforce* supervision, surveillance, superintendence, charge, care, administration, management, direction, control, handling.

**overt** adjective obvious, noticeable, observable, visible, undisguised, unconcealed, apparent, plain, manifest, patent, open, public, blatant, conspicuous.

**overtake** verb **1** *cars overtaking each other* pass, get/go past, go by, overhaul, outdistance, outstrip. **2** *misfortune overtook them* befall, hit, strike, fall upon, surprise, catch unawares, catch unprepared, catch off guard.

**overthrow** verb **1** *overthrow the government* cause the downfall of, remove from office, overturn, depose, oust, unseat, dethrone, disestablish. **2** *overthrow the army of occupation* conquer, vanquish, defeat, beat, rout, trounce, best, worst, subjugate, crush, quash, quell, overcome, overwhelm, overturn, overpower. **3** *squalls overthrowing boats* throw over, turn over, overturn, tip over, topple over, upset, capsize, knock over, upturn, upend, invert.

**overthrow** noun **1** *the overthrow of the government* downfall, deposition, ousting. **2** *the overthrow of the army* defeat, vanquishing, rout, subjugation, crushing, overwhelming, overturning.

**overtone** noun implication, innuendo, hint, suggestion, insinuation, association, connotation, undercurrent, nuance, flavor, coloring, vein.

**overture** noun *peace overtures* advances, move, opening move, conciliatory move, approach, proposal, proposition, offer, suggestion, motion.

**overturn** verb **1** *the boat overturned* capsize, keel over, tip over, topple over. **2** *high winds overturning trash cans* upturn, turn over. *See* OVERTHROW verb **3**. **3** *overturn the previous decision* reverse, rescind. *See* OVERRULE. **4** *overturn the government* depose, oust. *See* OVERTHROW verb

**1**. **5** *overturn the army of occupation* conquer, vanquish, defeat. *See* OVERTHROW verb **2**.

**overweight** adjective obese, fat, plump, stout, ample, chubby, tubby, corpulent, rotund, portly, pudgy, paunchy, heavy, on the heavy side, big, hefty, large, bulky, chunky, outsize, massive, gross; *inf.* well-padded, well-upholstered, roly-poly.

**overwhelm** verb **1** *the generous present overwhelmed her* move, daze, dumbfound, shake, take aback, leave speechless, stagger; *inf.* bowl over, knock for a loop, blow one's mind, flabbergast. **2** *overwhelmed with work* inundate, flood, deluge, engulf, submerge, swamp, bury, overload, overburden, snow under. **3** *overwhelm the army of occupation* overpower, conquer, vanquish. *See* OVERCOME.

**overwhelming** adjective **1** *an overwhelming desire to laugh* uncontrollable, irrepressible, irresistible, overpowering. **2** *an overwhelming amount of mail* profuse, enormous, immense, inordinate, massive, huge, stupendous, prodigious, staggering, shattering; *inf.* mind-boggling, mind-blowing. **3** *the overwhelming majority* vast, massive, great, large.

**overwrought** adjective **1** *overwrought mothers* tense, agitated, nervous, on edge, edgy, keyed up, highly strung, overexcited, beside oneself, distracted, jumpy, frantic, frenzied, hysterical; *inf.* in a state, in a tizzy, uptight, wound up. **2** *overwrought designs* overornate, overelaborate, overembellished, overblown, overcharged, florid, busy, fussy, strained, contrived, overworked, baroque, rococo.

**owe** verb be in debt to, be indebted to, be in arrears to, be obligated to, be beholden to.

**own** adjective personal, individual, particular, private.

**own** verb **1** *they own three cars* possess, have, keep, retain, maintain, hold, enjoy. **2** *I own that he is right* admit, allow, concede, grant, accept, acknowledge, recognize, agree. **own up** confess, admit; *inf.* come clean.

**owner** noun possessor, holder, keeper; proprietor/proprietress/proprietrix, landlord, landlady; master/mistress.

# Pp

**pace** noun **1** *take one pace toward her* step, stride. **2** *walk with an ambling pace* gait, walk, tread. **3** *unable to keep up with the pace of the race* speed, swiftness, quickness, rapidity, velocity, tempo; *inf.* clip. **4** *the fast/slow pace of life there* tempo, momentum, measure.

**pacific** adjective **1** *a pacific nation* peace-loving, peaceable, pacifist, nonviolent, non-aggressive, nonbelligerent, noncombative, dovish. **2** *pacific waters* calm, still, motion-less, smooth, tranquil, peaceful, placid, unruffled, undisturbed.

**pacify** verb calm, calm down, placate, con-ciliate, propitiate, appease, mollify, soothe, tranquilize, quieten.

**pack** noun **1** *carry a pack on his back* bag, backpack, rucksack, knapsack, haversack, duffel bag, kitbag, bundle, parcel, bale, truss; *inf.* bindle. **2** *buy a pack of cigarettes* packet, container, package, carton. **3** *a pack of animals* herd, drove, flock, troop. **4** *a pack of thieves* gang, crowd, mob, group, band, company, troop, set, clique; *inf.* crew, bunch. **5** *a pack of lies* collection, parcel, assortment, mass, assemblage, bunch; *inf.* load, heap.

**pack** verb **1** *pack a suitcase* fill, load, bun-dle, stuff, cram. **2** *pack clothes in a suitcase* put, place, store, stow. **3** *pack the glass in straw* package, wrap, wrap up, box, bale, cover, protect. **4** *people packing the stadium* fill, crowd, throng, mob, cram, jam, press into, squeeze into. **5** *snow packed by the wind against the wall* compact, compress, press, tamp, ram. **pack in 1** *a show that has been packing them in for years* draw in, pull in, attract, fill the theater (etc.) with. **2** *pack in one's job* resign, leave, give up, abandon; *inf.* chuck. **pack up 1** *pack up one's equipment* put away, tidy up, clear up, store. **2** *decided to pack up for the day* fin-ish, leave off, halt, stop, cease; *inf.* call it a day, pack it in.

**package** noun **1** *a Christmas package* par-cel, packet, container, box, carton. **2** *agree to some items but not the (whole) pack-age* lot, combination; agreement, contract, arrangement, deal.

**package** verb *package the gift* pack, pack up, wrap, wrap up, gift-wrap, box.

**packet** noun pack, carton, box, container, package, parcel.

**pact** noun agreement, treaty, deal, contract, settlement, bargain, compact, covenant, bond, concordat, entente, protocol.

**pad** noun **1** *a pad to prevent friction* padding, wadding, wad, stuffing, buffer. **2** *a pad to rest one's head on* cushion, pillow, bolster. **3** *write one's notes in a pad* notepad, writing pad, notebook; *inf.* memo pad.

**pad** verb *pad the package with tissue paper* pack, stuff, line, cushion, protect.

**paddle** noun *use the paddles to row ashore* oar, scull, sweep.

**paddle** verb *paddle one's way to the shore* row, pull, oar, scull, pole, punt.

**pagan** noun nonbeliever; heathen, infidel, idolater; pantheist, atheist, polytheist.

**pagan** adjective paganistic, heathen, hea-thenish, infidel, idolatrous, pantheistic, atheistic, polytheistic.

**page** noun **1** *a report 20 pages long* sheet, side, leaf, folio. **2** *his bravery will be recorded in the pages of history* report, account, anec-dote, book, volume, writing. **3** *a glorious page in American history* chapter, event, epi-sode, incident, time, period, stage, phase, epoch, era, point.

**pageant** noun display, spectacle, extrava-ganza, show, parade, scene, representation, tableau.

**pageantry** noun display, spectacle, magnifi-cence, pomp, splendor, grandeur, glam-our, flourish, glitter, theatricality, show, showiness; *inf.* pizazz.

**pain** noun **1** *a pain in her leg* soreness, hurt, ache, aching, throb, throbbing, smarting, twinge, pang, spasm, cramp, discomfort, irritation, tenderness. **2** *invalids enduring pain* suffering, agony, affliction, torture, torment. **3** *the pain of losing a loved one* hurt, sorrow, grief, heartache, sadness, distress, misery, wretchedness, anguish, woe. **4** *that job/person is a pain* nuisance, pest, bother, vexation, worry, source of aggravation; *inf.* pain in the neck, drag.

**pain** verb **1** *the memory of the event still pains her* hurt, grieve, sadden, distress, afflict, torment, torture. **2** *it pained him to tell him to go* worry, distress, trouble, hurt, vex, embarrass.

**painful** adjective **1** *a painful arm* sore, hurt-ing, aching, throbbing, smarting, cramped, tender, inflamed, irritating, agonizing, ex-cruciating. **2** *endure a painful experience* disagreeable, unpleasant, nasty, distress-ing, disquieting, disturbing, miserable, agonizing, harrowing. **3** *a painful climb* arduous, laborious, strenuous, rigorous, demanding, exacting, trying, hard, tough, difficult. **4** *it was painful to watch him work so slowly* irksome, tedious, annoying, vexatious.

**painkiller** noun *take painkillers for headaches* analgesic, anodyne, palliative, lenitive; aspirin, acetaminophen, ibuprofen, codeine, morphine.

**painstaking** adjective careful, thorough, assiduous, conscientious, meticulous, punctilious, sedulous, scrupulous.

**paint** noun **1** *buy paint for the walls* coloring, colorant, tint, dye, stain, pigment, gloss (paint), semigloss (paint), enamel, latex (paint), wash, whitewash. **2** *the paint required for his picture* colorant, tint, pigment, watercolor, oil, oil paint. **3** *apply paint to her face* makeup, cosmetic, greasepaint, maquillage; *inf.* warpaint.

**paint** verb **1** *paint the walls* decorate, color, tint, dye, stain, whitewash. **2** *paint slogans on the walls* daub, smear, plaster, spraypaint. **3** *painted the scene from her window* portray, depict, delineate, draw, sketch, represent. **paint the town red** celebrate; *inf.* go out on the town, whoop it up, carouse, party, step out.

**painting** noun picture, illustration, portrayal, depiction, delineation, representation, likeness, drawing, sketch, portrait, landscape, seascape, still life, oil painting, watercolor; *inf.* oil.

**pair** noun **1** *the pair walked down the road* twosome, two, couple, duo. **2** *a pair of pheasants* brace, couple. **3** *a pair of gloves* matched set, matching set. **4** *a coach and pair* team, yoke, span, two horses. **5** *the happy pair after their wedding* married couple, couple, husband and wife, partners, lovers.

**pair** verb **pair off** *pair off the children for games* arrange/group in pairs, pair up, put together. **pair up** *we paired up to search for clues* join up, link up, team up, unite, form a partnership.

**pal** noun friend, mate, companion, crony, comrade; *inf.* chum, buddy.

**palace** noun royal residence, castle; château, mansion, villa.

**palatial** adjective luxurious, deluxe, imposing, splendid, grand, magnificent, stately, majestic, opulent, sumptuous, plush; *inf.* posh.

**pale** adjective **1** *a pale complexion* white, white-faced, colorless, anemic, wan, drained, pallid, pasty, ashen, waxen. **2** *pale colors* light, light-colored, pastel, muted, low-key, restrained, faded, bleached, washed-out. **3** *the pale light of dawn* dim, faint, weak, feeble, thin.

**pale** verb **1** *she paled at the gruesome sight* blanch, grow pale, lose color. **2** *other problems paled beside their financial difficulties* fade, dim, diminish, lessen, lose significance.

**pall** verb lose its (etc.) interest, lose attraction, cloy, become tedious, become boring, grow tiresome.

**pall** noun **1** *a pall of darkness* shroud, mantle, cloak. **2** *the news cast a pall over the gathering* cloud, shadow, gloom, depression, melancholy, somberness, gravity.

**pallid** adjective **1** *pallid faces* pale, white, white-faced, colorless, anemic, wan, drained, pasty, peaked, ashen, waxen, sickly, ghostly, ghastly, lurid, like death. **2** *a pallid performance* colorless, uninteresting, dull, boring, tedious, unimaginative, lifeless, uninspired, spiritless, bland, vapid.

**pallor** noun paleness, whiteness, wanness, pallidness, pastiness, ashenness, sickliness, ghastliness, luridness.

**palpable** adjective **1** *a palpable swelling* tangible, feelable, touchable, solid, concrete. **2** *a palpable error* obvious, apparent, clear, plain, evident, manifest, visible, conspicuous, patent, blatant, glaring, definite, unmistakable.

**palpitate** verb **1** *with her heart palpitating* pulsate, pulse, throb, flutter, quiver, vibrate, pound, thud, thump, pump. **2** *palpitating with fear* tremble, quiver, quake, quaver, shake.

**paltry** adjective **1** *a paltry sum of money* small, meager, trifling, minor, insignificant, trivial, derisory; *inf.* piddling. **2** *a paltry excuse/trick* mean, low, base, worthless, despicable, contemptible, miserable, wretched, sorry.

**pamper** verb spoil, cosset, indulge, overindulge, humor, coddle, mollycoddle, baby.

**pamphlet** noun leaflet, booklet, brochure, circular, flyer.

**pan** noun **1** *pans simmering on the stove* saucepan, pot, frying pan, skillet, kettle, pressure cooker, casserole, wok. **2** *put a pan under the leak* container, vessel, receptacle.

**panacea** noun cure-all, elixir, nostrum, universal cure, universal remedy.

**pancake** noun hotcake, flapjack, griddle cake; crêpe, blintz; tortilla.

**pandemonium** noun uproar, tumult, turmoil, commotion, clamor, din, hullabaloo, hubbub, hue and cry, chaos, confusion, disorder, bedlam.

**pang** noun **1** *hunger pang* pain, twinge, spasm, ache. **2** *feel a pang of remorse* twinge, qualm, sensation.

**panic** noun alarm, fright, fear, terror, horror, trepidation, nervousness, agitation, hysteria, perturbation, dismay, disquiet.

**panic** verb **1** *panic at the sight of smoke* be alarmed, take fright, be scared, be terrified, be agitated, be hysterical, lose one's nerve, overreact, go to pieces; *inf.* lose one's cool, get the jitters, get/go into a tizzy. **2** *the crowd was panicked into a stampede* alarm, frighten, scare, terrify, petrify, startle, agitate, unnerve.

**panorama** noun **1** *the panorama from the top of the tower* view, vista, spectacle, aerial view, bird's-eye view. **2** *a panorama of political events* survey, overview, perspective, appraisal.

**pant** verb **1** *panting after climbing the hill* puff, huff and puff, blow, gasp, wheeze. **2** *panting for water/knowledge* long, yearn, pine, ache, hunger, thirst, burn; *inf.* have a yen.

**pants** plural noun trousers, slacks, jeans, blue jeans; Levis (*trademark*); *inf.* cords.

**paper** noun **1** *go for the morning paper* newspaper, journal, gazette, tabloid, scandal sheet, daily, weekly; *inf.* rag. **2** *lost the mortgage papers* legal paper, document, certificate, record, deed, instrument, assignment. **3** *write a paper on child development* essay, article, work, dissertation, treatise, thesis, monograph, study, report, analysis. **4** *put striped paper on the walls/shelves* wallpaper, wall covering, shelf paper. **on paper 1** *put your objections on paper* in writing, written down, in black and white. **2** *the plan was good only on paper* in theory, theoretically, hypothetically, in the abstract.

**papers** plural noun **1** *sign the adoption papers* document, certificate. *See* PAPER noun 2. **2** *escape using forged papers* identification papers, identification documents, identity card, ID. **3** *go through her papers after her death* personal papers, personal documents, letters, records, files.

**par** noun average, mean, standard, normal, norm. **below par** below average, substandard, inferior, lacking, wanting, second-rate, poor; *inf.* not up to scratch, not up to snuff. **on a par with** equal to, a match for, on a level with, on an equal footing with, of the same standard as, as good as. **par for the course** usual, normal, standard, typical, predictable, what one would expect. **up to par** satisfactory, acceptable, good enough, adequate, passable; *inf.* up to scratch, up to snuff.

**parable** noun allegory, morality tale/story, fable, lesson.

**parade** noun *parade of soldiers | Memorial Day parade* march, procession, progression, cavalcade, spectacle, pageant, array.

**parade** verb **1** *soldiers parading during the celebrations* march, go in columns, file by. **2** *parade their wealth/knowledge* display,

exhibit, show, demonstrate, air, make a show of, flaunt; *inf.* show off. **3** *parade up and down in her new hat* strut, swagger.

**paradise** noun **1** *believe in paradise after death* heaven, heavenly kingdom, kingdom of heaven, Elysium, the Elysian fields. **2** *Adam and Eve in paradise* the Garden of Eden, Eden. **3** *the resort island is a paradise* Eden, fairyland, Utopia, Shangri-la. **4** *it was paradise to be in love* heaven, bliss, ecstasy, seventh heaven.

**paradox** noun contradiction, self-contradiction, inconsistency, incongruity, anomaly, enigma, puzzle, absurdity, oxymoron.

**paragon** noun *a paragon of good behavior* ideal, model, pattern, exemplar, nonpareil, paradigm, standard, criterion, archetype, prototype, quintessence, epitome, apotheosis, acme.

**parallel** adjective **1** *parallel lines* side by side, equidistant, collateral. **2** *the judge considering a parallel case* similar, like, resembling, analogous, comparable, equivalent, corresponding, matching, duplicate. **3** *parallel processes* concurrent, coexistent, coexisting.

**parallel** noun **1** *find a parallel for the case* analog, counterpart, equivalent, correspondent, match, duplicate, equal. **2** *draw a parallel between the two cases* similarity, likeness, resemblance, analogy, correspondence, comparison, equivalence, symmetry.

**parallel** verb **1** *the case parallels the murder of her neighbor* resemble, be similar to, be like, bear a resemblance to, be analogous to, correspond to, compare with, be comparable/equivalent to. **2** *his account of the incident parallels the policeman's* match, correspond to, agree with, be in harmony with, conform to. **3** *his rowing feat has never been paralleled* match, equal, rival, emulate.

**paralyze** verb **1** *the spider's poison paralyzed the fly | he was paralyzed in the accident* immobilize, render/make powerless, numb, deaden, incapacitate, debilitate, disable, cripple. **2** *paralyze the transport system* immobilize, bring to a halt, bring to a standstill, freeze, put out of order/commission. **3** *paralyzed with fear* immobilize, render motionless, freeze, unnerve, terrify, shock, stun.

**parameter** noun *within the parameters of the budget* limit, limitation, limiting factor, restriction, constant, specification, guidelines, framework.

**paramount** adjective *financial considerations are paramount* most important, of greatest importance, of greatest significance, uppermost, supreme, predominant, foremost, first and foremost, preeminent, outstanding.

**paramour** noun lover, illicit lover; mistress, girlfriend, kept woman, inamorata; boyfriend, inamorato; *inf.* boy toy.

**paranoid** adjective suspicious, mistrustful, distrustful, fearful, insecure.

**parapet** noun 1 *the parapet of a balcony* wall, railing, handrail, fence, barrier. 2 *soldiers sheltering behind the parapet* fortification, barricade, rampart, bulwark, bank, embankment.

**paraphernalia** plural noun 1 *the artist's paraphernalia* equipment, gear, stuff, apparatus, implements, tools, materials, accoutrements, trappings, appurtenances. 2 *loaded down with all her paraphernalia* baggage, luggage, personal belongings, belongings, possessions, things, impedimenta; *inf.* stuff.

**paraphrase** verb reword, put in other words, rephrase, restate, rehash, interpret, gloss.

**parasite** noun hanger-on, sponge, sponger, cadger, leech, bloodsucker, drone; *inf.* scrounge, scrounger, freeloader.

**parcel** noun 1 *tie the parcel with string* package, packet, pack, bundle. 2 *a parcel of land* plot, tract, piece, lot, patch. 3 *a parcel of lies* pack, collection, assortment, mass, assemblage, bunch; *inf.* heap, load.

**parcel** verb **parcel out** *parcel out the food to the needy* distribute, dispense, allocate, allot, portion out, apportion, mete out, divide out, share out, hand out, deal out, dole out, carve up; *inf.* divvy up.

**parched** adjective 1 *parched ground/grass* dry, baked, burned, scorched, seared, desiccated, dehydrated, withered, shriveled, dried up, dried out. 2 *parched from walking in the heat* thirsty, dehydrated; *inf.* dry.

**pardon** noun 1 *seek their pardon* forgiveness, forbearance, indulgence, clemency, lenience, leniency, mercy. 2 *the accused received a pardon* reprieve, release, acquittal, absolution, amnesty, exoneration, exculpation.

**pardon** verb 1 *pardon me | could never pardon such an offense* forgive, excuse, condone, let off. 2 *the accused man was pardoned* reprieve, release, acquit, absolve, exonerate, exculpate.

**parent** noun 1 *resembles his parent* mother; father; procreator, progenitor, ancestor. 2 *the parent of all his misfortune* source, root, origin, originator, wellspring, fountain, cause, author, architect.

**parentage** noun *of humble parentage* family, birth, origins, extraction, ancestry, lineage, descent, heritage, pedigree.

**pariah** noun *a social pariah* outcast, leper, *persona non grata*, untouchable, undesirable.

**parish** noun 1 *local administrators of the parish* county, community, district; canton. 2 *the parish choosing a new minister* congregation, parishioners, churchgoers, flock, fold.

**park** noun 1 *children playing in the park* public park, green, recreation ground, playground, play area. 2 *park surrounding the estate* parkland, grassland, lawns, grounds. 3 *few fans left in the park* stadium, arena, ballpark, ball field, field, playing field.

**parliament** noun legislative assembly, legislature, lawmaking body, congress, senate, chamber, house, convocation, diet.

**parliamentary** adjective 1 *parliamentary assemblies* legislative, legislatorial, lawmaking, lawgiving, governmental, congressional, senatorial, democratic, representative. 2 *parliamentary behavior/language* orderly, proper, seemly, by the rules, according to the rule book.

**parlor** noun 1 *a beauty parlor* salon, shop, establishment, store. 2 *have tea in the parlor* sitting room, living room, drawing room, lounge.

**parochial** adjective *a parochial attitude to life* provincial, small-town, insular, narrow, narrow-minded, petty, small-minded, limited, restricted.

**parody** noun 1 *a parody of a Gothic novel* burlesque, lampoon, satire, caricature, mimicry, takeoff; *inf.* spoof, send-up. 2 *trial was a parody of justice* travesty, poor imitation, misrepresentation, perversion, corruption.

**parody** verb *parody an operatic aria* lampoon, satirize, caricature, burlesque, mimic; *inf.* send up.

**parrot** verb repeat, echo, copy, imitate, mimic, ape.

**parry** verb 1 *parry a blow* avert, deflect, block, rebuff, repel, repulse, ward off, fend off, stave off, turn aside, hold at bay. 2 *parry awkward questions* avoid, dodge, evade, elude, sidestep, circumvent; *inf.* duck.

**part** noun 1 *the early part of her life | part of an orange* portion, division, section, segment, bit, piece, fragment, scrap, slice, fraction, chunk, wedge. 2 *spare parts* component, bit, constituent, element, module. 3 *parts of the body* organ, member, limb. 4 *an unknown part of the country* area, region, sector, quarter, territory, neighborhood. 5 *a book/play in several parts* volume, book, episode. 6 *his part in the project* function, role, job, task, responsibility, capacity, participation, duty, charge. **7** *play the part of Hamlet* role, character. **8** *learn his part* lines, words, script, lyrics. **in part** *success due in part to good luck* partly, partially, to a certain extent/degree, to some extent/degree, somewhat, in some measure. **on the part of** *an error on the part of the instructor* made by, done by, carried out by, caused by, by. **take part in** *take part in the protest* participate in, join (in), engage in, play a part in, contribute to, associate oneself with, be involved in/with, share in, have a hand in. **take someone's part, take the part of** *take his mother's part in the quarrel | take the part of weaker candidates* take the side of, side with, support, lend/give support to, back, back up, abet.

**part** verb **1** *the crowd parted to let the police through* divide, separate, split, break up, disjoin. **2** *the police parting the crowd* divide, separate, split up, break up, sever, cleave. **3** *couples deciding to part* separate, split up, break up, part company, go their (etc.) separate ways, divorce, get divorced. **4** *exchange kisses before parting* take one's departure, take one's leave, leave, go, go away, say good-bye/farewell/adieu. **part with** *part with her last few dollars* give up, relinquish, forgo, surrender, let go of, renounce, sacrifice, yield, cede.

**partake** verb **partake of 1** *partake of Christmas cheer* consume, eat, take, receive, drink, share in. **2** *their manner partook of insolence* suggest, have the qualities/attributes of, hint at, evidence, demonstrate, exhibit, show.

**partial** adjective **1** *a partial solution/eclipse* limited, incomplete, imperfect, fragmentary. **2** *a partial witness* biased, prejudiced, partisan, colored, one-sided, discriminatory, preferential, unjust, unfair, inequitable. **be partial to** *be partial to dark chocolate* have a liking for, like, love, be fond of, be keen on, have a weakness/taste for, have a soft spot for, have a predilection/proclivity/penchant for.

**partiality** noun **1** *condemn the partiality of the judge* bias, prejudice, partisanship, discrimination, preference, favoritism, unjustness, unfairness, inequity. **2** *their partiality for chocolate* liking, love, fondness, keenness, taste, weakness, soft spot, inclination, predilection, proclivity, penchant.

**partially** adverb partly, in part, somewhat, not wholly, not fully, half, to a certain extent/degree, to some extent/degree, fractionally, slightly.

**participant** noun participator, member, contributor, associate, sharer, partaker.

**participate** verb **participate in** take part in, join in, engage in, play a part in,

contribute to, associate oneself with, be involved in, share in, have a hand in.

**participation** noun part, contribution, association, involvement, partaking.

**particle** noun **1** *particles of dust* speck, spot, mote, atom, molecule. **2** *not a particle of common sense* iota, jot, whit, grain, bit, scrap, shred, morsel, mite, atom, hint, touch, trace, suggestion.

**particular** adjective **1** *in this particular case* specific, individual, single, distinct, precise. **2** *a matter of particular importance* special, especial, singular, peculiar, exceptional, unusual, uncommon, notable, noteworthy, remarkable, outstanding. **3** *particular about hygiene/food* fastidious, discriminating, selective, fussy, painstaking, meticulous, punctilious, exacting, demanding, critical, finicky; *inf.* persnickety, choosy, picky. **4** *require a particular account of the incident* detailed, exact, precise, faithful, close, thorough, blow-by-blow, itemized, painstaking, meticulous, punctilious, minute.

**particularly** adverb **1** *a book that is particularly good* especially, specially, singularly, peculiarly, distinctly, markedly, exceptionally, unusually, uncommonly, notably, remarkably, outstandingly, surprisingly. **2** *ask for him particularly* in particular, specifically, explicitly, expressly, specially, especially.

**partisan** noun **1** *a partisan of the breakaway party* supporter, adherent, devotee, backer, champion, upholder, follower, disciple, fan, votary. **2** *partisans fighting against the ruling power* guerrilla, resistance fighter, underground fighter.

**partisan** adjective *a partisan attitude to the legal dispute* biased, prejudiced, colored, one-sided, discriminatory, preferential, partial, unjust, unfair, inequitable.

**partition** noun **1** *the partition of Germany* division, subdivision, separation, splitting-up, breakup, severance. **2** *erect a partition to divide the room* divider, dividing wall, screen, barrier, wall, fence.

**partition** verb **1** *the Allies partitioned Germany* divide up, separate, split up, break up, sever. **2** *partition the room to make two sleeping areas* divide, divide up, subdivide, separate.

**partly** adverb in part, partially, somewhat, not wholly, not fully, half, to a certain extent/degree, to some extent/degree, in some measure, fractionally, slightly.

**partner** noun **1** *his partner in business* associate, colleague, coworker, teammate, collaborator, ally, comrade, consociate. **2** *his partner in crime* accomplice, confederate, accessory, collaborator, fellow conspirator; *inf.* sidekick. **3** *bring your partner* *to the party* wife/husband, spouse, mate, companion, girlfriend/boyfriend; date.

**partnership** noun **1** *work in partnership with his brother* association, cooperation, collaboration, alliance, union, fellowship, companionship. **2** *a partnership in crime* collusion, connivance, conspiracy. **3** *the partnership was bought out* company, firm, corporation, cooperative, conglomerate, syndicate.

**party** noun **1** *invite guests to a party* social gathering, social function, reception, celebration, festivity, soirée, orgy, bacchanal; *inf.* get-together, bash, shindig. **2** *a hunting/search party* group, band, company, squad, team, crew, contingent, detachment, unit. **3** *belong to a left-wing party* alliance, affiliation, association, caucus. **4** *both parties declared that they were right* side, faction, camp, set. **5** *a certain party who shall be nameless* person, individual, somebody, someone; *inf.* character.

**pass**¹ verb **1** *traffic passing along the road* go, move, proceed, progress, run, travel, roll, flow, course. **2** *cars passing us* overtake, outstrip, outdistance. **3** *pass the frontier* cross, traverse, go across, get through. **4** *pass the butter* hand over, give, transfer. **5** *the title passes to his eldest son* be transferred, be turned over, be signed over, go, devolve. **6** *time passed slowly* go by, proceed, progress, advance, roll by, slip by, glide by, flow by, elapse. **7** *how to pass the time* spend, occupy, fill, take up, use, employ, while away. **8** *pass all understanding* exceed, surpass, transcend. **9** *let the matter pass* go, go unheeded, go unnoticed, go unremarked, go undisputed, go uncensored. **10** *students passing their exams* get a passing grade in, get through, succeed in, meet the requirements of, pass muster in. **11** *the examiners passed everyone* let through, declare acceptable/adequate/satisfactory, accept, approve. **12** *pass the motion* accept, approve, adopt, authorize, ratify, sanction, validate, legalize. **13** *pass judgment* pronounce, utter, express, deliver, declare. **14** *after all that has passed* happen, occur, take place, befall, supervene. **15** *the storm passed* blow over, run its course, ebb, die out, fade away, evaporate, disappear, finish, end, terminate. **16** *pass urine* discharge, excrete, eliminate, evacuate, expel, emit. **pass for** *he could pass for 30* be taken for, be regarded as, be mistaken for. **pass off 1** *the demonstration passed off without incident* take place, happen, occur, be completed. **2** *pass him off as her husband* present as genuine, give a false identity, have accepted as genuine.

**pass out 1** *passing out in the heat* faint, collapse, lose consciousness, black out, keel over, swoon. **2** *pass out the exam papers* hand out, distribute, give out, deal out, dole out, allot, allocate. **pass over 1** *pass over the interruption and proceed* ignore, disregard, overlook, forget, pay no attention to, gloss over, take no notice of, turn a blind eye to. **2** *he was passed over for promotion* overlook, ignore, disregard, forget, neglect, omit. **pass up** *pass up an opportunity* fail to take advantage of, waive, reject, refuse, decline, neglect, let slip, ignore, brush aside, forgo.

**pass**² noun **1** *a pass to leave the military base* warrant, permit, authorization, license, passport, visa, safe-conduct. **2** *a pass to the theater* permit, free admission, complimentary ticket; *inf.* freebie. **3** *object to his passes* sexual advance, advance, overture; *inf.* proposition. **make a pass at** *make a pass at his friend's wife* make sexual advances/overtures to; *inf.* make a play for, proposition.

**pass**³ noun *a mountain pass* gap, gorge, defile, col, canyon.

**passable** adjective **1** *a passable knowledge of the subject* adequate, tolerable, fair, acceptable, satisfactory, mediocre, middling, ordinary, average, run-of-the-mill, unexceptional, indifferent; *inf.* so-so, OK. **2** *roads scarcely passable in the snow* crossable, traversable, navigable, unblocked, unobstructed, open, clear.

**passage** noun **1** *the passage of time* passing, progress, advance, flow, course. **2** *passage through foreign lands* journey, voyage, transit, trek, crossing, trip, tour. **3** *denied passage to the country* access, entry, admission, safe-conduct, warrant, passport, visa. **4** *his passage from boyhood to manhood* change, changeover, transformation, transition, conversion, shift, switch. **5** *underground passages* road, route, path, way, track, trail, lane, channel, course, conduit. **6** *bicycles left in the passage* passageway, corridor, hall, hallway, vestibule. **7** *read aloud passages from the novel* extract, excerpt, quotation, citation, section, verse. **8** *the passage of the bill by Congress* acceptance, approval, adoption, authorization, ratification, sanction, validation, enactment, legalization.

**passé** adjective out-of-date, outdated, dated, outmoded, old-fashioned, obsolete, obsolescent, out of fashion, out of style, archaic, antiquated, antediluvian; *inf.* old hat, fuddy-duddy.

**passenger** noun rider, commuter, farepayer, traveler, fare.

**passion** noun **1** *do everything with great passion* intensity, fervor, fervidness, ardor, zeal, vehemence, fire, emotion, feeling, zest, enthusiasm, eagerness, excitement, animation. **2** *fly into a passion* rage, blind rage, fit of anger, temper, tantrum, fury, frenzy, paroxysm. **3** *his passion for her* love, desire, lust, concupiscence, ardor, infatuation. **4** *a passion for motorcycles* enthusiasm, fascination, keen interest, obsession, fixation, craze, mania.

**passionate** adjective **1** *a passionate entreaty/person* impassioned, intense, fervent, fervid, ardent, zealous, vehement, fiery, emotional, heartfelt, zestful, enthusiastic, eager, excited, animated. **2** *a passionate lover* ardent, aroused, desirous, hot, sexy, amorous, sensual, erotic, lustful; *inf.* turned-on.

**passive** adjective **1** *play a passive role in the business* inactive, nonactive, inert, nonparticipating, uninvolved. **2** *a passive attitude to their invaders* unresisting, nonresistant, unassertive, yielding, submissive, compliant, pliant, acquiescent, quiescent, resigned, obedient, tractable, malleable. **3** *look on with a passive expression | a passive person* impassive, emotionless, unmoved, unresponsive, undemonstrative, dispassionate, detached, distant, remote, aloof, indifferent.

**password** noun watchword, keyword, signal, word, open sesame, shibboleth.

**past** adjective **1** *in times past* gone by, gone, bygone, elapsed, over, ended, former, long ago. **2** *the past few months* recent, preceding, last, latter, foregone. **3** *past achievements/chairmen* former, previous, prior, foregoing, late, erstwhile, one-time, sometime, ex-.

**past** noun **in the past** in days gone by, in bygone days, in former times, formerly, previously, before.

**pastel** adjective *pastel colors* pale, soft, delicate, muted, subdued, faint, low-key.

**pastime** noun hobby, leisure activity, game, recreation, diversion, amusement, entertainment, distraction, relaxation.

**pastor** noun minister, vicar, parson, priest, rector, reverend, clergyman, clergywoman, churchman, churchwoman, ecclesiastic, cleric, divine.

**pastoral** adjective **1** *a pastoral scene* rural, country, rustic, simple, idyllic, innocent, Arcadian, bucolic, georgic. **2** *his pastoral duties* ministerial, vicarial, parsonical, priestly, rectorial, ecclesiastical, clerical.

**pastry** noun pie, strudel, tart, puff pastry, doughnut, cruller, Danish pastry; *inf.* Danish.

**pat** verb **1** *pat the child on the head | pat the dog* stroke, caress, pet. **2** *pat the mixture* tap, slap, dab. **pat someone on the back** *pat himself on the back for bringing off the deal* congratulate, praise, commend, compliment, applaud.

**pat** noun **1** *a pat on the cheek* stroke, touch, caress. **2** *flatten the mixture with a pat* tap,

slap, dab. **3** *a pat of butter* dab, lump, cake, portion.

**patch** noun **1** *put a patch over the hole* piece of cloth, scrap, piece of material. **2** *a patch over the eye* cover, covering, pad, shield. **3** *patch of ground* plot, area, piece, lot, tract, parcel.

**patch** verb **1** *patch the pants* cover, mend, repair, sew, sew up, stitch, stitch up. **2** *patch the roof* repair, reinforce, fix. **patch up** *patch up the quarrel* settle, resolve, set right.

**patchwork** noun *a patchwork of different styles* pastiche, hodgepodge, mishmash, jumble, medley, mélange, miscellany, potpourri, mosaic, blend, mixture.

**patent** noun license, copyright, registered trademark.

**patent** adjective **1** *her patent dislike of him* obvious, clear, plain, evident, apparent, manifest, transparent, conspicuous, blatant, unmistakable, unconcealed. **2** *patent medicine* patented, proprietary, licensed, branded, brand-name.

**paternal** adjective **1** *take a paternal interest in the boy* fatherly, fatherlike, patriarchal, protective, concerned, solicitous, kindly, benevolent. **2** *his paternal grandfather* patrilineal, patrimonial, on the father's side.

**path** noun **1** *a path through the forest* footpath, track, trail, walk, walkway. **2** *the moon's path around the earth* course, route, circuit, track, orbit, trajectory. **3** *unable to predict the path he will take* course of action, procedure, direction, approach, method, system, strategy. **4** *the path to success* way, road, avenue, route.

**pathetic** adjective **1** *children in rags were a pathetic sight* pitiful, pitiable, piteous, moving, touching, poignant, affecting, distressing, heartbreaking, heart-rending, sad, wretched, mournful, woeful. **2** *a pathetic attempt/performance* pitiful, lamentable, deplorable, miserable, wretched, feeble, woeful, sorry, poor, contemptible, inadequate, unsatisfactory, worthless.

**pathological** adjective **1** *a pathological condition* morbid, diseased. **2** *a pathological liar* irrational, compulsive, obsessive.

**pathos** noun poignancy, pity, piteousness, sadness, plaintiveness, sentiment, compassion.

**patience** noun **1** *wait in line with patience* calmness, composure, even-temperedness, equanimity, serenity, tranquillity, restraint, imperturbability, tolerance, indulgence, forbearance, resignation, stoicism, fortitude; *inf.* unflappability, cool. **2** *a task requiring patience* perseverance, persistence, endurance, tenacity, assiduity, diligence, staying power, indefatigability, doggedness.

**patient** adjective uncomplaining, serene, calm, composed, even-tempered, tranquil, restrained, imperturbable, inexcitable, tolerant, accommodating, long-suffering, forbearing, indulgent, resigned, stoical; *inf.* unflappable, cool.

**patio** noun terrace, veranda, deck, piazza.

**patriotic** adjective nationalistic, loyal, chauvinistic, flag-waving, jingoistic.

**patrol** verb *soldiers patrolling the border area* monitor, watch, make the rounds of, guard, range, police, keep watch on, keep guard on.

**patrol** noun **1** *make regular patrols of the border area* round, sentry duty, policing, watch, guard, vigil, monitoring. **2** *report the matter to the patrol* sentinel, sentry, garrison, guard, watchman, watch, policeman/policewoman.

**patron** noun **1** *a patron of the arts* sponsor, backer, benefactor/benefactress, promoter, friend, helper, supporter, upholder, champion, protector; *inf.* angel. **2** *parking for patrons only* customer, client, frequenter, shopper, buyer, purchaser; *inf.* regular.

**patronage** noun **1** *customers taking their patronage elsewhere* trade, custom, business, commerce, shopping, buying, purchasing. **2** *their patronage of the arts* sponsorship, backing, funding, financing, promotion, help, aid, assistance, support, encouragement, championship. **3** *under the patronage of the crime boss* power of appointment, aegis, protection.

**patronize** verb **1** *patronize her subordinates* condescend to, look down on, talk down to, treat with condescension/disdain, treat contemptuously, be snobbish to. **2** *patronize the new salon* frequent, shop at, buy from, be a customer of, be a client of, do business with. **3** *patronize the arts* sponsor, back, fund, finance, promote, help, aid, assist, support, encourage, champion, protect.

**patronizing** adjective *a patronizing attitude to younger people* condescending, supercilious, superior, haughty, lofty, lordly, disdainful, scornful, contemptuous, snobbish; *inf.* uppity, snooty.

**patter** verb **1** *mice pattering across the attic floor* scurry, scuttle, trip. **2** *rain pattering on the window* pitter-patter, tap, drum, beat, pound, pelt.

**patter** noun **1** *the patter of mice on the floor above* scurrying, scuttling, tripping. **2** *the patter of rain on the window* pitter-patter, tap, tapping, drumming, beat, beating, pounding, rat-a-tat.

**pattern** noun **1** *the pattern on the wallpaper* design, decoration, motif, marking, ornamentation, device, figure. **2** *study the rats' behavior pattern* system,

order, arrangement, method, sequence. **3** *a knitting pattern* guide, blueprint, model, plan, template, stencil, instructions.

**pattern** verb *pattern himself on his father* model, mold, style, form, shape.

**paucity** noun *a paucity of evidence* scarcity, sparseness, dearth, shortage, insufficiency, deficiency, lack, want, meagerness, paltriness.

**paunch** noun **1** *developing quite a paunch* potbelly, protruding stomach/abdomen, pot; *inf.* beer belly. **2** *a belt around his paunch* stomach, belly, abdomen; *inf.* gut.

**pauper** noun beggar, mendicant, down-and-out, penniless person, homeless person.

**pause** noun break, interruption, lull, respite, stay, discontinuation, gap, interlude, intermission, interval, rest, delay, hesitation; *inf.* letup, breather.

**pause** verb discontinue, break, stop, halt, cease, take a break, desist, rest, hold back, delay, hesitate, waver; *inf.* let up, take a breather.

**pave** verb *pave the front path* concrete, asphalt, flag, tile, tar, macadamize. **pave the way** *pave the way for radical change* prepare, clear the way, lay the foundations/groundwork.

**pawn** verb *pawn her necklace to pay the rent* pledge, give as security, mortgage; *inf.* hock, put in hock.

**pawn** noun *pawns in the leader's struggle for power* tool, cat's-paw, instrument, puppet, dupe; *inf.* stooge.

**pay** verb **1** *pay him for work done* remunerate, reimburse, recompense, reward, indemnify, requite. **2** *pay hundreds of dollars for his services* spend, expend, lay out, part with, disburse, hand over, remit, render; *inf.* shell out, cough up. **3** *pay his debts/bill* settle, discharge, meet, clear, square, honor, liquidate, foot, defray. **4** *the business does not pay* make money, be profitable, be remunerative, make a return. **5** *investments paying large sums of money* yield, return, produce, bring in; *inf.* rake in. **6** *pay compliments* give, bestow, extend, offer, proffer, render. **7** *make him pay for his mistakes* atone, suffer, pay a penalty, make atonement. **pay back 1** *pay back the loan* repay, return, reimburse. **2** *pay her back for her cruel behavior* repay, punish, avenge oneself on, get revenge on. **pay off 1** *pay off his debts* pay in full, settle, discharge, meet, clear, square, honor, liquidate. **2** *his hard work paid off* meet with success, be successful, be effective, work, get results, be profitable.

**pay** noun *get one's pay at the end of the month* salary, wages, earnings, fee, remuneration, recompense, reimbursement, reward, stipend, emoluments.

**payable** adjective *a bill that is payable now* due, owed, owing, outstanding.

**payment** noun **1** *receive payment for his services* wages, fee. *See* PAY noun. **2** *in payment of the account* settlement, discharge, clearance, squaring, liquidation. **3** *make twelve monthly payments* installment, premium, amount, remittance.

**peace** noun **1** *the peace of the countryside* tranquillity, restfulness, calm, quiet, quietness, stillness. **2** *a mind seeking peace* peacefulness, tranquillity, serenity, calmness, composure, placidity, rest, repose, contentment. **3** *hope for peace between the countries* harmony, accord, concord, amity, goodwill, friendship, cordiality, non-aggression, nonviolence, cease-fire. **4** *the Peace of Versailles* treaty, truce, agreement, armistice, cessation of hostilities.

**peaceable** adjective **1** *a peaceable person* placid, gentle, mild, nonaggressive, nonviolent, noncombative, easygoing, good-natured, even-tempered, amiable, pacific, pacifistic, dovish, irenic. **2** *a peaceable set of negotiations* harmonious, amicable, friendly, cordial.

**peaceful** adjective **1** *in a peaceful setting* tranquil, restful, quiet, calm, still, undisturbed. **2** *a peaceful mind* tranquil, serene, calm, composed, placid, at rest, untroubled, unworried. **3** *peaceful conditions between the two countries* harmonious, amicable, friendly, cordial, nonviolent.

**peacemaker** noun *call in a third party as a peacemaker* conciliator, mediator, arbitrator, pacifier, appeaser, peacemonger.

**peak** noun **1** *snow on the mountain peaks* top, summit, crest, pinnacle. **2** *at the peak of his career as a singer* height, high point, climax, culmination, zenith, acme, meridian, apogee, apex, prime.

**peak** verb *prices peak just before Christmas* climax, culminate, crest, reach the high point.

**peaked** adjective pale, wan, drained, drawn, pallid, pasty, white, anemic.

**peal** noun *hear the peal of the bells/thunder* ring, ringing, chime, clang, resounding, reverberation, tintinnabulation, roar, boom, rumble, crash, clap.

**peal** verb *bells/thunder pealing* ring, chime, clang, resound, reverberate, roar, boom, rumble, crash.

**peasant** noun farm worker/laborer, sharecropper, peon, rustic; serf; bumpkin, provincial.

**peck** verb bite, strike, hit, tap, rap, jab.
**peck at** nibble, pick at, eat sparingly of.

**peculiar** adjective **1** *a peculiar smell | peculiar clothes* strange, odd, queer, funny, curious, unusual, abnormal, eccentric, unconventional, bizarre, weird, quaint, outlandish, offbeat. **2** *have a peculiar walk* characteristic, distinctive, individual, distinguishing, special, unique, idiosyncratic. **peculiar to** *peculiar to that period of history* belonging to, characteristic of, typical of, representative of, indicative of, exclusive to.

**peculiarity** noun **1** *the peculiarity of the smell | the peculiarity of her clothes* strangeness, oddness, queerness, curiousness, abnormality, eccentricity, unconventionality, bizarreness, weirdness, outlandishness. **2** *a peculiarity of the breed* characteristic, feature, quality, property, trait, attribute, mark, stamp, hallmark.

**pedagogue** noun **1** *learning from a pedagogue* teacher, tutor, lecturer, instructor, educator. **2** *a pedagogue without inspiration* dogmatist, pedant.

**pedant** noun perfectionist, formalist, dogmatist, literalist, precisionist, quibbler, hairsplitter, casuist, sophist, pettifogger; *inf.* nitpicker.

**pedantic** adjective precise, exact, scrupulous, punctilious, meticulous, formalist, precisionist, dogmatic, literalistic, quibbling, hairsplitting, casuistic, sophistic, pettifogging; *inf.* nitpicking.

**peddle** verb *peddle goods around town* hawk, sell, tout, market, vend; *inf.* push.

**pedestal** noun *a bust of Shakespeare on a pedestal* base, support, stand, foundation, pillar, column, plinth. **put on a pedestal** *put his father on a pedestal* idealize, exalt, glorify, adulate, worship, deify.

**pedestrian** noun walker, stroller, hiker.

**pedestrian** adjective **1** *pedestrian traffic* on foot, walking. **2** *pedestrian prose* plodding, unimaginative, uninspired, unexciting, dull, flat, prosaic, stodgy, mundane, humdrum, banal, run-of-the-mill, commonplace, ordinary, mediocre.

**pedigree** noun **1** *proud of his aristocratic pedigree* ancestry, descent, lineage, line, extraction, heritage, parentage, birth, family, strain, stock, blood, stirps. **2** *draw up the dog's pedigree* genealogy, family tree, ancestral record, line of descent.

**peek** verb peep, glance, take a stealthy look; *inf.* sneak a look.

**peek** noun peep, glance, glimpse, secret look, sneaky look.

**peel** verb *peel the fruit | peel the wallpaper from the walls* pare, skin, decorticate, strip, remove, take off.

**peel** noun *the peel of the fruit* rind, skin, covering, zest, shell, husk, epicarp.

**peep**[1] verb **1** *peep through the keyhole* peek, glance, take a secret look; *inf.* sneak a look. **2** *crocuses peeping through the snow* appear, emerge, show, come into view, spring up, pop up.

**peep**[2] noun *take a peep at the secret document* peek, glance. *See* PEEK noun.

**peep**[3] verb *fledglings peeping in the nest* cheep, chirp, chirrup, tweet, twitter, pipe, squeak.

**peep**[4] noun **1** *the peep of a baby bird* cheep, chirp, chirrup, tweet, twitter, piping, squeak. **2** *not a peep out of the children* sound, noise, cry, utterance, word.

**peer** verb *peer at the faded handwriting* squint, look closely, stare, gaze, narrow one's eyes.

**peer** noun **1** *remained close to his peers from college* compeer, associate, colleague, fellow, equal, match, like, coequal, confrère. **2** *the peers of the realm* noble, nobleman, aristocrat, lord, patrician.

**peerless** adjective *a peerless performance* incomparable, matchless, unrivaled, unsurpassed, unequaled, unparalleled, superlative, nonpareil.

**peeve** verb *his behavior really peeved her* irritate, annoy, anger, vex, provoke, upset, exasperate, irk, pique, nettle; *inf.* aggravate, miff.

**peevish** adjective irritable, fractious, cross, crabby, cranky, petulant, sulky, moody, grumpy, ill-tempered, ill-natured, ill-humored, surly, churlish, touchy, testy, snappish, crusty, splenetic.

**peg** noun pin, nail, dowel, spike, skewer, brad, screw, bolt, post. **take down a peg or two** humble, humiliate, mortify, abase.

**pejorative** adjective *pejorative remarks* derogatory, disparaging, deprecatory, slighting.

**pell-mell** adverb *children rushing pell-mell from the school* helter-skelter, headlong, impetuously, recklessly, hurriedly, hastily.

**pelt** verb *pelt the fortress with gunfire* bombard, shower, attack, assail, batter, pepper.

**pelt** noun *a beaver's pelt* skin, hide, fleece, coat, fur.

**pen** noun *put animals in a pen* enclosure, fold, coop, pound, compound, corral, paddock.

**penal** adjective **1** *a penal institution* disciplinary, punitive, corrective, retributive. **2** *a penal offense* punishable, indictable, chargeable, impeachable.

**penalize** verb **1** *penalized for arriving late* punish, discipline, castigate, correct. **2** *people penalized for being poor* handicap, disadvantage.

**penalty** noun **1** *have to pay a penalty for his crime* punishment, retribution, castigation, penance, fine, forfeit, sentence,

mulct. **2** *one of the penalties of living in the city* handicap, disadvantage, drawback, snag, obstacle.

**penance** noun atonement, reparation, amends, mortification, expiation; punishment, penalty.

**penchant** noun *a penchant for bright colors* fondness, preference, taste, partiality, soft spot, inclination, bent, proclivity, predilection, love, passion, desire, fancy, whim, weakness, liking.

**pending** adjective **1** *the lawsuit then pending* undecided, unsettled, unresolved, uncertain, awaiting action, undetermined, up in the air. **2** *a decision is pending* imminent, impending, on the way, coming, approaching, forthcoming, near, nearing, close at hand.

**penetrate** verb **1** *penetrate the skin* pierce, bore, perforate, stab, prick, gore, spike. **2** *penetrate the dense forest* enter, infiltrate. **3** *terror penetrated her whole being* permeate, pervade, fill, imbue, suffuse, saturate. **4** *our explanation did not penetrate* register, be grasped, get through, have an impact. **5** *unable to penetrate the mystery* understand, comprehend, apprehend, fathom, get to the bottom of, make out, solve, resolve, work out, figure out, unravel, decipher; *inf.* crack.

**penetrating** adjective **1** *a penetrating wind* sharp, keen, biting, stinging, harsh. **2** *a penetrating voice* shrill, loud, strong, piercing, ear-piercing, intrusive. **3** *a penetrating mind* keen, sharp, sharp-witted, discerning, perceptive, percipient, intelligent, incisive, astute, shrewd, acute, discriminating. **4** *ask penetrating questions* searching, sharp, incisive, analytic, in-depth.

**penetration** noun **1** *the penetration of the skin* piercing, perforation, pricking, stabbing. **2** *the penetration of the forest* entry, infiltration. **3** *penetration of the mystery is difficult* comprehension, apprehension, fathoming, resolution, solution, understanding; *inf.* cracking. **4** *impressed by the penetration of their minds* keenness, sharpness, sharp-wittedness, discernment, perception, perceptiveness, insight, intelligence, incisiveness, astuteness, shrewdness, acuteness, acuity, discrimination.

**penitence** noun *show penitence for his sins* repentance, contrition, compunction, regret, remorse, ruefulness, self-reproach, shame, sorrow.

**penitent** adjective *feel penitent about his sin|penitent children apologizing* repentant, contrite, regretful, remorseful, sorry, apologetic, conscience-stricken, rueful, ashamed, abject.

**pennant** noun banner, banderole, streamer, flag, ensign, colors, bunting.

**penniless** adjective impecunious, penurious, impoverished, indigent, poor, poverty-stricken, destitute, bankrupt, hard up; *inf.* broke, flat broke, strapped.

**penny-pinching** adjective mean, miserly, parsimonious, niggardly, tight-fisted, close-fisted, penurious, scrimping, skimping, close, money-grubbing, Scroogelike; *inf.* stingy, tight.

**pensive** adjective *in a pensive mood* thoughtful, reflective, contemplative, meditative, pondering, cogitative, ruminative, absorbed, preoccupied, serious, wistful, melancholy.

**pent-up** adjective *pent-up feelings* bottled-up, repressed, suppressed, restrained, constrained, curbed, bridled.

**penury** noun *unemployment reduced them to penury* indigence, destitution, privation, pennilessness, impecuniousness, impoverishment, need, want, pauperism, bankruptcy, insolvency.

**people** noun 1 *too many people in the hall/country* persons, individuals, human beings, humans, mortals, living souls. 2 *a warlike people* race, tribe, clan, nation, country, population, populace. 3 plural noun *issue to be decided by the people* citizens, general public, public, populace, electorate, masses, rank and file, commonalty, multitude, hoi polloi, rabble.

**pep** noun *a performance full of pep* spirit, liveliness, animation, life, sparkle, effervescence, verve, ebullience, vivacity, fire, dash, zest, exuberance, élan, vigor, vim, brio; *inf.* zip, oomph, pizzazz.

**perceive** verb 1 *perceive someone walking down the hill* spot, observe, glimpse, notice, make out, discern, behold, espy, detect, witness, see, catch sight of. 2 *perceive the difference between right and wrong* discern, appreciate, recognize, be cognizant of, be aware of, know, grasp, understand, comprehend, apprehend.

**perceptible** adjective *no perceptible improvement* perceivable, discernible, noticeable, detectable, distinguishable, appreciable, visible, observable, distinct, clear, plain, evident, apparent, obvious, manifest, conspicuous, patent, palpable, tangible.

**perception** noun 1 *his perception of the problem* discernment, appreciation, recognition, cognizance, awareness, consciousness, knowledge, grasp, understanding, comprehension, apprehension, notion, conception, idea, sense. 2 *show great perception in his performance \ his analysis shows great perception* perspicacity, discernment, perceptiveness, understanding, discrimination, insight, intuition, feeling, sensitivity.

**perceptive** adjective 1 *a perceptive child noticed the fire* observant, alert, sharp-eyed, sharp-sighted, keen-sighted, vigilant. 2 *one of the more perceptive theater critics / a perceptive analysis* discerning, perspicacious, percipient, shrewd, discriminating, intuitive, responsive, sensitive, penetrating, astute.

**perch** noun pole, rod, branch, roost.

**perch** verb sit, rest, roost, settle, alight, land.

**percolate** verb 1 *liquid percolating through the strainer* filter, filtrate, drain, drip, ooze, seep, leach. 2 *percolate the coffee* strain, filter, filtrate, sieve, sift. 3 *coffee percolating in the pot* brew, bubble; *inf.* perk.

**perdition** noun damnation, hellfire, hell, spiritual destruction.

**peremptory** adjective 1 *receive a peremptory request from the boss | behave in a peremptory manner* imperious, high-handed, imperative, overbearing, dogmatic, autocratic, dictatorial, domineering, arbitrary, tyrannical, despotic, arrogant, overweening, supercilious, lordly. 2 *a peremptory judgment* incontrovertible, irreversible, binding, absolute, final, conclusive, decisive, definitive, categorical, irrefutable.

**perennial** adjective *a subject of perennial interest* perpetual, everlasting, eternal, never-ending, undying, ceaseless, abiding, enduring, lasting, persisting, permanent, constant, unfailing, unchanging, continuing, persistent, recurrent.

**perfect** adjective 1 *a perfect set of china* complete, full, whole, entire. 2 *a perfect fool* absolute, complete, out-and-out, thorough, thoroughgoing, downright, utter, sheer, consummate, unmitigated, unqualified. 3 *a perfect performance/mother* flawless, faultless, unmarred, ideal, impeccable, consummate, immaculate, exemplary, superb, superlative, supreme, excellent, wonderful, model. 4 *a perfect evening* superb, exquisite, superlative, excellent, wonderful, marvelous; *inf.* terrific, fantastic, fabulous. 5 *a perfect copy* exact, precise, accurate, faithful, correct, right, close, true, strict; *inf.* right-on. 6 *the perfect present* ideal, just right, right, appropriate, fitting, fit, suitable, apt.

**perfect** verb *perfect the technique* polish, refine, elaborate, complete, make perfect, render faultless/flawless, improve, better, consummate, put the finishing touches to.

**perfection** noun 1 *working on the perfection of their technique* improvement, betterment, polishing, refinement, completion, consummation. 2 *try to achieve perfection in his work* flawlessness, faultlessness, consummation, impeccability, immaculateness, exemplariness, superbness.

**perfectionist** noun precisionist, precisian, purist, formalist, stickler for perfection.

**perfectly** adverb **1** *perfectly happy/miserable* absolutely, utterly, completely, altogether, entirely, wholly, totally, thoroughly, fully. **2** *the cake turned out perfectly* to perfection, flawlessly, faultlessly, without blemish, ideally, impeccably, immaculately, superbly, exquisitely, superlatively, wonderfully.

**perfidious** adjective treacherous, traitorous, treasonous, false, untrue, disloyal, unfaithful, deceitful, double-dealing, duplicitous, dishonest, two-faced.

**perforate** verb **1** *perforate the skin* pierce, puncture, prick, stab, gore, bore, penetrate, spike. **2** *perforate paper* make holes in, punch holes in, punch, honeycomb.

**perform** verb **1** *perform acts of charity | perform feats of skill* carry out, execute, discharge, conduct, effect, bring about, bring off, accomplish, achieve, fulfill, complete. **2** *perform in Hamlet | perform a new symphony* act, play, appear, execute. **3** *a car performing well* function, work, operate, run, go.

**performance** noun **1** *faithful in the performance of his duty* execution, discharge, conducting, effecting, accomplishment, achievement, carrying out, fulfillment. **2** *watch a musical performance* concert, show, production, entertainment, act, presentation; *inf.* gig. **3** *his performance of Hamlet* representation, acting, playing, staging.

**performer** noun **1** *applaud the performers* actor/actress, player, entertainer, artist, artiste, thespian, trouper, musician, singer, dancer. **2** *performers of charitable acts | a performer of strange feats* executor, worker, doer, operator, architect, author.

**perfume** noun **1** *the perfume of roses* scent, fragrance, aroma, smell, bouquet, redolence. **2** *buy some French perfume* scent, fragrance, balm, essence, eau de toilette, toilet water, eau de cologne, cologne.

**perfunctory** adjective *take a perfunctory look at the contract* cursory, superficial, desultory, mechanical, automatic, routine, sketchy, brief, hasty, hurried, rapid, fleeting, quick, fast, offhand, casual, indifferent, careless, inattentive, negligent.

**perhaps** adverb *perhaps we will meet him on the way* maybe, possibly, it may be that, conceivably, feasibly; *lit.* peradventure.

**peril** noun danger, jeopardy, risk, hazard, menace, threat.

**perilous** adjective dangerous, menacing, risky, precarious, hazardous, chancy, threatening, unsafe, fraught with danger.

**perimeter** noun boundary, border, frontier, limits, confines, edge, margin, fringe, periphery, circumference.

**period** noun **1** *over a period of several years* time, space, spell, interval, term, stretch, span. **2** *absent for a period* time, while, spell. **3** *the period of the French Revolution* time, days, age, era, epoch. **4** *irregular periods* menstruation, menstrual flow, monthly flow, menses.

**periodic** adjective recurrent, recurring, repeated, cyclical, cyclic, regular, intermittent, occasional, infrequent, sporadic.

**periodical** noun *subscribe to periodicals* journal, publication, magazine, newspaper, newsletter, review, organ, almanac, yearbook, annual, quarterly, monthly, weekly, daily; *inf.* paper, rag.

**peripatetic** adjective itinerant, traveling, wandering, roving, roaming, nomadic, migrant, migratory.

**periphery** noun *on the periphery of the town/group* outskirts, boundary, border, outer limits, edge, margin, fringe, perimeter.

**perish** verb **1** *soldiers perishing in battle* die, be killed, lose one's life, breathe one's last; *inf.* bite the dust, kick the bucket. **2** *the old theories having perished* die away, disappear, vanish, disintegrate, be destroyed. **3** *food perishing in the heat* rot, decay, decompose, go bad, go sour.

**perk** verb **perk up 1** *perking up when his friends arrived* cheer up, brighten up, be gladdened, rally, revive, take heart; *inf.* buck up, pep up. **2** *the vacation perked them up* cheer up, brighten up, give someone a boost/lift.

**permanent** adjective **1** *the couple's separation is permanent | a permanent disability* everlasting, perpetual, eternal, enduring, perennial, abiding, constant, persistent, unending, never-ending, immutable, unchangeable, inalterable, invariable. **2** *a permanent job* lasting, long-lasting, stable, fixed, established, sound, firm.

**permeate** verb *cooking smells permeating the whole house | water permeating the soil* spread through, pervade, fill, saturate, be diffused through, imbue, penetrate, infiltrate, percolate through, pass through, soak through, seep through, leak through, leach through.

**permissible** adjective permitted, allowable, admissible, acceptable, tolerated, authorized, sanctioned, legal, lawful, legitimate, licit, within bounds; *inf.* legit.

**permission** noun authorization, sanction, leave, license, dispensation, empowerment, allowance, consent, assent, acquiescence, go-ahead, thumbs up, agreement, approval; *inf.* green light.

**permissive** adjective *a permissive parent/upbringing* indulgent, lenient, unrestricted, overindulgent, liberal, tolerant, broad-minded, open-minded, easygoing, forbearing, latitudinarian, lax, unprescriptive.

**permit** verb *parents not permitting the children to go | not permit talking in class* allow, let, authorize, give leave, sanction, grant, license, empower, enable, consent to, assent to, acquiesce in, give the go-ahead to, agree to, approve of, tolerate, countenance, suffer, brook; *inf.* give the green light to.

**permit** noun *a permit to sell food | a permit to enter the country* license, authorization, warrant, sanction, pass, passport, visa.

**pernicious** adjective *a pernicious influence on society* destructive, ruinous, injurious, damaging, harmful, hurtful, detrimental, deleterious, deadly, lethal, fatal, wicked, evil, bad, malign, malevolent, malignant, noxious, poisonous, venomous.

**perpendicular** adjective upright, vertical, at right angles, at 90 degrees.

**perpetrate** verb *perpetrate a crime* commit, carry out, perform, execute, effect, effectuate, bring about, be guilty of; *inf.* pull off.

**perpetual** adjective **1** *a state of perpetual bliss | the perpetual snow of the Arctic* everlasting, eternal, never-ending, unending, endless, undying, perennial, permanent, perdurable, lasting, abiding, persisting, enduring, constant, unfailing, unchanging, unvarying, invariable. **2** *work with perpetual noise* incessant, ceaseless, nonstop, continuous, uninterrupted, unbroken, unremitting. **3** *tired of their perpetual complaints* interminable, persistent, frequent, continual, recurrent, repeated.

**perpetuate** verb *perpetuate the myth that he was a hero* preserve, conserve, sustain, maintain, continue, immortalize, eternalize.

**perplex** verb *her behavior perplexed him* puzzle, baffle, mystify, stump, bewilder, confound, confuse, nonplus, disconcert, dismay, dumbfound; *inf.* bamboozle.

**perplexing** adjective **1** *her perplexing behavior* puzzling, baffling, mystifying, mysterious, bewildering, confusing, disconcerting, unaccountable, strange, weird. **2** *a perplexing problem* complicated, involved, intricate, complex, difficult, thorny, knotty, taxing, trying, vexing.

**perquisite** noun *a perquisite of the job* fringe benefit, benefit, advantage, bonus, dividend, extra, plus; *inf.* perk, freebie.

**persecute** verb **1** *persecute people for their beliefs* oppress, tyrannize, abuse, mistreat, maltreat, ill-treat, molest, afflict, torment, torture, victimize, martyr. **2** *celebrities persecuted by the press* harass, pester, hound, badger, vex, bother, worry, annoy; *inf.* hassle.

**perseverance** noun persistence, tenacity, pertinacity, determination, resolve, purposefulness, obstinacy, insistence, intransigence, patience, application, diligence, assiduity.

**persevere** verb persist, keep going, continue, carry on, struggle, work, be tenacious, be resolute, be purposeful, not give up, be diligent; *inf.* plug away, stick to one's guns, be determined.

**persist** verb **1** *persist in his efforts to win* continue, carry on. See PERSEVERE. **2** *the cold weather persisted* continue, last, remain, linger, hold, carry on, keep on, keep up.

**persistence** noun *with persistence he got a job* tenacity, determination. See PERSEVERANCE.

**persistent** adjective **1** *persistent people refusing to give up* tenacious, pertinacious, determined, resolute, purposeful, obstinate, stubborn, insistent, intransigent, obdurate, intractable, patient, diligent. **2** *persistent rain* constant, continual, continuous, interminable, incessant, endless, unremitting, unrelenting, relentless. **3** *a persistent cough* chronic, frequent, repetitive, repetitious.

**persnickety** adjective fussy, punctilious, finicky, fastidious, overparticular, particular; *inf.* nitpicking, choosy, picky.

**person** noun individual, human being, human, creature, living soul, soul, mortal; *inf.* character.

**personable** adjective pleasant, agreeable, amiable, affable, likable, charming, nice, presentable.

**personage** noun *events attended by political personages* public figure, dignitary, notable, celebrity, personality, VIP, luminary; *inf.* big shot.

**personal** adjective **1** *his reasons for leaving are personal* private, confidential, intimate, secret. **2** *a personal style of prose* individual, idiosyncratic, characteristic, unique, peculiar. **3** *receive the personal attention of the manager* individual, special.

**personality** noun **1** *an unassuming personality* nature, disposition, character, temperament, makeup, psyche. **2** *man with little personality* character, charisma, magnetism, charm.

**personification** noun *he is the personification of politeness* embodiment, incarnation, epitome, quintessence, essence, representation, image, portrayal, likeness, semblance.

**personify** verb *personify all that was good about the country* embody, epitomize, typify, exemplify, symbolize, represent, be the incarnation of.

**personnel** noun staff, employees, workers, workforce, labor force, manpower, human resources.

**perspective** noun **1** *young people have a different perspective of such matters* outlook, viewpoint, point of view, standpoint, vantage point, stand, stance, angle, slant, attitude, frame of mind. **2** *get a perspective of the whole valley* view, vista, bird's-eye view, prospect, scene, panorama, aspect, sweep.

**persuade** verb *persuade her to go* | *cannot be persuaded* induce, convince, influence, sway, prompt, prevail upon, win over, talk into, coerce, inveigle, cajole, wheedle; *inf.* sweet-talk.

**persuasion** noun **1** *their successful persuasion of the children to go* prevailing, winning over, inducement, convincing, coercion, inveiglement, cajolery, wheedling; *inf.* sweet-talking. **2** *use their powers of persuasion* persuasiveness, inducement, influence. **3** *Christians of different persuasions* denomination, belief, creed, credo, faith, school of thought, philosophy, sect, affiliation, camp, faction.

**persuasive** adjective *persuasive arguments* effective, effectual, convincing, cogent, plausible, compelling, forceful, eloquent, weighty, influential, telling.

**pert** adjective *a pert young girl* impudent, impertinent, saucy, forward, presumptuous, audacious, bold, brash, brazen, bumptious.

**pertinent** adjective *make a few pertinent comments* relevant, appropriate, suitable, fitting, fit, apt, apposite, applicable, material, germane, apropos, ad rem.

**perturb** verb disturb, make anxious, worry, alarm, trouble, upset, disquiet, discompose, disconcert, vex, bother, agitate, unsettle, fluster, ruffle, confuse.

**peruse** verb *peruse the document* study, scrutinize, pore over, inspect, examine; scan.

**pervade** verb *cooking smells pervaded the entire house* | *terror pervaded his whole being* spread through, permeate, fill, pass through, suffuse, be diffused through, imbue, infuse, penetrate, infiltrate, percolate.

**pervasive** adjective prevalent, suffusive, extensive, ubiquitous, omnipresent, permeating, rife, widespread, universal.

**perverse** adjective **1** *too perverse to get along with others* contrary, wayward, troublesome, unruly, difficult, unreasonable, disobedient, unmanageable, uncontrollable, rebellious, willful, headstrong, capricious, stubborn, obstinate, obdurate, pertinacious, mulish, pigheaded, bullheaded, querulous, fractious, intractable, refractory, intransigent, contumacious. **2** *take a perverse delight in annoying her* contradictory, unreasonable, irrational, illogical, senseless, abnormal, deviant.

**pervert** verb **1** *pervert the course of justice* turn aside, divert, deflect, avert, subvert. **2** *pervert the English language* misapply, misuse, distort, garble, warp, twist, misinterpret, misconstrue. **3** *pervert young minds* lead astray, corrupt, warp, deprave, debauch, debase, degrade, vitiate.

**perverted** adjective corrupt, corrupted, depraved, debauched, debased, vitiated, deviant, abnormal, aberrant, warped, distorted, twisted, sick, unhealthy, immoral, evil, wicked, vile; *inf.* kinky.

**pessimism** noun *his pessimism made everyone gloomy* hopelessness, gloom, gloominess, cynicism, defeatism, fatalism, distrust, doubt, suspicion, resignation, despair.

**pessimist** noun *pessimists forecasting disaster* prophet of doom, cynic, defeatist, fatalist, alarmist, doubter, doubting Thomas.

**pest** noun nuisance, bother, vexation, irritant, trouble, worry, inconvenience, trial, tribulation, the bane of one's life; *inf.* pain, pain in the neck, aggravation.

**pester** verb *photographers pestering the movie star* badger, hound, irritate, annoy, bother, irk, nag, fret, worry, harass, torment, plague, bedevil, harry; *inf.* bug, hassle.

**pestilence** noun **1** *villagers dying from a pestilence* plague, epidemic, pandemic, disease, contagion, bubonic plague, Black Death, sickness. **2** *the pestilence of war* bane, blight, affliction, scourge, curse, torment.

**pet** noun *teacher's pet* favorite, darling, idol, apple of one's eye; *inf.* fair-haired boy/girl.

**pet** adjective **1** *a pet lamb* domesticated, domestic, tame, tamed, housebroken. **2** *a pet theory* favorite, favored, cherished, prized, preferred, particular, special.

**pet** verb **1** *pet the cat* stroke, caress, fondle, pat. **2** *a couple petting romantically* kiss, cuddle, embrace, caress; *inf.* neck, smooch.

**peter** verb **peter out** fade, melt away, evaporate, wane, ebb, diminish, taper off, die out, fail, fall through.

**petition** noun **1** *sign a petition to save the building* appeal, protest document, list of protesters, round robin. **2** *make a petition to God* | *made petitions for leniency to the judge* entreaty, supplication, plea, prayer, appeal, request, application, suit.

**petition** verb *petition God* | *petitioned the court for mercy* entreat, beg, beseech, plead with, make a plea to, pray, appeal to, request, ask, apply to, call upon, press, adjure.

**petrify** verb **1** *the thought of speaking in public petrified her* terrify, horrify, frighten, panic, alarm, scare, paralyze, stun, stupefy, transfix. **2** *age had petrified the tree* turn to stone, fossilize, calcify, ossify.

**petty** adjective **1** *waste time discussing petty details* trivial, trifling, minor, small, slight, unimportant, inconsequential, inconsiderable, negligible, paltry; *inf.* piddling. **2** *do it out of petty spite* narrow-minded, narrow, small-minded, mean, grudging.

**petulant** adjective querulous, complaining, peevish, fretful, impatient, cross, irritable, moody, crabby, snappish, crotchety, touchy, bad-tempered, ill-tempered, ill-humored, irascible, sulky, sullen.

**phantom** noun ghost, apparition, specter, spirit, revenant, wraith, shadow, phantasm; vision, chimera; *inf.* spook.

**phase** noun *an exciting phase in history* stage, part, step, chapter, point, period, time, juncture, spell.

**phenomenal** adjective *enjoying phenomenal success* extraordinary, remarkable, exceptional, singular, uncommon, unheard-of, unique, unparalleled, unprecedented, amazing, astonishing, astounding, marvelous, prodigious, sensational, miraculous; *inf.* fantastic, fabulous, mind-boggling.

**phenomenon** noun **1** *a social phenomenon peculiar to our times* circumstance, fact, experience, occurrence, happening, event, incident, episode. **2** *the gymnast is a phenomenon* marvel, prodigy, rarity, wonder, sensation, miracle, nonpareil.

**philanderer** noun Casanova, Don Juan, womanizer, woman-chaser, ladies' man, flirt, lothario, dallier, trifler; *inf.* lady-killer, wolf, stud.

**philanthropic** adjective humane, humanitarian, public-spirited, socially concerned, solicitous, unselfish, selfless, altruistic, kindhearted, benevolent, beneficent, charitable, almsgiving, generous, kind, munificent, bountiful, bounteous, liberal, openhanded, giving, helping.

**philanthropist** noun altruist, humanitarian, benefactor, patron, sponsor, almsgiver, donor, contributor, backer, helper.

**philanthropy** noun humanitarianism, humanity, humaneness, public-spiritedness, social concern, unselfishness, selflessness, altruism, kindheartedness, brotherly love, benevolence, beneficence, charity, generosity, almsgiving, kindness, munificence, bounty, liberality, openhandedness, patronage, sponsorship, backing, help.

**philistine** noun lowbrow, ignoramus, boor, barbarian, vulgarian, yahoo, lout, clod, oaf.

**philosopher** noun scholar, metaphysicist, metaphysician, sage, wise man, guru, pundit, seeker after truth, philosophizer, thinker, theorist, theorizer.

**philosophical** adjective **1** *read philosophical works* philosophic, metaphysical. **2** *in a philosophical mood* thoughtful, reflective, pensive, meditative, contemplative. **3** *remain philosophical in the face of failure* calm, composed, cool, collected, self-possessed, serene, tranquil, stoical, impassive, phlegmatic, unperturbed, dispassionate, unruffled, patient, resigned, rational, logical, realistic, practical.

**philosophy** noun **1** *the philosophy of Aristotle | studying philosophy* thought, thinking, reasoning, logic, wisdom, metaphysics. **2** *his philosophy of life* beliefs, convictions, ideology, doctrine, tenets, values, principles, attitude, view, viewpoint, outlook.

**phlegmatic** adjective **1** *a phlegmatic disposition* calm, cool, composed, serene, tranquil, placid, impassive, imperturbable, dispassionate, philosophical. **2** *no enthusiasm in the phlegmatic students* apathetic, indifferent, uninterested, impassive, sluggish, lethargic, listless, languorous, dull, indolent, inert, inactive, stolid, placid, bovine.

**phobia** noun aversion, abnormal/obsessive fear, dread, horror, terror, hatred, loathing, detestation, distaste, antipathy, revulsion, repulsion; *inf.* thing, hang-up.

**phony** adjective **1** *phony documents* bogus, counterfeit, imitation, spurious, mock, ersatz, fake, forged, simulated, make-believe, false, fraudulent. **2** *a phony French accent* bogus, sham, imitation, fake, feigned, assumed, affected, contrived, false, mock, pseudo.

**phony** noun **1** *the doctor is a phony* impostor, pretender, sham, fraud, fake, faker, charlatan, mountebank; *inf.* quack. **2** *the diamond is a phony* counterfeit, fake, forgery, imitation, sham.

**photograph** noun photo, snap, snapshot, picture, likeness, shot, print.

**phrase** noun **1** *in phrases and sentences* word group, group of words. **2** *a few well-chosen phrases* expression, idiomatic expression, idiom, remark, saying, utterance, witticism, tag. **3** *an elegant turn of phrase* phraseology, style of speech/writing, style, usage, choice of words, idiom, language, diction, parlance.

**phrase** verb *phrase the instruction differently* put, word, express, formulate, couch, frame, put into words.

**physical** adjective **1** *physical and mental well-being* bodily, corporeal, corporal, somatic. **2** *novitiates rising above their physical concerns* nonspiritual, material, earthly, corporeal, carnal, fleshly, mortal. **3** *everything physical in the universe* material, substantial, solid, concrete, tangible, palpable, visible.

**physician** noun doctor, doctor of medicine, medical practitioner, general practitioner, GP, specialist, consultant; *inf.* doc, medic; *derog.* quack.

**pick** verb **1** *pick a new sofa from the showroom | pick him for the team* choose, select, pick out, single out, handpick, decide upon, settle upon, fix upon, prefer, favor, elect. **2** *picking apples* harvest, gather, collect, take in, pluck, pull, cull. **3** *pick a safe* break into, force open, pry/prize open, crack. **pick at** *picking at their food* nibble at, peck at, toy with, play with, eat like a bird. **pick off** *soldiers picked off by a sniper* shoot, shoot down, gun down, hit, take out. **pick on** *picking on a child* punish repeatedly, criticize, badger. **pick out 1** *picked out from a huge list of applicants* choose, select, single out, handpick. See PICK verb 1. **2** *pick out his face in the crowd* make out, distinguish, tell apart, discriminate, recognize, notice. **pick up 1** *pick up the suitcase* lift, take up, raise, hoist. **2** *business starting to pick up* improve, get better, recover, rally, make a comeback, perk up, make headway, make progress. **3** *manage to pick up a first edition* find, discover, locate, come across, stumble across, happen upon, unearth, obtain, get, acquire, purchase, buy. **4** *pick up tomorrow where we left off today* carry on, go on, continue, take up, begin, begin again. **5** *pick them up on the way* collect, call for, fetch. **6** *pick up a date at the party* strike up an acquaintance with, take up with, fall in with. **7** *pick up the basic skills | pick up the local language* learn, get to know, master; *inf.* get the hang of.

**pick** noun **1** *early shoppers have the pick of the bargains* choice, selection, option, preference. **2** *the pick of the litter/crop* best, choicest, prime, cream, flower, prize, elite, crème de la crème.

**picket** noun **1** *line of pickets outside the factory* picketer, demonstrator, protester, objector, rebel, dissident. **2** *drive pickets into the ground* stake, post, paling, pale, peg, upright, pike, stanchion, palisade.

**picket** verb **1** *picket the factory* demonstrate at, protest at, blockade. **2** *picket an area for the animals* enclose, fence off, box in, stake off, secure, rail off, palisade.

**pickle** noun *in a financial pickle* plight, predicament, mess, trouble, problem, straits, crisis, tight corner; *inf.* jam, fix, scrape, tight spot.

**picture** noun **1** *paint a picture of the house* painting, drawing, sketch, watercolor, print, canvas, delineation, portrait, portrayal, illustration, likeness, representation, similitude, semblance. **2** *take pictures at the wedding* photograph, photo, snapshot, shot, snap, slide, print, still. **3** *his report*

*painted a bleak picture* scene, view, image, impression, representation, vision, concept. **4** *write a graphic picture of his despair* description, portrayal, account, report, narrative, narration, story, tale, recital. **5** *the picture of health/happiness* personification, embodiment, epitome, essence, model, exemplar, archetype. **6** *he is the picture of his father* image, living image, double, exact likeness, duplicate, replica, carbon copy, twin; *inf.* spitting image, ringer, dead ringer.

**picture** verb **1** *I can picture them still* imagine, call to mind, visualize, see, evoke, conjure up an image of. **2** *in the drawing they were pictured against a snowy background* paint, draw, sketch, depict, delineate, portray, illustrate, reproduce, represent.

**picturesque** adjective **1** *a picturesque village/setting* beautiful, pretty, lovely, attractive, scenic, charming, quaint, pleasing, delightful. **2** *a picturesque description of the events | use picturesque language* vivid, graphic, colorful, striking.

**piddling** adjective **1** *ignore the piddling details* trivial, trifling, minor, small, unimportant, insignificant, petty, paltry, worthless, useless; *inf.* piffling. **2** *a piddling sum of money* meager, trifling, paltry, derisory, negligible, small; *inf.* measly, piffling, Mickey Mouse.

**piece** noun **1** *a desk delivered in several pieces* part, bit, section, segment, unit. **2** *a vase broken to pieces | a dress torn to pieces* bit, fragment, smithereens, shard, shred. **3** *buy a large piece of cheese/wood* bit, section, slice, chunk, lump, hunk, wedge. **4** *a piece of cloth* length, bit, remnant, scrap, snippet. **5** *a piece of his fortune | get a piece of the action* share, slice, portion, allotment, allocation, quota, percentage, fraction, quantity. **6** *a fine piece of Colonial furniture* example, specimen, sample, instance, illustration, occurrence. **7** *write a piece on modern theater | disagree with his latest piece* article, item, story, report, essay, review, paper, column. **8** *one of the finest pieces by the composer* musical work, work, composition, creation, opus. **9** *one of the artist's finest pieces* work of art, work, painting, canvas, composition, creation, opus. **all in one piece** *find the vase/car/child all in one piece* unbroken, undamaged, unhurt, uninjured, safe, safe and sound. **fall/go to pieces** *people going to pieces in an emergency* panic, lose control, lose one's head, fall apart, break down; *inf.* crack up.

**piecemeal** adverb *put the story together piecemeal* piece by piece, bit by bit, gradually, in stages, in steps, little by little, by degrees, in fits and starts.

**pier** noun *stand on the pier to watch the boats* wharf, dock, jetty, quay, promenade.

**pierce** verb **1** *the spear had pierced his shoulder* penetrate, puncture, perforate, prick, stab, spike, enter, pass through, transfix. **2** *pierce the leather to make a belt* perforate, bore, drill. **3** *a heart pierced by the suffering of others* wound, hurt, pain, cut to the quick, affect, move, sting.

**piercing** adjective **1** *a piercing glance* penetrating, sharp, keen, searching, alert, shrewd, perceptive, probing. **2** *a piercing shriek* penetrating, shrill, ear-piercing, ear-splitting, high-pitched, loud. **3** *a piercing pain* sharp, stabbing, shooting, intense, severe, fierce, excruciating, agonizing, exquisite. **4** *frostbitten in the piercing cold* biting, numbing, bitter, raw, keen, freezing, frigid, arctic.

**piety** noun **1** *a family noted for its piety* piousness, religiousness, religion, holiness, godliness, devoutness, devotion, veneration, reverence, faith, spirituality, sanctity, religious zeal. **2** *children who were taught filial piety* obedience, duty, respect, respectfulness, deference, veneration.

**pig** noun **1** *farmers keeping pigs* hog, boar, sow, porker, grunter, swine, piglet; *inf.* piggy, oinker. **2** *pigs who left hardly any food for the others* glutton, guzzler; *inf.* hog. **3** *they live like pigs* slob, messy/filthy/dirty person. **4** *her boss is a real pig* boor, brute, swine, animal, monster; *inf.* bastard, beast, louse.

**pigheaded** adjective obstinate, stubborn, mulish, bullheaded, obdurate, tenacious, dogged, single-minded, inflexible, uncompromising, adamant, intractable, intransigent, unmalleable, headstrong, self-willed, willful, perverse, contrary, stiff-necked.

**pile**[1] noun **1** *a pile of clothes* heap, bundle, stack, mound, mass, accumulation, collection, assemblage, store, stockpile, hoard, load, mountain. **2** *a pile of work to do* great deal, quantity, abundance, mountain; *inf.* lot, lots, heap, stacks, oodles, tons. **3** *make a pile on the black market* fortune, money, wealth; *inf.* mint, tidy sum.

**pile**[2] verb **1** *pile his plate with food* heap, fill, load, stock. **2** *commuters piling on to the train* crowd, charge, tumble, stream, flock, flood, pack, squeeze, crush, jam. **pile up 1** *pile up the cans/apples* heap, stack. **2** *pile up logs for the winter* accumulate, amass, collect, gather, stockpile, hoard, store up, assemble, lay by/in. **3** *snow piled up by the roadsides* heap up, amass, accumulate, form piles, form heaps.

**pile**[3] noun *the piles supporting the bridge* pillar, column, support, post, foundation, piling, pier, buttress, upright.

**pilfer** verb *pilfer money from the petty cash* steal, thieve, rob, take, filch, purloin, embezzle, misappropriate; *inf.* walk off with, swipe, lift.

**pilgrim** noun *pilgrims going to Bethlehem/Mecca* worshiper, devotee, traveler, hajji; Puritan.

**pilgrimage** noun *make a pilgrimage to Bethlehem/Mecca* religious expedition, holy expedition, trek, excursion, hajj.

**pill** noun **1** *take a pill for a headache* tablet, capsule, pellet, lozenge, bolus. **2** *she can be a real pill* nuisance, pest, bore, trial; *inf.* pain, pain in the neck, drag.

**pillage** verb *rival tribes invading and pillaging* plunder, rob, raid, loot, maraud, sack, ransack, ravage, lay waste, despoil, spoil, spoliate, depredate, rape.

**pillar** noun **1** *pillars supporting the temple* column, post, pole, support, upright, pile, piling, pilaster, stanchion. **2** *a pillar of the community* mainstay, backbone, tower of strength, support, upholder, rock.

**pillow** noun cushion, bolster, headrest.

**pilot** noun **1** *the pilot at the aircraft's controls* aviator, aviatrix, aeronaut, captain, commander; *inf.* flier. **2** *the pilot directing the ship into the harbor* navigator, guide, steersman, helmsman.

**pilot** verb **1** *pilot the aircraft* fly, drive, operate, control, handle, maneuver. **2** *pilot the ship into the harbor* navigate, guide, steer.

**pimple** noun spot, pustule, boil, swelling, papule; *inf.* blackhead, whitehead, zit.

**pin** verb **1** *pin the pieces of cloth together* fasten, join, attach, secure. **2** *pin the notice to the board* attach, fasten, affix, fix, stick, tack, nail. **3** *pinned under the fallen tree* pinion, hold, press, restrain, constrain, hold fast, immobilize. **pin down 1** *pinned down by the weight of the car* pinion, hold down, restrain, constrain, hold fast, immobilize. **2** *to get his decision, you must pin him down* force, compel, make, pressure, put pressure on, nail down. **3** *something I dislike about him but I cannot pin it down* define, specify, identify, put one's finger on, put into words, express in words, designate, name. **pin on** *pin the blame on him* lay on, place on, attribute to, impute to, ascribe to.

**pin** noun **1** *fasten the hem with a pin* straight pin, dressmaker's/dressmaking pin, safety pin. **2** *a broken pin in the machine* peg, bolt, rivet, screw, dowel, post.

**pinch** verb **1** *pinch her little brother's arm* nip, tweak, squeeze, compress. **2** *shoes pinching her feet* hurt, crush, squeeze, cramp, confine. **3** *have to pinch and scrape to live* scrimp, skimp, stint, economize, be sparing, be frugal, be economical; *inf.* be stingy, be tight. **4** *pinch money from her mother's purse* steal, thieve, rob, take, pilfer, filch, purloin, embezzle, misappropriate; *inf.* swipe, lift.

**pinch** noun **1** *give her arm a pinch* nip, tweak, squeeze. **2** *a pinch of salt* bit, touch, trace, soupçon; *inf.* smidgen, smidge, tad.

**pine** verb *pine away* *pine away with grief* decline, weaken, waste away, wilt, fade, languish, droop. *pine for* *pine for her old way of life* long for, yearn for, ache for, sigh for, hunger for, thirst for, hanker for/after, crave.

**pink** adjective **1** *pink dresses* rose, rose-colored, salmon, salmon-pink, shell-pink. **2** *pink cheeks* rosy, flushed, blushing.

**pinnacle** noun *the pinnacle of her success* peak, height, culmination, high point, acme, zenith, climax, crowning point, meridian, summit, apex, vertex, apogee.

**pinpoint** verb *pinpoint the cause of the trouble* identify, discover, distinguish, locate, spot, home in on, put one's finger on.

**pioneer** noun **1** *the pioneers of the Wild West* settler, colonist, colonizer, frontiersman/frontierswoman, explorer. **2** *a pioneer in/of cancer research* developer, innovator, groundbreaker, trailblazer, front runner, founder, architect.

**pious** adjective **1** *pious church members* religious, holy, godly, spiritual, devout, devoted, dedicated, reverent, God-fearing, righteous, faithful, dutiful. **2** *patronized by pious do-gooders* sanctimonious, hypocritical, self-righteous, unctuous, pietistic, religiose; *inf.* holier-than-thou, goody-goody.

**pipe** noun **1** *lay pipes under the street* tube, cylinder; conduit, main, duct, channel, conveyor, pipeline, drainpipe. **2** *smoke a pipe* brier, meerschaum, clay pipe, tobacco pipe, corncob pipe; peace pipe, calumet; hookah. **3** *playing a pipe* whistle, penny whistle, flute, recorder, fife. *pipes* plural noun *playing the pipes* bagpipes, panpipes.

**piquant** adjective **1** *a piquant sauce/flavor* spicy, highly seasoned, flavorsome, peppery, tangy, pungent, sharp, tart, zesty, biting, stinging. **2** *a piquant piece of gossip* stimulating, intriguing, interesting, fascinating, alluring, racy, salty, provocative. **3** *a piquant wit* lively, sparkling, animated, spirited, sharp, clever, quick.

**pique** verb **1** *her lack of interest piqued him* irritate, annoy, anger, displease, affront, put out, offend, irk, peeve, vex, nettle, gall, wound; *inf.* aggravate, miff, rile. **2** *pique her curiosity* arouse, rouse, awaken, excite, stimulate, kindle, stir, whet.

**pirate** noun *pirates boarded the ship* buccaneer, rover, sea robber, corsair, freebooter.

**pirate** verb *pirate his music/poetry* copy, poach, infringe the copyright of, plagiarize, illegally reproduce; *inf.* crib, lift.

**pit**[1] noun **1** *fall down a pit* abyss, chasm, crater, hole, cavity, excavation, quarry, mine. **2** *pits in the pottery/skin* depression, hollow, dent, dint, pockmark, indentation, dimple, pock, mark.

**pit**[2] noun *cherry pits* stone, pip, seed, kernel.

**pitch** verb **1** *pitch a baseball* | *pitch the bales on to the truck* throw, cast, fling, hurl, toss, heave, launch; *inf.* chuck, lob. **2** *pitch a tent* erect, raise, put up, set up. **3** *trip and pitch forward into the lake* tumble, topple, fall headlong, fall, plunge, dive. **4** *ships pitching in the storm* lurch, roll, reel, sway, rock, flounder, keel, list. *pitch in* **1** *everyone pitched in to finish the work* help, assist, lend a hand, join in, participate, play a part, cooperate, collaborate. **2** *everyone pitched in to buy a present* contribute, make a contribution; *inf.* chip in.

**pitch** noun **1** *with one pitch* throw, cast, fling, hurl, toss, heave; *inf.* chuck, lob. **2** *excitement reached such a pitch* level, point, degree, height, extent, intensity. **3** *the pitch of the roof* angle, slope, slant, tilt, cant, inclination. **4** *get the right musical pitch* tone, sound, tonality, modulation. **5** *the pitch of the ship* lurch, roll, reeling, swaying, rocking, keeling, list. **6** *taken in by the salesman's pitch* spiel, sales talk, patter; *inf.* line.

**pitcher** noun *a pitcher of water* jug, ewer, jar, crock.

**piteous** adjective *hear a piteous cry/tale* pitiable, pathetic, distressing. *See* PITIFUL 1.

**pitfall** noun *the pitfalls of running a small business* trap, snare, catch, stumbling block, hazard, peril, danger, difficulty.

**pithy** adjective *a pithy remark* | *a pithy piece of prose* terse, succinct, concise, condensed, compact, summary, epigrammatic, to the point, pointed, expressive, incisive.

**pitiful** adjective **1** *in a pitiful condition* | *a pitiful sight* pitiable, piteous, pathetic, wretched, distressing, affecting, moving, sad, woeful, deplorable, heart-rending, heartbreaking, poignant, emotional. **2** *a pitiful excuse/coward* contemptible, despicable, poor, sorry, miserable, inadequate, worthless, base, shabby; *inf.* pathetic.

**pitiless** adjective *a pitiless tyrant* merciless, ruthless, relentless, cruel, severe, harsh, heartless, callous, brutal, inhuman, inhumane, cold-hearted, hard-hearted, unfeeling, uncaring, unsympathetic.

**pittance** noun *earn a pittance* trifling amount, modicum, tiny amount; *inf.* peanuts, chicken feed.

**pity** noun **1** *show pity for her situation* commiseration, condolence, sympathy, compassion, fellow feeling, understanding, forbearance, mercy, clemency, kindness, charity. **2** *it is a pity that he left* shame, crying shame, misfortune, sin; *inf.* crime.

**pity** verb *pity the homeless* take pity on, feel sorry for, weep for, grieve for, commiserate with, be sympathetic toward, sympathize with, have compassion for, show mercy to, be merciful toward.

**pivot** noun **1** *the machine turning on a pivot* axis, fulcrum, axle, swivel, spindle, central shaft. **2** *his job was the pivot of his life* central point, center, focal point, focus, hub, heart, *raison d'être.*

**pivot** verb *the machine pivots on a central shaft* turn, revolve, rotate, spin, swivel, twirl.

**placate** verb *placate the angry customer* calm, calm down, pacify, soothe, appease, conciliate, propitiate, mollify, win over.

**place** noun **1** *the place where the accident happened* location, spot, scene, setting, position, site, situation, venue, area, region, whereabouts, locus. **2** *a sore place on her arm* spot, area, bit, part. **3** *visit a different place each year* town, city, village, hamlet, district, locality, neighborhood, quarter, country, state, area, region. **4** *have a place in town* residence, home, house, apartment, accommodation, abode, dwelling, domicile, property; *inf.* pad. **5** *occupy a lowly place in the company* | *win first place* position, status, grade, rank, station, standing, footing, role, niche. **6** *find a place in a law firm* position, post, job, appointment, situation, office. **7** *children asked to go back to their places* seat, position, space. **8** *put the book back in its place* position, correct position, space. **9** *not your place to criticize* function, job, role, task, duty, responsibility, charge, concern, affair, prerogative. **in place** *everything must be in position* in position, in order, set up, arranged. **in place of** *her sister went in place of her* instead of, in lieu of, in someone's place, in someone's stead, as a substitute for. **out of place** **1** *with not a hair out of place* out of position, out of order, in disorder, disarranged, in disarray, disorganized, in a mess. **2** *her remarks were quite out of place* inappropriate, unsuitable, inapposite, unseemly, improper, unfit. **3** *feel out of place at the party* out of one's element, uncomfortable, ill-at-ease, like a fish out of water. **put in (someone's) place** *he was trying to flirt with her but she put him in his place* humble, humiliate, mortify, take down a peg or two; *inf.* cut down to size. **take place** *where did the murder take place?* happen, occur, come about, transpire, crop up, befall, come to pass. **take the place of** *trying to take the place of her mother* replace, substitute for, be a substitute for, act for, stand in lieu of, cover for.

**place** verb **1** *place the books on the shelves* put, position, set, lay, deposit, rest, stand,

install, settle, station, situate. **2** *place the recruits according to their test scores* order, rank, grade, group, arrange, sort, class, classify, categorize, bracket. **3** *place her trust in him* put, lay, invest, consign. **4** *I know his face, but I cannot place him* identify, recognize, know, remember, put one's finger on, locate. **5** *try to place graduates* find employment for, find a job for, accommodate, find accommodation for, appoint, assign.

**placid** adjective **1** *the placid waters of the lake* still, calm, peaceful, pacific, tranquil, motionless, smooth, unruffled, undisturbed. **2** *of a placid temperament* calm, cool, coolheaded, collected, composed, self-possessed, serene, tranquil, equable, even-tempered, easygoing, unperturbed, imperturbable, unexcitable, unruffled.

**plagiarize** verb copy, pirate, poach, borrow, reproduce, appropriate; *inf.* crib, lift.

**plague** noun **1** *villagers dying from a plague* bubonic plague, Black Death, contagion, disease, pestilence, sickness, epidemic, pandemic. **2** *a plague of locusts* multitude, host, swarm, influx, infestation. **3** *famine and other plagues* affliction, evil, scourge, curse, blight, bane, calamity, disaster, trial, tribulation, torment, visitation.

**plague** verb **1** *plagued with/by poor health* afflict, torture, torment, bedevil, trouble. **2** *plagued by her little brother* annoy, irritate, bother, disturb, worry, pester, vex, harass, torment, tease; *inf.* hassle, bug.

**plain** adjective **1** *it was plain that he was guilty* clear, crystal-clear, obvious, evident, apparent, manifest, transparent, patent, unmistakable. **2** *plain indications of his guilt* clear, clear-cut, obvious, visible, discernible, perceptible, distinct, transparent, patent, noticeable, pronounced, marked, striking, unmistakable, conspicuous. **3** *a plain statement of the facts* clear, clear-cut, simple, straightforward, uncomplicated, comprehensible, intelligible, understandable, lucid, unambiguous. **4** *a plain lifestyle* | *plain furnishings* simple, austere, stark, severe, basic, ordinary, unsophisticated, spartan, restrained, muted, bare, unadorned, undecorated, unembellished, unornamented. **5** *a rather plain child* unattractive, ill-favored, ugly, unprepossessing, unlovely, homely. **6** *a plain man* simple, straightforward, ordinary, average, typical, unpretentious, unassuming, unaffected, artless, guileless, sincere, honest, plain-speaking, plain-spoken, frank, candid, blunt, outspoken, forthright, direct.

**plain** noun lowland, grassland, prairie, meadowland, pasture, savannah, flatland; steppe, tundra; tableland, plateau, mesa.

**plainspoken** adjective plain-speaking, frank, candid, blunt, outspoken, forthright, direct, downright, unequivocal, unambiguous.

**plaintive** adjective *plaintive cries* mournful, doleful, melancholy, sad, sorrowful, unhappy, disconsolate, wretched, woeful, grief-stricken, heartbroken, brokenhearted, pathetic, pitiful, piteous.

**plan** noun **1** *a plan to make money* scheme, system, procedure, method, program, schedule, project, way, means, strategy, tactics, formula. **2** *our plan is to relocate* idea, proposal, intention, intent, aim, hope, aspiration, ambition. **3** *the architect's plan for the new building* drawing, scale drawing, blueprint, layout, sketch, diagram, chart, map, illustration, representation, delineation.

**plan** verb **1** *plan a picnic for tomorrow* arrange, organize, line up, schedule, program. **2** *plan the reconstruction of the company* devise, design, plot, formulate, frame, outline, sketch out, draft, prepare, develop, shape, build, concoct, contrive. **3** *we are planning to relocate* intend, aim, propose, mean, contemplate, envisage, foresee.

**plane** noun **1** *on a different intellectual plane* level, stratum, stage, degree, position, rank, footing. **2** *planes taking off* airplane, aircraft, airliner, jet, jumbo jet.

**plant** noun **1** *buy plants for the garden* herb, shrub, flower, vegetable, weed. **2** *work at the textile plant* factory, works, foundry, mill, workshop, shop, yard.

**plant** verb **1** *plant tomatoes* put in the ground, implant, sow, scatter, transplant, bed (out). **2** *plant his feet firmly on the ground* place, position, set, situate. **3** *plant an idea in his head* put, place, fix, establish, lodge, embed, insert. **4** *plant a microphone in his bedroom* hide, conceal, secrete.

**plastic** adjective **1** *as plastic as clay* moldable, shapable, ductile, fictile, pliant, pliable, supple, flexible, malleable. **2** *a plastic charm* false, artificial, synthetic, spurious, sham, bogus, assumed, superficial, specious, meretricious, pseudo; *inf.* phony.

**plate** noun **1** *serve food on plates* dish, platter, dinner plate. **2** *a plate of spaghetti* plateful, helping, portion, serving. **3** *a book with colored plates* illustration, picture, photograph, print, lithograph. **4** *steel plates used in shipbuilding* sheet, panel, slab.

**plateau** noun *stand on the plateau to view the valley below* elevated plain, highland, upland, mesa, tableland.

**platform** noun **1** *deliver a speech from the platform* dais, rostrum, podium, stage, stand. **2** *nothing new in the candidate's platform* plan, program, policy, objectives, principles, tenets, manifesto, party line.

**platitude** noun *a speech rife with platitudes* cliché, truism, bromide, hackneyed/stock expression, trite/banal phrase, banality, stereotyped phrase, inanity.

**platoon** noun *the officer in charge of the platoon* squadron, squad, company, patrol, group.

**platter** noun serving plate, salver, plate, dish, tray.

**plaudits** plural noun *the plaudits of his colleagues* praise, acclaim, acclamation, applause, ovation, congratulations, compliments, cheers, approval, approbation, commendation, accolade, pat on the back.

**plausible** adjective *a plausible argument/excuse* tenable, cogent, reasonable, believable, credible, convincing, persuasive, likely, probable, conceivable, imaginable.

**play** verb **1** *time to play* amuse oneself, entertain oneself, enjoy oneself, have fun. **2** *playing in the park* play games, frolic, frisk, gambol, romp, cavort, sport. **3** *play a musical instrument* perform on. **4** *play Ophelia in Hamlet* act the part of, perform, portray, represent, execute. **5** *play a trick on* perform, carry out, execute, do, accomplish, discharge, fulfill. **6** *play football* take part in, participate in, engage in, be involved in. **7** *play the neighboring team* compete against, contend against, oppose, take on, challenge, vie with, rival. **8** *told not to play with the controls* fiddle, toy, fidget, fool around; *inf.* mess around. **9** *playing with her affections* trifle, toy, dally, amuse oneself. **10** *sunlight playing on the water* move lightly, dance, flit, dart. **play around** philander, womanize, have an affair, fool around, cheat; *inf.* mess around. **play ball** *want to do business, but they refused to play ball* cooperate, collaborate, play along, go along, be willing. **play down** *play down his part in the crime* make light of, gloss over, minimize, diminish, underrate, underestimate, underrate, think little of; *inf.* soft-pedal. **play it by ear** *we have no plans—we are going to play it by ear* improvise, extemporize, ad lib, take it as it comes. **play up** *car dealers playing up the new safety features* emphasize, accentuate, bring/draw/call attention to, point up, underline, underscore, highlight, spotlight, stress.

**play** noun **1** *children at play | prefer play to work* amusement, entertainment, recreation, diversion, leisure, enjoyment, fun, merrymaking, revelry. **2** *appear in a play by a local dramatist* drama, stage play, stage show, radio play, comedy, tragedy, farce. **3** *need more play on the fishing line* movement, freedom of movement, slack;

*inf.* give. **4** *made sarcastic remarks in play* fun, jest, joking, sport, teasing.

**playboy** noun pleasure seeker, man about town, socialite, rake, roué, womanizer, philanderer, ladies' man, lady-killer, lothario, Casanova, Don Juan, debauchee.

**player** noun **1** *one of the players in the game* competitor, contestant, participant, team member, athlete, sportsman/sportswoman. **2** *one of the players in the theater company* actor/actress, performer, entertainer, artist, artiste, trouper, thespian. **3** *several of the players in the orchestra* performer, musician, instrumentalist, artist, artiste, virtuoso.

**playful** adjective **1** *playful kitten | in a playful mood* fun-loving, full of fun, high-spirited, frisky, skittish, coltish, frolicsome, sportive, mischievous, impish, puckish. **2** *a playful remark* in fun, in jest, joking, jesting, humorous, facetious, waggish, tongue-in-cheek, arch, roguish.

**playwright** noun dramatist, dramaturge, scriptwriter.

**plea** noun **1** *make a plea to the governor to save his life* appeal, entreaty, imploration, supplication, petition, prayer, request, solicitation, suit, invocation. **2** *evidence in support of his plea against the accused* allegation, case, suit, action, claim.

**plead** verb *plead insanity as the reason for his crime* put forward, state, assert, argue, claim, allege. **plead with** *plead with the judge to show mercy* appeal to, beg, entreat, beseech, implore, petition, make supplication to, supplicate, importune, pray to, solicit, request, present one's case to.

**pleasant** adjective **1** *a pleasant experience* agreeable, enjoyable, entertaining, amusing, delightful, pleasing, pleasurable, satisfying, gratifying, nice, good, fine, welcome, acceptable; *inf.* lovely. **2** *a pleasant person/manner* agreeable, friendly, amiable, affable, genial, likable, nice, good-humored, charming, engaging, winning, delightful; *inf.* lovely.

**pleasantry** noun *exchange pleasantries with his neighbor* good-natured remark, polite remark, joke, jest, quip, witticism, bon mot.

**please** verb **1** *a gift that will please his mother* be agreeable to, gladden, delight, cheer up, charm, divert, entertain, amuse, tickle, satisfy, gratify, fulfill, content, suit; *inf.* tickle pink. **2** *do as one pleases* want, wish, see fit, will, like, desire, be inclined, prefer, opt.

**pleased** adjective *give a pleased smile* happy, glad, cheerful, delighted, thrilled, elated, contented, satisfied, gratified, fulfilled.

**pleasing** adjective **1** *a pleasing experience* agreeable, enjoyable. See PLEASANT adjective 1. **2** *he had a pleasing personality* agreeable, friendly, amiable. See PLEASANT adjective 2.

**pleasure** noun **1** *events that bring pleasure | the pursuit of pleasure* happiness, gladness, delight, joy, enjoyment, entertainment, amusement, diversion, satisfaction, gratification, fulfillment, contentment, recreation. **2** *what is your pleasure?* wish, desire, will, inclination, preference, choice, option, purpose.

**plebeian** adjective **1** *of plebeian origins* lower-class, low, lowborn, working-class, proletarian, common, peasant, mean, ignoble; *inf.* blue-collar. **2** *have plebeian tastes* uncultivated, uncultured, unrefined, coarse, common, base.

**plebeian** noun commoner, proletarian, peasant.

**pledge** noun **1** *give his pledge to look after the children* promise, word, word of honor, vow, assurance, oath, covenant, warrant. **2** *give his watch as a pledge* security, surety, guarantee, collateral, bond, earnest, deposit, pawn. **3** *give her a ring as a pledge of his love* token, symbol, sign, mark, testimony, proof, evidence.

**pledge** verb **1** *he pledged that he would support the children* promise, give one's word, vow, undertake, take an oath, swear, vouch, engage, contract. **2** *pledge one's house/ring as security* mortgage, put up as collateral, guarantee, pawn.

**plentiful** adjective abundant, copious, ample, profuse, lavish, liberal, generous, bumper, infinite.

**plenty** noun *the years of plenty* plenteousness, affluence, prosperity, wealth, opulence, luxury, abundance, copiousness, fruitfulness, profusion. **plenty of** *have plenty of money* enough, sufficient, a good deal of; *inf.* lots of, piles of, tons of.

**plethora** noun *a plethora of good advice* overabundance, superabundance, excess, superfluity, surplus, surfeit, glut.

**pliable** adjective **1** *a pliable substance* flexible, bendable, pliant, elastic, supple, stretchable, ductile, plastic. **2** *expect the army recruits to be pliable* malleable, yielding, compliant, docile, biddable, tractable, manageable, governable, controllable, amenable, adaptable, flexible, impressionable, persuadable.

**plight** noun *the plight of the homeless | the plight they are in* predicament, trouble, difficulty, dire straits, extremity, tight corner; *inf.* hole, pickle, spot, jam.

**plod** verb *plod along the road* trudge, clump, stomp, lumber, tramp.

**plot** noun **1** *a plot against the dictator* conspiracy, intrigue, secret plan, stratagem. **2** *the plot of the novel* action, theme, subject, story line, story, scenario, thread. **3** *a burial plot* patch, allotment, lot, parcel.

**plot** verb **1** *plot the new construction site* map out, make a plan/blueprint of, draw, draw a diagram of, draw the layout of, sketch out, outline. **2** *plot the battle sites on the map* mark, chart, map. **3** *rebels plotting against the dictator* scheme, conspire, intrigue. **4** *plot the dictator's downfall* plan, hatch, scheme, concoct, devise, frame, think up, dream up, conceive; *inf.* cook up.

**plow** verb **1** *plow the field* till, work, cultivate, break up, turn up. **2** *the car plowed into a snowbank* plunge, lunge, career, crash, smash, bulldoze, hurtle. **3** *plow through the mud* plod, trudge, wade, flounder.

**ploy** noun *a ploy to distract the teacher* dodge, ruse, scheme, trick, stratagem, maneuver.

**pluck** verb **1** *pluck the burning paper from the fire* pull, remove, extract. **2** *pluck blackberries for jam* gather, collect, pick, harvest, take in, pull, cull. **3** *pluck the string of the guitar* finger, strum, pick, plunk. **pluck at** *plucking at her mother's skirt* tug at, pull at, clutch at, snatch at, catch at, tweak; *inf.* yank (at).

**pluck** noun *took a lot of pluck to go into the jungle alone* courage, bravery, valor, heroism, intrepidity, fearlessness, mettle, nerve, backbone, determination, boldness, daring, spirit, audacity; *inf.* gumption, grit, guts, spunk.

**plug** noun **1** *put a plug in the bathtub/jug* stopper, bung, cork, stopple, seal. **2** *a plug of tobacco* cake, chew, twist, quid, wad. **3** *the talk-show host gave his book a free plug* advertisement, commercial, promotion, push, mention; *inf.* ad, hype.

**plug** verb **1** *plug the hole in the tank* stop up, bung, cork, dam up, block, stopper, stopple, seal off, pack, stuff. **2** *plug his new book on television* publicize, promote, advertise, play up, push, build up; *inf.* hype. **plug away** *keep plugging away* labor, slog away, persevere, grind away.

**plumb** verb *plumb the mysteries of computer technology* probe, search out, delve into, explore, scrutinize, investigate, inspect, examine, sound out, go into, fathom, unravel.

**plummet** verb **1** *the kite plummeted to the ground* plunge, hurtle, nosedive, dive, drop. **2** *prices plummeted* plunge, tumble, take a nosedive, drop rapidly.

**plump** adjective chubby, round, of ample proportions, rotund, buxom, stout, obese, corpulent, fleshy, portly, tubby, dumpy, pudgy, roly-poly.

**plunder** verb **1** *enemy forces plundering the villages* rob, pillage, loot, raid, ransack, rifle, strip, fleece, ravage, lay waste, despoil, spoil, spoliate, depredate, harry, maraud, sack, rape. **2** *plunder food* steal, thieve, rob, purloin, filch, make off with.

**plunder** noun **1** *the plunder of the village* robbery, robbing, pillaging, looting, raiding, ransacking, despoiling, laying waste, harrying, marauding, rapine. **2** *take their plunder back to camp* stolen goods, loot, booty, spoils, prize, pillage.

**plunge** verb **1** *plunge the dagger into his back* thrust, stick, jab, push, drive. **2** *the pelican plunged into the sea* dive, nosedive, jump, plummet, drop, fall, swoop down. **3** *plunge the house into darkness* throw, cast, pitch. **4** *plunge his burned hand into cold water* immerse, sink, dip, douse. **5** *plunge into matrimony* charge, lunge, rush, dash, hurtle, career. **6** *real-estate prices plunged* plummet, tumble, nosedive, take a nosedive.

**plunge** noun **1** *his plunge into the sea* dive, nosedive, jump, fall, drop, swoop, descent. **2** *the car's sudden plunge forward* charge, lurch, rush, dash. **3** *an unexpected plunge in prices* fall, drop, tumble, nosedive.

**plus** noun *use of the company car is a definite plus* bonus, extra, added advantage, fringe benefit, perquisite; *inf.* perk.

**plush** adjective *plush furnishings* luxurious, deluxe, sumptuous, lavish, gorgeous, opulent, rich, costly; *inf.* ritzy, classy.

**ply** verb **1** *plying the oars* wield, use, operate, work, utilize, employ, manipulate, handle. **2** *ply his trade as a plumber* practice, work at, engage in, pursue, follow. **3** *ply them with questions* bombard, assail, besiege, beset, harass, importune; *inf.* hassle. **4** *ply them with food and drink* supply, provide, lavish, shower, load, heap.

**pocket** noun **1** *pockets on the side of the suitcase* pouch, compartment, receptacle. **2** *isolated pockets of resistance to the government* small area, small region, district, zone.

**pocket** verb *pocketing money from the cash register* appropriate, misappropriate, steal, thieve, purloin, filch; *inf.* lift, swipe.

**pod** noun *pea pod* shell, husk, hull, case, shuck; pericarp.

**poem** noun verse, ode, sonnet, ballad, song, lyric, lay, elegy, rhyme, limerick, haiku, jingle.

**poetic** adjective **1** *write poetic works* metrical, rhythmical, lyrical, elegiac. **2** *poetic language* imaginative, creative, figurative, symbolic, flowery. **3** *a poetic rendering of the symphony* aesthetic, artistic, tasteful, graceful, elegant, sensitive.

**poetry** noun *write poetry rather than prose* poems, verse, verses, versification, metrical composition, rhythmical composition, rhymes, rhyming.

**poignant** adjective moving, affecting, touching, emotional, sentimental, heartfelt, sad, sorrowful, tearful, evocative.

**point** noun **1** *the point of the spear/tool* tapered end, tip, top, extremity, prong, spike, tine. **2** *ships sailing around the point* promontory, headland, head, foreland, cape, bluff. **3** *Gettysburg is a point of great interest* place, position, location, situation, site, spot, area, locality. **4** *abrupt to the point of rudeness* extent, degree, stage. **5** *reach an important point in her life* stage, position, circumstance, condition. **6** *have to go home at some point* time, juncture, stage, period, moment, instant. **7** *at the point where he could not face her* critical point, crux, moment of truth. **8** *explain the situation point by point* detail, item, particular. **9** *get to the point* focal point, salient point, keynote, heart of the matter, essence, nub, core, pith, marrow, meat, crux. **10** *miss the point of the story* meaning, significance, import, essence, gist, substance, drift, thrust, burden, theme, tenor, vein. **11** *raise various points during the discussion* subject, issue, topic, question, matter, item. **12** *the various points of the argument* part, element, constituent, component, ingredient. **13** *what is the point of it?* aim, purpose, object, objective, goal, intention, reason for, use, utility. **14** *kindness is one of his strong points* characteristic, trait, attribute, quality, feature, property. **beside the point** *their religious beliefs are beside the point* irrelevant, immaterial, incidental. **point of view 1** *listen to everyone's point of view* view, viewpoint, opinion, belief, attitude, sentiment, stand, standpoint, stance, position. **2** *look at the situation from a different point of view* angle, slant, perspective, standpoint, viewpoint, outlook. **to the point** *his remarks were very much to the point* pertinent, relevant, germane, applicable, apropos, apposite, appropriate, apt, fitting, suitable.

**point** verb *point the gun* direct, aim, level, train. **point out** *point out the disadvantages of the proposal* indicate, show, specify, designate, identify, mention, call/draw attention to. **point to** *all the evidence points to her* indicate, show, signify, suggest, be evidence of, evidence.

**point-blank** adverb **1** *shot him point-blank* at close range, close up. **2** *ask him point-blank for his reasons* bluntly, directly, plainly, straight, straightforwardly, frankly, candidly, forthrightly, openly, explicitly, unequivocally, unambiguously.

**pointed** adjective **1** *the pointed end of the stick* sharp, sharp-edged, cuspidate, acicular. **2** *a pointed remark* cutting, trenchant, biting, incisive, penetrating, forceful, telling, significant. **3** *treat her with pointed*

*indifference* obvious, evident, conspicuous, striking, emphasized, unmistakable.

**pointless** adjective **1** *it is pointless to go on* futile, useless, in vain, unavailing, unproductive, senseless, absurd, foolish, nonsensical, stupid, silly. **2** *a few pointless remarks* meaningless, senseless, vague, empty, worthless, irrelevant, senseless, fatuous, foolish, nonsensical, stupid, silly, absurd, inane.

**poise** noun **1** *admire her poise in difficulties* composure, equanimity, self-possession, aplomb, self-assurance, self-control, calmness, serenity, dignity, imperturbability, suaveness, urbanity, elegance; *inf.* cool. **2** *admire the poise of the ballet dancers* balance, equilibrium, control, grace, gracefulness.

**poise** verb **1** *poise oneself to jump* steady, brace, prepare. **2** *the hawk poised in midair* hang, hang suspended, float, hover.

**poised** adjective **1** *a very poised young woman* composed, serene, self-possessed, self-assured, self-controlled, calm, collected, dignified, imperturbable, unperturbed, unruffled, suave, urbane, elegant; *inf.* unflappable. **2** *poised to take over the president's job* ready, prepared, all set, standing by, waiting, waiting in the wings.

**poison** noun **1** *the snake's deadly poison* venom, toxin. **2** *a poison in our society* blight, bane, contagion, cancer, canker, malignancy, corruption, pollution.

**poison** verb **1** *poisoned the victim* administer poison to, give poison to, kill by poison. **2** *poison the environment/soil* contaminate, pollute, blight, spoil, infect, defile, adulterate. **3** *poison their minds* corrupt, warp, pervert, deprave, defile, debauch.

**poisonous** adjective **1** *poisonous snakes/chemicals* venomous, toxic, mephitic, noxious, deadly, fatal, lethal. **2** *a poisonous influence on society* cancerous, malignant, corrupting, polluting, harmful, injurious, noxious, pernicious, malicious, malevolent, vicious.

**poke** verb **1** *poke him in the ribs* jab, prod, dig, elbow, nudge, butt. **2** *poke a key through the hole* jab, push, thrust, shove, stick. **poke around** *poke around his possessions* rummage around, ransack, nose around, pry into. **poke fun at** *poking fun at his clumsiness* laugh at, mock, jeer at, ridicule, deride, tease, chaff, taunt; *inf.* rib, rag.

**poke** noun jab, prod, dig, nudge, butt, push, thrust, shove.

**police** noun *wanted by the police* police force, the law, policemen, policewomen, police officers, constabulary; *inf.* the cops, the boys in blue; *derog.* the fuzz, the pigs.

**police** verb **1** *police the school buildings* patrol, make the rounds of, guard, keep watch on, protect. **2** *police the soccer match* control, keep under control, regulate, enforce, administer, oversee, monitor.

**policy** noun *the government's educational policy* plan, scheme, program, schedule, code, system, approach, procedure, guideline, theory.

**polish** verb *polish the table* wax, buff, rub, burnish, shine. **polish off** *polish off his meal quickly* finish, eat up, consume, devour, wolf down, down, bolt.

**polite** adjective **1** *too polite to interrupt* well-mannered, mannerly, courteous, civil, respectful, deferential, well-behaved, well-bred, genteel, polished, tactful, diplomatic. **2** *things not done in polite society* well-bred, civilized, cultured, refined, polished, genteel, urbane, sophisticated, elegant, courtly.

**politic** adjective wise, prudent, sensible, advisable, judicious, sagacious, expedient, shrewd, astute, discreet, tactful, diplomatic.

**political** adjective **1** *hold a political position* governmental, ministerial, public, civic, administrative, bureaucratic. **2** *dismissed for political reasons* factional, partisan, power, status.

**politician** noun statesman, stateswoman, legislator, lawmaker, public servant; senator, congressman, congresswoman, representative; officeholder, bureaucrat.

**politics** noun **1** *a career in politics* government, affairs of state, party politics. **2** *study politics* political science, civics, statecraft, statesmanship. **3** plural noun *what are his politics?* political alliance, political belief. **4** plural noun *resigned because of the politics within the company* power struggle, manipulation, maneuvering, jockeying for position, Machiavellianism, opportunism, realpolitik.

**poll** noun **1** *organize a poll to decide on the best candidate* vote, ballot, canvass, headcount, show of hands, straw vote/poll. **2** *a poll heavily in favor of the present administration* returns, count, tally. **3** *conduct a poll to investigate people's eating habits* opinion poll, Gallup poll, survey, market research, sampling.

**poll** verb *poll one hundred people in a survey* canvass, question, interview, survey, sample, ballot.

**pollute** verb **1** *pollute the water with chemicals | pollute the environment* contaminate, adulterate, infect, taint, poison, befoul, foul, make dirty, make filthy. **2** *pollute the minds of the young* corrupt, poison, warp, pervert, deprave, defile, debauch.

**pollution** noun **1** *chemicals involved in the pollution of our water* contamination, adulteration, infecting, tainting, befouling,

fouling, foulness, dirtying, dirtiness, impurity, filthiness. **2** *the pollution of young minds* corruption, corrupting, poisoning, warping, depraving.

**pomp** noun **1** *the pomp of the coronation* ceremony, ceremoniousness, ritual, display, pageantry, show, spectacle, splendor, grandeur, magnificence, majesty, glory, brilliance, flourish, style. **2** *more interested in pomp than substance* ostentation, exhibitionism, grandiosity, glitter, show, showiness, pomposity, vainglory, fanfaronade.

**pompous** adjective **1** *a pompous official* self-important, presumptuous, imperious, overbearing, grandiose, affected, pretentious, arrogant, vain, haughty, proud, conceited, egotistic, supercilious, condescending, patronizing. **2** *pompous language* high-sounding, high-flown, bombastic, turgid, grandiloquent, magniloquent, euphuistic, pedantic, stilted, fustian.

**pond** noun pool, puddle, lake, tarn, millpond, duck pond, fishpond, lagoon.

**ponder** verb **1** *take time to ponder his previous behavior* consider, reflect on, mull over, contemplate, dwell on, weigh, review. **2** *sit in the dark and ponder* think, consider, reflect, meditate, contemplate, deliberate, brood, ruminate, cogitate, cerebrate.

**ponderous** adjective **1** *ponderous movements* heavy, slow, awkward, clumsy, lumbering, heavy-footed. **2** *a piece of ponderous prose* awkward, clumsy, labored, forced, stilted, turgid, stodgy, lifeless, plodding, dull, boring, tedious, monotonous, dry, dreary, pedantic, verbose.

**pool**[1] noun **1** *resting by a mountain pool* pond, water/watering hole, tidal pool, lake, tarn. **2** *a pool of blood* puddle.

**pool**[2] noun **1** *typing pool* consortium, syndicate, collective, combine, group, team. **2** *a pool of cars for the sales reps* common supply, supply, reserve.

**pool**[3] verb *pool their resources* put together, combine, amalgamate, merge, share.

**poor** adjective **1** *poor and homeless* poverty-stricken, penniless, hard up, needy, deprived, in need, indigent, impoverished, impecunious, destitute, penurious; *inf.* cash-strapped, broke, flat broke. **2** *poor dwellings* humble, lowly, mean, modest, plain. **3** *a poor diet/performance | goods of poor quality* inadequate, deficient, insufficient, unsatisfactory, inferior, imperfect, bad, low-grade, defective, faulty, second-rate; *inf.* junky, crummy. **4** *a poor crop of apples* sparse, scanty, meager, scarce, skimpy, reduced, paltry, miserable, exiguous. **5** *a diet poor in nutrients* deficient, lacking, wanting, insufficient. **6** *poor soil* unproductive, barren, unyielding, unfruitful, bare, arid, sterile. **7** *you poor thing* wretched, pitiable, pitiful, unfortunate, unlucky, luckless, unhappy, hapless, ill-fated, ill-starred. **8** *a poor specimen of a man* miserable, sad, sorry, spiritless, mean, low, base, disgraceful, despicable, contemptible, abject, pathetic.

**pop** verb *guns were popping* explode, go off, bang, crack, burst, detonate. **pop in** *pop in to see his mother* visit, stop by; *inf.* drop in/by. **pop up** *crocuses popping up all over the yard* appear, appear suddenly/abruptly, crop up.

**popular** adjective **1** *a popular choice | teachers popular with the students* well-liked, liked, favored, favorite, well-received, approved, admired, accepted. **2** *these items are so popular that we have run out* well-liked, in favor, sought-after, in demand, desired, wanted, fashionable, in fashion, in vogue, in. **3** *popular movie stars* well-known, famous, celebrated, renowned. **4** *popular music/science* accessible, simple, understandable, middle-of-the-road, middlebrow, lowbrow, readily understood; *inf.* pop. **5** *issues of popular concern* public, general, civic. **6** *popular beliefs* current, prevalent, prevailing, accepted, recognized, widespread, universal, general, common, customary, usual, standard, stock, conventional.

**popularity** noun **1** *teachers gaining in popularity* favor, approval, approbation, admiration, acceptance. **2** *restocking the items due to their popularity* demand, fashionableness, vogue, trendiness. **3** *ideas gaining popularity* currency, prevalence, recognition. **4** *the popularity of the entertainer* fame, renown, acclaim, esteem, repute.

**population** noun **1** *the population of the town* inhabitants, residents, community, people, citizenry, populace, society. **2** *the elderly population* people, folk, society. **3** *populations decreasing in rural areas* population count, numbers of inhabitants, census, headcount.

**populous** adjective *populous urban areas* densely populated, heavily populated, crowded.

**porch** noun veranda, portico, stoa, piazza.

**pore** verb **pore over** *poring over the map* study, read, peruse, scrutinize, examine, review, inspect.

**pornography** noun **1** *obsessed with pornography* obscenity, salaciousness, lewdness, prurience, erotica, indecency, smut, filth; *inf.* porn. **2** *selling pornography* obscene literature, erotica; *inf.* porn, hard porn, soft porn, porno.

**port** noun seaport, harbor, haven, anchorage.

**portable** adjective transportable, movable, conveyable, lightweight, compact, handy, manageable.

**portend** verb be a warning of, herald, bode, augur, presage, forebode, foreshadow, foretell, be an omen of.

**portent** noun *dark skies can be a portent of a storm* sign, indication, presage, warning, omen, harbinger, foreshadowing, augury.

**portentous** adjective **1** *portentous events warning of trouble* ominous, warning, threatening, menacing, foreboding, ill-omened. **2** *a portentous monument* marvelous, remarkable, prodigious, phenomenal, spectacular, wondrous, amazing, astounding.

**portion** noun **1** *serve generous portions* helping, serving, piece, quantity. **2** *give a portion of his estate to each child* share, division, quota, part, bit, piece, allocation, allotment; *inf.* cut.

**portion** verb *portion the estate among his children* share, divide, split, partition, carve up, parcel out; *inf.* divvy up. **portion out** *portion out pieces of cake* distribute, dispense, hand out, deal out, dole out, allocate, apportion, allot, parcel out, mete out; *inf.* divvy up.

**portly** adjective stout, plump, fat, corpulent, obese, tubby, of ample build, stocky.

**portrait** noun **1** *portraits of his ancestors hung on the walls* painting, picture, drawing, sketch, portrayal, representation, likeness, image, study, canvas. **2** *have the photographer take a portrait of his daughter* photograph, photo, picture, studio portrait, study, shot, snapshot, still. **3** *the writer's portrait of his childhood* description, portrayal, depiction, account, story, chronicle, profile.

**portray** verb **1** *the artist portrayed the girl in a simple blue dress* paint, draw, sketch, depict, represent, delineate. **2** *portray a scene of abject poverty* describe, depict, characterize. **3** *portray Hamlet's mother in the production* play, act the part of, act, perform, represent, execute.

**pose** verb **1** *ask him to pose for a portrait* sit, model. **2** *carefully pose the subjects for his still life* arrange, position, lay out, set out, dispose, place, put, locate, situate. **3** *her posing impressed no one* strike an attitude, posture, act, playact, put on airs, show off. **4** *pose a question* put forward, put, submit, advance, propound, posit. **5** *icy roads pose problems for drivers* present, set, create, cause, give rise to. **pose as** *the con artist posed as a stockbroker* pretend to be, impersonate, masquerade as.

**pose** noun *assume a pose for the photo session* posture, stance, position, attitude, bearing, carriage.

**posh** adjective luxurious, deluxe, sumptuous, opulent, lavish, rich, grand, elegant, ornate, fancy, plush; *inf.* classy, ritzy, swanky.

**position** noun **1** *a house in an isolated position* situation, location, site, place, spot, area, locality, locale, scene, setting. **2** *identify the ship's position* location, bearings, whereabouts. **3** *standing in an uncomfortable position* posture, stance, attitude, pose, bearing. **4** *in an unfortunate financial position* situation, state, condition, circumstance, predicament, plight. **5** *declared their position on tax reform* point of view, viewpoint, opinion, outlook, attitude, stand, standpoint, stance. **6** *apply for the position of manager* post, job, situation, appointment, role, office, place, capacity, duty. **7** *what is his position in the class* place, level, grade, grading, rank, status, standing. **8** *people of position in society* rank, status, stature, standing, prestige, influence, reputation, importance, consequence.

**position** verb *position the soldiers in rows* place, locate, situate, put, arrange, set, settle, dispose, array.

**positive** adjective **1** *given positive instructions* clear, clear-cut, definite, precise, categorical, direct, explicit, express, firm. **2** *no positive proof of his guilt* real, actual, absolute, concrete, conclusive, unequivocal, incontrovertible, indisputable, undeniable, incontestable, unmistakable. **3** *they are positive that they have the solution* certain, sure, assured, confident, convinced. **4** *the results of the blood test are positive* affirmative. **5** *positive criticism* constructive, productive, helpful, practical, useful, beneficial. **6** *positive thinking* confident, optimistic, assured, assertive, firm. **7** *positive progress* good, favorable, effective, promising, encouraging, heartening.

**positively** adverb **1** *she assured us positively that he had gone* with certainty, definitely, emphatically, firmly, categorically, absolutely, confidently, dogmatically. **2** *they were positively furious* absolutely, really, indeed, extremely.

**possess** verb **1** *they possess two cars* own, be the owner of, have, hold, enjoy. **2** *possess a good mind* have, be endowed with, be gifted with. **3** *as if demons had possessed them* influence, control, dominate, bewitch, enchant, obsess.

**possessed** adjective *like someone possessed* bewitched, enchanted, under a spell, obsessed, haunted, bedeviled, crazed, mad, demented, berserk, frenzied. **2** *a possessed young woman* self-possessed, poised, self-controlled, self-assured, self-confident, confident, calm, cool, eventempered, composed, imperturbable; *inf.* unflappable.

**possession** noun **1** *her possession of the jewels* ownership, proprietorship. **2** *their possession of the house* occupancy, occupation, holding, tenure, tenancy. **3** *a possession of which she was very fond* personal item, asset, personal article.

**possibility** noun **1** *discuss the possibility of the plan working* feasibility, practicability, attainability, likelihood, potentiality, conceivability, probability. **2** *buying a smaller house is one possibility* likelihood, prospect, chance, hope. **3** *a possibility of more violence* likelihood, prospect, potential, promise, chance, risk, hazard.

**possible** adjective **1** *it is not humanly possible to get there on time* feasible, practicable, doable, attainable, achievable, realizable, within reach. **2** *one of several possible outcomes* likely, potential, conceivable, imaginable, probable, credible, tenable.

**possibly** adverb **1** *he may possibly arrive tomorrow* perhaps, maybe, likely; *lit.* peradventure. **2** *he will arrive if he possibly can* conceivably, by any means, by any chance, at all.

**post**[1] noun *put up the posts for the fence* stake, upright, pole, shaft, prop, support, column, stanchion, standard, stock, picket, pillar, pale, palisade, baluster, newel.

**post**[2] verb **1** *post notices on the walls* put up, attach, affix, hang, display, stick, stick up, pin, pin up, tack, tack up. **2** *details of the exams will be posted* announce, advertise, publish, publicize, circulate, broadcast, make known.

**post**[3] noun *promoted to a more prestigious post* appointment, assignment, office, position, job, situation; work, employment.

**post**[4] verb *post guards at the front entrance* station, put, place, position, set, situate, locate.

**poster** noun **1** *posters advertising the carnival* placard, bill, notice, flyer, advertisement, announcement, bulletin; *inf.* ad. **2** *bedroom walls covered with posters* picture, print, reproduction.

**postpone** verb defer, put off, delay, hold over, adjourn, shelve, table, pigeonhole; *inf.* put on ice, put on the back burner.

**postulate** verb *postulate that the population will decrease* assume, presuppose, suppose, presume, posit, hypothesize, theorize.

**posture** noun **1** *in a reclining posture* position, pose, attitude. **2** *have an elegant posture* carriage, bearing, stance. **3** *adopted a critical posture toward the new policy* attitude, position, point of view, viewpoint, opinion, outlook, stand, standpoint, stance, angle, slant.

**potent** adjective **1** *potent drugs* powerful, strong, effective, efficacious. **2** *he was a* *potent force in the land* powerful, forceful, strong, vigorous, mighty, influential, authoritative, commanding, dominant, energetic, dynamic; *lit.* puissant.

**potential** adjective **1** *a potential star* budding, embryonic, developing, promising, prospective, likely, possible, probable. **2** *his potential musical ability* latent, dormant, inherent, embryonic, developing, promising. **3** *a potential disaster* likely, possible, probable.

**potential** noun **1** *recognize the potential of the young singer* promise, capability, capacity, ability, aptitude, talent. **2** *the potential of the broken-down house* possibilities, promise.

**potion** noun drink, beverage, brew, concoction, mixture, draft, elixir, philter.

**potpourri** noun medley, miscellany, mélange, pastiche, collage, blend, mixture, hodgepodge, mishmash, jumble, gallimaufry, farrago, olio, olla podrida.

**pouch** noun bag, purse, wallet, container.

**pounce** verb **pounce on** *the fox pounced on the mouse* swoop on, spring on, lunge at, leap at, jump at/on, bound at, make a grab for, take by surprise, attack.

**pounce** noun *the fox grabbed the mouse with one pounce* swoop, spring, lunge, leap, jump, bound, grab, attack.

**pound** verb **1** *pound the garlic to a paste* crush, beat, pulverize, smash, mash, grind, comminute, triturate. **2** *pound his opponent with his fists* beat, batter, pummel, strike, hammer, pelt, thump. **3** *with heart pounding* pulsate, pulse, throb, thump, pump, palpitate.

**pour** verb **1** *she poured cream over the fruit* decant, splash, spill. **2** *water poured from the burst pipe* gush, rush, stream, flow, course, spout, jet, spurt. **3** *it was pouring rain heavily*, come down in torrents/sheets, rain cats and dogs. **4** *people poured from the burning building* stream, swarm, crowd, throng, flood.

**pout** verb sulk, scowl, glower, lower, look sullen, look petulant.

**poverty** noun **1** *the poverty of the homeless people* penniless-ness, neediness, need, want, hardship, deprivation, indigence, impoverishment, impecuniousness, destitution, penury, privation, beggary, pauperism, straitened circumstances. **2** *the poverty of their surroundings* humbleness, lowliness, meanness, modesty, plainness. **3** *the poverty of their imagination* deficiency, dearth, shortage, scarcity, paucity, insufficiency, lack, want, meagerness. **4** *the poverty of the soil* poorness, barrenness, unfruitfulness, bareness, aridity, sterility.

**power** noun **1** *the power to corrupt* ability, capability, capacity, potential. **2** *lose*

*the power of speech* ability, capability, faculty, competence. **3** *the power behind the blow* strength, force, forcefulness, might, weight, vigor, energy, potency. **4** *have him in her power* control, authority, mastery, domination, dominance, rule, command, ascendancy, supremacy, dominion, sway, sovereignty, influence. **5** *have the power to veto the rule* authority, authorization, warrant, license, right, prerogative. **6** *power used for heating* energy, electricity, nuclear power, solar power. **7** *the power of her argument* potency, strength, force, forcefulness, eloquence, effectiveness, cogency, conviction, persuasiveness.

**powerful** adjective **1** *of powerful build* | *two powerful boxers* strong, sturdy, strapping, stout, stalwart, robust, vigorous, tough, mighty. **2** *powerful members of the committee* influential, controlling, dominant, authoritative, commanding, forceful, strong, vigorous, potent, puissant. **3** *a powerful argument against leaving* forceful, strong, effective, cogent, compelling, convincing, persuasive, eloquent, impressive, telling, influential.

**powerless** adjective **1** *formerly influential members of the committee now powerless* impotent, weak, feeble, debilitated. **2** *powerless to give them any assistance* helpless, unfit, impotent, ineffectual, inadequate.

**practicable** adjective feasible, possible, viable, workable, doable, achievable, attainable, accomplishable.

**practical** adjective **1** *practical experience* hands-on, active, seasoned, applied, empirical, pragmatic, workaday. **2** *practical clothing for walking* functional, useful, utilitarian, sensible. **3** *she is very practical* businesslike, sensible, down-to-earth, pragmatic, realistic. **4** *find a practical solution* expedient, pragmatic, matter-of-fact, sensible, realistic, utilitarian.

**practically** adverb **1** *practically every day* almost, nearly, virtually, all but, in effect. **2** *behave practically* sensibly, with common sense, realistically, reasonably, pragmatically.

**practice** noun **1** *put the plan into practice* action, operation, application, effect, exercise, use. **2** *go to tennis practice* training, preparation, study, exercise, drill, workout, rehearsal. **3** *it is standard practice* procedure, method, system, usage, tradition, convention. **4** *it was his practice to visit his mother on Sundays* habit, custom, routine, wont. **5** *he engaged in the practice of law* profession, career, business, work, pursuit. **6** *buy a medical practice* firm, business.

**practice** verb **1** *to practice self-control* carry out, perform, execute, follow, pursue, observe. **2** *practicing a musical piece* work at, run through, go over, rehearse, polish, refine. **3** *practice law* work at, pursue a career in, engage in, specialize in.

**practiced** adjective *a practiced liar* experienced, seasoned, skilled, skillful, accomplished, expert, proficient, able, adept, adroit.

**pragmatic** adjective *she is very pragmatic | a pragmatic approach to the problem* practical, matter-of-fact, down-to-earth, sensible, businesslike, realistic, utilitarian.

**praise** verb **1** *praise the musician's performance* applaud, acclaim, cheer, compliment, congratulate someone on, pay tribute to, extol, laud. **2** *praise God* worship, glorify, honor, exalt, adore, laud, pay tribute to, give thanks to.

**praise** noun **1** *receive praise for his efforts* approval, approbation, applause, acclaim, acclamation, cheers, compliments, congratulations, commendation, tributes, accolades, plaudits, eulogy, panegyric, encomium, extolment, laudation, ovation, bouquets. **2** *praise to God* worship, glory, honor, devotion, exaltation, adoration, tribute, thanks.

**praiseworthy** adjective commendable, laudable, admirable, honorable, estimable, creditable, deserving, meritorious, worthy, excellent, exemplary, sterling, fine.

**prank** noun trick, practical joke, joke, hoax, caper, stunt; *inf.* lark.

**prattle** verb chatter, jabber, babble, twitter, blather, run on, rattle on.

**pray** verb **1** *pray the leaders to seek peace* appeal to, call upon, beseech, entreat, implore, beg, petition, solicit, plead with, importune, supplicate, sue, invoke, adjure. **pray for** *pray for mercy* appeal for, call for, beg for, petition for, solicit, plead for, crave, clamor for. **pray to** *pray to God* offer prayers to.

**prayer** noun **1** *say a prayer to God* devotion, communion, litany, invocation, intercession. **2** *prayers for mercy* appeal, plea, entreaty, petition, solicitation, supplication, suit, invocation, adjuration.

**preach** verb **1** *ministers preaching on Sunday* give a sermon, sermonize, evangelize. **2** *preach the word of God* proclaim, teach, spread. **3** *preach economy* advocate, recommend, advise, urge, exhort. **preach at** *tired of being preached at by her father* lecture, moralize, admonish, harangue, sermonize.

**preacher** noun **1** *a Baptist preacher* minister, reverend, parson, clergyman, clergywoman, ecclesiastic, cleric, missionary, revivalist, evangelist, televangelist. **2** *preachers of economy* advocate, adviser, urger, exhorter.

**precarious** adjective **1** *a precarious way of earning a living* uncertain, unsure, unpredictable, undependable, unreliable, risky, hazardous, chancy, doubtful, dubious, unsettled, insecure; *inf.* dicey. **2** *sitting in a precarious position at the edge of the cliff* risky, hazardous, insecure, unstable, shaky, perilous, dangerous, touch-and-go; *inf.* dicey, hairy.

**precaution** noun **1** *take a few precautions to avoid accidents* preventative measure, safeguard, provision. **2** *a situation that demands precaution* foresight, forethought, anticipation, prudence, circumspection, caution, care, attentiveness, chariness, wariness.

**precede** verb **1** *his father preceded him as chairman* go before, be the predecessor of. **2** *she preceded him into the room* lead, usher in, go/come before, go/come ahead of. **3** *the events that preceded the murder/victory* antedate, antecede, lead up to, herald, pave the way for. **4** *precede her lecture with a few informal remarks* preface, prefix, introduce, begin, open, launch.

**precedence** noun *educational considerations should take precedence over financial considerations* priority, superiority, pre-eminence, supremacy, primacy, transcendence, ascendancy.

**precedent** noun *is there a precedent for such a punishment?* prior case, pattern, model, example, exemplar, paradigm, criterion, yardstick, standard, previous instance.

**preceding** adjective *as stated in the preceding paragraph* above, foregoing, previous, earlier, prior, antecedent, anterior.

**precept** noun **1** *follow the precepts of one's religion* rule, guideline, principle, code, law, tenet, canon, ordinance, statute, command, order, decree, mandate, dictate, dictum, directive, direction, instruction. **2** *precepts that her grandmother used to quote* maxim, axiom, saying, law, adage, aphorism.

**precious** adjective **1** *precious metals* valuable, costly, expensive, priceless, rare, choice. **2** *precious memories* valued, cherished, prized, treasured, favorite, dear, beloved, adored. **3** *her manners are too precious for words* affected, artificial, chichi, overrefined, effete.

**precipice** noun escarpment, scarp, cliff, crag, bluff.

**precipitate** verb *precipitate the crisis* hasten, accelerate, expedite, speed up, propel, trigger.

**precipitate** adjective **1** *his precipitate dash from the room* hurried, rapid, swift, speedy, headlong, abrupt, sudden, unexpected, breakneck, violent, precipitous. **2** *his precipitate action* hasty, hurried, rash, heedless, reckless, impetuous, impulsive, precipitous, harebrained.

**precipitous** adjective **1** *a precipitous cliff* steep, sheer, perpendicular, abrupt, high. **2** *his precipitous exit* hurried, abrupt. *See* PRECIPITATE adjective 1. **3** *his precipitous action* hasty, impetuous. *See* PRECIPITATE adjective 2.

**precise** adjective **1** *a precise record of events* exact, literal, actual, close, faithful, strict, minute, accurate, correct. **2** *at that precise moment she saw him* exact, very, actual, particular, specific, distinct. **3** *precise attention to detail* careful, exact, meticulous, scrupulous, conscientious, punctilious, particular, methodical, fastidious, strict, rigorous.

**precisely** adverb **1** *at 6 o'clock precisely* exactly, sharp, on the dot, on the button. **2** *write out instructions precisely* exactly, literally, strictly, minutely.

**precision** noun **1** *the precision of his prose* carefulness, exactness, meticulousness, scrupulousness, conscientiousness, punctiliousness, rigor. **2** *the precision of the mechanism* accuracy, exactness, reliability, regularity.

**preclude** verb **1** *the rules of the club preclude drinking* prevent, prohibit, debar, interdict, block, bar, hinder, impede. **2** *the findings preclude any doubt as to his guilt* rule out, eliminate.

**precocious** adjective advanced, gifted, talented, brilliant, bright, quick, intelligent, smart.

**preconception** noun assumption, presupposition, presumption, prejudgment.

**precursor** noun **1** *the attacks proved to be the precursors of a full-scale war* forerunner, prelude, harbinger, herald, curtain-raiser. **2** *a precursor of the modern computer* predecessor, forerunner, antecedent, ancestor, forebear, progenitor.

**predatory** adjective **1** *predatory birds* predacious, carnivorous, rapacious, raptorial. **2** *her predatory relatives have left her penniless* exploitative, exploiting, imposing, greedy, acquisitive, rapacious, vulturine.

**predestine** verb *he seemed predestined to lead a life of poverty* preordain, foreordain, predetermine, fate, destine.

**predetermined** adjective *everyone acted on a predetermined signal* prearranged, preplanned, agreed, settled, fixed, set.

**predicament** noun dilemma, quandary, plight, tight corner, mess, emergency, crisis; *inf.* jam, sticky situation, fix, pickle, scrape, tight spot.

**predict** verb forecast, foretell, prophesy, foresee, divine, prognosticate, forewarn, forebode, portend, presage, augur.

**prediction** noun prophecy, forecast, divination, prognostication, forewarning, augury.

**predilection** noun *a predilection for spicy food* fondness, preference, love, partiality, taste, weakness, soft spot, fancy, inclination, leaning, liking, bias, propensity, bent, proclivity, proneness, penchant, predisposition.

**predispose** verb **1** *his poverty-stricken childhood predisposed him to save* move, incline, dispose, persuade, influence, sway, induce, prompt. **2** *the child is predisposed to asthma* make susceptible, make prone, make vulnerable.

**predominant** adjective **1** *the predominant member of the alliance* dominant, controlling, ascendant, ruling, leading, principal, chief, main, supreme, superior. **2** *idleness is his predominant characteristic* chief, main, principal, preponderant, most prevailing.

**predominate** verb **1** *the largest country predominates in the policymaking* be dominant, rule, hold ascendancy, hold sway, have the upper hand, carry most weight. **2** *blue predominates in the decor* be prevalent, preponderate, be most prominent.

**preeminent** adjective outstanding, leading, foremost, chief, excellent, distinguished, prominent, eminent, important, famous, renowned, supreme, superior, unrivaled, unsurpassed, transcendent.

**preempt** verb **1** *preempt the sale of the building by buying it themselves* forestall, prevent, invalidate. **2** *a news bulletin preempting the regular broadcast* supplant, displace, supersede, replace, substitute for.

**preen** verb **1** *birds preening their feathers* clean, smooth, arrange, plume. **2** *preening himself in front of the mirror* groom, spruce up, beautify, prettify, primp; doll up.

**preface** noun introduction, foreword, front matter, preamble, prologue, prelude, proem, exordium, prolegomenon; *inf.* intro.

**preface** verb *preface her speech with a short introduction* precede, prefix, introduce, begin, open, launch.

**prefer** verb **1** *of the desserts, I prefer pie* favor, incline toward, choose, select, pick, opt for; *inf.* fancy. **2** *prefer to go by bus* would rather, would sooner, favor, choose, opt, elect, wish, want.

**preference** noun **1** *her preference is for a two-story house* choice, first choice, inclination, liking, fancy, desire, wish, partiality, predilection, leaning, bias, bent. **2** *of the desserts, what is your preference?* choice, selection, option, pick. **3** *applicants with experience will be given preference* priority, advantage, preferential treatment, favor, precedence.

**pregnant** adjective **1** *discover that she was pregnant* expectant, with child, enceinte; *inf.* expecting, in the family way. **2** *a* *pregnant pause following her announcement* meaningful, significant, eloquent, expressive, suggestive, loaded, charged, pointed, telling.

**prejudice** noun **1** *have a prejudice against young people* bias, partiality, jaundiced eye, preconceived idea, preconception, prejudgment, predetermination. **2** *racial prejudice* bigotry, bias, discrimination, intolerance, partisanship, partiality, chauvinism, narrow-mindedness, unfairness, unjustness, racism. **3** *without prejudice to any future judgment* detriment, disadvantage, damage, injury, harm, hurt, loss.

**prejudice** verb **1** *newspaper articles had prejudiced the attitude of the jury* bias, color, poison, jaundice, influence, sway, predispose. **2** *his conviction may prejudice his chances* be detrimental to, damage, injure, harm, hurt, mar, spoil, impair, undermine.

**prejudiced** adjective *have a prejudiced attitude about foreigners* biased, discriminatory, partisan, partial, one-sided, jaundiced, chauvinistic, bigoted, intolerant, narrow-minded, unfair, unjust, racist, sexist. ·

**preliminary** adjective **1** *a few preliminary remarks* introductory, prefatory, precursory, opening, initial, beginning, preparatory, initiatory. **2** *preliminary heats* prior, precursory, qualifying, eliminating. **3** *preliminary experiments* introductory, early, exploratory, pilot, test, trial.

**preliminary** noun **1** *dispense with the preliminaries and get on with the meeting* preparation, groundwork, introduction, preamble, prelude, opening. **2** *advance to the final round after passing the preliminaries* first round, heat, trial, preliminary exam/examination.

**prelude** noun **1** *the skirmishes were a prelude to full-scale war* precursor, forerunner, curtain-raiser, harbinger, herald, preliminary, introduction, start, beginning. **2** *the prelude to the narrative poem* introduction, preface, prologue, preamble, proem, exordium, prolegomenon; *inf.* intro. **3** *the prelude to the fugue* overture, introductory movement, voluntary.

**premature** adjective **1** *his premature death* early, untimely, too soon. **2** *it was premature of him to announce his plans* hasty, precipitate, impulsive, impetuous, rash. **3** *announce premature plans* incomplete, undeveloped, immature, embryonic.

**premier** noun *an international meeting of premiers* head of government, head of state, chief executive, president, prime minister, chancellor.

**premise** noun *financial advice based on the premise that the recession was over* hypothesis, thesis, assumption, presupposition, presumption, argument, postulation.

**premium** noun **1** *monthly premiums for life insurance* payment, installment. **2** *earned a premium of $60 on their investment* bonus, dividend. **3** *pay a premium for early delivery* surcharge, additional payment, additional fee. **at a premium 1** *cannot buy a house when real estate is at a premium* high-priced, expensive, costly, upmarket. **2** *parking spaces are at a premium in the city* rare, hard to come by, in short supply, scarce, in great demand, like gold, not to be had. **put a premium on 1** *the teacher puts a premium on creative work* set great store by, hold in high regard, appreciate. **2** *the risk of disease puts a premium on hygiene* make invaluable, make essential, make important.

**premonition** noun **1** *had a premonition that something terrible was going to happen* foreboding, presage, presentiment, intuition, feeling, hunch, suspicion, misgiving, apprehension. **2** *given a premonition that all was not well in the firm* forewarning, warning, sign, indication, omen, portent.

**preoccupied** adjective *she seemed rather preoccupied* absorbed, engrossed, pensive, absentminded, distracted, abstracted, distrait, oblivious, rapt.

**preoccupy** verb *his financial worries were preoccupying him* absorb, engross, distract, obsess.

**preparation** noun **1** *the preparation of their plans* arrangement, development, assembly, drawing up, production, construction, composition. **2** *finalize their preparations for battle* arrangement, provision, preparatory measure, groundwork, spadework. **3** *the preparation of the students for the exam* coaching, training, grooming, priming.

**prepare** verb **1** *prepare their plans* make ready, arrange, develop, assemble, draw up, produce, construct, compose, concoct, fashion, work up. **2** *prepare for the president's visit* make preparations, get ready, lay the groundwork, do the spadework. **3** *prepare for the soccer game* train, get into shape, practice, exercise, warm up. **4** *prepare for the exam* study, do homework. **5** *prepare the students for the exam/contest* coach, train, groom, prime. **6** *prepare herself for a shock* brace, steel. **7** *prepare a meal* cook, make, put together, assemble; *inf.* fix, throw together.

**preponderance** noun *a preponderance of men over women on the staff | a preponderance of red in the room's decor* predominance, dominance, prevalence, majority, bulk.

**preposterous** adjective *what a preposterous idea!* absurd, ridiculous, foolish, ludicrous, farcical, asinine, senseless, unreasonable, irrational, outrageous, shocking, astonishing, unbelievable, incredible, unthinkable; *inf.* crazy, insane.

**prerequisite** noun *experience is a prerequisite for the job* requirement, requisite, necessity, essential, precondition, condition, sine qua non; *inf.* must.

**prerogative** noun *he thinks it is his prerogative to make all the decisions* right, birthright, privilege, due, entitlement, liberty, authority, license.

**prescribe** verb **1** *the doctor prescribed antibiotics* write a prescription for, order, advise, direct. **2** *prescribe a vacation to cure her depression* advise, recommend, commend, suggest. **3** *the law prescribes strict penalties for drunk driving* lay down, require, direct, stipulate, specify, impose, decree, order, command, ordain, enjoin.

**presence** noun **1** *the presence of too much acid in the soil* existence, being. **2** *demand his presence at the meeting* attendance, company, companionship. **3** *in the presence of a great man* company, propinquity, proximity, vicinity, closeness, nearness. **4** *a woman of presence* magnetism, aura, charisma, personality, attraction, poise, self-assurance, self-possession, self-confidence, bearing, carriage, dignity. **presence of mind** composure, aplomb, levelheadedness, sang-froid, self-assurance, self-possession, calmness, calm, coolness, alertness, quickness, quick-wittedness.

**present**[1] adjective **1** *poison was present in the drink* existent, extant. **2** *in the present climate* present-day, existing, current, contemporary. **3** *a doctor had to be present* in attendance, nearby, available, at hand, ready.

**present**[2] noun *forget the past and think about the present* today, now, here and now, the time being. **at present** *at present he is unavailable* just now, right now, at the moment, currently, presently.

**present**[3] verb **1** *present a gift to the retiring chairman* award, grant, accord, give, confer, bestow. **2** *present his proposals to the committee* submit, set forth, put forward, proffer, offer, tender, advance. **3** *present my apologies* give, offer, send, tender. **4** *may I present my daughter?* introduce, make known. **5** *present their new product* exhibit, display, put on display, demonstrate, introduce, show, launch. **6** *present a new musical* produce, perform, stage, put on, mount. **7** *present a radio/television program* introduce, host; *inf.* emcee.

**present**[4] noun *a birthday present* gift, donation, offering, contribution, gratuity, handout, giveaway, presentation, largesse, award, premium, bounty, boon, benefaction.

**presentable** adjective *make yourself presentable for the interview* well-groomed, smartly dressed, tidy, spruce.

**presentation** noun **1** *the presentation of his retirement gift* conferral, bestowal, award, granting, according. **2** *the presentation of their proposals to the committee* submission, proffering, tendering, offering. **3** *the presentation of his fiancée to his family* introduction, making known, acquainting. **4** *the presentation of their new product* launch, launching, show, exhibition, display, demonstration. **5** *attend the drama club's presentation of Hamlet* production, performance, staging, mounting, showing, rendition. **6** *improve the presentation of his material* arrangement, organization, ordering, disposition, layout, scheme, system, structure.

**presently** adverb *he will be here presently* soon, shortly, momentarily, directly, in a moment.

**preservation** noun **1** *the preservation of the rain forest* conservation, protection. **2** *the preservation of the town from danger* protection, defense, guarding, safeguarding, safekeeping, safety, security, salvation, sheltering, shielding. **3** *the preservation of old traditions* conservation, maintenance, continuation, upholding, perpetuation.

**preserve** verb **1** *find a substance to preserve the wood* protect, safeguard, care for. **2** *preserve the town from danger* keep, protect, defend, guard, safeguard, secure, shelter, shield. **3** *preserve his work for posterity* save, keep, safeguard, maintain, perpetuate. **4** *preserve the old traditions* keep up, keep alive, maintain, uphold, prolong, perpetuate. **5** *preserve food* cure, smoke, dry, pickle, salt, marinate, kipper, freeze, freeze-dry, can; *inf.* put up, lay by.

**preserve** noun **1** *an animal preserve* sanctuary, reserve, reservation, game reserve. **2** *he regards the family finances as his preserve* area, domain, field, sphere, realm.

**preside** verb *the committee members elected him to preside* chair, officiate. **preside over** *preside over the company* be in charge of, head, manage, administer, control, direct, run, conduct, supervise, govern, rule, head up.

**president** noun **1** *president of the United States* chief of state, head of state, chief executive, commander in chief. **2** *president of the society* head, chief, director, leader, captain.

**press** verb **1** *press the button* depress, push down, bear down on. **2** *press grapes* crush, squeeze, compress, mash, reduce. **3** *press a pair of pants* iron, smooth out, put creases in, calender, mangle. **4** *press her hand/arm affectionately* squeeze, pat, caress. **5** *they are pressing him to make a decision* urge, entreat, exhort, implore, pressurize, force, compel, coerce, constrain. **6** *press a claim* plead, urge, push forward, advance. **7**

*press around the stage to see the performers* crowd, surge, cluster, mill, flock, gather, swarm, throng. **press for** *they are pressing for a quick decision* call for, demand, insist on, clamor for. **press on** *we must press on to reach the summit* push on, make haste, hasten, hurry, proceed, continue.

**press** noun **1** *advertise in the press* newspapers, papers, news media, journalism, the media, journalists, reporters. **2** *get good/bad press* press coverage, press reporting, newspaper articles, write-ups. **3** *he has set up a small press* printing firm, publishing firm, publishing house.

**pressing** adjective *pressing engagement* urgent, vital, crucial, critical, demanding, important, high-priority, exigent, pivotal.

**pressure** noun **1** *have to exert pressure on the door to open it | the pressure of the crowd against the barriers* force, weight, heaviness, compression, compressing, squeezing, crushing. **2** *police exerting pressure to get a confession* force, compulsion, coercion, constraint, duress. **3** *the pressure of the job* strain, stress, tension, burden, load, weight, trouble; *inf.* hassle. **4** *find it difficult to work under pressure* adversity, difficulty, urgency, strain, stress, tension.

**prestige** noun *suffered a loss of prestige when he lost his job* status, standing, stature, importance, reputation, fame, renown, esteem, influence, authority, supremacy, eminence, superiority, predominance.

**prestigious** adjective **1** *a prestigious school* respected, esteemed, eminent, distinguished, of high standing, well-known, celebrated, illustrious, renowned, famous. **2** *a prestigious job* prominent, impressive, high-ranking, influential, glamorous.

**presumably** adverb *presumably he will get the job* in all probability, probably, in all likelihood, on the face of it, as likely as not.

**presume** verb **1** *I presume that your new partner is honest* assume, take for granted, take it, suppose, presuppose, believe, imagine, judge, guess, surmise, conjecture, hypothesize, infer, deduce. **2** *do not presume to offer advice to a more experienced person* have the temerity, have the audacity, be so bold as, have the effrontery, go so far as, dare, venture. **presume on/upon** *presume on/upon his good nature* take advantage of, exploit, take liberties with.

**presumption** noun **1** *his request for an invitation was pure presumption* arrogance, egotism, boldness, audacity, forwardness, insolence, impudence, bumptiousness, temerity, effrontery. **2** *our presumption is that he has run away* assumption, supposition, presupposition, belief, thought, judgment, guess, surmise, conjecture, hypothesis, premise, inference, deduction.

**presumptuous** adjective *it was presumptuous to offer advice to someone of her experience* overconfident, cocksure, arrogant, egotistical, conceited, overbold, bold, audacious, forward, insolent, impudent, bumptious, self-assertive, overbearing, overweening; *inf.* pushy.

**pretend** verb **1** *she is not ill—she is only pretending* act, playact, dissemble, sham, feign, fake, fake it, dissimulate, posture. **2** *she is pretending that she knows nothing about it* make believe, affect, profess, fabricate. **3** *pretend illness* feign, fake, simulate, sham. **4** *pretend to the title* lay claim, make a claim, aspire. **5** *pretend to be her friend* claim, profess, purport.

**pretense** noun **1** *she is not ill—it is just pretense* acting, dissembling, shamming, faking, dissimulation, make-believe, invention, imagination, posturing. **2** *not taken in by their pretense of grief* false show, semblance, appearance, guise, façade, masquerade, mask, veneer, cover, charade. **3** *on the pretense that he was dying* sham, ruse, wile. See PRETEXT. **4** *I have no pretense to being expert* claim, aspiration, purporting, profession. **5** *lead humble lives without pretense* pretentiousness, display, ostentation, affectation, showiness, flaunting, posturing.

**pretentious** adjective **1** *a pretentious style of writing* affected, ostentatious, showy, overambitious, pompous, artificial, mannered, high-flown, flowery, grandiose, elaborate, extravagant, flamboyant, grandiloquent, magniloquent, bombastic, orotund; *inf.* highfalutin. **2** *a pretentious lifestyle* affected, ostentatious, showy, flaunting, flamboyant.

**pretext** noun *the thief got into the house on the pretext of checking the phone lines* pretense, false excuse, excuse, cover, guise, sham, ruse, wile, trickery, red herring, lie, falsehood, misrepresentation.

**pretty** adjective **1** *a pretty child* attractive, lovely, good-looking, nice-looking, comely, prepossessing, appealing, charming, delightful, nice, engaging, pleasing, winning, winsome, cute. **2** *a pretty pattern* attractive, lovely, appealing, pleasant, pleasing, charming, delightful, nice. **3** *cost a pretty penny | make a pretty profit* considerable, large, sizable, substantial, appreciable, fair, tolerable, goodly; *inf.* tidy.

**prevail** verb **1** *in the end, common sense prevailed* win, win out, triumph, be victorious, carry the day, prove superior, conquer, overcome, gain mastery, gain ascendancy, take the crown, rule. **2** *the economic conditions prevailing at the time* exist, obtain, occur, abound, hold sway, predominate, preponderate, be prevalent, be current, be widespread. **prevail on/upon** *prevail* *upon him to speak at the conference* persuade, induce, convince, sway, prompt, influence, urge, exhort, pressure, cajole, coax; *inf.* sweet-talk.

**prevailing** adjective **1** *the prevailing attitude toward criminals | the prevailing fashion in hats* prevalent, current, usual, common, general, widespread, established, accepted, popular, fashionable, in style, in vogue. **2** *the prevailing political party* prevalent, dominant, predominant, preponderant, ruling, governing, ascendant, principal, chief, main, supreme. **3** *the prevailing wind in the area* most frequent, most common, commonest.

**prevalent** adjective **1** *the prevalent opinion in the country is against the war* current, common, widespread. *See* PREVAILING 1. **2** *malaria is prevalent there* common, usual, endemic, widespread, universal, extensive, frequent, ubiquitous, rampant, rife. **3** *the prevalent political party* dominant, preponderant, governing. *See* PREVAILING 2.

**prevent** verb *prevent the spread of the fire | prevent his daughter from leaving school* stop, halt, arrest, avert, nip in the bud, fend off, turn aside, stave off, ward off, block, check, hinder, impede, hamper, obstruct, balk, foil, thwart, frustrate, forestall, inhibit, restrain, prohibit, bar, deter.

**prevention** noun *the prevention of crime* stopping, halting, halt, arresting, staving off, warding off, checking, hindrance, hampering, obstruction, balking, foiling, frustration, restraint, prohibition, barring, deterrence.

**previous** adjective **1** *the previous mayor* former, ex-, preceding, foregoing, past, sometime, onetime, quondam, erstwhile, antecedent, precursory. **2** *in the previous paragraph* preceding, foregoing, earlier, prior, above, precursory, antecedent, anterior. **3** *on a previous occasion* prior, earlier, former, preceding. **previous to** *previous to this everything was fine* before, prior to, until, up to, up until, earlier than, preceding.

**previously** adverb *previously they lived in Kansas* formerly, earlier on, before, until now/then, hitherto, heretofore, once, at one time.

**prey** noun **1** *lions looking for prey* quarry, game, kill. **2** *prey for any dishonest salesman* victim, target, dupe; *inf.* sitting duck.

**prey** verb **prey on 1** *lions preying on deer* eat, devour, hunt, catch, seize. **2** *con men preying on the unsuspecting* victimize, exploit, take advantage of, fleece, attack, bleed; *inf.* con.

**price** noun **1** *what is the price of the table in the window?* cost, charge, fee, payment, rate, amount, figure, value, valuation, outlay, expense, expenditure, bill. **2** *lack of privacy is the price of fame* consequence, result, cost, penalty, sacrifice, forfeiture, punishment. **3** *outlaws with a price on their heads* reward, bounty, premium, recompense, compensation.

**price** verb *price the items at $10 each* value, rate, cost, evaluate, assess, estimate, appraise, assay.

**priceless** adjective *priceless jewels/memories* invaluable, precious, rare, incomparable, expensive, costly, rich, dear, irreplaceable, treasured, prized, cherished, worth its weight in gold, worth a king's ransom.

**prick** noun **1** *give his finger a prick with a sharp needle* jag, jab, stab, nick. **2** *see the prick on the surface* puncture, perforation, hole, pinhole, nick. **3** *feel a prick on the surface of the skin* prickle, sting, smarting, tingle, tingling, pain. **4** *the pricks of his conscience* pang, twinge, gnawing. **5** *rosebushes with pricks* spike, thorn, barb, spine, prong, tine.

**pride** noun **1** *his pride was hurt by her criticisms* self-esteem, self-respect, ego, *amour propre*, self-worth, self-image, feelings, sensibilities. **2** *puffed with pride at his achievement* conceit, vanity, arrogance, haughtiness, self-importance, self-conceit, egotism, presumption, hauteur, superciliousness, disdain; *inf.* bigheadedness. **3** *take pride in his work* satisfaction, gratification, pleasure, joy, delight. **4** *the gold medalist is the pride of the swim team* prize, jewel, jewel in the crown, flower, gem, treasure, glory.

**pride** verb **pride oneself on** *she prided herself on her punctuality* take satisfaction in, congratulate oneself on, revel in, glory in, exult in.

**priest** noun clergyman, minister, vicar, ecclesiastic, cleric, churchman, churchwoman, man/woman of the cloth, man/woman of God, father, padre.

**prig** noun prude, puritan, killjoy; *inf.* goody-goody, Goody Two-shoes.

**priggish** adjective prudish, puritanical, prim, prissy, straitlaced, stuffy, starchy, self-righteous, sanctimonious, narrow-minded, censorious; *inf.* holier-than-thou, goody-goody.

**prim** adjective proper, demure, formal, precise, stuffy, starchy, straitlaced, prudish, prissy, priggish, puritanical.

**prima donna** noun diva, leading lady, star.

**primarily** adverb *his role is primarily an administrative one* basically, essentially, in essence, fundamentally, first and foremost, chiefly, mainly, principally, mostly, for the most part, on the whole, predominantly, predominately.

**primary** adjective **1** *the children's welfare is our primary consideration* prime, chief, main, principal, leading, predominant, paramount. **2** *finding food to eat is a primary need* basic, fundamental, elemental, rudimentary, essential, prime. **3** *the primary stages of the disease* earliest, original, initial, beginning, first, opening, introductory.

**prime** adjective **1** *his prime motive was self-interest* chief, main, principal, leading, predominant, major, paramount. **2** *the prime cause of the trouble* basic, fundamental, elemental, rudimentary, essential, primary. **3** *of prime quality* top-quality, highest, top, best, first-class, high-grade, grade A, superior, choice, select; *inf.* A-1. **4** *a prime example of what is wrong with modern society* classic, ideal, excellent, typical, standard.

**prime** noun *in the prime of his life* | *flowers in their prime* peak, pinnacle, height, zenith, acme, culmination, apex, heyday, full flowering, perfection, blossoming.

**prime** verb **1** *prime the machines for use* prepare, make ready, get ready, equip. **2** *prime the investigating officer* brief, inform, supply with facts; *inf.* fill in. **3** *the attorney was accused of priming the witness* coach, prepare.

**primeval** adjective *primeval rocks/species* ancient, earliest, prehistoric, primitive, primordial, primal, autochthonal, pristine.

**primitive** adjective **1** *in primitive times* | *the primitive church* ancient, earliest, primeval, primordial, primal, autochthonal. **2** *primitive farming tools* crude, simple, rudimentary, undeveloped, unrefined, rough, unsophisticated, rude. **3** *primitive tribes* uncivilized, barbarian, barbaric, savage, wild. **4** *primitive art* simple, natural, unsophisticated, naïve, undeveloped, childlike. **5** *primitive artists* unsophisticated, naïve, untaught, untrained, untutored.

**primp** verb *primp themselves for the photo* groom, tidy, smarten, spruce, preen, plume; *inf.* doll up.

**principal** adjective **1** *the principal members of the organization* chief, leading, preeminent, foremost, most influential, dominant, controlling, ruling, in charge. **2** *the principal issues on the agenda* chief, main, major, most important, leading, key, primary, prime, paramount.

**principal** noun **1** *the principals in the firm* chief, head, director, leader, manager, boss, ruler, controller; *inf.* honcho. **2** *the principals in the play* leading player, leading man/lady, lead, star. **3** *lend him the principal to start up the business* capital, capital funds, working capital, financial resources.

**principally** adverb *he is interested principally in higher education* chiefly, above all, first

and foremost, mainly, primarily, mostly, particularly, especially.

**principle** noun **1** *the basic principles of geometry* truth, philosophy, idea, theory, basis, fundamental, essence, assumption. **2** *believe in the principle of equal opportunity* rule, law, canon, tenet, code, maxim, axiom, dictum, postulate. **3** *a woman of principle* morals, ethics, integrity, uprightness, righteousness, probity, rectitude, honor, conscience, scruples. **in principle 1** *there is no reason in principle why such a machine could not be built* in theory, theoretically. **2** *they agree in principle to the plan* in essence, in general.

**print** verb **1** *print books/newspapers* set in print, publish, issue, send to press, run off, put to bed. **2** *print a design on the cloth* imprint, stamp, mark.

**print** noun **1** *see the story in print* type, letters, lettering, typeface, newsprint. **2** *buy a print of one of Monet's works* copy, reproduction, replica. **3** *buy a set of prints showing presidential homes* picture, design, engraving, lithograph, etching, silkscreen, woodcut. **4** *get enlarged prints* photograph, photo, snapshot. **5** *chairs covered in a print* patterned material/cloth, chintz. **in print 1** *likes to see his name in print* in black and white, on paper. **2** *are her novels still in print?* published, printed, available, on the market. **out of print** *looking for a biography that is out of print* no longer published/printed, unavailable, unobtainable.

**prior** adjective *a prior claim* earlier, previous, anterior. **prior to** *prior to the conference, they had never met* before, until, up to, preceding.

**priority** noun **1** *the children's safety is their priority* prime concern, most important thing. **2** *give priority to homeless people* precedence, preference, urgency, superiority.

**prison** noun jail, penitentiary, lockup, penal institution, dungeon; *inf.* clink, cooler, slammer, pen.

**pristine** adjective **1** *a pristine copy of the book* unmarked, unblemished, unspoiled, spotless, immaculate, clean, in mint condition. **2** *pristine snow* spotless, clean, fresh, virgin.

**private** adjective **1** *for her private use* personal, individual, own, particular, especial, special, exclusive. **2** *hold private talks* confidential, secret, unofficial, off-the-record, in camera, closet, privileged; *inf.* hush-hush. **3** *her private thoughts* personal, intimate, secret. **4** *a private place where the lovers meet* secluded, sequestered, quiet, secret, remote, out-of-the-way, withdrawn, retired. **5** *trespassing on private property* privately owned, off-limits. **6** *a private person* reserved, retiring, self-contained, uncommunicative, noncommunicative, diffident, secretive. **7** *the president on a private visit* unofficial, personal. **8** *private industry* privatized, independent.

**privation** noun *suffering a life of privation* deprivation, want, need, neediness, disadvantage, poverty, penury, hardship, distress, indigence, destitution.

**privilege** noun **1** *parking there is the privilege of the executives* right, prerogative, entitlement, due, sanction, advantage, benefit, birthright. **2** *enjoy diplomatic privilege* immunity, exemption, dispensation, concession, liberty, freedom. **3** *has always led a life of privilege* advantage, favor, favorable circumstances. **4** *he felt that it had been a privilege to meet her* honor, special benefit.

**privileged** adjective **1** *coming from a privileged background* advantaged, favored, elite, protected, sheltered. **2** *foreign diplomats are privileged* immune, exempt, excepted. **3** *punished for revealing privileged information* confidential, private, off-the-record, secret, top-secret; *inf.* hush-hush.

**prize** noun **1** *win a prize in the lottery* jackpot, stakes, purse, winnings. **2** *six prizes awarded in the flower show* trophy, medal, award, accolade, reward, premium, honor, laurels.

**prize** adjective *wind destroyed his prize roses* prizewinning, award-winning, champion, best, top, choice, select, first-class, first-rate, excellent; *inf.* top-notch, A-1.

**prize** verb *she prizes her freedom* value, treasure, cherish, hold dear, appreciate, esteem, hold in high regard.

**probability** noun **1** *what is the probability of the government losing the election?* likelihood, prospect, expectation, chance, chances, odds, possibility. **2** *snow at Christmas is a distinct probability* likelihood, prospect, possibility, reasonable bet.

**probable** adjective *the probable result is a win for the home team | it is probable that we will arrive late* likely, odds-on, expected, to be expected, anticipated, predictable, foreseeable, credible, possible.

**probably** adverb *they will probably win* in all probability, likely, in all likelihood, as likely as not, it is to be expected that, perhaps, maybe, possibly.

**probe** noun *order a probe into the company's accounting procedures* investigation, scrutiny, inquiry, inquest, exploration, examination, study, research, analysis.

**probe** verb **1** *probe the tooth with his tongue* feel, prod, poke, explore, check. **2** *probe the financial state of the company* investigate, scrutinize, inquire into, examine, study, research, analyze.

**problem** noun **1** *face a seemingly impossible problem* difficulty, complication, trouble, mess, predicament, plight, dilemma, quandary; *inf.* pickle. **2** *the car's mechanical problems* difficulty, trouble, complication. **3** *he and his wife have had a few problems* difficulty, dispute, bone of contention; issues. **4** *baffled by the word problems* question, puzzle, poser, enigma, riddle, conundrum; *inf.* teaser, brainteaser. **5** *the child is a real problem* source of trouble, bother, nuisance, pest, vexation; *inf.* hassle, aggravation.

**problem** adjective *a problem child* difficult, troublesome, delinquent, unmanageable, unruly, uncontrollable, intractable, recalcitrant, nuisance.

**problematic** adjective **1** *a problematic situation* difficult, troublesome, complicated, puzzling, knotty, thorny, ticklish, tricky. **2** *the likely result is still problematic* doubtful, uncertain, unsettled, questionable, open to question, debatable, arguable.

**procedure** noun **1** *the usual office procedure* course of action, policy, system, method, methodology, modus operandi, technique, means, practice, operation, strategy, way, routine, wont, custom. **2** *essential procedures for setting up the new system* action, step, process, measure, move, operation, transaction.

**proceed** verb **1** *proceed along Main Street* make one's way, go, advance, carry on, continue, move on, progress. **2** *how shall we proceed?* act, take action, take steps, take measures, go ahead, move, make a start, progress, get under way. **3** *noise proceeding from the floor below | the tragedy that proceeded from a family feud* arise, originate, spring, stem, come, derive, result, follow, ensue, emanate, issue, flow.

**proceedings** plural noun **1** *the evening's proceedings begin at 7 p.m.* activities, events, action, process, business, affairs, doings, happenings. **2** *the proceedings against him are likely to last several weeks* legal action, case, lawsuit, litigation, trial. **3** *the proceedings of the meeting were made available* minutes, report, account, record, transactions.

**proceeds** plural noun *donate the proceeds to charity* takings, profits, returns, receipts, gain, income, earnings.

**process** noun **1** *damaged during the manufacturing process* operation, action, activity, steps, stages. **2** *develop a new process for cleaning stone buildings* method, system, technique, means, practice, way, procedure. **3** *the aging process* development, evolution, changes, stages, steps. **4** *legal processes can be very slow* proceedings, legal action, case, lawsuit, trial. **in the process** *we are in the process of cataloging our* *books* in the midst, in the course, at the stage.

**procession** noun **1** *a candlelit procession as part of the celebration* parade, march, column, file, train, cortege. **2** *a procession of decorated vehicles* cavalcade, motorcade. **3** *a seemingly endless procession of houseguests* stream, string, succession, series, sequence, run.

**proclaim** verb **1** *proclaim the news of a royal birth* announce, declare, make known, notify, circulate, advertise, publish, broadcast, promulgate, pronounce, blazon, trumpet, shout something from the rooftops. **2** *proclaim him king* pronounce, announce, declare.

**proclamation** noun **1** *hear the proclamation of a royal birth* announcement, declaration, notification, circulation, advertisement, publishing, broadcasting, promulgation, pronouncement, blazoning. **2** *the king's proclamation was posted in each town* announcement, declaration, pronouncement, decree, edict, order, command, rule, manifesto.

**procrastinate** verb delay, stall, temporize, play for time, dally, dilly-dally, drag one's feet/heels.

**procure** verb **1** *procure a copy of the book from the library* obtain, acquire, get, pick up, find, come by, get hold of, secure, get possession of, gain. **2** *somehow procure the dismissal of his colleague* bring about, cause, contrive, manage, manipulate, rig; *inf.* fix.

**prod** verb **1** *prod him in the ribs* poke, jab, dig, nudge, elbow, butt, push, shove, thrust. **2** *prod the child into doing some work* urge, encourage, rouse, move, motivate, stimulate, incite, spur, impel, actuate, goad.

**prod** noun **1** *get a prod in the ribs from someone in the crowd* poke, jab, dig, nudge, elbow, butt, push, shove, thrust. **2** *use a prod to get the cows to go back to the farm* goad, stick, spike. **3** *giving the child a prod to get him to do some work* encouragement, prompt, motivation, stimulus, incitement, spur, goad.

**prodigal** adjective *a government accused of being prodigal* extravagant, spendthrift, squandering, improvident, imprudent, immoderate, profligate, excessive, wasteful, reckless, wanton.

**prodigious** adjective **1** *a prodigious achievement* amazing, astonishing, astounding, staggering, stupendous, marvelous, wonderful, phenomenal, miraculous, impressive, striking, startling, extraordinary, remarkable, exceptional, unusual; *inf.* fantastic, fabulous, flabbergasting. **2** *children frightened by the prodigious creatures on the screen* enormous, huge, colossal, gigantic, giant, mammoth, immense, massive, vast, monumental, tremendous, inordinate, monstrous. **3** *charge a prodigious amount of money* huge, large, colossal, immense, massive, considerable, substantial, sizable; *inf.* vast, tremendous.

**prodigy** noun **1** *the young musician is a prodigy* genius, gifted child, mastermind; *inf.* Einstein. **2** *the pyramids are among the prodigies of the world* wonder, marvel, phenomenon, sensation, miracle.

**produce** verb **1** *a factory producing high-quality work* make, manufacture, create, construct, build, fabricate, assemble, turn out. **2** *produce great works of art* compose, create, originate, prepare, develop, frame, fashion, turn out. **3** *produce new evidence* bring forward, set forth, present, offer, proffer, advance, show, exhibit, demonstrate, disclose, reveal. **4** *cows producing milk* yield, bear, give, bring forth, supply, provide, furnish. **5** *sows producing litters of piglets* give birth to, bring forth, bear, breed, procreate. **6** *his speech produced an angry reaction* cause, give rise to, evoke, bring about, set off, occasion, generate, engender, induce, initiate, start, spark. **7** *produce plays for television* mount, stage, put on, present, direct.

**produce** noun *organically grown produce* crops, fruit and vegetables, fruit, vegetables, greens.

**product** noun **1** *a factory specializing in electronic products* commodity, artifact, manufactured item/article. **2** *good health is the product of good nutrition | he is the product of a Victorian upbringing* result, outcome, effect, consequence, upshot, fruit, spin-off, legacy. **products** *marketing new products* goods, wares, merchandise.

**production** noun **1** *speed up the production of cars* manufacture, manufacturing, creation, construction, building, fabrication, making, assembly. **2** *his production of great works of literature/art* composition, creation, origination, preparation, development, framing, fashioning. **3** *the production of new evidence* presentation, offering, proffering, advancement, exhibition, demonstration, disclosure. **4** *an increase in production* output, yield. **5** *see a production of her latest play* performance, staging, mounting. **6** *several productions staged by the company* play, film, concert, show, performance, presentation, piece. **7** *this is the writer's/artist's latest production* work, publication, composition, piece, creation, opus.

**productive** adjective **1** *productive soil* fertile, fruitful, fecund, rich, high-yielding. **2** *a productive worker* prolific, energetic, vigorous, efficient. **3** *not a very productive* *day's work* profitable, gainful, valuable, fruitful, useful, constructive, effective, worthwhile, beneficial, rewarding.

**profane** adjective **1** *their profane behavior in setting fire to the altar* blasphemous, sacrilegious, impious, irreligious, ungodly, godless, irreverent, disrespectful. **2** *shocked by their profane language* blasphemous, obscene, foul, vulgar, crude, filthy, coarse.

**profanity** noun **1** *the profanity of brawling in church* profaneness, blasphemy, sacrilege, impiety, irreverence, disrespectfulness, disrespect. **2** *issue a stream of profanities* oath, swearword, swearing, obscenity, four-letter word, curse, execration, imprecation.

**profess** verb **1** *profess satisfaction with his work | profess one's faith* declare, announce, proclaim, assert, state, utter, affirm, avow, aver, confess, confirm, . **2** *he professed total ignorance of the situation* claim, lay claim to, allege, pretend, feign, fake.

**profession** noun **1** *a teacher by profession* career, calling, vocation, occupation, line of work, employment, position, situation, post, job, office, appointment, métier, walk of life, business. **2** *they were relieved by his professions of satisfaction | his profession of his faith* declaration, announcement, proclamation, assertion, statement, affirmation, avowal, testimony, averment, confession. **3** *not taken in by his profession of ignorance* claim, allegation, pretense, feigning, shamming, faking, dissembling.

**professional** adjective **1** *he has a professional job* white-collar. **2** *a very professional worker* skilled, skillful, proficient, expert, adept, competent, efficient, experienced. **3** *a very professional piece of work* skillful, expert, masterly, excellent, fine, polished. **4** *conduct that was hardly professional* ethical, fitting.

**professional** noun **1** *a new office for the young professional* professional worker, white-collar worker. **2** *this tennis player is a professional now* nonamateur, paid player; *inf.* pro. **3** *the singer/tailor is a real professional* expert, master, past master, adept, authority; *inf.* pro.

**proficient** adjective *a proficient swimmer | proficient at swimming | proficient in French* accomplished, skilled, skilled, adept, apt, expert, adroit, deft, able, capable, competent, experienced, effective, talented, gifted.

**profile** noun **1** *look better in profile* side-view, outline. **2** *the profile of the church against the sky* silhouette, outline, contour, lines, shape, form, figure. **3** *write a profile of the author* short biography, sketch, thumbnail sketch, portrait, vignette.

**profit** noun *the profit made from the sale of the house* takings, proceeds, gain, yield, return, receipts, income, earnings, winnings.

**profit** verb *it will not profit you to be openly critical of the company* benefit, be of benefit to, be advantageous to, serve, do (someone) good, help, be helpful to, assist, aid, stand (someone) in good stead. **profit from** *profit from his advice* benefit from, gain from, put to good use, learn from; *inf.* cash in on.

**profitable** adjective **1** *a profitable venture* moneymaking, commercial, gainful, remunerative, paying, lucrative. **2** *a profitable company* sound, solvent, in the black. **3** *find it a profitable experience* beneficial, advantageous, rewarding, helpful, productive, useful, worthwhile, valuable.

**profligate** adjective **1** *profligate people ending up in debt* extravagant, spendthrift, improvident, prodigal, immoderate, squandering, reckless, wasteful. **2** *a profligate cad* dissolute, dissipated, debauched, corrupt, degenerate, depraved, reprobate, unprincipled, immoral, promiscuous, loose, wanton, licentious, lascivious, lecherous.

**profound** adjective **1** *a profound thinker* discerning, penetrating, thoughtful, philosophical, deep, weighty, serious, learned, erudite, wise, sagacious. **2** *unable to understand such profound doctrine* learned, erudite, serious, deep, difficult, complex, abstract, abstruse, esoteric, impenetrable. **3** *a profound love for his country* deep, intense, keen, great, extreme, sincere, heartfelt. **4** *a profound silence* deep, pronounced, total, absolute, complete, utter. **5** *profound changes taking place* far-reaching, radical, extensive, exhaustive, thoroughgoing.

**profuse** adjective **1** *give profuse thanks* lavish, liberal, unstinting, generous, fulsome, extravagant, inordinate, immoderate, excessive. **2** *profuse blossom on the trees* abundant, copious, ample, plentiful, bountiful, luxuriant.

**profusion** noun *a profusion of roses on the bushes* abundance, superabundance, copiousness, quantities, scores, masses, multitude, plethora, wealth, plenitude, cornucopia; *inf.* heaps, stacks, piles, loads, mountains, tons, scads, oodles.

**progeny** noun **1** *the parents and all their progeny* children, offspring, young ones, family, issue. **2** *the progeny of John Adams* descendants, successors, lineage, scions, seed, posterity.

**program** noun **1** *refer to the conference program* agenda, calendar, schedule, syllabus, order of the day. **2** *buy a program at the theater* playbill, list of performers. **3** *the orchestra played a varied program* repertoire, repertory, performance. **4** *watch* *several television programs* production, presentation, show, performance, broadcast. **5** *get the program for next semester's courses* syllabus, prospectus, schedule, list, curriculum, literature. **6** *organize a program of financial investment* schedule, scheme, plan, project.

**progress** noun **1** *climbers making progress toward the summit* headway, going, passage, advancement. **2** *the company has made very little progress in the past few years* advancement, improvement, betterment, upgrading, development, growth. **in progress** *work in progress* under way, ongoing, occurring, taking place, proceeding, being done, being performed.

**progress** verb **1** *the climbers progressed up the mountain* advance, continue, proceed, make one's way, make headway, push forward, forge ahead. **2** *the talks are progressing* make progress, move forward, advance, make headway, make strides, develop, improve.

**progression** noun **1** *the progression from mail clerk to managing director* passage, advancement, development. **2** *a progression of applicants/jobs* succession, sequence, series, string, stream, parade, chain, train.

**progressive** adjective **1** *progressive movement* forward, onward, advancing. **2** *a progressive disease* increasing, growing, intensifying, accelerating, escalating. **3** *a progressive office system* modern, advanced, forward-looking, enlightened, enterprising, up-and-coming, innovative; avant-garde. **4** *progressive ideas on education* radical, reforming, innovative, revolutionary, revisionist.

**prohibit** verb **1** *a regulation to prohibit smoking* forbid, ban, bar, disallow, proscribe, veto, interdict, outlaw. **2** *low salaries prohibit them from buying a house* prevent, stop, rule out, preclude, hinder, impede, hamper, obstruct, restrict, constrain.

**prohibition** noun **1** *the prohibition of smoking in hospitals* forbidding, banning, barring, disallowing, proscription, vetoing, interdiction, outlawing. **2** *a prohibition on the sale of cigarettes to children* ban, bar, interdict, veto, embargo, injunction, proscription.

**prohibitive** adjective *the prohibitive cost of housing* prohibitory, forbidding, disallowing, proscriptive, restrictive, suppressive.

**project** noun scheme, plan, program, enterprise, undertaking, venture, activity, operation, campaign.

**project** verb **1** *a projected new mall* plan, propose, devise, design, outline. **2** *project missiles into space* launch, discharge, propel, hurl, throw, cast, fling, shoot. **3** *the*

*balcony projects over the garden* jut, jut out, protrude, extend, stick out, bulge out, beetle, obtrude. **4** *project sales figures for next year* extrapolate, calculate, estimate, gauge, reckon, forecast, predict.

**projection** noun **1** *a projection of rock* overhang, ledge, shelf, ridge, protuberance, protrusion, jut, bulge. **2** *their sales projection for next year* forecast, prediction, extrapolation, calculation, computation, estimate, estimation, gauge, reckoning.

**proletariat** noun workers, working class, wage earners, laboring classes, common people, commonalty, lower classes, lower orders, rank and file, masses, mob, rabble, hoi polloi.

**proliferate** verb multiply, mushroom, increase, extend, expand, burgeon, accelerate, escalate, snowball.

**proliferation** noun increase, growth, multiplication, spread, expansion, extension, burgeoning, acceleration, escalation, buildup, snowballing, mushrooming.

**prolific** adjective **1** *prolific vegetation* fertile, fruitful, fecund, luxuriant, abundant, profuse, copious, rank. **2** *a prolific writer* productive.

**prologue** noun *the prologue to the novel* introduction, foreword, preface, preamble, prelude, preliminary, exordium, proem, prolegomenon.

**prolong** verb *problems with the car prolonged the journey* lengthen, elongate, extend, stretch out, draw out, drag out, protract.

**prominence** noun **1** *a prominence on the flat countryside* protuberance, projection, protrusion, jutting, swelling, bulge. **2** *the prominence of the tower on the skyline* conspicuousness, obviousness, obtrusiveness. **3** *newspapers giving prominence to the scandal* importance, weight, conspicuousness, precedence, top billing. **4** *men of prominence in the community* importance, eminence, preeminence, distinction, note, prestige, stature, illustriousness, celebrity, fame, renown, acclaim.

**prominent** adjective **1** *a prominent feature of the landscape* conspicuous, noticeable, obvious, unmistakable, obtrusive, outstanding, eye-catching, striking. **2** *a prominent member of the local community* leading, outstanding, chief, main, top, important, eminent, preeminent, distinguished, notable, noted, illustrious, celebrated, well-known, famous, renowned, acclaimed.

**promiscuous** adjective sexually indiscriminating, dissolute, dissipated, fast, licentious, loose, profligate, abandoned, immoral, debauched, wanton, unchaste.

**promise** verb **1** *promise that he will be present* give one's word, give one's assurance, swear, vow, take an oath, pledge, contract. **2** *skies that promise good weather* augur, indicate, denote, signify, show signs of, hint at, suggest, betoken, presage.

**promise** noun **1** *a promise that he would be there* word, word of honor, assurance, guarantee, commitment, vow, oath, pledge, bond, contract, covenant. **2** *a promise of spring in the air* indication, hint, suggestion, sign. **3** *a young musician of promise* talent, potential, flair, ability, aptitude, capability, capacity.

**promising** adjective **1** *it is promising that you have a second interview* encouraging, hopeful, favorable, auspicious, propitious, optimistic, bright. **2** *a promising young writer* with potential, talented, gifted, able, apt; *inf.* up-and-coming.

**promontory** noun headland, point, cape, head, foreland, bluff, cliff, precipice, overhang, height, projection, prominence.

**promote** verb **1** *she has been promoted to sales manager* upgrade, elevate, advance, move up, give a higher position to, place in a higher rank, prefer, aggrandize. **2** *he promoted the cause of peace by his actions* advance, further, assist, aid, help, contribute to, foster, boost. **3** *the local council promotes equal rights for all* advocate, recommend, urge, support, back, endorse, champion, sponsor, espouse. **4** *companies promoting their new products* advertise, publicize, push; *inf.* plug, hype.

**promotion** noun **1** *get a promotion to a managerial post* upgrading, elevation, advancement, preferment, aggrandizement. **2** *his promotion of peace* advancement, furtherance, furthering, assistance, aid, help, contribution to, fostering, boosting. **3** *the council's promotion of equal rights for all* advocacy, recommendation, urging, support, backing, endorsement, championship, sponsoring, espousal. **4** *the company's promotion of their new products* advertising, advertising campaign, publicity, publicizing, push, pushing; *inf.* plug, plugging, hype.

**prompt** adjective *receive a prompt reply* swift, rapid, speedy, quick, fast, expeditious, early, punctual, timely; immediate, instant, instantaneous.

**prompt** verb **1** *what prompted them to leave?* cause, make, encourage, move, induce, urge, incite, impel, spur, motivate, stimulate, inspire, provoke. **2** *his actions prompted an angry response* cause, give rise to, induce, occasion, elicit, evoke, provoke. **3** *he forgot his lines, so she prompted him* remind, jog someone's memory, cue.

**promulgate** verb publicize, announce, spread, communicate, disseminate, circulate, broadcast, publish, proclaim, declare, herald, blazon, trumpet.

**prone** adjective **1** *lying prone for his rubdown | weary hikers lying prone at their campsite* face down, procumbent, lying down, flat, horizontal, full-length, supine, prostrate, stretched out, recumbent. **2** *prone to lose his temper* inclined, given, likely, liable, apt, disposed, predisposed. **3** *prone to headaches* subject, susceptible, disposed, predisposed.

**prong** noun point, tip, spike, tine.

**pronounce** verb **1** *have difficulty in pronouncing the letter 's'* enunciate, articulate, say, utter, sound, voice, vocalize. **2** *pronounce judgment* announce, declare, proclaim, assert, affirm, rule, decree.

**pronounced** adjective **1** *have a pronounced lisp* marked, noticeable, obvious, evident, conspicuous, striking, distinct, unmistakable. **2** *have pronounced views on the subject* decided, definite, clear, strong, positive, distinct.

**proof** noun **1** *produce proof of your identity* evidence, certification, verification, authentication, validation, confirmation, attestation. **2** *produce proof of his guilt* evidence, demonstration, substantiation, corroboration, confirmation, attestation, testimony. **3** *send the novelist proofs of her book* galley proof, galley, page proof, trial print.

**prop** noun **1** *a prop holding up the side of the shed* support, upright, brace, buttress, stay, bolster, stanchion, truss, column, post, rod, pole, shaft. **2** *a prop of the local arts league* pillar, mainstay, anchor, rock, backbone, supporter, upholder, sustainer.

**prop** verb *prop his bike against the wall* lean, rest, set, lay, stand, balance, steady. **prop up** *prop up the wall of the garage* shore up, bolster, buttress, support, brace, underpin, reinforce, strengthen.

**propagate** verb **1** *propagate plants* grow, breed. **2** *animals propagating* reproduce, multiply, proliferate, breed, procreate. **3** *propagate new political ideas* spread, communicate, circulate, disseminate, transmit, distribute, broadcast, publish, publicize, promulgate.

**propel** verb move, set in motion, push forward, drive, thrust forward, force, impel.

**propensity** noun *a propensity to lie | a propensity for getting into trouble* tendency, inclination, leaning, bent, bias, disposition, predisposition, proneness, proclivity, penchant, susceptibility, weakness.

**proper** adjective **1** *the proper equipment for the sport* right, suitable, fitting, appropriate, apt. **2** *the proper way to do things* right, correct, precise, accepted, acceptable, established, orthodox, conventional, formal, *comme il faut.* **3** *put the books in*

**property · prosper**

*their proper place* right, correct, own, individual, particular, respective, special, specific. **4** *have a very proper upbringing* seemly, decorous, respectable, decent, refined, genteel, gentlemanly/ladylike, formal, conventional, orthodox, strict.

**property** noun **1** *the books were her personal property* possessions, belongings, things, goods, effects, chattels, assets, resources. **2** *put his money in property* real estate, buildings, land, estates. **3** *the antiseptic properties of alcohol* quality, attribute, characteristic, feature, power, peculiarity, idiosyncrasy, quirk.

**prophecy** noun **1** *her prophecy came true* prediction, forecast, prognostication, divination, augury. **2** *the gift of prophecy* prediction, foretelling the future, fortune-telling, second sight, prognostication, divination, augury, soothsaying.

**prophesy** verb *the seer prophesied his death* predict, foretell, forecast, foresee, presage, prognosticate, divine, augur.

**prophet** noun seer, soothsayer, fortuneteller, diviner, clairvoyant, prognosticator, prophesier, oracle, augur, sibyl, Cassandra. **prophet of doom** pessimist, Cassandra.

**propitious** adjective *not a propitious time to try to sell one's house* auspicious, favorable, promising, optimistic, bright, advantageous, fortunate, lucky, rosy, beneficial, opportune, suitable, timely.

**proponent** noun *a proponent of socialism* advocate, supporter, upholder, adherent, backer, promoter, endorser, champion, defender, sponsor, espouser, friend, well-wisher.

**proportion** noun **1** *the proportion of women to men on the staff* ratio, distribution, relative amount/number, relationship. **2** *give a large proportion of his income to the poor* portion, part, segment, share, quota, division, percentage, fraction, measure; *inf.* cut. **3** *the pleasing proportions of the room* balance, symmetry, harmony, correspondence, congruity, agreement.

**proportional** adjective *more work to do, with a proportional increase in salary* proportionate, corresponding, commensurate, equivalent, comparable.

**proposal** noun **1** *the proposal of new terms of employment* putting forward, advancement, offer, proffering, presentation, submitting. **2** *draw up a financial proposal* scheme, plan, project, program, motion, bid, proposition, presentation, suggestion, recommendation, tender, terms.

**propose** verb **1** *propose changes in legislation* put forward, advance, offer, proffer, present, submit, tender, propound, suggest, recommend, advocate. **2** *they are proposing to leave now* intend, mean, plan,

aim. **3** *propose his cousin as president of the society* put forward, put up, nominate, name, suggest, recommend. **4** *propose to his girlfriend* offer marriage, ask for someone's hand in marriage, pay suit; *inf.* pop the question.

**proposition** noun **1** *an attractive business proposition* proposal, scheme, plan, project, program, motion, bid. **2** *getting into the building unnoticed is not an easy proposition* task, job, undertaking, venture, problem. **3** *make a proposition to the man at the bar* sexual advance, indecent proposal; *inf.* come-on.

**proprietor** noun owner, possessor, titleholder, deed-holder, landowner, landlord/landlady; host, innkeeper, hotelier, manager, restaurateur.

**propriety** noun **1** *behave with propriety* seemliness, decorum, respectability, decency, correctness, appropriateness, good manners, courtesy, politeness, civility, refinement, gentility, breeding, conventionality, orthodoxy, formality, etiquette, protocol. **2** *question the propriety of your decision* rightness, correctness, fitness, suitability, appropriateness, aptness.

**prosaic** adjective unimaginative, uninspired, matter-of-fact, dull, dry, humdrum, mundane, pedestrian, lifeless, spiritless, stale, bland, vapid, banal, hackneyed, trite, insipid, monotonous, flat, ordinary, everyday, common, routine, commonplace, workaday, tedious, boring.

**proscribe** verb **1** *proscribe the sale of alcohol on Sundays* prohibit, forbid, ban, bar, disallow, embargo, interdict, outlaw. **2** *he was proscribed for his part in the conspiracy* outlaw, exile, expel, expatriate, deport, boycott, blackball, ostracize.

**prosecute** verb *he was prosecuted for drunk driving* bring a charge against, charge, try, put on trial, sue, interdict, arraign.

**prospect** noun **1** *there is little prospect of success* likelihood, hope, expectation, anticipation, chance, chances, odds, probability, possibility. **2** *the prospect of being unemployed frightens him* thought, idea, contemplation, outlook. **3** *admire the prospect from the hill* view, vista, outlook, perspective, panorama, scene, spectacle.

**prospect** verb *prospect an area for diamonds* explore, search, inspect, survey, examine, check out. **prospect for** *prospect for gold* search for, seek.

**prospective** adjective **1** *her prospective father-in-law* future, soon-to-be, intended, expected. **2** *attract prospective customers* would-be, potential, possible, likely, hoped-for, awaited, anticipated.

**prosper** verb thrive, flourish, succeed, get ahead, progress, advance, make good, become rich, be in clover; *inf.* be on easy street, live the life of Riley.

**prosperity** noun success, good fortune, ease, plenty, affluence, wealth, riches, the good life, luxury, life of luxury.

**prosperous** adjective thriving, flourishing, successful, well-off, well-to-do, affluent, wealthy, rich, moneyed, opulent, in clover; *inf.* well-heeled, in the money, on easy street.

**prostitute** noun call girl, whore, woman of the streets, lady of the evening, street-walker, woman of ill repute, fallen woman, courtesan, *fille de joie*; *inf.* hooker, working girl, hustler.

**prostrate** adjective **1** *found prostrate on the floor* prone, lying down, flat, stretched out, horizontal, full-length, procumbent. **2** *prostrate before the emperor* bowed low, humbled. **3** *prostrate with grief* overcome by/with, overwhelmed by, overpowered by, brought to one's knees by, paralyzed by, laid low by/with, impotent with.

**protagonist** noun **1** *the protagonist in the new play* hero/heroine, central character, principal, leading man/lady, title role, lead. **2** *a protagonist of feminism* leader, standard-bearer, mainstay, spokesman, spokeswoman, spokesperson, advocate, supporter, upholder, adherent, backer, proponent, promoter, champion.

**protect** verb **1** *protect the child from injury* keep safe, save, safeguard, shield, preserve, defend, shelter, secure. **2** *soldiers protecting the castle* guard, defend, secure, watch over, look after, take care of. **3** *protect the surface of the table with a plastic sheet* preserve, shield, cover, cover up, conceal, mask.

**protection** noun **1** *provide protection against violence* safekeeping, safety, preservation, defense, security. **2** *under the protection of the police* safekeeping, care, charge, keeping, defense, protectorship. **3** *wear warm clothes as a protection against the cold* safeguard, shield, barrier, buffer, screen, cover.

**protest** verb **1** *protesting his treatment of the staff* object to, oppose, make/take a stand against, put up a fight against, take exception to, complain about, express disapproval of, demur at, remonstrate about, demonstrate against; *inf.* gripe about, grouse about, beef about, bitch about. **2** *protest his innocence* declare, announce, profess, proclaim, assert, affirm, argue, attest, testify to, maintain, insist on, aver, avow.

**protest** noun **1** *register a protest against/about his treatment of the children* objection, opposition, exception, complaint, disapproval, disagreement, dissent, demurral, remonstration, fuss, outcry, demonstration. **2** *listen to his protests that he was*

innocent protestation, declaration, profession, assertion, affirmation, attestation, assurance, avowal, proclamation.

**protester** noun *a crowd of protesters gathered outside the embassy* objector, opposer, opponent, complainer, demonstrator, dissenter, dissident, rebel, striker, agitator.

**protocol** noun *observe the protocol associated with royal visits* etiquette, rules of conduct, code of behavior, conventions, formalities, customs, propriety, decorum, manners, courtesies, civilities, good form, politesse.

**protract** verb *loves to talk at meetings and protract the discussions* prolong, extend, stretch out, draw out, lengthen, drag out, continue.

**protrude** verb *a piece of rock protruding from the cliff face* jut, jut out, stick out, stand out, project, extend, beetle, obtrude, bulge.

**protuberance** noun *a protuberance on the trunk of the tree* swelling, bulge, lump, bump, protrusion, projection, knob, growth, outgrowth, tumor, excrescence.

**proud** adjective **1** *proud parents* pleased, glad, happy, satisfied, gratified, content, appreciative. **2** *they were poor but proud* self-respecting, dignified, independent. **3** *he has become too proud to associate with his old friends* arrogant, conceited, vain, self-important, egotistical, boastful, haughty, disdainful, scornful, supercilious, snobbish, imperious, overbearing, lordly, presumptuous, overweening, high-handed; *inf.* high-and-mighty, stuck-up, uppity, snooty, highfalutin. **4** *it was a proud day when they won the cup* gratifying, satisfying, happy, memorable, notable, red-letter, glorious, marvelous. **5** *the ship was a proud sight sailing into the harbor* magnificent, splendid, grand, noble, stately, imposing, majestic, august.

**prove** verb **1** *prove that he was the murderer* determine, demonstrate, show beyond (a/the shadow of a) doubt, substantiate, corroborate, verify, validate, authenticate, confirm. **2** *the rumor proved to be correct* be found, be shown, turn out.

**proverb** noun saying, adage, maxim, saw, axiom, aphorism, gnome, dictum, apothegm.

**proverbial** adjective **1** *her proverbial meanness kept visitors away* legendary, notorious, infamous, famous, famed, renowned, well-known, acknowledged, accepted, traditional, time-honored. **2** *he has become the proverbial good Samaritan* axiomatic, epigrammatic, aphoristic, apothegmatic, well-known.

**provide** verb **1** *provide the guests with food and shelter* supply, furnish, equip, accommodate, provision, outfit, give, offer. **2**

351

# provident · prudish

*the novel provides insight into the war* give, bring, afford, present, offer, accord, yield, impart, lend. **3** *the contract provides that the tenants are responsible for repairs* stipulate, lay down, require, state, specify.

**provide against** *provide against an enemy attack* make provision for, take precautions against, guard against. **provide for 1** *provide for his family* support, maintain, keep, sustain, take care of, care for, look after. **2** *the organizers of the wedding tried to provide for every eventuality* allow for, prepare for, anticipate, plan for.

**provident** adjective *it was provident of them to take out accident insurance | provident people providing for their old age* farsighted, prudent, judicious, shrewd, circumspect, wise, sagacious, cautious, careful, canny.

**province** noun **1** *the administrative center of the province* state, territory, region, area, district. **2** *that part of the business is not my province* area of responsibility, field, business, line, charge, concern, duty. **3** *in the province of English literature* discipline, field, specialty, area.

**provincial** adjective **1** *provincial government* regional, local, municipal, state, county, district; topical. **2** *unfair in her assumption that all suburbanites are provincial* uncultured, uncultivated, unrefined, unpolished, unsophisticated, parochial, limited, small-minded, insular, naïve, uninformed, narrow-minded, bigoted, prejudiced, intolerant.

**provision** noun **1** *the provision of conference facilities* providing, supply, furnishing, equipping, outfitting, accommodation, affording. **2** *make provision for their old age* preparation, plan, prearrangement, arrangement, precaution. **3** *the housing policy makes no provision for single people* arrangement, allowance, concession. **4** *under the provisions of his will, his children inherit his estate* term, requirement, specification, stipulation, proviso, condition.

**provisional** adjective provisory, temporary, interim, stopgap, transitional, conditional, tentative, contingent; *inf.* pro tem.

**provisions** plural noun *stock up with provisions* supplies, stores, groceries, food, foodstuffs, staples, rations, provender, eatables, edibles, victuals, comestibles, viands.

**proviso** noun *they agreed to the change with the proviso that an investigation be held* condition, stipulation, provision, clause, rider, qualification, restriction, reservation, limitation, strings.

**provocation** noun **1** *react to the slightest provocation* annoyance, irritation, vexation, harassment, affront, insult, exasperation, infuriation, irking; *inf.* rile, aggravation. **2** *hit him under provocation* incitement, stimulation, stimulus, motivation,

prompting, inducement, goading. **3** *what was the provocation of their anger?* evocation, instigation, cause, occasioning, inducement, inspiration, kindling, production, generation, precipitation, promotion.

**provocative** adjective **1** *the fight was started by a provocative remark* annoying, irritating, exasperating, infuriating, maddening, vexing, galling, affronting, insulting, inflammatory, goading; *inf.* aggravating. **2** *wear a provocative, low-cut dress* alluring, seductive, sexy, tempting, suggestive, erotic, titillating.

**provoke** verb **1** *do not provoke the hornet* annoy, anger, incense, enrage, irritate, exasperate, infuriate, madden, pique, nettle, vex, harass, irk, gall, affront, insult; *inf.* rile, needle, aggravate. **2** *provoke her into shouting at them* incite, rouse, stir, move, stimulate, motivate, excite, inflame, prompt, induce, spur, goad, prod, egg on. **3** *his speech provoked laughter* evoke, cause, give rise to, occasion, call forth, elicit, induce, inspire, excite, kindle, produce, generate, engender, instigate, lead to, precipitate, promote, prompt.

**prowess** noun **1** *admire his prowess as a yachtsman* skill, skillfulness, expertise, facility, ability, capability, talent, genius, adroitness, adeptness, aptitude, dexterity, deftness, competence, proficiency, knowhow, *savoir faire.* **2** *the prowess of the soldiers in battle* courage, bravery, gallantry, valor, heroism, intrepidity, fearlessness, mettle, pluck, gameness, nerve, boldness, daring, fortitude, steadfastness, stoutness, sturdiness; *inf.* grit, guts, spunk.

**prowl** verb *prowling around the building* slink, skulk, steal, roam, range, sneak, stalk; *inf.* snoop.

**proximity** noun closeness, nearness, propinquity, adjacency, contiguity.

**prudence** noun **1** *question the prudence of his action* wisdom, judgment, judiciousness, sagacity, shrewdness, sense, circumspection, farsightedness, foresight, forethought. **2** *behave with prudence rather than rashness* caution, care, discretion, wariness, vigilance, heedfulness. **3** *her prudence allowed her to buy a house* providence, thrift, thriftiness, economy, canniness, sparingness, frugality, management, budgeting.

**prudent** adjective **1** *a prudent decision* wise, judicious, sagacious, sage, shrewd, sensible, circumspect, farsighted, politic. **2** *advised to be prudent* cautious, careful, discreet, wary, vigilant, heedful. **3** *prudent with her income* provident, thrifty, economical, canny, sparing, frugal.

**prudish** adjective puritan, puritanical, priggish, prim, straitlaced, prissy, stuffy, starchy, Victorian; *inf.* goody-goody.

**prune** verb **1** *prune the roses* trim, thin, thin out, cut back, shape. **2** *prune branches from the bushes* cut, lop, chop, clip, snip, remove. **3** *prune expenses* cut back, pare down, cut, trim, reduce, shorten, curtail.

**pry** verb *she resents it when he pries* interfere, meddle, intrude, be inquisitive, be a busybody; *inf.* snoop. **pry into 1** *pry into her private affairs* be inquisitive about, nose into, inquire into, interfere in, meddle in; *inf.* be nosy about. **2** *pry into her possessions* peer into, peek into, scrutinize, ferret around in, poke around in, nose around in, spy on; *inf.* poke one's nose into, snoop into.

**pseudo** adjective *a pseudo interest in the arts* feigned, pretended, simulated, imitation, false, artificial, ersatz, spurious, fake, bogus, sham, mock, fraudulent, counterfeit, forged; *inf.* phony.

**pseudonym** noun nom de plume, pen name, stage name, professional name, assumed name, alias, allonym, sobriquet, nickname, nom de guerre.

**psychic** adjective **1** *people thought to be psychic* clairvoyant, telepathic, telekinetic, spiritualistic. **2** *psychic powers* supernatural, preternatural, extrasensory, otherworldly, paranormal, occult. **3** *psychic disorder* spiritual, mental, psychological, psychogenic.

**psychological** adjective **1** *psychological studies* mental, cerebral, psychic, psychical. **2** *her inability to work is psychological* in the mind, psychosomatic, emotional, irrational, imaginary, subconscious, unconscious.

**public** adjective **1** *public health services* state, national, civic, civil, social. **2** *increase public awareness* popular, general, common, universal, widespread. **3** *public parks* accessible to all, open to the public, of free access. **4** *make his views public* known, acknowledged, overt, in circulation, published, publicized, plain, obvious. **5** *scandals about public figures* prominent, well-known, eminent, influential, prestigious, famous, celebrated, illustrious.

**public** noun **1** *the public has a right to know* people, everyone, population, country, nation, community, citizens, populace, masses, commonalty, electorate, voters. **2** *actors/authors worrying about what their public think* audience, spectators, readers, followers, following, fans, admirers, patrons, clientele. **in public** *refuse to appear in public* publicly, openly.

**publication** noun **1** *the publication of the book/newspaper* publishing, production, issuance. **2** *a widely read publication* book, newspaper, magazine, periodical, journal, daily, weekly, monthly, quarterly, booklet, brochure, leaflet, pamphlet, handbill. **3** *the publication of the committee's findings* publishing, announcement, notification, reporting, declaration, communication, imparting, proclamation, disclosure, divulgence, broadcasting, publicizing, distribution, spreading, dissemination, promulgation, issuance.

**publicity** noun **1** *his marriage prompted much publicity* notoriety, public interest, public notice. **2** *seeking publicity for her new book* promotion, advertising; *inf.* hype, buildup.

**publicize** verb **1** *publicize a description of the wanted man* announce, publish, broadcast, distribute, disseminate, promulgate. **2** *publicize her new book* promote, advertise; *inf.* hype, plug.

**publish** verb **1** *they publish reference books* produce, issue, print. **2** *publish the committee's findings* make public, announce, report, declare, communicate, impart, proclaim, disclose, divulge, broadcast, publicize, distribute, spread, disseminate, promulgate.

**pucker** verb **1** *a dress puckered at the waist* gather, shirr, pleat, ruck, ruffle, wrinkle, crease. **2** *the unhappy child's face puckered* screw up, wrinkle, crease, furrow, knit, crinkle, corrugate.

**pudgy** adjective stout, round, rotund, plump, roly-poly, dumpy, squat, stubby, stumpy, chubby, tubby.

**puerile** adjective childish, immature, infantile, juvenile, adolescent, foolish, silly, inane, asinine.

**puff** noun *a puff of wind* gust, blast, whiff, breath, flurry, draft.

**puff** verb *puffing while climbing the hill* pant, blow, gasp, gulp.

**puffy** adjective *puffy cheeks/eyes* swollen, distended, inflated, dilated, bloated, bulging, edematous.

**pugnacious** adjective *in a pugnacious mood* belligerent, bellicose, combative, fighting, battling, aggressive, antagonistic, quarrelsome, argumentative, disputatious, hostile, threatening, irascible, ill-tempered, bad-tempered.

**pull** verb **1** *the child was pulling a toy behind him* haul, drag, draw, trail, tow, tug. **2** *pull the rope to straighten it* haul, tug, jerk; *inf.* yank. **3** *pull teeth* extract, remove, draw out, take out, root out. **4** *pull a muscle* strain, sprain, wrench, stretch, tear, dislocate, damage. **pull back** *the army pulled back after the defeat* withdraw, retreat, draw back, fall back. **pull down** *pull down old buildings* knock down, demolish, raze, level, destroy, bulldoze, dismantle. **pull in 1** *the car pulled in to the driveway* drive in, draw in. **2** *plays pulling in large audiences* draw, bring in, attract, lure, entice. **3** *he pulls in $50,000 a year* earn, take home, bring in, make, clear, net, gross, pocket. **pull off 1** *pull the top off the can* remove, detach, tear off. **2** *pull off the export deal* bring off, carry out, accomplish, execute, succeed in. **pull oneself together** regain one's composure, get a grip on oneself; *inf.* snap out of it. **pull out 1** *pull out a gun* take out, withdraw. **2** *pull out of the contest* withdraw, leave, quit, abandon, give up, renege on. **pull someone's leg** *he was only pulling her leg* tease, make fun of, poke fun at, joke with, rag, chaff, twit; *inf.* rib. **pull through** *she was very ill but pulled through* recover, rally, survive, recuperate. **pull up 1** *pull up the weeds* root out, uproot, dig up, grub up, extract. **2** *the car pulled up to the curb* draw up, park alongside, drive up.

**pull** noun **1** *give a pull at the bell rope* tug, haul, yank, jerk. **2** *the pull of the current* tug, force, power, exertion, effort. **3** *the pull of the sea to sailors* attraction, lure, enticement, draw, magnetism, influence. **4** *he has pull with the boss* influence, weight, leverage, muscle; *inf.* clout.

**pulp** noun **1** *the pulp of the fruit* flesh, marrow. **2** *reduce the vegetables to a pulp* paste, purée, mush, mash, pap, triturate. **3** *make a fortune out of writing pulp* pulp fiction, rubbish, trash, trivia, drivel, pap.

**pulsate** verb *loud music pulsating throughout the building* beat, throb, vibrate, pulse, palpitate, pound, thud, thump, drum.

**pulse** noun *the compelling pulse of the music* beat, rhythm, throb, throbbing, vibration, pulsation, pounding, thudding, thud, thumping, thump, drumming.

**pulse** verb beat, throb. *See* PULSATE.

**pulverize** verb **1** *pulverize the solid foods* grind, crush, pound, crumble, powder, crunch, squash, pulp, purée, liquidize, mash, comminute, triturate. **2** *pulverize his opponent in the boxing ring* defeat utterly, overwhelm, trounce, rout, flatten, crush, smash, vanquish, destroy, annihilate; *inf.* hammer.

**pump** verb **1** *pump the bicycle tires* pump up, blow up, inflate. **2** *pump blood through the body* drive, force, push, send. **3** *pump him for information* question, quiz, interrogate, cross-examine; *inf.* grill.

**punch** verb strike, hit, knock, thump, thwack, box, jab, cuff, slug, smash, bash, slam, batter, pound, pummel; *inf.* sock, wallop, whack.

**punch** noun **1** *give his opponent a punch in the jaw* blow, hit, knock, thump, box, jab, cuff, slug, smash, slam; *inf.* sock, wallop, whack, clout, plug. **2** *the speech lacked punch* strength, vigor, force, verve, drive, impact, bite, effectiveness; *inf.* oomph, pizazz.

**punctilious** adjective careful, scrupulous, meticulous, conscientious, exact, precise, particular, strict, finicky, fussy; *inf.* persnickety.

**punctual** adjective prompt, on time, on the dot, timely, well-timed, early.

**puncture** noun *a puncture in the tire* perforation, hole, rupture, cut, nick, slit, leak, prick.

**puncture** verb *the piece of glass punctured the tire* perforate, pierce, bore, deflate, prick, spike, penetrate, rupture, cut, nick, slit.

**pungent** adjective **1** *a pungent smell* sharp, acrid, biting, stinging. **2** *a pungent taste* sharp, acid, sour, biting, bitter, tart, tangy, spicy, aromatic, piquant. **3** *pungent wit* caustic, acid, biting, cutting, sharp, incisive, piercing, penetrating, pointed.

**punish** verb discipline, penalize, castigate, chastise; beat, cane, whip, flog, lash, scourge; mistreat, abuse, manhandle.

**punishment** noun discipline, penalty, retribution, castigation, redress, chastisement; beating, caning, whipping, flogging, lashing, scourging; mistreatment, abuse, manhandling.

**punitive** adjective **1** *take punitive measures against the culprits* punishing, penalizing, disciplinary, corrective, castigating, castigatory, chastising. **2** *punitive rates of taxation* harsh, severe, stiff, taxing, cruel, savage.

**puny** adjective **1** *the bodybuilder claimed that he was once puny* weak, frail, feeble, undersized, underdeveloped, stunted, small, slight, little, dwarfish. **2** *a puny contribution* paltry, petty, trifling, trivial, insignificant, inconsequential, minor, meager; *inf.* piddling.

**pupil** noun **1** *pupils wearing school uniforms* student, schoolboy, schoolgirl, schoolchild, scholar. **2** *a pupil of Picasso* student, disciple.

**puppet** noun **1** *puppets amusing children* marionette, hand puppet, finger puppet. **2** *a puppet of management* tool, instrument, cat's-paw, pawn, dupe, mouthpiece; *inf.* stooge.

**purchase** verb *purchase a new car* buy, acquire, pick up, obtain, invest in, put money into.

**purchase** noun **1** *proud of her new purchase* acquisition, buy, investment. **2** *difficult to get any purchase on the slippery cliff face* grip, hold, foothold, footing, toehold, support, grasp, leverage, advantage.

**pure** adjective **1** *pure gold* unalloyed, unmixed, unadulterated, uncontaminated, flawless, perfect, genuine, real, true. **2** *pure water* clean, clear, fresh, unpolluted, untainted, unadulterated, uncontaminated, wholesome, natural. **3** *pure novitiates* virgin, virginal, chaste, virtuous, undefiled, unsullied. **4** *lead a pure life* uncorrupted, moral, righteous, honorable, virtuous, honest, upright, decent, good, worthy, noble, blameless, guiltless, pious, sinless. **5** *of pure character* stainless, spotless, unsullied, unblemished, impeccable, immaculate, blameless, sinless. **6** *pure madness* sheer, utter, absolute, downright, out-and-out, complete, total, perfect, unmitigated, unqualified. **7** *pure mathematics* theoretical, abstract, conceptual.

**purely** adverb *find out purely by accident* entirely, completely, totally, wholly, solely, only, simply, just, merely.

**purge** verb **1** *purge their souls of sin* cleanse, clear, purify. **2** *purge the party of dissidents* rid, clear, empty. **3** *purge the dissidents from the party* remove, expel, eject, dismiss, oust, depose, eradicate, root out, weed out.

**purge** noun **1** *the purge of their souls* cleansing, purification. **2** *the purge of the dissidents from the party* removal, expulsion, ejection, dismissal, ousting, deposal, deposition, eradication, rooting out, weeding out.

**purify** verb **1** *purify the water* clean, cleanse, decontaminate, depollute, filter, filtrate. **2** *purify the air* clean, cleanse, freshen, deodorize, decontaminate, depollute, refine. **3** *purify their souls* purge, cleanse, clear, absolve.

**puritanical** adjective ascetic, austere, straitlaced, rigid, stiff, prudish, prim, priggish, prissy.

**purity** noun **1** *test the purity of the gold* flawlessness, perfection, genuineness. **2** *the purity of the water* cleanness, clearness, freshness, wholesomeness. **3** *the purity of the novitiates* virginity, chasteness, chastity, virtue. **4** *the purity of her character* stainlessness, spotlessness, impeccability, immaculateness, blamelessness, sinlessness.

**purport** verb **1** *this report purports to be an official statement* claim, allege, profess, assert, pretend, feign. **2** *the document purports that changes are to be made* mean, signify, indicate, denote, suggest, imply, state, convey, express, show, betoken.

**purport** noun **1** *the purport of his message* gist, substance, drift, implication, meaning, import, tenor, thrust. **2** *his purport is to embarrass them* aim, intention, intent, object, objective, goal, plan, scheme, design, purpose.

**purpose** noun **1** *the purpose of his visit* reason, point, basis, motivation, cause, justification. **2** *his only purpose in life* aim, intention, object, objective, goal, end, target, ambition, aspiration, desire, wish, hope. **3** *to little purpose* benefit, advantage, use, usefulness, value, gain, profit, avail, result, outcome, effect. **on purpose** *cheated us on purpose* purposely, intentionally, deliberately, by design, willfully, wittingly, knowingly, consciously.

**purposeful** adjective determined, resolute, resolved, firm, steadfast, single-minded, persistent, persevering, tenacious, dogged, unfaltering, unwavering.

**purposely** adverb on purpose, intentionally, deliberately, by design, willfully, wittingly, knowingly, consciously.

**purse** noun **1** *carry money in her purse* wallet, pouch; bag, handbag, pocketbook. **2** *a purse of $50,000* prize, award, reward.

**pursue** verb **1** *the detective pursued the thief* chase, follow, hunt, stalk, track, trail, shadow; *inf.* tail. **2** *decide not to pursue the line of inquiry* follow, proceed with, carry on with, continue with, continue, persist in. **3** *pursue a career in science* follow, engage in, work at, practice, prosecute, conduct, ply, apply oneself to. **4** *pursue his goal of happiness* strive toward, work toward, seek, search for, aim at, aspire to. **5** *she pursued every eligible young man* chase after, chase; play up to.

**pursuit** noun **1** *take part in the pursuit of the thief* chase, hunt, stalking, tracking; *inf.* tailing. **2** *give up the pursuit of that line of inquiry* continuance, persistence, following, proceeding. **3** *his pursuit of a life of crime* engagement, occupation, work, practicing, prosecution, conducting, plying. **4** *his pursuit of happiness* striving toward, search, aim, goal, objective, aspiration.

**push** verb **1** *push his friend into the swimming pool* shove, thrust, propel, boost, drive, ram, butt. **2** *push one's way through the crowd* shove, thrust, force, press, squeeze, jostle, elbow, shoulder. **3** *push the button* press, depress. **4** *push him into applying for the job* encourage, prompt, press, urge, egg on, spur, prod, goad, incite, impel, dragoon, force, coerce, constrain, browbeat, strong-arm. **5** *pushing their latest products* promote, advertise, publicize, boost; *inf.* plug, hype. **push around** *older boys pushing him around* bully, trample on, tread on, browbeat, tyrannize, intimidate, domineer. **push off** *they told him to push off* go away, leave, depart, get out; *inf.* shove off, make oneself scarce, beat it, get lost, hit the road.

**push** noun **1** *gave his friend a push into the pool* shove, thrust, boost, butt. **2** *the army launched a big push* attack, assault, advance, onslaught, onset, charge, sortie, sally.

**pushy** adjective assertive, self-assertive, aggressive, forceful, forward, bold, brash, bumptious, presumptuous, cocksure, loud, obnoxious.

**put** verb **1** *put the books on the shelf* place, lay, set, deposit, position, rest, stand, locate, situate, settle, install, posit. **2** *put it in layman's terms* translate, transcribe, render, construe, interpret, word, express, phrase, frame, formulate, couch, say, utter, voice, speak, state, pronounce. **3** *put them to work* set, apply, employ, use, utilize, assign, allocate, devote. **4** *put to death* commit, consign, subject, condemn, sentence, convict, doom. **5** *put its worth at $500* assess, evaluate, value, estimate, calculate, reckon, guess, measure, establish, fix, place, set. **6** *put money on a horse* place, bet, wager, gamble, stake, risk, chance, hazard. **7** *put his fist through the window* thrust, drive, plunge, stick, push, force, lunge, knock, bang, smash, bash. **put across** *successfully put across the message* convey, communicate, explain, express, make understood, clarify. **put aside 1** *put aside money for a rainy day* lay by, save, reserve, keep in reserve, store, stockpile, hoard, deposit, salt away, squirrel away. **2** *put aside the newspaper* set aside, cast aside, discard, abandon, drop. **3** *put aside their differences* set aside, forget, disregard, ignore, bury. **put away 1** *put away food for a rainy day* lay by, set aside, save, keep in reserve, store, stockpile. **2** *put away the books* replace, tidy up, clear away. **3** *put away all thoughts of him* lay aside, discard, cast aside, forget, disregard, rid oneself of, jettison. **4** *put the criminal away* confine, lock up, shut away, commit, imprison, hospitalize, institutionalize, certify. **5** *put away quantities of food* consume, eat, swallow, gulp down, devour, down, gobble up, bolt, wolf down. **put down 1** *put down a rebellion* crush, suppress, quash, quell, stamp out, stop, repress, smash, extinguish. **2** *put their names down* write down, make a note of, jot down, take down, enter, list, record, register, log. **3** *put it down to experience* attribute, ascribe, impute, chalk up to, blame on. **4** *put down the sick animal* euthanize, put to sleep, put out of its misery, destroy. **5** *always putting down his wife* snub, disparage, deprecate, belittle, denigrate, deflate, slight, humiliate, mortify. **put forward** *his name was put forward for the candidacy* submit, present, suggest, advance, tender, propose, move, introduce, offer, proffer, recommend, suggest, nominate, name. **put off 1** *put off the meeting* postpone, defer, delay, adjourn, hold over, reschedule, shelve; *inf.* put on ice, put on the back burner. **2** *put off by his surly*

*behavior* discourage, dissuade, dishearten, distress, dismay, discomfit, daunt, repel, offend, disgust, revolt. **put on 1** *put on her new suit* get dressed in, change into, slip into, don. **2** *put on a play* stage, mount, present, produce. **3** *she is just putting on the grief* feign, fake, sham, simulate, affect. **4** *put the blame on the father* place on, attribute to, ascribe to, impute to, fix on, attach to, assign to, allocate to, lay on, pin on. **put one over on** *he really put one over on us* trick, deceive, hoodwink, mislead, delude, fool, take in, dupe, lead on, outwit, bamboozle; *inf.* pull a fast one on, con, make a sucker of. **put out 1** *she is easily put out* annoy, anger, irritate, exasperate, infuriate, provoke, irk, vex, gall, disturb, perturb, disconcert, agitate, harass. **2** *don't put yourself out* inconvenience, trouble, bother, impose upon, discommode, incommode. **3** *put out the fire* extinguish, quench, douse, snuff out, stamp out. **4** *put out a report on the drought* issue, circulate, release, disclose, publish, broadcast, publicize. **put to** *put it to the committee* set before, lay before, present to, submit to, tender to, offer to, proffer to, set forth to, advance to, posit to. **put up 1** *put up new houses* build, construct, erect, raise. **2** *put up his friends for the night* accommodate, house, give accommodations to, give a bed to, entertain. **3** *put his friend up for chairman* put forward, nominate, propose, recommend. **4** *put up the money for the campaign* provide, supply, furnish, give, donate, pay, advance, pledge. **5** *put up posters* post, display, exhibit. **put up to** *put his friend up to the burglary* egg on to do/commit/(etc.), persuade to do/commit/(etc.), goad to do/commit/(etc.). **put up with** *endure, tolerate, bear, stand, abide, suffer, take, stomach, brook, accept, swallow.* **put upon** *she is so obliging that she gets put upon* take advantage of, impose upon, exploit, overburden, saddle.

**puzzle** verb *he was puzzled by her behavior* perplex, baffle, stump, mystify, confuse, bewilder, nonplus, dumbfound, daze, confound; *inf.* flummox.

**puzzling** adjective perplexing, knotty, baffling, enigmatic, abstruse, nonplussing, mystifying, bewildering, unfathomable, inexplicable, incomprehensible.

**pygmy** noun **1** *insultingly called him a pygmy* midget, dwarf; *inf.* shrimp, munchkin, Tom Thumb. **2** *a pygmy among intellectual giants* nonentity, nobody, lightweight.

# Qq

**quack** noun *quacks selling fake medicines* charlatan, mountebank, impostor, fraud, fake, pretender, humbug; *inf.* con man, phony.

**quagmire** noun **1** *avoiding the muck of the quagmire* quag, bog, peat bog, marsh, swamp, morass, mire, slough, fen. **2** *in a quagmire with no place to live* quandary, dilemma, predicament, plight, tight corner, muddle, imbroglio, impasse; *inf.* jam, scrape, pickle, fix.

**quail** verb flinch, shrink, recoil, shy away, cower, cringe, shudder, shiver, tremble, shake, quake, blanch.

**quaint** adjective old-world, droll, curious, whimsical, attractive, charming, sweet.

**quake** verb shake, tremble, quiver, shiver, shudder, rock, vibrate.

**qualification** noun **1** *qualification to be a teacher* certification, training, competence, competency, accomplishment, eligibility, acceptability, suitability, preparedness, fitness, proficiency, skillfulness, adeptness, capability, aptitude; skill, ability, attribute, endowment. **2** *say what you mean without qualification* modification, limitation, restriction, reservation, stipulation, adaptation, adjustment; condition, proviso, provision, caveat.

**qualified** adjective **1** *a qualified doctor* certified, trained, fit, equipped, prepared, competent, accomplished, proficient, skilled, skillful, adept, practiced, experienced, expert, capable, able. **2** *a qualified approval* modified, limited, conditional, restricted, contingent, confined, circumscribed, reserved, guarded, equivocal, stipulated, adapted, adjusted.

**qualify** verb **1** *his training qualifies him to teach* certify, license, empower, authorize, allow, permit, sanction, warrant, fit, equip, prepare, train, educate, coach, teach, instruct. **2** *qualify her statement* modify, limit, make conditional, restrict. **3** *qualify her criticism* modify, temper, soften, modulate, mitigate, reduce, lessen, diminish.

**quality** noun **1** *the material is of poor quality* standard, grade, level, make, sort, type, kind, variety. **2** *his quality has been recognized* excellence, superiority, merit, worth, value, caliber, talent, eminence, preeminence, distinction. **3** *they have many good qualities* feature, trait, attribute, characteristic, aspect, property, peculiarity.

**qualms** plural noun **1** *have some qualms about going* doubt(s), misgivings, hesitation, hesitancy, reluctance, disinclination, anxiety, apprehension, disquiet, uneasiness, concern(s). **2** *have no qualms about having hurt them* pangs of conscience, scruples, compunction, remorse.

**quandary** noun dilemma, predicament, plight, tight spot, muddle, impasse; *inf.* jam, pickle, fix.

**quantity** noun **1** *what quantity of books/paper do you need?* number, amount, total, aggregate, sum, quota, weight. **2** *estimate the quantity* size, capacity, mass, volume, bulk, extent, length, area. **a quantity of** *found a quantity of books/paper* a number of, several, numerous, many, considerable amounts of.

**quarrel** noun **1** *the couple had a quarrel* argument, fight, disagreement, dispute, squabble, altercation, wrangle, tiff, row, misunderstanding; *inf.* falling-out, spat, scrap. **2** *I have no quarrel with him* bone of contention, complaint, grievance, resentment.

**quarrel** verb *the couple quarreled* argue, fight, dispute, squabble, bicker, spar, wrangle. **quarrel with** *I cannot quarrel with his logic* fault, criticize, object to, take exception to.

**quarrelsome** adjective argumentative, belligerent, disputatious, contentious, pugnacious, combative, bellicose, litigious, hot-tempered, irascible, choleric, irritable.

**quarter** noun **1** *live in the Latin quarter of the city* district, area, region, part, side, neighborhood, locality, zone, territory, province. **2** *accept help from any quarter* direction, place, point, spot, location.

**quarters** plural noun rooms, chambers, barracks; lodging(s), accommodations, billet, residence, abode, dwelling, domicile, habitation, cantonment; *inf.* digs, pad.

**quash** verb **1** *quash the jail sentence* annul, nullify, invalidate, void, cancel, overrule, override, overthrow, reverse, revoke, rescind, repeal. **2** *quash the rebellion* crush, put down, squash, quell, subdue, suppress, repress, quench, extinguish, stamp out, end, terminate, defeat, destroy.

**quaver** verb *his voice quavered* quiver, vibrate, tremble, shake, waver.

**queasy** adjective sick, nauseated, nauseous, ill, indisposed, dizzy.

**queen** noun **1** *the queen reigned for 50 years* monarch, sovereign, empress, ruler. **2** *she* *was the queen of Broadway* star, shining star, prima donna, idol, paragon, doyenne.

**queer** adjective **1** *queer behavior* odd, strange, unusual, extraordinary, funny, curious, peculiar, weird, outlandish, singular, eccentric, unconventional, unorthodox, atypical, abnormal, irregular, anomalous, deviant, outré, offbeat; *inf.* off-the-wall. **2** *something queer going on* strange, peculiar, suspicious, suspect, irregular, questionable, dubious, doubtful; *inf.* fishy, shady.

**quell** verb **1** *quell the rebellion* quash, defeat, conquer, vanquish, overpower, overcome, overwhelm, rout, crush, suppress, subdue, extinguish, stamp out, put down. **2** *quell their fears* allay, lull, put at rest, quiet, silence, calm, soothe, appease, assuage, abate, deaden, dull, pacify, tranquilize, mitigate, palliate.

**quench** verb **1** *quench one's thirst* satisfy, slake, sate, satiate. **2** *quench their desire* suppress, extinguish, stamp out, smother, stifle.

**query** noun *his behavior raises a query as to his sanity* question, doubt, uncertainty, inquiry, reservation, suspicion; skepticism.

**query** verb **1** *"where are we?" he queried* ask, inquire, question. **2** *he queried their fitness for the job* call into question, question, doubt, challenge, express reservations about.

**quest** noun **1** *in quest of a better life* search, pursuit, chase, hunt. **2** *their quest was the Holy Grail* goal, aim, objective, purpose. **3** *knights setting out on a quest* adventure, expedition, journey, voyage, exploration, crusade.

**question** noun **1** *answer her questions* query, inquiry, interrogation. **2** *there is no question that he is ill* doubt, dispute, argument, debate, controversy, reservation. **3** *there is the question of safety* issue, problem, matter, point, subject, topic, theme. **beyond question** without (a) doubt, undoubtedly, indisputably, incontestably, incontrovertibly. **in question** *the matter in question* under consideration, at issue. **out of the question** impossible, inconceivable, unthinkable, unimaginable, absurd, ridiculous, preposterous.

**question** verb **1** *question the witnesses* interrogate, cross-examine, cross-question, quiz, catechize, interview, sound out, examine, give the third degree to; *inf.* grill, pump. **2** *question his motives* call into question, query, challenge, express reservations about.

**questionable** adjective *his motive/ability is questionable* doubtful, dubious, uncertain, debatable, in dispute, arguable, controversial, controvertible.

**quibble** verb **1** *quibble about/over a minor detail* cavil, carp, pettifog, split hairs; *inf.* nitpick. **2** *he quibbles so that it is difficult to get a straight answer* be evasive, equivocate, hedge, fudge; *inf.* beat about the bush.

**quick** adjective **1** *a quick reader* fast, rapid, speedy, swift, fleet, express. **2** *a quick response* prompt, immediate, expeditious. **3** *a quick look at the map* brief, brisk, fleeting, momentary, hasty, hurried, cursory, perfunctory. **4** *the child is very quick* sharp-witted, alert, intelligent. *See* QUICK-WITTED.

**quicken** verb **1** *his pulse quickened* speed up, accelerate. **2** *they quickened their steps* speed up, accelerate, expedite, hasten, hurry, precipitate. **3** *the documentary quickened his interest in wildlife* stimulate, arouse, rouse, whet, inspire, kindle, fan, refresh, strengthen, revitalize, resuscitate, pique, sharpen.

**quickly** adverb **1** *run quickly* fast, rapidly, speedily, swiftly, on the double, post-haste; *inf.* hell-bent for leather, like a bat out of hell. **2** *respond quickly* promptly, without delay, immediately, expeditiously. **3** *read the letter quickly* rapidly, briskly, hastily, hurriedly, cursorily, perfunctorily.

**quick-tempered** adjective irascible, irritable, hot-tempered, fiery, hasty, impatient, touchy, testy, snappish, quarrelsome, petulant, choleric, splenetic, volatile; *inf.* on a short fuse.

**quick-witted** adjective quick, sharp-witted, nimble-witted, alert, intelligent, bright, lively, smart, perceptive, discerning, shrewd; *inf.* quick on the uptake.

**quiet** adjective **1** *the house was quiet* silent, hushed, noiseless, soundless, peaceful. **2** *a quiet voice* soft, low, inaudible. **3** *a quiet person* calm, serene, composed, placid, untroubled, peaceful, tranquil, gentle, mild, temperate, restrained, phlegmatic, reserved, uncommunicative, taciturn. **4** *quiet colors/clothes* unobtrusive, unostentatious, restrained, muted, understated, subdued, subtle, conservative, sober, modest, demure. **5** *live in a quiet village* peaceful, sleepy, undisturbed, unfrequented, private, secluded, sequestered, isolated; *inf.* off the beaten track. **6** *have a quiet word with him* private, confidential, secret, discreet, unofficial, off the record. **7** *we kept his presence quiet* secret, unrevealed, undisclosed, uncommunicated; *inf.* hush-hush.

**quiet** noun *in the quiet of the evening* stillness, silence, hush, noiselessness, peace, peacefulness, calmness, tranquillity, serenity.

**quiet** verb **1** *quiet the noisy children* silence, hush, shush. **2** *the children soon quieted* grow silent, settle down; *inf.* shut up. **3** *quiet the frightened horse | quiet their fears* calm, soothe, tranquilize, allay, appease, lull, pacify, mollify, palliate, suppress, quell, stifle, dull, deaden.

**quietly** adverb **1** *speak quietly* softly, in a whisper, in an undertone, inaudibly. **2** *creep out quietly* silently, noiselessly, soundlessly. **3** *tell him quietly that he must leave* privately, confidentially, secretly, discreetly. **4** *she is quietly confident* calmly, patiently, placidly, serenely, undemonstratively, unemotionally. **5** *dress quietly* unobtrusively, unostentatiously, with restraint, conservatively, soberly, modestly, demurely.

**quip** noun witticism, wisecrack, joke, jest, bon mot, epigram, aphorism; *inf.* crack.

**quirk** noun *it is one of his quirks to polish his car every day* idiosyncrasy, peculiarity, oddity, eccentricity, foible, whim, vagary, caprice, kink, mannerism, habit, characteristic, trait.

**quit** verb **1** *quit smoking* give up, stop, cease, discontinue, drop, leave off, abandon, abstain from, desist from. **2** *quit his job* leave, vacate, walk out on. **3** *he has decided to quit* leave, depart, take off; *inf.* call it quits, pack it in.

**quite** adverb **1** *he has quite recovered* completely, fully, entirely, totally, wholly, absolutely, in all respects. **2** *he is quite talented* extremely, exceedingly, considerably, hugely, enormously, very. **3** *it is quite delicious* truly, really, definitely, absolutely, certainly, unequivocally.

**quiver** verb *quiver with fear* tremble, shiver, vibrate, quaver, quake, shudder, palpitate.

**quiz** noun test, examination, questioning, interrogation, catechism, inquiry.

**quiz** verb *quiz them about their movements* question, ask, interrogate, cross-examine, cross-question, catechize; *inf.* pump, grill.

**quizzical** adjective *a quizzical look* questioning, puzzled, perplexed, baffled, mystified, mocking, teasing.

**quota** noun share, allowance, allocation, portion, ration, part, slice, measure, proportion, percentage; *inf.* cut.

**quotation** noun **1** *full of quotations from Shakespeare* citation, reference, allusion, excerpt, extract, selection, passage, line; *inf.* quote. **2** *give them a quotation for the work* estimate, cost, charge, figure; *inf.* quote.

**quote** verb **1** *quote verses from the sonnet* repeat, iterate, recite. **2** *he could not quote an example of what he meant* cite, name, refer to. **3** *quote the job at $800* estimate, price.

# *Rr*

**rabble** noun **1** *a rabble gathered to protest the verdict* mob, horde, swarm, crowd, throng. **2** *inciting the rabble to revolt* populace, commonality, rank and file, peasantry, hoi polloi, riff-raff; masses.

**rabid** adjective **1** *rabid dogs* rabies-infected, mad, foaming at the mouth, hydrophobic. **2** *rabid socialists/conservatives* fanatical, extreme, overzealous, overenthusiastic, fervent, unreasonable, frenzied, irrational, raging, raving, intolerant, bigoted.

**race**[1] noun **1** *the competitors in the race* competition, chase, pursuit, relay. **2** *the race for the presidency* contest, competition, rivalry, contention.

**race**[2] verb **1** *horses racing at Churchill Downs* run, contend, compete. **2** *race to the finish line* run, sprint, dash, dart, bolt, speed, fly, tear, zoom, accelerate, career.

**race**[3] noun **1** *humankind divided into races* people, ethnic group. **2** *discrimination on grounds of race* ancestry, racial type, blood, bloodline, stock, line, lineage, breed, strain, stirps, extraction, parentage.

**racism** noun racial discrimination, racial prejudice, bigotry, apartheid, segregation, racial bias.

**racist** adjective discriminatory, prejudiced, bigoted, intolerant, illiberal.

**rack** noun frame, framework, stand, form, trestle, structure, holder, shelf.

**racket** noun **1** *a racket coming from next door* noise, din, row, commotion, disturbance, uproar, hubbub, hullabaloo; clamor, pandemonium, tumult. **2** *he is involved in a drugs racket* illegal enterprise, fraud, scheme, swindle.

**racy** adjective risqué, suggestive, off-color, ribald, bawdy, vulgar, coarse, crude, rude, smutty, dirty, blue, indecent, indelicate, immodest, naughty; *inf.* spicy.

**radiance** noun **1** *the radiance of the sun* light, shining, brightness, brilliance, luminosity, effulgence, incandescence, glow, gleam, glitter, sparkle, shimmer. **2** *the radiance of the bride* joyfulness, joy, elation, rapture, blitheness, happiness, delight, pleasure, gaiety, warmth. **3** *the radiance of her beauty* resplendence, splendor, dazzlingness.

**radiant** adjective **1** *the radiant sun/light* shining, bright, brilliant, luminous, luminescent, effulgent, refulgent, incandescent, beaming, glowing, gleaming, glittering, sparkling, shimmering. **2** *the bride was radiant* joyful, elated, ecstatic, delighted, glowing; *inf.* in seventh heaven, on cloud nine. **3** *her radiant beauty* splendid, resplendent, magnificent, dazzling, glowing.

**radiate** verb **1** *radiating heat* emit, emanate, scatter, disperse, diffuse, spread. **2** *radiate joy* transmit, emanate; *inf.* be the picture of.

**radical** adjective **1** *radical change needed* thorough, complete, comprehensive, exhaustive, sweeping, far-reaching, profound, drastic, violent. **2** *radical views* extremist, extreme, immoderate, revolutionary, militant, fanatic, leftist, left-wing.

**rag** noun (piece of) cloth, scrap, remnant, fragment; dishrag, dishcloth, dustcloth, dust rag.

**rage** noun **1** *be filled with rage* fury, anger, wrath, ire, frenzy, madness. **2** *fly into a rage* frenzy, tantrum, rampage. **all the rage** *miniskirts are all the rage* ultrafashionable, ultrapopular; *inf.* trendy.

**rage** verb **1** *the dissatisfied customer is raging* seethe, lose one's temper, boil over, rant, rave, storm, fume, fulminate; *inf.* foam at the mouth, blow one's top, blow a gasket, hit the ceiling, flip one's lid. **2** *rage against the new rules* fulminate, storm, inveigh, rail. **3** *the storm is raging* be violent, be turbulent, be tempestuous.

**ragged** adjective **1** *ragged clothes* tattered, torn, rent, worn to shreds, threadbare, frayed. **2** *ragged children* in rags, shabby, unkempt, destitute, indigent. **3** *a ragged coastline* jagged, notched, serrated, sawtoothed, craggy, rugged, uneven, irregular. **4** *a ragged band of soldiers* straggling, straggly, disorganized, fragmented.

**raid** noun *make a raid on the enemy | a police raid* surprise attack, assault, onslaught, invasion, incursion, foray, charge, thrust, sortie, sally; *inf.* bust.

**raid** verb **1** *raid the enemy lines* attack, assault, invade, charge, assail, storm, rush, set upon. **2** *raid the enemy supplies | raid the refrigerator* plunder, pillage, loot, rifle, forage, ransack.

**rail** verb **rail against** *rail against the new rules* criticize, censure, condemn, inveigh against, rage against, protest; *inf.* lambaste.

**railing** noun balustrade, fencing, barrier.

**rain** noun **1** *farmers needing rain* rainfall, precipitation, drizzle, shower, rainstorm,

cloudburst, torrent, downpour, deluge, thunderstorm. **2** *a rain of arrows* shower, hail, deluge, volley.

**rain** verb *it is raining* pour, precipitate, shower, drizzle; *inf.* rain cats and dogs, come down in buckets.

**raise** verb **1** *raise one's eyes | raise the ship* lift, lift up, elevate, uplift, hoist, heave up. **2** *raise his prices* increase, escalate, inflate; *inf.* hike, jack up. **3** *raise the volume/temperature* increase, heighten, augment, amplify, intensify. **4** *raise a statue* construct, build, erect, put up. **5** *raise money/troops* collect, assemble, muster, levy, accumulate, amass, scrape together. **6** *raise objections* put forward, introduce, advance, bring up, broach, suggest, present. **7** *raise hopes* cause, engender, create, kindle, arouse, awaken, excite, provoke, activate, evoke, incite. **8** *raise three children* bring up, rear, nurture, educate. **9** *raise chickens* breed, rear. **10** *raise crops* grow, farm, cultivate, propagate, till, produce. **11** *raise him to captain* promote, advance, upgrade, elevate, exalt. **12** *raise a ghost* call up, call forth, summon, conjure up.

**raise** noun *a raise in salary* gain, (pay/wage) increase, growth, addition, appreciation; *inf.* rise.

**rake** noun roué, debauchee, playboy, libertine, profligate.

**rakish**[1] adjective *the playboy's rakish behavior* dissolute, debauched, dissipated, profligate, wanton, degenerate, depraved.

**rakish**[2] adjective *wears his hat at a rakish angle* dashing, jaunty, sporty, breezy, debonair, smart, dapper, spruce; *inf.* natty.

**rally** verb **1** *rally to support the school* come together, assemble, convene, unite. **2** *rally the forces* call together, assemble, summon, round up, muster, marshal, mobilize. **3** *they were defeated, but they rallied* regroup, reassemble, re-form, reunite. **4** *she was ill, but she rallied* recover, recuperate, revive, improve, perk up, pull through, turn the corner.

**rally** noun **1** *a political rally* mass meeting, gathering, assembly, convention, conference. **2** *a rally on the stock exchange* resurgence, recovery, recuperation, improvement, revival, comeback.

**ram** verb **1** *ram the tobacco into the pipe* force, cram, stuff, compress, thrust, tamp. **2** *ram fence posts into the ground* drive, hammer, pound, beat, hit. **3** *his car rammed ours* strike, hit, bump, slam.

**ramble** verb **1** *ramble through the countryside* wander, stroll, saunter, amble, roam, range, rove, traipse, jaunt. **2** *the speaker rambled on* digress, wander, go off on tangents, maunder, gibber, blather, babble, chatter, rattle on.

**ramble** noun wander, stroll, saunter, amble, roam, traipse, jaunt, trip, excursion, tour.

**rambling** adjective *rambling speeches* digressive, wandering, roundabout, circuitous, diffuse, periphrastic, disconnected, disjointed, maundering, long-winded, verbose, wordy, prolix.

**ramification** noun *the action had many ramifications* consequence, implication, aftermath, outcome, result, upshot.

**rampage** noun uproar, furor, mayhem, turmoil. **on the rampage** running amok, going berserk, out of control.

**rampant** adjective *rampant crime* uncontrolled, rife, unrestrained, unchecked, unbridled, widespread, pandemic, epidemic.

**rampart** noun *the ramparts of the fortress* embankment, earthwork, parapet, fortification, fort, stronghold, bulwark, bastion, barbican.

**ramshackle** adjective tumbledown, broken-down, rundown, dilapidated, derelict, decrepit, neglected, crumbling, rickety, shaky, unsteady, tottering, flimsy, jerry-built.

**rancor** noun resentment, malice, spite, ill will, hatred, malevolence, malignancy, animosity, antipathy, enmity, hostility, acrimony, venom, vindictiveness.

**random** adjective haphazard, chance, accidental, fortuitous, serendipitous, adventitious, arbitrary, hit-or-miss, indiscriminate, sporadic, stray, spot, casual, unsystematic, disorganized, unplanned, unpremeditated. **at random 1** *chose numbers at random* randomly, haphazardly, arbitrarily. **2** *trees planted at random* unsystematically, erratically, indiscriminately, sporadically.

**range** noun **1** *range of vision | the range of his influence* scope, compass, radius, span, scale, gamut, reach, sweep, extent, area, field, orbit, province, domain, latitude; limits, bounds, confines. **2** *a range of mountains* row, line, file, rank, string, chain, series, sequence, succession, tier. **3** *a wide range of flavors* assortment, variety. **4** *animals on the range* pasture, pasturage, grassland, grazing land.

**range** verb **1** *range from very hot to freezing* extend, stretch, reach, cover, go, run, pass, fluctuate, vary. **2** *sheep ranging over the hills* roam, rove, ramble, traverse, wander, meander, amble, stroll, stray, drift.

**rank** noun **1** *salary according to rank* grade, level, stratum, class, status, position, station, echelon, standing. **2** *persons of rank* nobility, aristocracy, high birth, eminence, distinction, influence, power, prestige, weight, importance. **3** *break rank* array, alignment, order, arrangement, organization. **rank and file 1** *the officers separated from the rank and file* ordinary soldiers, soldiers, men, troops. **2** *government ignoring the wishes of the rank and file* ordinary people, public, general public; populace, commonality, rabble.

**rank** adjective **1** *rank vegetation* lush, luxuriant, abundant, dense, profuse, flourishing, exuberant, vigorous, overgrown. **2** *a rank smell* strong, pungent, acrid, malodorous, foul-smelling, evil-smelling, stinking, rancid, putrid, fetid, offensive, revolting, sickening, noxious, mephitic. **3** *condemn his rank language* indecent, immodest, indecorous, coarse, gross, vulgar, shocking, outrageous, lurid, crass, scurrilous, nasty, foul, filthy, vile, obscene, smutty, profane. **4** *rank disobedience* utter, complete, total, absolute, out and out, downright, thorough, sheer, unqualified, unmitigated, arrant, flagrant, blatant, glaring, egregious.

**rankle** verb *their insults still rankle* fester, annoy, irk, vex, peeve, irritate, rile, chafe, gall; *inf.* get one's goat.

**ransack** verb **1** *raiders ransacking the area* plunder, pillage, raid, rob, loot, despoil, rifle, strip, fleece, sack, ravage, harry, maraud, devastate, depredate. **2** *ransack the house looking for the will* search, scour, comb, explore, turn inside out.

**ransom** noun **1** *pay the kidnappers a ransom* payoff, payment, price. **2** *obtain the kidnapped child's ransom* release, freedom, deliverance, liberation, rescue, redemption, restoration.

**ransom** verb *succeed in ransoming the kidnapped child* release, free, deliver, liberate, rescue, redeem, restore to freedom.

**rant** verb bluster, harangue, vociferate, declaim, hold forth, roar, bellow, bawl, rave; *inf.* spout.

**rap** noun **1** *a rap on the knuckles* tap, hit, blow, whack, bang, cuff, clip, clout. **2** *hear a rap at the door* knock, knocking, tap, bang, rat-a-tat. **3** *take the rap for the accident* blame, responsibility, accountability, punishment, penalty, castigation.

**rap** verb **1** *rap him on the knuckles* tap, hit, strike, whack, bang, cuff, clip, clout, batter; *inf.* bash. **2** *rap at the door* knock, tap, bang.

**rapacious** adjective **1** *rapacious moneylender* acquisitive, greedy, avaricious, covetous, insatiable, predatory, usurious. **2** *rapacious invaders* plundering, pillaging, robbing, marauding, looting, piratical.

**rapid** adjective quick, fast, swift, speedy, fleet, hurried, hasty, expeditious, express, brisk, lively, prompt, precipitate.

**rapidly** adverb quickly, fast, swiftly, speedily, hurriedly, in a hurry, hastily, in haste, expeditiously, briskly, promptly, precipitately, at full tilt; *inf.* before one can say Jack Robinson.

**rapport** noun affinity, bond, empathy, harmony, sympathy, understanding, link.

**rapt** adjective **1** *rapt attention* absorbed, engrossed, preoccupied, intent, concentrating, pensive, meditative. **2** *a rapt smile* enraptured, enchanted, entranced, charmed, thrilled, transported, blissful, ecstatic.

**rapture** noun joy, ecstasy, elation, exaltation, exhilaration, bliss, euphoria, rhapsody, enchantment, delight, delectation; *inf.* cloud nine, seventh heaven.

**rare** adjective **1** *a rare specimen* unusual, uncommon, extraordinary, exceptional, atypical, singular, remarkable, phenomenal, strange, recherché, unique. **2** *one of his rare appearances* infrequent, scarce, sparse, sporadic, scattered. **3** *exhibit a rare skill* outstanding, superior, first-rate, special, choice, excellent, incomparable, unparalleled, peerless, matchless; *inf.* A-1, top-notch.

**rarely** adverb seldom, infrequently, hardly, scarcely; *inf.* once in a blue moon.

**rascal** noun **1** *the child is a little rascal* imp, scamp, scalawag, mischief-maker, devil. **2** *that man is a real rascal* scoundrel, villain, rogue, blackguard, ne'er-do-well, wastrel, reprobate, cad.

**rash** adjective reckless, impetuous, hasty, impulsive, madcap, audacious, brash, daredevil, foolhardy, harum-scarum, devil-may-care, headstrong, hotheaded, incautious, careless, heedless, thoughtless, imprudent, ill-advised, ill-considered, foolish, hare-brained.

**rash** noun **1** *a rash on his face* outbreak, eruption, breaking out; erythema, hives, heat rash, nettle rash, diaper rash. **2** *a rash of burglaries* outbreak, spate, torrent, flood, wave, plague, epidemic, succession, series, run.

**rasping** adjective *a rasping noise/voice* grating, scratchy, jarring, discordant, creaky, harsh, rough, gravelly, croaking, croaky, gruff.

**rate** noun **1** *rate of interest* percentage, ratio, proportion, scale, degree, standard. **2** *the rate per day* payment, fee, remuneration, price, cost, charge, rent, tariff; *inf.* damage. **3** *walk at a rate of 4 miles per hour* pace, speed, tempo, velocity, measure. **at any rate** in any case, anyhow, anyway, nevertheless, in any event.

**rate** verb **1** *how would you rate his performance?* adjudge, judge, assess, appraise, evaluate, value, measure, grade, rank, classify, categorize. **2** *I rate him a complete fool* regard as, consider, count, deem, reckon, esteem. **3** *he rates re-*

*spect* be worthy of, deserve, merit, be entitled to.

**rather** adverb **1** *I would rather not go* sooner, preferably, more willingly, more readily. **2** *not a notebook, but rather a leaflet* on the contrary, instead, actually, in reality, strictly speaking, to be precise. **3** *he is rather outspoken* quite, fairly, a bit, a little, slightly, somewhat, relatively, to some degree/extent; *inf.* kind of, pretty.

**ratify** verb confirm, endorse, sign, countersign, corroborate, sanction, warrant, approve, authorize, authenticate, certify, validate, accept, consent to, uphold, bear out.

**ratio** noun proportion, correlation, correspondence, percentage, fraction, quotient.

**ration** noun allowance, quota, allotment, portion, share, measure, part, lot, amount, helping, proportion, percentage, budget.

**ration** verb *ration the amount per person* limit, restrict, control, conserve, budget. **ration out** *ration out the week's supplies* distribute, issue, allocate, allot, divide out, apportion, give out, hand out, dole out, measure out, mete out, parcel out.

**rational** adjective **1** *based on purely rational considerations* cognitive, mental, cerebral, logical, analytical, conceptual. **2** *a rational course of action* sensible, reasonable, logical, sound, intelligent, wise, judicious, sagacious, prudent, circumspect, politic, astute, shrewd, perceptive, well-advised. **3** *the patient does not always seem rational* lucid, coherent, sane, in sound mind, in one's right mind, *compos mentis*, well-balanced, normal; *inf.* all there.

**rationale** noun theory, hypothesis, thesis, logic, philosophy, reason, *raison d'être*; grounds.

**rationalize** verb *rationalize his behavior* explain away, account for, make excuses for, make plausible, justify.

**rattle** verb **1** *the windows/chain rattled* bang, clatter, clang, clank, jangle, clink. **2** *the car rattled along* bounce, bump, jiggle, jounce, shake, jolt, vibrate, jar. **3** *he rattled on about his job* chatter, babble, gabble, prattle, jabber, gibber, blather, prate; *inf.* yak. **4** *she was rattled by the experience* disconcert, disturb, fluster, upset, shake, perturb, discompose, discomfit, frighten, scare; *inf.* faze.

**raucous** adjective strident, shrill, screeching, piercing, ear-piercing, harsh, sharp, grating, rasping, discordant, dissonant, jarring.

**ravage** verb devastate, lay waste, ruin, wreak havoc on, destroy, level, raze, demolish, wreck, shatter, pillage, plunder, despoil, harry, maraud, ransack, sack, loot.

**rave** verb **1** *the invalid is raving* talk wildly,

babble, ramble. **2** *her parents raved at her* rant, rage, storm, fulminate, explode, lose one's temper, lose control, go into a frenzy, run amok; *inf.* fly off the handle, flip one's lid. **rave about/over** *rave about her performance | rave over his car* go into raptures over, rhapsodize over, gush over, acclaim; *inf.* go wild about, be mad about.

**rave** adjective *rave reviews* rapturous, ecstatic, enthusiastic, laudatory, excellent, favorable.

**ravenous** adjective starving, starved, famished; greedy, gluttonous, voracious, insatiable, insatiate, ravening, wolfish.

**ravine** noun chasm, gorge, canyon, abyss, gulf, gully, gulch, defile, pass, gap.

**raving** adjective **1** *raving patients* delirious, out of one's mind, irrational, frenzied, deranged, hysterical, frantic, berserk, demented, insane, mad, crazed, wild; *inf.* crazy. **2** *a raving beauty* extraordinary, singular, striking, outstanding, stunning.

**ravishing** adjective stunning, gorgeous, dazzling, radiant, enchanting, bewitching, charming.

**raw** adjective **1** *raw food* uncooked, fresh. **2** *raw sugar/silk* unrefined, crude, coarse, unprocessed, unprepared, untreated, unfinished. **3** *raw recruits* inexperienced, untrained, unskilled, untutored, unschooled, unpracticed, untried, untested, unseasoned, undisciplined, new, callow, immature, green, ignorant, naive, unsophisticated; *inf.* wet behind the ears. **4** *raw flesh/wounds* excoriated, skinned, grazed, abraded, scratched, chafed, open, exposed, unhealed, sore, tender. **5** *raw weather* damp, wet, cold, chilly, chilling, freezing, bitter, biting, nippy, piercing, penetrating.

**ray** noun **1** *rays of light* beam, shaft, streak, stream, gleam, glint, flash, glimmer, flicker, twinkle. **2** *a ray of hope* flicker, glimmer, spark, trace.

**raze** verb flatten, demolish, tear down, level, pull down, knock down, fell, bulldoze, ruin, wreck.

**reach** verb **1** *he reached out | reach out a hand* stretch, outstretch, extend, hold out. **2** *reach one's destination* get to, arrive at, come to, set foot on. **3** *reach perfection* attain, achieve, gain, accomplish. **4** *we could not reach him that day* contact, get in touch with, get through to. **reach for** *reach for the book* grasp, seize, grab at, clutch at.

**reach** noun **1** *the rope was beyond her reach | within reach of safety* stretch, spread, extension, extent, span, distance. **2** *within the reach of his influence* scope, range, compass, latitude, ambit, orbit,

sphere, area, field, territory, authority, jurisdiction.

**react** verb **1** *react to the drug* respond, behave in response to. **2** *how did she react on hearing the news?* behave, act, conduct oneself, proceed, operate, function, cope.

**reaction** noun **1** *receive a reaction to their proposal* response, answer, reply, feedback. **2** *his harsh regime was a reaction to total disorder* counteraction, counterbalance, counterpoise, recoil, reversal.

**reactionary** adjective ultraconservative, conservative, diehard, rightist, right-wing.

**read** verb **1** *read the book* peruse, study, scan, pore over, scrutinize, run one's eye over, look at, refer to, browse through; *inf.* wade through, dip into. **2** *read his silence as consent* interpret, construe, take to mean, decipher, understand, comprehend. **3** *the thermometer is reading zero* register, record, display, show, indicate. **read into** *read too much into their statement* infer from, interpolate from.

**readable** adjective **1** *readable exam papers* legible, decipherable, clear, intelligible, understandable, comprehensible. **2** *readable works of fiction* enjoyable, entertaining, interesting, gripping, enthralling, stimulating.

**readily** adverb **1** *he will readily help you* willingly, without hesitation, gladly, happily, cheerfully, with pleasure, eagerly. **2** *the sofa readily converts into a bed* easily, with ease, without difficulty, effortlessly.

**ready** adjective **1** *dinner is ready* prepared, completed, finished, organized. **2** *ready for battle | ready to go* prepared, equipped, organized, all set, fit. **3** *ready to help* willing, inclined, disposed, given, eager, keen, happy, glad; *inf.* game. **4** *a ready source of income* available, accessible, handy, convenient, on hand, present, near, near at hand, on call, at one's fingertips; *inf.* on tap. **5** *a ready answer* prompt, quick, rapid, swift, speedy, punctual, timely. **ready to** *ready to collapse* about to, on the verge/brink of, in danger of, liable to.

**real** adjective **1** *the real world* actual, existent, factual, unimaginary. **2** *real leather* authentic, genuine, bona fide, veritable. **3** *real emotion* sincere, heartfelt, earnest, fervent, unfeigned, unaffected, honest, truthful.

**realistic** adjective **1** *be realistic as to your prospects* practical, pragmatic, rational, down-to-earth, matter-of-fact, sensible, commonsensical, levelheaded, hardheaded, businesslike, sober; *inf.* with both feet on the ground, no-nonsense. **2** *a realistic model of a dinosaur* lifelike, true-to-life, true, faithful, close, representational, graphic, naturalistic, authentic.

**realize** verb **1** *realize that they are rich* grasp, know, comprehend, apprehend, be aware, appreciate, recognize, perceive, discern, conceive; *inf.* get it. **2** *realize one's dreams* fulfill, achieve, accomplish, bring to fruition, consummate, effect, effectuate, actualize, reify. **3** *realize a profit* make, clear, acquire, gain, bring in, obtain, earn.

**really** adverb **1** *the guard dog is really a gentle dog* in reality, actually, in fact. **2** *this is really useful* certainly, surely, truly, undoubtedly, indubitably, assuredly, unquestionably, indeed, absolutely, categorically. **3** *a really charming person* very, extremely, thoroughly, truly, decidedly. **4** *his career is really over* to all intents and purposes, virtually, for all practical purposes, just about, almost.

**realm** noun **1** *the realm of Denmark* kingdom, country, land, state, province, empire, domain, monarchy, principality. **2** *the realm of the imagination | the realm of science* world, field, sphere, area, department, region, province, orbit, zone.

**reap** verb harvest, gather in, take in, realize, obtain, acquire, secure, procure.

**rear** noun **1** *at the rear of the garage* back, back part, hind part. **2** *at the rear of the line* end, tail, tail end.

**rear** verb **1** *rear three children* raise, bring up, care for, nurture, parent, educate, train, instruct. **2** *rear one's head* raise, lift up, hoist, elevate.

**reason** noun **1** *the reason for his behavior* grounds, cause, basis, motive, motivation, impetus, actuation, instigation. **2** *give a reason for your absence* explanation, exposition, justification, argument, case, defense, vindication, apologia, rationalization, excuse, apology. **3** *follow reason not emotion* reasoning, intellect, intelligence, mind, judgment, logic, rationality, ratiocination; brains. **4** *he has lost his reason* sanity, mind, soundness of mind; senses. **5** *keep a sense of reason in your expenditure* common sense, sense, practicality, practicability, moderation, propriety. **within reason** *have anything you like within reason* in moderation.

**reason** verb **1** *unable to reason when upset* think, think straight, use one's head, analyze, cerebrate, intellectualize, ratiocinate. **2** *he reasoned that one could live as cheaply as one* deduce, infer, conclude, work out, reckon, think, surmise. **reason with** *try reasoning with him* use logic on, argue with, debate with, dispute with, try to persuade, plead with.

**reasonable** adjective **1** *he is a reasonable man* fair, just, equitable, impartial, aboveboard. **2** *it seemed a reasonable idea* logical, practical, rational, sensible, intelligent, wise, sound, judicious, advisable, well-thought-out, tenable, plausible. **3** *reasonable prices* moderate, inexpensive, modest.

**reasoning** noun **1** *let reasoning, not emotion, dictate your actions* thought, logic, rationalization, deduction, analysis, cerebration, ratiocination. **2** *his reasoning is faulty* argument, rationale, case, hypothesis, interpretation.

**reassure** verb encourage, hearten, put one's mind at rest, put at ease, restore confidence to, buoy up, cheer up.

**rebate** noun refund, repayment, deduction, discount, allowance, reduction.

**rebel** noun revolutionary, insurrectionist, insurgent, revolter, mutineer, seditionist, agitator, resistance fighter, anarchist; dissenter, nonconformist.

**rebel** verb *the troops are rebelling* mutiny, riot, revolt, rise up, take to the streets. **rebel against** *rebel against authority* defy, disobey. **rebel at** *his stomach rebelled at the thought of food* recoil from, shrink from, flinch from.

**rebellion** noun revolt, revolution, insurrection, insurgence, insurgency, uprising, mutiny, riot, civil disobedience, resistance; defiance, disobedience, dissent, nonconformity.

**rebellious** adjective **1** *rebellious children* unruly, ungovernable, unmanageable, disorderly, intractable, recalcitrant, incorrigible, contumacious. **2** *the rebellious protestors were imprisoned* revolutionary, insurrectionary, insurgent, mutinous, rioting. **3** *the rebellious students were expelled* defiant, disobedient, resistant, dissentient, nonconformist.

**rebuff** verb reject, refuse, decline, turn down, spurn, repudiate, repel, discourage, fend off, stave off, snub, slight; *inf.* brush off.

**rebuke** verb reprimand, scold, chide, admonish, reproach, reprove, lecture, reprehend, censure, berate, upbraid, castigate, take to task; *inf.* tell off, call on the carpet, lambaste, chew out, bawl out.

**rebuke** noun reprimand, scolding, admonition, reproach, reproof, reproval, remonstration, lecture, censure, upbraiding, castigation; *inf.* tongue-lashing, dressing-down, bawling out.

**recalcitrant** adjective intractable, refractory, unmanageable, ungovernable, disobedient, insubordinate, defiant, contrary, wayward, willful, headstrong, perverse, contumacious, obstinate, obdurate.

**recall** verb **1** *unable to recall his name* call to mind, remember, recollect, summon, evoke.

**recall** noun *have total recall* memory, recollection, remembrance.

**recant** verb disavow, disclaim, disown, deny, renounce, relinquish, abjure, forswear, repudiate, renege on, recall, revoke, retract, countermand.

**recapitulate** verb restate, repeat, reiterate, summarize, sum up; *inf.* recap.

**recede** verb **1** *the water receded* ebb, abate, subside, retreat, withdraw, fall back. **2** *the coastline receded as we sailed away* grow less visible, become distant, fade into the distance. **3** *danger receded in time* lessen, fade, diminish, decrease, dwindle, shrink, wane, fall off, taper off, peter out. **4** *his chin recedes* slant, slope backward, fall away.

**receipt** noun **1** *the receipt of the goods | receipt of his apology* receiving, recipience, arrival, reception, acceptance, obtaining, acquisition. **2** *get a receipt for the goods* sales slip, proof of purchase, stub, voucher. **3** *make a list of receipts for the auditor* payment received, income, proceeds, profits, gains, earnings.

**receive** verb **1** *he did receive the goods* accept, take possession of. **2** *receive good news* get, obtain, acquire, come by, gain, gather, collect, hear. **3** *receive bad treatment* undergo, experience, meet with, encounter, sustain, be subjected to, bear, suffer. **4** *receive guests* welcome, greet, entertain.

**recent** adjective **1** *recent developments* new, fresh, novel, latest, late, modern, contemporary, latter-day, current, up-to-date, up-to-the-minute. **2** *his recent illness* occurring recently, not long past.

**reception** noun **1** *the reception of the goods* receiving, acceptance. See RECEIPT 1. **2** *the reception of the guests* welcoming, greeting, entertaining. **3** *the show got a warm reception* response, acknowledgment, reaction, treatment, welcome. **4** *a wedding reception* party, function, entertainment, soirée; *inf.* do, bash.

**receptive** adjective open, flexible, willing, perceptive, sensitive, keen.

**recess** noun **1** *books arranged in a recess* alcove, niche, nook, corner, cavity, bay, oriel. **2** *in the recesses of my memory* interior, heart, retreat, refuge, sanctum; depths; *inf.* innards. **3** *Congress will resume discussions after the recess* break, respite, rest, interval, intermission, time off, vacation, holiday, closure, cessation of business; *inf.* breather, time out.

**recession** noun **1** *the recession cost many stockbrokers their jobs* economic downturn, depression, slump; hard times. **2** *the recession of floodwaters* receding, retreat, withdrawal, ebbing, subsiding, abatement.

**recipe** noun **1** *follow the recipe for pancakes* directions, instructions; guide. **2** *his suggestions are a recipe for disaster* method, technique, system, procedure, modus operandi, process, means, way, formula, prescription.

**reciprocal** adjective **1** *a reciprocal favor* return, in return, requited, retaliated. **2** *reciprocal affection* mutual, shared, common, exchanged, give-and-take, complementary, corresponding, correlative.

**reciprocate** verb return, requite, repay, give back; respond in kind.

**recital** noun **1** *the recital of the poem* rendition, declamation, reading, delivery. **2** *the recital of the events* enumeration, detailing, itemizing, specification; account, report, chronicle, recounting, relation, record, story, tale. **3** *a piano recital* performance, concert, show.

**recite** verb **1** *recite a poem* declaim, speak, render, say, repeat, deliver. **2** *recite a list of disasters* enumerate, detail, list, itemize, reel off, rattle off, specify, particularize, describe, recount, relate, narrate, recapitulate.

**reckless** adjective rash, careless, thoughtless, incautious, heedless, inattentive, daredevil, devil-may-care, madcap, harum-scarum, wild, precipitate, headlong, hasty, irresponsible, harebrained, foolhardy, ill-advised, imprudent, unwise, indiscreet, mindless, negligent, temerarious.

**reckon** verb **1** *he reckoned that she was lying* think, believe, suppose, assume, surmise, conjecture, imagine, fancy, guess. **2** *she was reckoned a good painter* regard as, consider, judge, hold to be, look upon as, account, deem, rate, evaluate, gauge, count, estimate, appraise. **3** *reckon the cost* count, calculate, add up, compute, total, tally. **reckon with** *he will have her father to reckon with* cope with, deal with, contend with, handle, face.

**reckoning** noun **1** *according to my reckoning, the total is wrong* calculation, addition, computation, total, tally, counting, summation, score. **2** *according to their reckoning, she is the best* opinion, judgment, evaluation, estimation, appraisal. **3** *the reckoning of the account* settlement, payment, discharging, defrayal, squaring, clearance. **4** *the day of reckoning* settlement, retribution, judgment, fate, doom.

**recline** verb lie, lie down, lean, be recumbent, rest, repose, loll, lounge, sprawl, stretch out.

**recluse** noun hermit, anchorite, ascetic, eremite, monk, nun, solitary, lone wolf, loner.

**recognition** noun **1** *recognition of the thief* identification, spotting, knowing, recollection. **2** *his recognition of his mis-*

*take* realization, awareness, consciousness, perception, appreciation, understanding, acknowledgment, acceptance. **3** *their recognition of his claim* acknowledgment, acceptance, admittance, granting, endorsement, sanctioning, approval, validation, ratification. **4** *receive recognition as an artist* acknowledgment, appreciation, reward, honor, homage, applause.

**recognize** verb **1** *recognize an old friend* know, identify, place, spot, recall, recollect, remember. **2** *recognize his own mistake* realize, see, perceive, discern, appreciate, understand, apprehend, acknowledge, accept, admit, concede, allow, grant, confess, own. **3** *recognize his claim* acknowledge, accept, admit, allow, grant, endorse, sanction, approve, validate, ratify, uphold. **4** *recognize his achievement* reward, honor, salute, applaud.

**recoil** verb **1** *recoil from him in terror* shrink, shy away, flinch, start, wince, cower, quail. **2** *the spring/gun recoiled* rebound, resile, kick back.

**recollect** verb *I cannot recollect his name* remember, recall, call to mind, think of, summon up, place; *inf.* put one's finger on.

**recommend** verb **1** *recommend this as a cure* advocate, commend, endorse, approve, vouch for, suggest, offer, put forward, propose, advance. **2** *recommend that you go home* advise, counsel, guide, urge, exhort, enjoin.

**recommendation** noun **1** *accept your recommendation as to the wine* endorsement, suggestion, tip, hint, proposal, commendation, praise; *inf.* plug. **2** *accept the judge's recommendation as to how to act* advice, counsel, guidance, exhortation, enjoinder. **3** *fast service is the restaurant's only recommendation* advantage, benefit, blessing, good point, boon.

**reconcile** verb **1** *mother and daughter have been reconciled* reunite, bring together, bring to terms, pacify, appease, placate, propitiate, mollify. **2** *reconcile themselves to her death* resign, come to accept, accept, accommodate, submit, yield. **3** *reconcile their differences* settle, resolve, square, put to rights, mend, remedy, patch up, rectify. **4** *reconcile his philosophy and his actions* harmonize, make compatible, adjust, attune, make coincide, make congruent.

**reconnaissance** noun survey, exploration, probe, scan, inspection, investigation, scrutiny, observation, scouting.

**reconsider** verb review, reexamine, revisit, reevaluate, reassess, think better of; think twice, have second thoughts, change one's mind.

**record** noun **1** *the records are missing* official document, register, log, logbook, file, chronicle, diary, journal; documentation; documents, minutes, notes, annals, archives. **2** *play a record* album, phonograph record, disc; compact disc; single, recording, release; *inf.* LP, CD. **3** *what do you know of his record?* employment history, past performance, curriculum vitae, history, background, reputation; *inf.* track record. **4** *does he have a record?* criminal record; *inf.* rap sheet. **5** *this is a record of his achievement* remembrance, souvenir, testimony, testimonial, witness; documentation, evidence. **6** *climate records* information, collected information; data, reports, accounts. **off the record** confidential, in confidence, unofficial, private, secret, sub rosa. **on record 1** *the wettest winter on record* registered, documented, officially noted. **2** *he is on record as promising improvements* officially noted, documented, publicly known.

**record** verb **1** *record the details* document, register, chronicle, set down, write down, take down, enter, put on file, docket, list, log, catalog, transcribe. **2** *record a very low temperature* register, read, indicate, show, display. **3** *record a music video* make, produce, cut, tape, videotape.

**recoup** verb *recoup the lost property* regain, recover, win back, retrieve, repossess, redeem.

**recover** verb **1** *recover their stolen possessions* regain, recoup, retrieve, reclaim, repossess, redeem, recapture. **2** *the invalid will recover in time* recuperate, convalesce, get well, heal, get back on one's feet, improve, mend, rally, revive, pull through, bounce back.

**recreation** noun **1** *for recreation he rows* relaxation, refreshment, leisure, amusement, entertainment, distraction, diversion, pleasure, enjoyment, fun, play, sport. **2** *his favorite recreation is reading* leisure activity, pastime, hobby, diversion.

**recruit** verb **1** *recruit new members* enlist, enroll, sign up, draft, conscript, levy, engage, obtain, acquire, procure, take on, round up, muster. **2** *recruit an army* form, raise, muster, assemble.

**recruit** noun **1** *army recruits* enlistee, draftee, conscript. **2** *new recruits to the industry* newcomer, initiate, beginner, learner, trainee, apprentice, novice, tyro, neophyte; *inf.* rookie, greenhorn.

**rectify** verb remedy, repair, right, correct, amend, emend, fix, make good, redress, reform, improve, better, ameliorate, adjust, square.

**recuperate** verb **1** *he is recuperating after an illness* recover, convalesce, improve, mend, rally, revive, pull through, bounce back. **2** *recuperate costs* recover, recoup, regain, retrieve, reclaim.

**recur** verb happen again, return, reappear, repeat itself, happen repeatedly.

**recurrent** adjective recurring, repeated, repetitive, reiterative, periodic, cyclical, regular, habitual, continual, frequent, intermittent, chronic.

**recycle** verb reuse, reprocess, salvage, save.

**red** adjective **1** *red dresses/flowers* crimson, scarlet, vermilion, cherry, ruby, cardinal, carmine, ruby-colored, maroon, wine, wine-colored, claret, russet, coral, cochineal, rose. **2** *she had a red face* flushed, blushing, florid, ruddy, rubicund, roseate. **3** *with red eyes* bloodshot, inflamed. **4** *red hair* flaming-red, flame-colored, auburn, copper, Titian, chestnut, carroty, ginger.

**redeem** verb **1** *redeem pawned goods* reclaim, regain, recover, retrieve, repossess, recoup, buy back, repurchase. **2** *redeem the vouchers* exchange, cash in, convert, turn in. **3** *he redeemed himself by helping his neighbor* vindicate, absolve, remove guilt from. **4** *redeem his obligations* fulfill, discharge, make good, carry out, execute, keep, adhere to, abide by, obey, meet, satisfy.

**redress** verb **1** *redress a wrong* rectify, remedy, make amends for, compensate for, make reparation/restitution for, recompense for, atone for. **2** *redress the balance of power* put right, even up, regulate, adjust, correct.

**redress** noun amends; compensation, reparation, restitution, recompense, atonement.

**reduce** verb **1** *reduce the size of the garden | reduce the volume* decrease, diminish, lessen, lower, cut, curtail, contract, shorten, abbreviate, moderate, dilute, mitigate, alleviate, abate. **2** *they were reduced to tears* bring to, bring to the point of, force to, drive to. **3** *they were reduced to a lower grade/rank* demote, downgrade, lower, humble. **4** *reduced yesterday's stock* lower, make cheaper, cut, mark down, slash, discount, put on sale. **5** *she is trying to reduce* slim down, lose weight, diet, shed some pounds, slenderize.

**redundant** adjective **1** *his presence was redundant* not required, unnecessary, inessential, unwanted, de trop, surplus, supernumerary, in excess, extra. **2** *redundant writings* padded, wordy, verbose, tautological, periphrastic, diffuse, pleonastic.

**reel** verb **1** *drunks reeling down the street* stagger, lurch, sway, stumble, totter, wobble, falter, waver, pitch, roll. **2** *reeling from the blow* feel giddy/dizzy, feel confused, be shaken, be in shock, be upset. **3** *her mind was reeling* whirl, spin, revolve, swirl, twirl, swim.

**refer** verb **refer to 1** *refer to his notes* consult, turn to, look at, look up in, have recourse to. **2** *refer the question/person to a higher court* pass (on) to, hand on to, send on to, transfer to, remit to, direct to. **3** *he referred to her death in his speech* mention, make reference to, allude to, touch on, speak of, cite, advert to, hint at. **4** *these figures refer to last year* apply to, be relevant to, concern, relate to, pertain to, have a bearing on.

**referee** noun umpire, judge, adjudicator, arbitrator, arbiter, mediator; *inf.* ref.

**referee** verb **1** *referee the game* umpire, judge, adjudicate. **2** *referee in the dispute* arbitrate, mediate, intercede.

**reference** noun **1** *a reference to her death in his speech* mention, allusion, citation, hint. **2** *with reference to yesterday's meeting* regard, respect, relation, bearing, application, relevance, pertinence, connection, correlation. **3** *give a list of your references for the book* source, citation, authority. **4** *the teacher gave her a reference* recommendation, character reference, testimonial, good word; credentials.

**refine** verb **1** *refine sugar* purify, rarefy, clarify, clear, cleanse, strain, sift, filter, distill, process. **2** *sent to a school that would refine them* civilize, make cultivated, polish, improve, make elegant. **3** *refine the art of conversation* improve, perfect, consummate, elaborate, hone, fine-tune, complete.

**refined** adjective **1** *refined sugar* purified, pure, rarefied, clarified, clear, filtered, distilled, processed. **2** *a refined lady/gentleman* cultivated, cultured, polished, civilized, civil, gracious, stylish, elegant, sophisticated, urbane, courtly, well-mannered, well-bred, gentlemanly, ladylike, genteel. **3** *refined tastes/manners* discriminating, discerning, tasteful, sophisticated, fastidious.

**refinement** noun **1** *the refinement of sugar* purification, processing, distillation, filtration. **2** *a person of refinement* cultivation, culture, taste, discrimination, polish, civility, grace, graciousness, style, elegance, finesse, sophistication, urbanity, courtliness, good breeding, politeness, gentility, politesse; good manners. **3** *the term paper needs refinement* revision, improvement, enhancement, correction, amendment. **4** *refinements of logic/language* subtlety, nicety, nuance, fine point.

**reflect** verb **1** *the surface reflects heat/light* throw back, send back, give back, scatter, diffuse. **2** *their faces reflected in the pool* mirror, image. **3** *reflect sound* bounce back, echo. **4** *his complexion reflects his state of health* indicate, express, bespeak, communicate, show, display, demonstrate, exhibit, reveal, manifest. **reflect on 1** *it will reflect on the school if he does badly* discredit, damage the reputation of, detract from. **2** *reflect on her problems* consider, mull over, contemplate, deliberate over, ponder, meditate about, muse about, ruminate about, cogitate about, cerebrate, dwell on, brood about.

**reflection** noun **1** *the reflection of sound/images* throwing back, echoing, mirroring, diffusion, radiation. **2** *look at her reflection* image, mirror image. **3** *the ring is a reflection of the way he feels about her* indication, expression, display, demonstration, manifestation. **4** *his behavior is a reflection on the school* imputation, slur, aspersion, source of discredit, derogation. **5** *on reflection, he decided to go* thought, second thought, consideration, contemplation, deliberation, meditation, rumination, cogitation, cerebration. **6** *write down your reflections on the subject* thought, opinion, view, idea, impression, comment; findings.

**reform** verb **1** *reform the system* improve, better, ameliorate, amend, mend, rectify, correct, rehabilitate, change, revise, revolutionize, reorganize, reconstruct, rebuild, refashion, remodel, remake, revamp, renovate. **2** *he has reformed since you knew him* mend one's ways, turn over a new leaf, improve; *inf.* go straight.

**reform** noun *the reform of the system* improvement, betterment, amelioration, amendment, rectification, correction, rehabilitation, change, revision, reorganization, reconstruction, rebuilding, refashioning, remodeling, renovation.

**refrain** verb *refrain from drinking* desist, abstain, forbear, forgo, avoid, eschew, cease, stop, give up, leave off, quit, renounce.

**refresh** verb **1** *refreshed by a long walk* invigorate, revitalize, revive, brace, fortify, enliven, stimulate, energize, exhilarate, reanimate, resuscitate, rejuvenate, regenerate, inspirit; *inf.* perk up. **2** *refresh one's memory* stimulate, prompt, prod, jog, activate, rouse, arouse.

**refreshments** plural noun *food and drink, sustenance; snacks, finger foods, drinks; *inf.* grub, nosh, chow.

**refuge** noun **1** *seek refuge from the elements* shelter, safety, security, protection, asylum, sanctuary. **2** *regard their house as a refuge* shelter, haven, retreat, sanctuary, harbor.

**refugee** noun displaced person, émigré, exile, fugitive, escapee.

**refund** verb *refund her deposit* return, repay, pay back, reimburse, make good, restore, replace.

**refund** noun *give the disappointed audi-*

*ence a refund* repayment, reimbursement, rebate.

**refurbish** verb renovate, revamp, overhaul, redecorate, spruce up, recondition, refit, reequip, remodel, repair, mend; *inf.* do up, fix up.

**refusal** noun **1** *four acceptances and one refusal to the invitation* rejection, spurning, decline, nonacceptance, dissent, no, demurral, negation, thumbs down, rebuff; regrets; *inf.* brush-off. **2** *you can have first refusal* option, choice, consideration, opportunity.

**refuse** verb **1** *refuse an invitation* turn down, decline, reject, spurn, rebuff, repudiate; *inf.* pass up. **2** *refuse to go* decline, be unwilling; balk at, demur at, avoid, resist, protest at. **3** *refuse permission to go* withhold, not grant.

**refuse** noun rubbish, garbage, trash, waste, debris, litter, dross; dregs, leavings, flotsam; *inf.* junk.

**regain** verb recover, recoup, retrieve, reclaim, repossess, redeem, retake, recapture, get back, win back.

**regal** adjective royal, majestic, noble, proud, stately, magnificent, sumptuous; kingly, queenly, princely.

**regard** verb **1** *he seldom regards her advice* heed, pay attention to, listen to, mind, take into consideration/account. **2** *regard the prospect with horror* look upon, view, consider, contemplate, reflect on. **3** *his work is well regarded* judge, adjudge, rate, value, estimate, gauge, appraise, assess, deem, consider, look upon.

**regard** noun **1** *pay no regard to his warning* heed, attention, notice, consideration, thought, mind. **2** *looked upon with regard* respect, esteem, admiration, approval, approbation, appreciation, favor, deference, affection, love. **3** *in this regard I disagree with you* respect, aspect, point, particular, detail, item, feature.

**regardless** adjective **regardless of** despite, notwithstanding, heedless of, indifferent to.

**regardless** adverb *he decided to go, regardless* anyway, anyhow, in any case, nevertheless, nonetheless.

**regime** noun government, rule, reign, command, administration, establishment, direction, management, leadership.

**region** noun **1** *the western region of the country* area, province, territory, division, section, sector, zone, tract, part, quarter. **2** *the lumbar region of the body* part, place, section, locality, site. **3** *work in the region of metaphysics* field, sphere, orbit, ambit, realm, domain, world.

**register** noun **1** *be in the medical register* official list, roll, roster, index, directory, catalog. **2** *historians consulting county reg-*

*isters* record, chronicle, journal, log; annals, archives, files. **3** *the register of her voice* range, compass, scope, scale, gamut, reach, spectrum.

**register** verb **1** *register a birth* record, put on record, enter, chronicle, enroll, inscribe, write down, note, list, catalog. **2** *the speedometer registered 50 miles per hour* read, record, indicate, show, display. **3** *her face registered surprise* show, express, display, exhibit, evince, betray, reveal, manifest, demonstrate, reflect. **4** *his danger did not register* make an impression, get through, sink in, penetrate.

**regress** verb retrogress, revert, relapse, lapse, backslide, degenerate, recidivate.

**regret** verb **1** *she regrets her action* repent, rue, feel contrite about, feel remorse about. **2** *she regrets their going* feel sorry about, lament, bemoan, mourn, grieve over, deplore.

**regret** noun **1** *she looks upon her actions with regret* remorse, contrition, repentance, compunction, ruefulness, self-reproach, penitence. **2** *she regarded their going with regret* sorrow, disappointment, lamentation, grief, mourning, pining.

**regrettable** adjective deplorable, reprehensible, blameworthy, unfortunate, unwelcome, distressing, ill-advised.

**regular** adjective **1** *his regular route to work* usual, normal, customary, habitual, routine, typical, everyday, daily, unvarying, common, average, commonplace. **2** *regular breathing* rhythmic, periodic, steady, even, uniform, constant, unchanging. **3** *trees placed at regular intervals* even, uniform, consistent, orderly, systematic, fixed. **4** *he is a regular charmer* real, thorough, absolute, utter, complete.

**regulate** verb **1** *regulate one's expenditure* control, direct, guide, govern, rule, manage, order, administer, handle, arrange, organize, conduct, run, supervise, oversee, superintend, monitor. **2** *regulate the mechanism* adjust, balance, set, synchronize, modulate.

**regulation** noun **1** *the regulation of expenditure* control, direction, guidance, government, rule, management, administration, organization, handling, supervision, monitoring. **2** *the regulation of the mechanisms* adjustment, balancing, synchronization, modulation. **3** *new government regulations* rule, ruling, order, directive, act, law, decree, statute, edict, ordinance, pronouncement, dictum, command, procedure, requirement, prescription, precept.

**rehabilitate** verb **1** *rehabilitate the injured athlete* restore to health, reintegrate, readapt, retrain. **2** *rehabilitate slum*

*areas/houses* restore, redevelop, recondition, renovate, renew, refurbish, redecorate, mend, repair, fix up, rebuild, reconstruct. **3** *rehabilitate the criminal* reform, reclaim, reeducate, redeem, transform.

**rehearse** verb **1** *rehearse the play* practice, prepare, try out, run through, go over. **2** *rehearse the actors* drill, train, prepare.

**reign** verb **1** *she reigned for thirty years* be king/queen, be monarch/sovereign, occupy the throne, wear the crown, wield the scepter. **2** *the present committee has reigned for years* govern, rule, be in command/charge/control, administer, hold sway; *inf.* be at the helm. **3** *chaos reigned* prevail, predominate, obtain, hold sway, be supreme, be rife, be rampant.

**reign** noun **1** *during the reign of the king* monarchy, sovereignty. **2** *under the reign of the present government* government, rule, command, control, administration, charge, influence, sway, ascendancy, dominion, power, supremacy.

**rein** noun *act as a rein on their expenditure* check, curb, restraint, constraint, restriction, limitation, control, bridle, brake.

**rein** verb *try to rein in his impatience | rein your expenditure* check, curb, restrain, constrain, restrict, control, bridle.

**reinforce** verb **1** *reinforce the bridge | reinforce his argument* strengthen, fortify, bolster, shore up, buttress, prop up, brace, support, back up, uphold, stress, underline, emphasize. **2** *reinforce the troops* augment, increase, add to, supplement.

**reiterate** verb repeat, restate, belabor, dwell on, harp on, stress.

**reject** verb **1** *reject an offer* refuse, turn down, decline, spurn, rebuff, repudiate, veto, deny; *inf.* pass up. **2** *reject the bill | reject his wife* cast aside, discard, jettison, renounce, abandon, forsake, scrap, exclude, eliminate.

**rejection** noun **1** *the rejection of their offer* refusal, turning down, declining, spurning; *inf.* brush-off. **2** *the rejection of the bill | his rejection of his family* casting out, discarding, jettisoning, renunciation. **3** *receive a rejection* refusal, no, demurral, negation, thumbs down; *inf.* brush-off.

**rejoice** verb **1** *people rejoicing on hearing the good news* celebrate, revel, be joyful, be delighted, be elated, be overjoyed, be jubilant, be euphoric, jump for joy, exult, glory, triumph, make merry. **2** *rejoice in her new baby* take delight/pleasure in, find joy in.

**rejoicing** noun jubilation, happiness, celebration, revelry, merrymaking, gladness, delight, elation, euphoria, exultation, glory, triumph.

**rejoinder** noun answer, response, reply, riposte, retort; *inf.* comeback.

**relapse** verb **1** *business improved but then relapsed* regress, retrogress, revert, backslide, degenerate, retrograde, recidivate. **2** *the patient relapsed* worsen, take a turn for the worse, sicken, deteriorate, sink.

**relapse** noun **1** *the business had a relapse after its improvement* regression, retrogression, reversion, recidivism. **2** *the patient suffered a relapse* turn for the worse, setback, deterioration.

**relate** verb **1** *relate the story of the accident* recount, tell, narrate, describe, report, impart, communicate, recite, present, detail, delineate, chronicle, set forth. **2** *it is sometimes difficult to relate cause and effect* connect, associate, link, correlate, ally, couple, join. **relate to** *this information does not relate to the matter in hand* concern, apply to, be relevant to, refer to, pertain to, bear on.

**relation** noun **1** *the relation of the story* recounting, telling, narration, description, reporting, reciting. **2** *the relation between cause and effect* connection, association, link, tie-in, correlation, alliance, bond, interdependence. **3** *have no relation to the problem in hand* applicability, application, relevance, reference, pertinence, bearing. **4** *he is my one Scandinavian relation* relative, kinsman, kinswoman.

**relationship** noun **1** *the relationship between cause and effect* connection, association, link, correlation, alliance, bond, parallel, correspondence, conjunction. **2** *enter into a new relationship* friendship, love affair, partnership, liaison.

**relative** adjective **1** *consider the relative merits of the candidates* comparative, respective, correlative, parallel, corresponding. **2** *the salary scale is relative to production* proportionate, in proportion/ratio, proportional. **3** *facts relative to the issue* applicable, relevant, pertaining, pertinent, germane, material, apposite, appropriate, apropos, appurtenant.

**relative** noun *a relative of his wife* relation, member of the family, kinsman, kinswoman, connection; kin.

**relax** verb **1** *relax one's grip* loosen, slacken, weaken, untighten, lessen, let up, reduce, diminish. **2** *relax the rules* moderate, make less strict, soften, ease. **3** *relax one's efforts* lessen, reduce, diminish, decrease, ease off, slacken off, let up on, abate. **4** *this will relax you* loosen up, calm, calm down, tranquilize, soothe, pacify; *inf.* unwind. **5** *he relaxes by playing the piano* loosen up, enjoy oneself, amuse oneself, entertain oneself, ease up, rest; *inf.* unwind, take it easy, let one's hair down. **6** *relax by the pool* rest, lounge, repose, take one's ease, idle, put one's feet up.

**relaxation** noun **1** *the relaxation of his grip* loosening, slackening, weakening, letting-up. **2** *relaxation of rules* moderation, softening, easing. **3** *relaxation of one's efforts* lessening, reduction, easing off, abatement. **4** *the relaxation of the patients* calming, tranquilization, soothing, pacification. **5** *for relaxation he plays the piano* leisure, recreation, enjoyment, amusement, entertainment, fun, pleasure, rest.

**release** verb **1** *release the prisoners* set free, free, let go, turn loose, liberate, deliver, emancipate, manumit. **2** *release those who had been tied up* set free, free, untie, unloose, unbind, unchain, unfetter, unshackle, extricate. **3** *release her from her promise* let off, excuse, absolve, acquit, exonerate, exempt. **4** *release the news* make public, issue, break, announce, reveal, divulge, unveil, present, disclose, publish, broadcast, circulate, disseminate, distribute, spread.

**release** noun **1** *the release of the prisoners* liberation, deliverance, emancipation, manumission, freedom. **2** *the release of the bound victims* freeing, untying, unbinding, unchaining, extrication. **3** *the release from her promise* absolution, acquittal, dispensation, exemption, excusing. **4** *the release of the news* issuing, breaking, announcement, divulging, publication, broadcasting, circulation. **5** *write a press release* announcement, bulletin, publication, proclamation. **6** *the artist's latest release* recording, record, disc, compact disc; single, album; book; movie, motion picture, film; *inf.* CD; flick.

**relent** verb **1** *the judge relented and reduced the sentence* soften, become lenient, show mercy/pity, melt, capitulate, yield, give in, forbear, change one's mind; *inf.* do a U-turn. **2** *the wind relented* let up, ease, slacken, relax, abate, drop, fall off, die down, weaken.

**relentless** adjective *a relentless tyrant* ruthless, merciless, pitiless, remorseless, unforgiving, implacable, inexorable, cruel, grim, harsh, hard, cold-hearted, fierce, strict, obdurate, unyielding.

**relevant** adjective applicable, pertinent, apposite, material, appurtenant, germane, admissible, appropriate, apt, fitting.

**reliable** adjective **1** *a reliable friend* dependable, trustworthy, true, faithful, steady, steadfast, constant, unfailing, certain, sure, responsible. **2** *reliable evidence* dependable, trustworthy, well-founded, well-grounded, authentic, genuine, credible, sound.

**reliance** noun **1** *place no reliance on what she says* confidence, trust, faith, belief, conviction. **2** *his total reliance on his colleagues* dependence, leaning.

**relic** noun **1** *relics on view in the museum* artifact, antique, heirloom. **2** *a tradition that is a relic of another age* vestige, trace, survivor, remnant. **3** *regard the ring as a relic of a former relationship* souvenir, memento, keepsake, remembrance, reminder.

**relief** noun **1** *the relief of the pain* alleviation, mitigation, allaying, soothing, dulling, lessening, reduction, assuagement, palliation, ease, abatement. **2** *bring relief to the starving people* aid, help, assistance, succor. **3** *relief from the monotony* respite, remission, interruption, break, variation, diversion; *inf.* letup. **4** *the soldier's relief* replacement, substitute, stand-in, fill-in, alternate, understudy; *inf.* sub. **5** *details bringing the story out in sharp relief* distinctness, vividness, intensity, sharpness, focus, clarity, precision. **6** *relief from his burden* freedom, release, liberation, deliverance, exemption, extrication, discharge.

**relieve** verb **1** *relieve his pain* alleviate, mitigate, assuage, allay, soothe, soften, palliate, appease, ease, dull, abate, reduce, lessen, diminish. **2** *relieve the victims* aid, help, assist, rescue, save, succor. **3** *relieve the monotony* interrupt, break up, vary, lighten. **4** *relieve the soldier on guard* take over from, take the place of, stand in for, substitute for. **5** *relieve them of their burdens* free, release, liberate, deliver, exempt, extricate, discharge, unburden, disencumber.

**religion** noun faith, belief, creed, persuasion, doctrine, theology, church, denomination.

**religious** adjective **1** *religious festivals/discussions* church, holy, divine, theological, doctrinal, spiritual, sectarian. **2** *religious people* churchgoing, God-fearing, godly, pious, devout.

**relinquish** verb **1** *relinquish her right to the title* renounce, resign, abdicate, surrender, give up, sign away. **2** *relinquish his position* leave, quit, vacate, abandon, forsake. **3** *relinquish the habit* give up, discontinue, stop, cease, drop, abstain from, forbear from, forgo, desist from. **4** *relinquish her grip* release, let go, loosen, unloose.

**relish** noun *tells a story with relish* gusto, enjoyment, delight, pleasure, satisfaction, gratification, appreciation, liking, zest.

**relish** verb *the children relish the beach* enjoy, delight in, fancy, like, love, adore, appreciate, revel in, luxuriate in.

**reluctant** adjective **1** *a reluctant hero* unwilling, hesitant, unenthusiastic, grudging. **2** *reluctant to go* unwilling, disinclined, loath, averse.

**rely** verb *you can rely on me* depend, count, bank, trust, lean, bet.

**remain** verb **1** *only a handful remained* be left, stay behind, survive, last, abide, endure, prevail. **2** *remain at home* stay, wait, linger, tarry; *inf.* stay put. **3** *remain calm* stay, continue, persist in being.

**remainder** noun remnant, residue, residuum, balance, surplus, excess, superfluity; remains, remnants, relics, vestiges, leavings, dregs.

**remark** verb mention, say, state, declare, pronounce, assert, observe. **remark on/upon** *she remarked on his appearance* comment on, mention.

**remark** noun **1** *ignore his nasty remarks* comment, statement, utterance, pronouncement, observation, reference, opinion. **2** *a performance worthy of remark* comment, attention, mention, notice, observation, heed, acknowledgment, recognition.

**remarkable** adjective extraordinary, unusual, uncommon, conspicuous, singular, signal, rare, exceptional, outstanding, striking, impressive, considerable, notable, noteworthy, memorable, preeminent, significant, important, momentous, phenomenal, wonderful, distinctive, peculiar, special, curious, unique.

**remedy** noun **1** *given a remedy for asthma* cure, treatment, medicine, medication, medicament, therapy, antidote, restorative, nostrum, panacea. **2** *find a remedy for the situation* corrective, solution, redress, panacea.

**remedy** verb **1** *unable to remedy her condition* cure, heal, treat, counteract, control. **2** *remedy the situation* rectify, solve, put right, redress, fix, sort out.

**remember** verb **1** *I cannot remember his name* recall, call to mind, recollect, think of. **2** *remember that it is raining* keep/bear in mind, not forget. **3** *remembering the past* recall, recollect, reminisce; reminisce about, look back on, hark back to, summon up.

**remembrance** noun **1** *their remembrance of times past* recollection, reminiscing, memory. **2** *give her a remembrance of their meeting* keepsake, souvenir, memento, token, commemoration, memorial.

**remind** verb cause one to remember, jog/refresh one's memory, prompt, awake one's memories of.

**remiss** adjective negligent, neglectful, lax, slack, slipshod, careless, forgetful, inattentive, heedless, thoughtless, unthinking, unmindful, culpable, delinquent; *inf.* sloppy.

**remit** verb **1** *remit a penalty* cancel, revoke, repeal, rescind, stop, halt. **2** *remit payment* send, dispatch, forward, transmit, post, mail. **3** *remit the case to another court* refer, pass on, hand on, send on, transfer, direct. **4** *remit the offense* pardon, forgive, excuse, overlook, pass over.

**remittance** noun payment, fee, transmittal.

**remnant** noun **1** *the remnant of the army* remainder, residue, balance; remains, vestiges. **2** *a remnant of material* piece, fragment, scrap.

**remorse** noun regret, sorrow, contriteness, compunction, penitence, repentance, guilty conscience, guilt, shame, self-reproach, ruefulness; pangs of conscience.

**remote** adjective **1** *the remote past* distant, far, far-off, faraway, far-removed. **2** *in remote mountain villages* out-of-the-way, outlying, inaccessible, off the beaten track, isolated, secluded, lonely. **3** *a remote possibility* outside, unlikely, improbable, implausible, negligible, insignificant, doubtful, dubious, inconsiderable, slight, slender, slim, small, poor. **4** *she is rather remote among strangers* aloof, distant, detached, withdrawn, reserved, uncommunicative, unapproachable, standoffish, cool, haughty, uninvolved, indifferent.

**remove** verb **1** *remove the dishes from the table* take away, shift, convey, transfer, transport. **2** *remove him from office* get rid of, dismiss, evict, eject, expel, cast out, oust, throw out, dislodge, relegate, unseat, depose, displace; *inf.* sack, fire. **3** *remove their coats* take off, doff, pull off. **4** *remove their privileges* withdraw, do away with, abolish. **5** *remove the errors* delete, eliminate, erase, rub out, cross out, strike out, blue-pencil, efface, obliterate. **6** *remove the weeds/opposition* take out, pull out, uproot, eradicate, extirpate, destroy, exterminate, annihilate. **7** *remove a branch* cut off, amputate, lop off, chop off, excise.

**remuneration** noun payment, pay, salary, fee, emolument, stipend, honorarium, income, profit, reward, recompense, reimbursement; wages, earnings.

**renaissance** noun rebirth, reemergence, reappearance, resurgence, renewal, reawakening, revival, resurrection, rejuvenation, regeneration.

**render** verb **1** *render them helpless* make, cause to become, leave. **2** *pay for services rendered* give, contribute, provide, supply, furnish; do, perform. **3** *render insult for insult* exchange, trade, swap, return. **4** *render a verdict* present, send in, submit, tender; deliver, hand down. **5** *the artist rendered her in a wistful mood* paint, portray, depict, represent. **6** *the piano solo was well rendered* play, execute, perform, interpret. **7** *render the passage into Russian* translate, transcribe, construe, put, express. **8** *they rendered their land to the emperor* hand over, deliver, turn over, give up, yield, cede, surrender, relinquish. **9**

## remittance · reparation

*render the lands (back) to the original owners* give back, return, restore.

**rendezvous** noun **1** *have a rendezvous with her lover* appointment, date, engagement, tryst, meeting, assignation. **2** *their rendezvous is the café* meeting place, venue, tryst.

**renegade** noun defector, deserter, turncoat, betrayer, traitor, dissenter, apostate, revolutionary, rebel, mutineer.

**renege** verb default, go back on one's word, break one's promise, back out, pull out; *inf.* cop out, welsh.

**renounce** verb **1** *renounce his claim* give up, relinquish, resign, abdicate, abnegate, surrender, waive, forgo. **2** *renounce his son* repudiate, disown, cast off, discard, reject, disinherit, spurn, shun. **3** *renounce strong drink* give up, abstain from, desist from, swear off, eschew. **4** *renounce one's religion* abandon, forsake, renege on, turn one's back on, abjure.

**renovate** verb modernize, recondition, refurbish, rehabilitate, overhaul, restore, revamp, remodel, repair, redecorate, refit; *inf.* do up, fix up.

**renown** noun fame, repute, acclaim, celebrity, distinction, illustriousness, eminence, preeminence, prominence, note, consequence, prestige.

**renowned** adjective famous, famed, well-known, acclaimed, celebrated, distinguished, illustrious, eminent, preeminent, prominent, noted, notable, prestigious.

**rent** noun *what is the rent for the boat?* rental, payment, fee.

**rent** verb *rent a boat from the owner* lease, hire, charter, let, lease, hire out. **rent out** *they rent out houses/boats* let, lease, hire out.

**renunciation** noun **1** *the renunciation of his claim* resignation, abdication, abnegation, surrender, waiving. **2** *the renunciation of his son* repudiation, disowning, discarding, rejection, disinheriting, shunning, spurning. **3** *the renunciation of strong drink* giving up, abstention. **4** *the renunciation of their friendship* abandonment, forsaking, reneging, abjuration.

**repair** verb **1** *repair the machine* fix, service, adjust, regulate, overhaul. **2** *repair the torn clothes* mend, darn, sew, patch. **3** *repair the rift in their friendship* mend, fix, patch up, heal. **4** *repair the omission* rectify, correct, redress, put right, make good, compensate for.

**repair** noun **1** *the repair of the car* fixing, restoration, servicing, overhaul. **2** *you will not notice the repair* mend, darn, patch. **3** *the car is in good repair* condition, state, form, fettle, kilter; *inf.* shape.

**reparation** noun redress, atonement, restitution, satisfaction, compensation, recompense, indemnity; amends, damages.

**repartee** noun witty conversation, badinage, banter, raillery, wordplay.

**repay** verb 1 *repay him for the money owed* refund, reimburse, recompense, remunerate, settle up with, indemnify. 2 *repay him for the crime against her family* retaliate against, get even with, settle the score with. 3 *repay the wrong* avenge, revenge.

**repeal** verb *repeal the bill* revoke, rescind, abrogate, annul, nullify, void, invalidate, cancel, countermand, retract, withdraw, recall, abjure, overrule, override, reverse.

**repeal** noun *the repeal of the bill* revocation, rescission, abrogation, annulment, nullification, voiding, invalidation, cancellation, countermanding, retraction, withdrawal, recall, abjuration, overruling, overriding, reversal.

**repeat** verb 1 *repeat the statement* say again, restate, retell, iterate, recapitulate; *inf.* recap. 2 *she repeated his words* restate, echo, parrot, quote, duplicate, copy, reproduce. 3 *repeat the task* do again, redo, duplicate.

**repeat** noun 1 *a repeat of his statement* repetition, restatement, retelling, iteration, recapitulation; *inf.* recap. 2 *a repeat of his actions* repetition, echoing, duplication, copy, reproduction. 3 *watch a repeat of the sitcom's first episode* rerun, replay, rebroadcast.

**repeated** adjective recurrent, frequent, continual, incessant, constant, endless.

**repel** verb 1 *repel attackers* repulse, drive back, beat back, hold off, ward off, fend off, stave off, parry, keep at bay, foil, check, frustrate, put to flight. 2 *repel his advances* repulse, reject, decline, rebuff. 3 *the sight of blood repels her* revolt, disgust, sicken, nauseate, turn one's stomach, offend, shock.

**repellent** adjective repulsive, revolting, disgusting, sickening, nauseating, distasteful, repugnant, abhorrent, offensive, obnoxious, loathsome, hateful, vile, nasty, shocking, despicable, reprehensible, contemptible, odious, abominable, horrible, horrid, foul, heinous, obscene.

**repent** verb regret, rue; be penitent, be sorry, be contrite, feel remorse/remorseful, reproach oneself, be ashamed; *inf.* see the light.

**repentance** noun penitence, sorrow, regret, contrition, contriteness, remorse, conscience, self-reproach, ruefulness, shame, guilt.

**repercussion** noun 1 *the repercussions of his action* effect, result, consequence, backlash. 2 *he heard/felt the repercussion* echo,

reverberation, reflection, recoil, rebound.

**repetition** noun 1 *a repetition of the statement* restatement, retelling, iteration, recapitulation; *inf.* recap. 2 *her repetition of his words* restatement, echoing, parroting, quoting, copying. 3 *a repetition of his actions* duplication, repeat, redoing. 4 *a lot of repetition in the essay* redundancy, tautology.

**repetitive** adjective *repetitive work* recurrent, unchanging, unvaried, monotonous, tedious, boring, mechanical, automatic.

**replace** verb 1 *replace the book on the shelf* put back, return, restore. 2 *he will replace the retired teacher* take the place of, succeed, supersede, follow after, supplant, substitute for, stand in for, act for, fill in for, cover for, understudy; *inf.* sub for.

**replacement** noun *find a replacement for the retired teacher* successor, substitute, stand-in, fill-in, understudy, proxy, surrogate, *inf.* sub.

**replenish** verb 1 *replenish one's plate* refill, top off, fill up, recharge, reload. 2 *replenish stocks of food* stock up, fill up, make up, replace, renew.

**replica** noun copy, carbon copy, duplicate, facsimile, model, reproduction, imitation.

**reply** verb answer, respond, rejoin, retort, return, riposte, come back, counter.

**reply** noun answer, response, acknowledgment, rejoinder, retort, return, riposte, comeback.

**report** noun 1 *a report of the accident* account, statement, record, exposition, delineation. 2 *newspaper/television reports* article, piece, account, story, write-up, communication, communiqué, dispatch, bulletin. 3 *a company's financial report* statement, record, register, chronicle. 4 *the report of a gun/explosion* bang, boom, crack, crash, rumble, reverberation, noise, echo.

**report** verb 1 *report the latest findings* announce, pass on, communicate, relay, relate, tell, recount, document, delineate, detail, divulge, disclose, circulate. 2 *report the child for cheating* tell on, inform on, expose, accuse, charge; *inf.* squeal on, rat on. 3 *they will report at noon* present oneself, appear, arrive, check in; *inf.* show up.

**reporter** noun journalist, newsman, newswoman, pressman, correspondent, writer, broadcaster, announcer, presenter, news commentator; *inf.* newshound, hack.

**repose** noun 1 *seek repose after work* rest, relaxation, leisure, ease, inactivity, respite, sleep, slumber. 2 *a place of repose in the mountains* quiet, quietude, calm, calmness, tranquillity, peace, peacefulness, stillness, silence, hush.

**reprehensible** adjective blameworthy, reproachable, censurable, condemnable, reprovable, culpable, errant, wrong, bad, shameful, disgraceful, discreditable, dishonorable, ignoble, objectionable, odious, opprobrious, unpardonable, indefensible, unjustifiable, inexcusable.

**represent** verb **1** *X represents the larger number* stand for, correspond to, equal, be equivalent to, symbolize. **2** *the Statue of Liberty represents the spirit of democracy* stand for, symbolize, personify, epitomize. **3** *he represents their idea of a Frenchman* embody, incorporate, typify, exemplify. **4** *Cupid is usually represented as a winged boy* depict, portray, delineate, illustrate, picture, denote, paint, draw, sketch, exhibit, show, display. **5** *he represented the children at the hearing* act for, appear for, speak for.

**representative** adjective **1** *a representative specimen* typical, archetypal, exemplary, characteristic, indicative, illustrative. **2** *the bald eagle is representative of the United States* emblematic, symbolic, evocative. **3** *a representative government* elected, elective, democratic, representational, delegated.

**representative** noun **1** *a typical representative of its class* example, exemplar, specimen, type, archetype, illustration, epitome, embodiment. **2** *he is the society's representative* spokesman, spokeswoman, spokesperson, agent, deputy, proxy. **3** *he is a sales representative* salesman, agent; *inf.* rep. **4** *our country's representative at the conference* delegate, commissioner, ambassador, envoy. **5** *the state's representative in Congress* congressman, congresswoman, member of Congress, senator.

**repress** verb **1** *tyrants repressing the people* subjugate, oppress, tyrannize, crush, master, dominate, domineer, bully, intimidate. **2** *repress a rebellion* put down, quell, quash, squash, subdue, suppress, extinguish, stamp out. **3** *repress a laugh* bite back, restrain, suppress, check, inhibit, bottle up, silence, muffle, stifle, smother.

**repressive** adjective *a repressive regime* tyrannical, despotic, dictatorial, authoritarian, oppressive, coercive, suppressive, harsh, severe, strict, cruel.

**reprieve** noun *the condemned man has had a reprieve* postponement of punishment, remission/cancellation of punishment, stay of execution, pardon.

**reprimand** noun *receive a reprimand from the teacher* rebuke, scolding, chiding, reproof, reproof, lecture, admonition, berating, upbraiding, castigation, tonguelashing; *inf.* talking-to, dressing-down, bawling-out.

**reproach** noun **1** *words of reproach* criticism, faultfinding, censure, admonition, condemnation, abuse, reprimand, scolding, reproof, reproval, upbraiding. **2** *her behavior brought reproach to the family* discredit, disgrace, shame, dishonor, disrepute, ignominy, opprobrium, odium, obloquy, stigma.

**reproduce** verb **1** *the copier can reproduce color photographs* copy, duplicate, replicate, photocopy, print, transcribe, clone; Xerox (*trademark*). **2** *reproduce the effect* recreate, repeat, redo, remake, imitate, emulate, echo, mirror, parallel, match, mimic, ape. **3** *the animals seem unable to reproduce* breed, procreate, bear young, produce offspring, multiply, propagate, proliferate, spawn.

**reproduction** noun **1** *the reproduction of color photographs* copying, duplicating, photocopying, printing; Xerox (*trademark*). **2** *a reproduction of the painting* copy, duplicate, replica, facsimile, imitation, print. **3** *a reproduction of the photograph* copy, duplicate, facsimile, fax, photocopy, mimeograph, print; Xerox (*trademark*). **4** *animal reproduction* breeding, procreation, multiplying, propagation, proliferation.

**reproof** noun **1** *without a word of reproof* reproval, disapproval, disapprobation, reproach, admonition, castigation, criticism, censure, blame, condemnation. **2** *ignore their reproofs* rebuke, scolding, chiding, reproach, lecture, admonition, berating, upbraiding, castigation, criticism, faultfinding, censure.

**reprove** verb rebuke, scold, chide, reproach, lecture, admonish, berate, upbraid, castigate, take to task, criticize, censure, blame, condemn; *inf.* tell off, bawl out.

**repudiate** verb **1** *repudiate one's son/faith* disown, cast off, cut off, abandon, forsake, desert, discard, reject, renounce, disavow, abjure. **2** *repudiate a charge/claim* deny, contradict, gainsay, disclaim, disavow. **3** *repudiate a treaty* reject, rescind, revoke, cancel, disregard, flout, spurn, dishonor, disobey.

**repugnant** adjective abhorrent, revolting, repulsive, repellent, disgusting, sickening, nauseating, disagreeable, distasteful, offensive, objectionable, obnoxious, loathsome, hateful, despicable, reprehensible, contemptible, abominable, horrible, horrid, foul, nasty, vile, ugly, odious, heinous.

**repulsive** adjective abhorrent, revolting, disgusting. *See* REPUGNANT.

**reputable** adjective respectable, respected, well-thought-of, esteemed, estimable, worthy, creditable, reliable, dependable, trustworthy, honest, honorable, aboveboard, legitimate, upright.

**reputation** noun **1** *have a dishonest reputa-*

*tion* name, estimation, character, repute, standing, position, status. **2** *she has lost her reputation* good name, good character, standing, respect, respectability, repute, status, stature, esteem.

**repute** noun **1** *a house of ill repute* character, estimation. *See* REPUTATION 1. **2** *they are companies of repute* good reputation, good name, high standing, stature, esteem, fame, renown, celebrity, distinction.

**repute** verb *he is reputed to be a good player* think, believe, consider, hold, suppose, reckon, judge, assume, presume.

**request** noun **1** *come at his request* asking, entreaty, solicitation, petitioning, application, imploration, pleading, behest, supplication, demand, summons, requisition. **2** *make several requests* entreaty, appeal, petition, plea, behest, demand, call, suit.

**request** verb *request a favor* ask for, solicit, seek, apply for, put in for, entreat, beseech, petition, implore, requisition.

**require** verb **1** *we require peace and quiet* need, lack, want, wish, desire, crave, miss. **2** *absolute obedience is required* demand, order, command, call for, insist on, ask for, request. **3** *they required him to go* order, instruct, command, oblige, enjoin, bid, compel. **4** *the job requires patience* call for, demand, necessitate, involve, take.

**required** adjective *required reading* compulsory, obligatory, mandatory, prescribed, recommended, set, essential, necessary, vital.

**requirement** noun **1** *list your travel requirements* need, want, lack, must, necessity, essential, demand. **2** *what are the requirements for the job?* prerequisite, requisite, precondition, specification, qualification, sine qua non, stipulation.

**requisite** adjective *the requisite amount* required, prerequisite, needed, necessary, essential, indispensable, vital, obligatory, mandatory.

**requisition** noun *put in a requisition for supplies* application, order, claim, request, call, demand, summons.

**rescind** verb repeal, revoke, reverse, abrogate, retract, countermand, overturn, annul, nullify, void, invalidate, cancel.

**rescue** verb save, deliver from danger, come to the aid of, free, release, liberate, emancipate, extricate, redeem, salvage, relieve.

**rescue** noun saving, deliverance, release, liberation, emancipation, extrication, redemption, salvage, relief.

**research** noun *carry out medical research* investigation, experimentation, fact-finding, testing, exploration, analysis, examination,

scrutiny; experiment, assessment, study, review, inquiry, probe, inspection; tests.

**research** verb *research the new drug* investigate, inquire into, look into, probe, explore, analyze, study, examine, scrutinize, review, inspect, experiment with, do tests on, assess.

**resemblance** noun likeness, similarity, similitude, sameness, uniformity, correspondence, parallelism, parity, analogy, affinity, closeness, nearness, agreement, congruity, concurrence, conformity.

**resemble** verb look like, bear a resemblance to, be similar to, remind one of, take after, echo, mirror, duplicate, parallel; *inf.* favor.

**resent** verb take offense/umbrage at, take exception to, take amiss, begrudge, dislike.

**resentment** noun offense, indignation, irritation, displeasure, annoyance, anger, ire, pique, grudgingness, bitterness, animosity, hostility; hard feelings.

**reservation** noun **1** *make a reservation* advance booking, booking, engagement, accommodation. **2** *have reservations concerning the plan* qualification, proviso, provision, condition, stipulation, limitation, qualm, scruple; hesitancy, doubt. **3** *an American Indian reservation* reserve, preserve, enclave, sanctuary, tract, area, territory.

**reserve** verb **1** *reserve some food for later* put/set aside, put away, keep, withhold, conserve, save, retain, store, hoard, stockpile; *inf.* hang on to. **2** *reserve a room* book, engage, arrange for, charter, hire. **3** *reserve judgment* put off, postpone, defer, delay, withhold. **4** *reserve the right to refuse* keep, retain, secure; *inf.* hang on to.

**reserve** noun **1** *we have reserves of steel* store, stock, supply, reservoir, pool, cache, fund, stockpile, accumulation, backlog, hoard. **2** *her reserve puts people off* restraint, aloofness, detachment, distance, remoteness, formality, coolness, reticence, unapproachability, unresponsiveness, shyness, diffidence, secretiveness, silence.

**reserved** adjective **1** *the table/room is reserved* booked, engaged, taken, spoken for, chartered, hired. **2** *she is reserved, but he is outgoing* aloof, detached, remote, formal, unemotional, undemonstrative, cool, reticent, unapproachable, uncommunicative, unsociable, unfriendly, unresponsive, unforthcoming, shy, retiring, diffident, secretive, taciturn, silent.

**reside** verb **1** *he resides in Utah* live, dwell, stay, sojourn, inhabit, occupy, be settled. **2** *the strength residing in his personality* be inherent, be intrinsic, rest, dwell, abide, exist.

**residence** noun **1** *his residence is in London*

house, home, place, dwelling, domicile, habitation; quarters. **2** *take up residence tomorrow* occupation, occupancy, habitation, inhabitation, tenancy.

**resident** noun *all residents pay taxes* inhabitant, occupant, householder, dweller, sojourner, tenant, local, denizen.

**residue** noun remainder, remnant, rest, surplus, extra, excess, balance; remains, leftovers, dregs, lees, residuum.

**resign** verb **1** *he resigned yesterday* give notice, leave, quit. **2** *resign his position* relinquish, give up, renounce, abdicate, surrender, cede. **3** *resign oneself to losing* reconcile, submit, yield, accede, bow.

**resigned** adjective **1** *resigned to the fact that he would fail* reconciled, acquiescent. **2** *take a resigned attitude* compliant, unresisting, passive, submissive, subdued, docile, patient, tolerant, stoical.

**resilient** adjective **1** *a resilient material* elastic, springy, rubbery, flexible, pliant, supple, pliable, plastic. **2** *she was usually resilient after disappointments* quick to recover, irrepressible, tough, strong, hardy.

**resist** verb **1** *resist the march of progress* check, stem, curb, obstruct, hinder, impede, block, thwart, frustrate, inhibit, restrain. **2** *resist fatty foods* abstain from, forgo, avoid. **3** *resist the invading army* stand up to, withstand, repel, defy, oppose, confront.

**resistance** noun *the invaders met with resistance* opposition, obstruction, hindrance, impediment, defiance, confrontation, struggle, contention.

**resolute** adjective determined, resolved, decided, firm, fixed, set, intent, steadfast, earnest, staunch, bold, courageous, serious, purposeful, deliberate, inflexible, unyielding, unwavering, unfaltering, unhesitating, unswerving, unflinching, obstinate, obdurate, strong-willed, dogged, persevering, persistent, tenacious, relentless, unshakable, dedicated.

**resolution** noun **1** *admire the resolution of the competitors* resolve, determination, firmness, intentness, steadfastness, staunchness, boldness, courage, seriousness, purpose, purposefulness, obstinacy, obduracy, willpower, doggedness, perseverance, persistence, tenacity, dedication. **2** *it is our resolution to proceed* resolve, decision, aim, intent, intention, purpose, object, plan, design, aspiration. **3** *the committee/court passed a resolution* motion, declaration, decree, verdict, judgment. **4** *the resolution of the problem will take time* solving, solution, sorting out, working out, unraveling, disentanglement.

**resolve** verb **1** *he resolved to leave* decide, make up one's mind, determine, undertake. **2** *resolve the problem* solve, sort out, work out, clear up, unravel, disentangle. **3** *resolve their doubts* dispel, remove, banish, clear up.

**resolve** noun **1** *their resolve is to win* aim, intent, purpose. *See* RESOLUTION 2. **2** *set out with resolve* determination, purposefulness. *See* RESOLUTION 1.

**resort** verb **resort to** *resort to force* fall back on, turn to, have recourse to, look to, use, utilize, exercise.

**resort** noun **1** *a health resort* vacation spot, retreat; spa. **2** *your only resort is to ask the police* recourse, expedient, measure, alternative, choice, chance, possibility, hope.

**resound** verb **1** *caves resounding with the noise of waves* reverberate, resonate, echo, ring. **2** *her fame resounded throughout Europe* spread, circulate, be proclaimed, be celebrated.

**resource** noun **1** *use any resource to find help* expedient, resort, course, way, device; means. **2** *draw on one's coal resources* reserve, reservoir, store, stock, supply, pool, fund, stockpile, accumulation, hoard. **3** *person of resource* resourcefulness, initiative, ingenuity, inventiveness, talent, ability, capability. **4** *rely on their country's resources* assets, reserves, materials; wealth.

**resourceful** adjective ingenious, inventive, creative, imaginative, bright, sharp, talented, gifted, able, capable.

**respect** noun **1** *their respect for their teacher* esteem, regard, admiration, appreciation, veneration, reverence, deference, honor, homage. **2** *treat the old lady with respect* deference, consideration, thoughtfulness, attentiveness, politeness, courtesy, civility. **3** *without any respect for/to rhythm* heed, regard, consideration, attention, notice. **4** *correct in all respects* aspect, facet, feature, way, sense, characteristic, particular, point, detail, matter. **5** *with respect to the matter in hand* reference, relevance, regard, relation, connection, bearing.

**respect** verb **1** *they respect their teacher* esteem, think highly of, admire, appreciate, venerate, revere, value, honor. **2** *respect her wishes | respect the treaty* heed, observe, comply with, follow, abide by, adhere to, obey.

**respectable** adjective **1** *a respectable person/background* reputable, upright, honorable, trustworthy, aboveboard, worthy, decent, good, virtuous, admirable, well-bred, proper, decorous. **2** *a respectable effort/salary* reasonable, fair, passable, tolerable, adequate, decent, worthy, considerable, substantial, satisfactory; *inf.* not bad.

**respite** noun rest, break, breathing spell, interval, intermission, recess, lull, pause, hiatus, halt; relief, relaxation; reprieve, stay, suspension, postponement, adjournment, deferment, delay, moratorium; *inf.* breather, letup.

**respond** verb *"no," she responded* answer, reply, rejoin, retort, riposte, come back, counter.

**response** noun **1** *they gave no response to the question* answer, reply, acknowledgment, rejoinder, retort, riposte, comeback. **2** *receive a good response to their questionnaire* reaction, feedback.

**responsibility** noun **1** *it is his responsibility to get us there* charge, duty, onus, task, role, liability, accountability, answerability. **2** *people of responsibility* maturity, reason, common sense, soundness, stability, reliability, dependability, trustworthiness, conscientiousness. **3** *a post of responsibility* authority, control, power.

**responsible** adjective **1** *he is responsible for the confusion* accountable, answerable, to blame, at fault, guilty, culpable. **2** *he is responsible to the president* answerable, accountable. **3** *the children are very responsible* mature, adult, levelheaded, rational, reasonable, sensible, sound, stable, reliable, dependable, trustworthy, conscientious. **4** *a responsible position* authoritative, executive, powerful, high, important.

**responsive** adjective *a responsive audience* receptive, sensitive, perceptive, sympathetic, impressionable, open, alive, awake, aware, sharp.

**rest**[1] noun **1** *seek rest after work* repose, relaxation, leisure, ease, inactivity, respite, time off. **2** *have a rest after work* sleep, nap, doze, slumber, siesta; *inf.* breather, snooze, forty winks. **3** *a place of rest in the mountains* repose, quiet, quietude, calm, calmness, tranquillity, peace, peacefulness, stillness, silence, hush.

**rest**[2] verb **1** *resting after work* relax, lie down, sleep, take a nap, doze, slumber; *inf.* take it easy, snooze. **2** *the result rests on the decision of the jury* depend, rely, hang, hinge.

**rest**[3] noun *some will go; the rest will stay* remainder, residue, residuum, balance, remnant, surplus, excess, remains, leftovers.

**rest**[4] verb *you may rest assured* remain, stay, continue, be left.

**restful** adjective **1** *a restful effect* calming, relaxing, soothing, tranquilizing. **2** *a restful place* quiet, calm, tranquil, relaxed, peaceful, placid, still, languid, undisturbed, unhurried, sleepy.

**restitution** noun reparation, redress, atonement, recompense, compensation, indemnification, indemnity, requital, retribution, remuneration, reimbursement, repayment; amends.

**restless** adjective **1** *pass a restless night* sleepless, wakeful, fitful. **2** *the crowd grew restless* uneasy, on edge, agitated. **3** *restless children* restive, fidgety.

**restore** verb **1** *restore the building* renovate, repair, fix, recondition, rehabilitate, refurbish, rebuild, reconstruct, remodel, revamp, redecorate, touch up; *inf.* fix up. **2** *a rest will help to restore him* build up, resuscitate, revitalize, refresh, revive, revivify. **3** *restore the vase to the shelf* put back, return, replace, reinstate. **4** *restore democracy* reestablish, reinstitute, reinstate, reimpose.

**restrain** verb **1** *restrain the unruly crowd* control, hold in check, curb, subdue. **2** *restrain one's anger* control, check, suppress, repress, contain, smother, stifle, rein in. **3** *restrain the boy from jumping* prevent, hold back, hinder, impede, inhibit. **4** *restrain the thieves* tie up, bind, chain up, fetter, pinion, confine, detain.

**restraint** noun **1** *he acts as a restraint on their impulsiveness* constraint, check, curb, barrier, block, hindrance, impediment, deterrent, inhibition. **2** *behave with restraint* self-restraint, self-control, self-discipline, moderation, temperateness, prudence, judiciousness. **3** *her restraint puts people off* self-possession, reserve, formality, aloofness, detachment, reticence. **4** *put the thieves in/under restraint* confinement, detention, imprisonment, incarceration, bonds, chains.

**restrict** verb **1** *restrict movement* hinder, impede, hamper, retard, handicap, cramp. **2** *restrict your food consumption* limit, regulate, control, moderate.

**restriction** noun **1** *impose currency restrictions* constraint, limitation, control, check, curb, regulation, condition, provision, proviso, stipulation, qualification. **2** *the restriction of the space* confinement, constraint. **3** *restriction of movement* hindrance, impediment, handicap.

**result** noun *pleased with the result of the talks* outcome, consequence, upshot, effect, reaction, repercussion, conclusion, termination, aftermath, product, by-product; fruits.

**result** verb **1** *a fight resulted from the discussion* follow, ensue, issue, develop, stem, arise, evolve, emerge, emanate, occur, happen, come about, eventuate. **2** *it resulted in a draw* end, culminate, finish, terminate.

**resume** verb **1** *resume after lunch* carry on, continue, proceed, go on, recommence, restart. **2** *resume negotiations* reopen, reinstitute, take up, carry on, continue, recommence.

**résumé** noun **1** *present a résumé of the events* summary, précis, synopsis, abstract, outline, sketch, abridgment, digest. **2** *send your résumé with your application* work history, curriculum vitae; *inf.* CV.

**resuscitate** verb **1** *resuscitate him after his collapse* administer CPR to, bring around, revive. **2** *resuscitate old practices* revive, resurrect, breathe new life into, restore, reintroduce.

**retain** verb **1** *retain his job* keep, hold on/fast to; *inf.* hang on to. **2** *retain the old system* keep, maintain, continue, preserve. **3** *retain the facts* memorize, remember, recall, recollect. **4** *retain a gardener* hire, employ, engage, commission, pay.

**retaliate** verb return like for like, make reprisal(s), take/exact revenge, avenge oneself, counter, reciprocate, even the score.

**retard** verb slow down, hold up, delay, hinder, hamper, obstruct, impede, check, arrest, thwart, frustrate.

**reticent** adjective reserved, restrained, taciturn, diffident, uncommunicative, secretive, tight-lipped, closemouthed, quiet, silent; *inf.* mum.

**retire** verb **1** *he retires at 65* give up work, stop working. **2** *the jury retired* withdraw, go out, depart, exit, leave, absent oneself. **3** *they retire at midnight* go to bed, go to one's room; *inf.* turn in, call it a day.

**retiring** adjective *a retiring young woman* shy, diffident, bashful, self-effacing, shrinking, unassuming, unassertive, reserved, reticent, timid, timorous, modest, demure.

**retract** verb *retract one's statement* take back, withdraw, revoke, repeal, rescind, annul, cancel, abrogate, disavow, abjure, renounce, recant, disclaim.

**retreat** verb *the army retreated* withdraw, pull back, fall back, give ground, decamp, depart, leave, flee, take flight, turn tail.

**retreat** noun **1** *the retreat of the army* withdrawal, departure, flight, evacuation. **2** *he has a retreat in the mountains* refuge, haven, shelter, den, sanctuary, sanctum sanctorum, hideaway, resort.

**retribution** noun punishment, justice, reckoning, reprisal, requital, retaliation, revenge, vengeance, redress, reparation, recompense, restitution; just deserts.

**retrieve** verb **1** *retrieve one's property* get back, recover, regain, recoup, redeem, reclaim, repossess, recapture, salvage, rescue. **2** *dogs retrieving sticks* fetch, bring back.

**retrospect** noun **in retrospect** on reflection, on reconsideration, with hindsight.

**return** verb **1** *they returned at dawn | the symptoms returned* go back, come back, reappear, reoccur, come again. **2** *return soda bottles | return his love letters* give back, send back, take back, remit. **3** *return the books to the shelves* put back, replace, restore, reinstate, reinstall. **4** *return her greetings* reciprocate, repay, requite. **5** *the firm returned a profit* yield, bring in, earn, make, net. **6** *return a guilty verdict* bring in, deliver, announce, submit.

**return** noun **1** *look forward to their return* homecoming, reappearance, reoccurrence. **2** *the return of the books to the shelf* replacement, restoration, reinstatement, reinstallment. **3** *the return on the investment* profit, yield, gain, income, revenue, interest, benefit. **4** *fill in a tax return* statement, report, account, summary, form. **5** *done in return for your help* reciprocation, repayment, response, exchange.

**reveal** verb **1** *the coat blew back to reveal a red dress* show, display, exhibit, expose. **2** *examination revealed a deep cut* bring to light, uncover, expose, lay bare, unearth, unveil, unmask. **3** *reveal the details of the affair* disclose, divulge, tell, let slip, give away, leak, betray, broadcast, publicize, publish.

**revel** verb *partygoers reveling all night* celebrate, make merry, party, carouse; *inf.* whoop it up, rave, paint the town red. **revel in** *revel in her victory* delight in, take pleasure in, bask in, rejoice in, relish, savor, luxuriate in, wallow in.

**revelation** noun *the revelation of the details* disclosure, divulgence, leak, betrayal, publication, communication.

**revelry** noun celebration, festivities; merrymaking, mirth, carousal.

**revenge** noun **1** *seek revenge* vengeance, retaliation, retribution, reprisal, requital, redress, satisfaction. **2** *a heart full of revenge* vengefulness, vindictiveness, spite, spitefulness, malice, ill will, animosity, hostility.

**revenge** verb *revenge an injustice | revenge oneself* avenge, retaliate, exact retribution for, requite.

**revenue** noun income, return, yield, interest, gain; profits, receipts, proceeds.

**reverberate** verb resound, echo, ring, vibrate.

**revere** verb admire, respect, esteem, defer to, honor, venerate, worship, adore, hold in awe, exalt, put on a pedestal, idolize.

**reverence** noun *regard the leader with reverence* admiration, respect, deference, honor, veneration, worship, homage, adoration, devotion, awe, exaltation.

**reverent** adjective respectful, deferential, admiring, adoring, loving, devoted, awed, submissive.

**reverse** verb **1** *reverse the collar* turn inside out, transpose. **2** *reverse the barrel* turn upside down, upend, invert. **3** *reverse roles* change, exchange, trade, swap. **4** *reverse the decision* alter, change, countermand, overturn, revoke, repeal, rescind, annul, nullify, void, invalidate.

**reverse** adjective *in reverse order* backward, inverted, transposed, opposite, inverse.

**reverse** noun **1** *the reverse is the case* opposite, contrary, converse, antithesis. **2** *write on the reverse* other side, back, flip side, verso. **3** *the firm has suffered reverses* reversal, upset, setback, failure, misfortune, mishap, misadventure, blow, disappointment; adversity, hardship, affliction, vicissitude, defeat.

**review** noun **1** *a review of the whole situation* survey, study, analysis, examination, scrutiny, assessment, appraisal. **2** *the salary structure is under review* reconsideration, reexamination, reassessment, reevaluation, reappraisal, revision. **3** *the general conducting a military review* inspection, parade, display, procession. **4** *his review of the play* criticism, critique, assessment, evaluation, judgment, rating.

**review** verb **1** *review the situation* survey, study, analyze, examine, scrutinize, assess, appraise. **2** *it is more than time to review salaries* reconsider, reexamine, reevaluate, reassess, reappraise, revise. **3** *review the troops* inspect, view, scrutinize. **4** *review the play* criticize, critique, evaluate, assess, appraise, judge.

**revile** verb criticize, rail, abuse, berate, vilify, vituperate.

**revise** verb **1** *revise the text* emend, amend, correct, alter, change, edit, rewrite, redraft, rework, update, revamp. **2** *revise our opinions* reconsider, review, reassess, alter, change.

**revive** verb **1** *revive the man who collapsed* bring around, resuscitate, administer CPR to, save. **2** *a cup of tea revived her* refresh, restore, enliven, revitalize. **3** *revive old traditions* breathe new life into, bring back, restore, resuscitate, resurrect, revitalize, reintroduce, reestablish.

**revoke** verb repeal, rescind, abrogate, countermand, annul, nullify, void, invalidate, cancel, retract, withdraw, recall, abjure, overrule, override, reverse.

**revolt** verb **1** *the citizens revolted against the army* rise up, take to the streets, take up arms, rebel, mutiny. **2** *the filthy sight revolted me* repel, disgust, sicken, nauseate, be repugnant to, put one off, offend, shock; *inf.* turn one off.

**revolting** adjective repulsive, repellent, disgusting, sickening, nauseating, distasteful, repugnant, abhorrent, offensive, obnoxious, loathsome, hateful, foul, vile, nasty, shocking, abominable, despicable, reprehensible, contemptible, odious, heinous, obscene.

**revolution** noun **1** *the French Revolution* rebellion, revolt, insurrection, uprising, insurgence, mutiny, riot, coup, coup d'état. **2** *a revolution in the fashion industry* drastic change, metamorphosis, upheaval, upset, transformation, innovation, reformation, cataclysm. **3** *a revolution of the wheel* rotation, whirl, spin.

**revolutionary** adjective **1** *revolutionary troops* rebellious, insurgent, insurrectionist, mutinous, seditious, factious, insubordinate, subversive, extremist. **2** *revolutionary changes in education* drastic, progressive, radical, innovative, avant-garde, experimental.

**revolve** verb **1** *the wheel revolved slowly* turn, rotate, spin, whirl. **2** *revolve around the sun* circle, orbit, gyrate, whirl.

**revulsion** noun repulsion, disgust, nausea, distaste, aversion, repugnance, abhorrence, loathing, hatred, detestation, contempt.

**reward** noun **1** *a reward for finding the wallet* recompense, payment, remuneration, bonus, bounty, present, gift, tip, gratuity, prize; *inf.* cut. **2** *the criminal got his (just) reward* retribution, requital, retaliation; just deserts, deserts; *inf.* comeuppance.

**reward** verb *reward them for their efforts* recompense, pay, remunerate, tip.

**rhetoric** noun **1** *the use of rhetoric to win over the crowd* oratory, eloquence, elocution. **2** *the literary work was spoiled by rhetoric* bombast, grandiloquence, hyperbole, pomposity, verbosity, wordiness, prolixity, turgidity, purple prose, fustian.

**rhyme** noun *a nursery rhyme* verse, ditty, poem, song, ode.

**rhythm** noun beat, cadence, meter, tempo, pulse, throb, lilt, flow.

**ribald** adjective bawdy, risqué, blue, smutty, vulgar, coarse, earthy, off-color, rude, naughty, racy, suggestive, indecent, indelicate, lewd, salacious, licentious, concupiscent.

**rich** adjective **1** *rich and powerful people* wealthy, affluent, well off, well-to-do, prosperous, moneyed, propertied; *inf.* well-heeled, loaded, flush, on easy street. **2** *rich furnishings* opulent, expensive, costly, precious, valuable, priceless, luxurious, lush, sumptuous, splendid, superb, resplendent, elegant, fine, exquisite, magnificent, grand, gorgeous. **3** *rich in talent* abounding, overflowing, replete, rife. **4**

*rich supplies of minerals* copious, abundant, ample, plentiful, plenteous, bountiful. **5** *a rich soil* fertile, productive, fecund, fruitful, lush. **6** *rich food* creamy, fatty, heavy, spicy. **7** *rich colors* strong, deep, intense, vivid, brilliant, warm, vibrant. **8** *rich voices* full, sonorous, resonant, deep, mellow, mellifluous, melodious.

**rid** verb *rid the park of litter* clear, cleanse, purge, purify, free, relieve, deliver. **get rid of** dispose of, do away with, throw away, remove, dispense with, eliminate, dump, unload, jettison, expel, eject, weed out.

**riddle** noun puzzle, poser, conundrum, brainteaser, problem, enigma, mystery.

**ride** verb **1** *ride a horse* sit on, mount, manage, control. **2** *ride in a car* travel, go, move, progress.

**ridicule** noun derision, mockery, laughter, scorn, jeering, gibing, teasing, taunting, banter, badinage, raillery, satire, sarcasm; *inf.* kidding, ribbing, ragging.

**ridicule** verb deride, mock, laugh at, scoff at, scorn, jeer at, gibe at, tease, taunt; *inf.* kid, rag.

**ridiculous** adjective **1** *telling ridiculous jokes* absurd, comical, funny, laughable, hilarious, humorous, droll, farcical, facetious, ludicrous. **2** *what a ridiculous thing to do* foolish, inane, nonsensical.

**rife** adjective **1** *disease is rife* rampant, prevalent, predominant, widespread, common, extensive, ubiquitous. **2** *the territory is rife with disease/vermin* abounding, overflowing, alive, swarming, teeming.

**riff-raff** noun rabble, mob, commonality, hoi polloi, scum.

**rifle** verb *looters rifling stores during the blackout* plunder, pillage, loot, ransack. **rifle through** *rifle through her belongings* ransack, rummage through, search.

**rift** noun **1** *a rift in the rock* fault, split, break, breach, fissure, cleft, crevice, gap, crack, cranny, slit, chink, cavity, opening, hole, aperture. **2** *a rift between family members* breach, division, estrangement, schism, split, alienation, quarrel, disagreement, conflict, feud; *inf.* falling-out.

**right** adjective **1** *his actions were not right* just, fair, equitable, righteous, proper, moral, ethical, honorable, honest, principled, lawful, legal. **2** *the right answer* correct, accurate, unerring, exact, precise, valid. **3** *he is the right owner* rightful, true, genuine, authentic, lawful, legal, legitimate. **4** *the right person for the job* suitable, appropriate, fitting, fit, proper, ideal. **5** *he came at the right moment* opportune, favorable, convenient, suitable, appropriate, propitious. **6** *in his right mind* sane, sound, rational, lucid. **7** *the engine does not sound right* fine, healthy, well, fit, nor-

mal, sound; *inf.* up to scratch. **8** *the right wing of politics* conservative, reactionary.

**right** adverb **1** *go right on* straight, directly. **2** *he will be right down* immediately, instantly, promptly, quickly, straightaway, without delay. **3** *come right off its hinges* all the way, completely, entirely, totally, wholly, altogether, utterly, quite. **4** *right in the middle* exactly, precisely, just, squarely; *inf.* smack-dab. **5** *if I remember right* accurately, correctly, exactly, precisely. **6** *treat them right* justly, fairly, properly, honorably, honestly, morally, ethically. **7** *it will come out right* well, for the best, favorably, advantageously. **right away** at once, immediately, straight away, this instant, promptly, directly, forthwith.

**right** noun **1** *know the difference between right and wrong* lawfulness, legality, goodness, righteousness, virtue, virtuousness, integrity, rectitude, propriety, morality, truth, honesty, honor, justice, fairness, equity. **2** *his position gives him the right to dismiss people* prerogative, privilege, authority, power, license, permission, warrant, sanction, entitlement.

**right** verb **1** *right the pole* stand/set upright. **2** *right the situation* put to rights, sort out, straighten out, rectify, fix, tidy up, repair. **3** *right a wrong* set/put right, rectify, redress, vindicate.

**righteous** adjective **1** *righteous people* good, virtuous, upright, moral, ethical, law-abiding, honest, honorable, blameless, guiltless, pure, noble, God-fearing. **2** *righteous indignation* rightful, justifiable, well-founded, defensible, admissible, allowable, reasonable.

**rigid** adjective **1** *a rigid substance* stiff, hard, taut, inflexible, unbending, unyielding, unmalleable. **2** *a rigid schedule* fixed, set, firm, inflexible, unalterable, unchangeable, unvarying, invariable, hard and fast. **3** *a man of rigid principles* strict, severe, stern, stringent, rigorous, uncompromising.

**rigorous** adjective **1** *rigorous discipline* strict, severe, stern, stringent, austere, spartan, tough, hard, harsh, rigid, inflexible, intransigent, uncompromising, demanding, exacting. **2** *rigorous attention to detail* meticulous, punctilious, painstaking, thorough, laborious, scrupulous, conscientious.

**rim** noun **1** *the rim of a cup* brim, lip. **2** *the rim of a lake* edge, border, brink, circumference.

**ring**¹ noun **1** *wore a ring on her finger* band, circlet. **2** *a ring around the moon* circle, circlet, loop, halo. **3** *a boxing ring* arena, enclosure. **4** *a spy ring* gang, syndicate, cartel, mob, organization, confederacy, league, cabal, junta.

**ring**² verb *a fence ringed the area* circle, encircle, circumscribe, encompass, enclose, surround, hem in, fence in, seal off.

**ring**[3] noun *the ring of the bells* ringing, toll, tolling, peal, pealing, knell, chime, clang, tinkle.

**ring**[4] verb **1** *ring the bells* toll, sound. **2** *the halls rang with music* resound, reverberate, resonate, echo. **ring in** *bells ringing in the new year* herald, signal, announce, usher in.

**riot** noun *there was a riot when he was arrested* rebellion, revolt, uprising, insurrection, insurgence, commotion, disturbance, uproar, tumult, melee, row, scuffle, fracas, fray, brawl, free-for-all.

**riot** verb *crowds rioting in the streets* rebel, revolt, take to the streets, rampage, run wild/amok, fight, brawl.

**ripe** adjective **1** *ripe fruit/cheese* mature, full-grown, ready, mellow, seasoned, tempered. **2** *the time is ripe* suitable, convenient, opportune, favorable, advantageous, auspicious.

**ripen** verb **1** *fruit ripening on the trees* mature, come to maturity, mellow. **2** *our plans are ripening* develop, come to fruition.

**rise** verb **1** *mountains rising above the town* tower, soar, loom. **2** *prices rose* increase, soar, rocket, escalate. **3** *standards have risen* improve, advance. **4** *her voice rose* grow, increase, swell, intensify. **5** *the children rose on the arrival of the guest* stand up, get up, jump up. **6** *he rose at dawn* arise, get up, wake up. **7** *rise from the ranks* climb, ascend, advance, be promoted. **8** *citizens rising against the troops* rebel, revolt, mutiny, take up arms. **9** *the river rises in the mountains | the argument rose from a misunderstanding* originate, begin, start, commence, issue, spring, flow, emanate. **10** *the ground rises here* slope/slant upward, ascend, climb.

**rise** noun **1** *the rise in prices* increase, escalation, upsurge, upswing. **2** *a rise in standards* improvement, advance, upturn. **3** *his rise to power* climb, ascent, advancement, promotion, aggrandizement. **4** *a rise in the ground* incline, elevation, upward slope, acclivity, hillock, hill.

**risk** noun *an element of risk in the game* chance, hazard, uncertainty, speculation, venture.

**risk** verb **1** *risk his life* endanger, imperil, jeopardize. **2** *risk $5 on the bet* gamble, hazard, chance, venture.

**risky** adjective dangerous, hazardous, perilous, unsafe, precarious, tricky, uncertain; *inf.* chancy, dicey.

**risqué** adjective off-color, indelicate, improper, suggestive, naughty, bawdy, spicy, racy, salacious, licentious, lewd, ribald.

**rite** noun ritual, ceremony, observance, service, sacrament, celebration, performance, act, practice, tradition, convention, formality, procedure, usage.

**rival** noun **1** *they are rivals for her love* opponent, adversary, antagonist, contestant, competitor, challenger, vier, contender. **2** *in tennis she has no rival* equal, match, equivalent, fellow, peer.

**rival** verb compete with, vie with, match, equal, emulate, measure up to, compare with.

**rival** adjective *rival teams* opposed, opposing, competing, contending, in conflict.

**road** noun street, avenue, roadway, boulevard, thoroughfare, highway, turnpike, expressway, parkway, freeway.

**roam** verb wander, rove, ramble, meander, drift, range, tramp, traverse, trek, peregrinate.

**roar** verb **1** *the sergeant roared at the recruits* bellow, yell, bawl, shout, howl, thunder, scream, cry, bay. **2** *roar at the comedian's jokes* howl with laughter, guffaw; *inf.* split one's sides, roll in the aisles.

**rob** verb **1** *rob a bank* hold up, stick up, burgle, burglarize, break into. **2** *rob a tourist* mug; *inf.* rip off. **3** *rob them of their savings* defraud, swindle, cheat, mulct; *inf.* bilk.

**robber** noun burglar, thief, mugger, pilferer, housebreaker, looter, raider, bandit, brigand, pirate, highwayman.

**robbery** noun **1** *commit robbery* burglary, theft, thievery, stealing, housebreaking, larceny, embezzlement, misappropriation, swindling, fraud. **2** *a robbery at the bank* mugging, holdup, break-in, raid.

**robe** noun **1** *judges' robes* vestment, habit, costume, gown. **2** *wearing a robe over pajamas* bathrobe, dressing gown, housecoat, kimono, peignoir.

**robust** adjective *robust young athletes* healthy, strong, vigorous, hearty, energetic, muscular, powerful, rugged, sturdy, stalwart, strapping, brawny, burly.

**rock** noun **1** *rocks dislodged from the cliff* boulder, stone. **2** *that department is the rock on which the company is built* foundation, cornerstone, support, prop, mainstay.

**rock** verb **1** *the cradle/boat was rocking* move to and fro, swing, sway, roll, lurch, pitch, reel, wobble, undulate, oscillate. **2** *the world was rocked by his death* stun, shock, stagger, astound, astonish, amaze, dumbfound, surprise, shake, take aback, bewilder, throw, unnerve, disconcert.

**rod** noun **1** *rods of iron* bar, stick, pole, baton, staff. **2** *spare the rod and spoil the child* cane, stick, birch, switch, wand.

**rogue** noun scoundrel, rascal, reprobate, wretch, cad, blackguard, ne'er-do-well, wastrel, good-for-nothing, scamp, imp, rascal, devil, mischief-maker.

**role** noun 1 *play the role of King Lear* part, character, representation, portrayal. 2 *in his role as mayor* capacity, function, position, place, situation, job, post, task.

**roll** verb 1 *the wheels rolled* turn, rotate, revolve, spin, whirl, wheel. 2 *roll up a newspaper* furl, coil, fold. 3 *roll the pastry* flatten, level, smooth, press down, crush. 4 *ships rolling on the ocean* toss, rock, pitch, lurch, sway, reel. 5 *waves rolling* billow, toss, tumble.

**roll** noun 1 *a roll of tape* spool, reel, bobbin, cylinder. 2 *buy rolls for lunch* bun; hard roll, croissant. 3 *on the electoral roll* register, list, file, index, roster, directory, catalog. 4 *a roll of drums* boom, reverberation, thunder, rumble. 5 *the roll of the sea* undulation, billowing, swell, tossing, pitching, rocking.

**romance** noun 1 *she wrote about a world of adventure and romance* fantasy, glamour, mystery, legend. 2 *their romance is over* love affair, affair, liaison, attachment, intrigue, courtship, amour. 3 *write romances* love story; romantic fiction, melodrama; *inf.* tearjerker.

**romantic** adjective 1 *present a romantic picture of his life* unrealistic, fanciful, idealistic, Utopian, starry-eyed, optimistic. 2 *romantic words* loving, amorous, passionate, fond, tender, sentimental; *inf.* mushy. 3 *a romantic figure in black* fascinating, mysterious, glamorous, exotic, exciting.

**room** noun 1 *take up a lot of room* space, area, territory, expanse, volume, elbowroom. 2 *room for improvement* scope, capacity, margin, leeway, latitude, occasion. 3 *she has a room in that building* bedroom, apartment, office.

**room** verb *we roomed together in college* board, stay, dwell, reside, lodge.

**roomy** adjective spacious, commodious, capacious, voluminous, ample, extensive.

**root** noun 1 *the plant's roots* radicle, radix, rhizome, tuber. 2 *the root of the problem* source, origin, fountainhead, basis, foundation, seat, nucleus, kernel, nub, cause, reason, rationale, occasion, motivation.

**root** verb 1 *the idea rooted* take root, become established, set. 2 *her fear was deeply rooted* fix, establish, embed, implant, entrench.

**rope** noun *tie the logs with a rope | hang the clothes on a rope* cord, cable, line, strand, hawser.

**roster** noun list, rota, roll, register, schedule, agenda, calendar, directory, index, table.

**rosy** adjective 1 *rosy cheeks* pink, red, ruddy, rubicund, blushing, glowing. 2 *a rosy future* optimistic, promising, auspicious, hopeful, encouraging, bright, favorable, sunny.

**rot** verb 1 *the material is rotting* decompose, decay, crumble, disintegrate, corrode. 2 *the food is rotting* spoil, molder, putrefy.

**rot** noun 1 *material suffering from rot* decomposition, decay, disintegration, corrosion, putrefaction, mold, blight. 2 *combating the rot of urban society* degeneracy, deterioration, decline, dissoluteness. 3 *talk rot* rubbish, nonsense, bunkum, claptrap, drivel, moonshine; *inf.* bunk, tommyrot, gobbledegook, hogwash, poppycock, bull.

**rotate** verb 1 *the wheels are rotating* turn, revolve, spin, whirl, swivel, reel, wheel, gyrate. 2 *the directorship rotates* alternate, take turns.

**rotten** adjective 1 *rotten food* bad, moldy, moldering, spoiled, tainted, rancid, rank, decaying, decomposed, putrid, putrescent, fetid; *inf.* off. 2 *rotten material/teeth* decomposing, decaying, crumbling, disintegrating, corroding. 3 *he is a rotten creep* corrupt, dishonorable, dishonest, untrustworthy, immoral, unprincipled, unscrupulous, villainous. 4 *that was a rotten thing to do* nasty, foul, mean, bad, dirty, filthy, contemptible, despicable, base, scurrilous. 5 *we had a rotten time* miserable, unpleasant, disagreeable. 6 *it is a rotten idea* ill-considered, ill thought out, ill-advised, injudicious. 7 *what a rotten selection of goods* poor, inadequate, inferior, substandard, unsatisfactory, unacceptable; *inf.* lousy, crummy. 8 *feeling rotten with the flu* ill, sick, unwell, unhealthy, below par; *inf.* under the weather, poorly, lousy, yucky.

**rotund** adjective plump, chubby, buxom, roly-poly, tubby, well-rounded, portly, stout, corpulent, pudgy, fat, obese, heavy, fleshy.

**rough** adjective 1 *rough surfaces* uneven, irregular, bumpy, broken, rugged, craggy, lumpy, nodulous. 2 *dogs with a rough coat* shaggy, hairy, bushy, fuzzy, bristly, hirsute. 3 *get involved in some rough play* boisterous, rowdy, disorderly, wild, violent, savage. 4 *rough seas* turbulent, tumultuous, choppy. 5 *rough weather* inclement, stormy, squally, tempestuous. 6 *he is a rough character* coarse, crude, uncouth, vulgar, unrefined, loutish, boorish, churlish, brutish, ill-bred, ill-mannered, impolite, discourteous. 7 *receive rough treatment* harsh, severe, hard, tough, difficult, unpleasant, disagreeable, nasty, cruel. 8 *he was rough on his son* harsh, hard, stern, unrelenting, merciless, unfeeling, unfair, unjust. 9 *rough wood* crude, raw, unpolished, undressed, uncut, rough-hewn, unrefined, unprocessed. **10** *rough voices* husky, gruff, hoarse, harsh. **11** *a rough sketch* hasty, quick, sketchy, cursory, crude, incomplete, rudimentary, basic, unpolished, unrefined. **12** *a rough estimate* approximate, inexact, imprecise, vague, hazy.

**round** adjective **1** *a round shape* circular, ring-shaped, annular, cycloid, discoid, spherical, spheroid, ball-shaped, globular, orblike, orbicular, balloonlike. **2** *spent, in round figures,* $600 approximate, rough; *inf.* ballpark.

**round** noun **1** *cut it in rounds* circle, circlet, ring, hoop, band, disk, cylinder, sphere, ball, globe, orb. **2** *a round of parties* succession, sequence, series, cycle. **3** *two rounds left in the gun* bullet, cartridge, shell. **4** *the first round of the competition* stage, level, division, lap, heat, game.

**round** verb *round Cape Horn* go around, travel around, sail around, circumnavigate. **round up** gather together, drive together, assemble, collect, group, muster, marshal, rally.

**roundabout** adjective *a roundabout route* indirect, circuitous, meandering, winding, tortuous.

**rouse** verb **1** *rouse the sleeping children* wake, wake up, call, awaken, get up. **2** *rouse the crowds to protest* stir up, excite, incite, egg on, inflame, agitate, whip up, galvanize, stimulate. **3** *rouse feelings of guilt* stir up, kindle, evoke, call up, conjure up.

**rout** noun **1** *troops put to rout* retreat, flight, headlong flight. **2** *suffer a rout at the hands of the enemy* defeat, drubbing, trouncing, conquest, subjugation, beating, thrashing; *inf.* licking.

**rout** verb **1** *they routed the enemy troops* put to flight, dispel, scatter. **2** *they easily routed their opponents* defeat, drub, trounce, worst, conquer, subjugate, overthrow, crush, beat, thrash; *inf.* lick.

**route** noun course, way, itinerary, road, path.

**routine** noun **1** *he hates to upset his routine* pattern, procedure, practice, custom, habit, wont, program, schedule, formula, method, system, order, way. **2** *have heard the comic's routine before* act, performance, piece, line; *inf.* spiel.

**routine** adjective **1** *carry out routine procedures* usual, normal, everyday, common, ordinary, typical, customary, habitual, conventional, standard. **2** *he finds the work too routine* boring, tedious, tiresome, monotonous, predictable, unexciting, uninspiring.

**row**[1] noun **1** *a row of people* line, column, queue, procession. **2** *a row of vegetables* column, sequence, series. **3** *a row of seats* tier, rank, bank.

**row**[2] noun argument, dispute, disagreement, controversy, quarrel, squabble, tiff, fight, altercation, scuffle, fracas, melee; *inf.* set-to, scrap.

**rowdy** adjective unruly, disorderly, noisy, boisterous, loud, obstreperous, rough, unrestrained, lawless.

**rowdy** noun ruffian, thug, hooligan, troublemaker, brawler; *inf.* tough.

**royal** adjective **1** *a royal wave* kingly, queenly, princely, regal, monarchical, sovereign. **2** *royal surroundings* majestic, magnificent, impressive, glorious, splendid, imposing, grand, superb. **3** *he is a royal pain in the neck* extreme, unmitigated, absolute, relentless, outright, sheer.

**rub** verb **1** *rub her sore neck* massage, knead. **2** *rub the silver lamp* polish, buff up, burnish. **rub in** *rub in the ointment* apply, smear, spread, work in.

**rubbish** noun **1** *throw out the rubbish* garbage, trash, waste, refuse, litter, junk, debris, detritus, dross, rubble. **2** *talking rubbish* nonsense, drivel, gibberish, balderdash, bunkum, twaddle; *inf.* rot, tommyrot, bunk, gobbledegook, hogwash.

**ruddy** adjective *a ruddy complexion* red, pink, rosy, rosy-cheeked, rubicund, flushed, blushing, glowing.

**rude** adjective **1** *offended by rude people* ill-mannered, impolite, discourteous, impertinent, insolent, impudent, uncivil, disrespectful, churlish, curt, brusque, blunt. **2** *rude tools* primitive, crude, rudimentary, rough, rough-hewn, simple. **3** *rude peasants* simple, artless, uncivilized, uneducated, ignorant, illiterate, uncultured, unrefined, rough. **4** *rude jokes* vulgar, coarse, indelicate, smutty, dirty, naughty, risqué, blue, ribald, bawdy, licentious. **5** *a rude awakening* sudden, abrupt, startling, harsh, unpleasant, disagreeable, nasty.

**rudimentary** adjective **1** *rudimentary arithmetic* elementary, basic, fundamental, introductory. **2** *rudimentary tools* primitive, crude, rough, simple.

**rue** verb *live to rue her actions* regret, be sorry about, feel remorseful about.

**ruffian** noun thug, villain, scoundrel, hoodlum, hooligan, rogue, rascal, miscreant; *inf.* tough, rowdy.

**ruffle** verb **1** *ruffle feathers* disorder, rumple, dishevel, tousle, tangle, mess up; *inf.* muss. **2** *she gets ruffled in a crisis* vex, exasperate, fluster, agitate, harass, upset, disturb, discompose, unsettle, disconcert, worry, trouble, confuse; *inf.* rattle, shake up.

**rugged** adjective **1** *rugged terrain* rough, uneven, irregular, bumpy, rocky, jagged, craggy. **2** *rugged features* wrinkled, furrowed, lined, weather-beaten. **3** *a rugged beauty* unrefined, unpolished, coarse, crude. **4** *you have to be rugged to survive there* tough, hardy, robust, sturdy, strong, vigorous, stalwart. **5** *a rugged way of life* tough, harsh, austere, spartan, exacting, taxing, demanding, difficult, hard, arduous, rigorous, strenuous.

**ruin** noun **1** *cities in a state of ruin* ruination, destruction, devastation, havoc, demolition, dilapidation, desolation, decay. **2** *the ruin of the army | the ruin of his hopes* ruination, downfall, overthrow, defeat, undoing, conquest, elimination, termination, end. **3** *businesses facing ruin* ruination, failure, bankruptcy, insolvency, disaster. **4** *castle ruins* remains, relics, remnants, vestiges.

**ruin** verb **1** *it ruined our plans* damage, spoil, wreak havoc on, mar, wreck, botch, shatter. **2** *the recession ruined him* bankrupt, make insolvent, impoverish, pauperize. **3** *invading armies ruining cities* destroy, devastate, lay waste, raze, demolish.

**ruinous** adjective disastrous, devastating, calamitous, catastrophic, cataclysmic, injurious, damaging, crippling, destructive.

**rule** noun **1** *obey the rules of the realm* law, bylaw, regulation, statute, ordinance, tenet, canon, order, decree, commandment, directive. **2** *it is a good rule to wait for others to speak* principle, precept, standard, axiom, truth, truism, maxim, motto. **3** *as a general rule, children are not allowed* practice, procedure, routine, custom, habit, convention. **4** *the rule of the present government* reign, dominion, sovereignty, regime, government, administration, jurisdiction, authority, control, direction, leadership, command, ascendancy, supremacy, power, sway, influence.

**rule** verb **1** *the last administration ruled for only a few months* be in power, reign, control, be in authority, administer, command, be in charge, govern; *inf.* be at the helm. **2** *the judge ruled that he be released* order, decree, direct, pronounce, decide, determine, resolve, settle, establish. **3** *let common sense rule* prevail, obtain, hold sway, predominate. **rule out** *rule out the possibility of arson* preclude, exclude, eliminate, reject, dismiss.

**ruler** noun sovereign, monarch, king, queen, emperor, empress, head of state, governor, president, overlord, chief, chieftain, lord, commander, leader.

**ruling** noun judgment, adjudication, finding, verdict, resolution, decree, pronouncement.

**ruminate** verb *sit and ruminate* think, contemplate, deliberate, ponder, brood, meditate, muse, cogitate. **ruminate on** *ruminating on her problems* give thought to, consider, mull over.

**rumor** noun **1** *rumor has it that he has gone* gossip, hearsay, talk; *inf.* the grapevine. **2** *hear a rumor that he has gone* report, story, whisper, canard; *inf.* buzz.

**rumor** verb *they are rumored to be wealthy* say, report, think, gossip, hint, suggest.

**rumple** verb **1** *rumple clothes* crumple, crease, wrinkle, crush, crinkle. **2** *rumple hair* disarrange, tousle, dishevel, ruffle, mess up.

**rumpus** noun disturbance, row, uproar, commotion, brouhaha, fracas, brawl, melee.

**run** verb **1** *she ran to catch the bus* race, rush, hasten, hurry, dash, sprint, bolt, dart, gallop, speed, scurry, scamper, scramble; *inf.* hotfoot it. **2** *the thief ran from the police* abscond, flee, take flight, make off, bolt, make a run for it, clear out, escape; *inf.* beat it, skedaddle, split, cut and run, hightail it. **3** *trains run on tracks* move, go, travel. **4** *leave the engine running* go, operate, function. **5** *the lease runs for 20 years* continue, operate, be valid, be current. **6** *the play runs until Christmas* be staged, be presented, be performed, be put on. **7** *the road runs along the coast* go, continue, proceed, extend, stretch. **8** *the horse will run* compete, take part, enter, race. **9** *run for president* stand, stand as candidate, campaign, put oneself forward. **10** *water running* flow, issue, stream, pour, gush, cascade, spurt, course, jet, trickle, leak. **11** *the dye from the shirt ran all over the pants* spread, be diffused, bleed. **12** *joggers running the course* travel, traverse. **13** *run an errand* go on, do, carry out, perform, fulfill, execute. **14** *the newspaper ran a story about the accident* publish, print, feature, carry. **15** *run a business* operate, conduct, carry on, direct, manage, administer, control, head, lead, look after, organize, coordinate, supervise, superintend, oversee. **16** *run them out of town* chase, drive, propel, hunt. **17** *ideas running through my mind* go, pass, dart, flow, slide. **18** *run your eye over the page* pass, slide, flick. **19** *stockings running* unravel, tear, be snagged. **20** *her eyes are running because of the cold* stream, water, tear. **run across** *run across an old friend* run into, come across, chance upon, stumble upon; *inf.* bump into. **run away** *the thieves have run away* abscond, flee. *See* RUN verb

2. **run away with 1** *run away with his daughter* run off with, elope with, abduct, make off with. **2** *run away with the race* win easily; *inf.* win hands down, win by a mile. **run into 1** *another car ran into ours* bump into, knock into, collide with, crash into, hit, strike, ram. **2** *I ran into an old friend* run across, chance upon, stumble upon; *inf.* bump into. **3** *the cost runs into thousands of dollars* reach, extend to, be as high/much as. **run low** *supplies are running low* dwindle, diminish, become depleted, become exhausted. **run off 1** *the dog ran off* run away, flee, bolt, clear out, escape; *inf.* beat it, hightail it. **2** *run off several copies* copy, duplicate; *Xerox (trademark).* **run off with 1** *run off with her daughter* run away with, elope, abduct, make off with. **2** *run off with the company funds* abscond with, snatch, steal, purloin; *inf.* pinch, swipe, lift. **run out** *supplies have run out | run out of food* be finished, give out, dry up, fail, be exhausted; exhaust. **run out on** *he has run out on his family* desert, abandon, forsake, jilt; *inf.* leave high and dry, leave in the lurch. **run over 1** *nearly ran over a rabbit with his car* run down, knock down, knock over, hit. **2** *the bathwater is running over* overflow, spill over. **3** *run over the figures for tomorrow* run through, look over, go over, go through. **run through 1** *run through the figures for tomorrow* run over, go over, look over, look through. **2** *run through money* squander, fritter away, dissipate, waste; *inf.* blow. **3** *sadness runs through the book* pervade, permeate, suffuse. **run to 1** *the cost runs to thousands* run into, reach, extend to, be as high/much as. **2** *the family runs to fat* tend to, be disposed/inclined to.

**run** noun **1** *break into a run* jog, sprint, dash, gallop, canter. **2** *the run from Providence to Boston* trip, route. **3** *a run of luck* period, spell, stretch, streak, chain, string, cycle, sequence, series, succession. **4** *a run on silver* demand, rush, clamor. **5** *different from the general run of applicants* kind, variety, type, sort, class. **6** *the chickens' run* enclosure, pen, coop. **7** *a run in her tights* rip, tear, snag.

**rundown** noun *give them the rundown on/of the situation* analysis, briefing, brief, review, summary, résumé, sketch, outline; *inf.* low-down.

**run-down** adjective **1** *run-down property* dilapidated, tumbledown, ramshackle, decaying, in ruins, seedy, shabby. **2** *feel run-down after an illness* debilitated, below par, drained, exhausted, fatigued, tired, enervated, worn-out; *inf.* under the weather.

**run-of-the-mill** adjective ordinary, average, common, middling, mediocre, commonplace, everyday, undistinguished, unexceptional, passable, tolerable, acceptable, fair, not bad; *inf.* so-so.

**rupture** noun **1** *a rupture in the defenses* break, fracture, crack, split, rent, tear, rift, fissure; breaking, cracking, splitting, bursting. **2** *ruptures exist within the party* rift, estrangement, schism, breach, division, alienation, variance, disagreement, quarrel, feud; *inf.* falling-out.

**rupture** verb **1** *rupture the defenses | rupture an organ* break, fracture, crack, split, breach, burst, rend, tear, puncture. **2** *rupture East-West relations* sever, cut off, break off, disrupt, breach.

**rural** adjective country, pastoral, rustic, agricultural, agrarian.

**ruse** noun trick, stratagem, subterfuge, artifice, device, wile, dodge, ploy, machination, maneuver, tactic, deception, hoax, blind.

**rush** verb **1** *rush to the door* hurry, hasten, run, race, dash, sprint, speed, scurry, scamper; *inf.* step on it, get a move on, hotfoot it. **2** *rush the enemy* attack, assault, charge, storm. **3** *rush the job through* hurry, hasten, expedite, speed up, accelerate, advance, hustle, press, push.

**rush** noun **1** *make a rush on the enemy* onslaught, attack, assault, charge. **2** *a rush of water* surge, flow, gush, stream, flood. **3** *no rush for the goods* hurry, haste, speed, swiftness, rapidity, dispatch. **4** *a rush for toys* demand, clamor, run (on). **5** *the Christmas rush* activity, bustle, hubbub, flurry.

**rustic** adjective **1** *rustic scenes* country, rural, pastoral, agricultural, agrarian, Arcadian, bucolic. **2** *rustic pleasures* unsophisticated, plain, simple, homely, homespun. **3** *rustic peasants* artless, plain, simple, naïve, ingenuous, unsophisticated, uncultured, unrefined, unpolished, homespun; coarse, rough, indelicate.

**rustic** noun countryman, countrywoman, peasant, country bumpkin, yokel; *inf.* hillbilly, hayseed.

**rut** noun **1** *farm roads full of ruts* furrow, groove, track, crack, hollow, hole, pothole, trough, gutter, ditch. **2** *in a rut in his job* humdrum existence, routine, boring pattern; *inf.* daily grind, treadmill, dead end.

**ruthless** adjective merciless, pitiless, unrelenting, remorseless, unsparing, inexorable, implacable, heartless, unfeeling, hard, harsh, severe, stern, grim, cruel, vicious, brutal, barbarous, callous, savage, fierce, ferocious.

# Ss

**sabotage** noun **1** *the fire at the factory was an act of sabotage* deliberate destruction/damage, vandalism, subversion, treachery. **2** *the sabotage of our plans* disruption, spoiling, ruination, wrecking; *inf.* fouling up.

**saccharine** adjective oversweet, cloying; mawkish, maudlin, sentimental; *inf.* sappy, mushy.

**sack** noun bag, pack, pouch; knapsack, backpack. **the sack** *delinquent workers getting the sack* a dismissal, a discharge, a termination; *inf.* one's walking papers, a pink slip, the boot, the ax.

**sack** verb *enemy soldiers sacking the city* plunder, ransack, raid, loot, rifle, pillage, maraud, harry, lay waste, wreak havoc on, destroy, ruin, devastate, ravage, vandalize, despoil, rape.

**sacred** adjective **1** *a sacred place* holy, blessed, blest, hallowed, consecrated, sanctified. **2** *sacred music* religious, spiritual, devotional, church, churchly, ecclesiastical. **3** *in Hinduism the cow is sacred* sacrosanct, inviolable, inviolate, unimpeachable, protected.

**sacrifice** noun **1** *the job was not worth the sacrifice of her principles* giving up, renunciation, abandonment, surrender, relinquishment, forfeiture. **2** *make many sacrifices to educate their children* renunciation, relinquishment, loss, self-sacrifice. **3** *give the goat as a sacrifice to their god* offering, gifts, oblation, burnt offering.

**sacrifice** verb **1** *sacrifice her principles for the job* give up, forgo, renounce, abandon, surrender, relinquish, yield, cede, forfeit. **2** *sacrifice the goat to the god* offer up, offer, immolate.

**sacrilege** noun *sacrilege to vandalize the cross* desecration, profanity, profanation, blasphemy, godlessness, disrespect.

**sad** adjective **1** *feeling sad about his departure* unhappy, miserable, sorrowful, gloomy, melancholy, blue, mournful, woebegone, wretched, dejected, downcast, despondent, in low spirits, low, downhearted, depressed, doleful, glum, cheerless, dispirited, disconsolate, heartbroken, sick at heart, grief-stricken; *inf.* down, down in the dumps, down in the mouth, in the pits. **2** *the sad events of the past* unhappy, unfortunate, sorrowful, miserable, sorry, depressing, upsetting, distressing, dispiriting, heartbreaking, heart-rending, grievous, tragic, disastrous, calamitous. **3** *the country is in a sad state* sorry, wretched, deplorable, lamentable, regrettable, unfortunate, pitiful, pitiable, pathetic, shameful, disgraceful.

**sadden** verb deject, depress, dispirit, dampen one's spirits, upset, distress, grieve, break one's heart, make one's heart bleed.

**safe** adjective **1** *the children are safe in bed* secure, protected, sheltered, guarded, safe and sound, out of harm's way. **2** *the flood victims are safe* unharmed, alive and well, unhurt, uninjured, unscathed, undamaged, out of danger. **3** *the building is quite safe* secure, sound, impregnable, unassailable. **4** *he is a safe person to leave the children with* reliable, dependable, responsible, trustworthy, upright, honest, honorable. **5** *he is a safe driver | on the safe side* reliable, cautious, circumspect, prudent, unadventurous, conservative, timid, unenterprising. **6** *these crayons are safe for children* harmless, innocuous, nontoxic, nonpoisonous.

**safe** noun *put jewelry in the safe* safe-deposit box, cashbox, depository, locker, vault, crypt.

**safeguard** noun *they need to have some safeguard against fraud* protection, defense, precaution, security, surety.

**safeguard** verb *you must safeguard your investment* protect, look after, defend, guard, preserve, secure.

**sag** verb **1** *the ceiling sags* sink, subside, curve down, slump. **2** *the hem of the skirt sags* hang unevenly, droop. **3** *his spirit sagged* fall, flag, fail, wilt, falter. **4** *industrial production has sagged* fall, decline, decrease, diminish, sink, plummet, tumble.

**saga** noun epic, chronicle, legend, history, myth, adventure.

**sage** adjective **1** *give sage advice* wise, judicious, prudent, sensible, shrewd, politic. **2** *a sage old man* wise, sagacious, learned, intelligent, acute, shrewd, discerning, perspicacious; *lit.* sapient.

**sage** noun wise man/woman, philosopher, thinker, savant, pundit, authority, expert, guru.

**sail** verb **1** *learn to sail* boat, cruise, yacht, ride the waves. **2** *we sail tonight* set sail, embark, put to sea, raise sail, shove off. **3** *he is sailing the ship* steer, captain, pilot, navigate.

**sailor** noun seaman, seafarer, mariner, marine, (old) salt, sea dog, yachtsman, yachtswoman; *inf.* tar, gob.

**saintly** adjective sainted, holy, godly, pious, God-fearing, religious, devout, blessed, virtuous, righteous, good, moral, ethical, sinless, blameless, pure, angelic.

**sake** noun **1** *stop smoking for the baby's sake* good, well-being, welfare, behalf, benefit, advantage, interest, gain, profit, consideration, regard, concern, account, respect. **2** *for the sake of peace we agreed* cause, reason, purpose, aim, end, objective, object, goal, motive.

**salary** noun pay, earnings, remuneration, fee, emolument, stipend, honorarium.

**sale** noun *not concerned in the actual sale of the cars* selling, vending, deal, transaction. **on sale** reduced, marked down, discounted.

**salient** adjective *discuss the salient points* important, main, prominent, conspicuous, striking, noticeable, obvious.

**sallow** adjective *a sallow complexion* yellowish, jaundiced-looking, pallid, wan, pale, waxen, anemic, colorless, pasty, pasty-faced.

**sally** noun **1** *enemy troops making a sally into our territory* charge, sortie, foray, thrust, offensive, drive, attack, raid, assault, onset, rush, onrush. **2** *coming out with a series of quick sallies* witticism, bon mot, quip, joke, jest, barb; *inf.* wisecrack, crack.

**salon** noun shop, boutique, parlor.

**salt** noun *conversation in need of a little salt* spice, flavor, piquancy, pungency, zest, bite, liveliness, vigor; *inf.* zing, zip. **with a grain of salt** with reservations, skeptically, cynically, doubtfully, suspiciously.

**salubrious** adjective *living in a salubrious climate* healthy, healthful, beneficial, wholesome, salutary, refreshing, invigorating, bracing.

**salute** noun *raise his hat as a friendly salute* greeting, salutation, address, welcome.

**salute** verb **1** *salute one's neighbor in passing* greet, address, hail, acknowledge. **2** *salute the director's achievement* pay tribute to, honor, recognize, acknowledge; *inf.* take one's hat off to.

**salvage** verb *succeed in salvaging the ship* / *salvage valuable articles from the fire* rescue, save, recover, retrieve, reclaim.

**salvation** noun **1** *the salvation of sinners* redemption deliverance, saving, rescue. **2** *regard his work as his salvation* lifeline, preservation, conservation.

**same** adjective **1** *the same person I saw yesterday* identical, selfsame, one and the same. **2** *family members having the same mannerisms* identical, alike, duplicate, twin, indistinguishable, interchangeable, corresponding, equivalent. **3** *the same old food/story* unchanging, unvarying, invariable, unfailing, constant, consistent, uniform.

**sample** noun **1** *a sample of his handwriting* specimen, example, instance, illustration, model, pattern. **2** *polled a sample of the population* cross section, sampling, test.

**sample** verb *sample the wine* try, try out, test, examine, inspect, taste.

**sanctify** verb **1** *sanctify the building* consecrate, bless, hallow, set apart, dedicate. **2** *sanctify sinners* free from sin, absolve, purify, cleanse. **3** *a practice sanctified by tradition* sanction, ratify, confirm, warrant, legitimize.

**sanctimonious** adjective self-righteous, holier-than-thou, overpious, pietistic, unctuous, smug, hypocritical, pharisaic; *inf.* goody-goody.

**sanction** noun **1** *receive the sanction of the church/authorities* authorization, warrant, accreditation, license, endorsement, permission, consent, approval, seal of approval, stamp of approval, go-ahead, approbation, acceptance, thumbs-up; backing, support; *inf.* the green light, OK. **2** *laws receiving sanction* ratification, validation, confirmation. **3** *sanctions imposed against certain crimes* penalty, punishment, penalization, penance, sentence. **4** *impose trade sanctions on the belligerent country* embargo, ban, boycott.

**sanction** verb *unwilling to sanction the sale* authorize, warrant, accredit, license, endorse, permit, allow, consent to, approve, accept, back, support; *inf.* OK.

**sanctuary** noun **1** *priests standing in the sanctuary* holy place, church, temple, shrine, altar, sanctum. **2** *find a sanctuary from his pursuers* refuge, haven, shelter, retreat, hide-out. **3** *seek sanctuary in the church* safety, safekeeping, protection, shelter, immunity. **4** *a bird sanctuary* preserve, reserve, reservation.

**sane** adjective **1** *patients not absolutely sane* of sound mind, in one's right mind, *compos mentis*, rational, lucid; *inf.* all there. **2** *a sane course of action* sensible, reasonable, sound, balanced, levelheaded, judicious, responsible, prudent, wise, politic, advisable.

**sanguine** adjective *a sanguine disposition* optimistic, confident, assured, hopeful, buoyant, cheerful, spirited.

**sanitary** adjective *sanitary conditions in the hospital* hygienic, clean, germ-free, antiseptic, aseptic, sterile.

**sanity** noun **1** *question the patient's sanity* saneness, soundness of mind, mental health, reason, rationality, lucidness. **2** *acknowledge the sanity of the decision* sense, common sense, reasonableness, rationality, soundness, judiciousness, prudence, wisdom, advisability.

**sap** verb *completely sapped by the heat* drain, enervate, exhaust, weaken, enfeeble, debilitate.

**sarcasm** noun derision, scorn, sneering, scoffing, irony, satire, causticness, acerbity, acrimony, mordancy, bitterness, spitefulness.

**sarcastic** adjective derisive, derisory, scornful, mocking, sneering, ironic, sardonic, satirical, caustic, trenchant, acerbic, mordant, bitter, spiteful.

**sardonic** adjective dry, wry, derisory, scornful, mocking, cynical, sneering, jeering, scoffing, contemptuous, sarcastic, caustic, trenchant, acerbic, mordant, bitter, spiteful.

**Satan** noun the Devil, the Evil One, Old Nick, Prince of Darkness, Lucifer, Beelzebub, Moloch, Belial.

**satanic** adjective diabolical, fiendish, devilish, demonic, hellish, infernal, accursed, wicked, evil, sinful, iniquitous, malevolent.

**satiate** verb *satiated with food/pleasure* sate, overfill, surfeit, glut, gorge, cloy.

**satire** noun 1 *write a satire* burlesque, parody, travesty, caricature, lampoon, skit, pasquinade; *inf.* takeoff, spoof, send-up. 2 *treat them with satire* mockery, ridicule, irony, sarcasm.

**satirical** adjective mocking, ridiculing, taunting, ironic, sarcastic, sardonic, caustic, biting, trenchant, mordant, acerbic, pungent, critical, cynical.

**satisfaction** noun 1 *derive satisfaction* fulfillment, gratification, pleasure, enjoyment, happiness, pride, comfort, contentment. 2 *the satisfaction of her demands* fulfillment, gratification, appeasement. 3 *demand satisfaction for the trouble caused* damages, compensation, recompense, amends, reparation, redress, indemnity, restitution, requital, atonement, reimbursement, remuneration, payment.

**satisfactory** adjective adequate, acceptable, sufficient, competent, up to standard, up to scratch, passable.

**satisfy** verb 1 *satisfy their appetites/thirst* satiate, sate, slake, quench. 2 *satisfy their desires* fulfill, gratify, appease, indulge. 3 *satisfy the qualification requirements* fulfill, meet, comply with, answer. 4 *satisfy a debt* pay, settle, discharge, square up. 5 *satisfy the police that he is innocent* convince, persuade, assure, reassure.

**saturate** verb 1 *the rain saturated our clothing* wet through, drench, soak, souse, douse. 2 *saturate the market* overfill, surfeit, glut, satiate.

**saucy** adjective impudent, impertinent, insolent, rude, disrespectful, audacious, presumptuous, bold, brazen, cheeky, pert, brash; *inf.* fresh.

**saunter** verb stroll, amble, wander, meander, traipse, walk, ramble, roam, promenade; *inf.* mosey.

**savage** adjective 1 *a savage blow* vicious, ferocious, fierce, brutal, cruel, bloody, murderous, inhuman, harsh, terrible, merciless, ruthless, pitiless, sadistic, barbarous. 2 *a savage animal* fierce, ferocious, wild, untamed, feral. 3 *explorers encountering savage tribes* primitive, uncivilized, uncultivated.

**savage** noun 1 *sailors attacked by island savages* barbarian, native, primitive, heathen. 2 *her attacker was a savage* brute, beast, monster, barbarian, ogre.

**save** verb 1 *save the children from danger* rescue, free, liberate, deliver, snatch, salvage, redeem. 2 *save them from their sinful desires* protect, safeguard, guard, keep, shield, screen, preserve. 3 *save a lot of trouble* prevent, obviate, forestall, spare, rule out. 4 *save some money* set aside, put by, keep, reserve, conserve, salt away, stockpile, store, hoard. 5 *time to save, not spend* economize, scrimp, budget, cut costs, cut expenditure.

**savings** plural noun capital, assets, resources, cache, reserves, funds, nest egg.

**savior** noun rescuer, liberator, deliverer, emancipator, champion, knight in shining armor.

**Savior** noun *worshiping the Savior* Christ, Jesus, Jesus Christ, the Redeemer, the Messiah, Our Lord.

**savoir faire** noun finesse, poise, aplomb, social graces, style, diplomacy, discretion, smoothness, urbanity, suaveness; *inf.* savvy.

**savor** verb *savor the taste of the soup | savor the joys of freedom* taste, enjoy, appreciate, delight in, take pleasure in, relish, revel in, luxuriate in.

**savory** adjective *savory smells from the kitchen | savory entrées* appetizing, mouthwatering, fragrant, flavorful, palatable, tasty, delicious, delectable, luscious, toothsome; *inf.* scrumptious.

**say** verb 1 *refuse to say his name* speak, utter, mention, voice, pronounce, give voice to, vocalize. 2 *"it is too expensive," he said* state, remark, announce, affirm, assert, maintain, declare, aver, allege, profess, avow; *lit.* opine. 3 *finding it difficult to say how one feels* express, put into words, tell, phrase, articulate, communicate, convey, reveal, divulge, disclose. 4 *say a short poem* recite, repeat, deliver, declaim, orate, read, perform. 5 *what do the instructions say?* indicate, specify, designate, tell, explain, suggest. **6** *people said to be spying* suggest, allege, claim, report, rumor.

**saying** noun *old sayings about the weather* proverb, maxim, aphorism, axiom, adage, saw, epigram, dictum, gnome, apothegm, platitude, cliché.

**scale**[1] noun *weigh it on the scale* scales, weighing machine, balance.

**scale**[2] noun **1** *on the Richter scale | social scale* graduated system, calibrated system, measuring system, progression, succession, sequence, series, ranking, register, ladder, hierarchy; *inf.* pecking order. **2** *a scale of a hundred miles to the inch* ratio, proportion. **3** *entertain on the grand scale* extent, scope, range, degree, reach.

**scale**[3] verb *scale the high wall* climb, ascend, mount, clamber up, escalade. **scale down** *scale down the extent of the alterations* reduce, cut down, cut back on, decrease, lessen, lower, trim.

**scamp** noun rascal, rogue, imp, devil, monkey, scalawag, mischief-maker, prankster, miscreant.

**scamper** verb scurry, scuttle, dart, run, rush, dash, race, sprint, hurry, hasten, scramble; *inf.* scoot.

**scan** verb **1** *scan the horizon/evidence* study, examine, scrutinize, survey, inspect, take stock of, search, scour, sweep. **2** *scan the pages of the document* skim, look over, glance over, run one's eye over, read through, leaf through, flip through.

**scandal** noun **1** *corruption scandals destroying political careers* impropriety, misconduct, transgression. **2** *caused a scandal in the village* outrage, disgrace, embarrassment. **3** *bring scandal on the family* disgrace, shame, dishonor, disrepute, discredit, odium, opprobrium, censure, obloquy. **4** *spread scandal about the politician* calumny, defamation, aspersion, gossip, rumors, dirt, muckraking, smear campaign.

**scandalous** adjective **1** *public figures guilty of scandalous behavior* disgraceful, shameful, dishonorable, shocking, disreputable, improper, unseemly, discreditable, opprobrious. **2** *spread scandalous rumors* slanderous, libelous, defamatory, scurrilous, malicious, gossiping.

**scant** adjective *pay scant attention* little, minimal, limited, insufficient, inadequate.

**scanty** adjective *scanty supplies of food* meager, sparse, small, paltry, slender, negligible, skimpy, thin, poor, insufficient, inadequate, deficient, limited, restricted, exiguous.

**scar** noun **1** *a scar left by the wound* mark, blemish, blotch, discoloration, disfigure-

ment, defacement. **2** *cruelty leaves an emotional scar* damage, trauma, injury.

**scarce** adjective **1** *money being scarce in short supply* meager, scant, scanty, sparse, paltry, insufficient, deficient, inadequate, lacking, exiguous. **2** *red squirrels being scarce* rare, infrequent, sparse, uncommon, unusual.

**scarcely** adverb **1** *I scarcely know them* hardly, barely, only just. **2** *I can scarcely expect them to believe that* hardly, certainly not, surely not, not at all, on no account, by no means.

**scarcity** noun **1** *scarcity of money in the recession* dearth, shortage, paucity, meagerness, sparseness, insufficiency, deficiency, inadequacy, lack, exiguity. **2** *the scarcity of red squirrels* rarity, infrequency, uncommonness.

**scare** verb frighten, alarm, startle, make fearful, make nervous, terrify, terrorize, petrify, horrify, appall, shock, intimidate, daunt, cow, panic, make one's blood run cold, make one's hair stand on end; *inf.* scare the living daylights out of.

**scare** noun *recovering from a scare* fright, alarm, start, fearfulness, nervousness, terror, horror, shock, panic.

**scarf** noun muffler, kerchief, cravat, bandanna, headscarf.

**scary** adjective *a scary experience* frightening, alarming, startling, nerve-racking, terrifying, petrifying, hair-raising, horrifying, appalling, daunting.

**scathing** adjective *scathing criticism* virulent, savage, fierce, ferocious, brutal, stinging, biting, mordant, trenchant, caustic, vitriolic, withering, scornful, harsh, severe, stern.

**scatter** verb **1** *scatter breadcrumbs for birds* disseminate, diffuse, spread, sow, sprinkle, strew, toss. **2** *the crowd scattered* break up, disperse, disband, dissolve.

**scatterbrained** adjective irresponsible, forgetful, dreamy, featherbrained, harebrained, erratic, giddy.

**scene** noun **1** *the scene of the accident* place, location, site, position, spot, setting, locale. **2** *against a scene of confusion* background, backdrop, setting, set. **3** *look out on beautiful rural scenes* scenery, view, outlook, landscape, vista, panorama, prospect. **4** *the scene created by the bickering couple* fuss, exhibition, outburst, commotion, to-do, upset, tantrum, furor, brouhaha.

**scenic** adjective **1** *the scenic route* picturesque, pretty, beautiful, pleasing. **2** *the scenic advantages of the area* landscape, panoramic.

**scent** noun **1** *the scent of new-mown hay* aroma, perfume, fragrance, smell, bouquet, redolence, odor. **2** *dogs losing the scent of the fox* track, trail, spoor.

**schedule** noun **1** *projects going according to schedule* timetable, plan, scheme, program. **2** *a busy schedule* list of appointments, diary, calendar, itinerary, agenda.

**schedule** verb *schedule the meeting for tomorrow* time, arrange, organize, plan, program, book.

**scheme** noun **1** *a scheme for recycling paper* plan, program, project, system, procedure, strategy, design, device, tactics, contrivance. **2** *an attractive color scheme* arrangement, system, organization, disposition. **3** *produce the scheme for the new shopping center* outline, blueprint, design, delineation, diagram, layout, sketch, chart, map, schema. **4** *police discovering his little scheme* plot, ruse, ploy, stratagem, maneuver, machinations, subterfuge, intrigue, conspiracy; *inf.* game, racket.

**scheme** verb *rebels scheming to overthrow the government* plot, conspire, intrigue, maneuver, plan, lay plans.

**scheming** adjective calculating, conniving, wily, crafty, cunning, sly, tricky, artful, foxy, slippery, underhanded, duplicitous, devious, Machiavellian.

**scholar** noun man/woman of letters, academic, intellectual, pundit, savant; *inf.* bookworm, egghead.

**scholarship** noun **1** *works showing scholarship* learning, knowledge, education, erudition, letters. **2** *on a scholarship to the college* fellowship, endowment, award, grant.

**school** noun **1** *attend the local school* educational institution, academy, nursery school, primary school, secondary school, grammar school, high school, seminary. **2** *belonging to the Impressionist school of art* group, set, proponents, adherents, devotees, circle, class, sect, clique, faction, following, disciples, votaries, pupils, students. **3** *teachers belonging to the old school* school of thought, outlook, persuasion, opinion, point of view, belief, faith, creed, doctrine.

**school** verb **1** *schooled locally* educate, teach, instruct. **2** *school oneself in patience* train, coach, instruct, drill, discipline, direct, guide, prepare, prime, verse.

**scientific** adjective *requiring a scientific approach* systematic, methodical, orderly, regulated, controlled, exact, precise, mathematical.

**scintillating** adjective *scintillating conversation* sparkling, dazzling, vivacious, effervescent, lively, animated, ebullient, bright, brilliant, witty, exciting, stimulating, invigorating.

**scion** noun *a scion of a noble family* descendant, heir, offspring, issue, child.

**scoff** verb *scoff at* revile, deride, belittle, jeer at, mock, sneer at, gibe at, taunt, laugh at, ridicule, poke fun at, make sport of, rag, pooh-pooh, scorn; *inf.* knock.

**scold** verb *scolded them for being late* rebuke, reprimand, chide, reprove, reproach, remonstrate with, upbraid, berate, censure, lecture, castigate; *inf.* tell off, bawl out.

**scope** noun **1** *within the scope of the inquiry* extent, range, sphere, area, field, realm, compass, orbit, reach, span, sweep, confine, limit. **2** *a job with much scope* latitude, capacity, room to maneuver, elbowroom, opportunity, freedom.

**scorch** verb **1** *scorched by an iron* burn, singe, char, sear. **2** *grass scorched by the sun* burn, parch, wither, brown.

**score** noun **1** *a score of five to two* result, outcome, total. **2** *a score on the table/wall* notch, mark, scratch, scrape, groove, cut, nick, chip. **3** *a score to settle* dispute, grievance, grudge, injury, a bone of contention.

**score** verb **1** *score a point/goal* win, gain, achieve; *inf.* chalk up, notch up. **2** *score the woodwork* notch, mark, scratch, scrape, cut, nick, chip, gouge.

**scorn** noun *treat the poor with scorn* contempt, disdain, haughtiness, derision, mockery, contumely.

**scorn** verb **1** *scorn their attempts at playing* hold in contempt, disdain, disparage, slight, deride, mock, scoff at, sneer at. **2** *scorn his invitation* rebuff, spurn, shun, refuse, reject, turn down.

**scornful** adjective contemptuous, disdainful, haughty, supercilious, disparaging, scathing, derisive, mocking.

**scoundrel** noun villain, rogue, rascal, miscreant, reprobate, cad, good-for-nothing, ne'er-do-well, wastrel.

**scour** verb **1** *scour the bathtub* scrub, cleanse, abrade, polish, buff, burnish. **2** *scour the countryside* search, comb, ransack, hunt through, rummage through.

**scourge** noun **1** *poverty was the scourge of her life* bane, curse, affliction, plague, trial, torment, burden, cross to bear. **2** *punished with a scourge* whip, horsewhip, bullwhip, switch, lash, cat-o'-nine-tails, thong, flail, strap, birch.

**scourge** verb **1** *scourge the offenders* whip, horsewhip, flog, lash, strap, birch, cane, thrash, beat. **2** *scourge them with cruel words* curse, afflict, plague, torment, burden, punish.

**scout** noun **1** *scouts returning with no information* advance guard, vanguard, lookout, outrider, spy. **2** *a scout in the* *audience* talent scout, talent spotter, re-cruiter.

**scout** verb **scout for** *scout for information* search for, seek, hunt for. **scout out** *scout out the territory* reconnoiter, make a reconnaissance of, survey, inspect, investigate, examine, scan, study, observe; *inf.* check out, case.

**scowl** verb frown, glower, glare, look daggers, grimace.

**scowl** noun frown, glower, glare, dirty look.

**scramble** verb **1** *scramble over the fence* clamber, climb, crawl. **2** *scramble to get there on time* hurry, hasten, rush, race, scurry. **3** *scramble for a place in the finals* jockey, struggle, jostle, strive, contend, compete, vie. **4** *the tools were scrambled together* mix up, jumble, tangle, disorganize.

**scramble** noun **1** *a scramble to get there on time* hurry, rush, race. **2** *a scramble for concert tickets* jockeying, struggle, tussle, jostle, competition.

**scrap**[1] noun **1** *a scrap of material* fragment, piece, bit, snippet, remnant, tatter. **2** *not a scrap of truth in it* bit, grain, iota, trace, whit, particle, sliver, snatch. **3** *collect scrap* waste, junk, rubbish, scrap metal.

**scrap**[2] verb *scrap the van/plans* throw away, get rid of, discard, toss out, abandon, jettison; *inf.* ditch, junk, throw on the scrap heap.

**scrap**[3] noun fight, quarrel, argument, squabble, wrangle, tiff, row, fracas, brawl, scuffle, clash; *inf.* set-to, run-in.

**scrape** verb **1** *scrape the surface to smooth it* scour, rub, scrub, file, sandpaper. **2** *scraping a knife across metal* grate, rasp, grind, scratch. **3** *fall and scrape one's knee* graze, scratch, abrade, skin, cut, lacerate, bark. **4** *scrape the side of a car* scratch, gouge, damage, deface, spoil, mark.

**scrape** noun **1** *the scrape of a knife on metal* grating, rasping, grinding, scratching. **2** *wash the scrape on the child's knee* graze, scratch, abrasion, cut, laceration, wound. **3** *a scrape on the woodwork* scratch, mark, defacement. **4** *a financial scrape* trouble, difficulty, straits, mess, muddle, predicament, plight, tight spot; *inf.* fix.

**scratch** verb **1** *skin scratched by rose bushes* graze, scrape, abrade, skin, cut, lacerate, bark. **2** *scratch an itchy part* rub, scrape, tear at. **3** *scratch a knife over metal* scrape, grate, rasp, grind. **4** *scratch his name from the list* cross out, strike out, delete, erase, remove, eliminate. **5** *runners being scratched from the race* withdraw, take out, pull out, remove, eliminate.

**scratch** noun **1** *a scratch on the skin* graze, scrape, abrasion, cut, laceration, wound.

**2** *a scratch on the paint* scrape, mark, line, defacement. **up to scratch** up to par, satisfactory, acceptable, passable, sufficient, adequate, competent; *inf.* OK, up to snuff.

**scrawny** adjective scraggy, thin, skinny, gaunt, bony.

**scream** noun *a scream of pain* shriek, howl, shout, yell, cry, screech, yelp, squeal, wail, squawk.

**scream** verb *scream in pain* shriek, howl, shout, cry out, call out, yell, screech, yelp, squeal, wail, squawk, bawl; *inf.* holler.

**screech** noun *a screech of fright* shriek, howl, squeal, squawk.

**screech** verb *screeching in pain* shriek, howl, shout, yell.

**screen** noun **1** *change clothes behind a screen* partition, (room) divider, curtain. **2** *a screen on a window* mesh, net, netting. **3** *act as a screen from the wind* shelter, shield, protection, guard, safeguard, buffer. **4** *coal put through a screen* sieve, strainer, colander, filter, winnow.

**screen** verb **1** *screen them from the wind* shelter, shield, protect, guard, safeguard. **2** *their activities screened by darkness* conceal, hide, cover, cloak, veil, mask, camouflage, disguise. **3** *employees screened by security* evaluate, check, test. **4** *screen people for cancer* check, test, examine, investigate, scan. **5** *screen coal* sieve, sift, strain, filter, winnow.

**screw** verb *screw the planks down* fasten, clamp, rivet, bolt, batten. **screw in** *screw in the bolt* tighten, turn, twist, work in. **screw up** **1** *screw up one's face in the sun* wrinkle up, pucker, contort, distort. **2** *screw up a business deal* make a mess of, bungle, botch, ruin, spoil.

**scrimp** verb skimp, economize, be frugal, be thrifty, tighten one's belt.

**script** noun **1** *written in a careful script* handwriting, hand, pen, calligraphy. **2** *read over the script of the play* text, book, libretto, score, lines, words, manuscript.

**Scripture** noun Holy Writ, the Bible, the Holy Bible, the Gospel, the Good Book, the Word of God.

**scrounge** verb *scrounge money* cadge, beg, borrow; *inf.* sponge, bum.

**scrub** verb **1** *scrub the floor/bathtub* rub, scour, clean, cleanse, wash. **2** *scrub the plans* cancel, drop, discontinue, abandon, call off, give up, discard, abort.

**scrub** noun *land covered in scrub* brushwood, brush, copse, coppice, thicket.

**scruffy** adjective untidy, unkempt, disheveled, ungroomed, shabby, ragged, tattered, slovenly.

**scruples** plural noun *have no scruples about stealing* qualms, twinge of conscience, compunction, hesitation, doubt, misgivings, uneasiness, reluctance, restraint.

**scrupulous** adjective **1** *pay scrupulous attention to detail* meticulous, careful, painstaking, thorough, rigorous, strict, conscientious, punctilious, exact, precise, fastidious. **2** *scrupulous in his business dealings* honest, honorable, upright, moral, ethical.

**scrutinize** verb examine, study, inspect, survey, scan, investigate, peruse, probe, analyze, dissect.

**scrutiny** noun examination, study, inspection, perusal, investigation, inquiry, analysis, dissection.

**scuffle** noun *involved in a barroom scuffle* struggle, fight, tussle, row, quarrel, fracas, brawl, disturbance.

**scuffle** verb *arrested for scuffling in the street* struggle, fight, tussle, brawl; *inf.* scrap.

**sculpture** noun *a sculpture of Jefferson* statue, bust, figure, figurine.

**sculpture** verb *sculpture his head in bronze* sculpt, chisel, model, fashion, shape, cast, carve, hew.

**scum** noun **1** *scum forming on the surface of the pond* froth, foam; algae, filth, dirt. **2** *regard his neighbors as scum* lowest of the low, dregs of society, riff-raff, rabble.

**scurrilous** adjective *a scurrilous attack on her character* abusive, vituperative, insulting, offensive, disparaging, defamatory.

**scurry** verb hurry, hasten, rush, race, dash, run, sprint, scamper, scramble.

**sea** noun **1** *sail on the sea* ocean, brine; *lit.* deep, main. **2** *rough seas* waves, swell, breakers. **3** *a sea of daffodils* expanse, mass, multitude, host, profusion, abundance, plethora.

**seal** noun *the presidential seal* emblem, symbol, insignia, badge, crest, token, mark, monogram.

**seal** verb **1** *seal the parcel/jars* fasten, secure, shut, close, cork, stopper, stop up. **2** *seal off the area* close, shut, cordon, fence. **3** *seal the bargain* secure, clinch, settle, decide, complete, confirm, validate.

**seam** noun **1** *the seam between the lengths of material* joint, join, junction. **2** *seams of coal* layer, stratum, vein, lode. **3** *seams on her brows* furrow, line, ridge, wrinkle.

**sear** verb **1** *cloth seared by an iron* burn, singe, scorch, char. **2** *grass seared by the sun* burn, scorch, wither.

**search** verb **1** *search the house* look through, scour, ransack, comb, rummage through, rifle, sift through, turn inside out. **2** *search one's soul* examine, explore, investigate,

inspect. **3** *search the prisoner* examine, inspect, check; *inf.* frisk. **search for** *search for clues* look for, seek out, hunt for, scout out; track down, uncover.

**search** noun **1** *conduct a search of the house* hunt, rummage, forage, rifling, ransacking. **2** *a search for truth* exploration, pursuit, quest, probe. **in search of** *in search of happiness* seeking, hunting for, in pursuit of.

**season** noun *in the warm season* period, time of year, spell, term. **in season** *when strawberries are in season* available, obtainable, common, plentiful.

**season** verb **1** *season the sauce* flavor, add salt/pepper/herbs/spice(s) to, spice; *inf.* add zing to. **2** *letters seasoned with gossip* enliven, leaven, spice, pep up. **3** *season the wood* mature, mellow, prime, prepare.

**seasoned** adjective *seasoned travelers* experienced, practiced, well-versed, established, habituated, veteran, hardened, battle-scarred.

**seasoning** noun *add seasoning to the sauce* flavoring, salt and pepper, herbs, spices.

**seat** noun **1** *enough seats for the spectators* chair, bench, settee, stool. **2** *the seat of government* headquarters, location, site, base, center, hub. **3** *fall on one's seat* bottom, buttocks, posterior, rump, hindquarters; *inf.* behind, backside, butt, tail, fanny, ass.

**seat** verb **1** *seat them next to each other* place, position, put, situate. **2** *the hall seats 500* hold, take, accommodate.

**secede** verb **secede from** *secede from the organization* withdraw from, break away from, sever relations with, quit, resign from, pull out of, drop out of, repudiate, reject, renounce.

**secluded** adjective *a secluded place | the cabin was secluded* concealed, hidden, private, unfrequented, solitary, lonely, sequestered, out-of-the-way, remote, isolated, sheltered, off the beaten path, tucked away, cut off.

**seclusion** noun *celebrities now living in seclusion* privacy, solitude, retreat, retirement, sequestration, isolation, concealment, hiding, secrecy.

**second** adjective **1** *take a second pair of climbing boots* extra, additional, other, alternative, backup, substitute, further. **2** *move from the second team to the first* secondary, lower, subordinate, lesser, lower-grade, inferior. **3** *regarded as a second Einstein* duplicate, replicate. **second to none** *as a player he is second to none* unparalleled, without equal, unmatched, unique, in a class of one's own.

**second** verb **1** *seconded in his research by a student* assist, help, aid, support. **2**

*second the proposal* support, back, approve, endorse, promote.

**second** noun *I will be with you in a second* moment, minute, instant, trice, twinkling of an eye; *inf.* sec, jiffy, two shakes of a lamb's tail.

**secondary** adjective **1** *ignore the secondary issues* lesser, subordinate, minor, ancillary, subsidiary, nonessential, unimportant. **2** *a secondary line of action* backup, reserve, relief, auxiliary, extra, alternative, subsidiary.

**second-rate** adjective **1** *regarded as second-rate citizens* second-class, inferior, lesser, unimportant. **2** *second-rate goods* inferior, substandard, poor-quality, low-grade, shoddy; *inf.* tacky.

**secrecy** noun **1** *the secrecy of the information* confidentiality, privateness. **2** *the secrecy of their love affair* clandestineness, furtiveness, surreptitiousness, stealth, covertness. **3** *the secrecy of their meeting place* seclusion, concealment, privacy, sequestration, remoteness.

**secret** adjective **1** *keep the matter secret* confidential, private, unrevealed, undisclosed, under wraps, unpublished; *inf.* hushhush. **2** *a secret drawer in the table* hidden, concealed, camouflaged, disguised. **3** *a secret love affair* clandestine, furtive, conspiratorial, undercover, surreptitious, stealthy, cloak-and-dagger, covert; *inf.* closet. **4** *a secret code/message* mysterious, cryptic, abstruse, recondite, arcane. **5** *a secret place* secluded, concealed, hidden, sheltered, private, solitary, sequestered, out-of-the-way, remote, tucked away. **6** *a secret person* reticent, uncommunicative. *See* SECRETIVE.

**secret** noun **1** *unable to keep a secret* confidential matter, confidence, private affair. **2** *the secrets of nature* mystery, enigma, puzzle, riddle. **3** *the secret of their success* recipe, formula, key, answer, solution. **in secret 1** *talks held in secret* behind closed doors, in camera. *See* SECRETLY 1. **2** *conduct their love affair in secret* privately, discreetly. *See* SECRETLY 2.

**secrete** verb **1** *secrete a watery discharge* discharge, emit, excrete, exude, ooze, leak, give off. **2** *secrete the package in a hidden drawer* hide, conceal, cover up, cache; *inf.* stash.

**secretive** adjective *a secretive nature* secret, reticent, uncommunicative, reserved, taciturn, silent, quiet, tight-lipped, closemouthed; *inf.* cagey.

**secretly** adverb **1** *committees meeting secretly* in secret, confidentially, privately, behind closed doors, in camera, sub rosa. **2** *conducting their love affair secretly* in secret, clandestinely, furtively, conspiratorially, surreptitiously, stealthily, on the sly, covertly; *inf.* on the q.t.

**sect** noun group, denomination, order, faction, camp, splinter group, wing, division.

**section** noun **1** *divide the fruit into sections* part, segment, piece, portion, bit, slice, fraction, fragment. **2** *the various sections of the book* part, division, component, chapter. **3** *the reference section of the library* part, division, department, branch.

**sector** noun **1** *the manufacturing sector of the economy* part, division, area, branch, category, field. **2** *forbidden to enter the military sector* zone, quarter, district, area, region.

**secular** adjective *secular music/matters* lay, nonreligious, nonspiritual, nonchurch, laical, temporal, worldly, earthly.

**secure** adjective **1** *the children/jewels will be quite secure there* safe, free from danger, out of harm's way, invulnerable, protected, sheltered, shielded. **2** *the windows are secure* fastened, closed, shut, locked, sealed. **3** *feeling secure in his job* safe, unworried, at ease, comfortable, confident, assured. **4** *look forward to a secure future* settled, fixed, established, solid.

**secure** verb **1** *secure the building from attack* make safe, fortify, strengthen, protect. **2** *secure the doors and windows* fasten, close, shut, lock, bolt, chain, seal. **3** *secure the boat* tie up, moor, anchor. **4** *secure their rights* ensure, guarantee, underwrite, confirm, establish. **5** *finally secure all they needed* acquire, obtain, gain, get, procure, get possession of.

**security** noun **1** *the security of the children/jewels* safety, invulnerability, protection, safekeeping, shielding. **2** *children losing their feelings of security* safety, certainty, confidence, assurance. **3** *the security of the job* reliability, dependability, solidity. **4** *tight security for the president's visit* safety measures, safeguards, surveillance, defense, protection. **5** *use one's house as security for a loan* collateral, surety, guarantee, pledge.

**sedate** adjective *remained sedate during the excitement* calm, composed, tranquil, placid, serene, unruffled, imperturbable, unflappable.

**sedative** noun tranquilizer, depressant, sleeping pill, narcotic, opiate.

**sedative** adjective *drugs with a sedative effect* calming, tranquilizing, soothing, calmative, relaxing, soporific, narcotic.

**sedentary** adjective *sedentary workers/people* sitting, seated, deskbound, inactive.

**sediment** noun lees, dregs, grounds, deposit, residue, precipitate.

**sedition** noun incitement to riot/rebellion, agitation, rabble-rousing, fomentation,

**seduce · self-confidence**

civil disorder, insurrection, insurgence, mutiny, subversion, treason.

**seduce** verb **1** *seducing the younger employees* lead astray, corrupt, deflower, ravish, violate. **2** *seduced into crime by the promise of wealth* attract, allure, lure, tempt, entice, beguile, ensnare.

**seductive** adjective **1** *seductive smiles* alluring, tempting, provocative, exciting, arousing, sexy. **2** *seductive salaries* attractive, appealing, inviting, alluring, tempting, enticing, beguiling.

**see** verb **1** *I can see the house* make out, glimpse, spot, notice, observe, view, perceive, discern, espy, distinguish, identify, recognize. **2** *see that man over there* look at, regard, note, observe, heed, mark, behold; *inf.* get a load of. **3** *saw a movie last night* watch, look at, view. **4** *see what they mean* understand, grasp, get, comprehend, follow, know, realize. **5** *go and see what he wants* find out, discover, learn, ascertain, determine, ask, inquire. **6** *we will have to see* consider, reflect, deliberate. **7** *see that the door is locked* see to it, take care, mind, make sure, make certain. **8** *see trouble ahead* foresee, predict, forecast, anticipate, envisage. **9** *see an old friend in the street* meet, encounter, run into, chance upon. **10** *see the doctor* visit, pay a visit to, consult. **11** *he is seeing someone else now* go out with, take out, court; *inf.* go steady with, date. **12** *see her to her car* escort, accompany, show, lead, take. **see through 1** *I see through his disguise* be undeceived by, not be taken in by, be wise to, fathom, penetrate; *inf.* not fall for, have someone's number. **2** *see the job through* keep at, persevere with, persist with; *inf.* stick (it) out. **3** *see a friend through misfortune* support through, help through, stand by through, stick by through. **see to** *see to the travel arrangements* deal with, arrange, organize, attend to, cope with, look after, take care of.

**seed** noun **1** *growing plants from seeds* ovule, germ. **2** *issue of his seed* sperm, semen, spermatozoa. **3** *the seed of her discontent* source, origin, root, cause, reason, grounds, basis, motivation. **go/run to seed** *the farm has gone to seed* deteriorate, decline, degenerate, decay; *inf.* go to pot.

**seedy** adjective *seedy little hotels* shabby, scruffy, shoddy, run-down, dilapidated, squalid, mean, sleazy, sordid, tatty; *inf.* crummy.

**seek** verb **1** *seek up-to-date information* search for, look for, hunt for, be in pursuit of. **2** *seek help from a counselor* ask for, request, solicit, entreat, beg for. **3** *seek to please* try, attempt, endeavor, strive, aim, aspire.

**seem** verb *seem a pleasant place* appear, appear to be, look, look like.

**seeming** adjective *his seeming charm* apparent, ostensible, outward, external, surface, superficial, pretended, feigned, assumed, supposed.

**seemly** adjective decorous, proper, decent, becoming, fitting, suitable, appropriate, meet, *comme il faut*, in good taste.

**seep** verb ooze, leak, exude, drip, drain.

**seer** noun prophet, soothsayer, augur, sibyl.

**seethe** verb *seething at the lateness of the bus* be furious, be livid, be incensed, rant and rave, storm, fume, foam at the mouth.

**segment** noun *divide the fruit into segments* section, part, piece, portion, slice, wedge.

**segregate** verb separate, set apart, isolate, dissociate, cut off, sequester, ostracize.

**seize** verb **1** *a drowning man seizing a lifeline | seize power/control* grab, grab hold of, take hold of, grasp, grip. **2** *police seizing a shipment of drugs* confiscate, impound, commandeer, appropriate, sequester. **3** *criminals seizing a hostage/van* snatch, abduct, kidnap, hijack. **4** *police seizing the criminals* catch, arrest, apprehend, take into custody; *inf.* collar, nab. **5** *seize the meaning of the message* grasp, understand, comprehend, discern, perceive.

**seizure** noun **1** *the vice squad's seizure of the drugs* confiscation, commandeering, appropriation, sequestration. **2** *the seizure of the hostage/van* snatching, abduction, kidnapping, hijacking. **3** *the seizure of the criminals* arrest, apprehension; *inf.* collaring, nabbing.

**seldom** adverb rarely, hardly ever, infrequently; *inf.* once in a blue moon.

**select** verb choose, pick, hand-pick, single out, opt for, decide on.

**select** adjective **1** *a select range of goods* choice, hand-picked, prime, finest, best, top-quality, supreme, superb, excellent. **2** *a select club* exclusive, elite, privileged, cliquish; *inf.* posh.

**selection** noun **1** *offer a wide selection of goods* choice, pick, option. **2** *publish a selection of his works* anthology, variety, assortment, miscellany, collection, range.

**selective** adjective *able to be selective about houses* particular, discriminating, discerning, fussy; *inf.* choosy, picky.

**self-assurance** noun self-confidence, assertiveness, positiveness.

**self-centered** adjective egocentric, egotistical, self-absorbed, self-seeking, selfish, narcissistic.

**self-confidence** noun self-assurance, self-possession, poise, aplomb, composure, sang-froid.

**self-conscious** adjective awkward, shy, diffident, bashful, timorous, nervous, timid, ill-at-ease, embarrassed, uncomfortable.

**self-control** noun self-restraint, restraint, self-discipline, willpower.

**self-esteem** noun self-respect, self-regard, self-confidence, pride.

**self-important** adjective pompous, vain, conceited, arrogant, egotistical, presumptuous, overbearing, overweening, haughty, swaggering.

**selfish** adjective self-seeking, self-centered, egocentric, egotistic, self-interested.

**selfless** adjective unselfish, altruistic, generous, self-sacrificing, magnanimous.

**self-respect** noun self-esteem, self-regard, pride, self-confidence.

**self-righteous** adjective sanctimonious, holier-than-thou, pietistic, pharisaic; *inf.* goody-goody.

**self-satisfied** adjective pleased with oneself, proud of oneself, complacent, smug.

**sell** verb 1 *sell their house* put up for sale, dispose of, vend, auction off, trade. 2 *selling fruit and vegetables* trade in, deal in, stock, carry, market, peddle, hawk. 3 *selling for $5* retail, go, be found. 4 *sell the idea of self-support* promote, win approval for, get support for. 5 *you have been sold!* betray, cheat, swindle, defraud, fleece, deceive, trick, double-cross, sell down the river; *inf.* con, stab someone in the back. **sell on** *try to sell him on the plan* persuade of, convince of, talk someone into. **sell out 1** *supplies of tickets sold out* be bought up, be depleted, be exhausted. 2 *he used to have principles but he sold out for money* prostitute oneself, sell one's soul.

**semblance** noun *only a semblance of honesty* appearance, show, air, guise, pretense, façade, front, veneer, mask, pretext.

**send** verb 1 *send a letter* dispatch, forward, mail, post, remit. 2 *send a message* transmit, convey, communicate, broadcast; e-mail. **send for** *send for a doctor* call for, summon, request, order.

**senior** adjective 1 *senior officer* high-ranking, superior. 2 *the senior of the two* older, elder.

**sensation** noun 1 *awake with a sensation of fear* feeling, sense, awareness, consciousness, perception, impression. 2 *their affair caused a sensation* stir, excitement, agitation, commotion, furor, scandal. 3 *the new show is a sensation* great success; *inf.* hit, smash.

**sensational** adjective 1 *a sensational news story* spectacular, exciting, startling, dramatic, amazing, shocking, scandalous, lurid. 2 *looking sensational in the evening dress* marvelous, superb, exceptional; *inf.* fabulous, out of this world.

**sense** noun 1 *a sense of touch* feeling, sensation, faculty, sensibility. 2 *detect a sense of hostility* atmosphere, impression, aura. 3 *a sense of guilt* feeling, awareness, consciousness, perception. 4 *a sense of humor* appreciation, awareness, understanding, comprehension. 5 *have the sense to keep quiet* practicality, wisdom, sagacity, discernment, perception, intelligence, understanding, logic, brains. 6 *a word with several senses* meaning, definition, signification, implication, nuance, drift, gist, purport, denotation. 7 *no sense in what she said/did* intelligibility, coherence, logic, rationality, purpose, point.

**sense** verb *sense their hostility* feel, be conscious of, perceive, discern, grasp, pick up, suspect, divine, intuit.

**senseless** adjective 1 *a senseless act/comment* nonsensical, stupid, foolish, silly, inane, idiotic, mindless, irrational, illogical, meaningless, pointless, absurd, ludicrous, fatuous. 2 *knocked senseless by the blow* unconscious, insensible, out cold, numb, insensate.

**sensibility** noun sensitivity, delicacy, taste, discrimination, discernment.

**sensible** adjective 1 *a sensible approach* practical, realistic, down-to-earth, grounded, wise, prudent; judicious, sagacious, discerning, perceptive, well-balanced, reasonable, rational, logical. 2 *a sensible rise in temperature* perceptible, discernible, appreciable, noticeable, observable, palpable.

**sensitive** adjective 1 *sensitive skin* delicate, fine, soft, fragile. 2 *sensitive rather than coarse people* responsive, perceptive, discerning, sympathetic, understanding, empathetic. 3 *too sensitive to withstand criticism* thin-skinned, touchy, temperamental. 4 *a sensitive issue* delicate, problematic ticklish. **sensitive to** *sensitive to unfriendly atmospheres* responsive to, susceptible to, reactive to, sentient of.

**sensual** adjective 1 *sensual rather than spiritual pleasures* physical, carnal, bodily, fleshly, animal, epicurean. 2 *sensual lips* voluptuous, sexy, erotic.

**sentiment** noun 1 *no room for sentiment in business* emotion, tenderness, softness. 2 *a revolutionary sentiment obvious in her writings* attitude, opinion, view, point of view. 3 *romantic novels full of sentiment* emotionalism, mawkishness. *See* SENTIMENTALITY.

**sentimental** adjective 1 *singing sentimental love songs* overemotional, romantic, mawkish, maudlin, soppy; *inf.* mushy, schmaltzy, corny. 2 *a sentimental attachment to the town* emotional, nostalgic, affectionate.

**sentimentality** noun *criticizing the sentimentality of the novels* emotionalism, overemotionalism, romanticism, mawkishness; *inf.* mush, corniness.

**separate** adjective **1** *have separate residences* individual, distinct, different, autonomous, independent. **2** *the problems being quite separate* unconnected, distinct, different, disconnected, unrelated, detached, divorced, divided, discrete.

**separate** verb **1** *separate the joined pieces of wood* detach, sever, disconnect, uncouple, divide, disjoin, sunder. **2** *old pipes separating at the joints* come apart, break off, divide. **3** *the fence separating the two gardens* divide, come between, stand between, partition. **4** *the roads separated at the foot of the hill* part, part company, diverge, split, divide. **5** *the couple separated last year* break up, split up, become estranged, divorce. **6** *separate the misbehaving child from the rest* set apart, segregate, single out, isolate. **separate from** *a splinter group separating from the society* break away from, secede from, withdraw from, sever relations with.

**separation** noun **1** *the separation of the pieces* detachment, disconnection, severance, uncoupling, division, disjunction, segregation. **2** *upset by her parents' separation* breakup, split, parting, estrangement, rift, divorce.

**sequel** noun *an unfortunate sequel of/to the party* follow-up, development, result, consequence, outcome, upshot, conclusion.

**sequence** noun *sequence of events* chain, course, cycle, series, progression, succession, order, pattern.

**serene** adjective calm, composed, tranquil, peaceful, placid, still, quiet, unperturbed, imperturbable, undisturbed, unruffled, unworried.

**serenity** noun calm, calmness, composure, tranquillity, peace, placidity, stillness, quietness.

**series** noun *a series of numbers* succession, progression, sequence, chain, string, set, row, arrangement.

**serious** adjective **1** *serious expressions* solemn, earnest, unsmiling, thoughtful, grave, somber, sober, stern, grim. **2** *serious problems* important, significant, consequential, momentous, urgent, pressing, crucial, vital, life-and-death. **3** *serious injuries* acute, grave, bad, critical, grievous, dangerous, perilous. **4** *serious about reforming* earnest, sincere, honest, resolute, determined.

**sermon** noun **1** *sermons from the pulpit* homily, preaching, teaching, speech, address, oration. **2** *her father gave her a ser-* mon on lateness lecture, tirade, harangue, diatribe, reprimand; *inf.* talking-to.

**servant** noun *kitchen servants* domestic, domestic help, maid, housekeeper, butler, steward, valet; menial, drudge; attendant, lackey.

**serve** verb **1** *willing to serve his fellow men* be of use to, help, assist, aid, lend a hand to, do a good turn to, benefit, support, minister to, succor. **2** *serve on the committee* sit, perform duties, fulfill duties. **3** *will the car serve us for another year?* be good for, be adequate for, suffice; *inf.* fill the bill for, do. **4** *serve three years as an apprentice* spend, carry out, complete, discharge. **5** *serve food* dish up, give out, distribute, set out, present, provide. **6** *serve a customer* attend to, take care of, assist. **serve as** *sofas serving as beds* act as, do duty as, function as.

**service** noun **1** *retire after fifty years' service* work, employment, labor, duties. **2** *do him a service by telling him* good turn, advantage, benefit. **3** *wedding service* ceremony, ritual, rite, sacrament. **4** *cars due for service* servicing, overhaul, maintenance check, repair. **5** *pay extra for service in a restaurant* serving, waiting at table. **6** *have had good service from it* treatment, behavior, conduct, handling.

**service** verb *service the washing machine* overhaul, maintain, repair.

**serviceable** adjective **1** *serviceable rather than fashionable shoes* functional, utilitarian, practical, plain, useful. **2** *machinery no longer serviceable* usable, of use, functional, operative.

**servile** adjective **1** *made to do servile tasks* menial, lowly, humble, mean, base. **2** *surrounded by servile employees* subservient, obsequious, sycophantic, fawning, toadying, groveling; *inf.* bootlicking.

**servitude** noun slavery, enslavement, subjugation, domination, bondage, serfdom.

**session** noun **1** *the afternoon sessions of the summit talks* meeting, sitting, assembly, conference, discussion. **2** *studied French during the fall session* semester, term.

**set** verb **1** *set the books (down) there | a house set in the woods* put, place, lay, deposit, position, situate, station, posit; *inf.* stick, park, plunk. **2** *set a jewel in the ring* fix, embed, insert, lodge, mount, arrange, install. **3** *set pen to paper* put, apply, touch. **4** *set your mind to it* apply, direct, aim, turn, address, focus. **5** *set one's watch* adjust, regulate, synchronize, coordinate, calibrate. **6** *set the table* lay, make ready, prepare, arrange. **7**

set her hair fix, style, arrange, curl. **8** *a dress set with sequins* decorate, adorn, ornament, deck, embellish. **9** *set things in motion | set it on fire* start, actuate, instigate. **10** *the gelatin/concrete will not set* solidify, stiffen, thicken, gel, jell, harden, congeal, coagulate. **11** *the sun setting* go down, sink, disappear. **12** *set them thinking* start, motivate, cause. **13** *set a new record* establish, fix, create, institute. **14** *set a date for the meeting* fix, settle (on), appoint, decide on, name, specify, stipulate, determine, designate, select, choose, arrange, schedule, confirm. **15** *set rules* impose, establish, define, stipulate, prescribe. **16** *teachers setting classroom tasks* assign, allocate, allot, give out, distribute, dispense, mete out. **17** *set her services at a high price* evaluate, value, assess, price, rate. **18** *footsteps set toward home* direct, steer, orientate, point, incline, train, aim. **set about** *set about clearing up* begin, start, commence, tackle, undertake; *inf.* get cracking on. **set apart** *behavior setting him apart from the rest* differentiate, distinguish, single out, demarcate, characterize. **set aside 1** *set aside money for later* lay by, put away, save, reserve, keep in reserve, store, stockpile, hoard, deposit, salt away, squirrel away; *inf.* stash. **2** *set aside the newspaper* put aside, discard, abandon, drop. **3** *set aside our differences* put aside, forget, disregard, ignore, bury. **4** *set aside the judge's ruling* overrule, overturn, reverse, nullify, annul, dismiss. **set back** *set back their progress* hinder, impede, obstruct, hold up, delay, retard, check, thwart. **set forth 1** *set forth for the city* start out, depart. *See* SET OUT 1. **2** *set forth their demands* declare, state, describe, detail, submit, present, advance. **set in** *winter has set in* begin, start, commence, arrive, come. **set off 1** *set off for the city* start out, depart. *See* SET OUT 1. **2** *set off a bomb* detonate, explode, blow up, ignite, light. **3** *set off a flurry of selling on the stock market* cause, start, initiate, prompt, touch off, stimulate. **4** *a dress setting off the blue of her eyes* enhance, bring out, heighten, intensify, emphasize. **set on** attack, assault, strike, beat, beat up, fall upon, pounce on, fly at. **set out 1** *they set out for the city early* set off, set forth, start out, depart, leave, get under way, embark, sally forth; *inf.* hit the road. **2** *I did not set out to hurt them* intend, aim, mean, aspire. **set up. 1** *they set up a statue in his memory* put up, erect, raise, construct, build. **2** *we set up a business/scholarship* establish, institute, found, create, start, initiate, inaugurate, organize. **3** *we must set up a meeting* arrange, organize, prepare, plan, devise, fix.

**set** *noun* **1** *a set of articles for sale* collection, group, assemblage, series, batch, array, assortment, selection. **2** *the golfing set* circle, crowd, clique, group, gang, coterie, faction, company; *inf.* crew. **3** *the set of his shoulder* bearing, carriage, cast, posture, position, inclination. **4** *paint the set* stage setting, scenery, backdrop, *mise en scène*.

**set** *adjective* **1** *set meals* fixed, prescribed, scheduled, specified, predetermined, prearranged, established. **2** *her set routine* customary, regular, normal, usual, habitual, accustomed. **3** *give a set speech* stock, standard, routine, hackneyed, conventional. **4** *people of set opinions | set in their ways* fixed, firm, rooted, immovable, deep-seated, ingrained, entrenched, rigid, inflexible, hidebound. **5** *all set for the journey* ready, prepared, equipped, primed, fit. **set on** *set on getting his own way* intent on, determined to be, resolute about.

**setback** *noun* *their progress/plans suffered a setback* reversal, stumbling block, hitch, hindrance, impediment, obstruction, disappointment, misfortune, blow.

**settle** *verb* **1** *settle in Chicago* make one's home, take up residence, put down roots, move to. **2** *the Mormons settled (in) Utah* colonize, occupy, people, inhabit, populate. **3** *the children will not settle after the excitement* calm down, be quiet, be still, relax. **4** *the sedative will settle her* calm, calm down, tranquilize, quiet, soothe, sedate. **5** *a butterfly settling on the leaf* alight, light, land, repose, rest. **6** *settle a dispute* resolve, clear up, patch up, reconcile. **7** *settle one's affairs* put in order, arrange, straighten out, organize, systematize. **8** *settle one's debts* pay, discharge, square, clear, liquidate. **9** *the dust settled* sink, subside, fall, gravitate. **settle for** *settle for a smaller sum* compromise on, accept, agree to, assent to. **settle on** *settle on a date* decide on, agree on, determine, confirm, arrange, fix, choose, appoint, select.

**settlement** *noun* **1** *the settlement of the area* founding, peopling, colonization. **2** *a remote settlement* community, colony, town, village, encampment, outpost. **3** *the settlement of the dispute* resolution, patching up, reconciliation, conclusion. **4** *reach a financial settlement with management* agreement, contract, pact, compact. **5** *the settlement of his finances* ordering, arrangement, organization, systematization. **6** *in settlement of debts* payment, discharge, defrayal, liquidation.

**settler** *noun* colonist, pioneer, frontiersman, immigrant.

**sever** *verb* **1** *sever a branch* cut off, chop off, lop off, hack off. **2** *sever the log in two pieces* divide, split, cleave, halve. **3** *sever* *relations with them* break off, discontinue, suspend, dissolve, terminate.

**several** adjective **1** *several people came* some, a number of, a few. **2** *go their several ways* separate, different, diverse, divergent, respective, individual, own, various, sundry.

**severe** adjective **1** *severe criticism* harsh, stringent, rigorous, unsparing, relentless, merciless, ruthless, painful, caustic, biting, scathing. **2** *a severe regime* harsh, hard, stern, stringent, strict, grim, inflexible, uncompromising, merciless, pitiless, ruthless, brutal, cruel, iron-handed, autocratic, tyrannical, despotic. **3** *a severe shortage of food* extreme, serious, grave, acute, critical, dire, dangerous, perilous. **4** *severe headaches* fierce, strong, intense, powerful. **5** *a severe test of their stamina* demanding, taxing, exacting, tough, difficult, arduous, rigorous, punishing. **6** *a severe expression* stern, grim, cold, austere, forbidding, dour, disapproving, tight-lipped, unsmiling, grave, sober, serious. **7** *a severe style of decoration* austere, stark, spartan, ascetic, plain, bare, unadorned, unembellished. **8** *a severe winter* harsh, extreme, inclement, cold, freezing, frigid.

**sew** verb stitch, seam, embroider, mend, darn.

**sex** noun **1** *identify the sex of the animal* gender. **2** *attraction based on sex* sexuality, sexual attraction, desire, sex drive, sexual appetite, libido. **3** *sex education* facts of life, reproduction; *inf.* the birds and the bees. **4** *have sex with him* intimacy, coitus, copulation, making love, mating, fornication.

**sexuality** noun **1** *differences based on sexuality* sex, gender. **2** *identifying one's sexuality* sexual desire, sexiness, eroticism, sensuality; sexual orientation, sexual preferences.

**sexy** adjective **1** *sexy pictures/clothes* erotic, titillating, suggestive, arousing, exciting, stimulating, provocative, seductive, sensuous. **2** *sexy women/men* sexually attractive, alluring, seductive.

**shabby** adjective **1** *shabby houses* dilapidated, broken-down, run-down, tumbledown, ramshackle, scruffy, dingy, seedy, squalid; *inf.* tacky. **2** *shabby clothes* worn, worn-out, threadbare, ragged, frayed, tattered, faded, scruffy. **3** *shabby treatment of the old lady* contemptible, despicable, dishonorable, disreputable, mean, base, low, shameful, ignoble, unworthy, shoddy.

**shackle** verb **1** *shackle the prisoner* chain, fetter, put in irons, manacle, tie up, bind, handcuff. **2** *no longer shackled by convention* deter, restrain, restrict, limit, impede, hinder, hamper, encumber, check, curb, constrain.

**shackles** plural noun **1** *prisoners in shackles* chains, fetters, bonds, irons, manacles, ropes, handcuffs. **2** *throw off the shackles of convention* restraint, impediment, hindrance, check, curb, constraint.

**shade** noun **1** *sit in the shade of a tree* shadow, shelter, cover. **2** *a darker shade for the carpets* color, hue, tone, tint, tinge. **3** *act as a shade against the light* screen, shield, curtain, blind, canopy, veil. **4** *a word with several shades of meaning* nuance, degree, gradation. **a shade** *a shade better* slightly, marginally, a bit, a touch.

**shade** verb **1** *trees shading the garden* cast a shadow over, screen, darken, dim. **2** *shading the light* cover, obscure, mute, hide, conceal, veil.

**shadow** noun **1** *sit in the shadow of the building* shade, cover. **2** *their shadows on the wall* silhouette, outline, shape. **3** *cast a shadow on their happiness* gloom, cloud, blight. **4** *her younger sister was her shadow* constant companion, intimate, alter ego; *inf.* sidekick. **5** *the policewoman acting as a shadow* watch, follower; *inf.* tail. **6** *not a shadow of a doubt* bit, shade, trace, modicum, hint, suggestion, ghost. **7** *a shadow of his former self* ghost, specter, phantom, remnant.

**shadowy** adjective **1** *shadowy parts of the garden* shady, shaded, dim, murky, crepuscular, tenebrous. **2** *shadowy shapes on the horizon* indistinct, indeterminate, unclear, nebulous.

**shady** adjective **1** *shady parts of the garden* shaded, shadowy, sheltered, covered, dim, dark, leafy, bowery, umbrageous, tenebrous. **2** *shady character* disreputable, suspicious, questionable, dishonest, untrustworthy, devious, shifty, slippery, underhanded, unscrupulous; *inf.* fishy.

**shaft** noun **1** *the shafts of the mine* passage, duct, tunnel, flue. **2** *shafts of light* ray, beam, gleam, streak, pencil. **3** *the shaft of a spade* pole, rod, staff, shank, stem, handle, upright.

**shaggy** adjective hairy, hirsute, long-haired, unkempt, untidy.

**shake** verb **1** *the truck shaking on the rough roads* jolt, bounce, roll, sway, wobble, rattle, vibrate. **2** *shaking with fear* shiver, tremble, quiver, quake, shudder. **3** *shake the can of coins* jiggle, joggle, jerk, rattle, agitate. **4** *shaken by the accident/news* agitate, upset, distress, shock, alarm, disturb, perturb, fluster, unsettle, disquiet, disconcert, unnerve, ruffle, jolt; *inf.* rattle. **5** *shake a stick at them* brandish, wave, flourish, swing, wield. **shake off** *shake off their pursuers* escape, elude, give the slip to, throw off. **shake up 1** *shake up the dressing/cocktail* mix, churn up, agitate. **2** *shaken up by the accident* agitate, upset, disturb, unsettle. **3**

*shake up the firm* reorganize, revolutionize, stir up.

**shake** noun **1** *the children had the shakes* shivering, trembling, tremor, quiver, quivering, convulsion. **2** *with one shake of the can* jiggle, joggle, jerk, rattle. **3** *get quite a shake from the accident/news* upset, shock, jolt. **4** *with a shake of his fist* brandish, wave, flourish, swing.

**shaky** adjective **1** *with shaky limbs* trembling, tremulous, quivering, shaking, unsteady, weak. **2** *take a few shaky steps* unsteady, faltering, wobbly, tottering, staggering. **3** *rather shaky reasoning* questionable, dubious, tenuous, flimsy, weak, nebulous, unsound, ungrounded, unfounded.

**sham** verb *shamming an illness* fake, pretend, feign, counterfeit, simulate, affect, imitate.

**sham** noun **1** *his charm is only a sham* pretense, feint, counterfeit, imposture, simulation. **2** *the doctor was a sham* impostor, fake, fraud, pretender, dissembler, charlatan; *inf.* phony. **3** *the document is a sham* counterfeit, fake, forgery, copy, imitation, hoax.

**sham** adjective **1** *sham sympathy* pretended, feigned, contrived, simulated, affected, insincere, false, bogus, spurious; *inf.* phony. **2** *sham gold watches* fake, counterfeit, imitation, artificial, synthetic, ersatz; *inf.* phony, pseudo.

**shame** noun **1** *feel shame at being imprisoned* humiliation, mortification, loss of face, remorse, compunction, embarrassment. **2** *bring shame on the family* disgrace, dishonor, scandal, discredit, degradation, ignominy, disrepute, infamy, odium, stigma, opprobrium. **3** *a shame he could not be there* pity, misfortune, bad luck, ill luck, source of regret. **put to shame** *put their efforts to shame* outshine, outclass, overshadow, eclipse, surpass, outdo.

**shamefaced** adjective *too shamefaced to appear after his crime* ashamed, embarrassed, remorseful, contrite, penitent, regretful, humiliated, mortified.

**shameful** adjective **1** *shameful behavior* disgraceful, base, mean, low, vile, outrageous, shocking, dishonorable, unbecoming, deplorable, despicable, contemptible, reprehensible, scandalous, atrocious, heinous.

**shameless** adjective **1** *shameless about his prison sentence* unashamed, unabashed, uncontrite, impenitent. **2** *shameless behavior* brazen, impudent, bold, brash, forward, audacious, immodest, unseemly, improper, unbecoming, wanton, indecent.

**shape** noun **1** *pieces of plastic in all shapes and sizes* form, figure, configuration, formation, contour, outline, silhouette. **2** *in*

*the shape of the devil* form, guise, appearance, likeness, semblance, image, aspect. **3** *athletes in good shape* condition, state, health, trim, fettle, kilter.

**shape** verb **1** *shape the clay into a figure* form, fashion, make, design, mold, model, cast, carve, sculpt. **2** *attitudes shaped by childhood experiences* form, mold, create, influence, determine, define. **shape up** **1** *new recruits shaping up* improve, make progress, show promise. **2** *plans shaping up* take shape, develop, crystallize, fall into place, come along, progress.

**shapeless** adjective **1** *shapeless hunks of clay* amorphous, formless, undeveloped, embryonic. **2** *shapeless clothes* formless, sacklike, ill-proportioned, inelegant.

**shapely** adjective *shapely legs* well-proportioned, elegant, curvaceous, curvy.

**share** noun *each receiving a fair share* division, quota, allowance, ration, allocation, allotment, portion, part, lot; *inf.* cut.

**share** verb *share the workload/profits* divide (up), split, distribute, apportion, parcel out; *inf.* divvy (up). **share in** *sharing in their good fortune* participate in, take part in, partake of, have a stake in.

**sharp** adjective **1** *a sharp utensil* razor-edged, pointed, keen. **2** *a sharp drop to the sea* steep, sheer, abrupt, precipitous, vertical. **3** *a sharp pain* intense, acute, piercing, stabbing, shooting. **4** *a sharp taste* pungent, biting, bitter, acid, sour, tart. **5** *a sharp smell* acrid, pungent, burning. **6** *a sharp noise* piercing, shrill, high-pitched, earsplitting, harsh, strident. **7** *exchange sharp words* harsh, curt, brusque, bitter, cutting, scathing, caustic, biting, barbed, acrimonious, hurtful. **8** *a sharp student* sharp-witted, intelligent, bright, clever, quick. **9** *sharp intelligence/wits* keen, acute, quick, shrewd, discerning, perceptive, penetrating. **10** *a sharp customer* unscrupulous, cunning, wily, crafty, artful. **11** *a sharp dresser* smart, stylish, fashionable, chic; *inf.* snappy, natty.

**sharp** adverb *arrive at 9 a.m. sharp* promptly, punctually, on the dot.

**sharpen** verb edge, whet, hone, strop, grind.

**shatter** verb **1** *shatter the windshield* smash, break into pieces, splinter, fracture, pulverize, crush, crack. **2** *shatter one's hopes* destroy, demolish, wreck, ruin, dash, blight, torpedo. **3** *shattered by their betrayal* devastate, crush.

**sheath** noun **1** *a sheath for a sword* scabbard, case, casing, cover. **2** *a contraceptive sheath* condom, contraceptive; *inf.* rubber.

**shed** noun hut, outhouse, lean-to, shack.

**shed** verb **1** *trees shedding their leaves* let fall, let drop. **2** *snakes shedding their skins* cast off, slough off. **3** *shed clothes* take off, remove, strip off, doff. **4** *shed blood* pour forth, spill, discharge. **5** *shed light* diffuse, radiate, disperse, scatter.

**sheen** noun shine, luster, gleam, gloss, patina.

**sheepish** adjective embarrassed, ashamed, shamefaced, blushing, abashed, bashful.

**sheer** adjective **1** *sheer folly* utter, complete, total, absolute, downright, out-and-out, unmitigated. **2** *a sheer drop to the sea* steep, abrupt, sharp, precipitous, vertical, perpendicular. **3** *sheer silk* transparent, diaphanous, see-through, translucent, filmy, gossamer.

**sheet** noun **1** *sheets and blankets* bedsheet, bed linen. **2** *a sheet of lacquered veneer on the table* layer, stratum, overlay, coating, coat, veneer, film. **3** *sheets of plastic* pane, panel, plate, slab. **sheet of paper** leaf, page, folio.

**shell** noun **1** *the shell of a crab* carapace, case. **2** *the shell of a nut* casing, husk, pod, integument. **3** *shells in the army magazine* bullet, shot, cartridge, case. **4** *the shell of a car/ship under construction* framework, frame, chassis, hull, skeleton.

**shell** verb **1** *shell peas* husk, shuck. **2** *troops shelling the city* bomb, bombard, blitz, strafe, fire on. **shell out** *shell out money* pay out, spend, disburse; *inf.* fork out.

**shelter** noun **1** *provide shelter from danger/cold* protection, shield, cover, safety, security, refuge, sanctuary, asylum. **2** *a shelter for battered wives* refuge, sanctuary, retreat, haven.

**shelter** verb **1** *shelter them from the weather* protect, shield, screen, safeguard. **2** *shelter the criminal from the police* guard, harbor, conceal, hide.

**sheltered** adjective **1** *a sheltered spot for the picnic* protected, shielded, secluded. **2** *lead a sheltered life* secluded, isolated, protected, cloistered, reclusive.

**shelve** verb *shelve expansion plans* lay aside, put off, postpone, defer, delay, suspend, table, mothball, put on the back burner.

**shepherd** verb *shepherd the children to their classes* escort, conduct, usher, guide, marshal, steer.

**shield** noun *a shield against disease* protection, defense, safeguard, bulwark.

**shield** verb *shield one's eyes from the dust* protect, screen, guard.

**shift** verb *shift one's position on the new project* alter, vary, modify, change, reverse.

**shift** noun **1** *a shift in public opinion* change, alteration, variation, modification, about-face, reversal. **2** *an eight-hour shift* work period, stint.

**shiftless** adjective lazy, idle, indolent, slothful, unenterprising, good-for-nothing.

**shifty** adjective evasive, slippery, devious, underhanded, wily, crafty, artful, sly, scheming, contriving.

**shilly-shally** verb vacillate, waver, hesitate, hem and haw.

**shimmer** verb glisten, flicker, twinkle, sparkle, gleam, scintillate, dance.

**shine** verb **1** *lights shining in the distance* gleam, glow, sparkle, twinkle, flicker, glitter, glisten, shimmer, flash, dazzle, beam, radiate, illuminate, luminesce. **2** *with face shining* glow, beam, radiate. **3** *shine the shoes* polish, burnish, buff, wax, gloss. **4** *shine in a crowd* stand out, be conspicuous, excel, dominate, star.

**shine** noun **1** *the shine of the street lights* brightness, gleam, glow, sparkle, twinkle, flicker, glitter, shimmer, flash, dazzle, glare, beam, radiance, illumination, luminescence, effulgence. **2** *put a shine on the table* polish, burnish, gloss, luster, sheen, patina.

**shiny** adjective polished, burnished, gleaming, glossy, lustrous.

**shirk** verb avoid, evade, dodge, sidestep, shun; *inf.* duck.

**shiver** verb *shiver with cold* tremble, quiver, shake, shudder, quake.

**shiver** noun *a shiver of fear* quiver, shake, quaver, shudder.

**shock**[1] noun **1** *the shock of the two cars hitting each other* impact, blow, concussion, jolt. **2** *the news came as a shock* surprise, blow, disturbance, revelation, bolt from the blue, bombshell. **3** *suffering from shock after the accident* trauma, stupor, stupefaction, collapse.

**shock**[2] verb *shocked by the scenes of famine* appall, horrify, outrage, astound, dumbfound, stagger, amaze, astonish, stun, flabbergast, overwhelm.

**shock**[3] noun *a shock of red hair* mass, mop, mane, thatch.

**shocking** adjective *a shocking sight* appalling, horrific, dreadful, awful, frightful, terrible, horrible, scandalous, outrageous, disgraceful, ghastly, hideous, repellent, revolting, repulsive, repugnant, disgusting, distressing, disturbing, staggering, amazing, overwhelming.

**shoddy** adjective poor-quality, inferior, tawdry, trashy, junky; *inf.* tacky.

**shoot** verb **1** *shoot a deer* hit, wound, injure, bring down, bag, fell, kill, slay; *inf.* pick off, plug. **2** *shoot a round of bullets/arrows* fire, discharge, launch, let fly. **3** *runners shooting past* race, dash, sprint, bound, charge, dart, fly, hurtle, bolt, streak, flash,

# shoot · show

speed. **shoot at** *shoot at the fugitives* fire at, open fire on, snipe at, shell. **shoot up** *plants shooting up* bud, burgeon, sprout, germinate, spring up.

**shoot** noun *shoots of a tree* bud, slip, scion, sucker, sprout, branch, twig, sprig, cutting, graft.

**shop** noun **1** *a dress shop* store, boutique. **2** *mechanics working in the shop* workshop; plant, factory.

**shop** verb *shop for a dress/house* go shopping, look to buy, browse.

**shore** noun *seaside*, beach, coast, waterfront, strand.

**shore** verb *shore up the broken wall* prop up, support, underpin, strengthen, brace, buttress.

**short** adjective **1** *short people* small, little, petite, tiny, squat, dwarfish, diminutive, Lilliputian; *inf.* pint-sized. **2** *short bushes* low, stubby, miniature. **3** *a short report* brief, concise, succinct, compact, terse, pithy, abbreviated, condensed, truncated. **4** *a short affair* brief, temporary, short-lived, short-term, cursory, fleeting, passing, transitory, transient, ephemeral. **5** *the short route* direct, straight. **6** *money is a bit short* deficient, lacking, wanting, scarce, scanty, meager, sparse, tight. **7** *he was short with her* curt, sharp, abrupt, brusque, terse, gruff.

**short** adverb *stop short* abruptly, suddenly, unexpectedly. **cut short** shorten, curtail, truncate, abbreviate, reduce, interrupt. **fall short** be deficient, be inadequate, disappoint, fail, not fulfill expectations. **in short** briefly, in a word, in a nutshell. **short of 1** *short of eggs* deficient in, lacking, wanting, in need of, low on. **2** *short of breaking a window, how will you get into your locked car?* other than, apart from, aside from, besides, except (for), without, disregarding.

**shortage** noun *dearth*, scarcity, lack, deficiency, insufficiency, paucity, deficit, shortfall, want.

**shortcoming** noun *forgive his shortcomings* defect, fault, flaw, imperfection, failing, drawback, weakness, foible.

**shorten** verb *shorten the text* abbreviate, condense, abridge, cut, compress, reduce, decrease, diminish, curtail, trim, pare down.

**shortly** adverb **1** *she will be with you shortly* soon, in a little while, presently, directly. **2** *he replied shortly* curtly, sharply, abruptly, bluntly, brusquely, tersely, gruffly.

**shortsighted** adjective **1** *wear spectacles because of being shortsighted* myopic, nearsighted. **2** *a shortsighted attitude to business* lacking foresight, ill-considered, imprudent, injudicious, unwise, ill-advised, thoughtless, unthinking, heedless.

**short-tempered** adjective quick-tempered, hot-tempered, irascible, touchy, testy; *inf.* on a short fuse.

**shot** noun **1** *hear a shot* gunfire, report (of a gun), crack, bang, blast, explosion. **2** *shot for the guns* bullets, slugs, projectiles, ammunition. **3** *got the ball through the hoop with one shot* throw, toss, lob, fling, hurl. **4** *a better shot than his brother* shooter, marksman, markswoman, rifleman. **5** *have a shot at getting there* attempt, try, effort, endeavor; *inf.* go, stab, crack. **6** *have shots before going to the tropics* injection, vaccination. **a shot in the arm** *a shot in the arm for the tourist industry* boost, fillip, lift, encouragement, stimulus. **a shot in the dark** *her answer was a shot in the dark* wild guess, random guess. **like a shot** *he flew out of here like a shot* without hesitation, immediately, instantly, like a flash.

**shoulder** verb **1** *shoulder a heavy responsibility* bear, carry, support, take on. **2** *shoulder his way to the front* push, shove, jostle, elbow. **give (someone) the cold shoulder** ostracize, shun, snub, ignore, rebuff. **put one's shoulder to the wheel** apply oneself, exert oneself, get down to work, strive; *inf.* buckle down. **rub shoulders with** associate with, socialize with, fraternize with, hobnob with.

**shout** verb *cry out*, call out, yell, roar, howl, bellow, bawl; *inf.* holler.

**shout** noun *a shout of pain* cry, call, yell, roar, howl, bellow.

**shove** verb *shove her out of the way* push, thrust, drive, force, jostle.

**shove** noun *give him a shove* push, thrust, jostle.

**shovel** noun spade, scoop.

**show** verb **1** *gray hairs beginning to show* be visible, appear. **2** *show the new merchandise* exhibit, display, present, demonstrate, reveal. **3** *show his grief* express, manifest, reveal, make plain, disclose, betray, divulge. **4** *show (them) the new procedures* demonstrate, point out, explain, clarify, teach, instruct in. **5** *show them to their seats* escort, accompany, usher, conduct, attend, guide, lead, direct, steer. **6** *he never showed* show up, appear, turn up, come, arrive. **show off 1** *models showing off the dresses* display, exhibit, demonstrate, parade, flaunt. **2** *showing off in front of the guests* put on airs, boast, brag, swagger. **show up 1** *sunshine showing up the dust* expose, reveal, make obvious, highlight. **2** *the red showing up well against the white* be visible, stand out, catch the eye. **3** *show him up in front of his rich friends* expose, shame, mortify, humiliate, embarrass. **4** *the guest did not show up* appear, turn up, come.

**show** noun **1** *a brilliant show of flowers / a boat show* display, array, arrangement, exhibition, demonstration, presentation, exposition, spectacle; *inf.* expo. **2** *put on a musical show* performance, production. **3** *a show of courage* appearance, air, guise, semblance, pretense, pose, affectation. **4** *doing it only for show* display, ostentation, affectation, window-dressing.

**shower** noun **1** *a shower of rain/snow* drizzle, flurry, sprinkling. **2** *a shower of arrows* volley, barrage, fusillade. **3** *a shower of gifts* abundance, profusion, plethora.

**shower** verb **1** *arrows showered on them* rain, fall. **2** *shower them with gifts* deluge, inundate, lavish, overwhelm.

**show-off** noun exhibitionist, braggart, boaster, braggadocio; *inf.* blowhard.

**showy** adjective *showy clothes/lifestyle* ostentatious, flamboyant, elaborate, fancy, pretentious, glittering; *inf.* bling, bling-bling.

**shred** noun **1** *shreds of material* scrap, fragment, sliver, bit, remnant, snippet. **2** *not a shred of evidence* bit, iota, whit, particle, atom, modicum, trace, speck.

**shred** verb *shred paper/cabbage* cut up, tear up, rip up, grate.

**shrew** noun virago, termagant, fury, harpy, nag.

**shrewd** adjective *a shrewd businessman* astute, sharp, clever, quick-witted, discerning, discriminating, canny, cunning, artful, crafty, wily, calculating.

**shriek** verb *shriek with laughter* scream, screech, squeal, howl.

**shriek** noun *a shriek of terror* scream, screech, squeal, howl, shout, cry, wail.

**shrill** adjective high-pitched, sharp, piercing, penetrating.

**shrine** noun **1** *a shrine in memory of the dead soldiers* memorial, monument, tomb, cenotaph. **2** *worship in the shrine* holy place, temple, church.

**shrink** verb **1** *markets shrinking* become smaller, contract, diminish, lessen, reduce, dwindle, narrow, decline, fall off, shrivel. **2** *shrinking in fear* draw back, pull back, shy away, recoil, retreat, flinch, cringe, wince.

**shrivel** verb *leaves shriveled by the sun* dry up, wither, desiccate, dehydrate, wrinkle.

**shroud** noun *a shroud of mist over the hills* covering, pall, cloak, mantle, blanket, cloud, veil.

**shroud** verb *hills shrouded in mist* cover, enshroud, swathe, envelop, cloak, blanket, veil, conceal, hide.

**shudder** verb *shudder in horror* shake, shiver, tremble, quiver, quake, convulse.

**shudder** noun *a shudder of horror* shake, shiver, tremor, quiver, convulsion, spasm.

**shun** verb avoid, evade, eschew, steer clear of, cold-shoulder.

**shut** verb *shut the doors* close, fasten, bar, lock, secure, seal. **shut down 1** *the factory has shut down* close, close down, cease production, come to a halt. **2** *shut down the machinery* switch off, stop, halt. **shut out 1** *shut out intruders* lock out, keep out. **2** *during negotiations, he was shut out* exclude, omit, keep out, bar, ostracize, blackball, banish. **shut up 1** *shut the sheep up in a pen* lock in, confine, imprison, coop up. **2** *please shut up* be quiet, keep silent; *inf.* hold one's tongue, pipe down. **3** *the sound of the siren shut up the crowd* quiet, silence, hush, shush.

**shy** adjective bashful, diffident, reserved, reticent, self-effacing, withdrawn, timid, timorous, hesitant, self-conscious.

**shy** verb **shy away from** shrink from, recoil from, flinch from, balk at, quail at.

**sick** adjective **1** *unable to work when sick* unwell, ill, ailing, indisposed, out of sorts, laid up; *inf.* under the weather. **2** *feel sick on a boat* nauseated, queasy, bilious; *inf.* green around the gills. **3** *be sick on the boat* vomit, retch, be sick to one's stomach; *inf.* throw up, puke. **4** *a sick joke* morbid, macabre, ghoulish, gruesome, sadistic, perverted, cruel. **sick of** *sick of that music* tired of, weary of, bored with, satiated with; *inf.* fed up with.

**sicken** verb *sickened by the smell of garbage* nauseate, revolt, disgust, repel, shock, appall.

**sickly** adjective **1** *a sickly child* unhealthy, delicate, frail, weak, feeble, puny. **2** *a sickly complexion* pale, wan, pallid, anemic, languid.

**sickness** noun **1** *a terminal sickness* illness, disease, ailment, affliction, malady, infirmity; *inf.* bug. **2** *a bout of sickness* vomiting, retching, upset stomach; *inf.* throwing up, puking. **3** *a feeling of sickness on the swaying boat* nausea, queasiness, biliousness.

**side** noun **1** *by the side of the lake/road* edge, border, verge, boundary, margin, rim, fringe, flank, brink, brim, periphery. **2** *on the east side of the city* part, quarter, section, sector. **3** *the upper side of the paper/wood* surface, face, facet. **4** *both sides of the question* aspect, angle, facet, point of view, standpoint, position, slant. **5** *on the chairman's side in the dispute* camp, faction, caucus, party. **6** *which side do you root for?* team, squad, group. **side by side** *walk/fight side by side* together, alongside each other, shoulder to shoulder, cheek by jowl, arm in arm. **take the side of**

*take the side of the likely winner* side with, support, favor.

**side** adjective **1** *on the side position of the battle* lateral, wing, flank. **2** *a side issue* minor, lesser, secondary, subordinate, subsidiary, ancillary, marginal.

**sideways** adverb **1** *walk sideways* crabwise, to the side. **2** *bring the table in sideways* side first, edgeways, edgewise. **3** *look sideways at her* obliquely, indirectly, sidelong.

**siege** noun blockade, beleaguerment.

**sieve** noun *use a sieve to strain the mixture* strainer, sifter, filter, colander, screen.

**sift** verb **1** *sift flour onto a board* shake, sprinkle, scatter, strew. **2** *sift the lumps from the flour* filter, strain, screen, winnow. **sift through 1** *sift through the evidence* examine, scrutinize, study, pore over, investigate, analyze, screen, review, probe. **2** *sift through the debris* search through, look through, rummage through.

**sigh** verb **1** *sigh with boredom* groan, exhale. **2** *the wind sighing through the trees* whisper, rustle. **3** *sigh for times past* yearn, pine, long, mourn.

**sight** noun **1** *have excellent sight* eyesight, vision. **2** *within (the) sight of her father* range of vision, view. **3** *love at first sight* view, glimpse, glance. **4** *in her father's sight, she was perfect* view, judgment, estimation, perception. **5** *memorable sights* spectacle, scene, display, curiosity, rarity, marvel. **catch sight of** glimpse, see, spot, sight, espy, set eyes on. **set one's sights on** aim at/for, aspire to, strive toward.

**sign** noun **1** *a sign of weakness* indication, symptom, hint, suggestion, mark, manifestation, token. **2** *signs indicating the offices in the building* signpost, notice, placard, marker. **3** *make a sign to follow him* gesture, signal, motion, gesticulation. **4** *mathematical signs | decipher the signs* symbol, mark, hieroglyph. **5** *look for a sign from above* omen, portent, warning.

**sign** verb **1** *sign one's name* write, inscribe. **2** *sign the agreement* autograph, initial, endorse, certify. **sign on/up 1** *soldier signing on for five years* enlist, join up. **2** *sign up for music classes* enroll, register. **3** *sign on new employees* employ, take on, engage, hire, recruit. **sign over** *sign over the estate to his son* transfer, hand over, turn over, assign, consign.

**signal** noun **1** *the signal to stop* sign, indicator, cue. **2** *a signal that winter is coming* sign, indication, token, hint.

**signal** verb **1** *signal to her to follow* give a sign, beckon, gesture, motion, gesticulate. **2** *signaled his displeasure* indicate, show, express, communicate.

**significance** noun **1** *not comprehend the significance of his remark* meaning, sense,

import, purport, point, gist, essence, implications. **2** *the significance of the medical discovery* importance, consequence, momentousness, magnitude, impressiveness, seriousness.

**significant** adjective **1** *a significant few words* meaningful, eloquent, expressive. **2** *make significant progress* important, momentous, material, impressive, vital.

**signify** verb **1** *dark clouds signifying rain* indicate, mean, betoken, suggest, portend. **2** *what do the symbols signify?* mean, denote, represent, symbolize. **3** *signify one's agreement* indicate, show, express, communicate.

**silence** noun **1** *in the silence of the night* still, stillness, quiet, hush, peacefulness, tranquillity, soundlessness. **2** *their behavior reduced him to silence* speechlessness, wordlessness, muteness, taciturnity. **3** *the need for silence about their whereabouts* secrecy, secretiveness, concealment, reticence.

**silence** verb **1** *silence the noisy children* quiet, hush, calm, pacify, subdue. **2** *silence the noise of the engine* muffle, deaden, extinguish. **3** *silence their complaints* put an end to, put a stop to, cut short.

**silent** adjective **1** *in their silent surroundings* still, quiet, hushed, peaceful, tranquil, noiseless. **2** *silent in the face of the opposition* speechless, wordless, dumb, mute, taciturn, tight-lipped; *inf.* struck dumb. **3** *silent criticism* unspoken, wordless, unvoiced, tacit, implicit, implied.

**silhouette** noun *see her silhouette on the wall* outline, contour, profile, form, shape.

**silly** adjective **1** *a silly person* foolish, stupid, idiotic, brainless, witless, thoughtless, reckless, foolhardy, irresponsible, scatterbrained, featherbrained, flighty, frivolous, giddy, inane, immature, childish, naïve. **2** *silly actions* foolish, stupid, senseless, mindless, idiotic, pointless, meaningless, irrational, thoughtless, foolhardy, irresponsible, harebrained, absurd, ridiculous, ludicrous, preposterous, asinine; *inf.* half-baked.

**similar** adjective *have similar houses* like, alike, comparable, corresponding, comparable, analogous, parallel, equivalent.

**similarity** noun *a degree of similarity* resemblance, sameness, similitude, correspondence, equivalence, closeness.

**simmer** verb **1** *a stew simmering on the stove* boil gently, bubble, stew. **2** *simmering with rage* fume, seethe, smolder.

**simple** adjective **1** *a simple task* easy, uncomplicated, straightforward, effortless, elementary; *inf.* like falling off a log. **2** *simple instructions* clear, plain, intelligible, comprehensible, lucid, straightforward, uncomplicated. **3** *simple clothes* plain, unelaborate, unadorned, undecorated, unembellished, austere, spartan. **4** *simple chemical substances* pure, basic, uncompounded, unmixed, unblended, unalloyed, single, elementary, fundamental. **5** *the simple truth* plain, straightforward, candid, honest, unvarnished, bald, unembellished. **6** *a simple country girl* unsophisticated, natural, unaffected, innocent, guileless, childlike, naïve, ingenuous. **7** *lead a simple life* ordinary, commonplace, unpretentious, modest, humble, rustic.

**simpleton** noun idiot, halfwit, dolt, fool, nincompoop; *inf.* nitwit, dope.

**simplicity** noun **1** *the simplicity of the task* simpleness, easiness, straightforwardness, effortlessness, facility. **2** *the simplicity of the directions* clarity, plainness, intelligibility, lucidity, straightforwardness. **3** *the simplicity of the clothes* clean lines, absence of adornment/decoration, plainness, absence of ornamentation/embellishment, austerity, starkness, restraint, naturalness. **4** *the simplicity of the statement* straightforwardness, frankness, directness, candor. **5** *the simplicity of their lifestyle* unpretentiousness, modesty, humbleness, lowliness.

**simplify** verb **1** *simplify the instructions* make simpler, make plainer, clarify, decipher, explain, paraphrase, translate, condense. **2** *simplify the procedure* make simpler, make easier, streamline.

**simulate** verb **1** *simulate grief* feign, pretend, fake, sham, affect. **2** *simulate flight landing conditions* reproduce, mimic, parallel, do a mock-up of.

**simultaneous** adjective *simultaneous events* concurrent, contemporaneous, concomitant, coinciding, coincident, synchronous, coexistent, parallel.

**sin** noun **1** *commit a sin in the eyes of the church* wrong, act of evil/wickedness, crime, offense, misdeed, transgression, lapse, fall from grace; *lit.* trespass. **2** *guilty of sin* wrongdoing, evil, evildoing, wickedness, iniquity, immorality, unrighteousness, ungodliness, impiety.

**sin** verb *sin against the church* commit a sin, do wrong, commit a crime/offense, transgress, go astray, stray from the straight and narrow, fall from grace.

**sincere** adjective **1** *sincere affection* genuine, real, true, honest, unfeigned, unaffected, honest, heartfelt, earnest. **2** *sincere people* honest, trustworthy, frank, candid, straightforward, genuine, guileless, ingenuous; *inf.* up-front.

**sincerely** adverb **1** *thank them sincerely* wholeheartedly, earnestly, fervently. **2** *mean it most sincerely* genuinely, truly, without pretense, honestly, in good faith.

**sincerity** noun **1** *doubt the sincerity of his beliefs* genuineness, truth, honesty, good faith, wholeheartedness, earnestness. **2** *misled by their seeming sincerity* openness, honesty, trustworthiness, frankness, candor, straightforwardness, genuineness, ingenuousness.

**sinful** adjective evil, wicked, bad, iniquitous, immoral, corrupt, unrighteous, ungodly, irreverent, profane, impious, dissolute, depraved.

**sing** verb **1** *children singing happily* carol, pipe, croon, chant, yodel. **2** *birds singing* trill, warble, chirp.

**singer** noun vocalist, soloist, songster, songstress, chorister, crooner, chanteuse, minstrel; balladeer, diva.

**single** adjective **1** *send a single rose* sole, lone, solitary, unique, isolated, exclusive. **2** *remove every single item* individual, particular, separate, distinct. **3** *preferring to remain single* unmarried, unwed, wifeless/husbandless, spouseless, partnerless, unattached, free.

**singular** adjective **1** *a singular talent* extraordinary, exceptional, rare, unusual, unique, remarkable, outstanding, notable, noteworthy. **2** *singular occurrences happening in the village* strange, unusual, odd, peculiar, curious, weird.

**sinister** adjective **1** *a sinister figure* evil-looking, menacing, threatening, frightening. **2** *sinister motives* evil, wicked, villainous, malevolent. **3** *sinister signs* ominous, inauspicious, portentous.

**sink** verb **1** *sink to one's knees | the sun sinking* fall, drop, descend, plunge, plummet, slump. **2** *ships sinking* go under, submerge, founder, capsize. **3** *feel the ground sinking* collapse, cave in, fall in. **4** *empires/patients sinking rapidly* decline, fade, fail, deteriorate, weaken, flag, degenerate, decay; *inf.* go downhill. **5** *would not sink to that level* stoop, lower oneself. **6** *sink a well/shaft* dig, bore, drill, excavate. **7** *having sunk their savings into the venture* invest, put, venture, risk.

**sinner** noun wrongdoer, evildoer, offender, miscreant, transgressor, reprobate; *lit.* trespasser.

**sip** verb *sip the drink* taste, sample, sup.

**sip** noun *take a sip* mouthful, swallow, drop, thimbleful, taste.

**sit** verb **1** *please sit* take a seat, settle down, be seated; *inf.* take a load off. **2** *the books sitting on the shelf* rest, perch. **3** *committees sitting until midnight* be convened, meet, assemble, be in session.

**site** noun **1** *the site of the battle* location, position, place, locality, setting, scene. **2** *the building site* ground, plot, lot.

**situate** verb *factories situated near the river* place, position, locate, site.

**situation** noun 1 *their financial situation* circumstances, affairs, state, state of affairs, condition, predicament, plight. 2 *from a lowly situation in life* status, station, standing, rank. 3 *apply for a situation in the new firm* post, position, place, job, employment.

**size** noun dimensions, measurements, proportions, magnitude, vastness, bulk, extent.

**skeleton** noun 1 *the skeleton of the building/car* framework, frame, structure, shell, bare bones, chassis. 2 *the human skeleton* bones.

**skeptic** noun 1 *supporters of his theories arguing with the skeptics* doubter, disbeliever, dissenter, cynic. 2 *ministers of the church challenging skeptics* agnostic, unbeliever, doubter, doubting Thomas, atheist.

**skeptical** adjective doubtful, distrustful, mistrustful, suspicious, disbelieving, incredulous, unconvinced, cynical.

**sketch** noun 1 *draw a rough sketch of the house* preliminary drawing, outline, diagram, plan, delineation. 2 *give a sketch of his plans* outline, summary, abstract, précis, skeleton, draft.

**sketch** verb *sketch the landscape on paper* draw, rough out, outline, pencil, delineate. **sketch out** *sketch out his plans* outline, summarize, précis, draft.

**sketchy** adjective 1 *plans still a bit sketchy* preliminary, provisional, unpolished, rough, crude. 2 *sketchy knowledge* slight, superficial, cursory, perfunctory, meager, skimpy, imperfect, incomplete.

**skill** noun *the skill of the performer* skillfulness, ability, accomplishment, adeptness, competence, adroitness, deftness, aptitude, expertise, talent.

**skillful** adjective *a skillful performer* skilled, able, accomplished, adept, competent, adroit, deft, masterly, expert, first-rate, practiced, talented, gifted.

**skim** verb *skim through the report* glance at, scan, run one's eye over, leaf through, thumb through.

**skimp** verb **skimp on** *skimp on food/material* be sparing with, economize on, be frugal with, scrimp on, limit; *inf.* be stingy with.

**skimpy** adjective 1 *skimpy meals* small, meager, scanty, insubstantial, inadequate, paltry. 2 *skimpy dresses* short, brief, insubstantial.

**skin** noun 1 *damage the skin* integument, epidermis, cuticle, corium, derma. 2 *fair skin* complexion, coloring. 3 *animal skin* hide, pelt, fleece, fell. 4 *banana skin* peel, rind, hull, husk. 5 *a skin forming on the* gravy film, coating, layer, crust. **by the skin of one's teeth** only just, narrowly, barely, by a hair's breadth; *inf.* by a whisker. **get under one's skin** *noisy neighbors getting under her skin* irritate, annoy, irk, vex, grate on, nettle; *inf.* needle.

**skin** verb *skin one's knee* scrape, graze, abrade, cut, bark, excoriate.

**skinflint** noun miser, penny-pincher, Scrooge; *inf.* cheapskate, tightwad.

**skinny** adjective thin, lean, scrawny, emaciated; *inf.* skin and bone.

**skip** verb 1 *children skipping along* hop, bounce, dance, caper, prance, trip, cavort, gambol, frisk. 2 *skip from subject to subject* pass quickly, flit, dart, zoom. 3 *skip the more boring parts of the text* omit, pass over, bypass, skim over. 4 *skip lectures* play truant from, miss; *inf.* cut, play hooky from.

**skirmish** noun battle, fight, clash, conflict, engagement, combat, contest, tussle, scrimmage, fracas, melee, altercation; *inf.* set-to, scrap.

**skirmish** verb fight, engage, combat, clash, tussle.

**skittish** adjective highly strung, nervous, restive, jumpy, fidgety, excitable.

**sky** noun upper atmosphere, heaven, firmament, blue, blue yonder; *lit.* ether.

**slab** noun 1 *a slab of cheese* hunk, chunk, lump, slice, wedge. 2 *a slab of wood/stone* plank, block, lump.

**slack** adjective 1 *slack clothes* loose, baggy, hanging, flapping. 2 *slack muscles* relaxed, limp, flaccid, flabby. 3 *a slack rope* not taut, relaxed, flexible, pliant. 4 *business a bit slack* slow, quiet, sluggish. 5 *rather slack about punctuality* lax, negligent, remiss, neglectful, careless, inattentive, slipshod, sloppy, disorderly.

**slack** noun 1 *take up the slack of the rope* looseness, play; *inf.* give. 2 *no more slack left in personnel* surplus, excess, leeway.

**slacker** noun idler, shirker, loafer, dawdler, layabout, malingerer, gold brick.

**slake** verb *slake one's thirst/desire* satisfy, quench, assuage, relieve, gratify.

**slander** noun defamation, misrepresentation, calumny, libel, aspersion, vilification, muckraking.

**slander** verb defame, libel, malign, vilify, smear, slur, disparage.

**slang** noun 1 *use slang rather than formal language* colloquialism, informal language. 2 *cannot understand the technicians' slang* jargon, lingo, cant, argot.

**slant** verb 1 *the old floor slants* slope, tilt, be askew, lean, dip, list. 2 *accuse the newspaper of slanting the news* give a slant to, give a bias to, angle, distort.

**slant** noun **1** *the slant of the floor/picture* slope, tilt, dip, inclination. **2** *giving a political slant to the news* bias, leaning, prejudice, angle, distortion. **3** *require a woman's slant on the new product* angle, point of view, opinion, attitude.

**slap** noun *a slap on the back* smack, blow, whack, thump, cuff, spank; *inf.* wallop. **slap in the face** *giving the job to his assistant was a slap in the face* snub, insult, rebuff, humiliation, blow to one's pride.

**slap** verb **1** *slap him on the back* smack, strike, hit, whack, spank; *inf.* belt. **2** *slap the money (down) on the table* plunk, plop, slam, fling, throw. **3** *slap paint on* daub, plaster, spread.

**slash** verb **1** *slash the fencing dummy* cut, gash, lacerate, hack, slit, score, knife. **2** *slash prices* reduce, lower drastically, cut, drop, mark down.

**slaughter** verb **1** *slaughter animals for food* kill, butcher. **2** *slaughter the enemy soldiers* massacre, murder, butcher, put to the sword, slay, exterminate, annihilate. **3** *slaughter the opposition* defeat utterly, rout, trounce, thrash, vanquish, conquer, crush, overwhelm, give a drubbing to.

**slaughter** noun massacre, murder, butchery, extermination, annihilation; bloodshed, carnage.

**slave** noun **1** *the master and his slaves* bondsman, bondswoman, bondservant, serf, vassal. **2** *slaves in the kitchen* drudge, laborer, menial worker, servant; *lit.* scullion.

**slave** verb *slaving (away) at the stove* toil, drudge, slog, labor, grind.

**slavery** noun **1** *sold into slavery* enslavement, bondage, servitude, subjugation. **2** *working there is sheer slavery* drudgery, toil, hard labor, grind.

**slavish** adjective **1** *slavish admiration* servile, subservient, obsequious, sycophantic, deferential, groveling, fawning, abject. **2** *slavish imitation* unoriginal, uninspired, unimaginative.

**slay** verb *slay his enemy* kill, murder; *slaughter*, put to death, assassinate.

**sleek** adjective *sleek hair* smooth, glossy, shiny, lustrous, silky, satiny, burnished.

**sleep** verb *sleep for a few hours* be asleep, slumber, doze, nap; *inf.* snooze, crash, catch some Z's, have forty winks.

**sleep** noun *have a short sleep* slumber, doze, nap, rest, siesta; *inf.* snooze, forty winks, (bit of) shut-eye.

**sleepy** adjective **1** *feeling sleepy* drowsy, tired, somnolent, languid, languorous, lethargic, comatose. **2** *sleepy little villages* inactive, quiet, peaceful, slumberous.

**slender** adjective **1** *slender figures* slim, thin, slight, lean, svelte, willowy. **2** *a*

*slender hope of success* small, slight, slim, faint, remote, feeble, flimsy, tenuous, fragile.

**slice** noun *a slice of cake* piece, portion, segment, sliver, wedge.

**slice** verb *slice the cake/meat* cut, carve, divide, segment, sever, separate.

**slick** adjective **1** *a slick presentation* smooth, well-organized, streamlined, efficient, polished. **2** *a slick reply* smooth, glib, fluent, specious. **3** *a slick operator* smooth, skillful, deft, adroit, sharp, shrewd, suave, urbane, sophisticated, polished.

**slide** verb **1** *slide on the ice* slip, skid, slither, skate. **2** *drawers sliding in easily* slip, glide, slither. **let slide** *let the housework slide* neglect, forget, ignore, gloss over.

**slight** adjective **1** *a slight change* small, little, tiny, minute, imperceptible, subtle, modest. **2** *of slight importance* little, minor, unimportant, petty, insignificant, inconsequential, negligible, trivial, trifling, scant. **3** *a slight figure* slim, slender, spare, delicate, frail.

**slight** verb *slight him by not inviting him* snub, insult, rebuff, give the cold shoulder to, disregard, ignore, neglect, scorn.

**slight** noun *upset by the slight* snub, insult, affront, rebuff, cold shoulder, disregard, neglect, scorn, disdain; *inf.* a slap in the face.

**slim** adjective **1** *slim girls* slender, thin, slight, lean, svelte, willowy. **2** *slim hopes of success* slight, faint. *See* SLENDER 2.

**slimy** adjective **1** *slimy surfaces* sludgy, mucky, oozy, muddy, slippery, viscous. **2** *a slimy character* despicable, contemptible, vile, low, scurvy.

**slink** verb *slinking around dark corners* steal, sneak, creep, skulk, lurk.

**slip**[1] verb **1** *slip on the ice* skid, slither, lose one's footing. **2** *slip from her hands* fall, slide, drop. **3** *slip from the room unnoticed* steal, creep, sneak, slink. **4** *slip through the police net* escape, evade, dodge. **5** *the standard of the work slipped* drop, fall off, decline, deteriorate, degenerate. **let slip** *let slip the secret* let out, reveal, disclose, divulge, give away, leak. **slip on** *slip on a sweater* put on, pull on, don. **slip up** blunder, miscalculate, err; *inf.* screw up.

**slip**[2] noun *accused of making a slip* slipup, mistake, error, blunder, miscalculation, oversight; *inf.* booboo. **give the slip** *the pickpocket gave the policeman the slip* lose, evade, dodge, elude, shake off.

**slip**[3] noun **1** *written on a slip* of paper scrap, shred; sales slip, receipt. **2** *a slip from the plant* cutting, offshoot, scion, sprout, sprig.

**slippery** adjective **1** *slippery surfaces* smooth, slick, oily, icy, glassy. **2** *a slippery character* shifty, devious, duplicitous, cunnings, foxy, tricky, sneaky, treacherous, unreliable.

**slipshod** adjective *slipshod methods* careless, slovenly, sloppy, slapdash, unsystematic.

**slipup** noun mistake, error, blunder. *See* SLIP².

**slit** verb *slit the material* cut, split open, slash, gash, rip, knife, lance.

**slit** noun *make a slit in the material* cut, gash, rip, incision, tear, split, rent, fissure, opening.

**silver** noun chip, flake, splinter, shred, fragment, scrap.

**slobber** verb slaver, drool, dribble.

**slogan** noun motto, catchword, jingle, rallying cry, mantra, shibboleth.

**slop** verb *water slopping over* spill, splash, slosh, splatter.

**slope** verb drop away, slant, incline, lean, tilt, dip.

**slope** noun **1** *floors on a slope* slant, inclination, angle, tilt, dip, gradient. **2** *grassy slopes* hill, hillock, bank, rise.

**sloppy** adjective **1** *a sloppy mixture* wet, soggy, slushy, sludgy. **2** *sloppy work* careless, slapdash, slipshod, disorganized, unmethodical, untidy, messy, slovenly.

**slot** noun **1** *money in the slot* slit, crack, hole, opening, aperture, groove, notch. **2** *broadcast a show in the noon slot* place, position, niche, space, opening, time, period.

**sloth** noun laziness, indolence, idleness, sluggishness, lethargy, languor, torpor.

**slothful** adjective lazy, indolent, idle, sluggish, inactive, lethargic, languid, torpid.

**slouch** verb slump, hunch, stoop, droop.

**slovenly** adjective **1** *of slovenly appearance* slatternly, untidy, messy, unkempt, disheveled, tousled, rumpled. **2** *slovenly methods* careless, sloppy, slapdash, slipshod.

**slow** adjective **1** *at a slow pace* slow-moving, unhurried, leisurely, measured, deliberate, ponderous, creeping, sluggish, snail-like. **2** *he was incorrectly labeled as slow* backward, retarded, slow-witted, dull-witted, stupid, dense; *inf.* dumb. **3** *the service being a bit slow* delayed, dilatory, unpunctual, tardy. **4** *a slow process* long-drawn-out, time-consuming, protracted, prolonged. **5** *a slow part of the world* sleepy, unprogressive, backward, stagnant. **6** *business being slow* slack, quiet, sluggish, dead. **7** *slow to make a decision* reluctant, hesitant, loath, unwilling, disinclined.

**slow** verb slow down **1** *slow down at the corner* reduce speed, decelerate, put the brakes on. **2** *weather slowed the runners down* hold back, keep back, delay, detain, restrain. **3** *workaholics told to slow down* take it easy, ease up, relax; *inf.* let up.

**sluggish** adjective **1** *feeling sluggish with a hangover* listless, slight, lethargic, languid, languorous, torpid, phlegmatic. **2** *business being sluggish* slow, slack, inactive, stagnant

**slumber** verb sleep, doze; *inf.* snooze; be in the land of Nod.

**slumber** noun sleep, doze; *inf.* snooze, shuteye.

**slump** noun *a slump in sales* plunge, falling-off, drop, downturn, slide, decline, decrease, depreciation, depression.

**slump** verb **1** *slump into a chair* collapse, sink, fall. **2** *prices slumped* plummet, plunge, nosedive, fall, drop, slide, decline, decrease.

**slur** verb *slur his words* mumble, stammer, drawl.

**slur** noun **1** *slurs made against/on her character* insult, slight, aspersion, imputation, smear, stain, stigma. **2** *avoid all suggestion of a slur* insult, affront, defamation, slander, libel, calumny.

**slut** noun trollop, hussy, prostitute, harlot, whore, streetwalker, *inf.* floozy, hooker.

**sly** adjective **1** *a sly character* cunning, crafty, wily, foxy, conniving, scheming, devious, shrewd. **2** *in a sly manner* furtive, underhand, stealthy, surreptitious, covert, clandestine. **3** *a sly smile* roguish, impish, mischievous, playful, arch. **on the sly** *have another job on the sly* secretly, stealthily, surreptitiously, covertly, clandestinely.

**smack** noun **1** *a smack on the face* slap, blow, whack, cuff, punch, rap, bang; *inf.* wallop, clout, swipe. **2** *the object hit the car with a smack* thud, thump, bang.

**smack** verb *smack him on the back* slap, hit, strike, whack, thump; *inf.* wallop, belt.

**smack** adverb *run smack into the police* headlong, right, straight, directly, bang, plumb.

**small** adjective **1** *a small toy* little, tiny, wee, petite, slight, minute, miniature, minuscule, diminutive, undersized, puny; *inf.* pocket-size, pint-sized. **2** *a small mistake* slight, minor, unimportant, trifling, trivial, insignificant, inconsequential. **3** *from small beginnings* humble, modest, lowly, simple, unpretentious. **4** *a small mind* narrow-minded, mean, petty.

**smart** adjective **1** *wedding guests looking smart* well-dressed, well turned out, fashionable, stylish, elegant, chic, spruce, trim; *inf.* natty, spiffy. **2** *smart children* clever, bright, intelligent, gifted, sharp, quick-witted, shrewd, ingenious. **3** *at a smart pace* brisk, quick, fast, swift, lively, energetic, spirited, vigorous.

**smart** verb *eyes smarting with the smoke* sting, burn, bite.

**smash** verb **1** *smash the dishes* break, shatter, pulverize, splinter. **2** *smash the car* crash, demolish, wreck. **3** *smash their hopes* destroy, ruin, shatter, devastate.

**smash** noun *hear the smash of dishes* breaking, shattering, crashing.

**smashing** adjective *a smashing time at the fair* marvelous, magnificent, sensational, stupendous, superb, wonderful, excellent, first-rate; *inf.* terrific, fantastic, super, great, fabulous.

**smattering** noun *a smattering of French* bit, modicum, rudiments.

**smear** verb **1** *children smearing paint on the walls* spread, daub, slap, plaster. **2** *smear the windows* smudge, streak, blur. **3** *smear his reputation* sully, tarnish, blacken, taint, stain, slur, defame, defile, vilify, slander, libel, calumniate.

**smear** noun **1** *a smear of paint on the walls* daub, spot, splotch. **2** *smears on the windows* smudge, streak. **3** *the smears on their reputation* taint, stain, slur, blot.

**smell** verb **1** *smell something rotten* sniff, get a whiff of. **2** *drains smelling* stink, reek, be malodorous.

**smell** noun **1** *the smells of the countryside* odor, scent, whiff. **2** *the smell of new-mown hay* scent, aroma, perfume, fragrance, bouquet, redolence. **3** *what a smell from the drains!* stink, stench, reek.

**smile** verb grin, beam.

**smirk** verb leer, sneer, simper, grin.

**smitten** adjective **smitten with** *smitten with the pretty girl* taken with, infatuated with, enamored of, captivated by, enchanted by; *inf.* bowled over by, swept off one's feet by.

**smog** noun haze, fog, pollution.

**smoke** verb **1** *fires smoking* smolder, reek. **2** *smoke the salmon* cure, dry, preserve.

**smoky** adjective **1** *a smoky atmosphere* smoke-filled, hazy, smoggy, murky. **2** *smoky walls* grimy, sooty.

**smolder** verb **1** *fires smoldering* smoke, reek. **2** *smoldering with resentment* seethe, fume, burn, boil, simmer.

**smooth** adjective **1** *paint smooth surfaces* even, level, flat, plane, flush, unwrinkled. **2** *smooth hair/tabletops* glossy, shiny, sleek, silky, satiny, polished, burnished. **3** *smooth sea* calm, still, tranquil, glassy. **4** *smooth progress* easy, effortless, trouble-free. **5** *the smooth running of the machine* steady, regular, rhythmic, uninterrupted, fluid. **6** *smooth young men* suave, urbane, courteous, gracious, glib, slick.

**smooth** verb **1** *smooth the surface* level, even, flatten, plane, steamroll. **2** *smooth the troubled situation* ease, soothe, pacify, calm, alleviate, appease, palliate. **3** *smooth his promotion* ease, facilitate, pave the way for, expedite, assist, help along.

**smother** verb **1** *nearly smothered by the fumes* suffocate, stifle, asphyxiate. **2** *smother them with kindness* overwhelm, shower, inundate, envelop. **3** *smother a fire* extinguish, dampen, snuff out. **4** *smother a laugh* stifle, muffle, suppress. **5** *smother the steak in onions* cover with, pile with, heap with.

**smudge** noun *smudges on the walls* mark, spot, smear, streak, stain, blotch, blot.

**smug** adjective self-satisfied, complacent, pleased with oneself, conceited.

**snack** noun light meal, refreshments, bite, tidbit; *inf.* bite to eat.

**snack** verb eat between meals, nibble, munch; *inf.* graze.

**snag** noun **1** *discover a snag in our plans* catch, drawback, hitch, stumbling block, obstacle, complication. **2** *a snag in her tights* rip, tear, run.

**snag** verb *snag one's tights* catch, rip, tear.

**snap** verb **1** *the rod/rope snapped* break, fracture, splinter, separate, crack. **2** *suddenly snap after years of stress* have a nervous breakdown, collapse, lose one's mind, go mad. **3** *snap one's fingers* | *burning logs popping and snapping* crack, click, crackle. **4** *dogs snapping* bite, nip. **5** *snap into action* hurry, hasten, rush, race. **6** *snapping at the children* speak sharply, bark, lash out; *inf.* fly off the handle. **snap out of it** get over it, recover, perk up; *inf.* pull oneself together, get a grip on oneself. **snap up** *snap up the bargains* snatch at, take advantage of, grab, seize, grasp, pounce upon.

**snap** noun **1** *a snap of one's fingers* | *the snap of twigs beneath our feet* crack, click, crackle. **2** *with a snap of its teeth* bite, nip. **3** *a snap of cold weather* spell, period, stretch, interval.

**snappy** adjective *a snappy dresser* smart, fashionable, stylish, chic, modish, dapper; *inf.* natty, spiffy, trendy. **make it snappy** hurry up, be quick, look lively; *inf.* get a move on, step on it.

**snare** verb **1** *snare rabbits* trap, catch, net. **2** *snare a rich spouse* ensnare, trap, catch, capture.

**snare** noun **1** *rabbits caught in a snare* trap, springe, net, noose. **2** *unaware of the snares set by the opposition* trap, pitfall, danger, hazard, peril.

**snarl**[1] verb **1** *dogs snarling* show one's teeth, growl. **2** *snarling at everyone first thing in the morning* snap, lash out; *inf.* fly off the handle.

**snarl**[2] verb **1** *ropes getting snarled* tangle, entangle, entwine, twist, knot. **2** *snarl plans for reorganization* complicate, confuse, muddle; *inf.* mess up.

**snatch** verb **1** *snatch the last sandwich from the plate* seize, grab, pluck. **2** *snatch the tourist's wallet* grab, steal, make off with, appropriate; *inf.* nab, swipe. **3** *snatch the millionaire's child* kidnap, abduct. **4** *snatch victory toward the end of the game* pluck, wrest, seize, secure.

**snatch** noun **1** *at one snatch* grab, pluck, grip, clutch. **2** *snatches of the broadcast* fragment, snippet, bit, scrap, piece.

**sneak** verb **1** *sneak out of the lecture* steal, creep, slip, slink. **2** *hear people sneaking around outside* creep, skulk, lurk, prowl. **3** *sneak a quick look* snatch, take, catch.

**sneer** verb *sneering rather than smiling* smirk, snicker, snigger. **sneer at** *sneer at their unsuccessful attempts* scoff at, scorn, disdain, mock, jeer at, ridicule, deride, insult.

**sneer** noun **1** *give a sneer* smirk, snicker. **2** *endure the sneers of her enemies* jeer, jibe, taunt, insult, slight.

**snicker** verb snigger, smirk, titter, giggle.

**sniff** verb **1** *people with colds sniffing* snuffle, sniffle. **2** *sniff the aroma of fresh-baked bread* smell, get a whiff of.

**sniff** noun **1** *the sniffs of people with colds* snuffle, sniffle. **2** *take a sniff of the sea air* smell, scent, whiff.

**snip** verb **1** *snip the piece of cloth* cut, nick, slit, notch, incise. **2** *snip off a lock of hair* cut, clip, dock, trim, crop, prune.

**snip** noun **1** *cut it with one snip* cut, nick, slit, notch, incision. **2** *snips of cloth* scrap, cutting, bit, piece, fragment, remnant, tatter.

**snobbish** adjective arrogant, proud, condescending, haughty, disdainful, supercilious, patronizing; *inf.* snooty, stuck-up, hoity-toity.

**snub** verb *snub him in public* ignore, disregard, shun, rebuff, repulse, spurn, slight, give the cold shoulder to; *inf.* give the brush-off to, put down.

**snub** noun *embarrassed by the snub* rebuff, slight, insult, affront; *inf.* brush-off, put-down.

**snug** adjective **1** *a snug little house* cozy, comfortable, warm, sheltered; *inf.* comfy. **2** *a snug fit* close-fitting, tight.

**snuggle** verb nestle, cuddle, nuzzle.

**soak** verb **1** *soaked by the rain* drench, saturate. **2** *soak the soiled dress in soapy water* steep, immerse, souse. **3** *ink soaking through the paper* permeate, penetrate, infuse, imbue.

**soar** verb **1** *birds/planes soaring into the air* fly, take flight, ascend, climb, rise. **2** *prices soaring* rise/increase rapidly, spiral, climb.

**sob** verb weep, cry, blubber, snivel, howl, bawl.

**sober** adjective **1** *he was drunk but is now sober* abstemious, teetotal, abstinent, temperate, moderate; *inf.* on the wagon, dry. **2** *sober speakers* serious, solemn, thoughtful, grave, earnest, composed, sedate, staid, dignified. **3** *discuss sober matters* serious, solemn, grave, important, crucial, weighty, ponderous. **4** *a sober account* factual, dispassionate, objective, rational, logical, circumspect. **5** *wearing sober clothes/colors* dark, somber, quiet, restrained, severe, austere.

**sociable** adjective social, friendly, affable, cordial, neighborly, companionable, gregarious, convivial, genial.

**social** adjective **1** *social problems* civic, public, societal. **2** *social clubs* entertainment, recreational, amusement. **3** *not a very social person* friendly, affable, gregarious. *See* SOCIABLE.

**society** noun **1** *enemies of society* civilization, the general public, the people, the community. **2** *urban and rural societies* community, culture, civilization. **3** *marry into society* high society, polite society, the aristocracy, the gentry, the upper classes, the elite; *inf.* the upper crust. **4** *enjoy the society of friends* company, companionship, fellowship, camaraderie. **5** *join a society* association, club, group, circle, fraternity, brotherhood, sisterhood, league, union, alliance, federation.

**sodden** adjective **1** *sodden clothes* soaking wet, drenched, saturated, sopping, dripping. **2** *sodden ground* saturated, soggy, boggy, swampy, waterlogged.

**soft** adjective **1** *soft ground* spongy, swampy, boggy, miry. **2** *pieces of a soft substance* pliable, supple, elastic, flexible, malleable. **3** *the soft surface of the curtains* smooth, velvety, cushiony, downy, silky, satiny; *inf.* like a baby's bottom. **4** *soft winds blowing* gentle, light, mild, calm, balmy, delicate. **5** *soft lights* low, faint, dim, subdued, muted, mellow. **6** *soft colors* pale, light, pastel, subdued, muted, understated. **7** *he spoke in soft tones* hushed, whispered, murmured, low, faint, quiet, mellow, melodious, mellifluous. **8** *soft words* sympathetic, kind, gentle, soothing, tender, affectionate, warm, sweet. **9** *teachers too soft with the students* easygoing, tolerant, lenient, indulgent, permissive, liberal, lax. **10** *too soft to be a good leader* tenderhearted, sensitive; spineless, feeble. **11** *soft muscles* flabby, flaccid, limp. **12** *lead a soft life* easy, comfortable; pampered, indulged; *inf.* cushy. **13** *soft in the head* feebleminded, simple, silly; *inf.* daft.

**soften** verb **1** *soften the blow* ease, cushion, temper, mitigate, assuage. **2** *the winds softened* abate, moderate, lessen, diminish, calm down. **3** *they softened their harsh approach* moderate, temper, tone down.

**soggy** adjective wet, saturated, sodden, boggy, swampy, waterlogged.

**soil** noun **1** *plant in light soil* earth, ground, dirt. **2** *on American soil* land, country, terra firma.

**soil** verb **1** *soil her white gloves* dirty, stain, muddy, spot, smudge. **2** *soil his reputation* sully, stain, taint, blot, smear.

**sojourn** noun stay, visit, stop, stopover; holiday, vacation.

**solace** noun *bring solace to the bereaved* comfort, consolation, condolence.

**soldier** noun fighter, warrior, trooper; *inf.* cannon fodder.

**solemn** adjective **1** *a solemn occasion* serious, grave, profound; formal. **2** *a solemn procession* dignified, ceremonious, stately, majestic. **3** *a solemn child* serious, somber, unsmiling; pensive, thoughtful. **4** *a solemn promise* earnest, sincere, heartfelt.

**solicit** verb **1** *solicit information* ask for, request, seek, beg, plead for. **2** *solicit him for financial help* ask, beg, beseech, implore, entreat, petition, importune, supplicate.

**solicitous** adjective *solicitous about your health* concerned, caring, attentive, anxious.

**solid** adjective **1** *a solid rather than liquid substance* firm, hard, dense, compressed. **2** *made of solid silver* pure, unalloyed, unadulterated, genuine. **3** *solid houses* sound, substantial, strong, sturdy, durable, well-built, stable. **4** *solid arguments* sound, well-founded, valid, logical, cogent, authoritative, convincing, plausible. **5** *a solid friendship* reliable, dependable, trustworthy, stable, steadfast. **6** *solid citizens* sensible, decent, law-abiding, upright. **7** *a solid company* financially sound, solvent, creditworthy, secure. **8** *a solid line of people* continuous, uninterrupted, unbroken, undivided. **9** *solid political support* unanimous, united, undivided.

**solidarity** noun *the solidarity of the workers* unity, unanimity, like-mindedness, team spirit, camaraderie, harmony, esprit de corps.

**solitary** adjective **1** *forced to lead a solitary life* reclusive, cloistered, lonely, companionless, friendless, antisocial, hermitical. **2** *seek a solitary spot for a honeymoon* lonely, remote, out-of-the-way, isolated, secluded, hidden, private, unfrequented, sequestered. **3** *a solitary tree on the horizon* lone, single, sole.

**solitude** noun loneliness, remoteness, isolation, seclusion, privacy.

**solution** noun **1** *the solution to the mathematical problem* answer, result, key, resolution. **2** *the solution of the problem will take years* solving, resolving, explanation, clarification, elucidation, unraveling. **3** *a solution of brine* suspension, emulsion, mixture, mix, blend, compound.

**solve** verb *solve the problem* answer, resolve, work out, figure out, fathom, decipher, clear up, unravel; *inf.* crack.

**solvent** adjective financially sound, debt-free, creditworthy; *inf.* in the black.

**somber** adjective **1** *dress in somber clothes* dark, dull, drab. **2** *in a somber mood* *a somber expression* gloomy, depressed, sad, melancholy, doleful, mournful, joyless, cheerless, lugubrious, funereal.

**sometimes** adverb *we see her sometimes* occasionally, on occasion, now and then, from time to time, once in a while, every so often, off and on.

**song** noun **1** *a beautiful song* tune, air, melody; ballad, ditty, chorus, chantey, carol, canticle. **2** *the song of the birds* warble, chirp, trill, whistle, pipe.

**sonorous** adjective **1** *the sonorous tones of the minister* deep, rich, full, round, resonant, ringing. **2** *a sonorous style of prose* majestic, lofty, grandiloquent, orotund.

**soon** adverb **1** *be there soon* shortly, in a little while, before long, in a moment, any minute, in the twinkling of an eye; *inf.* before you know it, before you can say Jack Robinson, pronto, in two shakes of a lamb's tale. **2** *How soon can you get here?* quickly, promptly, speedily.

**soothe** verb **1** *soothe the baby* quiet, calm, pacify, settle down, hush, lull, mollify. **2** *soothe the pain* ease, assuage, alleviate, allay, mitigate, palliate, lessen, reduce.

**soothsayer** noun seer, augur, prophet, diviner, sibyl.

**sophisticated** adjective **1** *sophisticated people* worldly, suave, urbane, cultured, refined, elegant, cosmopolitan. **2** *sophisticated production techniques* advanced, highly developed, ultramodern, complex, elaborate, intricate.

**soporific** adjective *soporific drugs* sleep-inducing, somnolent, sedative, tranquilizing, narcotic, opiate, somniferous.

**sorcery** noun black magic, magic, witchcraft, wizardry, necromancy, thaumaturgy.

**sordid** adjective **1** *a sordid creature* vile, foul, base, low, degenerate, despicable, ignoble. **2** *sordid moneylenders* mean, greedy, avaricious, mercenary. **3** *sordid hovels* filthy, dirty, foul, squalid, shabby, seedy, slummy.

**sore** adjective **1** *a sore leg* painful, aching, hurting, tender, inflamed, raw, irritated, bruised, injured. **2** *feel sore at her* distressed, upset, resentful, vexed, aggrieved, offended, hurt, annoyed, angry, irritated, irked, nettled; *inf.* peeved. **3** *in sore need of some food* dire, urgent, pressing, desperate, critical, acute, extreme.

**sore** noun *a sore on his leg* wound, scrape, abrasion, cut, laceration, abscess.

**sorrow** noun **1** *the sorrow of the widow* sadness, unhappiness, grief, misery, distress, heartache, anguish, suffering, wretchedness. **2** *one of the great sorrows of his life* worry, woe, misfortune, affliction, trial, tribulation.

**sorrowful** adjective *sorrowful expressions* sad, unhappy, tearful, woebegone, dejected, mournful, doleful, melancholy.

**sorry** adjective **1** *sorry for his actions* regretful, apologetic, repentant, penitent, remorseful, contrite, ashamed. **2** *feel sorry for them* sympathetic, full of pity, compassionate, moved, empathetic. **3** *sorry to hear about his accident* sad, unhappy, distressed, grieved, regretful. **4** *a sorry sight* wretched, miserable, pitiful, piteous, pathetic.

**sort** noun **1** *a different sort of plant/car* kind, type, variety, class, category, style, set, genre, genus, family, order, breed, make, brand. **2** *a good sort* person, individual, soul; *inf.* fellow, chap, guy. **out of sorts 1** *having been out of sorts with a bad cold* unwell, sick, ill, indisposed; *inf.* under the weather. **2** *avoid him when he is out of sorts* in a bad mood, ill-tempered, irritable, cross, testy, crotchety, grumpy, snappish. **3** *out of sorts after her broken engagement* in low spirits, dejected, depressed, downcast, glum, melancholy, miserable; *inf.* down.

**sort** verb *sort the potatoes according to size* classify, class, categorize, grade, group, divide, arrange, order, organize. **sort out 1** *sort out the weaker plants and dispose of them* separate out, segregate, sift, pick out, select. **2** *sort out the problem/mess* clear up, put right, solve, tidy up, put in order.

**so-so** adjective mediocre, average, indifferent, unexceptional, undistinguished, uninspiring, tolerable, passable.

**soul** noun **1** *the soul as opposed to the body* spirit, psyche, inner self, vital force. **2** *the soul of discretion* personification, embodiment, incarnation, essence, epitome. **3** *not a soul in sight* person, human being, individual, creature. **4** *the life and soul of the party* essence, heart, core, driving force. **5** *performed without soul* feeling, emotion, intensity, fervor, ardor, vitality, animation, energy, inspiration.

**sound** noun **1** *not a sound was heard* noise. **2** *she made not a sound* utterance, cry. **3** *the sound of the flute* noise, music, note, chord. **4** *they do not like the sound of her plans* impression, idea, tone, tenor. **5** *within sound of the church bells* hearing, distance, earshot, range.

**sound** verb **1** *sound the trumpet* play, blow. **2** *the trumpet sounded* resound, reverberate, resonate. **3** *sound the alarm* operate, set off, ring. **4** *sound the letter "f" or "t"* pronounce, utter, voice, enunciate, articulate, vocalize. **5** *sound a word of warning* utter, express, voice, pronounce, declare, announce.

**sound** adjective **1** *sound lungs* healthy, in good condition, physically fit, disease-free, undamaged, uninjured, in fine fettle. **2** *sound rafters in the building* solid, substantial, sturdy, well-constructed, intact. **3** *sound arguments* solid, well-founded, well-grounded, valid, reasonable, logical, cogent, authoritative, convincing, plausible. **4** *a sound judge of character* reliable, dependable, trustworthy, good, sensible, judicious, astute. **5** *sound business* solvent, creditworthy, solid, secure. **6** *a sound sleep* deep, undisturbed, untroubled. **7** *a sound thrashing* thorough, complete, out-and-out, severe.

**sour** adjective **1** *sour substances* tart, bitter, acid, acidulous, sharp, vinegary, pungent. **2** *sour milk* turned, curdled, fermented, rancid, bad. **3** *a sour old man* embittered, nasty, unpleasant, disagreeable, bad-tempered, irritable, crotchety, cross, peevish, grumpy; *inf.* grouchy.

**sour** verb *people soured by his treatment of them* embitter, disenchant, alienate; *inf.* turn off.

**source** noun **1** *the source of the river* wellspring, fountainhead, headwater. **2** *the source of the rumor* origin, derivation, cause, wellspring, fountainhead, provenance, originator. **3** *sources listed in the essay* reference, authority.

**souvenir** noun memento, keepsake, token, reminder, relic, memorabilia.

**sovereign** noun ruler, monarch, king, queen, emperor, empress, tsar, crowned head, potentate.

**sovereign** adjective **1** *sovereign power* supreme, absolute, unlimited. **2** *the children are her sovereign concern* chief, paramount, predominant, ruling. **3** *a sovereign state* independent, self-governing, autonomous. **4** *our sovereign lord* ruling, royal, regal, majestic, noble.

**sovereignty** noun **1** *hold sovereignty over adjoining states* supremacy, dominion, power, ascendancy, jurisdiction, control, sway. **2** *an island sovereignty* kingdom, realm, country.

**sow** verb **1** *sow seed* scatter, disperse, strew, disseminate, distribute, spread. **2** *sow a field with wheat* plant. **3** *sow doubt in their minds* implant, plant, lodge, instigate, foster.

**space** noun **1** *houses taking up a lot of space | not enough space for them all* room, expanse, capacity, area, volume, spaciousness, scope, elbowroom, leeway. **2** *a large space between houses* interval, gap, opening. **3** *write your name in the space provided* blank, gap. **4** *no spaces left in the theater* seat, place, berth, accommodation. **5** *green spaces at the edge of the city* expanse, stretch. **6** *within the space of three hours* time, duration, period, span, stretch, interval. **7** *staring into space* the blue, the vacuum, the void. **8** *travel in space* outer space, the universe, the galaxy, the solar system; infinity.

**space** verb **1** *space the trees around the garden* place at intervals, arrange, order. **2** *space out the plans* interspace, set apart.

**spacious** adjective *a spacious house | spacious grounds* roomy, commodious, capacious, sizable, large, ample, extensive, broad, wide, expansive.

**span** noun **1** *the span of the bird's wings* length, extent, reach, stretch, spread, distance. **2** *within a short span of time* duration, period, space, stretch, interval.

**span** verb **1** *a life spanning almost a century* extend over, stretch across, cover, range over. **2** *bridges spanning the Hudson* bridge, cross, traverse.

**spank** verb smack, slap, put over one's knee; *inf.* tan someone's hide, belt.

**spare** adjective **1** *a spare blanket* extra, additional, reserve, supplementary, auxiliary, surplus, supernumerary. **2** *have little spare time* free, leisure, unoccupied. **3** *of spare build* lean, thin, slim, slender, skinny, wiry, lank; *inf.* skin and bones. **4** *a spare helping* meager, frugal, scanty, skimpy, modest. **to spare** *a few plants to spare* left over, superfluous, surplus.

**spare** verb **1** *can you spare a few dollars?* afford, part with, give, provide, relinquish. **2** *spare the culprit* pardon, show mercy to, be lenient to; *inf.* let off. **3** *spare the tree from destruction* save, protect, guard, defend.

**sparing** adjective *be sparing with money* economical, frugal, thrifty, careful, prudent, cautious, parsimonious, niggardly; *inf.* stingy, tight-fisted.

**sparkle** verb **1** *lights/diamonds sparkling* twinkle, flicker, shimmer, flash, glitter, glint, wink, dance, shine, gleam, coruscate. **2** *people sparkling at the party* be vivacious, be animated, be effervescent, be witty. **3** *wine sparkling* bubble, effervesce.

**sparkle** noun **1** *the sparkle of lights on the river* twinkle, flicker, shimmer, flash, glitter, glint, winking, dancing, gleam, coruscation. **2** *require employees with some sparkle* vivacity, liveliness, animation, vitality, enthusiasm, dash, élan, panache; *inf.* pizzazz, zip, zing.

**sparse** adjective scanty, meager, slight, scattered.

**spartan** adjective *a spartan life* austere, harsh, stringent, rigorous, strict, severe, ascetic, abstemious.

**spasm** noun **1** *stomach spasms* contraction, convulsion, cramp, twitch. **2** *a spasm of coughing/laughter* fit, paroxysm, attack, bout, seizure, outburst.

**spasmodic** adjective intermittent, fitful, irregular, sporadic, periodic, recurrent.

**speak** verb **1** *speak the truth* utter, voice, express, say, pronounce, articulate, enunciate, state, tell. **2** *the lecturer spoke for two hours* talk, lecture, hold forth, discourse, orate. **3** *speak volumes with her eyes* convey, impart, suggest, communicate, express. **speak for** *a lawyer speaking for the accused* represent, act on behalf of, intercede for. **2** *speak for the motion* support, uphold, defend, advocate. **speak of** *speak of his faults* talk about, discuss, mention, refer to, allude to, comment on. **speak out/up** *speak up to be heard in the crowd* raise one's voice, make oneself heard. **2** *speak out against the cruelty* speak one's mind, sound off. **speak to 1** *she spoke to him angrily* address, talk to, converse with, have a word with. **2** *speak to the insubordinates* reprimand, rebuke, scold, lecture, admonish; *inf.* tell off. **3** *speak to the motion* comment on, touch upon, remark on.

**speaker** noun *an accomplished speaker* speech-maker, lecturer, orator, demagogue.

**spearhead** noun *the spearhead of the opposition* vanguard, forefront, driving force.

**spearhead** verb *spearhead the opposition* lead, head, initiate, launch, pioneer.

**special** adjective **1** *have a special talent* exceptional, remarkable, unusual, rare, extraordinary, singular, outstanding, unique. **2** *words with a special meaning* particular, individual, distinctive. **3** *take special care of it* especial, particular, exceptional. **4** *a special occasion* significant, momentous, memorable, festive, gala, red-letter. **5** *a special tool* specific, particular, custom-built. **6** *his special interest* particular, chief, main, major, primary.

**specialist** noun *a specialist in electronics* expert, authority, professional, consultant.

**specialty** noun **1** *many specialties in the field of medicine* area of specialization, field of study. **2** *putting people at ease is her specialty* forte, métier, talent, gift, claim to fame.

**species** noun *a species of plant* sort, kind, type, variety, class, category, genus, breed, genre.

**specific** adjective **1** *give very specific instructions* well-defined, clear-cut, unambiguous, unequivocal, exact, precise, explicit, express, detailed. **2** *for a specific purpose* particular, specified, fixed, set, distinct, definite.

**specify** verb *specify your housing requirements* state, name, stipulate, define, itemize, detail, list, spell out, enumerate.

**specimen** noun sample, representative, example, illustration, instance, exhibit.

**speck** noun **1** *specks of soot on the curtains* spot, fleck, stain, mark, smudge. **2** *not a speck of food left* particle, bit, atom, iota, grain, trace.

**speckled** adjective *speckled eggs/horses* mottled, flecked, spotted, dotted, dappled, brindled.

**spectacle** noun **1** *the spectacle of snow-capped mountains* sight, vision, scene, picture. **2** *the circus act was quite a spectacle* display, show, exhibition, extravaganza. **3** *making a spectacle of himself* laughingstock, fool, curiosity.

**spectacular** adjective striking, impressive, magnificent, splendid, breathtaking, glorious, dazzling, sensational, stunning, outstanding, extraordinary, dramatic, astonishing, singular.

**spectator** noun watcher, viewer, observer, onlooker, witness, bystander.

**specter** noun apparition, ghost, phantom, spirit, vision; *inf.* spook.

**speculate** verb **1** *speculate that he left unwillingly* conjecture, theorize, hypothesize, guess, surmise. **2** *speculate on their future* muse, reflect, deliberate, consider. **3** *speculate on the stock market* gamble, take a risk, venture.

**speech** noun **1** *express opinions in speech* communication, conversation, discussion, dialogue, colloquy. **2** *slurred speech* diction, articulation, enunciation, pronunciation. **3** *give an after-dinner speech* talk, lecture, address, discourse, oration, sermon, harangue. **4** *the speech of the Deep South* language, tongue, idiom, dialect, parlance; *inf.* lingo. **5** *given to obscene speech* utterance, remarks, comments.

**speechless** adjective **1** *speechless with rage* dumbstruck, dumbfounded. **2** *speechless with modesty* tongue-tied, inarticulate, dumb. **3** *speechless disappointment* silent, unspoken, tacit.

**speed** noun rapidity, swiftness, quickness, haste, expeditiousness, expedition, alacrity, celerity, velocity.

**speed** verb **1** *commuters speeding homeward* hurry, hasten, rush, race, dash, sprint, scurry, charge; *inf.* tear. **2** *speed their recovery* expedite, hasten, hurry up, accelerate, advance, facilitate, boost. **speed up 1** *I need to speed up to win the race* hurry up, rush, accelerate; *inf.* step on it. **2** *speed up the process* expedite, hasten. See SPEED verb 2.

**speedy** adjective **1** *a speedy form of transport | a speedy reply* rapid, swift, quick, fast, expeditious, fleet; prompt, immediate.

**spell**[1] noun **1** *recite a spell* incantation, conjuration, charm. **2** *put under a spell* trance, state of enchantment, enthrallment. **3** *fall under his spell* allure, charm, attraction, beguilement.

**spell**[2] noun **1** *a spell of warm weather* time, period, interval, stretch, span, patch. **2** *a spell of coughing* bout, fit. **3** *do a spell at the wheel* turn, stint, term, shift.

**spellbound** adjective riveted, entranced, enthralled, enraptured, rapt, bewitched, fascinated, captivated, mesmerized, hypnotized.

**spend** verb **1** *spend a great deal of money on clothes* pay out, lay out, expend, disburse; *inf.* fork out, shell out. **2** *spend hours on the task* occupy, fill, pass. **3** *spend a lot of effort* employ, apply, devote. **4** *soldiers having spent all their ammunition* use up, consume, exhaust, finish off, deplete.

**spendthrift** noun squanderer, prodigal, profligate, wastrel; *inf.* big spender.

**spendthrift** adjective *spendthrift habits* extravagant, prodigal, profligate, wasteful, improvident.

**spent** adjective **1** *a spent force* used up, consumed, exhausted, finished, depleted, drained; *inf.* played-out, burnt-out. **2** *feeling spent after the long walk* exhausted, worn-out, tired-out, fatigued, weary; *inf.* done in, bushed.

**spew** verb *lava spewing from the volcano* gush, pour, spurt, issue, discharge, spout.

**sphere** noun **1** *ornaments in the shape of spheres* globe, ball, orb, globule. **2** *spheres in the sky* planet, star, moon, celestial body. **3** *a limited sphere of influence* area, field, range, scope, extent, compass, jurisdiction. **4** *in the sphere of economics* field, discipline, specialty, domain, realm, province.

**spice** noun **1** *add spices to food* flavoring, seasoning, herb, condiment. **2** *add a bit of spice to food* flavor, piquancy, pungency, relish, tang, bite, zest, savor; *inf.* punch, kick. **3** *add spice to life* excitement, interest, color, zest, gusto, pep; *inf.* zip, zing.

**spicy** adjective **1** *spicy sauces* well-seasoned, sharp, tart, hot, peppery, piquant, pungent. **2** *spicy stories about her colleagues* lively, spirited, suggestive, risqué, racy, off-color; *inf.* raunchy.

**spill** verb **1** *milk spilling from the jug* pour, flow, overflow, brim over, slop. **2** *spill the scandalous details* reveal, disclose, divulge, leak; *inf.* blab.

**spin** verb **1** *wheels spinning* revolve, rotate, turn, circle, whirl, gyrate. **2** *spin around to face him* wheel, whirl, twirl, turn, twist, swivel, pirouette. **3** *spin a yarn about his successes* tell, relate, narrate, recount, concoct, invent, fabricate. **4** *her head was spinning* whirl, reel, swim. **spin out** *have to spin out his lecture* protract, draw out, drag out, prolong, extend, pad out.

**spin** noun **1** *a spin of the coin* turn, revolution, rotation, whirl, gyration. **2** *a spin in the car* drive, ride, trip, run, jaunt, journey, outing, turn; *inf.* joyride.

**spine** noun **1** *injure his spine* spinal column, vertebrae, vertebral column, backbone, dorsum. **2** *a weak man lacking spine* mettle, grit, pluck, determination, resolution, fortitude, courage, bravery, valor.

**spineless** adjective weak, feeble, indecisive, cowardly, timorous, timid, lily-livered; *inf.* chicken, yellow, yellow-bellied, gutless.

**spiral** adjective *spiral staircases* coiled, corkscrew, winding, twisting, whorled, helical, cochlear.

**spiral** noun *a spiral of smoke* coil, twist, whorl, corkscrew, curlicue, helix.

**spire** noun **1** *a church spire* steeple, belfry. **2** *mountain spires* peak, pinnacle, crest.

**spirit** noun **1** *a healthy body but a troubled spirit* soul, psyche, inner self, ego. **2** *the spirit of nature* vital spark, life force. **3** *haunted by spirits* apparition, ghost, phantom, specter, wraith; *inf.* spook. **4** *take the criticism in the wrong spirit* attitude, way, mood, frame of mind, humor. **5** *the spirit of the age* ethos, essence, quintessence, embodiment, quiddity. **6** *lack the spirit to carry out the task* courage, mettle, pluck, grit, willpower, motivation, backbone, stoutheartedness, vigor, energy, determination, resoluteness; *inf.* guts, spunk. **7** *play the song with spirit* animation, liveliness, vivacity, enthusiasm, fervor, fire, passion, energy, verve, zest, dash, élan; *inf.* pizzazz, zing, zip. **8** *the spirit of the new rule* implication, essence, gist, tenor, drift, meaning, sense, purport. **spirit away** *spirit away the celebrity from the photographers* whisk away, carry off, make off with, snatch, seize.

**spirited** adjective **1** *put up a spirited defense* courageous, brave, valiant, valorous, heroic, plucky, gritty. **2** *a spirited playing of the song* animated, lively, vivacious, enthusiastic, fiery, passionate, energetic.

**spiritual** adjective **1** *spiritual needs* incorporeal, ethereal, intangible, otherworldly, unworldly. **2** *spiritual music* religious, sacred, divine, holy, ecclesiastic, devotional.

**spit** verb **1** *not allowed to spit in public* expectorate, hawk. **2** *spit blood* discharge, issue, eject. **3** *"get out," he spat* hiss, rasp, snort.

**spit** noun spittle, saliva, sputum.

**spite** noun *say it out of spite* malice, illwill, malevolence, malignance, hostility, resentment, rancor, envy, hatred, vengefulness, vindictiveness. **in spite of** *happy in spite of being poor* despite, notwithstanding, regardless of.

**spite** verb *do it to spite her sister* annoy, harass, irritate, vex, provoke, peeve, pique, frustrate.

**spiteful** adjective malicious, malevolent, venomous, hostile, resentful, snide, rancorous, vengeful, vindictive, splenetic.

**splash** verb **1** *splash water/paint around* spatter, sprinkle, spray, shower, splatter, slosh, slop. **2** *waves splashing against the rocks* dash, beat, batter, buffet, break, wash, surge. **3** *children splashing about in water* paddle, wade, wallow, dabble. **4** *his name splashed across the newspapers* blazon, exhibit, plaster, broadcast, trumpet.

**splash** noun **1** *the splash of water against the rocks* dashing, beating, battering. **2** *splashes of mud on the walls* spot, splotch, smudge, smear. **3** *the scandal made a frontpage splash* display, exhibition, sensation. **4** *a splash of color* patch, burst, streak. **make a splash** cause a sensation, cause a stir, attract attention.

**spleen** noun *vent one's spleen on the innocent* bad temper, ill-humor, irritability, irascibility, peevishness, cantankerousness, resentment, spitefulness, bitterness, hostility, rancor, maliciousness, malevolence, bile.

**splendid** adjective **1** *splendid furnishings* magnificent, imposing, superb, grand, sumptuous, resplendent, opulent, luxurious, gorgeous, elegant. **2** *a splendid reputation* distinguished, impressive, illustrious, brilliant, notable, outstanding, eminent, celebrated, venerable. **3** *splendid colors* glorious, brilliant, gleaming, radiant, dazzling, refulgent. **4** *a splendid meal* excellent, fine, first-rate, marvelous, wonderful; *inf.* fantastic, terrific, fabulous.

**splendor** noun **1** *the splendor of the furnishings* magnificence, grandeur, sumptuousness, opulence, luxury, luxuriousness, elegance. **2** *the splendor of his reputation* illustriousness, brilliance, eminence, renown. **3** *the splendor of the colors* gloriousness, brilliance, radiance.

**splinter** noun *splinters of wood* sliver, fragment, shiver, shard, chip, shaving, shred, bit.

**splinter** verb *the glass splintered* break into fragments, shatter, shiver, fracture.

**split** verb 1 *split the material in two* break, chop, cut, hew, cleave, rip, tear, slash, snap, rive. 2 *split the party in two* divide, separate, sever, sunder, bisect, partition. 3 *split the profits* share, divide, halve, apportion, distribute, parcel out, allocate; *inf.* divvy. 4 *the road splits over the hill* divide, fork, bifurcate. 5 *her husband split* leave, depart, take off, decamp, exit; *inf.* push off, shove off. **split up** *the couple split up* break up, separate, part, part company, become estranged, divorce.

**split** noun 1 *a split in the material* break, cut, rent, rip, tear, slash, slit, crack, fissure, breach. 2 *a split in the political party* division, rift, schism, rupture, separation.

**spoil** verb 1 *spoil the material by washing it* damage, disfigure, injure, harm, ruin, destroy. 2 *spoil our plans* upset, mess up, ruin, destroy, wreck. 3 *spoil her little boy* pamper, overindulge, mollycoddle, cosset, coddle, baby, spoonfeed. 4 *the food will spoil* go bad, turn, rot, become tainted, decompose, decay.

**spoils** plural noun 1 *the spoils of high rank* benefit, advantage, gain, profit. 2 *divide up the spoils from the burglary* booty, loot, plunder, pickings.

**spoken** adjective oral, verbal, voiced, expressed, unwritten.

**spokesman** noun spokeswoman, spokesperson, mouthpiece, voice, negotiator, mediator, representative.

**sponsor** noun *a sponsor of the new art gallery* patron, backer, promoter, guarantor, supporter; *inf.* angel.

**sponsor** verb *companies sponsoring the softball teams* back, fund, finance, promote, subsidize, support.

**spontaneous** adjective 1 *spontaneous offers of help* voluntary, unforced, unconstrained. 2 *a spontaneous vote of thanks* unplanned, unpremeditated, unrehearsed, impromptu, extempore, spur-of-the-moment, extemporaneous. 3 *a spontaneous smile* instinctive, involuntary, automatic, impulsive.

**sporadic** adjective irregular, intermittent, scattered, occasional.

**sport** noun 1 *play a variety of sports* physical activity, game, physical exercise, recreation, pastime, athletics. 2 *flying kites for sport* amusement, entertainment, diversion, play, fun, pleasure, enjoyment. **make sport of** make fun of, laugh at, poke fun at, mock, jeer at, ridicule.

**sporting** adjective *a sporting gesture* sportsmanlike, fair, honorable, generous.

**spot** noun 1 *black spots on the cloth* mark, dot, speck, fleck, smudge, stain, blotch, splotch, patch. 2 *a spot on her face* pimple, blemish, pustule, boil, pock. 3 *a dark spot on her reputation* stain, blemish, flaw, brand, stigma. 4 *a picnic spot* area, place, site, location, scene, setting, situation. 5 *a regular spot on the program* place, position, niche. 6 *in a spot* difficulty, mess, plight, predicament, quandary, tight corner; *inf.* fix, jam.

**spot** verb 1 *spot someone following him* catch sight of, notice, observe, espy, discern, detect. 2 *the mud spotted her dress* mark, stain, dirty, soil, spatter.

**spotless** adjective 1 *spotless houses* clean, ultraclean, spick-and-span, immaculate, shining, gleaming. 2 *of spotless character* pure, flawless, faultless, unsullied, untainted, unimpeachable.

**spotted** adjective 1 *a spotted dog/horse* dappled, mottled, pied, piebald, speckled. 2 *a spotted dress* polka-dot, flecked.

**spout** verb 1 *oil spouting from the well* spurt, gush, spew, squirt, erupt, disgorge, pour, spray. 2 *tired of politicians spouting* declaim, orate, rant, harangue, speechify, sermonize.

**sprawl** verb 1 *people sprawling on the sofa* stretch out, lounge, repose, recline, flop, loll. 2 *suburbs sprawling out into the countryside* spread, stretch, spill, ramble.

**spray** noun 1 *a spray from the well* shower, jet, mist, drizzle, foam, froth. 2 *buy a deodorant spray* atomizer, vaporizer, aerosol.

**spray** verb disperse, disseminate, sprinkle, shower.

**spread** verb 1 *spread the map out* stretch, extend, unfurl, unroll. 2 *the town is spreading out* stretch out, extend, enlarge, widen, grow, develop, branch out. 3 *the view spread out before them* stretch out, unfold, be unveiled, be revealed. 4 *spread manure on the fields* lay, put, apply, smear; *inf.* plaster. 5 *spread the bread with butter* cover, coat, layer. 6 *the disease is spreading* mushroom, extend, advance, proliferate, escalate. 7 *spread rumors* disseminate, circulate, transmit, broadcast, publicize, propagate, promulgate, bruit.

**spread** noun 1 *measure the spread of the bird's wings* extent, stretch, span, reach, compass, sweep. 2 *the spread of the disease* advance, expansion, proliferation, escalation, diffusion. 3 *the spread of rumors* dissemination, circulation, transmission, broadcasting, publicizing, propagation. 4 *a birthday spread* feast, banquet, repast.

**spree** noun outing, fling, revel, orgy, debauch, bacchanal; *inf.* binge.

**sprightly** adjective spry, lively, energetic, agile, nimble, spirited, brisk, jaunty, perky.

**spring** verb **1** *springing to his feet* jump, leap, bound, vault, hop. **2** *her family springs from a relative of James Madison* descend, originate, derive, issue. **3** *disapproval springs from ignorance* originate, derive, stem, arise, emanate, proceed, start. **4** *spring his resignation on them* present unexpectedly, introduce suddenly. **spring back** *the branch sprang back* rebound, recoil. **spring up** *new houses springing up everywhere* appear, shoot up, mushroom, burgeon, crop up; *inf.* pop up.

**spring** noun **1** *reach her in one spring* jump, leap, bound, vault. **2** *a mattress with little spring* springiness, bounce, elasticity, resilience, flexibility, stretch, recoil, tensility. **3** *put a spring in his step* bounce, buoyancy, liveliness, lightheartedness.

**sprinkle** verb **1** *sprinkle water on the grass* spray, shower, splash, trickle, spatter. **2** *sprinkle salt on the icy steps* scatter, strew. **3** *sprinkle the cake with powdered sugar* dust, powder.

**sprinkling** noun **1** *a sprinkling of snow on the ground* scattering, dusting. **2** *only a sprinkling of people in the audience* handful, trickle.

**sprint** verb *sprinting for the bus* run, race, rush, dash; *inf.* scoot, tear.

**sprout** verb **1** *deer sprouting antlers* send forth, grow, develop. **2** *potatoes sprouting* bud, germinate. **3** *weeds sprouting up everywhere* shoot up, spring up, grow, develop, appear, mushroom, proliferate.

**spry** adjective sprightly, lively, energetic, active, agile, nimble, quick.

**spunk** noun courage, bravery, valor, pluck, mettle, daring, spirit, backbone; *inf.* guts.

**spur** noun **1** *the use of spurs to speed up the animals* goad, prick, prod. **2** *act as a spur to his ambition* stimulus, incentive, encouragement, impetus. **on the spur of the moment** impulsively, on impulse, impetuously, suddenly, unexpectedly, out of the blue.

**spur** verb **1** *spur the animal to go faster* goad, prick, prod. **2** *his early success spurred him on to try hard* stimulate, induce, encourage, motivate, prompt, urge, impel.

**spurious** adjective counterfeit, fraudulent, fake, bogus, sham, contrived, fictitious, deceitful, specious; *inf.* phony.

**spurn** verb reject, repulse, rebuff, repudiate, snub, slight, disdain, scorn.

**spurt** verb *oil spurting from the well* gush, squirt, shoot, surge, pour, stream, flow, issue, emanate.

**spurt** noun **1** *a spurt of water* gush, jet, spray. **2** *a sudden spurt of energy/speed* burst, fit, surge. **3** *put on a spurt at the end* burst of speed, sprint, rush.

**spy** noun *documents stolen by an enemy spy* enemy agent, foreign agent, secret agent, undercover agent, operative, informer; *inf.* mole.

**spy** verb *spy someone on the horizon* catch sight of, spot, see, notice, observe, discern. **spy on** *spy on the rival firm* keep under surveillance, watch, observe, shadow; *inf.* tail.

**squabble** noun quarrel, row, dispute, argument, tiff; *inf.* scrap, spat.

**squabble** verb quarrel, argue, bicker, wrangle; *inf.* scrap.

**squalid** adjective **1** *squalid hovels* dirty, filthy, grubby, grimy, slumlike, wretched, mean, nasty, seedy, slovenly, neglected, dilapidated, ramshackle. **2** *squalid tales of corruption* sordid, vile, nasty, shameful.

**squander** verb *squander his savings on bad investments* waste, misspend, dissipate, fritter away, run through; *inf.* blow.

**square** noun **1** *a band playing in the square* town square, village square, market square, quadrangle. **2** *regard parents as squares* old fogy, traditionalist, conformist; *inf.* stick-in-the-mud, fuddy-duddy.

**square** adjective **1** *a businessman square in all his dealings* fair, just, equitable, honest, straight, aboveboard; *inf.* on the level. **2** *regard her parents as being square* old-fashioned, behind the times, conservative, conventional, straitlaced, stuffy; *inf.* fuddy-duddy.

**square** verb **1** *the two accounts do not square with each other* tally, agree, correspond, fit, conform, harmonize. **2** *square the bill* settle, pay, discharge. **3** *square matters before we go* straighten out, set right, put in order.

**squash** verb **1** *squash the berries with a spoon* crush, squeeze, flatten, compress, smash, mash, pulverize. **2** *the audience was squashed into the hall* crowd, crush, cram, pack, jam, squeeze, wedge. **3** *squash the rebellion* put down, quash, quell, crush, suppress, squelch.

**squat** verb *squat behind the hedge* crouch, sit on one's heels.

**squat** adjective *a squat figure* dumpy, stubby, chunky, stocky.

**squeak** verb **1** *mice squeaking* squeal, peep, whimper. **2** *gates squeaking in the wind* creak, scrape, grate.

**squeal** verb **1** *children squealing with pain/excitement* shriek, yell, scream, howl, shout, cry, wail. **2** *the burglar squealing on his associates* inform, tell tales on; *inf.* blow the whistle on, rat, snitch.

**squeamish** adjective queasy, nauseous, sickish, sick.

**squeeze** verb 1 *squeeze the sweater to re-move moisture* wring, twist, press. 2 *squeeze the juice from the orange* extract, press, force, express. 3 *squeeze the oranges* compress, crush, squash, mash. 4 *squeeze his arm* grip, clutch, pinch, compress. 5 *the audience was squeezed into the hall* crowd, crush, cram, pack, jam, squash, wedge. 6 *squeeze his fiancée* embrace, hug, cuddle, clasp, hold tight. 7 *squeeze money out of them* extort, wring, wrest, pressure, strong-arm, blackmail; *inf.* bleed.

**squeeze** noun 1 *give his fiancée a squeeze* embrace, hug, cuddle. 2 *give her hand a squeeze* clasp, grip, grasp, clutch. 3 *it was a bit of a squeeze in the hall* crowd, crush, jam, press, congestion. 4 *a squeeze of lemon juice* drop, dash, bit.

**squirm** verb wriggle, wiggle, writhe, twist, turn, shift.

**squirt** verb 1 *squirt water from a water pistol* discharge, expel, shoot, spurt. 2 *water squirting from the water pistol* eject, discharge, spurt, spout, stream, spray, gush, surge. 3 *squirting people with water* splash, wet, spray, shower, sprinkle.

**squirt** noun 1 *a squirt of water* jet, stream, spray, flow. 2 *a nasty little squirt* insignificant person; *inf.* pipsqueak, twerp.

**stab** verb knife, pierce, puncture, stick, skewer, gash, slash.

**stab** noun 1 *receive a stab in the leg* puncture, gash, slash, incision. 2 *feel a stab in the chest* pain, shooting pain, pang, twinge, spasm. 3 *take a stab at writing a novel* try, attempt, endeavor, essay, effort, venture; *inf.* go, shot, crack.

**stability** noun 1 *the stability of the structures | the stability of their relationship* firmness, solidity, steadiness, secureness, strength, stoutness, sturdiness, sureness, durability, constancy, permanence, reliability, dependability. 2 *question her stability* soundness, sense, responsibility, self-control, sanity.

**stable** adjective 1 *stable structures* firm, solid, steady, secure, fixed, strong, fast, stout, sturdy, immovable. 2 *a stable relationship* secure, strong, sure, steadfast, unwavering, unfaltering, deep-rooted, well-grounded, abiding, durable, enduring, lasting, permanent, reliable, dependable. 3 *a stable person* well-balanced, sound, steady, sensible, responsible, sane.

**stack** noun 1 *a stack of logs* heap, pile, store, stock, stockpile, mound, mountain. 2 *a stack of money* abundance, amplitude; *inf.* load, heap, ton, scads.

**stack** verb *stack logs* heap, pile, accumulate, store, stockpile.

**stadium** noun arena, field, amphitheater, coliseum; ballpark.

**staff** noun 1 *a shepherd's staff* rod, pole; stick, cane, crook. 2 *the staff of office* rod, mace, scepter. 3 *reduce staff in the office* employees, workers, workforce, personnel.

**stage** noun 1 *a stage in the development* period, step, juncture, level. 2 *the last stage of a journey* lap, leg, phase. 3 *stand on a stage in the theater* platform, dais, rostrum, podium. 4 *the stage for many international meetings* setting, scene, site, arena, backdrop. **the stage** *a career connected with the stage* the theater, drama, show business.

**stage** verb 1 *stage a production of Shakespeare* produce, direct, perform, mount, present. 2 *stage a protest rally* arrange, organize, engineer, orchestrate.

**stagger** verb 1 *stagger drunkenly up the road* reel, sway, teeter, totter, wobble, lurch. 2 *staggered by the price of the toys* amaze, astound, dumbfound, astonish, flabbergast, shock, stupefy, stun. 3 *stagger the lines of bricks* alternate, vary, step.

**stagnant** adjective 1 *stagnant water* still, motionless, standing, stale, brackish. 2 *stagnant business economy* sluggish, slow-moving, inactive, static.

**staid** adjective sedate, quiet, serious, sober, proper, decorous, formal, prim, stiff.

**stain** verb 1 *fabric stained with rust* soil, discolor, smudge, smear. 2 *stain her reputation* blacken, tarnish, sully, blemish, mar, besmirch, taint. 3 *stain the wood* varnish, dye, paint.

**stain** noun 1 *the stains made by the blood* mark, spot, blotch, blemish, smudge, smear. 2 *stains on her character* blemish, taint, blot, slur, stigma. 3 *use a brown stain on the wood* varnish, dye, paint.

**stake**¹ noun *stakes for plants to grow up* post, pole, stick, upright, rod, spike.

**stake**² noun 1 *card players laying down $50 stakes* wager, bet, ante. 2 *have a stake in the firm* financial interest, share, investment.

**stake**³ verb *stake $10 on the race | stake his life on the outcome* wager, bet, gamble, chance, venture, risk, hazard.

**stale** adjective 1 *stale bread/cheese* dry, hard, hardened, moldy. 2 *stale air* stuffy, close, musty, fusty. 3 *stale beer* flat, sour, turned, spoiled. 4 *stale jokes* hackneyed, tired, worn-out, threadbare, banal, trite, stock, clichéd.

**stalemate** noun *reach a stalemate in their talks* deadlock, impasse, standstill, standoff.

**stalk** noun *the stalk of a plant* stem, branch, shaft.

**stalk** verb pursue, follow, shadow, hunt; *inf.* tail.

**stall** noun **1** *the vendor's stall* booth, stand, kiosk. **2** *animals in their stalls* pen, coop, sty, corral.

**stall** verb **1** *stall until he thinks of the answer* play for time, delay, hem and haw; *inf.* drag one's feet. **2** *stall his creditors* hold off, stave off, keep at bay, evade, avoid.

**stalwart** adjective **1** *stalwart young men* strong, sturdy, robust, hardy, brawny, strapping, burly, rugged. **2** *stalwart adventurers* brave, courageous, valiant, intrepid, heroic, bold, daring, adventurous.

**stamina** noun endurance, staying power, fortitude, strength, vigor, energy, robustness, toughness; *inf.* grit.

**stammer** verb stutter, stumble, mumble, splutter, hesitate, falter.

**stamp** verb **1** *stamp his name on the book* imprint, inscribe, engrave, emboss. **2** *her last words stamped on his mind* imprint, impress, fix. **3** *he was stamped a criminal* brand, characterize, categorize, style, term, label, dub, tag. **stamp out** *stamp out the rebellion* quash, suppress, put down, quell, crush, squelch, extinguish, eradicate, eliminate.

**stamp** noun have the stamp of genius mark, hallmark, label, quality.

**stampede** noun charge, rush, flight.

**stand** verb **1** *ask the children to stand* rise, get to one's feet, get up. **2** *a house once stood there* be situated, be located. **3** *stand the ladder against the wall* set, place, put, position. **4** *the orders stand* remain in force, remain valid, hold. **5** *unable to stand his attitude* put up with, tolerate, bear, take, endure, abide, suffer, brook, countenance, cope with; *inf.* stomach. **stand by 1** *stand by his friend* support, back, uphold, be loyal to, defend, stick up for, champion, side with. **2** *stand by his word* adhere to, stick to, observe. **3** *soldiers asked to stand by* wait, be prepared. **stand for 1** *what do the initials stand for?* represent, mean, signify, denote, imply, symbolize. **2** *he stands for all that is good* advocate, favor, support, uphold, promote. **3** *refuse to stand for her behavior* tolerate, bear. *See* STAND 5. **stand in for** *stand in for the leading lady* replace, act as substitute for, cover for, act as understudy for. **stand out 1** *sculptures standing out from the building* project, jut out, protrude, extend, stick out. **2** *she stood out in the crowd* be noticeable, be conspicuous, be striking, be distinctive, be prominent, attract attention, catch the eye. **stand up 1** *that argument will not stand up in court* be valid, have force, be effective, be plausible. **2** *stand her up on a date* fail to meet, let down. **stand up for 1** *stand up for his friend in trouble* support, defend, champion. *See* STAND BY 1.

**2** *stand up for what one believes* uphold, promote, argue for. **stand up to** *stand up to the bully* confront, face up to, brave, defy, challenge.

**stand** noun **1** *come to a stand* standstill, halt, stop. **2** *take a stand against the new policies* defensive position, resistance, opposition. **3** *take a liberal stand* stance, standpoint, position, line, policy, attitude. **4** *selling books in his stand* stall, booth, kiosk. **5** *put books in stands* display case, shelf, rack, frame. **6** *give a speech from the stand* platform, stage, dais, rostrum.

**standard** noun **1** *a standard by which quality is judged* yardstick, benchmark, gauge, measure, criterion, touchstone, paradigm, ideal, archetype, principle, law, canon. **2** *works of a low standard* level, grade, quality, worth, merit. **3** *raise the battle standard* flag, banner, pennant, streamer, ensign, colors. **4** *trees supported by standards* support, prop, post, upright. **5** *maintain old-fashioned standards* principle, code of behavior, code of honor, morals, ethics, ideals.

**standard** adjective **1** *standard shoe sizes* usual, ordinary, average, normal, common, regular, stock, conventional. **2** *the standard work on Shakespeare* definitive, classic, recognized, accepted, authoritative.

**standardize** verb make uniform, regulate, systematize, normalize.

**standing** noun **1** *his standing in the community* status, rank, position, station, footing, place, circumstances. **2** *people of standing in the community* reputation, repute, eminence, prominence, note. **3** *her husband of many years' standing* duration, continuance, endurance.

**standoffish** adjective aloof, distant, cool, remote, detached, unapproachable.

**standpoint** noun *from the standpoint of the customer* point of view, viewpoint, perspective, angle, frame of reference.

**staple** adjective *staple foods* primary, main, principal, basic, fundamental, essential, indispensable, necessary.

**star** noun **1** *stars in the sky* heavenly body; planet, asteroid. **2** *born under a lucky star* destiny, fate, fortune, lot. **3** *read his stars* horoscope, forecast, augury. **4** *one of the stars of the film* principal, leading lady, leading man, lead. **5** *some of the stars on the local council* celebrity, dignitary, notable, name; *inf.* VIP, big shot.

**stare** verb *stare into space* gaze, gape, look; *inf.* gawk.

**stark** adjective **1** *in stark contrast* sharp, obvious, evident, clear, clear-cut. **2** *a stark landscape* desolate, bare, barren, vacant, empty, forsaken, bleak, grim, harsh. **3** *stark madness* sheer, utter, absolute, downright, out-and-out, outright, total, complete, pure, unmitigated, unqualified, consummate, patent. **4** *the stark facts* bald, bare, simple, blunt, straightforward, unadorned, unembellished, harsh, grim.

**stark** adverb *stark (raving) mad* completely, totally, entirely, wholly, altogether, utterly, absolutely, quite. **stark naked** nude, bare, undressed, unclad, au naturel; *inf.* in the buff, in the altogether, in the raw, in one's birthday suit.

**start** verb **1** *when her illness started* commence, get underway, begin, appear, come into existence, arise, originate, crop up. **2** *have to start now to finish the job in time* begin, commence, get going, get things moving, buckle down, start the ball rolling; *inf.* get moving, get down to business, get the show on the road, kick off. **3** *start now to be there by tonight* set out, depart, leave; *inf.* hit the road, push off. **4** *start the machine* set in motion, turn on, activate. **5** *start the campaign* set up, establish, create, institute, initiate, launch, originate, pioneer, organize; *inf.* kick off. **6** *start in pain* jump, jerk, twitch, recoil, flinch, wince, shy. **7** *chipmunks starting out of the bushes* jump, leap, spring, bound, dart.

**start** noun **1** *present at the start of the event* beginning, commencement, opening, inception, inauguration, dawn, birth; *inf.* kickoff. **2** *at the start of her illness* beginning, onset, emergence. **3** *the start of the trouble* origin, source, root, basis, derivation, wellspring. **4** *at the start of the campaign* establishment, foundation, institution, launch, origination. **5** *get a start in the race* head start, advantage, edge, lead, jump. **6** *finally got her start in show business* opening, opportunity, chance, introduction; *inf.* break. **7** *give a start from the pain* jump, leap, jerk, twitch, wince.

**startle** verb disturb, agitate, perturb, unsettle, frighten, alarm, surprise, astonish.

**starvation** noun extreme hunger, famine, fasting, malnourishment.

**starving** adjective starved, famished, ravenous, malnourished, fasting; *inf.* able to eat a horse.

**state** noun **1** *in its previous state* condition, shape, situation, circumstances, state of affairs, position. **2** *in a nervous state* condition, mood, humor, frame of mind. **3** *she often gets into a state* state of agitation, panic, fluster, pother; *inf.* flap, tizzy. **4** *look at the state of this room* mess, chaos, disorder, disarray, confusion, clutter. **5** *a meeting of the world's states* country, nation, land, realm, kingdom, republic. **6** *feel the state is too powerful* government, administration, establishment. **7** *occasions of state* pomp, ceremony, display, majesty, grandeur.

**state** verb *state one's objections* express, voice, utter, declare, set out, assert, announce, pronounce, articulate, present.

**stately** adjective ceremonial, dignified, solemn, majestic, royal, regal, magnificent, grand, splendid, elegant, imposing, impressive, august, lofty, pompous; measured, deliberate.

**statement** noun *a statement of one's views* declaration, account, recitation, report, assertion, announcement, pronouncement, articulation, presentation.

**static** adjective unmoving, unvarying, changeless, constant, steady, stationary, motionless.

**station** noun **1** *get the bus at the bus station* terminus, terminal, stop, depot. **2** *police station* base, office, headquarters, seat. **3** *security staff at their stations* post, place, position, location. **4** *different stations in life* class, level, rank, grade, standing, status, caste.

**stationary** adjective **1** *stationary traffic* unmoving, motionless, at a standstill. **2** *stationary price patterns* unchanging, constant, unvarying.

**statuesque** adjective dignified, stately, majestic, magnificent, imposing, regal.

**stature** noun **1** *ill-developed in stature* height, tallness, size. **2** *catering to people of stature* status, importance, standing, consequence, eminence, prominence, note, fame, renown.

**status** noun *of uncertain social status* standing, rank, level, grade, position, importance.

**staunch** adjective *staunch supporters* loyal, faithful, dependable, reliable, steadfast, unswerving, unwavering, unfaltering.

**stay** verb **1** *stay there till we call you* remain, wait, continue, delay, tarry. **2** *stay loyal to him* remain, continue to be. **3** *stay judgment until tomorrow* put off, postpone, suspend, defer, delay. **4** *stay the progress of the disease* check, curb, arrest, stop, delay, hold, prevent, hinder, impede, obstruct. **5** *stay at a hotel* lodge, take a room, visit, reside, dwell.

**stay** noun **1** *a brief stay at a hotel* visit, sojourn, stop, vacation. **2** *a stay of judgment* postponement, suspension, adjournment, deferment, delay. **3** *a stay in his old age* prop, support, brace, bolster, buttress.

**steadfast** adjective **1** *a steadfast friend* faithful, loyal, true, constant, devoted, dependable, reliable, staunch. **2** *steadfast in his views* steady, firm, determined, resolute, unchanging, unwavering, unfaltering. **3** *a steadfast gaze* steady, fixed, intent, immovable, unwavering, unfaltering.

**steady** adjective **1** *make the posts steady* firm, fixed, stable, secure. **2** *a steady hand* still, unshaking, motionless, sure. **3** *a steady gaze* steadfast, fixed, immovable, unwavering, unfaltering. **4** *a steady faith* constant, unchanging, invariable, continuous, ceaseless, perpetual, persistent, unremitting, unending, endless. **5** *walk at a steady pace* uniform, even, regular, rhythmic, consistent. **6** *a steady boyfriend* regular, habitual, usual, customary. **7** *a steady young man* balanced, sensible, level-headed, rational, down-to-earth, calm, equable, reliable, dependable.

**steal** verb **1** *steal money* take, misappropriate, pilfer, purloin, filch, walk off with, embezzle, pocket, shoplift; *inf.* pinch, swipe, rip off. **2** *steal someone else's work* plagiarize, copy, pirate, appropriate, poach; *inf.* lift. **3** *steal a child* kidnap, snatch, abduct, seize, shanghai. **4** *steal a kiss* snatch, obtain surreptitiously. **5** *steal out of the room* slip, tiptoe, sneak, creep, slink, glide.

**stealth** noun *get into the house by stealth* secrecy, furtiveness, surreptitiousness, slyness, covertness.

**stealthy** adjective *stealthy maneuvers* secret, furtive, surreptitious, sly, sneaky, clandestine, covert, underhand, undercover.

**steep** adjective **1** *steep cliffs* sheer, abrupt, precipitous, perpendicular, vertical. **2** *a steep rise in share prices* sharp, rapid, sudden, precipitate. **3** *prices at that restaurant are a bit steep* high, costly, expensive, excessive, exorbitant.

**steep** verb **1** *steep the stained clothes in cold water* soak, saturate, immerse, submerge, souse. **2** *steep the meat in wine* marinate, souse. **steep in** *a family steeped in misery* imbue with, permeate with, pervade with, infuse with. **2** *they were steeped in the classics* submerge in, immerse in.

**steeple** noun spire, tower, bell tower, turret.

**steer** verb **1** *steer the car* guide, navigate, drive, pilot, be at the wheel of. **2** *steer the guests to the garden* guide, lead, direct, conduct, usher. **steer clear of** keep away from, give a wide berth to, avoid, evade, dodge, eschew, shun.

**stem** noun **1** *the stem of a bush* trunk, stock, peduncle. **2** *flowers on a stem* stalk, shoot, branch, twig.

**stem** verb **1** *stem the flow of blood* check, stop, halt, hold back, contain, curb, staunch. **2** *troubles stemming from poverty* arise, originate, derive, spring, emanate.

**stench** noun stink, foul smell, odor, reek.

**step** noun **1** *reach her in one step* stride, pace. **2** *hear steps on the stairs* footstep, footfall, tread. **3** *police examining steps in the mud* footprint, impression, track. **4** *walk with a cheerful step* walk, gait, bearing, carriage. **5** *live just a step away* pace,

stone's throw, spitting distance. **6** *the steps of a ladder* rung, tread. **7** *take a foolish step* course of action, move, act, deed. **8** *a step toward international peace* advancement, development, progression, stage, move. **9** *another step in his promotion* stage, level, grade, rank, degree. **in step** *in step with the views of the committee* in agreement, in accord, in harmony, in line, in conformity. **watch one's step 1** *watch your step on the broken pavement* step carefully, tread cautiously. **2** *watch your step when doing business with him* be careful, be cautious, be wary, be circumspect, take care, take heed, be on one's guard, look out. **out of step** *out of step with modern thinking* in disagreement, at odds, out of line, at variance. **step by step** *follow the instructions step by step* by stages, by degrees, progressively, gradually, bit by bit.

**step** verb *step lightly down the street* walk, tread, stride. **step down** *step down to make way for a younger person* resign, retire, abdicate. **step in** *the police had to step in* intervene, intercede, take action. **step up 1** *police stepping up their efforts* increase, boost, augment, intensify, escalate. **2** *step up the pace of production* increase, speed up, accelerate.

**stereotype** verb typecast, pigeonhole, label, tag, categorize.

**stereotyped** adjective *stereotyped images of a woman's role* typecast, conventional, hackneyed, clichéd, trite, platitudinous.

**sterile** adjective **1** *sterile female* infertile, barren. **2** *sterile soil* infertile, unproductive, unfruitful, unyielding, arid, dry, barren, unprolific. **3** *sterile discussions* unproductive, fruitless, useless, futile, vain, ineffectual, worthless. **4** *sterile conditions in the hospital* sterilized, germ-free, antiseptic, disinfected, aseptic, uncontaminated.

**sterling** adjective **1** *have done sterling service* excellent, first-rate, exceptional, outstanding, splendid, superlative. **2** *sterling friends* genuine, real, true, dependable, trustworthy, faithful, loyal.

**stern** adjective **1** *a stern regime* strict, harsh, severe, rigorous, stringent, rigid, exacting, demanding, relentless, unsparing, inflexible. **2** *a stern expression* severe, forbidding, unsmiling, sober, austere.

**stew** verb **1** *stew the meat* simmer, fricassee. **2** *stewing in the doctor's waiting room* be anxious, be nervous, be agitated, worry, fret, agonize.

**stew** noun **1** *make a beef stew* casserole, ragout, fricassee. **2** *get in a stew about the lost document* state of agitation, fluster, panic, dither, pother; *inf.* flap, tizzy.

**stick** noun **1** *gather sticks for kindling* branch, twig, switch. **2** *sticks supporting plants* cane, pole, post, stake, upright. **3** *punished with a stick* cane, birch, switch, rod. **4** *beaten with a stick* cudgel, truncheon, blackjack, baton. **the sticks** *bored with living in the sticks* the backwoods, the hinterland, the backwater; *inf.* the middle of nowhere, the boondocks, boonies.

**stick** verb **1** *stick a fork in the potato* thrust, push, insert, jab, poke. **2** *stick the pictures to a sheet of paper* glue, paste, tape, fasten, attach, fix, pin, tack. **3** *events that stick in the mind* remain, stay, linger, dwell, lodge, persist, continue. **4** *the car stuck in the mud* become bogged down, become embedded, become immobilized. **5** *machines sticking* jam, come to a standstill, stop, halt, cease to work. **6** *stick it in the drawer* put, place, lay, deposit, drop; *inf.* plunk, stuff. **7** *a needle sticking his finger* pierce, penetrate, puncture, prick, stab. **stick by** *stick by his friend in his misfortune* stand by, be loyal to, remain faithful to, support, back, defend. **stick it out** *the work is hard but he can stick it out* see it through, endure it, grin and bear it, soldier on; *inf.* take it, hang in there, tough it out. **stick out 1** *sculptures sticking out from the wall* stand out, jut out, project, extend, protrude, bulge. **2** *she stuck out in the crowd* stand out, be noticeable, be obvious.

**sticky** adjective **1** *sticky tape* adhesive, gummy, tacky. **2** *sticky substances* gluey, glutinous, viscous; *inf.* gooey. **3** *a sticky summer day* humid, muggy, clammy, sultry, sweltering, oppressive. **4** *a sticky situation* awkward, difficult, tricky, ticklish, delicate, thorny; *inf.* hairy.

**stiff** adjective **1** *stiff cardboard* rigid, inflexible, firm, hard, brittle. **2** *stiff muscles* tight, tense, taut, aching, arthritic, rheumatic. **3** *a stiff climb* difficult, arduous, tough, laborious, demanding, formidable, challenging, Herculean. **4** *a stiff penalty* severe, harsh, stringent, rigorous, heavy. **5** *put up a stiff resistance* strong, vigorous, determined, resolute, dogged, tenacious. **6** *a stiff occasion* formal, ceremonious, dignified, proper, decorous, pompous. **7** *stiff behavior* formal, prim, punctilious, chilly; *inf.* starchy. **8** *a stiff drink* strong, potent. **9** *a stiff breeze* vigorous, brisk, fresh.

**stiffen** verb **1** *the mixture needs time to stiffen* thicken, set, gel, jell, solidify, harden, congeal, coagulate. **2** *something to stiffen their resolve* strengthen, harden, fortify, brace, steel, reinforce. **3** *his muscles have stiffened* tighten, tense, become taut.

**stifle** verb **1** *stifle a yawn* smother, check, keep back, withhold, choke back, muffle, suppress, silence. **2** *stifle a rebellion* suppress, quash, quell, put down, extinguish, stamp out, crush, subdue, repress. **3** *it is stifling in here* suffocating, sweltering, airless, close.

**stigma** noun shame, disgrace, dishonor, stain, taint.

**still** adjective **1** *completely still bodies* motionless, unmoving, immobile, inert, lifeless, stock-still, stationary. **2** *the house was completely still* quiet, silent, hushed, soundless, noiseless. **3** *a still evening* calm, mild, tranquil, peaceful, serene, windless.

**still** noun *in the still of the night* quiet, silence, hush, calm, tranquillity, peacefulness, serenity.

**still** verb **1** *try to still her fears* quiet, calm, pacify, soothe, allay, assuage, appease, silence, subdue. **2** *the wind stilled* abate, die down, moderate, slacken.

**stilted** adjective **1** *a stilted way of speaking* stiff, unnatural, wooden, forced, labored, awkward. **2** *stilted prose* pompous, pretentious, high-flown, grandiloquent, pedantic.

**stimulant** noun **1** *a stimulant to the system* tonic, restorative, energizer, analeptic; *inf.* pep pill, upper, pick-me-up, bracer. **2** *a stimulant to further economic growth* incentive, impetus, fillip. See STIMULUS.

**stimulate** verb *stimulate economic activity* encourage, prompt, spur, stir up, excite, kindle, incite, fan.

**stimulus** noun *a stimulus to economic growth* stimulant, incentive, fillip, spur, push, drive, encouragement, incitement, goad, jog, jolt; *inf.* shot in the arm.

**sting** noun **1** *get a sting from a bee* prick, wound, injury. **2** *take the sting out of the burns* irritation, smarting, tingle, pain. **3** *the sting of unrequited love* pain, hurt, distress, anguish, agony, torment. **4** *crooks planning a sting* swindle, fraud; *inf.* rip-off.

**sting** verb **1** *stung by a jellyfish* prick, wound, injure, hurt. **2** *eyes stinging in the smoke* smart, tingle, burn. **3** *stung by their son's treatment of them* hurt, wound, distress, grieve, torment. **4** *stung by the dishonest dealer* swindle, defraud, cheat, fleece; *inf.* rip off.

**stingy** adjective mean, miserly, parsimonious, niggardly, tight-fisted, penny-pinching; *inf.* tight, cheap.

**stipulate** verb *stipulate a delivery date* specify, set down, demand, require, make a condition of.

**stir** verb **1** *stir the mixture* mix, blend, beat, whip. **2** *stirred in his sleep* move, quiver, tremble, twitch. **3** *wind stirring the leaves* disturb, agitate, rustle. **4** *refuse to stir from the fireside* move, budge, get up. **5** *stirring early on Christmas Day* get up, rise, be up and about; *inf.* shake a leg, look lively. **6** *stir his imagination* stimulate, excite, rouse, kindle, inspire. **7** *speakers stirring the men to action* rouse, incite, provoke, inflame, goad, spur, egg on, urge, motivate, drive, impel.

**stir** noun *their arrival caused a stir* excitement, commotion, disturbance, fuss, to-do, bustle.

**stock** noun 1 *a stock of goods for sale* store, supply, range, selection, assortment, variety, 2 *run out of stock before Christmas* supplies, goods, merchandise, wares, commodities. 3 *lay in a stock of wood for the winter* store, supply, stockpile, reserve, reservoir, accumulation, load, hoard, cache. 4 *employed to look after the farm stock* livestock, cattle, beasts, herd. 5 *have stock in the company* shares, investment, holding, capital. 6 *his stock in the company is rising* standing, status, reputation, position. 7 *born of good stock* descent, lineage, ancestry, extraction, family, parentage, pedigree. 8 *stock for soup* bouillon, broth. 9 *the stock of an implement* handle, haft, grip, shaft, shank, **in stock** *a range of goods in stock* for sale, on sale, available; *inf.* on tap. **take stock of** *take stock of the situation* review, weigh, appraise; *inf.* size up.

**stock** adjective 1 *stock sizes of clothes* standard, regular, average, readily available. 2 *stock items in a kitchen cupboard* regular, common, customary, staple, basic, fundamental, essential, indispensable. 3 *stock responses to his requests* usual, routine, run-of-the-mill, commonplace, conventional, traditional, clichéd.

**stock** verb 1 *stores stocking children's clothes* sell, deal in, market, supply. 2 *stock the factory with modern machinery* equip, fit, outfit, furnish, supply, provide, **stock up** 1 *stock up the shelves* fill, fill up, load, replenish. 2 *stock up (on) cans of soup* collect, gather, accumulate, amass, lay in, stockpile, hoard; *inf.* squirrel away.

**stockings** plural noun hosiery, hose, nylons; panty hose, tights.

**stocky** adjective heavyset, thickset, squat, chunky, solid, sturdy.

**stodgy** adjective 1 *a stodgy young man* staid, sedate, stuffy. 2 *stodgy prose* dull, uninteresting, boring, tedious, dry, wearisome, unimaginative, uninspired, monotonous, labored, wooden, turgid.

**stoical** adjective impassive, unemotional, self-disciplined, forbearing, patient, long-suffering, resigned, philosophical, fatalistic.

**stomach** noun 1 *a pain in the stomach* abdomen, belly, paunch, potbelly; *inf.* tummy, gut, bread basket. 2 *have no stomach for rich food | have no stomach for the battle* appetite, taste, hunger, desire, inclination, liking, fancy, fondness, relish, gusto.

**stomach** verb 1 *unable to stomach rich food* eat, digest, swallow. 2 *unable to stomach his arrogance* stand, bear, tolerate, abide, endure, suffer; *inf.* weather.

**stony** adjective 1 *stony ground* rocky, pebbly, gravelly, gritty, rough. 2 *a stony stare* cold, frosty, icy, rigid, fixed. 3 *a stony heart* unfeeling, uncaring, unsympathetic, insensitive, callous, heartless, unmoved, unresponsive, severe, harsh, hard, cruel, cold-hearted, merciless, pitiless, ruthless, unforgiving.

**stoop** verb 1 *stoop to pick something up* bend down, lean over, crouch down. 2 *stoop his head to get into the car* bend, bow, lower, duck. 3 *very tall people often stoop* slouch, slump, hunch one's shoulders. 4 *never stoops to talk to her inferiors* condescend, deign, lower oneself. 5 *refuse to stoop to crime* sink, descend, resort.

**stop** verb 1 *stop the fight* halt, end, put an end to, finish, terminate, discontinue, interrupt. 2 *unable to stop laughing* cease, refrain from, leave off, quit; *inf.* knock off. 3 *work has stopped for the day* come to a halt, end, finish, come to a close, cease, conclude, terminate. 4 *stop their getaway flight* prevent, hinder, obstruct, impede, block, check, curb, frustrate, thwart, foil, restrain. 5 *stop off at Newport on the way to Boston* stay, sojourn, lodge, rest. **stop up** *stop up a leak* plug (up), seal (up), block (up), bung up, stem.

**stop** noun 1 *come to a stop* halt, end, finish, close, cessation, conclusion, termination, standstill, stoppage. 2 *there are ten stops on the bus route* terminus, terminal, depot, station. 3 *aim for a stop at Miami* stopoff, stopover, stay, sojourn, overnight.

**stopgap** noun substitute, fill-in, makeshift, improvisation, expedient, last resort.

**stoppage** noun 1 *the stoppage of some forms of welfare* end, discontinuation, cessation, termination. 2 *another stoppage at the factory* strike, walkout, shutdown. 3 *a stoppage in the pipe* blockage, obstruction, occlusion. 4 *a stoppage in the supply* obstruction, obstacle, impediment, check, snag.

**store** noun 1 *a store of logs for the winter* supply, stockpile, reserve, accumulation, pile, cache, reservoir. 2 *get supplies from the store* storeroom, storehouse, warehouse, repository. 3 *buying shoes/food/books at the store* shop, mart, department store, supermarket, retail outlet, emporium. **set store by** think highly of, hold in regard, admire, appreciate, value, prize, esteem.

**store** verb *store food in case of a shortage* stock up on, stockpile, collect, gather, accumulate, amass, put away, deposit; *inf.* salt away, stash.

**storm** noun 1 *ships damaged in the storm* gale, hurricane, cyclone, tempest, squall, cloudburst, downpour, torrent. 2 *a storm of protest* outcry, outburst, commotion, furor, clamor, tumult, disturbance; *inf.*

to-do. **3** *a storm on the castle* assault, attack, offensive, onslaught, charge, raid, foray, sortie. **4** *a storm of missiles* shower, deluge, volley, salvo.

**storm** verb **1** *storm the castle* attack, charge, rush. **2** *storm out of the room* charge, rush headlong, stamp; *inf.* stomp. **3** *storming at the incompetent recruits* rage, rant, rave, fume, bellow, thunder; *inf.* raise the roof, raise hell.

**stormy** adjective blustery, windy, gusty, squally, tempestuous, turbulent.

**story** noun **1** *have a story published|read the children a story* short story, tale, fairy tale, fable, legend; *inf.* yarn. **2** *their stories of the accident did not agree* account, report, record. **3** *the novel's complicated story* story line, plot. **4** *journalists looking for a story* news item, article, feature; *inf.* scoop. **5** *told a story when she was caught* lie, untruth, falsehood, fib.

**stout** adjective **1** *stout people advised to lose weight* fat, plump, portly, tubby, obese, corpulent, rotund, heavy, thickset, overweight, burly, fleshy; *inf.* beefy. **2** *a stout stick* strong, heavy, solid, substantial, sturdy. **3** *a stout defender of the city* stouthearted, valiant, gallant, intrepid.

**stouthearted** adjective *stouthearted defenders of the city* courageous, valiant, valorous, gallant, fearless, plucky, intrepid, brave, bold.

**straight** adjective **1** *in a straight line* direct, undeviating, unswerving, uncurving. **2** *three straight wins* successive, consecutive, in a row, running, uninterrupted, nonstop. **3** *is the picture straight?* level, symmetrical, even, true, in line, aligned. **4** *get the room straight* in order, orderly, neat, tidy, spruce, shipshape, organized, arranged, sorted out. **5** *a straight answer* direct, honest, sincere, frank, candid, forthright, straightforward, plainspoken, plain, unequivocal, unambiguous, unqualified. **6** *incapable of straight thinking* logical, rational, sound, intelligent, unemotional, dispassionate. **7** *straight spirits* unmixed, undiluted, pure, neat.

**straight** adverb **1** *go straight there* directly, by a direct route, without deviating; without delay. **2** *tell them straight* directly, honestly, frankly, candidly, plainly, straight from the shoulder, with no holds barred, unequivocally, unambiguously. **3** *not thinking straight* logically, rationally, intelligently, dispassionately. **straight away** *the work must be done straight away* right away, immediately, at once, without delay; *inf.* pronto. **straight out** *tell him straight out that he is fired* directly, honestly, frankly, candidly.

**straightforward** adjective **1** *a straightforward answer* direct, honest, frank, candid.

*See* STRAIGHT adjective 5. **2** *a straightforward task* uncomplicated, simple, elementary, undemanding, routine.

**strain** verb **1** *strain a rope till it snaps* tighten, make taut, stretch, extend, distend. **2** *strain a muscle* pull, wrench, twist, sprain. **3** *strain one's eyes by reading too much* tax, overtax, overwork, fatigue, tire. **4** *strain to win* make every effort, strive, struggle, labor. **5** *strain at the rope* pull, tug, heave, haul, jerk; *inf.* yank. **6** *strain the mixture* sieve, filter, sift, screen, riddle, separate.

**strain** noun **1** *the rope snapped under the strain* tension, tightness, tautness. **2** *suffer muscle strain* wrench, twist, sprain, pull. **3** *the strain of his job* demands, exertions, burdens, pressure, stress, tension. **4** *suffer from strain* stress, tension, overwork, exhaustion, anxiety.

**strainer** noun *put the food through a strainer* sieve, colander, filter, sifter, screen, riddle.

**strait** noun *the boat crossing the strait* sound, narrows, channel, inlet, arm of the sea.

**straitlaced** adjective puritanical, prudish, prim, proper, priggish, stuffy; *inf.* fuddy-duddy.

**straits** plural noun *in dire straits* predicament, plight, difficulty, trouble, crisis, mess; *inf.* tight corner, hot water, jam, hole, scrape.

**strand**[1] noun **1** *the strands of the wool* thread, fiber, filament. **2** *strands of hair* lock, wisp, tress. **3** *the last volume drawing together the strands of the trilogy* element, component, strain, story line, theme.

**strand**[2] noun *walk on the strand* shore, seashore, beach, coast, seaside, waterfront.

**stranded** adjective **1** *she was stranded when her purse was stolen* left helpless, abandoned, forsaken, in dire straits, left in the lurch, left high and dry. **2** *stranded ships* grounded, beached, shipwrecked, wrecked, marooned.

**strange** adjective **1** *he had a strange expression on his face* peculiar, odd, bizarre, unusual, atypical, abnormal, weird, funny, unfamiliar. **2** *a strange land* unknown, unfamiliar. **3** *a strange phenomenon* inexplicable, anomalous, unexpected, extraordinary.

**stranger** noun **1** *he was a complete stranger to her* unknown person, alien. **2** *strangers being welcomed into the community* new person, outsider, newcomer, foreigner. **a stranger to** *a stranger to the area* unfamiliar with, unacquainted with, unaccustomed to, new to, unused to, inexperienced in, unversed in.

**strangle** verb **1** *he strangled his victim with a scarf* throttle, choke, garrotte. **2** *strangle artistic expression* suppress, inhibit, repress, restrain, curb, stifle, gag.

**strap** noun *straps fastening the trunk* band, belt, thong, cord, tie.

**strap** verb **1** *strap the trunk with leather thongs* fasten, secure, tie, bind, lash, truss, pinion. **2** *strap the naughty children* flog, lash, whip, scourge, beat; *inf.* belt.

**stratagem** noun trick, ruse, plot, scheme, maneuver, plan, tactic, artifice, machination, wile, subterfuge, dodge, deception.

**strategic** adjective **1** *strategic schemes* tactical, diplomatic, calculated, planned, plotted, cunning, wily. **2** *strategic bases in the war* crucial, key, vital, critical.

**strategy** noun **1** *the government's economic strategy* policy, approach, program, scheme, plan of action, blueprint, game plan. **2** *the general's strategy* art of war, military science, military tactics.

**stray** verb **1** *cows straying into the neighbor's field* wander, roam, rove, go astray. **2** *strayed in later life* go astray, go wrong, stray from the straight and narrow, err, sin, transgress. **3** *stray from the point* digress, wander, deviate, get sidetracked, go off on a tangent.

**stray** adjective **1** *a stray dog* lost, homeless, wandering, vagrant, abandoned, unclaimed. **2** *a stray bullet* odd, random, isolated, scattered, occasional, incidental, accidental, chance, freak.

**streak** noun **1** *a streak of light in the dark sky* line, band, strip, stripe. **2** *a streak of cowardice* strain, vein, element, trace. **3** *a streak of lightning* bolt, flash, beam. **4** *streaks on the windows* smear, smudge, mark. **5** *on a winning streak* spell, period, course, stretch, series.

**streak** verb **1** *a blue sky streaked with white* striate, fleck, band, stripe. **2** *dirty cloths streaking the glass* smear, smudge, mark. **3** *runners/cars streaking past* race, rush, speed, dash, sprint, hurtle, fly, flash, zoom, zip; *inf.* whiz.

**stream** noun **1** *mountain streams* river, brook, creek, rivulet, rill, freshet. **2** *a stream of blood* flow, rush, gush, surge, efflux, current, cascade. **3** *people going with the stream* flow, current, tide, drift.

**stream** verb **1** *water streaming from the pipe* flow, run, pour, course, spill, gush, surge, flood, cascade. **2** *flags streaming in the breeze* float, swing, flap, flutter. **3** *people streaming out of the building* surge, pour, crowd.

**street** noun road, thoroughfare, boulevard, avenue, drive, lane.

**strength** noun **1** *men of great physical strength* power, might, force, brawn, muscle, stamina. **2** *regain his strength* health, robustness, vigor. **3** *adversity gave him inner strength* fortitude, courage, firmness, stamina, backbone. **4** *test the strength of the castle doors* solidity, toughness, resistance, impregnability. **5** *the strength of the feeling against him* intensity, force, forcefulness, vehemence, ardor, fervency. **6** *the strength of their argument* cogency, potency, weight, soundness, validity. **7** *workers who are the strength of the firm* mainstay, support, anchor, foundation stone. **8** *the firm's reliability is its main strength* advantage, asset, strong point, forte. **9** *the strength of the workforce* size, extent, magnitude.

**strengthen** verb **1** *strengthen children's bones* make stronger, make healthy, nourish, build up. **2** *the wind strengthened* gain strength, intensify, heighten. **3** *strengthen their determination* fortify, harden, stiffen, toughen, steel. **4** *his evidence strengthened their argument* reinforce, support, back up, bolster, substantiate, corroborate.

**strenuous** adjective **1** *a strenuous task* arduous, laborious, taxing, demanding, exhausting, tiring, fatiguing. **2** *make strenuous efforts to reach the top* energetic, active, vigorous, forceful, strong, spirited, determined, zealous.

**stress** noun **1** *the stress of his new job* strain, pressure, tension. **2** *in times of stress* worry, anxiety, trouble, difficulty, distress, trauma. **3** *place stress on education* emphasis, priority, importance, weight, significance, value, worth. **4** *place stress on the first syllable* emphasis, accent, accentuation.

**stress** verb **1** *stress the importance of education* emphasize, accentuate, underscore, highlight, spotlight, dwell on. **2** *stress the first syllable* place emphasis on, place the accent on, accentuate. **3** *discover that the workers have been stressed for years* overtax, pressurize, overwork, overburden, push too far.

**stretch** verb **1** *the material stretches* be elastic, distend, be tensile, enlarge, expand. **2** *stretch the piece of elastic* extend, elongate, lengthen, expand, draw out. **3** *stretched a hand out* reach out, hold out, proffer, offer. **4** *the forests stretched for miles* extend, spread, unfold, range. **5** *a job that will stretch her* challenge, tax, push to the limit. **6** *stretch the truth* strain, exaggerate, overdraw, push too far. **stretch out** *stretch out on the sofa* lie down, recline, sprawl (out), lounge.

**stretch** noun **1** *stretches of forest* expanse, area, tract, extent, spread. **2** *a four-hour stretch* period, time, spell, term, stint.

**strict** adjective **1** *a strict interpretation of the rules* precise, exact, close, faithful, scrupulous, meticulous, conscientious, punctilious. **2** *a strict upbringing* stringent, rigorous, authoritarian, rigid, austere, inflexible, unyielding, uncompromising. **3**

*in strict confidence* absolute, utter, complete, total, perfect. **4** *strict members of the religious sect* orthodox, fundamentalist.

**stride** verb *stride along swinging their arms* step, pace, walk.

**stride** noun *take huge strides* long/large step, pace.

**strident** adjective shrill, loud, harsh, raucous, rough, grating, discordant, jarring, screeching.

**strife** noun conflict, friction, discord, dissension, dispute, bickering, controversy, contention.

**strike** verb **1** *strike the gong* bang, beat, hit, pound. **2** *struck his opponent* hit, slap, smack, beat, batter, thump, punch, cuff, box, knock, rap; *inf.* wallop, belt, clout, whack, clobber, bop, sock. **3** *the ship struck a rock* run into, bang into, bump into, smash into, collide with, dash against. **4** *strike the ball a good distance* hit, drive, propel. **5** *strike a match* light, ignite. **6** *the enemy struck our army at dawn* attack, charge, assault, storm, fall upon. **7** *disaster struck the family* come upon, afflict, smite. **8** *strike a balance* reach, achieve, arrive at, find, attain. **9** *strike a bargain* agree on, settle on, sign, endorse, ratify, sanction. **10** *strike a dramatic pose* assume, adopt, affect, feign. **11** *strike oil/gold* discover, find, happen upon, stumble upon, unearth, uncover, turn up. **12** *an idea struck him* occur to, come to, dawn on. **13** *the house strikes me as unfriendly* seem to, appear to, impress, affect. **14** *workers striking for higher wages* go on strike, protest, walk out. **15** *strike the disputed clause from the record* delete, cross out, erase, rub out, obliterate. **strike up 1** *the band struck up* commence playing, begin/start to play. **2** *they struck up an acquaintance* begin, start, commence, embark on, initiate.

**strike** noun **1** *stunned his opponent with one strike* hit, slap, smack, thump, punch, cuff, box, knock; *inf.* wallop, whack. **2** *a lucky strike* discovery, find. **3** *an unexpected enemy strike* attack, assault, blitz. **4** *declare a strike* walkout, protest.

**striking** adjective **1** *a striking resemblance* obvious, conspicuous, prominent, unmistakable, remarkable, extraordinary. **2** *a striking floral display* impressive, splendid, magnificent, superb, marvelous, dazzling; *inf.* smashing. **3** *married to a striking woman* beautiful, glamorous, stunning, gorgeous.

**string** noun **1** *tie the package with string* twine, cord, yarn, rope, line. **2** *own a string of stores* chain, series, succession. **3** *a string of people waiting to get in* line, row, queue, procession, file, column, succession, sequence. **4** *a string of beads* strand, necklace.

**stringent** adjective **1** *a stringent ban on smoking* strict, firm, rigid, severe, harsh, tough, exacting, demanding, inflexible, uncompromising. **2** *stringent economic conditions* difficult, tight, hard, tough.

**strip** verb **1** *they stripped and got into dry clothes* undress, take one's clothes off, disrobe. **2** *strip the wet child* undress, unclothe. **3** *strip the bark from the tree* peel, pare, skin, excoriate. **4** *strip paint from the doors* remove, take off, peel off, flake off. **5** *strip a machine* dismantle, break down, take apart. **6** *the burglars stripped the house* empty out, clean out, plunder, ransack, rob. **strip of** *strip him of his rank* take away from, deprive of, confiscate from.

**strip** noun *strips of paper* piece, bit, band, belt, ribbon, stripe, swathe, slip.

**stripe** noun *a white stripe on a black background* strip, band, belt, bar.

**strive** verb *strive to succeed* try, attempt, endeavor, make an effort, exert oneself, strain, struggle, bend over backward; *inf.* go all out, give it one's best shot. **strive against** *strove all his life against oppression* struggle against, fight, battle, combat, contend with, grapple with.

**stroke** noun **1** *felt the stroke of his opponent* blow, hit, slap, smack, thump, punch, cuff, knock; *inf.* wallop, clout, whack. **2** *swimming strokes* movement, action, motion. **3** *a stroke of genius/diplomacy* accomplishment, achievement, feat, attainment, coup. **4** *with one stroke of the pen* movement, action, mark, line. **5** *put the finishing strokes to the plan* touch, detail, bit, addition. **6** *hear five strokes of the church bell* striking, peal, ring, knell. **7** *in the hospital since he had a stroke* thrombosis, embolism, seizure, apoplexy.

**stroke** verb *stroke the cat* caress, fondle, pat, touch, rub, massage, soothe.

**stroll** verb *stroll (along) in the sunshine* saunter, amble, wander, meander, ramble, promenade, stretch one's legs; *inf.* mosey (along).

**stroll** noun *go for a stroll* saunter, walk, amble, wander, turn, constitutional, promenade.

**strong** adjective **1** *strong men lifting heavy weights* powerful, mighty, brawny, muscular, strapping, sturdy, burly. **2** *invalids becoming strong again* healthy, well, robust, vigorous. **3** *strong enough to refuse the blackmailer's demands* courageous, brave, resolute; *inf.* gutsy. **4** *intimidated by strong individuals* determined, forceful, high-powered, tough, formidable. **5** *the vault's strong doors* solid, well-built, heavy, secure, well-fortified, impregnable, impenetrable. **6** *strong material* heavy-duty, sturdy, durable, long-lasting. **7** *arouse strong feelings* forceful, intense, acute, vehement, passionate, fervent. **8** *a strong supporter of the local team* keen, eager, enthusiastic, dedicated, staunch, loyal, steadfast, passionate, fierce, fervent. **9** *a strong argument* powerful, cogent, potent, weighty, compelling, convincing, plausible, effective, sound, valid, well-founded. **10** *a strong resemblance* marked, pronounced, distinct, definite, obvious, unmistakable, remarkable. **11** *strong colors* deep, intense, vivid, graphic. **12** *in strong light* bright, brilliant, intense, dazzling, glaring. **13** *strong measures to reduce crime* firm, energetic, active, forceful, severe, drastic, extreme. **14** *strong coffee* concentrated, undiluted. **15** *strong drink* alcoholic, intoxicating, heady. **16** *strong garlic* sharp, pungent, biting, spicy.

**stronghold** noun **1** *assault the enemy stronghold* fortress, fort, castle, citadel. **2** *a conservative stronghold at the last election* bastion, center, refuge, hotbed.

**structure** noun **1** *wooden structures* building, edifice, construction, erection, complex. **2** *the structure of the firm* construction, form, configuration, shape, constitution, composition, makeup, organization, system, arrangement, design.

**struggle** verb **1** *struggle to obtain power* strive, endeavor, exert oneself, battle, labor, toil, strain. **2** *boys struggling with each other* fight, grapple, wrestle, scuffle, brawl; *inf.* scrap. **3** *rivals struggling for supremacy* fight, compete, contend, vie, lock horns, cross swords.

**struggle** noun **1** *his struggles to obtain power* battle, endeavor, effort, exertion, labor, pains. **2** *a barroom struggle* fight, wrestling match, scuffle, brawl, tussle; *inf.* scrap, set-to. **3** *opposing armies engaged in a struggle* battle, fight, combat, conflict, contest, hostilities, clash, skirmish. **4** *a struggle on the committee for supremacy* competition, contention, vying, rivalry. **5** *a struggle just to survive* effort, fight, trial, labor; *inf.* grind, hassle.

**strut** verb swagger, prance, parade, flounce, sashay.

**stub** noun end, butt, stump, remnant.

**stubborn** adjective obstinate, headstrong, willful, strong-willed, pigheaded, mulish, dogged, persistent, adamant, inflexible, uncompromising, unbending, unyielding, obdurate, intractable, refractory, recalcitrant, contumacious.

**stuck** adjective **1** *posters stuck to the wall* glued, fixed, mired, fastened. **2** *stuck in the mud* immobile, fast, fixed, mired, rooted. **3** *the problem has her stuck* baffled, stumped, at a loss, perplexed. **stuck on** *stuck on the new girl* attracted to,

infatuated with, fond of, in love with, obsessed by; *inf.* mad about, hung up on.

**student** noun pupil, schoolboy, schoolgirl; undergraduate; trainee, apprentice.

**studied** adjective *with studied indifference* deliberate, willful, conscious, calculated, purposeful, forced.

**studio** noun workshop, workroom, atelier.

**studious** adjective *a studious pupil* scholarly, academic, intellectual, bookish, serious, earnest.

**study** noun **1** *a life devoted to study* learning, scholarship, education, academic work, research, reading. **2** *make a study of rural transport* investigation, inquiry, examination, analysis, review, survey. **3** *writing in his study* office, workroom, studio, library. **4** *write a study on/of Shakespeare's late plays* paper, work, essay, review.

**study** verb **1** *study history* learn, read, work at; *inf.* bone up on, cram. **2** *study the effects of sleeplessness* investigate, inquire into, research, examine, analyze, review, survey, scrutinize. **3** *study the suspect's movements* watch, observe, keep an eye on, keep under surveillance.

**stuff** noun **1** *made out of durable stuff* material, fabric, matter, substance. **2** *get rid of the stuff in the hall* things, objects, articles, items. **3** *travelers carrying their stuff* luggage, baggage, belongings, possessions, paraphernalia.

**stuff** verb **1** *stuff a pillow* fill, pack, pad. **2** *too much furniture stuffed into the room* pack, cram, squeeze, crowd, stow, press, force, compress, jam, wedge. **3** *stuff the money into his wallet* thrust, shove, push, ram. **4** *stuff themselves with turkey* fill, gorge, overindulge, satiate.

**stuffing** noun **1** *stuffing for cushions* filling, filler, packing, padding, wadding. **2** *stuffing for the duck* filling, dressing, forcemeat.

**stuffy** adjective **1** *a stuffy atmosphere* airless, close, muggy, stifling, suffocating. **2** *a stuffy young man* staid, stiff, formal, pompous, starchy, prim, priggish, straitlaced, conservative, stodgy; *inf.* fuddy-duddy, square. **3** *a stuffy nose* stuffed-up, blocked.

**stumble** verb **1** *stumble and fall* trip, lose one's balance, slip. **2** *drunks stumbling home* blunder, lumber, lurch, stagger, reel. **3** *stumble a little when giving her speech* stammer, stutter, hesitate, falter; *inf.* fluff one's lines. **stumble upon** *stumble upon an unpublished work of the novelist* chance upon, happen upon, come across, find, discover, encounter.

**stump** noun end, stub, butt, remnant, remains.

**stump** verb *the last question stumped him* baffle, outwit, foil, perplex, puzzle, confound, bewilder; *inf.* flummox, stymie.

**stun** verb **1** *the blow stunned him* daze, stupefy, knock senseless. **2** *stunned by the news of his death* shock, astound, dumbfound, stupefy, overwhelm, devastate, stagger, take one's breath away, confound, bewilder; *inf.* flabbergast.

**stunning** adjective **1** *a stunning range of electronic equipment* impressive, extraordinary, staggering, incredible, amazing, astonishing, marvelous; *inf.* mind-boggling. **2** *looking stunning in a new evening dress* sensational, ravishing, dazzling, wonderful, magnificent, glorious, exquisite, beautiful; *inf.* gorgeous, fabulous, smashing.

**stunt** verb *stunt the child's growth* retard, slow, impede, hamper, hinder, check, curb, restrict, arrest.

**stupefy** verb **1** *a boxer stupefied by the first blow* stun, daze, knock senseless. **2** *stupefied by the news* shock, astound, dumbfound. *See* STUN 2.

**stupendous** adjective **1** *a stupendous achievement* amazing, astounding, astonishing, extraordinary, wonderful, phenomenal; *inf.* fantastic, mind-boggling. **2** *a stupendous beast* colossal, immense, gigantic, massive, huge, enormous.

**stupid** adjective **1** *a stupid fellow* dense, brainless, mindless, dull-witted, slow-witted, slow, simpleminded, halfwitted; *inf.* thick, dim, dumb, dopey, moronic, imbecilic. **2** *stupid error/behavior* foolish, silly, idiotic, mindless, senseless, irresponsible, unthinking, ill-advised, ill-considered, unwise, injudicious, shortsighted, inane, absurd, ludicrous, ridiculous, asinine, pointless, meaningless, insane.

**stupor** noun *in a drunken stupor* daze, insensibility, oblivion, coma, blackout.

**sturdy** adjective **1** *sturdy young men* well-built, muscular, athletic, strong, strapping, brawny, powerful, solid, substantial, robust, vigorous, tough, hardy, stalwart. **2** *put up a sturdy resistance* strong, vigorous, stalwart, firm, determined, resolute, tenacious, staunch, steadfast, unyielding, unwavering, uncompromising.

**stutter** verb stammer, stumble, hesitate, falter, splutter.

**style** noun **1** *an unusual style of house* kind, type, variety, sort, design, pattern. **2** *try to copy the style of her favorite artist* technique, method, approach, manner, way, mode, system. **3** *a young man with style* elegance, polish, suaveness, urbanity, flair, dash, panache, élan; *inf.* pizzazz. **4** *used to living in style* comfort, elegance, affluence, wealth, luxury. **5** *styles popular in the 1920s* fashion, trend, vogue, mode.

**6** *criticize both the content and style of the novel* mode of expression, phraseology, wording, language.

**style** verb **1** *style the clothes to suit a warm climate* design, fashion, tailor. **2** *he styled himself professor* designate, call, term, name, dub, label, tag.

**stylish** adjective *stylish clothes* fashionable, smart, elegant, chic, modish, à la mode; *inf.* trendy, natty, classy, snazzy.

**suave** adjective smooth, glib, sophisticated, urbane, worldly, charming, polite, diplomatic, polished.

**subconscious** adjective subliminal, latent, suppressed, repressed, hidden, underlying, deep, intuitive, instinctive.

**subdue** verb **1** *subdue the rebel forces* conquer, defeat, vanquish, overpower, subjugate, master, crush, quell, tame. **2** *subdue one's desire to hit him* control, curb, restrain, check, inhibit, repress, suppress, stifle.

**subject** noun **1** *the subject of the discussion* topic, theme, question, gist, thesis. **2** *subjects studied at university* course of study, course, discipline. **3** *a suitable subject for hypnosis* case, client, patient, participant; *inf.* guinea pig. **4** *his disappearance was the subject of much speculation* occasion, basis, grounds, source. **5** *a British subject* citizen, national. **6** *the king's subjects* liege, subordinate, underling, vassal.

**subject** adjective **subject to 1** *subject to the terms of the contract* conditional upon, contingent upon, dependent on. **2** *subject to colds in the winter* susceptible to, liable to, prone to, vulnerable to. **3** *subject to the laws of the land* bound by, constrained by, accountable to.

**subject** verb **subject to** *subjected us to his anger* put through, expose to, lay open to, submit to.

**subjective** adjective *a highly subjective view of the situation* personal, individual, biased, prejudiced.

**sublime** adjective **1** *sublime devotion/beauty* noble, exalted, awe-inspiring, majestic, imposing, glorious, supreme, virtuous, high-principled. **2** *a sublime meal* excellent, outstanding, first-rate, first-class, superb, perfect, ideal, wonderful, marvelous; *inf.* fantastic, fabulous. **3** *a sublime lack of concern for the truth* total, complete, utter, arrogant.

**submerge** verb **1** *watch the submarines submerging* go under water, dive, sink, plummet. **2** *submerge the dress in soapy water* immerse, dip, plunge, dunk. **3** *floodwaters submerged the streets* flood, inundate, deluge, engulf, swamp. **4** *submerged in a backlog of correspondence* inundate, deluge, swamp, bury, engulf.

**submission** noun **1** *he sought their submission to his demands* yielding, capitulation, agreement, acceptance, consent, accession, compliance. **2** *the submission of our army to the enemy forces* surrender, laying down one's arms. **3** *the submission of a planning proposal* presentation, tendering, entry, proposal, introduction. **4** *accept his submission that his client is innocent* argument, assertion, contention, claim. **5** *after years of submission, they rebelled* passivity, obedience, submissiveness, compliance, acquiescence, tractability, nonresistance, docility, meekness, resignation, humility, deference, subservience, servility, subjection.

**submissive** adjective yielding, compliant, acquiescent, tractable, nonresisting, passive, obedient, dutiful, docile, meek, resigned, humble, deferential, obsequious.

**submit** verb **1** *submit a planning proposal* put forward, present, proffer, tender, advance, propose, introduce. **2** *submit a claim* put in, enter, refer. **3** *submit that his client was innocent* argue, assert, contend, state, claim, aver, propound. **4** *submit to his demands* give in, yield, bow, capitulate, agree, accept, consent, accede, acquiesce, conform. **5** *submit to the enemy forces* surrender, yield, lay down one's arms, raise the white flag, bend the knee.

**subordinate** adjective **1** *his subordinate officers* lower-ranking, junior, lesser, inferior. **2** *subordinate issues* lesser, minor, secondary, subsidiary, ancillary, auxiliary.

**subordinate** noun *be patronizing to his subordinates* junior, assistant, second, deputy, aide, underling, inferior; *inf.* sidekick.

**subscribe** verb **subscribe to 1** *subscribe to several learned journals* pay a subscription to, contract to buy. **2** *subscribe to several charities* donate to, give to, pledge money to, contribute to. **3** *subscribe to the theory of evolution* agree with, accede to, consent to, accept, believe in, endorse, back, support.

**subsequent** adjective *on subsequent visits* following, ensuing, succeeding, later. **subsequent to** *subsequent to his illness* following, after, in the wake of.

**subservient** adjective servile, submissive, deferential, obsequious, sycophantic, groveling, fawning, ingratiating, toadying, unctuous; *inf.* bootlicking.

**subside** verb **1** *storms subsiding* abate, let up, moderate, calm, slacken, die down/out, peter out, taper off, recede, lessen, diminish. **2** *water levels subsiding* go down, recede, sink, fall back.

**subsidiary** adjective *discuss subsidiary issues* subordinate, secondary, ancillary, auxiliary, minor.

**subsidy** noun *government subsidies for the arts* grant, contribution, backing, support, aid, sponsorship, funding, subvention.

**subsist** verb **1** *subsist on bread and water | old customs still subsist* live, exist, survive, be in existence, continue, last. **subsist in** *her attractiveness subsists in her personality* lie in, reside in, be attributable to.

**subsistence** noun **1** *their subsistence on bread and water | the subsistence of old customs* existence, survival, continuance. **2** *contribute to the child's subsistence* keep, support, maintenance, livelihood; sustenance, provisions.

**substance** noun **1** *a hard substance* matter, material, stuff, mass. **2** *ghostly figures with no substance* solidity, body, corporeality, materiality, concreteness, tangibility. **3** *an argument with little substance* meaningfulness, significance, weight, soundness, validity. **4** *a person of very little substance* character, backbone, mettle. **5** *the substance of the novel* subject matter, theme, topic, content, essence, gist, sense, import. **6** *born poor, he became a man of substance* wealth, affluence, prosperity, capital, means, resources, assets, property.

**substantial** adjective **1** *confuse the substantial world with the world of the imagination* material, real, actual, concrete. **2** *make a substantial contribution to the project* sizable, considerable, meaningful, significant, important, major, material, marked, valuable, useful, worthwhile. **3** *substantial houses* solid, sturdy, strong, well-built, durable. **4** *a substantial figure of a man* large, big, solid, sturdy, stout, hefty, bulky. **5** *put forward a substantial argument* solid, meaningful, weighty, powerful, sound, valid. **6** *run a substantial business* successful, prosperous, wealthy, affluent, well-to-do. **7** *in substantial agreement* essential, basic, fundamental.

**substantiate** verb support, uphold, back up, bear out, validate, corroborate, verify, authenticate, confirm.

**substitute** noun *act as a substitute for the manager* replacement, deputy, relief, proxy, surrogate, fill-in, stand-in.

**substitute** verb **substitute for 1** *substitute sparkling wine for champagne* replace with, use instead of, exchange for, switch with; *inf.* swap for. **2** *she substituted for him when he was ill* replace, relieve, fill in for, cover for, take over from, hold the fort for.

**subterfuge** noun **1** *think of a subterfuge to get past the doorman* trick, ruse, wile, ploy, stratagem, artifice, dodge, maneuver, pretext, intrigue, scheme, deception. **2** *use subterfuge to gain entry* trickery, intrigue, deviousness, evasion, deception, duplicity.

**subtle** adjective **1** *a subtle flavor* elusive, delicate, understated, low-key, muted, toned down. **2** *a subtle distinction* fine, nice, slight, minute, indistinct. **3** *a subtle intelligence* perceptive, discerning, sensitive, discriminating, penetrating, astute, keen, acute, shrewd, sagacious. **4** *subtle devices to trap the unwary* clever, ingenious, intricate, crafty, artful, devious.

**subtract** verb take away, take, deduct; *inf.* knock off.

**subversive** adjective *spread subversive rumors about the boss* inflammatory, seditious, revolutionary, treasonous, disruptive.

**subvert** verb **1** *subvert the government* overthrow, overturn, sabotage, destroy, wreck, disrupt, undermine, weaken. **2** *subverted by gifts from the enemy* corrupt, pervert, warp, deprave, contaminate, vitiate.

**succeed** verb **1** *plans that succeed* be successful, turn out well, work; *inf.* pan out. **2** *he succeeded him as chairman* come after, follow, replace, supplant. **3** *he succeeded as a lawyer* achieve success, make good, prosper, flourish, thrive, triumph; *inf.* make it, arrive. **succeed in** *succeed in his ambition* accomplish, achieve, bring off, attain, reach, arrive at, complete, fulfill, realize. **succeed to** *succeed to the throne* accede to, inherit, assume, take over, come into.

**succeeding** adjective *grow weaker in the succeeding days* subsequent, following, ensuing, next.

**success** noun **1** *gain success in his endeavor* accomplishment, achievement, attainment, fulfillment, victory, triumph. **2** *envy his success* prosperity, affluence, wealth, fame, eminence. **3** *the book/play was a success* best seller, box-office success, winner, sellout, triumph; *inf.* hit, box-office hit, smash hit, sensation. **4** *became a success in Hollywood* celebrity, big name, somebody, VIP, star.

**successful** adjective **1** *successful in his endeavor* victorious, triumphant. **2** *envying successful people* prosperous, affluent, wealthy, well-to-do, famous, eminent. **3** *a successful business* flourishing, thriving, profitable, moneymaking, lucrative.

**succession** noun **1** *a succession of events leading to disaster* sequence, series, progression, course, cycle, chain, train. **2** *his succession to the throne* accession, inheritance, assumption, elevation. **3** *the succession is through his eldest son* line of descent, ancestral line, dynasty, lineage. **in succession** *several firms closed in (quick) succession* successively, one after the other.

**successor** noun **1** *the successor to the throne* heir, heir apparent, next-in-line. **2** *select the chairman's successor* heir, replacement, supplanter.

**succinct** adjective short, brief, concise, compact, crisp, terse, to the point, pithy.

**succor** noun *give succor to the wounded* assistance, aid, help, comfort, relief, support.

**succor** verb *succor the wounded* assist, aid, help, minister to, comfort, bring relief to, support.

**succumb** verb **1** *succumb to temptation* give in, yield, submit, surrender, capitulate, fall victim. **2** *succumb to his injuries* die, pass away, expire.

**sudden** adjective **1** *a sudden change in the temperature* immediate, instantaneous, abrupt, unexpected, unforeseen, unanticipated. **2** *his sudden rise to fame* rapid, swift, speedy, quick, meteoric.

**suddenly** adverb all of a sudden, instantaneously, abruptly, unexpectedly, without warning; *inf.* out of the blue.

**sue** verb take one to court, bring an action against, bring charges against, charge, bring a suit against, prosecute, summons, indict.

**suffer** verb **1** *suffered from the illness* be in pain, endure agony, hurt, ache. **2** *the divorce caused him to suffer* be distressed, experience hardship, be miserable, be wretched. **3** *suffer loss* experience, undergo, sustain, encounter, endure. **4** *his work suffered because of tardiness* deteriorate, fall off, decline, be impaired. **5** *cannot suffer his arrogance* put up with, tolerate, bear, stand, abide. **suffer from** *suffer from headaches* be affected by, be afflicted by, be troubled with.

**suffering** noun **1** *distressed by the patient's suffering* pain, agony, torment. **2** *endured the suffering of poverty* distress, hardship, misery, wretchedness, hurt, pain, anguish.

**suffice** verb be enough, be sufficient, be adequate, do, serve, meet one's needs; *inf.* fill the bill, hit the spot.

**sufficient** adjective enough, adequate, plenty of, ample.

**suffocate** verb *was nearly suffocated by the fumes* smother, stifle, asphyxiate.

**suffuse** verb spread over, cover, bathe, mantle, permeate, pervade, imbue.

**suggest** verb **1** *suggest him as a replacement* propose, put forward, move, submit, recommend, advocate. **2** *an aroma suggesting fresh-baked bread* bring to mind, evoke. **3** *an appearance suggesting that he lived rough* indicate, lead (one) to believe, give the impression. **4** *a letter suggesting that he is lying* insinuate, hint, imply, intimate.

**suggestion** noun **1** *put forward a suggestion that we leave* proposal, proposition, plan, motion, submission, recommendation. **2** *a suggestion of a French accent in* her speech hint, trace, touch, suspicion. **3** object to the suggestion that he was making insinuation, hint, implication, intimation.

**suggestive** adjective **1** make suggestive remarks provocative, sexual, indelicate, improper, off-color, racy, risqué. **2** an aroma suggestive of freshly cut grass redolent, indicative, evocative, reminiscent.

**suit** noun **1** a woman wearing a blue suit set of clothes, outfit, costume, ensemble. **2** bring a suit against his employers lawsuit, court case, action, proceedings, prosecution. **3** take one's suit to the king petition, appeal, request, plea, entreaty. **4** pay suit to his friend's sister courtship, wooing, attentions.

**suit** verb **1** a color that suits her become, look attractive on, go well with. **2** the suggested attire does not suit him be suitable for, be convenient for, be acceptable to, meet requirements. **3** rich food does not suit him agree with, be good for, be healthy for. **4** suit your speech to the occasion make appropriate, tailor, fashion, accommodate, adjust, adapt, modify.

**suitable** adjective **1** find a suitable date convenient, acceptable, satisfactory. **2** shoes suitable for dancing right, appropriate, fitting, ideal, apt. **3** not suitable behavior appropriate, fitting, becoming, seemly, decorous, proper. **suitable for** a speech suitable for the occasion suited to, befitting, appropriate to, in keeping with, in character with.

**suitcase** noun case, grip, valise, overnight bag.

**suitor** noun **1** unable to choose among her suitors admirer, beau, wooer, boyfriend; lit. follower. **2** the king giving audience to several suitors petitioner, supplicant, plaintiff, appellant.

**sulk** verb mope, pout, be sullen, be put out, be grumpy.

**sullen** adjective morose, uncommunicative, resentful, sulky, sour, glum, gloomy, surly, cross, glowering, grumpy.

**sultry** adjective **1** a sultry day stuffy, stifling, close, oppressive, muggy, humid, sticky, hot, sweltering. **2** a sultry singer sensual, sexy, voluptuous, seductive, alluring, passionate, erotic.

**sum** noun **1** find the sum of the figures total, grand total, tally, aggregate. **2** a large sum of money amount, quantity. **3** look at the problem in its sum entirety, totality, whole. **sum up 1** when the judge sums up review the evidence, summarize the argument. **2** sum up the situation form an opinion of, form an impression of, get the measure of; inf. size up. **3** sum up the facts summarize, précis, abstract, encapsulate, put in a nutshell.

**summarily** adverb summarily dismissed when caught stealing immediately, straight away, on the spot, directly, forthwith, promptly, speedily, suddenly, abruptly, peremptorily, without discussion, without formality.

**summarize** verb sum up, give a synopsis of, précis, abstract, abridge, condense, outline, sketch, give a rundown of, review.

**summary** noun a summary of the plot synopsis, précis, résumé, abstract, abridgment, digest, epitome, outline, sketch, rundown, review, summing-up.

**summary** adjective **1** summary dismissal immediate, instantaneous, prompt, speedy, swift, rapid, sudden, abrupt, hasty, peremptory. **2** a summary account of the long debate abridged, abbreviated, shortened, condensed, brief, concise, succinct, thumbnail.

**summit** noun **1** the summit of the mountain top, peak, crest, crown, apex, vertex, apogee. **2** the summit of her stage career peak, height, pinnacle, climax, zenith, acme.

**summon** verb **1** summoned by the principal send for, call for, bid. **2** summon a committee meeting order, call, convene, assemble, convoke, muster. **3** summon a witness summons, serve with a summons, cite, serve with a writ, subpoena. **summon up 1** summon up the courage to act gather, collect, muster, rally. **2** summon up half-forgotten memories call to mind, call up, conjure up, evoke, recall, revive.

**summons** noun **1** a summons to give evidence in court citation, writ, subpoena. **2** obey the principal's summons to attend order, directive, command, instruction, dictum.

**sumptuous** adjective lavish, luxurious, opulent, magnificent, splendid, costly, expensive, extravagant; inf. plush, ritzy.

**sundry** adjective **1** sundry items various, varied, miscellaneous, assorted, diverse. **2** on sundry occasions several, some, various, different.

**sunny** adjective **1** a sunny day sunlit, bright, clear, fine, cloudless. **2** a sunny nature cheerful, lighthearted, bright, gay, merry, joyful, buoyant, bubbly, blithe, hopeful, optimistic.

**sunrise** noun dawn, daybreak, sunup, first light; lit. aurora.

**sunset** noun sundown, nightfall, close of day, evening, twilight, dusk, gloaming.

**superb** adjective superlative, excellent, first-rate, first-class, outstanding, remarkable, dazzling, brilliant, marvelous, magnificent, wonderful, splendid, exquisite; inf. fantastic, fabulous, A-1.

**supercilious** adjective arrogant, haughty, conceited, proud, vain, disdainful, scornful, condescending, patronizing, lordly, snobbish; *inf.* hoity-toity, high-and-mighty, uppity, snooty, stuck-up.

**superficial** adjective **1** *superficial damage* surface, exterior, peripheral, slight. **2** *a superficial examination* cursory, perfunctory, hasty, hurried, slapdash. **3** *a superficial similarity* outward, apparent, ostensible. **4** *rather a superficial person* shallow, trivial, frivolous, silly. **5** *a superficial book* lightweight, insignificant, trivial.

**superfluous** adjective **1** *sell off the superfluous furniture* spare, surplus, extra, excess, supernumerary. **2** *their presence was superfluous* unnecessary, unneeded, unwarranted, gratuitous.

**superhuman** adjective **1** *require a superhuman effort* Herculean, phenomenal, prodigious, heroic, extraordinary. **2** *superhuman intervention* divine, godlike, holy. **3** *a cry that seemed superhuman* supernatural, preternatural, otherworldly.

**superintendent** noun director, administrator, manager, supervisor, overseer, boss, chief.

**superior** adjective **1** *the superior player* better, greater, more skillful, more advanced. **2** *hold a superior position* higher, higher-ranking, higher-up. **3** *goods of superior leather* high-quality, first-rate, top-quality, high-grade, choice, select, prime, fine. **4** *give her a superior look* haughty, disdainful, condescending, supercilious, patronizing, lordly, snobby; *inf.* high-and-mighty, hoity-toity, uppity, snooty, stuck-up.

**superior** noun boss, manager, chief, supervisor, foreman.

**superlative** adjective best, greatest, supreme, consummate, first-rate, first-class, excellent, magnificent, outstanding, unsurpassed, unparalleled, unrivaled, peerless.

**supernatural** adjective **1** *supernatural beings* otherworldly, unearthly, spectral, ghostly, magical. **2** *supernatural powers* paranormal, supernormal, psychic, miraculous, extraordinary.

**supersede** verb **1** *workers superseded by machines* replace, displace, supplant, oust. **2** *supersede him as chairman* replace, take over from, succeed.

**supervise** verb **1** *supervise the factory* superintend, direct, administer, manage, run. **2** *supervise the trainees* oversee, watch, observe, guide.

**supervision** noun **1** *the supervision of the factory* administration, management, direction, control. **2** *children playing under supervision* observation, guidance.

**supervisor** noun **1** *the supervisor of the factory* director, administrator, manager, overseer, boss, chief, superintendent. **2** *the supervisors of the children* overseer, observer, guide, adviser.

**supplant** verb replace, displace, supersede, oust, overthrow, unseat.

**supple** adjective **1** *supple gymnasts* lithe, loose-limbed, limber. **2** *supple leather* pliant, pliable, flexible, bendable.

**supplement** noun **1** *dietary supplement* addition, additive, extra. **2** *add a supplement to the book/document* appendix, addendum, codicil, rider. **3** *a newspaper supplement* pullout, insert.

**supplement** verb *supplement his salary with an evening job* add to, augment, increase, complement.

**supplicate** verb plead, entreat, beseech, beg, implore, petition, appeal, solicit, pray.

**supplies** noun provisions, stores, rations, food, victuals, provender; equipment, materials, matériel.

**supply** verb **1** *supply the necessary money* provide, give, furnish, contribute, donate, grant; *inf.* shell out. **2** *supply him with tools* provide, equip, outfit.

**supply** noun **1** *organize the supply of wood* provision, furnishing. **2** *a supply of logs* stock, store, reserve, reservoir, stockpile, hoard, cache.

**support** verb **1** *beams supporting the roof* bear, carry, hold up, prop up, bolster up, brace, underpin, buttress. **2** *work to support his family* maintain, provide for, sustain, take care of. **3** *support him in his hour of need* comfort, help, sustain, encourage, fortify. **4** *bring evidence to support his argument* back up, substantiate, corroborate, confirm, verify, validate, authenticate, endorse, ratify. **5** *support several charities* contribute to, donate to, subsidize, fund, finance. **6** *support the candidate* back, champion, side with, vote for, stand behind, stand up for. **7** *support conservation measures* back, advocate, promote, further, champion, espouse, recommend, defend.

**support** noun **1** *the supports of the bridge* base, foundation, pillar, post, prop, underpinning, substructure, brace, buttress, abutment, bolster, stay. **2** *pay toward his family's support* keep, maintenance, sustenance, subsistence, aliment. **3** *discouraged and in need of support* friendship, encouragement, fortification. **4** *give support to charities* contribution, donation, money, subsidy, funding, funds, capital. **5** *give his support to the candidate* backing, assistance, vote. **6** *in support of conservation measures* backing, advocacy, promotion, championship, espousal, recommendation. **7** *he was a great support to his mother* help, assistance, comfort, tower of strength, prop, backbone, mainstay.

**supporter** noun **1** *supporters of the charity* backer, contributor, donor, sponsor, patron, friend, well-wisher. **2** *the candidate's supporters* backer, helper, adherent, follower, ally, voter. **3** *supporters of animal welfare* adherent, advocate, promoter, champion, defender, apologist. **4** *football supporter* fan, follower.

**suppose** verb **1** *I suppose you are right* dare say, assume, presume, expect, imagine, believe, suspect, guess, surmise, reckon, conjecture. **2** *suppose we arrive late* take as a hypothesis, hypothesize, postulate, posit; *inf.* let's say. **3** *creation supposes a creator* presuppose, require, imply.

**supposition** noun **1** *his suppositions proved correct* assumption, presumption, suspicion, guess, surmise, conjecture, speculation, theory. **2** *on the supposition that he is right* assumption, hypothesis, postulation.

**suppress** verb **1** *suppress the rebellion* conquer, vanquish, crush, quell, squash, stamp out, extinguish. **2** *suppress his anger* restrain, keep a rein on, hold back, check, curb. **3** *suppress the information* keep secret, conceal, hide, withhold, cover up, smother, stifle.

**supremacy** noun **1** *a country holding supremacy over its neighbors* ascendancy, predominance, dominion, sway, authority, mastery, control, power, rule, sovereignty, lordship. **2** *challenge her supremacy as top tennis player* preeminence, dominance, superiority, ascendancy, inimitability, matchlessness, peerlessness.

**supreme** adjective **1** *the supreme commander* highest-ranking, chief, foremost, principal. **2** *a supreme effort* extreme, utmost, maximum, extraordinary, remarkable. **3** *the supreme sacrifice* final, last, ultimate.

**sure** adjective **1** *we cannot be sure that he is honest* certain, definite, positive, confident, assured. **2** *a sure success* assured, certain, guaranteed, inevitable. **3** *in the sure knowledge* true, certain, absolute, categorical, proven, unquestionable, indisputable, incontestable, irrefutable, incontrovertible, undeniable. **4** *a sure remedy* unfailing, infallible, reliable, dependable, trustworthy, tested, tried and true, foolproof, effective, efficacious; *inf.* sure-fire. **5** *sure friend* true, reliable, dependable, trusted, trustworthy, loyal, faithful, steadfast. **6** *with a sure hand* firm, steady, stable, secure, confident, unhesitating, unfaltering, unwavering. **be sure** *be sure to arrive on time* be certain, be careful, take care, remember.

**surely** adverb **1** *they will surely fail* certainly, definitely, assuredly, undoubtedly, without doubt, indubitably, unquestionably, irrefutably, incontrovertibly, undeniably, inevitably. **2** *walk slowly but surely* firmly, steadily, confidently, unhesitatingly.

**surface** noun outside, exterior, top, façade. **on the surface** *on the surface, the business seems profitable* at first glance, to the casual eye, outwardly, to all appearances, apparently, superficially.

**surge** noun **1** *a surge of water* gush, rush, outpouring, stream, flow, efflux. **2** *a sudden surge in prices* increase, rise, upswing, escalation.

**surge** verb *the water surged from the broken pipe* | *crowds surging from the hall* gush, rush, stream, flow.

**surly** adjective bad-tempered, ill-natured, grumpy, crotchety, grouchy, cantankerous, irascible, gruff, churlish, sullen.

**surmise** verb guess, conjecture, suspect, deduce, assume, presume, gather, think, believe, imagine.

**surmount** verb **1** *many obstacles to surmount* get over, overcome, conquer, triumph over, prevail over, beat. **2** *climbers struggling to surmount the mountain* climb, ascend, scale, mount.

**surpass** verb beat, exceed, excel, transcend, outdo, outshine, outstrip, overshadow, eclipse.

**surplus** noun *get rid of the surplus* excess, remainder, residue, surfeit.

**surplus** adjective *surplus food going to waste* excess, superfluous, leftover, unused, remaining, extra, spare.

**surprise** verb **1** *their sudden appearance surprised him* astonish, amaze, nonplus, take aback, startle, astound, flabbergast. **2** *surprise the burglars opening the safe* take by surprise, catch unawares, catch off guard, catch red-handed.

**surprise** noun **1** *look up in surprise* astonishment, amazement, incredulity, wonder. **2** *it was a surprise when she left* shock, bolt from the blue, bombshell.

**surrender** verb **1** *surrender his right to the title* give up, relinquish, renounce, forgo, forsake, cede, abdicate, waive, hand over, let go of. **2** *surrender to the enemy* give oneself up, yield, submit, capitulate, lay down one's arms, raise the white flag. **3** *surrender all hope* give up, abandon, lose.

**surrender** noun **1** *the surrender of his title* relinquishment, renunciation, forgoing, ceding, cession, abdication, waiving. **2** *their surrender to the enemy* yielding, capitulation, submission.

**surreptitious** adjective stealthy, clandestine, secret, sneaky, furtive, underhand, covert.

**surround** verb encircle, enclose, encompass, ring, gird, fence in, hem in.

**surroundings** plural noun *brought up in squalid surroundings* environment, setting, milieu, element.

**surveillance** noun *under surveillance* observation, watch, scrutiny, espionage.

**survey** verb **1** *survey the burned building* observe, view, regard, examine, inspect. **2** *survey the evidence* scan, study, consider, review, examine, scrutinize, take stock of; *inf.* size up. **3** *survey a building* make a survey of, value, appraise, assess, prospect, triangulate.

**survey** noun **1** *undertake a survey of the evidence* study, consideration, review, overview, examination, inspection, scrutiny. **2** *carry out a survey of the building* valuation, appraisal. **3** *a survey of TV viewing habits* investigation, inquiry, research, study, review, probe, questionnaire.

**survive** verb **1** *old customs surviving in the village* live on, continue, remain, last, persist, endure, exist. **2** *fathers surviving their sons* outlive, outlast; live longer than. **3** *people surviving in the freezing conditions* remain alive, live, subsist.

**susceptible** adjective **1** *con artists preying on susceptible people* impressionable, gullible, vulnerable. **2** *susceptible to colds* subject, liable, prone, inclined, predisposed.

**suspect** verb **1** *I suspect that you are right* feel, fancy, surmise, guess, conjecture, speculate, have a hunch, suppose, believe, think. **2** *suspect the truth of his statement* doubt, harbor suspicions about, have misgivings about, distrust, mistrust.

**suspend** verb **1** *suspend a light from the tree* hang, swing, dangle. **2** *suspend the proceedings* adjourn, interrupt, discontinue, break off, put off, postpone, delay, defer, shelve, pigeonhole, table; *inf.* put on ice. **3** *suspend him from his job* debar, shut out, exclude, keep out, remove.

**suspense** noun uncertainty, doubt, anticipation, expectation, excitement, tension, anxiety, nervousness, apprehension.

**suspicion** noun *his suspicion is that she will appear* feeling, surmise, guess, conjecture, speculation, hunch, supposition, belief; *inf.* gut feeling, **suspicions** *have suspicions about his motives* doubts, misgivings, qualms, skepticism; *inf.* a funny feeling.

**suspicious** adjective **1** *give him suspicious looks* doubtful, wary, chary, skeptical, distrustful, mistrustful. **2** *police observing a suspicious character* guilty-looking, dishonest-looking; *inf.* shifty, shady. **3** *suspicious circumstances* questionable, doubtful, odd, strange, irregular, queer, funny; *inf.* fishy.

**sustain** verb **1** *beams sustaining the weight of the roof* bear, support, carry, prop up, shore up. **2** *sustain one's courage* keep up, continue, carry on, maintain. **3** *sustain him in his hour of need* support, comfort, help, assist, encourage. **4** *enough food to sustain them* keep alive, keep going, maintain, preserve, feed, nourish. **5** *sustain defeat* experience, undergo, suffer, endure. **6** *the court sustained his claim* uphold, validate, ratify, vindicate. **7** *evidence sustaining his allegations* confirm, verify, corroborate, substantiate.

**swagger** verb *swagger down the street in his new coat* strut, parade, prance; *inf.* show off.

**swallow** verb **1** *swallow the meat with difficulty* gulp down, eat, consume, devour, ingest. **2** *swallow two drinks in quick succession* gulp down, drink, swill; *inf.* swig, chug. **3** *swallow one's pride* repress, restrain, choke back, control; stifle, smother, bottle up; eat. **swallow up 1** *the waves swallowed him up* engulf, swamp, overwhelm. **2** *big companies swallowing up small ones* take over, absorb, assimilate, overrun.

**swamp** noun *get stuck in a swamp* marsh, bog, quagmire, mire, morass, fen, quag.

**swamp** verb **1** *heavy rains swamping the town* flood, inundate, deluge, wash out, drench, saturate. **2** *swamped with applications* inundate, flood, deluge, overwhelm, engulf, snow under, besiege.

**swap** verb **1** *children swapping toys* exchange, trade, barter, switch. **2** *swap jokes* exchange, trade, bandy.

**swarm** noun *a swarm of people* crowd, multitude, horde, host, mob, throng, mass, army, drove.

**swarm** verb *shoppers swarming to the sales* flock, crowd, throng. **swarming with** *a barn swarming with flies* overrun with, teeming with, bristling with, crawling with, infested with.

**swarthy** adjective dark, dark-skinned, dark-complexioned, dusky.

**sway** verb **1** *trees swaying in the breeze* swing, shake, bend, lean, incline. **2** *drunks swaying on their way home* roll, stagger, wobble. **3** *swaying her hips* swing, shake. **4** *swaying between emigrating and staying* waver, hesitate, fluctuate, vacillate, oscillate. **5** *swayed by their arguments* influence, affect, persuade. **6** *swayed by ambition* rule, govern, control, direct, guide.

**sway** noun *colonies under the sway of the monarchy | under the sway of her parents* jurisdiction, rule, government, sovereignty, dominion, control, command, power, authority, influence, guidance, direction. **hold sway** *the aged emperor still holds sway* hold power, rule, be in control, predominate, have the upper hand.

**swear** verb **1** *swear to take care of the child* solemnly promise, pledge oneself, vow, give one's word, take an oath. **2** *he swore that he was fit to drive* vow, insist, declare, assert, maintain, contend, aver. **3** *swear* *at the other driver* curse, blaspheme, utter profanities, swear like a trooper/sailor; *inf.* cuss. **swear by 1** *swear by Almighty God* call as one's witness, appeal to, invoke. **2** *swear by her remedy for colds* have faith in, have trust in, place reliance on, depend on, believe in.

**sweat** noun **1** *sweat pouring from his brow* perspiration; *Med.* diaphoresis. **2** *in a sweat until the results came through* fluster, dither, fuss, panic; *inf.* tizzy, stew, lather.

**sweat** verb **1** *sweating in the heat* perspire, drip with perspiration. **2** *they were sweating until the results came through* fret, dither, fuss, panic, worry, agonize, lose sleep; *inf.* be on pins and needles. **3** *sweat to get the work done* work like a Trojan, labor, toil, slog.

**sweep** verb **1** *sweep the floor* brush, whisk, clean. **2** *swept away by the waves* carry, pull, drag. **3** *fire sweeping through the building* race, hurtle, streak, whip; *inf.* tear. **sweep aside** *sweep aside their objections* cast aside, discard, disregard, ignore, dismiss.

**sweep** noun **1** *with one sweep of her hand* gesture, movement, action, stroke, wave. **2** *the sweep of the road* curve, curvature, bend, arc. **3** *within the sweep of his power* span, range, scope, compass, reach. **4** *a sweep of pasture lands* stretch, expanse.

**sweeping** adjective **1** *sweeping reforms* extensive, wide-ranging, global, broad, comprehensive, far-reaching. **2** *make sweeping statements* blanket, wholesale, unqualified, indiscriminate. **3** *a sweeping victory* decisive, overwhelming, thorough, complete, total, absolute, out-and-out.

**sweet** adjective **1** *sweet types of food* sugary, honeyed, syrupy, saccharine. **2** *sweet fruit* ripe, mellow, luscious. **3** *the sweet smell of roses* fragrant, aromatic, perfumed, scented, balmy. **4** *the sweet sound of children's voices* musical, tuneful, dulcet, mellifluous, harmonious, euphonious. **5** *the sweet sight of home* pleasing, delightful, welcome. **6** *have a sweet nature* good-natured, amiable, pleasant, agreeable, friendly, kindly, charming, engaging. **7** *sweet faces* attractive, beautiful, lovely, comely. **8** *his sweet wife* dear, darling, beloved, cherished, precious, treasured. **sweet on** *sweet on the boy next door* fond of, taken with, in love with, enamored of, keen on.

**sweetheart** noun **1** *his teenage sweetheart* girlfriend, boyfriend, lover, suitor, admirer, beau, paramour, inamorato, inamorata; *inf.* steady, flame. **2** *good-bye, sweetheart* dear, dearest, darling, love, beloved; *inf.* honey, sweetie.

**swell** verb **1** *his ankle swelled up* expand, bulge, distend, inflate, dilate, become bloated, blow up, puff up, balloon. **2** *the numbers have swelled* increase, rise, mount, escalate, snowball, mushroom. **3** *the music swelled* grow louder, intensify, heighten.

**swell** noun **1** *the swell of the sea* billowing, undulation, surging. **2** *a swell in numbers* increase, rise, escalation, mushrooming.

**swelling** noun *treat the swelling on his head* bump, lump, bulge, inflammation, protuberance.

**swerve** verb veer, turn aside, skew, deviate, sheer.

**swift** adjective **1** *a swift runner* fast, rapid, quick, speedy, fleet. **2** *at a swift pace* fast, rapid, brisk, lively, expeditious. **3** *a swift change of plan* rapid, sudden, abrupt, hasty, hurried. **4** *a swift reply* rapid, prompt, immediate, instantaneous.

**swill** verb *swill bottles of beer* gulp down, drink, quaff, swallow, down, drain, guzzle; *inf.* swig, knock off.

**swill** noun *remove the swill from the pigsties* waste, slop, refuse, scourings.

**swindle** verb *swindle the old lady* defraud, cheat, trick, fleece, dupe, deceive; *inf.* con, rip off, pull a fast one on, bilk.

**swindle** noun *get the money through a swindle* fraud, trick, deception, scam; *inf.* con, rip-off.

**swindler** noun fraud, cheat, trickster, rogue, mountebank; *inf.* con man, con artist, shark.

**swing** verb **1** *lights swinging from the roof* hang, be suspended, dangle. **2** *the pendulum swings* sway, undulate, oscillate. **3** *he swings from optimism to despair* change, fluctuate, oscillate, waver, seesaw, yo-yo. **4** *manage to swing an interview with the chairman* achieve, obtain, acquire, get, maneuver.

**swing** noun **1** *the swing of the pendulum* swaying, oscillation, undulation. **2** *music with a swing* rhythm, beat, pulse. **3** *a swing to the left at the election* move, change, turn-around.

**swirl** verb *water swirling round and round* whirl, eddy, circulate, spin, churn, swish.

**switch** noun **1** *a switch from a tree* shoot, twig, branch. **2** *hit the mutineer with a switch* cane, rod, stick, whip. **3** *a sudden switch in direction* change, shift, reversal, about-face, swerve, U-turn. **4** *the switch from one method to another* change, changeover, transfer, conversion. **5** *get a new book in a switch with his friend* exchange, trade; *inf.* swap.

**switch** verb **1** *switch directions* change, shift, reverse. **2** *switch cars* exchange, interchange, trade, barter; *inf.* swap.

**swollen** adjective bulging, distended, inflated, dilated, bloated, puffy.

**swoop** verb *hawks swooping on their prey* pounce, dive, descend. **swoop up** *swoop* *up the baby in her arms* take up, pick up, scoop up, seize, grab.

**sword** noun blade, rapier, saber, cutlass. **cross swords** fight, do battle, quarrel, engage in conflict, lock horns. **put to the sword** *put the traitor to the sword* put to death, execute, kill, slay, murder.

**sycophant** noun toady, flatterer, Uriah Heep; *inf.* bootlicker, yes-man.

**symbol** noun **1** *the dove is the symbol of peace* emblem, token, sign, badge, representation, image. **2** *mathematical symbol* sign, character, mark. **3** *the symbol of the company* stamp, emblem, trademark, logo, monogram.

**symbolic** adjective **1** *the dove being symbolic of peace* emblematic, representative. **2** *a symbolic dance* representative, illustrative, figurative, allegorical.

**symbolize** verb stand for, represent, personify, exemplify, betoken, denote, signify.

**symmetrical** adjective **1** *symmetrical features* balanced, well-proportioned, even, harmonious. **2** *the two sides of the building must be symmetrical* regular, even, uniform, proportional, consistent, in agreement.

**symmetry** noun **1** *the symmetry of her features* balance, proportions, regularity, harmony. **2** *the symmetry of the two sides of the building* regularity, evenness, uniformity, consistency, congruity, conformity, agreement, correspondence.

**sympathetic** adjective compassionate, commiserating, pitying, consoling, comforting, supportive, caring, concerned, solicitous, considerate, kindhearted, warmhearted, understanding, charitable, empathetic. **sympathetic to** *not very sympathetic to their cause* favorably disposed to, approving of, supportive of, encouraging of.

**sympathize** verb **sympathize with 1** *sympathize with the bereaved* be sympathetic toward, show compassion for, commiserate with, offer condolences to, console, comfort, be supportive of, empathize with. **2** *sympathize with their cause* be sympathetic toward, be in favor of, approve of, commend, back, support, encourage.

**sympathy** noun **1** *express their sympathy to the bereaved* compassion, commiseration, pity, condolence, consolation, support, concern, consideration, charity, understanding, empathy. **2** *a bond of sympathy between them* empathy, harmony, compatibility, closeness. **3** *show sympathy for their cause* favor, approval, approbation, good will, support, encouragement.

**symptom** noun **1** *a symptom of the disease* sign, indication, warning, mark, characteristic, feature. **2** *his bad behavior was a symptom of his unhappiness* expression, sign, indication, signal, token, evidence, demonstration, display.

**synthetic** adjective manufactured, manmade, fake, artificial, mock, ersatz.

**system** noun **1** *the railroad system* structure, organization, arrangement; *inf.* setup. **2** *a new system for teaching languages* method, methodology, technique, procedure, approach, means, way, modus operandi. **3** *absolutely no system in his accounting methods* method, order, planning, logic.

**systematic** adjective *a systematic approach to the problem* structured, organized, methodical, orderly, logical, efficient, businesslike.

# *Tt*

**table** noun **1** *put the plates on the table* counter, bar, buffet, bench, stand. **2** *table of data* list, catalog, tabulation, inventory, digest, itemization, index; chart, diagram, figure, graph, plan.

**table** verb postpone, defer, suspend, shelve; *inf.* put on ice.

**taboo** adjective forbidden, prohibited, banned, proscribed, vetoed, ruled out, outlawed.

**tabulate** verb chart, systematize, systemize, arrange, order, dispose, organize, catalog, list, classify, class, codify, group, range, grade.

**tacit** adjective implicit, understood, implied, unstated, undeclared, unspoken, unexpressed, unmentioned, unvoiced, silent, wordless.

**taciturn** adjective unforthcoming, uncommunicative, reticent, secretive, untalkative, tight-lipped, closemouthed, quiet, silent, mute, dumb; reserved, withdrawn, aloof, cold, detached.

**tack** noun **1** *attach the notice with a tack* nail, pin, staple, rivet. **2** *take an unusual* *tack* course/line of action, method, approach, process, way, policy, tactic, plan, strategy, attack.

**tack** verb **1** *tack the picture to the wall* nail, pin, staple, fix, fasten, affix, put up/down. **2** *in politics it is necessary to know when to tack* change course/direction, alter one's approach, change one's mind/attitude, have a change of heart, do an about-face; *inf.* do a U-turn. **3** *tack a postscript on the letter* add, attach, append, tag, annex.

**tackle** noun *fishing tackle* gear, equipment, apparatus, outfit; tools, implements, accoutrements, paraphernalia, trappings; *inf.* things, stuff.

**tackle** verb **1** *tackle the task/problem* undertake, attempt, apply/address oneself to, get to grips with, set/go about, get to work at, take on. **2** *tackle the intruder* grapple with, seize, take hold of, confront, accost, waylay.

**tacky** adjective tasteless, garish. *See* TAWDRY.

**tact** noun diplomacy, *savoir faire*, sensitivity, delicacy, subtlety, finesse, skill, adroitness, perception, judgment, prudence.

**tactful** adjective diplomatic, politic, discreet, sensitive, understanding, subtle, skillful, adroit, prudent, judicious.

**tactic** noun maneuver, device, stratagem, trick, scheme, plan, ploy, method, approach, tack. *See* TACTICS.

**tactics** plural noun strategy, campaign, policy; plans, battle/game plans.

**tactless** adjective undiplomatic, impolitic, indiscreet, insensitive, crude, clumsy, awkward, inept, bungling, maladroit, gauche.

**tag** noun label, ticket, sticker, docket.

**tag** verb **1** *tag the items* label, put a ticket/sticker on, mark. **2** *tag him Lefty* name, call, nickname, title, entitle, label, dub, term, style, christen. **3** *tag a postscript to the letter* add, attach, append, affix, tack. **tag along with** accompany, follow, trail behind, tread on the heels of, dog.

**tailor** noun outfitter, dressmaker, couturier, clothier, costumier.

**tailor** verb *tailor the schedule to your needs* fit, suit, fashion, style, mold, shape, adapt, adjust, modify, convert, alter, accommodate.

**taint** verb contaminate, pollute, adulterate, infect, blight, befoul, spoil; tarnish, sully, blacken, stain, besmirch, smear, blot, blemish, muddy, damage, injure, harm.

**take** verb **1** *take the book from her* get/lay hold of, grasp, grip, clutch. **2** *take first prize* get, receive, obtain, gain, acquire, secure, procure, come by, win, earn. **3** *take prisoners* seize, catch, capture, arrest, carry off, abduct. **4** *who took my pen?* remove, appropriate, make off with, steal, filch, pilfer, purloin, pocket; *inf.* pinch, swipe. **5** *she showed me several dresses but I took the blue one* pick, choose, select, decide on, settle on, opt for. **6** *take some nourishment* consume, eat, devour, swallow; drink, imbibe. **7** *the vaccination did not take* be effective/efficacious, work, operate, succeed. **8** *the journey takes three hours* use, use up, require, call for, need, necessitate. **9** *take the box home with you* carry, fetch, bring, bear, transport, convey, cart; *inf.* tote. **10** *will you take his sister home?* escort, accompany, conduct, guide, lead, usher, convoy. **11** *take the child's temperature* find out, discover, ascertain, determine, establish. **12** *I take it that you agree* understand, interpret as, grasp, gather, comprehend, apprehend, assume, believe, suppose, consider, presume. **13** *take the news badly* receive, deal with, cope with. **14** *take the offer* accept, receive, adopt. **15** *take a course of study* enter upon, undertake, begin, set about. **16** *take French at school* study, learn, be taught, take up, pursue. **17** *take an oath/look* perform, execute, effect, do, make, have. **18** *the bucket takes three gallons* hold, contain, have the capacity for, have space/room for, accommodate. **19** *I cannot take his rudeness* bear, tolerate, stand, put up with, stomach, brook. **20** *the machine takes its name from the inventor* derive, obtain, come by. **21** *the passage is taken from the Bible* extract, quote, cite, excerpt, derive. **22** *take three from five* subtract, deduct, remove. **23** *taken by her beauty* captivate, enchant, charm, delight, please, attract, win over, fascinate. **take after** resemble, look like, be like, favor; *inf.* be a chip off the old block, be the spitting image of. **take back 1** *take back the accusation* retract, withdraw, renounce, disclaim, unsay, disavow, recant. **2** *the store will not take the goods back* give a refund for, exchange, trade, swap. **3** *his wife has taken him back* accept back, welcome back, forgive. **4** *take back the land won by the enemy* regain, repossess, reclaim, recapture, reconquer. **take down 1** *take down the details* write down, note down, make a note of, jot down, set down, record, put on record, commit to paper, document. **2** *take down the scaffolding/fence* remove, dismantle, disassemble, take apart, take to pieces, demolish, tear down, level, raze. **3** *take down the flag* pull down, let down, haul down, lower, drop. **4** *that should take him down a bit* humble, deflate, humiliate, mortify, take down a peg or two; *inf.* put down. **take for** regard as, consider as, view as, look upon as. **take in 1** *take in paying guests* admit, let in, receive, welcome, accommodate, board. **2** *he didn't* *seem to take the news in* grasp, understand, comprehend, absorb, assimilate. **3** *said nothing but took everything in* observe, see, notice, take note of, note, perceive, regard. **4** *they were completely taken in by the con man* deceive, delude, hoodwink, mislead, trick, dupe, fool, cheat, defraud, swindle, gull; *inf.* con, bilk, pull the wool over someone's eyes. **5** *the court's jurisdiction takes in these three districts* include, encompass, embrace, contain, comprise, cover. **6** *try to take in a concert there* go to, go to see, attend, visit. **take off 1** *take the lid off the jar* remove, detach, pull off. **2** *take off one's clothes* remove, discard, strip off, peel off, throw off, divest oneself of, doff. **3** *take money off the bill for poor service* deduct from, subtract from, take away from. **4** *the children took off when they saw the police* run away, take to one's heels, flee, decamp, disappear, leave, go, depart; *inf.* split, beat it, skedaddle, vamoose, hightail it. **5** *the business/scheme has really taken off* succeed, do well, become popular, catch on. **take on 1** *take on extra work* undertake, accept, tackle. **2** *take on extra staff* employ, engage, hire, enroll, enlist; *inf.* take on board. **3** *take him on at chess* compete against, oppose, challenge, face, pit/match oneself against, contend with, vie with, fight. **4** *suddenly his words took on new meaning* acquire, come to have, assume. **take out 1** *take out a tooth* remove, extract, pull out, yank out. **2** *take out the girl next door* go out with, escort; *inf.* date. **take over** take/assume/gain control of, take charge/command of, assume responsibility for. **take to 1** *she's taken to smoking* start, commence, make a habit of, resort to. **2** *he did not take to her friend* like, get on with. **3** *he has really taken to swimming* develop an ability/aptitude for, develop a liking for, like, enjoy, become interested in. **take up 1** *take up surfing* become involved/interested in, engage in, begin, start, commence. **2** *practicing the piano takes up a great deal of time* use, use up, occupy, fill, consume, absorb, cover, extend over. **3** *take up the story where they left off* resume, recommence, restart, begin again, carry on, continue, pick up. **4** *take up with the wrong sort of people* become friendly/friends, go around; *inf.* hang around.

**take** noun takings, proceeds, returns, receipts, profits, winnings, purse, pickings, earnings; gain, income, revenue.

**tale** noun **1** *a fairy tale* story, short story, narrative, anecdote, legend, fable, myth, parable, allegory, epic, saga; *inf.* yarn. **2** *hear tales of her wild behavior* talk, rumor, gossip, hearsay; report, allegation. **3** *don't believe her story—it's just a tale* lie,

fib, falsehood, untruth, fabrication; *inf.* tall story, cock-and-bull story, whopper.

**talent** noun gift, flair, aptitude, facility, knack, bent, ability, faculty, endowment.

**talented** adjective gifted, accomplished, able, capable, apt, deft, adept, proficient, brilliant.

**talk** verb **1** *talk incessantly* speak, chat, chatter, gossip, prattle, prate, gibber, jabber, babble, rattle on; *inf.* yak, gab. **2** *talk nonsense* speak, say, utter, voice, express, articulate, pronounce, enunciate, verbalize. **3** *they do not talk any more* communicate, converse, confer, parley, palaver, confabulate; *inf.* have a confab, chew the fat, jaw, rap. **4** *torture made the prisoner talk* tell, reveal all, tell tales, give the game away, open one's mouth, let the cat out of the bag; *inf.* blab, squeal, spill the beans, sing. **5** *if they divorce, people will talk* gossip, spread rumors, pass comment, make remarks, criticize. **6** *the professor is talking tonight* give a talk, speak, lecture, discourse. **talk back** answer defiantly/impertinently, answer back, be sassy; *inf.* give lip. **talk big** brag, boast, crow, exaggerate; *inf.* blow one's own horn, shoot one's mouth off. **talk down to** speak condescendingly to, condescend to, speak haughtily to, patronize. **talk into** persuade to, cajole to, coax into, influence. **talk of** speak about, discuss, mention, make mention of, refer to, make reference to. **talk out of** dissuade from, persuade against, discourage from, deter from, stop.

**talk** noun **1** *their noisy talk kept me awake* talking, speaking, chatter, chatting, gossiping, prattling, gibbering, jabbering, babbling, gabbling; *inf.* yakking, gabbing. **2** *baby/seamen's talk* words; speech, language, dialect, jargon, cant, slang, idiom, idiolect, patois; *inf.* lingo. **3** *have a talk about their future* conversation, chat, discussion, tête-à-tête; dialogue; *inf.* confab, rap. **4** *give a talk to the society* lecture, speech, address, discourse, oration, sermon, disquisition. **5** *there is talk of a merger* gossip, rumor, hearsay.

**talkative** adjective loquacious, garrulous, voluble, chatty, gossipy, conversational, long-winded, gushing, effusive, gabby, mouthy; *inf.* bigmouthed.

**talker** noun **1** *the talker bored the audience* speaker, lecturer, orator. **2** *they are a family of talkers* conversationalist, chatter, chatterbox, gossip.

**tall** adjective **1** *tall people/buildings* lanky, rangy, gangling, high, lofty, towering, soaring, sky-high, skyscraping. **2** *a tall story* exaggerated, unlikely, incredible, far-fetched, implausible.

**tally** noun count, record, running total, reckoning, enumeration, register, roll, census, poll; score, result, total, sum.

**tally** verb *the two accounts do not tally* agree, accord, concur, coincide, conform, correspond, match, fit, harmonize.

**tame** adjective **1** *tame animals* domesticated, gentle, docile. **2** *the supposedly rowdy children were quite tame* subdued, docile, submissive, compliant, meek, obedient, tractable, manageable. **3** *the horror movie turned out to be quite tame* unexciting, uninteresting, dull, bland, flat, insipid, vapid, run-of-the-mill, mediocre.

**tame** verb **1** *tame the wild cat* domesticate, break, train, gentle. **2** *tame the unruly element in the class* subdue, discipline, curb, control, master, overcome, suppress.

**tamper** verb **tamper with 1** *tamper with the exam papers* meddle with, interfere with, monkey around with, mess about with, tinker with, fiddle with. **2** *tamper with the jury* influence, get at, rig, manipulate, bribe, corrupt; *inf.* fix.

**tang** noun **1** *the tang of orange* flavor, taste, savor; smell, odor, aroma. **2** *add some tang to the occasion* spice, spiciness, piquancy, relish, sharpness, zest; *inf.* ginger, punch, zip.

**tangible** adjective **1** *tangible changes to the skin* touchable, palpable, tactile. **2** *tangible proof* concrete, real, actual, solid, substantial, hard, definite, clear, distinct, unmistakable.

**tangle** verb **1** *the net became tangled in the rose bush* entangle, intertwine, twist, snarl, ravel, knot. **2** *do not tangle with the authorities* come into conflict, dispute, argue, quarrel, fight, wrangle, squabble, contend, cross swords, lock horns.

**tantalize** verb tease, torment, make one's mouth water, lead on, entice, titillate, allure, beguile.

**tap**[1] noun spigot, faucet, stopcock, valve. **on tap** at/on hand, available, ready, in reserve, standing by.

**tap**[2] verb **1** *tap cider from a cask* draw off, siphon off, drain, bleed. **2** *tap a cask* broach, open, pierce. **3** *tap sources of information* use, make use of, draw on, exploit, milk, explore, probe. **4** *tap their telephone calls* wiretap, eavesdrop on; *inf.* bug.

**tap**[3] noun knock, rap, beat, touch, pat.

**tap**[4] verb knock, rap, strike, beat, drum, touch, pat.

**tape** noun **1** *the first-place runner breaking the tape* band, strip, string, ribbon. **2** *play a tape* tape recording, cassette, videotape, videocassette, video, audiotape, audiocassette.

**tape** verb **1** *tape the pieces together* bind, tie, fasten, stick, seal, secure; Scotch (*trademark*) tape. **2** *tape the concert/conversation* record, tape-record, videotape.

**taper** verb narrow, thin. **taper off** dwindle, diminish, lessen, decrease, reduce, subside, die off, die away, fade, peter out, wane, ebb, wind down, slacken off, thin out.

**target** noun objective, goal, object, aim, end, intention, desired result.

**tariff** noun tax, duty, toll, excise, levy, impost.

**tarnish** verb **1** *time had tarnished the brass* dull, dim, discolor, rust. **2** *tarnish his reputation* sully, besmirch, blacken, stain, blemish, blot, taint, befoul.

**tart** adjective **1** *a tart dessert* sour, tangy, piquant, pungent, bitter, acid, acidulous, vinegary. **2** *a tart remark/wit* astringent, caustic, sharp, biting, cutting, stinging, mordant, trenchant, incisive, piercing, scathing, sardonic.

**task** noun job, duty, chore, charge, odd job, assignment, mission, undertaking, errand, quest. **take to task** rebuke, reprimand, reprove, reproach, upbraid, scold, berate, lecture, castigate, censure, criticize, blame; *inf.* tell off.

**taste** noun **1** *the taste of fresh raspberries* flavor, savor, relish, tang. **2** *a taste of the pudding/sauce* bit, morsel, bite, mouthful, spoonful, sample, sip, drop, swallow, touch, soupçon. **3** *a taste for the unknown* liking, love, fondness, fancy, desire, preference, penchant, predilection, inclination, partiality. **4** *furnish the house with taste* discrimination, discernment, judgment, cultivation, culture, refinement, polish, finesse, elegance, grace, stylishness. **5** *her remark lacked taste* decorum, propriety, tact, tactfulness, diplomacy, delicacy, nicety, discretion.

**taste** verb **1** *taste the sauce while cooking it* sample, test, try, nibble, sip. **2** *I cannot taste the garlic* make out, perceive, discern, distinguish, differentiate. **3** *not taste food for days* eat, partake of, consume, devour. **4** *taste success/defeat* experience, undergo, encounter, meet, come up against, know.

**tasteful** adjective **1** *a tasteful display* in good taste, pleasing, elegant, graceful, discriminating, refined, restrained. **2** *tasteful behavior* decorous, proper, seemly, fitting, refined, cultivated.

**tasteless** adjective **1** *tasteless food* flavorless, savorless, bland, insipid, unappetizing, vapid. **2** *tasteless decorations* vulgar, crude. *See* TAWDRY. **3** *tasteless behavior* indecorous, improper, unseemly, rude, unfitting, unrefined, uncultured, uncultivated, vulgar, crude, uncouth, crass.

**tasty** adjective flavorsome, flavorful, full-flavored, appetizing, palatable, toothsome, delectable, delicious, luscious, mouthwatering, piquant, pungent, spicy; *inf.* scrumptious, yummy.

**tatter** noun **in tatters 1** *clothes in tatters* ragged, torn, in shreds, in bits. **2** *his career in tatters* in ruins, ruined, destroyed, demolished.

**tattle** verb gossip, chatter, prattle, prate, babble, rattle on; *inf.* gab.

**taunt** noun gibe, jeer, sneer, insult, barb, dig, catcall; provocation, derision, mockery; *inf.* put-down.

**taunt** verb gibe at, jeer at, sneer at, insult, chaff, tease, torment, provoke, ridicule, deride, mock.

**taut** adjective **1** *taut ropes/muscles* tight, stretched, rigid, tightened, flexed, tensed. **2** *a taut expression* tense, strained, stressed, drawn; *inf.* uptight. **3** *run a taut ship* orderly, shipshape, tight, trim, neat, tidy, spruce.

**tawdry** adjective showy, gaudy, flashy, garish, loud, tasteless, cheap, cheapjack, shoddy, meretricious; *inf.* tacky, kitsch.

**tax** noun **1** *a tax on imports* levy, charge, duty, toll, excise, tariff; customs. **2** *they became a tax on her resources* burden, load, weight, encumbrance, strain, pressure, stress, drain.

**tax** verb *the work taxes his strength* make demands on, weigh down, burden, load, encumber, overload, stretch, strain, try, wear out, exhaust, sap, drain, enervate, fatigue, tire, weary, weaken.

**teach** verb instruct, educate, school, tutor, coach, show, guide, train, drill, ground, enlighten, edify.

**teacher** noun schoolteacher, instructor, educator, tutor, coach, trainer, lecturer, professor, pedagogue, guide, mentor, guru.

**team** noun band, bunch, party, gang, crew, troupe, set, squad, side, lineup.

**tear**[1] noun rip, split, hole, rent, run, rupture.

**tear**[2] verb **1** *tear the paper/cloth* rip, pull apart, split, rend, sever, rive, sunder, rupture. **2** *tear the flesh* lacerate, gash, slash, pierce, stab, scratch, cut, mutilate, hack. **3** *tear off the cover* wrench, yank, wrest, extract, peel, snatch, pluck, grab, seize. **4** *torn by guilt* distress, upset, harrow, torture, torment. **5** *children tearing down the street* run, race, sprint, gallop, rush, dash, bolt, career, dart, fly, shoot, hurry, speed, hasten, whiz, zoom, zip; *inf.* hotfoot it.

**tear**[3] noun teardrop, drop, droplet, globule, bead. **in tears** crying, weeping. *See* TEARFUL 1.

**tearful** adjective **1** *in a tearful state* in tears, crying, weeping, weepy, sobbing, blubbering, sniveling, whimpering, wailing; emotional, upset, distressed. **2** *a tearful parting* heartbreaking, heart-rending, sad, poignant, mournful, melancholy, lamentable, dolorous.

**tease** verb **1** *tease the cat* torment, provoke, badger, bait, goad, needle, aggravate, pest, bother, worry, vex, irritate, annoy, gibe, rag, twit, mock, ridicule. **2** *he was only teasing her* joke (with), fool (with); *inf.* kid, rib, put on.

**technical** adjective *technical training* mechanical, practical, scientific, nontheoretical.

**technique** noun **1** *new business techniques* method, modus operandi, system, procedure, manner, way, course of action, mode, fashion; means. **2** *admire the violinist's technique* execution, performance, skill, proficiency, expertise, mastery, artistry, art, craftsmanship, craft, ability, adroitness, deftness, dexterity, knack.

**tedious** adjective wearisome, wearying, tiresome, tiring, fatiguing, long-drawn-out, overlong, long-winded, prolix, dull, boring, uninteresting, dry, uninspired, flat, monotonous.

**teem** verb abound, swarm, crawl, bristle, seethe, brim; be abundant, be plentiful, be copious.

**teeter** verb **1** *teeter down the street on high heels* totter, wobble, stagger, stumble, reel, sway, roll, lurch. **2** *teeter between accepting and refusing* waver, vacillate, fluctuate, oscillate, dither, hesitate, shilly-shally, seesaw.

**tell** verb **1** *tell the news to everyone* make known, impart, communicate, announce, proclaim, broadcast, divulge, reveal, disclose, declare, state, mention, utter, voice, say, speak. **2** *tell a story* narrate, relate, recount, report, chronicle, recite, rehearse, describe, portray, sketch, delineate. **3** *tell them tomorrow that you are going* inform, let know, make aware, apprise, notify. **4** *I tell you that he is guilty* assure, promise, guarantee, warrant. **5** *tell them to go home* instruct, bid, order, command, direct, charge, enjoin, require. **6** *he knows, but he promised not to tell* talk, tell tales, blab, give the game away, open one's mouth, let the cat out of the bag, spill the beans. **7** *his friend told on him* report, inform; *inf.* sing, squeal, rat, blow the whistle. **8** *his expression told how he felt* reveal, disclose, show, display, exhibit, indicate. **9** *unable to tell his reaction from his expression* deduce, make out, discern, perceive, recognize, discover, understand, comprehend. **10** *unable to tell one from the other* distinguish, differentiate, discriminate. **11** *breeding tells* have an effect, count, carry weight, have influence/force, register.

**telling** adjective significant, important, striking, impressive, forceful, effective, effectual, cogent, influential, decisive.

**temerity** noun effrontery, impudence, audacity, cheek, gall, presumption, presumptuousness, brazenness, rashness, recklessness, foolhardiness.

**temper** noun **1** *he is of an equable temper* disposition, nature. See TEMPERAMENT 1. **2** *the temper of the times* tenor, tone, attitude, vein. **3** *he is in a temper* fury, rage, passion, fit of pique, tantrum. **4** *a display of temper* anger, annoyance, fury, rage, irritation, irascibility, hotheadedness, resentment, surliness, churlishness. **5** *lose one's temper* composure, equanimity, self-control, coolness, calm, tranquillity; *inf.* cool.

**temper** verb **1** *temper the metal* toughen, anneal, harden, strengthen, fortify. **2** *temper justice with mercy* moderate, soften, tone down, modify, mitigate, alleviate, allay, palliate, mollify, assuage, lessen, weaken.

**temperament** noun **1** *of a nervous temperament* disposition, nature, humor, mood, makeup, constitution, complexion, temper, spirit, mettle, frame of mind, cast of mind, mind, attitude, outlook, stamp, quality. **2** *actors often are people of temperament* excitability, volatility, capriciousness, moodiness, oversensitivity, touchiness, petulance; moods.

**temperamental** adjective **1** *temperamental differences between them* constitutional, inherent, innate, deep-rooted, ingrained. **2** *actors are often temperamental* excitable, emotional, volatile, mercurial, oversensitive, touchy, moody, hotheaded, explosive, impatient, petulant.

**temperate** adjective **1** *lead a temperate life* moderate, self-restrained, restrained, abstemious, self-controlled, continent, austere, self-denying. **2** *temperate winds* mild, gentle, clement, balmy, pleasant, agreeable.

**tempest** noun **1** *ships buffeted by the tempest* storm, gale, hurricane, squall, cyclone, tornado, typhoon, whirlwind. **2** *their squabble erupted into a tempest* uproar, commotion, furor, disturbance, tumult, turmoil, upheaval.

**tempestuous** adjective **1** *tempestuous weather* stormy, turbulent, blustery, squally, windy, gusty, breezy. **2** *a tempestuous affair* tumultuous, turbulent, wild, uncontrolled, unrestrained, emotional, intense, fierce, heated, feverish, hysterical, frenetic.

**tempo** noun beat, rhythm, cadence, pulse; pace, rate, speed, measure.

**temporal** adjective *temporal affairs* secular, nonspiritual, worldly, material, earthly, carnal.

**temporary** adjective short-term, impermanent, interim, provisional, pro tem, pro

*tempore*; passing, short-lived, transient, transitory, ephemeral, evanescent.

**tempt** verb **1** *she is tempted to run away* entice, incite, induce, egg on, urge, goad, prompt, sway, influence, persuade, cajole, coax. **2** *displays to tempt buyers* allure, lure, entice, attract, whet the appetite of, make one's mouth water, captivate, appeal to, beguile, inveigle, woo, seduce, tantalize. **3** *tempt fate* fly in the face of, risk, bait, provoke.

**temptation** noun allurement, lure, attraction, draw, bait, pull, enticement, inducement, invitation, decoy, snare; *inf.* come-on.

**tempting** adjective alluring, enticing, attractive, captivating, appealing, beguiling, fascinating, tantalizing, appetizing, mouthwatering.

**tenacious** adjective **1** *a tenacious grip* clinging, fast, tight, strong, forceful, powerful, unshakable, iron. **2** *tenacious efforts/individuals* persistent, pertinacious, determined, dogged, resolute, firm, steadfast, purposeful, unswerving, relentless, inexorable, unyielding, inflexible, stubborn, obstinate, intransigent.

**tenant** noun occupier, occupant, resident, inhabitant, renter, leaseholder, lessee, holder, possessor.

**tend** verb *tend the sick/cows* look after, take care of, care for, attend to, minister to, see to, cater to, nurse, wait on, watch over, watch, guard, keep an eye on, keep.

**tendency** noun **1** *a tendency to dishonesty* inclination, disposition, predisposition, proclivity, propensity, proneness, aptness, bent, leaning, penchant, susceptibility, liability. **2** *the upward tendency of the graph* movement, direction, course, drift, bias, trend.

**tender** adjective **1** *tender meat* succulent, juicy, soft. **2** *tender blossoms/shoots* fragile, frail, delicate, sensitive, slight, feeble. **3** *they are still of tender years* young, youthful, early; immature, callow, inexperienced, green, raw. **4** *a tender heart* compassionate, softhearted, kind, kindly, sympathetic, warm, caring, humane, gentle, solicitous, generous, benevolent, loving, affectionate. **5** *a tender spot on her arm* sore, painful, aching, smarting, throbbing, inflamed, irritated, red, raw, bruised. **6** *a tender subject requiring tact* delicate, sensitive, tricky, ticklish.

**tender** verb *tender a proposal* offer, proffer, present, extend, give; volunteer, put forward, propose, suggest, advance, submit.

**tenderness** noun **1** *the tenderness of the blossoms/shoots* fragility, frailness, frailty, delicacy, sensitivity, sensitiveness, slightness, feebleness. **2** *the tenderness of their years* youthfulness, immaturity, callowness, inexperience, greenness. **3** *the tenderness of her heart* compassion, compassionateness, softheartedness, kindness, kindliness, sympathy, warmth, humaneness, gentleness, solicitousness, generosity, benevolence, sentimentality, emotionalism; fondness, love, affection, emotion, amorousness. **4** *the tenderness of the topic* delicacy, delicateness, sensitivity, sensitiveness, difficulty, trickiness, ticklishness. **5** *the tenderness of the wounded area* soreness, pain, painfulness, ache, aching, smarting, throbbing, inflammation, irritation, redness, rawness, bruising.

**tenet** noun doctrine, creed, credo, principle, belief, conviction, persuasion, view, opinion.

**tense** adjective **1** *tense ropes* tight, taut, rigid, stretched, strained. **2** *feeling tense about the interview* nervous, keyed up, worked up, overwrought, distraught, anxious, uneasy, worried, apprehensive, agitated, jumpy, edgy, on edge, restless, jittery, fidgety; *inf.* uptight, wound up, strung out. **3** *there were some tense moments in the negotiations* nerve-racking, stressful, worrying, fraught, exciting, cliff-hanging.

**tension** noun **1** *the tension of the ropes* tightness, tautness, rigidity, stretching, straining. **2** *the tension of waiting* stress, stressfulness, pressure, anxiety, unease, disquiet, worry, apprehensiveness, agitation, jumpiness, edginess, restlessness; nerves. **3** *the tension between the two sides grew* strain, unease, ill feeling, hostility, enmity.

**tentative** adjective **1** *a tentative plan* experimental, exploratory, trial, provisional, test, pilot. **2** *take a few tentative steps* hesitant, hesitating, faltering, wavering, uncertain, unsure, doubtful, cautious, diffident, timid.

**tenuous** adjective **1** *a tenuous connection between the two events* fragile, slight, flimsy, weak, insubstantial, shaky, sketchy, doubtful, dubious, nebulous, hazy, vague, unspecific, indefinite. **2** *a tenuous thread* fine, thin, slender.

**term** noun **1** *fail to understand the technical term* word, expression, phrase, name, title, denomination, appellation, designation. **2** *the chairman's term of office* period, time, spell, interval, stretch, span, duration, space.

**terminal** adjective fatal, deadly, mortal, lethal, killing; dying, on one's deathbed, near death, in the throes of death.

**terminal** noun **1** *the terminal of the railroad line* terminus, last stop, depot. **2** *the computer terminal* workstation, visual display unit, monitor; *inf.* VDU.

**terminate** verb close, end, conclude, finish, stop, wind up, discontinue; cease, cancel, expire, run out, lapse; abort, put an end to.

**termination** noun **1** *the termination of the meeting* closing, close, ending, end, conclusion, finish, winding-up, wind-up. **2** *the termination of his contract* cessation, discontinuance, expiration, lapse, cancellation.

**terms** plural noun **1** *tell them in no uncertain terms* words, phrases, expressions, language. **2** *on good terms with their neighbors* relations; standing, footing, relationship. **3** *under the terms of the will* stipulations, specifications, conditions, provisions, provisos, particulars. **4** *offer reduced terms in the winter* prices, rates, charges, costs, fees. **come to terms with 1** *they finally came to terms with the neighbors* come to an agreement/understanding with, reach a compromise with. **2** *come to terms with her loss* become reconciled with, reach an acceptance of, learn to live with.

**terrible** adjective **1** *he is a terrible tennis player* bad, poor, incompetent, useless, talentless; *inf.* rotten. **2** *hostages enduring terrible experiences* dreadful, terrifying, frightening, frightful, horrifying, horrible, horrific, horrendous, harrowing, hideous, grim, unspeakable, appalling, awful, gruesome. **3** *the terrible heat/pain* extreme, severe, harsh, unbearable, intolerable, insufferable. **4** *what is that terrible smell?* nasty, foul, offensive, odious, obnoxious, vile, revolting, repulsive, abhorrent, loathsome, hateful, unpleasant, disagreeable, dreadful, awful, horrible, horrid.

**terrific** adjective **1** *a terrific bang/speed* tremendous, great, huge, sizable, considerable, intense, extreme, extraordinary, excessive. **2** *she is a terrific singer* excellent, superb, ace, remarkable, magnificent, wonderful, marvelous, great, super, sensational, fabulous; *inf.* fantastic, A-1, unreal, awesome. **3** *there has been a terrific accident* dreadful, frightful, horrible, horrific, hideous, grim, appalling, awful.

**terrify** verb terrorize, frighten to death, frighten, scare stiff, scare, petrify, horrify, make one's blood run cold, make one's flesh crawl, make one's hair stand on end, alarm, panic, intimidate, dismay, appall, shock, paralyze with fear, put the fear of God into; *inf.* spook.

**territory** noun **1** *territories governed by the same ruler* country, state, domain, county, district. **2** *an unexplored territory* region, area, terrain, tract. **3** *leave me out of it—that's your territory* area of concern, province, field, sector, department, bailiwick, beat.

**terror** noun **1** fright, fear, fear and trembling, dread, alarm, panic, shock, horror.

**2** *imagining all manner of terrors* bogeyman, bugbear, monster, demon, fiend, devil. **3** *that child is a little terror* hooligan, ruffian, hoodlum, rogue, rascal, troublemaker, holy terror.

**terrorize** verb **1** *terrorize the hostages* strike terror in/into, petrify. *See* TERRIFY. **2** *terrorize them into leaving their homes* coerce, browbeat, bully, intimidate, menace, threaten, bulldoze; *inf.* strong-arm.

**terse** adjective **1** *a terse description of the event* concise, succinct, compact, brief, short, to the point, crisp, pithy. **2** *she sounded terse on the phone* abrupt, curt, brusque, blunt.

**test** noun **1** *a test to distinguish the competent from the incompetent* examination, check, assessment, evaluation, appraisal, investigation, inspection, analysis, study, probe. **2** *take the bike out for a test* trial, tryout, try, probation, assay. **3** *studying for a test* exam, quiz, questionnaire. **4** *the test of a good cake* criterion, touchstone, yardstick, standard, measure, model.

**test** verb **1** *test their knowledge of local history* put to the test, examine, check, assess, evaluate, appraise, investigate, scrutinize, study, probe. **2** *their behavior tested his patience* try, tax, strain. **3** *test the water for pollution* analyze, assay, check, investigate, scrutinize, explore, probe.

**testament** noun *the sculpture was a testament to his skill* attestation, testimony, evidence, proof, witness; demonstration, indication, exemplification, tribute.

**testify** verb **1** *she testified to his honesty* swear to, attest to, corroborate, substantiate, verify, vouch for, endorse, support, back up, uphold. **2** *testify that she had witnessed the accident* swear, declare, assert, affirm, state, allege, pledge, profess, avow. **testify to** *tears that testified to her guilt* be evidence/proof of, confirm, bear out, show, demonstrate, indicate.

**testimony** noun **1** *challenge the testimony of the witness* evidence, attestation, sworn statement, deposition, affidavit; statement, declaration, assertion, protestation, affirmation, profession, allegation. **2** *her academic record was a testimony to her ability* proof, evidence, verification, corroboration, support; demonstration, manifestation, indication.

**testy** adjective touchy, irritable, irascible, petulant, cross, ill-tempered, crotchety, crabby, crabbed, snappish, querulous, peevish, grouchy, grumpy, cantankerous, fractious.

**tether** noun rope, cord, chain, lead, leash, line.

**tether** verb tie, tie up, fasten, secure, chain, rope.

**text** noun **1** *the text of the speech* words, wording, script, transcript. **2** *the speaker took foreign policy as his text* theme, subject matter, topic. **3** *the texts chosen for the funeral service* passage, verse, quotation, extract, line, abstract, paragraph.

**texture** noun **1** *the texture of her skin* feel, touch, appearance, surface, grain. **2** *fabrics of varying texture* weave, structure, composition, constitution, constituency.

**thankful** adjective **1** *she was thankful to reach home safely* grateful, appreciative, pleased, relieved. **2** *she was thankful to them for taking her in* indebted, obliged, beholden.

**thankless** adjective **1** *thankless children* ungrateful, unappreciative, ungracious. **2** *thankless tasks* unappreciated, unrewarded, unrewarding, unacknowledged.

**thanks** plural noun gratitude, gratefulness, appreciation, acknowledgment, recognition.

**thaw** verb defrost, unfreeze, melt, soften, liquefy; relax, loosen up.

**theater** noun drama, dramatic art, dramaturgy, the stage, show business, thespian art; *inf.* showbiz.

**theatrical** adjective **1** *theatrical careers* dramatic, stage, dramaturgical, show business, thespian. **2** *theatrical gestures* dramatic, melodramatic, histrionic, exaggerated, overdone, ostentatious, showy, affected, mannered, stilted, forced, stagy; *inf.* hammy.

**theft** noun stealing, robbery, thieving, thievery, burglary, larceny, misappropriation, pilfering, purloining, shoplifting, embezzlement, swindling, fraud; *inf.* swiping, rip-off.

**theme** noun **1** *the theme of the speech* topic, subject, subject matter, matter, thesis, text, argument, burden, idea, keynote. **2** *play the theme from the TV series* theme song, melody, tune, air, leitmotif. **3** *students writing themes in French* essay, composition, paper, dissertation.

**theoretical** adjective conceptual, abstract, hypothetical, conjectural, suppositional, speculative.

**theorize** verb speculate, conjecture, suppose, hypothesize.

**theory** noun hypothesis, thesis, conjecture, supposition, speculation, guess, notion, postulation, assumption, presumption, opinion, view.

**therapy** noun treatment, remedy, cure.

**thereafter** adverb afterward, after that, then, next, subsequently.

**therefore** adverb and so, so, then, thus,

**thesis** noun **1** *his thesis is that the territory is uninhabited* theory, hypothesis, contention, argument, proposal, proposition, premise, postulation. **2** *present a thesis for his doctorate* dissertation, paper, treatise, disquisition, essay, composition, monograph.

**thick** adjective **1** *two feet thick* across, wide, broad, deep. **2** *thick legs* large, big, bulky, solid, substantial, fat, beefy. **3** *a thick forest* dense, close-packed, concentrated, crowded, condensed, compact, impenetrable, impassable. **4** *thick cream* coagulated, heavy, firm. **5** *thick mists* dense, heavy, opaque, smoggy, soupy, murky, impenetrable. **6** *too thick to understand* stupid, dense, unintelligent, dull-witted, dull, slow-witted, slow, doltish; *inf.* dim, dimwitted, boneheaded. **7** *a voice thick with emotion* husky, hoarse, throaty, guttural, rough, indistinct, muffled. **8** *a thick accent* broad, pronounced, marked, strong, rich, obvious, distinct, decided. **9** *those two are thick these days* intimate, close, devoted, hand and/in glove, inseparable, familiar; *inf.* palsy-walsy, chummy. **lay it on thick** flatter, overpraise, toady; *inf.* butter up. **thick with 1** *the ground thick with ants* teeming with, swarming with, crawling with, alive with. **2** *the room thick with smoke* full of, filled with; *inf.* chock-full of.

**thicken** verb set, gel, solidify, congeal, clot, coagulate, cake.

**thicket** noun dense growth, tangle, copse, grove, wood.

**thickset** adjective burly, brawny, muscular, bulky, sturdy, stocky, beefy.

**thick-skinned** adjective insensitive, unfeeling, tough, unsusceptible, impervious, invulnerable, hardened, case-hardened, callous, hard-boiled.

**thief** noun robber, burglar, housebreaker, larcenist, pilferer, stealer, purloiner, filcher, shoplifter, pickpocket, embezzler, bandit, swindler, fraudster, mugger.

**thin** adjective **1** *thin lines* narrow, fine, attenuated. **2** *thin materials* fine, light, delicate, flimsy, diaphanous, gossamer, unsubstantial, sheer, transparent, see-through, gauzy, filmy, translucent. **3** *their models have to be thin* slim, slender, lean, slight, svelte, light, spare. **4** *thin and ill-looking* skinny, spindly, lank, lanky, scrawny, scraggy, bony, skeletal, wasted, emaciated, shrunken, anorexic, undernourished, underweight. **5** *thin hair* sparse, scanty, wispy, skimpy. **6** *the audience was rather thin* sparse, scarce, scanty, meager, paltry, scattered. **7** *a thin mixture* dilute, diluted, weak, watery, runny. **8** *a thin voice* weak, small, low, soft, faint,

feeble. **9** *a thin excuse* flimsy, unsubstantial, weak, feeble, lame, poor, shallow, unconvincing.

**thin** verb **thin down** *thin down the mixture* dilute, water down, weaken. **thin out** lessen, decrease, diminish, dwindle.

**thing** noun **1** *people matter more than things* object, article, item. **2** *where did you get that thing?* object; *inf.* what-d'you-call-it, whatchamacallit, what's-its-name, whatsit, thingamabob, thingamajig. **3** *what a silly/difficult thing to do* action, act, deed, exploit, feat, undertaking, task, job, chore. **4** *what a silly thing to think* idea, thought, notion, concept, theory, conjecture. **5** *say silly things* statement, remark, comment, declaration, utterance, pronouncement. **6** *a terrible thing to happen* event, happening, occurrence, incident, episode. **7** *patience is a useful thing* quality, characteristic, attribute, property, trait, feature. **8** *the poor thing has no home* soul, creature, wretch. **9** *there is another thing you should know* fact, point, detail, particular, aspect. **10** *the latest thing in swimwear* style, fashion, specimen, example. **have a thing about 1** *have a thing about spiders* phobia of, fear of, aversion to/toward; *inf.* hang-up about. **2** *have a thing about champagne* liking for/of, love for/of, fancy for, predilection for, penchant for, preference for, taste for, obsession with, fixation on/with/about. **the thing 1** *the thing is to avoid annoying him* the aim, the intention, the idea, the objective, the object, the purpose. **2** *the thing is that he has no money* the fact, the fact of the matter, the point, the issue, the problem.

**things** plural noun **1** *put on dry things | take night things* clothing, attire, apparel; clothes, garments, gear; *inf.* togs. **2** *I will watch your things while you get a ticket* belongings, possessions, paraphernalia; *inf.* stuff. **3** *her painting things* equipment, apparatus, gear, tackle; implements, tools. **4** *things are getting worse* matters, affairs, circumstances, conditions, relations; the state of affairs, the situation.

**think** verb **1** *I think they will come* believe, suppose, expect, imagine, surmise, conjecture, guess, fancy. **2** *he is thought to be clever* consider, deem, hold, reckon, regard as, assume, presume, estimate. **3** *he is sitting thinking* ponder, meditate, deliberate, contemplate, muse, cogitate, ruminate, cerebrate, concentrate, brood, rack one's brains, be lost in thought, be in a brown study. **think better of** have second thoughts about, reconsider, change one's mind about, decide against. **think over** contemplate, consider, deliberate about, muse over, mull over, ponder, reflect on, weigh up, consider the pros and cons of.

**think up** dream up, come up with, devise, invent, create, concoct.

**thinking** noun *the latest thinking on tax reform* view, opinion, outlook, judgment, assessment, appraisal, evaluation, position, theory, reasoning; conclusions, thoughts.

**thin-skinned** adjective sensitive, hypersensitive, supersensitive, easily offended/hurt, touchy.

**thirst** noun **1** *dying of thirst in the desert* thirstiness, dryness, parchedness, dehydration. **2** *a thirst for knowledge* desire, craving, longing, hankering, yearning, avidity, hunger, lust, appetite; *inf.* yen.

**thirst** verb **thirst for/after** desire, crave, long for, hanker after, yearn for, hunger after, lust after.

**thorn** noun prickle, spike, barb, spine, bristle.

**thorny** adjective **1** *thorny branches* prickly, spiky, barbed, spiny, spined, bristly, sharp, pointed. **2** *a thorny situation/issue* problematic, awkward, ticklish, difficult, tough, troublesome, bothersome, trying, taxing, irksome, vexatious, worrying, harassing, complicated.

**thorough** adjective **1** *a thorough investigation* in-depth, exhaustive, complete, comprehensive, full, intensive, extensive, widespread, sweeping, all-embracing, all-inclusive, detailed. **2** *he is slow but thorough* meticulous, scrupulous, assiduous, conscientious, painstaking, punctilious, methodical, careful. **3** *he is a thorough villain* thoroughgoing, out-and-out, utter, downright, sheer, absolute, unmitigated, unqualified, complete, total, perfect.

**thoroughbred** adjective purebred, pure, pure-blooded, full-blooded, pedigreed; well-bred, highborn, aristocratic, blue-blooded, elegant, graceful, refined.

**thoroughfare** noun road, roadway; main road, street; highway, freeway, turnpike, parkway, expressway, throughway; *inf.* pike.

**thoroughly** adverb **1** *search the place thoroughly* exhaustively, completely, fully, intensively, extensively, meticulously, scrupulously, assiduously, conscientiously, painstakingly, methodically, carefully. **2** *she is thoroughly spoiled* completely, utterly, absolutely, totally, entirely.

**thought** noun **1** *lost in thought* thinking, reasoning, pondering, meditation, deliberation, cogitation, rumination, musing, mulling, reflection, introspection, contemplation. **2** *a thought came to me about how to do it* idea, notion, theory, opinion. **3** *I had no thought of going* intention, plan, design, purpose, aim. **4** *what are your thoughts on this?* judgment, stance, stand, feeling, sentiment. *See* THINKING. **5** *give the matter thought* consideration, attention, heed, regard, scrutiny, care, carefulness. **6** *give up all thought of winning* expectation, anticipation, hope, prospect, aspiration, dream. **7** *he has no thought for his widowed mother* thoughtfulness, consideration, care, regard, concern, solicitude, kindness, kindliness, compassion, tenderness.

**thoughtful** adjective **1** *a thoughtful mood* pensive, reflective, introspective, meditative, contemplative, ruminative, cogitative, absorbed. **2** *a thoughtful essay* profound, deep, serious, pithy, meaty, weighty. **3** *every action he takes is thoughtful* considered, circumspect, prudent, careful, cautious, heedful, wary, guarded. **4** *he is a thoughtful son* considerate, attentive, caring, solicitous, helpful, kind, kindly, compassionate.

**thoughtless** adjective **1** *thoughtless remarks* tactless, undiplomatic, indiscreet, insensitive, inconsiderate, impolite, rude. **2** *his thoughtless actions* unthinking, heedless, careless, absentminded, injudicious, ill-advised, ill-considered, imprudent.

**thrash** verb **1** *rebels thrashed by the dictator's guards* beat, whip, horsewhip, flog, lash, birch, cane, flagellate, scourge, spank, chastise; *inf.* belt, wallop, lambaste, tan. **2** *the home team thrashed the opposition* trounce, rout, vanquish, drub, crush; *inf.* lick, clobber, hammer, slaughter, wipe (up) the floor with. **3** *thrashing around in pain* thresh, flail, jerk, twitch, squirm, writhe.

**threadbare** adjective **1** *threadbare upholstery* worn, frayed, tattered, ragged, holey, shabby; *inf.* tatty. **2** *threadbare arguments* hackneyed, tired, stale, worn-out, trite, banal, platitudinous, clichéd, cliché-ridden; *inf.* played out.

**threat** noun warning, menace, risk, danger, hazard, omen, foreboding, portent.

**threaten** verb **1** *bullies threatening younger children* make threats to, menace, intimidate, browbeat, bully; *inf.* lean on. **2** *rain is threatening* be imminent, impend, hang over, loom, foreshadow. **3** *a sky threatening rain* warn of, presage, portend, augur. **4** *pollution threatening the environment* be a threat to, endanger, imperil, put at risk, jeopardize.

**threshold** noun **1** *guests standing at/on the threshold* doorway, doorstep, entrance, entry. **2** *on the threshold of a new era* beginning, commencement, start, outset, inception, opening, dawn, brink, verge, debut; *inf.* kickoff.

**thrift** noun thriftiness, economy, frugality, scrimping, parsimony, penny-pinching, miserliness.

**thrifty** adjective economical, economizing,

frugal, sparing, scrimping, parsimonious, penny-pinching, miserly.

**thrill** noun **1** *seeing his hero gave him a thrill* glow, tingle, joy, delight, pleasure; *inf.* buzz, charge, kick. **2** *a thrill of terror ran through him* throb, tremble, tremor, quiver, flutter, shudder, vibration.

**thrill** verb excite, stimulate, arouse, stir, electrify, move, give joy/pleasure to; *inf.* a buzz/charge/kick to. **thrill to** tingle from, feel joy from; *inf.* get a buzz/charge/kick out of.

**thrilling** adjective **1** *a thrilling experience* exciting, stirring, stimulating, electrifying, hair-raising, rousing, moving, gripping, riveting, joyful, pleasing. **2** *a thrilling sensation through the body* throbbing, trembling, tremulous, quivering, shivering, fluttering, shuddering, vibrating.

**thrive** verb flourish, prosper, boom, burgeon; succeed, advance, get ahead.

**throb** verb beat, pulse, pulsate, palpitate, pound, vibrate, go pit-a-pat, thump.

**throes** plural noun **1** *the throes of childbirth* agony, suffering, excruciation, pain, torture, distress; pangs. **2** *in the throes of changing jobs* turmoil, upheaval, disruption, tumult.

**throng** noun crowd, horde, mob, mass, host, multitude, swarm, flock, pack, herd, drove.

**throng** verb **1** *people thronged to see the play* flock, troop, swarm. **2** *fans thronging around the star* crowd, mill, congregate, converge. **3** *fans thronging the stadium* pack, cram, jam, fill.

**throttle** verb choke, strangle, strangulate, garrotte; gag, muzzle, silence, stifle, suppress, control, inhibit.

**through** adverb **through and through** thoroughly, completely, utterly, altogether, totally, to the core, entirely, wholly, fully, unreservedly, out and out.

**through** adjective finished, completed, done, ended, terminated; *inf.* washed up.

**throw** verb **1** *throw a brick* hurl, toss, cast, sling, pitch, shy, lob, propel, launch, project, send, heave, chuck. **2** *throw an opponent/rider* fell, floor, prostrate; unseat, dislodge. **3** *his question threw me* disconcert, discomfit, disturb, confound, astonish, surprise, dumbfound. **4** *threw the switch* operate, turn/switch on, move. **5** *the potter throwing a vase* shape, form, mold, fashion. **6** *she threw on her clothes* pull/put on quickly, don, slip into. **throw away 1** *throw away his textbooks* throw out, discard, get rid of, dispose of, jettison, scrap, reject, dispense with; *inf.* dump, ditch. **2** *throw away a good opportunity* waste, squander, fritter away, lose; *inf.*

blow. **throw off 1** *throw off their shackles* cast off, shake off, abandon. **2** *throw off one's pursuers* evade, escape from, get away from, elude, give someone the slip, lose.

**throw out 1** *throw out the troublemakers* eject, evict, expel, show the door to, put out; *inf.* kick out. **2** *throw out a proposal* reject, dismiss, disallow. **3** *fires throwing out heat* emit, radiate, give off, diffuse, disseminate.

**throw** noun hurl, toss, cast, sling, pitch, lob, heave, chuck. **a throw** *jackets at $50 a throw* each, apiece; *inf.* a pop.

**thrust** verb **1** *thrust open the door | thrust their way through the crowd* push, shove, drive, press, prod, propel, force, shoulder, elbow, jostle. **2** *thrust responsibility on him* force, impose, push, press, urge. **3** *fencers learning to thrust* stab, pierce, stick, jab, lunge at.

**thrust** noun **1** *with one thrust of his fist* push, shove, ram, drive, press, prod. **2** *surprised by the enemy's sudden thrust* advance, drive, attack, offensive, assault, charge, onslaught, incursion, raid. **3** *upset by her nasty thrust* criticism, censure. **4** *the thrust of the speech* gist, drift, substance, essence, theme, subject, thesis.

**thud** noun thump, clunk, crash, smack, wham.

**thug** noun ruffian, tough, rough, hoodlum, bully, hooligan, villain, gangster, robber, bandit, murderer, killer, assassin; *inf.* hood, goon, mobster, hit man.

**thumb** verb *thumb through the book* leaf, flick, flip, riffle, browse, skim, scan.

**thump** verb **1** *he thumped her attacker* strike, hit, punch, thwack, wallop, smack, slap, batter, beat, cudgel, knock, thrash; *inf.* whack, belt, clout, lambaste. **2** *my heart/head is thumping* pound, thud, pulse, pulsate, throb, palpitate. **3** *thumping on the table* bang, batter, beat, crash, knock, rap.

**thump** noun **1** *give the attacker a thump* blow, punch, thwack, wallop, smack, slap; *inf.* whack, belt, clout, lambasting. **2** *give the table a thump* bang, knock, rap. **3** *the shoe landed with a thump* thud, clunk, crash, smack, wham.

**thunder** verb **1** *his voice thundered in my ear* boom, rumble, roar, blast, resound, reverberate. **2** *thundering at the crowd to be quiet* roar, bellow, bark, yell, shout.

**thus** adverb **1** *hold the apparatus thus* like this, in this way, so, like so. **2** *he is the eldest son and thus inherits the estate* so, therefore, accordingly, hence, consequently, as a result, ergo.

**thwart** verb frustrate, foil, balk, check, block, stop, prevent, defeat, impede, obstruct, hinder, hamper, stymie.

**tic** noun twitch, spasm, jerk.

**tick** noun ticking, click, beat, tap, tapping, tick-tock.

**tick** verb click, beat, tap, sound, tick-tock. **tick off** annoy, irritate, rile, aggravate, peeve.

**ticket** noun pass, token, stub, coupon, card.

**tickle** verb **1** *tickle one's fancy* interest, excite, stimulate, arouse, captivate, please, gratify, delight. **2** *tickled by the antics of the children* amuse, entertain, divert, cheer, gladden.

**ticklish** adjective *a ticklish situation* difficult, problematic, awkward, delicate, sensitive, tricky, thorny, knotty, touchy, risky, uncertain, precarious; *inf.* sticky.

**tide** noun *the tide of events* course, movement, direction, trend, current, drift, run, tendency.

**tidings** plural noun news, notification, word, communication, information, intelligence, advice; reports; *inf.* info, low-down.

**tidy** adjective **1** *a tidy room/garden* neat, trim, orderly, in order, in good order, well-ordered, spruce, shipshape, well-kept, clean, spick-and-span. **2** *people who are tidy by nature* organized, well-organized, methodical, systematic, businesslike. **3** *leave a tidy sum* considerable, sizable, substantial, goodly, handsome, generous, ample, largish, large.

**tidy** verb clean, clean up, put to rights, put in order, straighten, make shipshape, spruce up, groom, smarten, neaten.

**tie** verb tie up, fasten, attach, fix, bind, secure, tether, moor, lash, join, connect, link, couple, rope, chain. **tie down** restrict, confine, curb, limit, constrain, restrain, hamper, hinder, impede, cramp. **tie in** fit in, tally, concur, conform, dovetail. **tie up 1** *tie up the package* wrap, wrap up, bind, truss. **2** *his capital is tied up* invest, commit. **3** *the meeting will tie him up all morning* occupy, engage, keep busy, engross, take up one's attention. **4** *we should tie up the arrangements* finalize, conclude, wind up, complete, finish off; *inf.* wrap up.

**tie** noun **1** *trash bags fastened with a tie* ligature, link, fastening, fastener, clip, catch. **2** *business ties* bond, connection, relationship, kinship, affiliation, allegiance. **3** *the game ended in a tie* draw, dead heat, deadlock, stalemate.

**tier** noun row, level, bank, line; layer, echelon, rank.

**tight** adjective **1** *keep a tight grip* fast, secure, fixed, clenched, clinched. **2** *tight ropes/muscles* taut, rigid, stiff, tense, stretched, strained. **3** *a tight mass of fibers* compact, compacted, compressed. **4** *space was a* bit tight with so many people cramped, restricted, limited, constricted. **5** *the box must be tight* impervious, impenetrable, sound, sealed, hermetic, watertight, airtight. **6** *money is a bit tight just now* scarce, scant, sparse, in short supply, limited, insufficient, inadequate. **7** *security was tight at the press conference* strict, rigorous, stringent, tough, rigid, uncompromising, exacting. **8** *in a tight situation* problematic, difficult, precarious, hazardous, dangerous, perilous, tricky, ticklish, worrying, delicate; *inf.* sticky. **9** *a piece of tight prose* concise, succinct, terse, crisp, pithy, epigrammatic. **10** *it was a tight race* close, even, evenly matched, neck and neck. **11** *tight with his money* tight-fisted, mean, miserly, parsimonious, stingy, niggardly.

**tighten** verb **1** *she tightened the leash* secure, make fast, tauten, stretch, make rigid, stiffen, tense. **3** *tighten security* increase, make stricter, make rigorous/stringent. **3** *his throat tightened* narrow, constrict, contract.

**till** verb cultivate, farm, plow, dig.

**tilt** verb lean, list, slope, slant, incline, tip, cant.

**timber** noun wood, lumber; beam, spar, pole.

**time** noun **1** *in the time of the dinosaurs* age, era, epoch, period. **2** *he worked there for a time* while, spell, stretch, span, period, term. **3** *the last time I saw him* occasion, point, juncture. **4** *now is the time to act/leave* moment, point, instant, stage. **5** *the places I have been in my time* lifetime, life, life span. **6** *have a hard time* condition, circumstance; situation, experience. **7** *in waltz time* rhythm, measure, tempo, beat, meter. **8** *he never has any time to himself* freedom, leisure, leisure time, spare time; moments, odd moments. **ahead of time** early, in good time, with time to spare. **all the time** *he works all the time* constantly, always, at all times, perpetually, continuously, continually. **at one time 1** *at one time he worked there* once, previously, formerly, hitherto. **2** *several matches going on at one time* simultaneously, concurrently, at once, at the same time, together. **at the same time** *he is wealthy; at the same time, he lives frugally* nevertheless, nonetheless, however, but, still, yet, just the same. **at times** from time to time, every now and then, periodically, on occasion, occasionally. **behind time** late, running late, behind schedule. **behind the times** old-fashioned, out-of-date, dated, outmoded, obsolete, passé, antiquated; *inf.* old hat. **from time to time** now and then, now and so often, at times. **in no time** rapidly/quickly/swiftly, speedily, at great speed, expeditiously, with dispatch. **in good time** punctually, on time; early, ahead of time, with time to spare. **in time** *they will forget in time* eventually, ultimately, as time goes on/by, by and by, one day, someday, sooner or later, in the long run. **many a time** often, frequently, many times, on many occasions. **on time** punctually, early enough, in good time, sharp, on the dot. **time after time** again and again, many times over, repeatedly, time and again, time and time again, recurrently.

**time** verb **1** *time the meeting for the afternoon* schedule, fix, set, arrange, program. **2** *time his progress* clock, measure, calculate, regulate, count.

**timeless** adjective ageless, enduring, lasting, permanent, abiding, unending, ceaseless, undying, deathless, eternal, everlasting, immortal, changeless, immutable, indestructible.

**timely** adjective opportune, well-timed, convenient, appropriate, seasonable, felicitous.

**timetable** noun schedule, program, calendar, list, agenda.

**timid** adjective **1** *too timid to stand up to the bully* timorous, fearful, apprehensive, afraid, frightened, scared, faint-hearted, lily-livered, cowardly, pusillanimous; *inf.* chicken, yellow. **2** *too timid to speak to strangers* shy, diffident, bashful, reticent, unselfconfident, timorous, shrinking, retiring, coy, demure.

**tinge** verb color, tint, shade, dye, stain, suffuse, imbue, flavor.

**tinge** noun **1** *a tinge of silver in the wallpaper* color, tint, shade, tone, tincture, cast, dye, stain, wash. **2** *a tinge of sadness in her attitude* hint, suggestion, trace, touch, bit, dash, soupçon.

**tingle** verb prickle, prick, tickle, itch, sting, quiver, tremble.

**tingle** noun **1** *the tingle in her fingers* tingling, prickling, pricking, tickle, itch, quiver, trembling, pins and needles. **2** *feel a tingle of excitement* quiver, tremor, thrill, throb.

**tinker** verb fiddle, play, toy, tamper, fool (around), mess (about).

**tinkle** verb ring, chime, peal, ding, jingle.

**tint** noun **1** *several tints to choose from* shade, color. *See* TINGE noun 1. **2** *a hair tint* dye, rinse, colorant, coloring.

**tiny** adjective minute, diminutive, miniature, mini, minuscule, infinitesimal, microscopic, dwarfish, midget, pocket-sized, Lilliputian, wee, petite, small, little, insignificant, trifling, negligible, inconsequential; *inf.* teeny, teeny-weeny, itsy-bitsy, pint-sized.

**tip**[1] noun point, peak, top, summit, apex, crown.

**tip**[2] verb *the table tends to tip* tilt, lean, list, cant, slant. **tip over** topple (over), overturn, fall over, turn topsy-turvy, capsize, upset, upend.

**tip**[3] noun **1** *give the waiter a tip* gratuity, pourboire, baksheesh; *inf.* little something. **2** *tips on how to take out stains* hint, suggestion, recommendation, piece of advice; advice.

**tip**[4] verb **tip off** warn, forewarn, advise, inform, notify, caution, alert.

**tipsy** adjective drunk, intoxicated, inebriated; *inf.* tiddly, tight, under the influence.

**tirade** noun diatribe, harangue, lecture, upbraiding, denunciation, obloquy, philippic; invective, vituperation, fulmination.

**tire** verb **1** *climbing the hill tired him* tire out, fatigue, wear out, weary, exhaust, drain, enervate, debilitate; *inf.* take it out of. **2** *he tires easily* flag, droop; *inf.* poop out. **3** *their constant boasting tires me* bore, weary, irk, irritate, get on one's nerves, annoy, exasperate; *inf.* get to.

**tired** adjective **1** *feel tired after the climb* fatigued, worn out, weary, wearied, exhausted, drained, enervated, debilitated; *inf.* done in, all in, beat, dog-tired, bushed, pooped (out), dead on one's feet, ready to drop. **2** *tired children ready for bed* sleepy, drowsy, weary; *inf.* asleep on one's feet. **3** *tired jokes* stale, hackneyed, familiar, worn-out, outworn, well-worn, clichéd, stock, platitudinous, trite, banal. **4** *made tired by their chatter* bored, wearied, irked, irritated, annoyed, exasperated.

**tireless** adjective untiring, unflagging, indefatigable, energetic, industrious, vigorous, determined, resolute, dogged.

**tiresome** adjective **1** *tiresome work* wearisome, laborious, wearing, tedious, boring, monotonous, dull, uninteresting, unexciting, humdrum, routine. **2** *she is a tiresome child* troublesome, irksome, vexatious, irritating, annoying, exasperating, trying.

**titillate** verb excite, arouse, stimulate, thrill, fascinate, tantalize, seduce; *inf.* turn on.

**titillating** adjective exciting, arousing, stimulating, provocative, tantalizing, suggestive, seductive, erotic.

**title** noun **1** *picture/illustration titles* credit, caption, legend, inscription, heading, name. **2** *what is the title of the ship's officer?* designation, appellation, name, denomination, epithet, sobriquet; *inf.* moniker, handle. **3** *disputing his title to the land* entitlement, right, claim, ownership, proprietorship, possession, holding. **4** *boxers contending for the title* championship, first place, crown; laurels.

**title** verb entitle, name, call, designate, label, tag, style, term.

**titter** noun snicker, snigger, giggle, tee-hee, laugh, chuckle, cackle, chortle.

**titular** adjective *the titular head of state* nominal, so-called, self-called, self-styled, *soi-disant*, token, puppet, putative.

**toady** noun sycophant, fawner, flatterer, groveler, lackey, flunky, minion; hanger-on, parasite, leech, jackal; *inf.* yes-man, bootlicker.

**toady** verb **toady to** bow and scrape to, be obsequious to, fawn on, flatter, grovel to, kowtow to, curry favor with; *inf.* butter up, fall all over, suck up to.

**toast** verb **1** *toast the bread* brown, crisp, grill. **2** *toast the winner* drink (to) the health of, drink to, pledge, salute.

**toddle** verb totter, teeter, wobble, falter, dodder. **toddle off** go, leave, depart.

**together** adverb **1** *friends who work together* in conjunction, jointly, conjointly, in cooperation, as one, in unison, side by side, hand in hand, hand and/in glove, shoulder to shoulder, cheek by jowl. **2** *they arrived together* simultaneously, concurrently, at the same time, at once, all at once, synchronously. **3** *they have got it together at last* organized, sorted out, straight, to rights, settled, fixed, arranged.

**toil** verb labor, slog, struggle, slave, push oneself, drive oneself, strive, drudge, work like a dog/slave/Trojan; *inf.* work one's fingers to the bone, sweat, grind.

**toil** noun labor, slaving, drudgery, striving, industry, effort, exertion, travail, sweat of one's brow; *inf.* elbow grease, grind.

**toilet** noun lavatory, bathroom, rest room, washroom, men's room, ladies' room, powder room, convenience, urinal, latrine, privy, outhouse; *inf.* john, can.

**token** noun **1** *a token of friendship* symbol, sign, emblem, badge, representation, indication, mark, manifestation, expression, demonstration. **2** *keep the menu as a token of the celebration* memento, souvenir, keepsake, remembrance, reminder, memorial.

**token** adjective *offer token resistance* perfunctory, superficial, nominal, minimal, slight, hollow.

**tolerable** adjective **1** *the pain/noise level was scarcely tolerable* endurable, bearable, sufferable, supportable, acceptable. **2** *his work was only tolerable* fair, passable, adequate, so-so, mediocre, middling.

**tolerance** noun **1** *treat the young with*

*tolerance* toleration, open-mindedness, forbearance, patience, magnanimity, understanding, charity, lenience, indulgence, permissiveness, complaisance, laxness. **2** *his tolerance of pain* endurance, sufferance, acceptance, fortitude, stamina, hardiness, resilience, toughness.

**tolerant** adjective open-minded, unprejudiced, unbiased, unbigoted, broad-minded, liberal, magnanimous, sympathetic, understanding, charitable, lenient, indulgent, permissive.

**tolerate** verb **1** *tolerate other people's views* permit, allow, admit, sanction, warrant, countenance, brook, recognize, acknowledge. **2** *unable to tolerate the pain/noise* endure, bear, suffer, take, stand, put up with, abide, accept, stomach, submit to.

**toll** noun **1** *pay a toll to use the road* charge, fee, payment, levy, tariff. **2** *the death toll* cost, damage, loss.

**tomb** noun grave, burial place/chamber, sepulcher, vault, crypt, catacomb, mausoleum.

**tomfoolery** noun horseplay, mischief, fooling, foolery, clowning, skylarking, buffoonery, nonsense; pranks, tricks, capers, antics, larks; *inf.* shenanigans, monkey business.

**tone** noun **1** *the pleasant tone of the flute* sound, color, pitch, timbre, tonality. **2** *speak in an angry tone* intonation, inflection, modulation, accentuation. **3** *the tone of his letter was optimistic* mood, air, attitude, character, manner, spirit, temper, tenor, vein, drift, gist.

**tongue** noun *speak in a foreign tongue* language, speech, parlance, dialect, idiom, patois, vernacular; *inf.* lingo.

**tonic** noun restorative, refresher, stimulant, analeptic, pick-me-up, boost, fillip; *inf.* shot in the arm, picker-upper.

**too** adverb **1** *the dog came, too* as well, also, in addition, besides, furthermore, moreover, to boot. **2** *she is too busy* excessively, overly, unduly, inordinately, extremely.

**tool** noun **1** *the tools of his trade* implement, instrument, utensil, device, apparatus, gadget, appliance, machine, contrivance, contraption, aid. **2** *he is the manager's tool* puppet, pawn, minion, lackey, flunky, henchman, toady.

**top** noun **1** *the top of the hill* summit, peak, pinnacle, crest, crown, tip, apex, vertex, apogee. **2** *he is at the top of his career* height, zenith, acme, culmination, climax, crowning point, prime, meridian. **3** *put the top on the jar* cap, lid, stopper, cork, cover. **4** *she wore a blue top* shirt, T-shirt, blouse, jersey, sweater, sweatshirt.

**top** adjective **1** *the top drawer/floor* topmost, uppermost, highest. **2** *top scientists* foremost, leading, principal, preeminent, greatest, finest. **3** *the top positions in the firm* leading, chief, principal, main, highest, ruling, commanding. **4** *top goods* top-quality, top-grade, best, finest, prime, choicest, quality; *inf.* A-1, top-notch. **5** *at top speed* maximum, maximal, greatest, utmost.

**top** verb **1** *ice cream topped with chocolate sauce* cap, cover, finish, garnish. **2** *she tops the list of candidates* head, lead. **3** *he topped his previous record* surpass, exceed, go beyond, transcend, better, best, beat, excel, outstrip, outdo, outshine, eclipse.

**topic** noun subject, subject matter, theme, issue, matter, point, question, argument, thesis.

**top-notch** adjective first-rate, top-grade, excellent, ace, choice, superior; *inf.* A-1, crack.

**topple** verb **1** *the load was unstable and toppled* fall over, tip over, keel over, overturn, capsize. **2** *the rebels toppled the tyrant* overthrow, oust, unseat, bring down.

**topsy-turvy** adverb/adjective in disorder, in confusion, in a muddle, in chaos, in disarray, in a mess, upside down.

**torment** noun **1** *the torment of grief* agony, suffering, torture, pain, excruciation, anguish, hell, misery, distress, affliction, wretchedness. **2** *he was a torment to them* scourge, curse, plague, bane, affliction, thorn in the flesh, irritation, irritant, annoyance, worry, nuisance, bother.

**torment** verb **1** *tormented by conscience* afflict, harrow, plague, torture, distress, worry, trouble. **2** *tormented the new teacher* tease, irritate, vex, annoy, pester, harass, badger, bother.

**torn** adjective **1** *torn clothes* ragged, tattered, ripped, split, slit, cut, lacerated, rent. **2** *I am torn between the two dresses* divided, wavering, vacillating, irresolute, uncertain, undecided.

**torpid** adjective sluggish, slow-moving, slow, dull, lethargic, heavy, inactive, stagnant, inert, somnolent, sleepy, languorous, languid, listless, apathetic, passive, slothful, indolent, lazy.

**torrent** noun **1** *torrents of floodwaters* flood, deluge, inundation, spate, cascade, rush, stream, current; downpour, rainstorm. **2** *a torrent of abuse* stream, volley, outpouring, barrage, battery.

**torrid** adjective **1** *the torrid conditions in the desert* hot, arid, sweltering, scorching, boiling, parching, sultry, stifling. **2** *torrid love scenes* passionate, impassioned, ardent, fervent, fervid, amorous, erotic; *inf.* steamy.

**tortuous** adjective **1** *a tortuous mountain path* twisting, winding, curving, curvy, sinuous, coiling, serpentine, snaking, snaky, zigzag, meandering. **2** *a tortuous description of the incident* convoluted, roundabout, circuitous, indirect, involved, complicated, ambiguous. **3** *his tortuous policy* devious, cunning, tricky, deceptive.

**torture** noun **1** *use torture to extract a confession* persecution, pain, suffering, abuse, ill-treatment, punishment, torment. **2** *the torture of a toothache* agony, anguish. *See* TORMENT noun 1.

**torture** verb **1** *torture the hostages* persecute, abuse, ill-treat, punish, torment; *inf.* work over. **2** *tortured by his conscience* rack, afflict. *See* TORMENT verb 1.

**toss** verb **1** *toss the book over here* throw, hurl, cast, sling, pitch, shy, lob, propel, launch, project, heave, chuck. **2** *tossing around unable to sleep* thrash, wriggle, writhe, squirm, roll, tumble. **3** *ships tossing around on the waves* rock, roll, sway, undulate, pitch, lurch, heave.

**total** noun sum, sum total, aggregate, whole, entirety, totality.

**total** adjective **1** *the total number of votes* complete, entire, whole, full, comprehensive, combined, aggregate, composite, integral. **2** *a total disaster* complete, thorough, thoroughgoing, all-out, utter, absolute, downright, out and out, unmitigated, unqualified.

**total** verb **1** *these figures total more than $1,000* add up to, come to, amount to. **2** *total these figures rapidly* add up, sum, count up, count, calculate, reckon.

**totalitarian** adjective one-party, monocratic, undemocratic, autocratic, authoritarian, absolute, despotic, dictatorial, tyrannical, oppressive, fascist.

**totally** adverb completely, entirely, wholly, fully, thoroughly, utterly, absolutely, quite.

**totter** verb **1** *tottering on high heels* teeter, wobble, stagger, stumble, reel, sway, roll, lurch. **2** *tables/buildings tottering in the explosion* shake, sway, rock, lurch, shudder. **3** *the regime is tottering* be unstable, be unsteady, be shaky, be on the point of collapse, falter.

**touch** verb **1** *the wires are touching* be in contact, meet, converge, be contiguous, adjoin, abut. **2** *he touched her arm* tap, brush, graze, feel, stroke, pat, fondle, caress. **3** *do not touch the glassware* handle, hold, pick up, move, play with, toy with, fiddle with. **4** *she did not touch her meal* eat, consume, drink, take, partake of. **5** *they were touched by the child's plight* affect, move, influence, upset, disturb, sadden; *inf.* get to. **6** *the recession did not touch him* affect, concern, involve. **7** *they would not touch anything illegal* be associated with, have dealings with, deal with, handle, be a party to. **8** *no one can touch him at tennis* come near (to), come up to, compare with, be on a par with, equal, match, be in the same league as, rival, hold a candle to. **9** *they touched rock bottom* reach, attain, arrive at. **touch off 1** *touch off the explosive* ignite, trigger, explode, detonate. **2** *the statement touched off a storm of protest* set off, start, begin, set in motion, initiate, instigate, trigger, launch. **touch on/upon 1** *touch on the subject in his speech* refer to, mention, comment on, remark on, allude to. **2** *his actions touched on treason* come close to, verge on, be tantamount to. **touch up** patch up, fix up, repair, refurbish, renovate, revamp, give a face-lift to, improve, enhance.

**touch** noun **1** *feel a touch on his arm* pressure, tap, strike, hit, blow, brush, stroke, pat, caress. **2** *sense its presence by touch* feel, feeling, tactility. **3** *material with a velvety touch* feel, texture, grain, finish, surface, coating. **4** *a touch of garlic* bit, trace, dash, taste, spot, drop, pinch, speck, smack, suggestion, hint, soupçon, tinge, tincture, whiff, suspicion. **5** *admire the player's touch* craftsmanship, workmanship, artistry, performance, dexterity, deftness, skill, virtuosity, adroitness. **6** *the room needs a few extra touches* detail, feature, addition, accessory. **7** *I think the teacher is losing his touch* skill, skillfulness, expertise, technique, knack, adeptness, ability, talent, flair. **8** *the house needs a woman's touch* influence, effect, hand, handling, direction, management, technique, method. **9** *in touch with old friends* contact, communication, correspondence.

**touch-and-go** adjective uncertain, precarious, risky, hazardous, dangerous, critical, suspenseful, cliff-hanging.

**touching** adjective moving, impressive, affecting, warming, heartwarming, emotive, stirring, upsetting, disturbing, saddening, pitiful, piteous, poignant.

**touchy** adjective **1** *he is very touchy about his height* sensitive, oversensitive, hypersensitive, easily offended, thin-skinned; testy, irascible, irritable, grouchy, grumpy, peevish, querulous, cross, surly. **2** *a touchy situation* tricky, ticklish, delicate, precarious, chancy, risky.

**tough** adjective **1** *a tough substance* strong, durable, resistant, resilient, sturdy, firm, solid, hard, rigid, stiff. **2** *tough meat* chewy, leathery, gristly, stringy, fibrous, sinewy. **3** *have to be tough to survive those conditions* hardy, strong, fit, sturdy, rugged, stalwart, vigorous, strapping, robust. **4** *a tough job managing the firm* difficult, hard, arduous, onerous, heavy, uphill, laborious, strenuous, exacting, taxing, stressful. **5** *teachers getting tough with the children* firm,

strict, stern, severe, harsh, hard-hitting, adamant, inflexible. **6** *a tough way of life* hard, harsh, austere, bleak, grim, dire, rough. **7** *led astray by tough kids* rough, rowdy, unruly, disorderly, violent, wild, lawless, lawbreaking, criminal.

**toughen** verb **1** *toughen the glass* strengthen, fortify, reinforce, harden. **2** *toughen the laws* stiffen, tighten; *inf.* beef up.

**tour** noun **1** *a world tour* trip, excursion, journey, expedition, jaunt, outing, peregrination. **2** *on a golfing tour* circuit, ambit, round, course, beat. **3** *troops doing a tour in the Persian Gulf* tour of duty, stint, stretch, turn.

**tour** verb travel, journey, explore, vacation, visit, sightsee.

**tournament** noun competition, contest, series, meeting, event, match, tourney.

**tousled** adjective rumpled, disheveled, unkempt, disordered, untidy, messy; *inf.* mussed up.

**tow** verb pull, draw, drag, haul, tug, trail, lug.

**tower** noun steeple, spire, belfry, bell tower, turret, column, pillar, obelisk, minaret.

**tower** verb soar, rise, ascend, mount, rear. **tower above** surpass, excel, outshine, outclass, outdo, leave behind, overshadow, cap, top, transcend, eclipse, be head and shoulders above, put in the shade, run circles around.

**towering** adjective **1** *towering skyscrapers* high, tall, lofty, elevated, sky-high. **2** *in a towering rage* extreme, mighty, fierce, terrible, intense, violent, vehement. **3** *one of the towering intellects of his age* outstanding, extraordinary, preeminent, surpassing, incomparable, unrivaled, peerless.

**town** noun community; borough, municipality, township.

**toxic** adjective poisonous, venomous, virulent, noxious.

**toy** noun **1** *children's toys* plaything, game. **2** *the rich woman surrounds herself with toys* trinket, bauble, knickknack, gewgaw, trifle.

**toy** verb **toy with 1** *he is just toying with her* amuse oneself with, play around with, flirt with, dally with, sport with, trifle with. **2** *the child was toying with his food* play around with, fiddle with, fool/mess around with.

**trace** noun **1** *there was no trace left of the picnic* mark, sign, vestige, indication; evidence; remains, remnants, relics. **2** *traces of poison in the drink* bit, touch, hint, suggestion, suspicion, trifle, drop, dash, tinge, tincture, shadow, jot, iota.

**trace** verb **1** *unable to trace the letter* find,

discover, detect, unearth, uncover, track down, turn up, dig up, ferret out, hunt down. **2** *trace the bear to the forest* follow, pursue, track, trail, tail, shadow, stalk, dog. **3** *trace out the policies for the year* draw up, sketch, draft, outline, delineate, rough out, map, chart.

**track** noun **1** *follow the tracks of the burglar/bear/motorbike* marks, impressions, prints, imprints, footprints, footsteps; trail, spoor, scent. **2** *follow in the track of the great explorers* trail, path, pathway, way, course, route, line, orbit, trajectory. **keep track of** keep up with, follow, monitor, record. **lose track of** forget about, be unaware of, misplace, lose/cease contact with.

**track** verb *track the bear to the forest* follow, pursue. See TRACE verb 2. **track down** hunt down/out, run to earth, unearth, uncover, turn up, dig up, ferret out, nose out, bring to light, expose, discover, find out, detect.

**tract**[1] noun area, region, zone, stretch, expanse, extent, plot.

**tract**[2] noun pamphlet, booklet, leaflet, brochure, monograph, essay.

**trade** noun **1** *he is in the export trade* commerce, buying and selling, dealing, traffic, trafficking, business, marketing, merchandising. **2** *what trade is his father in?* line of work, line, occupation, job, career, profession, craft, vocation, calling, métier; work, employment. **3** *I will do a trade of my car with yours* swap, trade-off, exchange, switch, barter.

**trade** verb **1** *the firm is trading at a loss* do business, deal, run, operate. **2** *they trade in diamonds* buy and sell, traffic, market, merchandise. **3** *he traded his stamps for comics* swap, exchange, switch, barter. **trade on** take advantage of, exploit, capitalize on.

**trader** noun merchant, dealer, buyer, seller, buyer and seller, marketer, merchandiser, broker.

**tradition** noun custom, belief, practice, convention, ritual, observance, habit, institution; oral history, lore, folklore.

**traditional** adjective **1** *traditional holiday fare* customary, accustomed, conventional, established, ritual, habitual, routine, usual, wonted, old, time-honored, familiar, ancestral. **2** *keeping alive traditional customs* handed-down, folk, unwritten, oral.

**traffic** noun *drug traffic* trafficking, trade, trading, dealing, commerce, business, peddling, smuggling, bootlegging.

**traffic** verb **traffic in** trade in, deal in, do business in, peddle, smuggle.

**tragedy** noun disaster, calamity, catastrophe, misfortune, misadventure, affliction, adversity.

**tragic** adjective **1** *a tragic accident* disastrous, calamitous, catastrophic, fatal, terrible, dreadful, appalling, dire, awful. **2** *listen to her tragic tale* pitiful, piteous, melancholy, doleful, mournful, dismal, gloomy. **3** *it is tragic what they have done to the river* dreadful, deplorable, lamentable, regrettable.

**trail** noun **1** *follow the trail left by the leader* track, scent, spoor; traces, marks, signs, footprints, footmarks; path, pathway, footpath, track, road, route. **2** *the rock star had a trail of young admirers* line, queue, train, file, column, procession, following, entourage. **3** *leave a trail of disaster behind them* chain, series. See TRAIN noun 2.

**trail** verb **1** *the child trailed the toy behind him* tow, pull, drag, draw, haul. **2** *her long skirt trailing on the floor* drag across, sweep, dangle, hang down, droop. **3** *children trailing behind their parents* trudge, plod, dawdle, straggle, loiter, linger, lag. **4** *plants/creatures trailing along the ground* creep, crawl, slide, slink. **5** *they trailed him to his lair* follow, pursue. See TRACE verb 2. **6** *his voice trailed away* fade, fade away/out, disappear, vanish, peter out, die away, melt away.

**train** noun **1** *leaving a train of vapor* trail, stream, track, path, wake, wash. **2** *a train of disasters followed* trail, chain, string, series, sequence, set, progression. **3** *a train of people climbing the mountain* procession, line, file, column, convoy, caravan. **4** *the princess and her train* retinue, entourage, cortege, following.

**train** verb **1** *train the students in reading* instruct, teach, coach, tutor, school, educate, drill, prepare, ground, guide, indoctrinate, inculcate. **2** *she is training to be a teacher* study, qualify, learn, prepare. **3** *athletes train daily* exercise, do exercises, work out, practice, prepare. **4** *train the binoculars on the bird* aim, point, focus, direct, level, line up.

**trait** noun characteristic, attribute, feature, quality, property, idiosyncrasy, peculiarity, quirk.

**traitor** noun betrayer, backstabber, turncoat, double-crosser, double-dealer, renegade, defector, deserter, apostate, Judas, quisling, fifth columnist; *inf.* snake in the grass, two-timer.

**tramp** verb **1** *hear him tramping upstairs* trudge, plod, stamp, stump, stomp. **2** *spend the day tramping over the hills* trek, hike, march, slog, walk, ramble, roam, range, rove; *inf.* traipse.

**tramp** noun **1** *tramps sleeping on freight trains* vagrant, vagabond, hobo, derelict, down-and-out, itinerant, drifter. **2** *hear* *the tramp of the soldiers* footstep, footfall, tread, stamp, stomping. **3** *labeled her a tramp* loose woman, slut, wanton, trollop, prostitute, whore.

**trample** verb **1** *trample on the grass* tramp on, tread on, walk over, stamp on, squash, crush, flatten. **2** *trample on other people* ride roughshod over, treat with contempt, disregard, show no consideration for, encroach on, infringe.

**trance** noun daze, stupor, dream, reverie, brown study.

**tranquil** adjective **1** *a tranquil life* peaceful, restful, reposeful, calm, quiet, still, serene, placid, undisturbed. **2** *a tranquil person* calm, placid, composed, even-tempered, unexcitable, unflappable, unruffled, unperturbed.

**tranquillity** noun **1** *love the tranquillity of the place* peace, peacefulness, restfulness, reposefulness, calm, quiet, quietness, quietude, stillness, serenity, placidity. **2** *her tranquillity is never disturbed* composure, coolness, serenity, equanimity, even-temperedness, unexcitability, unflappability.

**transact** verb carry out, conduct, do, perform, execute, enact, manage, handle, negotiate, take care of, see to.

**transaction** noun **1** *the transaction took less than an hour* business, deal, undertaking, affair, bargain, negotiation; proceedings. **2** *the transaction of business in private* conducting, performance, execution, enactment, handling, negotiation.

**transcend** verb **1** *transcend human belief* go beyond, exceed, overstep, rise above. **2** *her performance transcended that of her opponents* surpass, excel. *See* TOWER ABOVE (TOWER *verb*).

**transcendental** adjective mystical, mystic, mysterious, preternatural, supernatural, otherworldly.

**transfer** verb **1** *transfer the material from the house to the garage* convey, move, shift, remove, take, carry, transport, change, relocate. **2** *transfer his property to his son* turn over, sign over, hand on, hand down, pass on, transmit, convey, devolve, assign, delegate.

**transfer** noun move, shift, relocation, change.

**transfix** verb *transfixed with/in terror* root to the spot, paralyze, petrify, stop dead, hypnotize, mesmerize, rivet, spellbind, fascinate, engross, stun, astound.

**transform** verb change, alter, convert, metamorphose, revolutionize, transfigure, remodel, redo, reconstruct, rebuild, reorganize, rearrange, renew, translate, transmute; *inf.* transmogrify.

**transgression** noun **1** *transgression of the law* overstepping, infringement, breach, breaking, contravention, violation, defiance, disobedience. **2** *punished for their transgressions* wrong, misdemeanor, misdeed, lawbreaking, crime, offense, lapse, fault, sin; wrongdoing, misbehavior.

**transgressor** noun wrongdoer, lawbreaker, criminal, miscreant, delinquent, villain, felon, offender, culprit, sinner, trespasser, malefactor.

**transient** adjective short-lived, impermanent. *See* TRANSITORY.

**transition** noun passage, change, transformation, conversion, changeover, metamorphosis, shift, switch, jump, leap, progression, gradation, development, evolution.

**transitory** adjective transient, short-lived, short-term, impermanent, temporary, brief, short, ephemeral, evanescent, momentary, fleeting, flying, passing, fugitive, fugacious, mutable.

**translate** verb **1** *translate the jargon into plain English* construe, interpret, render, convert, transcribe, transliterate, paraphrase, reword, decipher, decode, explain, elucidate. **2** *translate ideas into action* turn, change, convert, transform, alter, metamorphose, transmute.

**transmission** noun **1** *the transmission of mail* sending, conveyance, transport, dispatch, remission. **2** *the transmission of information/disease* transference, transferal, passing on, communication, imparting, dissemination, spreading. **3** *a radio transmission* broadcasting, relaying, sending out; broadcast, program.

**transmit** verb **1** *transmit the package by air* send, convey, transport, dispatch, forward, remit. **2** *transmit information/disease to others* transfer, pass on, hand on, communicate, impart, disseminate, spread, carry, diffuse. **3** *transmit late-night programs* broadcast, air, relay, send out, put on the air.

**transparent** adjective **1** *transparent plastic/streams* clear, see-through, translucent, lucid, pellucid, crystal-clear, crystalline, limpid, glassy, transpicuous. **2** *made of transparent material* sheer, diaphanous, filmy, gauzy. **3** *his transparent dishonesty* obvious, patent, manifest, undisguised, unmistakable, clear, plain, visible, noticeable, evident. **4** *done with transparent sincerity* frank, open, candid, direct, forthright, plainspoken, straight, ingenuous, artless.

**transpire** verb **1** *it transpired that he had been married before* become known, come to light, emerge, come out. **2** *tell me what transpired at the meeting* come about, take place, happen, occur, turn up, arise, chance, befall.

**transport** verb **1** *transport the goods to the warehouse* convey, take, transfer, move, shift, bring, fetch, carry, bear, haul, lug, cart, run, ship. **2** *transport criminals to an island* banish, exile, deport, drive away, expatriate. **3** *she was transported by the music* enrapture, entrance, enchant, enthrall, captivate, delight, ravish, carry away.

**transport** noun transportation, conveyance, transit, carriage, freight; vehicle, car.

**trap** noun **1** *rabbits caught in a trap* snare, net, mesh, ambush, pitfall, booby trap. **2** *the question was a trap to get him to confess* stratagem, setup, artifice, ruse, wile, trick, device, deception, subterfuge. **3** *lay a trap for the criminal* ambush, lure, decoy, bait.

**trap** verb **1** *trap the rabbits* snare, ensnare, enmesh, entrap, catch, corner. **2** *trapped into making a confession* trick, dupe, deceive, lure, inveigle, beguile, set up. **3** *they were trapped in the building* cut off, corner, confine, imprison.

**trappings** plural noun accoutrements, appurtenances, appointments, trimmings, paraphernalia, fittings, things; equipage, equipment, apparatus, gear, livery, adornment, ornamentation, decoration, finery, frippery; panoply.

**trash** noun **1** *talk trash* rubbish, garbage, nonsense, drivel, poppycock, balderdash, bunkum, twaddle; *inf.* bunk, tripe, bilge, rot, tommyrot. **2** *empty out the trash* rubbish, waste, refuse, litter, garbage. **3** *he regards his neighbors as trash* riff-raff, scum, rabble, canaille, vermin; dregs, good-for-nothings.

**traumatic** adjective agonizing, shocking, scarring, disturbing, distressing, damaging, injurious, harmful.

**travel** verb **1** *she plans to travel after she retires* journey, take a trip, tour, voyage, sightsee. **2** *news travels fast* proceed, progress, advance, be transmitted, carry. **3** *travel the length of the country* cross, traverse, cover, wander, ramble, roam, rove, range, wend, make one's way over. **4** *the car was certainly traveling* speed, go at breakneck speed; *inf.* hellbent for leather, go like a bat out of hell, tear up the miles.

**traveler** noun tourist, vacationer, excursionist, explorer, passenger, voyager, sightseer, globe-trotter.

**traverse** verb **1** *traversing the desert* cross, go across, travel over, journey over, make one's way across, pass over, wander, roam, range. **2** *beams traversing the ceiling* go across, lie across, stretch across, extend across, cross, cut across, bridge. **3** *traverse all aspects of the subject* consider, examine, check, study, review, investigate, inspect, scrutinize, look into.

**travesty** noun misrepresentation, distortion, perversion, corruption, poor imitation, mockery, parody, caricature, sham, burlesque, satire, spoof, lampoon, takeoff; *inf.* send-up.

**treacherous** adjective **1** *betrayed by a treacherous follower* traitorous, backstabbing, double-crossing, double-dealing, disloyal, faithless, unfaithful, perfidious, duplicitous, deceitful, false-hearted, false, untrue, untrustworthy, unreliable, undependable; *inf.* two-timing. **2** *the weather conditions can be treacherous* precarious, unreliable, undependable, unstable, unsafe, risky, hazardous, dangerous, perilous, deceptive; *inf.* dicey.

**treachery** noun traitorousness, backstabbing, double-crossing, double-dealing, disloyalty, faithlessness, unfaithfulness, perfidy, perfidiousness, treason, duplicity, deceit, deceitfulness, deception; *inf.* two-timing.

**tread** verb **1** *tread softly so as not to wake the baby* walk, step, go, pace. **2** *tread the long road home* hike, tramp, stride, step out, trek, march, trudge, plod. **3** *tread grapes* trample, tramp on, step on, stamp on, squash, crush, flatten, press down. **tread on** ride roughshod over, oppress, repress, suppress, subdue, subjugate, quell, crush.

**tread** noun step, footstep, footfall, walk, tramp.

**treason** noun high treason; betrayal, traitorousness, treachery, disloyalty, perfidy, sedition, subversion, mutiny, rebellion, lese-majesty.

**treasure** noun **1** *find buried treasure* riches, valuables; wealth, fortune, hoard; jewels, gems, coins, gold, money, cash. **2** *she is her father's treasure* darling, pride and joy, apple of one's eye, jewel, jewel in the crown, gem, pearl, precious, prize.

**treasure** verb **1** *she treasures her friendship/children* value, prize, set great store by, think highly of, hold dear, adore, cherish, love, worship, revere, venerate, dote on. **2** *treasure the souvenirs of their travels* save, collect, accumulate, hoard, store up, lay by, stow away, squirrel away, salt away; *inf.* stash away.

**treat** noun **1** *think of a treat for her birthday* surprise, celebration, entertainment, amusement, diversion. **2** *bringing a treat for the child* gift, present, tidbit, delicacy; *inf.* goodie. **3** *it was a treat to see her again* pleasure, delight, thrill, joy, gratification, satisfaction; fun.

**treat** verb **1** *treat his car recklessly* deal with, handle, cope with, contend with, manage, use. **2** *treat his remarks as jokes* regard, consider, view, look upon, deal with. **3** *treat the sick patient* medicate, doctor, nurse, care for, attend to, minister to, cure, heal. **4** *her book treats the question of religious doubt* deal with, discuss, go into, discourse upon, be concerned with, touch upon, refer to, consider, study, review, analyze. **treat to 1** *treat (them) to dinner* pay for, buy for, pay/foot the bill for, finance, take out to. **2** *we were treated to a wonderful performance* entertain by, amuse by, divert by, cheer by, gratify by, delight by, regale by. **treat with** *treat the wood with creosote* apply to, put on, use on, ply with.

**treatise** noun discourse, exposition, dissertation, thesis, disquisition, study, essay, paper, monograph, tract, pamphlet.

**treatment** noun **1** *his treatment was fair/cruel* action, behavior, conduct, handling, management, use; dealings. **2** *patients/wounds responding to treatment* medication, medicament, therapy, doctoring, nursing, first aid, care, ministration; cure, remedy; drugs, therapeutics.

**treaty** noun agreement, pact, deal, compact, covenant, bargain, pledge, contract, alliance, concordat, convention, entente.

**trek** verb trudge, tramp, plod, travel, journey. *See* TRAMP verb 2.

**trek** noun expedition, trip, journey, hike, march, walk, odyssey.

**tremble** verb **1** *fingers trembling with excitement* shake, quiver, shiver, quake, twitch, wiggle. **2** *buildings trembling in the earthquake* shudder, teeter, totter, wobble, rock, vibrate, oscillate, rattle. **3** *I tremble at the thought* fear, be frightened, be apprehensive, worry, be anxious.

**tremendous** adjective **1** *people of tremendous girth* great, huge, enormous, immense, massive, vast, colossal, prodigious, stupendous, gigantic, gargantuan, mammoth, giant, titanic; *inf.* whopping. **2** *she is a tremendous cook* excellent, marvelous, extraordinary, exceptional, wonderful, incredible, fabulous; *inf.* fantastic, terrific, super.

**tremor** noun tremble, trembling, shake, shaking, shiver, quiver, quaver, vibration, twitch, spasm, paroxysm.

**trench** noun ditch, excavation, earthwork, furrow, duct, trough, channel, conduit, cut, drain, waterway, moat, fosse.

**trenchant** adjective **1** *a trenchant wit* incisive, cutting, pointed, sharp, biting, pungent, caustic, piercing, penetrating, razor, razor-edged, mordant, scathing, acrid, acid, tart, acidulous, acerbic, astringent, sarcastic. **2** *trenchant divisions between the political parties* clear, clear-cut, distinct, defined, well-defined, sharp, crisp, unequivocal, unambiguous.

**trend** noun **1** *an upward trend in prices* tendency, drift, course, direction, bearing, current, inclination, bias, leaning, bent, swing. **2** *they like to follow the trend* fashion, vogue, style, mode, look, craze, fad.

**trespasser** noun **1** *trespassers will be prosecuted* intruder, interloper, encroacher, infringer, invader, obtruder. **2** *trespassers asking for forgiveness* wrongdoer, evildoer, criminal, offender, transgressor, sinner, malefactor.

**trial** noun **1** *the murder trial lasted several weeks* court case, case, hearing, inquiry, tribunal, litigation. **2** *give the applicant/car a trial* probation, test, audition, testing, tryout, check, assay; *inf.* dry run. **4** *climb the mountain at the third trial* try, attempt, endeavor, effort, venture, go; *inf.* shot, stab, crack. **5** *she was never a trial to her mother* nuisance, pest, bother, worry, vexation, annoyance, irritant, irritation, bane, curse, burden, cross to bear, thorn in one's flesh; *inf.* pain in the neck. **6** *the trials of life* trouble, worry. *See* TRIBULATION.

**tribe** noun **1** *the tribes of Israel* family, dynasty, clan, sept. **2** *a tribe of doctors at the conference* group, crowd, company, party, band, number, collection; *inf.* bunch.

**tribulation** noun trouble, worry, anxiety, vexation, load, burden, cross to bear, blow, affliction, trial, adversity, hardship, ordeal, pain; suffering, distress, misery, wretchedness, unhappiness, sadness, woe, grief.

**tribute** noun **1** *give tributes to the heroes* gift, present, accolade, commendation, testimonial, paean, eulogy, panegyric, encomium; gratitude, applause, praise, homage, honor, exaltation, laudation, extolment, glorification; congratulations, compliments, bouquets. **2** *the success is a tribute to their hard work* acknowledgment, recognition, testimonial, indication, manifestation; evidence, proof. **3** *foreign governments paying tributes to the emperor* charge, tax, duty, levy, tariff, ransom.

**trick** noun **1** *he got the job by a trick* stratagem, ploy, artifice, ruse, dodge, wile, device, maneuver, trick of the trade, deceit, deception, subterfuge, swindle, fraud; *inf.* con. **2** *he has the trick of making guests feel welcome* knack, art, gift, talent, technique, ability, skill, expertise, know-how. **3** *play tricks on the old man* hoax, practical joke, leg-pull, prank, jape, antic; *inf.* gag, put-on. **4** *he has an annoying trick of repeating himself* idiosyncrasy, habit, mannerism, quirk, peculiarity, foible, eccentricity, characteristic, trait, practice.

**trick** verb deceive, delude, mislead, take in, cheat, hoodwink, fool, outwit, dupe, hoax, gull, cozen, defraud, swindle; *inf.* con, pull a fast one on, put one over on.

**trickery** noun guile, artifice, wiliness, deceit, deception, cheating, subterfuge, craft, craftiness, chicanery, pretense, dishonesty, fraud, swindling, imposture, double-dealing, duplicity; *inf.* conning, monkey/funny business, hanky-panky.

**trickle** verb drip, dribble, leak, ooze, seep, exude, percolate.

**tricky** adjective **1** *a tricky situation* difficult, problematic, awkward, delicate, sensitive, ticklish, thorny, knotty, touchy, risky, uncertain, precarious; *inf.* sticky. **2** *a tricky character* cunning, crafty, wily, artful, devious, scheming, foxy, sly, slippery, deceitful, deceptive.

**trifle** noun **1** *her mind is occupied with trifles* trivia, inessentials; triviality, bagatelle. **2** *buy a few trifles for gifts* bauble, knickknack. *See* TRINKET. **3** *it cost a mere trifle* next to nothing, hardly anything, pittance, piddling sum. **4** *a trifle confused* bit, touch.

**trifle** verb **trifle with 1** *he is just trifling with the young woman* amuse oneself, dally with. *See* TOY WITH (TOY verb). **2** *he is not a man to be trifled with* treat lightly, deal with casually, treat in a cavalier fashion, dismiss.

**trifling** adjective **1** *discuss trifling matters* petty, trivial, unimportant, insignificant, inconsequential, shallow, superficial, frivolous, silly, idle, foolish, empty. **2** *cost a trifling amount* small, tiny, minuscule, infinitesimal, negligible, paltry, piddling.

**trim** adjective **1** *looking trim in her uniform* neat, tidy, neat and tidy, smart, spruce, well-groomed, well-dressed, well-turned-out, dapper, natty. **2** *trim gardens* orderly, well-maintained, shipshape, well-looked-after, well-cared-for, spick-and-span. **3** *have a trim figure* slim, slender, lean, svelte, streamlined, willowy, lissome, sleek, in good shape, fit, physically fit.

**trim** verb **1** *trim one's hair/beard* cut, clip, snip, shear, prune, pare, even up, neaten, tidy up. **2** *trim the fat from the meat | trim the branches from the tree* chop, hack, remove, take off. **3** *trim the annual budget* cut down, decrease, reduce, diminish, cut back on, curtail, dock, retrench. **4** *trim the Christmas tree* decorate, adorn, ornament, embellish, festoon. **5** *trim the dress with lace* edge, pipe, border, fringe.

**trim** noun **1** *admire the trim on the dress* trimming, decoration, adornment, ornamentation, embellishment, edging, piping, border, fringe, frill, embroidery. **2** *give the boy/hedge a trim* haircut, cut, clip, snip, shearing, pruning, paring. **3** *the old man is still in trim* good health, good

condition, good shape/form, fine fettle, shape.

**trinket** noun bauble, ornament, knickknack, trifle, gimcrack, gewgaw, piece of bric-à-brac, bibelot, doodad, whatnot.

**trip** noun **1** *go on a trip to China* excursion, tour, expedition, voyage, jaunt, outing, run. **2** *the trip on the sidewalk* stumble, misstep, false step, slip, slide, fall, tumble, spill.

**trip** verb **1** *she tripped on the broken pavement* stumble, lose one's footing/balance, stagger, totter, slip, slide, misstep, fall, tumble. **2** *she tripped across the dance floor* skip, dance, hop, prance, bound, spring, gambol, caper, frisk, cavort, waltz. **trip up 1** *she tripped up when she tried to alter the accounts* make a mistake, blunder, go wrong, err, lapse, bungle, botch, slip up. **2** *the defending lawyer tripped the witness up* trap, outwit, outsmart, confuse, disconcert, unsettle, discountenance; *inf.* throw.

**trite** adjective hackneyed, banal, commonplace, ordinary, common, platitudinous, clichéd, stock, stereotyped, overused, overdone, stale, worn-out, threadbare, unimaginative, unoriginal, uninspired, dull, pedestrian, run-of-the-mill, routine, humdrum.

**triumph** noun **1** *his triumph over his opponent* conquest, victory, win, ascendancy, mastery, success. **2** *it was a triumph of American engineering* coup, tour de force, feat, masterstroke, achievement, attainment, accomplishment, supreme example, sensation, hit. **3** *expressions of triumph on their faces* exultation, jubilation, jubilance, elation, rejoicing, joy.

**triumph** verb **1** *the better team triumphed* win, succeed, be the victor, be victorious, gain a victory, carry the day, take the honors/prize/crown. **2** *the defeated team watching the winners triumph* exult, rejoice, jubilate, celebrate, revel, glory, gloat, swagger, brag, boast. **triumph over** beat, defeat, conquer, vanquish, best, worst, overcome, overpower, get the better of, prevail against.

**triumphant** adjective **1** *the triumphant team took a bow* winning, victorious, successful, prizewinning. **2** *giving triumphant shouts* exultant, jubilant, elated, rejoicing, joyful, joyous, proud, gloating, boastful.

**trivial** adjective unimportant, insignificant, inconsequential, flimsy, insubstantial, petty, minor, of no account/matter, negligible, paltry, trifling, foolish, frivolous, worthless, piddling.

**troop** noun band, group, company, assemblage, gathering, body, crowd, throng, multitude, horde, host, mob, squad, pack, drove, flock, swarm, stream, gang, crew.

**troop** verb flock, stream, swarm, surge, crowd, throng, mill.

**troops** plural noun armed forces, army, military, services, soldiers, soldiery, fighting men/women.

**trophy** noun cup, prize, award, laurels; spoil, booty; souvenir, memento, keepsake, relic.

**tropical** adjective hot, torrid, sweltering, boiling, sultry, steamy, humid, sticky.

**trouble** noun 1 *his car is causing him trouble* worry, bother, anxiety, disquiet, unease, irritation, vexation, inconvenience, annoyance, agitation, harassment, difficulty, distress; problems. 2 *there has been a lot of trouble in her life* difficulty, misfortune, adversity, hardship, bad luck, ill luck, burden, distress, pain, suffering, affliction, torment, woe, grief, unhappiness, sadness, heartache. 3 *please do not go to any trouble* bother, inconvenience, disturbance, fuss, effort, exertion, work, labor, attention, care, thoughtfulness; *inf.* hassle. 4 *the trouble with him is he's too nice* problem, difficulty, failing, weakness, shortcoming, fault, imperfection, defect, blemish. 5 *he has stomach trouble* disorder, disease, illness, dysfunction. 6 *the bartender does not want any trouble* disturbance, disorder, unrest, fighting, strife, conflict, tumult, commotion, turbulence, lawbreaking. **in trouble** in difficulty, having problems, in dire straits, in a predicament, in a tight corner, in hot water, in a jam/pickle, in a mess/spot.

**trouble** verb 1 *he is troubled by neighbors/finances* worry, annoy, irritate, vex, irk, fret, pester, torment, plague, upset, perturb, agitate, discompose, harass, distress; *inf.* hassle. 2 *he is troubled by back pain* afflict, oppress, weigh down, burden, incapacitate. 3 *I am sorry to trouble you, but may I use your phone?* bother, disturb, inconvenience, put out, impose upon, discommode, incommode.

**troublesome** adjective worrying, worrisome, bothersome, tiresome, disturbing, annoying, irritating, irksome, upsetting, perturbing, harassing, distressing, difficult, problematic, demanding, taxing.

**trounce** verb 1 *they trounced the other team* rout, drub, thrash, crush, overwhelm; *inf.* make mincemeat (out) of, walk all over, wipe the floor with, hammer, clobber, slaughter, give a pasting to. 2 *trounced for disobeying the emperor* thrash, beat, whip, flog, lash, birch, cane, spank, chastise; *inf.* belt, wallop, lambaste, tan the hide of.

**truce** noun cease-fire, armistice, suspension/cessation of hostilities, peace, respite, moratorium.

**truculent** adjective belligerent, pugnacious, bellicose, combative, contentious, hostile, obstreperous, violent, fierce, defiant, sullen, surly, cross, bad-tempered, ill-natured.

**trudge** verb plod, lumber, shuffle, drag one's feet, clump, slog, trek, tramp, hike.

**true** adjective 1 *what you say is true* | *a true account* truthful, accurate, correct, right, valid, factual, exact, precise, faithful, genuine, reliable, veracious, honest. 2 *a true witch doctor* real, genuine, authentic, actual, bona fide, valid, legitimate; *inf.* honest-to-goodness. 3 *a true friend* loyal, faithful, trustworthy, trusty, dependable, staunch, firm, fast, steady, constant, unswerving, unwavering, devoted, sincere, dedicated.

**truly** adverb 1 *she is truly his daughter* in truth, really, in reality, actually, in fact, genuinely, certainly, surely, definitely, decidedly, positively, absolutely. 2 *tell me truly what you think* truthfully, honestly, frankly, candidly, openly. 3 *truly, I did not know* indeed, veritably. 4 *they are truly grateful* sincerely, very, extremely, exceptionally. 5 *the novel does not truly depict the era* exactly, precisely, faithfully, closely, accurately, correctly, unerringly.

**truncate** verb shorten, reduce, diminish, decrease, cut short, prune, trim, lop, curtail, abbreviate.

**trunk** noun chest, case, portmanteau, crate, storage box, box, coffer.

**truss** verb tie up, wrap up, bind up, bundle up.

**truss** noun support, brace, prop, strut, buttress.

**trust** noun 1 *have trust in the surgeon* faith, confidence, belief, conviction, credence, assurance, certainty, reliance, hope, expectation. 2 *a position of trust* responsibility, duty, obligation. 3 *the money is kept in trust* trusteeship, guardianship, care, custody.

**trust** verb 1 *you can trust him to behave well* have faith/confidence in, rely on, depend on, bank on, count on, be sure of, swear by. 2 *I trust you will come* hope, assume, presume, expect, believe, suppose. 3 *he trusted his son to her* entrust, put in the hands of, turn over, assign, consign, commit, delegate.

**trustful** adjective trusting, unsuspicious, unquestioning, credulous, ingenuous, naive.

**trustworthy** adjective reliable, dependable, stable, staunch, loyal, faithful, trusty, responsible, honest, honorable, upright, ethical, righteous, principled.

**truth** noun 1 *no truth in what she says* truthfulness, accuracy, correctness, rightness, validity, fact, genuineness, veracity, verity, honesty. **2** *truth is stranger than fiction* reality, actuality, factuality. **3** *he is a man of truth* integrity, uprightness, righteousness, honor, honorableness, sincerity, candor. **4** *cite an old truth* truism, axiom, maxim, proverb, adage, aphorism.

**truthful** adjective **1** *a truthful child* honest, trustworthy, veracious, candid, frank, open, forthright, straight. **2** *a truthful account* true, accurate, correct, right, valid, factual.

**try** verb **1** *try to do well* attempt, aim, endeavor, make an effort, exert oneself, undertake, strive, seek, struggle, do one's best; *inf.* have a go/shot/crack/stab. **2** *try a new brand* try out, test, put to the test, experiment with, investigate, examine, appraise, evaluate, assess, experience, sample, check out. **3** *the children try her patience* tax, strain, sap, drain, exhaust. **4** *she has been sorely tried by the children* irk, vex, annoy, irritate, harass, afflict, nag, pester, plague, torment. **5** *try the case* hear, adjudge, adjudicate. **try out** test, appraise. *See* TRY 2.

**trying** adjective **1** *the visitors were very trying* troublesome, bothersome, tiresome, irksome, vexatious, annoying, irritating, exasperating. **2** *have a trying day* taxing, demanding, stressful, difficult, arduous, hard, tough, tiring, fatiguing, exhausting, upsetting.

**tuck** verb **1** *tuck the shirt into the skirt* gather, push, ease, insert, stuff. **2** *tuck the material* gather, fold, ruck, ruffle, pleat. **tuck in** cover up, wrap up, put to bed, make snug/comfortable.

**tuck** noun gather, fold, ruck, ruffle, pleat.

**tug** verb **1** *tug the rope hard* pull, jerk, yank, wrench, wrest. **2** *the dog was tugging him along the road* draw, drag, haul, tow.

**tumble** verb **1** *the toddler tumbled suddenly* fall over, fall down, fall headlong, topple, fall head over heels, fall end over end, lose one's footing/balance, stumble, stagger, trip up; somersault, flip. **2** *share prices have tumbled* plummet, plunge, slump, dive, drop, slide, fall, decrease, decline. **3** *ships tumbling about on the waves* roll, toss, pitch, heave, thrash. **4** *tumble out of bed* blunder, stumble. **5** *the wind had tumbled her hair* dishevel, ruffle, disarrange, disorder, mess up; *inf.* muss up.

**tumbledown** adjective dilapidated, ramshackle, crumbling, disintegrating, decrepit, ruined, in ruins, rickety, shaky, tottering, teetering.

**tumult** noun **1** *we cannot hear you above the tumult* din, uproar, commotion, racket, hubbub, hullabaloo, clamor, shouting, yelling, pandemonium, babel, bedlam. **2** *the meeting ended in tumult* disorder, disarray, disturbance, chaos, upheaval. **3** *police sent to deal with a tumult* riot, protest, insurrection, rebellion, brawl, fight, fracas. **4** *emotions in tumult* turmoil, confusion, ferment.

**tumultuous** adjective **1** *tumultuous applause* loud, noisy, clamorous, ear-shattering, deafening, ear-piercing, blaring, uproarious, unrestrained. **2** *a tumultuous crowd* rowdy, unruly, boisterous, disorderly, obstreperous, wild, violent, lawless, vociferous. **3** *tumultuous emotions* raging, unrestrained, uncontrolled, frenzied, in turmoil, turbulent.

**tune** noun **1** *play a folk tune* melody, air, song, theme, strain, motif. **2** *his ideas are not in tune with modern thinking* agreement, accord, accordance, harmony, correspondence, congruence, conformity, sympathy.

**tune** verb adjust, regulate, pitch, attune.

**turbulent** adjective **1** *turbulent seas* tempestuous, stormy, raging, foaming, rough, choppy. **2** *turbulent crowds* rowdy, agitated. *See* TUMULTUOUS 2. **3** *turbulent emotions/moods* disturbed, agitated, unsettled, unstable, troubled, distraught, in turmoil.

**turgid** adjective **1** *turgid ankles* swollen, enlarged, puffy, puffed up, bloated, distended, tumescent. **2** *turgid prose* bombastic, high-flown, high-sounding, grandiloquent, magniloquent, extravagant, pretentious, pompous, flowery, orotund, fustian.

**turmoil** noun agitation, ferment, confusion, disorder, disarray, upheaval, chaos, pandemonium, bedlam, tumult; disturbance, bustle, flurry, commotion.

**turn** verb **1** *the wheel is turning* go around/round, rotate, revolve, circle, roll, spin, wheel, whirl, twirl, gyrate, swivel, pivot. **2** *he turned in the driveway* turn around/round, change direction/course, go back, return, reverse direction, make a U-turn. **3** *he turned toward her* veer, wheel around/round, swing around/round. **4** *turn the meat* turn over, reverse, invert, flip over, turn upside down, turn topsy-turvy. **5** *turn the hose on them* aim, direct, point, train, level, focus. **6** *his expression turned from amusement to horror* change, alter, transform, metamorphose, mutate. **7** *he turned nasty* become, come to be, get, go. **8** *the milk/butter turned* go/turn sour, curdle, spoil, become rancid, go bad. **9** *the sight turned my stomach* nauseate, sicken, upset, unsettle. **10** *my head is turning* spin, feel dizzy/giddy. **11** *turn the corner* go/come around, round, negotiate, take. **12** *turn somersaults* perform, execute, do, carry out. **13** *turn a profit* make, bring in, gain, acquire, obtain, get, procure, secure. **14** *turn a pot* shape, mold, fashion, form, cast, construct. **15** *he used to be a loyal follower, but he turned* change sides, go over, defect, desert, renege, turn renegade, break faith, apostatize, tergiversate. **turn away** send away, reject, rebuff, repel, cold-shoulder; *inf.* give the brush-off to. **turn back** *go back if the weather is bad* go back, retrace one's steps, return, retreat. **turn down** **1** *he turned down the proposal* reject, decline, give the thumbs down to, rebuff, repudiate, spurn, veto. **2** *turn down the gas* lessen, lower, reduce, decrease, diminish. **turn in** **1** *turn in your homework* hand in, submit, tender, hand over, deliver. **2** *it is time to turn in* retire, call it a day; *inf.* hit the hay/sack. **3** *turn him in to the police* hand over, turn over, deliver, inform on, betray; *inf.* squeal on, blow the whistle on, rat on, finger, put the finger on. **turn off** **1** *turn off the heater* switch off, shut off, flick off, unplug. **2** *the driver suddenly turned off the main road* branch off, leave, quit, depart from, deviate from. **3** *she was turned off by his table manners* put off, turn against; disenchant, alienate, repel, disgust, nauseate, sicken. **turn on** **1** *turn on the electricity* put on, switch on, flick on, plug in, operate. **2** *the dog turned on his master* attack, launch an attack on, fall on, set upon, become hostile to; *inf.* lay into, tear into. **3** *the result turns on the number voting* depend on, hang on, hinge on, be contingent on. **4** *she is turned on by muscular men* arouse, excite, titillate, stimulate, thrill, attract, please. **turn out** **1** *turn her out of her house* put out, throw out, kick out, eject, evict, oust; *inf.* chuck out, bounce. **2** *turn out the delinquent workers* dismiss, discharge, ax; *inf.* fire, sack. **3** *turn out the light* turn off, put off, switch off, shut off, flick off, unplug. **4** *turn out thousands of toys per year* bring out, put out, produce, make, manufacture, fabricate, yield, process. **5** *a big crowd turned out to hear him* go, come, be present, attend, put in an appearance, appear, turn up, arrive, assemble, gather; *inf.* show up, show. **6** *it turned out that she was right* happen, occur, come about, end up, transpire. **7** *she turned out a beautiful girl* develop into, end up, emerge as. **turn over** **1** *the boat turned over* overturn, topple, upturn, capsize, keel over, turn turtle. **2** *turn over the pages* flick over, flip over, leaf over. **3** *turn over the pros and cons* consider, think about, ponder, reflect on, mull over, muse on, ruminate about. **4** *turn over the estate to his brother* hand over, transfer, consign, assign, commit. **turn to** **1** *turn to drink* have recourse to, resort to, take to. **2** *turn to him for help* look to, apply to, approach, appeal to, have recourse to. **turn up** **1** *turn up*

*the volume* increase, raise, amplify, make louder, intensify. **2** *turn up some interesting information* uncover, unearth, discover, bring to light, find, hit upon, dig up, ferret out, root out, expose. **3** *he has mislaid the book, but it will turn up* be found, be located, come to light. **4** *they did not turn up at the party* appear; *inf.* show up. See TURN OUT 5 (TURN *verb*). **5** *he hopes a job will turn up* present itself, crop up, pop up, arise, come on the scene.

**turn** noun **1** *give the wheel a few turns* rotation, revolution, circle, spin, whirl, twirl, gyration, swivel. **2** *take a turn to the left* deviation, divergence, veer. **3** *a road full of turns* turning, bend, curve, corner, twist, winding. **4** *dislike the turn of events* trend, tendency, bias, leaning, direction, drift. **5** *a turn for the better/worse* change, alteration, variation, difference, deviation, divergence, shift. **6** *he is of an academic turn of mind* bent, tendency, inclination, bias, propensity, affinity, leaning. **7** *it is your turn to play* time, opportunity, chance, stint, spell, move, try. **8** *take a turn in the park* walk, stroll, airing, constitutional, promenade, drive, ride, outing, jaunt; *inf.* spin. **9** *do him a good/bad turn* act, action, deed, service, gesture, favor. **10** *you gave me quite a turn* shock, start, surprise, fright, scare.

**turning point** noun crossroads, crisis, crux, moment of truth/decision.

**turnout** noun number, gathering, crowd, assembly, assemblage, audience, attendance, gate.

**tussle** noun struggle, wrestle, conflict, fight, battle, skirmish, scuffle, brawl; *inf.* set-to, scrap.

**tutor** noun teacher, instructor, coach, lecturer, educator.

**tutor** verb teach, instruct, coach, educate, school, train, drill, direct, guide.

**twig** noun branch, stick, offshoot, shoot, spray, stem.

**twilight** noun **1** *walk home at twilight* dusk, gloaming. **2** *scarcely able to see her in the twilight* half-light, semidarkness, dimness. **3** *in the twilight of his career* decline, ebb, waning.

**twin** noun **1** *where is the twin of that glove?* mate, match, fellow, counterpart, complement. **2** *she is an absolute twin for the queen* double, look-alike, likeness, image, duplicate, clone; *inf.* spitting image, ringer, dead ringer.

**twine** noun **1** *a ball of twine* cord, string, yarn, thread. **2** *vines in a twine* coil, spiral, whorl, convolution, twist, tangle.

**twinge** noun **1** *a twinge of rheumatism* spasm, pain, pang, ache, throb, tweak, tingle, cramp, stitch. **2** *a twinge of conscience* pang, uneasiness, discomfort, qualm, scruple, misgiving.

**twinkle** verb glitter, glint, sparkle, flicker, shimmer, glimmer, gleam, dazzle, flash, wink, blink, shine, scintillate, coruscate.

**twinkle** noun twinkling, glitter, glint, sparkle, flicker, shimmer, glimmer, gleam, dazzle, flash, wink, blink, shining, scintillation, coruscation.

**twirl** verb **1** *she twirled around/round to the music* spin, whirl, turn, pirouette, wheel, gyrate, revolve, rotate, pivot, twist. **2** *twirl a curl of hair around/round her finger* twist, coil, wind, curl.

**twist** verb **1** *twist the metal rod | twist it off the wall* bend, warp, misshape, deform, contort, distort; wrench, wrest. **2** *his face twisted in agony* contort, screw up. **3** *he twisted his ankle* wrench, turn, sprain. **4** *the plant had twisted itself around the tree* twine, entwine, coil, wind, weave, wrap. **5** *twist a garland* twine, weave, plait, braid. **6** *twist a curl of hair around/round her finger* twirl, coil, wind, curl. **7** *the path twisted around/round the mountain* wind, curve, bend, twine, zigzag, meander, snake, worm. **8** *the child twisted out of his grasp* wriggle, writhe, squirm, wiggle. **9** *twist their words* distort, pervert, warp, garble, misrepresent, falsify, misquote, misreport, change, alter. **10** *she twisted her head around* swivel, turn, rotate, spin, pivot.

**twist** noun **1** *with a twist of his arm* wrench, wrest, turn, contortion, pull, jerk, yank. **2** *try to repair the twist in the wire* bend, warp, kink, contortion, distortion. **3** *a painful twist of the ankle* wrench, turn, sprain. **4** *a twist of hair* coil, twirl, curl, braid. **5** *the twists in the mountain path* bend, turn, curve, winding, arc, zigzag, meander. **6** *a slight twist to his character* aberration, peculiarity, quirk, oddity, eccentricity, idiosyncrasy, foible.

**twitch** verb jerk, jump, quiver, shiver, quaver, blink, flutter.

**twitch** noun spasm, jerk, jump, quiver, tremor, shiver, quaver, blink, flutter, jump, tic.

**twitter** verb chirrup, cheep, tweet, trill, warble, whistle, sing.

**two-faced** adjective hypocritical, insincere, deceitful, deceiving, dissembling, duplicitous, false, untrustworthy, treacherous, perfidious, double-dealing, Janus-faced.

**tycoon** noun magnate, baron, captain of industry, industrialist, financier, merchant prince, mogul; *inf.* fat cat.

**type** noun **1** *a rare type of plant* kind, sort, variety, form, class, classification, category, group, order, set, genre, strain, species, genus, ilk. **2** *they regard her as the very type of womanhood* example, exemplar, model, pattern, essence, personification, epitome, quintessence, archetype, prototype. **3** *set in a different kind of type* print, font, face, character.

**typical** adjective **1** *a typical New England winter* representative, classic, standard, stock, orthodox, conventional, true-to-type, quintessential, archetypal. **2** *what would be your typical day?* normal, average, ordinary, regular, general, customary, habitual, routine. **3** *it is typical of him to be rude* characteristic, in character, in keeping, to be expected, usual.

**typify** verb **1** *he typifies the self-made man* exemplify, characterize, personify, epitomize, symbolize, embody, sum up, incarnate. **2** *they have tried to typify the various sectors of society* represent, indicate, illustrate, denote.

**tyranny** noun despotism, absolutism, authoritarianism, arbitrariness, high-handedness, imperiousness, oppressiveness, oppression, coercion, bullying, severity, cruelty, brutality, unjustness, unreasonableness; autocracy, dictatorship.

**tyrant** noun despot, autocrat, dictator, absolute ruler, authoritarian, oppressor, martinet, slave driver, bully.

# *Uu*

**ubiquitous** adjective everywhere, omnipresent, ever-present, in all places, all over, all over the place, pervasive, universal.

**ugly** adjective **1** *ugly people/buildings* ill-favored, hideous, plain, unattractive, unlovely, homely, unprepossessing, unsightly, displeasing; *inf.* not much to look at. **2**

*an ugly sight met their eyes* hideous, horrible, horrid, frightful, terrible, disagreeable, unpleasant, foul, nasty, shocking, distasteful, disgusting, revolting, repellent, repugnant, loathsome, hateful, nauseating, sickening. **3** *he is an ugly character* objectionable, offensive, obnoxious, foul, vile, base, dishonorable, dishonest, rotten. **4** *an ugly situation* threatening, menacing, ominous, sinister, dangerous, nasty, unpleasant, disagreeable. **5** *the crowd grew ugly* nasty, angry, bad-tempered, ill-natured, hostile, surly, sullen, mean, sour, spiteful, malevolent, evil.

**ulterior** adjective hidden, concealed, unrevealed, undisclosed, undivulged, secret, covert.

**ultimate** adjective **1** *take ultimate responsibility* last, final, eventual, concluding, conclusive, terminal, end, furthest. **2** *ultimate truths* basic, fundamental, primary, elemental, radical. **3** *the ultimate gift* supreme, superlative, paramount, greatest, highest, unsurpassed, unrivaled.

**umbrella** noun *under the corporate umbrella* agency, aegis, cover, protection, support, patronage, backing.

**umpire** noun adjudicator, arbitrator, arbiter, judge, moderator, referee; *inf.* ref.

**umpire** verb adjudicate, arbitrate, judge, moderate, referee; *inf.* ref.

**unabridged** adjective uncut, unshortened, unreduced, uncondensed, unexpurgated, full-length, complete, entire, whole, intact.

**unacceptable** adjective unsatisfactory, inadmissible, unsuitable, insupportable, intolerable, objectionable.

**unaccompanied** adjective alone, on one's own, by oneself, unescorted, solo, lone, solitary, single.

**unaccountable** adjective **1** *an unaccountable increase in births* inexplicable, unexplainable, insoluble, unsolvable, incomprehensible, unfathomable, puzzling, baffling, mysterious, inscrutable, peculiar, unusual, curious, strange. **2** *she is unaccountable for the error* not responsible, not answerable, not liable, free, clear, exempt, immune.

**unaccustomed** adjective unusual, unfamiliar, uncommon, unwonted, new, exceptional, out of the ordinary, extraordinary, special, remarkable, singular. **unaccustomed to** unused to, new to, unpracticed at/in, unfamiliar with, inexperienced at/in, unversed in.

**unaffected** adjective **1** *unaffected children* artless, guileless, ingenuous, naive, unsophisticated, unassuming, unpretentious, down-to-earth, without airs, natural, plain, simple. **2** *unaffected sincerity* unfeigned, unpretended, genuine, real, sincere, honest, true, candid. **unaffected by** unchanged by, unaltered by, uninfluenced by, untouched by, unmoved by, impervious to, unresponsive to, insensible to, invulnerable to.

**unanimity** noun agreement, accord, concord, unity, consensus, like-mindedness, solidity, concertedness, uniformity, consistency, congruence.

**unanimous** adjective in complete agreement/accord, of one mind, like-minded, with one voice, united, concordant, concerted, uniform, consistent, congruent.

**unapproachable** adjective **1** *unapproachable places* inaccessible, remote, out-of-the-way, out of reach, beyond reach, unreachable, off the beaten path/track. **2** *the new teacher is unapproachable* aloof, standoffish, distant, remote, detached, reserved, uncommunicative, unsociable, cool.

**unassuming** adjective modest, self-effacing, humble, meek, retiring, demure, restrained, reticent, diffident, shy, bashful, unassertive, unobtrusive, unostentatious, unpretentious, unaffected, natural, genuine, simple.

**unattached** adjective **1** *she is still unattached* unmarried, unwed, uncommitted, free, available, footloose and fancy free, partnerless, single, on one's own, by oneself, unescorted. **2** *a merger was discussed, but the firm is still unattached* independent, unaffiliated, unassociated, autonomous, nonaligned, self-governing, self-ruling.

**unauthorized** adjective uncertified, unaccredited, unlicensed, unofficial, unsanctioned, unwarranted, unapproved, disallowed, prohibited, forbidden, illegal.

**unavoidable** adjective inescapable, inevitable, bound to happen, inexorable, ineluctable, certain, fated, predestined, necessary, compulsory, required, obligatory, mandatory.

**unaware** adjective unknowing, unconscious, ignorant, heedless, unmindful, oblivious, uninformed (about), unenlightened (about), undiscerning, incognizant; *inf.* in the dark.

**unawares** adverb **1** *come upon him unawares* unexpectedly, by surprise, without warning, suddenly, abruptly, unprepared, off guard; *inf.* with one's pants down. **2** *I must have dropped my keys unawares* unknowingly, unwittingly, unintentionally, unconsciously, inadvertently.

**unbalanced** adjective **1** *unbalanced since the death of her husband* unstable, of unsound mind, mentally ill, deranged, demented, crazed, distracted, insane, mad, crazy, lunatic; *inf.* not all there, off one's head. **2** *an unbalanced report of the events* one-sided, biased, prejudiced, partisan, partial, inequitable.

**unbearable** adjective intolerable, insufferable, unsupportable, unendurable, unacceptable, more than flesh and blood can stand; *inf.* too much, enough to try the patience of a saint.

**unbeatable** adjective invincible, indomitable, unconquerable, unstoppable, unsurpassable.

**unbecoming** adjective **1** *an unbecoming hat* unflattering, unattractive, unsightly. **2** *unbecoming behavior* unfitting, inappropriate, unsuitable, inapt, improper, indecorous, unseemly.

**unbelievable** adjective beyond belief, incredible, unconvincing, far-fetched, implausible, improbable, inconceivable, unthinkable, unimaginable, astonishing, astounding, preposterous.

**unbending** adjective **1** *an unbending material/manner* rigid, stiff, inflexible, unpliable, inelastic, unmalleable, hard-line, uncompromising, tough, harsh, strict, stern, severe, firm, resolute, determined, unrelenting. **2** *an unbending person* formal, stiff, aloof, reserved; *inf.* uptight.

**unbiased** adjective impartial, unprejudiced, nonpartisan, neutral, objective, disinterested, dispassionate, detached, evenhanded, open-minded, equitable, fair, fair-minded, just.

**unbounded** adjective boundless, unlimited, limitless, infinite, unrestrained, unconstrained, uncontrolled, unchecked, unbridled, vast, immense, immeasurable.

**unbridled** adjective unrestrained, unconstrained, uncontrolled, unchecked, uncurbed, ungoverned, rampant, excessive, intemperate.

**unbroken** adjective **1** *unbroken china/sets* intact, whole, undamaged, unimpaired, complete, entire. **2** *an unbroken series* uninterrupted, continuous, unremitting, ceaseless, unceasing, endless, incessant, constant, nonstop. **3** *unbroken sleep* undisturbed, untroubled, sound.

**unburden** verb **1** *unburden the horse* unload, disburden, unpack, disencumber. **2** *unburden one's sins/guilt* confess, confide, acknowledge, disclose, reveal, divulge, expose, lay bare, make a clean breast of; *inf.* come clean.

**uncalled-for** adjective **1** *uncalled-for advice* unsought, unasked, unsolicited, unrequested, unprompted, unwelcome, gratuitous. **2** *uncalled-for rudeness* unnecessary, needless, undeserved, unmerited, unjustified, unreasonable, inappropriate.

**uncanny** adjective **1** *uncanny happenings in the old house* strange, mysterious, odd, queer, weird, eerie, unnatural, preternatural, supernatural, unearthly, ghostly; *inf.* creepy, spooky. **2** *bear an uncanny resemblance to the president* remarkable, striking, extraordinary, exceptional, astounding, astonishing, incredible.

**uncertain** adjective **1** *the outcome is uncertain* unknown, undetermined, unsettled, pending, in the balance, up in the air. **2** *feel uncertain about what to do* unsure, doubtful, dubious, undecided, unresolved, indecisive, irresolute, hesitant, wavering, vacillating, equivocating, vague, hazy, unclear, ambivalent, of two minds. **3** *the future is uncertain* unpredictable, unforeseeable, incalculable, speculative, unreliable, untrustworthy, undependable, risky, chancy. **4** *uncertain weather* changeable, variable, irregular, fitful, unpredictable, unreliable.

**uncharitable** adjective uncompassionate, unsympathetic, ungenerous, unfeeling, unkind, hard-hearted, censorious, unforgiving, merciless.

**uncharted** adjective unmapped, unsurveyed, unexplored, unresearched, unplumbed, unfamiliar, unknown, strange.

**uncivil** adjective discourteous, rude, impolite, unmannerly, bad-mannered, ill-bred, ungracious, disrespectful.

**uncivilized** adjective **1** *uncivilized tribes* barbarian, barbarous, barbaric, primitive, savage, wild. **2** *some of their friends are so uncivilized* uncouth, coarse, rough, boorish, vulgar, philistine, uneducated, uncultured, uncultivated, unsophisticated, unrefined, unpolished.

**uncomfortable** adjective uneasy, ill-at-ease, nervous, tense, edgy, self-conscious, awkward, embarrassed, discomfited, disturbed, troubled, worried, anxious, apprehensive, distressing, disturbing.

**uncommon** adjective **1** *an uncommon name* unusual, rare, uncustomary, unfamiliar, strange, odd, curious, out of the ordinary, novel, singular, peculiar, queer, bizarre, weird. **2** *those birds are uncommon here* rare, scarce, infrequent, few and far between, occasional. **3** *an uncommon resemblance* remarkable, extraordinary, exceptional, singular, outstanding, notable, noteworthy, distinctive, striking.

**uncommunicative** adjective taciturn, reserved, shy, retiring, diffident, reticent, quiet, unforthcoming, unconversational, untalkative, silent, tight-lipped, secretive, unresponsive, close, distant, remote, aloof, withdrawn, standoffish, unsociable, antisocial.

**uncompromising** adjective unyielding, immovable, dogged, obstinate, obdurate, tenacious, relentless, inexorable, intransigent. *See* UNBENDING 1.

**unconcerned** adjective unworried, untroubled, unperturbed, unruffled, insouciant, nonchalant, carefree, blithe, relaxed, at ease. **unconcerned with** indifferent about, apathetic about, uninterested in, uninvolved with/in, dispassionate about, detached from, aloof from, remote from.

**unconditional** adjective complete, total, entire, full, outright, absolute, downright, out-and-out, utter, all-out, thoroughgoing, unequivocal, conclusive, definite, positive, indubitable, incontrovertible, categorical, unqualified, unlimited, unreserved, unrestricted.

**unconscious** adjective **1** *fall unconscious* senseless, insensible, comatose, knocked out, stunned, dazed; *inf.* blacked out, KO'd, out like a light, out cold, out. **2** *unconscious of the noise* unaware, heedless, ignorant, incognizant, oblivious, insensible. **3** *deliver an unconscious insult* unintentional, unintended, accidental, unthinking, unwitting, inadvertent, unpremeditated. **4** *unconscious prejudice* instinctive, automatic, reflex, involuntary, inherent, innate, subliminal, subconscious, latent.

**unconventional** adjective unorthodox, irregular, unusual, uncommon, uncustomary, rare, out of the ordinary, atypical, singular, individual, individualistic, different, original, idiosyncratic, nonconformist, bohemian, eccentric, odd, strange, bizarre; *inf.* edgy, left-field, offbeat, way-out.

**uncoordinated** adjective clumsy, awkward, inept, maladroit, butterfingered, all thumbs, bungling, blundering, bumbling, lumbering, heavy-footed, graceless, ungainly; *inf.* like a bull in a china shop, klutzy.

**uncouth** adjective rough, coarse, uncivilized, uncultured, uncultivated, unrefined, unpolished, unsophisticated, provincial, crude, gross, loutish, boorish, oafish, churlish, uncivil, rude, impolite, discourteous, unmannerly, bad-mannered, ill-bred, vulgar.

**uncover** verb expose, lay bare, bare, reveal, discover, detect, unearth, dig up, bring to light, unmask, unveil, make known, divulge, disclose.

**unctuous** adjective **1** *unctuous behavior* sycophantic, ingratiating, obsequious, fawning, servile, toadying, honey-tongued, gushing, effusive, suave, urbane, glib, smooth. **2** *unctuous substance* oily, oleaginous, greasy, soapy, saponaceous.

**undaunted** adjective undismayed, unalarmed, unafraid, unflinching, unfaltering, indomitable, resolute, unflagging, intrepid, bold, valiant, brave, courageous.

**undecided** adjective **1** *the result is as yet undecided* uncertain, unsettled, unresolved, indefinite, unknown, unestablished, unascertained, pending, in the balance, up in the air. **2** *they are undecided as to what to do* unsure, doubtful, dithering. *See* UNCERTAIN 2.

**undeniable** adjective indisputable, indubitable, unquestionable, beyond doubt/question, inarguable, incontrovertible, incontestable, irrefutable, unassailable, certain, sure, definite, positive, proven, clear, obvious, evident, manifest, patent.

**under** preposition **1** *under the tree* below, beneath, underneath, at the foot/bottom of. **2** *prices under $5* | *numbers under 20* below, less than, lower than, smaller than. **3** *ranks under major* inferior to, subordinate to, junior to, secondary to, subservient to, reporting to, subject to, controlled by, at the mercy of, under the heel of. **4** *under the water* submerged by, immersed in, sunk in, engulfed by, inundated by, flooded by, drowned by. **5** *it is under his mother's name* listed under, classified under, categorized under, placed under, positioned under, included under, subsumed under. **6** *living under threat* subject to, liable to, bound by.

**undercover** adjective secret, hidden, concealed, masked, veiled, shrouded, private, confidential, covert, clandestine, underground, surreptitious, furtive, stealthy, sly; *inf.* hush-hush.

**undercurrent** noun *an undercurrent of discontent* undertone, overtone, hint, suggestion, implication, whisper, murmur, atmosphere, aura, tenor, flavor; *inf.* vibes.

**undercut** verb undersell; weaken, impair, damage. *See* UNDERMINE 1.

**underestimate** verb miscalculate, misjudge, underrate, undervalue, set little store by, not do justice to, misprize, minimize, hold cheap; *inf.* sell short.

**undergo** verb go through, experience, sustain, be subjected to, submit to, endure, bear, tolerate, stand, withstand, put up with, weather.

**underground** adjective **1** *underground shelters* subterranean, subterrestrial, belowground, buried, sunken, hypogeal. **2** *an underground organization* secret, clandestine, surreptitious, covert, undercover, concealed, hidden. **3** *underground literature* unconventional, unorthodox, experimental, avant-garde, alternative, radical, revolutionary, subversive.

**underhand, underhanded** adjective deceitful, devious, sneaky, furtive, covert, dishonest, dishonorable, unethical, immoral, unscrupulous, fraudulent, dirty, unfair, treacherous, double-dealing, below the belt, two-timing; *inf.* crooked.

**underline** verb underscore, emphasize, stress, highlight, point up, accentuate, call attention to, give prominence to.

**undermine** verb **1** *undermine their authority* weaken, impair, damage, injure, sap, threaten, subvert, sabotage; *inf.* throw a monkey wrench in/into the works of, foul up. **2** *undermine the foundations* tunnel under, dig under, burrow under, excavate.

**underprivileged** adjective disadvantaged, deprived, in need, needy, in want, destitute, in distress, poor, impoverished, impecunious, badly off.

**understand** verb **1** *understand his meaning* comprehend, apprehend, grasp, see, take in, perceive, discern, make out, glean, recognize, appreciate, get to know, follow, fathom, get to the bottom of, penetrate, interpret; *inf.* get the hang/drift of, catch on, latch on to, figure out. **2** *I understand your feelings/position* appreciate, accept, commiserate with, sympathize with, empathize with. **3** *I understand that he has left* gather, hear, learn, believe, think, conclude.

**understanding** noun **1** *it depends on your understanding of his meaning* comprehension, apprehension, grasp, perception, discernment, appreciation, interpretation. **2** *his powers of understanding are limited* intelligence, intellect, mind, brainpower; brains; *inf.* gray matter. **3** *it is my understanding that he has gone* belief, perception, view, notion, idea, fancy, conclusion, feeling. **4** *treat the difficult problem with understanding* compassion, sympathy, empathy, insight. **5** *we have an understanding, although not a signed contract* agreement, gentleman's agreement, arrangement, bargain, pact, compact, (verbal) contract.

**understanding** adjective compassionate, sympathetic, sensitive, considerate, kind, thoughtful, tolerant, patient, forbearing, lenient, merciful, forgiving.

**understate** verb downplay, play down, make light of, minimize, de-emphasize; *inf.* soft-pedal.

**understudy** noun substitute, replacement, reserve, stand-in, fill-in, locum, backup, relief.

**undertake** verb take on, set about, tackle, shoulder, assume, enter upon, begin, start, commence, embark on, venture upon, attempt, try.

**undertone** noun *undertones of unrest* murmur, whisper, undercurrent, hint, suggestion, intimation, inkling, insinuation.

**underwater** adjective submarine, subaqueous, undersea, submerged, immersed.

**underwear** noun underclothes, undergarments; underclothing, lingerie, underthings; *inf.* undies, unmentionables.

**underworld** noun **1** *the underworld revenged my death* (crime) syndicate, organized crime; criminals, gangsters; Mafia, Cosa Nostra, gangland; *inf.* mob. **2** *Orpheus in the underworld* abode of the dead, nether/infernal regions, hell, Hades.

**underwrite** verb **1** *underwrite the agreement* agree to, approve, sanction, confirm, ratify, validate; *inf.* OK. **2** *underwrite the new project* fund, finance, back, support, sponsor, subsidize, contribute to, insure.

**undesirable** adjective unwanted, unwished-for; unpleasant, disagreeable, objectionable, offensive, repugnant, repellent, distasteful, unsavory.

**undisciplined** adjective unruly, disorderly, disobedient, obstreperous, wild, willful, wayward; disorganized, erratic, lax.

**undisguised** adjective open, obvious, evident, patent, manifest, transparent, overt, unconcealed, unhidden, unmistakable.

**undisputed** adjective uncontested, unchallenged, unquestioned, not in question/doubt, accepted, acknowledged, recognized, incontestable, unquestionable, incontrovertible.

**undo** verb **1** *undo buttons/laces* unfasten, untie, loosen, loose, disentangle, release, free, open. **2** *undo the agreement* cancel, annul, nullify, invalidate, revoke, repeal, rescind, reverse, set aside, wipe out. **3** *undo all his work/hopes* destroy, ruin, wreck, smash, shatter, annihilate, eradicate, obliterate.

**undoing** noun destruction, ruin, ruination, downfall, defeat, overthrow, collapse.

**undoubtedly** adverb indubitably, doubtless, doubtlessly, beyond a doubt, unquestionably, beyond question, undeniably, positively, absolutely, certainly, decidedly, definitely.

**undress** verb strip, disrobe, unclothe.

**undue** adjective unwarranted, unreasonable, inappropriate, improper, excessive, immoderate, disproportionate, inordinate, fulsome, uncalled-for, unnecessary, nonessential, unrequired.

**unduly** adverb excessively, overly, disproportionately, immoderately, inordinately, unnecessarily.

**undying** adjective deathless, immortal, eternal, infinite, perpetual, unending, never-ending, unceasing, ceaseless, incessant, permanent, lasting, abiding, constant, unfading, imperishable, inextinguishable.

**unearth** verb **1** *dogs unearthing bones* dig up, excavate, exhume, disinter, unbury. **2** *unearth new evidence* uncover, discover, find, come across, hit upon, bring to light, reveal, expose, turn up, root up, dredge up, ferret out.

**unearthly** adjective **1** *unearthly sounds* otherworldly, not of this world, supernatural, preternatural, ghostly, spectral, phantom, haunted, uncanny, eerie, strange; *inf.* spooky, creepy. **2** *come home at an*

**unearthly** *hour* unreasonable, preposterous, abnormal, extraordinary, absurd, ridiculous; *inf.* ungodly, unholy.

**uneasy** adjective **1** *feel uneasy about what was happening* ill at ease, troubled, worried, anxious, apprehensive, alarmed, disturbed, agitated, nervous, on edge, edgy, jittery, restive, restless, unsettled, discomposed, discomfited. **2** *an uneasy peace* strained, constrained, tense, awkward, precarious, unstable, insecure. **3** *an uneasy suspicion that all was not well* dismaying, disturbing, perturbing, disquieting, unsettling, upsetting.

**unemotional** adjective undemonstrative, passionless, cold, frigid, cool, reserved, restrained, self-controlled, unfeeling, unresponsive, unexcitable, unmoved, impassive, apathetic, indifferent, phlegmatic, detached.

**unemployed** adjective jobless, out of work, out of a job, workless, laid off, idle, on the dole.

**unending** adjective endless, never-ending, interminable, perpetual, ceaseless, incessant, unceasing, nonstop, uninterrupted, continuous, continual, constant, unremitting, relentless.

**unequal** adjective **1** *unequal in size/talent* different, differing, dissimilar, unlike, unalike, disparate, varying. **2** *unequal to the task* not up to, inadequate, insufficient. **3** *the sides of the box are unequal* asymmetrical, unbalanced. *See* UNEVEN 3. **4** *unequal contest* unfair, one-sided. *See* UNEVEN 4.

**unequaled** adjective peerless, unmatched, unrivaled, unparalleled, unsurpassed, incomparable, beyond compare, inimitable, second to none, nonpareil, unique.

**unequivocal** adjective unambiguous, clear, clear-cut, crystal-clear, unmistakable, plain, well-defined, explicit, unqualified, categorical, outright, downright, direct, straightforward.

**unethical** adjective immoral, unprincipled, unscrupulous, dishonorable, dishonest, disreputable, dirty, unfair, underhand, underhanded; *inf.* shady.

**uneven** adjective **1** *uneven surfaces* rough, bumpy, lumpy. **2** *his work is uneven* variable, varying, changeable, irregular, fluctuating, erratic, patchy. **3** *the sides of the box are uneven* unequal, asymmetrical, unsymmetrical, unbalanced, lopsided, irregular, disproportionate, not matching. **4** *an uneven contest* unequal, unfair, unjust, inequitable, one-sided, ill-matched.

**unexpected** adjective unforeseen, unanticipated, unlooked-for, unpredicted, not bargained for, surprising, out of the blue.

**unfair** adjective **1** *unfair treatment* unjust, inequitable, partial, partisan, prejudiced, biased, one-sided, unequal, uneven, unbalanced. **2** *the punishment was unfair* undeserved, unmerited, uncalled-for, unreasonable, unjustifiable, disproportionate, excessive, immoderate. **3** *unfair play* foul, unsporting, unsportsmanlike, dirty, below-the-belt, underhanded, unscrupulous, dishonorable; *inf.* crooked.

**unfaithful** adjective **1** *unfaithful friends* disloyal, false, false-hearted, faithless, perfidious, treacherous, traitorous, untrustworthy, unreliable, undependable. **2** *unfaithful spouses* adulterous, fickle, untrue, inconstant; *inf.* cheating, two-timing.

**unfamiliar** adjective unknown, new, strange, alien, unaccustomed, uncommon. **unfamiliar with** unacquainted with, unused to, unaccustomed to, unskilled in, uninformed of, uninitiated in.

**unfavorable** adjective **1** *unfavorable reviews* adverse, critical, hostile, inimical, unfriendly, negative, discouraging, poor, bad. **2** *unfavorable circumstances* disadvantageous, adverse, unfortunate, unhappy, detrimental. **3** *come at an unfavorable moment* inconvenient, inopportune, untimely, untoward.

**unfeeling** adjective uncaring, unsympathetic, hard-hearted, hard, harsh, heartless, apathetic, cold, callous, cruel, pitiless, inhuman.

**unfit** adjective *too unfit to compete in the race* out of condition, in poor condition/shape, flabby, unhealthy, debilitated, weak. **unfit for** unsuited for/to, ill-suited for/to, unsuitable for, unqualified for, unequipped for, unprepared for, untrained for, incompetent for, not up to, not equal to, not good enough for; *inf.* not cut out for.

**unfold** verb **1** *unfold the map* open out, spread out, stretch out, flatten, straighten out, unfurl, unroll, unravel. **2** *unfold a tale of horror* narrate, relate, recount, tell, reveal, make known, disclose, divulge, present. **3** *when our plans unfold* develop, evolve, grow, mature, bear fruit.

**unforeseen** adjective unpredicted, unanticipated. *See* UNEXPECTED.

**unforgettable** adjective memorable, impressive, striking, outstanding, extraordinary.

**unfortunate** adjective **1** *unfortunate circumstance* adverse, disadvantageous, unfavorable, untoward, unpromising, disastrous, calamitous. **2** *the unfortunate girl* unlucky, luckless, ill-starred, hapless, wretched, miserable. **3** *an unfortunate remark* regrettable, deplorable, ill-advised, inappropriate, unsuitable, inapt, tactless.

**unfounded** adjective groundless, baseless, unsubstantiated, unproven, unsupported, uncorroborated, speculative, conjectural, spurious.

**unfriendly** adjective **1** *unfriendly neighbors* unamicable, uncongenial, unsociable, inhospitable, unneighborly, unkind, unsympathetic, aloof, cold, cool, distant, disagreeable, unpleasant, hostile, antagonistic, aggressive, quarrelsome. **2** *an unfriendly climate* unfavorable, disadvantageous, unpropitious, inauspicious.

**ungainly** adjective awkward, clumsy, ungraceful, graceless, inelegant, gawky, gangling, maladroit, inept, bungling, bumbling, lumbering, uncoordinated, hulking, lubberly.

**ungodly** adjective **1** *ungodly people/acts* godless, irreligious, impious, blasphemous, profane, immoral, sinful, wicked, iniquitous. **2** *come home at an ungodly hour* unreasonable, preposterous. *See* UNEARTHLY 2.

**unhappy** adjective **1** *feeling unhappy* sad, miserable, wretched, sorrowful, dejected, despondent, disconsolate, brokenhearted, down, downcast, dispirited, crestfallen, depressed, melancholy, blue, gloomy, glum, mournful, woebegone, long-faced, joyless, cheerless. **2** *unhappy circumstances* unfortunate, disadvantageous, unlucky, adverse. **3** *an unhappy choice of phrase* unfortunate, regrettable, inappropriate.

**unhealthy** adjective **1** *unhealthy children* in poor health, unwell, ill, ailing, sick, sickly, indisposed, unsound, weak, feeble, frail, delicate, debilitated, infirm. **2** *an unhealthy diet* unwholesome, unnourishing, detrimental, injurious, damaging, deleterious, noxious, insalubrious.

**unholy** adjective **1** *unholy people/acts* godless, irreligious. *See* UNGODLY 1. **2** *an unholy commotion* unreasonable, preposterous, outrageous, appalling, shocking, dreadful; *inf.* ungodly.

**unidentified** adjective nameless, unnamed, unknown, anonymous, incognito.

**unification** noun union, junction, merger, fusion, alliance, amalgamation, coalition, combination, consolidation.

**uniform** adjective **1** *a uniform temperature* constant, consistent, invariable, unvarying, unvaried, unchanging, undeviating, stable, regular, even, equal, equable. **2** *all of uniform length* same, alike, like, selfsame, identical, similar, equal.

**uniform** noun livery, regalia, habit, suit, dress, costume, garb.

**unify** verb unite, bring together, merge, fuse, amalgamate, coalesce, combine, blend, mix, bind, link up, consolidate.

**unimaginable** adjective unthinkable, inconceivable, incredible, unbelievable, unheard-of, unthought-of, implausible, improbable, unlikely, impossible.

**unimaginative** adjective unoriginal, uninspired, commonplace, pedestrian, mundane, ordinary, prosaic, vapid, insipid, bland.

**unimportant** adjective insignificant, inconsequential, of no account, nonessential, immaterial, irrelevant, not worth mentioning, minor, slight, trifling, trivial, petty, paltry; dinky.

**uninhabited** adjective vacant, empty, unoccupied, untenanted, unpopulated, unpeopled, unsettled, abandoned, deserted, forsaken, desolate.

**uninhibited** adjective unreserved, unrepressed, unconstrained, unselfconscious, spontaneous, relaxed, informal, open; unrestrained, uncontrolled, uncurbed, unchecked, unbridled.

**unintelligible** adjective incomprehensible, meaningless, unfathomable, incoherent, indistinct, inarticulate, confused, muddled, jumbled.

**unintentional** adjective unintended, accidental, inadvertent, unpremeditated, uncalculated, unconscious, involuntary, unwitting, unthinking.

**uninterested** adjective indifferent, unconcerned, uninvolved, apathetic, blasé, unresponsive, impassive, dispassionate, aloof, detached, distant.

**uninteresting** adjective unexciting, dull, unentertaining, boring, tiresome, wearisome, tedious, dreary, flat, monotonous, humdrum, dry, pedestrian, prosaic, hackneyed, stale.

**uninviting** adjective unappealing, unattractive, unappetizing, repellent, revolting, repugnant.

**union** noun **1** *the union of three firms* joining, merging. *See* UNIFICATION. **2** *the union is made up of several organizations* association, alliance, league, coalition, consortium, syndicate, guild, confederation, federation. **3** *the union of the man and the woman* marriage, wedding, coupling, intercourse, coition, coitus, copulation. **4** *we are all in union about the plans* agreement, accord. *See* UNITY 3.

**unique** adjective **1** *a unique specimen* only, one and only, single, sole, lone, solitary, *sui generis*, exclusive, in a class by itself. **2** *a unique opportunity* unequaled, unparalleled, unmatched, matchless, peerless, incomparable, beyond compare.

**unit** noun **1** *the family regarded as a unit* entity, whole. **2** *the course is divided into units* component, part, section, element, constituent, subdivision, portion, segment, module, item, member. **3** *a unit of length* measurement, measure, quantity.

**unite** verb **1** *unite the two parties/firms* join, link, connect, combine, amalgamate, fuse, weld, splice. **2** *unite the two substances* combine, mix, commix, admix, blend, mingle, homogenize. **3** *unite this man and this woman* marry, wed, join in wedlock, tie the knot between. **4** *they united to fight the common enemy* join together, join forces, band together, ally, cooperate, work/act/pull together.

**united** adjective **1** *a united effort* combined, amalgamated, allied, cooperative, concerted, collective, pooled. **2** *united in their opinion of the plan* in agreement, agreed, in unison, of the same opinion/mind, of like mind, like-minded, at one, in accord, unanimous.

**unity** noun **1** *detract from the unity of the painting* oneness, singleness, wholeness, entity, integrity. **2** *their strength lies in their unity* union, undividedness. *See* UNIFICATION. **3** *strive for political unity* agreement, harmony, accord, concord, concurrence, unanimity, consensus, concert, togetherness, solidarity.

**universal** adjective general, all-embracing, all-inclusive, comprehensive, catholic, across the board, worldwide, global, widespread.

**unjust** adjective **1** *an unjust verdict* inequitable, prejudiced. *See* UNFAIR 1. **2** *an unjust accusation* wrongful, wrong, undue, unwarranted. *See* UNFAIR 2.

**unkempt** adjective untidy, disheveled, disordered, disarranged, tousled, rumpled, windblown, uncombed, ungroomed, messy, messed up, scruffy, slovenly, sloppy; *inf.* mussed up.

**unkind** adjective **1** *unkind remarks* unfriendly, unamiable, uncharitable, inhospitable, ungenerous, nasty, mean, cruel, vicious, spiteful, malicious, pitiless, unsympathetic, unfeeling, hard-hearted. **2** *an unkind climate* inclement, harsh, intemperate.

**unknown** adjective **1** *the results of the test are as yet unknown* unrevealed, undisclosed, undivulged, undetermined, undecided, unestablished, unsettled, unascertained, up in the air. **2** *the donor is unknown* unnamed, nameless. *See* UNIDENTIFIED. **3** *unknown territory* unfamiliar, unexplored, uncharted, untraveled, undiscovered. **4** *unknown poets* unheard-of, little-known, obscure, undistinguished, unrenowned, unsung.

**unlawful** adjective illegal, illicit, illegitimate, criminal, felonious, actionable, prohibited, banned, outlawed, proscribed.

**unlike** adjective unalike, dissimilar, different, distinct, disparate, contrary, diverse, divergent, incompatible, ill-matched, incongruous; *inf.* like day and night.

**unlikely** adjective improbable, doubtful, dubious, faint, slight, remote.

**unlimited** adjective **1** *unlimited freedom* unrestricted, unconstrained, uncontrolled, unrestrained, unchecked, unhindered, unhampered, unimpeded, unfettered, untrammeled; absolute, total, unqualified, unconditional. **2** *unlimited supplies of money* limitless, boundless, unbounded, immense, vast, great, extensive, immeasurable, incalculable, untold, infinite, endless.

**unlucky** adjective **1** *an unlucky young man* luckless, out of luck, down on one's luck, unfortunate, hapless, ill-fated, ill-starred, star-crossed, wretched, miserable. **2** *an unlucky set of circumstances* adverse, disadvantageous, unfavorable, unfortunate, untoward, unpromising, inauspicious, unpropitious.

**unmarried** adjective single, unwed, unwedded, spouseless, partnerless, divorced, unattached, bachelor, celibate; husbandless, wifeless.

**unmistakable** adjective clear, plain, obvious, evident, manifest, patent, palpable, distinct, conspicuous, well-defined, pronounced.

**unmitigated** adjective absolute, unqualified, unconditional, categorical, complete, total, thorough, thoroughgoing, downright, utter, out and out, veritable, perfect, consummate.

**unmoved** adjective **1** *unmoved from their purpose* firm, steadfast, unshaken, staunch, unwavering, unswerving, undeviating, determined, resolute, resolved. **2** *unmoved by the sad sight* unaffected, untouched, unstirred, unconcerned, uncaring, indifferent, impassive, unfeeling, impervious.

**unnatural** adjective **1** *his face turned an unnatural color* unusual, uncommon, extraordinary, strange, queer, odd, bizarre, preternatural. **2** *an unnatural laugh | unnatural behavior* affected, artificial, forced, labored, studied, strained, mannered.

**unnecessary** adjective needless, unneeded, inessential, nonessential, uncalled-for, unrequired, gratuitous, useless, dispensable, expendable, redundant, superfluous.

**unnerve** verb discourage, dishearten, demoralize, daunt, alarm, frighten, dismay, disconcert, perturb, upset, unsettle, disquiet, fluster, agitate, shake; *inf.* rattle.

**unobtrusive** adjective low-key, restrained, subdued, quiet, unostentatious, unshowy, inconspicuous, unnoticeable.

**unoccupied** adjective **1** *unoccupied houses/places* vacant, unpopulated. *See* UNINHABITED. **2** *he is unoccupied just now* not busy, at leisure, idle, inactive, unemployed.

**unofficial** adjective informal, casual, unauthorized, unsanctioned, unaccredited, unconfirmed, unsubstantiated.

**unorthodox** adjective **1** *unorthodox beliefs* heterodox, uncanonical, heretical, nonconformist. **2** *unorthodox methods* unconventional, unusual, uncommon, out of the ordinary, irregular, abnormal, divergent, aberrant, anomalous.

**unparalleled** adjective matchless, peerless. *See* UNEQUALED.

**unperturbed** adjective calm, composed, cool, collected, serene, tranquil, self-possessed, placid, unruffled, unflustered, unexcited, undismayed, untroubled, unworried; *inf.* laid-back.

**unpleasant** adjective disagreeable, disgusting, repugnant, revolting, nauseating, sickening, offensive, obnoxious, foul.

**unpopular** adjective disliked, unliked, unloved, friendless, unwanted, unwelcome, avoided, ignored, rejected, shunned, out in the cold, out of favor.

**unprecedented** adjective unparalleled, unheard-of, uncommon, out of the ordinary, unusual, exceptional.

**unpredictable** adjective **1** *unpredictable results* unforeseeable, undivinable, uncertain, unsure, in the balance, up in the air; *inf.* iffy. **2** *unpredictable behavior* erratic, fickle, capricious, whimsical, mercurial, volatile, unstable, undependable, unreliable.

**unpretentious** adjective simple, plain, modest, ordinary, humble, unostentatious, unshowy, unimposing, unassuming, unaffected.

**unprincipled** adjective immoral, amoral, unethical, dishonorable, dishonest, unprofessional, deceitful, devious, unscrupulous, corrupt, crooked.

**unproductive** adjective fruitless, futile, vain, idle, useless, worthless, valueless, ineffective, ineffectual, inefficacious, unprofitable, unremunerative.

**unprofessional** adjective **1** *unprofessional conduct* unethical, unprincipled, improper, unseemly, indecorous, lax, negligent. **2** *unprofessional workers* amateur, amateurish, unskilled, inexpert, untrained, unqualified, inexperienced, incompetent.

**unqualified** adjective **1** *unqualified teachers* uncertificated, unlicensed, untrained. **2** *unqualified to comment* ineligible, unfit, incompetent, incapable, unequipped, unprepared. **3** *unqualified approval* without reservations, utter, perfect, consummate. *See* UNCONDITIONAL.

**unquestionable** adjective undoubted, indisputable. *See* UNDENIABLE.

**unravel** verb **1** *unravel knots* untangle, disentangle, straighten out, unknot, undo.

**2** *unravel the problem* solve, resolve, work out, clear up, get to the bottom of, fathom; *inf.* figure out.

**unreal** adjective imaginary, make-believe, fictitious, mythical, fanciful, fantastic, fabulous, hypothetical, nonexistent, illusory, chimerical, phantasmagoric.

**unrealistic** adjective impractical, impracticable, unworkable, unreasonable, irrational, illogical, improbable, foolish, wild, absurd, quixotic; *inf.* half-baked.

**unreasonable** adjective **1** *unreasonable demands* excessive, immoderate, undue, inordinate, outrageous, extravagant, preposterous, unconscionable, exorbitant. **2** *unreasonable people* irrational, illogical, opinionated, obstinate, obdurate, willful, headstrong, temperamental, capricious. **3** *unreasonable behavior* unacceptable, inappropriate.

**unrelenting** adjective **1** *unrelenting demands/rain* relentless, unremitting, continuous, continual, constant, incessant, unceasing, nonstop, endless, unending, perpetual, unabating. **2** *unrelenting judge* implacable, inexorable, inflexible, rigid, hard, strict, harsh, stern.

**unreliable** adjective undependable, irresponsible, untrustworthy, suspect, questionable, open to question/doubt.

**unrepentant** adjective impenitent, unrepenting, unremorseful, shameless, unregenerate.

**unresolved** adjective undecided, to be decided, unsettled, undetermined, pending, unsolved, unanswered, debatable, open to debate/question, doubtful, in doubt, moot, up in the air; *inf.* iffy.

**unrest** noun dissatisfaction, discontent, discontentment, unease, disquiet, dissension, dissent, discord, strife, protest, rebellion, agitation, turmoil.

**unruly** adjective unmanageable, uncontrollable, refractory, recalcitrant, intractable, contumacious, disobedient, rebellious, mutinous, insubordinate, defiant.

**unsavory** adjective **1** *unsavory food/smell* unpalatable, unappetizing, unpleasant, disagreeable, disgusting, loathsome, repugnant, revolting, nauseating, sickening. **2** *unsavory characters* objectionable, offensive, disreputable, degenerate, coarse, gross, vulgar, boorish.

**unscrupulous** adjective unprincipled, unethical, amoral, immoral, conscienceless, shameless, corrupt, exploitative.

**unseemly** adjective unbecoming, unfitting, unbefitting, indecorous, improper, inappropriate, undignified, unrefined, indelicate, tasteless.

**unselfish** adjective altruistic, self-sacrificing, selfless, kind, self-denying, openhanded, generous, liberal, unsparing, ungrudging, unstinting, charitable, philanthropic.

**unsettle** verb **1** *the move unsettled the children* disturb, discompose. See UPSET verb 2. **2** *unsettle the smooth workings of the firm* throw into confusion/disorder, disrupt, disorganize, disarrange, derange.

**unsightly** adjective ugly, unattractive, unprepossessing, hideous, horrible, repulsive, revolting, offensive, distasteful.

**unskilled** adjective untrained, unqualified, inexpert, inexperienced, amateurish.

**unsociable** adjective unfriendly, unamiable, unaffable, uncongenial, reclusive, reticent, withdrawn, aloof, distant, remote, standoffish.

**unsolicited** adjective unsought, unasked-for, unrequested, uninvited, unwelcome, gratuitous, volunteered.

**unsophisticated** adjective **1** *unsophisticated country girls* naive, simple, innocent, childlike, artless, guileless, ingenuous, natural, unaffected, unrefined, unpolished, provincial. **2** *unsophisticated tools* crude, basic, rudimentary, primitive, undeveloped. **3** *unsophisticated approach to the problem* simple, straightforward, uncomplicated, unspecialized.

**unsound** adjective **1** *in unsound health* unhealthy, unwell, ailing, delicate, weak, frail. **2** *of unsound mind* disordered, diseased, deranged, demented, unbalanced, unhinged. **3** *unsound furniture* defective, disintegrating, broken, broken-down, rotten, rickety, flimsy, shaky, wobbly, tottery, insubstantial, unsafe. **4** *unsound reasoning* flawed, defective, faulty, weak, unreliable, unfounded, untenable, specious, spurious, false, fallacious, erroneous.

**unspeakable** adjective **1** *unspeakable joy* beyond words, inexpressible, unutterable, indescribable, ineffable, overwhelming, marvelous, wonderful. **2** *an unspeakable crime* appalling, abominable, despicable, contemptible, repellent, loathsome, odious, monstrous, heinous, execrable.

**unspoken** adjective **1** *unspoken criticism* unexpressed, unstated, tacit, implicit, implied, understood. **2** *unspoken plea for mercy* mute, silent, wordless, unuttered.

**unstable** adjective **1** *unstable chairs* unsteady, infirm, rickety, shaky, wobbly, tottery, unsafe, unreliable, insecure, precarious. **2** *emotionally unstable* unbalanced, volatile, moody, mercurial, capricious, giddy, erratic, unpredictable. **3** *unstable prices* changeable, variable, unsettled, fluctuating, inconstant, unpredictable.

**unsuccessful** adjective failed, vain, unavailing, futile, useless, worthless, abortive, ineffective, ineffectual, inefficacious,

fruitless, unproductive, unprofitable, unprosperous; frustrated, thwarted, foiled.

**unsuitable** adjective inappropriate, inapt, inapposite, unfitting, unbefitting, incompatible, incongruous, out of place/keeping.

**unsure** adjective **1** *he was a bit unsure at first* unselfconfident, insecure, hesitant, diffident. **2** *unsure what to do* undecided, irresolute, of two minds, ambivalent. **3** *unsure about his motive* uncertain, unconvinced, dubious, doubtful, skeptical, distrustful, suspicious.

**unsuspecting** adjective unwary, off guard, trusting, trustful, gullible, credulous, ingenuous.

**unsympathetic** adjective uncompassionate, compassionless, unpitying, pitiless, uncaring, unfeeling, insensitive, unconcerned, indifferent, unresponsive.

**untenable** adjective indefensible, undefendable, insupportable, unsustainable, refutable, unsound, weak, flawed, defective, faulty, implausible, specious.

**unthinkable** adjective **1** *it is unthinkable that the territory is unexplored* inconceivable, unimaginable, unbelievable, beyond belief. **2** *it is unthinkable that he should represent us* out of the question, absurd, preposterous, outrageous.

**unthinking** adjective **1** *hurt by an unthinking remark* thoughtless, inconsiderate, tactless, undiplomatic, injudicious, indiscreet, insensitive, blundering, careless, rude. **2** *an unthinking kick of the ball* mechanical, automatic, instinctive, involuntary.

**untidy** adjective **1** *untidy children* disheveled, rumpled. See UNKEMPT. **2** *untidy desks/rooms* disordered, disorderly, disarranged, disorganized, chaotic, confused, muddled, jumbled, topsy-turvy, at sixes and sevens, higgledy-piggledy, every which way.

**untimely** adjective **1** *an untimely visit* illtimed, mistimed, inconvenient, inopportune. **2** *his untimely death* premature, early.

**untiring** adjective tireless, indefatigable, unfailing, unfaltering, unwavering, unflagging, unremitting, constant, resolute, steady.

**untold** adjective **1** *her untold story* unrecounted, unrelated, unnarrated, unreported, unmentioned, unstated, unspoken, unrevealed, undisclosed, undivulged, unpublished, secret. **2** *untold joy* unspeakable, indescribable, inexpressible, unutterable, ineffable, unimaginable, inconceivable. **3** *untold millions* countless, innumerable, myriad, incalculable, immeasurable, measureless.

**untrue** adjective **1** *untrue stories* false, fallacious, fictitious, fabricated, erroneous, in error, wrong, incorrect, inaccurate, unsound, distorted, misleading. **2** *untrue friends* disloyal, faithless, unfaithful, false, treacherous, perfidious, deceitful, untrustworthy, double-dealing, insincere, unreliable, inconstant.

**untrustworthy** adjective treacherous, two-faced, double-dealing, duplicitous, deceitful, dishonest, dishonorable, unreliable, undependable, slippery.

**unusual** adjective uncommon, out of the ordinary, atypical, abnormal, rare, singular, extraordinary, exceptional, remarkable, outstanding; odd, strange, curious, queer, bizarre, different, unconventional, unorthodox, irregular; *inf.* weird.

**unveil** verb uncover, reveal, lay open/bare, expose, bring to light, disclose, divulge, make known/public.

**unwarranted** adjective unauthorized, unsanctioned, unapproved, unjustifiable, unjustified, indefensible, inexcusable, uncalled-for, gratuitous.

**unwelcome** adjective unwanted, undesired, uninvited; displeasing, distasteful, undesirable.

**unwieldy** adjective cumbersome, unmanageable, unmaneuverable, awkward, clumsy, massive, hefty, bulky, hulking.

**unwilling** adjective reluctant, disinclined, averse, loath, opposed.

**unwind** verb **1** *unwind the balls of yarn* undo, unravel, uncoil, unroll, untwist, disentangle. **2** *unwind by watching television* wind down, relax, calm down, slow down, loosen up.

**unwise** adjective imprudent, injudicious, inadvisable, ill-considered, ill-judged, ill-advised, impolitic, indiscreet, irresponsible, foolish, unintelligent, mindless.

**unwitting** adjective **1** *an unwitting offender* unknowing, unconscious, unaware, ignorant. **2** *an unwitting slight* unintentional, unintended, inadvertent, unplanned, accidental, chance.

**unwonted** adjective unusual, uncommon, uncustomary, atypical, abnormal.

**unworldly** adjective **1** *unworldly considerations* spiritual, spiritualistic, nonmaterial, religious. **2** *too unworldly to cope on her own* naive, inexperienced, uninitiated, unsophisticated, gullible, ingenuous, trusting, credulous, idealistic. **3** *unworldly beings* otherworldly, unearthly, extraterrestrial, ethereal, ghostly, spectral, phantom, preternatural, supernatural.

**unworthy** adjective **1** *unworthy conduct for a teacher* unsuitable, inappropriate, unbefitting, unseemly, improper, incompatible, incongruous, degrading. **2** *an unworthy cause* worthless, inferior, second-rate, undeserving, ignoble, disreputable.

**3** *an unworthy wretch* disreputable, dishonorable, base, contemptible, reprehensible.

**upbraid** verb scold, rebuke, reproach, reprove, chide, reprimand, berate, remonstrate with, castigate, criticize, censure.

**upgrade** verb improve, better, ameliorate, enhance, promote, advance, elevate, raise.

**upheaval** noun disruption, disturbance, revolution, disorder, confusion, turmoil, cataclysm.

**uphill** adjective **1** *an uphill path* upward, ascending, climbing, mounting, rising. **2** *an uphill job* arduous, difficult, laborious, strenuous, hard, tough, taxing, grueling.

**uphold** verb **1** *uphold the committee's decision* confirm, endorse, support, back up, stand by, champion, defend. **2** *uphold the old traditions* maintain, sustain, hold to, keep.

**upkeep** noun maintenance, running, preservation, conservation, repairs, keep, support, subsistence.

**uplift** verb raise, upraise, lift, elevate; improve, edify, inspire.

**upper** adjective higher, loftier; superior, higher-ranking, elevated, greater.

**uppermost** adjective **1** *the uppermost shelf* highest, furthest up, loftiest, top, topmost. **2** *uppermost in our minds* foremost, greatest, predominant, dominant, principal, chief, main, paramount, major.

**upright** adjective **1** *upright posts* erect, on end, vertical, perpendicular, standing up, rampant. **2** *upright members of the community* honest, honorable, upstanding, decent, respectable, worthy, reputable, good, virtuous, righteous, law-abiding, ethical, moral.

**uprising** noun rebellion, revolt, insurrection, insurgence, mutiny, riot, revolution, coup, coup d'état, overthrow, putsch.

**uproar** noun tumult, turmoil, turbulence, disorder, confusion, commotion, mayhem, pandemonium, bedlam; din, noise, clamor, hubbub, racket; row, rumpus, brouhaha, hullabaloo, furor, fracas, brawl, scuffle, conflict.

**uproarious** adjective **1** *an uproarious party* noisy, loud, rowdy, disorderly, unruly, boisterous, wild, unrestrained, rollicking. **2** *an uproarious show* hilarious, sidesplitting; *inf.* rib-tickling.

**upset** verb **1** *upset the bucket/boat* overturn, knock over, push over, upend, tip over, topple, capsize. **2** *the news upset them* perturb, disturb, discompose, unsettle, disconcert, dismay, disquiet, trouble, worry, bother, agitate, fluster, ruffle, shake, frighten, alarm, anger, annoy, distress, hurt, grieve; *inf.* rattle. **3** *upset the* *smooth running of the firm* disturb, disarrange, mess up, mix up, turn topsyturvy. **4** *upset Napoleon's army* defeat, beat, conquer, vanquish, rout, overthrow, overcome, triumph over, get the better of, worst.

**upset** adjective **1** *the upset bucket* overturned, upturned, upended, toppled, capsized, upside down. **2** *upset by the news* perturbed, disturbed, discomposed, unsettled, disconcerted, dismayed, disquieted, troubled, worried, bothered, anxious, agitated, shaken, annoyed, distressed, hurt. **3** *an upset stomach* queasy, ill, sick. **4** *our upset plans* disordered, confused, in confusion, disarranged, in disarray, jumbled up, messed up, chaotic, in chaos, topsy-turvy, higgledy-piggledy.

**upshot** noun result, outcome, conclusion, issue, end, end result, denouement, effect, repercussion, reaction; *inf.* payoff.

**up-to-date** adjective modern, current, present-day, up-to-the-minute, fashionable, in fashion, in vogue, voguish; *inf.* all the rage, trendy, with-it, now.

**urban** adjective city, cityish, citified, innercity, metropolitan, municipal, civic.

**urbane** adjective suave, debonair, sophisticated, smooth, worldly, elegant, cultivated, cultured, civilized, polished, refined, gracious, courtly, polite, courteous, wellmannered.

**urge** verb **1** *urge the horses on* push, drive, propel, impel, force, hasten, hurry. **2** *urge the contestants to greater effort* spur, incite, stir up, stimulate, prod, goad, egg on, encourage, prompt; *inf.* psych up. **3** *urged him to go* entreat, exhort, implore, appeal, beg, beseech, plead. **4** *urge caution* advise, counsel, advocate, recommend, suggest, support, endorse.

**urge** noun desire, need, compulsion, longing, yearning, wish, fancy, impulse, itch; *inf.* yen.

**urgent** adjective **1** *it is urgent that we operate* | *urgent matters* imperative, vital, crucial, critical, essential, exigent, top-priority, high-priority, necessary, important, pressing, serious, grave. **2** *an urgent whisper/demand* importunate, insistent, clamorous, earnest, pleading, begging.

**usage** noun **1** *damaged by rough usage* treatment, handling, management. *See* USE noun 1. **2** *old usages now forgotten* custom, practice, habit, way, procedure, method, mode, form, tradition, convention.

**use** verb **1** *use tools* make use of, utilize, employ, work, operate, wield, ply, maneuver, manipulate, avail oneself of, put to use, put into service. **2** *use him roughly* treat, handle, deal with, act/behave toward. **3** *he just uses people for his own ends* exploit,

take advantage of, impose upon, abuse. **4** *we have used up all the food* consume, get through, exhaust, deplete, expend, spend, waste, fritter away. **used to** accustomed to, at home with, habituated to, inured to.

**use** noun **1** *for external use* usage, application, utilization, employment, operation, manipulation, maneuvering. **2** *fall to pieces from use* using, usage, wear, wear and tear. **3** *his use of other people for his own ends* exploitation, manipulation. **4** *what use is this to you?* usefulness, good, advantage, benefit, service, help, gain, profit, avail. **5** *established by long use* practice, custom, habit, wont. **6** *we have no use for this machine* need, necessity, call, demand, purpose, reason.

**used** adjective secondhand, cast-off, handme-down.

**useful** adjective **1** *a useful tool* of use, functional, utilitarian, of service, practical, convenient. **2** *a useful experience* beneficial, advantageous, of help, helpful, worthwhile, profitable, rewarding, productive, valuable.

**useless** adjective **1** *a useless attempt* vain, in vain, to no avail/purpose, unavailing, unsuccessful, futile, purposeless, ineffectual, inefficacious, fruitless, unprofitable. **2** *he is a useless player* worthless, ineffective, ineffectual, incompetent, incapable, inadequate; *inf.* no good.

**usher** noun escort, guide, attendant.

**usher** verb escort, show, conduct, direct, guide, lead. **usher in** herald, pave the way for, announce, introduce, bring in, get going, get under way, launch.

**usual** adjective **1** *his usual route* habitual, customary, accustomed, wonted, normal, regular, routine, everyday, established, set, familiar. **2** *not usual behavior* common, typical, ordinary, average, run-of-the-mill, expected, standard, stock, regular.

**usually** adverb generally, as a rule, normally, by and large, in the main, mainly, mostly.

**utilize** verb use, put to use, make use of, employ, avail oneself of, have recourse to, resort to, take advantage of, turn to account.

**utmost** adjective **1** *have the utmost confidence in them* maximum, supreme, paramount, greatest, highest, most. **2** *the utmost ends of the earth* uttermost, furthest, farthest, remotest, outermost, extreme, ultimate.

**utter** adjective absolute, sheer. *See* UNMITIGATED.

**utter** verb voice, say, speak, pronounce, express, enunciate, articulate, verbalize, vocalize.

**utterly** adverb absolutely, completely, totally, entirely, thoroughly, positively, extremely, perfectly.

# Vv

**vacancy** noun **1** *a vacancy in the firm* opening, position, post, job, opportunity, slot. **2** *the vacancy of his expression* blankness, expressionlessness, emotionlessness, vacuousness.

**vacant** adjective **1** *a vacant space* empty, void. **2** *a vacant position/seat* unoccupied, unfilled, free, empty, available, unengaged, not in use, unused; *inf.* up for grabs. **3** *a vacant house* uninhabited, untenanted, tenantless, to let, abandoned, deserted. **4** *a vacant expression* blank, expressionless, inexpressive, deadpan, poker-faced, emotionless, uninterested, vacuous, inane.

**vacate** verb leave, quit, depart from, evacuate, abandon, desert.

**vacation** noun break, recess, furlough, holiday, rest, respite; leave, time off.

**vacillate** verb shilly-shally, waver, dither, hesitate, equivocate, hem and haw, keep changing one's mind, beat about the bush; *inf.* blow hot and cold.

**vacuum** noun emptiness, void, nothingness, vacuity; gap, empty space, lacuna, need, want.

**vagabond** noun wanderer, itinerant, nomad, wayfarer, traveler, rover, gypsy, hobo, tramp, vagrant, derelict, beachcomber, down-and-out, bird of passage, rolling stone; *inf.* bum.

**vagrant** noun tramp, hobo, beggar. *See* VAGABOND noun.

**vague** adjective **1** *a vague shape* indistinct, indeterminate, ill-defined, unclear, nebulous, amorphous, shadowy, hazy, dim, fuzzy, foggy, blurry, bleary, out of focus. **2** *a vague description* imprecise, inexact, unexplicit, nonspecific, loose, generalized, ambiguous, equivocal, hazy, woolly. **3** *she is rather vague about her plans* uncertain, unsure, hesitant, wavering, shilly-shallying, blowing hot and cold. **4** *her plans are rather vague* undecided, indefinite, indeterminate, doubtful, open, speculative, conjectural; *inf.* up in the air. **5** *she is rather vague* absentminded, abstracted, dreamy, vacuous; *inf.* with one's head in the clouds.

**vain** adjective **1** *vain people* conceited, narcissistic, self-admiring, peacockish, egotistical, proud, haughty, arrogant, boastful, swaggering, imperious, overweening, cocky, affected, vainglorious; *inf.* stuck-up, bigheaded, swellheaded. **2** *vain triumphs* futile, worthless, insignificant, pointless, meaningless, valueless, meritless, empty, hollow,

idle. **3** *vain attempts* unsuccessful, futile. *See* USELESS 1.

**valiant** adjective brave, courageous, valorous, heroic, stouthearted, lionhearted, gallant, manly, intrepid, fearless, undaunted, undismayed, bold, daring, audacious, staunch, stalwart, indomitable, resolute, determined.

**valid** adjective **1** *valid reasons/objections* sound, well-founded, well-grounded, substantial, reasonable, logical, justifiable, defensible, authentic, bona fide. **2** *the ruling is still valid* lawful, legal, licit, legitimate, binding, contractual, in force, in effect.

**validate** verb **1** *validate the contract | validate his appointment* ratify, legalize, legitimize, authorize, sanction, warrant, license, approve, endorse, set one's seal to. **2** *validate a statement* verify, prove, authenticate, substantiate, confirm, corroborate, justify.

**valley** noun dale, dell, hollow, vale, glen, depression.

**valor** noun bravery, courage, heroism, stoutheartedness, gallantry, manliness, intrepidity, fearlessness, boldness, daring, staunchness, fortitude.

**valuable** adjective **1** *a valuable watch* costly, high-priced, expensive, priceless, precious. **2** *a valuable contribution/lesson* useful, helpful, beneficial, advantageous, worthwhile, worthy, important.

**value** noun **1** *place a value on the ring* price, market price, cost. **2** *the value of a healthy diet* worth, merit, usefulness, advantage, benefit, gain, profit, good.

**value** verb **1** *value the watch* set a price on, price, evaluate, assess, appraise. **2** *we value his contribution greatly* rate highly, appreciate, esteem, hold in high regard, think highly of, set store by, respect, admire, prize, cherish, treasure.

**values** plural noun *moral values* principles, ethics, morals, standards.

**vanguard** noun advance guard, forefront, front, front line, front rank, leading position, van; leaders, spearheads, trailblazers, trendsetters.

**vanish** verb **1** *she vanished in the mist* disappear, be lost to sight/view, be/become invisible, evaporate, dissipate, fade, fade away, evanesce, melt away. **2** *hopes of success have vanished* pass away, die out, come to an end, end, become extinct/obsolete.

**vanity** noun **1** *his vanity about his looks/achievements* conceit, conceitedness, self-conceit, self-admiration, self-love, narcissism, egotism, pride, haughtiness, arrogance, boastfulness, braggadocio, vainglory; airs; *inf.* bigheadedness, swellheadedness, showing off. **2** *the vanity of human triumphs* worthlessness, futility, futileness, insignificance, pointlessness, meaninglessness, emptiness, hollowness.

**vanquish** verb conquer, defeat, triumph over, beat, overcome, best, worst, master, subdue, subjugate, put down, quell, quash, repress, rout, overwhelm, overrun, overthrow, crush, trounce, thrash, drub; *inf.* clobber.

**variable** adjective varying, changeable, changeful, changing, mutable, chameleonic, protean, shifting, fluctuating, wavering, vacillating, inconstant, unsteady, unstable, fitful, capricious, fickle; *inf.* blowing hot and cold.

**variation** noun **1** *subject to variation* change, alteration, modification, diversification. **2** *noted for its variation* variability, changeability, fluctuation, vacillation, vicissitude. **3** *show variation from the norm* deviation, divergence, departure, difference.

**varied** adjective diversified, diverse, assorted, miscellaneous, mixed, motley, heterogeneous.

**variety** noun **1** *introduce variety into your selection* variation, diversification, diversity, multifariousness, many-sidedness, change, difference. **2** *a variety of flowers were exhibited* assortment, miscellany, range, mixture, medley, motley, collection, multiplicity. **3** *a variety of rose/humor* strain, breed, kind, type, sort, class, category, classification, brand, make.

**various** adjective **1** *come in various shapes* varying, different, differing, dissimilar, unlike, disparate, assorted, mixed, miscellaneous, variegated, heterogeneous. **2** *for various reasons* varied, sundry, diverse.

**varnish** noun coating, lacquer, shellac, enamel, glaze, veneer.

**vary** verb **1** *they tend to vary in size* differ, be different, be dissimilar. **2** *the sky varies constantly* change, alter, metamorphose, suffer a sea change, vacillate, fluctuate. **3** *our opinions vary* be at variance, disagree, conflict, clash, be at odds, be in opposition, diverge. **4** *vary the speed/appearance* change, alter, modify, transform, permutate. **5** *vary from the norm* deviate, diverge, depart.

**vast** adjective **1** *a vast shape loomed* immense, huge, enormous, massive, bulky, tremendous, colossal, prodigious, gigantic, monumental, elephantine, hulking. **2** *vast forests* extensive, broad, wide, expansive, boundless, limitless, infinite.

**vault** noun **1** *hide in the vault* cellar, basement, underground chamber, tomb. **2** *valuables stored in the vault* safe, strongbox, strongroom, repository, depository. **3** *take a vault over the fence* jump, leap, spring, bound.

**vault** verb jump, leap, jump over, leap over, spring over, bound over.

**veer** verb change course/direction, shift direction, turn, swerve, swing, sidestep, sheer, tack.

**vegetation** noun plant life, herbage, greenery, verdure; plants, flora.

**vehement** adjective passionate, ardent, impassioned, fervent, fervid, strong, forceful, forcible, powerful, emphatic, vigorous, intense.

**vehicle** noun **1** *park the vehicle* transportation, conveyance; car, bus, truck. **2** *a vehicle for their propaganda* channel, medium, means, agency, instrument, mechanism, organ, apparatus.

**veil** noun *a veil of secrecy* covering, cover, screen, curtain, film, mantle, cloak, mask, blanket, shroud, canopy, cloud.

**veil** verb **1** *try to veil his contempt* hide, conceal, cover up, camouflage, disguise, mask, screen. **2** *mist veiling the mountains* cover, envelop, mantle, cloak, blanket, shroud, canopy.

**vein** noun **1** *a vein of ore* lode, seam, stratum. **2** *veins of blue in the white marble* streak, stripe, line, thread, marking. **3** *there was a vein of wickedness in him* streak, strain, trait, dash, hint. **4** *a humorous vein* mood, temper, attitude, inclination, tendency, tenor, tone.

**velocity** noun speed, swiftness, fastness, quickness, rapidity, celerity.

**vendor** noun seller, salesperson, dealer, trader, merchant, peddler, hawker.

**veneer** noun **1** *a veneer of mahogany* facing, covering, coat, finishing coat, finish. **2** *a veneer of politeness* façade, front, false front, show, outward display, appearance, semblance, guise, mask, pretense, camouflage.

**venerable** adjective venerated, respected, revered, reverenced, worshiped, honored, esteemed, hallowed.

**veneration** noun respect, reverence, worship, adoration, honor, esteem.

**vengeance** noun revenge, retribution, requital, retaliation, reprisal, an eye for an eye, tit for tat, measure for measure, blow for blow, quid pro quo. **with a vengeance 1** *the rain came down with a vengeance* forcefully, violently, vehemently, furiously, wildly. **2** *go at the job with a vengeance* to the utmost, to the limit, all out, flat out.

**venom** noun **1** *suck the venom of the snake bite* poison, toxin, toxicant. **2** *speak with venom about his rival* spite, spitefulness, rancor, vindictiveness, malice, malevolence, malignity, ill will, animosity, bitterness, resentment, acrimony, virulence, hostility, enmity.

**venomous** adjective **1** *a venomous snake/bite* poisonous, toxic, lethal, deadly, fatal, noxious. **2** *a venomous remark/look* spiteful, rancorous, vindictive, malicious, malevolent, malignant, baleful, bitter, resentful, grudging, virulent, antagonistic, hostile, hate-filled, vicious.

**vent** noun **1** *an air vent* opening, aperture, hole, gap, orifice, duct, flue. **2** *give vent to his anger* outlet, expression, release.

**vent** verb *vent his anger* give vent to, express, air, utter, voice, verbalize, let out, release, pour out, emit, discharge, come out with.

**ventilate** verb **1** *ventilate a room* air, aerate, oxygenate, air-condition, freshen, cool, purify. **2** *ventilate one's views* air, give an airing to, bring into the open, discuss, debate, talk over.

**venture** noun **1** *explorers engaged in a new venture* adventure, exploit, mission. **2** *a business venture* enterprise, undertaking, project, speculation, fling, plunge, gamble.

**venture** verb **1** *venture to voice an opinion* dare, be so bold as, presume. **2** *venture an opinion* volunteer, advance, put forward, chance, risk. **3** *venture his life for her* risk, put at risk, endanger, hazard, put in jeopardy, jeopardize, imperil, chance, gamble.

**verbal** adjective *a verbal account* oral, spoken, said, uttered, articulated.

**verbatim** adjective word for word, literal, verbal, exact.

**verbatim** adverb word for word, literally, to the letter, faithfully, exactly, precisely.

**verbose** adjective wordy, loquacious, garrulous, long-winded, prolix, diffuse, pleonastic, circumlocutory, periphrastic, tautological.

**verdict** noun decision, judgment, adjudication, finding, conclusion, ruling, opinion.

**verge** noun **1** *the verges of the lake* edge, border, margin, rim, limit, boundary, end, extremity. **2** *on the verge of a discovery* brink, threshold.

**verify** verb confirm, substantiate, prove, corroborate, attest to, testify to, validate, authenticate, bear out, justify, give credence to.

**versatile** adjective **1** *a versatile member of staff* all-around, multifaceted, resourceful, ingenious, clever. **2** *a versatile tool* adaptable, adjustable, multipurpose, all-purpose, handy.

**verse** noun **1** *a poem in several verses* stanza, strophe, canto, couplet. **2** *a verse about the countryside* poem, lyric, sonnet, ode, limerick, piece of doggerel, ditty, song, lay, ballad.

**version** noun **1** *tell us your version of the events* account, report, story, rendering, interpretation, construction, understanding, reading, impression, side. **2** *published in several versions* adaptation, interpretation, translation. **3** *there are several versions of the song going around* variant, variation, form, copy, reproduction.

**vertical** adjective upright, erect, on end, perpendicular.

**vertigo** noun dizziness, giddiness, light-headedness; *inf.* wooziness.

**verve** noun enthusiasm, vigor, force, energy, vitality, vivacity, liveliness, animation, sparkle, spirit, life, élan, dash, brio, fervor, gusto, zing, vim; zip, punch, get-up-and-go, pizzazz.

**very** adverb extremely, exceedingly, to a great extent, exceptionally, uncommonly, unusually, decidedly, particularly, eminently, remarkably, really, truly; *inf.* awfully, terribly.

**very** adjective **1** *his very words* actual, exact, precise. **2** *that is the very thing for the task* ideal, perfect, appropriate, suitable, fitting, right, just right. **3** *its very simplicity appeals to us* sheer, utter, simple, pure, plain, mere. **4** *at the very beginning* extreme, absolute.

**vessel** noun **1** *a seagoing vessel* ship, boat, yacht, craft, argosy. **2** *pour the milk into several vessels* container, receptacle.

**vest** verb *vest in* *the power vested in him* bestow on/upon, confer on/upon, endow, entrust to/with, invest in, lodge in/with, place in/on/with, put in the hands of.

**vestige** noun **1** *see vestiges of a pack of wolves* trace, mark, sign, indication, print, imprint, impression, track. **2** *vestiges of a lost civilization* remains, relics; evidence. **3** *not a vestige of proof* scrap, hint, suggestion, touch, tinge, suspicion, soupçon, inkling, drop, dash, jot, iota.

**veteran** noun old hand, old-timer, past master, master; *inf.* pro, warhorse.

**veteran** adjective long-serving, seasoned, old, adept, expert; *inf.* battle-scarred.

**veto** verb reject, turn down, give the thumbs down to, prohibit, forbid, interdict, proscribe, disallow, outlaw, embargo, ban, bar, preclude, rule out; *inf.* kill, put the kibosh on.

**veto** noun rejection, prohibition, interdict, proscription; embargo, ban.

**vex** verb anger, annoy, irritate, incense, irk, enrage, infuriate, exasperate, aggravate, pique, provoke, nettle, disturb, upset, perturb, discompose, put out, try one's patience, try, bother, trouble, worry, agitate, pester, harass, fluster, ruffle, rile, hound, nag, torment, distress, tease, fret, gall, molest, peeve; *inf.* miff, bug, hassle, get one's goat, drive up the wall, get to.

**viable** adjective *a viable plan* workable, sound, feasible, practicable, applicable, usable.

**vibrant** adjective **1** *vibrant music* throbbing, pulsating, resonant, reverberating, ringing, echoing. **2** *vibrant with excitement* trembling, quivering, shaking, shivering. **3** *a vibrant personality* lively, energetic, spirited, vigorous, animated, sparkling, vivacious, dynamic, electrifying. **4** *vibrant colors* vivid, bright, strong, striking.

**vibrate** verb **1** *the pendulum vibrated* oscillate, swing. **2** *the noise vibrated through the house* throb, pulsate, resonate, resound, reverberate, ring, echo. **3** *vibrating with excitement* pulsate, tremble, quiver, shake, quaver, shiver, shudder.

**vibration** noun **1** *the musical vibration* throb, pulsation, resonance, reverberation. **2** *the vibration of the engine* pulsating, trembling, tremble, quivering, quiver, shake, shaking, quaver, shiver, shivering.

**vicarious** adjective indirect, secondhand, surrogate, by proxy.

**vice** noun **1** *vice is rampant* sin, sinfulness, wrong, wrongdoing, wickedness, badness, immorality, iniquity, evil, evildoing, venality corruption, depravity, degeneracy; transgression, offense, misdeed, error, violation. **2** *chocolate/shopping is one of her vices* failing, flaw, defect, imperfection, weakness, foible, shortcoming.

**vice versa** adverb conversely, inversely, the other way around, contrariwise.

**vicinity** noun **1** *he lives in the vicinity* neighborhood, locality, area, district; environs, precincts, purlieus; *inf.* neck of the woods. **2** *the town's vicinity to Nashville* nearness, closeness, proximity, propinquity. **in the vicinity of** *in the vicinity of $3000* in the neighborhood of, near to, close to.

**vicious** adjective **1** *vicious dogs* fierce, ferocious, savage, dangerous, ill-natured, bad-tempered, surly, hostile. **2** *vicious remarks* malicious, malevolent, malignant, spiteful, vindictive, venomous, catty, backbiting, rancorous, caustic, mean, cruel; *inf.* bitchy. **3** *a vicious attack* violent, brutal, inhuman, barbarous, fiendish, sadistic, monstrous, heinous. **4** *a vicious band of*

*people* corrupt, degenerate, depraved, debased, wicked, evil, immoral, unprincipled, disreputable.

**victim** noun **1** *they were victims of his sales patter* dupe, easy target/prey, fair game; *inf.* sitting duck, sucker, sap, fall guy, pushover. **2** *track down their victim(s)* prey, quarry, game, the hunted, target. **3** *a sacrificial victim for the gods* offering, sacrifice, scapegoat.

**victimize** verb **1** *bullies victimizing their classmates* persecute, bully, pick on, discriminate against, punish unfairly. **2** *con artists victimizing the naïve couple* exploit, prey on, take advantage of, swindle, dupe, cheat, trick, hoodwink.

**victor** verb conqueror, vanquisher, winner, champion, prizewinner, conquering hero; *inf.* champ, top dog, number one.

**victorious** adjective conquering, vanquishing, triumphant, winning, champion, successful, prizewinning, top, first.

**vie** verb compete, contend, contest.

**view** noun **1** *come into view* sight, field/range of vision, vision, eyeshot. **2** *the view from the mountain* outlook, prospect, scene, spectacle, vista, panorama; landscape, seascape. **3** *radical views* viewpoint, opinion, belief, judgment, thinking, thought, notion, idea, conviction, sentiment. **4** *a private view of the exhibition* viewing, sight, look, contemplation, observation, inspection, scrutiny, scan. **in view of** considering, taking into consideration, bearing in mind, taking into account. **on view** on display, on exhibition, on show.

**view** verb **1** *view the birds through binoculars* look at, watch, observe, contemplate, regard, behold, scan, survey, inspect, gaze at, stare at, peer at. **2** *view the house* survey, examine, scrutinize, take stock of. **3** *view the prospect with dismay* look on, consider, contemplate, think about, reflect on, ponder. **4** *view himself as an upright man* see, consider, judge, deem.

**viewpoint** noun point of view, way of thinking, frame of reference, perspective, angle, slant, standpoint, position, stance, vantage point.

**vigilance** noun watchfulness, observation, surveillance, attentiveness, attention, alertness, guardedness, carefulness, caution, wariness, circumspection, heedfulness, heed.

**vigilant** adjective watchful, attentive, alert, on the alert, on the qui vive, awake, wide awake, unsleeping, on one's guard, cautious, wary, circumspect, heedful.

**vigor** noun **1** *the natural vigor of country children* robustness, healthiness, strength, sturdiness, fitness, toughness. **2** *return to* *work with renewed vigor* energy, vitality, vivacity, vim, verve, animation, dynamism, sparkle, zest, dash, élan, gusto, zing, pep; *inf.* zip, oomph.

**vigorous** adjective **1** *vigorous children brought up in the country* robust, healthy, in good health, hale and hearty, strong, sturdy, fit, in good condition/shape. **2** *feel more vigorous after exercise* energetic, lively, active, spry, sprightly, vivacious, animated, dynamic. **3** *a vigorous attempt at winning* strenuous, forceful, forcible, spirited, keen, enthusiastic, ardent, fervent, vehement, intense.

**vile** adjective **1** *a vile taste/smell* foul, nasty, unpleasant, disagreeable, horrid, horrible, offensive, obnoxious, odious, repulsive, repellent, revolting, repugnant, disgusting, distasteful, loathsome. **2** *a vile creature | a vile thing to do* base, low, mean, wretched, dreadful, disgraceful, appalling, shocking, ugly, abominable, monstrous, wicked, evil, iniquitous, sinful, vicious, corrupt, depraved, degenerate, contemptible, despicable, reprehensible.

**villain** noun rogue, scoundrel, blackguard, wretch, cad, reprobate, evildoer, wrongdoer, ruffian, hoodlum, hooligan, criminal, miscreant; *inf.* baddy, crook, rat, louse.

**vindicate** verb **1** *he was vindicated when his alibi was proved* acquit, clear, absolve, free from blame, exonerate, exculpate. **2** *time vindicated his suspicions* justify, warrant, substantiate, testify to, verify, confirm, corroborate. **3** *vindicate his claim* defend, support, back, fight for, champion, uphold, maintain, sustain, stand by.

**vindictive** adjective vengeful, out for revenge, revengeful, avenging, unforgiving, resentful, implacable, unrelenting, spiteful.

**vintage** noun year, harvest, crop; era, epoch, period, time, generation.

**vintage** adjective **1** *vintage wines* high-quality, quality, prime, choice, select, superior, best. **2** *vintage comedy* classic, ageless, enduring. **3** *this story is vintage Poe* characteristic, typical, supreme, at his/her/its best.

**violate** verb **1** *violate a law/treaty* break, breach, infringe, contravene, infract, transgress, disobey, disregard, ignore. **2** *violate a grave* desecrate, profane, defile, blaspheme. **3** *violate their privacy* disturb, disrupt, intrude on, interfere with, encroach on, invade, upset, shatter, destroy. **4** *he was accused of violating his niece* rape, ravish, abuse, molest.

**violence** noun **1** *the violence of his temper* strength, forcefulness, wildness, passion. **2** *the violence of the blow* forcefulness, powerfulness, might, savagery, ferocity, destructiveness, brutality. **3** *the violence of his*

*dislike* strength, intensity, vehemence. **4** *use violence to get his way* force, brute force, roughness, ferocity, brutality, savagery; strong-arm tactics.

**violent** adjective **1** *a violent temper* strong, powerful, forceful, uncontrolled, unrestrained, unbridled, uncontrollable, ungovernable, wild, passionate, raging. **2** *he is a violent person* brutal, vicious, destructive, savage, fierce, wild, intemperate, hotheaded, hot-tempered, bloodthirsty, homicidal, murderous, maniacal. **3** *a violent blow* forceful, powerful, mighty, savage, ferocious, destructive, damaging, brutal. **4** *a violent dislike* strong, great, intense, extreme, vehement, inordinate, excessive, acute.

**virgin** adjective *virgin territory* pure, immaculate, unblemished, spotless, stainless, unused, untouched, untainted, unspoiled, untarnished, unadulterated.

**virile** adjective manly, masculine, male, all-male, strong, vigorous, robust, powerfully built, muscular, rugged, strapping, sturdy, red-blooded; *inf.* macho.

**virtual** adjective near, effective, in effect, tantamount to, for all practical purposes, in all but name; functioning as, operating as.

**virtually** adverb more or less, nearly, practically, as good as, effectively, essentially, for all practical purposes, to all intents and purposes.

**virtue** noun **1** *admires the virtue of workers* goodness, righteousness, morality, uprightness, integrity, rectitude, honesty, honorableness, honor, incorruptibility, probity, decency, respectability, worthiness, worth, trustworthiness. **2** *the virtue of youth* virginity, celibacy, purity, pureness, chastity, chasteness, innocence, modesty. **3** *generosity is one of her virtues* good point, merit, asset, credit, attribute, advantage, benefit, strength, plus. **4** *there is no virtue in the use of such drugs* merit, usefulness, efficacy, efficaciousness, power, potency. **by virtue of** by reason of, by dint of, on account of, as a result of, owing to, thanks to.

**virtuoso** noun master, genius, expert, artist, maestro, wizard.

**virtuous** adjective **1** *virtuous, hardworking people* good, righteous, moral, ethical, upright, upstanding, honest, honorable, incorruptible, decent, respectable, worthy, trustworthy. **2** *virtuous youth* virginal, celibate, pure, chaste, innocent, modest.

**visible** adjective **1** *hills scarcely visible in the mist* perceptible, perceivable, discernible, detectable, seeable. **2** *his distress was visible to all* apparent, evident, noticeable, observable, recognizable, manifest, plain, clear, obvious, unconcealed, undisguised, conspicuous.

**vision** noun **1** *have good vision* eyesight, sight, eyes. **2** *the prophet saw a vision* apparition, specter, phantom, ghost, wraith, phantasm, chimera, revelation. **3** *saw wild horses in one of his visions* dream, hallucination, optical illusion, mirage, illusion, delusion, figment of the imagination, daydream, pipe dream, fantasy. **4** *artists must have vision* perception, perceptiveness, insight, intuition, imagination. **5** *in need of political vision* foresight, farsightedness, prescience, breadth of view, discernment. **6** *she was a vision in white* dream, spectacle, picture, feast for the eyes, beautiful sight.

**visionary** adjective **1** *visionary schemes* idealistic, impractical, unrealistic, utopian, romantic, quixotic, starry-eyed, unworkable, unfeasible, theoretical, hypothetical. **2** *visionary artists* perceptive, intuitive, insightful, imaginative. **3** *visionary politicians* farsighted, discerning, wise, prescient. **4** *visionary figures* unreal, imaginary, imagined, fanciful, fancied, illusory, phantasmagoric, spectral, ghostly, wraithlike.

**visionary** noun **1** *ancient visionaries* mystic, seer, prophet. **2** *too much of a visionary to run a business* dreamer, daydreamer, idealist, romantic, romanticist, fantasist, theorist, utopian.

**visit** verb **1** *visit his aunt* pay a visit to, go/come to see, pay a call on, call on, look in on, stop by (to see); *inf.* pop/drop in on, look up. **2** *a city visited with the plague* attack, assail, afflict, smite, descend on, trouble, harrow, torture.

**visit** noun call, social call; stay, sojourn, stopover.

**visitor** noun caller, guest; tourist, traveler, pilgrim.

**visualize** verb conjure up, envisage, picture in the mind's eye, picture, envision, imagine.

**vital** adjective **1** *the vital organs* life-giving, life-preserving, life-sustaining, basic, fundamental. **2** *matters of vital importance* essential, necessary, key, important, significant, urgent, critical, crucial, life-and-death. **3** *such a vital person* lively, animated, spirited, vivacious, vibrant, zestful, dynamic, energetic, vigorous, forceful. **4** *a vital error* deadly, lethal, fatal, fateful.

**vitality** noun life, liveliness, animation, spirit, spiritedness, vivacity, vibrancy, zest, zestfulness, dynamism, energy, vigor, forcefulness.

**vitriolic** adjective caustic, mordant, bitter, acerbic, astringent, acid, acidulous, acrid, trenchant, virulent, scathing, withering, sarcastic, sardonic.

**vituperation** noun invective, condemnation, denunciation, castigation, chastisement, rebuke, abuse, vilification, denigration.

**vivacious** adjective lively, full of life, animated, effervescent, bubbling, ebullient, sparkling, scintillating, lighthearted, spirited, high-spirited, gay, merry, jolly, vibrant, dynamic, vital.

**vivid** adjective **1** *vivid colors* strong, intense, colorful, rich, glowing, bright, brilliant, clear. **2** *a vivid description* graphic, clear, realistic, lifelike, true to life. **3** *a vivid personality* strong, striking, flamboyant, memorable, dynamic, lively, animated, spirited, vibrant, vital.

**vocal** adjective **1** *vocal noises* voiced, vocalized, spoken, said, uttered, expressed. **2** *people vocal in their criticism* vociferous, outspoken, forthright, clamorous, strident, loud, noisy.

**vocation** noun profession, calling, occupation, walk of life, career, life's work, métier, trade, craft, job, work, employment, business, line, specialty.

**vociferous** adjective loud, noisy, clamorous, vehement, strident, vocal, outspoken.

**vogue** noun **1** *the vogue for short skirts* fashion, mode, style, trend, taste, fad, craze, rage, latest thing, last word. **2** *a hairstyle in vogue in the 1920s* fashionableness, modishness, popularity, currency, prevalence, favor, acceptance.

**voice** noun **1** *give voice to her feelings* expression, utterance, verbalization, vocalization, airing. **2** *the voice of the people* opinion, view, comment, feeling, wish, desire, vote. **3** *he is the voice of the company* spokesman, spokeswoman, spokesperson, mouthpiece, organ, agency, medium, vehicle.

**voice** verb express, give utterance to, utter, articulate, enunciate, mention, talk of, communicate, declare, assert, divulge, air, ventilate, come out with.

**void** adjective **1** *a void space* empty, vacant, bare, clear, free, unfilled. **2** *the ticket is now void* null and void, invalid, canceled, inoperative, ineffective, not binding, not in force.

**void** noun emptiness, blankness, vacuum; space, gap, lacuna, hole, hollow, chasm, abyss.

**void** verb **1** *void the decision* annul, nullify, disallow, invalidate, quash, cancel, repeal, revoke, rescind, reverse, abrogate. **2** *void the bowels* empty, drain, evacuate; excrete, eject, expel, emit, discharge.

**volatile** adjective **1** *a volatile person* mercurial, changeable, variable, capricious, whimsical, fickle, flighty, giddy, inconstant, erratic, unstable. **2** *a volatile international situation* explosive, eruptive, charged, inflammatory, tense, strained.

**volition** noun **of one's own volition** of one's own free will, of one's own choice, by one's own preference, voluntarily.

**volley** noun barrage, cannonade, battery, broadside, salvo, fusillade, shower, stream, deluge.

**volume** noun **1** *a volume on butterflies* book, publication, tome. **2** *measure the volume* bulk, capacity, quantity, amount, mass. **3** *turn down the volume* loudness, sound, amplification.

**voluminous** adjective capacious, roomy, commodious, ample, full, big, vast, billowing.

**voluntary** adjective **1** *attendance is voluntary* of one's own free will, volitional, of one's own accord, optional, discretional, at one's discretion, elective, noncompulsory, nonmandatory. **2** *undertake voluntary work* unpaid, honorary, volunteer.

**volunteer** verb offer, tender, proffer, present, put forward, advance; offer one's services, present oneself, step forward.

**voluptuous** adjective **1** *voluptuous pleasures* hedonistic, sybaritic, epicurean, pleasure-loving, self-indulgent, sensual, carnal, licentious, lascivious. **2** *a voluptuous woman* curvy, shapely, full-figured, buxom, seductive; *inf.* curvaceous.

**vomit** verb **1** *he suddenly vomited* be sick, retch, heave, spew, throw up; *inf.* puke, barf, toss one's cookies, lose one's lunch, upchuck, hurl. **2** *vomit blood* bring up, regurgitate, spew up, spit up. **3** *chimneys vomiting smoke* belch, eject, emit, send forth.

**voracious** adjective **1** *a voracious eater* gluttonous, greedy, ravenous, ravening,

starving, hungry. **2** *a voracious reader* insatiable, insatiate, unquenchable, prodigious, compulsive, enthusiastic, eager.

**vortex** noun whirlpool, maelstrom, eddy, swirl, whirlwind.

**vote** noun **1** *have a vote on who should be mayor* ballot, poll, election, referendum, plebiscite. **2** *get the vote* franchise, suffrage.

**vouch** verb **vouch for 1** *vouch for his honesty* attest to, bear witness to, give assurance of, answer for, be responsible for, guarantee. **2** *vouch for the painting's authenticity* certify, warrant, confirm, verify, validate, substantiate.

**vow** noun oath, pledge, promise.

**vow** verb swear, state under oath, pledge, promise, undertake, give one's word of honor.

**voyage** noun crossing, cruise, passage; journey, trip, expedition; travels.

**vulgar** adjective **1** *vulgar language/jokes* indecent, indecorous, indelicate, unseemly, offensive, distasteful, obnoxious, risqué, suggestive, off-color, blue, ribald, bawdy, obscene, lewd, salacious, licentious, concupiscent, smutty, dirty, filthy, pornographic, scatological; *inf.* raunchy. **2** *vulgar table manners* rude, impolite, ill-mannered, unmannerly, ill-bred, common, coarse, boorish, rough, crude. **3** *vulgar decorations* tasteless, gross, crass, unrefined, tawdry, ostentatious, showy, flashy, gaudy. **4** *the vulgar masses* common, ordinary, low, lowborn, ignorant, unsophisticated, unrefined, uneducated, illiterate, uncultured, uncouth.

**vulnerable** adjective open to attack, attackable, assailable, exposed, liable, subject, unprotected, unguarded, defenseless, easily hurt/wounded/damaged, powerless, helpless, weak, sensitive, thin-skinned.

# *Ww*

**wade** verb **1** *wade the stream* ford, cross, traverse. **2** *wade through piles of papers* plod, plow, labor, toil/plug/peg away.

**wag** verb swing, sway, vibrate, quiver, shake, rock, twitch, waggle, wiggle, wobble, wave, nod, bob.

**wag** noun *he's quite a wag* wit, humorist, jester, joker, jokester, comic, comedian, comedienne, wisecracker, punner.

**wage** noun pay, remuneration. *See* WAGES 1.

**wage** verb carry on, conduct, execute, engage in, pursue, undertake.

**wager** noun bet, gamble, stake, pledge, hazard.

**wager** verb lay a wager, bet, place/make/lay a bet, lay odds, put money on, speculate.

**wages** plural noun **1** *collect one's wages* pay, payment, fee, remuneration, salary, emolument, stipend; earnings. **2** *the wages of sin* recompense, requital, retribution; returns, deserts.

**waif** noun stray, foundling, orphan.

**wail** verb cry, lament, weep, sob, moan, groan, whine, complain, howl, yowl, ululate.

**wait** verb **1** *wait here* stay, remain, rest, linger, tarry, abide. **2** *you will just have to wait and see* be patient, hold back, stand by, bide one's time, hang fire, mark time, cool one's heels; *inf.* sit tight, hold one's horses, sweat it out. **3** *wait his arrival* await, wait for, look/watch out for, anticipate, expect, be ready for, be in readiness for.

**wait** noun *have a wait of two hours for the bus* period of waiting, interval, stay, delay, holdup.

**waive** verb **1** *waive one's right to appeal* relinquish, renounce, give up, abandon, surrender, yield, cede. **2** *waive the rules* set aside, forgo, disregard, ignore. **3** *waive the decision until tomorrow* postpone, defer, put off, delay, shelve; *inf.* put on the back burner.

**wake** verb **1** *wake at dawn* awake, awaken, waken, wake up, rouse, stir, come to, get up, arise. **2** *wake him out of depression* rouse, stir up, activate, stimulate, spur, prod, galvanize, provoke. **3** *wake to the fact that he is dishonest* become aware/conscious, become alert, become mindful/heedful. **4** *wake old memories* evoke, call up, conjure up, rouse, stir, revive, resuscitate, revivify, rekindle, reignite.

**wakeful** adjective **1** *wakeful children* unsleeping, restless, tossing and turning, insomniac. **2** *wakeful security staff* alert, on the alert, vigilant, on the lookout, on one's guard, on the qui vive, watchful, observant, attentive, heedful, wary.

**walk** verb **1** *we walked rather than take the car* go by foot, travel on foot; *inf.* hoof it. **2** *walk, don't run* stroll, saunter, amble, plod, trudge, hike, tramp, trek, march, stride, step out. **3** *walk her home* accompany, escort, convoy. **walk off/away with 1** *walk off with the firm's money* make/run off with, snatch, steal, filch, pilfer, embezzle. **2** *walk off with the prize* win easily, win hands down. **walk out 1** *he had a fight with the boss and walked out* storm out; *inf.* take off. **2** *the workers walked out at lunchtime* go on strike, call a strike, stop work. **walk out on** desert, abandon, forsake, leave, leave in the lurch, throw over, jilt.

**walk** noun **1** *go for a walk* stroll, saunter, amble, promenade, ramble, hike, tramp, march, constitutional, airing. **2** *he has a distinctive walk* gait, pace, step, stride. **3** *the walk up to the house* promenade, path, pathway, footpath, track, lane, alley. **4** *the postman's usual walk* route, beat, round, run, circuit. **walk of life** social status, sphere, area, line of work, profession, career, vocation, job, employment, trade, craft, métier.

**wall** noun **1** *areas of the house separated by walls* partition, divider. **2** *the city walls are still standing* fortification, rampart, barricade, parapet, bulwark, stockade, breastwork.

**wallow** verb **1** *a hippopotamus wallowing in mud* roll, tumble about, lie around, splash around. **2** *wallow in self-pity* luxuriate, bask, indulge oneself, delight, revel, glory.

**wan** adjective **1** *looking wan after illness* pale, pallid, ashen, white as a sheet/ghost, anemic, colorless, bloodless, waxen, pasty, peaked, washed out, sickly. **2** *a wan light* dim, faint, weak.

**wand** noun baton, stick, rod, staff, twig, sprig.

**wander** verb **1** *wander over the hills* ramble, roam, meander, rove, range, prowl, saunter, stroll, amble, peregrinate, drift; *inf.* traipse. **2** *rivers wandering along* wind, meander, curve, zigzag. **3** *wander from the straight and narrow* stray, depart, diverge, veer, swerve, deviate. **4** *the narcotics make him wander* babble, talk nonsense, rave, be delirious. **wander off** lose one's way, get lost, go off course, go astray, go off on a tangent.

**wanderer** noun rambler, roamer, rover, drifter, traveler, itinerant, wayfarer, nomad, bird of passage, rolling stone, gypsy; vagabond, vagrant, hobo, tramp, derelict; *inf.* bum.

**wane** verb decrease, decline, diminish, dwindle, shrink, contract, taper off, subside, sink, ebb, dim, fade away, vanish, die out, draw to a close, evanesce, peter out, wind down, be on the way out, abate, fail.

**want** verb **1** *the child wants candy* wish, wish for, desire, demand, call for, long for, hope for, yearn for, pine for, fancy, crave, hanker after, hunger for, thirst for, lust after, covet, need; *inf.* have a yen for. **2** *he wants to emigrate* wish, desire, long, yearn. **3** *the garden wants weeding | the poor wanting food* need, be in need of, require, lack, be without, be devoid of, be bereft of, be short of, be deficient in.

**want** noun **1** *for want of time* lack, absence, dearth, deficiency, inadequacy, insufficiency, shortness, paucity, shortage, scarcity, scarceness, scantiness. **2** *children expressing their wants* wish, desire, demand, longing, yearning, fancy, craving, hankering, hunger, thirst. **3** *give aid to* *people in want* need, neediness, privation, poverty, destitution, penury, indigence.

**wanting** adjective **1** *find the service wanting* lacking, deficient, inadequate, imperfect, not up to standard/par, not good enough, disappointing, not acceptable, not up to expectations, flawed, faulty, defective, inferior, second-rate. **2** *something wanting in the machine/organization* lacking, missing, absent, not there, short.

**wanton** adjective **1** *wanton behavior* promiscuous, fast, immoral, loose, immodest, shameless, unchaste, impure, lustful, lecherous, lascivious, libidinous, licentious, libertine, dissolute, dissipated, debauched, degenerate. **2** *wanton destruction* willful, malicious, malevolent, spiteful, cruel, unmotivated, arbitrary, groundless, unjustified, uncalled-for, unprovoked, gratuitous, senseless, pointless. **3** *a wanton wind* capricious, playful, sportive, careless, heedless, devil-may-care. **4** *weeds growing in wanton profusion* wild, unrestrained, uncontrolled, immoderate, lavish, extravagant, abundant, profuse, luxuriant.

**war** noun **1** *a state of war between the nations* conflict, strife, hostility, enmity, antagonism, animus, ill will, bad blood. **2** *the war lasted five years* warfare, combat, fighting, struggle, battle, fight, confrontation, skirmish; hostilities. **3** *the war against poverty* battle, fight, campaign, crusade.

**war** verb wage/make war, be at war, do battle, fight, take up arms, cross swords, quarrel, wrangle.

**ward** verb ward off fend off, stave off, parry, avert, deflect, turn aside, drive back, repel, repulse, beat back, put to flight, keep at bay, keep at arm's length, rebuff, foil, frustrate, thwart, checkmate.

**warden** noun custodian, keeper, guardian, protector, guard, watchman.

**wares** plural noun goods, products, commodities, lines; merchandise, produce, stuff, stock.

**warfare** noun conflict, strife. *See* WAR noun 1, 2.

**warlike** adjective aggressive, belligerent, bellicose, pugnacious, combative, militaristic, militant, martial.

**warm** adjective **1** *warm water* heated, tepid, lukewarm. **2** *a warm day* sunny, balmy. **3** *a warm person* kindly, kind, friendly, affable, amiable, genial, cordial, sympathetic, affectionate, loving, tender, caring. **4** *a warm welcome* hearty, enthusiastic, eager, sincere, heartfelt, ardent, vehement, passionate, intense, fervent. **5** *the international situation is getting rather warm* heated, tense, strained, dangerous, perilous, hazardous, tricky, difficult, unpleasant, uncomfortable.

**warm** verb *warm the food in the oven* warm up, make warm, heat, heat up, reheat.

**warm up 1** *warm the party up* liven, enliven, put some life into, cheer up, animate; *inf.* get going. **2** *warm up for the race* loosen up, limber up, condition, prepare, exercise, practice, train.

**warmth** noun **1** *feel the warmth of the fire/sun* warmness, heat, hotness. **2** *the warmth of her personality* kindliness, friendliness, affability, amiability, geniality, cordiality, sympathy, tenderness, charitableness, charity, sincerity, genuineness. **3** *the warmth of the welcome* heartiness, hospitality, enthusiasm, eagerness, sincerity, ardor, vehemence, passion, intensity, fervor.

**warn** verb **1** *call to warn them of the coming storm* inform, notify, give notice, let know, alert, acquaint, give fair warning, forewarn; *inf.* tip off, put wise. **2** *warn them to be careful* advise, exhort, urge, counsel, caution, forewarn.

**warrant** noun authorization, consent, sanction, permission, validation, license, imprimatur, seal of approval.

**warrant** verb **1** *the law warrants the procedure* authorize, sanction, permit, license. **2** *her interference was not warranted* justify, vindicate, excuse, be a defense of, explain away, account for. **3** *unable to warrant the truth of the statement* guarantee, swear to, vouch for, testify to, bear witness to, support, endorse.

**warrior** noun fighter, fighting man, combatant, soldier, mercenary; champion.

**wary** adjective **1** *be wary when you walk alone at night* careful, cautious, circumspect, chary, on one's guard, alert, on the alert/look out, on the qui vive, attentive, heedful, watchful, vigilant, observant. **2** *you should be wary of strangers* suspicious, distrustful, mistrustful, leery.

**wash** verb **1** *I must wash before breakfast* wash oneself, bathe, shower, take a bath/shower. **2** *wash ones face | wash the floor* clean, cleanse, sponge, scrub. **3** *waves washing against the rocks* splash, dash, break, beat. **4** *his story just won't wash* hold up, hold water, stand up, bear scrutiny. **5** *the current washed the boat away* carry, bear, sweep, convey, transport. **6** *wash , away the riverbank* erode, abrade, wear, denude.

**wash** noun washing, clean, cleaning, cleansing; bath, shower, laundry.

**waspish** adjective petulant, peevish, querulous, touchy, testy, irritable, cross, snappish, splenetic, ill-tempered, crabby, crabbed, cantankerous, ornery.

**waste** verb **1** *waste resources/money* squander, dissipate, fritter away, misspend, misuse, spend recklessly, throw away, go through, run through; *inf.* blow. **2** *the disease had wasted his legs* weaken, enfeeble, sap the strength of, wither, debilitate, atrophy, emaciate, shrivel, shrink. **3** *the invading army wasted the land* destroy, devastate, wreak havoc on, pillage, plunder, sack, spoliate, loot, maraud.

**waste** noun **1** *a waste of money/time* squandering, dissipation, frittering away, misspending, misuse. **2** *dispose of the waste* rubbish, refuse, garbage, trash, debris, dross; dregs, leavings. **3** *lost in the waste of Antarctica* desert, wasteland, wilderness, barrenness, emptiness.

**waste** adjective **1** *waste material* left over, unused, superfluous. **2** *the land was waste* desert, barren, uncultivated, unproductive, arid, bare, desolate.

**wasteful** adjective prodigal, profligate, thriftless, spendthrift, extravagant, lavish.

**watch** verb **1** *watch the moon* look at, observe, view, eye, gaze at, stare at, gape at, peer at, contemplate, behold, inspect, scrutinize, survey, scan, examine. **2** *watch the children* mind, take care of, look after, supervise, superintend, tend, guard, protect, keep an eye on. **watch out 1** *watch out and don't get mugged* look out, pay attention, take heed/care, be careful, be on the alert/lookout, be vigilant, be wary; *inf.* keep one's eyes peeled. **2** *watch out for the delivery truck* look (out) for, wait for; *inf.* keep an eye open for. **watch over** look after, tend. *See* WATCH verb 2.

**watch** noun **1** *the time by my watch* wristwatch, pocket watch, timepiece, chronometer. **2** *on watch at night* guard, vigil, surveillance.

**watchful** adjective observant, alert, vigilant, attentive, heedful, sharp-eyed, eagle-eyed, wary, circumspect.

**watchman** noun security guard, guard, custodian, caretaker.

**water** noun **1** *drink water* $H_2O$; tap water, drinking water, mineral water, bottled water. **2** *have a picnic by the water* sea, ocean, sound, bay, river, lake, pond, pool, reservoir. **hold water** be tenable, ring true, bear examination, work out.

**water** verb **1** *water the garden* sprinkle, moisten, dampen, wet, water down, douse, hose, spray, drench, saturate, sodden, flood. **2** *water the drinks* water down, dilute, thin, weaken, adulterate. **water down** *water down the extent of the disaster* play down, downplay, tone down, soft-pedal, understate, underemphasize.

**waterfall** noun cascade, cataract; falls.

**watery** adjective **1** *a watery substance* aqueous, liquid, liquefied, fluid, hydrous. **2** *watery terrain* wet, damp, moist, sodden, soggy, saturated, waterlogged, marshy, boggy, swampy, miry. **3** *a watery soup/batter* thin, runny, weak, dilute, diluted, watered down, adulterated, tasteless, flavorless.

**wave** verb **1** *wheat waving in the breeze* undulate, ripple, stir, flutter, flap, sway, swing, shake, quiver, oscillate. **2** *wave one's hand/flag* wag, waggle, flutter. **3** *wave a sword in the air* brandish, swing, shake. **4** *wave to them to follow* gesture, gesticulate, signal, sign, beckon, indicate.

**wave** noun **1** *children playing in the waves* breaker, billow, roller, ripple, whitecap; swell, surf. **2** *a wave of visitors* stream, flow, rush, surge, flood. **3** *a wave of enthusiasm* surge, upsurge, groundswell, welling up, rush, outbreak, rash.

**waver** verb **1** *his gaze did not waver* falter, wobble, hesitate. **2** *waver between staying and leaving* hesitate, dither, hem and haw, vacillate, shilly-shally. **3** *lights wavering* flicker, quiver, tremble.

**wavy** adjective undulating, curvy, curling, squiggly, rippled, curving, winding.

**wax** verb **1** *his power waxed in time of war* increase, develop, enlarge, magnify, extend, widen, broaden, spread, mushroom. **2** *wax lyrical about his achievements* become, grow.

**way** noun **1** *walk along the paved way* road, roadway, street, thoroughfare, track, path, pathway, lane, avenue, drive. **2** *is this the way to their house?* route, course, direction. **3** *the right way to cook the meat* method, procedure, technique, system, plan, scheme, manner, modus operandi; means. **4** *the American way* conduct, behavior, practice, wont, manner, style, nature, personality, temperament, disposition, character; habit, custom, characteristic, trait, attribute, mannerism, peculiarity, idiosyncrasy. **5** *a long way from here* distance, length, stretch, journey. **6** *things are in a bad way* state, condition, situation, shape. **7** *can I help in any way?* feature, aspect, detail, point, particular, respect, sense. **by the way** incidentally, by the by, in passing. **give way 1** *the bridge gave way* collapse, give, fall to pieces, crumble, cave in. **2** *he refused to help but finally gave way* yield, back down, acquiesce. **on the/one's way** coming, going, proceeding, journeying, traveling.

**waylay** verb lie in wait for, ambush, hold up, attack; accost, intercept, pounce on, swoop down on.

**wayward** adjective **1** *wayward children* willful, contrary, uncooperative, refractory, recalcitrant, contumacious, unruly, ungovernable, unmanageable, incorrigible, intractable, difficult, fractious, disobedient, insubordinate. **2** *wayward fancies* capricious, whimsical, fickle, inconstant, changeable, unpredictable, mercurial, volatile, flighty.

**weak** adjective **1** *too weak to walk* weakly, frail, fragile, delicate, feeble, infirm, shaky, debilitated, incapacitated, ailing, indisposed, decrepit, puny, faint, enervated, tired, fatigued, spent. **2** *too weak to stand up for his rights* timid, spineless, ineffectual, powerless, impotent, namby-pamby, soft, weak-kneed. **3** *weak eyesight* defective, faulty, poor, inadequate, deficient, imperfect, substandard. **4** *weak excuses* unsound, feeble, flimsy, lame, unconvincing, untenable, implausible. **5** *a weak sound/signal* faint, low, muffled, stifled, muted. **6** *weak coffee* diluted, watery, thinned down, thin, adulterated, tasteless, flavorless, insipid; *inf.* wishy-washy.

**weaken** verb **1** *the illness had weakened her* enfeeble, debilitate, incapacitate, sap one's strength, enervate, tire, exhaust, wear out. **2** *weaken the force of the argument* lessen, reduce, decrease, diminish, moderate, temper, sap. **3** *the force of the storm weakened* abate, dwindle, ease up, let up. **4** *weaken the argument* impair, undermine, invalidate. **5** *they first refused to help but weakened later* relent, give in, yield, give way, accede, come around. **6** *too much milk weakened the coffee* dilute, water down, thin, adulterate.

**weakling** noun coward, mouse, milksop, namby-pamby, sissy; *inf.* wimp, chicken, yellowbelly, fraidy-cat, scaredy-cat.

**weakness** noun **1** *the weakness of the invalid* frailty, fragility, delicateness, delicacy, feebleness, infirmity, debility, incapacity, indisposition, decrepitude, puniness, enervation, fatigue. **2** *despise his weakness* cowardliness, timidity, spinelessness, ineffectuality, ineptness, powerlessness, impotence. **3** *the weakness of her eyesight* defectiveness, faultiness, inadequacy, deficiency. **4** *the weakness of the excuses* unsoundness, feebleness, flimsiness, lameness, untenability, implausibility. **5** *the weakness of the sound/light* faintness, mutedness, dimness. **6** *the weakness of the coffee* wateriness, thinness, tastelessness, flavorlessness; *inf.* wishy-washiness. **7** *extravagance is one of her weaknesses* weak point, failing, foible, fault, flaw, defect, shortcoming, imperfection, blemish, Achilles' heel, chink in one's armor. **8** *a weakness for chocolate* soft spot, fondness, liking, partiality, preference, leaning, inclination, proclivity.

**wealth** noun **1** *amass wealth* money, cash, capital, treasure, fortune, finance, property; riches, assets, possessions, resources, goods, funds, wherewithal; *inf.* dough, bread. **2** *people of wealth* richness, money, affluence, prosperity, substance; means. **3** *a wealth of opportunities* mass, abundance, profusion, plenitude, amplitude, bounty, cornucopia.

**wealthy** adjective rich, well off, well-to-do, moneyed, affluent, prosperous, of means, of substance; *inf.* well-heeled, rolling in it/money, in the money, made of money, filthy/stinking rich, loaded, flush, on easy street.

**wear** verb **1** *wear beautiful clothes* be dressed in, dress in, be clothed in, cloth oneself in, have on, put on, don, sport. **2** *she wore an anxious expression* have, assume, present, show, display, exhibit. **3** *wind and rain have worn the rock* erode, corrode, abrade, wash away, rub away, rub down, grind away, wear down/away. **4** *the carpet is starting to wear* become worn, show signs of wear, wear thin, fray, become threadbare. **5** *she is worn by the whole experience* fatigue, exhaust. *See* WEAR OUT 2 (WEAR verb). **6** *this carpet has worn well* last, endure, hold up, survive, bear up, stand up to wear, prove durable. **wear down 1** *the steps have become worn down* wear away, erode. *See* WEAR verb 3. **2** *wear down their resistance* erode, undermine; *inf.* chip away at. **wear off** *the novelty will soon wear off* fade, peter out, dwindle, decrease, diminish, disappear, subside, ebb, wane. **wear on** *as time wore on* pass, go by, move on, roll on. **wear out 1** *children wear out their clothes quickly* wear thin, make threadbare, fray. **2** *the job has quite worn her out* fatigue, tire, weary, exhaust, drain, strain, stress, weaken, enfeeble, prostrate, enervate; *inf.* wear to a frazzle, poop out.

**wear** noun **1** *clothes/items for everyday wear* use, service, employment. **2** *pack away her winter wear* clothing, attire, apparel, wardrobe; clothes, garments, outfits; *inf.* gear. **3** *showing signs of wear and tear* erosion, corrosion, abrasion, deterioration, degeneration, damage.

**weary** adjective **1** *weary at the end of a hard day's work* fatigued, tired, exhausted, drained, worn, worn out, spent, wearied; *inf.* dead tired/beat, dead on one's feet, dog-tired, all in, done in, pooped (out), bushed. **2** *a weary journey* wearisome, fatiguing, tiring, exhausting, wearing, trying, taxing, irksome, tiresome, laborious, boring, tedious, dull. **3** *she is weary of the job* bored, fed up, discontented, jaded.

**weary** verb fatigue, tire, exhaust, drain, wear out; *inf.* wear to a frazzle, poop out.

**weather** noun **under the weather** below par, unwell, out of sorts, indisposed, ailing, ill, sick.

**weather** verb **1** *weather the wood* dry, season, expose. **2** *rocks weathered by storms* erode, wear, bleach. **3** *weather the recession* survive, withstand, bear up against, stand, endure, ride out; *inf.* stick out.

**weave** verb **1** *weave flowers into garlands* interlace, intertwine, interwork, entwine, braid, plait. **2** *weave a story* make up, fabricate, put together, construct, invent, create, contrive. **3** *weave in and out of the crowds* zigzag, wind, crisscross.

**web** noun lacework, lattice, latticework, mesh, net, netting; network, tissue, tangle, knot.

**wed** verb **1** *they wed tomorrow* get married, marry; *inf.* get hitched, tie the knot. **2** *the two firms have been virtually wedded for years* unite, join, merge, amalgamate, fuse, link, ally.

**wedded** adjective married, marital, matrimonial, connubial, conjugal, nuptial.

**wedge** noun chunk, lump, block.

**wedge** verb *wedged himself into the crowded backseat* thrust, stuff, pack, ram, force, cram, squeeze, jam.

**weep** verb cry, shed tears, sob, blubber, snivel, whimper, whine, moan, lament, grieve, mourn, keen, wail; *inf.* boo-hoo.

**weigh** verb **1** *the child weighs 50 pounds* have a weight of; *inf.* tip the scales at. **2** *weigh one plan against the other* balance, compare, evaluate. **weigh down** load (down), overload, burden, overburden, weigh on, bear down on, press down on, oppress, trouble. **weigh up** *weigh up the situation* consider, contemplate, think over, mull over, ponder, deliberate upon, meditate on, muse on, brood over, reflect on.

**weight** noun **1** *what is the weight of the flour?* heaviness; poundage, tonnage. **2** *lack of money is a weight on his mind* burden, load, onus, millstone, albatross, strain, millstone around one's neck, cross to bear. **3** *how much weight is attached to his statement?* importance, significance, consequence, value, substance, force, influence; *inf.* clout.

**weighty** adjective **1** *weighty loads* heavy, massive, burdensome, cumbersome, ponderous, hefty. **2** *weighty responsibility* burdensome, onerous, oppressive, worrisome, stressful. **3** *weighty matters* important, of great import, significant, momentous, of moment, consequential, of consequence, vital, crucial, serious, grave. **4** *weighty arguments* cogent, powerful, potent, forceful, effective, persuasive.

**weird** adjective **1** *weird things were happening* strange, queer, uncanny, eerie, mysterious, mystifying, unnatural, unearthly, ghostly; *inf.* spooky, creepy. **2** *she wears weird clothes* odd, eccentric, bizarre, outlandish, freakish, grotesque; *inf.* offbeat, far-out, way-out.

**welcome** noun *receive a welcome from their hostess* greeting, salutation, reception.

**welcome** verb bid welcome to, greet, receive, embrace, receive with open arms, roll out the red carpet for, meet, usher in.

**welcome** adjective *welcome guests/news* wanted, appreciated, desirable, pleasant, agreeable, to one's liking.

**welfare** noun **1** *concern for the welfare of the firm* well-being, health, soundness, security, prosperity, success, good fortune. **2** *poor families on welfare* state aid, public assistance; social security, dole.

**well** adverb **1** *behave well* satisfactorily, correctly, rightly, properly, fittingly, suitably, nicely. **2** *get on well* agreeably, pleasantly, happily; *inf.* capitally. **3** *he plays the piano well* ably, competently, proficiently, adeptly, skillfully, expertly, admirably, excellently. **4** *treat their guests well* kindly, in a kind/kindly way, genially, affably, generously, hospitably, civilly, politely. **5** *polish it well* thoroughly, completely, efficiently, effectively, conscientiously, industriously, carefully. **6** *we don't know her well* fully, deeply, profoundly, intimately, personally. **7** *listen to it well* closely, attentively, carefully, conscientiously. **8** *speak well of him* highly, admiringly, with praise, glowingly, approvingly, favorably, warmly. **9** *live well* comfortably, in comfort, prosperously. **10** *you may well be right* probably, possibly, likely, undoubtedly, certainly. **11** *he is well over forty* considerably, markedly, substantially. **12** *it bodes well for the future* auspiciously, propitiously. **as well** too, also, in addition, besides, into the bargain, to boot.

**well** adjective **1** *the patient is quite well now* healthy, in good health, fit, strong, robust, hale and hearty, able-bodied. **2** *all is well now* satisfactory, all right, (just) fine, good, thriving, flourishing; *inf.* OK, fine and dandy. **3** *it would be well to leave early* advisable, fitting, proper, wise, prudent, sensible.

**well-being** noun good health, happiness, comfort. *See* WELFARE 1.

**well-bred** adjective well brought up, mannerly, well-mannered, courteous, polite, civil, ladylike, gentlemanly, gallant, chivalrous, cultivated, refined, polished, cultured.

**well-known** adjective known, familiar; famous, famed, renowned, celebrated, noted, notable, illustrious, eminent.

**well off** adjective **1** *his parents are poor but he is very well off* rich, well-to-do. *See* WEALTHY. **2** *he doesn't know when he is well off* fortunate, lucky, comfortable, thriving, successful, flourishing.

**well-spoken** adjective articulate, eloquent, fluent, silver-tongued, smooth-talking.

**wet** adjective **1** *wet clothes/ground* damp, dampened, moist, moistened; soaked, drenched, saturated, sopping/dripping/wringing wet, sopping, dripping, soggy, waterlogged. **2** *a wet day* rainy, raining, pouring, showery, drizzling, damp, humid, dank, misty. **wet blanket** killjoy; *inf.* party pooper, gloomy Gus.

**wet** noun **1** *the wet damaged the table/land* wetness, damp, dampness, moisture, condensation, humidity, water, liquid. **2** *get in out of the wet* rain, drizzle, damp.

**wet** verb dampen, damp, moisten, sprinkle, spray, splash, water, irrigate, douse, wet through, soak, saturate.

**wharf** noun pier, quay, dock, jetty; mooring(s).

**wheedle** verb coax, cajole, beguile, charm, flatter, inveigle, win over, talk into, persuade, induce, entice, influence; *inf.* butter up.

**wheel** noun disk, hoop, circle, ring. **at the wheel** driving, steering; in charge, in command, in control; *inf.* at the helm, in the driver's seat.

**wheel** verb **1** *birds wheeling around* circle, rotate, revolve, spin. **2** *wheel a stroller* push, shove, trundle.

**wheeze** verb gasp, whistle, hiss, rasp.

**whet** verb **1** *whet a blade* sharpen, put an edge on, edge, hone, strop, file, grind, rasp. **2** *whet the curiosity* stimulate, excite, arouse, rouse, kindle, quicken.

**whiff** noun **1** *a whiff of air* puff, breath, gust, draft. **2** *a whiff of the perfume* smell, scent, odor, aroma, stink, reek. **3** *a whiff of scandal* hint, suggestion, trace, suspicion, soupçon.

**while** noun time, spell, period, interval.

**whim** noun **1** *have a sudden whim* notion, fancy, idea, impulse, urge, caprice, vagary. **2** *behavior ruled by whim* whimsy, capriciousness, caprice, volatility, fickleness.

**whimper** verb whine, cry, sniffle, snivel, moan, wail, groan.

**whimsical** adjective fanciful, fantastical, playful, waggish, quaint, unusual, curious, droll.

**whine** verb whimper, cry; complain, grumble, moan, groan, fuss, lament; *inf.* grouse, gripe, bellyache, beef.

**whip** verb **1** *condemned for whipping his crew* lash, flog, scourge, flagellate, birch, switch, strap, cane, thrash, beat, strike, castigate; *inf.* belt, tan, give a hiding to, beat the living daylights out of. **2** *whip a handkerchief from his pocket* whisk, flash, snatch, pull, yank, jerk, produce, remove. **3** *he whipped around the corner* dart, dash, dive, dodge, shoot, tear, rush, fly, bolt, zoom. **4** *whip the opposition at football* defeat, overcome, overpower, overwhelm, thrash, trounce, crush, rout. **5** *whip them into a frenzy* rouse, stir up, incite, goad, prod, spur, prompt, agitate.

**whip** noun lash, scourge, flagellum, horsewhip, bullwhip, cat o'nine tails, knout, birch, switch, thong, crop, riding crop, cane.

**whirl** verb **1** *dancers whirling* circle, spin, rotate, revolve, wheel, twirl, swirl, gyrate, reel, pirouette, pivot. **2** *buses whirling past* speed, rush, race, shoot, tear, charge, whip. **3** *my head is whirling* go round, spin, reel.

**whirl** noun **1** *give the wheel a whirl* turn, spin, rotation, revolution, wheel, twirl, swirl, gyration, reel, pirouette, pivot. **2** *the social whirl* activity, bustle, flurry, to-do, hurly-burly. **3** *a whirl of parties* round, succession, series, sequence, progression, string, chain, cycle. **4** *with heads in a whirl* spin, dither, daze, muddle, jumble. **5** *give the new game a whirl* try, tryout, test, go; *inf.* shot, stab.

**whirlpool** noun vortex, maelstrom, eddy.

**whirlwind** noun cyclone, tornado, twister, dust devil.

**whirlwind** adjective lightning, swift, rapid, quick, speedy, hasty, headlong, impulsive.

**whisk** verb **1** *the horse whisked its tail* wave, flick, brandish. **2** *whisk the table clean | whisk away the crumbs* brush, sweep, wipe. **3** *whisk a handkerchief out of his pocket* snatch, pull. See WHIP verb 2. **4** *the cat whisked around the corner* dart, dash. See WHIP verb 3.

**whisper** verb **1** *whisper endearments* murmur, mutter, breathe, say under the breath. **2** *trees whispering in the wind* rustle, sigh, sough, swish, swoosh.

**whisper** noun **1** *speak in a whisper* murmur, mutter, hushed tone, undertone. **2** *the whisper of trees in the wind* rustle, sigh, sough, swish, swoosh. **3** *there is a whisper that he has been promoted* rumor, report, insinuation, suggestion, hint; gossip, word. **4** *a whisper of hostility about the room* whiff, trace, tinge, hint, suggestion, suspicion.

**white** adjective **1** *a white face* white as a ghost/sheet, chalk-white, pale, wan, pallid, ashen, waxen, pasty, peaky. **2** *white hair* gray, silver, hoary, snow-white.

**white-collar** adjective office, clerical, professional, executive, salaried.

**whittle** verb cut, hew, pare, shave, trim; carve, shape, model. **whittle away 1** *inflation whittled away their savings* wear away, eat away, erode, consume, use up, undermine, destroy. **2** *the number of employees has been whittled away* reduce, lessen, decrease, diminish, cut back.

**whole** adjective **1** *three whole days* entire, complete, full, total, solid, integral, unabridged, unreduced, undivided, uncut. **2** *he came home whole* intact, sound, flawless, in one piece, unimpaired, undamaged, unharmed, unhurt, uninjured, unmutilated.

**whole** noun entity, unit, ensemble, totality, entirety. **on the whole 1** *on the whole, he is perfect for the job* all in all, all things considered, by and large. **2** *on the whole, he works late* as a rule, as a general rule, generally, in the main, for the most part.

**wholehearted** adjective enthusiastic, zealous, earnest, committed, unreserved, unqualified, unstinting, complete, sincere, genuine.

**wholesome** adjective health-giving, healthful, good for one, salubrious, salutary; uplifting, edifying, helpful, beneficial.

**wholly** adverb **1** *wholly in favor of the scheme* completely, fully, entirely, totally, utterly, thoroughly, altogether, unreservedly, heart and soul; *inf.* one hundred percent. **2** *the burden rests wholly on his shoulders* only, solely, exclusively, purely.

**whoop** noun cry, call, shout, yell, scream, shriek, hoot, cheer, hurrah; *inf.* holler.

**whore** noun prostitute, call girl, streetwalker, harlot, lady of the evening/night, *fille de joie*, woman of ill repute, wanton, loose woman, trollop, slut, fallen woman, courtesan; *inf.* tart, hooker, hustler.

**wicked** adjective **1** *a wicked man* evil, sinful, bad, black-hearted, villainous, base, vile, vicious, dishonorable, unprincipled, unrighteous, criminal, lawless, perverted, immoral, amoral, unethical, corrupt, dissolute, abandoned, dissipated, degenerate, reprobate, debauched, depraved, unholy, impious, irreligious, ungodly, godless, devilish. **2** *his wicked deeds* sinful, iniquitous, wrong, foul, mean, gross, odious, obnoxious, nefarious, heinous, flagitious, infamous, dreadful, dire, grim, horrible, hideous, gruesome, monstrous, atrocious, abominable, abhorrent, loathsome, hateful, detestable, reprehensible, dishonorable, disgraceful, shameful, ignoble, ignominious, unlawful, illicit, illegal, villainous, dastardly, blackguardly, profane, blasphemous, irreverent, damnable, demonic, diabolic. **3** *hurt by her wicked remarks* spiteful, malicious, malignant, nasty, offensive, hurtful, distressing, galling, vexatious. **4** *aim a wicked blow* dangerous, perilous, destructive, harmful, injurious, ferocious, fierce, terrible, mighty. **5** *a wicked sense of humor* mischievous, impish, roguish, arch, rascally, naughty. **6** *the weather has been wicked* nasty, unpleasant, disagreeable, dreadful, terrible, awful.

**wide** adjective **1** *a wide river/building* broad, extensive, spacious, spread out, ample. **2** *a wide range of subjects* extensive, vast,

far-ranging, immense, wide-ranging, expansive, sweeping, encyclopedic, comprehensive, general, all-embracing, catholic, compendious.

**wide** adverb **1** *open your mouth wide* as far as possible, fully, completely. **2** *he shot wide* wide of the mark/target, off target, off course, astray. **wide awake 1** *still wide awake at dawn* fully awake, open-eyed. **2** *you have to be wide awake to do business with them* alert, vigilant, wary, chary, watchful, observant, attentive, heedful, aware; *inf.* on one's toes, on the ball. **wide open 1** *with eyes wide open* fully, dilated, gaping. **2** *with arms wide open* outspread, spread open, outstretched. **3** *wide open to attack* exposed, vulnerable, unprotected, unguarded, defenseless, at risk, in danger. **4** *the outcome of the game was wide open* uncertain, unsure, indeterminate, unsettled, unpredictable, in the balance, up in the air, anyone's guess.

**widen** verb broaden, expand, extend, enlarge, increase, augment, add to, supplement.

**widespread** adjective universal, common, general, far-reaching, far-flung, prevalent, rife, extensive, sweeping, pervasive, epidemic.

**width** noun wideness, breadth, broadness, span, diameter, thickness, ampleness, scope, range, span, extensiveness, vastness.

**wield** verb **1** *wield a sword* brandish, flourish, wave, swing, shake, use, put to use, employ, handle, ply, manipulate. **2** *wield the power in the country* exercise, exert, be possessed of, have, hold, maintain, command, control, manage.

**wife** noun spouse, mate, consort, woman, helpmate, squaw, bride; *inf.* better/other half, missus; *derog.* old woman/lady, the little woman, the lady of the house.

**wild** adjective **1** *wild cats/horses* untamed, undomesticated, unbroken, feral, savage, fierce, ferocious. **2** *wild plants* uncultivated, natural, native, indigenous. **3** *wild peoples/tribes* uncivilized, primitive, ignorant, savage, barbaric, barbarous, brutish, ferocious, fierce. **4** *wild countryside* unpopulated, uninhabited, unsettled, unfrequented, empty, barren, waste, desolate, forsaken, godforsaken, isolated. **5** *a wild night* stormy, tempestuous, turbulent, blustery, howling, violent, raging, furious, rough. **6** *a wild life* undisciplined, unrestrained, unconstrained, uncontrolled, out of control, uncurbed, unbridled, unchecked, chaotic, disorderly. **7** *a wild crowd* rowdy, unruly, disorderly, noisy, turbulent, violent, lawless, riotous, unmanageable, ungovernable. **8** *the crowd went wild* beside oneself, berserk, frantic, frenzied, in a frenzy, hysterical, crazed, mad, distracted, distraught; *inf.* crazy. **9** *lost his temper and was wild* angry, infuriated, incensed, exasperated, in a temper, seething, mad. **10** *wild schemes* extravagant, fantastical, impracticable, foolish, ill-advised, ill-considered, imprudent, unwise, madcap, impulsive, reckless, rash, outrageous, preposterous. **11** *wild about rock music* enthusiastic, eager, avid, agog; *inf.* crazy, mad, nuts. **12** *a wild guess* arbitrary, random, hit-or-miss, haphazard, uninformed, unknowledgeable. **13** *wild hair* uncombed, unkempt, disheveled, tousled, windblown, disarranged, untidy.

**wilderness** noun **1** *the Arctic wilderness* desert, wasteland, waste, jungle, no-man's land; wilds. **2** *a wilderness of cars* confusion, tangle, jumble, muddle, clutter, miscellany, hodgepodge.

**wile** noun trickery, craftiness, craft, cunning, artfulness, slyness, guile, chicanery, fraud, deception; trick, dodge, ruse, subterfuge, ploy, stratagem, lure, artifice, maneuver, device, contrivance.

**will**[1] verb *come when you will* wish, want, desire, please, see/think fit, think best, choose, prefer, opt, elect.

**will**[2] verb **1** *God willed it* decree, order, ordain, command, direct, bid, intend, wish, desire. **2** *will him all her books* bequeath, leave, give, hand/pass down to, pass on to, transfer to.

**will**[3] noun **1** *freedom of will* volition, choice, option, decision, discretion, prerogative, desire, wish, preference, inclination, fancy, mind. **2** *it is the will of God* decree, ordinance, dictate. **3** *he lacks the will to succeed* willpower, determination, resolution, resolve, firmness of purpose, purposefulness, doggedness, single-mindedness, commitment, moral fiber, pluck, mettle, grit, nerve. **4** *bear him ill will* feeling, disposition, attitude. **at will** *come and go at will* as one wishes/pleases, as one thinks fit, to suit oneself.

**willful** adjective **1** *willful neglect* deliberate, intentional, intended, conscious, purposeful, premeditated, planned, calculated. **2** *coping with willful children* headstrong, strong-willed, obstinate, stubborn, stubborn as a mule, mulish, pigheaded, bullheaded, obdurate, intransigent, intractable, refractory, recalcitrant, contrary, perverse, wayward.

**willing** adjective **1** *willing helpers* ready, eager, keen, enthusiastic, avid. **2** *willing to accept responsibility* prepared, ready, disposed, agreeable, amenable, in the mood, compliant; *inf.* game. **3** *willing help* cooperative, accommodating, obliging.

**willpower** noun strength of will, determination. *See* WILL[3] 3.

**wilt** verb **1** *plants wilting* droop, wither, shrivel, sag, languish. **2** *their courage wilted* diminish, dwindle, lessen, grow less, flag, fade, melt away, ebb, wane, weaken, fail.

**wily** adjective crafty, cunning, artful, sharp, astute, shrewd, scheming, intriguing, shifty, foxy, sly, guileful, deceitful, deceptive, underhanded.

**win** verb **1** *win first prize* achieve, attain, earn, gain, receive, obtain, acquire, procure, get, secure, collect, pick up, come away with, net; *inf.* bag. **2** *may the best side win* be victorious, gain the victory, overcome, achieve mastery, carry the day, finish first, come out ahead, come out on top, succeed, triumph, prevail, win out. **win over** bring around, persuade, induce, influence, sway, prevail upon, convert.

**win** noun victory, conquest, success, triumph.

**wince** verb grimace, start, flinch, blench, quail, shrink, recoil, cringe, squirm.

**wind** noun **1** *a day almost entirely without wind* zephyr, breeze, gust, blast, gale. **2** *need a lot of wind to play the trombone* breath, respiration; *inf.* puff. **3** *a pompous fool full of wind* empty talk, talk, babble, blather, boasting, bluster, braggadocio; *inf.* hot air, baloney, gas. **4** *wind of a scandal* rumor, gossip, hint, suggestion, inkling, intimation; news, information, report, intelligence. **in the wind** about to happen, in the offing, on the way, coming near, close at hand, approaching, impending, looming, in the cards.

**wind** verb **1** *the road winds up the hill* twist, twist and turn, curve, bend, loop, zigzag, snake, spiral, meander, ramble. **2** *smoke winding up into the sky* curl, spiral, wreathe, snake. **3** *wind the yarn into a ball* twist, twine, coil, wrap, roll. **wind down 1** *the runners need to wind down after a race* unwind, relax, ease up, calm down, cool off. **2** *schoolwork is winding down for the summer* slacken off, taper off, dwindle, diminish, lessen, decline, come to an end/close. **wind up 1** *he gets wound up easily* make tense, strain, make nervous, work up, put on edge, agitate, fluster, disconcert, discompose. **2** *it's time to wind up the meeting* end, conclude, terminate, finish; *inf.* wrap up. **3** *we wound up in a remote village* end up, finish, find oneself.

**windy** adjective **1** *a windy day* breezy, blowy, blustery, blustering, gusty, gusting, boisterous, squally, stormy, wild, tempestuous, turbulent. **2** *a windy speech* long-winded, loquacious, wordy, verbose, rambling, meandering, prolix, diffuse, turgid, bombastic.

**wing** noun **1** *the extreme wing of the party* arm, side, branch, section, segment, group, grouping, circle, faction, clique, set, coterie, cabal. **2** *the east wing of the house* extension, annex, addition, ell.

**wing** verb **1** *birds winging through the air* fly, glide, soar. **2** *winged to the finish line* zoom, speed, race, hurry, hasten. **3** *the bullet winged the bird/soldier* wound, hit, clip.

**wink** verb **1** *wink an eye* blink, flutter, bat, nictitate. **2** *lights winking across the water* flash, twinkle, sparkle, glitter, gleam. **wink at** *wink at the child's mistakes* turn a blind eye to, close/shut one's eyes to, blink at, ignore, overlook, disregard, let pass, condone, tolerate.

**winner** noun champion, victor, vanquisher, conqueror, conquering hero, prizewinner.

**wintry** adjective **1** *a wintry day* cold, chilly, icy, frosty, freezing, frozen, snowy, arctic, glacial, biting, piercing, nippy. **2** *a wintry look* unfriendly, cool, chilly, cold, distant, remote, bleak, cheerless.

**wipe** verb rub, brush, dust, mop, sponge, swab, clean, dry. **wipe off** rub off, brush off, mop up, sponge off, clean off, remove, get rid of, take off, take away, erase, efface. **wipe out** destroy, demolish, annihilate, exterminate, eradicate, eliminate, extirpate, obliterate, expunge, erase, blot out, extinguish.

**wiry** adjective **1** *wiry youths* lean, spare, sinewy, tough, strong. **2** *wiry brushes* bristly, prickly, thorny, stiff, rigid.

**wisdom** noun **1** *the wisdom of the old man* sageness, sagacity, enlightenment, reason, philosophy, discernment, perception, insight. **2** *admire their wisdom in leaving early* sense, common sense, prudence, judiciousness, judgment, shrewdness.

**wise** adjective **1** *she is a wise woman* sage, sagacious, enlightened, philosophic, deepthinking, discerning, perceptive, experienced. **2** *a wise decision* sensible, prudent, well-advised, judicious, politic, shrewd, astute, smart, reasonable.

**wish** verb **1** *wish to travel abroad* want, desire, long, yearn, aspire. **2** *they wish you to go now* demand, bid, ask, require, instruct, direct, order, command. **wish for** fancy, crave, hunger for, thirst for, lust after, covet, sigh for, set one's heart on; *inf.* hanker after, have a yen for.

**wish** noun desire, longing, hope, yearning, want, fancy, aspiration, inclination, urge, whim, craving, hunger, thirst, lust; *inf.* hankering, yen.

**wishy-washy** adjective **1** *he is a bit wishy-washy* weak, feeble, puny, ineffectual, effete, spineless, irresolute, weak-kneed. **2** *wishy-washy soup* tasteless, flavorless, insipid, watery, weak, diluted.

**wistful** adjective yearning, longing, melancholy, sad, mournful, dreaming, dreamy, daydreaming, in a reverie, pensive, reflective, musing.

**wit** noun **1** *he did not have the wit to understand* intelligence, intellect, cleverness, wisdom, sageness, sagacity, judgment, common sense, understanding, comprehension, reason, sharpness, astuteness, shrewdness, acumen, discernment, perspicacity, perception, percipience, insight, ingenuity; brains. **2** *a person of great wit* wittiness, humor, jocularity, drollery, waggishness, repartee, badinage, banter, raillery. **3** *one of the great wits of his time* humorist, wag, comic, jokester, farceur; *inf.* card.

**witch** noun **1** *the witch cast a spell* sorceress, enchantress, magician, necromancer. **2** *dressed up as an ugly old witch* hag, ogress, crone, gorgon; virago, termagant, shrew, harridan.

**witchcraft** noun witchery, sorcery, black art/magic, magic, necromancy, wizardry, occultism, the occult, sortilege, thaumaturgy.

**withdraw** verb **1** *withdraw the poker from the fire* take back, pull back, take away, extract, remove. **2** *asked to withdraw their remarks* retract, recall, unsay. **3** *Congress withdrew the bill* revoke, annul, nullify, declare void, rescind, repeal, abrogate. **4** *withdraw from the group* draw back, go back, absent oneself, detach oneself. **5** *the troops withdrew* pull back, fall back, retire, retreat, disengage, depart, go, leave.

**withdrawn** adjective retiring, reserved, uncommunicative, unsociable, taciturn, silent, quiet, introverted, detached, aloof, distant, private, shrinking, timid, timorous, shy, bashful, diffident.

**wither** verb dry up/out, desiccate, shrivel, go limp, wilt; fade, ebb, wane, die.

**withhold** verb **1** *unable to withhold their laughter* hold back, keep back, restrain, check, curb, repress, suppress. **2** *withhold permission* refuse, decline.

**without** preposition **1** *they were three days without food* lacking, short of, wanting, requiring, deprived of, destitute of. **2** *he arrived without her* unaccompanied by, unescorted by, in the absence of. **3** *that is the price without tax* exclusive of, excluding, not including, not counting.

**withstand** verb hold out against, resist, fight, combat, oppose, endure, stand, tolerate, bear, put up with, take, cope with, weather, brave, defy.

**witness** noun **1** *a witness to the accident* eyewitness, observer, spectator, onlooker, looker-on, viewer, watcher, beholder, bystander. **2** *his ragged clothes were witness* of his poverty evidence, testimony, confirmation, corroboration, proof. **bear witness to** testify to, attest to, be evidence of, confirm, corroborate, be proof of, prove, bear out, vouch for, betoken.

**witness** verb **1** *they witnessed the accident* see, observe, view, watch, look on at, behold, perceive, be present at, attend. **2** *witness his will/signature* endorse, countersign, sign. **witness to** testify to, attest to. *See* BEAR WITNESS TO (WITNESS noun).

**witty** adjective clever, ingenious, scintillating, humorous, amusing, jocular, funny, facetious, droll, waggish, comic.

**wizard** noun **1** *wizards casting spells* sorcerer, warlock, enchanter, witch, necromancer, magician. **2** *he is a wizard at the piano* expert, master, genius, virtuoso, maestro, star, ace, whiz.

**wobble** verb **1** *the table/runner wobbled* rock, sway, seesaw, teeter, shake, vibrate, totter, stagger, waddle, waggle. **2** *her voice wobbled with emotion* shake, tremble, quiver, quaver. **3** *the politicians were wobbling* waver, vacillate, hesitate, dither, shilly-shally.

**woe** noun **1** *a tale of woe* misery, wretchedness, grief, anguish, affliction, suffering, pain, agony, torment, sorrow, sadness, unhappiness, distress, heartache, heartbreak, despondency, desolation, dejection, depression, gloom, melancholy. **2** *she told everyone her woes* trouble, misfortune, adversity, trial, tribulation, ordeal, burden, affliction, disaster, calamity, catastrophe; trials and tribulations.

**woeful** adjective **1** *woeful tales of poverty* sad, saddening, unhappy, sorrowful, miserable, dismal, wretched, doleful, gloomy, tragic, pathetic, grievous, pitiful, plaintive, heart-rending, heartbreaking, distressing, anguished, agonizing, dreadful, terrible. **2** *the army will meet a woeful fate* disastrous, ruinous, calamitous, catastrophic. **3** *a woeful piece of work* poor, bad, inadequate, substandard, lamentable, deplorable, disgraceful, wretched, appalling, terrible, shocking; inf. rotten, lousy.

**woman** noun **1** *women and children first* female, lady, girl, she; derog. inf. chick, dame. **2** *he has a new woman* girlfriend, female friend, lady love, sweetheart, partner, lover, wife.

**womanizer** noun lady-killer, ladies' man, philanderer, seducer, lecher, lech, Casanova, Don Juan, lothario; inf. wolf.

**wonder** noun **1** *children gazing with wonder at the Christmas tree* wonderment, awe, surprise, astonishment, amazement, bewilderment, stupefaction, fascination, admiration. **2** *one of the wonders of the world* marvel, phenomenon, miracle, prodigy, curiosity, rarity.

**wonder** verb **1** *she wondered what to do next* think, speculate, ponder, muse, ask oneself, puzzle. **2** *they wondered at the beauty of the church* marvel, stand in awe, gape, gawk, look agog; inf. be flabbergasted.

**wonderful** adjective **1** *the church ceiling was wonderful to behold* marvelous, awe-inspiring, awesome, remarkable, extraordinary, phenomenal, prodigious, miraculous, fantastic, amazing, astonishing, astounding, surprising, incredible, unprecedented, unparalleled, unheard-of; lit. wondrous. **2** *a wonderful mother* superb, marvelous, magnificent, brilliant, sensational, stupendous, excellent, first-rate, fabulous, outstanding, terrific, ace, tremendous, admirable, very good; inf. great, super, fantastic, tip-top, A-1.

**woo** verb **1** *woo the boss's daughter* court, pay court/suit to, seek the hand of, set one's cap at, make love to. **2** *woo fame* seek, seek to win/gain, pursue, chase after. **3** *wooing consumers into buying their goods* importune, press, urge, entreat, beg, implore, supplicate, solicit, coax, wheedle.

**wood** noun lumber, timber; firewood, kindling, fuel.

**wooden** adjective **1** *a wooden performance* stiff, stolid, stodgy, graceless, inelegant, ungainly, gauche, awkward, clumsy, maladroit. **2** *a wooden expression* expressionless, inexpressive, blank, deadpan, empty, vacant, impassive, lifeless, spiritless, unanimated.

**woods** plural noun forest, woodland, wood, copse, thicket, grove; trees.

**word** noun **1** *what's another word for "fame"?* term, expression, name. **2** *he said not a word* remark, comment, statement, utterance, expression, declaration. **3** *she gave him her word* word of honor, solemn word, promise, pledge, assurance, guarantee, vow, oath. **4** *have a word with the teacher* chat, chitchat, talk, conversation, discussion, tête-à-tête, consultation, exchange of views; inf. confab, powwow. **5** *they have had word of his death* news, notice, communication, information, intelligence; tidings; message, report, account, communiqué, dispatch, bulletin; inf. lowdown. **6** *word has it that he is a spy* rumor, talk, hearsay, gossip, grapevine. **7** *give the word to begin* command, order, signal, go-ahead, thumbs up; inf. green light. **8** *the king's word is law* decree, edict, mandate, bidding, will. **9** *our watch word now must be success* slogan, watchword, password, catchword. **in a word** in short, in a nutshell, briefly. **word for word** verbatim, literal, exact, precise, accurate.

**word** verb express, phrase, couch, put, say, utter, state.

**words** plural noun **1** *the words of the song/opera/play* lyrics, libretto, book, text, script. **2** *she has had words with her sister* argument, disagreement, row, altercation.

**wordy** adjective long-winded, verbose, loquacious, garrulous, voluble, prolix, protracted, discursive, diffuse, rambling, digressive, maundering, tautological, pleonastic.

**work** noun **1** *building a house involves a lot of work* effort, exertion, labor, toil, sweat, drudgery, trouble, industry; *lit.* travail; *inf.* grind, elbow grease. **2** *your work is to answer the phone* job, task, chore, undertaking, duty, charge, assignment, commission, mission. **3** *out of work* employment, occupation, business; job, profession, career, trade, vocation, calling, craft, line, field, métier, pursuit. **4** *he regards it as his life's work* achievement, accomplishment, deed, feat, handiwork, fulfillment, performance, production. **5** *a work of art* composition, creation, opus, piece, oeuvre, masterpiece. **6** *admire the work that has gone into the statue* art, craft. *See* WORKMANSHIP.

**work** verb **1** *he works in industry* be employed, have a job, hold down a job, be engaged, earn one's living, do business, follow/ply one's trade. **2** *work hard to pass the exam* exert oneself, put in effort, labor, toil, sweat, drudge, slave, peg away; *inf.* grind, plug away, knock oneself out. **3** *work the machine* operate, control, drive, manage, direct, use, handle, manipulate, maneuver, ply, wield. **4** *this machine will not work* go, operate, function, perform, run. **5** *your idea/plan will not work* succeed, go well, be effective. **6** *work the land* cultivate, till, dig, farm. **7** *they can work miracles* bring about, achieve, accomplish, perform, carry out, execute, create, cause, contrive, effect, implement. **8** *they worked it so that the criminal got off* arrange, handle, manipulate, maneuver, contrive, bring off, carry off, pull off; *inf.* fix, swing. **9** *work the clay* knead, shape, form, mold, fashion, model. **10** *work the peg into the hole* maneuver, manipulate, negotiate, guide, engineer, direct, edge. **11** *work one's way through the crowd* maneuver, progress, penetrate, move, make, push, elbow. **work on** coax, cajole, wheedle, pester, press, nag, importune, persuade, influence, sway. **work out 1** *work out the puzzle* solve, resolve, figure out. **2** *work out a plan* develop, evolve, formulate, devise, arrange, organize, elaborate, construct, put together, plan, contrive. **3** *the plan did not work out* work, succeed, go well. **4** *things worked out well/badly* go, turn out, come out, develop, evolve, result; *inf.* pan out. **5** *work out to keep fit* exercise, do exercises, train, drill, warm

up. **work up 1** *work up to a climax* advance, progress, proceed, make headway. **2** *unable to work up any enthusiasm* stir up, arouse, rouse, awaken, excite, instigate, prompt, generate, kindle, foment. **3** *the speaker worked up the crowd* agitate, stir up, arouse, excite, animate, inflame.

**worker** noun **1** *workers and employers* employee, hand, workman, working man/woman/person, blue-collar worker, white-collar worker, laborer, artisan, craftsman, craftswoman, wage-earner, proletarian. **2** *workers of miracles* doer, performer, perpetrator, executor, operator. **3** *he is a real worker* hard worker, toiler, workhorse, busy bee; *inf.* workaholic.

**working** adjective *working machines* functioning, operating, going, running, in working order.

**working** noun **1** *understand the working of the machine* functioning, operation, modus operandi. **2** *the working of miracles* doing, performing, performance, perpetration, execution, operation. **3** *the workings of the clock* mechanism, machinery; works.

**workmanship** noun craftsmanship, craft, artistry, art, handicraft, handwork, expertise, skill, technique, work.

**workout** noun exercises, gymnastics, aerobics; *inf.* daily dozen.

**workshop** noun **1** *the car is still in the workshop* factory, plant, mill; garage. **2** *craftsmen in their workshop* workroom, studio, atelier, shop. **3** *hold a workshop in self-assertiveness* seminar, study/discussion group, class.

**world** noun **1** *travel around the world* earth, globe, sphere, planet. **2** *The world was shocked by the nuclear attack* whole world, mankind, man, humankind, humanity, people everywhere, people, everyone, everybody, public, general public. **3** *God created the world* universe, creation, cosmos. **4** *the earth and other worlds* planet, satellite, moon, star, heavenly body, orb. **5** *the academic world* society, sector, section, group, division. **6** *he works in the world of finance* area, field, department, sphere, province, domain, realm. **7** *the world of the Roosevelts* age, epoch, era, period; times. **8** *it made a world of difference* vast/huge amount; *inf.* great deal, immensity.

**worldly** adjective **1** *worldly pleasures* earthly, terrestrial, secular, temporal, material, materialistic, human, carnal, fleshly, corporeal, physical. **2** *traveling has made her more worldly* worldly-wise, experienced, knowing, sophisticated, cosmopolitan, urbane.

**worn** adjective **1** *worn clothes* worn-out, threadbare, tattered, in tatters, ragged,

# worry · wrench

488

frayed, shabby. **2** *worn furniture* dilapidated, crumbling, broken-down, run-down, tumbledown, decrepit, deteriorated, on its last legs. **3** *rescue workers looking worn* haggard, drawn, strained, careworn; *inf.* all in, done in, dog-tired, dead on one's feet, played out, bushed, pooped. **4** *workers worn by long hours* exhausted, over-tired, tired out, fatigued, weary, wearied, spent. **5** *worn ideas/jokes* obsolete, antiquated, old, hackneyed, stale, played out. **worn-out** worn, dilapidated, exhausted.

**worry** verb **1** *she worries too much* be worried, be anxious, fret, brood. **2** *his absences worry her* make anxious, disturb, trouble, bother, distress, upset, concern, disquiet, discompose, fret, agitate, unsettle.

**worry** noun anxiety, disturbance, trouble, bother, distress, concern, care, upset, uneasiness, unease, disquiet, fretfulness, agitation, edginess, tenseness, apprehension, fearfulness.

**worsen** verb **1** *his statement worsened the situation* aggravate, exacerbate, damage, intensify, increase, heighten. **2** *the financial situation worsened* take a turn for the worse, deteriorate, degenerate, retrogress, decline, sink, slip, slide, go downhill.

**worship** noun **1** *acts of worship* reverence, veneration, homage, respect, honor, adoration, devotion, praise, prayer, glorification, exaltation, laudation, extolment. **2** *the fans' worship of the star* adulation, admiration, adoration, devotion, idolization, hero-worship.

**worship** verb **1** *worship God* revere, venerate, pay homage to, honor, adore, praise, pray to, glorify, exalt, laud, extol. **2** *he worships his wife* be devoted to, cherish, treasure, admire, adulate, idolize, hero-worship; *inf.* be wild about.

**worth** noun **1** *the jewels are of little worth* value, price, cost; valuation, assessment, appraisal. **2** *his advice is of little worth to you* use, usefulness, advantage, benefit, service, gain, profit, avail. **3** *persons of great worth in the community* worthiness, merit, credit, eminence, importance.

**worthless** adjective **1** *the jewels are worthless* valueless, of little/no value, rubbishy, trashy. **2** *his advice was worthless* useless, of no benefit, to no avail, futile, ineffective, ineffectual, pointless. **3** *their worthless son ended up in prison* good-for-nothing, useless, despicable, contemptible, base, low; *inf.* no-good, no-account.

**worthwhile** adjective worth it, worth the effort, valuable, of value, useful, of use, beneficial, advantageous, helpful, profitable, constructive, justifiable.

**worthy** adjective virtuous, good, moral, upright, righteous, honest, decent, honorable, respectable, reputable, trustworthy,

reliable, irreproachable, blameless, unimpeachable, admirable, praiseworthy, laudable, commendable, deserving, meritorious.

**wound** noun **1** *a wound in the leg that is not healing* lesion, cut, graze, scratch, gash, laceration, tear, puncture, slash, injury, sore. **2** *a wound to his pride* blow, insult, slight, offense, affront; hurt, harm, damage. **3** *mental/emotional wounds* pain, pang, ache, distress, grief, trauma, anguish, torment, torture.

**wound** verb **1** *the shot wounded his arm* cut, graze, scratch, gash, lacerate, tear, puncture, pierce, stab, slash, injure, hurt, damage, harm. **2** *their words wounded his pride* harm, damage, insult, slight, offend, affront. **3** *his actions wounded her feelings* distress, grieve, mortify, pain, shock, traumatize.

**wrap** verb **1** *wrap the child in blankets* envelop, enfold, fold, encase, enclose, cover, swathe, bundle up, swaddle. **2** *wrap the present* wrap up, package, do up, tie up, gift-wrap. **wrap up** *try to wrap up the meeting early* finish, conclude, terminate, wind up.

**wrap** noun shawl, stole, cloak, cape, mantle.

**wrapper** noun wrapping, cover, covering, packaging, paper; jacket, casing, case, sheath; capsule, pod, shell.

**wrath** noun anger, ire, rage, fury, annoyance, indignation, exasperation, dudgeon, high dudgeon, bad temper, ill humor, irritation, crossness, displeasure, irascibility.

**wreath** noun **1** *wreaths of flowers* garland, chaplet, circlet, coronet, crown, diadem, festoon, lei. **2** *wreaths of smoke* ring, loop, circle.

**wreck** noun **1** *the wreck of the car/house/dreams* wreckage, debris, rubble, detritus; ruins, remains, remnants, fragments, pieces, relics. **2** *upset by the wreck of their car/house/dream* wrecking, destruction, devastation, ruination, ruin, demolition, smashing, shattering, disruption, disintegration, undoing.

**wreck** verb **1** *wreck the car* smash, demolish, ruin, damage; *inf.* write off. **2** *wreck their plans/hopes* destroy, devastate, smash, shatter, disrupt, undo, spoil, mar, play havoc with. **3** *the new crew wrecked the ship* shipwreck, sink, capsize, run aground.

**wrench** noun **1** *remove the root with one wrench* twist, pull, tug, yank, wrest, jerk, jolt. **2** *the wrist injury is just a wrench* sprain, twist, strain. **3** *the wrench of a broken heart* pain, ache, pang, anguish, distress, trauma.

**wrench** verb **1** *wrench the root from the ground* twist, pull, tug, yank, wrest, jerk, tear, rip, force. **2** *wrench one's ankle/wrist* sprain, twist, strain.

**wrest** verb twist, wrench, pull, snatch, take away, remove.

**wrestle** verb **wrestle with** struggle with, grapple with, fight with, contend with, battle with, combat with, come to grips with, face up to, pit oneself against.

**wretch** noun **1** *pity the wretches living on the streets* poor creature/soul/thing, unfortunate, poor devil. **2** *the wretch who stole her purse* scoundrel, villain, ruffian, rogue, rascal, blackguard, reprobate, criminal, delinquent, miscreant; *inf.* rat, swine, skunk.

**wretched** adjective **1** *feeling wretched at leaving home* miserable, unhappy, sorry, sad, brokenhearted, sorrowful, distressed, disconsolate, downcast, down, downhearted, dejected, crestfallen, cheerless, depressed, melancholy, gloomy, mournful, doleful, forlorn, woebegone, abject. **2** *feeling wretched during the sea voyage* ill, unwell, sick, sickly, ailing, below par; *inf.* under the weather, out of sorts. **3** *lead a wretched existence* hard, harsh, grim, difficult, unfortunate, sorry, pitiful, tragic. **4** *wretched people living in poverty* unfortunate, unlucky, hapless, pitiable. **5** *the wretched drug dealer is back in prison* contemptible, despicable, base, low, vile. **6** *the food was wretched* poor, bad, substandard, low-quality, inferior, pathetic, worthless.

**wring** verb **1** *wring the clothes* twist, squeeze. **2** *wring the information from him* extract, force, coerce, exact, extort, wrest, wrench, screw.

**wrinkle** noun crease, fold, pucker, gather, furrow, ridge, line, corrugation, crinkle, crumple, rumple, crow's-foot.

**write** verb **1** *write their names* write down, put in writing, put in black and white, commit to paper, jot down, note, set down, take down, record, register, list, inscribe, scribble, scrawl. **2** *write an essay/letter* compose, draft, create, pen, dash off. **3** *don't forget to write* write a letter, correspond, communicate; *inf.* drop a line/note. **write off** forget about, disregard, dismiss, give up for lost, cancel, annul, nullify, wipe out.

**writer** noun author, wordsmith, penman, hack; novelist, essayist, biographer, journalist, columnist, scriptwriter; scribe; *inf.* scribbler, pen/pencil pusher.

**writhe** verb twist about, twist and turn, roll about, squirm, wriggle, fidget, jerk, thrash, flail, toss, struggle.

**writing** noun **1** *the writing is illegible* handwriting, hand, penmanship, script, print, calligraphy, scribble, scrawl. **2** *have his writing published* work, opus, book, volume, publication, composition.

**wrong** adjective **1** *the wrong answer* incorrect, inaccurate, erroneous, mistaken, inexact, imprecise, unsound, faulty, false, wide of the mark, off target; *inf.* barking up the wrong tree. **2** *chose the wrong moment to speak* unsuitable, inappropriate, inapt, inapposite, undesirable, unacceptable, unfitting, improper, unseemly, indecorous, unconventional. **3** *it is wrong to steal* unlawful, illegal, illicit, lawless, criminal, delinquent, felonious, dishonest, dishonorable, corrupt, unethical, immoral, bad, wicked, evil, sinful, iniquitous, blameworthy, culpable; *inf.* crooked. **4** *something wrong with his phone/heart* amiss, awry, out of order, not right, faulty, defective. **5** *iron the dress on the wrong side* inside, reverse, opposite, inverse.

**wrong** adverb **get wrong** misunderstand, misinterpret, misapprehend, misconstrue. **go wrong 1** *you cannot go wrong if you follow the instructions* make a mistake, go astray, err; *inf.* slip up, make a booboo. **2** *things went wrong from the start* go badly, go amiss, go awry. **3** *when did he go wrong?* go astray, err, stray from the straight and narrow, fall from grace; *inf.* go to the dogs.

**wrong** noun **1** *not know right from wrong* badness, immorality, sin, sinfulness, wickedness, evil, iniquity, unlawfulness, crime, dishonesty, dishonor, injustice, transgression, abuse; *inf.* crookedness. **2** *commit a wrong | do us a wrong* misdeed, offense, injury, crime, infringement, infraction, injustice, grievance, outrage, atrocity. **in the wrong** in error, mistaken, at fault, to blame, blameworthy, culpable, guilty.

**wrong** verb **1** *he wronged his wife* abuse, mistreat, maltreat, ill-treat, ill-use, harm, hurt, do injury to. **2** *you wrong him by calling him a thief* malign, dishonor, impugn, vilify, defame, slander, libel, denigrate, insult; *inf.* bad-mouth.

**wrongdoer** noun lawbreaker, criminal, delinquent, culprit, offender, felon, villain, miscreant, evildoer, sinner, transgressor, malefactor.

**wry** adjective **1** *make a wry face* twisted, distorted, contorted, crooked, lopsided, askew. **2** *a wry wit* ironic, sardonic, mocking, sarcastic, dry, droll, witty, humorous.

#  Xx

**Xerox** (trademark) verb *Xerox the document* photocopy, copy, duplicate, reproduce; Photostat (trademark).

#  Yy

**yank** verb *yank the weeds out* pull, tug, jerk, wrench.

**yardstick** noun measure, standard, gauge, scale, guide, guideline, touchstone, criterion, benchmark, model, pattern.

**yarn** noun **1** *use a fine yarn* thread, fiber, strand. **2** *tell a good yarn* story, tale, anecdote, fable; *inf.* tall tale/story, cock and bull story.

**yearn** verb long, pine, crave, desire, want, wish, hanker, have a fancy, hunger, thirst; *inf.* have a yen.

**yearning** noun longing, craving, desire, want, wish, hankering, fancy, hunger, thirst, lust, ache, burning; *inf.* yen.

**yell** verb shout, cry out, howl, scream, shriek, screech, squeal, roar, bawl, whoop; *inf.* holler.

**yell** noun shout, cry, howl, scream, shriek, screech, squeal, roar, bawl, whoop; *inf.* holler.

**yen** noun hankering, desire. *See* YEARNING.

**yet** adverb **1** *he has not appeared yet* as yet, so/thus far, up till/to now. **2** *there is yet more to come* still, in addition, besides, into the bargain, to boot. **3** *I was not expecting him yet* now, just/right now, by now, already, so soon.

**yield** verb **1** *fields yielding a good crop* produce, bear, give, give forth, supply, provide. **2** *investments yielding a good profit* return, bring in, fetch, earn, net, produce, supply, provide, generate, furnish. **3** *yield the crown to the conqueror* give up, relinquish, part with, deliver up, turn over, give over, remit, cede, renounce, resign, abdicate, forgo. **4** *the army yielded*

after a long battle surrender, capitulate, submit, lay down one's arms, give in, give up the struggle, succumb, raise/show the white flag; *inf.* throw in the towel, cave in. **5** *the material yields on pressure* give, bend, stretch, be flexible/pliant.
**yield to** submit to, bow down to, comply with, accede to, agree to, consent to, go along with.

**yoke** noun **1** *the yoke of the oxen* harness, collar, coupling. **2** *under the yoke of the tyrant* oppression, tyranny, enslavement, slavery, servitude, bondage, thrall. **3** *the yoke of marriage* tie, link, bond.

**yokel** noun rustic, countryman, countrywoman, peasant, country bumpkin, provincial, country cousin; *inf.* hayseed, hillbilly.

**young** adjective **1** *young people* youthful, juvenile, junior, adolescent, in the springtime of life, in one's salad days. **2** *young industries* new, recent, undeveloped, fledgling, in the making.

**young** noun *bear young* offspring, progeny, family, issue; little ones, babies; litter, brood.

**youngster** noun young adult/person, youth, juvenile, teenager, adolescent, young hopeful; lad, boy, young man/woman, lass, girl; *inf.* kid, shaver, young 'un.

**youth** noun **1** *in their youth they were beautiful* young days, early years, teens; early life, adolescence; boyhood, girlhood. **2** *the coach was a good friend to the youths* juvenile, teenager. *See* YOUNGSTER. **3** *the youth of today* young people, young, younger generation; *inf.* kids.

**youthful** adjective *he is a youthful sixty-five* young, active, vigorous, spry, sprightly.

# Zz

**zany** adjective eccentric, weird, peculiar, daft, odd, ridiculous, absurd, comic, clownish, madcap, funny, amusing; *inf.* wacky, screwy, kooky.

**zeal** noun **1** *his zeal for life/hockey* ardor, fervor, fervency, passion, fire, devotion, vehemence, intensity, enthusiasm, eagerness, keenness, earnestness, vigor, energy, verve, gusto, zest. **2** *put off by their religious/political zeal* fanaticism, extremism. *See* ZEALOTRY.

**zealot** noun enthusiast, fanatic, extremist, radical, militant; *inf.* fiend.

**zealotry** noun zeal, fanaticism, extremism, single-mindedness, radicalism, militancy.

**zealous** adjective ardent, fervent, fervid, passionate, impassioned, devoted, intense, enthusiastic, eager, keen, earnest, vigorous, energetic, zestful, fanatical.

**zenith** noun crowning point, height, top, acme, peak, pinnacle, climax, prime, meridian, apex, apogee, vertex.

**zero** noun **1** *a series of zeros | win absolutely zero* naught, nothing, cipher, nil; *inf.* zilch, nada, goose egg, zippo. **2** *economic growth is at zero* lowest point, nadir, rock bottom.

**zest** noun **1** *approach the project with zest* relish, gusto, enthusiasm, zing, eagerness, zeal, vigor, liveliness, energy, enjoyment, joy, delectation, appetite; *inf.* oomph. **2** *add zest to the dish/occasion* piquancy, spice, pungency, flavor, relish, tang, savor, interest; *inf.* kick.

**zip** noun zest, enthusiasm, zing, eagerness, gusto, life, liveliness, spirit, animation, sparkle, pep, élan, brio; *inf.* oomph, pizzazz.

**zip** verb rush, dash, hurry, speed. *See* ZOOM.

**zone** noun area, sector, section, belt, district, region, province.

**zoom** verb rush, dash, pelt, race, tear, shoot, fly, scurry, speed, hurry, hasten, whiz, zip.

# Writer's Toolkit

# Punctuation Guide

Punctuation is an essential element of good writing because it makes the author's meaning clear to the reader. Although precise punctuation styles may vary somewhat among published sources, there are a number of fundamental principles worthy of consideration. Discussed below are these punctuation marks used in English:

> comma
> semicolon
> colon
> period
> question mark
> exclamation point
> apostrophe
> quotation marks
> parentheses
> dash
> hyphen

## Comma

The comma is the most used mark of punctuation in the English language. It signals to the reader a pause, which generally clarifies the author's meaning, and establishes a sensible order to the elements of written language. Among the most typical functions of the comma are the following:

1. It can separate the clauses of a compound sentence when there are two independent clauses joined by a conjunction, especially when the clauses are not very short:

> *It never occurred to me to look in the attic, and I'm sure it didn't occur to Rachel either.*

> *The Nelsons wanted to see the Grand Canyon at sunrise, but they overslept that morning.*

2. It can separate the clauses of a compound sentence when there is a series of independent clauses, the last two of which are joined by a conjunction:

> *The bus ride to the campsite was very uncomfortable, the cabins were not ready for us when we got there, the cook had forgotten to start dinner, and the rain was torrential.*

3. It is used to precede or set off, and therefore indicate, a nonrestrictive dependent clause (a clause that could be omitted without changing the meaning of the main clause):

> *I read her autobiography, which was published last July.*

They showed up at midnight, after most of the guests had gone home.

The coffee, which is freshly brewed, is in the kitchen.

4. It can follow an introductory phrase:

Having enjoyed the movie so much, he agreed to see it again.

Born and raised in Paris, she had never lost her French accent.

In the beginning, they had very little money to invest.

5. It can set off words used in direct address:

Listen, people, you have no choice in the matter.

Yes, Mrs. Greene, I will be happy to feed your cat.

6. The comma can separate two or more coordinate adjectives (adjectives that could otherwise be joined with *and*) that modify one noun:

The cruise turned out to be the most entertaining, fun, and relaxing vacation I've ever had.

The horse was tall, lean, and sleek.

Note that cumulative adjectives (those not able to be joined with *and*) are not separated by a comma:

She wore bright yellow rubber boots.

7. Use a comma to separate three or more items in a series or list:

Charlie, Melissa, Stan, and Mark will be this year's soloists in the spring concert.

We need furniture, toys, clothes, books, tools, housewares, and other useful merchandise for the benefit auction.

Note that the comma between the last two items in a series is sometimes omitted in less precise style:

The most popular foods served in the cafeteria are pizza, hamburgers and nachos.

8. Use a comma to separate and set off the elements in an address or other geographical designation:

My new house is at 1657 Nighthawk Circle, South Kingsbury, Michigan.

We arrived in Pamplona, Spain, on Thursday.

9. Use a comma to set off direct quotations (note the placement or absence of commas with other punctuation):

"Kim forgot her gloves," he said, "but we have a pair she can borrow."

There was a long silence before Jack blurted out, "This must be the world's ugliest painting."

"What are you talking about?" she asked in a puzzled manner.

"Happy New Year!" everyone shouted.

10. A comma is used to set off titles after a person's name:

Katherine Bentley, M.D.

Martin Luther King, Jr., delivered the sermon.

# Semicolon

The semicolon has two basic functions:

1. It can separate two main clauses, particularly when these clauses are of equal importance:

> *The crowds gathered outside the museum hours before the doors were opened; this was one exhibit no one wanted to miss.*

> *She always complained when her relatives stayed for the weekend; even so, she usually was a little sad when they left.*

2. It can be used as a comma is used to separate such elements as clauses or items in a series or list, particularly when one or more of the elements already includes a comma:

> *The path took us through the deep, dark woods; across a small meadow; into a cold, wet cave; and up a hillside overlooking the lake.*

> *Listed for sale in the ad were two bicycles; a battery-powered, leaf-mulching lawn mower; and a maple bookcase.*

# Colon

The colon has five basic functions:

1. It can introduce something, especially a list of items:

   *In the basket were three pieces of mail: a postcard, a catalog, and a wedding invitation.*

   *Students should have the following items: backpack, loose-leaf notebook, pens and pencils, pencil sharpener, and ruler.*

2. It can separate two clauses in a sentence when the second clause is being used to explain or illustrate the first clause:

   *We finally understood why she would never go sailing with us: she had a deep fear of the water.*

   *Most of the dogs in our neighborhood are quite large: two of them are St. Bernards.*

3. It can introduce a statement or a quotation:

   *His parents say the most important rule is this: Always tell the truth.*

   *We repeated the final words of his poem: "And such is the plight of fools like me."*

4. It can be used to follow the greeting in a formal or business letter:

   *Dear Ms. Daniels:*

   *Dear Sir or Madam:*

5. In the U.S., use a comma to separate minutes from hours, and seconds from minutes, in showing time of day and measured length of time:

   *Please be at the restaurant before 6:45.*

   *Her best running time so far has been 00:12:35.*

# Period

The period has two basic functions:

1. It is used to mark the end of a sentence:

   *It was reported that there is a shortage of nurses at the hospital. Several of the patients have expressed concern about this problem.*

2. It is often used at the end of an abbreviation:

   *On Fri., Sept. 12, Dr. Brophy noted that the patient's weight was 168 lbs. and that his height was 6 ft. 2 in.* (Note that another period is not added to the end of the sentence when the last word is an abbreviation.)

# Question Mark and Exclamation Point

The only sentences that do not end in a period are those that end in either a question mark or an exclamation point.

Question marks are used to mark the end of a sentence that asks a direct question (generally, a question that expects an answer):

*Is there any reason for us to bring more than a few dollars?*

*Who is your science teacher?*

Exclamation points are used to mark the end of a sentence that expresses strong feeling, typically surprise, joy, or anger:

*I want you to leave and never come back!*

*What a beautiful view this is!*

# Apostrophe

The apostrophe has two basic functions:

1. It is used to show where a letter or letters are missing in a contraction:

   *The directions are cont'd [continued] on the next page.*

   *We've [we have] decided that if she can't [cannot] go, then we aren't [are not] going either.*

2. It can be used to show possession:

   a. The possessive of a singular noun or an irregular plural noun is created by adding an apostrophe and an s:

   *the pilot's uniform*

   *Mrs. Mendoza's house*

   *a tomato's bright red color*

   *the oxen's yoke*

   b. The possessive of a plural noun is created by adding just an apostrophe:

   *the pilots' uniforms* [referring to more than one pilot]

   *the Mendozas' house* [referring to the Mendoza family]

   *the tomatoes' bright red color* [referring to more than one tomato]

# Quotation Marks

Quotation marks have two basic functions:

1. They are used to set off direct quotations (an exact rendering of someone's spoken or written words):

> *"I think the new library is wonderful," she remarked to David.*

> *We were somewhat lost, so we asked, "Are we anywhere near the art gallery?"*

> *In his letter he had written, "The nights here are quiet and starry. It seems like a hundred years since I've been wakened by the noise of city traffic and squabbling neighbors."*

Note that indirect quotes (which often are preceded by that, if, or whether) are not set off by quotation marks:

> *He told me that he went to school in Boston.*

> *We asked if we could still get tickets to the game.*

2. They can be used to set off words or phrases that have specific technical usage, or to set off meanings of words, or to indicate words that are being used in a special way in a sentence:

> *The part of the flower that bears the pollen is the "stamen."*

> *When I said "plain," I meant "flat land," not "ordinary."*

> *Oddly enough, in the theater, the statement "break a leg" is meant as an expression of good luck.*

> *What you call "hoagies," we call "grinders" or "submarine sandwiches."*

> *He will never be a responsible adult until he outgrows his "Peter Pan" behavior.*

Note that sometimes single quotation marks (the 'stamen.'), rather than double quotation marks as above (the "stamen."), may be used to set off words or phrases. What is most important is to be consistent in such usage. Single quotation marks are also used to set off words or phrases within material already in double quotation marks, as:

> *"I want the sign to say 'Ellen's Bed and Breakfast' in large gold letters," she explained.*

# Parentheses

Parentheses are used, in pairs, to enclose information that gives extra detail or explanation to the regular text. Parentheses are used in two basic ways:

1. They can separate a word or words in a sentence from the rest of the sentence:

   *On our way to school, we walk past the Turner Farm (the oldest dairy farm in town) and watch the cows being fed.*

   *The stores were filled with holiday shoppers (even more so than last year).* (Note that the period goes outside the parentheses, because the words in the parentheses are only part of the sentence.)

2. They can form a separate complete sentence:

   *Please bring a dessert to the dinner party. (It can be something very simple.) I look forward to seeing you there.* (Note that the period goes inside the parentheses, because the words in the parentheses are a complete and independent sentence.)

# Dash

A dash is used most commonly to replace the usage of parentheses within sentences. If the information being set off is in the middle of the sentence, a pair of dashes is used; if it is at the end of the sentence, just one dash is used:

> *On our way to school, we walk past the Turner Farm—the oldest dairy farm in town—and watch the cows being fed.*

> *The stores were filled with holiday shoppers—even more so than last year.*

# Hyphen

A hyphen has three basic functions:

1. It can join two or more words to make a compound, especially when so doing makes the meaning more clear to the reader:

> *We met to discuss long-range planning.*

> *There were six four-month-old piglets at the fair.*

> *That old stove was quite a coal-burner.*

2. It can replace the word "to" when a span or range of data is given. This kind of hyphen is sometimes also called a dash:

> *John Adams was president of the United States 1797-1801.*

> *Today we will look for proper nouns in the L-N section of the dictionary.*

> *The ideal weight for that breed of dog would be 75-85 pounds.*

3. It can indicate a word break at the end of a line. The break must always be between syllables:

> *It is important for any writer to know that there are numerous punctuation principles that are considered standard and proper, but there is also flexibility regarding acceptable punctuation. Having learned the basic "rules" of good punctuation, the writer will be able to adopt a specific and consistent style of punctuation that best suits the material he or she is writing.*

# Usage Guide

Even the best writers are sometimes troubled by questions of correct usage. A guide to some of the most common questions is provided below, with discussion of the following topics:

## singular or plural

1. When subject and complement are different in number (i.e., one is singular, the other plural), the verb normally agrees with the subject, e.g.,

(Plural subject)
*Their wages* were *a mere pittance.*

*Liqueur chocolates* are *our specialty.*

(The Biblical *The wages of sin is death* reflects an obsolete idiom in which *wages* took a singular verb.)

(Singular subject)
*What we need* is *customers.*

*Our specialty* is *liqueur chocolates.*

2. A plural word or phrase used as a name, title, or quotation counts as singular, e.g.,

*Sons and Lovers has always been one of Lawrence's most popular novels.*

3. A singular phrase (such as a prepositional phrase following the subject) that happens to end with a plural word should nevertheless be followed by a singular verb, e.g.,

*Everyone except the French* wants (not *want*) *Britain to join.*

*One in six* has (not *have*) *this problem.*

See also *-s plural or singular; nouns ending in -ics*

# -s plural or singular

Some nouns, though they have the plural ending -s, are nevertheless usually treated as singular, taking singular verbs and pronouns referring back to them.

1. *News*

2. Diseases:

   | | |
   |---|---|
   | *measles* | *rickets* |
   | *mumps* | *shingles* |

*Measles* and *rickets* can also be treated as ordinary plural nouns.

3. Games:

   | | |
   |---|---|
   | *billiards* | *craps* |
   | *dominoes* | *quoits* |
   | *checkers* | *darts* |

4. Countries:

   | | |
   |---|---|
   | *the Bahamas* | *the Netherlands* |
   | *the Philippines* | *the United States* |

These are treated as singular when considered as a unit, which they commonly are in a political context, or when the complement is singular, e.g.,

   *The Philippines is a predominantly agricultural country.*

   *The United States has withdrawn its ambassador.*

*The Bahamas* and *the Philippines* are also the geographical names of the groups of islands that the two nations comprise, and in this use can be treated as plurals, e.g.,

   *The Bahamas were settled by British subjects.*

See also nouns ending in *-ics*.

## comparison of adjectives and adverbs

The two ways of forming the comparative and superlative of adjectives and adverbs are:

(*a*) Addition of suffixes *-er* and *-est*. Monosyllabic adjectives and adverbs almost always require these suffixes, e.g., *big* (*bigger, biggest*), *soon* (*sooner, soonest*), and normally so do many adjectives of two syllables, e.g., *narrow* (*narrower, narrowest*), *silly* (*sillier, silliest*).

(*b*) Use of adverbs *more* and *most*. These are used with adjectives of three syllables or more (e.g., *difficult, memorable*), participles (e.g., *bored, boring*), many adjectives of two syllables (e.g., *afraid, awful, childish, harmless, static*), and adverbs ending in *-ly* (e.g., *highly, slowly*).

Adjectives with two syllables sometimes use suffixes and sometimes use adverbs.

There are many that never take the suffixes, e.g.,

| | |
|---|---|
| *antique* | *bizarre* |
| *breathless* | *constant* |
| *futile* | *steadfast* |

There is also a large class that is acceptable with either, e.g.,

| | |
|---|---|
| *clever* | *pleasant* |
| *handsome* | *tranquil* |
| *solemn* | *cruel* |
| *common* | *polite* |

The choice is largely a matter of preference.

# nouns ending in *-ics*

Nouns ending in *-ics* denoting subjects or disciplines are sometimes treated as singular and sometimes as plural. Examples are:

| | |
|---|---|
| *apologetics* | *mechanics* |
| *genetics* | *politics* |
| *optics* | *economics* |
| *classics* (as a study) | *metaphysics* |
| *linguistics* | *statistics* |
| *phonetics* | *electronics* |
| *mathematics* | *obstetrics* |
| *physics* | *tactics* |
| *dynamics* | *ethics* |

When used strictly as the name of a discipline they are treated as singular:

> *Psychometrics* is *unable to investigate the nature of intelligence.*

So also when the complement is singular:

> *Mathematics* is *his strong point.*

When used more loosely, to denote a manifestation of qualities, often accompanied by a possessive, they are treated as plural:

> *His politics* were *a mixture of fear, greed, and envy.*

> *I don't understand the mathematics of it, which* are *complicated.*

> *The acoustics in this hall* are *dreadful.*

So also when they denote a set of activities or pattern of behavior, as commonly with words like:

| | |
|---|---|
| *acrobatics* | *athletics* |
| *dramatics* | *gymnastics* |
| *heroics* | *hysterics* |

E.g., *The mental gymnastics required to believe this* are *beyond me.*

## group possessive

The group possessive is the construction by which the ending -'s of the possessive case can be added to the last word of a noun phrase, which is regarded as a single unit, e.g.,

*The king of Spain's daughter*

*John and Mary's baby*

*Somebody else's umbrella*

*A quarter of an hour's drive*

Expressions like these are natural and acceptable.

## *may* or *might*

There is sometimes confusion about whether to use *may* or *might* with the perfect tense when referring to a past event, e.g., *He may have done* or *He might have done*.

1. If uncertainty about the action or state denoted by the perfect remains, i.e., at the time of speaking or writing the truth of the event is still unknown, then either *may* or *might* is acceptable:

> *As they all wore so many different clothes of identically the same kind . . . there* may *have been several more or several less.*

> *For all we knew our complaint went unanswered, although of course they* might *have tried to call us while we were out of town.*

2. If there is no longer uncertainty about the event, or the matter was never put to the test, and therefore the event did not in fact occur, use *might*:

> *If that had come ten days ago my whole life* might *have been different.*

> *You should not have let him come home alone; he* might *have gotten lost.*

It is a common error to use *may* instead of *might*, as here:

> *If they had not invaded, then eventually we* \*may\* *have agreed to give them aid.*

> *I am grateful for his intervention, without which they* \*may\* *have remained in the refugee camp indefinitely.*

> *Schoenberg* \*may\* *never have gone atonal but for the breakup of his marriage.*

In each of the three sentences above *might* should be substituted for *may*.

## *I* or *me*, *we* or *us*, etc.

There is often confusion about which case of a personal pronoun to use when the pronoun stands alone or follows the verb *to be*.

1. When the personal pronoun stands alone, as when it forms the answer to a question, strictly formal usage requires it to have the case it would have if the verb were supplied:

> *Who called him?*—I (in full, *I called him* or *I did*).
>
> *Which of you did he approach?*—Me (in full, *he approached me*).

Informal usage permits the objective case in both kinds of sentence, but this is not acceptable in formal style. However, the subjective case often sounds stilted. One can avoid the problem by providing a verb, e.g.,

> *Who likes cooking?*—I do.
>
> *Who can cook?*—I can.
>
> *Who is here?*—I am.

2. When a personal pronoun follows *it is, it was, it may be, it could have been*, etc., formal usage requires the subjective case:

> *Nobody could suspect that it was* she.
>
> *We are given no clues as to what it must have felt like to be* he.

Informal usage favors the objective case (not acceptable in formal style):

> *I thought it might have been* him *at the door.*
>
> *Don't tell me it's* them *again!*

When *who* or *whom* follows, the subjective case is obligatory in formal usage and quite usual informally:

> *It was* I *who painted that sign.*

The informal use of the objective case often sounds incorrect:

> *It was* her *who would get into trouble.*

In constructions that have the form *I am* + noun or noun phrase + *who*, the verb following *who* agrees with the noun (the antecedent of *who*) in number (singular or plural)

> *I am the sort of person who* likes *peace and quiet.*
>
> *You are the fourth of my colleagues who's told me that.*
> (*'s* = *has*, agreeing with *the fourth*.)

## we (with phrase following)

Expressions consisting of *we* or *us* followed by a qualifying word or phrase, e.g., *we Americans, us Americans*, are often misused with the wrong case of the first person plural pronoun. In fact the rules are exactly the same as for *we* or *us* standing alone.

If the expression is the subject, *we* should be used:

> (Correct)
> *Not always laughing as heartily as we Americans are supposed to do.*

> (Incorrect)
> *We all make mistakes, even us judges* (substitute *we judges*).

If the expression is the object or the complement of a preposition, *us* should be used:

> (Correct)
> *To us Americans, personal liberty is a vital principle.*

> (Incorrect)
> *The president said some nice things about we reporters in the press corps* (substitute *us reporters*).

## I who, you who, etc.

The verb following a personal pronoun (*I, you, he,* etc.) + *who* should be the same as what would be used with the pronoun as a subject:

> *I, who have no savings to speak of, had to pay for the work.*

> *They made me, who have no savings at all, pay for the work* (not *who has*).

When *it is* (*it was*, etc.) precedes *I who,* etc., the same rule applies: the verb agrees with the personal pronoun:

> *It's I who have done it.*

> *It could have been we who were mistaken.*

## *you and I* or *you and me*

When a personal pronoun is linked by *and* or *or* to a noun or another pronoun, there is often confusion about which case to put the pronoun in. In fact the rule is exactly as it would be for the pronoun standing alone.

1. If the two words linked by *and* or *or* constitute the subject, the pronoun should be in the subjective case, e.g.,

> *Only* she *and her mother cared for the old house.*
>
> *That's what we would do, that is, John and* I *would.*
>
> *Who could go?—Either you or* he.

The use of the objective case is quite common in informal speech, but it is non-standard, e.g.,

> *Perhaps only* her *and Mrs. Natwick had stuck to the christened name.*
>
> *That's how we look at it,* me *and Martha.*
>
> *Either Mary had to leave or* me.

2. If the two words linked by *and* or *or* constitute the object of the verb, or the complement of a preposition, the objective case should be used:

> *The afternoon would suit* her *and John better.*
>
> *It was time for Kenneth and* me *to go down to the living room.*

The use of the subjective case is very common informally. It probably arises from an exaggerated fear of the error indicated under 1 above. •It remains, however, non-standard, e.g.,

> *It was this that set Charles and* I *talking of old times.*
>
> *Why is it that people like you and* I *are so unpopular?*
>
> *Between you and* I . . .

This last expression is very commonly heard. *Between you and me* should always be substituted.

# collective nouns

Collective nouns are singular words that denote many individuals, e.g., *audience, government, orchestra, the clergy, the public*.

It is normal for collective nouns, being singular, to be followed by singular verbs and pronouns (*is, has, consists*, and *it* in the examples below):

> *The government* is *determined to beat inflation, as* it has *promised.*

> *Their family* is *huge:* it consists *of five boys and three girls.*

> *The bourgeoisie* is *despised for not being proletarian.*

The singular verb and pronouns are preferable unless the collective is clearly and unmistakably used to refer to separate individuals rather than to a united body, e.g.,

> *The cabinet* has *made* its *decision.*

but

> *The cabinet* are *sitting at* their *places around the table with the president.*

The singular should always be used if the collective noun is qualified by a singular word like *this, that, every*, etc.:

> This *family* is *divided.*

> Every *team* has its *chance to win.*

## *none* (pronoun)

The pronoun *none* can be followed either by singular verb and singular pronouns, or by plural ones. Either is acceptable, although the plural tends to be more common.

Singular: *None of them was allowed to forget for a moment.*

Plural: *None of the orchestras ever* play *there.*

*None of the authors expected* their *books to become best-sellers.*

## *as*

In the following sentences, formal usage requires the *subjective* case (*I, he, she, we, they*) on the assumption that the pronoun would be the subject if a verb were supplied:

*You are just as intelligent as* he (in full, *as he is*).

*He . . . might not have heard the song so often as* I (*in full, as I had*).

Informal usage permits *You are just as intelligent as* him.

Formal English uses the *objective* case (*me, him, her, us, them*) only when the pronoun would be the object if a verb were supplied:

*I thought you preferred John to Mary, but I see that you like her just as much as* him (which means . . . *just as much as you like him*).

# Diacritical Marks

*(to distinguish sounds or values of letters)*

´   acute (as in the French word *née*)
`   grave (as in the French word *père*)
~   tilde (as in the Spanish word *piñata*)
^   circumflex (as in the word *rôle*)
¯   macron (as used in pronunciation: *āge, īce*)
˘   breve (as used in pronunciation: *tăp, rĭp*)
¨   dieresis (as in the word *naïve*)
,   cedilla (as in the word *façade*)